The Evolution of
THE BRITISH EMPIRE AND COMMONWEALTH
From the American Revolution

THE EVOLUTION OF

The
British Empire
and
Commonwealth

FROM THE AMERICAN REVOLUTION

By Alfred LeRoy Burt

D. C. Heath and Company Boston

MAPS BY DONALD T. PITCHER

Library of Congress Catalog Card Number
56-6105

Foreword

I HAVE attempted to explain a subject that is admittedly much too large and complicated to be mastered by anyone in a whole lifetime. It began to intrigue me forty-five years ago, when I was a student of the late Professor Egerton and lived in daily contact with other students drawn to Oxford from all over the empire. It provided the theme of my first book, which came out as I "went down," and it has been a major interest ever since.

The present volume begins with the success of the American Revolution because this has had an enormous and far-reaching effect on the evolution of the British Empire. I have sought to present this evolution as an organic whole, arranged around dominant ideas and forces, rather than as a collection of unrelated episodes. Personalities, however interesting in themselves, have been kept to a minimum; and so also have the details of internal history of each part of the empire.

As no man can really understand his own country until he looks at it from the outside, nor understand another country until he somehow gets inside it, I have tried to combine both views in this account of what has happened to the British Empire since the thirteen colonies broke away from it.

I am indebted to so many scholars and friends for help in writing this book that a list of them would fill another. To all those who have read portions of the manuscript, I give my special thanks.

A. L. B.

University of Minnesota

Table of Contents

LIST OF MAPS

I THE ERA OF
THE AMERICAN REVOLUTION

Chapters

CHAPTER I

How the American Revolution Released a British Revolution

THERE IS something important about the American Revolution that recalls Shakespeare's famous comment upon mercy:

> *It is twice blest;*
> *It blesseth him that gives, and him that takes.*

Little did Americans think that by wresting liberty from Britain they would also confer it upon her. Yet this was the very thing they did. As children occasionally help their parents more by resisting them than by submitting to them, so did the thirteen colonies unwittingly rescue the mother country by their successful revolt against her. They rescued her from the stifling clutches of the king, thereby earning the gratitude of many Britons then, and more since, for the American war precipitated a British revolution. George III had hamstrung parliament and captured the cabinet. The British government was his government in fact as well as in name until the complete failure of his policy in America broke his power in Britain. Though he continued to reign, he could no longer rule, nor could any of his successors. This was a great revolution, but to understand it we have to glance back at what had been happening in the government of the country.

After a long struggle between king and parliament, in which one king lost his head and another his throne, the supremacy of parliament had been established at the end of the previous century. Then the struggle for power became one for the control of parliament, and the balance wavered between the two historic parties, the Whigs and the Tories. Then also the cabinet form of government began to take shape, not as the result of any theory but out of practical necessity.

Parliament did not claim the right to choose the king's ministers or to direct their actions. That was still recognized to be the king's business; but now he had to be careful how he did it, because the opposition of parliament could at any time bring the wheels of government to a full stop. To keep them going he had to have the continuing support of a majority in the legislature; and experience soon demonstrated that the only way he could carry on was by governing through ministers selected from the leaders of that majority.

Thus without any specific law requiring it—there is none to this day for the simple reason that none is needed—the executive, instead of being separated from the legislature, was embedded in it. Legally the ministers were responsible to the king, who appointed them and invested them with his powers of government; but practically the ministers were responsible to their fellow members of parliament for the way they exercised these powers. In other words, parliament, through its principal committee, conducted the government for the king. This became more apparent shortly after George I, a German prince, succeeded to the British throne in 1714. His predecessors had regularly presided over the meetings of the ministers, or cabinet, and so retained some personal influence. But the new king could not speak English, and therefore he early abandoned the practice of attending cabinet meetings. The precedent he thus established has never been broken, not even by his great-grandson George III.

The office of prime minister, the crowning feature of the cabinet system, could not arise until the departure of the king left a vacant seat at the head of the table. Though one of the ministers then had to preside, years passed before one came to dominate his colleagues. That was Sir Robert Walpole, who really ruled the land, for he was the leader of the legislature and the effective head of the executive. He was the first prime minister—and the last for a long time.

Strange as it may seem today, one of the chief accusations that were hurled at Walpole by the growing opposition in parliament, which finally forced his resignation by an adverse vote in 1742, was that he had made himself "prime and sole minister." Equally strange today appears a charge that he confidently aimed at his attackers to rout them. It was that their attempt to remove him, one of the king's servants, "without so much as alleging any particular crime against him," constituted "one of the greatest encroachments ever made on the prerogative of the Crown." Here we have the prime minister openly denouncing in parliament the first essential principle of cabinet government, and being himself denounced for introducing the second essential! Clearly the new system of government was far from being established. Indeed it ceased to develop and began to degenerate with the fall of Walpole.

During the next forty years, which brings us to the end of the American Revolution, the degeneration passed through two stages. Both were marked by the use of political jobbery—modern politicians prefer to call it patronage—to control parliament and, through parliament, to run the government. It had been used before, but never so thoroughly as during this period, when parliament virtually lost its independence. For the first two decades, a small number of baronial Whig families ruled the land. The ministries they formed had only nominal heads, sometimes improperly called prime ministers, and were as inefficient as they were corrupt. When at last the country stood in dire need of a strong and able man to direct the war that smashed the old French Empire, an overwhelming tide of public opinion forced the admission of the elder William Pitt into the cabinet. Yet one of the old crowd was still nominal head of the cabinet and real manager of the whole business of patronage.

The second stage began with the accession of George III in 1760, and it was worse than the first. He turned things upside down. Instead of being the puppet of his ministers, he made them his puppets. The Whig bosses had shown him how to do it—by patronage. That was the key to power, and by law it belonged to him. He took it back from the hands into which his predecessors had allowed it to fall, and he used it to break the Whig oligarchy and to put himself in their place.

By a most shameless distribution of rewards and punishments, George III built up his own party in parliament. It was composed of Tory remnants and Whig refuse, and was known as the King's Friends—"as if the body of the people were the king's enemies," said one of the leading writers of the day. With this block of votes at his command, the king could turn out of office any ministry he did not like. None suited him exactly until he got Lord North to form a government for him in 1770, the government against which America appealed to arms, the government that fought and lost the American war.

Now we are in a position to examine the British revolution that came at the end of the war. The war shattered George III's system of personal direction and control, and it freed parliament. This was of more momentous significance than it seems, unless we remember how the British constitution was formed.

Unlike the American Constitution, the British constitution was not the conscious creation of any body of men, nor was it ever set forth in a written document—and so it is spelled without a capital. The British constitution was an unconscious growth, and a slow one, taking its shape from the force of circumstances—like a tree, which accommodates its roots and branches to the room it finds in soil and air. No law established the cabinet or the office of prime minister; no law has ever defined them or their powers; no law has ever said they must be responsible to parliament. They just grew to be what they are. And so is it with the constitution as a whole, which is simply what worked and continued to work. But it did not always work as it does now.

George III's personal system, though a complete perversion of what we know as parliamentary and cabinet government, was working so well that it might have been established as the permanent constitution if the colonies had not revolted, or if their resistance had been crushed. Then Britain might have settled down to be ruled by the king draped in the robes of parliament, instead of by parliament draped in the robes of the king.

It is difficult for us to imagine that this might have occurred, because our whole thinking is so deeply colored by the established fact. But we should not forget that government by the people has been, and still is, a rather rare exception in the world. The eighteenth century was an age of absolute monarchy. It is true that since that time, during the hundred years between the fall of Napoleon and the outbreak of the First World War, parliaments at last became fashionable; but even then they were commonly used to cover the nakedness of irresponsible power. The Prussian diet, the German reichstag, the Russian duma, and the Japanese diet were striking examples. And after the First World War, a new generation of dictators arose who shamelessly scorned to wear anything but a bare minimum of clothing and sometimes discarded even that. We who have been born and nurtured in freedom are apt to think of ourselves as following the rule rather than the exception, or to thank God we are not as other men when we see the difference. In this, we are just like the British—and for that matter like other peoples too.

But to return to the point of our discussion, the liberty gained when one king lost his head and a second his throne was finally secured when a third lost his colonies; and so the British owe a tremendous debt to their American cousins, whose ancestors precipitated this British revolution. If some British are inclined to forget it, so are many of us inclined to forget an enormous debt over which the American Revolution has cast a veil—the debt we owe to earlier generations of Englishmen who, from the days of Magna Carta, slowly and painfully evolved the tradition of self-government and personal liberty that was transplanted to American soil by English colonists. There is something deeply satisfying in the sight of British liberty being unintentionally rescued by its American offspring.

The significance of this British revolution becomes more apparent when we look at it more closely and follow it through. Though many people in Britain, notably Edmund Burke and Charles James Fox, warmly sympathized with the American cause from the very beginning —as did many Americans with the British cause—the king and his policy were by no means unpopular at home until after the war began to turn against the British at Saratoga. Indeed it is very probable that if a democratic election could have been held at any time between 1770 and 1777, Lord North would have lost none of his large majority in parliament. At it was, he could count on the votes of members who were neither bought nor coerced—the not inconsiderable body of independent country gentlemen who would support any administration that was not too obviously incompetent. They were quite content with the royal management of parliament and direction of the government. Of course the Whigs, who formed the opposition, did not like it at all; but they were a divided and discouraged minority.

Such was the situation until growing failure in the conduct of the war discredited the government, as it would have discredited almost any government. The Whigs helped by a furious and sustained attack upon the royal policy for causing as well as mismanaging the war; and outside parliament—something that had never been seen in the country before—public meetings were held to demand reform that would cut at the roots of the king's evil system, and to thank the politicians who had tried to prevent or arrest the American war.

In the spring of 1780, a Whig member of the House of Commons moved "that the influence of the Crown has increased, is increasing, and ought to be diminished," and the resolution was carried. The country gentry were deserting to the opposition. In the following September the king suddenly dissolved parliament to repair his shaking majority; and he spent at least twice as much money on the ensuing election, so he told his minister, as he had on any other. Nor was this all he spent. Windsor was persuaded not to re-elect Admiral Keppel, a member of the opposition, after George III visited a local silk merchant's shop and there announced: "The queen wants a gown, wants a gown. No Keppel! No Keppel!"

Lord North hung on for another year and a half, subordinating his own judgment to that of the king; but he knew he was losing the political battle as well as the war. When the news of Yorktown hit him, he behaved as if he had been shot—throwing up his arms and repeatedly crying, "Oh, God! It is all over." It was nearly all over for him and his royal master. They suffered a worse defeat, if that were possible, early in March 1782, when the House of Commons adopted a resolution branding as enemies of the country all who should advise or attempt the further prosecution of the war in America. A fortnight later North resigned, and with him fell the king's personal system of government.

It was the third time the royal power had fallen, and now its revival was made impossible. This was the work of the Whigs, upon whom George III had to call to form a ministry. The party that had once taught him how to rule had since been taught by him that this was not the way to rule. It was too dangerous, and they promptly passed three much-needed reforms. One was a law excluding government contractors from the House of Commons, where North had bought too many votes with fat government jobs. A second limited the pension list and abolished a large number of salaried offices that required no real duties other than voting for the government. "Placemen," as those who held them were called, occupied a quarter of the seats in the lower house. The third reform disfranchised revenue officers, who had been required to vote for government candidates under pain of dismissal—a serious thing when they formed almost a sixth of the limited electorate and could swing the election in about seventy constituencies. These three measures effectively ended the flagrant corruption that had perverted the parliamentary system of government.

The reform of the system itself, to make it more representative of the nation, was also considered at this time. There was a certain public demand for it, expressed by renewed public meetings and by quite a number of petitions to the House of Commons; and within parliament it had strong advocates among the Whigs. But the majority of that party were opposed to it, and a succession of what might be called political accidents put it off for half a century. Yet the failure to change the basis on which the House of Commons was elected did not prevent an interesting and most important development in the government of the country.

The slow growth of the British constitution, which had only begun to take its modern shape in Walpole's day and then had been twisted out of all recognition, soon revived. The constitution, however, possessed no more than the potentialities of what it has since come to be. Though the king had lost his controlling power, he still exercised more than a little influence, which was recognized as quite proper; and the problem of how to carry on the government had yet to be worked out by experience. The legal theory did not fit the facts.

If we could go back and question intelligent Englishmen of that day about their constitution we should get many astonishing answers. They would tell us that it was the freest and best in the world, and that its supreme virtue lay in its mixture of the three historic principles underlying all government: monarchy, aristocracy (the House of Lords), and democracy (the House of Commons). They might also tell us something that would sound strangely familiar about the balance and separation of powers. America got the idea from Montesquieu, the most penetrating political philosopher of eighteenth century France, who took it from the English and thought it was the essence of their form of government. They still believed it was. But if we asked them to explain it, we should find ourselves suspecting that it was very like a divine mystery to them; and so it was. Indeed, not until well on in the nineteenth century were the facts of cabinet government so firmly established that a recognizable theory of its functioning was at last formulated. So we come to a conclusion that has startled many people: the British constitution, though compounded of ancient elements, is really more modern than the American, which, by the way, is much older than any other in the world today.

Political confusion followed the fall of the king's political system. For two years it continued, until a decisive general election cleared it up. Then at long last the development of parliamentary government was resumed under the leadership of a most remarkable young man, who definitely established the office of prime minister, gave the cabinet a solidity it had never possessed, and based his power upon a well-organized parliamentary majority supported by public opinion.

This man was William Pitt the younger. From his earliest years he had been carefully trained by his illustrious father for a parliamentary career, and this was his consuming ambition. While still a lad in his teens he haunted the gallery of the House of Commons, and he was already master of its ways when, at the age of twenty-one, family influence provided him with a seat in it. That was in January 1781, and almost at once his genius elevated him above his fellows.

After his first speech, one of his seniors called him "a chip of the old block," which immediately drew from one of the greatest members the retort: "He is not a chip of the old block: he is the old block itself!" Aligned with his late father's friends in opposition, he denounced the American war as "most accursed, wicked, barbarous, cruel, unnatural, unjust, and diabolical." In the summer of 1782, when only twenty-three, he became chancellor of the exchequer and government leader in the House of Commons. As no administration could remain long in office during this period of confusion, he was out again in the spring, but only for a few months.

In December 1783, when the king dismissed the next ministry, a strange and unpopular coalition of Fox and North, he called upon this young man of twenty-four to form a government. Pitt at once accepted though it meant severing his connection with most of the Whigs and facing a hostile majority in the House of Commons with the brilliant Charles James Fox to lead them. They regarded Pitt's taking office as "a boyish freak" and laughed at his "mince-pie administration which would end with the Christmas holidays," but they underestimated his courage and his ability. He fought them almost single-handed, for all the other members of his cabinet were in the House of Lords, where he had a safe majority; and the way he conducted himself won the admiration of the country as well as the eternal gratitude of the king, who loathed Fox as the inspired child of the devil.

In the general election that was held in the spring of 1784, the nation rallied back of Pitt, giving him a thumping majority; and "Fox's Martyrs" became a byword of derision. For seventeen more years Pitt remained in office—longer than any successor. When he resigned, it was over a difference not with parliament but with the king, whose will he would not cross; and then, after an interval of three years, public opinion thrust him back into office. He died, still in office, at the early age of forty-six. What a record! Is it any wonder that no other man had more, if as much, to do with shaping the constitution?

Pitt shaped the constitution—without, of course, being conscious of doing so—by working it as it had never been worked before, and getting better results. Until his day only one minister had ever made himself the real master of his colleagues, and he had been turned out of office with curses for having monopolized such power. During the forty years that elapsed between the fall of Walpole and the accession of the younger Pitt, the title of prime minister gathered respectability, but the men to whom it was given did not rule. Lord North refused the title. Pitt accepted it, and he soon packed it full of meaning. He made the office a permanent institution.

Thenceforth the cabinet was not just a collection of ministers picked from parliament to manage the executive departments of government, each more or less independent of the others; it was an organic body that was coordinated by its head, the prime minister. Far from being divided, as in the United States, all power was concentrated, and responsibility for its exercise was focused in this one man. As the real head of the executive, he was responsible for the administration of the laws. And he could never plead that the laws tied his hands, for he was also the real leader of the legislature and as such he was responsible for the making of the laws. Conversely, he could never excuse himself as the leader of the legislature for any faulty application of a law without condemning himself as head of the executive.

Many Americans have found it difficult to understand how such a strange system could work—just as many an Englishman has wondered how it was possible to get anything done under the American system with its separation of powers, its divided responsibility, and its dependence on the interpretation of the courts. Here we hit upon another striking and most fundamental difference between the two constitutions. When explained, it removes a common American obstacle to an understanding of the British system. No act of the British parliament is ever subjected to judicial review. That would be unthinkable to the people of Britain. Their courts naturally have to interpret the law as enacted by parliament, but they can never question its constitutional validity. The nation assembled in parliament is absolutely supreme. It can do anything except make a man a woman or a woman a man, as the old saying goes. Its nominal head is the king, but its effective head is the prime minister. Hence his enormous power.

Another peculiar feature of the British system, which further explains the position of the prime minister, is that general elections are not held at fixed intervals as in America. At any time parliament can be dissolved, which means that a new House of Commons has to be elected before parliament can sit again. There is, however, a legal limit to the life of any parliament, and it is set by its own act. For almost two centuries it was seven years, being reduced to the present limit of five years in 1911. Two parliaments have since extended their own lives—in the two World Wars, because the British did not wish to be upset by a general election in wartime—but the seven years of the older law were never exceeded until the Second World War.

From Pitt's day it has been the rule for the prime minister, acting through the king, to dissolve parliament whenever he sees fit, and this contributes greatly to the smooth working of the British system. It gives the prime minister a disciplinary check upon members of the House of Commons, for at any time he can turn them all out to face their electors. Pitt, however, had little if any occasion to crack this whip, which had always been in the hands of the king. At first glance it looks like a dangerous weapon in the hands of the prime minister, but it is not, for the House has a corresponding check upon him. By refusing to follow him, the Commons can force him out of office unless he, by appealing to the people in a general election, can get a new house that will follow him.

In practice, this balance of checks makes for greater and more continuous responsibility all round, and preserves the essential harmony between executive and legislature. Though the prime minister is thus all-powerful, and though he holds office for an indefinite period without ever being elected to it by the people, he can be removed at any time and not just at stated intervals. Some of Pitt's successors have not been able to last a year.

Pitt never lost the public confidence given him in the spring of 1784, but he recognized that this was not enough to maintain him in power. He freely admitted that he also had to have the royal confidence, a condition that did not pass away until the Reform Bill of 1832. Rarely, however, did the king interfere, as he did when he caused Pitt's one resignation by opposing the grant of the franchise to Roman Catholics. What kept the royal influence to a minimum was practical necessity; and, as we shall see in a later chapter, practical necessity finally eliminated it. This was characteristically British.

A cheap wit once said that statesmen can be distinguished from politicians by the fact that the former are dead. It is doubtful if this was any truer in Pitt's day than it is in ours. He was a great statesman and a consummate politician. Though he entered public life as a Whig, his position as prime minister rested upon the support of the Tory party, which he recreated in 1784. No longer did it stand, as it had done, for the controlling power of the Crown; and not yet had it become what the French Revolution made it, a party of blind reaction.

Pitt was by nature a reformer. When he came into power he was already known as the most hopeful champion of parliamentary reform, and as such he won the votes of many independent electors in the spring of 1784. But the politician in him doubted whether he could persuade parliament to reform its electoral system, even if he made this the issue in a new general election; and so, after an ineffectual effort to introduce reform in the following year, he dropped the subject.

Another reform that he espoused, with much greater persistence, was the abolition of the slave trade. It was Pitt who directed Wilberforce, his old Cambridge friend and fellow member of the Commons, to lead the cause and thereby win fame. It was Pitt's parliamentary committee whose investigations lifted the lid off the traffic and let loose an awful smell. This helped him to pass an act curbing the abuses of the trade; and it inspired several bills, including one of his own, to suppress it entirely. He dared not make it a government measure, on which he would stand or fall, for the West Indian planters' influence was too strong in parliament and even in the cabinet. As it was, his pressing for this reform alienated quite a number of his followers. It was not until 1807, the year after his death, that the cause finally triumphed.

Pitt was also a firm believer in the gospel according to Adam Smith. In 1785 he strove, though unsuccessfully, to establish free trade with Ireland, a subject that we shall discuss by itself; and in the following year he concluded with France a treaty that went very far in this direction and he jammed the implementing legislation through parliament, stirring bitter cries that still have a familiar ring.

But the great fame of Pitt the reformer springs from a Herculean task that he achieved. He found the administration of the country a veritable Augean stable, and he cleansed it. Public funds to the amount of £40,000,000 had not been accounted for. Officials had continued from year to year, and died or otherwise departed, without closing their accounts, which were audited loosely or not at all. This was only one manure pile he removed.

The tariff was a tangled mess, a single article being burdened with numerous customs duties, each of which was paid into a separate fund, requiring multiple bookkeeping. He swept away this hopeless complexity and confusion by imposing a single duty to be paid into one consolidated fund, on which the national debt was secured. Hence the British abbreviation "consols" for government bonds.

Wholesale smuggling was robbing the country of £2,000,000 a year, when the revenue was only £14,000,000. Tea was already a national institution, and more than half of it never saw a customs officer, except when he drank it, so small was the risk and so great the profit of importing it illegally. This ceased to pay when Pitt passed a "hovering act" for the confiscation of suspected vessels within four leagues of the coast and when he cut the tea duty from 119 per cent to 12.5 per cent; and then the many things that had floated in with the illicit tea had to come the proper way, encouraged by Pitt's reduction of other excessive duties.

By these and a host of other drastic reforms, Pitt substituted an annual surplus of £1,000,000 for an annual deficit of £3,000,000; he increased the revenue to £22,000,000, with scarcely any addition to the cost of collection; he restored the public credit, which had fallen so low that government bonds were quoted at 56 in 1783; and he helped Britain to recover from the strain of the last war and prepare for the much more terrible strain of the next one, which killed him.

Pitt also purified public life by purging it of many means of corruption that the reforming Whigs had left untouched. For example, he abolished a whole batch of sinecures that he accumulated by not filling them when they fell vacant. Such measures cut down the patronage that was at the government's disposal, and anyone who has even dabbled in politics knows that patronage has its uses as well as its abuses. The politician therefore had to find some substitute.

Pitt found this substitute in the generous distribution of peerages and lesser honors, for which he has been criticized. Though dukes did not fall to the Gilbertian low of "two a penny," all honors were more or less cheapened. We may dismiss as of no consequence the conferring of minor honors for political ends; but we cannot ignore the creation of peers for that purpose, because it gave them seats in the House of Lords and so affected that body. Pitt increased its size by more than half, he reduced the average of its intelligence, and he completely transformed its character. He found it a Whig preserve and he left it a Tory stronghold. It has never recovered from what he did to it.

Looking back over this British revolution that the American Revolution precipitated, we see a new form of government evolving that was not to be limited to that country. It has since been copied by freedom-loving people in other lands, and nowhere more successfully than in the British colonial empire. But before we examine what the American Revolution did to this empire, it will be well to notice another contemporary revolution that was to transform the mother country and the new empire that grew in the nineteenth century.

CHAPTER II

New Life in Old England

BRITISH PRESTIGE reached its lowest ebb at the end of the American Revolution. The loss of the best part of the empire seemed positive proof that Britain's day was done. European observers were convinced that it was, and many Englishmen thought so too. The national self-confidence was rudely shaken, and everybody knows that Englishmen do not easily lose their self-confidence. Yet the days of British greatness, far from being ended, were about to begin. New life was stirring in the land, new life that was to make Britain lead the world.

A silent revolution, which had nothing to do with the American Revolution, was transforming the life of the country into something new and dynamic. The process, which had commenced long before and was to gather marvelous momentum in the nineteenth century, was at this time becoming quite noticeable. Modern industrial society was being born, and it is a striking fact that this occurred in England long before it did elsewhere—half a century or more.

Why were all other countries so far behind England in working out this new phase of our western civilization? Part of the answer is to be found in the French Revolution, which generally retarded industrial development on the continent and stimulated it in England. But this European upheaval merely magnified the lead that England had already gained and was increasing. Her advantage was clearly demonstrated in her commercial relations with the infant United States.

What made many Englishmen fear that they had passed their peak as a nation was not only the loss of the war and the loss of their colonies but also the loss of their rich American trade, which they thought was almost sure to follow. It was therefore most encouraging for them to discover that peace restored this trade. Indeed, with the exception of a few particulars in which European rivals supplanted England, it was soon brisker than ever. Why? Because she had the best industries in the world and there were practically none in America; because Americans demanded credit, which her merchants could and did give, as Europeans could not; and because she offered the best market for American produce. But what enabled her to gain this advantage?

One important factor was natural resources. England had a better combination of them than was to be found under any one government on the continent of Europe. She had long produced the best wool that was known. Her rivers and streams provided power adequate to the needs of the day and, what was then of great importance, water of a quality best suited for the manufacture of textiles, which has always been one of the world's greatest industries. For this particular purpose, also, even the climate was an asset, for in certain parts of England the atmosphere contained the optimum amount of moisture. England also had as good pottery and china clays as had been found anywhere, and she possessed an abundance of coal and iron. Though these last two items had not yet assumed anything like the massive proportions of the twin pillars supporting nineteenth century industrialism, they were already beginning to play that essential role. But all these things together would have been of little avail if there had not been something else.

Private enterprise had much greater freedom in England than on the continent, thanks to the nature of society and of government in the little island. English society was not, like that of Europe, divided into watertight compartments, hereditary castes. All the sons of a continental noble were nobles too and could never touch business lest it contaminate their lily-white hands; whereas in England all but the eldest son were commoners and were destined to remain commoners, and there was no corresponding social stigma attached to money making. As the great Dr. Johnson once remarked, English primogeniture had the advantage of making only one fool in the family. Coming down the scale, we find that commerce and industry had long since escaped from the monopolistic control of the surviving mediaeval guilds in England, but not on the continent; and that the people living on the land had been emancipated from feudalism in England as they had not been on the continent.

Equally great was the difference in government. European society had fallen under the bondage of absolute monarchy since the close of the middle ages, while the overthrow of the despotic Stuart rulers had effectively ended the central government's attempt to control and regu-

late the economic life of England. It is therefore not in the least surprising that continental visitors were most surprised by the spirit of
freedom that pervaded eighteenth century England. Moreover, since
the union of England and Scotland to form the kingdom of Great
Britain, this was the largest free trade area in the Old World. Germany
and Italy were still divided into many small fragments, and countless
internal customs barriers clogged the economic life of France and
Spain.

The economic revolution that was transforming life in England was
threefold. An agricultural revolution went hand in hand with the
industrial revolution, each supporting the other when they got going.
Agriculture supplied the food and the labor needed in industrial centers, and in return was accelerated by the growing appetite of the new
industrial towns. These two revolutions were scarcely under way when
a third began—one in transportation, without which the other two
would have been stunted—and then all three helped one another along.

The mainspring of the agricultural revolution was the enterprise of
great landlords—the country gentry and the nobility, who wanted to
improve their estates. Here we notice a great difference from the
society of France, then the leading European state, a much bigger and
wealthier country, with a population about three times that of England
in the 1780's. The larger landlords in France were not at all interested
in their estates, on which they seldom resided, except as a source of
revenue to support them in the luxurious life of the royal court. They
scorned country life as a boorish existence, and they seldom traveled
abroad. The English upper classes, on the other hand, loved life in
the country, where they spent most of their time. They also loved travel
on the continent, where as young men just out of college they habitually went on a grand tour of a year or two.

One of the most fruitful improvements ever made in the production
of field crops came as an inspiration to an English gentleman watching
Frenchmen cultivating the soil between their vines. Why not sow the
seed in rows and hoe between the rows? It would save seed and produce a richer harvest. So he invented a drill and a horse hoe. That
was Jethro Tull in the first quarter of the eighteenth century, but it
was a long time before his new method became common. A few years
before Tull's death, in the second quarter of the century, an English
nobleman was kicked out of the cabinet by Walpole, and the expelled
lord took his revenge on the soil. Much of his estate was a miserable
waste, but in Holland he had seen men make something of just such

land. He did the same with his own, dressing the sandy stretches with marl, adopting the seed drill and the horse hoe, working out a new and better rotation of crops, and introducing the turnip. This kept the land clean, supported more stock, and gave him the name "Turnip" Townshend. In the third quarter of the century another gentleman farmer, Robert Bakewell, produced such phenomenal results by his experiments in mating carefully selected sheep, cattle, and horses that he became famous as the father of modern animal breeding.

The example set by these and many other innovators made experimental farming a fashionable hobby in the early years of George III's reign, and the king himself pursued it so enthusiastically on his Windsor estate that he was called "Farmer George." Unlike most other hobbies in which only wealthy men can indulge, experimental farming was profitable and patriotic as well as pleasurable. It put England ahead of the rest of the world in scientific agriculture.

The one great obstacle that blocked the general adoption of the new methods was being cleared away. This was the ancient arrangement of the village, the normal agricultural community. Most of the land was owned by the villagers and not by the squire or lord, whose hall stood off to one side of their cluster of cottages, though he was by far the largest holder. Behind the dwellings lay the arable land in great open fields, divided into acre strips by lines of unplowed turf, and each inhabitant's land was scattered all over in separate strips. Beyond was the uncultivated waste, on which each inhabitant had the right to pasture stock in rough proportion to the number of strips he owned. The intermingled ownership of the strips made it impossible for a man to do what he liked with his own land. It had to be worked according to a common system, which required the cooperation of all and was regulated by custom. As the system could be changed only by general agreement, one obstinate villager—an eternal breed—could prevent the introduction of new crops and techniques. Similarly the right of common pasture allowed a promiscuity among beasts that was the despair of the disciples of Bakewell.

To clear the way for improvements in the growing of crops and the raising of stock, there came a reshuffling of the ownership of the land to give each holder a compact block which he could enclose and use as he liked. This is known as the enclosure movement. It had been going on for a long time, at first very slowly because for each village the consent of all who had a stake in the village was required. Then a new device was found—a private act of parliament to reapportion the lands of a village. This was easy to get when interest in agricultural improvements became fashionable, for the members of parliament were themselves large landowners who stood to gain most by the change. Around the time of the American Revolution such acts were being passed at the rate of forty a year—ten times as many as a generation or so before—and this rate was soon doubled.

This agricultural revolution, which made for much greater efficiency, improved the lot of some villagers, but not of the majority. It shook them down to a lower economic and social level, and many of them it shook out entirely. Few small holders had the money to pay for enclosing their land, and fewer still the capital and knowledge to improve it. Those who could not take advantage of the new arrangement sold out to those who could, and the many sank to be mere agricultural laborers for hire or drifted off to the towns. The few rose to be capitalist farmers, and the one man who could afford most got most—the man who lived in the hall. This was characteristic of the coming age, in which the rich grew richer and the poor poorer. Rural society was splitting. The old system had fostered the community spirit and protected the small man, but this old system was going because it penalized enterprise.

Turning to the industrial revolution, we find that the first great lead came in the making of textiles, and there particularly in cotton. The beginning was an invention that recalls what every woman knows, though she may not be able to explain it. By far the commonest width of woven fabrics has been three quarters of a yard. The measure is many centuries old, being the limit around which a weaver could reach when he had to pass the shuttle through the warp by hand. For anything wider he had to have another man to help him—until 1733, when John Kay, a maker of loom parts, invented the flying shuttle, which was flipped from side to side along a board. The use of the flying shuttle spread very slowly, like contemporary improvements in agriculture. One important reason was that it constricted an industrial bottleneck that was already bad, for one weaver had required the output of several spinners to keep him busy and now he would require more.

In spite of all the efforts of Kay and many others, spinning did not catch up until a generation later. Then James Hargreaves, a weaver, patented his spinning jenny, a sort of multiple spinning wheel that produced eight, and soon many more threads at once. The jenny was so simple and so easy to turn that a child could operate it. About the same time Richard Arkwright, a wig maker who stole other people's ideas and ultimately became a millionaire factory owner, produced his "water frame," so called from the power that ran it, which employed rollers to spin a finer and firmer thread, much desired in weaving. Within a decade, in the midst of the American war, Samuel Crompton, a spinner who used the jenny, crossed it with the water frame and got the spinning mule, which combined the best features of both parents.

Now the balance was upset the other way, since all weaving was still done with the hand loom. The industry needed a power loom badly, and this came from an unexpected source. One day a country parson named Edmund Cartwright, a literary man who had never seen a loom in his life, heard some despondent manufacturers say that a power loom could not be made. Roused by the challenge, he made one himself with the aid of a cabinetmaker and a smith, and he patented it in 1785. That was only a few months after a copper-plate printer invented the cylindrical printing of cotton goods, which was incidentally the origin of the process now used in turning out our newspapers. Another fundamental innovation followed in 1786, when chemical bleaching was introduced.

In the manufacture of pottery, England could not compare with the continent until the industry was revolutionized by Josiah Wedgwood, by far the greatest and most influential figure in the whole history of the business. At the tender age of nine this son of a potter left school to learn the family trade, and when he established his own works twenty years later, in 1759, his original mind and his ceaseless experimentation began to bring startling results. He was ever trying out new clays, new glazes, new ovens, new firing controls, new colors, new designs, new artists, new perfection. He was blessed by poor and rich alike. He supplied the cottages of the former with dishes that were cheap as well as serviceable, something they had never had before; and he furnished the mansions of the wealthy with finer and more artistic wares than they had ever seen, wares of all kinds from dinner sets to snuff boxes and cameos. His London showroom was a fashionable resort; and the European fame of his products was such that Catherine the Great of Russia ordered from him a service of nearly a thousand pieces, each depicting a different English scene.

Iron was also coming into its own in England, though at the beginning of the century she had been lagging behind the Continent in this industry. Charcoal was then necessary for smelting, and England's supply of this fuel was disappearing with the exhaustion of her forests. Then a small local ironmaster came to the rescue, Abraham Darby, the first of three of that name. He discovered that he could use coal by coking it, and later without coking it. Around the middle of the century his son, Abraham Darby II, developed this newer method with great success when he harnessed water to provide a more powerful blast. His son, Abraham Darby III, made no striking improvement in production; but in 1779 he pointed the way to future expansion by building the first iron bridge, something that would have been inconceivable only a few years before.

Of the many large iron works that had by this time grown with the introduction of improved methods, perhaps the most famous was that established in 1760 by an English physician in Scotland. This foundry of Dr. John Roebuck on the little river Carron made a specialty of turning out guns. It was the birthplace of the "carronade," which was adopted by the British navy during the American war and afterward by other navies, including the American.

It was immediately after that war that Henry Cort gave the iron industry two big boosts. One was the introduction of grooved rollers operating in pairs, which squeezed out the dross and formed the hot metal into plates or rods or rails or other desired shapes. The other was simplifying the conversion of the brittle cast iron into the tougher wrought iron and steel. Cort did this by devising the reverberatory puddling furnace, in which a flame was made to play upon the iron from above and the molten metal was stirred so that the surplus carbon was burned out of it.

Power was of course necessary to make the iron industry what it had become, and the steam engine could not have become what it already was without the earlier improvements in the production of iron. The steam engine was not fathered by the legendary teakettle, nor was it conceived by James Watt sitting by the fire. It was a child of the mines, born a generation before Watt was.

Around 1700, when the shallow mines of England were being exhausted and the traditional pump could not cope with flooding at lower levels, the operators were saved from ruin by the invention of a pump worked by steam power. A vertical cylinder open at its upper end was fitted with a piston, which was pushed up by steam injected below the piston. Then the steam was cut off and cold water from a cistern above was squirted into the cylinder, condensing the steam within to form a vacuum that pulled the piston down. This Newcomen engine, so called after the blacksmith who made the original model, was soon at work all over the coal fields, for there it was quite indispensable. But nowhere else was it indispensable, or of any use at all. The power it developed was not worth the fuel it devoured, except at a pit head.

What Watt did, more than half a century afterward, was to take this crude device and make a real engine out of it. He was able to do this because he was no ordinary man. This son of a Scottish ship-wright first attracted attention as the maker of scientific instruments in the University of Glasgow. Determined to improve upon what had been done anywhere, he mastered three foreign languages to learn what had been done abroad; but the wide knowledge he gained was as nothing compared with his rare scientific attainment. As a mechanical engineer, he was the wizard of the age.

Watt began to work upon the Newcomen engine about 1763 and within twenty years, by dint of many inventions, he gave us the modern steam engine. By adding a separate condenser, he eliminated the enormous waste of cooling and reheating the cylinder each time the piston moved back and forth. By closing the open end of the cylinder and injecting steam there too, he made half an engine into a whole one, and he made it work much faster. By converting the straight motion within the cylinder to a circular one outside, he endowed the engine with almost infinite possibilities. Of his less notable but still very important inventions, we may notice two that he made quite early. One was steam-tight packing for pistons and piston rods, and the other was the method of preserving the heat of the cylinder by enclosing the cylinder in a steam jacket with insulation on the outside.

Watt built his first engine for Roebuck of the Carron works, who provided the capital in return for a share in the profits on the engine. But it was not successful. The best mechanics could not yet produce a true cylinder; and the packing of the piston could not make up for a variation of nearly half an inch in diameter. When Roebuck failed, he turned over his interest in the steam engine, which Watt had pat-ented, to an enterprising creditor. This was Matthew Boulton, whose iron works at Soho near Birmingham had recently become famous. Watt and his engine Beelzebub migrated to Soho in 1774, the very year when true cylinders became possible with the invention of an im-proved borer for cannon; and the new firm of Boulton and Watt began the new industry of manufacturing steam engines. At first the engines were used chiefly for pumping, particularly in Cornwall where they rescued the tin mines from drowning; but in 1785 they began to be used in industry generally.

The third revolution, that in inland transportation, was likewise the work of private enterprise, but it was not unique, as were the agricultural and industrial revolutions. In the 1780's there was still, as there had long been, a much better road and canal system in France, where the government had assumed responsibility. Yet without the new English system, there would have been much less profit in improved agricultural production and England's industrial development would have been stunted.

In 1760 England had not a single canal; and most of the roads, left to the care of negligent local authorities, were in a shocking state. A road was often "a mere horse track across a miry common, or a watery hollow lane twisting between high banks." Once a whole hunting party chased a stag over the top of a loaded wagon without touching the vehicle. It was not uncommon in winter for communication between districts to be halted for months at a time. Indeed, the roads were generally so bad that the usual means of inland transportation was the backs of horses or donkeys, not wheels. Imagine coal, grain, ironware, potteries, and cloth having to be "shipped" this way! Small wonder Wedgwood threw much of his remarkable public spirit into agitating for road improvements and canal construction!

Here and there a turnpike road had been built by a private company that collected tolls for its use; but it was not until this time that turnpike roads began to be common. They now began to multiply so fast that a law was passed in 1773 to obviate the necessity of a separate act of parliament for each one. The general condition of the roads was much improved by the end of the next decade. The metaled surface had yet to be invented by Macadam but a better solution of England's transportation problem had already been found.

England's first canal was opened in 1761 and was only seven miles long. It connected Manchester with the collieries of the Duke of Bridgewater. This progressive nobleman, on finding that the cost of getting his coal to Manchester in sacks on the backs of horses was nine or ten shillings a ton, had the canal built at his own expense. The construction was quite a feat for, among other difficulties, the new waterway had to be carried over a river by means of an aqueduct about forty feet high; but the man who planned and executed it was a genius, though he could neither read nor write—Richard Brindley. The great success of this canal, which cut the Manchester price of coal in half, encouraged the duke to have Brindley extend the canal to the Mersey River, thus connecting Manchester with Liverpool and reducing freight rates between them to one sixth of what land carriers charged.

These wonders worked by the combination of Bridgewater's "brass" and Brindley's brains inaugurated the great canal-building era in England. Before the illiterate genius died in 1772, he designed nearly four hundred miles of canals; and by the end of the next decade little England had between two and three thousand miles of canals, the digging of which has given us the name "navvy," because the armies of men who toiled with pick and shovel were working on the navigation system. What railways did for America in the last hundred years, canals did for England in this earlier day. They opened the country and made its development possible. Over the network of artificial waterways, the bulkiest and the heaviest freight of the new industrial era was easily and cheaply borne by long barges drawn by horses on the towpaths.

England was being made over into a new country. The old and relatively stable order was undergoing a rapidly accelerated change. Things were in a state of flux, new developments were coming thick and fast, and the future offered boundless opportunities. A new creative spirit was abroad in the land. It makes one think of the spirit that permeated American society several generations afterward, in the most expansive years of the nineteenth century when immigrants and capital were pouring into the United States, when the West was filling with a rush, and when giant industries were springing up in the East to supply the demands of the enormous new domestic market.

Yet the earlier English experience was in a way even more remarkable; for England got no new population, no new capital from other lands, and it had no West. It was an old country and a small one. But its own inventive genius was ushering in a new age in the history of the world: the age of machines, the age of power, the age of marvelous production, the age of phenomenal wealth, the great age of individual enterprise. Of course England had to pay the price of the pioneer, as we shall see, but the complicated social and political problems produced by maturing industrialism had not begun to press, and the dead weight of the older society was gone in this transitional period when a new England was arising—at the very time when a new America was finding its feet. The average educated Englishman, however, had little confidence in the future when the empire, built by several generations of his people until it was greater than any rival, had just crashed in ruins.

CHAPTER III

Fragments of Empire

THE AMERICAN REVOLUTION had an effect upon the British colonial empire that was the very opposite of what it had upon the mother country. It turned back the hands of the clock. Generations were to pass before the empire was again as large, as mature, and as self-governing as it had been; and a reactionary colonial policy prevailed for more than half a century. How greatly the development of the empire was set back, we may see by observing that the old empire had grown ripe for some such fundamental change as that which has only recently produced the British Commonwealth of Nations.

The reduction in the size of the empire is striking. What was left in 1783 was almost entirely confined to the North American continent and its neighboring islands. True, the East India Company had begun to establish British rule in India, but as yet it had acquired scarcely more than a foothold in that subcontinent; and the only other British possessions in the whole of the eastern hemisphere were two square miles of rock known as Gibraltar, and a small handful of trading posts on the west coast of Africa which had little or no value except to America, since they existed to supply slave labor for plantations in the New World. The Negro colony of Sierra Leone was not begun until 1787, when a few hundred blacks discharged from the army and navy were planted at Freetown. South Africa still belonged to the Dutch; it was not until 1786 that a merchant captain raised the British flag in Penang, from which the Straits Settlements grew in later years; and all of Australia was a no man's land until, as a by-product of the American Revolution,[1] the convict settlement of New South Wales was

---

[1] Convicts had been deported to the southern colonies, where they fetched about £10 a head.

founded in 1788. The British empire was still an American empire, but its solid central body had been torn away, leaving behind only the outlying fragments, the disjointed northern and southern extremities, British North America and the British West Indies.

Britain had come very close to losing all her West Indies, but not by their revolt. Though they felt much sympathy for the American cause, it was physically impossible for them to join in the Revolution. They were individually too weak and too isolated, and no effective American aid could have reached them. What nearly broke their British connection was foreign conquest, for it should not be forgotten that the American war grew into a world war in which Britain fought without any ally against a ring of enemies. Of these, France was by far the strongest; her naval strength was then at its peak, while that of Britain, though not neglected or mismanaged as much as tradition has asserted, was not yet near its peak. French sea power was therefore able to tip the scales of war against the British. The result was not only the crowning American victory of Yorktown but also the French capture of island after island in the West Indies until Britain held only Jamaica, Barbados, and Antigua in the early spring of 1782. A combined French and Spanish expedition was on the way to conquer Jamaica, the biggest and strongest of these three surviving colonies, when Admiral Rodney intercepted and broke up the French fleet in the "Battle of the Saintes" between Guadeloupe and Dominica. That turned the tide in those waters, but the damage then inflicted on the French fleet was not sufficient to establish the supremacy of British sea power. The French navy was still so strong that, as Mahan has pointed out, France might have been able to keep her island conquests at the peace settlement, already being negotiated, if her treasury had not become so hopelessly bankrupt. What Britain had lost in the West Indies as a consequence of French naval strength she was able to recover at the peace table as a consequence of French financial weakness—all save Tobago, which she recovered finally in 1803.

The British West Indies on the morrow of the American Revolution included the Bahamas, an archipelago of small islands strung out for 630 miles along a line between Florida and Haiti; most of the Leeward Islands, beginning with the Virgins, just east of Puerto Rico, and ending with Dominica, 300 miles to the southeast; to the south again, the Windward Islands of St. Vincent, the Grenadines, and Grenada; Barbados, off by itself, 150 miles to the east; and 1,200 miles to the west, just south of Cuba, the island of Jamaica, which had a few small outlying dependencies. Most of the islands were known as "old colonies," having been acquired by England in the second and third quarters of the previous century—all by settlement except Jamaica and the Virgin group, which had been taken from the Spaniards and the Dutch respectively. The remainder were known as the "ceded islands," which Britain had gained from the French by conquest during the Seven Years' War and by formal cession at the close of it—Dominica and the Windwards.

The total area of all the British West Indies was about 10,000 square miles, of which Jamaica, by far the largest, accounted for nearly 4,300 and the Bahamas nearly 4,500. The most thickly settled was Barbados, which had early been a base for the colonization of other islands. Its 166 square miles contained about 16,000 whites and 55,000 blacks. The most populous of all these colonies was, of course, Jamaica, which had approximately 18,000 whites and 215,000 blacks. Of the other islands, the largest populations were in three of the Leewards: Antigua, with some 40,000, more than 90 per cent of them black; Dominica, about 3,500 whites and 20,000 blacks; and St. Christopher, better known as St. Kitts, which had about 5,000 whites and four times as many blacks. The Bahamas were the most sparsely settled, and at the close of the war their population was some 4,000. With the arrival of the Loyalists, mostly southern planters accompanied by their slaves, the population of the Bahamas leaped to 10,000, only a third of which were whites. These newcomers introduced cotton cultivation, which was the staple industry of the colony for the next quarter of a century. Jamaica attracted the only other considerable Loyalist migration to the West Indies. This migration was likewise from the planter South and so brought twice as many slaves as whites. These newcomers were two or three times as numerous as those in the Bahamas. They wrought no corresponding change in Jamaica, however, for they added only a small minority to its population. A few of them tried to raise indigo, and some of them coffee; but they were only repeating the rather discouraging experience of other Jamaican planters.[2]

Sugar was king and his rule was a curse. With the exception of the Bahamas, the soil of which was not suitable for the growth of cane, the British West Indies were given over almost entirely to the pro-

---

[2] W. H. Siebert, *The Legacy of the American Revolution to the British West Indies and the Bahamas* (Columbus, Ohio, 1913).

duction of sugar. The reasons for this specialization lie in the fiscal arrangements of the mother country, which gave to British Caribbean sugar—but to no alternative crop—a monopoly in the home market, and then milked this monopoly through the collection of heavy customs duties on the sugar.[3] Not all the profits of the monopoly, extracted from consumers in the mother country in the form of higher prices than prevailed in France and other continental countries, were gathered into the British Treasury. Enough was left to the planters to keep the precious sugar flowing—and the curse operating.

British colonization in the West Indies had long since been blighted. Time was—in the previous century—when these islands contained a population that was predominantly white and considerably larger than that of the mainland colonies. Now the slave population of these same islands was well over 400,000, the white about 50,000; and the former was swelling while the latter was shrinking, for sugar fostered slavery. The small freeholders had been pretty well crowded out by large estates owned by single families and worked by gangs of servile labor, and the planters themselves were disappearing from the islands. Most of those who could afford it—and many who could not—were living in England, where the amenities of life were much more abundant. There they spent all the income they could drain from their West Indian estates through agents who had no interest in preserving the property and less in improving it. The plantations were running down, the soil was running down, the society was running down, the West Indies were running down.

The deepening shadow cast by sugar had also perverted the nature of British political institutions in the West Indies. These colonies all had assemblies, the largest with about two dozen members; and these assemblies, which had been democratic when they were established in the early days of British settlement, came to be filled with slaveowners. As might be expected, the councils, which were never intended to be democratic, were also soon dominated by slaveowners. Government of free men by free men had degenerated into government of slaves by their masters. Because the whites were a small minority of the population, they were haunted by a feeling of insecurity. This bred fear, and fear bred cruelty; and because their minority position was steadily growing worse, so was this reaction. According to Adam Smith, it was

---

[3] The tariff also blocked the development of a refining industry in the colonies, the rate on the finished article being prohibitive — for the benefit of the London refiners.

generally conceded that the evil institution was not so evil in the French sugar colonies, where, under an "arbitrary" form of government, the planters neither enacted nor administered the laws, as they did in the British colonies. It should also be observed that government in these colonies was being more or less crippled by the absentee habits of assemblymen, councilors, and other local functionaries, and by the growing difficulty of finding residents who were fit for public office.

That Great Britain should curb rather than encourage self-government in her West Indian colonies was obviously in the interest of the large black majority and even of the little white minority, though the latter could not see it, for slavery corrupts the masters no less than the slaves. As slavery was already beginning to trouble the conscience of the mother country—and was to trouble it more as the years passed by—imperial control over the governments of these colonies was bound to grow tighter. Of course this outside interference was resented, but resistance by force was out of the question. Being small and divided, and sprinkled widely over the sea, the colonies were helpless against the power on which they were dependent for protection not only against foreign foes, who had convenient bases all around them, but also against a domestic upheaval of blacks, the worst nightmare of all. The economy of these islands also bound them tightly to the mother country. If they lost the monopoly of the British sugar market, they would face financial ruin. The best the planters could do to guard their interests was to buy their way into parliament, which was then possible, and there work in combination with the wealthy British merchants who handled the West Indian trade. Already there was a strong West Indian pressure group in England, and it exerted a powerful political influence until the purge of parliament by the great reform of 1832.[4]

One small fragment of the British Empire in the New World was neither in the West Indies nor in British North America. This was Bermuda, or the Bermudas, for it is a little cluster of islands with an area of not quite twenty square miles, a population of scarcely 15,000, and the second oldest colonial assembly, dating from shortly after that of Virginia. Tobacco had once been the mainstay of the Bermudian colony of freeholders; but agriculture had long been neglected and left to slaves, while the white settlers took to building ships and trading in American waters, the principal article of com-

---

[4] L. J. Ragatz, *The Fall of the Planter Class in the Caribbean, 1763–1833* (New York, 1928).

merce being salt from the Bahamas and Turks Islands. At the close
of the Revolutionary War, the prosperity and population of Bermuda
began to decline, and a whole century was to pass before they were
up again to where they had been.

British North America in 1783 comprised the old Province of
Quebec, not to be confused with the modern province of that name,
though it covered much the same territory; Nova Scotia, which then
included what soon became New Brunswick; the Island of Saint John,
now Prince Edward Island; Newfoundland; and Rupert's Land, or the
domain of the Hudson's Bay Company. These British possessions were
as different as they could be from the West Indies. The latter belonged
to the past, the former to the future. The tropical climate had forced,
and the small size of the islands had cramped, the growth of the Caribbean colonies, and their value was steadily falling. Nevertheless, they
were then worth many times the whole of British North America,
which had not yet begun to disclose the enormous potentialities in its
continental expanse. Because these northern parts of the empire in
America were the land of the future, they merit closer attention; and
because there was much more diversity between them than between
the British West Indies, it is impossible to describe them collectively.

The territory of the Hudson's Bay Company was a vast land of
emptiness. It was a commercial game preserve that stretched from the
Rockies to the Atlantic and from the frozen Arctic to the northern
parts of the present Minnesota and North Dakota, for it was coexten-
sive with the drainage basin of Hudson Bay and Strait. The monopoly
of the trade, the ownership of the land, and the right of government
throughout all this region were vested in this company of London
merchants by its royal charter which the first governor or head of the
company, Prince Rupert, had procured from his cousin Charles II in
1670. But as yet the land had no value; the government was merely
what was necessary for the management of the company's servants, and
the fur trade was all that mattered. The only reason white men were
in this wild country was to get the pelts gathered by the Indians, and
there were many traders there who had nothing to do with this English
company. The establishment of the company had commenced the historic rivalry between the fur trade based on Hudson Bay and the fur
trade already based on the St. Lawrence, a bitter struggle that ended
only a century and a half afterward with the complete victory of the
former in 1821.

It was now half a century since French traders, who could not recognize the English charter, had penetrated beyond their rivals into the richer fur region of the West, along the Saskatchewan. The conquest of Canada checked this invasion. It was soon renewed more vigorously, however, by British enterprise, which was attracted to Montreal by visions of fortunes in furs and was equally scornful of the old charter. Then the Canadian trade also indulged in fierce internal competition, which caused much liquor and not a little blood to flow in the West, until the Montreal leaders ended this fratricidal strife in 1784 by combining their interests in the North West Company.

This new Canadian company, possessing a driving power and a ruthless efficiency seldom if ever surpassed in the later history of business corporations in America, roused the old English company to fight for its life. Within a decade the intense competition between them planted fur-trading posts along the waterways of the far Northwest, even beyond the watershed of Hudson Bay. It was spreading British influence and control over this immense no man's land and was laying the foundations for the Canadian acquisition of the West nearly a century afterward. As the only way into the country was over Hudson Bay or the long canoe trail from Montreal, no settlement was yet possible, nor any real government. The white men were ruled by their respective companies, and neither organization attempted to exercise jurisdiction over the red men.

Newfoundland was little more developed than Rupert's Land in 1783. Ten years afterward it was described by William Knox, former undersecretary of state, as "a great English ship moored near the Banks during the fishing season for the convenience of fishermen." The mother country had long discouraged settlement there, lest it undermine the fishing industry conducted from England; and the land itself was too rocky and barren to offer a living by agriculture. All its population of 15,000, chiefly Irish, lived along the coast on the southeast corner of the island; and fishing, principally cod, was almost the sole occupation. There was no settled government in the colony. An admiral or other naval officer of approximate rank held a commission as governor for three or four years, but he resided there only for some four months in the summer when fishing activities were at their height. He had power to appoint judges and justices of the peace, and this system was used from 1763 to provide a rudimentary judicial system. Its incompetence and corruption, and also the lack of any authority to try cases involving property, caused such complaints that the naval governor created a court of common pleas in 1789. As the legality of this action met a prompt challenge that was sustained at home, parliament had to repair the fault by an act of 1791 establishing a court with a resident chief justice. There was no resident governer until 1818, and no council or assembly until 1832.

The explanation of all this apparent neglect is that Newfoundland was very much more than the little colony in it. The fishermen who dwelt there were greatly outnumbered by others who swarmed around its shores and over its Banks every summer. Of these there were, in 1783, some 9,000 whose homes were in England. They alone were more numerous than the resident fishers and, what was of paramount importance, they alone represented the sole interest in Newfoundland that England had always regarded as worth fighting for—the fisheries as a nursery of seamen essential to maintain her sea power. Fishermen who resided on the island confined their operations to small boats in which they rarely ventured far from shore. They were lost to the Royal Navy.

Newfoundland was also a bone of international contention, though in 1713 France had surrendered to Britain all claim to sovereignty over it. Again and again, as the price of peace, France had forced Britain to share the use of the shores of Newfoundland, for France too would fight rather than be excluded from this valuable training ground for sailors. Treaty definitions of what part of the shore French fishermen could use led to troublesome disputes over the extent of this "French shore" and over the French attempt to exclude British fishermen from it. Now the disruption of the empire added a third party to the international problem of Newfoundland; for New Englanders, as British subjects, had played a large part in the development of these fisheries and they insisted, against French as well as British pressure, on retaining a share in them. The diplomatic triangle of forces thus pulling on Newfoundland during the peace negotiations was resolved as follows: The French shore was redefined as extending along all the west side of the island, around the north, and down the east as far as Cape St. John. France failed to get from Britain a treaty recognition of her exclusive right to this shore, which she had already exacted from the United States as a condition of the alliance of 1778; but the British government, again as the price of peace, gave France a solemn assurance that British subjects would not be allowed to interfere with Frenchmen on the French shore. British fishermen could therefore use only the south shore, off which the French retained the two little islands of St. Pierre and Miquelon, and the east shore up to Cape St.

John; and these shores they had to share with Americans. There the latter could catch fish but could not land to dry or cure. Newfoundland was caught in an international tangle that became more complicated as a result of the American Revolution and was not finally unraveled until the early years of the twentieth century. In 1783, and for many years afterward, the chief responsibility of the naval governor of Newfoundland was not the management of the little colony but the preservation of British interests in this tangle.

The Island of Saint John, better known by its later name of Prince Edward Island,[5] was an infant colony that already had been delivered into bondage. In 1767, shortly after the island was ceded by France, the British government granted the whole of it to a few favored friends, among whom it was parceled out in big estates. The grantees possessed such political influence that two years later they had their island severed from the government of Nova Scotia, to which it had been annexed after the cession, and erected into a separate colony with its own governor, council, and assembly, though it had scarcely any population. When the land became British, it had only two or three hundred Acadians left in it; by 1783 its English-speaking settlers had risen to only about a thousand, and then it attracted a mere six hundred Loyalists. There was nothing wrong with the soil or the climate of the island, which later became known as the smiling "garden of the Gulf." The little colony was simply suffering from the proverbial curse of absentee proprietors, who were loath to spend money in developing their estates and apparently thought they could make more by merely holding them for speculation. Moreover, these privileged persons were allowed to keep their titles even though they did not pay their quit rents, which were to have financed the administration of the island. The curse was not lifted until 1873.

Nova Scotia was a real colony and had just acquired a definite British character after seventy years of continuous British possession. It was the land of the Acadians, until 1749 a French colony held by a little British garrison and without any English-speaking settlers. In that year the mother country sent out 2,500 colonists to found Halifax. But Nova Scotia still remained predominantly French. These original Haligonians (residents of Halifax) and the few other newcomers were only half as numerous as the Acadians when the governor and his

---

[5] Given in honor of the Duke of Kent, Queen Victoria's father. The change of name from saint to sinner occurred in 1798.

council decided to expel the latter. The tragic deportation of 1755 effected a permanent revolution in the character of Nova Scotia, which thenceforth was an English-speaking land. It also wrought two other important changes there: the establishment of an assembly and a further alteration in the character of the population. The removal of the Acadians, who had refused to take the oath of allegiance and were legally incapacitated from holding any public office and even from exercising the franchise because they were Roman Catholics, made officials in London think that Nova Scotia was ready for government as an ordinary English colony. The governor in Halifax did not think so, but he bowed to peremptory orders from the secretary of state and called an assembly in 1758. The other change began as soon as the Acadians were driven from the homes they had built and the lands they had improved. These were inviting berths, and settlers arrived from New England to appropriate them. Thus began a stream of immigration that swelled when the British capture of Louisburg in 1758 made Nova Scotia a safer place to live in. By 1775, when the outbreak of hostilities stopped this immigration, three quarters of the population were New Englanders.

Why did not these newly arrived Yankees who formed such a large majority in Nova Scotia throw this colony into the American Revolution? They would have done it if they could, but they could not. They were living in little isolated communities that were scattered around the coast of what, for all practical purposes, was then an island. No American aid could reach them, and without it they were helpless against the power that the mother country could bring to bear upon them at any time. They were trapped, as the Acadians had been before them; and they reacted in the very same way, begging to be allowed to remain neutral. Like the British West Indies, the colonies of Nova Scotia, Prince Edward Island, and Newfoundland were beyond the grasp of the American Revolution; and, unlike the West Indies, they were never seriously threatened by French capture in this war. The sugar islands of the Caribbean were then much richer prizes.

The American Revolution gave Nova Scotia its definite British character. The "Neutral Yankees" were not expelled, nor did they seek to depart when the war ended. They were swamped by the immigration of Loyalists in 1783. The arrival of these people—some 30,000 of them—increased the population threefold. About 9,000 settled on the St. John River, forming the nucleus of the province of New Brunswick, between 2,000 and 3,000 in Cape Breton Island, and almost all the rest on the mainland of what is still Nova Scotia. For the most part they were city-bred folk from the northern colonies, chiefly New England, and a high proportion of them had belonged to the upper class of the society they left behind—judges, doctors, lawyers, and business leaders. It has been said that a list of them reads very like an honor roll of Harvard graduates. They had lost all their property but they retained their education and their spirit. It was this select stock that really made the two provinces of Nova Scotia and New Brunswick, which have supplied an extraordinarily large proportion of the professional, political, and business leaders of the Dominion of Canada. In 1784 New Brunswick was cut off from Nova Scotia and made a separate colony with its own governor, council, and assembly. At the same time Cape Breton was severed too, but it had a much smaller population and was not given an assembly. It was finally reannexed to Nova Scotia in 1820.

In 1783 the old Canada, whose official name from 1763 to 1791 was the Province of Quebec, had a settled white population of about 125,000—twice as many as all the rest of British North America and more than twice as many as all the British West Indies—and it was almost entirely confined within the limits of the modern province of Quebec. This population was also solidly French and Roman Catholic, except for an English-speaking minority of scarcely more than 10,000. A third of the latter had fitted themselves into the life of the towns of Quebec and Montreal during the fifteen years before the Revolution. The remaining two thirds were Loyalist refugees who were waiting to be assigned land on which to live. In the following year these loyalists received land and became the first body of non-French people settled on the soil of the country.

Almost all the French drew their living directly from the land, even the seigneurs. These seigneurs were often little better off than their sturdy tenants, the habitants, whose feudal payments were a mere pittance, for frontier conditions had emasculated the feudal system introduced by France in the beginning. With the growth of population, the holdings of the habitants were squeezed together along the banks of the great St. Lawrence and a few miles up its tributaries, giving the colony the appearance of a continuous village that stretched for nearly 250 miles. Its upper end was just above Montreal, where the rapids had checked the climb of settlement. In the other direction the line of cottages gradually died away below the city of Quebec, where the climate grew harsher and the land poorer. Though the habitant and his family produced practically everything they consumed, Canada had a thriving commerce, for Montreal was the North American capital of the fur trade, and this trade had to be fed with imports to supply the Indians with the manufactured goods they demanded in exchange for furs. But more interesting and much more important was the peculiar problem posed by Canada and how this problem was being handled.

The national character of the colonial empire was fundamentally altered by the Revolution. Now it contained practically an equal number of French and English settlers. Here lies the problem, which began with the acquisition of Canada by the treaty of 1763. Hitherto the empire had grown gradually by more or less peaceful expansion and the settlement of Englishmen overseas. An occasional conquest had added a foreign colony, such as Dutch New York and French Acadia; but it had always been a young and small one, to which the conqueror had been able to give an English character. When Britain conquered Canada, it was already an old colony, only one year younger than Virginia, her oldest; it was a big one, with a European population of some 65,000; and it was utterly alien in language, religion, laws, political institutions, and culture. Never had the empire swallowed anything like this. How could it be assimilated?

The problem was so foreign to British experience that officials in London could not grasp it when they approached the task of providing for the administration of the newly conquered colony. They were also blinded by two expectations that, if realized, would have obviated the necessity of facing the problem. They had grounds, not wholly unreasonable, for believing that Canada might soon lose its French character and its Roman Catholic religion. The migration of New Englanders was changing the face of things in Nova Scotia, and London looked for a much larger movement of surplus population, English-speaking and Protestant, from the old colonies into Canada. Then too, the Catholic Church in Canada was without a head, its bishop having died on the eve of the French surrender; and without a bishop to ordain priests the church might die with its clergy. Moreover, reports from the St. Lawrence confidently asserted that the people might easily be converted. So the British government proceeded to deal with Canada on the assumption that it would conform to the traditional pattern of an English colony.

This assumption soon turned out to be quite false. The French of Canada, fearful of their fate under the rule of an alien conqueror and a heretic, instinctively rallied behind their church, their only possible shield; and the lands of Canada, though officially advertised in the newspapers of the old colonies, attracted no settlers from the south or anywhere else. The only British immigrants were those who went to engage in trade, a pushing urban minority. To this day that part of the country is still overwhelmingly French and Roman Catholic.

It was impossible to govern Canada as an ordinary English colony, and the attempt to do it was a tragic blunder. The penal laws of the mother country, which expressly applied to all British possessions, rigidly excluded all Roman Catholics from public office and from voting. These English laws made a mockery of English forms of government in Canada. The establishment of these forms began with the appointment of a governor, a council, and other ordinary officials, all but the chief of whom the governor had to pick from the handful of adventurers who had followed the army into the country and hoped to make their fortunes out of it. The governor was also directed to call an assembly as soon as possible, but this was too much for him. The surviving senior military officer after the capture of Quebec in 1759, he had become a warm friend of the Canadians, and he would never subject them to an assembly elected by and from this little band of newcomers. His resolute refusal threw these newcomers into such an uproar that they soon forced the home government to recall him, only to find that his successor, Guy Carleton, was equally resolute and more capable of bridling them. But if an assembly was impossible, so also was the situation created by the governor's refusal to call one, for the colony was thus left without a legislature[6] and without a revenue. The penal laws also struck at the jurisdiction, the revenue, and the property of the Roman Catholic church in Canada—the institution most precious to the vast mass of the population. Another impossible situation arose in the administration of justice, where courts modeled after those of England were to apply English law to a society that had been cast in the very different mold of Roman law. The change from French to English criminal law caused little trouble—it affected only a few persons—but the attempt to substitute English for French civil law produced hopeless confusion and threatened all the property in the colony.

Almost at once the inequity, or iniquity, of the whole governmental system prescribed from England started a reaction that began with the governor in Quebec and spread to the government in London. The governor picked councilors and judges who sympathized with the Cana-

---

[6] Though the council operated as such, it had not been empowered to do so.

dians, and the home government shrank from forcing him to call an assembly. He backed the eager prayers of the Canadians for a bishop; and the home government, after swallowing hard, winked at the consecration of their candidate and his return to Canada from France, where the ceremony was quietly performed. The governor countenanced some continuance of the old laws, and the home government disavowed the intention of sweeping them all away. He objected stoutly to the exclusion of Canadians from the administration of their own country, and the home government promised to open the doors of office to them. More and more it became evident that this old French colony could not be made over into a new English one and would have to be given a constitution that fitted its character. Only thus could the Canadians become loyal British subjects; otherwise they would yearn after their old mother country and seize the first opportunity to deliver Canada back to France. That such an opportunity might come at any time was then clear. Britain and France were still chronic foes and any year might see them at war again. The urgency of the Canadian problem also grew with the gathering of the storm that was soon to burst in the American Revolution.

The solution adopted was the Quebec Act of 1774. It provided the colony with a legislature by empowering the council, which it enlarged to become more representative, with authority to pass laws for the country. This authority did not extend to taxation and was limited in other ways as well, because it was to be exercised by an appointed, not an elected body. At the same time another act of parliament, the Quebec Revenue Act, imposed customs duties and license fees to provide the colony with a revenue. The rejection of an assembly caused much heart searching in England, much bitterness in the British minority on the St. Lawrence, and much alarm in the old colonies; but it is difficult to see how the British government could have decided otherwise. The little British minority in Canada, who had clamored for an elected chamber, would not have one at all unless they could control it, which was an intolerable condition. As for the French population, an assembly was an English institution which they neither understood nor desired; and even if they had wanted one, they were not to be trusted with it, for they were newly conquered subjects whose loyalty to Britain was doubtful in the event of another French war. Though an assembly was thus out of the question, the British government was anxious to give the Canadians a legislature that would satisfy them. The enlarged council was to include some of their leading men.

This of course meant admitting Roman Catholics, which the government had decided should be a general principle in the Canadian public service. Therefore, by the Quebec Act, Roman Catholics gained political emancipation in Canada more than half a century before they got it in the mother country. The act also confirmed the clergy's old legal right to collect the tithe—but only from their own people—and the right of their church to retain its property. This the act did by restoring the civil law as it was on the eve of the conquest, which covered all property in the country. English criminal law was retained.

Having regard for the exasperatingly complex and novel problem that the conquest of Canada had thrust upon Britain, the Quebec Act stands out as one of the greatest pieces of statesmanship in the history of the empire. It embodied a complete reversal of traditional policy. Though the French of Canada could never become English, they might develop into loyal British subjects if Britain won their hearts by guaranteeing them their religion, their laws, their customs, by opening public offices to them on equal terms with British-born, and by giving them a government that would understand them and protect their interests—in short, by freely according to them the liberty to be themselves. Such was the vision that inspired this remarkable act of parliament. The Canadians were the first non-British people to taste this new collective liberty which we may well call British, to distinguish it from the old English liberty of the individual, because this larger liberty became a basic principle of the greater British Empire of the future and a major reason for its success.

As British officials had to wrestle for years with the problem of Canada before they worked out this solution of 1774, it is not surprising that the whole business was beyond the comprehension of people in the old colonies; and as the latter were then suffering from British statesmanship at its worst, they were all the more incapable of understanding this act of British statesmanship at its best. That the same government at the same time should show so much consideration for strangers within the imperial family and so little for old members of it still puzzles some people, who conclude that the good policy was not so good. But the opposite conclusion, that the bad was not so bad, is just as logical—and as inconsequential, for such glaring incongruity is a common failing of governments all over the world, even in our own enlightened age. Very naturally, though quite mistakenly, Americans at once saw in the Quebec Act the design of a dastardly blow aimed through Canada at the back of the old colonies. Therefore, at the very outset, the Revolution thrust a fiery arm up into Canada, the only surviving colony into which it could reach.

If the American forces that laid siege to the fortress of Quebec at the close of 1775 had been able to take it and hold it, there can be little doubt that the old Province of Quebec would then have become part of the United States. But the invaders were not strong enough to take it, and if by some accident or blunder they had got it, they could not have held it against the powerful expedition that arrived from Britain in the spring of 1776 and quickly swept them out of the country. Yet this is not the whole explanation of why Canada survived the American Revolution as a British colony. If the newly conquered Canadians had risen in revolt when the invasion gave them a chance, there might have been a different story to tell; but they preferred to remain neutral, because they had less love for the Americans than they had for the British.

As the scope of the war widened, it was something else that governed the fate of Canada. The entry of France into the war shook the foundations of British rule in this French colony and simultaneously raised the prospect of a combined French attack by sea and American attack by land to conquer Canada. Whenever such a plan was proposed, however, one ally or the other vetoed it. It was first put off by American suspicion that it would establish French control of the St. Lawrence, which would work with Spanish control of the Mississippi to throttle the United States. When the American desire for Canada overcame this suspicion and revived the project, France vetoed it—twice—fearing it would establish the United States on the St. Lawrence. The French government calculated that Canada in the hands of Britain would keep the Americans dependent on France just as, when in the hands of France, it had made them cling to Britain. As neither ally would help the other to get it, preferring to let Britain hold it, she kept it. Thus the alliance that rendered Canada almost fatally vulnerable was politically, though not physically, incapable of striking the combined blow that might have torn it from the British Empire.

At the close of the war the Canadian problem entered upon a new phase. The settlement of the Loyalist refugees upon lands above the region inhabited by the French was the beginning of what grew to be Ontario. In contrast to those of the Maritime Provinces, these Loyalists were mostly backwoods farmers from the old colonies, just the people to open new country; and they were only the vanguard of a swelling migration of pioneers from the American frontier, which they pulled north of the border. At last, a quarter of a century after the conquest, a rapidly growing English-speaking population appeared beside the French but separated geographically from them. The colony was assuming a dual character that called for a radical revision of the Quebec Act, but the loud cries that arose in Canada were so conflicting that the government in London was again puzzled by what should be done in this strange colony.

The British mercantile minority on the lower St. Lawrence once more clamored lustily for an assembly. They knew that the great majority of the electorate would be French; yet they thought they could manage the chamber, for they counted on the solid backing of the new settlers in the southwest and on winning enough support from the French. Indeed, they got many of the latter to join in their chorus. On the other hand, the seigneurial class shouted against an assembly, and they too gathered a large following. Most of the French in each camp seem to have been stirred up by the leaders and to have had no clear notion of what they were doing. Then there were the Loyalists on the upper St. Lawrence and beyond. They demanded a separate government for their part of the country, while the opposing camps below united in denouncing this demand.

The consideration that finally brought the home government to a decision was finance. The proceeds of the Quebec Revenue Act had fallen far short of what the colony needed, and the governor had to meet the growing deficit by falling back upon the method used before that act, which was to draw bills on the British Treasury. This could not be continued indefinitely, for the taxpayer in the mother country would object. Nor could parliament impose additional levies by a repetition of what it had done in 1774. It had made this impossible in 1778 when, in a vain effort to stop the American Revolution, it had enacted that thenceforth it would lay no tax on any colony except such duties as might be necessary for the regulation of trade, in which event the net proceeds were to be turned over to the colonial legislature for disposal as it might please. The only way left to provide what was needed was to have the people tax themselves through their elected representatives. An assembly had to be established. This conclusion led to another: that the colony would have to be divided because one assembly for the whole would be unworkable. The country was too large, and the difference between the older French society on the lower St. Lawrence and the new English-speaking society above was too great. Therefore, in 1791, an imperial order in council divided the country into Lower and Upper Canada, and parliament endowed each with a legislative council and a legislative assembly.[7] The only part of the Quebec Act that was repealed was its provision for the council. Each of the two Canadas was thus freed from the other so that it could maintain and develop its own individuality.

---

[7] The passage of the act preceded the issuance of the order in council. The concession of an assembly to Lower Canada is in striking contrast to the exclusion of the French inhabitants of Grenada in 1784 from seats in the island legislature, which had been opened to them. This exclusive measure was the work of their British-born fellow colonists, who were embittered by the attitude of the French inhabitants when France recovered the island for the duration of the war.

CHAPTER IV

Salvaging What Was Left of the American Wreck

IT HAS BEEN the fond belief of many Americans that their Revolutionary ancestors taught Britain a wholesome lesson on how to govern colonies, but the lesson that Britain drew from the wreck of the first empire was the very opposite of what these Americans have supposed. Instead of loosening the bonds of empire, the mother country tried to tighten them in order to preserve what was left; and the reason for this was quite natural. The great reduction in the size of the empire had wrought a corresponding change in the character of it. From being an empire composed chiefly of colonies that were populous, wealthy, and politically mature enough for the fullest measure of self-government, it suddenly became an empire of small, poor, and weak colonies that were unable to stand on their own feet. From maturity it was plunged back into immaturity. The grown-up family was gone, and the mother was starting over again with a family of little children. But she was not the same parent, for a great change had been wrought in her too. Something had been burnt in upon her mind and heart. It was the fear of another American Revolution, which would rob her of still more colonies as they grew up.

This fear inspired a reactionary colonial policy that lasted for two generations. The home government was determined to avoid the mistakes that had produced the tragedy and that might, if repeated, reproduce it. What were these mistakes, and how could they be summed up? To the British official mind the answer was simple and obvious. It was first letting the colonies develop practically free of control and then attempting to tax them. Never again would the mother country tax a colony. Never again would she let her children get out of hand.

These two resolves then became cardinal principles of colonial management. The first, which had already been proclaimed by statute in 1778, was of course not reactionary at all; but the second was wholly so. How were the colonies to be kept in leading strings? By falling back upon the traditional methods that had been laxly applied, and by making them more efficient: particularly the old colonial system, which would confine the trade of the colonies to the empire, and the old machinery of government in the colonies, which would ensure political control from London.

The old colonial system, to which Britain clung as a potent means of holding her fragments of empire, survived the American Revolution by a narrow margin. It seemed to have expired during the peace negotiations, when the Americans suggested and the British agreed that there should be complete commercial reciprocity between the United States and the British Empire. The Americans were loath to lose their privileged position in the British imperial trading system, for most of the world's trade was then tied up in this and other similar systems. They also feared French and Spanish intrigues to combine with the British to exclude the United States from the interior of the continent. That was why John Jay, not long after he joined Benjamin Franklin in Paris, held out to the British the tempting offer of the commercial empire of America if they would be generous in drawing the new international boundary. The British were no less alarmed over the possibility of losing the best part of their trade along with the best part of their empire; and they were most anxious to pull the United States away from the alliance with France, the ancient foe of Britain. In their mutual eagerness for a lasting peace and reconciliation, both American and British negotiators were of one mind in believing that any lingering seeds of discord should be smothered by a generous application of reciprocity. Therefore the fourth article of the terms they drafted in October 1782 provided for the free navigation of the Mississippi from its source to its mouth, mutual free navigation of other British and American waters, and free trade between the United States and the British Empire.

This interesting article would have buried the old colonial system in the peace treaty. Why did it not? In the first place, more careful examination in London revealed that it would make Britain give much more than she would get. It would turn the navigation laws inside out—to the injury of British trade and the ruin of British shipping—by leaving the British to bear all the burden of these laws while allowing the Americans to gather all the benefits. Therefore the article was struck out,[1] but with no intention of discarding reciprocity. The purpose was to guard it by placing it upon a more equitable footing in a supplementary commercial treaty. That this would shortly follow was the understanding of both parties when they signed the preliminaries of 30 November 1782, the preamble of which retained a reference to the establishment of reciprocity; and when this draft of the treaty was submitted to parliament in January 1783, the omission of any provision to carry out the promise of the preamble at once roused great uneasiness.

The House of Commons, backed by the insistent demands of mercantile interests outside, was so impatient to get the freest possible trade with the United States that the government soon yielded, promising a bill to make provisional regulations pending the preparation of a permanent system. Then the government fell from power, for other reasons; and a few days afterward William Pitt, who continued in office until a new administration could be formed, presented the bill. It offered the United States substantially all the advantages, free of any of the disadvantages, of being included in the charmed circle of the British commercial system; therefore it was open to all the objections that had been raised against the eliminated article of the treaty. Nevertheless it was very much what "the whole house" had wanted, according to the admission of the member who opened the fight against it. The shipping interests were of course stoutly hostile because the bill spelled the doom of their monopoly, but the commercial and West Indian interests fought hard for it. During the weeks of warm debate that followed, various objections forced the house to adopt drastic amendments. In the end, the bill, though mutilated, was not killed; it was merely laid aside in the hope that a better solution was at hand.

The new ministry, of Fox and North, reverted to the original plan and hoped a solution might be worked out for insertion in the peace treaty. Again the negotiators tried to find a satisfactory formula; again the difficulty lay in Britain, with the navigation laws; and again London decided to put off the question for settlement in a supplementary treaty, for Fox was impatient to conclude peace. When he cut short the discussions and thrust forward the provisional treaty of November 1782, slightly reworded to make it definitive, the Americans were

---

[1] Except the provision for the navigation of the Mississippi, which the Americans desired in order to enlist British interest in preventing Spain from closing the mouth of the river.

reluctant to accept it because their signatures would terminate their commission without their having gained reciprocity. But they too would rather have an earlier peace without it than a later one with it. Thus it happened that the mutual eagerness of the American commissioners and the British government to end the war postponed the burial of the old colonial system.

The corpse was revived to vigorous life before it could be laid away in the commercial treaty that was to have supplemented and completed the peace. The revival was largely the work of one man, who was no shipping magnate but a patriotic soldier, accomplished scholar, wealthy landowner, and member of parliament: Lord Sheffield. He blew a trumpet call that reverberated throughout the land, rallying the nation behind the threatened navigation laws. Rarely has a book had such a great and rapid influence upon public opinion and public policy as his *Observations on the Commerce of the United States*, which ran through two editions in 1783 and reached a sixth in 1784.

There was no need, Sheffield asserted, to go courting the Americans to win back their trade. They would still have to buy most of their manufactured goods from Britain, because they had practically no industries whereas she had the best in the world, and because only her merchants could give the credit they needed. They would still have to sell to her, since she offered the best market for their produce. By holding fast to her navigation laws, under which she had grown great, Britain could make the Americans pay her for their own political independence. These laws would deprive them of their West Indian trade, the most valuable part of their commerce, and give it to Canada, Nova Scotia, Newfoundland, and Ireland. They would also shift this trade from American to British bottoms, giving more employment to the latter than they took away from the former because the voyages would be longer. Sheffield's arguments could not be dismissed as vain boasting, for he supported them with a wealth of facts and figures gathered by painstaking research that made him an outstanding authority on matters of trade. But the power of his appeal on behalf of the navigation laws was more than logical. It was psychological. It did much to revive this countrymen's self-confidence, which had been rudely shaken by the wreck of the empire.

The old colonial system, thus preserved for another two generations, never completely enclosed the colonial empire. The old colonies, which had burst through from the inside before the Revolution, burst through from the outside at the close of the Revolution. Britain was unable to

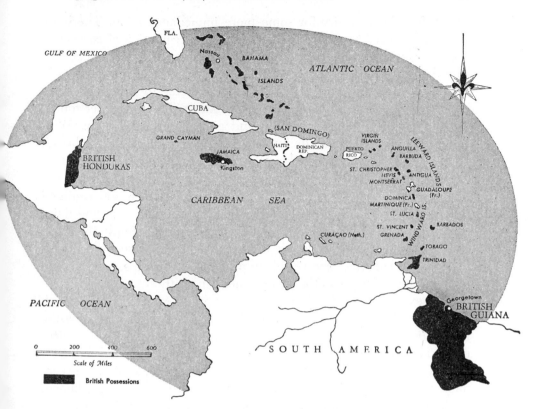

The British West Indies

get peace without opening all her North American inshore fisheries—not just those of Newfoundland—to citizens of the United States and, in addition, allowing them to use any unsettled parts of the coasts of Nova Scotia, Labrador, and the Magdalen Islands for purposes of drying.

American trade with the West Indies was also reopened even before the peace, but there the effective pressure was West Indian, not American. Before the Revolution the island planters had long been vitally dependent on New England, whence came their lumber, fish, and other foodstuffs in little New England vessels. The war cut off this source of supply, causing much distress in the islands; and the approach of peace fed West Indian impatience to resume such an essential trade. Hence the loud West Indian cries in the general chorus for Pitt's bill. When this bill was abandoned, the new ministry of Fox and North, while hoping to find a reciprocity formula to put in the peace

treaty, felt the necessity for some more immediate action. Therefore
an act was passed to authorize temporarily the regulation of commerce
between the United States and the British Empire by orders in council.
The first order, issued in May 1783, modified a basic rule of the old
law by opening the ports of the mother country to American ships
importing American unmanufactured produce. The first order touching the colonies followed in July and aimed at relief for the West
Indies. It allowed them to import American lumber, flour, bread,
grain, vegetables, and livestock; and to export to the United States rum,
sugar, molasses, coffee, nuts, ginger, and pimento. But it forbade the
importation of American meat, dairy produce, and fish and confined
this American trade to British ships. The exclusion of meat and dairy
produce was to protect Ireland, which had begun to supply the West
Indies with these articles during the war;[2] of fish to protect the British
fisheries; and of American vessels to protect British ships, which could
not operate as cheaply as the small American craft.

This exclusion of American vessels was an unexpected blow to both
the United States and the West Indies. It queered the pitch for the
negotiation of reciprocity then proceeding in Paris, and it shot prices
up 100 per cent in the islands. The planters were aghast, and the West
India Committee in England leaped into action. The coalition government would not yield; but West Indian hopes rose when Pitt, known
as the friend of free intercourse, became prime minister in December
1783. The new administration intimated a willingness to compromise
by admitting to West Indian ports American vessels of less than eighty
tons—in other words, vessels too small to engage in trade with Europe
or to feed an American navy. The West Indians then overshot the
mark by rejecting any limitation of tonnage, whereupon the government referred the whole question to the new Committee of the Privy
Council for Trade and Plantations on the very day it was organized in
March 1784.[3]

For nearly three months this privy council committee investigated
the problem of West Indian trade, patiently seeking and weighing all
the available evidence. There were three main considerations. The
West Indian merchants and planters did their best to prove that high
costs of production would ruin the islands if they could not get American supplies and if their trade with the United States was confined to

---

[2] In 1778 parliament opened colonial trade to Ireland.

[3] For its origin see *infra* p. 56.

British bottoms. Sir Guy Carleton and all others in England who were best informed on conditions in British North America testified that these colonies, if given a proper advantage over the United States, would soon be able to supply the West Indies at reasonable prices with all the North American products they needed; and that here was a good opportunity to stimulate the development of British North America at the expense of the colonies that had revolted and to give much-deserved encouragement to the new Loyalist settlements. The evidence collected on shipping was strong: over sixty thousand seamen discharged from the navy on the return of peace; "a vast number" of merchant vessels, with all their crews, released from transport and other public service; the fall of transatlantic freight rates to prewar levels; and the temptation of idle sailors to seek foreign employment, thereby draining Britain's naval reserve and building up the maritime strength of her competitors, particularly the United States. Another consideration was the possibility of American retaliation, but this was lightly dismissed for several reasons. The flourishing condition of American trade was deflating American indignation over the restriction of West Indian trade to British shipping, and neither the weak central government nor the several states were capable of applying any effective pressure. The question was therefore decided on grounds that were wholly intraimperial.

The West Indians suspected that the Loyalists prejudiced the committee in favor of British North America; and there is no doubt that from this time until its fall two generations later, the old colonial system, on balance, worked for British North America and against the West Indies. But regard for the Loyalists was not responsible for this preference, nor did it have any practical effect upon the decision of the committee. Its conclusion that British North America could supply immediately a large proportion, and within about three years the whole of the West Indian requirements of lumber and provisions, though quite wrong on both counts, did not visit any injury upon the West Indies. They were already getting American supplies in British ships, which had brought prices down from the recent peak; and the committee would let these supplies continue to flow as long as necessary, but it would not allow American vessels, even of small tonnage, to carry these supplies. That was the real issue, and it was decided in favor of British shipping. Britain could and should retain the monopoly of the carrying trade of her empire.

The report of the privy council committee thus upheld the existing arrangement, which had been made without any regard for British North America; and these northern colonies constituted only one of several factors that might dictate a future change. Meanwhile this compromise of the old colonial system was continued on a year to year basis until 1788. By that time it was fairly evident that the concession to the West Indies could not be withdrawn or curtailed, and need not be enlarged. The islands were still dependent on the United States for the great bulk of their supplies. On the other hand, the exclusion of American vessels was not strangling them, for their trade with the mother country, both export and import, was 25 per cent larger than before the war, and some six hundred British ships were employed in carrying it. Therefore Pitt's government introduced a bill to make the existing regulations permanent, and parliament passed it with only a flicker of opposition. But the time was not far off when it would be impossible to keep American vessels out of the British West Indies. The adoption of the Constitution of the United States provided for a central government that could retaliate; and the great war with France, which began in 1793, created new conditions that upset the act of 1788.

Meanwhile, how did the closing in of the old colonial system apply in British North America? Newfoundland had drawn so much of its food from New England before the Revolution that the return of peace brought pressure to reopen access to this source of supply. The problem of the fishing colony thus resembled that of the sugar islands, though it was on a much smaller scale and was complicated by the necessity of sharing the "British shore" with American fishermen, which created a greater possibility of smuggling. Here too there was a vain hope that the Loyalist settlements would obviate the necessity of relying on the United States. A temporary act of 1785 permitted specially licensed British ships to import American bread, flour, and livestock into Newfoundland; and the act of 1788, mentioned above, authorized the governor to continue this trade under the same limitation, though only on a temporary basis. No vessel could get a license more than seven months after it had cleared from a port in the mother country.

The Maritime Provinces, whose population had been suddenly trebled by the influx of Loyalists, were more dependent on New England. During the first winter of the peace, the governor of Nova Scotia, acting on no authority save necessity and the advice of his council, admitted supplies from Boston in small American craft. This freedom

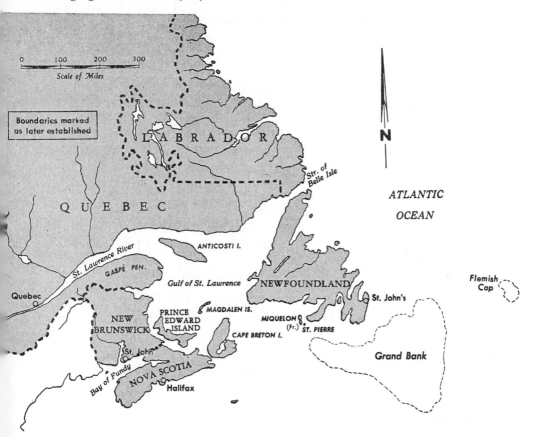

Maritime Provinces of British North America, 1784

was continued by him and by the governor of New Brunswick, when that province was carved out of the old Nova Scotia, until 1785. The home government then intervened with an order in council which, issued under a temporary renewal of the act of 1783, decreed that only livestock, grain, and lumber could be imported into the Maritime Provinces from the United States, and then only in British bottoms and under a governor's proclamation that their admission was necessary for the inhabitants. By the time the permanent act was passed in 1788, London was beginning to see that the necessity, instead of being only occasional, was a chronic condition in Nova Scotia and New Brunswick. Indeed, the governors of both provinces stretched the necessity to cover American lumber for shipment to the West Indies when they found that their own people were getting it anyway for this

purpose. Necessity and opportunity also gave rise to an illicit importation of American pitch, tar, and turpentine, which the governors
could not prevent and which the home government made licit by an
act of 1793. London, however, neither would nor could do anything
about the American rum that poured into Nova Scotia and New Brunswick during these years. It was cheaper than the domestic manufacture, which in turn was cheaper than the British West Indian product
laid down in Halifax. There was no keeping it out when American
fishermen were allowed by treaty to hover around these British shores
and even land on them. These conditions suggest a heaven for smugglers. Such was the intimacy between the Maritime Provinces and
New England that the governor of Nova Scotia asked permission to
provide himself with an armed vessel to keep this intimacy within
legal bounds. He got the permission from England and the vessel from
the United States.

No such trade, legitimate or illegitimate, linked the old Province of
Quebec with the United States during the first four years of their
peaceful separation, because there was neither necessity nor opportunity for it. The first chink in the wall was opened from the British
side in response to temptation from the other side—from Vermont;
and meanwhile the temptation started a highly interesting investigation
into the whole question of economic relations between Canada and the
neighboring Republic. Vermont was imprisoned in the interior and
threatened with economic suffocation, for the treaty of 1783 severed
it from the British Empire and the hostility of New York excluded it
from the United States until 1791. During the Revolution its leaders
had flirted with the British in Quebec, discussing the possibility of a
return to the old allegiance. Both parties dropped this discussion when
peace came, but the Vermonters could not end the flirtation. Their
economic plight was too pressing. They had to get an outlet, and the
one provided by nature was down Lake Champlain and the Richelieu
River to the St. Lawrence. So they knocked at the door of Quebec
with proposals of commercial reunion with the empire. Quebec
referred the matter to London, and there the peculiar position of
Vermont provoked an inquiry early in 1785 that revealed the peculiar
position of Canada.

Here was something quite new and very puzzling in the commercial
system of the British Empire. Cut off from the sea for five months out
of every twelve, the old Province of Quebec was really an inland colony.
Only through a foreign country, the United States, could it have con-

tact with the outside world the year round. This was a condition never contemplated by the navigation laws. Having been framed for only maritime colonies, these laws were silent on land communication and inland navigation. Hence the striking contrast between an order in council of April 1785 forbidding the importation of any American produce into the province by sea, and an additional instruction to the governor in May drawing his attention to this order in council and stating that it was necessary to regulate the foreign intercourse of Canada by land and inland navigation. How was this to be done? It could be by order in council, under the temporary enabling act; but the only intimation given by the instruction was in two directions to the governor. One was to have his legislative council pass an ordinance prohibiting the export of peltry; the other was to enforce the laws that prohibited the importation of any foreign rum or spirits or, except from Great Britain, any foreign European or Asiatic manufactured goods into the colonies. In approaching this novel inland frontier of the empire, London was evidently groping in the dark.

The possibility of the breakdown of the old colonial system in the interior of America, and the need for guidance from Canada, were clearly recognized by the home government in the following year, when the division of the colony into Upper and Lower Canada was already contemplated. Though Upper Canada would still be connected with Lower Canada geographically by the St. Lawrence and politically by allegiance to the same Crown, they would have little else in common, and there were reasons for thinking that the natural economic affiliation of Upper Canada might be with the United States. Thence had come its people; they were still coming; and they would continue to come. It could expect to receive few from the mother country, whose government continued to frown on emigration until after the Napoleonic wars. Moreover, as the years passed, this new colony would come to be half surrounded by American settlements; and the boundary, being a line along a natural highway, might tend to unite rather than divide the people on either side.

It is not very surprising, therefore, that the governor in Quebec was asked to give his opinion on whether "the inhabitants of the province so to be erected may not be supplied with European and other produce and manufactures with greater facility and upon easier terms by the subjects and through the territories of the United States of America than by our subjects and through our Province of Quebec, and thereby a connection and intercourse between the subjects of the two countries be unavoidably promoted and encouraged." Though we may here detect lingering hopes of reciprocity along the inland border, the vision of 1786 was different from that of 1782. British trade was to follow another course to another end. Instead of curving round to the American interior via the St. Lawrence, it would cut through the United States from the Atlantic seaboard to the British interior. This highly interesting suggestion apparently drew no direct reply from Quebec, perhaps because American settlement was still too remote from the western Loyalist communities to make it seem a practical issue.

The Vermont proposal, bogged down in London, was renewed in Quebec where it brought local action. In the spring of 1787, the governor took matters into his own hands and issued an order opening commercial intercourse with the "neighboring states" by way of Lake Champlain and the Richelieu, permitting the free import of lumber, naval stores, hemp, flax, grain, provisions, and livestock—the produce of those states—and the free export of any product, save furs, of Canada or of any other dominion of Great Britain. A few days later he had his council pass an ordinance allowing the free import of leaf tobacco and of pot and pearl ashes from the same source for re-export to Britain. In exchange for the above articles, Vermont of course took British manufactures. The reaction of London was a mild rebuke, not for what the governor had done but for the way he had done it—by his own order.

London now clearly stated what the instructions of 1785 had left unsaid, possibly because it was then undecided, that the regulation of intercourse with the United States by land and inland navigation was the function of the governor and council, limited naturally by the prohibition of the export of furs and the import of spirits, rum, and foreign manufactures. On receiving this direction, the governor corrected himself by having the council transform his order into an ordinance in 1788, which prohibited the import of all goods not specifically admitted. In the following year a serious shortage of food in the colony moved the governor to admit for that season American foodstuffs by sea as well as by land and inland navigation. He knew he was violating an imperial statute and an imperial order in council, but he trusted the home government to provide the necessary legal cloak, which it did by act of parliament.

Local necessity was not the reason for opening the regular trade across the inland border. The prime purpose was to make Canada a profitable entrepôt between Britain and the American interior, and it soon proved to be less profitable than anticipated. The local merchants blamed the foreign duties collected in Britain, for only what was certified as the produce of British colonies could enter the mother country free of duty in British ships; and, working through the council, these merchants inspired the governor in 1790 to plead for the removal of this discrimination. If, he wrote to the secretary of state, the mother country admitted on the same terms as colonial goods "all the produce of America . . . which shall come into the ports of Quebec and Montreal by land or inland navigation . . . three considerable advantages" would surely follow: "Canada must gain by the passage of all commodities through the country, Great Britain by an increase of her carrying trade, and both by interesting our neighbors to preserve in the hands of Great Britain this outlet to the sea and to the most profitable markets for all their produce." Quebec rather than London should control the extension of the indulgence. It should be gradual, he thought, so "that our settlers on the north side of the lakes may acquire strength and get the start of those on the opposite shore." He even looked forward to the time when there would be no restriction whatever on the importation of American produce across the border. His reference to the lakes shows that he was thinking of much more than Vermont, and his concluding words recall the query of the neglected instructions: "It appears to me highly proper to form alliances with our neighbours, as soon as all things are well matured . . . Their own interest alone can render them zealously attached to us." His appeal was superfluous. Three weeks before he penned these words in Quebec, London had removed the discrimination.

A Vermont agent had been busy in England, with Spain as his unwitting ally. The Nootka Sound affair, stirring British fears of latent American hostility, had moved the secretary of state to urge the governor to cultivate the friendship of Vermont; and parliament had passed an act, which came into force on 1 July 1790, giving American produce legally imported into the province the same favorable treatment as colonial produce on entering Britain. Here, however, we should observe that temporary expediency only hastened an action that the government favored on general principle, the privy council committee having advised the encouragement of this inland intercourse as a means of promoting the sale of British manufactures and increasing British commerce and navigation, the prime purpose of the old colonial system. To this end, also, the British government was soon, under new conditions created by the war with Revolutionary France, to negotiate a reciprocity agreement for traffic across this novel inland frontier, where reciprocity did not conflict with the sacred navigation laws.

Turning to the machinery of government, we find a distinct retrogression in London at the close of the American Revolution. The previous century had seen a considerable development that culminated in the creation of a real colonial department. Colonial affairs were long the charge of the Secretary of State for the Southern Department, who had other important duties to perform. He was one of the two principal secretaries of state who were responsible for foreign policy, his province being southern Europe while that of his colleague was northern Europe. Differentiation of function within the Southern Department, to look after colonial affairs, was not necessary. The old Board of Trade and Plantations, an advisory body established in 1696, had general supervision over colonial administration; and as colonial affairs grew in importance, so did this board. By 1768, however, the pressure of colonial business had so increased that it produced a reorganization. A third principal secretary of state was then added to the cabinet, the Secretary of State for the American Department, to look after the colonies, and he became president, or first lord of the Board of Trade. At last the imperial government had a colonial department headed by a member of the cabinet—but not for long. The need for it seemed to disappear with the loss of the best part of the colonial empire; and so out of regard for economy at home, the reforming Whigs had parliament abolish the new American secretaryship and the old board in 1782. What colonial business remained was transferred back to one of the two historic principal secretaries of state, whose duties were then rearranged. The Northern Department became the Foreign Office; and the Southern, the Home Office, to which was attached responsibility for Ireland and the colonies. The reorganization act also provided for a Committee of the Privy Council for Trade and Plantations, which has already been mentioned. Two years later, in 1784, its members were appointed; and in 1786 it was reorganized on a permanent basis, with an efficient clerical staff. This committee is the lineal ancestor of the modern Board of Trade of the British government, which has nothing to do with colonies, but in those days it performed much the same services as the defunct Board of Trade, except that the new body rarely conducted a direct correspondence with colonial governors. It was a long time before there was another specialized colonial secretary. Meanwhile the colonies were a minor care of the Home Office until 1801, when they were transferred to the War Office.

The only reform in colonial government that was made at the close of the American Revolution was another piece of Whig legislation in 1782, an act of parliament "for preventing certain offices in the plantations from being executed by deputy or granted for life."[4] It had been a recognized custom for secretaries of state to give lucrative colonial offices to relatives and friends as permanent sinecures, the duties being performed by deputies appointed by the principals who made private arrangements for their emolument. The act struck at this abuse but hardly scratched it, for the law was inapplicable to previous appointments and was commonly evaded in subsequent ones. The abuse, however, was by no means peculiar to colonial offices; there the burden rested more on the mother country than on the remaining colonies because they paid only part of the cost of their governments and the imperial exchequer had to make up the difference.

In the colonies themselves there was remarkably little change of governmental forms and practices on the morrow of the Revolution. There was no denying in governmental circles at home that something had gone wrong with the working of the traditional system of governor, council, and assembly. Nor was there much doubt of what this was: the machine had broken down and jumped the imperial track in the lost colonies because there the assembly, by gaining too much power, had upset the balance. One might have expected, therefore, a movement to improve the machine by discarding the troublesome part. Yet no such movement followed, despite appearances in Cape Breton, which was severed from Nova Scotia in 1784 without being given an elected chamber. The self-denying ordinance adopted by parliament in 1778 made assemblies more necessary than ever, for colonies must have revenues. This, as we have seen, was the prime cause of the establishment of representative government in the two Canadas by the act of 1791. Thus the American Revolution, instead of eliminating the popular chamber, actually fixed it more firmly in the system of British colonial government. The acceptance of this fact was easy because it harmonized with the prevailing conception of the British constitution. Britons believed it was the best in the world because it held the three great principles of government—monarchic, aristocratic,

---

[4] 22 George III, c. 75.

and democratic—in perfect balance. To them it seemed that there could be nothing better in the colonies, where the governor represented the king, the council the House of Lords, and the assembly the House of Commons. This opinion was repeatedly expressed, without challenge, in the parliamentary debates on the bill providing for the government of the two Canadas.

What was required, according to the lesson drawn in London from recent experience in America, was greater care to preserve the proper proportion between the three elements of government in the colonies, so that the democratic would never again encroach upon the aristocratic and the monarchic. Wherever possible, these two were to be strengthened as a check upon the other one; and the opportunity seemed greater in British North America, where new settlements necessitated new provisions for government, than in the West Indies, where British institutions were much older and more fixed.

To make the monarchical principle more effective, there was a union of North American colonies under one executive head, first on a small scale in 1784, and then on a larger one in 1786. In the former year Prince Edward Island had its governor demoted to the rank of lieutenant governor and placed under the governor of Nova Scotia; and Cape Breton, though erected into a separate colony, was made subordinate to the government in Halifax. In the latter year, 1786, the governors of Nova Scotia and New Brunswick were likewise demoted; and Sir Guy Carleton, raised to the peerage as Lord Dorchester, was sent back to Quebec as governor in chief of all the North American colonies except Newfoundland and commander-in-chief of all the forces in them, including Newfoundland. London regarded him very highly as the one man who might consolidate the imperial power in this half of the colonial empire; and five years later, when Upper and Lower Canada were established, each was given a lieutenant governor while Dorchester remained governor of all. Another device to uphold the authority of the Crown was introduced into the two Canadas when they were separated. It was the reservation of two sevenths of the land in every new township as an endowment that would increase in value with the growth of settlement. One of these sevenths was for the Church of England, whose constitution was monarchical, and the other seventh was to provide the executive with an independent income.

Concern for the aristocratic principle appears clearly in the careful preparation of the legislation of 1791 for the two Canadas. It was the work of Pitt's cousin and cabinet colleague, William Grenville, who observed that the colonial counterpart of the House of Lords had never been allowed to develop properly because it had been bound in its infancy by the imposition of another and quite incompatible function —that of an executive council whose function was to advise the governor. In this capacity its members had been necessarily subject to removal at will, which made it impossible for them to become an independent upper chamber of a legislature after the English pattern. Therefore he sought to free the aristocratic element by cutting it loose from the executive incubus. He also proposed to elevate the prestige of this body by attaching hereditary titles to holders of seats in it. Dorchester, who was more familiar with new world conditions, scoffed at the idea of a title aristocracy in an American colony, and therefore the act's provision for this distinction was merely permissive, not compulsory. But the differentiation according to function was adopted. When Upper and Lower Canada began their existence, they were the first colonies in which the legislative council was separated from the executive council, and the members of the former were appointed for life. This innovation was later copied in other colonies.

A further check upon the democratic element was the partial application of the principle of *divide et impera* which, in contrast to the consolidation of the monarchical element in 1784 and 1786, granted the Loyalists' prayers for a separate New Brunswick before ever these prayers were heard by the government in London. Two small assemblies with a long distance between them would be less dangerous than one big chamber. The same calculation, though inspired by a more distant prospect, seems to have been at least partly responsible for the simultaneous amputation of Cape Breton; and it may have assisted in bringing about the division of the old Province of Quebec into Upper and Lower Canada, which was dictated by other considerations. This calculation also explains what happened to an interesting plan that Dorchester forwarded to London before the act of 1791 was passed. The author of the plan was his alter ego whom he had brought out as chief justice of Quebec. He was William Smith, a Loyalist from New York, where he and his father before him had been chief justice. Long pondering over the American tragedy had convinced him that it might have been avoided if a common government for the colonies had been formed. While he was in London he seems to have been the prime inspiration of the design to draw the remaining North American colonies together under one resident head; but he would go much further. He would endow the whole of British North America with a superlegislature. Naturally this plan met with short shrift in the empire's capital.

The American Revolution thus induced the British government to tune up the old machine in the North American colonies so that it would operate more perfectly in the days to come. The new adjustments, which were specifically designed to give freer action to the monarchical and aristocratic parts, seem to have made no more practical difference than those of many a wayside mechanic to a modern traveler's car. The appointment of one governor for all the colonies, each with a lieutenant governor to act during his absence, accomplished nothing because conditions held the former official in his principal province. The endowment of the executive in the two Canadas acquired no value until too late to be of use; and the only political effect of the clergy reserves was the very opposite of what was intended, for they became a popular grievance against the Church of England and the government. The Canadian divorce of the legislative from the executive council was largely deceptive, because the members of the latter body were almost always the leaders in the former. But all these failures took years to prove, and meanwhile the practice of fission and the prohibition of fusion undoubtedly provided an effective brake upon the democratic part of the machine.

The effect of the American Revolution upon colonial policy is less evident in the government of the West Indies, not only because there was less scope for adjustments such as were attempted in the North American colonies, but also because there was less need for them. The society of British North America was wholly one of freemen, and the Loyalists who had so greatly reinforced it loved British liberty no less than the British Crown. Indeed their attachment to the king was largely a loyalty to British institutions, which they believed guaranteed the truest liberty. The society of the Caribbeans, on the other hand, was predominantly one of slaves; and the Loyalists who went thither did not make it less so, for they too were slave owners and they took their black property with them. Liberty in the West Indies was the privilege of the few to oppress the many, and this perversion of liberty was itself such a blight upon the popular element in government that the latter could not grow to subvert British control. Nevertheless, the problem of maintaining imperial guidance over the administration of these islands was a real one, for there the assemblies were older and stronger—notably in Barbados and Jamaica—and the power of the governor was weaker than in British North America.

On the whole, the policy of the mother country was not so much to introduce, as it was to prevent constitutional innovations in the colonies—particularly on the part of assemblies. It was essentially a conservative policy that would improve upon the past by adhering more strictly to what was regarded as the old ideal of colonial government, though some compromises might still be tolerated out of necessity or convenience. This old ideal, or theory, was a growth rather than a creation. It had taken shape through generations of commissions and instructions issued to colonial governors, and its features were plainly discernible in these and other official documents related to them. Because it was the ideal after which official London strove until well on into the nineteenth century, a summary sketch of it is essential for an understanding of colonial policy during this period.

According to this model, the assembly, elected by a liberal franchise, voted the necessary taxes and appropriations for the support of the colony and passed other legislation to meet the needs of the people. This assembly was nothing more than the lower chamber of the legislature. The upper chamber was the council, whose members were appointed by the home government on the recommendation of the governor and might be suspended by him. Every bill passed by the assembly, even one imposing taxes or appropriating public funds, had also to pass the upper chamber and receive the assent of the governor before it acquired the force of law; even then the home government might disallow it. Moreover, the governor was forbidden to give his assent to certain types of bills. These included bills touching a specified subject, such as shipping or the royal prerogative; any bill re-enacting one that had been disallowed, or repealing one that had been specifically sanctioned by the home government; and, except in emergencies, any measure that was to expire within two years, because otherwise it might defeat the purpose of the third hurdle—in London. Any bill of which the governor was doubtful, he would refer to the home government to decide whether it should become law or not. London would thus keep a tight rein on colonial legislation. It could guide as well as check, for a governor was occasionally instructed to have some particular piece of legislation passed in his colony.

London, according to this model, would also keep a tight rein in the administration of each colony. The assembly was to have no voice whatever in it. That was the business of the governor, who was appointed and sent out for this purpose and invested with ample authority for it. To assist him, he had the council which, because of

subsequent developments, deserves special attention. In striking contrast to the assembly, it was much more than just the upper chamber
of the legislature. It had also an executive and even a judicial function.
It was the highest civil court of appeal in the colony, from which there
was no recourse except to the privy council in London. There was no
criminal appeal from the regular courts, the only hope of a condemned
man being a petition to the governor to exercise the royal prerogative
of pardon or reprieve. To return to the council, most of the business it
handled was executive. Its concurrence was necessary for the exercise
of some gubernatorial powers, such as the erection of courts of justice,
the issuance of warrants for payment of monies out of the public purse,
and the granting of public lands; and its advice, though not essential,
was commonly sought by the governor on other matters pertaining to
the civil administration. The membership of this important body was
small, and there was seldom any change in it. Most, if not all, of the
few principal civil officials in the colony, notably the chief justice and
the receiver general, or treasurer, were ex officio members; while the
other members, who usually formed the majority, were selected from
the community for their personal merits and were commonly allowed
to retain their seats for life, though their tenure was legally at will.
One and all, they were answerable to the governor, who could suspend
any of them, even those who sat ex officio. He could also dismiss and
appoint any government official in the colony except the few top ones,
who received their commissions or delegations from London; and even
these he could suspend and replace temporarily, as he could the councilors, pending a final decision by the secretary of state, to whom he
had to report. As all were thus responsible to him, so was he responsible for all to the government in London, which might recall him at
any time.

The weakest point in this theory was finance. How could British
colonists, bred in the tradition of parliament, be expected to tax themselves without attempting to control the government that spent the
proceeds? The example of the old colonies, where assemblies had
effectively used the power of the purse over local administrations, was
a warning of what might happen in the remaining colonial empire.
Here was a problem that the mother country was never able to solve
satisfactorily but managed to put off by various makeshift arrangements.

Bungling in past generations had ruined what might have been a
solution in the Leeward Islands and Barbados. More than a century
before the American Revolution, these islands had got rid of proprie-

tory claims upon them by imposing a perpetual charge of 4.5 per cent upon the export of their produce. The colonists later claimed that their assemblies had granted this revenue to the Crown to provide for the government of the islands, for which it would have been ample, but the home government squandered most of it in pensions at home and used some of it to pay governors' salaries in other colonies. In 1764, by an exercise of the royal prerogative, the home government imposed the same duties on the ceded islands, just acquired from France. There they were collected for ten years, until a court in England declared them illegal. On the restoration of British rule in these islands at the close of the American Revolution, the home government proposed to straighten out the whole business of the 4.5 per cent duties. The governors of the ceded islands were instructed to press their assemblies to make the duties legal by enacting them, in return for which two thirds of the proceeds would be applied for the benefit of these islands. The Barbados and the Leewards were to receive the same concession. But they did not get it because the assemblies of the other islands refused to adopt the duties, thereby upsetting the nice plan. Already the 4.5 per cent fund was bankrupt, the pensions and governors' salaries charged against it being much greater than the income; the only reform was the restoration of its solvency in 1785 by a parliamentary grant to discharge the arrears and by the removal of a very heavy pension to another fund. More than fifty years were yet to pass before this millstone was removed from the neck of the Leewards and Barbados.

Three other colonies had permanent revenues enacted by their legislatures and earmarked for the support of their governments. Bermuda had a small one, granted in 1698 and administered by a joint committee of the council and the assembly under the presidency of the governor, but it fell short of what it was supposed to cover. The provision in Jamaica, dating from 1728, was somewhat different. In return for the assembly's granting of a permanent revenue from import duties and wine licenses, and its promise to make good any deficit, the government had turned over the quit rents and casual revenues of the Crown to form a combined fund. The whole was charged with permanent appropriations, and any surplus was placed at the joint disposal of governor, council, and assembly. But quarrels arose, and were renewed in 1783, over whether the assembly should share with the governor and council the disposal of its annual grants. The home government prudently refrained from intervening, and a compromise was reached in 1788, when the assembly increased the permanent revenue and got control of any surplus. In 1785 Prince Edward Island became the third colony where a local act established a permanent revenue. It was very small and was administered by the governor.

The British Treasury paid a goodly share of the cost of government in a number of the colonies in either of two ways. In 1748 parliament had begun to appropriate money for Nova Scotia, the settlement of which served an imperial strategic purpose; and now the principal official salaries of the Bahamas and all the North American colonies except Lower Canada were provided for in this fashion, partly out of regard for the Loyalists. The other method was by allowing governors to draw bills on the British Treasury, which paid them out of the annual grant for army extraordinaries. This practice was born of necessity during the Seven Years' War as the only way to meet emergencies, and it was continued afterward out of convenience. To prevent abuses, certain regulations were laid down in 1764 and again in 1785. It was used in the ceded islands, the Leewards, Barbados, the old Province of Quebec, and Lower Canada.

In every colony the court fines and other casual revenues were at the sole disposal of the executive, except in Jamaica. This income, however, never amounted to much; nor did quit rents or other land revenue payable to the Crown give much security to the local administration. But there was another custom of those days that did make it unnecessary to apply to the assemblies for grants that would have given these bodies more power. Public officials from high to low had a legal right to collect fees for services they performed, and with few exceptions they availed themselves of this right to the utmost. While fees were only an incidental part of the emolument that governors received, they were a large part and sometimes the whole of what other public servants got; and while some fees might be charged to the government, the bulk came from the private purses of the community in return for specific services rendered.

By one or more of all the above arrangements, the permanent civil list in almost every colony was pretty well provided for; and this constituted the main cost of government, which was then expected to do little more than preserve law and order. Here and there in the West Indies an assembly might refuse to vote some salaries, but the recalcitrant members made their own public pay for this parsimony by having to put up with incompetent functionaries, such as judges who had never studied law even as amateurs. In any colony it was not the government but their own constituents who suffered if assemblymen did not make necessary appropriations for roads, bridges, and other public works of a civilian nature. To sum up, there was little or no financial lever that assemblies could pull to gain control over the government.

On the whole, the system of colonial government worked tolerably well for some years after the American Revolution, for the simple reason that it suited the character of the colonial empire as it had been altered by that upheaval. The West Indian colonies might be old in years and mature in physical development, but slavery had so blighted their political growth that they were very far from being capable of standing on their own feet. The North American colonies, on the other hand, were all, with the single exception of Lower Canada, still infants who would take a long time to find their feet; and Lower Canada did not get an assembly, which was a new and strange institution to the vast majority of its population, until the French Revolution was beginning to turn the world upside down.[5]

---

[5] There is no evidence that the outbreak of the French Revolution had any appreciable effect upon the framing of the constitution given to Lower Canada in 1791.

II THE FRENCH REVOLUTIONARY AND NAPOLEONIC ERA

Chapters

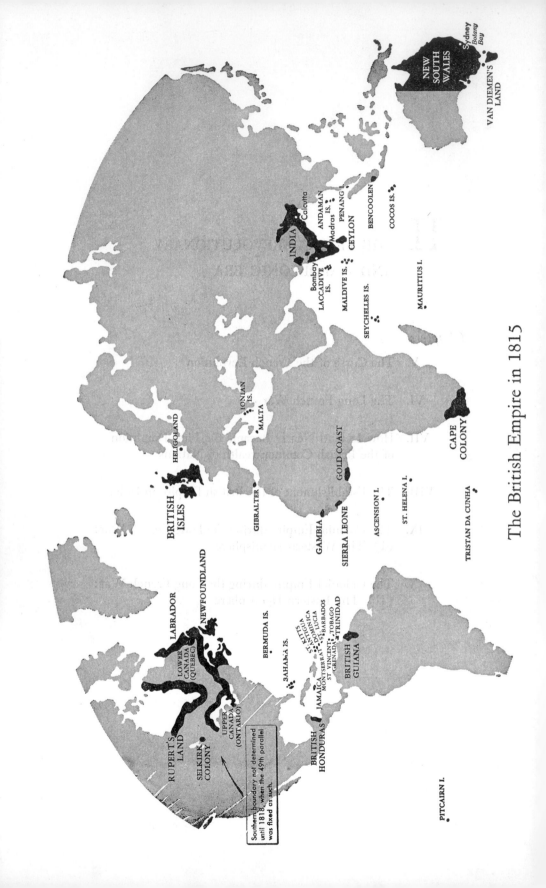

The British Empire in 1815

NEW SOUTH WALES

Sydney
Botany Bay

VAN DIEMEN'S LAND

Calcutta
ANDAMAN IS.
Madras IS.
PENANG I.
INDIA
CEYLON
BENCOOLEN
COCOS IS.
Bombay
LACCADIVE IS.
MALDIVE IS.
SEYCHELLES IS.
MAURITIUS I.

HELIGOLAND
IONIAN IS.
MALTA
BRITISH ISLES
GIBRALTER
GOLD COAST
CAPE COLONY

GAMBIA
SIERRA LEONE
ASCENSION I.
ST. HELENA I.
TRISTAN DA CUNHA

LABRADOR
NEWFOUNDLAND
BERMUDA IS.
LOWER CANADA (QUEBEC)
UPPER CANADA (ONTARIO)
RUPERT'S LAND
SELKIRK COLONY

Southern boundary not determined until 1818, when the 49th parallel was fixed as such.

BAHAMA IS.
ST. KITT'S
BRITISH GUIANA
ANTIGUA
DOMINICA
ST. LUCIA
BARBADOS
JAMAICA
MONTSERRAT
ST. VINCENT
TOBAGO
GRENADA
TRINIDAD
BRITISH HONDURAS
BRITISH GUIANA

PITCAIRN I.

CHAPTER V

The Curse of the French Revolution

THE FRENCH REVOLUTION distorted the history of Britain. To France, and to most other countries that felt the impact of that explosion, it was both a blessing and a curse. To Britain it was only a curse.

It was Revolutionary France that made the startling discovery of liberty for Europe as well as herself. But not for Britain any more than for America. It was Revolutionary France that proclaimed the flaming gospel of democracy to the modern world. But British democracy owes no more to French preaching than does American democracy. It was Revolutionary France, the greatest power on the continent of Europe, that restored and exalted the republican ideal by breaking the tradition that the republican form of government, though it had long existed in a few minor states, was impossible for a great power. The United States, of course, was not yet a great power. What France did for the republican form of government meant nothing to Britain, whose people remembered their unsuccessful experiment with it in Cromwell's day. It was in Revolutionary France that the mighty force of modern nationalism awoke, a dynamic force that remade Europe and spread to other continents. France, however, contributed nothing to nationalism in Britain, where it was already well established, or to the nationalism that was yet to grow within various parts of the empire, as it had already grown in the part that was lost.

On the other hand, it was the French Revolution that, by turning on the church and rending it, began the feud that has plagued the Latin world to our own day—the bitter feud between revolution and religion. This was no part of the curse that was laid upon Britain. That curse was a fear that blighted Britain for a generation. America scarcely felt it, but no country in the Old World could escape it and, bad as it was in Britain, it was worse on the continent. It was an evil phenomenon that we can understand today more easily than we could a generation ago. The French Revolution was a sort of combination of the Communist revolution in Russia and the Nazi revolution in Germany, and it ushered in a quarter of a century of tumults and wars culminating in a military despotism more widespread than Hitler's at its greatest—all springing, so it seemed, from the innocent seed of much-needed reforms. The French Revolution conjured up a terrifying vision of revolution in the abstract. Men thought of it as an all-devouring monster that had to be kept chained beneath the surface of society, or as the burning lava pushing upward against the fragile crust of a volcano; hence the dread of any yielding to pressure from below.

At first there was no sign of the curse in Britain. Even the Tories, whom the French Revolution was to turn into the party of blind reaction, felt relief rather than alarm at the strange news that began to come from across the Channel in the early summer of 1789. They thought that the disturbances in the capital and the provinces of France would eliminate that country as an international factor for some time, and the prospect pleased them. France was England's traditional foe, and had been for so many centuries that the hostility between these two countries was much more historic than any other in the Old World. Moreover, France seemed to be turning over a new leaf with her abolition of feudalism, her enunciation of liberty, and her establishment of a constitutional monarchy. Was she not, in her own way of course, following the English example? Imitation is the sincerest form of flattery, and even Tories are quite susceptible.

Among the Whigs, who were becoming a reform party and as such were soon to be smashed by the French Revolution, there was even more rejoicing over what was happening in France. Not a few of them hoped that the principles of the French Revolution would spread and triumph throughout the world. Their warmhearted leader, Charles James Fox, was the most enthusiastic of all. He declared that the taking of the Bastille was the greatest and best event that had ever happened in the world; and he loudly applauded every step in the progress of the French Revolution, though he regretted the shedding of blood that accompanied it.

Democratic societies were formed in British towns and cities, and they entered into correspondence with the political clubs that were springing up all over France. The British press poured out pamphlets advancing radical views inspired by events in France. In all this there was precious little to suggest that the people were trembling on the verge of rebellion. England was very far from that. The king had recovered the popularity he had lost in the American war, and the prime minister had the solid backing of the public. Scarcely any of the English advocates of French principles would follow French practice. That was not the way of the country, which was to proceed by law and order.

The first note of warning was sounded at the end of 1790, when Edmund Burke published his celebrated *Reflections on the French Revolution*. Earlier than anyone else he saw the danger in the mob violence that was driving the Revolution along, and with uncanny insight he predicted that the movement could not stop with reform but would rush headlong into anarchy, bloodshed, war, and military despotism, and that it would imperil all existing institutions of society in France and elsewhere. He was a magnificent writer and many people read him, but few believed him until developments in France seemed to prove that he was a true prophet.

Within a few months this ultraconservative blast was answered by an ultrademocratic blast—*The Rights of Man,* written by that stormy petrel of three countries, Tom Paine, who had returned to England a few years before. This too gained a wide circulation, and most of the program it contained was so good that it anticipated many later reforms. But the good quickly assumed the aspect of the worst evil. Rarely has a book so defeated its own purpose. English opinion was beginning to take alarm at the way the French Revolution was galloping along, and Paine had overshot the mark by urging republicanism for Britain. It was like calling upon Americans to abolish the flag and the Constitution; for the monarchy was the living personification of the state, and the whole theory of government revolved around the king, the ultimate source of all legal authority. By associating republicanism with democracy, Paine damned democracy. As one eminent English historian has put it, "For years he stuck to everything Liberal like a burr."

The mounting hatred of the new French ideas was not confined, as many later writers have supposed, to the government or the ruling classes. It was, if anything, stronger among the masses. In the summer of 1791, as a protest against local plans to celebrate the second anniversary of the fall of the Bastille, it burst forth in popular tumults in several towns. The worst was in Birmingham, where dwelt Dr. Joseph Priestley, a venerable Unitarian divine, a scientist of international reputation, a man of high public spirit—and an outstanding friend of the French Revolution. Upon him the wrath of the mob descended, burning his chapel, sacking his house, destroying his scientific equipment, and wiping out his experiments of years. He and his family escaped, and shortly afterward they migrated to America. The French Revolution was going into reverse in England.

In accord with public opinion, the government developed a policy of repression—not of such riots but of all reformers because they were regarded as revolutionaries. The most famous of these "incendiaries" was Tom Paine, who was indicted for treason in the spring of 1792. He saved his neck from the hangman's noose by escaping to France, where he nearly lost his head to the guillotine for attacking the Terror and trying to prevent the execution of the king.

Meanwhile the September Massacres of 1792, the gruesome work of the frenzied Parisian mob, sent a chill of horror down the English spine; and in the weeks that followed, the English terror was heightened by French decrees that offered the aid of French armies to all peoples who desired to throw off their rulers and threatened them with French armies if they did not. The European war had begun in the spring, and now French armies, intoxicated by revolutionary spirits and welcomed as apostles of liberty, were overrunning the eastern borders of France. They were openly preparing to invade Holland, where there was a strong republican party, and England was more relieved than surprised when France declared war on her, 1 February 1793.

Already the Tories had become reactionaries, and so had most of the Whigs. Their party was finally broken in the spring of 1792, when one of the youngest members, Charles Grey, organized the "Friends of the People," a society to force parliament to reform itself by stirring up an irresistible popular demand for a democratically elected House of Commons. This young aristocrat's public career culminated forty years later when, as Earl Grey and prime minister, he carried the great Reform Bill of 1832. When he formed this futile society he seemed to be committing political suicide as well as the more heinous crime of wrecking his party. That summer saw the Whig majority working in cooperation with the Tory government, which they openly joined two years later, leaving Fox with only a corporal's guard in opposition; yet he never lost courage—or gained discretion. Even in time of war his undying passion for liberty constantly betrayed him into the utterance of sentiments that, to say the least, were unpatriotic. He never missed an opportunity to attack the government or to praise the enemy, and so this most lovable man in British public life aggravated the unlovely nervous temper of his time.

The curse under which the country had fallen was naturally intensified by the long war, and it cast a dark shadow over the heroic age of Britain's mighty struggle against Revolutionary and Napoleonic France. The government used spies to hunt revolutionaries, and caught quite a number of reformers. In the early years of the war, the courts were filled with prosecutions, and it seems to have been easy to get convictions for charges that were no heavier than sedition. A billsticker was given six months in jail for posting an address calling for parliamentary reform; one lawyer was sentenced to fourteen years' transportation because he had promoted reform societies and had visited France; and another was condemned to prison and the pillory for remarking in a public place that he was "for equality and the rights of man." Some prisoners were held for years without trial, for the Habeas Corpus Act was suspended by parliament, something that had not been done for half a century even in wartime.

There were a few trials for treason and one man was hanged for it—a former spy who plotted to seize Edinburgh Castle. But trial by jury, that priceless gift of England to the world, checked the abuse of this charge when it was brought against a batch of a dozen leaders of reform societies. The first of these to come up was Thomas Hardy, a shoemaker who had founded the London Corresponding Society, memorable as the first political and educational club of workingmen in England. The second was Horne Tooke, a political parson and a terrible tartar who mocked the court. The evidence against him was his advocacy of parliamentary reform, and he summoned Pitt as witness to prove that the prime minister himself had used just such language ten years before. When Hardy and Tooke and one other were acquitted, the rest were discharged.

But if liberalism was not to be treated as actual treason, it was tainted with treason; and the persecution continued with the application of penalties which, though short of death, were bad enough. The societies that had corresponded with France were broken up as nests of dangerous conspirators. There was no doubt that this was what they were, when enemy leaders proudly boasted that thousands in England were just waiting for the word to revolt. Later generations have bitterly denounced the Tory government of that day for its policy of stern repression, but what evidence we have makes the whole nation share the blame. Francis Place, a tailor in Hardy's organization, the man who became the father of nineteenth century radicalism, later testified that "the mass of the shopkeepers and working people" approved the government's actions, "such was their terror of the French regicides and democrats." Indeed, the tyranny of the majority is the worst of all tyrannies when it is inspired by fear.

Here is the great tragedy. It was not the punishment of a small and unpopular minority for holding liberal views. It was the national approval of the punishment. It was the hysterical state of mind into which the whole country was thrown by the French Revolution. It was the phobia of all reform as incipient revolution. It was the gaping gulf that France caused in English history.

If we trace the development of reform in England, we find a clean break of thirty years around this time. The movement that begins in 1822, with a liberal Tory government urged on by a rather weak Whig opposition, fits on to the end of the promising movement when Pitt and his party were liberal Tories and the Whigs were conservative reformers. If we could stretch out the later reforms by pulling 1822 back to the place of 1792, we would get an unbroken and pretty even continuity.

Now let us look at the damage done by this violent break. For one thing, it gave the Irish problem a fatal twist at the very time when it was being straightened out. We shall see this later when we examine that problem by itself. Here we shall confine our attention to social and economic conditions in England, and they tell a tragic tale. It is a tale of growing strains and stresses in a rapidly changing society, of new and painful conditions that called loudly for sympathetic and intelligent treatment by remedial legislation, of the complete failure to provide such a cure for the mounting ills, and actually of measures that cruelly aggravated the evil.

For the first time in her history, England was unable to feed herself from the produce of her own soil. Though new agricultural methods were steadily increasing the domestic supply of food, the population was increasing faster still. With the exception of the fourteenth century spurt after the Black Death, the population had never grown so fast as it did in the latter part of the eighteenth century, when the acceleration that marks the nineteenth century began. The cause seems to have been a declining death rate rather than a rising birth rate.

Until the second half of the eighteenth century, England was a grain-exporting country, but the balance swung the other way at the time of the American Revolution. By the end of the century, when the population of England and Wales was slightly more than nine million and that of Scotland was somewhat over a million and a half, approximately a fifth of the country's requirements of food had to be imported. This, by the way, had to come from Europe, for it was roughly another half century before the Old World needed much food from the New World and the latter could supply it.

To reduce this dependence on foreign supplies, which was felt to be dangerous, parliament tried to encourage home production by the Corn Law of 1791. This offered a bounty on export when the price was no more than 44 shillings a quarter, which was slightly less than the average of the previous three decades; it imposed prohibitive duties up to 50 shillings; and it allowed practically free importation only when the price exceeded 54 shillings. Here a few words of explanation may be necessary. Being a conservative people, the English have kept the original meaning of the word "corn." It is "kernel" or "grain," as Americans know who read their Bibles carefully—the familiar King James version. And as we commonly use the general term for the specific, saying "the price of grain" when we really mean the price of wheat, so do they commonly mean wheat when they say "corn." The English "quarter" of grain is eight bushels—a quarter of a ton. Thus corn at 54 shillings a quarter meant about $1.65 for a bushel of wheat, which was two and a half times the daily wage of a London carpenter.

This looks bad; but what followed was worse, and it was not due to the act at all. A succession of bad harvests, beginning in 1792, and the interference of the war with importations made the price of wheat jump to higher levels. It reached $2.45 a bushel in 1795, with the government offering bounties on import. It hit $3.80 in 1800, and $4.65 in the next year. Wages rose, but nothing like the cost of living; and the poor suffered terrible distress, which occasionally found expression in bread riots, while the landlords' profits swelled.

The stimulus of high prices expanded the domestic production of food, so that perhaps it saved England from being starved into surrender by Napoleon. Cultivation of the soil became more intensive, with the speeding up of the agricultural revolution; and it also became more extensive, for a lot of land that had never been tilled before was plowed up for crops. Though much of it was good, there was much that was not profitable except at prices that pinched the poor.

The structure of society was rapidly changing as a result of the combined influence of the agricultural and industrial revolutions. The multiplication of enclosures, facilitated by a general Enclosures Act of 1801, enabled the landlords to get more land and reduced the mass of the rural population to the position of a proletariat. The rural population lost more than the land off which they had lived, and with it the right to use the common pasture. They lost another source of support, another side of life; for the handicrafts that they and their families had pursued in their own cottages—notably spinning—were being destroyed by the competition of more efficient machines in the new factories. They lost their independence, and there was nothing left for them save the miserable wages of agricultural laborers. One may wonder why these wages were so bad when prices were so good; but the new methods of agriculture were creating a greater supply than demand in the village labor market, and the good prices were bad for those who had to pay them, as ordinary villagers now had to do.

In the towns a new capitalist class was arising, born of the industrial revolution. They were men who started life as poor apprentices and ended it as rich manufacturers, self-made men and proud of it; men who had risen by breaking with tradition, men who were transforming England into the workshop of the world, men of wealth, men of power, men of the future. Their mills, or factories, formerly small units strung out along the limited power-giving streams of the North, were now, thanks to James Watt, more and more concentrated as bigger units in the new and large industrial centers of the Midlands and the North; and this concentration was forming another new class, a class that was to swallow up the greater part of English society.

This was the urban proletariat, spawned by the industrial revolution. By 1811, less than 35 per cent of the families in England were employed in agriculture, and more than 45 per cent in trade and industry. There was thus a great shift of population from country to town, from cottage and field to tenement and factory. The commonest type of Englishman was no longer a villager engaged in subsistence farming with the aid of his family. He was a propertyless industrial slave. His wages, though better than those of his country cousin, could scarcely supply his own individual needs; so his wife and all their children above the age of five or six were likewise condemned to toil in the mills from morning till night. It was the only way they could exist—one can hardly say live.

All over the land, in town and country alike, the few were thriving on the misery of the many. The landlords and the millowners were not at all conscious of this. What caused them to rise and the others to fall were great impersonal forces pushing society about—the unprecedented growth of population, the European war, the revolution in agriculture, and the revolution in industry. These inexorable forces were bound to produce widespread suffering.

This suffering cried out for sympathetic and intelligent treatment, and England could have found it if the French madness had not seized hold of the nation. The age of humanitarianism had begun. Witness the labors of Wilberforce and many others for the abolition of the slave trade, finally accomplished in 1807. Witness the work of John Howard, the father of prison reform and one of the outstanding social reformers of the modern world. He had just died, in 1790, while investigating hospital conditions in Russia. In addition to the humanitarian spirit, we can see in the legislation of the 1780's a distinct tendency of both Whigs and Tories to favor reform. It looks like the beginning of a movement that would broaden in scope and quicken in pace to meet the growing needs of the day. Then, in the early years of the next decade, it was blighted—at the very time when it was becoming most urgent.

When wages and prices spelled starvation for the poor, the authorities were gravely concerned. The humanitarian instinct was aroused; so were recent memories of rural disorders in France, where the early days of the Revolution saw starving peasants storm noble chateaux all over the country. In 1795 and 1796, the plight of the poor was aired in parliament; Pitt, who was less prone to panic than were most of his fellows, was prepared to relieve the public distress by legislation of a socialist character.[1]

Parliament, however, was incapable of doing anything effective to meet the crisis, and the local magistrates were already coming to the rescue with a palliative that had most disastrous consequences. The sessions of the justices of the peace, mostly country gentry, were still and for many years to come the only real local government outside the old chartered towns and cities; and it was at a session of the Berkshire justices in 1795 that the new policy was inaugurated.

Instead of fixing wages at a reasonable level, by the exercise of an old power long neglected, the assembled magistrates ordered wages to be supplemented out of parish rates[2] to guarantee to every family a minimum income calculated at so much per head according to the price

---

[1] Though it was not so called because the word "socialism" was not coined for another forty years.

[2] We would say taxes, but the English confine the use of this word to national levies.

of the standard loaf. For example, with the gallon loaf then at one shilling, the weekly income of a family was to be three shillings for the head and half as much for each other member. This measure was soon widely copied throughout rural England, and it was also adopted in some industrial districts. It came to be known, after the little village where the meeting was held, as the Speenhamland Act, though properly speaking it was not an *act* because it was not passed by parliament.

Much nonsense has been written about this system of relief. Because the extra money was drawn for all children, even bastards, it has been accused of fostering immorality, of encouraging the poor to multiply like rabbits, and of discouraging their sense of parental responsibility. The system has also been blamed for spreading other vices, such as drunkenness, and even crime. Recent research has discredited all these charges, however, and has supported the view that the people at that low level of existence would have done what they did without this pitiful subsidy.

The undoubtedly disastrous consequences of the Speenhamland Act were bad enough in all conscience. This act aggravated existing evils and added new ones. It subsidized the payment of lower instead of higher wages, and it magnified the employer's interest in keeping them down. It increased the squeeze on the small farmer who worked his own land; for he now had to help pay the labor bill of his big competitor, who thus got back more than he paid to support the system. Because the parish was responsible for the unemployed, it led also to the vicious practice of hiring out gangs of paupers—men, women, and children—under conditions that closely resembled slavery.

Apart from this pernicious system of dealing with poverty, the only treatment the authorities had for the sickness of English society at this time was repression or neglect. Repression was applied when any symptom seemed dangerous. One was poaching. As the squire grew more prosperous and the humble villager more miserable, the former improved his stock of game while the latter felt an increasing temptation to kill and eat it. Therefore, in 1800, a sport-loving parliament tightened the game laws by decreeing imprisonment with hard labor for anyone caught under suspicious circumstances. This made matters worse, for poachers then took to operating in armed gangs in order to resist capture. The consequence was that in 1803 the penalty of death was prescribed for even a threat of resistance in arms, which only intensified the nightly warfare in the English woods. There gentlemen and their servants exchanged volleys with poachers turned into ruffians

by a savage law and such inhuman devices as the concealed spring gun
and the steel mantrap.

The industrial workers took to forming small friendly societies, of
which a large crop sprang up in the war years. The individual, by
pooling his pennies, arranged for sick benefit and other mutual aid;
and the government encouraged the movement by passing a Friendly
Societies Act in 1793. But when the workmen took to forming rudimentary trade unions, which were helping them to bargain with their
employers, this was interpreted as another dangerous symptom of incipient revolution, and the government came down with a heavy hand.
In 1799 Pitt introduced a bill to prohibit under severe penalties any
combination to raise wages. Parliament passed this bill with practically
no discussion, and in the following year this Combination Act was
stiffened. Even the godly and philanthropic Wilberforce urged the
duty of adopting this legislation, which outlawed the trade union movement for a quarter of a century and so taught the town worker the
absolute necessity for parliamentary reform.

The slaves in the mills, thus prohibited from protecting themselves
against oppression by their employers, got no protection from the
government. Sir Robert Peel, the father of the great statesman and
himself a great cotton manufacturer, persuaded parliament in 1802
to pass the first Factory Act; but its purpose was limited to regulating
the conditions of work for poor-law apprentices, and this purpose was
defeated for lack of machinery to enforce it. The first effective Factory
Act did not come for another thirty years.

To cap the climax of a suffering England, the curse of the French
Revolution lived on for years after the fall of Napoleon; for the reactionary Tories whose government in the end triumphed over him
were, by this very triumph, entrenched in power. But the story of the
postwar reaction is better told as the prelude to the great reform era
which it precipitated. And now we must turn to the war itself.

CHAPTER VI

The Long French War

In 1940, when Britain without an ally stood at bay against the Nazis, her cities pounded to pieces by the Luftwaffe in preparation for the invasion that was hourly expected, many Americans wondered how soon British surrender would end the agony. But it was not the first time that the stubborn people of that little island refused to admit defeat when the overwhelming might of the European conqueror seemed to blot out all hope for them. During the long war unleashed by the French Revolution they had again and again seen all their allies fall by the wayside, leaving them alone to face France running amuck in Europe; and repeatedly—once for two years on end—they had been threatened with invasion by French armies that many times outnumbered their own.

This long French war, which offers a suggestive parallel to the Second World War, is one of a series of struggles that have shaken Europe about once a century since the close of the Middle Ages. The same issue has run through them all: the domination of the continent by one great power. This issue has always been most vital to England, a small country separated from the mainland by only twenty-one miles of water. Out of sheer self-defense, England has always had to throw her weight against the European power that menaced the others. Their independent existence and hers have been tied together inextricably.

This whole condition, the danger of domination by one and the combination of the others to prevent it, has been rationalized as the Balance of Power. But it should not be forgotten that the fact preceded the theory, and that when people came to talk of the necessity of preserving the Balance of Power this was really only a means to an end, the end being their own national independence. Moreover, we have been forced to face on a world scale the very same issue, with our own interests tied to those of other nations—a combination fortunate for us as well as for them.

Three times before the First World War, England played a role comparable to that which has since been thrust upon the United States. Back in the days of Queen Elizabeth I, when Spain bestrode the world like a colossus, English aid to the Dutch and the English destruction of the Spanish Armada turned the tide. A century later Louis XIV of France lorded it over Europe until he was brought to his knees by the greater power of an alliance organized and sustained by England. She provided the leadership, she contributed the most efficient army under the great Duke of Marlborough, she was the paymaster of the allies, and she threw her decisive sea power into the scale. The third time was when she was the one consistent foe of the much more powerful and dangerous France inspired by the Revolution and led by Napoleon, who was perhaps the greatest military genius of all time.

The Britain against which France declared war in the beginning of 1793 had the strongest fleet in the world, but she had scarcely any army—a bare twenty-seven thousand men. Her whole tradition was naval rather than military because of her island position. Here we come upon such an important influence in the development of the country—a development of which the United States has been the unconscious heir—that we may turn aside for a moment to consider it.

Casting a sweeping glance back through the centuries, we see that the problem of defense was for seagirt England quite different from what it was for continental countries with land frontiers separating them from dangerous foes. These countries were more open to invasion and had to maintain armies for their own protection, as England did not. Broadly speaking, it was possible in England but not on the continent for the people to oppose the king without endangering their country, and it was possible on the continent but not in England for the king to use against his own people the instrument that the necessity of national protection had placed in his hands. Armies can be used at home to build up and maintain absolute rule, but ships cannot. So it is not surprising that absolute monarchy became the normal form of government on the continent, whereas it could not grow in England. The tradition of liberty that she developed was sea-born. Her parliament was only one of many that began to appear at the same time in Europe, but hers alone survived, with the result that later generations in other lands looked to it as a sort of model. Thus it came to be known as the mother of parliaments; and because, as we have just seen, the

English Channel was the mother of the English parliament, we might call that protecting arm of the sea the grandmother of parliaments.

To return to the long French war, we find that it developed with strange surprises, like all great wars. Though the end did not come for another twenty-two years, Pitt told his friends it would be over in a campaign or two, and there seemed to be good reasons for his confident belief. The government of France was bankrupt. This was not a new condition for France, and it had invariably forced that country to turn from war to peace. Moreover, her armies appeared to be on the verge of dissolution. They had lost almost all their officers, for only nobles had been allowed to hold commissions and the Revolution had scattered their class like chaff before the wind. The French armies had also lost their discipline, blown to pieces by the explosion of liberty. Yet France was about to step forth on a career of conquest such as the Old World had never seen since the days of the Roman Empire.

Britain fought with her navy, as we shall presently see; with her gold, which she poured out like water to sustain her allies; and with her army, which she finally developed into a first-class fighting force when, after many years of vain efforts, she found on the continent a place where she could use it with effect. Pitt began by organizing an impressive coalition of powers, great and small, from Russia to Portugal, and by sending small military expeditions to the continent, chiefly to cooperate with French royalists. These expeditions were more than wasted. Like the attempts the continental allies made at the same time to take advantage of dissension in France, they riveted the Revolution more tightly on that country, just as in a later day European intervention to aid the White Russians to overthrow the Red regime only consolidated that regime by rallying patriotism back of it.

Half the British army was sent thousands of miles away to the Caribbean, the seat of by far the largest military operations of the British during the first three years of the war. The primary objective was the conquest of the French West Indies, which constituted a danger to the neighboring British islands and provided bases for French privateers preying on British commerce. The secondary purpose, which proved to be of more importance, was the suppression of the blacks whose revolt, instigated by French republican agents preaching freedom, spread from San Domingo through the English as well as the French islands and threatened the existence of the white race in the Archipelago. The servile rising was ultimately crushed except where it began. Campaigning in that vile climate cost the British, in these first three years, many times the number of the original expedition—forty thousand dead and as many invalids. Not long afterward, when the Netherlands and Spain were brought within the French system, the first as a satellite republic and the second as a subservient ally, the British began to reap a greater harvest of their overseas possessions.

Meanwhile the war in Europe was a miserable failure for the allies. In 1795, Belgium, the Netherlands, and the Rhineland had been "liberated" by the French, and the valuable Dutch navy had been taken by the French cavalry riding over the ice. Prussia and Russia had withdrawn to share with Austria in partitioning what was left of Poland; and though Austria was still in the war, all the other continental allies had retired from the struggle. When British military forces, having tried a jab here and a jab there with never more than momentary success, were compelled to pull out of the Netherlands early in this year, they practically disappeared from the continent until 1806.

The next couple of years were terribly dark for Britain. In 1796 Napoleon Bonaparte, in one of the most brilliant campaigns of military history, swept through northern Italy, routing the Austrian armies there; and in the following spring, crossing the Alps from northeastern Italy, he coerced Britain's one remaining ally to make peace. Already Britain was in a very critical position. In the summer of 1796, Spain, her ally of only a year before, was so impressed by Bonaparte's brilliant successes in Italy that she re-entered the war—now on the French side. This meant the addition of the considerable Spanish navy to the already impressive combination of the French and the Dutch fleets; and it obliged the British to evacuate the Mediterranean, which then became a French lake until 1798.

Early in 1797, the British got a bad scare when they learned that they had nearly lost Ireland to the French; for around Christmas time, 1796, a French fleet bearing a French army had crossed from Brest to Bantry Bay on the Irish coast, had there waited five days for weather that would make a landing possible, and had then returned to its base without encountering a hostile British force. Ireland, denuded of troops and ready to welcome an invasion, would have been easy prey for that army if foul weather had not prevented a landing. In February a smaller expedition from the same base demonstrated that a French landing in Wales was not impossible, though the troops that got ashore and the frigates that brought them were captured.

A few days after this landing a financial crises forced England off gold. It was the first time in her history that this had happened, and it was felt as a catastrophe. There had been a long and heavy drain of specie to the continent for the payment of subsidies to the allies and the purchase of supplies necessitated by the bad harvests at home. What brought things to a head was a run on the banks—caused by a dread of invasion.

Almost immediately afterward the greatest mutiny in British naval history paralyzed the fleets in home waters, the country's only defense against invasion from France, and for a while the mutineers blockaded the mouth of the Thames. The sailors had many just grievances, one being that the cost of everything had gone up while their pay had not been raised for more than a century. In two months the mutiny was ended with most of the seamen's demands granted and with less than a score of their ringleaders strung at the end of a yardarm. During this intensely anxious time, sheer luck prevented the launching of another invasion, which was to have been covered by the Dutch fleet in the Texel and the French fleet in Brest. Meanwhile, of course, Britain was badly alarmed. This year, 1797, was the blackest of the whole war, but the dawn was still many years off.

In 1798, when rebellion flamed in Ireland, Napoleon's expedition, eluding the British fleet that re-entered the Mediterranean, took Malta from the old crusading Order of the Knights of St. John, and conquered Egypt; French control in Italy was extended over almost the whole of the peninsula; and French plundering tyranny provoked a Swiss revolt that the French drowned in a bath of blood. In the following year, French aggressions enabled Pitt to organize a second coalition, supported by English gold and including Russia, Turkey, Austria, Naples, and Portugal. It began auspiciously but ended disastrously. By 1801 it had completely broken up, again leaving Britain all alone against France, now ruled by the indomitable Napoleon; and already, inspired by him, the Baltic powers, including Russia, were leagued against Britain to exclude her from the region on which she was dependent for vital naval supplies. But, as we will see, her sea power enabled her to force her way into the Baltic, and down into the Mediterranean to take both Malta and Egypt.

The short peace of Amiens, concluded in 1802, was almost as bad as the war, and it soon turned out to be no peace at all but only a truce. The British, supreme at sea, and the French, victorious on land, were both weary of the struggle; but the terms arranged at Amiens did not represent a draw, for that was impossible with Napoleon as one of the parties. The British agreed to return the whole harvest of conquests their sea power had gathered, except Trinidad and Ceylon, captured from the Spaniards and the Dutch respectively; while France not only regained her colonies but also remained mistress of Belgium, the Netherlands, the left bank of the Rhine, Switzerland, and Italy.

Napoleon had gained for France position and power such as even the ambitious Louis XIV had never attained, but the more he got the more he wanted. As he later admitted, he could not keep the peace because he had to keep his glory warm. Like Hitler in a later day, the demon within him would not let him stop. Having set his foot on the path of aggression, the unscrupulous master of France pressed on, characteristically trying to browbeat England with blustering threats and with accusations that she was a warmonger, until in the spring of 1803, seeing that he was bent on war, she declared it.

Never again could England trust Napoleon. Never would she make peace with him. She would fight till he was done or she went under. It was a life and death struggle for her, and he realized it was for him too. Through the dozen years of war that followed, he saw in England his principal foe, the one power that he had to destroy or it would destroy him. One by one the continental powers that dared to face him in the field had to bite the dust until in five years' time he brought the whole of the continent, including the Russian Empire, within his system. But he knew he could never consolidate it so long as he could not subdue England. He knew that, while she continued to defy him, his vassal states would look to her for aid and get it. Her submission was essential for their submission. To hold them down until he could bring her down, he had to press more and more heavily upon them, until the time came when he had not enough power to maintain his position.

With the directness of genius, Napoleon concentrated his attention for the first two years of the war upon plans for a gigantic invasion of England. At the Channel ports nearest to that island, he collected the largest army that western civilization had ever seen and built enough flat-bottomed boats to carry it all across the narrow Strait of Dover—so many boats that they had to be piled in tiers when not in use for training maneuvers on the beaches. All he needed to get this enormous army to its destination, where it could have made short work of any resistance, was command of that little body of water for a couple of days or so; this he calculated was possible by concentrating at that point a French fleet that would be just sufficient to hold off the

British navy during the short time necessary for the operation. This concentration upon which everything turned was the one thing he could not accomplish because British sea power prevented him. And now it is time we turned to examine that vital factor.

It was British sea power that, in the last analysis, dragged Napoleon down to his doom, and he never understood it. This greatest master of land warfare, in which he could read his enemy's mind like an open book and could even make his enemy do what he wanted, was utterly baffled when he applied himself to the problems of warfare on the sea. That was not his element. Indeed, until Captain (later Admiral) A. T. Mahan began to expound the influence and principles of sea power in 1890, they were clothed in mystery; and it is rather curious that the British, the greatest maritime people of all time, had to wait for an American naval officer to explain the secrets of their own power. His classical works, by the way, have been translated into many languages and have been very much better known and appreciated outside the United States than in it. He is an outstanding modern example of the prophet "not without honor save in his own country."

Mahan it was who revealed that, from the ancient wars between the Greeks and the Persians, the history of western civilization has been profoundly changed by conflicts at sea more often than by the much more frequent clash of arms on land. It was sea power that saved the fine flower of Athenian civilization from being destroyed in the bud by oriental despotism. It was sea power that gave Rome the victory over Carthage. It was sea power that enabled Islam to sweep across northern Africa, over Spain, and up into France. It was sea power that transferred the fight between Christian and Moslem back into the east with the Crusades. And so it continued down through the ages to our own time.

The French Revolution was fatal to French sea power, which was nearly a match for the British in the summer of 1789, the proportion being roughly five to six. Then the French navy lost almost all its officers and all its discipline, and this loss was much more serious than that suffered by the land forces. The navy was a much more highly trained technical service; it required a much longer training; and this training could not be conducted, like that of a new army, safely out of reach of the enemy, for it had to be on the open sea. Therefore, though the French still had the ships, which were often better than the British, the companies that manned these ships were now inferior as fighting units, despite all French efforts at recovery. Spain was the next strongest power at sea, with about half as many good ships-of-the-line as Britain, and the Dutch were not far behind the Spaniards. It will thus be seen that the British had something to think about when the French got the use of these two navies in addition to their own.

Unlike the continental fleets, the Royal Navy of Britain grew in size and efficiency as the war progressed; and at this time it had the supreme genius of its history: the naval genius that balances the military genius that commanded France, the man whom Mahan has called the embodiment of sea power. In all English history by far the greatest national hero is Horatio Nelson.

This son of a country parson entered the navy when he was twelve years old—in 1770, the year after Napoleon was born—and during the next twenty-odd years his training, spread widely over the ocean, was comparatively uneventful. The proverbial sailor, he was always falling in love, and once in the West Indies he went so far as to marry a young widow, but it was not a serious affair. More serious, he won the confidence of those above him and the devotion of those under him. When war came in 1793, the Admiralty fitted out a fleet for the Mediterranean. There Nelson served as captain of a battleship, and it was during an attack on Corsica in 1794 that he lost his right eye, which kept him off duty for just one day. But it was not until after Spain had deserted England and joined France, forcing the British to abandon the Mediterranean, that the first major battle was fought at sea and Nelson leaped into fame.

Nelson was the deciding factor in the four most important naval engagements of the whole war, and this was the first of them. It was the Battle of Cape St. Vincent, off the southwest corner of Portugal, which occurred in February 1797 in the midst of England's darkest hour. Half the effective Spanish ships-of-the-line, twenty-seven in all, having emerged from the safety of the Mediterranean, fell in with fifteen British under Admiral Jervis. Despite his numerical inferiority, he flew at them. The Spaniards fled and all might have escaped had not Nelson, who commanded a ship in the British line, caught them by a bold stroke. To execute it he had to disobey a general order of the admiral. At the end of the day, which he thus saved, Nelson was accused of disobedience by a jealous rival; and the wise Jervis curtly replied: "It certainly was so, and if you commit such a breach of your orders, I will forgive you also." The Spaniards had lost five vessels and the British none, but much more important was the revelation of the fact that the British had nothing to fear from the Spaniards. The rejoicing in Britain was immense, and Nelson became a rear-admiral.

A year and a half later, Nelson won another triumph, which raised him high above all his contemporaries. In the spring of 1798, the Admiralty ordered a return to the Mediterranean, with Nelson in command, to check the great maritime expedition that Napoleon was preparing in Toulon. Unfortunately the order was given a fortnight too late to prevent the escape, and when Nelson arrived to find the French gone—he knew not whither—heavy weather had blown away his frigates, the eyes of his fleet. Nelson had Napoleon's uncanny power of knowing what his enemy would do. Though most of the reports had credited the French with aiming their blow at the British Isles, he discarded this possibility because the prevailing winds would prevent them from making for Gibraltar, and he calculated that Egypt must be the objective. Straight as an arrow he sped to the mark, and he beat the French to it. When he found no trace of them there, he feared he had made a fatal blunder. So back he doubled to Sicily, where he got information that convinced him he was right in the first place. Again he pressed all sail for Egypt. Being still without scouting vessels, he had twice passed his prey. This time there was no escaping him. In the Battle of the Nile, on 1 August 1798, the French admiral was killed and his fleet was annihilated. Napoleon and his army were marooned in Egypt, while Nelson's fleet was at last free to scatter and "mop up" the Mediterranean. Nelson had changed the whole course of the war. Incidentally, on the way back, he met his Cleopatra in Lady Hamilton, the wily wife of the aged British ambassador in Naples; but Nelson was more a Caesar than an Antony, for he did not lose his head with his heart.

Nelson's third great exploit was to break open the Baltic in the spring of 1801. Though he was now a vice-admiral, considerations of rank made him second in command of this expedition. Yet everyone knew who was the real leader, and it is characteristic of the confidence reposed in him that when he sought instructions from the head of the Admiralty the latter replied, "Damn it, Nelson, send them to the devil in your own way." The Danes had erected strong fortifications at Copenhagen to keep the British out, and when Nelson began the attack according to his own plans, his superior thought it such a hopeless task that he signaled to leave off action. Nelson refused. Turning to the captain of his flagship, he remarked that he had a right to be blind sometimes, and then to the amusement of all around he put the glass to his right eye and exclaimed, "I really do not see the signal." Contrary to the popular interpretation of this famous incident that led to a famous victory, he was not playing the British bulldog—hanging on with his teeth. He was using his brain. The movement of his force was so confined by shoal water and the direction of the wind that he could not obey without facing almost certain destruction.

The fourth and final triumph of Nelson was the Battle of Trafalgar, just outside the Strait of Gibraltar. Long and highly important maneuvers preceded it, and in these Nelson's part was as decisive as in the battle itself. Napoleon thought to cover his invasion of England by an intricate scheme, the main features of which were quite simple. His various fleets, the chief of which were in Brest and Toulon, would dash out and away as if bound for the East Indies. Much of the Royal Navy would then go off on this wild-goose chase around Africa, while the French would secretly rendezvous in the West Indies and return to seize temporary control of the Strait of Dover. The Brest fleet never got out, however, and the British were not to be deceived.

Admiral Villeneuve escaped from Toulon in the spring of 1805 and by a succession of lucky breaks not only eluded Nelson, then commanding in the Mediterranean, but also got clear of Gibraltar long before Nelson could follow. Then, with unerring judgment, Nelson penetrated the enemy's design, chased the French to the West Indies and back again, once more outstripping them. Villeneuve, on returning, had a stiff brush with the British and did not dare make for Brest to release the French fleet there. He put into Spain, on the northwest corner, where he effected a junction with a Spanish squadron on which Napoleon counted, for Spain was again the subservient ally. In the middle of August, Villeneuve sailed with his enlarged fleet. But instead of steering north, to carry out Napoleon's plan, he headed south for Cadiz because the swarming British left him no alternative.

This move turned the crisis, for when Napoleon heard of it he could wait no longer lest he be caught in the rear. Pitt had recently organized the third coalition, and already Russian and Austrian armies, for which England paid so much per man per year, were on the move. The Grand Army that had been destined for England was suddenly snatched away from the Channel ports and marched across the continent to smash Austria at the great Battle of Ulm on 20 October 1805.

Not until the following day was the Battle of Trafalgar fought, which may suggest that it was unnecessary. It was for the French, but not for the British. Until a decision was reached at sea, Napoleon could resume his plans for an invasion of England. The reason for the battle was Villeneuve's desperation. He knew he was a ruined man because the wrathful emperor held him responsible for wrecking the great plan to conquer England. So the French admiral came out of Cadiz with thirty-three French and Spanish ships-of-the-line to face Nelson, who was waiting for him with twenty-seven British ships. About noon, when the opposing fleets were almost within range, a string of flags on Nelson's ship *Victory* fluttered out a signal that was greeted with loud cheers and has ever since been celebrated: "England expects that every man will do his duty." In a few hours the battle was finished, and so was the combined sea power of France and Spain. But Nelson lay dead in the cockpit of his flagship, having been carried below when shot through the spine. For three hours he had lingered in agony until he knew the battle was won, and then he died.

The leaden coffin in which the body was brought home was cut up and distributed as "relics of Saint Nelson," as a gunner of the *Victory* reverently called them; his flag, when about to be lowered into the grave, was suddenly rent in pieces by the sailors, that each of them might preserve a precious fragment as long as he lived. What these sacred relics were to those rough but honest men, Nelson's flagship *Victory* has been to the whole nation. To our own day his ship has ridden at anchor in Portsmouth harbor, whence he sailed for his last and most glorious fight. National heroes are the greatest asset a country can have, and England is rich in possessing Nelson. To all English people he still lives, for the truly great hero never dies. He is immortal, living on in the lives of his countrymen whom he inspires from generation to generation.

Nelson's final triumph changed the course of history. As Mahan has pointed out, "Moscow and Waterloo are the inevitable consequences of Trafalgar." This battle shattered all possibility of Napoleon's conquest of England, and without the conquest of England his empire was doomed. He knew he had to take the citadel of sea power in order to hold his empire together; therefore, when he saw he could not take it by quick assault, he determined to take it by slow siege, by the steady pressure of his great land power. Hence his Continental System, which only hastened his own downfall by stretching his power until it broke.

The Continental System aimed at the economic strangulation of England. Theoretically this was possible, because her most valuable market by far was on the continent and there Napoleon was supreme. If he could only shut her out of this market, he might choke her into submission. Such was the plan that Trafalgar forced upon him as the only means of encompassing the fall of his archenemy.

It was impossible to enforce this system without causing widespread distress on the continent, because Britain possessed a practical monopoly of supplying the people of Europe with some very important articles. Her monopoly sprang partly from her unique industrial development and partly from her naval supremacy. The list included products of her own manufacture, such as textiles, and also the produce of her own or conquered possessions, sugar being a prominent item. Even Napoleon himself could not refrain from violating his own system, and that rather frequently. On one occasion he procured from Britain a consignment of fifty thousand greatcoats for his troops.

How could Napoleon seal the whole continent? How could he deprive all the people of Europe of British goods? He might clamp his system upon France, but what about the other countries? He had to persuade them to adopt and, what was much more difficult, to enforce his decrees that outlawed all trade with Britain, whether in British or neutral ships. How could he persuade them? Only by force. Thus he was led on, step by step, to extend his power and to make it more oppressive everywhere. By 1808, having got even Russia into his system after thoroughly defeating Czar Alexander in the field, he saw only one area on the continent where British goods were leaking in badly. That was the Iberian peninsula, and he could not tolerate the breach. To plug the leak effectually, he at once overran the peninsula with his armies.

There Napoleon's empire began to crack. There occurred the first national uprising on the continent to shake off the yoke of the conqueror. By overthrowing the governments of Spain and Portugal, he opened the markets of all Latin America to the British, affording a welcome relief from the pressure of the Continental System; and he gave the British a foothold on the mainland from which he was never able to dislodge them—because he had overreached his own power.

That this was what he had done, soon became more and more apparent. In the following year, 1809, the Spanish revolt encouraged Austria to rise again. To suppress Austria—for the fourth time—he had to withdraw troops from Spain, with the result that the revolt there, aided by the British, flamed up worse than ever. When the suppression of Austria freed him on the east, he threw mightier forces into the southwestern peninsula to crush the national resistance and expel the invader. He smothered the rising and pushed the British back to Lisbon, but he could not penetrate the strong lines of defense prepared by Wellington. While Napoleon's army was held there, he heard that his Continental System had broken down in the east, with the defection of Russia. That was many times worse for him than leaving a little corner of Portugal to the British, and so he turned to force his system back upon Russia in 1812. Thus Trafalgar drove him into a course of action that involved him in ever-widening difficulties.

In the mighty struggle between the sea giant and the land monster, neutrality was quite impossible. It had disappeared from Europe, and no nation that had dealings with Europe could preserve it. Hence the American War of 1812, to which more attention will be given in another chapter. Here we need only observe its place in the larger setting. Though the United States had plenty of justification for declaring war on Britain—and for that matter against Napoleon too—the British could see things then only in relation to the much greater European struggle that had so long absorbed them and seemed to be approaching its climax. What they saw was the United States stabbing them in the back to rob them of Canada and relying on Napoleon to finish them off when he had finished Russia. Naturally they were very bitter at the time; but they soon got over it. The United States was so unprepared to fight, and contained so many people who would have preferred to fight on the other side, that the War of 1812 never amounted to much. Though it is still well remembered in the United States—and better still in Canada—it has long since been so forgotten on the other side of the Atlantic that today only a very small percentage of even well-educated Englishmen have ever heard of it. What pushed it into the background almost immediately was the victory over the greatest power that had ever risen on the European continent.

To return to our story, Napoleon had to withdraw many of his best troops from Spain for his new Russian campaign, with the result that the British penetrated Spain while he invaded Russia. There he completely lost the largest army he ever commanded; and though he rushed back to France and collected another army, he had left his strength behind him. Prussia, having waited years for this opportunity, leaped to arms and joined the advancing Russians. Austria soon joined too. Meanwhile Wellington, the British "Iron Duke," having developed the most efficient army then in existence, completed his liberation of Spain and, mercifully dismissing his insurgent Spanish forces at the border, pushed on into France. That was in 1813, when Napoleon lost everything east of the Rhine. In the following spring, the armies of the reformed European alliance, again cemented with British gold, closed in on Paris, and Napoleon abdicated under pressure from his marshals.

Napoleon's overthrow in 1814 had to be repeated in 1815, when he escaped from Elba, his first place of exile, and France rallied to him again. The end came on June 18 just south of Brussels, at Waterloo, where the Duke of Wellington and his peninsular veterans won a resounding victory. Again the emperor abdicated, and this time he fled to the west coast of France. He hoped to escape to the United States, and one is tempted to speculate on what might have happened had he managed to reach it. But British ships were waiting for him, and when he heard that the allies had again occupied his capital, he threw himself on the mercy of his archenemy by going on board H.M.S. *Bellerephon.* So began his long last journey into exile at St. Helena.

The terms of peace were dictated to France—as they always are to any enemy that is completely crushed, which France had to be. Prussia demanded the dismemberment of France, beginning with the northeast corner and the provinces of Alsace and Lorraine. This is what would have happened to the prostrate country if the governments of the allied powers had been democratic—such was the popular passion against France, particularly after she had torn up the treaty of 1814 by welcoming the conqueror back again. Even the majority of the British cabinet favored this policy for a while. The greatest living Briton, whom Waterloo had made the most influential person in Europe— the Duke of Wellington—would have none of it, however, and this was decisive. The policy adopted was security without vengeance. France was occupied for three years—the treaty allowed five—by an international army commanded by Wellington; a moderate war indemnity was imposed, for the collection of which he was also made responsible; and the country was left with the boundaries of 1789. More than that, she got back almost everything she had lost overseas.

Britain was the only great power that gave up any territory held at the end of the war, and what she restored was enormous. It was almost all the harvest of possessions reaped by her sea power during the Napoleonic struggle. She kept only a few little French islands, Mauritius and the Seychelles in the Indian Ocean and Tobago and St. Lucia in the Caribbean; the Danish Heligoland, which she ceded to Germany in 1890; the Ionian Islands, which she presented to Greece in 1864; Malta, an invaluable base in the Mediterranean; and three former Dutch possessions, British Guiana, Cape Colony, and Ceylon, for which she paid the Dutch £6,000,000. She restored to France her

West India Islands, her fishing rights and possessions on the coast of Newfoundland, and her trading posts in West Africa and in India. She restored to the Dutch their enormously wealthy empire in the East Indies.

Britain could well afford to be generous.[1] She had got something no treaty could give her, even by way of compensation. Her prestige was the greatest in the world. She had never bowed the knee to Napoleon, and she had saved Europe. Her naval supremacy was absolute—so absolute that another world war was impossible for a century.

---

[1] For a discussion of why Britain was so generous see *infra*, Chapter IX.

CHAPTER VII

How Ireland Nearly Became the First Dominion of the British Commonwealth of Nations

IRELAND WAS England's oldest overseas possession, the senior dependent member of the empire; and toward the close of the eighteenth century it gained such a large measure of independence within the empire that it showed distinct promise of becoming the first dominion of the British Commonwealth of Nations. Then occurred one of the greatest tragedies in the history of Ireland and of the empire. The curse of the French Revolution descended upon Anglo-Irish relations. The emergence of the modern British Commonwealth was postponed for generations, until the Dominion of Canada grew into the position that Ireland had so nearly attained; and Ireland was thrust back into subjection, to become the festering sore of British politics.

To understand the Irish problem, it is well to compare Ireland with Wales and Scotland in their relations with England, which incorporated all three of them to form the United Kingdom under one government seated in London. Wales and Scotland were no more English than was Ireland. Why, then, have there not been corresponding Welsh and Scottish problems? Obviously Wales and Scotland were as reconciled to union with England as Ireland was not. Why this striking difference?

Much of the explanation lies far in the past, and a swift glance back at each of the three in turn is very enlightening. Wales, the nearest and weakest, was the first to fall under English control, by a piecemeal conquest in the middle ages. But the Welsh were not treated as a subject race. They kept their own language without question—and they still do—and only gradually were English laws and institutions introduced among them. It was characteristic of the official English attitude that in 1301 the title "Prince of Wales" was conferred upon the eldest son of the king. Wales turned Protestant with England, and at the same time it was formally merged with England, whose parliament was enlarged to include Welsh members. Welshmen then became the political equals of Englishmen. It is also worth noting that the Tudor line, which ruled England at that time, was Welsh in origin and this was flattering to Welsh pride.

Scotland at that time was still an independent kingdom, and for several hundred years had been a nasty thorn in the flesh of England, as Ireland was later to become. Ever since the twelfth century Scotland had been the ally of France, England's chronic foe. England had tried to conquer both enemies but had been less successful in Scotland than in France. It was the triumph of the Reformation in Scotland that severed the historic Franco-Scottish alliance and first drew the two kingdoms of Great Britain together in defense of their common Protestantism, which in turn made it possible for the king of Scotland to ascend the throne of England when the Tudor line died with Elizabeth I in 1603. This union of the two crowns was acceptable to both kingdoms because it catered to the national pride of Scotland without offending that of England. The latter country was so much greater in wealth, power, and development that it could have no fear of being annexed by Scotland. Each country still had its own independent government, and more than a century passed before they were finally joined to form one realm, and then not by conquest but by negotiated agreement. Meanwhile they were associated as constitutional equals under the common Crown, like the dominions and the mother country today. But the modern British Commonwealth could not grow out of this loose Anglo-Scottish connection because the two kingdoms, sharing one little island, found that they had to unite as one on terms that were mutually satisfactory. Englishmen were able to plant flourishing colonies, to develop a great shipping interest, and to build a rich commerce—foreign as well as colonial—for the benefit of England, while the people of Scotland could not do the same for their country because it was relatively poor and weak. Scotland, therefore, wanted to share England's larger life. England, on the other hand, was alarmed by Scottish threats to choose a separate king, which would have revived the mediaeval danger to England's rear. Hence the bargain of 1707, by which the two countries were united under ᴠ common parliament and a common government as well as a common

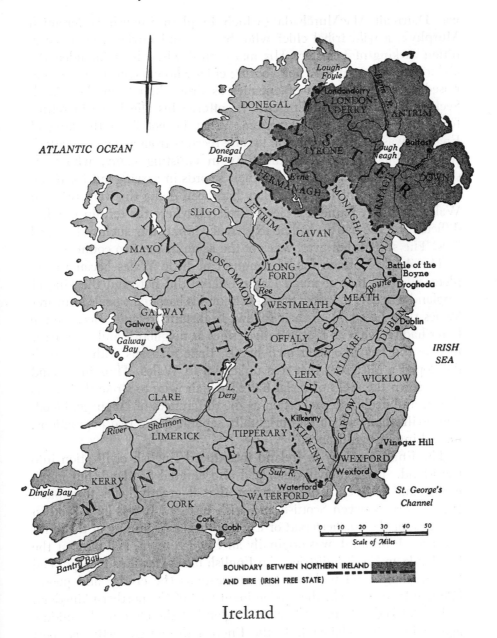

Ireland

sovereign, each, however, retaining its own church and its own legal system.

Ireland became an English possession by conquest. This began in the twelfth century, and an Irishman was at the bottom of it. He was Dairmait MacMurchada (which in plain English is Jeremiah Murphy), a wild tribal chief who, by war and intrigue, won recognition as king of Leinster. His many misdeeds, which included the abduction of the wife of a neighboring chief whose territory he coveted, raised up such a swarm of enemies as drove him from the island. Seeking out the king of England, he offered his allegiance in return for aid in recovering his kingdom. What he got from the king of England was merely permission to raise recruits from among the latter's subjects; but he had little difficulty in enlisting many, who were spoiling for such a chance to use their swords in carving out for themselves broad baronial estates. They had been doing this very thing in Wales, and they found it easier in Ireland, where the terrain was less difficult and the natives had no experience in meeting such well-armed foes. The sequel, however, was not the same in the two countries.

The Anglo-Norman feudal conquest of little Wales became complete, whereas that of much larger Ireland did not; and the king of England was able to keep a tighter rein on his baronial vassals in nearer Wales than he could on their fellows in distant Ireland. Because the latter had to live with hostile native tribes as neighbors, and were freer to take the law into their own hands, their relations with the Irish developed a bitterness that was unknown in Wales. Thus in Ireland were "sown the seeds of racial hatred which were to strike their roots deeper and deeper in proportion as the differences of language, blood, and civilization, which had originally separated the two populations, melted into insignificance."

The English colony in Ireland introduced English civilization into the island. English civilization had also entered Scotland, but much earlier and in such a different way that it greatly helps to explain the contrast between Scottish and Irish history. It was by a Scottish conquest of the northern part of England in the beginning of the tenth century. Edinburgh was originally an English town, and most of the Lowlands an English district. An English block was thus incorporated into Scotland, and within a few generations the cruder and poorer Highlands ceased to be the predominant part of the northern kingdom.

Ireland began to be a threat to England at the close of the middle ages, when rival claimants to the English throne got active support from the semi-independent Anglo-Irish barons. The king then dispatched Sir Edward Poynings with an army to establish the royal authority in Ireland, but the forces at the disposal of this official were barely sufficient for the task of confirming the English government's control of the Pale, an English district around Dublin. Beyond lay the great estates of the Anglo-Irish magnates who were accustomed to wage private war among themselves and with their Irish neighbors. All Poynings could do to check them was to restrict their power over the Irish parliament, which had been set up in the English colony after the English pattern, by having it pass what came to be known, and in later generations execrated, as Poynings' Laws. These subjected all Irish legislation to the will of the English government.

The Irish tragedy deepened in the sixteenth and seventeenth centuries. The Tudor rulers of England forced the Reformation on Ireland. At first this caused little trouble, for in Ireland the old church had fallen into sad decay. But during Elizabeth I's reign Roman Catholic missionaries, mostly Jesuits, poured into Ireland, effecting a revival which injected a religious fervor into the hatred between the Irish and the English. Meanwhile the English government tried to assimilate the Irish tribal system by transforming the chiefs into great landlords, like the descendants of the Anglo-Norman conquerors, with their clansmen as simple tenants toiling for them. Supported by grants of nobility and of confiscated church property, the attempt was more or less successful, but it produced some fierce uprisings. Another novelty of the time was the resumption, under the Roman Catholic Queen Mary, of English colonization in Ireland. Lands swept clean of Irish rebels were settled with an English population for the express purpose of strengthening the English interest in the island. This was the beginning of the plantation policy which was to be carried much further in the next century.

As Elizabeth I's reign wore on and England drifted into an undeclared war with Spain, the turmoil in Ireland increased and disclosed a new menace to England. The hands of Spain and Rome became more and more evident in Ireland, seeking to use it as a convenient base from which to effect the overthrow of Protestant England. After the destruction of the Spanish Armada, Philip of Spain relied chiefly on Ireland to encompass England's fall; and the old tribal Ireland, forgetting the bitter feuds that had always divided it, united in a flaming revolt. At last the English government did what it had never done before. It sent to Ireland sufficient forces to complete the conquest of the island, which was essential for England's security. Though Spain backed the Irish with a promise of aid, this was slow in coming. In 1601 a Spanish fleet landed a Spanish army in Ireland. It was too late. The back of the rebellion was already broken. The conquest of Ireland had also come too late, having been postponed until it entailed a terrific struggle in which both sides fought with savage ferocity. Government troops even destroyed crops with the express purpose of reducing the peasants by starvation.

The present division of Ireland dates from the settlement that followed this subjugation of Ireland—from the great Ulster plantation of 1608 on lands forfeited for treason. A company of Londoners got the town of Derry, which then became Londonderry, and thousands of dour Presbyterians from Scotland were settled as tillers of the soil in this part of Ireland. These Scots therefore took much firmer root than English landlords who lived on the rents paid by Irish tenants. It was then too that the Irish parliament received the shape it preserved until it disappeared with the Union of 1800. It was enlarged and packed with a majority of Protestants to bridle the political power of the Catholic nobility and gentry, Anglo-Irish as well as Irish.

In 1641, fearing further confiscations of land and religious persecution, Catholic Ireland rose in arms and fell upon the Protestants, massacring many of them. England was horrified but helpless, for she was trembling on the brink of her own civil war, which this Irish rebellion precipitated. Charles I vainly tried to draw a Catholic army from Ireland to crush the Puritans and establish his despotism in England, but his efforts only hastened his own execution and then visited an additional English curse on Ireland. There Cromwell and his fanatical veterans crushed the rebels mercilessly, killed all the priests they could lay their hands on, and sought to drive the whole Celtic population into Connaught so that the rest of the land might be settled by English Protestants. Though he failed to achieve this wholesale removal, he planted large numbers of his own soldiers as yeomen, and he well-nigh completed the destruction of the Irish gentry, whose estates were turned over to Englishmen. Outside Ulster, which became more intensely Protestant, Cromwell's soldier settlers were geographically too scattered and socially too cut off from the Protestant gentry to preserve their English character and their religion for more than a generation, and the destruction of the native gentry delivered the Irish peasants wholly into the hands of the persecuted priests. Cromwell's conquest of Ireland was more thorough than Elizabeth's, and again was the price that Ireland had to pay for England's security, this time against the danger of a royalist reconquest of England from Ireland, which would have destroyed liberty in England. Scotland likewise threatened England at this time, and, as a consequence, experienced its only real conquest by England. But the English army was soon withdrawn, when the Stuarts were peacefully restored in 1660, and Scotland recovered its independence under the same crown.

Ireland, on the other hand, suffered new disabilities. It was regarded as a colony, whose economic interests should be sacrificed for those of England. This, of course, was a basic principle of the old colonial system, which was then being developed; but Ireland was singled out for special treatment because it was the only colony that offered serious economic competition with England. Selfish interests in the English parliament insisted on excluding Ireland from the benefits of the navigation laws, thereby ruining a promising Irish shipping, and on prohibiting the importation of livestock, meat, butter, and cheese from Ireland, to the infinite damage of producers in that unhappy island.

Much worse was the fate that befell Ireland on the morrow of the English Revolution of 1688, because England's security was again at stake in Ireland. King James II, driven from his throne because he tried to force Roman Catholicism and despotism upon England, fled to France for aid, and with French troops turned up in Ireland to rally that country for the reconquest of his throne. He called a Roman Catholic Irish parliament that enacted a wholesale attainder of Protestants and the confiscation of their property; and he made war upon them to extirpate them, as a preliminary step to his invasion of England with a Roman Catholic army at his back. The Protestants were cornered in a little bit of Ulster and were nearly exhausted before they were saved by relief from England. William of Orange, the new king of England, followed with a strong army to reconquer Ireland before he could turn on his principal foe, which was France. For a while the issue was in doubt because the French defeated the English fleet and were, therefore, free to land a French army. It came in 1691 but, like the Spanish army of ninety years before, it was too late, for William had already won a decisive victory over the Irish. Before the year was out the Irish war was over, and for a third time, out of self-defense, England had completely conquered Ireland.

The fright that Ireland had again given England, and the nightmare of terror from which Irish Protestants had just recovered, inspired a grim determination to crush Catholic Ireland forever; to this end, law was piled upon law during the next half generation. The Roman Catholics, who formed at least three quarters of the population, were deprived of all civil rights, their property was confiscated, their education was proscribed, and their clergy were outlawed. These penal laws were almost as monstrous as the measures that had recently harried the Huguenots out of France. Catholic Ireland was so prostrate that it did not stir during the rest of England's long struggle against Louis XIV or her wars with France in the middle of the eighteenth century.

Even Irish Protestants suffered, though much less severely, from legislation passed by the newly sovereign parliament in London, under the influence of Anglican religious intolerance and English commercial jealousy. It excluded from every public office the loyal Presbyterians of Ulster, who were reinforced by immigration from Scotland until they perhaps equalled in number the Episcopalian Protestants in Ireland; and it forbade the export of Irish woolen goods to any country except England, which had earlier imposed prohibitive duties upon them. Irish landowners, mostly members of the established church, when hit by the closing of the English market to their livestock and meat, had turned to the production and manufacture of wool on a large scale, which profitable business was now strangled.

The only prosperous part of Ireland was Protestant Ulster, the home of the linen industry, which England encouraged, having practically none of her own. The rest of the country was in a deplorable state, and the economic plight of the Irish peasants was the worst of all. Crowded on diminutive holdings and without any security of tenure, they had to pay rackrents forced up by their own competition for land, the only thing that stood between them and certain starvation. They also had to support two churches, their own and a hated one, hated all the more because the tithe-jobbers, who bought the rights of the clergy, were a race of harpies. Already "Raleigh's fatal gift" was the staple food, which meant three "meal months" or "hungry months" before there were new potatoes to dig. The blight of absentee proprietorship rested heavily upon the country. Jonathan Swift declared that at least one third of all the Irish rent was spent in England. Rarely was any revenue from an estate put back into it. The land was usually leased and subleased by Protestant middlemen who battened on the half-starved, half-naked peasants living in mud hovels of their own construction. English colonization exhibited no more concern for the Irish natives than it did for the red men it encountered in North America or the black men it imported into the Caribbean colonies.

By the time of the American Revolution new life was stirring in Ireland. The previous decade had seen the beginning of two movements that were to color Irish history down to our own day. Though later they ran together, there was yet no connection between them.

One was organized agrarian violence, which then had no religious or political motive but was simply the blind outburst of a wretched peasantry against the extension of pasture land and the exactions of the tithe collectors. Bands of men, often several hundred strong, marched around, usually by night, destroying enclosures, cutting up grass lands, killing or maiming cattle, burning houses, breaking open jails where their fellows were incarcerated, and otherwise practicing intimidation, but generally stopping short of murder, a crime their nineteenth century successors frequently committed. Catholic priests opposed the outbreaks, and in the North they were chiefly the work of Protestant tillers of the soil. These disturbances were pretty well suppressed before the American revolt began.

The other movement was purely political and Protestant. Even so, it sought to embrace Roman Catholics rather than to oppress them. Its object was to emancipate the country from English control, to make Ireland a self-governing dominion; and the seat of the movement was the Irish parliament, the preserve of the Protestant minority who belonged to the established church. The fear of a Catholic uprising, which had made their grandfathers feel the need of English supremacy, was dying out. Since the beginning of the century, the subject race "had done nothing more dangerous than endure wrong." The local atmosphere of security and the general spirit of the age encouraged the growth of religious tolerance or indifference, and the penal laws that were most iniquitous had fallen into desuetude. The Catholic population, once regarded as steeped in disloyalty, was now free of that taint. The Catholic clergy were no longer molested, the Catholic townsfolk were quite a respectable body, and the surviving Catholic gentry and nobility were coming out of retirement to attest their attachment to the Crown.

When this relaxation of tension between religions had undermined the ruling oligarchy's reliance on English supremacy, a new influence made that oligarchy wish to throw off the English yoke. Their entrenched position was endangered by George III, who, having broken the power of the Whigs at home, was anxious to do the same to the little group who ran the government of Ireland by monopolizing the spoils of office and controlling a majority of the three hundred seats in the Dublin House of Commons. The lord lieutenant, who represented the king in Ireland, had been little more than a figurehead, visiting Ireland only for the sessions of parliament, held once in two years. Now he was required to reside there during his term of office, to take the business of patronage out of the hands of the Undertakers, as they were called because they had "undertaken" to manage parliament, and to manage the government himself under direction from London. Thus the problem of imperial control was coming to a head in Ireland at the same time as in the American colonies.

The American Revolution had a profound effect upon Ireland. Yet there it produced no sign of a revolutionary uprising, even among the Presbyterians in Ulster, who were "fiercely American." The Catholics were never quieter; their principal noblemen responded eagerly to a government request for aid in raising troops, the old ban on Catholic enlistments having been ignored for many years; and their gentry seized the occasion to present addresses of loyalty condemning the violence of the Americans. The Anglican minority, however, were far from unanimous in backing British authority in America, for many of them realized that the American cause was theirs too. Still they would use only constitutional means to get rid of British authority in Ireland.

The strength of the Irish parliamentary opposition grew, reinforced by the election of Henry Grattan, under whose eloquent leadership it concentrated upon the removal of trade restrictions and the establishment of Irish legislative independence; and the Irish political struggle led both sides to cultivate the favor of the Catholics. Grattan would grant them the same legal and political rights as Protestants, and the government of Lord North was not unfriendly to Catholic claims, with the result that an Irish act of 1778 repealed invidious limitations upon Catholic purchase and inheritance of land, and the preamble of the new law enunciated the general principle "that all denominations should enjoy the blessings of our free constitution." It was a good augury that real reform began in Ireland with a concession to Catholics and a promise of more to come. In the same year a British act admitted Irish vessels to the privileges of British vessels under the navigation laws. Ireland was drawing together and becoming a nation.

When the American war widened into a European one with the entry of France and Spain, and their navies qualified the British command of the sea, a hostile invasion of Ireland seemed imminent. Neither the British nor the Irish government could provide the forces to meet it, while the French government hoped for an Irish rebellion to aid the invasion; but the nascent Irish nation rallied to the defense of the country. Under the direction of the leading gentry, the people flew to arms, elected their own officers, met regularly for military drill, and without any legal obligation submitted to strict military discipline. Until the end of the war only Protestants were enrolled, for they alone could legally possess arms; but the Catholics who could afford it gladly bore their share of the expense. Such were the famous Volunteers, an intensely patriotic army, which sprang into being spontaneously to meet an urgent need that the government could not supply. From the rise of the Volunteers to the close of the war, when their numbers reached eighty thousand, the maintenance of law and order in Ireland was really in their hands, and it was better than it had ever been before or was to be for generations afterward.

This large unofficial military force, which had virtual control of the country, inevitably became also a political organization, to whose demands London was obliged to bow. That was why an Irish bill was passed to relieve Protestant dissenters from the Anglican sacramental test for office and allowed to become law in 1780, almost half a century before their coreligionists in England got political equality with members of the established church. By 1780, also, the British government passed legislation which, though not establishing free trade between the two countries, gave Ireland equal rights with Britain in imperial and foreign trade—and without requiring anything in return. This presents a striking contrast to the price England had exacted from Scotland, which was the surrender of her separate parliament. Instead of being swallowed up, the Irish parliament proceeded on a motion by Grattan to debate its own independence under the British Crown. Though the question was shelved by government influence, it was significant that during the discussion scarcely a member defended the supremacy of the British parliament. Then the Volunteers spoke out, and the result was decisive. In the spring of 1782 Grattan again moved his declaration of independence, the Irish House passed it unanimously, and London yielded to the Irish demand for legislative independence. Poynings' Laws, which had made the Irish parliament a puppet of the English government, were repealed in Dublin; and the British parliament renounced its right, formally asserted early in the century, to legislate for Ireland.

Thus was launched a constitutional experiment of an association between equals; but it was only an experiment and, as frequently happens with experiments, it posed problems that had to be solved if it was going to work. At the very outset the British ministry faced the problem of how to effect an imperial coordination of the two realms. Like Scotland before 1707, and unlike the distant dominions that arose generations afterward, Ireland was too close a neighbor for the government in London to contemplate the possibility of complete independence under the same Crown.

Another tie still connected the governments of the two countries. This, however, was too precarious to serve as anything more than a temporary solution. Though in legal theory the legislature of Ireland had now become independent, the executive had not. It had never been responsible to the parliament in Dublin and was still under the government in London. Yet this legal theory of legislative independence and administrative dependence was only partly operative because it did not fit some important political facts. The Irish parliament was not a free body, and Irish officialdom enjoyed a large measure of independence. The great majority in the Dublin Commons sat for pocket boroughs in the possession of local magnates or the Crown, or held government jobs, or were otherwise bought. The result was that the executive could pass anything with the cooperation of the Undertakers and nothing without it, which meant that the old ruling oligarchy still held a strong position against dictation from London. These men controlled enough seats in their parliament to give them a veto over legislation and, in addition, a strangle hold on office. They would serve British interests, but not beyond the point where these interests would override their own.

When conceding the supremacy of the Irish parliament in Irish affairs, the ministry in London announced the necessity of placing the connection between the two countries "by mutual consent upon a solid and permanent footing." The plan was to negotiate a treaty, to be adopted by both sovereign legislatures, which would recognize and define the right of Great Britain to regulate all foreign and imperial affairs. In other words, it was assumed that Ireland, assured of autonomy, would voluntarily accept British authority in matters that were not specifically Irish. But no treaty was forthcoming. The mere suggestion of it roused Irish suspicions of British sincerity in granting independence, and the government in London postponed the project for a more auspicious occasion. Irish gratitude for the new freedom recovered its first enthusiasm and expressed itself in a parliamentary grant of £100,000 toward supplying twenty thousand additional sailors for the British navy and in pledges of the Volunteers to help in recruiting them.

The more auspicious occasion seemed to be at hand in the spring of 1784, when Irish manufacturers, particularly of woolens, were in

such a distressed state that the Irish House of Commons unanimously
called for relief by a liberalizing of commercial relations with Britain.
In response to this request, negotiations were opened in London, and
there Pitt offered what amounted to an imperial treaty between the
two countries. In return for perpetual free trade between them, which,
while benefiting both, would be a much greater boon to Ireland than
to Britain, Ireland was to contribute to the defense of the empire. The
agreement was to be implemented by parallel legislation, and early in
1785 it was accepted by the Irish parliament only to encounter such
a storm in the British Commons, blown up by protectionist manufacturers, that Pitt had to withdraw it to avoid outright rejection. Still
hopeful, he redrafted the conditions to make them more favorable to
Britain, and in spite of fierce opposition he carried them, only to find
that his altered proposals could not be got through the Irish House
and that the whole project had therefore to be abandoned.

This failure was ominous. It was more than the collapse of an
attempted permanent solution for the basic problem in the relations
between the two countries. It was also the breakdown of the cooperation of the Undertakers, the temporary solution and the only means of
reaching a permanent solution. Three years later, in 1788, the inherent
danger in the situation was thrust forward by an unexpected domestic
crisis. George III suddenly went insane and the Prince of Wales, an
irresponsible fellow, was impatient to assume the full exercise of the
royal power that he might turn out the government and install his boon
companion Fox as prime minister. Pitt therefore passed a Regency Bill,
which recognized the Prince as Regent, but with greatly curtailed
prerogatives; and the Irish parliament was called upon to do the same.
But again the managers of the Irish House balked, insisting on a regency for Ireland without these new limitations. Ireland and Britain
were approaching the parting of the ways, like Scotland and England
in the beginning of the century, when the providential recovery of
the king terminated the crisis. The immediate effect of the episode was
a marked extension of the corruption that characterized the Irish parliament. By distributing more places, pensions, and titles, and by new
bargains with borough owners, the government consolidated its shaky
following among the members.

Meanwhile the grant of legislative independence, into which this
process of corruption was eating, had raised the question of parliamentary reform. It did not matter very much what Irish hands pulled
the strings that made the Dublin puppet dance, so long as the motions

were imprisoned in an English groove; but the passing of this condition in 1782 made the control of the Irish House a pressing issue. The
manipulating hands had suddenly acquired a power over Ireland that
they had never possessed, the power to dictate all Irish legislation.
According to a contemporary calculation, 124 borough seats in the
Irish Commons were at the absolute disposal of 53 peers, and another
91 were the property of 52 commoners. In other words, 105 individuals returned 215 of the 300 members, the remainder being the
only representatives of real constituencies—in the counties and larger
towns. As might be expected, there was quite a traffic in this artificial
representation. The ordinary price of a borough seat was £2,000 a
parliament, and four or five times this amount if the seat was sold outright. Could Irish freedom be safely entrusted to the guardianship of
an assembly so composed? Might not the Irish parliament be induced
to sell its independence, or even its separate existence? Patriotic Irishmen who asked such questions had a gloomy foreboding of what was
actually to happen in 1800, and they strove to make it impossible by
a thoroughgoing reform.

    There is a suggestion of Greek tragedy in the way the ancient reli-
gious division of the country divided the reformers and thereby paralyzed their strenuous efforts to rescue the national legislature from the
clutches of the little group of Irishmen who were to betray it. To effect
the rescue, it was necessary to substitute genuine elections by real constituencies for nomination by borough owners; the fatal disagreement
was over how representative the new parliament should be. The larger
body of active reformers would extend the electoral system to include
the whole of Protestant Ireland, Presbyterian as well as Anglican, and
there they would stop. Though they were willing to treat Roman Catholics as equals in other respects, they would never allow them to share
political power. Grattan, on the other hand, would heal the deep
schism of the nation by granting political rights to Roman Catholics
on equal terms with Protestants. He realized, of course, that it would
be suicidal folly to give the vote to the ignorant peasantry of those
days, so he advocated a rather limited franchise. All the Roman Catholics whom he would have embraced in the political system were too
discreet to take any part in the agitation for reform, and none of the
lower classes who belonged to the same faith showed the slightest
interest in the agitation. The debate was wholly between Protestants.

    If the reforming minority in the Irish House had been united on
either program, and had proceeded cautiously, they might have carried

it with one more push from the Volunteers. The latter were impatient for reform, and they looked to this minority of parliamentarians to lead them in the way they should go. Many of them, even of the Ulster Presbyterians, who were the backbone of the organization, decried the bigotry of the past and talked of a united nation that knew no religious discrimination. But Grattan would not pull them his way. A scrupulous constitutionalist, he saw grave danger in the pressure of armed force upon the sovereign parliament of Ireland. Therefore the Volunteer movement was easily captured by the leaders who would reform parliament on a strictly Protestant basis and were less squeamish about the means of accomplishing their end. It was not long before the sword broke in their hands.

Toward the close of 1783 these leaders got a convention of Volunteer delegates elected from the whole country and assembled in Dublin to dictate a drastic reform bill to parliament. This open attempt at intimidation defeated itself, in spite of the fact that it was directed by some of the most respectable men in the land including not a few members of parliament, lords as well as commoners. It alarmed Grattan and his friends, it emboldened the Commons to reject the measure forthwith by a vote of 157 to 77, and it destroyed the political influence of the Volunteers. The convention was persuaded to adjourn sine die, and in the following March the reform bill was again presented to parliament, this time without any suggestion of armed force behind it. Instead it was backed by petitions from most of the counties, and again it was thrown out, by almost as large a majority. Most of the little group of borough owners were no exception to the general rule that those who possess power will not surrender it except under compulsion.

Thenceforth, said Lecky, "the conviction sank deep into the minds of many that reform in Ireland could only be effected by revolution, and the rebellion of 1798 might be already foreseen."[1] But he also admitted that if the course of the world for the next fifty years "had been as peaceful as it had been during the first three quarters of the century, reforms might probably have been introduced by slow steps, and no great catastrophe would have occurred."[2] What made this evolution impossible was the French Revolution, which was a curse to Ireland even more than to England. In both countries it inspired hopes and fears that clashed and led to a stern reaction; but in Ireland

---

[1] W. E. H. Lecky, *History of Ireland in the Eighteenth Century,* II, 377.
[2] *Ibid.,* p. 381.

the disturbance and the repression were much more violent, the conflict inflamed racial and religious passions that had long been dying down, and the awakening nation lost even the symbol of its independence.

The spirit of the French Revolution entered Ireland in Ulster, a province of strange contradictions and explosive elements. There the American Revolution had roused much sympathy for the colonial cause and not a little republican feeling, and then had given rise to the main movement of the loyal Volunteers, many of whom, now Catholic as well as Protestant, were still under arms, the government having shrunk from the danger of attempting to dissolve them. There, too, some Protestants were now fighting with Roman Catholics while other Protestants were reaching out for political union with them. This fighting, which began in 1785 and seems to have originated in a private quarrel that had no religious flavor, was between bands of Peep-o'-Day Boys, mostly Presbyterians, who terrorized Catholic peasants by bursting into their cottages in the early hours of the morning to search for and seize illegally possessed arms, and bands of Defenders, Catholic peasants organized professedly to check such outrages. Furious as was the hatred on both sides of this sporadic rural strife among the poorest classes, it did not infect their betters. They were inoculated against it in that age of "enlightenment," and they realized that they had common interests that should draw them together. The compulsory payment of the tithe to support the Anglican Church was as objectionable to Presbyterians as it was to Roman Catholics, and so was the political monopoly of the ruling clique. Though the Roman Catholic leaders were still shy about demanding emancipation, they were encouraged by the politically-minded Presbyterians, who were not at all shy. They were more than ever impatient for the reform of parliament, but saw little chance of getting it except in alliance with the Roman Catholics and on equal terms with them. Great was the encouragement that came from Paris in the news that the French had abolished all religious disqualifications and the whole tithe system, and the revolutionary example of France awakened ominous echoes in the north of Ireland.

In July 1791, the second anniversary of the taking of the Bastille was the occasion of a great celebration in Belfast. Democratic toasts were downed with enthusiasm, an address of fulsome flattery was sent to France, a resolution in favor of religious equality was passed by Presbyterian Volunteers, and Catholic bodies formally returned their warmest thanks. In September, a startling pamphlet appeared and gained wide circulation. It summoned the whole nation to unite in demanding a parliament that would truly represent it and redress all Irish grievances. The author was Wolfe Tone, an able young lawyer of Dublin, a nominal Presbyterian and a real free thinker. In October, at Belfast, he launched the Society of United Irishmen, which soon had branch organizations in every part of Protestant Ulster. Its original purpose was to combine Protestants and Roman Catholics in such a powerful political organization that it would compel parliament to reform itself in accordance with the national will. Before long, however, despair of achieving this end by constitutional methods, and the contagious example of France, began to drive the movement along the road that Tone wanted it to follow, toward the establishment of an independent Irish republic by armed rebellion supported by a French invasion.

Catholic Ireland was repelled rather than attracted by the French Revolution, which confiscated all church property and essayed to reorganize the church as a democratically governed national institution having no ties with Rome. This being so, it is not surprising that the United Irishmen won scarcely any Catholic recruits until 1795, a fateful year in Irish history. Nevertheless, there was meanwhile a growing ferment among the Catholics. Defenderism was spreading to other parts of Ireland and it was changing in character, becoming an organized anarchic movement of desperate poverty-stricken peasants who knew nothing and cared nothing about politics. Of much more concern to the authorities in Dublin and London was the novel political activity of educated Catholics. Their old aristocratic leaders, whose loyalty to the Crown was unquestioned and whose shyness of politics was proverbial, were nudged out by new men of less certain loyalty and more aggressive disposition born of success in commerce. They were greatly encouraged by Protestant sympathy and the general unrest of the times. In 1791 they openly demanded equal rights for Roman Catholics. In 1792, under their guidance and against the opposition of prelates and priests, elected delegates from all over the country held a Catholic Convention in Dublin, which appealed over the heads of the Irish government to the king in London. It was an astoundingly bold step for Irish Roman Catholics to take. They had never dared do anything like this before. If they did not get satisfaction by constitutional means, would they not fall into the embrace of the republican United Irishmen, and with them throw Ireland into a wild revolution?

To avert this danger, Pitt's government pressed the Irish administration to buy off the Catholics with concessions and urged that these should include the franchise because without it all other concessions would be unavailing. But the ministers in Dublin objected so vehemently to anything that threatened Protestant ascendancy—by which they meant their own—that they persuaded London to be satisfied for 1792 with a relief bill that opened the legal profession to Roman Catholics and repealed restrictions on their intermarriage and education. Before the end of that year, which saw the European war begin and spread until it was on the point of dragging Britain in, London recognized more clearly than ever the urgent necessity of granting the vote to the Irish Catholics and again pressed Dublin to yield. There was a bitter argument between the two governments, the Irish accusing the British of stirring up the Catholics, and the British blaming the Irish for antagonizing the Catholics by resisting their just demands, and each believing that the other would betray its interests. As the Dublin ministers, with almost all Ireland against them, had to rely on British armed force in the event of an uprising, they had to obey the dictate of London. Early in 1793, just after France had declared war on Britain, a sullen Irish parliament passed a bill that extended the franchise to Roman Catholics, removed the legal ban on their possession of arms, and admitted them to grand juries and the magistracy.

There was a fatal flaw in this relief bill of 1793. Though Catholics then got the vote, they could not use it to elect Catholics. Their admission to parliament was moved as an amendment, opposed by the government, and defeated by 163 to 69. In the light of what followed, it seemed an almost insane thing to give political equality to Irish democracy, the possessors of forty-shilling freeholds, most of whom were too ignorant to realize the value of their new right, and at the same time to withhold political equality from the Catholic gentry, who, if allowed to sit in the House of Commons, would have exerted a most wholesome influence there and in the country generally. The number of independent members who favored their admission leaves little doubt that official pressure could have carried it easily. Why did not London insist upon it? There were several reasons. The Catholic spokesmen themselves had intimated, apparently to avoid prejudicing their cause, that they would be content without it; the Irish ministers asserted that their parliamentary following would revolt if required to pass it; and the British government, becoming involved in the European war, was reluctant to renew a long controversy with Dublin over a new Irish question.

Much evil was also done during the passage of the bill when the

Irish chancellor,[3] who loathed it but had to vote for it, explained his position to the House of Lords over which he presided. After a fierce denunciation of Catholic claims and principles, he said:

> If Papists have a right to vote for representatives in a Protestant Parliament, they have a right to sit in Parliament—they have a right to fill every office of the State—they have a right to pay tithes exclusively to their own clergy—they have a right to restore the ancient pomp and splendour of their religion—they have a right to be governed exclusively by the laws of their own Church—they have a right to seat their bishops in this House—they have a right to seat a Popish prince on the throne—they have a right to subvert the established Government and to make this a Popish country, which I have little doubt is their ultimate object.

Sheer madness! That was what he thought the bill was, and that was what his making such a speech was. It was an incendiary utterance. Other passages were a thinly veiled attack on the British government for driving such a measure through the Irish parliament. The obvious inference, that the legislative independence of Ireland was a fraud, was insulting to Irish sensibilities; and nothing could have been more cleverly contrived to poison Irish minds, of whatever party, against the British government as directly responsible for everything that was done or not done in Ireland.

The following year saw the United Irishmen forcibly suppressed as definitely treasonable, because they were conspiring with the French enemy. It also saw the rise of a vigorous agitation for the admission of Roman Catholics, who as a body were still solidly loyal, to the legislature in Dublin. The movement had strong Protestant as well as Catholic support. Grattan and his reforming friends in the house were all for it, and the government in London seemed to be back of it too. The leader of the Whigs who joined Pitt in that year was known to favor this completion of Catholic emancipation; so was one of his group, Lord Fitzwilliam, who went to Ireland as the new lord lieutenant in January 1795. He was instructed to avoid encouraging it and to postpone it, if possible, until the end of the war; but if the pressure was too great, he was to accept and support it.

What Fitzwilliam found on his arrival was that the Catholic question could not be put off. The Catholic leaders, old as well as new, had their hearts set on full emancipation and were looking to Grattan

---

[3] John Fitzgibbon, later Earl of Clare. Quoted in Lecky, *op. cit.,* III, 172.

to champion it in parliament. Protestant Ireland as a whole believed that it should be granted. Though borough owners disliked it, they were prepared to yield if the government declared for it; and the Protestant gentry feared that unless their Catholic brethren got it the restless masses would be swept away by revolutionary leaders and ideas. Defenderism was not yet political in character, but it was spreading anarchy throughout the countryside and the government lacked means to cope with it. The lord lieutenant was convinced, and on this the chancellor agreed with him, that the only remedy for such a dangerous condition was the organization of "an armed constabulary composed of the better orders of the people," which in three of the four provinces of Ireland meant Roman Catholics. But this force would be unreliable and even dangerous unless the government first granted Catholic emancipation. Quick action was also necessary because the war took an ugly turn in this January, when the French swarmed over Holland and captured the Dutch fleet. As Ireland was the Achilles' heel of Britain, Fitzwilliam had to face the prospect of an early invasion, and he saw little chance of successful defense unless he could rally the Irish as one people, which would be impossible without Catholic emancipation.

Ireland seemed to be on the point of becoming a united nation with the passage of the bill introduced by Grattan and backed by Fitzwilliam, when the noble work of these two statesmen was shattered by a bolt of lightning from London. Pitt's government ordered the bill stopped and Fitzwilliam home—only seven weeks after his landing in Dublin. The reason for this stunning blow is still somewhat obscure. By interfering with the shameless political jobbery that characterized the Irish administration, he had incurred the wrath of powerful interests. He was also the victim of political differences within the cabinet arising from the coalition of the previous year. Apparently the Catholic question was only a secondary consideration and may have been merely a pretext. But whatever the causes, the effects were undoubtedly disastrous.

The British repudiation of Fitzwilliam let the revolutionary movement run wild in Ireland. The United Irishmen, reconstituted as a conspiratorial society that aimed at a general rebellion in conjunction with a French invasion, set out to capture the Catholic peasantry, without whose support no such rising was possible. The blow from London paralyzed the political influence of the Catholic gentry and clergy over the masses, who were thereby exposed to the appeals of the mad schemers. Defenderism also helped the latter by providing a ready-made organization for them to take over and expand. This they did, not by preaching democracy and republicanism, neither of which meant anything to the peasants, but by promising them the abolition of the tithe and by playing on their fears of what was in store for them. The fighting in Ulster was growing in intensity. Protestants, now organized in Orange Lodges, were expelling Catholics; the fugitives spread the rumor that Orangemen were preparing to exterminate all Catholics; and United Irishmen fanned the rumor into a burning flame. Ireland was fast ripening for rebellion. It nearly came at the end of 1796, when only the winds of heaven prevented the landing of the French army that the French fleet had brought to Bantry Bay. In the following year, when mutiny paralyzed the Royal Navy, two hundred thousand prospective insurgents were drilling in Ireland and a greater French expedition to that unhappy land was projected.

To cut the claws of the impending insurrection, the Irish government decided to disarm the population, commencing in Ulster. There the United Irish leaders, by deserting the cause of religious brotherhood for that of religious hatred, had frightened away all their Presbyterian supporters except the few who were fanatical believers in the new French political gospel. The result was that the government, though lacking sufficient regular soldiers to carry out the disarmament, could recruit local Protestant yeomen for much of the work; and they, inspired by fear and hatred, did it in such savage fashion as to create the impression on many other Irish minds that this was the beginning of the Orange fury. The government also gathered up enough United Irish leaders to hamstring their organization, but not enough to destroy it; and measures designed to prevent a rebellion actually precipitated it.

The rebellion of 1798 was big only in its consequences. It was pretty well confined to Wexford, in the southeast corner of Ireland; and there the rising had no more than a momentary success, when a mob of distraught peasants wandered about, burning and slaying, until troops from England and yeomanry from Ulster were rushed to the camp of the rebels and cut them down on Vinegar Hill. The rising occurred in May. This miserable battle was fought in June, and all resistance was over by August, without any French landing. Afterward, when too late to be of any avail, two little French forces did invade Ireland and were quickly disposed of. With the second came Wolfe Tone, who was captured, tried, and condemned to death. He cheated the gallows by committing suicide in prison.

The Irish parliament was now doomed. Such fierce passions had been aroused as Ireland had not known for a whole century—passions that made it impossible for the Irish parliament to grant any concession to Catholics and also impossible for England to leave the Catholics of Ireland at the mercy of the enraged Protestants who formed the Irish parliament. Pitt's government, which had been coming to the conclusion that legislative union with Great Britain was necessary, could now see no alternative. Some of his wisest advisers believed that such a union would be neither justifiable nor even possible unless accompanied by a provision for the complete political emancipation of Roman Catholics, that this emancipation was essential for the healing of Ireland, and that it could be adopted only with union. The prime minister refused to make emancipation a condition of union, but he let it be understood that it would be one of the first measures of the new united parliament. A definite promise, far from facilitating union, would have made it more difficult. The Irish parliament had to be persuaded to vote itself out of existence, and its members would not do this for the benefit of Catholics. Of course they hated union, but a majority of them voted for it because they were beaten at their own game of parliamentary corruption. They sold out to the British government in return for twelve hundred thousand pounds, spent in buying up pocket boroughs, and for a lavish distribution of peerages, offices, and pensions.

The Act of Union, passed by both parliaments in 1800, combined them by adding one hundred Irish members to the British House of Commons and thirty-two Irish peers to the British House of Lords. The proportion of representation was not unjust to Ireland. Neither were the financial terms, which made allowance for the lower level of the national debt and of wealth in Ireland. The sacrifice imposed on Ireland was the loss of a parliament dominated by men who would keep the great majority of the Irish people in perpetual subjugation, a parliament that might stand as the symbol of Irish nationhood but could never make the adjustment necessary to represent it. The Union might well have been a blessing to both partners in the new United Kingdom of Great Britain and Ireland if Pitt had then carried out the implied promise of admitting Roman Catholics to sit in the united parliament. What stopped him was the bigotry and the mental instability of George III. Some of Pitt's enemies easily persuaded the king that his coronation oath bound him to veto any such concession, and the prime minister resigned rather than attempt to force it at the risk of driving the obstinate monarch out of his mind again. The Act of Union thus came to be associated in Irish minds with a British breach of faith such as neither Wales nor Scotland ever experienced. The French Revolution had undone what the American Revolution had previously done for Ireland.

CHAPTER VIII

The Establishment of
the British Empire in India

THE BRITISH EMPIRE gained immeasurably by the long war against Revolutionary France and Napoleon, when it reaped a harvest of colonies from France and her satellites. It was then too that the British Empire was definitely established in India, but this was not part of that harvest. The British conquest of India had begun before the Revolution. The French had already lost their chance of winning an empire there, and what the British won in that ancient land, they took neither from Europeans nor from the people of India. Nor did either the British government or the directors of the East India Company seek an empire there. They actually sought to avoid it. Against their will it was conquered for them by native Indian troops, sepoys, under British officers. It was a strange process that becomes intelligible only when we look at conditions in India, which was a world apart.

Ever since their first conquests in the eleventh century, Mohammedans had ruled India, though they were only a small minority of the population. The Hindus, the great majority, were easily subjugated because they had no unity. There were greater differences between them than between the peoples of Europe. They spoke a Babel of tongues; they were divided into many races; they belonged to different stages of civilization, from the highly cultivated to the most primitive; and they were split into a multitude of hereditary castes. As invasion after invasion swept down over them from the Afghan passes, there was a dreary succession of bloody wars between the conquerors, empires rose and fell, and smaller states appeared and disappeared. Never was the land united politically. The nearest it came to that was when the Mogul Empire was at its height, which was a generation before the

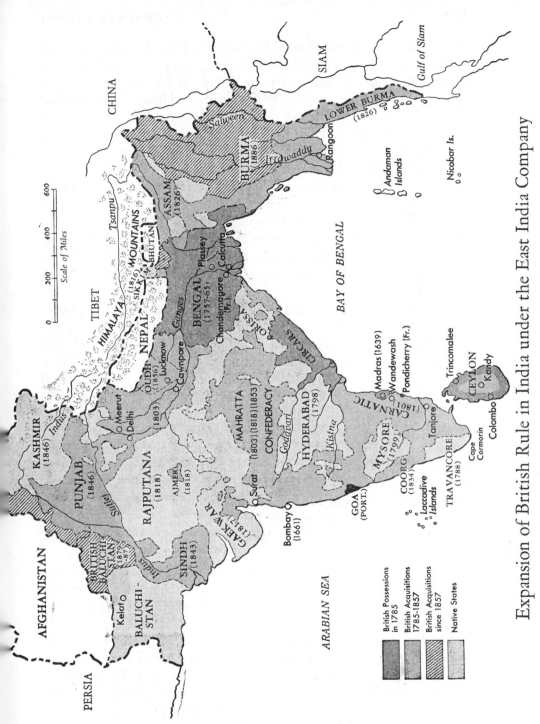

Expansion of British Rule in India under the East India Company

CHINA

SIAM

Gulf of Siam

LOWER BURMA
(1826)

Salween

BURMA
(1886)

Irrawaddy

Rangoon

Andaman Islands

Nicobar Is.

TIBET

Tsanpu

HIMALAYA MOUNTAINS

SIKKIM (1816)

BHUTAN

NEPAL

ASSAM
(1826)

BAY OF BENGAL

600

400

200

Scale of Miles

0

Ganges

BENGAL
(1757-65)

Plassey

Calcutta

Chandenagore (Fr.)

ORISSA

OUDH
(1856)

Lucknow

Cawnpore

CIRCARS

Godavari

KASHMIR
(1846)

Indus

PUNJAB
(1846)

Sutlej

Meerut

Delhi

Ajmer
(1803)

RAJPUTANA
(1818)

AJMER
(1818)

MAHRATTA
(1803) (1818) (1853)
CONFEDERACY

HYDERABAD
(1798)

Kistna

Madras (1639)

Wandewash

Pondicherry (Fr.)

CARNATIC
(1801)

Trincomalee

CEYLON

Kandy

Colombo

Cape Cormorin

MYSORE
(1799)

COORG
(1834)

TRAVANCORE
(1788)

Tanjore

Laccadive Islands

GOA
(PORT.)

Surat

Bombay
(1661)

GAEKWAR
(1817)

AFGHANISTAN

BRITISH BALUCHISTAN (1879)

KELAT (1877)

Kelat

BALUCHISTAN

SINDH
(1843)

Indus

PERSIA

ARABIAN SEA

British Possessions in 1785

British Acquisitions 1785-1857

British Acquisitions since 1857

Native States

first English colony was planted in America. From his splendid court at Delhi, the emperor ruled, an oriental despot, over most of India except the south. A hundred years afterward his successor tried to conquer the south, but in doing so he overreached himself and wrecked his empire. India disintegrated into a mass of warring states, and anarchy was rampant. Then the first Hindu power to arise for many centuries appeared in the west. This was the confederacy of Mahratta tribes, whose fierce horsemen subdued much of central India and threatened to dominate the whole country. In the middle of the eighteenth century it looked as if they might create a new empire—until a new horde of invaders from Afghanistan smashed the Mahratta host in the mighty battle of Panipat near Delhi in 1761. Instead of gathering up the heritage of the Moguls, the victors gathered up their loot and withdrew to their home across the mountains, leaving India in worse chaos.

Compared with these titanic struggles, the fighting between European trading companies at a few points around the coast was petty squabbling, but the outcome of these greater struggles was that it cleared the way for the winning trading company to establish a European empire in India. The Portuguese, Dutch, French, and British all had trading stations, but already the last two stood out as the great rivals. Both had found it necessary, in the disordered state of the country, to protect themselves by organizing small bodies of native troops and by gaining influence over the native states adjacent to their stations. The French began this game of native politics, but the British won it. In the very year of Panipat, they chased the French from India. By the Peace of Paris in 1763, the British restored the French posts on the condition that they were never to be fortified; and every subsequent war between Britain and France has seen the conquest and restoration of the latter's little bits of territory on the coast of India.

At the close of the Seven Years' War, the English East India Company, a private trading concern, possessed more than its main "factories" of Bombay, Madras, and Calcutta. In self-defense against the French company and native princes who aided the French, it had acquired a shadowy political control over the Carnatic, which lay around Madras, a firmer hand on the native ruler of the Circars, a coastal strip farther north, and complete power over the nawab of Bengal. Immediately afterward the nawab of neighboring Oudh, accompanied by the refugee Mogul emperor, invaded Bengal and met crushing defeat, which delivered Oudh and the emperor to the Company. Thereupon, in 1765, the Company took the homeless emperor under its protection, established him at Allahabad in territory severed from Oudh for this purpose, and promised this penniless potentate an annual tribute of £260,000 out of the taxes to be collected in Bengal; while he, the only shadow of legitimate authority, formally invested the Company with the right to collect this revenue. The Company also restored the nawab of Oudh, with whom it formed an alliance that lasted for nearly a century.

But the Company was soon threatened with the loss of all that it had just gained. Though the taxes wrung from the people of Bengal, thus burdened by the tribute to the Mogul, were all really needed to provide for the government of Bengal, greedy eyes in England saw an enormous surplus flowing into the coffers of the Company. This golden vision inspired the shareholders to insist on an increase of their dividends. It so tempted the Chancellor of the Exchequer, Charles Townshend of evil American fame, that in 1767 he procured an act of parliament exacting from the Company an annual payment of £400,000 to the British Treasury. This was the first interference of parliament in the affairs of India, and it was nothing less than a demand for a share of the plunder. It was not long before the Company found that it was worse off, instead of better off. The tax income in Bengal shrank under the native administration to which the Company left this business. In a desperate effort to retrieve the situation, the Company in 1769 appointed English district supervisors over the zemindars, the hereditary officials who gathered the land revenues. These appointments were the origin of the office of collector, which in later generations grew to great importance, and the first direct English interference with local administration in India. The result was disappointing. The golden eggs were not forthcoming; and on top of financial pressure from England, which would have killed the goose, came hot attacks from native states, which nearly cooked it alive.

Down in the south the Nizam of Hyderabad, who had deserted the French for the English, dragged the Company's governor and council of Madras into a disastrous war against his powerful foe, Hyder Ali, who had usurped the throne of Mysore. Up in the north, the Mahrattas, having recovered much of their strength, were again on the rampage. They seized Delhi, persuaded the Mogul to return there, made him their puppet, and used him to order the payment of the Bengal tribute to them and to demand the surrender of Allahabad to them also. At the same time they threatened to gobble up Rohilcund, the northwestern neighbor of Oudh which they also menaced from the south; the Rohillas sought aid from Oudh, which was obviously next on the list; and Oudh turned to the Company in Bengal, which stood ready to honor its alliance. In 1772, when the dreaded Mahratta attack still hung fire, the Company was facing ruin. The war with Hyder Ali had so exhausted its finances that, instead of meeting its payment to the British government, it had to borrow £1,000,000 from that government to avoid bankruptcy.

The British were facing a great crisis in India as well as in America. But while they were losing an empire in America, one man saved the East India Company and solidified its small beginning of the British Empire in India. He was Warren Hastings, an old servant of the Company, who landed in Bengal as governor in 1772. His first task was to introduce order and justice into the government of that native state, a typical oriental despotism that was crumbling to pieces because power had passed from the native despot to the English Company and the latter had recoiled from the responsibility of exercising it. Native tradition favored the worst corruption, which the Company had done nothing to check and many of its irresponsible servants had done much to preserve for their own private advantage. Hastings radically reformed the tax system, curbing the abuses and the profits of the zemindars, primarily to increase the revenue but also with an eye to prevent oppression of the poor peasants. He established an efficient administration of justice with entirely new courts manned by British magistrates, for whose guidance he had learned Hindus and Moslems prepare manuals of their respective laws. Though Hastings' work was far from perfect, within two years of his arrival in Calcutta he had given Bengal a government vastly superior to that of any other state in India.

For the next two years Hastings' intelligent reforming zeal was balked by the unintelligent reforming zeal of others. Tales of real and imaginary iniquities of the Company had wrought a change of heart in the British government toward India. Lord North's Regulating Act of 1773 was the second interference of parliament in the affairs of this unhappy land, and there was little good in this measure except its intention. By this act,[1] the Company had to submit to the British government all dispatches dealing with political matters; the governor of

---

[1] Another act of the same time suspended the £400,000 annual tribute to the British government.

Bengal became governor general with authority over the presidencies of Madras and Bombay, and he could do nothing without the consent of a council of five, including himself. Three members of this new and powerful council had no Indian experience, and from their arrival in 1774 they set out to tie his hands and undo his work. Two years later one of them died and Hastings recovered his authority by means of his casting vote. This was fortunate, for the hostility of the great native powers was growing and war with them was liable to break out at any time.

Hastings neither sought nor made a single conquest;[2] but from 1779, when the Nizam of Hyderabad engineered a confederacy with the Mahrattas and with Hyder Ali of Mysore, he had to fight a terrific war for five years. As the American war precluded any possibility of his getting aid from England, he had to rely wholly upon the resources of the Company in India, including its single ally Oudh; and the odds against him were tremendous. It was only the strength given by his earlier work that made resistance possible, and it was only his superb leadership that pulled the Company through the fiery ordeal without any loss. But if British rule in India was still confined to Bengal and the factories of Madras and Bombay, it had gained enormously in prestige, not only in its own territory but also among the native princes and their peoples.

The reward meted out to the man who thus rescued British rule in India from corruption and then saved it from military destruction is the greatest personal tragedy in the history of the empire. Philip Francis, the chief of the hostile triumvirate that had dominated the council, was a clever snake in the grass. He was determined to ruin Warren Hastings and was most ambitious to become governor general himself. During the war he returned to England, and there he spread his venom, persuading Burke and Fox and most of the other Whigs that Hastings was a poisonous monster. They demanded his recall but the Company refused it. Then, in 1783, they introduced into parliament a bill that would have forced it. This was a substitute for North's Regulating Act, which had become recognized as impossible; but the measure proposed by the Whigs was in some respects worse, and the only thing that prevented its passage was an unconstitutional action of the king, who privately intimidated the House of Lords into rejecting the bill.

---

[2] Except the French posts which he promptly seized when France declared war and which the British restored on the return of peace.

In the following year, 1784, Pitt passed an India Act that provided the main framework of British government in India during the next three quarters of a century—until the Company ceased to exist. This act made the British government responsible for the direction of Indian policy. It created a Board of Control, a branch of this government, whose function was to control the political, military, and financial affairs of the Company; and it greatly enlarged the powers of the governor general and his council who, with the presidents of Madras and Bombay and the members of their councils, were all to be appointed and removable by the Crown. The act also prescribed two doctrines that emanated from Francis and were to cause much mischief. One was that there should be no mingling in native politics, no treaty relations with native princes. The other was that the zemindars should be accepted as the owners of the land from which they and their forbears for many generations had gathered the income.

The tide of opinion in England was rising so high against Hastings, even in government circles, that Pitt was about to recall him when the governor general, realizing that his day in India was done, resigned and returned home. He was impeached by the House of Commons, and his trial by the House of Lords, which began in 1788, dragged on for seven long years. No one could impugn his private life, for it was above reproach; but in his public capacity he had done many things that, to people unfamiliar with the facts of life in India, could be made to appear as heinous crimes by the heated imagination and withering invective of such powerful orators as Burke and Fox and Sheridan, to say nothing of the many others who hurled torrents of abuse at him. In the end he was acquitted of every charge. Even though he left the bar with his reputation cleared, he was ruined in fortune, all of it having been swallowed up by the costs of the defense. This most protracted and famous of all impeachments was a shameful business, yet not entirely. There was a noble motive behind the vindictive prosecution of this great man. It was a high resolve to preserve the name of Britain from being contaminated by deeds of injustice or oppression in the government of subject peoples. This trial marked the vigorous awakening in the British public of a sense of imperial responsibility to match imperial power. It was an object lesson for all time that even the greatest Briton would be held strictly to account for the way he exercised British authority in any land, however distant.

Meanwhile Lord Cornwallis, whom Pitt picked in 1786 as the successor of Hastings in India, had there won much more honor than he may have lost at Yorktown. His appointment was a new departure, in keeping with the India Act of 1784 and the public purpose in the impeachment of Hastings. Not a Company man at all but a leading noble who, both in and out of parliament, had long devoted his life to the service of his country, the new governor general embodied the new sense of responsibility. High above the reach of Company jealousies, he had a free hand to develop the administrative reforms of his predecessor. His separation of the functions of collector and judge was only one of the many improvements he made in the system of government of Bengal, which then became a sort of model for other Indian territories when, in later years, they came under British rule.

One reform that Cornwallis effected, however, was to be given little application elsewhere because it did more harm than good. For this he was not to blame, because in this particular he was simply carrying out the orders of parliament and the home government. These orders, which called for a permanent settlement of the land revenues, were well intentioned but wholly mistaken. The error was not peculiar. It has been common in America, Africa, and the East, wherever westerners have imported their notions of private property in land into their dealings with a native society. Private property in land was utterly foreign to India. There from time immemorial the state shared with the cultivator the right to appropriate the produce of the soil; the Moslem conquerors had added a third party, the zemindar; and it was the custom, from time to time, to make a new assessment of what the land could produce and a new division of the income. Now, on the supposition that the zemindar was the familiar landlord who would develop his property best if his taxes were not to be raised every few years, there was a new assessment and a "permanent settlement" of what he had to pay to the government. The latter thus got a secure revenue and put an end to the possibility of oppression by its own agents, while it delivered the poor peasants over to worse native oppression at the hands of a new class of rapacious landlords.

The other principle laid down in 1784—that there was to be no intervention in native Indian politics—was likewise good in intention and bad in effect. Tipu Sahib, the son and successor of Hyder Ali in Mysore, had made peace with Hastings in 1784, but he was itching to break it. He threatened other native states even more than he did the British Company, and they appealed to Cornwallis for defensive alliances, which the governor general had to refuse in obedience to the act of parliament and instructions from the home government. His enforced isolationism, designed to prevent the British from becoming involved in war, had the very opposite result. It led the lawless Tipu to think he had nothing to fear, and he plunged ahead on the road of conquest. His aggressions provoked a two years' war in which the Nizam of Hyderabad and the Mahrattas were leagued with the British, whose forces were led by Cornwallis in person. It ended in 1792 when Tipu, besieged in his own capital, had to sign a punitive treaty. It stripped him of half the realm which he and his father had greatly expanded, and this was divided among the allies. It also bound him to pay £3,000,000 sterling toward the cost of the war. Though the British thus gained some territory, it was nothing to what they were soon to add.

The news of the French declaration of war against Britain in 1793 reached India about the time Cornwallis left it, and at once French influence became a disturbing factor that within five years threatened to undermine if not to destroy the British position in India. What made this threat serious was the British doctrine of nonintervention, from which Cornwallis had departed only temporarily and under necessity. His successor followed it faithfully, thereby driving the rival native powers to the conclusion that none could place any faith in the British as a possible ally against attack. Each then turned to the French, from whom they got officers and equipment with which they developed modern armies—and a disdain for the British. Such was the explosive situation in 1798, when Napoleon sailed for Egypt with India as one of his contemplated goals, and there the tide began to turn with the arrival of a new British governor general, who threw the paralyzing doctrine to the four winds and boldly grasped the empire of India.

This outstanding empire builder was Lord Wellesley, the eldest brother of Arthur Wellesley, the future Duke of Wellington, who accompanied him and supported him most ably during the next five momentous years in the East. Almost at once Lord Wellesley broke the hostile ring by winning over the Nizam of Hyderabad, who was wedged in between dangerous neighbors—the Mahrattas on the north and Tipu of Mysore on the south. In return for a guarantee of British protection, the Nizam bound himself to support the Company in war, disbanded his French battalions, and undertook never to take any European into his service without British consent—a condition that thenceforth became the rule in British treaties with native princes. By making this pact, which became tighter as the years passed, and by

from the responsibility he was incurring, the directors of the Company and the British government had firmly decided to call a halt. Wellesley was summoned home and threatened with impeachment, while Cornwallis was sent back to India with instructions to make peace at any price. Two months after his arrival in Calcutta, an old man broken in health, he died while rushing up country to take command. His authority devolved upon a civil servant of the Company, who obeyed the instructions literally. He restored all Holkar's territories and independence to him, even pledging the Company to give no aid to the princes of Rajputana who, having long been the prey of the Mahrattas, had joined the British against Holkar.

This sudden return to the policy of nonintervention, and its rigid enforcement for almost a decade, released in central India the wild anarchy that Wellesley had just chained. The Mahratta powers had always existed by plunder, and now they harbored new swarms of marauders. Some of these were Pathans, fierce Moslem warriors from the hill country of the northwest. More numerous and destructive were the Pindaris, outlaws of diverse races and religions. These murderous gangs, sometimes of many thousands, spread their terror far and wide for hundreds of miles, not only in territories beyond British control but also in native states under British protection. They did it with impunity, for orders from London sternly forbade any measures against them, out of fear of provoking another Mahratta war. At the same time and because of the same British policy, the ravages of the Gurkhas, who some forty years previously had migrated from the west and conquered Nepal, became a nightmare in Oudh and northern Bengal. Conditions in India being what they were, London's insistence on nonintervention, though designed to avert war with native states and to stop the expansion of British power, was actually inviting war which would lead to a new British advance.

Again the tide of empire was reversed in India with the arrival in 1813 of a new governor general, whose ten years of office saw the completion of Wellesley's work of conquest and reform. He was Lord Hastings, apparently no relative of Warren Hastings, and at once he examined what the little Gurkhas had done with their big knives. They had wrested territory from Oudh, and he demanded its return. Their reply was war. It was a difficult war, along a frontier of 600 miles and in mountainous terrain on the edge of the Himalayas. It lasted until 1816 when, with most of their country overrun, these sturdy tribesmen made peace by abandoning the lands they had taken from Oudh, ceding some of their own territory, accepting a British resident, and becoming an ally of the British, whom they staunchly supported from that day.

Meanwhile the havoc wrought by the Pindaris grew until, in this year, one of their raids destroyed some three hundred villages in the British-ruled Circars, and the governor general got permission from home to deal with this pest once and for all. At the same time he was cautioned to avoid, if possible, any war with the Mahrattas, and he tried his best to win their cooperation in stamping out the nests of marauders in their midst. The peshwa of Poona, Bhonsla of Nagpur, Holkar of Indore, and Sindhia of Gwalior, representing a combination of two hundred thousand fighters, all promised their aid and then, at the end of 1817, they[4] struck—at the British. But the British were fully prepared for such treachery. In a few months they completely crushed its authors and wiped out the Pindaris.

The peshwa paid with all his lands, most of which were annexed to form the modern presidency of Bombay, and he was paid with a pension of £80,000 a year. The other princes were restored, with substantial territorial losses and as vassals of the Company. Lord Hastings followed up his victories by treaties with all the numerous princes of Rajputana and central India, whom his predecessor had perforce betrayed to the Mahrattas in 1805. Now these rescued princes, in return for a guarantee of British protection, willingly accepted British supremacy.

At last the whole of India, with the exception of Sindh on the Indus, was brought under effective British control right up to the line of the Sutlej, two thousand miles north of Cape Cormorin. Once more the directors in London grumbled at the additional responsibility and criticized the governor general for driving their organization along the path of empire. They were never reconciled to following this course, but this time it was too late for them to act. The deed was done, the war was won, and for the first time in all its long history peace was established in this teeming ancient land. Nor was peace the only boon brought by British conquest. There was a vast change in the nature of government. This was little evident in the remaining native states, where oriental despotism was still rampant, but there the worse abuses of this evil kind of rule were liable at any time to be checked by the

---

4 Bhonsla having just died, his place was taken by the murderer of his imbecile son and heir. The earlier Holkar was also dead, and this Holkar was a minor for whom a regent was acting.

overlord. The great change was in the other parts of India. There the British conquest swept away the old corrupt native despotism, substituting for it the reign of law and an efficient administration that interfered with the time-honored customs of the population as little as possible, that employed native officials as much as possible, and that consciously and conscientiously preserved the only self-government existing in India—that of the village community.

CHAPTER IX

The Colonial Empire during the
Long French War:
(I) The Western Hemisphere

THE LONG FRENCH WAR wrought a profound change in the size and the character of the British Empire. It was the third such change in little more than half a century. The Seven Years' War had enlarged the old English empire into a British empire; the War of American Independence had cut it down again, leaving it an empire that was still American in extent but no longer predominantly English in population; and now the struggle against Revolutionary and Napoleonic France expanded it into a world empire.

The harvest of colonial spoils that Britain gathered from her European foes during those tumultuous years was immense. All of these foes, with the exception of Spain[1] whose people became allies of the British against Napoleon, lost all of their overseas possessions before he was overthrown. At the end of the war, however, Britain restored most of these possessions in order to consolidate the peace. What she kept was for security reasons rather than for economic exploitation. This was particularly true in the eastern hemisphere, where the conquered colonies to which she clung had then no value to her except as strategic supports of her empire in India. This was the one really profitable part of the empire; and its rise, which both the government and the East India Company in London vainly tried to check, was pulling imperial interest from the west to the east.

The transformation that the long French war effected in the character of the British Empire was a continuation and enlargement of the

---

[1] Portugal was not one of these foes.

change that began with the conquest of Canada and became pronounced with the loss of the old thirteen colonies. The new additions to the empire made it even less English. It became multiracial and polylingual, a world empire demographically as well as geographically. The problem presented by the acquisition of Canada in 1763, that of incorporating a foreign body, was multiplied manifold. This gave rise to a new form of British colonial government—that of the crown colonies—which, borrowed from the despoiled empires, greatly accentuated the tendency to concentrate control in London. It appeared even in Australia, the only quarter where the British Empire was gaining new territory by settlement instead of by conquest; the peculiar nature of that English settlement assimilated it to the new type of rule.

Meanwhile repercussions of the French Revolution were felt throughout the British Empire, and nowhere more than in North America. The effect on French Canada was deep and lasting. It took the form of a revulsion first from France and then from Britain. The French of Canada have never recovered from the shock administered by Revolutionary France when it turned on their beloved church and rent it. That completed their alienation from their old mother country and so, as it were, set the seal to the British conquest of Canada. The validity of the seal was soon tested by the war against France. French emissaries entered Canada via the United States and sought to revolutionize the French on the St. Lawrence, but they might as well have tried to reverse the flow of that mighty river. The desire of these French subjects of Britain to return to their former allegiance was forever dead. Their other revulsion, which was no less distinct and permanent, began during the Napoleonic period, when they were caught in a world movement that the French Revolution precipitated. It was the spread of a new phase of nationalism, whose dynamic force was to become dominant in the nineteenth century, substituting the national state for the dynastic state and the divine right of nations for the divine right of kings. Though French Canadian nationalism has not been so violent as the nationalism of some other peoples, its awakening split Canada forever.

The local condition that precipitated this awakening was a political revolution released by the introduction of representative government. The English-speaking minority in Lower Canada had long aspired to rule through an assembly, which had been denied them until its control was placed permanently beyond their reach by the separation of Upper Canada, with its British-American electorate. The prospect of having to live under a French assembly frightened the minority. Their fear turned their political principles inside out and welded them into a Tory party. Rallying behind the administration in Quebec, which was composed chiefly of men of their own blood who were likewise apprehensive of what the French assembly might do, the leaders of the minority captured the ear of the governor and entrenched themselves in the executive and legislative councils. Thus, at long last, by a complete reversal of principle, they came into power.

While this revolution was occurring, the French majority felt no particular alarm. For nearly a generation a British government had ruled them much as the previous French government had done—as a benevolent autocracy. They knew no other kind of rule until the British took them into partnership by granting an assembly. Their political education was just beginning, and it took them nearly fifteen years to discover that they were worse off instead of better off than before. Then they too were frightened by what they saw. Their assembly was blocked by the upper chamber of the legislature, and the administration was no longer their sympathetic friend. The actual rulers of the colony were hostile to their language, their religion, their laws, their economic interests, and would treat them as an inferior conquered people.

In 1806 the newly established minority organ, *The Mercury,* boldly declared that the province was too French for a British colony and ought to be made English; and in the same year the French founded their first national newspaper, *Le Canadien,* whose defiant motto was "Nos institutions, notre langue et nos lois." There is nothing like strife for inflaming national feeling, and the strife was on. It continued until the middle of the century with only one short respite, in the early years, but with no resort to physical violence except in the thirties. It was a bitter political struggle between the French in possession of the assembly and the British oligarchy in possession of the other branches of government, each side being convinced that it was fighting for self-preservation. The conflict obstructed the erection of a public school system for half a century, retarded the economic development of the province, and hardened French Canadian nationalism. The only respite was during the War of 1812, when the two factions in Lower Canada pulled together against the United States; for French Canadians had no desire to jump out of the British frying pan into the American fire, and much as they might revile the British, they relied on them for defense against a foreign foe. The French Canadians then gave the lie to the accusation that they were traitors at heart, which their domestic enemies had already leveled against them and were to renew in the years to come.

The chain of reactions set up by the French Revolution in North America was by no means confined to Lower Canada. It profoundly affected the whole of British North America. The French declaration of war in 1793 helped to pull Britain back from the verge of war with the United States over the division of the North American continent. Britain had not given up all the territory that she had signed away in 1783. In agreeing to run the international boundary through the Great Lakes, she neglected to protect her Indian allies who occupied the region south of this line. On learning that their lands had been included in the United States, they accused the British of betraying them, and they continued the war on their own account; while the British, out of regard for them, retained the garrisons established in strategic posts along the south of the lakes, thereby violating their own peace treaty and aggravating the native war with the United States. It was an ugly situation that grew uglier as the years passed—the years of the so-called "critical period" of the young Republic, when there were grave signs that it might break up. By 1793 the Indians were still fighting savagely and successfully against American forces sent to subdue them, and the British garrisons still held the keys of the American Northwest with orders to fight if attacked. London had no fear of such an explosion, which would blow up the boundary agreement of ten years before and lead to a new division of the continent. At this juncture, France unwittingly came to the rescue of the United States. The American people, now sure of an ally, shouted for war. President Washington, still alarmed by the possible outcome, dispatched John Jay to London where he found the government, with a French war on its hands, less willing to face an American war. The result was Jay's Treaty of 1794, by which Britain promised to evacuate the posts in return for an American promise not to interfere with the British fur trade in the United States.

Anglo-American relations, so vital to British North America, thus passed a dangerous crisis; and for the next few years they grew steadily closer, again thanks to the French war. Jay's Treaty infuriated the government in Paris, which regarded it as the betrayal of France by the United States; and the consequent reactions between these two former allies tended to push the United States into the war on the side of Britain. The reconciliation effected by the Franco-American treaty of 1800 reversed the movement of the United States, the Peace of Amiens checked it, and the breach of this peace in 1803 would have drawn the United States and Britain together again if it had not been for the Louisiana Purchase.

The effects that the Louisiana Purchase had upon the history not only of the United States but also of the British Empire in America are so important and far-reaching that it is difficult to appraise them fully. Here we should note that it was the first step the United States took toward the War of 1812—quite unconsciously. This was as Napoleon planned it. That Louisiana was then for sale was utterly beyond the imagination of the American government and people. What they wanted, and that very badly, was only one little corner of it, New Orleans, because it controlled the navigation of the Mississippi. Spain was closing this outlet and France threatened to shut it tight, with results that would be disastrous to the United States. Therefore the American government sought to buy New Orleans and, if this was impossible, was prepared to seek an alliance with Britain to pull the plug from the mouth of the great river. At the same time Britain was preparing to seize this strategic spot as soon as hostilities with France broke out again, in order to keep it out of French hands and ultimately to turn it over to the United States. Such was the situation when Napoleon surprised the American mission in Paris into purchasing a whole empire in order to buy a city. It was one of the shrewdest deals of his career. By selling what he had not yet got and could not hope to keep, he placed this rich prize forever beyond the reach of his great foe; he strengthened the United States, his prospective great friend and counterweight against Britain; and he inserted a wedge to split the two English-speaking powers apart.

The War of 1812, which left its mark upon British North America and through British North America upon British policy, was a by-product of the titanic war in the Old World. Belligerents are no respecters of neutrals, especially when the former are powerful and the latter are weak. In the life-and-death struggle between Britain and Napoleon, neither side could tolerate any neutral right that might aid the other, and so between them they subjected the United States to intolerable pressure. Neither side would yield to American protests, even to gain an American alliance, which was offered in the vain hope of playing one off against the other; for they equally scorned the potential resistance of the United States, which therefore had abundant provocation for making war on both. This was unthinkable. The only possible escape from such an impossible position was to make war on one or the other. Which would it be? Napoleon finally tricked the American government into a declaration against Britain, but we can see this end coming independently of his deception. Britain, being in command of the sea, pressed much harder than France upon American neutral rights; and France, having no foothold on the continent after the cession of Louisiana, was much less vulnerable to American attack.

Contrary to a persistent tradition, British tampering with American Indians was not a cause of the war. True, there was growing trouble with the western tribes; but this was of American origin and a careful examination of the Canadian archives reveals that British officials, using what influence they still had, were doing their best to check it. Another common mistake has been the assertion that the war was unnecessary and might have been averted if there had then been an Atlantic cable, because Congress voted for war not knowing that Britain had just repealed the offending orders in council. As a matter of fact the repeal was not effective, for it was loaded with conditions that the American government could not accept. Moreover, Britain refused to budge on the other great ground for quarrel, the right of search and impressment. Indeed, there is now little doubt that the war would have come long before it did if the United States had been better prepared for it.

The issues on which the United States went to war were maritime, and yet it is a notorious fact that the maritime interests of the country, which were concentrated in New England, were almost solidly opposed to the war. The apparent contradiction, which has given rise to the erroneous but plausible theory that the effective cause of the war was an American desire to conquer Canada, is easily explained and has an important bearing on the conduct of the war. New England faced economic starvation unless her ships were free to ply the ocean, and was therefore willing to submit to the conditions imposed by the mistress of the seas. In the eyes of the South, whose superior voting strength carried the resolution for war, New England would betray the country's honor, which had to be maintained. Also, the South's bread was buttered on the other side. Being engaged in the production of staples that were mostly consumed on the continent of Europe, the South faced economic suffocation if it could not get its goods through the British barrier to the markets controlled by Napoleon. Here was another reason for championing the maritime interests in their own despite. To New England, on the other hand, it was the South that was betraying the honor and ruining the prosperity of the United States.

The war itself was one of the strangest ever waged, and stranger still have been the conflicting accounts of it in the school texts of Canada and the United States, which until recent years taught the children on each side of the line that their country won the war. The nature of the war at sea was simple. No battle between fleets was possible because the United States navy was then negligible and the Royal Navy invincible. So each side struck at the other in the only way it could, the Americans by raiding and the British by blockade; and the one was as futile as the other was decisive. Americans have fondly cherished the memory of single-ship engagements in which their government's frigates captured a handful of British war vessels and American privateers gathered a harvest of British merchantmen, but these engagements had no military value because the consequent reduction of British sea power and ocean-born commerce was infinitesimal. From early in the conflict the British blockade of the American coast, with the exception of friendly New England, grew steadily tighter, paralyzing the American economy and thereby strangling the ability of the American government to continue the war on land; and, what has sometimes escaped attention, this effect was nearing completion when the fall of Napoleon released a mighty British army of veterans for use in America. Nor should it be overlooked that, as a last resort, British sea power could have been applied to make the United States disgorge even a considerable land conquest. Here was an ultimate guarantee, not called upon because not needed, that British North America would survive the war.

It was not at sea but on land that the war was a strange affair. In the United States there had been great confidence, and in England grave fears, that American forces would swarm over most of British North America, conquering it easily. At the outbreak of hostilities the British North American colonies had less than five thousand regulars in scattered garrisons, and they could get no reinforcements from the mother country while she was locked in a death grapple with the European monster. These colonies had a total population of scarcely half a million, as against seven and three quarters million in the United States; and of this half million the majority were French, who were now openly resenting the rule of their British masters, while the minority contained a large proportion of Americans, who formed the bulk of the Upper Canadian population. Moreover, British North America was a thin line of settlement that was not even continuous, and it stretched for a thousand miles and more along an indefensible border.

Here was the vulnerable part of the great power that the United

States had challenged, but the United States was incapable of seizing it. New England's bitter opposition to the war shielded the Maritime Provinces and withheld the support of the most solid part of the Republic. This, together with the British blockade, crippled the American war effort, while an almost unbelievable incompetence in Washington weakened this effort still further and misdirected it completely. Instead of being all focused in a drive on Montreal, the capture of which would have delivered everything above, the military resources at the disposal of the American government were dissipated over the wide region of the Lower Lakes, where there should have been no fighting at all. Such weakness and folly redressed the balance on land. The extent of the American conquest was the little southwest corner of Upper Canada, whereas the British were able to take and hold the whole territory between the Great Lakes and the Mississippi.

This small American war, thus brought to a stalemate, was turned upside down by the collapse of the big European war in 1814. Now the military issue was not whether the United States would conquer some of British North America, but whether Britain would reconquer some of the United States. The government in London was set on this reconquest, partly as a punishment for the attack on the empire in its hour of peril and partly to gain a more defensible North American frontier. The great Duke of Wellington was invited to undertake the task, and a large army of his veterans was sent across the Atlantic. But Wellington persuaded his government to end the war in another fashion. He suggested that he might soon be wanted in Europe, a possibility that became a reality in the Hundred Days; and he frankly stated that a conquest of any value to British North America would require considerable time and effort. It was better, he advised, to make peace right away by accepting the old frontier. This was done six weeks later, on Christmas Eve, 1814, when the Treaty of Ghent was signed. So, in a way, France came to the rescue of the United States for a third and last time.

The effect of the War of 1812 upon British North America was most evident in Upper Canada. The war suddenly stopped the peaceful American invasion of that province, and it checked a renewal of this invasion afterward, for it opened British eyes to what had been happening. It also stifled the potentially American character of the Upper Canadian population by purging it of the small minority who were incorrigible republicans and by corraling within the British fold the great majority who were not. These changes draw added significance from the fact that the tide of British immigration to this province was relatively small until fifteen years or so after the outbreak of hostilities in America. Then it might have been too late for these newcomers, themselves not very self-conscious politically, to impress a British character upon Upper Canada if the war had not cut, as with a knife, its growing connection with the United States.

Taking British North America as a whole, the war accentuated its British spirit by reinforcing the anti-American prejudice that dates from the American Revolution and the settlement of the Loyalists. To this very day Canadians have not been able to forget the fight to save their country from the United States, and they react against the anti-British prejudice that American memories of this war have strengthened in the United States.

Nevertheless, the experience of the war brought into clear relief a fundamental condition that made another war between the British Empire and the American Republic something to be avoided at almost any cost. The American commissioners at Ghent pointed it out in a reply to the British demand, later withdrawn, for a drastic revision of the boundary. The British said they must have it in order to give security to British North America, exposed as it was to an American attack by land. The reply pointed out that this was not necessary because Britain already had ample security in her undoubted ability to strike a more damaging blow on the Atlantic seaboard of the United States. That this balance of vulnerability governed the relations of the United States with British North America and through it the relations between Washington and London, becomes more apparent if one glances at the relations between the United States and its neighbors on the southwest, where there was no such balance. Thus did the revelation of the War of 1812 dictate permanent peace between the British Empire and the United States until the latter became a world power, when world considerations confirmed it.

The British West Indies were much more affected by the French Revolution than by the long French war that followed. The terrible explosion in San Domingo, which the explosion in France touched off in 1791, struck terror into the hearts of the British island planters— and put enormous profits into their pockets. The western third of San Domingo, which belonged to France, has been called the jewel of the French colonial empire. It was the richest tropical colony that any country possessed until this revolution ruined it by releasing perhaps the most hideous race war in history and by producing chronic anarchy.

The whites who did not escape were exterminated. Some of the leading fugitives sought a refuge in England, and there they begged for intervention that would make the island British. The British lent their ears but not their arms until after the outbreak of the Anglo-French war in 1793. In the autumn of that year an expedition from nearby Jamaica invaded the turbulent Negro republic, gaining a promising foothold; but the yellow fever wrecked this army and others sent after it until their miserable remnants were withdrawn from a much-shrunken foothold in 1798.

Whatever danger there was that the dreaded black contagion might spread to the British islands was checked by the dispatch of naval and military forces from England to eliminate French power from the West Indies. Jamaica, however, had a bad scare in 1795, when the flame of revolt burst forth in its own mountains. There dwelt the Maroons, descendants of runaway English slaves and, more particularly, of the Spanish slaves who had fled thither when the English took the island nearly a century and a half before. They were savage outlaws who defied all attempts to subdue them until nearly 1740, when their freedom was guaranteed and they were settled on reserves under their own chiefs assisted by white superintendents. Now, in 1795, occurred the last Maroon war, in which some but not all of these wild men joined, and as in previous generations English troops could make little headway against the rebels in their mountain fastnesses.

Would this fire in the interior, so much closer than San Domingo, which was dangerously near, drop sparks into the huge powder keg of the Jamaican slave population? In desperation the authorities at once procured effective fire extinguishers from the sympathetic governor of neighboring Cuba—a hundred man-hunting bloodhounds. These ferocious beasts turned the terror inward, and before the year was out the rebel chiefs concluded a treaty which, in return for the immediate surrender of their followers, promised that they would not be banished. Scant time was allowed for all to make their formal submission, and several bands failed to appear on the appointed day. Their delay served as a pretext for the lieutenant governor to declare the treaty broken. When the stragglers arrived they were promptly imprisoned, and shortly afterward they were deported to Nova Scotia, six hundred of them. Feelings in England were outraged by the inhuman method of cowing the rebels, and orders were sent out to extirpate from the island the whole breed of the horrible animals. From England pity also went out to the exiles in Nova Scotia, where many of these sons of the tropics succumbed to the harsh climate of the north, and in 1800 English humanitarians had the survivors removed to the more congenial environment of Sierra Leone. So strong was the storm of disapproval in the mother country that it stung the Jamaican legislature into publishing a set of official papers to present a complete justification of the whole nasty business.

The only British West Indian colonies that were touched by the fighting in the French war were Dominica, St. Vincent, and Grenada, which had been ceded by France in 1763 and reoccupied by France during the American Revolutionary War. This reoccupation had not improved the relations between the French and the English elements in their population, and the new war made them worse. In all three colonies the French residents appealed to arms in the very year of the Jamaican Maroon war. In Dominica the rising coincided with a French attack from Guadeloupe, but a small body of British troops, aided by British planters, quickly repelled the attack and repressed the rebellion. In Grenada and St. Vincent, however, the French insurgents found local allies—the free colored people in the former and the Caribs in the latter—and the British had to fight with their backs to the wall until they regained control in the following year. Meanwhile civil war ruined the crops and blighted the trade of these two little colonies. With these two exceptions, the British West Indies were enjoying a period of abounding prosperity.

What caused this prosperity was the fury in San Domingo. The normal production of this French colony was about equal to that of all the British Caribbean colonies combined, and the sudden destruction of this source of supply of tropical produce created a void that took years to fill. Prices on the continent of Europe, which had been steadily lower than those in England, jumped above them, pulling them upward. The British planter economy, which had been barely saved from bankruptcy by its monopoly of the British market, was called upon to help supply the continental market at scarcity prices. As there was little new land to be exploited in the British West Indies, they expanded their production by introducing superior varieties of cane, with the result that their average annual sugar export to the mother country increased by about 70 per cent in ten years. Coffee production, particularly in Jamaica, also leaped up to meet the unprecedented demand caused by the destruction of the plantations in San Domingo. That destruction gave the British West Indies a decade of high returns which injected new life into their tottering economy and thus "delayed its total collapse by a quarter of a century."[2]

Great as were their profits, the British planters reaped nothing like the full advantage of the havoc wrought by the blacks in San Domingo. The British government had to think of the British consumer, whom it had long forced to pay monopoly prices for colonial sugar, and so it felt no compunction in passing legislation to check the export of this article to the continent as the price soared. Also, the East India Company began to import sugar from Bengal, and this in considerable quantity despite a much higher duty than that charged on British Caribbean sugar.

This sweet invasion from the Orient alarmed the West Indians, as well it might, for it demonstrated how much cheaper production was in the East, and it started an ominous argument. The Company, backed by British consumers, pressed the government to eliminate or reduce the tariff discrimination that favored the West Indian product. To this end it was pointed out that the British Caribbeans could not meet the demand for sugar whereas India could; that their demand for British manufactures had reached its limit whereas the Indian market was insatiable; that their defense was a heavy burden on Britain whereas native troops guarded India at no expense to the mother country; and that the much longer voyage to India would give more employment to British shipping, and training to British seamen. Such reasoning threw the West Indians on the defensive. They appealed to the unwritten compact that gave mutual monopolies to the mother country and the colonies, and they asserted that they would be ruined if they lost the existing preference. Apparently they were in little danger of losing it, for they were strongly entrenched in the political life of the mother country, public opinion there was decidedly prejudiced against the Company, and the producer mentality did not yield the control of policy to the consumer mentality until the coming of free trade.

What the war added to the British West Indies raises a nice question. The British conquered all the French West Indies except San Domingo, on which they turned their back in 1798, all the Caribbean possessions of the Danes and the Dutch when Denmark and Holland were French satellites, and the Spanish island of Trinidad when Spain

---

[2] L. J. Ragatz, *The Fall of the Planter Class in the Caribbean, 1763–1833* (New York, 1928), p. 206.

was a subservient French ally. At the close of the long struggle Britain could have easily kept all these conquests, which had been in her possession for years and were being exploited by British capital; but she did not. She deliberately restored all the Danish and Dutch islands, Dutch Guiana, and most of the French islands including the rich ones of Martinique and Guadeloupe. Why did she return such valuable spoils of war? This question becomes very much bigger when we consider that she also restored the Dutch East Indies, which were worth many times everything she yielded in the West Indies. In magnitude at least, it was a splendid renunciation.

The answer to the question is simple and there is no mistaking it. It is plainly set forth in the confidential British government documents of the day—the minutes of the cabinet and the correspondence between the prime minister and the foreign secretary, who represented the British government in the peace negotiations. It was to get a lasting peace. The government, said a cabinet minute of early in 1814, "do not desire to retain any of these colonies for their mere commercial value—too happy if by their restoration they can give other states an additional motive to cultivate the arts of peace."[3] Britain had just signed a treaty with Denmark, which then deserted Napoleon for the allies, whereby all the Danish islands were to be returned and Danish troops were taken into British pay. Sweden had been promised Guadeloupe to bring her into line, but was later persuaded to accept a million pounds instead, which Britain paid, in order that this island might be given back to France. Why any consideration for France, the scourge of Europe for a quarter of a century? First, to persuade her to release her hold on Belgium, so that it might be annexed to Holland to make a strong kingdom that would stand on guard against France; and then, to bolster the restored Bourbon monarchy, which was regarded as a guarantee against future French aggression. The restoration of the Dutch colonies was to strengthen this new and greater Holland, the creation of which was one of the two cardinal points of British policy in the peace settlement. The other was the perpetuation of the warborn alliance as an international peace agency. To this end it was necessary to prevent mutual jealousies from dissolving the victorious

---

[3] Quoted in C. K. Webster, *Foreign Policy of Castlereagh* (2nd ed.; London, 1934), pp. 195–196. There is no evidence that the British West Indian planters, whose desire to preserve their vested interest opposed them to any permanent acquisition of sugar islands, had any influence upon British policy in the peace settlement.

combination, which would be impossible unless Britain took the lead by a generous restitution of conquests.

Another important, though secondary, influence on British policy was the humanitarian drive against the slave trade. Though Britain alone had abolished it—in the midst of the war—her action had been pretty effective as long as the war lasted. But now that peace was coming, it was obvious that the trade would flourish again unless she could persuade the other powers to abolish it too. In the spring of 1814 the House of Commons passed a resolution against the surrender of colonies without abolition, and the ministry assured Wilberforce and his friends that it would get general abolition. The Dutch, glad to get their colonies back, readily issued the necessary decree; but the French, suspicious that Britain was trying to cripple the colonies she was restoring, would promise abolition only after a few years when their islands were restocked with slaves and thus able to compete with the British. Anxious to placate French opinion, and to get at least some French concession of the principle, the British accepted the French condition.

Though Britain thus bargained her colonial conquests to get the sort of world she wanted, she did not give everything back to the former owners. Of the French West Indian islands, she retained two small ones. One was Tobago, which had been British from 1763 until it was lost during the American Revolution, by which time it had acquired a definite British character, much more so than perhaps any other of the ceded islands. The inhabitants of Tobago rejoiced when a British force recaptured it in 1793, lamented when it was returned to France by the Treaty of Amiens in 1802, and when it was finally taken in 1803 they earnestly petitioned that it should never be alienated again. In 1814, there were no French settlers left in Tobago and there was no question about its retention. The other French island was St. Lucia, which also had once been English. Its only value was its harbor, and for this it was kept at the behest of the Admiralty, which otherwise would have had none in that part of the West Indies.

Britain also kept the South American territory that contained the three little Dutch colonies of Essequibo, Demerara, and Berbice, which were united in 1831 to form British Guiana. These settlements had attracted British planters and merchants from the close of the American Revolutionary War, when a number of British planters went there from Tobago and prospered. During the years of British occupation, from 1796 to 1802 and from 1803, still more British went and Liverpool merchants invested heavily there. Even so, the British government did not decide to keep these Dutch settlements until very late in the day, but contemplated substituting them for Guadeloupe when France insisted on recovering that island and something else had to be found for Sweden. Then Sweden agreed to accept the offer of a million pounds instead, and this was to have been a charge upon the Dutch, until the British government assumed it as part of the arrangement with the Dutch when the latter formally ceded the territory to Britain in 1814. Another provision of this arrangement allowed the Dutch to continue trading in the little South American colonies they thus abandoned.

The only territory acquired from Spain was Trinidad, which was captured early in 1797 and formally ceded in 1802, so that it did not come under review in the general peace settlement of a dozen years later. Spain had neglected the development of this island until the 1780's, and then had tried to make something of it by attracting foreign Roman Catholics with the offer of land. From the Caribbean islands to the north, French and Irish went, and some English too because the religious qualification was not seriously enforced. There was a still greater influx from the French islands when they were infected by the fever of the French Revolution. The population of Trinidad, numbering nearly eighteen thousand in 1797, was thus mostly French. In addition to being a refuge for Frenchmen, who were enemies of the British, Trinidad was also a haven for fraudulent debtors from the West Indies generally and the home of outlaws who raided the other islands to carry off slaves. It was only natural, therefore, that the British should want to seize Trinidad; the capture was easy because the Spaniards who were there were quite bitter in their attitude toward the French. The British retention of the island by the Treaty of Amiens was inspired chiefly, if not entirely, by the fact that it offered a most convenient base for contraband trade with the Spanish Main, which had been an object of British policy for generations. Britain did not even try to take any other Spanish possession in the New World, Trinidad being the only one that harbored any French menace.

In the provisions for the government of these additions to the British Empire in America, there is a striking contrast between Tobago and the others. The former, because of its history and character, was treated as one of the old family that had been unfortunately lost for a while. Each time it fell into British hands, they at once reclothed it with British laws and institutions after the traditional pattern, and it behaved just as one of the old colonies. For example, its assembly was asked to enact the 4.5 per cent Leeward Islands duty on exports, and the characteristic refusal followed. The other new colonies, however, were foreign in character, and there the authorities in London again faced the problem that they had bungled on a large scale in Quebec and on a smaller one in Grenada. This time it was not taken for granted that foster children would be just the same as those that had always been in the family. Slowly and tentatively the British government worked out a new system for these acquisitions, and a new type of British colony arose—the crown colony, in which the complete control of legislation and of all administrative officers is in the hands of the Crown, meaning of course the cabinet in London.[4]

This development had an unconscious beginning in the disposition of the conquered French colonies, with the exception of Tobago, at the very outset of the long French war; and it sprang from a desire to give every possible satisfaction to the French royalists, on whom the British government then relied for valuable cooperation in these colonies. The British commanders, as instructed by London, included in the terms of capitulation an undertaking to preserve the government as it had been under the French monarchy, particularly in the administration of justice and the collection of taxes, until the restoration of peace. British governors were then sent out to restore civil government, and their instructions enjoined "conformity to the ancient laws and institutions" of the conquered people, with the exception that the British navigation laws were to be enforced. Each governor was also directed to form a small council of the leading landowners, whose advice he should seek but not necessarily follow; not to exclude Roman Catholics from this body, but to require of them the oath prescribed by the Quebec Act; not to interfere with the Roman Catholic religion, except to restrain its clergy from making converts and to establish toleration for other churches; not to impose any new taxes; and to follow British Treasury instructions in applying the revenues, which would be collected by a receiver general appointed by the Treasury. The commissions, which endowed the governors with authority, were framed after the common British model but departed from it by omitting every

---

[4] Though the empire already had two crown colonies, Gibraltar and Newfoundland, they were regarded as atypical because of the peculiar circumstances of each, the former being merely a naval station and the latter a land in which settlement was officially discouraged. The old Province of Quebec had also been a crown colony, but this too had been regarded as exceptional and the condition disappeared in 1791.

reference to a council or an assembly, so that there would be no independent local check upon a governor. He would rule as directed from London.

This autocratic form of government, imposed on captured French colonies as a war measure, was destined to have a larger and more permanent application. As the war widened and the British scooped up colonial possessions of France's allies, these other acquisitions were treated in the same way, apparently as a matter of course. It was not until the Treaty of Amiens in 1802, when Britain returned all her French conquests and all the others except Trinidad and Ceylon, which were then permanently ceded to her, that what had been adopted as an expedient for the duration of the war was projected beyond it and began to assume permanence as a new type of government in the British Empire. The transition was much less difficult in Ceylon, which we shall consider presently, than it was in Trinidad, where it was accepted only gradually and after much deliberation.

The government in London did not know what to do with Trinidad, now that it was definitely a British possession. Having an area of some seventeen hundred square miles, it was half as big again as all the British Leeward and Windward islands. Its virgin soil was as rich as their land had long ceased to be, and its climate was reported to be not unfavorable to Europeans. Its population had increased to more than twenty-eight thousand, and its development was only beginning. For its further development the government advised that there would have to be a great increase in its working population; but the prospect made parliament restive, for though that body did not abolish the slave trade for another five years it was already very sensitive about anything that might increase it. Nor was this the only embarrassment the ministry faced as a result of the retention of Trinidad. British merchants interested in the obvious possibilities of the island were agitating for the introduction of English laws and the traditional British form of government; but British confidence in this form of government for tropical colonies, where climate had discouraged white labor, was being undermined as the result of experience in the old West Indian islands. Moreover, the governor was pointing out the dilemma that the establishment of an assembly would raise because the majority of the population were "free people of color." It was their control of that body if they were allowed to vote, and their permanent alienation if they were not. The secretary of state assured the governor that there was no intention of making any such change until it was clear that this would be advanta-

geous to both mother country and colony. A commission, composed
of the governor and two other officials from England, was created to
investigate conditions and report on how the colony should be governed
and settled. The commission quarreled over charges that one of the
members made against the governor's administration of justice.[5] All
three members were recalled, and a new governor was sent out in 1804.

The new governor was expected to find a solution for the complicated problem of Trinidad. His instructions, while admitting that the
existing circumstances of the island would not then warrant the general
introduction of British laws and institutions, urged the adoption of
measures that would make this progressively possible, and definitely
suggested that the best course might be to follow the example of Canada under the Quebec Act. The governor and his advisory council got
the attorney general, an Englishman who had held this office for some
years, to work out a constitution as a draft of an act of parliament, and
sent him home with it. It resembled the Quebec Act but differed from
it by giving taxing power to the legislative council. When the author
reached England a new government was in power, and it was too absorbed by the war against Napoleon to give much attention to Trinidad
for some years. Meanwhile the administration of Spanish laws under
an English chief justice produced growing confusion, which helped to
stir up a new agitation in the colony and among the interested merchants in England.

This movement came to a head in 1810, when a meeting in London
voted to petition the House of Commons and to press the secretary of
state for the establishment of British laws and political institutions in
the island. Again the secretary of state professed anxiety for the adoption of English law and doubts of the wisdom of granting an assembly,
but he would not act until he could get from the governor the best
opinion in the island. This time the governor collected a committee of
leading colonists and they strongly backed the demands made in London. But petitions from others and an emphatic letter from the chief
justice opposed the change. This conflict of views left the ministry free
to follow its own inclination, which was to leave things as they were;
and toward the end of the year the secretary of state wrote to the governor explaining this decision.

An assembly, said the secretary of state in this dispatch, was out of

---

[5] Which led to the prosecution of the governor in England, reminiscent of the proceedings against Warren Hastings.

the question because of the peculiar conditions in Trinidad—the preponderance of "people of color" and the small proportion of British among the whites—and so was any other kind of legislature in the island. The reason he gave for this was the recent abolition of the slave trade, which made it essential for the Crown to retain full power of legislation for the colony. Some of this power might be delegated to the governor, but his exercise of it would always be subject to review in London. The secretary of state reserved judgment on the modification of the laws as an "extensive and complicated" business that could not be undertaken without more investigation. In conclusion he expressed the belief that this form of government which was at last being imposed permanently on Trinidad had proved its advantages elsewhere. The obvious reference is to Ceylon, but he may also have been thinking of the interim administrations in Guiana and the Cape Colony and even, perhaps, of the other empires from which Britain had taken this example of colonial administration.

"This dispatch is of the utmost importance in the history of the British Empire, for it closed the doors to any fundamental change in the system of government, not only in Trinidad but in all the conquered colonies, for a good many years to come."[6] There had been some thought of getting parliament to legislate a constitution for Trinidad; but the ministry preferred to keep its own hands free to deal with that colony as might seem best, and parliament acquiesced in the decision. The dispatch just quoted was printed for the information of parliament without raising any objection in that body.

The issue having been settled in Trinidad, there was no question of any change of laws and governmental institutions in St. Lucia and the settlements in Guiana when the peace settlement at the close of the Napoleonic struggle transformed British occupation into British possession. For some obscure reason the authorities in London thought that the terms granted to the Dutch when they capitulated were still binding after peace had been signed, but it is doubtful if this made any real difference. There had been no such thought about Trinidad and there was none about St. Lucia, yet they experienced no more alteration in government. In St. Lucia, however, the British governor had more power than his French predecessor because the French office of intendant was combined with that of governor at the time of the conquest.

---

[6] Helen Taft Manning, *British Colonial Government After the American Revolution* (New Haven, 1933), p. 362. This is a masterly treatise.

On the other hand, the British had there set up a court of appeal, or superior court, after the French model because this island, as a dependency of Martinique, had not possessed one of its own. For a while this colonial counterpart of a parlement in France claimed that no legislation could be valid until registered by it; but when, shortly after the cession, this court balked at registering orders in council and acts of parliament, the governor told its members, on orders from the secretary of state, that their authority was confined to the administration of justice. During the war a similar incident had occurred in Guiana, where the Dutch had combined Demerara and Essequibo under one governor with a "court of policy" to assist him. In 1812 this court objected to a proclamation sent out from London for the governor[7] to issue, and he held it up until the secretary of state administered a "stinging rebuke" for his lack of obedience.

In all these nascent crown colonies the prerogative of the Crown was supreme. Legislation was by imperial order in council, though only when important, and by gubernatorial proclamation. Occasionally, as we have just seen, a proclamation was actually drafted in London; sometimes a governor was ordered to prepare as well as issue it; usually it was the work of a governor acting on his own authority, but then it was always liable to be overruled by the home government. Taxation was a more delicate matter. At first it was supposed that the old taxes, which were continued, would suffice. They did in Guiana but not in Trinidad or St. Lucia, where there was a growing deficit. Though there was no legal doubt of the Crown's right to levy new taxes in the conquered colonies,[8] it was ten years after the cession of Trinidad before the home government admitted the necessity and decided how to meet it in that island. The method was to consult the governor on what taxes would be best and then to authorize him by order in council to impose them. The same thing was done in St. Lucia a few years afterward. The administration of justice was purged of torture, with the result that criminal procedure developed "grievous delays" and lost some of its certainty in Trinidad and Guiana, for torture had been embedded in the old Spanish code and continued with it by the Dutch. English criminal law and trial by jury would have cured these faults and were

---

[7] A Dutchman, the second whom the British entrusted to carry on the administration. It was not until after this incident that British military men were appointed to the government there.

[8] Except in Demerara, where the Dutch had given taxing power to a semi-representative body, the "combined court" mentioned above.

suggested, but the ministry rejected them as inapplicable, especially trial by jury because it denied justice to the blacks in the old West Indian colonies. Therefore minor adjustments that served as palliatives had to be found. There were also difficulties in the application of the old French, Spanish, and Dutch civil laws in these colonies, but they were gradually reduced after English judges took over the courts and as some features of English laws were introduced.

CHAPTER X

The Colonial Empire during the Long French War: (II) The Eastern Hemisphere

THE TWO most important colonial prizes that Britain won in the long French war were east of the Atlantic: Cape Colony and Ceylon. Both were taken from the Dutch for purely strategic reasons, but otherwise these two additions to the empire were as different as they could be.

As soon as the French Revolution threatened to engulf the Netherlands, the British government resolved to beat the French to the Cape of Good Hope lest this one key to the whole of the Orient fall into the hands of the enemy. That it was also the door leading into the treasure house of the South African interior was a dream yet unborn; and no one could see any commercial value in the colony that had spread from Cape Town when the British expedition took possession of it in 1795. There seemed to be nothing to develop in that country. Its soil was too poor, its climate too dry, and its geographical position too remote to attract European settlers; and its native population was so backward that it had never suggested any possibilities of profitable trade.

It was nearly a century and a half since the Dutch East India Company, discovering that some crops could be grown near Table Bay and that cattle could be procured from the Hottentots, planted a few settlers there to provide the company's ships with fresh food for the long voyage to and from the East; and the only other colonists that had come to the country had been brought for this very purpose by the company in the next couple of generations—two hundred Huguenot refugees and perhaps four times as many Dutch. During the eighteenth century this French element reluctantly yielded to absorption by the majority. The stern Calvinism that they had in common helped to draw them together; and the old High Dutch tongue of the original burghers, though surviving as the written language of their descendants, had broken down as the ordinary conversational medium, giving rise to a new language, Afrikaans, which was more acceptable to the Gallic portion of the population. Dutch and Huguenots were now one people—Boers speaking their own distinctive tongue and attached to the land in which they lived rather than to that from which most of them had come. This century also saw the complete failure of all the efforts of the company, which ruled autocratically, to keep the colonists close to the port and apart from the natives.

The marauding Bushmen, the lowest type, to whom the settlers' cattle were fat and easy prey, were hunted down and driven off. Racial segregation was impossible with the Hottentots, a mild pastoral people who inhabited the better-watered territory along the southern coast. Their society disintegrated almost at a touch. The whites took their flocks and their lands, transformed them into a half-caste race, and reduced them to a position of menial but still genial servants. The mixture of blood was wholly one-sided, the white community preserving its ethnic purity. Here we should also notice that slavery was developed in the colony. This was "by circumstance rather than by necessity." The Cape did not need to import slaves, for its climate was not inimical to white labor and its economy was largely self-sufficient; but it "lay between the two great slave-trading coasts of the world."[1] Moreover, contact with the Dutch East Indies was responsible for the introduction of Malays, who were the skilled workers of the colony and "ranked themselves above all other slaves and free Hottentots."[2] Finally, toward the end of the century, the Boers who had been trekking far to the eastward came into permanent contact with the Kaffirs, the vanguard of the fierce Bantu race who were pressing down from the interior; and then began a series of bitter Kaffir wars that lasted for a hundred years.

The expansion of the colony, which defied repeated decrees of the company to stop it, was the combined product of the soil and the climate. It was eastward rather than northward, because the interior was arid. In the vicinity of Cape Town, where the rainfall was usually plentiful, was the "land of corn and wine," with wheat fields and vineyards cultivated by slaves. But it was no lush country. It was a poor one, providing practically nothing for export except as ships' stores;

---

[1] C. W. De Kiewiet, *A History of South Africa* (Oxford, 1941), p. 21.

[2] Eric A. Walker, *A History of South Africa* (2nd ed.; New York, 1940), p. 87.

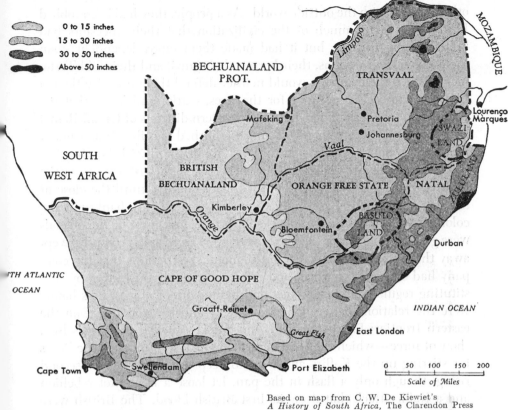

0 to 15 inches
15 to 30 inches
30 to 50 inches
Above 50 inches

BECHUANALAND PROT.

TRANSVAAL

MOZAMBIQUE

Limpopo

Mafeking

Pretoria

Johannesburg

Lourenço Marques

SWAZI LAND

SOUTH WEST AFRICA

Vaal

BRITISH BECHUANALAND

ORANGE FREE STATE

NATAL

ZULULAND

Kimberley

Orange

Bloemfontein

BASUTO LAND

Durban

SOUTH ATLANTIC OCEAN

CAPE OF GOOD HOPE

INDIAN OCEAN

Graaff-Reinet

Great Fish

East London

Cape Town

Swellendam

Port Elizabeth

0   50   100   150   200
Scale of Miles

Based on map from C. W. De Kiewiet's
A History of South Africa, The Clarendon Press

South African Rainfall

and it extended for no more than a three days' trek, about sixty miles, which was the limit of profitable hauling to the only market. The population of this more compact area of settlement, including the town which had grown up around the port, numbered scarcely more than thirteen thousand whites, considerably more slaves, and nobody knows how many detribalized Hottentots. Beyond lay the cattle country, into which sons of the first burghers began to push more than a hundred years before the trekking Boers clashed with the Kaffirs on the Fish River, four hundred miles to the east. It was a thirsty land, where some eight thousand whites were scattered—about one to every ten square miles. Each family, with its colored dependents and its herds of sheep and cattle, was a solitary community. Once a year some of the stock carried its own meat to the distant market, where it was traded for the few things the owners needed. There was practically no other contact with the outside world. As a people, they had been robbed by the frontier of much of the civilization that their ancestors had brought from Europe; but it had made them more dependent upon themselves, their wagons, their horses, their guns, and their Old Testament. When the company would neither defend them nor give them a free hand to seek vengeance for the lives, cattle, and lands that the Kaffirs had taken, the Boers in the two eastern districts of Graaff Reinet and Swellendam rose in revolt and established the first independent republics in South Africa—on the very eve of the British landing.

When the British took the Cape in 1795, with authority from the fugitive Prince of Orange to hold it for his country until the close of the war, the Dutch East India Company was already bankrupt, the colonists welcomed the end of its selfish rule, and most of the officials were glad to serve under the new sovereign. The British promptly swept away the system of monopoly and economic restrictions that the company had carefully guarded, and reformed the administration by substituting regular salaries for fees and perquisites of office. Less happy were the relations between the conqueror and the conquered on the eastern frontier; for the British, who quickly quelled the rebels by a show of force—which they had to do again in 1799—blamed the Boers for stirring up the Kaffirs and tried to keep them apart. This second rising, though only a flash in the pan, let loose a Hottentot rebellion and a Kaffir attack that drew its first British blood. The British were discovering that the Cape was more than a port and a filling station, and they were getting an unpleasant introduction to the complicated problems peculiar to South African society. The first British governor, an excellent man, had a poor opinion of the colony and its future; he reported that it would be a considerable expense to the mother country, which the government there expected.[3] He agreed, however, that it was worth it because of its strategic value as "the master link of connection between the Western and Eastern Worlds."

Though there is good reason to believe that the secretary of state, if not the whole cabinet, looked forward to keeping the Cape permanently, by some bargain with the Prince of Orange, the Treaty of Amiens provided for its restoration to the Batavian Republic and it was accordingly given up in 1803. Three years later, however, the British were back, this time to stay. Public opinion in Britain would not toler-

---

[3] It had been costing the Dutch company more than all its other East Indian stations combined. (Walker, *op. cit.*, p. 111.)

ate a second restoration of this vital link of communication with India, and the government said so to the Prince of Orange. During the peace negotiations at the close of the war his government made no claim and did not even express a desire to get the colony back, while the British were prepared to pay whatever was necessary for it. The amount agreed upon was £2,000,000,[4] which the Dutch were to spend in fortifying the French border of Belgium, which was then annexed to Holland.

Contrary to West Indian practice, neither the capitulation of 1795 nor that of 1806 contained any guarantee to preserve the existing form of government; and during both occupations the governors, though instructed to administer the colony in accordance with its established laws and customs, were directed and empowered to make such im' provements as they deemed fit. For all practical purposes, therefore, the Cape was treated as part of the British Empire before it was formally annexed, which of course reflects the intention to keep it. The reforms of the first occupation were continued in the second, with less direction from London, which had been largely responsible for the few changes made before 1803. As the colony held little attraction for British traders and none for British settlers, there was no pressure, either there or at home, for the introduction of English laws and institutions. The Roman Dutch law, which has prevailed to the present day in South Africa, was continued with scarcely any question; the established institutions of government were maintained with little alteration, manned mostly by experienced Dutch officials; nothing was done, or even attempted, to impair the full prerogative of the British Crown over the colony, so that even before it was determined that Trinidad should become this new and strange thing called a crown colony, the Cape was one.

What was introduced was more efficiency in the administration and publicity in the courts. The English mind distrusted the secrecy of Dutch criminal procedure and insisted upon the examination of witnesses and the accused in open court. The old court of policy was split, the burgher half becoming a sort of municipal council and the official half a bench of salaried judges, while the governor exercised legislative and executive authority, under the control of the secretary of state, without having to consult any officially constituted body of

---

[4] In addition to this £2,000,000 and the payment of £1,000,000 to Sweden in lieu of the Guiana settlements, the British government assumed a debt of £3,000,000 that the Russian government had incurred in Holland and could not or would not meet. Hence the £6,000,000 total mentioned on page 93.

advisers in the colony. In his judicial capacity, however, he had two legal "assessors" to help him decide appeals, both civil and criminal, and had to allow more important civil cases to be carried to the privy council in England. One of the best innovations of the time was the institution of circuit courts conducted annually throughout the colony by judges of the high court, who had to report not only on all the civil and criminal cases they tried but also on "all matters touching the morality and good Government of the Country Districts." Because they had keen eyes for such things as the work of the Landdrosts, or local magistrates, the state of the jails and roads, the treatment of slaves and colored dependents, and education both religious and secular, these judges did much to consolidate the sprawling colony and to improve conditions in it.

Economically the Cape was decidedly better off than it had been under Dutch rule. Trade was much freer and there was much more of it. A resident garrison of several thousand and a great increase in the number of ships calling at Cape Town enlarged the demand for provisions. Even the distant frontier felt the effect of a better market for meat. The "corn and wine" country had never known such prosperity. At last Cape wine had a real sale abroad, thanks to a tariff discrimination against foreign wines in Britain. For a quarter of a century beginning in 1806, the wine trade flourished, providing most of the colony's exports. Even the abolition of the slave trade in 1807 brought profit to South African owners by increasing the value of their black capital. It is also worthy of note that, as a consequence of the stopping of this trade, the free burgher population soon outstripped the servile; and the human lot of the slave, which had always been better here than in the West Indies, improved with his commercial value. But slavery was only a minor phase of the race question in South Africa, and this began to be more complicated as a consequence of the transfer of the country from one empire to another.

The coming of the British opened the door for an influence that struck at the foundations of Cape society and produced a serious internal strain, the effect of which is still felt in South Africa. The Boers would keep the colored races down, while the British would help them up; and because the whites have always been greatly outnumbered in that country, their conflicting attitudes toward the nonwhite minority of the population has bred no end of trouble. Before the arrival of the British, the Boers had severely frowned on the teaching of Christianity to the shaded majority. In this they resembled the British Caribbean planters, who were stoutly opposed to having missionaries tamper with their slaves. But now a vigorous missionary movement, closely allied to that against slavery, was springing up in the mother country. The London Missionary Society, by a rather striking coincidence, was formed in the very year of the first capitulation of Cape Town. Soon the emissaries of this organization began to invade the colony, and it was not long before the Boers came to regard them as something very like the emissaries of the devil who would turn South African society upside down.

However many souls they saved and lives they lifted, the missionaries had a bad effect on relations between whites and nonwhites, and between Boer and British. They were always siding with the underdog, and they were always writing home. Their letters home gave heartrending accounts of how miserably the slaves, Hottentots, Bushmen, and Kaffirs, were treated; and these accounts were broadcast from Evangelical and Nonconformist pulpits. The result was a strong and steady pressure on the government in London, which passed the pressure back to the governor, to have the inhuman conduct of the Boers investigated and punished. This constant prodding, which the governor in turn had to pass on to his officials, roused the resentment of the Boer farmers, who were generally innocent of the crimes with which they were thus charged. Again and again the governor reported back to London that there was little or no foundation for these evil stories and that the colonists were a well-behaved lot, but he was impotent to check the poisonous stream. British rule in South Africa was getting off to a bad start.

Ceylon was taken from the Dutch at the same time and for the same reason as the Cape of Good Hope. Its strategic value to the British in India was comparable to that of the Panama Canal to the United States. Ceylon controlled the communications between the east coast and the west coast; and the English East India Company had had its eye on this island ever since the main seat of the Company's power had shifted from Bombay on the west to Bengal on the east. Its only dockyards were at Bombay, and on the Bay of Bengal it had not a single harbor that seemed capable of development into a naval base. This lack was serious because the dangerous hurricanes of the northeastern monsoon season obliged the fleet to withdraw to the west coast, leaving the whole of the east coast at the mercy of any hostile squadron that might enter the Bay of Bengal between October and March. On the east side of the island of Ceylon, however, at Trincomalee, nature had formed perhaps its most perfect harbor in the whole of the East. Ceylon was, therefore, the inner key, as the Cape was the outer, to the defense of India against European rivals of the British. Which they should keep, if they had to choose, was not an easy question. The preference seems to have been for Ceylon on strategic grounds alone.

Economic considerations also favored the retention of the island rather than the Cape, for the latter had then no economic value, whereas the former was supplying the world with all its cinnamon and many of its pearls. That the cost of Ceylon was greater than its profit to the Dutch East India Company was probably unknown to the British when a dispatch from London directed the governor of Madras to undertake the seizure of the island; but the British had the same experience during the years that elapsed before the formal cession by the Treaty of Amiens in 1802, though they hoped to redress the balance with time.

Until 1798, from the capitulation of 1796, Ceylon was administered as an appanage of the Madras presidency. Madras troops had conquered Ceylon at an expense of some £12,000, and at first it seemed a most profitable venture. The pearl fisheries, which were off the northern part of the west coast, brought a total revenue of nearly £400,000 during the three seasons from 1796 to 1798, but then the banks were exhausted. It is impossible to tell how much the Company made out of the cinnamon. The amount exported during these years was worth about £650,000 in London, but captured Dutch stores accounted for almost half this amount and the rest was got by overexploiting the plantations. The Company also tried to make the government of the island yield a surplus, with disastrous results. Instead of taking over the native officials and land system, as the Dutch had done and the Portuguese before them, the Company imported a full complement of Indian assistants, whom it recruited in Madras, and imposed the revenue and land system of that presidency. Such violence to a society that possessed an ancient civilization, and the depredations of this flock of "harpies," who knew nothing of the languages or the customs of the country and were under no effective control, provoked the Singhalese to revolt within eighteen months.

Even before the rising, which was quickly suppressed, unpleasant accounts from Ceylon moved the governor of Madras to appoint an investigating commission, whose report in 1798 condemned the folly of 1796; and before the news of the revolt could reach England the cabinet decided to place the island directly under the Crown. As the directors of the Company objected, a compromise was reached and a governor was sent out from England to establish dual control. He did some healthy housecleaning, but his hands were too tied to establish efficient order. The directors required him to fill vacancies in his civil service by drawing from the Madras service, whence he could not get the men he needed. He had to accept the dregs, for Ceylon was too small and poor—its government ran deeply in the red—to offer the salaries and chances of promotion that able officials enjoyed on the mainland. Moreover, the island was so different in languages and problems that it had to have its own civil service. The governor soon persuaded the secretary of state that dual control was impossible. The decision to change was made late in 1800, and on 1 January 1802— before the formal cession—Ceylon became a crown colony.

That the new type of colonial government was adopted permanently and deliberately for Ceylon before it was for Trinidad or the Cape, appears clearly in what the secretary of state wrote to the governor at Colombo when he sent him his new commission and instructions. He definitely stated that the government of Ceylon was not to be assimilated to that of the West Indian colonies, but was rather to be modeled on experience in India, incorporating as far as feasible the principles that had been found wise in its presidencies. To protect the natives and the trade monopoly of the East India Company, whose charter excluded British competitors from eastern waters, all Europeans were to be excluded from permanent settlement except those who were in the service of the government or were specially licensed by the secretary of state. This was only natural, for Ceylon, like India, had no room for European settlers except as exploiters of native labor, and these were to be excluded as far as possible.

It was also in Ceylon that the British government inaugurated its regular colonial civil service, patterned more or less after that of the East India Company. Like the writers of the Company, promising young men were sent out from England to serve an apprenticeship in the colony and ultimately to fill all but a few of the highest offices. Pensions were guaranteed so that the civil servants need not think of lining their pockets by extraofficial activities, and promotion was to be by merit as determined by the governor, not by influence at home. In practice this system did not come up to the best of more modern standards, but it was a great improvement upon the system, or lack of it, that still prevailed in the other colonies and even at home. Unlike the Dutch officials in the Cape and British Guiana, those in Ceylon were rarely employed, and then only in a minor capacity. They were not anxious to serve the British, and the latter had little use for them. As in India, there was a swarm of lesser government servants who dealt directly with the people and were selected from them after the custom of the country.

There was a strong feeling among the British residents that the whole body of their own laws should be introduced; but this received no encouragement from the home government, which contemplated the use of the old Singhalese laws and called for a report upon them. A careful investigation then revealed that these laws had been pretty well obliterated by generations of enforcement of Roman Dutch law. Therefore the Roman Dutch law was continued with one important modification in favor of the English system, which was made in 1810 on the advice of the able second governor. Trial by jury, which was denied in the other foreign colonies acquired during this war, was then introduced into this ancient eastern land. There was no plantation slavery in Ceylon to make it objectionable there, and it was desirable because it would relieve the supreme court of considerable responsibility and make trials by one judge more acceptable. The bench was to decide whether a jury was to be composed of natives or Europeans, and a verdict by majority vote was allowed.

Ceylon was a heavy financial burden on the mother country. Not counting the cost of the new naval base at Trincomalee or the garrison of the island, which numbered four or five thousand, there was a chronic deficit. From 1802 to 1815 it averaged over £100,000 a year.[5] The civil establishment was more elaborate and expensive than that of any other colony, and quite out of proportion to any possible revenue. There was little to be got by way of direct taxation, because the system of land tenure was a sort of feudalism, labor services taking the place of money payments. With the failure of the pearl fisheries, the principal source of income was cinnamon, about half of which was stripped from government plantations established by the Dutch. The cinnamon was sold to the East India Company, which by its charter held a monopoly of the trade until 1813.[6] The Company contracted in 1802 to buy it for £60,000 a year, and in 1814 signed a new contract raising

---

[5] It has been suggested (Helen Taft Manning, *British Colonial Government After the American Revolution* [New Haven, 1933], pp. 460–461) that the East India Company may have made about as much out of the cinnamon during the same time.

[6] With the renewal of the charter in this year, the Company's monopoly was confined to the China trade. Hence the 1814 increase in the contract.

the payment to £100,000 for a slightly increased quantity, which was the limit of what the colony could supply.

Another problem was the native kingdom of Kandy, which covered the mountainous interior of the island and which neither the Portuguese nor the Dutch had been able to reduce. In 1803 the first governor foolishly allowed himself to be drawn into a war for its conquest. Ghastly failure followed. Malaria and massacre wiped out a garrison he managed to put in the town of Kandy, and London ordered an end to the expensive and futile war. Attempts to negotiate a peace failed, but hostilities ceased in 1805 and were not resumed for another ten years. Then the native king provoked a renewal of the war and the campaign of 1815 was over in a trice with practically no fighting. This time the British had taken every precaution to avoid a repetition of the fiasco, and the king had thorougly alienated his nobles,[7] who eagerly welcomed the invaders. This last of a long line of sovereigns, whose rule began more than two thousand years before, was captured, exiled, and pensioned. His realm was annexed; the nobles, whom he had deposed, were restored to the rule of their provinces under the supervision of British officials; and the people were promised that their "laws, institutions and customs" would be respected and their "religion of Boodhoo" would be maintained inviolate. George III may not have known it, but he then succeeded the exiled monarch as the spiritual and temporal head of the Buddhist church of Kandy. His functions as such were performed by his deputy, the governor, and included the appointment and dismissal of priests until the missionaries raised a storm against this official sanction of "idolatry" by a Christian government and the colonial secretary in 1844 instructed the governor to sever all connection with Buddhism.

Next in strategic importance to Ceylon and the Cape was the little island of Mauritius, which lay halfway between them and possessed a

---

[7] He seems to have been popular except with his nobles, against whom he protected the people. But he was a fierce tyrant. Unable to catch his rebellious prime minister, the king had the latter's young children beheaded, and he "compelled their mother to witness the executions and to pound the severed heads with a pestle, or else be publicly raped." He provoked the renewal of the war by seizing ten native merchants from British territory, having their noses, right ears, and right arms cut off, and sending them back to Colombo with the amputated members tied around their necks. Nine died on the way. (L. A. Mills, *Ceylon Under British Rule* [London, 1933], pp. 156–157, citing John Davy, *An Account of the Interior of Ceylon and Its Inhabitants*, pp. 320–322, 324. Davy, whose book was published in 1821, served in Ceylon as a member of the Army Medical staff from 1816 to 1820.)

fine natural harbor. When the French were expelled from India, they made Mauritius the seat of their trade, government, and power in the East, and in time of war it enabled them to take a heavy toll of the British, for every European vessel bound to or from India had to sail past Mauritius. In the single month of October 1807, privateers and warships operating from this base snapped up eighteen British East Indiamen. Finally, in 1810, an expedition from India took it and the neighboring French island of Bourbon, now Réunion. At the close of the war the British government restored Bourbon, which though larger and richer had no harbor, but would not consider giving up Mauritius for the simple reason that it had been too dangerous in enemy hands.

Already this little speck in the Indian ocean was a crown colony, having been taken over in 1811 from the Company, to which it was of no value; and its budget was regularly unbalanced, chiefly because of military expenditure. No attempt was made to change its laws, customs, and religion, which had been guaranteed by the capitulation, and to this day it remains largely French in character. Severed from Bourbon and other islands which it had served as a commercial capital, Mauritius naturally lost much of its prosperity. But it was not as dead as the dodo, which it had preserved until toward the end of the seventeenth century. It had a population of some 16,000 whites who had begun to raise tropical produce, mostly sugar, from a soil that was much better than was yet realized, with slaves imported from Madagascar, only five hundred miles to the west. Though the abolition of the slave trade had destroyed the advantage of being so close to the source of black labor, this new colony could produce sugar so much more cheaply than the old Caribbean colonies that its exports of this commodity leaped up to 25,000 hundredweight in 1815 and to more than three times that amount in 1816. Then out of compassion for the desperate West India planters, the home government granted them a customs preference of 10 shillings per hundredweight. This checked the rise of Mauritian shipments for three years, at the end of which they resumed their upward flight more rapidly than ever.

New South Wales, a quarter of the way around the globe from Mauritius, was too remote to be touched by the long French war; but peace and plenty were not the lot of the first British colony in Australia for many a long year. It was only finding its feet as the war drew to a close. When the fleet of convict ships, after a seven months' voyage, entered Botany Bay in January 1788 to establish the colony there, it was discovered that this was no place for it. The rich soil and the

Torres Strait

Gulf of
Carpentaria

GREAT BARRIER REEF

WESTERN
AUSTRALIA

SOUTH
AUSTRALIA

Moreton
Bay

Norfolk Island

Perth • Swan

Great Australian
Bight

NEW SOUTH
WALES

Darling

Lachlan

Murrumbidgee

Murray

BLUE MTNS.

Newcastle
• Sydney
Botany
Bay

• Adelaide

Port Phillip

Bass Strait

0   200   400   600
Scale of Miles

VAN DIEMEN'S
LAND

Hobart

The Beginning of Settlement in Australia

luxuriant vegetation described by the explorer Cook and the botanist
Banks, who had visited the bay eighteen years before, turned out to be
sand and swamps. In a few days the whole company moved a little way
up the coast to "the finest harbor in the world" and founded Sydney.
The settlement began with a population of just over a thousand—seven
hundred convicts to provide labor, two hundred marines to guard them,
and about one hundred other people including wives and children of
the marines. It had supplies for a year—at the end of which it was
supposed to become self-supporting—and about a hundred and sixty
head of livestock: horses, cattle, sheep, and pigs. But man and beast
fared ill. The land in the neighborhood was too poor for good crops; the
livestock dwindled, many a beast being lost through disease or in the
bush; while the number of mouths to be fed increased with an unnatural rapidity as convict ships continued to dump their cargoes on

the shore. During the early years vessels had to be hurried off to fetch food from the Cape, Batavia, and China in order to avert starvation, and severe rationing was a common experience. Though better land was shortly found and cultivated at the head of the harbor and also further up the coast, it was nearly twenty years before the importation of food became unnecessary.

To say that the British government was trying to build a colony with the wrong kind of material is to miss the whole point of this settlement. The *raison d'être* of New South Wales was transportation, not colonization. The only alternative at that time was more expensive and less humane. It was to keep the convicts in the mother country where, since the American Revolution had stopped transportation to the old colonies, congestion in the jails and prison ships had grown until they could hold no more. The whole colony was a prison from which there was practically no escape. The Blue Mountains, forty miles to the west, defied all efforts of white men to cross them until a quarter of a century after the founding of Sydney, by which time the prison camp was growing into a real colony; and over the sea no other land was near enough for fugitives to reach in small boats. Of course men and women who were condemned to serve for seven years or more, some of them for life, and who knew that the government was obliged to provide them with food, shelter, and clothing, had little incentive to labor. The lawyers insisted that they were not slaves because their persons were not the property of the government, though their services were. This was a distinction without a difference. Where they did differ from slaves was in their being more intelligent and less docile. They were a strange assortment of people drawn from many walks of life including the learned professions, and they had little in common except that all had been caught in the toils of the law. Most of them were not what we would call jailbirds, Many were victims of the unreformed criminal law, which prescribed heavy penalities for what are now light offenses. A few were radicals whose only crime was to be mistaken for revolutionaries. The most troublesome by far were some two thousand Irish rebels who had been captured after the rising of 1798.

More uncontrollable than the convicts were those who were sent out to keep them under control. The first governor had some trouble with the marines, who were as guardian angels compared with those who soon came to replace them permanently. The New South Wales Corps was recruited in England for this special purpose and therefore lacked the traditional military appeal of glory and honor. Its officers and men were soldiers in name but not in character. The rank and file were men whom no self-respecting regiment would have; and the officers, lured by promises of land, were bent on making their fortunes out of the colony. Quite a number of them did, for they got convicts to work their land and they monopolized the local trade, which was chiefly in spirituous liquors. They debauched the colony, and with their men behind them they defied governor after governor, all naval officers, until at last in 1808 they deposed and imprisoned Captain William Bligh, of mutinous *Bounty* fame, who had been appointed to bridle them. As the year 1809 drew to an end, the rule of this unruly corps came to an end with the arrival of orders for the New South Wales Corps to return to England. A Highland regiment was sent to garrison the colony, and the commander of this regiment was made the new governor. He was the first of a line of military governors, and his unit was the first of a succession of regular regiments that maintained order in this distant corner of the empire.

Drink and the devil did not have it all their own way during the days of naval governors and the New South Wales Corps. These governors, being men of the sea, pushed exploration around the coast of the continent; and the appearance of an odd French vessel, raising fears of a French attempt at occupation, inspired the planting of two subcolonies in Tasmania, then still known as Van Diemen's Land, in 1804. Meanwhile the wool industry of Australia was born. Its father was John Macarthur, who arrived as a lieutenant of the corps in 1790 and soon gave up his commission in order to take up sheep raising. By careful breeding, particularly with some merino stock he procured from South Africa in 1797, he proved that fortunes could be made in wool. In 1788 the number of sheep in the colony shrank from the original forty-four to twenty-nine; but by 1800, when Macarthur sailed for England to learn more about the business, the number had grown to more than six thousand. In 1810 there were more than twenty-five thousand, and the following decade saw a tenfold increase. Sheep provided the pressure that burst through the forbidding barrier on the west of the narrow coastal region. All who had tried to penetrate the Blue Mountains failed because they followed the valleys, which ended in blank walls. It was by following the ridges that a party got across in 1813 and discovered the great grasslands beyond. This was the beginning of inland exploration and expansion, and was the work not of government servants, as the coastal exploration had been, but of private individuals seeking room for sheep, which could now multiply indefinitely. Hence the tenfold increase of the second decade of the century. The colony had at last found its feet.

A social emancipation was also proceeding. Though free immigration was not allowed until after the war and then took many years to become relatively important, and though the transportation system continued to augment the population until well on in the century, the colony contained a declining proportion of convicts, and from being primarily a prison for their confinement was growing into a home for their reformation. Convicts were being graduated from their hard school, some at the end of their terms and some before it as a reward for good behavior or valuable service. The former were properly called "expirees" and the latter "emancipists," but both were often lumped together under the latter denomination. As these ex-convicts swelled in number, their place in society presented a nice problem; for the free settlers, who had entered the country through the New South Wales Corps or as civil servants, arrogated unto themselves the position of a moral aristocracy. The first military governor, Lachlan Macquarie, who restored discipline in the colony and ruled until 1821, tackled this problem boldly, some still think too boldly. He insisted that once a convict became a free man he was entitled to be treated as such in every respect; and being as much of an autocrat as his naval predecessors, he did not hesitate to appoint qualified emancipists to the magistrates' bench or other civil office. An aristocrat but no snob, this proud Highland laird also entertained at his own table ex-convicts whom he found socially respectable; but free settlers, whom he invited at the same time, would not compromise themselves by sitting down to dinner with such companions even in Government House. London received many bitter charges against him for favoring emancipists, and he may have patronized some who were still rascals. But there was no denying the fact that the best doctor, the only lawyer, and some of the soundest businessmen in Sydney were ex-convicts. Good was coming out of evil.

Macquarie was the last of the "tyrants," as all the first governors were called because they ruled with little check from far-off London and with none in the colony except from the lawless New South Wales Corps. These governors did not have even an advisory council. They legislated as they saw fit and conducted the administration accordingly. There was a criminal court designed by an act of parliament in 1787 to mete out justice in a community of condemned criminals where trial by jury was simply out of the question. It was military in composition and procedure. After the successful rising against Bligh, however, a trained lawyer was sent from England to preside over this court. The civil courts, erected by the governor on royal rather than parliamentary authority, were long manned by only amateurs who should have followed the laws of the mother country but knew little about them. Their decisions commanded equally little respect, with the result that from the year 1800 appeals were commonly carried to England whenever the amount involved warranted the expense—until 1812, when a local court of appeals with an English chief justice was set up. In parliament, which passed an annual grant to cover the bills drawn by the governor to pay the expenses of his government, there were occasional complaints of the cost, to which the ministers always replied that no cheaper method of disposing of criminals could be found. The amount for 1815 was £80,000, when the population was about 15,000. The home government seems to have thought it was getting its money's worth, and was pleased with the way the Australian enterprise was developing.

This very development was framing an awkward question for the ministers in London, who did not begin to see it until after the war was over. By what right was the governor exercising such despotic power over free Britons? This was no conquered colony where, by constitutional law, the authority of the Crown was supreme until it was renounced or parliament intervened to regulate it. Here the governor was legally invested with power to rule a society of convicts and their guardians, but not of freemen.

III THE APPROACH TO REFORM

Chapters

Overthrow of the Landed Oligarchy

WITH A REACTIONARY Tory party entrenched in power by the long
war which it had conducted to a triumphant conclusion, Great Britain
entered a period of internal strain and stress. The foundations of the
country's life had shifted from beneath the old landed ruling class,
which represented an age that had gone and yet clung tenaciously to a
system of government that excluded other classes from power. Sooner
or later the new industrial society, which was growing stronger year by
year, would throw off the yoke of the past. This is what happened in
1832, after a struggle that shook the country like an earthquake. It
was a veritable revolution, and it brought in its train sweeping measures
of reconstruction.

The curse of the French Revolution was not banished with Napoleon. It still brooded over the Old World, which is not surprising after
the terrible experiences that Europe had suffered during the previous
quarter of a century. A fierce reaction ruled on the continent. Down
in Rome, street lighting and vaccination were abolished as revolutionary, having been introduced by the French. Everywhere the authorities
were in mortal terror of revolution breaking out again, and they acted
accordingly, with the result that they only increased the danger of
explosion. Revolutions soon began to pop, and they got worse until at
last in 1848 almost all Europe seemed to be blowing up. Britain came
through these trying years without a revolution of violence, but apparently by rather a slim margin.

The repressive policy of the government in Britain, though mild in
comparison with what was common on the continent, was no longer
the persecution of an unpopular minority. Now the working class as a
whole felt that it was directed against them, and this was dangerous.
Now more than ever, the few throve on the misery of the many, and
the many knew it.

British democracy was awakening slowly and painfully. In origin and character, it was the same as that which later grew on the European continent, but quite different from American democracy of that time. The North American environment emancipated the individual. For little or nothing, the common man could get good land on which he and his family could lead an independent life. The cornerstone of American democracy was the farmer who worked his own farm. Democracy in Britain was the child of the industrial revolution, which uprooted people from the soil and herded them, a great mass of propertyless wage earners, into crowded urban centers where they inevitably became class conscious. There conditions kept the common man down, and there was no escape until, by organization and struggle, he gradually emancipated himself. There democracy was a difficult achievement of man, rather than a gift of nature; and it is a nice question whether democracy in America, where the condition that created and sustained it has passed away, can survive unless it conforms to the Old World type, which appears to be more permanent.

Though British democracy was awakening, it was not yet coherent, it did not know how to express itself; and half a century was to pass before the ordinary workingman won the right to vote. For several years after Waterloo the plight of the toiling masses in Britain was truly miserable. The return of peace did not bring prosperity. It broke the war boom, throwing many workingmen out of employment, and at the same time it turned loose a flood of discharged soldiers and sailors. The only relief it might have brought—cheap food—was quickly denied by the Corn Law of 1815. This prohibited importation when the domestic price was less than 80 shillings a quarter, which meant wheat at $2.50 a bushel—nearly twice the daily wage of a carpenter and more than twice the cost of a pair of shoes. The law was passed to save agriculture, which war pressure had extended to unprofitable land, from being ruined by the collapse of prices. It was class legislation with a vengeance. It taxed the multitude of consumers for the benefit of the few who possessed the means of production, the few being the landed class who constituted parliament. Another condition that increased the hardships of the time was the continuance of the industrial revolution, now speeding up, which substituted machines for hand labor.

The misery of the masses burst forth in riots all over the country. The people were desperate and they struck at those whom they held responsible for their suffering—at butchers and bakers whose shops they attacked, at landlords whose barns and stacks they burned, and at manufacturers whose machinery they smashed. The popular unrest was inflamed by rabble rousers of all kinds, from dirty scoundrels to simple cranks, who were all lumped together as Radicals—a new name then coming into common use. Though it later gained respectability as a label for those who sought radical reform, at this time it was synonymous with rebels. Sir Walter Scott, for example, regularly referred to rebels in arms as Radicals.

The Tories were as filled with alarm as the people were with misery. Parliamentary committees investigated, and they reported the existence of a widespread conspiracy to destroy government and to plunder property, with the result that severe legislation was passed to crush the incipient revolution, which in those days meant anarchy. The Habeas Corpus Act was suspended, public meetings were prohibited except when called by the authorities, and the magistrates were given summary powers. Still the disturbances continued, rising and falling with the fluctuation of economic conditions; the panicky government, unable to read this clear sign of what was the root of the trouble, continued to strike at a phantom and hit the people. One of the most odious features of the odious system of repression was the government's employment of stool pigeons, at least one of whom—the infamous "Oliver the Spy"—helped to stir up popular risings. The only remedial measure adopted was the vote of a million pounds for new churches, in the belief that society was breaking down for lack of sufficient religious education.

The worst incident in these troubled years was Peterloo in 1819, and it is most interesting as a revelation of how British tradition was drawing the popular movement in the right direction—to get representation in parliament for the people. Manchester, being one of the new industrial towns, had not a seat in the old unreformed parliament; and to protest against this injustice a crowd of some fifty thousand assembled in St. Peter's Field, an open space on the outskirts of the town. The magistrates, who had forbidden the meeting, used cavalry to disperse it, with the result that half a dozen people were killed and half a hundred wounded. This "Manchester massacre" of Peterloo, as the field then came to be called to bring out the shameful contrast to glorious Waterloo, gave an immense stimulus to the cause of parliamentary reform as the way to remedy the ills of the nation.

British tradition also restrained the government from going to the extremes that were only too common on the continent. The freedom of public meeting might be suppressed, but only by temporary legislation.

Freedom of speech and freedom of the press were too sacred to be taken away, even temporarily. And no one dared to question two features of English law that preserved the freedom of the individual. One was the principle that a man is presumed to be innocent until he is proven guilty—the very opposite of what prevailed on the continent. The other, of course, was the right to trial by jury.

Nevertheless, the country was in a bad way as long as the reactionary Tories ruled parliament. The Whigs, also an aristocratic body, were in a hopeless position, being divided between those who favored repression, which discredited them with the masses, and those who openly sympathized with the masses, which discredited them with all others. Another tragic twist in this twisted time was the attitude of the new capitalist class, the industrial and commercial leaders. Their economic power was eclipsing that of the landed class, and yet they were excluded from political power by the antiquated representative system. Though this was a condition they could not long tolerate, they shrank from attacking it as long as the radical movement seemed to threaten all property, for property has a marvelous way of guiding men's political principles.

The nation's confidence in its institutions was seriously shaken, and the spirit of revolution was in the air. Instead of being the protector of the people, government was appearing to be the enemy of the people; and the most ancient institution of all, the one around which all others were gathered, had ceased to command respect. The king who had lost his colonies had since lost his sight, his hearing, and his mind. From 1810, George III had been a hopeless lunatic. The Prince of Wales, who acted as regent until he succeeded to the throne as George IV in 1820, was a man whose character was as mean as his morals were notoriously loose. His wife had left him, and their only child, a gentle princess to whose succession people looked forward with hope, died in 1817. His six younger brothers were such objectionable creatures, none of whom had legitimate issue until Princess Victoria was born to the Duke of Kent in 1819, that many thinking Englishmen anticipated the early extinction of the monarchy; and this might very well have happened if the new princess had not lived to rehabilitate the institution.

But the days of the old Tory government were numbered. It never recovered from the damage it suffered at Peterloo in 1819. It suffered more on the death of the mad king in 1820, for it then became involved in a mad scheme to satisfy the new king's demand for a divorce. The necessary act of parliament could not be passed because the majority were frightened by a tremendous flame of national anger against such an unjust proceeding. Though the evidence against the queen looked bad, everyone knew that her husband was much worse. All decent people were disgusted with the king, who soon retired from public view; and the prestige of the government was seriously impaired, while that of the Whigs, who had stoutly opposed the divorce, rose considerably. In the next year Napoleon died, and with him the lingering fear that he might again escape to turn the Old World upside down. Meanwhile trade had been picking up and the price of bread had been dropping, with the result that the epidemic of popular disturbances disappeared.

Reaction was no longer possible. It ended in 1822, with a reorganization of the government that gave the upper hand to progressive Tories. Though opposed to parliamentary reform, they believed the only way to preserve the political ascendancy of the landed class was to follow a liberal and reforming policy. The new leaders, instead of belonging to the old aristocracy, represented the rising well-to-do class. This was reflected in the fact that now nearly half the cabinet, including its most influential members, sat in the House of Commons, whereas in 1815 three quarters had been in the House of Lords. It is also interesting to observe that the Whig opposition was shrewd enough not to attack the new Tory program but to encourage it even to the extent of offering really helpful suggestions.

One of the first of the Tory reforms was to sweep away the whole system of government espionage. This was followed by a reform of the criminal law to purge it of its savage harshness, which had often led juries to shut their eyes to undoubted evidence of guilt. For over a hundred crimes—including picking a pocket of such a small amount as a shilling—the death penalty was abolished. Sir Robert Peel, who as home secretary was responsible for this doubly welcome change, also inaugurated the modern police system. This civilian force, armed with only batons, soon became so popular that its members were endearingly called after the statesman who founded it, and to this day a policeman in Britain is known as a "bobby."

Other memorable reforms of the Tory ministry included the repeal of the unjust combination laws, and a number of enactments that gave new liberty to trade. Some of the worst rigidities of the navigation laws disappeared, and the old colonial system was liberalized, as we shall see in a later chapter. Greater still was the overhauling of the fiscal system, which was distinctly in the direction of free trade. Duties on raw materials, which had been burdensome to industry, were nearly eliminated; and the new scale on other articles ran from 15 to 30 per cent, in place of the old one that ran from 40 to 180 per cent, and with a duty of 20 per cent on nonenumerated articles in place of the old 50 per cent. This reform was helped through the House of Commons by an anecdote of a gentleman who imported a mummy from Egypt and had to pay £200 on it because the customs officers, after long deliberation, found that such "remains of mortality, muscles and sinews, pickled and preserved three thousand years ago, could not be deemed a raw material." The reforming Tories even tried to amend the Corn Law when it again pinched the people, but this was going too far and they failed.

Instead of saving the Tory party, reform wrecked it. The decisive issue was Catholic Emancipation. Back in the sixteenth and seventeenth centuries a whole train of tragic circumstances had taught the English public to identify Roman Catholicism with tyranny and the foreign foe, with the result that parliament then passed severe legislation against all members of that faith. The worst disabilities imposed by these old penal laws had gone, but Roman Catholics were still disqualified by law from sitting in parliament, from holding any office, and even from voting, with the single exception that in Ireland they had been allowed to vote since 1793. The most progressive Tories wanted to end this hoary injustice but found the great majority of the party hysterically opposed to any such change; and a reactionary Tory ministry was organized under the Duke of Wellington, whose great military reputation had thrust him into a political position for which he was quite unfitted. Then a sudden Irish crisis, to be noted in a later chapter, convinced him that there would be civil war in Ireland unless Roman Catholics got political equality at once, and he jammed through parliament the very measure that his government was formed to prevent. His followers never forgave him, and their fury finished the old party. Their thirst for revenge was not slaked until the following year, 1830, when they helped to turn him out of office and to bring their old political foes, the Whigs, into power. But their spiteful votes only hastened a change of government that a much greater question was making inevitable.

The question of the reform of parliament itself was throwing the country into a political convulsion, the like of which it never experienced again and had not seen since the days of Oliver Cromwell, when Royalists and Roundheads fought their civil wars. A glance at the representative system, which had long ceased to represent, will suffice to show the need for drastic reform.

Of 658 members of the House of Commons, little more than a quarter were elected by independent constituencies—the counties and some old towns—and even there the electorate was usually very restricted. The other members, the great majority, held borough seats that in bygone centuries had been created by the Crown, a practice that had been dead for a century and a half. By one means or another, the filling of these seats had fallen into the hands of wealthy landowners. One great nobleman, for example, now had eleven seats at his disposal. This system explains why ambitious young men of good connection, such as the younger Pitt, could enter Parliament when they turned twenty-one; and why certain wealthy interests, such as the West Indian planters, could buy their way in. Meanwhile the new industrial population, centered chiefly in the Midlands and the North, the new England that had arisen and was rapidly growing, had no representation at all.

The difficulty in the way of parliamentary reform was that this antiquated system would have to be abolished by the very men to whom it gave control of the sovereign parliament. In other words, the ruling oligarchy would have to vote for their own overthrow. Impossible as this might seem, it was precisely what they did. But why did they do it? The answer lies in a shifting of fears.

In place of the old fear that had blocked reform because it meant revolution, a new fear had arisen, a fear that urged reform as the only alternative to revolution. The reason for this was the state of the country. Trade was again bad, and there was a crop failure in 1829. Unemployment was up, wages were down, and bread was dear. Once more the popular misery burst forth in popular disturbances. Revolution was in the air. Radical leaders were shouting for all sorts of reforms to cure the distress of the nation—from free trade and factory acts to playing with the currency and abolishing capitalism. But however much they differed on these things, they all agreed that nothing effective could be done without a reform of parliament. Therefore the national discontent was focused upon this as its own immediate object.

Startling news from across the Channel in the summer of 1830 greatly stimulated the seething unrest. In July a revolution broke out in the French capital, and the reactionary government of the restored Bourbons fell like a house of cards, blown down by the workmen of Paris in only two days of street fighting. This was a powerful demonstration of how futile it was to resist a determined people. It gave vast encouragement to workmen in England and a solemn warning to other classes. With the warning also came comforting reassurance, for this new French revolution was quite different from the old one. It quickly ended with the substitution of a popular king for an unpopular one, and the rule of the bourgeoisie for that of the old aristocracy. Such was the background that explains why one section of the British ruling class espoused the popular cause and made it triumph over the other section. The final and decisive struggle, therefore, was not between the government and the people, nor between classes. It was between members of the same class, the class that enjoyed a monopoly of political power.

The struggle began in the summer of 1830, when a general election was held—under the influence of the July revolution in France. The Whigs, who had long flirted with parliamentary reform, were at last definitely pledged to it. There were doubts of how far they were willing to go with it, for they were no less aristocratic than the Tories, being likewise great landowners and possessors of boroughs. There were also doubts if they would be able to do anything with it, for the House of Lords was strongly against them, and in the new House of Commons, where there were quite a number of independent members, they could not count on a majority.

When parliament met in the autumn, the balance in the lower chamber was soon upset by a few words spoken in the upper. Replying to Earl Grey, who pled for reform, the Duke of Wellington roundly denounced it in any shape or form, to the amazement of his listeners. On resuming his seat, he asked a neighboring peer, "I have not said too much, have I?" and got the reply, "You have announced the fall of your own government, that is all." In a few days an adverse vote in the Commons forced his resignation, and Grey succeeded him.

In forming his government, the new prime minister had as his main object the passage of a reform bill that would restore peace to the land, and he was joined by a number of liberal Tories. This new combination, which was the beginning of the transformation of the Whig into the Liberal party, assured the support of a majority in the Commons and a large minority in the Lords.[1]

Grey's cabinet, which included four future prime ministers, was actually more aristocratic than any Tory cabinet before or after. With only two exceptions, the members were all peers or sons of peers. They

---

[1] "The old aristocracy still produced very able men, and most of the able aristocrats were reformers. It is remarkable that the peers of old creation were about equally divided on the Reform Bill; and the dissentient majority of the Upper House was due to the bishops and to Pitt's lavish creations of Tory partisans and borough-owners." G. M. Trevelyan, *British History in the Nineteenth Century* (2nd ed.; New York, 1937), p. 232.

were an unusually able and public-spirited lot of men, the best available; their blue blood was of great advantage in the performance of the task ahead. They could go further along the path of reform than could a less aristocratic body, which would have encountered more difficulty in persuading parliament and the king, whose support was still recognized as necessary. As it was, the famous bill that revolutionized the constitution was barely able to squeeze through.

The Reform Bill was drafted by a cabinet committee of which the chairman was Grey's son-in-law, the Earl of Durham, one of the wealthiest men in England, about the ablest in public life, and notoriously one of the most radical. He was the principal author of the measure. When it was introduced in the House of Commons in March 1831, by Lord John Russell, a younger son of the Duke of Bedford, it astounded parliament and delighted the people. It was much more drastic than had been expected. In addition to providing for a sweeping redistribution of seats to fit the distribution of population, it extended the franchise, and—what caused the greatest furore—it abolished all "nomination" boroughs without any compensation. The Tory opposition was struck dumb, and this was fortunate. Many government supporters were hesitant or hostile, but before the Tories could confirm their doubts and fears, they were converted by the explosion of national enthusiasm. The second reading was carried, amidst tremendous excitement, by a majority of only one vote in a House of 603, the largest number that had ever taken part in a division. A defeat in the committee stage followed, and the fate of reform hung in the balance.

The prime minister had to resign unless he could persuade the king to grant him a dissolution; and William IV, who had succeeded his brother in the previous year, now wavered. Grey had convinced him that the bill was aristocratic, its purpose being to prevent more revolutionary changes; but the rage of the Tories and the rejoicing of the Radicals had shaken this conviction. What saved the bill, the government, and perhaps the throne, was the majority of one vote that had carried the second reading. It decided the king to dissolve parliament as Grey desired. Throughout the land there was one unanimous cry: "The Bill, the whole Bill, and nothing but the Bill!" The government won almost every open constituency, and in September the new House passed the bill by a majority of over a hundred. In October, on the second reading, the House of Lords threw it out.

The leading newspapers appeared with black borders in mourning for the bill that the Lords had killed; and well might they mourn, for the national anger was roused to a dangerous pitch. All over the country, riots broke out. The worst disturbance was in Bristol, the center of which was destroyed by a mob that ran wild for two days. In the industrial north, workmen were arming and drilling, and through the agricultural south the night sky was again lurid with burning stacks. A false step on the part of the government might easily have plunged England into anarchy, but the government picked its way carefully.

The bill was modified, but not weakened, to meet certain criticisms; and in December 1831 it was again introduced into the Commons. By March 1832 it was ready for the Lords, where many opponents of reform were by this time less courageous in their defiance of the nation. The bill passed the second reading with a small majority, but on 7 May 1832 it was mutilated in committee.

Grey asked the king to create enough new peers—at least fifty, he calculated, were necessary—to bring the upper chamber in line with the lower. Only once had this been done, and that was a hundred and twenty years before. The king refused, for he had grown hostile, and the prime minister had to resign. The whole country was now in an uproar, and a grave crisis was at hand. It was over in a week. Wellington tried to form a government but could not get the necessary support in the Commons, where no government could carry on except that of Grey; therefore the king was compelled to capitulate by recalling Grey and promising to create the necessary number of peers. The royal surrender forced the Lords' surrender without the king's having to carry out his promise, and the bill became law in June 1832. Two months later the last unreformed House of Commons separated never to meet again; for in December a general election was held, the third in three years, under the new system.

The least satisfactory part of this great Reform Bill was the extension of the franchise. In the county constituencies, where only freeholders had been allowed to vote, copyholders and leaseholders were added; but until the new voters gained the protection of the secret ballot, which was yet a long way off, they could be influenced by their landlords, whose hold on the country seats was thus strengthened. In the towns, the vote was given to every occupant of a house or shop worth £10 a year if he paid certain rates, or local taxes. All this meant that about half the middle class and, with rare exceptions, the whole of the working class, in town and country alike, were still unenfranchised.

Nevertheless, the mere fact that the franchise, which had not been changed for centuries, was now widened by the action of parliament under popular pressure established a precedent that was to lead progressively to further widening until it was completely democratic; and the fact that half the middle class were left without votes was to lead them to combine with the working class in demanding further reform. In short, the act of 1832 made the achievement of democracy possible, though this was only dimly perceived at the time.

The great achievement of this great act was deliberate and immediate. It lifted parliament from its old and rotten foundation and set it down on a new and solid foundation. The distribution of seats, which had long since ceased to have any relation to the distribution of population, was at last made representative. The crying injustice of leaving such important places as Manchester and Birmingham without any members in parliament was now ended. Industrial England was admitted to the national legislature.

More revolutionary was the change the act made in the method by which the great majority of the House of Commons were elected. It had been a shameful farce. Now it was a genuine reality. Not a borough survived that did not have, or was not given a fairly numerous electorate. Now every constituency was open, not just one in about four; and this made a world of difference, not in the type of man who sat in the House of Commons, but in the political control of that House, in the ultimate seat of power. Instead of some 485 out of 658 members of the House being put there by 270 wealthy landlords, all the members were now chosen by popular election. The power that had been monopolized by a little oligarchy within the landed class was transferred to the whole landed class and half the middle class. In practice, this meant that the control of the House of Commons, though it was still largely composed of country gentlemen, passed into the hands of middle class voters of quite moderate means, for they were now the great majority of the electorate.

Most revolutionary, also, were certain implications in the act and in the circumstances of its passage. The king then lost the power to influence the composition and the policy of the government, a power that he had exercised through the members of the fallen oligarchy. The House of Lords lost power too. Not only were some 145 peers deprived of the right to nominate a much larger number of the House of Commons, but the manner in which the act was passed permanently shifted the balance between the two chambers. Thenceforth the upper house was definitely subordinate to the lower, and this subordination became more pronounced as the lower house became more representative.

Moreover, the whole concept of government and its functions was profoundly changed. The representative principle took a great leap forward in 1832, and this upset the prevailing notion of what was the purpose of government. From being merely the preservation of law and order, a negative concept that kept government activities down to a bare minimum, it gradually became social justice, a positive concept that has progressively extended and intensified the functions of government.

Nor should we forget that the act was not an end in itself. It was a revolutionary change designed to clear the way for further revolutionary changes, and this is precisely what it did. The reform of parliament burst the dikes and let loose a spate of reforms such as the country had never seen.

CHAPTER XII

The Rise of the Colonial Office and the Fall of Slavery

THE WAR-BORN political reaction in the mother country had its counterpart in the empire. The war brought great additions to the empire, and the nature of all these additions was such that the government in London assumed full control of their administration. In other words, the war-born expansion of the empire made for an enormous extension of imperial authority. At the same time, but for a different reason, this authority was being extended in the oldest parts of the colonial empire, which from almost their very beginning, back in the seventeenth century, had enjoyed self-government. There, in the West Indies, its abuse by the whites was leading to growing interference by the home government to protect the blacks, an interference that was to culminate in the abrogation of self-government in the third quarter of the nineteenth century. The only other colonial assemblies were in British North America, where they were relatively new and untried; there the behavior of the largest of these bodies, that of Lower Canada which comprised the great bulk of the British North American population, was undermining the confidence of London in its usefulness, for the cessation of military hostilities brought a renewal and intensification of the French Canadian assembly's hostility to British rule. Since the beginning of the long war with France in 1793, not a single British colony had been invested with representative institutions; and in 1815, when peace was at last secure, the British government had not the slightest intention of introducing them anywhere. It was a far cry from the age when it was taken for granted that every British colony should have a government modeled after that of the mother country.

As a matter of fact, Britain was not the mother country of most of the lands now under her sway. She had not given birth to their people.

She had conquered them, and she ruled them. She had been a great colonizing country and was to be again, but at this time she was not and had long since ceased to be one. She was a great imperial power, the only one left in the world, now that the Spanish Empire was in process of disintegration; and the authority she wielded over her far-flung empire was many times greater than it had ever been in any preceding age.

How could London handle the burden of managing an empire so centralized in control and so diversified in character? Out of the war, which raised this question, came the answer. It was the Colonial Office. The transfer of the colonies from the Home Office, where they were a very minor care, to the War Office in 1801 was not intended to benefit the colonies. It was an obscure political job. To the two historic secretaries of state in the cabinet, the pressure of the war had added a third in 1794, the Secretary of State for War; and the promise of peace at Amiens threatened to deflate his office, which did not embrace the older military offices—those of the ordnance, the commander in chief, and the secretary-at-war—until the middle of the nineteenth century. If the motive of the transfer was to provide a peacetime justification for the continuance of this third secretary of state in the cabinet by giving him new duties, which enlarged his title to be Secretary of State for War and the Colonies, the early rupture of the peace rendered this justification superfluous and relegated the colonies to the neglect of a minister absorbed in the war. Strange as it may seem, this neglect came to a rather abrupt end in 1812, the very year when the war assumed its most menacing proportions with the Napoleonic invasion of Russia and the outbreak of hostilities in America. Apparently the change was a personal matter. It occurred when the Earl of Liverpool, on becoming prime minister, chose Earl Bathurst to be his successor as Secretary of State for War and the Colonies, and Bathurst picked Henry Goulburn as his undersecretary.

Bathurst was a seasoned politician and administrator. Ever since 1783, when as a young man of twenty-one he had been elected to the House of Commons and his friend William Pitt had made him a lord of the admiralty, he had sat in parliament—from 1794 in the House of Lords—and almost always he had held some ministerial office. Now for the first time he entered the cabinet, and there, much respected by his colleagues, he remained as secretary of state for the next fifteen years—the first real colonial secretary. Goulburn, nearly a generation younger and one of Sir Robert Peel's closest friends, had just commenced a long and rather distinguished public career in the House of Commons and in almost every Tory government until his death in the middle of the century. For nine years—until 1821, when he was appointed Chief Secretary for Ireland—he served under Bathurst, often managing him and always running the department with fine efficiency. As parliamentary secretary of the Colonial Office, Goulburn overshadows his successors. There was also a permanent undersecretary from 1825, but he had little or no influence upon policy until a most remarkable man was appointed to this post eleven years later.

"Bathurst and Goulburn unquestionably created a Colonial Office where none existed before, and in so doing they performed a task which was essential if the British Empire was to survive."[1] Under these two men the whole balance of the Department of War and the Colonies was quickly reversed and within the department there was a specialization according to function. When the return of peace brought a Treasury demand for a reduction in the establishment of the department, which until 1812 had been almost wholly absorbed in war business, the minister could dispense with only nine or ten of his considerable staff, and none from the larger of the two branches into which it was already divided, for this was fully occupied with rapidly growing colonial business.

The importance of this business and of the office that handled it won public recognition in parliament during the early years of peace. On two separate occasions an opposition leader in the House of Commons pressed for the abolition of the third secretaryship of state as no longer necessary. He would turn back at least the American colonies to the Home Office, where, he said, Goulburn and his clerks could work as well as their predecessors had done; and if the new colonies in the eastern hemisphere should be excluded from this arrangement, he would put them under the Indian Board of Control. Such a disposal of the eastern colonies was of course suggested by the fact that, with the exception of the convict settlements, they had been acquired as subsidiary to the Indian Empire. There is little point in considering how the success of this motion to split the empire would have affected its history, for the proposal had little chance of success against the arguments of Goulburn and other members of the government. They did not stoop to pretend that the third secretary of state still had important military duties. They took their stand on high grounds, insisting that the colo-

---

[1] Helen Taft Manning, *British Colonial Government After the American Revolution* (New Haven, 1933), p. 483.

nies, not being represented in parliament and some of them being without local legislatures, had to have a responsible cabinet minister to look after their interests. The government thus committed itself to the maintenance of the Colonial Office as a major department in its own right, and the opposition was fully converted.

The Colonial Office grew in power from the very beginning, as its chiefs tackled a rather awkward problem of central administration. The secretary of state was not the only head of a department who could give orders to officials in the colonies; for the Customs, the Treasury, the Post Office, and the Ordnance each had local staffs scattered about the empire, and these local staffs were answerable only to their respective departments in London. Hitherto there had been no coordination of these independent services, with the result that each had gone its own way with little or no regard for the interests of any colony as a whole; and the local governor could do nothing about it, no matter how seriously he might be embarrassed by the actions of local officials over whom neither he nor anyone else in the colony had any control. This was intolerable to Bathurst and Goulburn. They were determined to get cooperation of all the services in each colony, and by degrees they got it. From his vantage point in the cabinet, Bathurst was able to assert an authority over the other departments to bring their regulations and their colonial agents into line. The Colonial Office thus gained a general supervision over all official matters pertaining to colonies, and, in addition, it absorbed various functions that it could perform more effectively than those who had been responsible for them.

It was also during Bathurst's regime that we see the Colonial Office coming under the influence of the humanitarian movement, which was to leave an indelible stamp upon British colonial policy. Bathurst was reputed to be friendly toward the "Clapham sect," so called because the original members of the group, which included Wilberforce, had lived as close neighbors in the suburban community of Clapham and were evangelical churchmen whose piety was as strict as it was unpretentious. They were men of independent means and outstanding ability who devoted their fortunes and their lives to the humanitarian cause. They were often called "the saints," and there was as much truth as jest in the nickname. They were the core of the awakening national conscience, which has been mentioned earlier. It was they who provided the driving leadership in the antislavery movement and in the founding of missionary societies, which inaugurated the modern British missionary movement. One of the ablest of this remarkable group was James Stephen, Wilberforce's brother-in-law, a lawyer and a member of parliament, who was recognized as such an authority on matters of slavery and the cause of the black race generally[2] that his advice was constantly sought by government officials at least as early as 1807. It was perhaps only natural therefore that Bathurst and Goulburn should cultivate such a valuable established connection when they took charge of the colonies five years later. This connection undoubtedly led to another and, in time, a more famous one—with the second generation of the Clapham sect.

James Stephen had a son, also James and a chancery lawyer, who in 1813 took on the duties of counsel to the Colonial Office in addition to the good legal practice he had already built, though he was then only twenty-four. Two years later the elder Stephen seems to have fallen out with Bathurst on a matter of policy, but the Colonial Office leaned more and more on the younger Stephen. In 1825 he gave up the bar and was appointed full-time counselor.[3] In this capacity he gradually dominated the department, which was already his department before he was made its permanent undersecretary in 1836 and remained his department until he retired eleven years later. A born administrator, he greatly improved the organization that Bathurst and Goulburn had created, and he really ruled the colonial empire. No other man before or since has ever wielded such power over it. In him the centralization of the empire reached its climax. "Mr. Oversecretary" and "Mr. Mother Country," his enemies called him, but that was because they were impractical reformers who could not bend him to their will. He was more enlightened than they were, though only now is this coming to be fully realized. His guiding motive was not the concentration of authority over the colonies, nor any selfish interest of the metropolitan state. A deeply religious and highly conscientious man, he was above all else, from first to last, the champion of the colored races against oppression by the whites. He was the vigorous personification of the new principle of trusteeship, which thenceforth characterized British colonial policy.

Another healthy change that appeared during Bathurst's administration was in the relations between the Colonial Office and parliament. At first the ministry was strongly reluctant to consult parliament on

---

[2] As a young man he had practiced his profession in the West Indies, and there he had gained a firsthand knowledge of slavery.

[3] Also to the Board of Trade.

colonial affairs, and parliament was little inclined to pry into them except in so far as they touched the sensitive subject of slavery. The normal desire of a specialized governmental agency to manage its business without interference by uninformed legislators and the remoteness of colonial business from almost all the members of parliament do not wholly explain this mutual shyness. There was also a constitutional reason. The Colonial Office was little beholden to parliament for authority to govern. The legal authority exercised by the secretary of state over the colonies was that of the royal prerogative, which was unlimited in the crown colonies and very considerable in the others. Of course the colonial secretary was far from being an absolute autocrat. He wielded this enormous power only on the sufferance of his cabinet colleagues and of his fellow members of parliament, who could at any time force his removal from office. Moreover, parliament could at will, by ordinary legislation, curtail the royal prerogative; but it has been chary of doing so, lest it impair the efficiency of government in the future.

It was Australia that began to bring the Colonial Office and parliament closer together on the management of the colonies. The effective pressure was not financial, though by 1815 parliament was required to make an annual grant of £80,000 to support the penal settlements of New South Wales and Van Diemen's Land, for it was generally conceded that the convicts would have cost more to maintain at home. What forced the change was, as suggested in a previous chapter, a growing realization that there was something constitutionally wrong in Australia. The governor there had undoubted authority, derived from parliament, to rule a society of convicts and their guardians. His power was more or less despotic, a condition dictated by the very nature of this society and reinforced by the enormous distance that separated Australia from England. But he was also exercising this power over the free settlers, who were growing in number; and though he did not know it, and the Colonial Office had not realized it, he had no legal authority to rule over them. Parliament had not given him this authority, and the Crown could not give it. The oversight on the part of the Colonial Office may be explained by the small and slow beginning of this new society under the shadow of the older one, by its location on the far side of the earth, by the distractions of the long French war, and by the false analogy of the conquered colonies, where the royal prerogative was supreme. Nevertheless, the Colonial Office was responsible for allowing the governor, who simply followed in the footsteps of his predecessors, to levy taxes he had no right to collect, to make and enforce laws that were invalid, and to impose on free Englishmen an arbitrary administration of justice which denied the precious right of trial by jury and sometimes punished without any trial.

In 1817 the highhanded behavior of Governor Macquarie was aired in the House of Commons, following a free settlers' petition to that body for his recall; and it began to dawn on the Colonial Office and the ministry that they would have to ask parliament to supply Australia with a proper constitution. This entailed considerable preliminary investigation, and meanwhile Bathurst warned Macquarie to walk warily. In 1819, while still wondering what should be done, the ministry suffered a withering attack from the opposition benches for what had been done in Australia. The ministers sought to soften the blow by declaring that a radical change was contemplated, that a royal commissioner was appointed and would soon depart to examine the whole situation in New South Wales, and that further action should await his recommendations. As an emergency measure, the government had parliament provide a legal sanction for the taxes raised in the colony.[4]

From this time forth the relations between the Colonial Office and parliament were the opposite of what they had been. The ministers had learned a wholesome lesson. Never again would the Colonial Office shield itself behind the royal prerogative, much less stretch the prerogative beyond the legal limits. The department would rather look to parliament for support in administering the colonies, and to this end it undertook the education of parliament. In 1822 Bathurst inaugurated the policy of publishing an annual "Blue Book" for each colony. It was he also who, under the impulse of this Australian crisis, developed the valuable practice of sending out specially selected royal commissioners as the need arose to tackle on the spot peculiarly difficult problems in the colonial world.[5]

The commissioner dispatched to New South Wales in 1819 had power to overrule the governor, who resented this interference with his authority and resigned in a huff; and the voluminous reports of the commissioner were the basis of the first Australian constitution, which was framed in the Colonial Office and then enacted by parliament in 1823. The act reformed the judicial system, invested the existing taxes

---

[4] By an act that was renewed annually until the new constitution was completed.

[5] Commissioners were sent to Trinidad in 1802, West Africa in 1811, Malta in 1812, New South Wales in 1819, the Cape, Mauritius, and Ceylon in 1823, and West Africa again in 1824.

with a permanent legality, gave a limited legislative authority to the governor and a small legislative council, and provided for the separation of Van Diemen's Land from New South Wales with the same form of government.

It will be observed that there was no provision for an assembly, which is in marked contrast to what had been done for Canada a generation previously, when Pitt's government felt bound by the Declaratory Act of 1778 to create an assembly as the only remaining means of raising the necessary colonial revenue. But the times had changed; there had been no popular demand in Australia for an assembly, and there was no pressing need to levy new taxes there. The old ones sufficed and though originally unconstitutional they were no longer so, parliament having leaped into the breach to cover them with its own authority, which no British law court could question. What seems to have forestalled any agitation for representative government among the free people of Australia, who by this time outnumbered the rest of the population and possessed most of the wealth in the country, was Macquarie's bitter quarrel with the rest of local officialdom over his policy of favoring emancipists and the continuance of this quarrel by his successor. Why should the emancipists seek to hobble the gubernatorial authority when it was their powerful ally against the class of entrenched "exclusives," who insisted that they could never be anything but outcasts? As for the Canadian precedent of 1791, Canadian experience had robbed it of much of its value in English eyes.

Canada was giving the Colonial Office a headache. The restoration of peace with the United States released the suspended strife in Lower Canada, and it flamed up more fiercely than ever. The conflict between the French majority who controlled the assembly and the British minority who monopolized the other branches of government affected more than Lower Canada. It injured Upper Canada by depriving that province of most of its revenue. As the upper province was dependent on the lower for access to the sea, and the latter was therefore in a position to tax the trade of the former, the two had made an agreement whereby Lower Canada would collect customs duties on imports without regard for their destination and turn over to Upper Canada a certain proportion of the proceeds. This payment stopped in 1819 when the local political discord prevented the renewal of the necessary Lower Canadian statute. Upper Canada appealed to London for redress by parliament. But the French province was in an even worse plight, for there the lower chamber of the legislature was at loggerheads with the upper chamber and the executive, and beneath this political deadlock burned the fires of racial and religious hatred. Because the intense nationalism that grew until it dominated western civilization in the nineteenth century was yet a novel phenomenon, London could not understand the strange fever that had gripped French Canada and made the assembly so intractable.

Therefore Bathurst welcomed a proposal that came from Lower Canada and promised, at one stroke, to remove the exasperating difficulties of both provinces. The plan was to pass an act of parliament, of which the Lower Canadian solicitor general prepared the first draft, to provide an arbitration system for the division of the duties collected at the port of Quebec, and to effect a legislative union of the two provinces, which would in other respects remain distinct. The new legislature was to have power to legislate for either or both, and representation was to be divided equally between them—though the population of Upper Canada was a bare 150,000 while that of Lower Canada was about 450,000—so that the new assembly would have a guaranteed English-speaking majority. The French Canadians were also to be bridled by other features of the bill, which was presented to parliament in the early summer of 1822. Much to the surprise of the government, which expected a prompt passage, the measure roused a violent storm in the House of Commons. The objections were not to the principles of the bill, but to the introduction of such an important measure so late in the session and without any effort to consult the provinces concerned. Thereupon the contentious union feature was dropped for that session, and the financial provisions, which were urgently needed to rescue Upper Canada, were rushed through.

It was well that parliament blocked this union, a scheme long cherished by influential leaders of the British minority in Lower Canada who seized the opportunity of Upper Canada's distress to launch it in parliament with ministerial support. They wanted to combine English-speaking Upper Canada with the English-speaking part of Lower Canada to crush the French, who still formed the great majority of the population of the two Canadas. Upper Canada knew nothing of the bill until after it was introduced, and then people in that province did not relish the thought of being used as a makeweight. Many of them suspected that the wrong party might be crushed, and the government of Upper Canada denounced the union in no uncertain terms. The news from London threw Lower Canada into an uproar. Everywhere, even in the smallest communities, there were meetings, speeches, resolutions, and petitions; for the French and British alike realized that their whole future was at stake in the decision to be made in the empire's capital, and each party was determined to make its voice heard over the other. Early in the winter their opposing petitions to king and parliament were carried across the Atlantic by special delegations, who were welcomed at the Colonial Office. Wilmot Horton, the new parliamentary undersecretary, admitted to Papineau, one of the delegates and the speaker of the assembly, that the government had expected opposition from the French Canadians but had favored union as best for them in the end. When Horton went on to criticize the Montreal committee's attack on the bill as destructive of French Canadian laws, language, and religion, the future rebel leader dissociated himself from such an expression and declared that his people had the fullest confidence in the government of the mother country. Papineau and his colleague remained for some time in London, using all the arguments and influence that they could, until they were satisfied that the union project was dead.

After Bathurst's retirement in 1827 there was a more or less rapid succession of colonial secretaries; but the Colonial Office was then well established and, on the whole, these later secretaries of state were abler than the first of the line. William Huskisson was perhaps the best statesman and administrator of them all, and he did much for the colonial empire by liberalizing its trading relations. This, however, was a service that he had already accomplished in another capacity, as we shall see in the next chapter. He was only eight months in the Colonial Office, just long enough to indicate that he might have done much more for the colonies if an unfortunate split with his colleagues over a domestic political matter had not forced his withdrawal from the cabinet.

Before Huskisson left the Colonial Office in May 1828, he had to face a new crisis in Lower Canada, whence came more delegates with monster petitions to the king for relief from an internal situation that seemed intolerable. After considerable study of the complicated problem, Huskisson analyzed it in a speech to the Commons and asked for a select committee of the House to investigate and report. It would not be surprising, he said, if the constitution given to the province a generation before was now found to be "extremely defective." Therefore he posed the question: What changes in form or operation are necessary to get a workable government? He deplored the constitutional deadlock, pointing out some of the crying evils it had wrought. The

British minority had to live under a system of French civil laws so antiquated that they had long been discarded in France, laws that knew nothing of commerce or freehold tenure.[6] The Eastern Townships, whose population was English-speaking, had not a seat in the assembly because they had been settled after the original establishment of electoral constituencies and these had remained unaltered. In order to strangle the executive into submission, the assembly had refused to vote supplies, with the result that "all improvement was at a stand, the roads were neglected, education was overlooked, the public buildings were suffered to fall to decay, and the country generally . . . was brought to such a state that there was not a Canadian whose interests did not suffer." Moreover, the executive had struck back. Unable to meet the minimum needs of government out of the £40,000 annual revenue which was not derived from provincial statute and therefore not legally subject to the assembly's control,[7] the governor, on his own authority, had met the deficit by drawing on the proceeds of the £100,000 revenue at the disposal of the assembly. He had no legal right to do this, but he felt that the assembly had forced him to it.

In conclusion, Huskisson rebuked some fellow members of parliament, and some other people outside, who had become so impatient with the troubles of Canada that they would get rid of them by getting rid of it. He poured forth his scorn upon the idea. Discarding all argument over material advantages, he declared that justice and honor forbade any such desertion of loyal British subjects. "We have carried our language, our free institutions, and our system of laws, to the remote corners of the globe . . . what we now foster as colonies will be, no doubt, one day or other, themselves free nations, the communicators of freedom to other countries. . . . Whether Canada is to remain forever dependent on England, or is to become an independent state—not, I trust, by hostile separation, but by amicable arrangement—it is still the duty and interest of this country to imbue it with English feeling, and benefit it with English laws and institutions."

Huskisson failed, as his words reveal, to reach the root of the problem in Lower Canada, and the French Canadian leaders did their best to keep it hidden from English eyes. What these leaders said in French

---

[6] Here Huskisson appears to have overlooked the fact that in 1826 parliament had mitigated this evil by passing the Canada Tenures Act, which made English law the rule for the regulation of real property in the Eastern Townships. But that district was still without law courts for the adjudication of property and without registry offices for the registration of deeds.

[7] All but £5,000 of this revenue was derived from the Quebec Revenue Act of 1774.

to their own people was not what they said to the rest of the world in English, and this for very natural reasons. While rousing their followers by unrestrained appeals to narrow national prejudice, they were most careful to pose before the British, particularly in England, as the righteous champions of constitutional government and popular freedom. His Majesty had no subjects more loyal than the French Canadians, according to the petitions and delegations they sent to London. They appealed to the British government to end the un-British rule of the British rulers in their midst. French Canadian nationalism was concealing itself beneath the cloak of British constitutionalism.

Small wonder the Commons committee could not penetrate the disguise. The failure of the committee becomes more understandable when we take into account two other facts of the time. As we look back today, we see how nationalism, in its new dynamic phase, shook nineteenth century Europe to its very foundations and later spread throughout the world; but all this, being yet in the future, was beyond the ken of Englishmen in 1828. The real nature of the troubles in Lower Canada was also obscured by what was happening next door, in Upper Canada, where a genuine constitutional struggle was developing. There the first assembly that was not in general harmony with the upper chamber and the executive was elected in 1824; and the popular party was appealing to the Colonial Office, with not a little success, against specific actions of the local ruling oligarchy. The Commons committee, which was appointed "to inquire into the state of the civil government of Canada" as established in 1791, submitted a well-meaning but rather innocuous report. It proposed no radical change, but it did lay down a principle that reflected the growing liberal outlook of the age. It was that such alterations as might be desirable should, as far as possible, be effected by the local legislatures working in cooperation with the local government, rather than by the paramount authority of parliament. The committee recommended some detailed concessions on both sides and a more conciliatory disposition in the operation of the constitution in the two Canadas.

One recommendation, suggested by Huskisson and based on domestic British experience, was that the assembly should have control of the whole revenue and provide a permanent civil list to preserve the independence of the judges and other principal officers of government. This compromise was possible in Upper Canada but not in Lower Canada, where party division cut too deep. The difference was demonstrated in 1831, when the new Whig government surrendered financial control to the two Canadian assemblies and asked them to reciprocate. The Upper Canadian house obliged, while the Lower Canadian body took all and gave nothing, not even its thanks.

The tension in the lower province was rising to a dangerous pitch. The spring of 1832 saw an election riot in Montreal, where three men were killed and many were wounded when a nationalist crowd clashed with the troops called out to preserve order. Papineau then shrieked that Craig, governor before the War of 1812, had only imprisoned men whereas Aylmer, the governor of the day, shot them down in the street. Lower Canada, which contained by far the largest white population of any colony in the empire, was ripening for the rebellion of 1837. But the problem of government in this one colony could not compare in magnitude, or in appeal to the British public, with the problem of the blacks in the whole series of old colonies that had long since ceased to be predominantly white.

The issue of slavery progressively overshadowed all other colonial questions in the first third of the nineteenth century. When parliament abolished the British slave trade in the spring of 1807, eight months before the United States slave trade became illegal under the Constitution, the promoters of the measure had no intention of following up their success by demanding the abolition of slavery. They believed that the Negroes were unfit for it, but they did look forward to the gradual amelioration of the lot of the slaves. Would not self-interest drive the planters to preserve and improve their slave stock, now that they could not replenish it, instead of wearing it out, as they had been wont to do because it was cheaper to import fresh stock? In the words of James Stephen the elder, the friends of the blacks anticipated "an emancipation of which not the slaves but the masters themselves would be the willing authors." It was not in the colonies but in Africa that the friends of the blacks sought to follow up their success. In the summer of 1807 they founded the African Institution, the original purpose of which was to encourage merchants and missionaries who would bring civilization and Christianity to Africa and thus "repair the ruin and degradation which we have contributed to bring upon her."

This organization, in which the elder Stephen and Wilberforce played the leading roles, soon found that it had more urgent work to do in the colonies, because the act of 1807 did not operate as expected. The iniquitous traffic had to be stopped in fact as well as in law, and the slaves had to be protected against their masters. These then became the two chief objects of the African Institution. In 1811 it got new teeth put into the law, which had prescribed nothing more severe than heavy fines and confiscation, by making slave trading a criminal offense for which the punishment was transportation. But this was not enough for Stephen. He insisted that illicit importation would continue until a rigid registration law, requiring a clearly identifiable description of every individual slave, prevented masters from acquiring legal title to any black property that might be smuggled in; and he persuaded the prime minister, his friend and patron, to try the experiment in the new colony of Trinidad. This was just before Bathurst entered the cabinet; and apparently it was Stephen who prepared the first draft of the order and selected the registrar to implement it in the island.

Until the close of the war, the Royal Navy could and did give almost universal application to the British law against the slave trade, but the return of peace made this no longer possible and raised the prospect of a revival of the traffic in the hands of other powers. Thereupon a tremendous wave of feeling swept over England to force the government to use its strong international position to make abolition universal. According to the Duke of Wellington the people were willing to go to war for abolition. During seven weeks in the early summer of 1814 no less than 772 petitions bearing almost a million signatures (the total population of Great Britain was only thirteen million) were addressed to the House of Commons. Under such pressure the British government was embarrassingly importunate at the Congress of Vienna. Other countries suspected some hidden British design; and France, Spain, and Portugal held out resolutely. It was this vehement outburst of British public opinion and its failure to get complete international cooperation to wipe out the traffic in slaves that provides the background for the efforts then made to mitigate the evils of slavery in the British colonies.

There was quite a tussle over the extension of Stephen's registration scheme, which had been confined to Trinidad. In 1815 it was applied to St. Lucia and Mauritius without any difficulty because they were crown colonies too. But it was a different matter to thrust it upon the old colonies, for there it meant riding roughshod over long-established rights of self-government. It was on this point, apparently, that Bathurst broke with the elder Stephen in 1815. The crusading lawyer knew full well that the legislatures of these colonies, being filled with slaveowners, were bitterly opposed to any such reform; and he could not suppose for a moment, as he said, "that the Government of this country will ever admit or countenance in Parliament the monstrous pretension of those petty assemblies to exclude in such a case the controlling and regulating hand of the supreme legislature." But the colonial secretary balked at the idea of imposing a registration law upon them by act of parliament.

Stephen's famous brother-in-law tried to force the issue by introducing into the House of Commons a bill to establish registry offices in all the West Indian colonies and a registry office in England where duplicates of the island registers would be kept for inspection. No master could then have any property right over a black who was not properly registered. The bill provoked two heated debates, not over the principle of registration, which was generally accepted, but over the method of adopting it. The ministry fought for legislation by the colonies, while Wilberforce was easily able to prove that they had consistently rejected measures for the benefit of their slaves even when recommended by the House of Commons or their own committees in England. Though he and his fellows had the better of the argument, he was persuaded to withdraw the bill until replies could be got from the colonies, Bathurst pledging himself to urge the reform upon them.

The Colonial Office was thus prodded into coercing the colonial legislatures by threatening them with parliamentary action if they did not do as desired. The circular dispatch that shook this big stick at the West Indies went out in the summer of 1816, when resentment in the islands had been forced to fever heat by an Easter rising of slaves in Barbados. Only one white was killed, but many estates were wrecked and hundreds of blacks were slain or executed. Of course Stephen and his African Institution were cursed for instigating the revolt; but the Caribbean legislatures bowed to their will and passed registration acts. Then the government had parliament crown the system in 1819 by setting up a central registry office in London.

The constitutional aspect of this struggle over registration is interesting. The real victory lay with the Colonial Office, and it was a double victory—over parliament as well as the colonies. The ministry had held off parliament from asserting its supremacy over elected colonial legislatures, which therefore might and did for a while believe they had preserved their independence. But the fact of their submission belied their belief. What they preserved was a rather hollow form. The power exercised by the Colonial Office over the crown colonies was now being definitely extended over the old colonies that had long managed their own internal affairs. Thenceforth they were subject to growing dictation from London until they too became crown colonies. On the othe hand, the ministers could count on the West Indian interest in the House of Commons to back their resistance to parliamentary interference in colonial administration, and on the "African" party to uphold the prerogative of the Crown to legislate for the conquered colonies.

Registration was not the only phase of the slavery question that was changing the relations between the colonies and the mother country. Sentiment in England was outraged to discover that British slaves had almost no protection in law and less in the application of it. They could not be legally married or baptized, nor could they own property or purchase their redemption from bondage, nor could they expect much justice from white judges and juries. They were neglected by the Church of England, which confined its activities to the whites; and when missionaries of other denominations tried to give them a little Christian education, these bearers of the Gospel commonly met with short shrift from the masters, who would tolerate no tampering with their slaves.

Slavery in the British West Indies, as in the United States, was much harsher than in Latin America, primarily because of a difference in legal and religious tradition.[8] When the Spaniards and Portuguese settled in the New World, they carried with them a law, inherited from the Roman Empire, that recognized and regulated the institution of slavery; and the Roman Catholic Church, by insisting that slaves had souls to save and must be regarded as members of the Christian community, gave a strong religious sanction to the slave codes in the Spanish and Portuguese colonies. English law, on the other hand, knew nothing of slavery when the English colonists brought the two together; and as it had no other category for slaves than that of chattels, this is what they became in the eyes of the law. Victims of a defective law, the slaves in the English colonies[9] were also victims of a weakness in Protestantism, which felt little or no responsibility for the salvation of nonwhite races until the rise of the humanitarian movement.

From almost the turn of the century the correspondence between the secretary of state and the governors of the various British Caribbean islands was more and more concerned with improving the lot of the slave by humanizing the law and its administration. Conditions were so bad that almost any change would have been for the better; yet it

---

[8] On this subject see Frank Tannenbaum, "The Destiny of the Negro in the Western Hemisphere," *Political Science Quarterly*, March 1946, pp. 1–41.

[9] This of course does not include the conquered colonies, such as Trinidad, where the British continued the Roman law.

was very difficult to effect a change. The Barbadian assembly balked at making murder of a slave a felony until a special message was sent in the king's name, and in another island martial law had to be proclaimed to bring about the execution of a council member who delighted in torturing Negroes to death. The "Africans" in the House of Commons made great capital out of the atrocities of this particular monster, and local resistance to the reform of slavery cured more than one West Indian governor of any faith in West Indian self-government. Still the ministry was loath to appeal to parliament against it, and the legislative colonies remained sullenly deaf to the repeated urgings of the Colonial Office to purge slavery of its evils.

In 1823 the crusade of the "Africans" changed its course. The slave trade, though banned by most countries, was as great an evil as ever, and so were the conditions of slavery in the British colonies. The labors of a generation seemed to have gone for nothing because they had been directed along impossible channels. Therefore the champions of the blacks at last decided to drive for the abolition of an institution that could not be reformed. In January 1823 they organized the Anti-Slavery Society[10] in London, which within a year had a couple of hundred branches all over the country. In March, the old and ailing Wilberforce fired the opening shot in the new campaign by presenting a Quaker petition to parliament to abolish slavery in all British possessions; and in May, Thomas Fowell Buxton, whom he had chosen to be his successor as parliamentary leader of the cause, followed it up by moving "that the state of slavery is repugnant to the principles of the British constitution, and of the Christian religion, and that it ought to be abolished gradually throughout the British colonies, with as much expedition as may be found consistent with a due regard to the well-being of the parties concerned."

The plan then propounded by Buxton had two parts, to the first of which he pinned his faith. It was that every child born after a certain date should be free. As parliament had made it piracy to enslave a full-grown Negro, it should sweep away the law that made slaves of children by the mere fact of birth. Then slavery would slowly but surely die out. The second part concerned existing slaves. Buxton said he could not demand their immediate emancipation because they were not ready for it, but he called for a series of drastic reforms that he had already communicated to Bathurst. Among other things, the law

---

[10] The official name was the "Society for the Mitigation and Gradual Abolition of Slavery throughout the British Dominions," but this was popularly shortened as above.

should cease to regard slaves as chattels; it should admit their testimony in the courts; it should shift the burden of proof from them to masters who claimed their services; it should remove all obstructions to manumission and should follow Spanish precedent by allowing them to purchase freedom at a just price; it should not permit any slaveowner to be governor, judge, or attorney general; it should recognize and protect the marriage of slaves; it should make provision for their religious instruction and give them Sundays to themselves; and it should restrain the masters' power of punishment.

Buxton's attack precipitated a parliamentary battle between the West Indians and the "Africans" that lasted until well into the next morning, when it was ended by the unanimous passage of a compromise advanced by the government. This shelved the first part of Buxton's plan, the government asserting that the emancipation of infants whose parents would remain in bondage was unwise; but it committed the House and the ministry to gradual emancipation by the progressive mitigation of slavery, on the understanding that it would be on such lines as were set forth in the second part of the plan. The government also explained that it would adhere to the policy it had pursued on the registration question, enforcing the program in the crown colonies and recommending it to the other colonies. If the latter were contumacious, the ministers "would not hesitate to come down to Parliament for counsel."

Behind the government compromise were several important considerations that are clearly evident. Almost everybody admitted that the sugar colonies were suffering acute economic distress and therefore deserved sympathetic handling. This was also good politics because there were many members of parliament, in both houses, who were financially interested, directly or indirectly, in these islands whose whole economy was on the brink of ruin. Moreover, the West Indians and the East Indians in London were at this time taking steps that promised to make the obdurate assemblies fall into line. During the three weeks prior to Buxton's attack, knowing it was coming and greatly fearing its effect upon the slave population of the Caribbeans, the Society of West India Planters and Merchants formulated a program of reform so thorough-going that it was almost the same in many particulars as the second part of Buxton's plan. The society then importuned the colonial legislatures to go all the way with the government, and that promptly, lest it be too late to head off the antislavery drive in Britain and dangerous trouble with the Negroes on the plantations. The East Indians were clamoring for a reduction of the duties on their sugars to give them the same preference as the West Indians enjoyed, and just a week after Buxton's attack there was a motion in the House of Commons for a select committee to investigate the rates on East and West India sugar. The threat of equalization, which would make it impossible for the old colonies to compete, was a sword of Damocles suspended over the West Indies.

Bathurst lost no time in attempting to apply the policy of gradual emancipation to which the government was now pledged. It was easy to get a program of reform because it had been pretty well worked out for him by Buxton and the London West Indians, but it was hard to get it carried out. Instead of generous cooperation, the colonial secretary encountered bitter obstruction in the colonies. They were soon in an angrier uproar than that with which the continental colonies had begun the American Revolution. The island planters, however, were in such a helpless position that they could not appeal to arms against the mother country. They were in mortal terror of a British San Domingo; and they resorted to not a little violence, sometimes naked and sometimes cloaked in legality, to cow the restless Negroes and to get rid of the missionaries, whom they naturally but unjustly suspected of fomenting insurrection.

The most notorious case was that of John Smith in Demerara. The slaves in that crown colony, hearing that some "good thing" ordered from London was being withheld from them by local authorities, which was true, went on a spree of liberty in August 1823. They neither looted nor burned, but they killed two whites who resisted their search for arms, and they were mercilessly suppressed. Not content with taking many black lives, the vengeance of the planters, of whom the governor was one, turned on Smith, in whose chapel they said the plot was hatched. Though absolutely innocent, he was condemned to death by court martial. The sentence was referred to England, where it was quashed—too late. While still in close confinement, he died of tuberculosis. Opinion in Britain reacted to the martyrdom of John Smith much as it reacted in the Northern States to the execution of John Brown a generation afterward.

In the crown colonies, where the authority of London was not open to question, the reform of slavery ran into countless snags. These colonies had different laws—Dutch, Spanish, and French—all foreign to the English system; and these divergencies were paralleled in many other conditions surrounding slavery. The Colonial Office had therefore to rely on the local officials not only to enforce the desired measures but also to adapt them to local conditions, all of which meant that the planters in the crown colonies had plenty of opportunity for obstruction. Naturally they made the most of it. In the chartered colonies, the assemblies would not comply with the recommendations of the Colonial Office even though the latter had the strong backing of the London West Indians, who were then constrained to defend at home the resistance in the colonies. At first the assemblies adopted a policy of evasion. Instead of accepting or rejecting the prescribed program, they reviewed their slave laws, made some ineffectual little changes in them, and then professed that in so doing they were giving every possible satisfaction to the desires of the home government. Thus flouted, Bathurst sent out drafts of legislation with orders for the law officers of each colony to frame them as bills to be introduced into the local legislature. When this was done, the little colony of Nevis accepted the bills; but with this single exception every legislature either threw them out or would not allow them to be brought in.

The whole business, dragging on year after year, was most exasperating. The slaves were exasperated, their masters were exasperated, the Colonial Office was exasperated, the whole government was exasperated, the antislavery leaders and their followers in parliament and out of it were exasperated, and the British public was exasperated. The emancipationists, unable to muster a majority of votes in parliament, were determined to bring outside pressure to bear upon that body, and to this end they bombarded the people with their propaganda, while the slavery interests bombarded them with counterpropaganda. The press, the pulpit, and the public platform thundered. The agitation at home aggravated feeling in the colonies, and news from the colonies fed the flaming controversy at home.

In 1830 the antislavery crusaders, despairing of getting gradual emancipation by colonial action, raised the cry of immediate emancipation by act of parliament; and in the elections of that and the following year, they pledged parliamentary candidates and appealed to the people to elect them. Though by this time public interest was chiefly focused on the great question of parliamentary reform, this was not so much an end in itself as it was a means to effect other reforms, of which the abolition of slavery was not the least; reports from the colonies then drew startling attention to the need for quick and strong action on slavery. In January 1831, a public meeting of planters and merchants in Grenada called for a West India congress; two months later such a congress, comprising members of the several legislatures who had been chosen by public meetings for this purpose, met in Barbados and passed some vigorous resolutions. These set forth the grievances of the Caribbean colonies and denounced any interference with their property. Never before had anything like this occurred in the West Indies. It recalled the ominous beginning of the American Revolution, and it was followed by angrier outbursts in crown and chartered colonies alike. The climax came toward the end of the year and in Jamaica, with wild talk of hoisting the American flag and appealing to the United States for protection, and with a destructive servile insurrection, which the irresponsible language of the white leaders did not a little to provoke. It seemed as if the whole of the British West Indies might blow up at any moment.

What brought this Caribbean crisis to a head was the crisis at home over parliamentary reform; for it was common knowledge that the passage of the Reform Bill, by routing the West India interest from its entrenched position in the House of Commons, would deliver parliament to the abolitionists. As the crisis over parliamentary reform passed in May 1832, when Wellington failed to form a ministry and Grey returned to power with a royal promise to create enough peers to carry the Reform Bill, the West Indians lost their final battle to save slavery, and they knew it. Thenceforth their interest was in getting the best possible terms of surrender.

The working out of a scheme for emancipation that would be both "safe and satisfactory" was a slow and difficult task entailing much investigation and negotiation. Not until a year afterward, in the first session of the first reformed parliament, did the government present its detailed proposals to the House of Commons. The institution of slavery was to be abolished throughout all British possessions. Slaves under six years of age were to be free immediately. All others were to work their way to freedom through a period of twelve years, bound as apprentices to give three quarters of the day or week to their old masters, from whom the power of punishment was transferred to magistrates answerable to the home government. During the remaining quarter of their time, the apprentices would serve as free laborers for wages, which were to be fixed at one twelfth of their value as slaves and to be used as compensation to the owners. Meanwhile, the latter, to offset the immediate loss of one quarter of the slaves' time, were to receive a government loan of £15,000,000, which was calculated to be ten times their annual profit on sugar, rum, and coffee; and if parliament desired to relieve the slaves from paying compensation, it could change this loan into a gift. The government admitted that, as slavery was a national wrong for which the whole nation was responsible, the people of the mother country should share with the slaves and their masters the cost of extinguishing it.

These proposals drew cross fire from the abolitionists and the West Indians. The former would eliminate or at least reduce the period of apprenticeship, and they attacked compensation; while the latter, who fiercely resisted every attempt to cut down apprenticeship, fought for more adequate compensation. The upshot was a compromise. The government agreed to make an outright grant of £20,000,000, and to limit apprenticeship for field hands to six years and for others to four years. The grant amounted to nearly half the national revenue for a year and about the same proportion of the total market price of the slaves. Toward the end of the summer the Abolition Bill, which was drafted by James Stephen, became law. It came into effect eleven months later, on 1 August 1834.

As the day of deliverance drew near, there was tense anxiety in the mother country and the West Indies lest the slave population break loose in an orgy of blood and fire. There was an explosion, but not of the kind that had long been dreaded. It was an outburst of delirious jubilation unaccompanied by violence. For this happy restraint much credit goes to the self-control of the planters who knew their day was done, to the strenuous efforts of the missionaries who had won the confidence of the slaves, and still more to the Negroes themselves. The legislatures of Antigua and Bermuda did away with apprenticeship at once. Elsewhere the system worked tolerably well except in Jamaica. There it was so shockingly abused that the antislavery agitation flared up in England again and forced the abandonment of apprenticeship in all the colonies on 1 August 1838.

So ended the liberation of some three quarters of a million blacks from bondage. How they would use their freedom had long been a matter of bitter dispute between the antislavery leaders and the planters, the former insisting and the latter vehemently denying that free labor would prove more profitable than slave labor. The event proved the planters right; for the liberated blacks, able to sustain life with a minimum of toil in their tropical islands, were little tempted by wages. But the planters themselves had conditioned the event by their successful resistance to the gradual reform of slavery; and they paid for it with their own ruin, which was now nearly complete.

CHAPTER XIII

The Growth of Anti-Imperialism

THE RISE of the Colonial Office and the fall of slavery reflected a changing concept of empire. The tide of British imperialism, which had reached its first flood in the Seven Years' War, its first great ebb in the American Revolutionary War, and its second flood in the Napoleonic Wars, was again receding. The turn came in the hour of Britain's most resounding imperial triumph when, as the only great world power in existence, she went to the Congress of Vienna and there made an unprecedented renunciation of colonial conquests in order to buy a lasting peace.

The international rivalry for colonial possessions, which had embroiled European powers ever since the discovery of America, had come to an end with the practical elimination of all Britain's competitors; and until the last quarter of the nineteenth century, when new conditions precipitated a new and more feverish scramble for colonies, neither Britain nor any other power was much interested in this game of grab. It was an anti-imperialist age, which reached its climax around the middle of the century, when most people in Britain who gave any thought to their empire actually anticipated, some with complacency and some with impatience, its early dissolution. Paradoxically this attitude of indifference or aversion prevailed in the midst of the long and only period when British sea power, without which the sprawling British Empire could not have been built up or held together, was absolutely supreme.

The burden of empire was beginning to weigh upon Britain when a special department of government was organized to help bear it and when a new sense of responsibility found expression in the victorious struggle against slavery. In the arguments that flew back and forth, the planters made strong appeals to imperial sentiment and interest, thinking this would embarrass their opponents by rallying public opinion against them, while the champions of the blacks did not hesitate to use anti-imperial language to further their cause. Emancipation, it is true, was effected by an exercise of imperial power; but the end was regarded as justifying the means, and the end was the very opposite of imperialistic. Britain would free the slaves even if it ruined her West Indian colonies and even though it was at a heavy cost to her own exchequer.

Whence came the growing idea that colonies were a burden rather than a benefit to the mother country? It sprang from the economic teaching of Adam Smith. In the long chapter on colonies in his *Wealth of Nations,* which was published in the same year as the American Declaration of Independence, he exploded the fallacy on which the old colonial system rested. According to this fallacy, the profits accruing from the monopoly of colonial trade compensated the parent state for the outlays it incurred in protecting the colonies and this monopoly. His closely reasoned analysis showed that these profits were collected by a few at the expense of the many, and that from a national point of view the monopoly produced loss instead of gain. This was because the artificial restraints which the system imposed on the freedom of trade operated to divert capital and labor from more to less profitable uses, thereby cramping the prosperity not only of the colonies but of the mother country as well. He also pointed out how enormous were the expenses incurred to support this injurious system. In addition to the cost of the ordinary peacetime military establishment in the colonies— twenty regiments of foot and auxiliary services—and the cost of maintaining a considerable naval force to keep away from the colonies "the smuggling vessels of other nations," there was the mountainous cost of past wars waged for the sake of the colonies. "Great Britain derives nothing but loss from the dominion which she assumes over her colonies."

Adam Smith thus came to the conclusion that, as the colonies were a source of weakness rather than of strength, it would be to Britain's advantage to give them up. Yet he admitted that this was a counsel of perfection, which "never was, and never will be, adopted by any nation in the world" because it would be too mortifying to national pride and too injurious to the personal interests of those who formed the government. Therefore he proposed, as others were then doing, that the rising American difficulty might be solved by introducing colonial representation into the imperial parliament. As a consequence, some later imperialists of lesser mind have asserted that he opposed a policy of separation. That he actually favored it is borne out by a memorable passage in which he cast a longing glance at the future it disclosed to him in 1776. By voluntarily surrendering all authority over the colonies and allowing them to be completely independent, he said:

> Great Britain would not only be immediately freed from the whole annual expense of the peace establishment of the colonies, but might settle with them such a treaty of commerce as would effectually secure to her a free trade, more advantageous to the great body of the people, though less so to the merchants, than the monopoly which she at present enjoys. By thus parting good friends, the natural affection of the colonies to the mother country, which, perhaps, our late dissensions have well nigh extinguished, would quickly revive. It might dispose them not only to respect, for whole centuries together, that treaty of commerce which they had concluded with us at parting, but to favour us in war as well as in trade, and instead of turbulent and factious subjects, to become our most faithful, affectionate, and generous allies; and the same sort of parental affection on the one side, and filial respect on the other, might revive between Great Britain and her colonies, which used to subsist between those of ancient Greece and the mother city from which they descended.

Here is the wisdom of a great seer whose prophetic vision, more penetrating than that of Lord Durham two generations later, embraced the British Commonwealth of Nations, which has come into being only in our own time, and the Anglo-American alliance that has been and still is the fond dream of many English-speaking people on both sides of the Atlantic. Unfortunately this wisdom was entirely wasted. The only contribution that Adam Smith made to British thinking on matters of empire was his thesis that the colonies were an economic burden to the mother country. It was years before this contribution was widely accepted, and meanwhile more compelling influences were driving British minds in an anti-imperialist direction.

The loss of the American colonies was a blow to British thinking from which it never recovered. The immediate effect was to shatter the British faith in empire. Englishmen then remembered ruefully what the great Frenchman Turgot had said about colonies: that, like fruit, they ripened and fell. In a few years, also, the collapse of the British Empire was followed by the collapse of every other colonial empire. This made the American Revolution stand out as the beginning of a world movement away from empire, and the lesson of universal experience was not lost upon people in Britain. Another sequel to the

American Revolution tended more specifically to reconcile the British to the recent loss of their colonies and to encourage them to face a future in which they could see little hope for their empire. It was the development of their trade with the United States, which soon proved much more valuable than their trade with the thirteen colonies had ever been. When the thriving commercial intercourse with the new Republic was temporarily stopped as a consequence of the British struggle against Napoleon, by the American embargo of 1808 and the War of 1812, another by-product of the European conflict brought relief to the British. This was the opening of the Latin American market, from which they have never since been excluded. Meanwhile Napoleon's Continental System had brought home to them how much they were dependent on the European market. In other words, the importance of extraimperial trade was growing so that it was beginning to eclipse that of intraimperial trade, and here we find yet another powerful influence at work. The industrial revolution was expanding British production beyond the capacity of British lands to absorb it, thereby building up a pressure that sooner or later would destroy the old colonial system.

On the morrow of Waterloo the climate of opinion in Britain grew less favorable to colonies. Then, a quarter of a century after Adam Smith was laid in his grave, arose the new school of classical economists in England—notably Ricardo, James Mill, and J. R. McCulloch— who built on the foundations that the remarkable Scot had laid. These new masters of the new science reflected and stimulated a widening and deepening interest in its principles and their application; and though they were only incidentally concerned with colonies, as bound up in the mercantile system which they vigorously assailed, their teachings spread the idea that colonies were an economic burden. That they were an economic burden, from the standpoint of public finance, was at the same time gaining recognition in government circles. There was scarcely a colony that did not have to be subsidized out of the Treasury, and the newly acquired ones were the most expensive of all. The drain could not escape attention because the government was then in such desperate financial straits that every item of expenditure was open to question. The staggering cost of the long French war had unbalanced the budget almost hopelessly, parliament revolted against the peacetime continuance of the war-imposed income tax, and the Chancellor of the Exchequer was borrowing heavily to meet the chronic deficit.

The British Empire, however, was not approaching dissolution; for it was something more than a profit and loss account, and those who would reduce it to such terms can never understand it. In an important way that has been too little seen, it resembled, and has continued to resemble, some better-class families. In these families children are an economic liability rather than an asset, yet the parents prefer to spend their money in having and raising them. So was it with Britain. Materially she might be richer without colonies, but they gave her a sort of parental satisfaction which she, being a wealthy country, could afford—even in those years of economic strain and stress. No one in responsible position, and few others, then suggested that the colonies should be cast off.

British opinion, however, was pretty solidly opposed to any increase in the imperial family. More colonies meant more burdens, and Britain did not want them. Again and again she rejected them by repudiating the actions of her own subjects or by refusing the offers of native rulers in various parts of the world, particularly Africa and the islands of the Pacific. The government's policy was definitely nonexpansionist even though there were some extensions of the empire during this period. In 1815 Britain took possession of Ascension and Tristan da Cunha, but these were little volcanic specks in the South Atlantic and they were occupied in order to lock Napoleon more securely in St. Helena. Also, as we have seen, British conquests in India continued despite the desire of London to halt them, until 1818, when they led to a stabilization of the frontier that lasted for nearly a generation, except in the East.

Beyond the confines of India proper, racketeering Burmese conquerors had been erecting a formidable power; and, by seizing the Burmese coastal district of Arakan and overrunning the Indian territory of Assam, they closed in on Bengal from the southeast and the northeast. Scorning the efforts of British embassies to establish friendly relations with them, they swore they would conquer Bengal and sack Calcutta. In the fall of 1823 they attacked; and in the following spring the British, unable to get any reply to repeated demands for redress, declared war against them. It lasted for two years and ended with the British annexation of the two Burmese provinces of Arakan and Tenasserim, which extended right down the eastern shore of the Bay of Bengal, and the creation of a British protectorate over Assam, which gave control of the great Brahmaputra River.

One might imagine that the British were proud of the empire they had gained in India, but they were not. It had ceased to be a paying concern for the Company, and it had become a heavy load of responsibility for the home government. The East India Company had lost the monopoly of trade with India, though not with China, when parliament renewed its charter in 1813; the volume and the profits of its Indian trade had since shrunk while those of its China trade had swelled until the latter were several times larger than the former; and its government of India was being run at a loss that could not be met without drawing on the profits from China. In official British circles there was much skepticism about the future of the British Empire in India. Its early demise was actually prophesied by no less a person than the governor general himself, Lord Hastings. "A time, not very remote, will arrive when England will, on sound principles of policy, wish to relinquish," he wrote in 1818, "the domination which she has gradually and unintentionally assumed over this country."

In the following year, 1819, Singapore was added to the British Empire, but this was a move that surprised and embarrassed both the East India Company, for which it was purchased, and the British government. It was the work of one man, Sir Stamford Raffles. His object in buying from the sultan of Jahore what was then a practically uninhabited mangrove island was to protect the Company's trade with the Malay states and more particularly to secure the vital trade with China. The route of this trade ran through the possessions of the only surviving rivals of the British in the Far East, the Dutch, who threatened to close it. Raffles' master stroke gave the British potential control of it, and his reward was characteristic of that anti-imperialistic age. For this crowning achievement of a remarkably fine career, the governor general of India reproved him, the ministry in London condemned him, and after his death seven years later the Company made his widow pay the expenses of the expedition with which he took possession of Singapore. He had committed a triple indiscretion. He had made a strategic move against the Dutch, he had risked war, and he had acted without specific authority. London was determined to avoid any danger of war, especially with the Dutch, because British policy regarded a strong Netherlands as one of the main pillars of European peace, and to this end positive orders had been sent to the governor general not to provoke the Dutch.

Promptly and vigorously the Dutch challenged the British right to occupy Singapore, the most strategic point within the bounds of their island empire, but it was soon evident that they would not go to war about it. Nevertheless, George Canning, the President of the Board of Control, was prepared to yield the point and evacuate the place if they insisted. The question was not settled until 1824, when an Anglo-Dutch treaty, which took four years to negotiate and was concluded by Canning as foreign secretary, disposed of all outstanding differences between the two powers. Then, in return for writing off £300,000 of a £400,000 debt still owing by the Dutch and for abandoning an old foothold in Sumatra, the British acquired the Dutch posts in India, regained Malacca, which they had twice taken and restored, and got recognition of their title to Singapore. As they already had the island of Penang and a strip of territory, Province Wellesley, on the adjacent mainland, they now possessed, with the islands of Malacca and Singapore, three separate bases on which the future British Malaya was built; but the only man who then had the slightest vision of it was Sir Stamford Raffles, and he was broken for his temerity. Incidentally Penang, which was valued chiefly because it commanded the northern end of the Straits of Malacca, though not so completely as Singapore did the southern end, was costing the Company about £80,000 a year.

There were few other changes in the territorial limits of the British Empire between the fall of Napoleon and the abolition of slavery. Suspicion that France, then recovering from the collapse of her European empire and beginning to erect an empire in Africa, was casting covetous eyes on unappropriated parts of Australia inspired a British assertion of title to the whole of that continent in 1829. In South Africa, the frontier of Cape Colony moved northward with trekking Boers and advanced eastward to provide a narrow unoccupied buffer against hostile native invasions. The Cape was an expensive liability, which the possession of Mauritius and St. Helena rendered less essential than it had been as a station on the way to India. In tropical Western Africa, the Sierra Leone settlement of free blacks became the "white elephant of the colonial empire," as its cost to the British Exchequer rose to be about £100,000 annually; and the posts on the Gold Coast and the Gambia were so worthless, either as centers of trade or as bases for the suppression of the slave trade, that during the 1820's their abandonment was seriously considered.

In the middle of the North American continent a new British colony began to appear in 1812, but it was on what was already British soil and the British government refused to accept responsibility for it. This was the Red River Settlement, which later grew to be the Canadian province of Manitoba. It was a proprietory colony founded as a philan-

thropic and patriotic enterprise by Lord Selkirk on land that the
Hudson's Bay Company deeded to him for the purpose. To the only
rival fur-trading organization, the North West Company of Montreal,
the project was nothing but a mortal blow aimed at it by the English
company; for a successful colony on the Red River would cut the life
line of the Canadian company. As there was no effective government
in that distant region, the leaders of the North West Company took the
law into their own hands and ordered the destruction of the colony.
Twice their half-breed minions drove the settlers off by force—the
second time, in 1816, after considerable bloodshed. Meanwhile, in
spite of Selkirk's appeals for protection, the authorities in Canada and
in England looked the other way; and afterward he found it impossible
to get justice in either country, where there was a strong prejudice in
favor of the North West Company.[1] The whole tragedy has left a stain
on British and Canadian history.

There has been a suspicion that official London was loath to interfere on the prairie because the North West Company was serving imperial interests on the Pacific coast where, between the Russians in the
north and the Spaniards in the south, it was transforming a no man's
land, claimed by the United States as well as by Britain, into a British
fur-trading region. The suspicion appears to be groundless, for out
there it was the Canadian company that had reason for feeling betrayed
by the home government. In 1814 British neglect allowed the Treaty
of Ghent to be so worded that the United States could demand a return
of the Columbia River post that John Jacob Astor had founded in 1811,
to break into the fur business on the west coast, and his agent on the
spot had sold to the Montreal firm in the autumn of 1813.[2] When the
American demand was made in 1815, official London turned a deaf
ear not to Washington but to the Canadian company, which petitioned
in vain for assurance of protection; and early in 1818 Britain hastened
to make formal delivery of the place to the United States, though with-

---

[1] It had great political influence in Canada, where the English company was regarded
as a foreign concern inimical to Canadian interests. One might expect the English
company to enjoy corresponding favor in the mother country; but there the Canadian
company had the general advantage of standing for free enterprise against the trade
monopoly granted to the Hudson's Bay Company by an ancient royal charter, and the
particular advantage of having gained, by astute politics, the ear of the Colonial Office.

[2] On the ratification of the Treaty of Ghent, Simon McGillivray of the North West
Company had an interview with Bathurst and then reported him as declaring "decidedly
that the country in question was not considered as a conquest to be restored under the
treaty, but as a British territory to which the Americans had no just claim."

out any disturbance to the company, in order to forestall an American reoccupation by force. The question of ultimate title to the whole territory was still unsettled, and later in the same year it was adjourned for a decade. This was by the Anglo-American convention of 1818, which made the forty-ninth parallel the international boundary out to the Rocky Mountains and declared that the region beyond should be equally free and open to the nationals of both powers for ten years. A year before this time limit expired, it was extended indefinitely. Evidently London was not much interested in pushing what was an old British claim to the Pacific coast.

London was much more interested in the conditions governing colonial trade than in extending the bounds of the empire, with the result that there was a considerable revision of the old colonial system during the 1820's. This revision was more or less incidental to, and part of, the general movement to revive British trade by liberating it from artificial restrictions. The free trade teachings of the economists were influencing commercial circles and percolating into the minds of those who controlled public policy; and the effect was becoming apparent before the reorganization of the cabinet in 1822, which marked the definite turning of the Tory government from reaction to reform.

In the spring of 1820, when peace had still brought no economic recovery, the House of Commons received a petition from London merchants urging free trade as the proper cure for the depression. The man who framed the petition and gathered its signatures was Thomas Tooke, a disciple of Ricardo, a successful businessman, an able scholar, and later famous as the author of the classic six-volume *History of Prices;* and the man whom he easily persuaded to present the petition was a distinguished member of the Commons and the leading banker of England, Alexander Baring, later Lord Ashburton. The petition declared that freedom from restraint would "give the utmost extension to foreign trade, and the best direction to the capital and industry of the country"; that "the maxim of buying in the cheapest market and selling in the dearest, which regulates every merchant in his individual dealings, is strictly applicable as the best rule for the trade of the whole nation"; that such a policy "would render the commerce of the world an interchange of mutual advantages, and diffuse an increase of wealth and enjoyments among the inhabitants of each state" and that the contrary policy, universally followed, of each country "trying to exclude the productions of other countries, with the specious and well-meant design of encouraging its own productions," inflicted "on the bulk of its subjects, who are consumers, the necessity of submitting to privations in the quantity or quality of commodities" and rendered "what ought to be the source of mutual benefit and harmony among states, a constantly-recurring occasion of jealousy and hostility."

Baring's speech in support of the petition drew "loud cheers from all sides of the House," and in the ensuing debate most of the members who participated, of whom Ricardo was one, eulogized the petition and its principles. On receiving a deputation of the signers, the prime minister concurred with their argument, and shortly afterward he did the same in the House of Lords when, as in the Commons, a select committee was appointed to inquire into the subject; but on both occasions Lord Liverpool held out small hope of government action, for he saw all sorts of obstacles in the way, including the opposition of strong vested interests. Nevertheless, his public endorsement of the theory of free trade and the appointment of these parliamentary committees signalled the beginning of the end of the old mercantilist system, and with it the old colonial system.

Disturbing drafts began to blow with this opening of the door of investigation, and one phase of the colonial system was particularly exposed to attack. It was the colonial timber trade, a child of the Napoleonic War. When the Russian czar met the French emperor at Tilsit and agreed to join in the struggle against Britain, she could no longer depend on the Baltic for naval supplies. As these were as vital to her sea power as *it* was to her independent existence, she turned to her North American colonies and bought security from them. She had to pay heavily for it. Colonial timber was inferior in quality; the longer voyage across the Atlantic tripled the freight charges; and colonial production, which was almost nothing because of these severe handicaps, had to be expanded enormously and quickly. To force capital and labor into the colonial business, the British government clapped heavy duties on foreign timber in 1809, doubled them in 1810, and pushed them still higher in the next two years, thereby giving the colonies a practical monopoly of the timber market in the mother country—at three times the old prices. Under the stimulus of high profits, the woodsman's ax bit furiously into the virgin forests of the colonies, particularly New Brunswick and Upper Canada; and a large North Atlantic timber trade sprang up, which lifted British North America to a new level of prosperity and a new importance in the empire.

On the return of peace the British government continued to buy security in this manner, apparently out of fear of the country's being caught again in the uncertain future and out of justice to the vested interests. Of these, by far the most important in government eyes was shipping, which faced a slump when peace put an end to the need for transports in the public service and to the delays of the convoy system. The maintenance of the preference, together with the increasing British demand for timber, which the industrial revolution doubled in the first two decades of the century, produced a further expansion of the colonial timber trade. By 1820 it employed nearly one quarter of all the tonnage clearing from the ports of the mother country and almost half as much again as the whole West Indian trade. This, however, was not the only result. After Waterloo the heavy price that Britain was still paying for security came more and more under question. When the London merchants prodded parliament into investigating the injuries wrought by artificial restraints on commerce, this new trade, lacking the sanction of long usage and acceptance that other features of the restrictive system had acquired, was particularly vulnerable. It was the exclusive subject of a Commons committee report in 1821.

The shipping interest rushed to the defense of the threatened colonial trade with an imposing battery of arguments. The Baltic trade would employ only half as many ships and sailors, and those mostly foreign. Its resumption would be a betrayal of Britain and her colonies. British shipping would suffer a major disaster. British sea power would be gravely imperiled; for experience had demonstrated the danger of depending upon the Baltic as a source of materials for naval building and repairs, and the other essential of those days—a plentiful supply of skilled seaman—would be greatly reduced by the elimination of the colonial timber trade, which bred them. British manufacturers would lose heavily, because British North America would be deprived of its principal means of paying for imports. These British colonies would have their economy wrecked and their loyalty ruined by the mother country's breach of faith with them, and they would turn to the outstretched arms of their great neighbor, the United States.

None of these evils befell, for the Commons committee, though set on paring down the colonial preference, had no mind to destroy the trade that this preference had called into being. Considerations of justice and security forbade it. What the committee recommended and parliament enacted was a 10 shilling reduction of the foreign timber duty and the imposition of a 10 shilling colonial timber duty, a change which was calculated to raise the revenue and lower the upper limit on prices. It cut the preference to 45 shillings a load or, if allowance was made for the difference in freight charges, to 30 shillings, which still gave colonial timber an ample protection of about 275 per cent in the British market. But the significance of the Timber Act of 1821 should not be measured by its negligible effect on trade. A Tory government and a Tory parliament had begun to shape the national policy according to the requirements of the new industrial society.

The following year, 1822, saw the first revision of the sacred navigation laws, and this too before the reorganization of the cabinet gave greater political power to the rising commercial interests. In so far as this revision modified the old colonial system, it did so only in the New World and largely as the result of pressure from the United States. The trade of Ceylon, Mauritius, and the Cape of Good Hope was comparatively free, and the trade of the East India Company's territories had never been shackled by the navigation system, the outstanding exception being that the traffic between the mother country and these possessions was confined to British vessels. The old colonial system was much more rigid in the western hemisphere, where it had grown up. It excluded foreign ships from British possessions in the West Indies and North America, and it would not allow these colonies to trade with foreign countries even in British ships. Here too there were exceptions, but these had been made only temporarily and to meet emergencies, mostly wartime.

From 1815 the American government sought to extend to British colonies the commercial convention of that year, which reopened the ports of the United Kingdom to American vessels and cargoes free of any discriminating charges on them as such, and American ports to British ships and cargoes on reciprocal terms. London was determined to preserve the colonial monopoly not so much for the sake of the trade as for the shipping that carried it, for the very essence of the British navigation system was the sacrifice of trade on the altar of maritime power. The United States was equally determined to break the colonial monopoly in order to recover the old trade with the West Indies, and likewise for the sake of the freight rather than the exchange of goods. On other matters the two governments were coming together in a spirit of friendly compromise, establishing disarmament on the Great Lakes in 1817 and negotiating the convention of 1818 to settle boundary disputes and a nasty quarrel over American fishing rights in neighboring British territorial waters, all of which throws into grim relief the uncompromising attitude of both governments over this question of navigation. For them the principle at stake was too important for either to yield until it was definitely beaten, and the outcome was a foregone conclusion. The British North American trade was no temptation to Americans because its carriage was beyond their grasp, but they had a lever with which they could pry open the British West Indies.

This lever was the island planters' indispensable need for American supplies, substitutes produced in British North America having proven too scanty and costly. When more than half the tonnage of the United States lay dismantled while American ports were filled with British vessels—many of them engaged in bringing American supplies to the West Indies—Washington grew more importunate in London for a relaxation of the colonial system. When threats of retaliation failed to budge the British government, congress began to pull on the lever. There was a little tug in 1817, and a bigger one in the next year.

The American Navigation Act of 1818 imposed a nonintercourse in British vessels between the United States and ports closed by British law to American vessels. No British ship could enter an American port if, on the way, it had called at a British West Indian or North American colony; and every British ship sailing with cargo from the United States was put under heavy bond not to land any of it in any such colony. The British government immediately readjusted its position to avoid the pressure, by making Halifax and St. John free ports, to which, over a short voyage, American vessels could carry American produce for British vessels to bear to the West Indies over a longer voyage than the prohibited one from the United States. This diversion of the traffic dropped showers of blessing on Nova Scotia and New Brunswick, which had not expected them, and imposed a new burden on the West Indies, which had to pay more for their supplies. British shipping also felt the pinch, for American bottoms got more and more of the direct trade between the United States and the United Kingdom, apparently more than half by 1819. The next pull on the lever, the American Navigation Act of 1820, severed intercourse between the United States and the British West Indies over the new and circuitous route. The pressure on the British sugar colonies then became intolerable, and the British government yielded.

The revision of 1822 permitted importation into designated free ports in the British West Indian and North American colonies of grain, flour, vegetables, livestock, lumber, and naval stores,[3] the produce of

---

[3] But not sugar or fish.

any foreign colony or country in the western hemisphere in vessels of the producing colony or country on equal terms with British vessels. This gave United States shipping a privilege still denied to other foreign shipping, by law if it was European and by fact if it was not, because there was practically no other foreign shipping belonging to this hemisphere. At the same time and by another act, the British West Indian and North American colonies were permitted to have direct trade with foreign ports in Europe and Africa, but under conditions that almost nullified the concession. One confined this traffic to British ships, and another limited colonial imports to a list of specified commodities that would not compete with British goods.

There was nothing enforced or grudging in the reform of the old colonial system that followed. It was the work of William Huskisson, who entered the cabinet during the reorganization of the ministry and, as President of the Board of Trade, had charge of the country's commercial system. He made no secret of the fact that his policy was a return to and development of the commercial liberalism of William Pitt before the French Revolution twisted the Tories into being reactionaries. Huskisson was an eminently practical man, distrustful of doctrinaire ideas, but he was also a statesman with vision. He would allow no rigid subordination of trade to navigation or of colonies to the mother country, formulae of little minds that would defeat their own ends. He would enlarge the ends, which he accepted without question, by enlarging the means. The only sound foundation for a great mercantile marine was an extensive commerce, and the best way to foster such a commerce was to cast off restrictions upon it. Likewise, whatever would tend to increase the prosperity of the colonies was bound, in the long run and in equal degree, to advance the general interests of the parent state. Proceeding on such principles, this liberal imperialist remade the old colonial system.

Huskisson launched his new colonial system, for such it may well be called, in 1825. In the navigation laws as they applied to the colonial empire, he took what had been an unwelcome exception in favor of the United States and elevated it into a desirable general rule. Now the ships of any foreign country that would grant reciprocal rights to British shipping could bring its own produce to any British colony and could carry away the latter's produce to any part of the world that was not British, all intercourse between different parts of the empire being regarded as coasting trade reserved for British bottoms. As the President of the Board of Trade explained to the House of Commons, it was high time to grant this liberty to British colonial trade, if only because nearly all the rest of the New World trade had ceased to be colonial. Its emancipation, having begun in the United States and having recently swept through Latin America, threw an invidious light on the situation of the British colonies. These were still in economic chains, while almost all the other colonies in the western hemisphere had got rid of their corresponding chains by becoming independent. When Huskisson left the Board of Trade, the commerce of the British colonies was virtually as free as that of Scotland.

This Tory reformer also overhauled the imperial tariff structure. He brought the duty on Mauritius sugar down to that levied on the West Indian; and he reduced the duties on many of the minor productions of the West Indies, which were generally raised by free blacks and small white proprietors. He amended the Corn Law so that Canadian wheat, which had been completely shut out of the mother country when the price was low, would always be admitted on the payment of a moderate duty. Otherwise he left intact the preferences enjoyed by colonial produce in the home market. But he made the preferential system bilateral, or rather multilateral, by throwing an imperial tariff ring around the colonies in the New World and the island of Mauritius, but not other British possessions. Mauritius was included out of justice to the West Indies, which had objected to equalization of the sugar duties on the ground that this East Indian colony had greater freedom of commerce. The new duties on the importation of foreign goods into the colonies were a mild substitute for the absolute prohibitions that were part of the monopoly system now discarded; they gave nothing like the protection accorded to colonial goods in the home market, for they were generally low, being only 15 per cent on nonenumerated articles; they were in addition to the small revenue tariffs enacted by the local legislatures, which were on imports irrespective of whether they were British or not; and in accordance with the act of 1778, the proceeds of the new duties were placed at the disposal of the local legislatures. At the same time Huskisson extended to the colonies in the New World the bonded warehousing system as it then existed in the mother country, by which goods could be imported without payment of duty if stored for re-export; and he freed the colonial ports of a heavy burden on their trade, by abolishing the fees collected on ships and cargoes by local officials, from governor down, who had been responsible for the enforcement of the navigation laws, which could now be entrusted to the customs officers.

Viewing these reforms as a whole, Huskisson assured the Commons that the opening of the sugar colonies to traffic with all other countries would afford the West Indies, "in the increased competition and economy of direct trade, a better chance of supplying their wants on reasonable terms, and of finding a demand for their surplus productions." He was more enthusiastic over the contemplated effect on British North America, "an immense country" with great potentialties and a white population that was growing rapidly and had already approached the million mark.

> I cannot doubt, that without any other encouragement than freedom of trade, and a lenient administration, these Provinces will, henceforward, make the most rapid strides towards prosperity;—that connecting their prosperity with the liberal treatment of the Mother Country, they will neither look with envy at the growth of other States on the same Continent, nor wish for the dissolution of old, and the formation of new, political connexions. With a tariff of duties, accounted for to their own treasury, and moreover far lighter than those paid by their neighbours,—with a trade as free,—with their shipping in possession of greater privileges,—themselves in the enjoyment of the same civil rights,—they will not be easily moved to acts by which all these advantages may be placed in jeopardy or danger.

Here he was referring to the pull of the United States, which he feared would be overwhelming if his reforms were not adopted. Even if these colonies were destined to break away from the empire, as then commonly prophesied in England, still would he press on with his policy. It was what the mother country owed to herself and to her children beyond the sea.

> At any rate, let us, as the parent state, fulfil our duties with all proper kindness and liberality. This is true wisdom; affording us, on the one hand, the best chance of perpetuating a solid and useful connexion, and on the other, the best hope if (which God avert!) in the progress of human events, that connexion is ever to be dissolved, that the separation may not be embittered by acrimony and bloodshed; and the certain consolation that, however brought about, it will not have been hastened or provoked, by vexatious interference or oppressive pretensions on our part.

Huskisson was obviously troubled by the shadow of the American Revolution that darkened the minds of Englishmen when they contemplated the empire, and he fought against it. He denied the prevailing British belief that the attempt to tax the old colonies was the primary cause of their revolt. The train of that explosion, he insisted, "had long been laid, in the severe and exasperating efforts of this country, to enforce, with inopportune and increasing vigour, the strictest and most annoying regulations of our Colonial and Navigation Code." His interpretation, shared by contemporary economists, became that of the whole free trade school which regarded the colonies as millstones round the neck of the mother country, and of Americans who looked back and saw the mother country as a millstone round the neck of the colonies. Whether he was right or wrong in this reading of the past, which is a debatable question, his reforms undoubtedly guarded the future against the possibility of another British colonial revolt inspired by such imperial restrictions.

Though British faith in the value and the survival of the empire continued to sink under the pressure of the industrial society that was rising in the mother country, a mass movement had already started that was to regenerate the empire. It was the outpouring of the surplus population of the British Isles to find a larger life in British lands beyond the sea. It contributed enormously to the development of the colonies and to the human ties that bound them to the mother country. But this strengthening of the empire was the unconscious result rather than the conscious purpose of the movement, and it was not until the last quarter of the nineteenth century that the people of Britain discovered that the empire was not on the road to disintegration. Meanwhile, so strong was the influence of the American Revolution, they took for granted that the colonies would break away as soon as they were able to stand by themselves.

The mass migration from the British Isles to the British colonies in the nineteenth century, which transformed the empire, dwarfs into relative insignificance the contribution of population made by any other European power to its colonies. The nearest parallel, which is on a much smaller scale, is that of England in the seventeenth century, when more Englishmen settled overseas than did the combined total of Spaniards, Portuguese, French, and Dutch. Then England ceased to be a colonizing country for several generations. During the eighteenth century, when English emigration was little more than a trickle, the Scottish Highlands and Northern Ireland began to send forth emigrants in considerable numbers. It has been calculated that they were moving to the colonies at the rate of 20,000 a year before the outbreak of the American Revolutionary War. When that war was over this migration was resumed, apparently at a reduced rate. Some Highlanders then turned to British North America, but more seem to have preferred the United States, as did almost all the Irish; and the movement continued fitfully during the long struggle against Revolutionary and Napoleonic France.

The exodus during the years that followed the peace of 1815 was much greater than any that had been known before, and it was only a fraction of what it became in the middle of the century. Unfortunately it is impossible to give even approximate figures for the emigration of the postwar period, because the official records of it are extremely defective. According to these records the two ports of Quebec and New York received thousands more emigrants from the British Isles than the total number who sailed thence for all ports, and there is good reason for believing that the returns of arrivals in Quebec and New York are incomplete. The records of departures from the British Isles covered sailings only from the ports that had customs houses, which means that the figures for England are as accurate as those for Scotland and Ireland are not. It was notorious that untold thousands of Scots and Irish embarked in countless little bays and harbors where no prying official was at hand to enforce customs laws and shipping regulations.

Bearing in mind how grossly inadequate are the customs house returns, we can get from them some idea of the outward movement. They show an emigration of nearly 200,000 during the first ten years of peace (1815–1824), more than 120,000 during the next five years, and over 240,000 during the next three years, a total of more than 550,000 down to the end of 1832. Nearly 340,000 of them are entered as going to British North America, where Upper Canada absorbed the largest number, and a little over 200,000 to the United States. There was no British emigration to South Africa until 1820 when, according to these records, a thousand went to the Cape where, according to more reliable sources, this year saw the arrival of five thousand to form the new settlement at Albany on the eastern frontier. Few others followed them, for this experiment was very discouraging. Australia attracted an annual immigration of less than a thousand until 1828, and the official figure was temporarily raised to just over two thousand in 1829 by the likewise discouraging establishment of the Swan River Colony, the beginning of Western Australia. The pull of North America was immensely greater because of its population and proven wealth, its constant and large traffic with Britain which provided the only facilities for much emigration overseas, the cheapness of the passage which was sometimes as low as 40 shillings in a timber vessel, and the shortness of the voyage, the trials of which were then a serious consideration for all but the favored few.

No one cause was responsible for this outpouring of population. The demobilization of the armed forces was a factor, but apparently only a minor one. More important was the distress occasioned by the withdrawal of the enormous stimulus that war had given to economic activity, and the unemployment produced by the continuance of the industrial revolution with its substitution of machines for men in production. Here, however, we have to exercise caution, because the people who were most oppressed were the least numerous among the emigrants, and as the century wore on emigration became a flood though the country was much more prosperous. From Waterloo to the Reform Bill there was some pauper emigration, subsidized by the government and by voluntary societies organized for the purpose; and because it was thus publicized, it has attracted attention out of all proportion to its relative size. The unassisted emigration was at least ten times greater, and in so far as the pressure of hard times drove these people forth it was by persuading them that they had better use at least some of their capital in getting out while they could still afford it.

The overwhelming proportion of emigrants who paid their own way also upsets the old theory that the Irish and the Scots were still migrating in larger numbers than the English because England had a poor relief system, Scotland only the rudiments of one, and Ireland none at all. Another mistaken notion has been that a difference in the rate of population growth largely explains the disparity in the rate of emigration from the different parts of the British Isles. From 1821, the date of the first reliable census of all the United Kingdom,[4] the Irish rate of population increase was slightly less than the English and more than the Scottish; and careful investigation indicates that the same was true before this time. How then can we account for the disparity in the emigration rate? England could best support its annual increase because it was by far the richest of the three countries and it was the most industrialized. In Scotland most of the people lived in the Lowlands, where industrialization had pretty well kept pace with that of England;

---

[4] England	11,261,437
Ireland	6,801,827
Scotland	2,093,456
Wales	717,438
Army, Navy, etc.	319,300
Total	21,193,458

but the Highlands were untouched by this development, and there the land was very poor. Ireland was in the worst way of all. English policy had long since blighted its industries and absentee landlords its agriculture, and its population was rapidly outgrowing the means of subsistence. Indeed, for many years Irishmen had been migrating in large numbers not only across the Atlantic but also to England and Scotland where, as cheap labor, they kept wages down but got more than they could have earned at home.

Conditions in the British Isles are only half the reason for the swelling emigration from them. People were drawn as well as pushed out, and what attracted them was the opportunity to improve their lot across the sea. To the average emigrant it was the call of a new world where wages were higher and the ownership of land was within the reach of all, where a few years of hardship and toil offered an economic independence that was denied at home. It was the appeal of adventure and hope for themselves and their children and their children's children. Though many emigrants, having spent their all on the voyage, needed assistance when they landed, they almost always found it—and their feet—for they arrived in a land where they were more needed than they had been at home, and they were of the stuff that made good. Their more fortunate fellows, who included a surprising number of Highlanders, each of whom managed to take out £150 or more, were of course no less welcome. At the end of this period, the British government's agent for emigrants in Quebec reported that in one year the new settlers brought into Canada a total capital of £1,000,000. Whether this be an exaggeration or not, it is clear that those who were migrating from the mother country were benefiting themselves and the land to which they went, and this double benefit increased the human pull across the Atlantic. With temporary spurts and lags due to passing conditions, emigration from the British Isles was gathering momentum from its own success.

What was the government's policy on emigration, which had long been officially discouraged on the ground that it would weaken the mother country, whose interests were paramount over those of the colonies? In the last decade of the eighteenth century private individuals at home, and more or less official voices in some of the colonies, began to urge the government to divert to British North America the stream of population that was flowing from the British Isles to the United States. It was not until the War of 1812 revealed the need for British settlers in Upper Canada, however, that official London began to discard the traditional policy of frowning on emigration. In 1813 Bathurst proposed a plan to take advantage of the Scottish urge to emigrate. As soon as peace returned and he could find the money, he would strengthen the British position in Upper Canada by planting Highlanders there. Parliament had not been consulted when this scheme was launched in 1815, with the interesting result that in the House of Commons the government was called upon to refute the charge of encouraging emigration and two members of the ministry denied it, asserting that the object was merely "to direct those determined to emigrate and change their destination from the United States to His Majesty's possessions." This was the first of several experiments in government colonization with Scots and Irish in Canada down to 1825. Each was humanly successful but too expensive to be adopted on a large scale.

The man who came nearest to working out a positive and coherent policy of emigration was Goulburn's successor as parliamentary under-secretary of state for the colonies, R. J. Wilmot Horton. His industry was tireless, and unfortunately often tiresome to others. On taking office he soon discovered what a load the mother country was bearing in the colonial establishments. The cause, he found, was "the utter inefficiency of our colonies, as to self-support and self-defense," and the obvious remedy was "to give them an addition of population more rapid than their natural rate of increase."

Like other public-spirited men of the day, Horton was also gravely concerned over the problem of population in the British Isles, the great discussion of which had been started by Malthus, whose famous *Essay*, first published in 1798, ran through six editions before his death in 1834. The discussion was, of course, immensely stimulated by the widespread popular distress of the times and the staggering cost of poor relief, which was steadily rising. It was almost universally admitted that there was a "redundant population," but there was no consensus of opinion on what should be done about it. The most generally accepted solution was emigration; but Malthus and others argued that this would only create a vacuum soon to be filled by the natural increase, which was ever pressing beyond the point of subsistence, and as a rule the advocates of emigration were so intent on getting rid of the surplus population that they cared naught whither it went.

Horton put the domestic and the colonial problems together, the surplus of population at home and the deficit of population in the overseas possessions, and sought by emigration to make "the redundant

labour and the curse of the mother country, the active labour and blessing of the colonies." Those who could not find employment at home
would find it waiting for them in the colonies or, if it did not exist there,
they could create it there by taking up virgin land. He would not dump
paupers on the colonies, but would transplant them, supplying them
with capital—not in money but in kind—with which to become established so that they would not only support themselves but would also
provide labor for others. The cost, he calculated, would be much less
than the six million pounds or so that were annually poured down the
drain of poor relief at home, which would then be stopped, and the investment of the smaller sum would pay perpetual dividends to British
society as a whole. Horton could see no limits to the possibilities of his
system, which, once set in motion, might go on indefinitely transforming a social liability into a social asset and giving an imperial direction
to the stream of voluntary emigration, "until all the colonies of the
British Empire are saturated, and millions added to those who speak the
English language, and carry with them the liberty and the laws and
the sympathies of their native country."

Parliamentary committees, over which the guiding hand of Horton
was more and more evident, made exhaustive inquiries into the state of
the poor at home and collected voluminous evidence of enormous latent potentialities in the colonies. But the undersecretary of state could
not convince his fellow members of the House of Commons that he had
the right policy—that the redundant population of the mother country
should be used to develop the colonies. Neither could he convert his
seniors in the ministry. Why did he fail? It may be said that the fault
lay in him, for the task demanded qualities that he did not possess. His
ideas were much bigger than his personality, his powers of exposition
were as weak as his persistence was strong, and his contemporaries
thought him a bore. But it would have taken a marvelous man to get
the action he wanted.

The spirit of the times was against Horton. When he encountered
the argument that the addition of population to British North America
would only hasten its annexation to the United States of America, this
was believed rather than his prophetic reply that the effect would be
the very opposite. Though the colonies wanted more population, they
objected to schemes of "shoveling out paupers" upon them, and this
criticism was caught up at home. Indeed there were not a few who
were skeptical or even hostile to the whole idea of emigration. Michael
Sadler, the Christian socialist, voiced the opinion of many when he

fought it as "unnatural, impolitic, and cruel." Was poverty a crime, and did it have to be punished by transportation? William Cobbett, the radical leader, attacked emigration as a mean and dishonest substitute for domestic reforms that were long overdue. Still others saw in emigration no permanent relief for Scotland or England until they could somehow be protected against the invasion of cheap Irish labor. Of the many who favored emigration, Horton was almost if not quite alone in maintaining that it should be at public expense. This seemed like a frightful gamble. If there had been much faith in the colonial empire, there might have been more willingness to run the risk, but this faith was lacking. The day of the Little Englander was dawning, when the concept of British interests was confined to the interests of the British Isles as separate from the British Empire. It was so characteristic of that day that even Sir Robert Peel wrote in 1824: "Extensive settlement in South America might as effectually serve British interests as if they were formed in North America." It was also characteristic of the age that the men who served on the committees mentioned above were much less interested in building up the colonies than they were in reducing the distress at home, and that when at last Horton got a favorable committee report in 1827 it was almost immediately shelved because a return of prosperity relieved the pressure of this distress. Horton could not succeed because he was struggling against the rising tide of anti-imperialism.

IV THE ERA OF REFORM

VI THE ERA OF REFORM

CHAPTER XIV

The Flood of Reforms in Britain

BRITAIN HAD never seen such a flood of reforms as came tumbling after the reform of parliament in 1832, and never did it see the like again. There was scarcely any phase of the nation's life that was not seriously affected. Indeed, it is very doubtful if any other country at any time has carried through such a mass of sweeping reforms without a violent overthrow of the existing government. Taken in conjunction with the reform of parliament, it was a stable and orderly British version of the unstable and disorderly French Revolution that began in 1789.

It is also worthy of note that these reforms stirred little bitterness between the two political parties, for they too were profoundly changed. The Tories, with the exception of a few rare fossils that managed to survive, had enough sense to realize that they had to move with the times, which were moving pretty fast. Under the wise leadership of Sir Robert Peel, the Tory party was quickly transformed into the Conservative party, which competed on fairly even terms with the Whigs, now becoming Liberals, for the support of the enfranchised middle class. So it came to pass that one party was about as liberal as the other, they alternated in office, and the great reforms of this era were not carried by party divisions. Therefore we need not bother with party politics in considering the radical reconstruction of these stirring years.

The reforms that distinguish this period, which lasted from the early thirties to the late forties, are so numerous and so varied that it almost makes one dizzy to look at them as they come pouring forth. But we can reduce them to some semblance of order by grouping them according to their general character under the following heads: the reform of local government; social reform, including labor legislation; economic reform, by which the new industrial society was freed and organized for its more efficient functioning; and the reform of the empire, in which we can see the modern British Commonwealth of Nations beginning to take shape. In this chapter we shall consider each of these in turn until we come to the last, which will be examined in the next chapter.

Municipal government was revolutionized, and it was high time that this was done. We have sometimes blushed over the corruption in our own American cities, but we never saw anything so bad as what was common in England until this great reform. The government of the old towns rested upon royal charters that were centuries old and had been seldom if ever revised. As a consequence, the old towns had almost all fallen into the hands of petty local oligarchies that were utterly irresponsible and thoroughly corrupt. The council was commonly a self-perpetuating body with full control over the property and finances of the corporation. The new towns, created by the industrial revolution, were in a worse predicament. They had no charters and, therefore, no municipal government. This was such an intolerable condition that in many of them local authorities with taxing power had been created by private acts of parliament for specific purposes, such as caring for the streets and the drains.

The reform of parliament made the reform of municipal government inevitable, for the majority in the House of Commons then came to depend on the support of the urban middle class; and one of the first steps taken by the government after the election at the end of 1832 was to appoint a royal commission to explore the problem. In America there is nothing quite like this favorite and most useful British device for approaching a difficult and complicated problem of government. A royal commission is an independent body of men picked for their special competence to undertake the required investigation and to advise on what should be done. It usually includes members of both houses and all parties, and also men from outside parliament. Its recommendations, which are made public, do not bind the government in any way; but as a general rule the government follows them because they are the best advice available.

After an exhaustive inquiry that continued until 1835, a report was submitted that served as the basis of the Municipal Corporations Act of the same year. With the exception of London, whose citizens had preserved their democratic freedom from mediaeval times, the act established a uniform system of self-government for all towns and cities: a council elected by all the ratepayers, and a mayor and aldermen chosen by the councilors from their own body. Now that parliament had taken in hand the regulation of municipal government, it was easy, by subsequent legislation, to enlarge and vary the powers of these corporations to meet their particular needs. From the very beginning the new system was a huge success, and thenceforth municipal government in Britain has been as efficient and pure as it had been the reverse. Indeed, it seems to have attracted a finer type of citizen than it has in the British dominions and in the United States.

This revolution in local government was confined to the towns and cities, where the growing majority of the population dwelt. For another half century rural society continued to be ruled by justices of the peace, who were local squires. It was not until 1888, shortly after the rural laborer was enfranchised, that parliament endowed the counties with elected councils. Nevertheless, rural self-government began to appear in this earlier period as a by-product of the reform of the poor law. For this reason, and more particularly because the reform of the poor law was undertaken to substitute efficiency for inefficiency in local administration, the subject fits in here better than in social reform, to which of course it also belongs.

The administration of poor relief had become like a millstone around the neck of England. The vicious Speenhamland policy of supplementing wages out of the local rates had not only kept wages down but had also pushed rates up to an alarming degree and had pauperized an enormous section of the population. In one parish the annual levy had risen from £10 in 1801 to £367 in 1832; and in another, 104 of the 139 inhabitants were paupers. Taking the country as a whole, we find one seventh of the people had become dependent on the rates, which totaled £8,500,000 a year. The evil was not wholly the result of the Speenhamland system. It also grew out of the law, which was centuries old, that made each parish responsible for its own poor and prevented them from leaving it in search of work.

Something drastic had to be done, and there were many remedies proposed; but the problem was so involved and politically so dangerous that responsible statesmen felt baffled by it. Therefore the government appointed a royal commission, which tackled the problem in a most thorough manner. The result was a new poor law that completely changed the whole system.

The pauperization of the working class was rigorously stopped to the immense relief of the ratepayer by this act of 1834, which revived a principle that had been followed without question for two centuries

until discarded for that of Speenhamland. It denied public relief to
able-bodied poor unless they submitted to the test of confinement in a
workhouse, where conditions of life and labor were so hard that any
other employment seemed good in comparison; and it allowed aid to be
given outside the workhouse only to those who were incapable of working. The law provided that this principle should come back into full
operation, not immediately but at the end of two years in order that
able-bodied paupers might have time to find their own feet. Out of
justice to them, the law also repealed the restriction upon their freedom
of movement to find employment.

The act created a new set of units and a new set of authorities for
the administration of poor relief. The old units, the parishes, were too
small to provide proper workhouses; and the burden of the poor rested
most unequally upon them, almost in inverse ratio to their ability to
bear it. The old authorities, the justices of the peace and the parish
vestries, had likewise proved to be very unsatisfactory for this business.
They had made such a sorry mess of it. Now the whole country was
organized in larger units known as "unions," for they were unions of
neighboring parishes, and each union had a "board of guardians" to
administer the poor law. Unlike the justices and the vestries, from
whom they took over this function, the poor law guardians were elected
by the ratepayers; thus, in the interest of efficiency, local representative
government made its first appearance throughout rural England.

Very striking is yet another feature of this poor law reform of 1834,
a feature that reflects a new and most important development in government. Some guiding hand was necessary to arrange the grouping of
the parishes in unions and to start the new system working properly.
For this purpose a central body of poor law commissioners was created.
It was intended to be only temporary. But the functions it performed
in advising and supervising the local boards of guardians were so valuable that it grew into a permanent department of the national government. Here was something new and vital in modern administration:
local representative bodies operating under the general control of a
central bureaucracy. It was the marriage of two principles that people
have often thought were irreconcilable—liberty and order.

Among the social reforms of this era, one of the most outstanding
has been described in a previous chapter—the abolition of slavery in
the British Empire a generation before it came in the United States.
It was very fitting that the aged Wilberforce, whose failing health
had obliged him to retire from the House of Commons and the leader-

ship of the long crusade against slavery, lived long enough to see the triumph. While the emancipation bill was being passed, he died content and was buried amid the other great in Westminster Abbey. His mantle descended on the shoulders of a young man, another Tory member of the House of Commons, who had just assumed the leadership in a new crusade, for which he sacrificed all other ambition. This was Anthony Ashley Cooper, who bore the courtesy title of Lord Ashley until, on the death of his father in 1851, he became the seventh Earl of Shaftesbury. His crusade, which made him the most venerated social reformer of the nineteenth century, was to redeem the lot of the oppressed white workers in industrial England.

Britain blazed the trail of modern labor legislation, which is what one might expect of the first country to be industrialized, and Ashley was chiefly responsible for forcing the pace of this legislative activity. The going was never easy, and at first it was particularly difficult. The opposition was large and strong. Manufacturers opposed out of interest, Whigs out of principle, and Tories out of instinct. Though some of the more enlightened millowners welcomed the reform, most of them fought bitterly against this legislative interference with their business. Many Whig or Liberal members of parliament were such firm believers in the gospel of free enterprise, then commonly called *laissez faire,* that it made them defend even the industrial slavery of children; and many members of the other party were still blinded by their Tory distrust of all change. But conscience and pity prevailed over profits, principle, and prejudice.

The new crusade was launched with an attack on the crying abuse of child labor. Contrary to a popular notion, child labor was not an innovation of the industrial revolution, which only gathered it together, like adult labor, under new conditions that attracted attention as the old conditions could not. Children were commonly toiling in the factories for thirteen or fourteen hours a day—a longer average than that of slaves in the West Indies—from the time they were six years old. This practice looks much worse now than it did then. Parents were glad to have their children enter the mills to eke out the family income—the larger the family, the better. Moreover, there were then no schools for such youngsters to go to. Popular education had yet to be developed, to take care of them when legislation shut them out of the factories. It was their social betters who, under the influence of the humanitarian movement, were so aroused by the plight of the poor children that they forced parliament to legislate against this evil.

The Factory Act of 1833, based on the work of another royal commission, was the beginning of the modern statutory code that regulates the conditions of labor in all industries. It prohibited the employment of any children under the age of nine and limited the hours of labor for all who were under eighteen—to nine hours if they were not thirteen years old, and to twelve if they were over. This was the first act of its kind to have teeth in it. The act of 1802, mentioned in an earlier chapter, and another act that had been passed in 1819 had remained quite harmless because the responsibility for their enforcement had been left to the justices of the peace, country squires who had neither the interest nor the capacity that was required for this purpose. The act of 1833 introduced a principle that was new in the English-speaking world—by providing for the inspection of factories by a staff of paid government officials who had power to enforce the regulations.

This provision was not regarded as a temporary expedient, like the creation of the poor law commissioners in the following year. It was intended to be permanent. It was the real beginning, the first in any self-governing country, of a central bureaucracy that was to carry effective state intervention into the daily life of the nation.

Further labor legislation was simply a question of time and pressure. In 1840, Ashley secured a law prohibiting the employment of children as chimneysweeps, a ghastly business; and he succeeded in getting a royal commission appointed to investigate conditions in the mines, which proved to be even blacker. Down in the bowels of the earth, where the atmosphere was so bad that a candle would not burn, women and children had to crawl through water along passages scarcely more than two feet high—the thickness of many seams—dragging heavy loads of coal to which they were harnessed like beasts of burden. Brute force commonly ruled in the mines, many of which were veritable pits of iniquity.

The revelations of the commission's report, submitted early in 1842, were so horrible that parliament lost no time in responding to Ashley's appeal. He demanded the exclusion of all women and of all children under thirteen from employment underground and the extension of government inspection to the mines. The owners stoutly resisted this interference with their industry, asserting that they would be ruined unless they could use boys as young as eight, and they were able to force an amendment of Ashley's bill so that boys from ten to thirteen could be employed for three days a week.

Turning back to the factories, Ashley wrung from parliament in

1844 a law limiting women's work to twelve hours a day, reducing from nine to six and a half those of children under thirteen, and imposing regulations to prevent injury by dangerous machinery. Two years later he lost his seat in the House of Commons for supporting free trade, but his troublesome ghost was still there and was largely responsible for the enactment of what has always been regarded as an outstanding landmark in the history of labor legislation. This Ten Hours Bill of 1847 was so framed that, in reducing to ten the hours for women and "young persons" under eighteen, it had the practical effect of likewise limiting the working day for most men in factories, since these could not be run by men's labor alone.

During these same years the state began to "meddle" in education too. The schooling of poor children had been left almost entirely to the churches. It began in 1780 when Robert Raikes, a newspaper proprietor in Gloucester, started a school on Sunday, the only free day, for youngsters engaged in industry. He used the columns of his newspaper to spread the idea, and soon there were Sunday schools all over the country. They had little resemblance to our modern anemic Sunday schools. Though they gave religious instruction, their main function was to teach reading and writing, and generally to impart the rudiments of an education to poor children and also to their elders. It was an expression of the humanitarian movement of the time.

Having thus entered the field of popular education, the churches soon began to open schools on weekdays; during the Napoleonic wars two rival systems were established, one sponsored by the established Church of England and the other by the Nonconformists. Both depended on pupil teachers, an easy solution of the problem of expense. Their rivalry attracted benefactions and stimulated their growth but discouraged state activity in the field. The state entered in 1833, very modestly, with a small annual grant for the school buildings of the two societies. This was steadily increased, and in 1839 a government committee was appointed to supervise the distribution of the money, which meant the introduction of a staff of inspectors to visit the schools and report on them. And thus, in this age of breathless reform, we see the beginning of the later system of national education, with its combination of local management and central control.

It was then, also, that the state began to take an active interest in public health, thanks to the cholera epidemics of 1831 and 1848 and to the agitation of Edwin Chadwick. This outstanding poor law commissioner, who had been the principal author of the reform of 1834, knew as no other man how appalling were sanitary conditions in all urban centers, and he was consumed with reforming zeal. When the dread Asiatic disease hit England a second time, he had little difficulty in persuading parliament to pass the first Public Health Act. This measure of 1848 set up a central Board of Health authorized to establish local Boards of Health with extensive powers. Here again we see the new development of administration: a central bureaucracy assisting and assisted by local bodies.

Many other reforms of the time were effected by the growing humanitarian spirit. It would be tedious to list them all, but we should notice a few. By the early thirties the milder criminal code that Peel had so recently inaugurated came to be regarded as too severe, with the result that by 1841 parliament had abolished the death penalty for all but the gravest crimes. Persons accused of felonies were at last permitted to be represented by counsel, and imprisonment for debt disappeared almost entirely. Impressment for the navy was abandoned, and flogging in the army practically ended. Even dumb creatures found legislative pity, which prohibited such cruel sports as cockfighting and the baiting of bulls, bears, badgers, or other animals.

Of the economic reforms of this era, one group of measures dealt with the organization of capital. This was a highly important matter in Britain, then the industrial, commercial, and financial center of the world. It was at this time that the British banking system received its modern form. The heart of it is the Bank of England, the oldest bank in existence anywhere, having been founded in 1694. In return for advancing a large loan to the government, it received a monopoly. Private banks were also allowed, but none could get a charter, and none could be operated by a company or by a partnership of more than six members.

By 1800, when the United States had twenty-eight banks, Britain had them by the hundred. Among them was the largest merchant-banking house in the world, run by the Baring brothers, grandsons of a Lutheran pastor in the German city of Bremen, and sons of an immigrant who had made a fortune in the manufacture of cloth. Most of the private banks, however, were small local concerns. As the Bank of England was content to be a bankers' bank and the financial agent of the government, private banks handled practically all the ordinary business of commerce and industry, and they issued their own notes. Because the country was off gold from 1797 to 1821, and the Bank of England abandoned the issue of notes for £1 and £2 while the private banks continued to issue them, these smaller notes became common currency, filling the gap between silver and the Bank of England's £5 notes.

Everything went well until the depression precipitated by the ending of the long war with France. Then within two years about 240 banks failed, a quarter of the total number. But it was not until after another blow—a financial panic that ruined some 70 banks in 1825—that the reform of the law governing banking began. It continued until the middle forties, by which time the principles of a much stronger system were established.

One weakness had been that most banks were too small to provide adequate security. Larger banks with more capital were needed. Therefore the ban on joint-stock banks was removed. At first they were permitted only beyond a radius of sixty-five miles from London, to protect the monopoly of the Bank of England; but in 1833 this restriction was also lifted, under a condition to be noted presently. The result was that big banks multiplied, they ate up the little ones, and branch banking became the rule. This reorganization was a healthy process that was continued in the relation between the new company banks, as weaker ones were absorbed by their stronger rivals. In 1844, also, parliament prescribed regulations for the organization and operation of banks, such as requiring a minimum capital of £100,000 and the periodic auditing and publication of accounts.

The other great weakness in the system had been an excessive issue of bank notes. The very first reform, that of 1825, cut at this by stopping the issue in denominations of less than £5. The return of gold into circulation had made possible this elimination of the great bulk of the paper currency; and it was not until the First World War, when gold was again withdrawn from circulation, that smaller notes reappeared in England.[1] The right of issue was also withheld from joint stock banks in the London circle from the time they were permitted there, the condition of the 1833 law referred to above; and eleven years later, in 1844, the law was greatly tightened for all banks, including the Bank of England. Its issue business was then divorced from its banking business, the demands of which had regulated the issue, in order to base its note circulation on a firmer foundation. Now the volume of its notes was not to exceed the value of the bullion in its coffers plus a fixed amount covered by government securities. The

---

[1] They had continued in Scotland.

new law restricted the issues of other banks to existing amounts and required these banks to publish weekly reports. It also provided that if any bank failed, or was amalgamated, or changed its character, its right of issue would automatically pass to the Bank of England. This provision, together with the prohibition of new banks of issue, gradually eliminated all issues save that of the Bank of England.

Even before this great reform of 1844, the banking system had gained such strength that there were scarcely any bank failures in Britain during the international financial crisis of 1837–38, which caused all the banks in the United States to stop payment and 180 of them to fail completely. Many other British firms, however, crashed in that panic; and the result was another valuable reform. It gave birth to the limited liability company in Britain.

The industrial and commercial development of the country had been achieved in spite of severe handicaps that were now to be removed. Back in 1720, England had a terribly bad headache from indulging in the worst fit of commercial speculation in her history; to prevent the like from ever happening again, parliament passed the "Bubble Act," so called after the South Sea Bubble that burst at that time. This act imposed severe penalties on all who got mixed up with joint stock speculations, and it prohibited the formation of companies with transferable shares unless they were incorporated by royal charter or act of parliament, which was a very difficult and expensive procedure. In time this act became a dead letter—long before it was repealed in 1825—and unincorporated companies flourished; but they had no legal existence, which meant that they could neither sue nor be sued, and they were governed by the common law, which made each member liable to the whole extent of his fortune for all the debts of a firm.

Incorporation, which gave a company legal existence, was made easier in 1826, and much more so in 1844, when it became a relatively cheap and simple process of registration in a government office. Yet neither of these reforms altered the law concerning liability. Limitation of liability to the actual investment in shares was introduced in 1837 under certain special conditions, which became general twenty years later; and every company organized on this principle was required to have its name end with the word "Limited," a provision that was later adopted throughout the British Empire.

Other economic reforms of this period had to do with communications, and one of these measures was so enormously valuable and yet so extremely simple that from Britain it "spread like wildfire over the civilized world." The centenary of its inauguration in 1840 would doubtless have seen world-wide celebrations in honor of the benefactor who conceived this reform—if Hitler had not rudely intervened.

Rowland Hill had a strong mind in a weak body. When sickness obliged him to retire from a short but brilliant career as a schoolmaster, he studied postal statistics. He then discovered that distance made practically no difference in the cost of the mail service, the chief expense being at the two ends; and he also calculated that the purpose of the government monopoly, which was taxation, was defeating itself by the imposition of heavy charges. Therefore he began to urge a uniform and low rate—one penny—for all letters within the country, and he suggested the postage stamp as a cheap and convenient device. The postal authorities ridiculed the ideas of this outsider, but the public backed them and the government adopted them, appointing him to supervise the introduction of the new system. For the great boon he conferred on mankind, he was later knighted and pensioned and buried in Westminster Abbey.

It is also interesting, in light of the problems raised in our own days, to see how that age of British reform reacted to the coming of the railways in the thirties and forties. They were all built wholly by private enterprise, which presents quite a contrast to developments on the continent of Europe, where government railways have been common from the very beginning, and in America, where public subsidies were most generous. Nevertheless, the idea of state control was strongly present in Britain, and it was written into the statute book. In 1840 a government department was established to supervise the railways, and its powers were soon enlarged. These included authority to validate railway by-laws, to inspect accounts and lines, to prevent the operation of lines that did not pass inspection, and to regulate rates and fares. There was even legislative provision for nationalizing the railways, though it was not carried out.

The crowning economic reform of the era was a complete reversal of the country's fiscal policy—the abandonment of protection in favor of free trade. It was the economic counterpart, and sequel, of the political and constitutional revolution of 1832; for protection was the policy of the dethroned landed class, and free trade was in the interest of the new industrial society.

The core of protection was the Corn Law, which taxed the food of the many for the profit of the few. Though maintained for the benefit of agriculture, this law was a burden even upon most of the people engaged in agriculture because, as we have seen, they were merely hired laborers. There would have been a different story to tell if Britain had been, like France, a country of peasant proprietors. As it was, the agricultural revolution had narrowed the so-called agricultural interest to a small class who could no longer control parliament.

To industrial Britain the Corn Law was a grievous burden. It increased the cost of production and it restricted markets. Free importation of foreign food would enable both employer and employee to get more for the wages that the one paid and the other received, and it would benefit both by increasing the foreign demand for British goods. Every restraint on purchases from abroad was a restraint on sales abroad. This consideration, of course, hit more than the Corn Law. It hit the whole protective system, and with growing force for another reason. Britain was taking the lead as the one great creditor nation of the world. As payment could be made only in goods, her policy of protection was making it more difficult for her debtors to pay what they owed, as well as to buy what she could sell to them. In short, it was cramping her prosperity. Here and there it might profit a few, but only at the expense of the many. British goods that could not stand against foreign competition at home could much less meet it abroad, and the country would be better off to let others produce such goods in exchange for what she could produce more economically.

The conversion of Britain to free trade came as a result of two movements that were unrelated until they reached their climax at the same time. One was a popular agitation started by a group of manufacturers who formed the Anti-Corn Law League in 1838. The leaders were Richard Cobden and John Bright, a remarkable team, for the one appealed to the head while the other appealed to the heart, Cobden being a master of calm persuasive reason and Bright of moving oratory. For eight years, until the victory was won, the League conducted a publicity campaign that has never been equalled in Britain or perhaps in any other country, denouncing the iniquity of the Corn Law and preaching the gospel of free trade. With ample financial resources, and aided by the new penny post, the League sent out speakers everywhere and all the time, and it flooded the country with its pamphlets, until it became a great power in the land.

The other movement that pushed Britain into adopting free trade was of a very different character. Its mainspring was the financial need of the government, and here we have to touch upon party politics. The Whig, or Liberal, administration that ruled through the thirties sank into a desperate position because it could not balance the budget. To get out of the hole, the government increased the customs and excise rates by 5 per cent, but the revenue did not respond; and so in the spring of the following year, 1841, the Whigs made a timid move to raise the revenue by lowering the tariff on sugar and corn, or wheat. This led to defeat in the House of Commons and in the general election that followed. Then Peel came into office as head of a protectionist government. The accumulated deficits of five successive years were a challenge to him, and he tackled the problem boldly, taking charge of the budget himself.

Peel sought a solution in a careful revision of the tariff to make it yield more. He began where the Tory revision of the twenties had left off, and so had a good precedent; but before he knew it he was moving pretty straight toward free trade. The reason was that he was after revenue, and the principle of a revenue tariff is quite contrary to the principle of a protective tariff, though many politicians and other interested parties have done their best to confuse them—and the public. The purpose of a protective tariff is to keep goods out, goods that might be taxed if allowed to come in; whereas the purpose of a revenue tariff is to collect as much money as possible, which means encouraging goods to come in so that they may be taxed. Any protection discourages importation; and to avoid protection while raising a revenue by customs, the same rates should be levied in the form of excise duties on articles produced at home, so that if a tax is laid on any article it will be collected equally on all that is consumed in the country irrespective of origin, foreign or domestic. As this was the system that Britain was to adopt, and to maintain with slight modification until the great depression of the 1930's, it will be seen that she did not abolish the tariff when she abandoned protection. She simply took the protective principle out of the tariff so that the tariff would produce the greatest possible revenue.

Peel's first budget, that of 1842, assured a surplus by reviving the income tax repealed at the end of the Napoleonic war; under this cover it abolished almost all export duties and effected a general reduction of import duties. The rates on raw materials, some of which had been considerable, were cut almost to nothing; the new upper limit was 5 per cent, while the new maximum for partly manufactured goods was 12 per cent, and on fully manufactured, 20 per cent, in place of the 30 prescribed in the twenties. It was frankly an experiment for three years, and the result was most encouraging. Trade picked up and the

revenue jumped up. Therefore, early in 1845, Peel decided to go
further and, getting a renewal of the income tax for another three
years, he vigorously slashed away more duties.

This budget of 1845 was carried only after a bitter struggle, for the
Anti-Corn Law League, now near its climax, had roused the protectionists and there was grave uneasiness in the Conservative ranks over the
course their leader was taking. Though in theory still a protectionist,
in practice Peel was abandoning the principle upon which he had come
to power. The malcontents, who staged a revolt, were headed by a man
who had hitherto attracted attention only as a fop and a fashionable
novelist and now leaped into political fame. This was Benjamin Disraeli, born a Jew and brought up a Christian, who was to be the most
brilliant Conservative leader of the century. He raised a laugh at Peel's
expense by declaring that he "had caught the Whigs in bathing and
walked away with their clothes." The jibe was dishonest, for, as we
have just seen, the downward revision of the tariff was based on Tory
precedent. But desperate politicians are apt to be reckless, and Disraeli
was championing a lost cause. The violence of his attacks grew savage,
as he accused the prime minister of betraying parliament and called his
government "an organized hypocrisy."

Meanwhile Peel was assailed from the opposite side of the house,
particularly by Cobden, for his adherence to protection; and it was
obvious that the Conservative leader was on the edge of conversion.
While listening to one of Cobden's finest appeals, his face grew more
and more solemn. At length he crumpled up the notes that he had
been making, and turning to a colleague he said, "You must answer
this, for I cannot."

The Corn Law was doomed, and the end came sooner than was
expected. Peel planned to get released from his pledge of 1841 by
holding a general election in which he would appeal to the country to
support him on a free trade policy. But he had no time to do it. Nature
intervened and forced him to act quickly. That very summer, after
parliament had closed its session, the potato blight brought Ireland face
to face with starvation, and the protectionists' hope that a good English
harvest would alleviate the crisis without heavy importations was
washed away by a month of rain that left English wheat rotting in the
ear. The Corn Law was "rained away." "Open the ports!" the League
cried, and everyone knew that once they were opened it would be impossible to close them again.

To meet the emergency, Peel opened the Irish ports, which created tremendous popular pressure to get similar relief for England and Scotland. He urged his cabinet to back him in a repeal of the Corn Law, but the majority balked. Then the leader of the opposition, Lord John Russell, came out openly for free trade and for a concerted public movement to make the government yield. Again Peel tried and failed to budge his colleagues. Their obstinacy forced his resignation early in December. But a fortnight later, Russell having attempted without success to form a government, Peel was back in power with his old cabinet, now broken to his will.

Parliament was called for January 1846, and a furious battle ensued over two bills introduced by the government. One was a customs bill that practically eliminated protection from the general tariff, and the other was a bill to repeal the Corn Law. The protectionists fought with all the exasperation of men who believed they were undone by the treachery of their chiefs. It was the last desperate stand of the landed interest. Only with the aid of Liberal votes was Peel able to get these measures through the Commons, and he needed all the great influence of the Duke of Wellington, government leader in the Lords, to persuade the peers to pass them. The old soldier, now nearly eighty, was still a protectionist—he could never be anything else—and believed, as he said to a friend, that "rotten potatoes have done it all; they put Peel in his damned fright." But he knew that free trade was inevitable; and as in 1829 during the storm over Catholic Emancipation, he was convinced that it would be dangerous to resist a reform which he personally detested.

The triumph of free trade in 1846 was completed by the repeal of the navigation laws in 1849, and the country entered upon an era of prosperity such as it had never known. This confirmed the faith of those who had preached the new doctrine and caused the scales to drop from the eyes of those who had opposed it. Thus free trade became a British religion, and it was much more of a religion than protection later became to America, for the British gospel embraced all mankind and held out the promise of establishing international peace and good will by knitting the world together.

CHAPTER XV

The British North American Revolution

WHEN BRITAIN threw protection overboard, she was consciously throwing out the old colonial system, which had been so modified that, on balance, it had come to benefit the colonies at the expense of the mother country. Commercially speaking, she was casting off the colonies that she might have economic freedom for herself; she was making her own declaration of independence. The logical sequel was the abandonment of her effort to control the governments of her maturing colonies, and it followed almost immediately. But such prompt obedience to simple logic seems too good to be true, especially in Britain, and closer examination suggests that this sequence was fortuitous. Though the free trade movement undoubtedly contributed to the concession of colonial autonomy, it did not give rise to the colonial demand for autonomy, and that demand was already so strong that London could no longer resist it. Indeed, the concession of colonial autonomy might well have preceded the victory of free trade if there had then been no rotten potatoes in Ireland or excessive rain in England.

It was in North America that the British Commonwealth of Nations began to emerge from the British Empire. There the policy of colonial self-government, which was later applied to other parts of the empire as a matter of course, was first worked out. There conditions forced it, conditions peculiar to North America, and the most compelling of these was the American Revolution. There, at long last, Britain found the solution to the colonial problem that had once wrecked the best part of her empire, but she did not know she had found it until many years afterward. Meanwhile she regarded the granting of colonial self-government as the dissolution rather than the regeneration of the empire.

In the history of the empire, this British North American Revolution stands next in importance to the American Revolution, with which it is more closely connected than most people realize. As observed in an earlier chapter, the fear of another American Revolution that would tear away still more colonies as they grew up had dictated a reactionary colonial policy. This policy, designed to keep the remaining colonies in leading strings, relied upon a more careful application of the traditional methods of controlling them. Their trade was to be confined to the empire and their governments were to be guided from London. Here we can dismiss trade, for it had nothing to do with creating the demand that led to the British North American Revolution. It was the mother country, not the colonies, that wanted to end the imperial trading system. They would much rather have kept it for the sake of the commercial privileges it gave them, and they resented the loss of these privileges. The demand of British North America was for political emancipation from a system of government that these colonies had once accepted without question but now found more and more objectionable. They found it so because neither it nor they had remained the same. It had degenerated and they had developed. Either of these changes would have been enough to cause serious friction, and together they produced such an intolerable strain that some kind of revolution was inevitable.

The degeneration of the governmental system was quite different from what had been allowed to occur in the "old thirteen" colonies. Then, by a neglect that was not to be repeated, the assembly had got out of hand. Now it was something else, and the resulting condition was much less healthy. There was an ossification in the executive department. The disease had appeared in the old colonies before the American Revolution, which eradicated it there, but it became much more pronounced in the remaining colonies afterward. Its seat was the council, whose members, other than the ex officio ones, were appointed by London on the nomination of the governor. Like all other colonial officials, even the judges, they were removable at will but were permitted by a hardening custom to hold their places during good behavior. In practice this meant permanent tenure for them as well as for all other officials save one—the most important of all in each colony. It was almost impossible for the governor, who was then regularly picked from the senior ranks of the armed services, to be much more than a temporary sojourner. If his administration was a failure, he was recalled; if it was a success, he was rewarded by promotion to a more important command elsewhere. As each new governor was thus a stranger to the land and its people, he naturally leaned on the permanent officials, who had acquired the necessary local knowledge and experience, for advice on how he should rule—in other words, on how he should carry out his orders from London. These orders, moreover, had to be based on some definite information about the colony, and this was secured from him and his predecessors, who in turn had got it largely from this very group of advisers.

So it came to pass that the government of each colony, though theoretically controlled by the mother country through the governor aided by the councilors, whom he could select and remove, slipped gradually and almost imperceptibly into the hands of a close little oligarchy in each provincial capital: the members of the council, who, with their friends and relatives, filled every important office except that of the chief executive. Legally they were responsible to him and through him to the home government, but practically they were not, because he was a stranger and London was afar off; and neither legally nor practically were they responsible to the assembly. To whom, then, were they responsible?

In other words, the council got out of hand, with the result that it prevented the struggle for self-government from being a straight conflict between the colonies and the mother country. The struggle was rather a three-sided affair between the home government, the local oligarchy, and the assembly; therefore the issue was commonly confused. As the people in the colonies discovered that they were really ruled by a favored few individuals in their midst, the demand for self-government arose and party strife became endemic in the political life of British North America. The members of each ruling clique of course clung to office and power, but their motives were by no means wholly selfish. They held two honest convictions which, being shared by many others in the community and by the home government, made them the leaders of a sizable Tory party and gave them the support of the authorities in Britain. One of these convictions was that self-government would be bad government because the majority of the people could never be entrusted with the control of public affairs, and to prove this the contemporary antics of American democracy were freely cited. This attitude of mind is not surprising if we remember that, in the awakening and triumph of democracy, the colonies lagged behind the United States but anticipated the mother country, where the mass of the people did not get the vote until the latter part of the nineteenth century. The other conviction was that colonial self-government would lead straight to colonial independence—the breakup of the empire. Here was the greatest obstacle in the path of the Reformers, as the members of the other party were generally called. They had to fight the invulnerable ghost of the American Revolution.

The constitutional struggle in British North America was also intensified, quite unconsciously, by the United States, which stiffened the demand for self-government as well as the resistance to it. The people living right next door in the former colonies were fully self-governing, and this ever-present contagious example greatly stimulated political discontent among their cousins in British North America. It could not be otherwise, particularly in that age of exuberant Jacksonian democracy. This is worth emphasizing because the British tradition in Canada and the rise of Canadian nationalism have since conspired to cover up the infection of British North America by Jacksonian democracy—just as nationalism in the United States has drawn a veil over the fact that Jacksonian democracy was an American expression of a general movement that was stirring in western civilization. The awakening of political democracy in British North America also derived some inspiration from contemporary developments in the Old World, especially from British radicalism; but this inspiration from across the ocean was much less than that which came from across the neighboring border. Though immigrants from the mother country began to pour into British North America about 1825, the motives that impelled them were economic and social rather than political, and as a rule they became politically conscious only after they had spent a generation establishing themselves in the new land, by which time the British North American Revolution was over. On the other hand, it would be a great mistake to suppose that the constitutional struggle in these colonies was chiefly the product of the Jacksonian ferment. The spirit of democracy was fostered by conditions that were North American, not just American in the narrow sense of the word; and as these British colonies approached what might be called the adolescent stage, the ancient traditions of political liberty that they had inherited from the mother country urged them to demand self-government.

Here it is well to glance at the development of these colonies, for it explains much in the coming of the British North American Revolution. By the middle of the century, when the mother country capitulated to their demand, their total population was multiplied to approximately 2,500,000, five times what it had been at the time of

the War of 1812, and nearly as large as that of the United States when
the Declaration of Independence was signed. Prince Edward Island
had about 63,000, Newfoundland nearly 150,000, New Brunswick a
little over 180,000, Nova Scotia 275,000, Lower Canada 890,000, and
Upper Canada 950,000.

Of the maritime group, Newfoundland was the least mature. Its
people dwelt along the coast, chiefly in and near St. John's, and the
fisheries provided their only means of livelihood. Prince Edward
Island, the "Garden of the Gulf," was well settled with a solid agricultural population. New Brunswick was less dependent on its timber
than it had been. The southern third of the province was pretty well
occupied by farms, and there was continuous settlement up the main
river valleys and around the coast. On the last there was considerable
fishing and not a little shipbuilding, while the port of St. John had a
thriving commerce. In none of these three colonies did the actual
struggle for self-government amount to much. Newfoundland was too
backward; politics in Prince Edward Island were obsessed by the old
problem of the absentee proprietors; and until the Webster-Ashburton
Treaty of 1842 terminated the long and bitter dispute over the location
of the boundary between Maine and New Brunswick, the people of
New Brunswick would not shake a finger at the mother country, whose
active support they might need at any time.

Nova Scotia was different. Its life was more mature than that of any
other colony. Around the much indented coast, fishing villages flourished; the land, though not so good as that of its little island neighbor,
was quite productive; and rich coal deposits supported a prosperous
mining industry, the only one in British North America. But the
golden age of Nova Scotia, which was then well begun, was based
chiefly upon shipping. Like New England of the same time, Nova
Scotia had developed into one of the principal shipbuilding centers of
the world. The vessels that came off its stocks included many of the
finest clippers that plowed the ocean in the era of wood and sail, and
they carried a goodly share of the world's commerce. When steam
began to supplant sail, it was an enterprising Halifax merchant, Samuel
Cunard, who in 1840 inaugurated the first line of transatlantic steamships. Nova Scotia had also produced in Joseph Howe, a native son
whose parents were Loyalists, the most intelligent and effective British
North American champion of self-government.

The two Canadas, which became Canada East and Canada West on
their reunion by an act passed in the same year as the Cunard Line was

founded, could also boast of a large commerce and an extensive ship-building industry, centered in Montreal and Quebec respectively, and controlled by English-speaking people. Montreal, now one third English and approaching the 60,000 mark, had greatly outgrown every other British North American city; for its strategic position at the head of ocean navigation made it the commercial capital of the two Canadas, which contained three quarters of the population of British North America. But the shipbuilding and trading activity of the St. Lawrence, which winter closed for five months out of every twelve while it never locked up the ports of the Maritime Provinces, played a relatively smaller part in the much larger life of the Canadas, which was overwhelmingly agricultural.

Lower Canada, whose population in 1815 outnumbered that of all the other British North American colonies combined, had fallen behind Upper Canada by 1850. The older colony had much less good arable land, and most of this had long been occupied. The one exception was in the Eastern Townships, the settlement of which had been only begun by Americans from across the line in Vermont and New Hampshire before the War of 1812—pioneer farmers like those then pressing into Upper Canada—and was completed after the war by British people from across the ocean at the very time when the French Canadians were begining to need this space for their own expansion. This particular development added not a little to the domestic political strife, for the rise of a new English-speaking and Protestant block in the old French and Catholic colony was highly offensive to the ancient inhabitants and it was a most welcome reinforcement to those whom the French regarded as intruders—the racial minority who were entrenched in power, economic as well as political.

But the most important development in Lower Canada was not physical. It was psychological. It was the inflation of the new French Canadian nationalism, whose political principles were as radical as its ultimate object was the reverse. The French Canadians strove to get control of the government in order to preserve their society, which was intensely conservative, from contamination by English influences. Their fears were not wholly imaginary, for the government in Quebec was directed by men who would undermine the position of their church, substitute freehold tenure for their antiquated seignioral system, purge their equally antiquated legal code of its anticommercial bias, make them as landholders shoulder the burden of taxation borne by the traders in the towns, increase this burden by a program of expensive public works in which they were not interested, train their children in lay schools to speak a strange tongue, and generally bustle their country into a new way of life. Small wonder the French were frightened into being fanatical reactionaries in everything save the principle of self-government, and into being just as fanatical in their pursuit of this principle! Small wonder the constitutional struggle began in Lower Canada much earlier and there grew much bitterer than in any other colony, for in this old French country the issue was much more than constitutional! It was primarily a question of whether the English would dominate the French, or the French the English.

The phenomenal growth of Upper Canada—its population increased about tenfold between the War of 1812 and the middle of the century—together with the conditions under which it occurred made this the one English-speaking colony in which the struggle for self-government developed an explosive intensity. Here the American influence was most felt. Indeed, Upper Canada had less in common with any other part of British North America than it had with the neighboring states of the American Union, then filling up with a rush. It shared with them the rich soil of the continent's interior plain, it had much the same kind of life as they had, and it was more than half surrounded by them. The war that saved this province for the empire retarded the progress of its settlement for a decade or more, by damming the old tide of immigration from the United States before the new tide from the British Isles began to flow in any volume. Meanwhile the settlement of the neighboring states was accelerated by this diversion of the human flood; and the contrast in development naturally injected into Upper Canada a feeling of frustration and envy, fruitful seed of political discontent.

This feeling was all the more natural because the war had only dampened, not quenched, the predominantly American character of the people there, and the resumption of peaceful intercourse with the land of their origin tended to preserve this character. Except in matters of trade, which was relatively small, and of government, from which they were excluded, almost their only external ties were with the United States. By far the largest and most vital religious body in Upper Canada was the Methodist, and until well on in the twenties it was an integral part, not just an offshoot, of the church south of the border. Its clergy, who were itinerant, came from the United States and returned to the United States. There was their home, as well as in heaven, and they were not always careful to distinguish between the two places when they were guiding their flocks in rustic Upper Canada. This was only one of the countless ways in which the sociological affiliation of the province with the United States was being preserved. Even when immigrants from the mother country were crowding in, Upper Canada was much more responsive than any other colony to the moods and ideas of society in the adjoining states. To the minds of the Family Compact, the name given to the Upper Canadian oligarchy, any popular agitation against their rule was American democracy and republicanism, which had to be crushed lest it subvert this British colony.

It was in the 1820's, two decades after Lower Canada and a decade before Nova Scotia, that Upper Canada became the scene of regular party strife. Here the political cleavage was not, as has sometimes been supposed, between the two classes of Americans who had laid the foundations of the province, the Loyalists and the post-Loyalists. It cut through both. Though the ruling clique included none of the latter, it was not particularly associated with the former. The most dominant member of the Family Compact, John Strachan, the poor Presbyterian schoolmaster who gained wealth and power as an Anglican parson, was a Scottish immigrant. So also was the toughest champion of the popular cause, William Lyon Mackenzie, whose political principles were those of a British Radical until he was converted to Jacksonian democracy. Nor was party allegiance anything like so rigid as it was in Lower Canada where, with rare exceptions, it was a matter of blood, or rather of native tongue. As long as Upper Canada had its own assembly, the Reformers could never do better than take turn about with the Tories in winning a majority of the seats.

Until late in the 1830's the British North American struggle for self-government was embarrassed for want of a clear practical program. The French Canadians tried to use successively, and then simultaneously, the clumsy and obsolete English weapon of impeachment and the newer and more effective one of supply to make their assembly supreme; when these failed to work, they cried out for an elected upper chamber which, by being an echo of the assembly, would make these instruments work to produce the desired end. An elected upper chamber was American; but their notion that it would duplicate the lower chamber, instead of being a check upon it, was not American. It was just naïve. How their supreme assembly would actually conduct the government, seems not to have concerned them very much. When Louis Joseph Papineau assumed the leadership of his people, he contributed more heat than light to the public controversy. His constitutional ideas were a confused international jumble of English, French, and American elements with a strong leaning toward republicanism. In Upper Canada, William Lyon Mackenzie was no better. He too was incapable of thinking things through; he could blast but he could not build. Until by rebellion he blew himself out of the country and the leadership of the Reformers, he was more and more inclined to copy the American pattern of government with its election of the executive as well as of both houses of the legislature, its separation of powers, and its checks and balances.

There was no such fumbling in the Maritimes, not so much because the people there were endowed with superior intelligence as because they were more British than the French Canadians and less American than the Upper Canadians, and especially because they were slower in facing the problem. By the time it began to worry them seriously, the colonial demand for self-government was being focused upon securing a form of government like that of the mother country with its fusion of powers in the cabinet, its executive chosen from the legislature and responsible to the lower chamber of it. Hence the technical name thenceforth applied to it—responsible government.

Looking back, it may seem strange that this solution was not urged from the beginning, at least in Upper Canada; but going back, it is the cry for it that seems remarkable. Much more natural was the popular impulse to wrest control of the upper chamber from the irresponsible executive, which sat in it and used it to thwart the will of the assembly. Also it should be remembered that the responsibility of the cabinet to the House of Commons alone, and not also to the House of Lords, was finally established only in 1832. Nor was the cabinet system, which was an unconscious growth shaped by necessity rather than a conscious creation based on recognized principle, much understood in England itself until long afterward. Walter Bagehot's classic exposition of it, when first published in 1867, was hailed as an important revelation. How then could colonials of a generation before be expected to grasp its value? Yet this is the very thing they did, following the lead of William Warren Baldwin, a wealthy and highly respected Irish doctor who settled in Toronto and who was the father of Robert Baldwin, one of the first to apply the system in Canada. Responsible government in the colonies stems from the elder Baldwin's definite proposal of it in 1828. But it was one thing to propound the principle in North America and another to get it put in practice there. The difficulty was, of course, the intellectual obstacle mentioned early in this chapter. To persuade any government in London that the grant of responsible government to the colonies was compatible with the continuance of the empire was an impossibility until long after the grant was made in the belief that the dissolution of the empire would surely follow.

The issue of colonial self-government was also confused by a curious exchange of roles between the opposing parties in the colonies and the imposition of a new role upon the home government—that of arbiter between the colonial parties. Assembly appeals to London called for the exercise of imperial authority to redress specific grievances against the local administration, while the latter countered by denouncing the idea of imperial interference in internal colonial affairs, and neither party seems to have been aware of its own inconsistency. The home government was instinctively reluctant to meddle, but felt such a responsibility for the proper management of colonial affairs that colonial delegations could count on finding the Colonial Office door open, an attentive ear within, and an occasional remedial order.

This feeling of responsibility helps to explain another paradox in the colonial struggle for self-government. The anti-imperialist movement was stronger than ever, and it was growing. There was an almost universal belief in Britain, shared by members of parliament, cabinet ministers, and even Colonial Office officials, that these colonies were heading for independence and it was impossible to stop them. At the same time, however, the home government repelled the idea of responsible government in the colonies on the very ground that it would lead to what was thus admitted to be inevitable—colonial independence. It would therefore appear that public policy defied public belief until it could do so no longer and, by surrendering to it, put an end to the struggle. But man fights against death though he knows it is inevitable, and only a most exceptional Englishman even at that time believed that the loss of the colonies would occasion no damage to the prestige or the material interests of his country.[1] Also there was in high places, where it influenced policy, this high sense of duty to the people in the colonies,

---

[1] Which also explains why British policy, when strongly opposed to imperial expansion, would tolerate no imperial contraction under external pressure. It is doubtful if Ashburton could have got more territory from Webster without at least a threat of war, which neither power desired; and the windy cry of "fifty-four-forty or fight" rallied Russell behind Peel in a preference for "fight," with the result that the Oregon Treaty of 1846, which completed the division of the continent between the United States and Britain, was a diplomatic victory for neither side.

such as Huskisson so well expressed during his short tenure of the Colonial Office.[2]

As Britain was settling down to enjoy Christmas in 1837, a rude shock came from Lower Canada, in the news that armed revolt had broken out there; not long afterward this was followed by intelligence that the same thing had happened in Upper Canada. Shades of Lexington and Concord at once exaggerated the seriousness of the outbreaks, and in later years Canadians and Americans have made the same mistake—assisted by the poverty of the English language. Because there is no English equivalent for the French *émeute,* which exactly describes these little disturbances, the word "rebellion," suggesting something much bigger, has been applied to them. Americans dipping into the history of Canada or of the British Empire have been prone to see these rebellions as the Canadian counterpart of the American Revolution, though they were nothing of the kind; and both French and English Canadians have been so impressed by what they thought, rightly or wrongly, were the political and constitutional consequences of their ancestors' appeal to arms in 1837 that they have each made their own rebellion a great national event for which they would take credit.

From the bloodstained election of 1832 in Montreal,[3] the prospect of an armed clash poisoned the atmosphere of Lower Canada, and soon a few extremists on both sides were drilling quietly. Of course each side began it—according to the other—and it is not easy to prove otherwise. Early in 1837 the persistent refusal of the assembly to vote supplies until the constitution was changed persuaded the home government to break the deadlock by invoking the sovereign power of parliament, and both houses passed by large majorities a series of resolutions presented by Lord John Russell. These flatly refused the French Canadian demands and authorized the governor to draw on the provincial treasury without the consent of the legislature. The blow dismayed and enraged French Canada, and might have provoked a general rising if the Church had not intervened with admonitions to the faithful against the sin of insurrection. The mass of the French Canadians stayed home with their curés when the rebellion broke. This was the work of only a few hundred, and they were soon crushed. The rebellion in Upper Canada was an echo of that in Lower Canada. A considerable stock of arms and ammunition in Toronto was left un-

---

[2] *Supra,* p. 195.

[3] *Supra,* p. 197.

guarded by the dispatch of troops to restore order on the lower St. Lawrence, and the temptation was too much for Mackenzie. He decided to seize the capital, overthrow the government, and set up a republic. Between four and five hundred deluded farmers gathered at a nearby country tavern in answer to his call, while more than twice that number of loyal men volunteered to disperse them, which they did a few days later.

These two miserable little affairs so startled London that the government appealed to Lord Durham, and he agreed, to go out to British North America as governor general and high commissioner with exceptionally wide powers to deal with the whole situation there. The dispatch of a leading statesman of England on a colonial mission was something unheard of, and so was the result. The report submitted by him early in 1839, shortly after his return from a five months' stay in Canada, is perhaps the most famous government report in the English language. It is the cornerstone of the present British Commonwealth of Nations.

Responsible government in the colonies, which parliament had roundly rejected in one of Lord John Russell's resolutions of less than two years before, was the great and startling recommendation of the *Report on Canada*. Seeing how the traditional form of government had broken down in Lower Canada and was going the same way in the other colonies under his charge, and casting about for some remedy that would place it upon a stable foundation, Durham turned to the Baldwins and asked them for their ideas. Apparently Robert then converted him to the belief that the cabinet system of the mother country could and should be applied in the colonies.

By adopting this proposal, Durham lifted it out of colonial obscurity into the limelight of British imperial politics and invested it with his own enormous prestige. He also improved the proposal when he made it his own. Robert Baldwin spoke of the executive council acting as a provincial cabinet composed of men enjoying the public confidence, sitting in one or the other chamber, and agreeing in "opinions and policy" with "the Representatives of the People," but he said nothing about heads of departments. Durham, on the other hand, did not use the word "cabinet" in his *Report* but, being much more familiar with the institution in practice, he emphasized heads of departments as forming an administration. Another difference was in the position of the governor or lieutenant governor, whom neither would make a mere figurehead. On even purely provincial affairs, Robert Baldwin would leave him, after getting his ministers' advice, to make the final decision himself; whereas Durham, whose greater boldness here made him more modern, laid down the rule that the home government should not support him against the assembly in any difference not involving the relations of the colony with the mother country. To reduce doubts to a minimum, he defined the classes of subjects that did not concern the mother country as well as those that did. The latter he limited to four: the constitution of a colony, foreign relations, the regulation of external trade, and the disposal of public lands. This division between reserved and transferred powers was part of Durham's answer to the question how responsible government in the colonies could be reconciled with their continuance in the empire.

Durham's insistence on a radical reversal of colonial policy came out in the other half of his answer. This too he seems to have got in Canada, though not so much from Baldwin or any other individual as from his general experience there. It was very simple, much too simple for almost all his fellow countrymen in that age: that the only real hope of retaining the colonies was to trust them with responsible government. The fear of letting them have too much freedom lest this freedom destroy the empire, he argued, was both false and dangerous. Trying to hold them in would only irritate them into wishing to break away, and their people would cease to be British if their British birthright were withheld from them. There was only one way to keep them attached to the mother country, and that was to give them the same liberty to govern themselves that the people at home enjoyed. Instead of a policy of force inspired by fear, he demanded a policy of freedom inspired by faith. This, he proclaimed, was the sovereign cure for the ills that had been troubling British North America, this was the magic that would bind the empire together.

Durham's *Report* also advocated the federation of British North America. In this too he was the prophet following a colonial lead. Every now and then some British North American had proposed a plan for such a union; but none of them had made it appear anything like so desirable as did this Englishman of genius, who offered no such plan. Federation, he said, would enable the colonies to attack their common problems together; it would give their public men a wider outlook and higher ambitions; it would inspire the people with self-confidence; and it would make them grow into a real nation. He realized, however, that the time had not yet come for the fulfillment of this dream. Hence the absence of a plan for it. The Maritime Provinces were not yet willing to be united with the Canadas, and the tense situation in Lower Canada precluded a simple policy of waiting until the Maritimes were ready. The only combination then possible—and it seemed to him to be imperatively urgent—was the reunion of the Canadas, which therefore was his practical advice in place of the ideal that he preached.

The great defect of the *Report* is its prescription for French Canada. Durham was a false prophet and a blind reactionary when he wrote it. Before sailing for Canada he was convinced that the French on the St. Lawrence would have to be made thoroughly British; and the British minority in Lower Canada, finding him in this a Daniel come to judgment, reinforced his conviction. As long as these French retained their separate nationality, he would exclude them from his healing gospel of self-government, for he could not trust them with so precious a gift. Nor could he contemplate the restoration of the French assembly, which parliament had suspended before he set out. The strife between "two nations warring in the bosom of a single state" had been too bitter. "Never again will the present generation of French Canadians yield a loyal submission to a British Government; never again will the English population tolerate the authority of a House of Assembly, in which the French shall possess or even approximate to a majority." On the other hand, there was little prospect of success for a government without an assembly, particularly under the very noses of the Americans. So the only way out that he could see was through a reunion of the Canadas, whose combined English-speaking population would provide a majority in the new and larger assembly, which in turn would make self-government safe. It would also hasten the extinction of French Canadian nationalism, which he thought was inevitable as well as desirable—not because he had risen above nationalism but because he too had fallen under its sway. French Canadians have never forgiven him, and they still resent the Union Act of 1840, which, implementing the threat of 1822, reduced them to the position of an artificial minority[4] in the legislature, saddled them with debts incurred by Upper Canada, and deprived their language of the official position it shared with English.

Durham could persuade the cabinet to unite the Canadas but not to grant responsible government, for he had not removed the logical difficulty in the way of the latter. He had proposed that the colonies have the same kind of government as Britain: that just as the king followed

---

[4] Durham had warned against this very thing.

the advice of his ministers, who were the leaders of parliament, so should a governor follow the advice of ministers who were leaders of his legislature. But a governor could not be like the king, because he was in a very different position. There was no one above the king, whereas the king was above a governor, who was only his representative. When the ministers in London told the king what to do, his course was clear, because no one else had any authority to advise him. But ministers in a colony might advise their governor to do something that conflicted with his orders from London. Then what should he do? "If he is to obey his instructions from England, the parallel of constitutional responsibility entirely fails; if, on the other hand, he is to follow the advice of his council, he is no longer a subordinate officer, but an independent sovereign." So did Lord John Russell, Durham's old colleague and the new colonial secretary, and also a great Liberal, dispose of "what is absurdly called responsible government."

While rejecting Durham's great principle because it would disintegrate the empire, the cabinet determined to give the people in the colonies every possible satisfaction, on the avowed principle that this was "the best security for permanent dominion." To this end, in October 1839, Lord John Russell launched a shattering blow at the provincial oligarchies of British North America. In a dispatch that was immediately published there, he condemned the custom of permanent tenure of office for heads of departments and executive councilors. Thenceforth the governor was to be free to change any of them as he saw fit; and he was expected, by judicious dismissals and appointments, to keep his executive in harmony with the will of the people as expressed in the assembly. In other words, he was to be prime minister as well as governor of his colony. But the two offices were so disparate that they were about as difficult to combine as oil and water. Only a man of political ability much greater than was required to fill either could hold both together, and then only temporarily.

The new policy soon broke down. Early in 1840, the year that Durham died, Joseph Howe persuaded a majority of the Nova Scotian assembly to declare that they had no confidence in the executive, and when the lieutenant governor replied that *he* had, Howe carried a motion demanding his recall. London recalled him but would not admit the principle of responsible government. The new policy had its best chance of success in United Canada, where the governor general who followed Durham was Charles Poulett Thomson, like Durham a civilian and an ex-cabinet minister, but much more adroit. In the

midst of his Canadian career he was deservedly rewarded with a peerage. Lord Sydenham, as he was then called, was the only man who did
manage to combine the functions of governor and prime minister, and
he had reached the end of the road as prime minister when death
released him in September 1841. The only government that would
satisfy the people was one controlled by them through their elected
representatives, not by the mother country through a governor. This
became more and more evident under Sydenham's successors. They
managed to limp along; the first, Sir Charles Bagot, by virtually conceding responsible government, to the great annoyance of the cabinet
in London; and the second, Sir Charles Metcalfe, who was sent out to
recover the lost ground, by defying the Reform majority in the assembly
until an appeal to the electorate, influenced by his promise of patronage
and appeals to patriotism, gave him a bare Tory majority. Meanwhile
the Tories were in power at home, but this made little difference, for
their policy on colonial government was the same as that of the fallen
Whigs. The great change came when the Whigs returned to office
in 1846.

At last the home government decided to let the British North American colonies have what they wanted, and it is interesting to probe into
the motives that prompted the concession. The colonial secretary was
Earl Grey, brother-in-law of Lord Durham and son of the Earl Grey
who had been prime minister. As Lord Howick and parliamentary
undersecretary in his father's administration, he had sponsored the
surrender of crown revenues to the colonies in 1831; and he was one
of the few men in Britain who were inspired by Durham's faith. His
colleagues in the cabinet, including the prime minister, Lord John
Russell, were still obsessed by the logical conflict between imperial
unity and colonial self-government. They had not conquered their fear
of another American Revolution. It had finally conquered them and
turned them face about. They realized that continued resistance to the
colonial demand would sooner or later drive the colonies into revolt,
and that no imperial force could then hold them within the empire
because they were too close to the United States. As the colonies were
apparently destined to go, was it not much better to have a peaceful
and friendly parting than a violent and bitter one? Such, it seems, was
the decision these men of little faith thought they were making when
they agreed to Grey's new policy. Then Durham's magic began to work,
though it took some years to show its strength.

As Durham had pointed out in his *Report,* no legislation was necessary to effect this momentous transformation in the government of the colonies. A simple instruction from the Colonial Office that the will of the assemblies should no longer be resisted was sufficient to establish the cabinet system of government in the colonies, and this was done quietly in the Maritime Provinces. When the Nova Scotian legislature met in January 1848, it was known that the lieutenant governor was directed to accept any government that the assembly desired. At once the members passed a resolution of no confidence, the executive resigned, and a real cabinet was formed—the first in any colony. The same year saw the government of New Brunswick reorganized as a coalition to satisfy the assembly, but it was not until 1854 that this province got a cabinet composed of one party with a majority in the House. Grey thought that Prince Edward Island and Newfoundland were too immature, but the former got responsible government in 1851 and the latter in 1854.

In United Canada the transition precipitated another convulsion, because there it meant much more than it did in the provinces down by the sea. It meant the end not only of the governor's control of the administration but also of the effort to keep the French Canadians down. English-speaking politicians in Canada had been coming to see that they could not have responsible government without sharing it equally with the French. The reason was one of simple arithmetic. The English-speaking majority in the assembly was so small that only a very few of the English members could turn out any government that was unacceptable to the French, and no government would be acceptable to the French that did not include them on a parity with English Canadians. The extreme Tories, however, still believed with bitter intensity that no French Canadian could be trusted with the affairs of government. The convulsion, which occurred in Montreal, the capital of the united province, was the work of these Tories.

To inaugurate the new era in the colony that was by far the largest and then also the most difficult, the Liberal Grey picked the Tory Earl of Elgin, an ideal choice. He was a young man of great ability and tested experience, having just returned from a successful administration of Jamaica during a trying time; and he had imbibed Durham's faith, an advantage advertised by his marriage to Durham's daughter, Grey's niece, which took place shortly before he sailed for Canada; and in one vital particular his vision was much clearer than his father-in-law's had been. Elgin saw that the French Canadians could never be Anglicized and that any attempt to crush their nationality would only strengthen it. With a noble vision that recalls Carleton at his best, he maintained that there might be no British subjects more loyal than the French Canadians if their loyalty were only rooted in real British liberty, the liberty to be themselves.

On arriving in Canada in 1847, Elgin found that the Tory government in office was tottering; but he would not lift a finger to push it over, for that would violate the principle he had come to establish. This government, unable to face the assembly again, asked for an election and he granted the request—again faithful to the new principle—with the result that the Tories were badly defeated at the polls. When the new assembly met in February 1848, it turned out the government, and Elgin called in Robert Baldwin and Louis Hippolyte Lafontaine, who had been cooperating in opposition and were now the leaders of the two wings of the majority, to form an administration. Grey was more anxious than Elgin over how the French Canadians would conduct themselves in office; but he was prepared, as he wrote Elgin, to see the new cabinet include even Papineau, who had returned from exile and re-entered the assembly, if his inclusion was necessary to satisfy his people. They, however, had deserted him for Lafontaine, who had opposed his appeal to force in 1837. To carry further the principle of racial equality, now respresented in the composition of the cabinet, Elgin persuaded Grey to have the Union Act amended to restore French as an official tongue, so that in 1849 the legislature was formally opened in both languages.

Then came the real test of responsible government. To the extreme Tories the sight of French Canadians in the government was like a red rag to a bull; and their rage mounted when the government introduced the Rebellion Losses Bill in 1849 to compensate people for the destruction or damage of their property during the rebellion in Lower Canada, provision having already been made for losses in Upper Canada. As the measure excluded from its benefits only those who had been convicted or transported for rebellion, it was plain that many would get payment who did not deserve it. The government knew this but preferred not to reopen old sores by an examination into the loyalty of every claimant. The Tories thus found an opening to accuse the government of scheming to pay rebels for rebelling, and there was a terrific political battle over the bill. When the legislature passed it, the Tories clamored for the governor general to veto it. Elgin did not like the details of the bill but, true to the principle of responsible government, he signed the bill. At once the loyal rage of the Tories exploded in disloyalty. They stirred up a mob that burned the provincial parliament buildings, wrecked Lafontaine's house, and threatened the governor general's life as he drove through the streets of Montreal. From Canada the storm shifted to England, where prominent speakers in both houses of parliament vehemently demanded that the measure be disallowed unless amended to make sure that no rebel would benefit by it. But Grey and Russell would not yield, and though the Lords were almost equally divided on the issue, the Commons by a large majority sustained the government's refusal to go back on its policy of granting responsible government.

The Montreal riots of 1849, though they cost that city the political capital of Canada, were a blessing in disguise, for they discredited the old Tory chiefs as the risings of a dozen years before had discredited the men of the opposite extreme. Though it is not true in arithmetic, it is true in Canadian history that forty-nine equals thirty-seven. As if to remove any doubt of it, some Tory leaders almost immediately took another step that gave the lie to their much-vaunted loyalty. They openly declared for annexation to the United States. But it was much more than blind fury against Elgin, or determination to remain English even at the expense of ceasing to be British, which Durham had noted in the racial minority of Lower Canada, that moved a thousand businessmen and politicians of Montreal to sign this Annexation Manifesto of 1849.

The something much more was economic. These men and their predecessors had long striven against American competition, French Canadian obstruction, and Upper Canadian opposition, to make Montreal the commercial capital not only of Canada but of the whole St. Lawrence and Great Lakes basin, and their last visible hope of achieving this goal was through a liberal stretching of the preference accorded to Canadian produce in the home market, a process that drew through Montreal more than a little trade between Britain and the interior of the United States. This and a great deal more trade—all that depended on this preference—Montreal lost when the mother country abandoned protection, with the result that the merchants of that city came face to face with what seemed to be the ruin of their own and the country's prosperity. The only hope of economic salvation that they could see in the dark days of depression was to cut the tie with Britain and join the neighboring republic.

The Annexation Manifesto was a striking pendant to the concession of self-government in British North America. The mere juxtaposition of the United States guaranteed to these colonies an escape from the British Empire at any time they wanted it; and this in turn guaranteed to them what had been denied to the "old thirteen" colonies—all the freedom they wanted within the empire without having to fight for it. As an appeal to Canadians for action, the Manifesto was a failure; but as a warning for the future, it was a success, which may be seen in what happened ten years later. When responsible government was granted, the recent conversion of Britain to free trade apparently blinded people there to the fact that the colonies might use their new freedom to impose protective duties against the mother country. This was precisely what United Canada proceeded to do in 1859, and it stirred great surprise and indignation in the Old Country. Manufacturing interests vigorously condemned the new Canadian tariff and called upon the government in London to kill it by an exercise of the imperial power of disallowance. The British government protested hotly to the Canadian government, which refused to back down, and there was quite a little tempest in the imperial teapot. The outcome was inevitable. London had to submit because, in the last analysis, the two million people of Canada were living in the shadow of the United States. If they could not go their own way in the empire, they could go their own way out.

The British North American Revolution, which sprang from the American Revolution and spread its influence around the globe, came in the nick of time. The principle of this revolution was conceded in 1846, applied in 1848, and tested in 1849. Meanwhile the Old World was blowing up with that chain reaction of revolutions that, beginning in Paris with the sudden overthrow of the July monarchy and erection of the Second Republic, pushed the republican movement to its nineteenth century peak. The last spasm of the Chartist agitation in England, that of 1848, and the pitiful attempt at revolution in Ireland in the same year, were part of this chain reaction. But no European spark touched off the British North American Revolution. It had started first, and so the substitution of a stable for an unstable political order in these colonies was carried out from above, not from below, and in an atmosphere free of the compulsion of violence.

Two loose ends still hang from the discussion in this chapter, and before concluding it we should tie them up. One is what happened to the chronic conflict between the legislative council and the assembly. This automatically disappeared with the grant of responsible government, which shifted the legislative seat of the executive from the nominated to the elected chamber and so removed the great cause of the conflict. It should also be remembered that, once this shift took place, the legislative council could not assert the independence of a House of Lords, for it had no history to give it prestige and self-confidence, and every member who died was replaced by a nominee of the provincial ministry, which meant the leaders of the assembly.

The other loose end is much more important. What happened to the division between the transferred and the reserved powers? In the colonies that were concerned as well as in the mother country, it was generally assumed that the grant of responsible government applied only to internal colonial affairs and that London would still manage other colonial affairs; but the actual transfer, being based on an administrative order rather than a legislative act, was made without any legal definition of what were to be colonial powers or what were not. This omission was intentional and thoroughly British. Who could then foretell what should be the boundary between colonial and imperial authority in the uncertain future? Like other British constitutional problems it was left free to work itself out, and this has meant that the colonies took over more and more responsibility from the mother country in proportion as they were prepared to shoulder it. This continuing transfer was, of course, the operation of the North American guarantee to these colonies that they could have all the liberty they wanted at any time.

To point the moral and adorn the tale of the peaceful British North American Revolution, we may conclude this chapter with a glance at the contemporary Irish contrast. From being constitutionally in advance of the North American colonies, Ireland had fallen away behind them with the loss of its legislature. Many years passed before there was even an audible Irish demand for its restoration, without which the Irish could not go on, as the people in the colonies did, to formulate a practical demand for an executive responsible to it instead of to the government in London.

The first stage of Irish political agitation in the nineteenth century was confined to a movement for Catholic Emancipation. Its leader was Daniel O'Connell, a Roman Catholic barrister of good family, fine education, moving eloquence, and no mean skill as an organizer and manager of public opinion. Far from being a revolutionary, he was an enemy to violence and a friend of the British connection. This he would consolidate by making Irishmen the legal equals of Englishmen, and he bent every effort to keep the movement strictly within constitutional channels. Being no demagogue, he long refrained from appealing to the masses, who meanwhile displayed no interest in the cause. After seventeen years of his leadership the movement was still a middle class affair and apparently no nearer its goal, when he suddenly saw the need and the opportunity to enlist the peasants in a sweeping national drive for Catholic Emancipation. His new vision was born of disaster—the Irish famine of 1822.

The first half of the nineteenth century, which witnessed the rise of the North American colonies, saw Ireland sinking under its own weight, for the balance between population and resources was favorable in the former and adverse in the latter. Indeed, Ireland had already sunk far below the level of a wheat culture and was reaching the limit of a potato culture, by which the same land is capable of supporting four times as many people; and the industrial solution that Britain had found for the problem of her own population pressure was inapplicable in Ireland for the simple reason that Ireland lacked the necessary raw materials. So Ireland was living ever closer to the edge of starvation, and every now and then slipped over the edge, because food crops could not be stored more than a few months and were subject to blight that left little or none to be harvested. Hence the famine of 1822 which, though nothing so severe as the one that was to follow in the forties, had important consequences. One was a new outbreak of agrarian violence bordering on anarchy, which then became chronic. Another was, as already suggested, the bridging of the gulf between politician and peasant. Thenceforth Irish politics had mass momentum.

The Catholic Association, formed by O'Connell in 1823, embraced the people under the leadership of their priests. Never had there been such a nationwide public agitation in any land under the British Crown. It reached a startling climax in 1828 when O'Connell, though ineligible as a Catholic to sit in parliament, became a candidate in an Irish by-election against a member of the British ministry and won an overwhelming victory without the slightest display of physical force by his followers. This was the crisis that convinced Wellington it was high time to grant Catholic Emancipation lest the Irish movement burst its peaceful bounds and plunge Ireland into a bath of blood. By forcing the passage of the Catholic Emancipation Act in the following year as a measure of necessity rather than of justice, he unwittingly suggested that the way to win Irish concessions from the British government was by violence or the threat of violence. The lesson was not lost on Ireland, as future years were to show.

When political discontent in the colonies was being focused in the demand for responsible government, the Irish cry for a repeal of the Union was being raised. On the morrow of his triumph in 1829 O'Connell started this new agitation, and in 1832 forty Irish members of the House of Commons were avowed Repealers. During the thirties, however, the Irish leader refrained from throwing his whole weight into the cause, and it made little headway. Two other Irish grievances were pressing and he hoped for more immediate results by working with the Whigs, who were in power. They were in a generous reforming mood, and he could help them by wagging his tail—the name applied to the block of votes that he commanded in the Commons.

Ireland was in an uproar over the tithe, a mass grievance that Catholic Emancipation did not touch. The growing resistance of the poverty-stricken peasants to its collection by the officers of the law produced a condition that has been well described as a tithe war. On one occasion it took two pieces of artillery and three companies of soldiers to effect the sale of a single cow that had been impounded to enforce payment. The other grievance was the continued Protestant monopoly of public offices in Ireland. The new law permitted, but did not require, the appointment of Roman Catholics; and the lord lieutenant and the chief secretary, who ruled in Dublin Castle under direction from London, picked only Protestant officials as they had always done of old. By a bargain with the Whigs, which both sides honored faithfully, O'Connell got a share of this patronage in return for Irish votes in the House of Commons. But parliament would not consider the abolition of the tithe, and all he could do to relieve his people of the physical burden imposed by the established church was by procuring the passage of legislation that merely nibbled at it.

By 1840, when it was obvious that the weak Whig ministry was about to give way before a strong Tory one, the Irish leader was losing patience with the British government, and younger Irish politicians were losing patience with him and his constitutional methods. Thereupon O'Connell revived his tactics of the twenties. He organized a Repeal Association on the model of the Catholic Association, and its almost immediate success restored his ascendancy. In 1843 he seemed to be on the point of winning another great triumph for Ireland. He planned a huge national demonstration that would impress Peel as he had once impressed Wellington. But Peel, unlike his predecessor, did not wait to be caught by such a crisis in Ireland. He prohibited the meeting, sent troops to occupy the place, and dispatched ships to guard the coast. This time it was O'Connell the constitutionalist who was caught, for to go on with his plan meant committing himself and his followers to open rebellion. He called off the demonstration, and by doing so he committed political suicide. The Repeal cause was now dead too. It was killed by Peel's bold stroke, which left Ireland no alternative but submission or rebellion.

With the collapse of the Repeal movement, political agitation in Ireland turned to violence as its only hope. The modern fever of nationalism, which was soon to throw Europe into the violent convulsions of 1848, had already infected Ireland. One symptom was the founding, by a group of fanatical young Irishmen in 1842, of a newspaper with the significant title of *The Nation* and the characteristic appeal to die fighting for national liberty rather than live in subjection. Now the fever mounted, producing delirious dreams of revolution.

But the next phase of the Irish tragedy was precipitated by the complete failure of the potato crop in 1845 and again in 1846. Though the British government and the British people poured immense quantities of food into the island, this relief was pitifully inadequate. Starvation and attendant disease mowed down Irishmen by the thousands. So began the depopulation of Ireland, which continued on a more gigantic scale as haunted survivors of the catastrophe fled from the land of death. They swarmed across the narrow sea to the slums of Glasgow, Liverpool, and Manchester, and in much greater numbers across the ocean to North America, where many settled in Canada, though the huge majority found the United States more inviting. The population of Ireland fell from 8,300,000 in 1845 to 6,600,000 in 1851.

In the desperate agony of their country, a few Irish revolutionaries plotted a national uprising in 1848, the year in which Canada got responsible government. The plotters sent to France, then in the throes of revolution, for aid that did not come; the government laid some of them by the heels; and the remnant made a pathetic attempt at an Irish revolution. It was snuffed out in a little skirmish known as Widow McCormick's Potato Patch. The futility of rebellion matched that of peaceful agitation, and Ireland seemed utterly helpless.

No power, European or American, could do for Ireland what the United States had unconsciously done, and was still doing, for British North America. Nor could Ireland share the benefit that the British North American example conferred upon other colonies. Ireland lay too close to England.

CHAPTER XVI

South Africa, a Workshop
of Native Policy

OF THE two principles that have largely shaped, and to that extent
explain, the modern British Commonwealth and Empire—self-government for the people capable of it and trusteeship in the government of
those who are not—the second owes nearly as much to South African
experience as the first does to North American conditions. The beginning of trusteeship may be traced back to the later days of the First
British Empire, when London tried to check the colonial settler's encroachment upon the red man's hunting grounds. But the motive then
was not humanitarian; it was plain common sense—to save the money,
the scalps, and the lives of whites. A truer beginning was the British
government's interference with the East India Company's administration in India; for there the purpose was to save Indians from Englishmen, not Englishmen from Indians. Yet the intervention was negative
rather than positive—to restrain rather than to lead, to prevent abuses
rather than to evolve and apply a practical policy; for the latter was still
the task of the Company, which continued to exercise the functions of
ruler in India. The British government, on the other hand, was directly
responsible for how the natives were treated in South Africa, because
the Cape was a crown colony; and the struggle to work out a proper
native policy in this part of the empire was a projection of the crusade
against slavery.

Emancipation, which shook the West Indies to their very foundations, was little more than an incident in the life of the Cape. There
society did not rest on slavery. Nature saw to that, for it was too harsh
to tolerate the plantation system with its use of black gangs for mass
production. The slaves in this colony, all of foreign origin, were domestic servants or skilled artisans; and as a rule they were neither op-

pressed, nor despised, nor feared. They were a superior laboring class and were paid about as much before the removal of their chains as they were able to get after their removal. It was not slavery but the native problem that was the dark shadow over South Africa.

Ranking far below the slaves were the Hottentots, who supplied the cheap labor, especially in the frontier regions, and inspired in the colonists no feeling but contempt. It used to be thought that they were roughly equal in number to either the slave or the European population in the late 1820's, each being then some thirty thousand; but now there is reason for believing that the Hottentots were more numerous—far too numerous for their own good. Pastoral nomads who had lost their grazing lands, their flocks and their herds, they had almost no means of subsistence. The majority of them were at the mercy of the white farmers, who employed them and found them much cheaper than slaves. A Hottentot cost nothing to get; he could be replaced any day; his wages were no more than a slave's keep; the maintenance of his aged and infirm, his childbearing women, and his little children was his burden, not his master's; and he was helpless against a master who withheld his pay or abused him physically. The Hottentots were the oppressed and despised.

The feared were the Bantus, of various tribes, who in addition to fighting among themselves were the perennial scourge of the eastern frontier, where alone nature tempted the white settlers to expand. There is no telling how many times these natives outnumbered all the Europeans in South Africa, but it was certainly much more than contemporaries imagined; and an untold number of other warlike tribes in the background contributed to this hostile pressure on the frontier. There the savages were in a much worse plight than the white men, though this was little realized at the time. Both wanted more land, neither could get it without dispossessing the other, and the need of the Boers was nothing so desperate as that of the Bantus, who, though also agriculturalists as well as pastoralists, were so crowded that they could not support themselves on the land they had without overworking and overgrazing it. Under such circumstances it is not surprising that there was chronic war.

The Boer instinct was to exploit the Hottentots and exterminate the Bantus, while the British was to protect them; and the clash of instincts aggravated the problem. The rescue of the Hottentots began almost with the century, when, following a lead given by the Moravians, the missionaries of the London Missionary Society founded the first of

their stations, or Institutions, as they were called, on public land provided for the purpose.[1] Within twenty years or so, they gathered into
these Institutions thousands of uprooted and detribalized Hottentots,
who thus were at last provided with a home and with a chance to find
a better life in this world as well as in the next. To improve the lot of
the much larger number whom they could not collect in such havens
of refuge, the missionaries continued to prod the government into
action with tales of how the burghers mistreated the natives. The
results of these efforts were not so happy. The Boers, who viewed with
a jealous eye the withdrawal of cheap labor into the Institutions, were
enraged rather than reformed by the talebearing and the credence the
government gave to it; the government lost face by countenancing the
charges, very few of which could be proven in court; and the missionaries paid for it by incurring official distrust and even hostility.

A new day dawned for the natives of South Africa with the arrival
of the Rev. Dr. John Philip at Cape Town in 1819. This middle-aged,
hardheaded, farseeing Scot was picked from the Congregational pulpit
in Aberdeen and sent out by the London Society as its superintendent
to give a much-needed intelligent leadership to the missionary work in
the colony. Within a few weeks he set out on a long tour of the stations
in the interior, and in the years that followed he was commonly absent
from his home in Cape Town for months at a time on such journeys of
investigation. Philip soon acquired an unrivaled knowledge of native
conditions in South Africa and did more than any other man to improve them. Instead of repeating the blunder of playing up individual
hard cases and pressing for prosecutions that could not succeed because
of a very defective law regarding natives, he concentrated his attention
upon getting a drastic revision of the law.

The worst defect in the legal system of the country came from a
governor's proclamation of 1809, which embodied a number of good
features and has been complacently called the Magna Carta of the
Hottentots. For their protection it limited wage contracts to one year,
required regular payment of wages, outlawed claims to personal service
based on debts, and did a number of other commendable things; but all

---

[1] The Society, nondenominational but largely Congregational, supported most of the
missionaries in the colony. The Moravian Brethren were there before them and they
remained, but they were few in number and their work was mostly in the older part
of the colony. The Wesleyan missionary activity in South Africa began later, about
1820, and was chiefly outside the colony, beyond the region of the Hottentots.

the good features of the proclamation were more than offset by its regulations to prevent "vagrancy." These regulations required every Hottentot to have a fixed place of abode, registered with the landdrost; forbade removal without a certificate from the same official or a field cornet, a sort of militia officer; and prescribed arrest and treatment as a vagrant—forced labor at the arbitrary will of the local authorities—for any Hottentot who ventured off his master's premises and failed to produce such a certificate or "pass" on the demand of any European. This pass system checked, though it did not stop, admissions to the Institutions and kept the bulk of the Hottentots under the control of the farmers. The following decade saw the tightening of this control by an amendment that authorized landdrosts to bind children from their eighth to their eighteenth year as "apprentices" if the master had maintained them during their infancy, or if they were orphans. Here, because the obligation was wholly one-sided, "apprentice" was a euphemism for long-termed indentured servant. Actually slavery was growing in South Africa.

Determined to win for the Hottentots the same legal freedom as the whites enjoyed, Philip appealed to the governor, the Colonial Office, and parliament, in which he enlisted the support of Wilberforce and Buxton. In 1823 the home government sent out a commission of inquiry to report on native conditions, but its main purpose was to review the whole administration of the colony, where a first-class political storm was brewing, and until this storm blew over Philip could do little for the benighted people he championed.

The center of the storm was the governor, Lord Charles Somerset. He had more power than judgment and overplayed the role of autocrat. On issues big and little, from the freedom of the press, which he could not stomach, to the management of a relief fund for distressed settlers, he ran foul of most of the leading men in the colony, including Philip. So loud and persistent was the outcry against Lord Charles that it could not go unheeded at home. Early in 1825, at Bathurst's orders, he was given an advisory council, the first step away from absolutism, and in June it was announced in parliament that he had been given leave of absence. The news of Lord Charles' virtual recall had a calming effect at the Cape until he surrendered the government to his successor early in 1826. Then the fight was renewed for the freedom of the press, but without the bitter personalities that Somerset had injected into it. A year later John Fairbairn, Philip's son-in-law, the boldest editor in the colony, carried the battle to London, and there he won it.

Other South African reforms of the time flowed from the commission of inquiry. The Charter of Justice, 1827, did away with amateur half-time judges and established a supreme court. Incidentally, it was a second and longer step from autocracy toward constitutionalism, for it took away the governor's authority to sit on appeals. The Roman-Dutch law remained the foundation of the legal system, criminal as well as civil; but now English influences softened the excessive hardness of many penalties in the old Dutch criminal code, and the introduction of the English jury system carried with it the English law of evidence. Around this time, too, the English language ousted High Dutch from its official position in the courts. In later generations Boer national bias blamed English national bias for this change; it was rather the result of practical necessity, the Boers having ceased to speak High Dutch, and their Afrikaans being still in a formative state. In 1828, also following a recommendation of the commission, the divergence of character and interest between the older and the newer districts led to the division of the colony into two provinces, Western and Eastern, with Captain Andries Stockenstrom as commissioner general for the latter. This descendent of a Swede was one of the finest South Africans of the nineteenth century. For years he had been landdrost of Graaff-Reinet, as his father had been before him; and he knew his country as few other men then living. He thoroughly agreed with Philip on the Hottentot question; as did the commissioners from England, but their agreement was to be of less consequence.

Meanwhile in London, whither he had gone for the purpose in 1826, Philip was pressing the cause of the Hottentots. With tireless energy he toiled on his two volumes of *Researches in South Africa,* which appeared in the spring of 1828; and if the influential people who then read them were many fewer than he had hoped, he soon had the satisfaction of knowing that his campaign was successful. That summer, in the House of Commons, the colonial secretary accepted a motion of Buxton's calling for the issuance of directions "for effectually securing to all the natives of South Africa the same freedom and protection as are enjoyed by other free persons residing at the Cape, whether they be English or Dutch." These directions were unnecessary. Two days later the acting governor at Cape Town, General Bourke, promulgated the emancipating Fiftieth Ordinance. He might have done it sooner if the commission of inquiry, whose advice on this point he sought, had not withheld it until later. It was Stockenstrom who persuaded him to move. Then Philip wisely had the home government give an imperial clinch to this provincial measure, by the addition of a clause prohibiting its repeal or amendment without the express sanction of the Crown.

This ordinance of 1828 "for improving the condition of Hottentots and other free persons of colour at the Cape" wiped a sponge over the pass law and over practically all other legal discriminations against them. Now there was no doubt whatever that they could even possess land—if they could find the means to buy it, or if they were given it. Here was the rub. Legal equality was no cure for economic helplessness. In the following year a new governor assigned a stretch of attractive land in the Kat River Valley for the settlement of some two thousand Hottentots, but this good beginning of a constructive policy was also the end. As the settlers were London Missionary Society people, they naturally "called" one of Philip's men to be their pastor. The Cape government tried unsuccessfully to stop his going, and then stood sullenly aloof; for the new governor was swinging with the tide of opinion in the colony, and it was running strongly against Philip and his Society.

The reaction of most of the white settlers to the Fiftieth Ordinance was out of all proportion to the material benefit it conferred upon the Hottentots by giving them freedom to leave bad employers for better. This reaction was an abhorrence of racial equality, a feeling that needs no explanation for those who share it and cannot be explained to others except as a form of hysteria. In South Africa resentment against the emancipation of 1828 was all the greater because of its bearing upon the question of self-government. In 1827, and again in 1830, Cape petitions for an elected assembly reached the House of Commons, only to bring out the dilemma arising from the fundamental conflict between the two principles mentioned in the beginning of this chapter, self-government and trusteeship. The grant of any measure of colonial self-government was intolerable to the mother country if such a grant would give whites power over nonwhites, and intolerable to these whites if it did not. A scapegoat was needed and soon found in Philip. His *Researches* got the blame for the denial of an assembly; and the reflections he there cast, or was supposed to have cast, upon white masters made the colony boil with bitterness. Shortly after Philip's return to the colony late in 1829, he was successfully prosecuted for publishing in his *Researches* a libel on a frontier official; later he became entangled in a dispute with the government over the withdrawal of certain public lands from the use of one of the Institutions.

The battle won in 1828 had to be fought over again in 1834. By that time the rising resentment against the Fiftieth Ordinance was focused upon its virtual undoing by the enactment of a new vagrancy law. This vagrancy law was one of the earliest measures passed by the legislative council, which, along with the executive council,[2] replaced the advisory council in 1834—a further step away from autocracy. At once the missionaries, led by Philip and backed by Fairbairn and his paper, were up in arms. The new governor, Sir Benjamin D'Urban, had been governor in the West Indies for more than a dozen years and was reputed to be the friend of the planters there, which suggested that he was also friendly to this bill. Philip and his followers bombarded him with protests and petitions until he reserved the bill for the royal pleasure. There could be little doubt of what the decision in London would be. The bill was disallowed in the spring of 1835.

This imperial veto had far-reaching consequences. It sealed the emancipation of the Hottentots; and it was the emancipation of the Hottentots, rather than the abolition of slavery, that precipitated the Great Trek, which has dominated the subsequent history of South Africa. There was little slavery in the part of the colony that was the base of that memorable migration, and there were very few slaveowners among the Boers who took part in it. But there were still fewer Boers, if any at all, who had no Hottentot servants. The veto of the vagrancy bill killed the Boers' last hope of restoring their old way of life in the colony, and left the irreconcilables no alternative but to rebuild outside what had been destroyed inside. They were also driven forth by the way the frontier problem was handled, and here too we see the missionaries at work.

In the rough jostling on the frontier, where the pressure for land was greatest, and was between savage tribes as well as between them and whites, everybody was punished for the sins of others, and the story of what happened might be called a comedy of errors if it had not been all so terribly tragic. It was impossible to find any eastern line that separated the land of the Boers from the land of the Bantus. The Dutch took the Fish River to be this boundary, though west of it there still lived a considerable Bantu population. As the Dutch were neither able to expel them from the colony nor willing to admit their presence in it, these people constituted an awkward problem for the British when

---

[2] The executive council included only officials, and these together with nominated unofficial members formed the legislative council.

they took over the country. They tried expulsion in 1812, little realizing how impossible it was for the chiefs on the east side of the Fish to make room for so many refugees, whose number was about twenty thousand. The natural result was the outbreak of war in that old Kaffirland, or Kaffraria, where the fighting came to a head in 1818 with the triumph of the refugee host over the army of Gaika, whom, for the sake of security on the frontier, the British governor, like his Dutch predecessor, had treated as "paramount" chief. Gaika appealed to his friend Somerset, who felt obliged to rescue him, and so the "fifth" Kaffir war began with the white invasion of Kaffir territory. A savage counterthrust penetrated the colony to the very gates of its new eastern capital, Grahamstown, before it was hurled back; and then a colonial drive to the Kei River, a hundred miles east of the Fish, brought the war of 1819 to a close.

Somerset's victory over Gaika's and his own foes put him in a position to try a new frontier policy that experience had recently been suggesting. It was the substitution of a vacant space for a mere line, which was quite unsatisfactory, between the colonists and the Kaffirs. The space was, of course, to be provided by the Kaffirs, and to this end Somerset persuaded Gaika, in an "amicable agreement" or unwritten "treaty" of October 1819, to cede the country between the Fish and the Keiskamma rivers, a belt of variable width averaging about twenty-five miles.

This arrangement only aggravated the problem it was intended to solve—a common happening in white dealings with colored races. Somerset did not know, and could not know, that he was forcing Gaika to stretch his authority beyond the Bantu limit by giving away his people's lands; and that by this action he, Somerset, was breaking the very authority on which he relied to keep the border tribes in hand. The fact that he was making his ally pay for their common enemy's sins—to say nothing of the tangled chain of responsibility going back to the Dutch regime—did not occur to him or to any other white man until the missionaries stumbled upon it some years later. Another fatal weakness in the agreement was that it was not put down on paper, which explains Philip's later policy. Without any written record to which either party to the treaty could appeal against the other's breach of faith, what was at first a "neutral belt" gradually and insensibly became "ceded territory," where pasture rights were allocated to natives who had not been cleared out and land was granted with growing freedom to white settlers. Thus an arrangement designed to stabilize the frontier by keeping the two races apart led to the advance of the frontier and the overlapping of the races on what had been native territory. Right or wrong, treaty or no treaty, missionaries or no missionaries, white settlers would dispossess the natives. It was a law of human nature that seemed almost as inexorable as a law of physical nature.

Meanwhile another device, likewise the subject of an agreement between Somerset and Gaika with the purpose of pacifying the frontier, was also being perverted. This was the spoor law, a custom of the Bantus that restrained cattle thieving among themselves, and was practically the same remedy as a tenth century king of England and earlier Franks prescribed for the same trouble. If a Bantu lost any of his cattle but found their tracks and followed them to another kraal, the headman of that kraal then became responsible for making good the loss unless he could prove that the spoor went beyond. In 1817 Somerset got Gaika's consent to the extension of this law to cover losses by white settlers, who thus acquired a right that soon ran wild in its new social environment. Divorced from Bantu customs that kept its application within just bounds, the right was now married to a century-old Boer tradition that made it vicious. The Boer tradition was that of the commando, an armed band of frontiersmen called out to protect their country by striking lightning-like blows at marauding tribesmen. An appalling example of what the spoor law could do when joined with this tradition was given by the "blundering commando" of 1825, which twice raided the wrong native village, carrying off its cattle and killing a number of its women and children.

Two adjustments that became noticeable in the 1820's gave some relief from the growing pressure between white and Bantu society. One was that white society began to soak up labor from Bantu society. Many a Kaffir abandoned as utterly hopeless the struggle to support life in his own country and found employment with the colonists, to whom they were even cheaper than Hottentots. This indicates how terrible conditions must have been in Kaffraria. That the white man contributed, though not alone, to the making of these conditions, there can be no doubt. But he was not at all responsible for conditions that presumably were quite as bad in the interior, far beyond his influence. Here the wholesale destruction wrought by Bantu plunderers, notably the Mantatees, drove other Bantus, Bechuanas, to seek work for a pittance in Cape Colony. So considerable was the infiltration of colored "displaced persons" that in 1828 General Bourke felt he had to provide for their regulation by a special ordinance, the Forty-ninth, which ironically applied the pass system to natives entering the colony in search of work. The very next ordinance, as we have seen, abolished the pass system for Hottentots.

The other adjustment was the diversion of Boer expansion to the north, where drought and distance seemed less forbidding than the human resistance on the east. The government made no effort to check this migration until 1824, when the Orange River became the recognized boundary beyond which no man could get a grant of land. Along this river expanding white society came in contact with the Griquas, half-civilized Hottentots of very mixed blood who recently had been retribalized and also resettled largely under the guiding influence of the missionaries. The two principal centers of these people were north of the river, at Griquatown in the west and Philippolis in the east. To preserve order in this wild region, where half-tamed Griquas shaded off into roving bands of bandits, the missionaries wished to see the government assume authority; but they shrank from urging annexation, fearing that it would betray their flocks to the Boers, and this even after the emancipation of 1828. When the missionaries were in such a quandary, the most that the government would, and perhaps could, do was to issue repeated prohibitions of any crossing of the line by burghers. The burghers, however, were not to be so easily deterred. They continued to cross, first temporarily for pasture and later for permanent settlement, seizing the all too scanty waterholes and purchasing land for next to nothing from the Griquas.

In justice to the whites—Boer as well as British—and the natives with whom they had to deal, we should here note in passing that by far the greatest disturbance in the balance of population at that time in what is now South Africa was not their work, but that of a bloodthirsty Bantu tyrant, the Zulu chief, Chaka. His armies spread fire and slaughter over much of the country covered by the modern Natal and even beyond, taking a terrific toll of human life. It has been said that the victims numbered "more nearly two millions than one." From this holocaust arose Basutoland, beginning with a band of refugees who fled to a natural fortress. Another repercussion was the intensification of the pressure upon the Kaffirs from behind, which aggravated the problem of the eastern frontier. Yet another result was the creation of a human vacuum that was soon to pull in the Boers of the Great Trek.

The conditions noted above, together with years of drought, brought the problem of the frontier to a new head at the very time the missionaries turned to it as the next great challenge after that of the Hottentots within the colony. In 1829 the raids of desperate Kaffirs upon white settlers' cattle-byres became a plague. In 1830, and again two years later, Philip spent much time in Kaffraria, studying the situation on the spot.

Returning in 1833 via the Orange River, Philip came out strongly in favor of extending the colony to include Griqualand, in order to give the Griquas the protection of Cape laws, to restrain their lawlessness, and to use them as a shield against the Matabele, Zulus whose wild behavior was echoing that of Chaka's followers. On the eastern frontier Philip's conclusions were very much to the point: that the Kaffirs, whom he well knew were no angels, were the victims of advancing white settlement; that the prevailing method of handling them, by military patrols, commandos, and reprisals, was not only useless but also dangerous; that there should be a new agreement with them, "something written," to give them effective guarantees; and that, most important of all, the administration of the frontier should be civil instead of military. He pressed these views in a series of letters written during and after his grand tour. They were addressed to Buxton, and through him they apparently exerted considerable influence upon the government in London. The colonial secretary vetoed an ordinance that the governor of the day issued to reinforce the commando system, and he sent out a new governor who, in addition to inaugurating a new constitution in the colony, was to work out a new policy for the frontier. His instructions suggested that the commando system was "brutal" and called for the devising of "such other measures as may appear calculated to protect colonists against unprovoked aggression."

Sir Benjamin D'Urban was the new governor. He arrived at the Cape in January 1834, and until almost the end of the year he showed promise of dealing with the frontier problem as cautiously as with the Hottentot problem that was presented to him in the form of the vagrancy bill. Unlike his predecessor, he seemed to have no prejudice against Philip. In March the missionary superintendent sent the governor a long memorandum on the causes and cure of the frontier troubles, and in May D'Urban invited the author to come and discuss it with him. For months thereafter they were in close collaboration. The result on the northern frontier was a treaty of December 1834 with Andries Waterboer, whereby this Griqua chief of Griquatown was officially made responsible for maintaining law and order in his region and was given a salary, some arms, and an adviser—a missionary who was appointed government agent. In the more strategic Philippolis district, disorders blocked a similar arrangement.

Meanwhile, in August, the two men concerted a plan for establishing a new regime on the crucial eastern frontier. Philip went ahead to "prepare the way" for D'Urban, who was to follow and conclude the negotiation with the natives. Philip carried out his part of the plan, and the promise of a personal visit from the governor to make a treaty with them kept the Kaffirs unusually quiet. But D'Urban, who was always coming "next month," did not follow, and so he let slip an irrevocable opportunity. In November Philip turned back toward the colony, convinced that only the governor could do anything more on the frontier. Before he left it, the missionary saw kraals burning. The reprisal system, released by the theft of three European-owned horses and a foal, was operating again. Violence quickly begat more violence, and before the year was out hostile Kaffirs were pouring into the colony.

Thus began the "sixth" and fiercest of the Kaffir wars at the very time when it looked as if these wars might cease. It ended in May 1835 with a triumphant D'Urban devoid of common sense, an estranged Philip dejected over the shipwreck of fine hopes, the vanquished natives in a more impossible situation than ever, the relieved colonists in a savage mood, and the home government determined to undo as much as possible of the terrible mischief that had been done and was being done.

When dictating peace, Sir Benjamin annexed the country out to the Kei, which he thought was a more defensible line, and he decreed the expulsion of all the tribes who inhabited the region thus acquired. According to his proclamation, these tribes were "treacherous and irreclaimable savages" who had "wantonly provoked" the war, their territory was justly forfeited, and their removal "to a safe distance" was "absolutely necessary to provide for the future security of the colony." It was horrible. Four months later Sir Benjamin contradicted himself and vindicated his critics by reversing his policy, though not the annexation part of it. Finding that the forcible removal of the Kaffirs was a task far beyond the military strength at his command, which he might have realized before, he decided to settle and civilize them on part of the land he had conquered from them, leaving large tracts open for Europeans; accordingly, in September 1835, he negotiated a new settlement with the natives whom he had so recently outlawed as incapable of civilization. How they, who had been badly squeezed for lack of land, could be expected to live on less and still be good neighbors to the Europeans settled on the land that had been taken from them, was a question that Sir Benjamin avoided.

It was not easy for London to catch up with D'Urban, six thousand miles away, three months by mail; and the governor made it more difficult by neglecting his official correspondence for weeks and even months at a time, and then by writing warped dispatches. The chase began in the spring of 1835. Stimulated by the news of the outbreak of the Kaffir War, Fowell Buxton pressed, and the House of Commons passed, a motion for a select committee to consider the state of the aborigines in British possessions. By the end of the summer the committee had collected from Andries Stockenstrom and other witnesses evidence that damned the old frontier system. The Colonial Office, run by Stephen and now headed by another child of the Clapham Sect, the much maligned Lord Glenelg, was disturbed in September by the arrival of D'Urban's report of his May peace settlement, but hesitated to condemn that strange work and its author without fuller information. This the secretary of the London Missionary Society then began to supply in quantity, drawn of course from Philip; and the condemnation was embodied in the famous 150-page dispatch dated the day after Christmas and addressed by Glenelg to D'Urban.

Admitting that hostilities with neighboring tribes might occasionally be inevitable for the protection of the king's subjects, this dispatch of 26 December 1835 maintained that the natives "had an ample justification of the war into which they rushed with such fatal imprudence at the close of last year," and it declared that the territorial conquest growing out of this war must be renounced by the end of 1836. Glenelg qualified the severity of this condemnation by conceding that he might be wrong because he lacked knowledge in the possession of the governor, who was therefore to follow his own judgment if still convinced that he was right. But in any event he was to send home a full explanation of all that had happened. For this the colonial secretary waited more than another year before he dismissed the governor.

Philip has often been pictured as the villain of the piece, Glenelg as his dupe, and D'Urban as his victim. That was how they appeared in the heated atmosphere of contemporary white society at the Cape, but South African scholarship has since corrected the distortion. The governor, who was treated very considerately, was the victim of his own folly; the secretary of state's dispatch might be fat but it was not at all fatuous; and the missionary superintendent was too honest to make any man his dupe. Contrary to the old assertion, sometimes repeated even today, Philip did not idealize the natives or villify the colonists. It was not men but the system that he blamed for provoking the war. Far from persuading Glenelg to cancel the annexation, he agreed with D'Urban in believing that to secure peace the government had to assume full control right up to the Kei, but not on D'Urban's terms. The condition that Philip would attach as essential was that the government should secure the natives in the possession of their lands. He wanted the Kaffirs to be accepted as British subjects so that they could be protected as such. He was an imperialist for purely humanitarian reasons. Unlike the anti-imperialist Glenelg, who was also a strong humanitarian, he did not have to reckon with the British taxpayer.

The utmost that the home government was then willing to do to protect natives from predatory whites beyond the old boundary was to pass the Cape of Good Hope Punishment Act of 1836, which extended the criminal jurisdiction of the colony's courts to cover the actions of British subjects up to 25° South. That this law would also hold whites responsible for what they did to whites was incidental. There was to be no British protection against crimes committed by natives in this wide region, whether their victims were natives or whites. To regulate relations between white and native on the frontier, London sent back Stockenstrom as lieutenant governor.[3] In December 1836, following his instructions from the Colonial Office, he concluded a series of treaties with the Kaffir chiefs, restoring to them the conquered territory, surrendering even the old ceded territory between the Fish and the Keiskamma rivers to be held as a "loan in perpetuity," and renouncing the commando system or anything else that would interfere with the autonomy of the tribes. The chiefs, assisted by government advisers, were to shoulder the burden of maintaining peace and order on the frontier. It was a bold experiment dictated by a home government that trusted in God and the chiefs; and it was far too bold for the average colonist, who also put his trust in God but could no more associate Him with the chiefs than with the devil.

A report that has been compared with Durham's emerged from the South African troubles at this stage. It was the report of the committee on aborigines, which was held up and altered by D'Urban's long delay in submitting his full explanation of what had happened. When his "papers a yard high" reached London in the summer of 1837, it was then too late for the committee to incorporate such a mass of material. Therefore, for the sake of consistency, Buxton cut away all the support-

---

[3] He had resigned his earlier appointment in 1833 because he could not work with the antinative governor of that time.

ing detail already in the report, reducing it to a summary indictment of European colonization for what it had done to native races and a statement of high-sounding principles that should guide the conduct of relations with these races anywhere in the empire or along its frontiers.

The protection of aborigines, so the statement ran, should be the duty of the executive and not be entrusted to colonial legislatures. Contracts for labor services should be so limited as to prevent a relapse into slavery. Alcohol should be kept from the natives because it would destroy them. Private persons should not be allowed to purchase native lands within the empire, or to have any claim on the Crown for protection in the possession of native lands they might acquire outside the empire. Governors should be forbidden to secure any new territory "either in sovereignty or in property, without the previous sanction of an Act of Parliament." Colonial revenues should be charged with the cost of the education, religious instruction, and protection of the natives as a debt owed to them. Punishment of crimes committed by natives within the empire should be tempered by regard for their own customs and traditions and, beyond the borders of the empire, should be regulated by treaties with the local chiefs. Otherwise treaties should be discouraged because they were bound to be unequal. The welfare of uncivilized races required that their contacts with whites "should be diminished rather than multiplied." Yet missionaries should be encouraged, and their essential qualifications were not only "piety and zeal" but also capacity to improve the physical, social, and political conditions of the tribes to which they ministered. The report was a crystallization of current humanitarian ideals and an expression of the sense of imperial trusteeship that Britain then felt. The report also greatly helps to explain the Boer upheaval that had already begun.

The Great Trek, the central event in South African history, was like the wandering of the Children of Israel, the voyage of the Pilgrim Fathers, the Secession of the South, and the opening of the American West, all rolled into one. The trekkers, religious fanatics nurtured on the Old Testament, fled from British rule as from Egyptian bondage. They wandered in the wilderness for years, looking for a place where they could build a community, a commonwealth of their own. Believing that God made colored men to be the servants of white men, they pulled out of the Cape rather than live under a government that was dangerously color-blind. They were also driven forth by land hunger. They doubled the area of European occupation, and the frontier doubled its stamp upon them. This stamp was not quite the same as that of the North American frontier. Life on the veld was more lonely and dangerous, less hopeful and civilized than life on the prairie; for the South African frontier was a poor and dry land that offered no prospect for any settlement other than a very thin one, with 6,000-acre farms and Bantus about, who showed no sign of fading away like the redskins. The exodus of irreconcilable burghers magnified the native problem. It spread as they spread, spilling over the interior. The geographical separation of Boer and Bantu was gone forever, now that the former body had exploded into the latter; the numerical balance of South African society was drastically and permanently altered in favor of the blacks; and the issue of white supremacy, thus intensified, set Boer against Briton.

Some twelve thousand Boers, mostly from the eastern and the northern frontier, left Cape Colony to go on the Great Trek. Their movement began toward the end of 1835, gathered momentum through the rest of the thirties, and slowed up during the early forties. They traveled in parties numbering anywhere from fifty to four hundred—enough for mutual protection and support, and not too many for the proper pasturing of their flocks and herds. Their organization was loose and shifting, for they were intense individualists seeking to get away from government; and it was years before experience led them to establish stable political structures of their own, in Orange Free State and the Transvaal. They also created another republic, that of Natal, but it disappeared before the other two took definite shape.

The main body left the High Veld in November 1837 to go down into Natal. This their able leader, Piet Retief, acquired by a fair bargain with the Zulu king, Dingaan, Chaka's brother and murderer, who thereupon wiped out the bargain by another foul deed. He lured Retief with a hundred followers unarmed into his presence and slaughtered every one of them. In the fighting that followed, the savage impis soon lost the only advantage they possessed, which was surprise. A handful of Boers with smoothbore flintlocks, firing from their mounts in the open or from behind their heavy wagons formed in laager, proved more than a match for a cloud of tribesmen who had no better weapons than assegais. The arrival of Boer reinforcements and a new leader, Andries Pretorius, led to the invasion of Zululand and a decisive battle by Blood River, which cost the Boers three men wounded and the Zulus three thousand slain. The anniversary of this destruction of the main Zulu army on 16 December 1838 is still celebrated in South Africa as Dingaan's Day. Upon the cornerstone of this victory the trekkers estab-

lished their ephemeral republic and its lasting capital, Pietermaritz-
burg, in 1839; and with poetic justice Pretorius helped to remove
Dingaan in 1840 by supporting his brother Panda, who then became a
vassal king paying a heavy tribute to the Boers.

British intervention cut short the life of the Natal republic. Unable
to prevent the Great Trek, which violated the policy inherited from
the Dutch, British authority could not at first make up its mind whether
to follow the emigrants or leave them alone. When the trekkers descended from the Drakensberg Mountains, British ivory traders, by
agreement with the Zulu king, had been in Port Natal for more than a
dozen years and they had just received a magistrate under the act of
1836. Stirred by the massacre perpetrated by Dingaan, they tried to
aid the Boers, with the result that they suffered defeat and lost their
base. Sir George Napier, D'Urban's successor, was anxious to throw a
military contingent into Port Natal, not to recover it for these people,
but to use it as a check upon the emigrant Boers who were stirring up a
hornets' nest and endangering the British frontier. The home government, on the other hand, favored curtailing rather than expanding its
commitments in South Africa, as elsewhere; and there was quite an
argument between London and Cape Town. In 1839 Napier dispatched a contingent too small and too late to control the situation, and
he withdrew it at the end of the year. It was the native policy of the
Natalians that decided the issue. They attacked the natives to the
southwest, back toward the Kaffir frontier of the colony; their unchecked pass law and apprenticeship system was reducing to slavery
the blacks whom they employed.

The second and final British occupation of Port Natal began in May
1842, the troops having been ordered up by the governor to give security to the Cape frontier. This time the Boers attacked the British and
were compelled to disperse only when the latter were reinforced. Instead of concurring in the occupation, the Colonial Office ordered a
withdrawal and proposed to control the trekkers by prohibiting intercourse with them. Napier then won the argument by pointing out that
such a prohibition would be impolitic and impossible, and that the
recall of the troops would be abandoning Natal to the Boer invaders
and its natives to slavery. In the following spring the governor formally
proclaimed the annexation of Natal, and sent Henry Cloete, a lawyer of
Cape Town, a son of one of the oldest Cape Dutch families, and a member of the new legislative council, to negotiate a settlement with the trekkers in the new possession. On condition that there be no slavery, no

color bar of any kind, and no attacks on the neighboring natives, the Boers were to be allowed to remain in occupation and, until other provision was made for their government, to continue their existing institutions unaltered. The threefold condition barred the main object of the trek, but after bitter debates and quarrels the Volksraad accepted the authority of the government from which its members had fled. The republican government lingered on until late in 1845, when a lieutenant governor arrived to administer Natal as a detached dependency of Cape Colony.

With the submission of 1843, the Great Trek retreated back over the mountains, the exodus from the colony fell off, and the pressure of the movement was confined to the High Veld. There too the Trek had caused confusion, native chiefs looked to the British for protection against the Boers, and Napier felt the need to intervene in some manner in order to restore and preserve order. He moved troops up to the Orange, but something more than the power of suggestion was called for, and along with permission to annex Natal he got permission to negotiate treaties with chiefs north of the border river. Late in that year of 1843, he concluded with Adam Kok, the Griqua chief of Philippolis, and Moshesh,[4] the leading Basuto, treaties similar to that of nine years before with Waterboer, which meant that the government of the Cape was more or less committed to intervene on their behalf whenever the Boers threatened them, as the Boers were sure to do the moment either of these chiefs tried to assert his newly recognized powers against a white man. In 1845, British troops had to rush in to rescue Kok after he had attempted to arrest a Boer; a new governor crossed the Orange, which no predecessor had ever done, and tried to untangle the conflict of color; and the most hardened of the trekkers pushed beyond the limits of the Cape Punishment Act (25°), drawing after them their leader, Hendrik Potgieter, founder of the Transvaal.

The new governor was Sir Peregrine Maitland. It was getting on toward thirty years since he had been sent to govern Upper Canada, and he was an old man with a new idea. This new idea, possibly suggested by the disposition of the Mohawk lands in Upper Canada, he presented to a conference of chiefs. It was that each should divide his territory into two parts, one an inalienable reserve for his tribe and the other to be alienable to Europeans for quit rents; and that white and colored jurisdictions could then be segregated, each chief ruling his

---

[4] The treaty with Moshesh was the beginning of the definition of Basutoland.

own people on their reserve, and a British resident managing the Europeans on the lands they leased. Accordingly Adam Kok partitioned his principality, and a British resident was established at Bloemfontein in the alienable part of Philippolis. If Maitland's refined version of an old theme—the white man's appropriation of the colored man's scanty lands—had any chance of adoption elsewhere, it was spoiled by the outbreak of another Kaffir war, which required the substitution of a younger soldier as governor.

The Kaffir war that began early in 1846 is known by a name, not a number—the War of the Ax. An old Kaffir thief, accused of stealing an ax, was being brought to Grahamstown for trial when some natives from across the border forcibly rescued him. Thereupon colonial troops invaded Kaffirland, and the war was on. Another incident might just as well have started it, for the chronic trouble of the eastern frontier was again coming to a head in one of its periodic climaxes. The settlement negotiated by Stockenstrom late in 1836 had broken down, as was inevitable. The Kaffirs were savages and too numerous for the land on which they lived;[5] and the effective policing of the border, across which there was considerable coming and going for peaceful purposes, was impossible because the colony could not pay for it and the mother country would not. In 1840 Napier reported the mounting tension arising from the constant plunder of farmers' cattle and the not infrequent murder of their armed herdsmen. To avoid the danger of war precipitated by outraged farmers' taking the law into their own hands and crossing the border in commandos, he persuaded the Kaffir chiefs to accept a modification of the Stockenstrom treaties. Maitland went further in the same direction and for the same reason, with the result that the 1836 system gradually disappeared and the extension of white power into Kaffirland, intended to prevent hostilities, tended to provoke them. The War of the Ax was much like the "sixth" war of a dozen years before, except that it cost more, was waged on a wider scale, and lasted longer—almost to the end of 1847, nearly two years in all.

This war faced Lord Grey when he took charge of the Colonial Office, and it taught him the necessity for a new frontier policy in South Africa. Though agreeing with his predecessors that territorial acquisitions in this quarter, considered by themselves, "would not be merely worthless, but pernicious—the source not of increased strength but of weakness," he was nevertheless prepared to accept annexation as the

---

[5] By 1843 many Kaffirs were destitute of cattle.

lesser of two evils. In shouldering additional responsibility instead of shrinking from it, he saw the only hope of putting an end to all this anarchy and bloodshed and recurrent war, so disastrous to the natives, injurious to the colonists, and burdensome to the mother country. Maitland's successor was significantly made Her Majesty's high commissioner for South Africa as well as governor of Cape Colony, but he was too busy with the war to exercise his wider powers. The first to make use of them was the man to whom he turned over in December 1847, Sir Harry Smith, Grey's chosen instrument to work out and apply the new policy.

Smith knew South Africa well, particularly the frontier, for he had served in the country for eleven years, during which he conducted the operations of D'Urban's war against the Kaffirs. Since then he had been in India, where he became the hero of the First Sikh War. His initial task on returning to the colony was to liquidate the new Kaffir war, which he did by liquidating Kaffir independence, a step that Grey had already suggested. In the north of the ceded territory, the high commissioner settled some natives (Fingos) behind a belt of retired veterans' villages, and he had the south sold as farms. The country between the Keiskamma and the Kei was erected into a separate dependency under British sovereignty and known as British Kaffraria, the separation serving to preserve it as a native reserve; and beyond the Kei, in order to secure land communication with Natal, he insisted upon a recognition of the Crown's authority.

Turning to the regions north of the Orange, Sir Harry could find no settled government, and the prevailing confusion convinced him that he must either cancel or complete the partial British sovereignty implicit in the treaties with the natives. In other words, he must either let the trekkers fight it out with them or assert control over the trekkers too. For a man of his dynamic nature and of his fighting experience on the eastern frontier, which endeared him to many a trekker, there could be only one choice. In February 1848 he proclaimed the sovereignty of Queen Victoria over all people of every color in the country between the Orange and Vaal rivers and the Drakensberg Mountains. He had persuaded Pretorius to sound out his fellows beyond the Vaal on their willingness to be gathered into the British fold again; but the embittered Boer leader, surprised by this precipitate annexation, turned to undo it. Unable to persuade annexed Boers to rebel, he gathered a body from the Transvaal to force them. As he marched south, his force swelled and he encountered no resistance. He picked up the British resident in Bloemfontein and deposited him on the south side of the Orange. Then Sir Harry Smith rushed north with a stout body of regulars. In August there was a smart clash at Bloomplaats, halfway back to Bloemfontein; Pretorius fled across the Vaal; and the high commissioner repeated his proclamation of the Orange River Sovereignty. Grey was a little startled by this addition to the empire, and he feared that it would "excite some alarm" at home; but he acquiesced, being persuaded by Smith's argument that there was no alternative and his assurance that the inhabitants of the new territory, white, colored, and black, desired annexation and would pay for their own simple government.

Sir Harry Smith's South African house, so promising for a while, began to collapse with the outbreak of yet another Kaffir war in December 1850, the "seventh," which dragged on until 1853. The main cause of this war was his sudden reduction of the powers of the chiefs, whose every decision he made subject to revision by magistrates planted in their midst. This war surprised him in more ways than one. To his dismay the Kaffir rebels were joined by many Hottentots, their hereditary foes, who were disappointed with their treatment after they had fought for the British in the War of the Ax; and to his greater embarrassment the commando system refused to work, the burghers offering various excuses for not turning out in arms. To cap the climax, the revolt in Kaffraria shook the British hold on the Orange River Sovereignty and absorbed the British resources that might have been used to preserve and strengthen that hold.

The Orange River Sovereignty was precariously poised, as might be surmised from the events of 1848. The British resident, who returned to Bloemfontein, was personally and institutionally a poor substitute for a governor. He was a good military officer whose political judgment was not good. He had a legislative council to tie him down, but no executive council to help him up with its advice; he had little revenue and less garrison; and to maintain the peace he had only native levies and burghers who elected their own officers. If the burghers backed him and the authority that he represented, the Sovereignty might survive, but otherwise it could not. They failed him in 1851 when he called them out to deal with Moshesh, whose supercession as head chief of the Basuto people Smith had unwisely ordered because he suspected him of conspiring with the Kaffir rebels.

In Britain the unpleasant news from South Africa stirred a hue and cry, led by the London *Times* and caught up by the opposition in parliament, against the colony, against Kaffir wars, against throwing away millions on both, against the Colonial Office, and against the government. Grey sent Smith more troops with which to extricate himself from his difficulties on the north as well as the east, but he sent them very grudgingly and with a warning that it might be necessary to withdraw from beyond the Orange. If the inhabitants would not support British authority there, "but on the contrary desire to be relieved from it, there is no British interest to be served by endeavouring to maintain it." He admitted that "the check which would be given to the progress of civilization, and the anarchy and bloodshed which would too probably follow . . . would no doubt be greatly to be lamented," but this could not be helped because the British people would not pay, and could not be expected to pay, for the imposition of the alternative. As a further warning of a change in policy, the colonial secretary appointed two assistant commissioners "for the settling and adjusting of the affairs of the eastern and northern boundaries" without having to report through the high commissioner.

Sir Harry was eager to save the Sovereignty as the keystone of the whole South African structure, lying as it did between the Cape, Natal, and the Transvaal. So he rushed the assistant commissioners north, hoping that they would preserve his work by completing it with the addition of the Transvaal, which had yet to achieve political unity and stability. But Smith was praying for the impossible. The Boers of the Transvaal were the most irreconcilable of all Boers, and the most remote—between 750 and 1000 miles from Cape Town. Their independence could not be denied; and unless the British would recognize it, Pretorius threatened to overturn the Sovereignty again. The upshot was the Sand River Convention of January 1852, which recognized the independence of the Transvaal, banned slavery in it, prohibited British alliances with "coloured nations" in it, provided for mutual extradition of criminals and facilities for trade, guaranteed to the Transvaalers the freedom to purchase ammunition from the British, and outlawed the sale of it to natives on either side of the Vaal.

The imperial tide that began to ebb at the Vaal was soon back to the Orange. Grey was prepared for this retreat before he left office early in 1852; and his successors, Tory and Whig, were likewise resigned to the surrender of the Sovereignty because it did not seem worth what it would cost to keep it. By the Bloemfontein Convention of February 1854, it was turned over to its burgher leaders on terms that were an expansion of those of the Sand River Convention. As the United States was then split over the colored population, so was South Africa, only more deeply. It was as if the American North lacked the strength of body and of will to challenge the secession of the South. The two halves of South Africa, now quite independent of each other, were to pursue radically different policies that would make their common and greatest problem still more difficult.

Meanwhile in Cape Colony the conflict between the two basic principles of colonial self-government and imperial trusteeship was being resolved in favor of the former though not wholly so. When Durham wrote in his report that French Canada had been introduced to self-government at the wrong end, at the top instead of the bottom, self-government at the Cape was beginning to grow from below—as it had done centuries before in England. The legislative council planted the seed in an ordinance of 1836 that authorized as few as twenty-five householders who formed a village to initiate an elected municipal government, and by 1840 there was a healthy crop of such institutions. Three years later two other ordinances furthered the cause of self-government in the colony. One provided for local roads under the direction of elected road boards. The other conferred a large measure of autonomy upon the church of the great majority, the Dutch Reformed Church, which had been more or less under the thumb of the administration.

Petitions for an assembly were again sent to London in 1841, this time backed by the governor and citing the success of municipal self-government as justification. Stanley, the colonial secretary, replied in the following year, accepting the general principle but raising all manner of practical objections to its application at the Cape, particularly the cleavage between the white and the colored populations. But the improvement of relations between them undermined Stanley's argument. This same year saw the passage of the Master and Servants Ordinance, which scrupulously avoided any reference to color and rendered the Fiftieth Ordinance obsolete. The old hostility between the mission stations and the colonists, caused by the racial issue, was dying down. Colored people qualified for the municipal franchise and exercised it; and one of them was elected in Cape Town with such little fuss that the colonial secretary of the Cape did not hear about his election—and withdrawal—until some time afterward and then by mere accident.

In 1846 the House of Commons called for a return of all applications from the Cape for representative government and of the answers thereto; and Grey sent the printed report to the governor, a new one, asking him if the principle might not be applied. The War of the Ax and another change of governor put off the question until 1848. Then the million pounds that this war cost made Lord Grey warn Sir Harry Smith that in the future the colony would have to pay for its own Kaffir wars, which of course implied self-government; and the energetic Smith got his advisers to work upon a plan.

There were some differences over details but not on the broad feature of representative without responsible government, the latter to be excluded by the reservation of a large civil list. When Grey got this plan, he feared it was too liberal for the Cape, and he thought of emasculating it by reserving the whole colonial revenue, not just a civil list, to be controlled by the Crown. Sir James Stephen, whose advice was still sought though he had retired, said this would never do because tradition had married taxation and representation. He frankly admitted that representative government at the Cape would be bad government but that opinion at home and in the colony had made it inevitable. Submitted to the Board of Trade Committee of the Privy Council, the plan re-emerged in 1850 with an elected in place of a nominated upper chamber—the nominated legislative council had been very unpopular in South Africa—with provision for dissolution by the governor of both chambers or just the lower one, and with the exclusion of officials from election to either house, though they might attend and speak there, the exclusion being designed to keep the executive aloof from party strife.

By this time crown colony government was thoroughly damned at the Cape by the home government's attempt in 1849 to dump convicts on the colony. The attempt, which was based on a misunderstanding, was defeated by the solid opposition of South Africans, British and Boer, Easterner and Westerner. "Passive resistance had gained the day: a surer indication of a people's fitness for self-government than open rebellion." Like the War of the Ax, the even more expensive "Seventh" Kaffir War, which began in 1850, increased the mother country's impatience with South Africa and the home government's desire to make the colony pay the piper and call its own tune; also, it delayed the implementation of the new constitution, which was ordered to be passed as a Cape ordinance. But Grey could not tolerate the thought of casting off the natives, and his two successors felt the same responsibility to them. The upshot was that representative government was enacted in 1853, but responsible government was not granted for nearly another twenty years.

CHAPTER XVII

Australasia and Systematic Colonization

EDWARD GIBBON WAKEFIELD and his theory of systematic colonization had a powerful influence in building the empire in Australasia during the 1830's and 1840's. Though a social and political outcast, he succeeded where the highly respectable and strategically placed Wilmot Horton had just failed, in pushing a rationalized policy of emigration, because the parliamentary undersecretary lacked the gift of persuasion that the scapegrace possessed in abundance. Wakefield had slipped and fallen when, in his eagerness to get money that he might enter upon a parliamentary career, he had grasped at a fortune by abducting an heiress from school and going through the form of marrying her. Sentenced to three years' imprisonment in Newgate, he found himself in the company of convicts bound for Australia, including some who had already been there as convicts and were professedly anxious to return. From them he learned all he could of conditions in that distant land, and at the same time he devoured a large mass of literature on colonies. It was then that he pieced together his theory from the ideas of others and began to expound it, under the name of another man, in "Letters from Sydney," published first in the *Morning Chronicle* and later in the same year, 1829, as a volume entitled *Letter from Sydney*.

Wakefield insisted that land in the colonies should be made available only as it was really needed; otherwise, as had been all too common, there would be a scramble for it, and private greed would retard the development of the country by dissipating the supply of labor and of working capital and by dispersing settlement in a most uneconomical fashion. The proper formula was to hold the land for sale at a price high enough to prevent these evils but not so high as to discourage desirable purchasers or to cripple their resources. The money derived from the sales was to be spent in sending out new settlers from the mother country, thus assuring a steady supply of labor and sale of land. The emigrants were to be carefully selected, so that they would be of the right age and class, and there would be no surplus of either sex. The whole concept was one of balance and harmony, as befitted that age of Utopian schemes, and the automatic feature struck people as an attractive revelation.

On his release from prison in 1830 Wakefield formed a colonization society to promote his plan. He realized that he would have to remain in the background because of the stigma attached to his name; but he had a genius for working through others, and he gathered a group of converts remarkable for their ability and influence. Chief among them were Lord Durham, Charles Buller, and Sir William Molesworth, all young and radical. The last named had no particular brilliance; but his wealth, industry, and voice in the House of Commons were very useful to the cause of systematic colonization. His political reward came years afterward, in 1855, when just before his death at the age of forty-five he was colonial secretary for a few months. Durham, unlike the other two, did not owe his interest in colonies to Wakefield, for he had already displayed it in 1825 by organizing a New Zealand Company; but he was so impressed by Wakefield that the latter became a principal member of his staff in Canada and the author of the public lands section of the famous *Report*. Buller, outstanding in the House of Commons for his brilliance, was Durham's secretary on this mission, was greatly instrumental in getting the Canadian Union Act passed, and is best remembered as the author of the classic *Responsible Government in the Colonies*. The contemporary rumor about Durham's *Report*— that "Wakefield thought it, Buller wrote it, and Durham signed it"—was a malicious fabrication; but it was also a genuine reflection of the recognized abilities of Wakefield and Buller. As a further indication of Buller's power, we may note that it was he who created the long-current false picture of James Stephen mentioned in an earlier chapter. It was the price this worthy official paid for raising sensible objections to Wakefieldian colonization plans, and for his strict observance of the principle that a civil servant should not participate in public controversy even to defend himself against unjust attack.

This little knot of men, of whom Wakefield was the inspiring center, exerted an influence out of all proportion to their number. This influence, however, has often been exaggerated, partly because of the name commonly applied to them—"radical imperialists" or "colonial reformers." As such they have been credited with being the prophets and

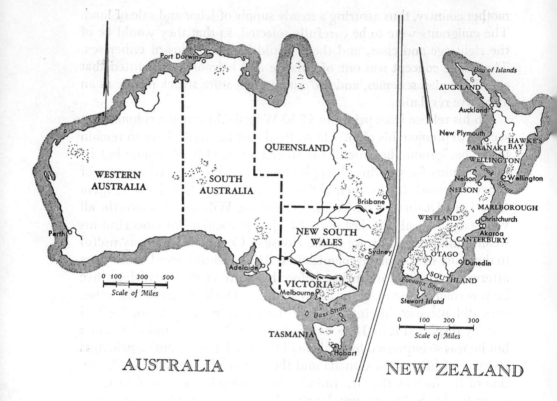

AUSTRALIA   NEW ZEALAND

The Settlement of Australia and New Zealand

even the architects of the twentieth century British Commonwealth. Of course their radical political principles and instincts made them champion colonial self-government and attack the Colonial Office for denying it. But these believers in the empire were greatly outnumbered by the skeptics who, also influential, would grant complete autonomy; and this was becoming inevitable. Wakefield knew little and cared less about government. He was a man of one idea. Through Durham's *Report* he tried to get its application extended to British North America, where it was neither necessary nor possible because emigrants were streaming thither of their own accord and lavish grants had robbed remaining public lands of any market value. What Wakefield and his supporters accomplished was to speed the settlement of Australia and New Zealand by providing them with a population that otherwise would have remained in England or have found another home in North America.

The application of the Wakefield system began in January 1831 as the result of the early conversion of Lord Howick, the future Lord Grey and colonial secretary, who was at this time parliamentary undersecretary.[1] A dispatch was then sent to the governor of New South Wales directing him to substitute, in place of the old methods of granting lands, sale by auction at an upset price of 5 shillings an acre, which was to be the new system for Australia generally; and the Treasury advanced £10,000 against the security of future sales, in order to commence subsidized emigration as soon as possible. More than this amount was realized from sales in 1832, and many times more in the years that followed. Thus the barrier was breached that the high cost of the ocean passage to Australia had raised against emigration in that direction.[2]

New South Wales was the chief beneficiary. There, down to 1831, the Crown had disposed of some three and a third million acres for a song; and then, from 1832 to 1842, it sold two million acres for over £1,000,000, most of which went to bring out 50,000 new settlers. The result was that the population, which in 1828 had been some 36,000, nearly half of them convicts, grew by 1841 to be about 130,000, more than five sixths of them free. Van Diemen's Land, because it was more devoted to convicts, was so much less attractive to free settlers that some were leaving it for the mainland, where in 1835 a party of them founded the Port Phillip settlement, which later grew to be Melbourne. In 1840 the island colony had 27,000 convicts and 40,000 free inhabitants. Of the latter, however, two thirds were under twenty-one. As for the infant Western Australia, child of a capitalist venture, nearly starved by a sterile soil and strangled by a stubborn forest, and a favorite butt of jokes by systematic colonizers, that was a place to stay away from. So much of its more eligible land was in private hands and for sale at 4.5 pence an acre that the 5 shilling price for less eligible land seemed ridiculous. It had 850 residents in 1829, and 2,300 in 1840. Meanwhile another Australian colony had been founded because Wakefield willed it.

South Australia was conceived as a model colony by Wakefield and

---

[1] The new regulations have often been called the Ripon regulations, after the secretary of state who signed them.

[2] The breach made it possible for Australia to benefit from adverse conditions in North America. In 1837 financial panic in the United States and rebellions in Canada frightened many prospective emigrants away from those countries and caused a trebling of the stream to Australia in 1838. This did not fall off again until four years later.

his followers. They were coldly critical of the 1831 regulations as a partial and distorted application of his system; they were burning with enthusiasm to work it out themselves, free of interference and encumbrances. The first scheme, for a joint stock company chartered by parliament, where it had many friends, and empowered to rule the colony, was demolished by the criticism of James Stephen in 1832. He may have suspected what one of the promoters later confessed, that most of them "intended to make money by it." The company was replaced by an association, which proposed the establishment of South Australia as a crown colony with the usual officials, under the direction of the Colonial Office, and with special commissioners appointed by the Crown to manage the land sales and emigration business. Official resistance to any new colonial venture that might increase the burden on the mother country—Western Australia was a fresh warning—was overborne by the pressure of the Wakefield interest in parliament, which passed the South Australia Act of 1834 to set up the colony.

This Foundation Act, as it is also called, never worked satisfactorily. The trouble was not with the location of the basic settlement, for no better place than Adelaide could have been selected. Nor could any fault be found with the colonists, the first of whom were sent out in 1836, for they were distinctly superior to the average emigrant of that age and might even rank with the best of any age. Much of the difficulty arose from the gross incompetence of the board of three commissioners, who were picked by the theorists at the behest of the government; from the division of authority between this board, which sat in London and was answerable to parliament, and the governor, who was responsible to the Colonial Office; and from the natural shyness of capital, which saw little chance of making a killing in this remote colony. By 1840, when the population was just 15,000, enough land had been sold for a population of 100,000, and the government of the colony was bankrupt. But two years later South Australia was at last finding its feet, the old board of commissioners having disappeared, the division of power having been followed by a concentration of it in the hands of a new and strong governor, and the imperial government having contributed £225,000 to restore the solvency of the colonial government, which was considerably less than what was paid for the same purpose in Western Australia with its much smaller population.

Wakefield lost no prestige through the tribulations of South Australia. Disgusted with the way it was being managed, he had washed his hands of the colony almost as soon as it was planted; and his remarkable ability for advertising spread the faith in his system. In 1836 he contrived to have the House of Commons appoint a Select Committee on the Disposal of Colonial Lands, to put one of his disciples in the chair, to appear as the principal witness, and virtually to shape the report. It was before this committee that he launched his more successful campaign for the colonization of New Zealand, which began when the fortunes of South Australia were reaching their lowest ebb; and his association with the Durham mission to Canada, which came in the midst of his New Zealand campaign, gave him a grand pulpit for preaching his doctrine.

It was in response to this preaching and with an eye on defective South Australian practice, rather than principle, that the tottering Whig ministry created the Board of Colonial Land and Emigration Commissioners in 1840, and that the new Tory government passed the Waste Lands Act in 1842. This board, which lasted until the seventies,[3] was designed to do for the colonies generally what the South Australian board, at once superseded by it, had been supposed to do for one colony. It was never able to function in British North America, and it had little scope in South Africa, to which it sent some 3,500 settlers by the end of 1850. Its chief concern was with Australia and New Zealand. The Waste Lands Act, applying to all Australia and New Zealand, made 20 shillings an acre the uniform minimum price for land. Wakefield had been horrified by the adoption of only 12 shillings in South Australia, but the price there and in much of New South Wales was already 20 shillings. The act also liberalized the prescription of how the proceeds of the sales should be spent. The South Australia Act had allocated all to emigration, leaving nothing for other expenses. The new law released up to half for the latter purpose. Wakefield had reached the zenith of his influence. But this was not in Australia. It was twelve hundred miles away to the east.

Wakefield has often been regarded as the father of New Zealand, and in a sense he was. It would be truer, however, to describe him as the doctor who presided at its birth; yet he was something more than this, for he determined the shape and the character of the colony. God and the devil had long been competing for New Zealand; and the struggle between them had reached the point where, to prevent the exploitation of the natives by evil white men uncontrolled by any government, it was necessary for some civilized power to step in. The whole business

---

[3] By which time the growth of colonial autonomy had pretty well eaten away its jurisdiction.

shows up those who can see no good in imperialism, placing them in the category of the willfully blind, along with the Marxists who refuse to admit any virtue in capitalism.

The native problem of New Zealand was much more difficult than that of Australia, which hardly existed at all. On the other hand, it was nothing so complicated and baffling as that of South Africa. The Maoris might be more formidable fighters than any Bantus, and hearty cannibals to boot; but their numbers were limited, and as a race they were far superior to almost any other savages anywhere. British and American whalers and traders provided their first regular white contacts, which were not very civilizing. These adventurers were only too glad to sell them firearms, thereby feeding native wars, and to buy a very special Maori manufacture—preserved human heads—for sale in the curio markets of the world. The first missionaries arrived in 1814, and these men of God found the natives remarkably apt pupils.

Both classes of white men, for their respective purposes, bought parcels of land from native chiefs; and the idea of buying large stretches of it for profitable development by white settlement became current in the twenties. The first to pursue it was a Belgian baron settled in England, Charles de Thiery, who bought through an agent and then vainly sought government support. Among others who followed was J. G. Lambton, the future Lord Durham, whose New Zealand Company of 1825 actually sent out a few settlers. Terrified by the Maoris, most of them departed as quickly as they could.

Meanwhile other whites—generally the offscourings of the earth and particularly escaped convicts—were attracted to the islands, with the result that wild iniquities were wrought there. These so scandalized the governor of New South Wales that in 1831 he struck at the gruesome and growing traffic in heads by forbidding their importation into his colony,[4] and shortly afterward he planted a British resident among the Maoris to protect them. They dubbed this official "the man-of-war without guns" because he was armed with only moral authority, which was not very effective against the sinners he was sent to check. Yet no other authority was possible while the British government was unwilling to assume any responsibility in or for New Zealand, and there the anti-expansionist policy of the era was reinforced by the missionaries, out of regard for the welfare of the Maoris.

Wakefield's New Zealand Association, formed in the spring of 1837

---

[4] Most of the vessels haunting New Zealand waters were fitted out in Sydney.

to force the government to undertake the colonization of the country, included in its committee a most formidable array of public men. This association ran into stiff opposition from the secretary of the Church (of England) Missionary Society, which had cultivated the New Zealand field, and also from the Colonial Office, the two chiefs of which, Lord Glenelg and James Stephen, were pillars of this society. The report of the House of Commons Select Committee on the Aborigines was adverse too, and in the following year, 1838, a committee of the House of Lords echoed the condemnation by the Church Society. But already the missionaries on the spot had come round to the view that official British intervention was necessary to preserve the Maoris from destruction, and Glenelg himself had arrived at the conclusion that the only alternative was "between a colonization, desultory, without law, and fatal to the natives, and a colonization organized and salutary." The reason for the change was, of course, the growing anarchy in New Zealand, where some two thousand British subjects, including two hundred fugitive convicts, were living without any government.

Having agreed in principle with the New Zealand Association, the colonial secretary offered to turn the practical task over to it with a royal charter, if the Association would reorganize as a joint stock company and give the government a veto over its principal personnel. One might expect that, following this proposal, they married and lived happily ever after; but the offer was at once rejected and later, when the Association voted to take it up, Glenelg's successor said that the refusal had canceled it. The feud between the Wakefield pressure group and the Colonial Office was feeding itself by the mutual suspicion it generated. Then the Baron de Thiery, who had reappeared on the horizon with French backing, loomed up as a menace; this precipitated action by both parties, each seeking to forestall the other and the French in New Zealand.

The Wakefield interest, reorganized as the New Zealand Company,[5] dispatched a preliminary expedition in the spring of 1839. It was commanded by the promoter's brother, Colonel William Wakefield, who made extensive purchases of land. Later in the year the first lot of

---

[5] Headed by Durham and including the company of the same name that he had formed years before. On Durham's death in 1840, Wakefield tried to persuade Molesworth to take the vacant chair. Molesworth, who had invested heavily in the company but distrusted Wakefield personally, refused to be a "decoy duck" to attract prospective colonists or a "pigeon" to be plucked. Wakefield then persuaded the deputy governor of the company to become governor. He was Joseph Somes, the greatest shipowner in London.

settlers embarked for New Zealand. They landed at Port Nicholson, later Wellington, in January 1840. A week later, Captain William Hobson of the Royal Navy arrived in the Bay of Islands, several hundred miles to the north, to negotiate with the Maoris for the recognition of British sovereignty. Another week later, with the decisive aid of the missionaries, of whom Henry Williams, a former naval officer, was outstanding, Hobson persuaded the assembled chiefs to sign the Treaty of Waitangi. Thereby the chiefs formally ceded the sovereignty of their territories; the Crown guaranteed them and their people the possession of their lands and other property; the chiefs bound themselves to sell no land except to the Crown; and the natives acquired the rights of British subjects. In May, for further security, Hobson established an alternative British title to the islands by proclaiming British sovereignty over them. In August a French expedition that had sailed in March arrived to plant a colony on the South Island but withdrew, after landing some settlers, because the commander shrank from challenging the British title.[6] Still the Colonial Office would not recognize the New Zealand Company. But before the end of the year Wakefield's astute publicity and wire-pulling produced an agreement by which the company was to receive a royal charter and land at the rate of one acre for every 5 shillings it spent on colonization.

The settlement of New Zealand was slower and less systematic than its planners anticipated. This was partly the result of their own bad management. As in South Australia, much land was sold to absentees for speculation and much to settlers before it was surveyed. The greatest cause of confusion and delay was the company's inability to deliver titles, and this in turn arose from the government's solicitude for the Maoris. For their protection Hobson's instructions required him, on his arrival, to proclaim that no private title to land would be valid unless granted or confirmed by the Crown. This struck at all purchases by private individuals from the Maoris before as well as after annexation, and it necessitated a review to determine what should be confirmed and what should not. Conflicting claims to the same land, different natives having sold it to different whites, also called for adjudication. A commission was appointed to straighten out the tangle, and the work began nicely. Then the second governor, an injudicious man, magnified the difficulty by creating a whole new class of claimants. Alarmed by growing Maori resentment against the treaty ban on sales to private

---

[6] The English company eventually bought out the land claims of the French company for £4,500.

individuals, he first lifted the ban on condition of a payment of 10 shillings an acre to the land fund; shortly afterward, when it was obvious that this fee operated as a prohibition, he reduced it to one penny. London stopped the business and recalled him in 1845, sending as his successor the strong man who had rescued South Australia and was to do even more for New Zealand, Captain (later Sir) George Grey.

Meanwhile the company, out of patience with the government's deference to native rights, took more than one shot at the Treaty of Waitangi. "We have always had very serious doubts whether the Treaty of Waitangi made with naked savages by a Consul invested with no plenipotentiary powers, without ratification by the Crown, could be treated by lawyers as anything but a praiseworthy device for amusing and pacifying the savages for the moment." These were the words of the governor of the company in a letter of January 1843 to Lord Stanley, the colonial secretary, whose reply was a stinging rebuke. In the following year the company again appealed to parliament against the Colonial Office, and got support from a committee of the House of Commons. As this failed to bring any result, Charles Buller in 1845 led a parliamentary assault, likewise in vain, upon the treaty and the government that fathered it.

Perhaps the best comment on this renewed feud in England was then written in New Zealand—in blood. The first serious fighting between the British and the Maoris was at the northern end of the South Island over some land claimed by both. The whites were routed and some of them, taken prisoner, were massacred in accordance with Maori custom. The frightened settlers cried out for vengeance, while the excited natives were pacified by their own victory and by an official assurance that there would be no vengeance. There was none. The injudicious governor, for once judicious, found that the English had been in the wrong, and on this point the Colonial Office agreed with him. The next outbreak was in the North Island early in 1845, and land was at the bottom of it too, in partial accordance with the old Maori saying, "By woman and land are men lost." It was a real war, the last ember of which was not stamped out until more than two years later; and again there was no vengeance, though this time the natives who fought the British had been wrong and had lost. Confiscation of land might seem a just punishment for rebellion. Yet there was none of it, thanks to the wise forbearance not of the settlers or of the company but of Governor George Grey and the Colonial Office. It is also noteworthy that many Maoris were British allies in this struggle.

Systematic colonization was at its best when resumed after these rough interruptions, and this happy phase had its origin in a shrewd idea that early occurred to Wakefield. Why not convert church people at home from enemies into friends by establishing church colonies in New Zealand? Two such were planted, both in the South Island, which for some strange reason had been almost entirely neglected. It was much more inviting than the North Island, for it was not nearly so crowded with trees and Maoris. Down in the south of the island, commencing in 1848, Scottish Presbyterians of the Free Kirk formed the Otago settlement with its capital Dunedin, which name is the Gaelic for Edinburgh. More than halfway up the east coast, the Church of England followed suit in the Canterbury settlement with its city, Christchurch. The first "Canterbury Pilgrims" arrived late in 1850. While these two settlements, whose population was most carefully selected, were struggling onto their feet, the New Zealand Company was wobbling on its last legs. Hopelessly in debt to the government, which refused to carry it any longer, it had to surrender to the Crown its lands and its charter. Its fall marks the end of the era of the systematic colonizers. Their greatest monument, New Zealand, already had a white population of about thirty thousand.

By a curious irony Wakefield's system was designed for an agricultural economy such as prevailed in British North America, from which it was excluded, rather than the economy that conditions dictated in a large part of the empire where it was applied; and there, as a consequence, a dominant sector of the rural economy had to be left outside the system. Wakefield forgot wool, the staple product and chief wealth of Australia; and this at the very time when British industry had awakened to its dependence upon the Australian raw material, and the rapidly swelling flocks of the sheepmen had burst the bounds of settlement prescribed by the government.[7] Whatever the theorist might say about the concentration of settlement, there was no stopping this dispersion over the interior of Australia. Three acres were needed to feed a sheep, and wool would bear a land carriage of three hundred miles.

The "squatters" were outside the law, and the regulations of 1831 threatened to lock the door behind them. The government in London was as blind as Wakefield, but the governor on the spot[8] saw the prob-

---

[7] Roughly a semicircle around Sydney and a hundred miles from it, embracing Governor Darling's nineteen counties as he defined them in 1829.

[8] Sir Richard Bourke, who had earlier been acting governor at the Cape.

lem clearly. In 1835 he wrote home pointing out the impossibility and the undesirability of stopping a movement so essential to the welfare of Australia and England, and the danger inherent in letting it run wild. He proposed to give it legal recognition, and to assert the rights of the Crown over the waste lands thus being appropriated, by granting annual leases at a nominal rent, such as had been the rule for stockmen within the pale. Glenelg agreed, and the legislative council of New South Wales enacted an annual fee of £10 for each squatter irrespective of the number of acres he stocked. Three years after this face-saving measure of 1836, the courts of the colony began to defend, though they would not define, the squatter's right of occupancy as good against anybody but the Crown. In 1839, also, the legislative council of New South Wales broke away from the uniform payment by adding an assessment varying with the size of the flocks, and assigned the new levy to the support of a new arm of the law in the wilderness—the border police.

The Land Sales Act of 1842 legalized for all Australia and New Zealand the annual licenses of occupation that New South Wales had developed, and at the same time it stimulated an agitation among the squatters for better terms to match their better conditions. From being land freebooters living in sod huts, they were becoming self-conscious capitalists with decent houses and other buildings. Their increasing investment in improvements made them impatient with their annual tenure. They sought the security of something more permanent. After much consultation between London, Sydney, and the back country, during which a bill was drafted in London, given its first reading in the House of Commons, and then sent to Australia for further criticism, an act embodying a compromise between public and private interests was passed by parliament in 1846 and brought into operation by an imperial order in council of March 1847. The new law left the yearly limit on leases in "settled lands" but allowed leases for eight years in "intermediate lands"—the populated pastoral districts—and for fourteen years in the "unsettled lands" of the farther interior; it provided for purchase, at the 20 shillings per acre minimum, the lessee to have the first option to buy.

Wakefield and his circle were from the beginning the staunch foes of transportation. Its shadow, which at one time or another darkened every other Australasian colony, was never allowed to rest on either of the two colonies founded by the ex-convict. Transportation to South Australia was expressly prohibited by the founding act. New Zealand, however, owed its immunity to the resolution of the Colonial Office. The original instructions to Hobson asserted "as a fundamental principle of the new colony that no convict is ever to be sent thither to undergo punishment." Hobson objected that it might be impossible to construct public works in New Zealand without convict labor, only to be told that the decision was "fixed and unalterable." But this resolution was perhaps largely a reflection of the strong public opinion that had grown during the thirties in the mother country.

Transportation was accepted with scarcely a question until the year of the Great Reform Bill, and from that time it was assailed by reformers who could not often agree on much else. The humanitarians attacked it on moral grounds and the Benthamites on utilitarian grounds, while the systematic colonizers were determined to destroy it because it poisoned the atmosphere for healthy colonization. As an illustration of how it failed to punish or reform, the witty Whig parson, Sydney Smith, cited "a wicked little tailor" who wrote home boasting that he was "as comfortable as a finger in a thimble, . . . had several wives, and was filled every day with rum and kangaroo." The attacks led to a searching investigation during 1837 and 1838 by a House of Commons committee headed by Molesworth and including among its members such outstanding men as Russell, Howick, Peel, and Buller. The report, largely the work of the Wakefieldians, strongly condemned the system and recommended its abolition. The government was not prepared for such a sweeping change; and the contemporary reaction in Australia to the report was hostile, for the report gave an unflattering picture of colonial society and would take away the supply of cheap labor. The threat was all the more resented because these same English theorists had already deprived the colony of cheap land. Nevertheless, in 1840—just after the founding of New Zealand—an imperial order in council abolished transportation to New South Wales.

The system was becoming more objectionable. More of the convicts were real criminals, now that the age of political reaction was left behind; and the crimes for which they were transported were more serious, now that the reform of the criminal law had cut down the work of the gallows. But the problem of what should be done with the convicts sentenced to transportation—then numbering between four and five thousand a year—was a difficult one that took years to work out. At first it was thought that Van Diemen's Land could accommodate them all, but the swelling of the polluted stream to that colony soon began to operate like a Gresham's law of colonization, driving out free settlers. Some relief was found in the new Port Phillip settlement, where labor was in great demand. But the convicts who were sent thither were given "conditional pardons"[9] as graduates of Pentonville, the model prison established at the behest of Jeremy Bentham and opened in 1842. Here was the real solution—penal reform, which obviated the need for transportation—but this was not yet fully seen.

Meanwhile Australian opinion, with one notable exception, was swinging so strongly against the admission of "expatriated villains" from England that it hastened the end of transportation. In 1849 the people of Melbourne forced a shipload of "Pentonvillains" to sail on to Sydney; and the people of Sydney being equally determined to prevent a landing there, the unwanted were sent on to Moreton Bay, a subsidiary penal settlement commenced some years before.[10] Also, in 1849, the people in Cape Colony, as we have seen, blocked the extension of transportation to their country by refusing to allow the landing of a cargo of "conditional pardon" exiles, who then had to go on to Van Diemen's Land. There the free settlers were already so desperate that their London agent was trying to insist that not one more convict should be sent to their colony. At the very same time Western Australia, the one exception, appealed for what the others were rejecting. It seemed to be the only possible salvation of that infant colony, where land was not yet worth the minimum price imposed by imperial statute in accordance with the principles of the systematic colonizers. Transportation to Van Diemen's Land was finally stopped in 1852, and in the following year the colony symbolically closed the door on its hateful past by adopting the new name Tasmania. The first convicts were sent to Western Australia in 1850, and the last in 1868, when this one vestige of the system was eliminated in the interest of the colony and its neighbors and because it was no longer useful to the mother country or tolerated by the Colonial Office. It had given a much-needed economic stimulus to Western Australia, but at the price of retarding its constitutional development.

Indeed, if we consider Australia as a whole, we see on a much larger scale the compensating reaction of which this in Western Australia was a belated example. It was transportation that was primarily responsible for the British colonization of that continent, and it was transportation that long withheld free institutions from it. The Australian demand for

---

[9] Therefore their dispatch to what was still part of New South Wales did not contravene the order in council that stopped transportation to that colony.

[10] In 1824, when Norfolk Island was revived.

them became audible in the 1820's, when the emancipists under the leadership of W. C. Wentworth, one of the first whites born in Australia[11] and about the ablest man in the country, appealed to the government in London for an assembly and trial by jury, and against the monopoly of power by the exclusives. But the greatest reform of the constitution then and for years afterward was the 1828 enlargement of the legislative council to include nonofficial appointed members—who were picked from the exclusive ranks.

Real constitutional reform did not come until the emancipists had reversed their political principles and joined the exclusives against the popular cause. This political conversion, or perversion, is another illustration of how interest may govern principle. It was brought about by the influx of free settlers, who were wage earners, and by the economic success of the leading emancipists, big merchants, squatters, and landowners, who were employers of labor. The new popular party was all for pushing wages up by cutting off the competition of convict labor, while the new reactionaries were so eager to have cheap labor that they cried out against the abolition of transportation and talked even of introducing coolie labor. During the late thirties conditions in Australia were changing so fast that the home government postponed from year to year a parliamentary revision of the constitution of New South Wales. It was a foregone conclusion that the termination of transportation would precipitate the introduction of popular government, and so the order in council of 1840 led to the enactment of a new constitution in 1842.

The New South Wales Act of 1842 transformed the legislative council by increasing its membership to thirty-six and making twenty-four of the seats elective with a low property franchise. It thus became a sort of combined assembly and council. The act also prescribed a rather elaborate scheme of local self-government, based on Canadian experience but still more on English experience in the reform of municipal government. Other provisions placed the disposal of the Crown lands and the revenue derived from them beyond the competence of the colonial legislature, since the Waste Lands Act of earlier in the same year regulated all this business; and there was provision for a permanent civil list, to bridle the popular element in the legislature, following the lesson learned in Canada. Crown colony government was then left without change in the rest of Australia—in Van Diemen's

---

[11] Norfolk Island, 1790.

Land because of its convicts, and in the other colonies because they were still mere infants.

New South Wales, by far the oldest, richest, and most populous Australian colony, rushed through the transitional stage of representative without responsible government, trying to make up for time lost under the penal regime and to catch up with the British North American example. The governor, who controlled the executive, soon found, as he feared, that the elected majority of the legislature would not accept his leadership nor be content until they controlled him; and the failure of the local self-government scheme, which was not at all suited to Australian conditions, concentrated the demand for self-government on the higher level. When Grey took over the Colonial Office in 1846, a deadlock between executive and legislature had been reached in Sydney. But he was not willing to make in Australia a surrender that seemed inevitable in America. The executive in New South Wales possessed a financial independence that had been lost in Canada, and there was no neighboring United States "down under." Responsible government was not conceded there until shortly after Grey left office. Yet he contributed much and would have contributed more to the constitutional development of Australia.

The memorable Australian Colonies Government Act of 1850 was several years in the making. It first took visible shape in proposals that Grey sent to New South Wales in 1847 for criticism. With the consequent amendments, they were referred to a privy council committee, whose report was drafted by Sir James Stephen on whom, though now retired because of ill health, Grey leaned heavily for advice. The report was circulated among the Australian governors for further testing by local opinion before the act was finally passed. The act severed the Port Phillip District from New South Wales and erected it into a separate colony named Victoria, after the queen; and provided for a similar separation in the north—the future Queensland—when the time was ripe. The act also extended the representative system of New South Wales to all the other Australian colonies[12] and gave all their legislatures, including that of New South Wales, certain constituent powers. They might amend the way in which they were constituted, and also their civil lists, under the condition that every such amendment had to be submitted to parliament before it could receive the royal assent. Grey

---

[12] Immediately to Victoria, Van Diemen's Land, and South Australia; and to Western Australia as soon as a third of its householders petitioned for it.

had hoped to make the Australian legislatures conform to the traditional bicameral type, and, what was much more important, to establish a federal government for the whole of Australia. In both respects Australians did for themselves, but much later, what the colonial secretary would have done for them in 1850.

Whatever the rejoicing in other parts of Australia, where the act was a new charter of political liberty, there were loud and angry protests in New South Wales because the act did not give responsible government. After the fall of the Russell administration early in 1852, Grey's Tory successor granted the principle, but his government was out of power before the end of the year and a new Whig or Liberal colonial secretary confirmed and implemented the policy. What was given to Canada could not be withheld from New South Wales, and what was given to New South Wales could not be withheld from the other Australian colonies except Western Australia, which, for the special reason already noted, had to wait until 1870.

In New Zealand, as in South Africa, the native problem impeded constitutional development, but even so this development was remarkably rapid. Charles Buller, addressing the House of Commons in 1845, demanded representative government for the New Zealanders, and Peel was ready to grant it. In the following year, shortly after entering the Colonial Office, Lord Grey had an act passed that did grant it; but Governor Grey held up its application and then persuaded the home government to suspend it for five years. London had thought the provisions of the act were sufficient to protect the Maoris; but the governor, from his much fuller knowledge, pointed out convincingly that the measure would deliver the native majority into the hands of the white minority and that this would be highly dangerous as well as unjust. A new act was passed in 1852, the New Zealand Constitution Act, which granted a large measure of self-government with six provincial legislatures for the six principal settlements[13] and a federal legislature, and surrendered control of the revenue. When the first general assembly met in 1854, it adopted with only one dissentient voice a resolution moved by Wakefield himself demanding responsible government. London yielded without question, for the control of native policy had been reserved for the Crown to exercise through the governor. Before it was finally handed over, in the following decade, there was another Maori war.

---

[13] Auckland, New Plymouth, Wellington, Nelson, Canterbury, and Otago.

CHAPTER XVIII

The Tropical Colonies under the Impact of Emancipation and Free Trade

HOWEVER GREAT were the colonial grievances that led to the American Revolution, they were small compared with what the British West Indies suffered at the hands of the mother country in the first half of the nineteenth century, particularly in the fourth and fifth decades of it.[1] Yet no corresponding revolution followed, nor was there even a threat of one, for these colonies were helpless. They were individually too weak, collectively too scattered, and sociologically too unstable to think of forcible resistance by themselves; and they were geographically too cut off from the United States for them to dream of getting any outside aid. Had they lain as close as the British North American colonies to the great Republic, there would have been a different tale to tell, but exactly what this tale would have been is an idle and uncertain speculation.

The sugar colonies were the only part of the empire upon which emancipation fell as a heavy blow, and it has commonly been said that they were ruined by it. This statement, however, needs qualification. Though the whites, the small minority of the population, were worse off, the blacks as a whole were much better off—so much so that it is noticeably reflected in the improvement of the quality and the increase of the quantity of imported foodstuffs, clothing, and other merchandise. Also it should be observed that the blow was not so serious in the few newly acquired colonies as it was in the many old ones—the historic

---

[1] One hoary grievance was then removed. The 4.5 per cent export duty on the produce of the Leeward Islands was repealed in 1838.

British West Indies. There it was crushing because dry rot had eaten through their economic structure.

Absentee proprietors, long the rule, had been drawing everything they could out of the plantations and putting nothing back. Without knowing it, they had been living on capital. For the management of their estates they depended upon resident agents, called attorneys, whose regular remuneration was 6 per cent of the gross value of the produce that they shipped. This was a heavy burden even when the attorney was both able and honest, and it was augmented in various ways when, as was common, he was simultaneously responsible for a number of estates. Then there were the charges of the London or Bristol merchant to whom the sugar was consigned for sale, through whom all stores were purchased, and by whom the whole business of the plantation was financed. This man usually held a strangling mortgage on the property and made a lot more out of it than the 6 per cent interest on it. He collected his commission of 2.5 per cent on the gross selling price of the sugar, including the customs duty, for which he advanced the money; and in the beginning of the 1830's the inclusion of the duty in the calculation made this selling cost approximate the managerial cost, which the merchant remitted to the attorney. In addition, the merchant charged his commission on all the supplies he bought, and made a still further gain by paying cash for the goods and entering the credit price in his account with the plantation.

More and more was taken from less and less. The fat profit once guaranteed by the monopoly of the home market had been shrinking away under the competition of expanding production on fresh land in the new colonies—Trinidad, British Guiana, and Mauritius—and under the pressure of hard times in the mother country. By 1831 the price of British colonial sugar in bond in London had fallen to 23s. 8d. a hundredweight, which was 4d. less than the specific duty it still had to pay and was not a third of what the price had been in 1814. Meanwhile British consumption instead of increasing with the cheapness of the article had actually decreased by more than a pound to about 17 pounds a head yearly. The marvel is not that sugar estates changed hands with great frequency and that British capital was disappearing down the West India drain, but that a few plantations could show a net profit until 1831, when it was wiped out by the last fall in price. From this low the market recovered, and the rise continued through emancipation. By 1836 the price was up to 40s. 10d., the 1819 level. But costs were also up and profits down. Indeed, the price seems to have climbed chiefly because production fell, production fell because it did not pay, and emancipation made it more difficult to pay.

The antislavery agitation wrung loud wails of impending ruin from the planters, who thereby completed the ruin of their own credit, for the lending public took them at their word when parliament passed the Emancipation Act. The damage the planters thus did to themselves was quickly repaired by the compensation paid by the Treasury. Though creditors gobbled up a large proportion of it, what they took meant lifting that much from the load of debt that was dragging down the planters. Some of the compensation money, and a lot of other fresh capital subscribed in England, went into the establishment of banks in the sugar colonies, where such institutions had been scarcely known until the substitution of a free for a slave economy made them necessary. But the revival of the planters' credit was only temporary, and it was soon followed by a long period of financial reorganization, during which old capital was written off as gone forever and some new capital was also lost.

Unfortunately there was a narrow legal limit, since removed, to this cancellation of debt; for the old English law of real property, as applied in the colonies, made the purchaser of an estate liable for obligations attached to it even though they might exceed the revenue from it. St. Lucia dipped into its French past and pulled out a French formula whereby sixty-nine of the eighty-one sugar estates of the island were freed of their mortgages by judicial sale. No other British Caribbean colony adopted a solution of this kind until a few years after the middle of the century. Nevertheless, the old sugar colonies as a whole had traveled a good way along the painful road to financial salvation when the mother country struck them down in her own interest by adopting free trade. But more of this anon.

There were great differences between the sugar colonies in the way they adjusted themselves to the abolition of slave labor. One of them, little Antigua, by its own legislative action skipped the apprenticeship stage, which elsewhere proved to be disappointing and even annoying to all who were concerned. The thirty thousand slaves of Antigua had reached an exceptionally high level of development, their relations with their masters were correspondingly good, and they had to go on working for them or starve, because the colony was densely populated, had no undeveloped land, and imported all its provisions. Here the adjustment was easiest, and there was little change in the volume of production. There was likewise little change in the other small and thickly populated islands, where the alternative of starvation kept Negroes at their old tasks even after apprenticeship was abruptly ended in 1838.

Piecework was extensively employed, though not in Barbados, because it was more satisfactory than daily wages for certain operations; incidentally, it revealed that freedom could compress into four or five hours a whole day's work for a slave. Wages were lowest in Barbados and some of the other crowded and impoverished islands, where 9d. a day was common. They were highest in Trinidad and British Guiana,[2] where a serious shortage of labor and a great surplus of rich land maintained a rate between 1s. 8d. and 2s. 6d. There and in other colonies that had unoccupied land, such as Jamaica and St. Vincent, there was a sort of wage dilemma or unstable equilibrium. If the rate fell, the Negro would disappear from the plantation because he could make more by cultivating a little plot for himself; if it rose, he would appear less frequently because he could earn enough in less time to satisfy his limited wants. When making the early plunge into full freedom, Antigua copied from rural England the customary law that recognized payment of a week's wages as proof that the recipient was hired for a year, subject to withdrawal by either party on giving a month's notice; but when other colonies tried to do the like four years later, the home government would not let them curtail the newborn freedom of the blacks in this fashion. The same jealous guardianship blocked the colonial enactment of laws against squatting and vagrancy.

There were fewer hands to work the estates even in the crowded colonies. On the termination of apprenticeship almost all the children and a majority of the women were withdrawn; and their menfolk, as if stricken by the weariness of centuries of toil, absented themselves whenever they did not absolutely need to earn the current wage. The revulsion from field labor was greatest in Mauritius, where the slave trade had lingered longest. There, out of an apprentice force of some thirty thousand, only five thousand, all males, could be persuaded to continue for wages. The revulsion was also very strong in Jamaica and British Guiana, where masters with singular shortsightedness had extracted the uttermost from their apprentices, often making their lot worse than it had been under slavery.

One compensation for the contraction of the old labor force was the recruiting of local substitutes. Many free blacks and colored people,

---

[2] But not in Mauritius, for a reason that will be noted presently.

who during slavery would not touch field work lest they compromise their status, were now attracted to it by the wages offered, and so also were quite a number of former domestic slaves. These new hands were few compared with the need, and more hope centered upon immigration. Jamaica got a few hundred Germans and a few thousand Irish and Scots, but soon abandoned the experiment as hopeless because these laborers perished like flies under the combined influence of the island's climate and drink. Some Portuguese went from Madeira to British Guiana, with little more success.

British Guiana, Trinidad, and St. Lucia attracted many blacks from the more heavily populated islands, of which Barbados was the principal loser; and there would have been a wholesale redistribution of labor between the British possessions in the Caribbean if the home government had not intervened in 1839 with an order in council outlawing the importation of contract labor lest it revive servile conditions. As planters would pay the passage only of those already bound to them by contract, and the blacks were incapable of moving themselves, the promising intra-Caribbean migration fell away. What was left of it depended on subsidization by the governments of the newer colonies; and this, after another three years, the older colonies persuaded the home government to stop.

No other source of immigration seeming possible, the labor-hungry planters turned their eyes to West Africa and India. Only a few liberated Africans were sent, for the Colonial Office was mortally, and perhaps rightly, afraid of encouraging the nefarious traffic that Britain had been trying to suppress for a whole generation. Humanitarian objections in Britain also limited to a few hundred the introduction of Indian coolies into the Caribbean. But Mauritius, to which the voyage was much shorter and in which conditions were not so strange to them, received them by the tens of thousands. Their migration, in the thirties and forties, solved the pressing labor problem of this one sugar island—and made its population predominantly Indian.

The introduction of laborsaving devices, for which very little of the compensation money was used, helped the West Indies to limp along under emancipation. The commonest substitution was that of horsepower for manpower—of the plow for the hoe—in the preparation of the soil for cane planting. Wheelbarrows and occasionally even wagons on rails replaced heads for carrying loads, and some machinery came into use for other operations. But the new methods were only slowly adopted. The planters as a class were steeped in conservatism, and the

Negroes were no less prejudiced. Native ignorance and carelessness could finish tools before the job. They also caused much wastage of horses. Hilly land in the islands and the open drains and canals that intersected the plantations of British Guiana limited the use of the plow. The steam engine scarcely appeared in the islands, though it had long been the common motive power of the sugar mills in this mainland colony. There, however, the industry was much younger than in the islands, it was organized in much larger units, and it had always faced a labor shortage.

Jamaica, with its 312,000 apprentices out of a total of 670,000 in all the British colonies, made the least adjustment to the abolition of slavery, and paid the natural penalty for failure. This is reflected in sugar production. The average during the five years before emancipation was 3,917,912 hundredweights for the British Caribbean colonies, of which Jamaica accounted for 1,384,111. The corresponding figures for the four years after emancipation are 3,487,801 and 1,040,070. In the early forties these averages fell to 2,583,291 and 677,896. The output of Jamaica had been cut in half. By way of contrast, it may be observed that the average production of Mauritius during these three periods was 470,155, 549,872, and 605,763 hundredweights respectively.

Emancipation precipitated a political and constitutional crisis in the West Indies that, to the embarrassment of the Whigs in power at home, happened to coincide with the crisis in Canada. The strain that the abolition of slavery imposed on the relations between the mother country and the colonies whose economy had rested on slave labor, was aggravated by the colonial enactment and imperial disallowance of legislation touching Negroes, and by the mere presence of the stipendiary magistrates. These magistrates were excellent officials, but they were hated as intruders who personified the deep distrust with which the government and the public in Britain viewed the ruling class in the plantation colonies. The latter's feelings toward London were very much like those of the planters in the Southern States toward Washington in the era of the Civil War, and London reciprocated.

As might be expected, these feelings came to a head in Jamaica. The protest of its assembly in 1838 reads like the envenomed charge of an oppressed nation against an oppressor nation. Parliament had "usurped the legitimate powers of the Assembly" with "monstrous pretexts" supported by "falsehoods and slander"; and was guilty "either of imbecility and cowardice," if yielding to popular pressure, "or of fraud and malice, and a thirst for omnipotent power, if the injustice was the result of deliberation and design." Jamaica, according to this hysterical document, would never consent to be ruled by men who had failed to give England decent government, were responsible for Ireland's woes, and had just provoked rebellion in Canada. The assembly went on strike, and essential laws expired.

The home government, following its own recent precedent in dealing with deadlock in Lower Canada, in 1839 introduced into parliament a bill to suspend the constitution of Jamaica for five years. But Peel's strenuous opposition frustrated this desperate Whig measure, and Lord Melbourne became the first head of an administration since Lord North to resign over a colonial question. The following month saw the Whigs back in office with a milder measure, which parliament made milder still before passing it. This empowered the governor and council to revive laws that the assembly allowed to lapse.

Lord John Russell, the colonial secretary at this time, began to try the effect of the genial sun instead of the harsh wind in dealing with Jamaica. He recalled the governor to whom, as the victim of circumstance, clung all the evil associations of the bitter quarrel between the assembly and the Crown; and in his place he sent out Sir Charles Metcalfe, who had made an enviable reputation as an administrator in India, with instructions to conciliate the colonials and win their cooperation. In this he was extraordinarily successful.

Metcalfe persuaded the assembly to act so that he did not have to use his emergency power of legislation, the exercise of which, in the explosive atmosphere of the time, might have wrecked his mission. He also cultivated a better spirit in Jamaica by impressing upon London the wisdom of trusting the planters and their assembly instead of insisting that they should be above reproach, of preferring minor evils wrought by the assembly's enactments to the major evil of interfering with self-government. In September 1841, two years after the new governor was sent out, Stephen drew up an important minute in which he admitted that for twenty-three years the practice of the Colonial Office had been to scrutinize all Jamaican legislation to catch anything that might injure labor, but that now the time had come to adopt the generous policy urged by Sir Charles. What Metcalfe began, his successor, Lord Elgin, developed; and Jamaica might well have called them blessed, for they turned the West Indian crisis that had centered in this colony. But the good they did was soon forgotten under the heaviest blow of all that fell on the West Indies as the age of anti-imperialism was reaching its climax.

Free trade was worse than emancipation or the abolition of the slave traffic. Much as the planters howled over the stopping of their supply of servile labor and over the liberation of their slaves, they knew in their hearts that their house, though sadly shaken and torn, had not yet fallen and could not fall so long as it was held up by their monopoly of the home market. Also, it was openly admitted in the mother country that by destroying the slave economy of her sugar colonies she was incurring a new and heavy moral obligation to maintain the prohibitive duties on foreign sugar, especially that which was slave-grown, which meant the great bulk of it. Everybody knew that the cost of production was much lower in Cuba and Brazil because they had an abundance of slave labor kept replenished by a thriving slave trade. Therefore, when the Sugar Duties Act of 1846 scaled down the foreign duty so that it would equal the colonial duty at the end of five years, this action of the mother country struck the Caribbean colonies as the Great Betrayal.

Britain was sacrificing her own principle and her own colonies in order to get cheaper and more sugar, and she got it. Within ten years the price her people paid was almost halved and their consumption per head was exactly doubled—to 34 pounds a year—while the specialized economy of her old sugar colonies was ruined beyond repair. In this respect there was no comparison between the impact of free trade and that of emancipation. The inevitable collapse of prices, precipitated and accentuated by the commercial panic of 1847, wiped out banks and merchants as well as planters; and this time the havoc was not limited to white men. The old rate of wages became impossible, and by the summer of 1848 there was a forced reduction that averaged about 25 per cent and in some thickly populated islands, such as Antigua, was 50 per cent. Estates by the score were abandoned as not worth cultivating. Some Jamaican owners who threw up their properties managed to salvage a little out of the wreck by selling their machinery to planters in Cuba! Not until some time after the middle of the century was there any recovery in the West Indies.

Meanwhile despair and fury filled the planters, who were not at all mollified by an imperial act of 1848 postponing from 1851 to 1854 the equalization of duties; and another constitutional crisis flared up, angrier than the last one. Last time the Combined Court of British Guiana had refused to vote supplies and the conflict had ended in a draw. This time labor strife, with incendiarism and other violence, provided an ugly background for the constitutional struggle, the control of the government was at stake, and there was no draw. The Combined Court demanded that the Crown pare 25 per cent from the fixed civil list, while the Colonial Office insisted that the reduction should be made first in the other six sevenths of the public expenditure. Grey sent out a new governor, Sir Henry Barkly, an able member of the House of Commons and the son of a West India planter. He was expected to conciliate but the opposition would only be coerced, and they helped to bring about their own defeat. Their stoppage of supplies for almost a year so damaged the colony that they lost popular support. When Barkly cut £80,000, or almost half, from the estimate of the above other expenses, and proposed a widening of the franchise, the Combined Court voted the necessary taxes in the latter part of 1849.

In Jamaica, when an acrimonious dispute with the governor had dragged on for months, the assembly passed a bill reducing the salaries paid to him and other officials of the colony, the council threw out the bill, and there was deadlock. In the following year, 1850, a temporary accommodation was made, which lasted until 1853. The planters were counting on a change of administration at home to restore the preference for colonial sugar—until their hopes were dashed by the Conservative government of Derby and Disraeli, which came into power early in 1852 and fell from it before the year was out. The assembly then made another slash at official salaries, the council blocked it, and the lower chamber went on strike. Barkly was promoted to Kingston and he broke the deadlock by intimating, on behalf of the home government, that the assembly could not expect to retain power it abused.

Turning from the British sugar colonies to their British neighbors, we find them relatively little affected by emancipation and free trade. The Bahamas, unable to compete with the Southern States, had abandoned the cultivation of cotton introduced by the Loyalists; their trade was very small—mostly the export of some salt, sponges, and other local produce to the United States. The islanders' most important source of income was the salvage of vessels wrecked on their reefs. Because these rocks were legion, the currents treacherous, the winds often sudden and violent, and the islands lying athwart common trade routes, there were several hundred wrecks each year—mostly American and British. Such being the economic activity of the Bahamas, the slavery issue meant little to them except as a chronic cause of quarrel between the executive and the assembly before emancipation but not afterward—when there was little serious friction—and the tariff policy of the mother country touched no Bahaman interest.

Bermuda had lost almost all its entrepôt trade, which had once been very profitable. But it still had some shipbuilding and general carrying trade; and it was coming to rely heavily upon the deep sea and the devil—its naval establishments, dockyard and hospital, and its convict settlement, the inmates of which toiled only for the government and could not be discharged in the colony. Here too slavery was of little consequence, which somewhat detracts from Bermuda's honor of being the only colony beside Antigua to emancipate its slaves outright in 1834. To prevent them from sharing political power, the property qualification for the vote, which was higher than in any other British island, was raised to more than twice the old height.

British Honduras lived by the logwood and mahogany it shipped to England. The former article, used for dyeing, had lost most if its importance because cheaper substitutes had appeared. Around 1830 the export of logwood was some 1800 tons a year, one tenth of what it had been three quarters of a century before; and the price, which had once reached £100 a ton, was now only £5. 10s. What saved the little settlement from dying with logwood was the passion of Victorians for furniture and fittings[3] made of mahogany, and this passion assured handsome profits on all the mahogany that British Honduras was capable of supplying. The limiting factor was the labor that was available. Most of the work was done by slaves until 1834, and by the same hands afterward. Here emancipation caused no such disruption as was common in the colonies where the plantation system prevailed and, what was much more important, production was marginal. The substitution of annual hiring under a local law acceptable to master and servant alike, and tolerated by the Colonial Office, might not have been possible if profits had been much slimmer. As it was, the trade had no difficulty in sustaining heavy duties on the importation of this valuable wood into England until 1846, and then the abolition of these duties seems to have made little difference except to purchasers in the mother country.

Politically and constitutionally, British Honduras was emerging from an obscure and anomalous position. The Spanish government had recognized it as a separate British settlement on territory that the British government admitted was nominally under Spanish sovereignty.

---

[3] Particularly on ships and railways.

Now it was becoming a regular British crown colony, and this rather cautiously because there was no present prospect of a formal surrender of Spanish sovereignty to accord with the actual withdrawal of it from the American mainland. The head of the executive was the superintendent, who was formally commissioned by the governor of Jamaica but was directly responsible to the Colonial Office. The other executive officials were seven magistrates, who were elected annually. All the free settlers, not just the electors,[4] formed the legislature, which was called the Public Meeting. It voted the taxes and prescribed how the magistrates should spend the revenue. The institutional balance had long tended to shift in favor of the superintendent, with his help of course; and in 1832 he helped still more by taking over the appointment of the magistrates and by asserting his right to legislate by proclamation whenever necessary and to prevent debate in the Public Meeting of any motion not approved by him. By the middle of the century he had pretty well established his ascendency, and it was obvious that the Public Meeting was too unsatisfactory to last much longer. The Colonial Office, frequently invoked as arbiter, recognized the authority of custom and ruled in favor of efficiency.

The British possessions on the tropical west coast of Africa were poor weak things that had no slaves to liberate or sheltered production to expose to world competition. Yet they too were caught in the currents of public opinion that insisted upon emancipation and free trade. In 1830 liberated Africans were still pouring into Sierra Leone, which had been established as a haven for them and was recently revealed, by official investigation, to be very different from the heaven that had been contemplated. It was, in fact, a growing failure, and before the end of the decade Stephen, for all his championing of the blacks, was hard put to it to provide his political chief with a justification of the parliamentary grant for this colony. The other British posts—on the Gambia, four hundred miles to the north, and along the Gold Coast, nearly a thousand miles to the east—were under the governor of Sierra Leone, which suggests their importance in the eyes of the home government. It had little interest in them except as possible bases for the war on the slave trade, and as such they had been almost worthless. After twenty years of British efforts to stop the trade, more slaves, not fewer, were being exported from this region by foreigners. Nor were these posts very attractive to British merchants, who after the abolition of their

---

4 The numbers in 1848 were 64 and 59 respectively.

slave trade had to seek new African commodities for which they could find a ready market. The industrial revolution helped them by making more people dirtier, so that they wanted more soap, which meant more fats. That is where—and for candles—palm oil came in. But the trade in this and other innocent African produce was severely limited by the prevalent native anarchy.

In an earlier or a later age the merchants or their government might have stepped in with force and imposed order for the sake of trade— but not in that anti-imperialist era. The Colonial Office was glad to get rid of the four forts on the Gold Coast by paying a mere pittance of three or four thousand pounds a year to a committee of merchants to take over all responsibility for them; and the merchants were glad to get rid of the burden of government and defense by placing and leaving it on the shoulders of a certain junior army officer. This George Maclean assumed command in 1830 and during the fourteen years of his *de facto* rule he demonstrated that he had a genius for managing natives and no regard for Colonial Office regulations. By sheer character and ability, for he had practically no other resources, he imposed a Pax Maclean such as had been unknown in that part of the wicked world. The Colonial Office had sternly forbidden treaties with native chiefs, yet he freely entered into them and made no formal report of them. They were all verbal agreements, and so far as is known none committed his government to assume responsibility for any territory or for the defense of any tribe against another. These highly irregular proceedings outraged the legal mind of Stephen when he discovered them late in the thirties; but in 1842, when more was known about them, a committee of the House of Commons paid generous tribute to the remarkable achievement of Maclean and recommended that his informal arrangements should be given proper legal clothing. The prohibition of native treaties was thereupon abandoned; and this decade saw the creation of a whole series of treaties that, without extending British territorial commitments, enlisted the native tribes in the cause of peace and order, and particularly in stamping out the slave trade over wide areas. In 1850 a much-strengthened Gold Coast was separated from Sierra Leone and given a government of its own with executive and legislative councils.

Ceylon had slaves but no slavery problem. They were not Africans, nor were they the property of Europeans. They were mostly domestic slaves, there were relatively few of them, and they were rarely abused. Slavery was gradually extinguished in the maritime provinces by manumission encouraged by the government, while in the Kandyan districts it lingered on, and there it was abolished in 1845. The island was of interest to the British chiefly as a strategic asset and an economic liability; and at first attention was concentrated on the asset, to make it secure. The conquest of Kandy in 1815 had to be repeated three years later, and with such difficulty that it required additional troops from India. The revolt was led by the nobles, who resented the rule of the British as they had that of the native king; and for trying to seize more power they lost most of what they had to newly installed resident agents of the government. During the next few years, also, military roads were driven into the interior, riveting the British hold on the country. After 1818 there were only petty risings.

Being an important military station and naval base, it would be rather surprising if Ceylon paid its own way. There was almost nothing to tax in the island, and the main source of its revenue was drying up. The fine cinnamon of Ceylon was losing value under the competition of coarser grades and of cassia grown in other parts of the East. The sale of the crop to the East India Company continued until 1821, when the government of the colony began to send it to London for sale there. This practice came to an end in 1833, when the government abandoned the monopoly, the preservation of which had been a very irritating business, and threw the cultivation and the trade open to all, requiring in return the payment of an export tax of 3 shillings per pound. This impost was suicidal, in view of the competition of production elsewhere.

Meanwhile peace made the chronic deficit more and more objectionable to the home government, and year after year the Colonial Office and the Treasury prodded Ceylon to perform the impossible feat of balancing its budget. Finally a special commissioner was sent out to wrestle with the problem, and after an investigation of two years he submitted some drastic recommendations. The Colonial Office, in desperation, applied them in 1833, with disastrous results. The civil service was wrecked, and still the budget was not balanced. The service ceased to attract able men because all pensions were abolished, the salary scale was cut away down, and some of the prize senior posts were eliminated. Deterioration was progressive, with officials no longer required to be versed in native languages and now permitted to supplement their meager salaries by devoting much of their time to managing their estates. Governor after governor warned the Colonial Office of the evil until at last in 1845 London reversed the errors of 1833, and then it took years for the service to recover from its demoralization.

Some changes made in 1833 were not shortsighted. That was the year in which the governor's advisory council was made an executive council and the governor was given a legislative council, composed of official and unofficial nominated members, whose concurrence was necessary for legislative and financial measures. The unofficial members were intended to represent local public opinion and to be divided equally between Europeans and natives. It was easy to get the former but not the latter, because most natives with the necessary education were already employed by the government and therefore excluded.

The modern prosperity of the island began in the second quarter of the century, when commercial blight was killing the cinnamon trees. The coconut industry, now the third most valuable in Ceylon, began then to grow from almost nothing. But what transformed Ceylon "from a sluggish military cantonment into an enterprising British colony" was coffee, the production of which dominated the island's economy for forty years before it was killed by a physical blight. The Dutch and the British had tried to introduce the cultivation of coffee but had failed because the lowlands, where they conducted their experiments, were quite unsuited to it. Following the second conquest of Kandy and the opening of the hilly interior by the construction of roads, it was found that the very finest coffee could be grown there. Whether it would be a profitable business was another question. This was decided in the middle thirties, when emancipation destroyed what was left of the West Indian coffee industry, forcing up prices in England, with the consequence that the duty on the East Indian article was reduced to the West Indian level, 6d. instead of 9d. a pound.

During the ten years from 1837 there was a coffee "boom" in Ceylon. It attracted capital to the amount of £3,000,000 and turned jungles into plantations. It also revived Indian immigration, for the Kandyans clung to their primitive agriculture, unwilling and unable to do the necessary work on the new estates of the Europeans. Overspeculation was bound to cause a reaction, and the general commercial crisis of 1847 paralyzed the coffee industry in the island, but only for a very few years. Ceylon was not in the parlous economic state of the West Indies. The great days of British Caribbean sugar were long past, whereas the great days of Ceylon coffee were still to come.

CHAPTER XIX

Reform and Expansion in India

"THE INTERESTS of the native subjects are to be consulted in preference to those of Europeans whenever the two come in conflict." This was "recognized as an indisputable principle," according to the report of a thorough parliamentary investigation, conducted from 1829 to 1832, into the affairs of the East India Company prior to the renewal of its expiring charter. The same report condemned the practice, begun by Cornwallis and prescribed by the Charter Act of 1793, of excluding Indians from responsible office. It urged the adjustment of government in India to fit the character of the people, in accordance with the lesson that the British first learned in Canada before the American Revolution, and insisted that "the principles of British law could never be made the basis of an Indian code." It also asserted that, if the Company was to continue exercising its powers of government, it must cease to be a trading organization, lest the pursuit of commercial profit for its shareholders in England interfere with the welfare of the people over whom it ruled in India. The alternative, that the Company should give up the business of government, was faced and rejected, as it had been at the last renewal in 1813, because neither the ministry nor parliament was prepared to assume the direct responsibility for the administration of British India.

The act that renewed the charter in 1833 for another twenty years embodied these ideas. It took away not only that part of the old monopoly that had survived 1813, but also the right to engage in trade. The Company, still a private corporation though now confined to the work of a government department, had its dividends fixed at the current 10.5 per cent, a charge on the revenues of India corresponding to the financial obligations that democratic governments of today assume when they take over businesses built by private enterprise. The act also provided for the codification of Indian law, which was to take account of "the rights, feelings and peculiar usages of the people," for which purpose it added a fourth member, a legal one, to the governor general's council; and for greater efficiency of administration it made the governor general supreme over the presidencies of Bombay and Madras, and conferred upon him, when acting with his council, full power to enact laws for the whole of British India. Of course he was still under the sovereignty of parliament and subject to orders from the Court of Directors, who in turn had to bow to the will of the President of the Board of Control, the minister of the Crown who was responsible for the Indian Empire as the colonial secretary was for the colonies. In addition to what it did for the unfication of India, the act laid down the famous rule "that no native of India, nor any natural-born subject of His Majesty, should be disabled from holding any place, office, or employment, by reason of his religion, place of birth, descent or color."

The Charter Act of 1833 was one of the first reform measures of the reformed parliament, but it did not inaugurate a reform era in India. This had already begun there years before, with the organization of the extensive territories conquered during the Napoleonic period and shortly afterward. It was the work of a remarkable group of brilliant officials, military as well as civilian, who devoted their talents to the land and its people: men like Mountstuart Elphinstone, the pacifier of the provinces of the former peshwa, the creative governor of Bombay, and the author of a classic history of India; or Sir Thomas Munro, whose ryotwari settlement, with its direct dealings between government and peasant, gave the Presidency of Madras a land revenue system far superior to that of Bengal, with its zamindar intermediaries; or Sir Charles Metcalfe, who established order in the North-West Provinces. All three were covenanted servants of the Company who rose to be governors, a rank usually filled, like the office of governor general, by outside appointment in England with the object of getting men of outstanding ability and independent position; and it is worthy of note that at the end of their careers in India, Metcalfe became governor general for a short while and Elphinstone was offered the succession but had to refuse it because his health was broken.

Men of this type were beginning to distinguish the covenanted service of the Company by 1800; and after the fall of Napoleon, when reaction was at its height in England as well as on the continent, the liberal-minded Marquis of Hastings was a reforming governor general. He reversed the Cornwallis policy of refusing to employ Indians in any but the meanest capacities; and, openly encouraging education for the natives, he denounced as "treason to British sentiment" the mere thought of trying to keep them down by keeping them ignorant. Munro would render them eligible for almost every office and, to quote his own words, would regard India "not as a temporary possession, but as one which is to be maintained permanently, until the natives shall have abandoned most of their prejudices, and become sufficiently enlightened to frame a regular government for themselves, and to conduct and preserve it." This statement might have come from almost any one of his fellow administrators of the Indian Empire, and it bears a striking resemblance to Huskisson's confession of faith in the developing colonies.

A new and more vigorous phase of the reform movement in India began in 1828, when Lord William Bentinck became governor general. This second son of the third Duke of Portland, who had led the Whigs into a coalition with Pitt's Tories, was a true liberal. It was more than twenty years since, as governor of Madras, he had learned much from Munro, then on his staff, and had declared that "British greatness should be founded upon Indian happiness." At that time an unfortunate local mutiny had caused his recall, which left him impatient to return and prove himself. Now that he had his chance, Bentinck made up for lost time. He conducted such a thorough housecleaning of the whole administration that in the space of his seven years' tenure of office he transformed a deficit of a million into a surplus of a million and a half pounds, while at the same time he made the service more efficient and more Indian. For example, he increased the number, the authority, and the salaries of the native judges, and he substituted the vernacular tongue for Persian, a relic of Moghul rule, as the language of the courts. Much, though not all, of the adverse criticism that long clung to his memory was the backbiting of European servants who hated him for cutting down their extravagant emoluments to make the average of the civilians, including members of the council, a beggarly £2,000 a year. Almost the only other cause of his unpopularity with the European services does more credit to his heart than to his head. As commander in chief Bentinck issued two important orders to improve the lot of the sepoys, one raising their pay after long service and the other abolishing the penalty of flogging. Both reforms were excellent in themselves, but the second gave rise to an "odious distinction" of race because troops sent out from Britain, being disciplined under a law that was beyond his reach, could still be flogged.

The most famous of Bentinck's reforms was the abolition of suttee or, more properly, *sati*. This immolation of widows on the funeral pyres of their husbands was a common but by no means universal Hindu rite that was sanctioned by immemorial custom, having been practiced in India for more than two thousand years, and was commended by authoritative ancient scriptures. In a single year, 1818, Bengal had 839 officially reported, and nobody knows how many unreported, cases of this inhuman burning of women alive. Bentinck's predecessors had often discussed, and the Court of Directors had recently urged, the proposal "to wash out this foul stain upon British rule"; but nothing had been done about it because it cut across the generally wise principle, rigidly observed by the Company, that there should be no interference with religion, and because it might shatter the loyalty of the native army and thereby release the forces of anarchy. The new governor general, while determined to stop the atrocious custom if he could, combined caution with courage. Canvassing the risk quickly and thoroughly, he got the unanimous approval of the judges of the highest criminal court; he found that though some of his best and most trusted advisers dreaded the consequences, the preponderant opinion of the army officers, police officials, civil administrators, and native leaders whom he consulted, favored abolition. He decreed it in 1829, the privy council upheld it in 1832 against the appeal of some influential Bengalis, and Hindu societly accepted it with no more resentment than rejoicing.

Another memorable social and moral reform that began almost at the same time was the stamping out of thuggee, or *thagi,* from which we get the word "thug." It was an ancient system of murder practiced by Moslems as well as Hindus organized in a society that was hereditary, secret, and semireligious. Their technique had an oriental finish that western gangsters could never approach. An innocent traveler fell in with what seemed to be a group of pious pilgrims and when they reached a spot where some of them had dug a fresh grave for his reception, they strangled and buried him—a human sacrifice to the goddess of destruction, Kali, who was thereby bound to protect them—and then divided the goods of the victim. The evil was probably at its height in the early part of the nineteenth century, when thousands vanished annually in this fashion. The government was baffled by an inverted morality, the influence of Kali, until at last one thag turned informer. He drew others after him, and the awful secrets were spilled. One man confessed to 719 murders of this kind. The officer who cracked the system and then directed the long but successful campaign against it was "Thuggee" Sleeman, also known as Sir William Sleeman, K. C. B.

The introduction of English education has been called the greatest thing that happened to India under British rule, and it was at the very close of Bentinck's administration that the crucial decision was made. There had long been general agreement that the spread of enlightenment in the country was a British responsibility, and there had also been a growing recognition that education to fit Indians for responsible employment by the Company was a British necessity. The first government provision for education was the grant of a lakh of ruppees, then worth a little more than £10,000, which Wilberforce got inserted in the Charter Act of 1813. The money went to assist some of the many native schools where Hindus and Moslems struggled to preserve their ancient lore in classic Sanscrit, Arabic, and Persian, and not for the support of the handful of modest schools of western learning that had appeared under various auspices. A controversy, with both Europeans and Indians on each side, arose over whether to build a public educational system on oriental or occidental writing and thought; and the dispute grew so tense that the government shrank from adopting either course until after the passing of the 1833 Charter Act, when the declaration against racial discrimination in the public service made a decision more urgent, and the appointment of T. B. (later Lord) Macaulay as legal member of the governor general's council introduced the man who broke the deadlock.

To Macaulay, who could see only one side of a question and knew nothing of oriental literature, the issue was between stagnation and progress, between the mentality of despotism and that of liberty; and he could not hesitate between them. England should bestow the most precious treasure of her heritage, the living conscious spirit of her civilization, upon India. He was not indifferent to the possibility that this might lead India to demand political freedom. If it did, that would be "the proudest day in English history." That was what this great Whig historian had declared to the House of Commons not two years since, and apparently so many of his compatriots were of the same mind that few saw anything startling in such a prophecy. It was as chairman of the committee of public instruction that, in March 1835, Macaulay wrung from the council this decisive resolution:

> The great object of the British Government ought to be the promotion of European literature and science among the natives of India; and that

all the funds appropriated to education would best be employed on English education alone.

And it was in the same capacity that, for the next three years, he gave shape and substance to the policy thus laid down.

There have been many criticisms of this policy. The exclusion of oriental studies from official support in a land of oriental civilization was an error that had to be corrected. So also was the attempt to make English the only language of instruction. But there was nothing wrong and much that was right in making it the regular language of instruction in a subcontinent which, with its two hundred different languages, was a Tower of Babel much worse than Europe. English became in modern India what Latin was in mediaeval Europe—a common medium of communication between educated people. Most of those who have thought it unfortunate that English was established as the official and literary language of India have really been condemning the selection of material for the curricula of the schools and colleges. Intellectual fare that might be wholesome for a young generation of Englishmen, phlegmatic by nature and law-abiding by social habit, might be food too strong for orientals of quicker blood and imagination, less inclined to toleration, and not so suspicious of extremes. Such, for example, were the prose models prescribed for Indian education: Edmund Burke, Jeremy Bentham, John Stuart Mill, and the philosophical radicals. But it is difficult to see how England could have done otherwise than teach India the ideas as well as the language of liberty.

Something else that Englishmen often admit their forbears did to India before 1840 was that they destroyed the native cotton manufacture. It was still flourishing in 1813, when the English merchants agitating against the Company's monopoly were thinking in terms of getting Indian cotton goods for sale on the English market. But already English machines had begun to compete with Indian fingers, and within twenty-five years the flow of cotton goods between the two countries was almost entirely from England to India. Meanwhile, as the chief means of paying for her imports, India had developed a large export trade in indigo to Britain and opium to China—the development of Indian tea production was much later. Already the great superiority of American raw cotton had severely limited trade in the Indian article; Lancashire and the American South had together struck the blow that killed the old Indian industry; and it should not escape attention that this Anglo-American combination of efficiency also did untold damage to the old Chinese industry. "When I first went to Java in 1811, they were almost exclusively clothed in Chinese manufactures, and I witnessed a revolution there which almost clothed them in European manufactures during the time I was there." These words, referring to conditions in southeast Asia generally, are those of a trader when examined by the parliamentary committee in 1830; and they tell only part of the story. Machine-made textiles, because they were much cheaper, were supplanting Chinese goods in the Chinese market; and China was taking the place of Britain as the feeder of bullion to India.

With the departure of Bentinck in 1835, interest shifts from the work of reform, which continued with little interruption, to the northwest frontier of India and the question of British expansion, which was then revived. This time the impetus came from London and sprang from fear of Russia. This fear had first seized Britain when Czar Alexander met Napoleon at Tilsit and they talked of partitioning the world; it disappeared when the French emperor attacked Russia and she perforce became Britain's ally; after Napoleon's fall it tended to rise again, as Russian and British policy diverged and clashed in Europe, the Near East, and the Middle East; and by 1830 it had become the chronic British obsession that it has since remained, with short exceptions of which the longest was from 1907 to 1917. The favorite British nightmare of the nineteenth century was a Russian attack on India, which was not so wild a dream as some people have since supposed. In 1830 it was less than a hundred years since Nadir Shah of Persia had invaded India, supervised the organized slaughter of untold thousands in Delhi, and annexed all the territory west of the Indus; his successor in Afghanistan had repeatedly invaded India, the second time annexing the Punjab and the fourth time smashing the Mahratta host at Panipat, where the number of Hindus slain has been reputed to be nearly two hundred thousand. Now Russia, having taken some big bites of Persian territory, had just concluded another war with Persia by dictating peace on humiliating terms. In other words, Russia was creeping up into a position from which a predatory spring into India was a demonstrated possibility.

The northwest frontier of the British Empire in India had approximately followed the line of the Sutlaj ever since the young Metcalfe had negotiated a treaty with Ranjit Singh in 1809. This Sikh ruler was a remarkable man: an illiterate, drunken, cruel, and unscrupulous genius who kept faith with the British and found compensation in conquests beyond, greatly at the expense of Afghanistan. He created a

compact though composite kingdom comprising the Punjab and Kashmir. There the Sikhs, a fighting minority, ruled a population divided
almost equally between Hindus and Moslems. To the southwest lay
Sind, the land of the lower Indus, separated from the rest of the
country on the east by the Thar or Indian desert.[1] Sind was a strategic
region, containing the crossroads of the northwest, for at right angles to
the great river ran the roads to the southern mountain passes into
Afghanistan; it was held by rather weak hands, being divided among
chieftains or amirs, one of whom had a shadowy claim to a shadowy
suzerainty over the others. Ranjit Singh coveted Sind, and in 1831 he
proposed partitioning it with the East India Company. Bentinck repelled the proposal and made a treaty with the amirs in 1832, which
gained for Indian merchants and traders the right of passage for themselves and their goods along the rivers and roads of Sind on condition
that no military stores or armed vessels pass through the country and
no English merchant settle in it, and which bound the two contracting
parties "never to look with the eye of covetousness on the possessions of
each other." From 1834 to 1836 Ranjit Singh threatened to seize Sind
by himself, but the Indian government blocked him with a warning
and early in 1838 persuaded Sind, in return for the protection given,
to admit a British resident.

   Afghanistan, which lay beyond these two states, had fallen upon evil
days. After being long a prey of anarchy, which left it divided into
three principalities, it was caught in a double squeeze between Ranjit
Singh on the one side and the shah of Persia on the other, each seeking
to recoup himself there for territory denied by Britain or lost to Russia.
Persia having fallen under Russian sway, a Persian army that was
trained and officered by Russians invaded Afghanistan and laid siege
to Herat, the seat of the western principality, late in 1837. The ruler
of the eastern principality of Kabul, Dost Mohammed, had already
appealed to the British for aid against Persia and against Ranjit Singh,
from whom he wanted to recover the state of Peshawar; and getting
an unfavorable reply from Calcutta, he threw himself on the side of the
Russo-Persian combination. If Herat fell, the whole of Afghanistan
might fall to the Russians, and this might shake the British position in
India by damaging the prestige on which it was built. Lord Auckland,
Bentinck's inept successor, determined to restore the lost balance in
Afghanistan by backing a scheme to restore Shah Shuja to the throne

---

[1] Also isolated on the west by a desert.

from which Dost Mohammed had driven him many years before. In the summer of 1838 the governor general entered into the Tripartite Treaty with Shah Shuja and Ranjit Singh, the plan being that the exile's adherents with the aid of Sikh allies would effect the restoration. But when Auckland learned, as he soon did, that these means were inadequate, he decided to send a British army to do the work—at the very time when British pressure in Moscow and on the Persian Gulf persuaded Russia to abandon Kabul and Tehcran and to call off the siege of Herat.

The First Afghan War, in which Auckland persisted, was therefore without justification from its beginning; and in the end it proved to be as disastrous as it was immoral. British bayonets put Shah Shuja back on his throne in 1839; but they had to remain in order to keep him there even though his rival surrendered in 1840, to be treated as an honored prisoner in India. The British occupation, disgracefully mismanaged, roused Afghan hostility to an explosive pitch by the winter of 1841–42, when a Kabul mob murdered the British resident; his successor negotiated a humiliating agreement for evacuation, and he too was murdered; a new and equally bad treaty for withdrawal was made; and Afghan treachery turned the British retreat into a sickening massacre. A new governor general retrieved the disaster, the worst that British arms had suffered in India. He sent in a fresh army which retook Kabul, rescued the British who had been held as hostages, did much unnecessary damage to property, and effected a complete withdrawal from the Afghan hornets' nest. Dost Mohammed was allowed to return to his throne unconditionally; and for the rest of his long life he remained, with one inconsequential lapse, on good terms with the British, who had wasted twenty thousand lives and fifteen million pounds to get rid of him.

The conquest of Sind was a sequel of the Afghan War. The strategic location of this territory tempted Auckland to send troops through it in flagrant violation of the treaty of 1832. Having decided that, he had to secure his communications through the country of the amirs, and to this end he imposed a new treaty upon them early in 1839. It took them formally under British protection and bound them to pay an annual tribute of three lakhs of rupees to help defray the cost of maintaining a British force in their midst. They were too weak to resist but not to resent this highhanded treatment. Though the Afghan explosion against the British did not release a rising in Sind, it magnified the rumors of disaffection there and moved the British to strengthen their hold upon the lower Indus. The chosen instrument was Sir Charles Napier, who dictated a new treaty late in 1842, substituting cessions of territory for the annual tribute, requiring the provision of fuel for British steamers on the river, and transferring to the British the right of uttering coinage, a recognized attribute of sovereignty. Early in 1843 continued British goading at last produced the rising that the Afghan example could not; Napier got his desired excuse for war; British forces soon smashed all resistance; and Sind was annexed in August.

Napier's famous telegram *peccavi*—I have sinned—was more than an innocent pun; for he had earlier written in his diary, "We have no right to seize Sind, yet we shall do so, and a very advantageous, useful, humane piece of rascality it will be." The whole transaction has been condemned, often in unmeasured terms, by almost every British writer from that day to this. Yet, if judged by the practical results, which Napier could not help foreseeing, it stands in a very different light. The amirs, who were sent packing, were degenerate despots whose only idea of ruling was to plunder and oppress and whose only right to rule rested on a conquest of sixty years before. The people of Sind benefited enormously from the substitution of civilized government by Napier, who administered the province until 1847 and of whom the following illustrative anecdote is told. When Brahmins objected that his prohibition of suttee was interference with a pious religious custom, he replied that if this was so the custom must be allowed to continue, but his own people also had a custom that would have to be observed with it: "When men burn women alive we hang them." His rejoinder effectively removed the objection. It may also be noted that the annexation of Sind coincided with the abolition of slavery in British India. Provision for emancipation by 1837 had been dropped from the Charter Act of 1833 because slavery in India, being complicated by caste and by both Hindu and Moslem law, was different from slavery in the West Indies; but the act directed the governor general and council to do away with it as soon as possible. Another humane reform that was being successfully pushed at that time was the stopping of female infanticide.

After Sind came the Punjab, but that is a different story. Ranjit Singh had forged a powerful instrument in his army. In size, training, and equipment, it resembled the British army in India and was its only possible rival. Trouble ensued when this instrument became the master. For five years before the Sikh ruler died in 1839, his control over the army and the government was slipping. His health was wrecked by drink and debauchery, he suffered two strokes of paralysis, and everyone knew that he had no heir fit to succeed him—only an imbecile son and a vicious grandson. The next six years were a nightmare in the Punjab. Murder soon wiped out son and grandson. Then came the turn of the imposters, the first of whom implored Auckland in 1841 to rescue him from his own soldiers. The last of his successors—all puppets—was a five-year-old son of a wicked woman who fawned upon the army in order to remain regent. She and some other highly placed individuals, who were afraid of being devoured by the headless military monster, saw their best hope in turning it against the British, while the monster's natural appetite for new conquests and fresh plunder also urged it to pounce upon the British. Two other influences were the encouragement offered by the Afghan War and the warning of what happened to Sind; but these seem to have played little part in hurling the Sikh army across the Sutlaj in December 1845. It was a clear case of unprovoked attack. The Sikhs thought to surprise the British and march on Delhi.

Though the First Sikh War lasted only fifty-four days, it was by far the stiffest military test that the British had ever faced in India. It was a breath-taking revelation of the magnificent fighting qualities of the Sikhs and of their skill as artillerymen and engineers. During a "night of horrors" in the middle of a fierce two-day battle, "the fate of India trembled in the balance." In the last pitched battle the British artillery shot away all its ammunition without silencing the opposing guns, and the British infantry had to take them with a desperate bayonet charge. That day cost the Sikhs 10,000 lives as well as all their guns, and it was decisive. It opened the road to Lahore, their capital, where the governor general dictated peace in March 1846. He did not annex the country, partly out of respect for the memory of a faithful ally of former days and partly because he doubted if he had enough strength to take over such a large and difficult prize. He trimmed off the southern edge of Sikh territory—everything on the British side of the river and some pieces on the other. He cut off Kashmir, which he sold to a friendly rajah for a million pounds. He exacted an indemnity of half a million from the Sikhs; and he limited their army to 20,000 infantry and 12,000 cavalry, less than half what it had been. The Sikh government was allowed to continue, its autonomy being qualified by the presence of a British resident and a British garrison.

The Second Sikh War, 1848–1849, was the inevitable result of this compromise settlement, which was essentially unstable. The Sikhs were determined to reverse the decision of 1846, and it was not by much that they failed to do so. Somehow they managed to put considerable artillery in the field; and with Peshawar as bait they hooked Dost Mohammed, once their bitterest foe, as their ally. Their own guns were much more useful. The account of the first big battle, which was almost a draw, roused consternation in England and caused the recall of the commander in chief and the promotion of Napier to take his place. In the final great battle, the Sikhs numbered 50,000—much more than the British—but the British were then for the first time superior in artillery, and without much cost to themselves they inflicted a crushing defeat on their foes. They pursued them as far as the Afghan frontier and clinched the conquest by the occupation of Peshawar.

The annexation of the Punjab was proclaimed in March 1849, a fortnight after the remnants of the Sikh army laid down their arms. It was Lord Dalhousie, governor general from early in 1848, who took this momentous step, and he did it on his own authority without consulting his council and without getting the consent of the directors or the home government. Of all who have held that high office, he was the youngest, being only thirty-five when appointed, and he was one of the ablest. He remade the Punjab into a model province, with the aid of a remarkable group of brilliant administrators of whom the Lawrence brothers, Henry and John, are the most famous. The rule of Ranjit Singh at its best had only one object, which was to build and keep the strongest possible army, and it exacted a land revenue that was about half the value of the cultivator's produce. Now that army was entirely disbanded, the people were disarmed, the land tax was cut in half, and the proceeds were spent upon providing enlightened government. The result was that within three years of the annexation, Sikh soldiers of their own free will fought under the British in Burma; and five years later, when the Mutiny shook the British raj in India, the Punjab remained steadfast in its new loyalty. The Second Sikh War carried the Indian Empire up to its natural limit in the barrier of mountains and deserts on the northwest, and so completed the unifying of India by conquest, a process that Clive had begun nearly a century before.

V THE MID-VICTORIAN ERA

CHAPTER XX

Britain on Top of the World and Turning to Democracy

IN THE Mid-Victorian era Britain sat on top of the world, and she was complacently conscious of that fact. Pride of empire played no part in supporting this serene consciousness, for such pride had vanished almost completely. She rather felt that she had outgrown the empire, that it was a thing of the past. The main foundation for her self-complacency was the position of industrial, commercial, and financial primacy that she then enjoyed. It has never been equaled before or since by herself or any other single country, not even by the United States after the Second World War, for Britain in this earlier age faced no rival such as America has since encountered in Soviet Russia.

British economic supremacy was overwhelming, and there were many reasons for it. Britain had an enormous lead over all other countries in the development of the industrial revolution. The first European country to become industrialized was Belgium, and there the process was not well under way until the 1840's. France and Germany followed in the next two decades, and the United States later. To establish their own industries, these other countries had to buy their machinery from Britain, and from her also they had to get mechanical experts and skilled workmen to install it and show how to work it. This demand greatly stimulated British heavy industry, and its efficiency was enormously increased by the introduction of the new Bessemer method of steel production in the fifties. Meanwhile Britain was the great supplier of other manufactured goods to the rapidly expanding markets of the world.

Britain was leading the world in transportation. Gladstone, the inscrutable master of figures, once said that 70 per cent of his country's abounding prosperity was due to her policy of free trade and 30 per cent to her railways. This nice calculation is open to serious question; but of the important contribution to Britain's economic growth made by her railways, there can be no question. By the middle of the century the little island had about 8,000 miles of railway with a paid-up capital of nearly £280,000,000 sterling and annual earnings of £20,000,000, of which more than half was net profit. At this time Belgium was the next best served with this new method of transportation, while France and Germany were still laying out their trunk lines and the gigantic American system was only in its infancy. During the next generation the mania of railway building spread all over the world; and the lead that Britain had already taken made her contracting firms the principal constructors, her industries the main producer of rails, locomotives, cars, and other railroad equipment, and her financial houses the chief source of capital for the expensive enterprise.

In 1850 British shipping was by far the largest in the world. The second largest mercantile marine was that of the United States, which then totalled 1,500,000 tons against the British 3,250,000. The next quarter of a century saw the British pre-eminence leap away up. British tonnage was doubled while the American stood still and then declined, the French rose to the American level and then fell off too, and the German climbed to a weak second place. Iron and steam were supplanting wood and sail. This substitution operated like a double godsend to British shipping, but we cannot call it a godsend because it was the conscious work of British enterprise. It removed an old handicap and gave a new advantage. Britain was the only shipbuilding country that had used up her forests and was therefore obliged to bear the extra cost of bringing timber from foreign lands. On the other hand, she alone was industrially prepared to turn out iron and then steel steamships that could take business away from wooden sailing ships. At the beginning of the last quarter of the century, about half the world's shipping was British owned and a larger proportion was British built, for she had added ships to the list of her principal exports.

Britain was mining much more coal than all the rest of the world, and coal was the very foundation upon which industrial society was built. Her production in 1851 was doubled in 1871, when it was almost twice as much as that of Belgium, France, and Germany combined. Germany had greater resources, and the United States much greater still; but their comparable exploitation was only beginning. Coal was already a valuable British export; what went out of the country, however, was only a crumb compared with what fed the fires of British industry.

British commerce was supreme, which was only to be expected when the country that was the workshop of the world was also the country that did most of the carrying trade of the world. Yet another of the many powerful factors that stimulated one another and worked together for the peculiar benefit of Britain in that age was her creation of capital. From the great profits of her industry, shipping, and trade, she was piling up new capital at a prodigious rate. Much of it she applied to expand these enterprises. Much of it she sent abroad for investment in other lands all over the world, quickening their development and enriching herself by enriching them. Few people in the United States now realize how greatly their country, to say nothing of others, was then dependent upon the the life-giving stream of capital flowing from Britain. Bills on London, and they alone, were universally acceptable; sterling was the only international currency; and the hub of the British Empire was the financial center of the world.

While Britain faced no competition from abroad, she had plenty of it at home. With unlimited markets to conquer, there was no temptation to adopt the restrictive business practices of a later age, when national jealousies raised high barriers around national markets. There was, rather, every incentive to translate into lower prices each successive improvement of production and distribution. This meant that the country as a whole, not just the business leaders, shared the benefits. Real wages rose by 20 per cent during the fifties and sixties. Then and there, in the only great industrial society that yet existed, it was no longer true that the poor were becoming poorer while the rich were growing richer, though Karl Marx was busy in the British Museum trying to prove that it must be true in all modern industrial society. It was a time of full employment, except when the American Civil War caused a cotton famine that threw Lancashire operatives out of work. It was also a time of increased emigration. During these two decades, when the population of the United Kingdom rose from some 27,000,000 to more than 30,000,000, more than half the natural increase, or approximately 4,000,000, sought greater prosperity for themselves in lands beyond the sea, thereby increasing the opportunity for their fellows who remained at home.

By her conversion to free trade, Britain had done much to build the world economy that she then dominated. It was a free, self-regulating economy; and it became more so as other countries, seeking to share her prosperity, cut down governmental restraints upon their trade. Prussia followed a substantially free trade policy, and so did quite a number of other European states. Piedmont did it to gird up her loins for the heavy task of uniting Italy. Even France, which had always been stoutly protectionist, moved in the same direction by concluding a commercial treaty with Britain in 1860. The man whom the government in London sent to negotiate this agreement, and after whom it is popularly called, was appropriately Richard Cobden. He personified the school of economic thought—then supreme in Britain and embracing almost every European economist of any standing—that insisted on the maximum economic freedom as the only way to achieve for all in every land the greatest and healthiest prosperity and to effect such an economic integration of the world that self-interest would make war impossible. Until the seventies, when the world turned in its tracks and began to rush down the slope of economic nationalism, it seemed to be following Britain's lead up the easy road to salvation. The gospel of free trade, free enterprise, was the British contribution to the list of modern ideologies; and Britons were then confident that it would triumph.

In political institutions, to a much greater degree than in fiscal policy, Britain seemed to be guiding the world in the third quarter of the century. Two classical treatises then appeared, John Stuart Mill's *Representative Government* in 1860 and Walter Bagehot's *English Constitution* in 1867, which taught the British that they were wiser than they knew, that they had evolved a political system as nearly perfect as any political system could be; and the extent to which their parliamentary system was being imitated abroad was almost startling. Not only were the colonies copying it as fast as they could, but, what was much more striking, European countries were doing the same thing. At the beginning of this period, genuine popular government scarcely existed on the European continent outside three of the smaller states—Belgium, the Netherlands, and Switzerland. By the end of the period, parliamentary government in some form was established in every European country, great and small, with the exception of Russia and Turkey. The change swept over the continent almost like an epidemic, as one country after another remodeled its political institutions after the British pattern. The nearest parallel to this European borrowing from Britain was the Latin American copying from the United States, and the contemporary breakdown of the American model in the

Civil War only heightened the international prestige of the British system.

Meanwhile British foreign policy altered its tone as public interest shifted from the international scene to internal reform. The turn came in 1865, with the death of Lord Palmerston. From 1830, except during the few years when his party was out of power, this old-fashioned Whig, who sat in the House of Commons because his peerage was Irish, not English, practically dictated British foreign policy. He never hesitated to intervene anywhere when he saw a chance to aid the struggling cause of liberalism or nationalism in Europe, thereby incurring the hatred of continental reactionaries which was expressed in the German couplet:

> *Hat der Teufel einen Sohn*
> *So ist er sicher Palmerston.*

> If the devil has a son,
> He surely is Palmerston.

He was also the truculent guardian of British interest, and as such he struck in 1850 the most strident note of nineteenth century British foreign policy.

The occasion was an Easter riot in Athens, when a mob sacked the house of Don Pacifico, a Portuguese Jew who was a British subject because he was born in Gibraltar. He immediately appealed to the British government for redress; Palmerston promptly demanded it of the Greek government, and when that government demurred, he quickly exacted it by dispatching a British fleet which occupied Piraeus, the port of Athens, and seized Greek shipping. This highhanded application of British might provoked a storm in parliament. But Palmerston was more than a match for his adversaries there. He won a thumping vote of confidence from the House of Commons after a five-hour speech that worked up to a proud climax. Referring to Paul the Apostle, he asserted that "as the Roman in the days of old held himself free from indignity when he could say '*civis Romanus sum*,' so also, a British subject, in whatever land he may be, shall feel confident that the watchful eye and strong arm of England will protect him against injustice and wrong." For the sublime insolence of his implication that Britain was then mistress of the world, as Rome had once been, British writers of a soberer age have unanimously condemned him. The immediate reaction, however, was the very opposite. It lifted him, the darling of the people, to the peak of his popularity.

The other members of the cabinet found "Palm" an uncomfortable colleague, and Queen Victoria detested him; for he was undiplomatic, uncontrollable, and unpredictable. So they shoved him out of office early in 1852, but he soon retaliated by swinging a parliamentary vote that turned out the government; and at the end of the year, when his old friends returned to power, they could not keep him out, though they would not let him be foreign secretary. It might have been better if they had let him, for in 1854 the country drifted into a war that might have been avoided if the cabinet had been more certain of the course it would steer.

The Crimean War, the only European war that Britain fought between Waterloo and the German invasion of Belgium a century afterward, grew out of Russian demands upon Turkey. The sultan rejected them because, in addition to French support, he counted on British backing; and the czar pressed his demands because he counted on British acquiescence. While the two eastern autocrats were reaching this deadlock, the cabinet in London was divided between the followers of the prime minister, who had talked things over with the czar and would negotiate an accommodation with him, and the supporters of Palmerston, who was the stoutest opponent of Russia as a dangerous aggressor and a reactionary despot. When the Russians and the Turks fell to fighting, the British public stampeded the government into an alliance with France and Turkey to stem the Russian advance. The focus of hostilities was the fortress of Sebastopol in the Crimea. There the Russians had begun a naval base upon which they might first erect a power that would dominate the Black Sea behind the protection of the Dardanelles, and then burst through the Dardanelles to challenge the British command of the Mediterranean and threaten the shortest British communication with the empire in the east. The British would nip this danger in the bud, and the war gave them a chance to do it, because the Turk was only too glad to open the straits for the passage of the forces sent by his allies. It was in one of the battles near Sebastopol that the British Light Brigade charged into the valley of death and the immortality of Tennyson's poem. The siege of the fortress was at first so miserably mismanaged that in 1855 the British public forced the resignation of the government and the elevation of Palmerston to the office of prime minister, where he remained, with but one short interval, until he died. The fall of Sebastopol knocked the bottom out of the war. Peace was made in Paris, where a general European conference met in 1856. There the powers formally took Turkey under their protection, bound its government to reform its treatment of Christian subjects, and decreed the demilitarization of both the Black Sea and the Dardanelles.

In the Far East Britain was breaking down the barriers raised by China to prevent all contact with the outside world, and she might have anticipated the United States in doing the same to Japan if the Chinese business had not dragged on so long. What precipitated the breach of China was the termination of the East India Company's trading monopoly in 1833. China still had a practical monopoly of the production of tea, which had become a British necessity and even an American necessity, for it was not until later that the United States became addicted to coffee; and the export of tea was all from the port of Canton, where it was paid for by the import of opium. Canton was the only door through which China had any external trade, and it was almost all with the British, which meant the English company until 1833. On the Chinese side the trade was wholly illegal, but the local mandarins winked at it, for a handsome profit, and the local officials of the East India Company conducted the trade in an orderly manner. When the Company lost its right to exclude British competitors, the competitors rushed in and the trade fell into confusion. Thereupon the British government sent an official representative to restore order. This was impossible for him because, as an agent of the British government, he could make the necessary arrangements only with some responsible official of the Chinese government, and none would have anything to do with him. The trade of Canton grew enormously, and so did the attendant chaos and corruption. It was common for Chinese smugglers to unload opium from one side of a ship while a Chinese patrol boat lay along the other side. Traders who boggled at the bribes demanded by the mandarins saw their opium seized to swell the roaring trade of these same mandarins.

Finally Peking sent down a new mandarin who swept British traders into prison and gathered up their stocks of opium. That was in 1839, and though Palmerston was then writing to the British commissioner that his government would not intervene to enable British subjects to violate the law of the land with which they traded, he dispatched gunboats to impress upon Chinese officialdom the necessity of dealing justly with them. The upshot was a miserable little war, known popularly as the Opium War in spite of the fact that the British government never questioned the right of China to prohibit the import of opium. Hostilities ceased in 1842, when the Celestial Empire condescended to treat. Britain then won for all westerners the legal right to trade in five treaty ports, and for herself the cession of the little desert island of Hong Kong which, as a free port under British government, became in a few years the main seat of western trade and influence in that part of the world.

China did not live up to the terms of the treaty. The government was still obstinately exclusive and the mandarins shamelessly predatory, causing growing disputes with the traders, who could get neither justice nor mercy at the hands of the native officials. The result was a second miserable little war with China. The incident that touched it off was the boarding of a vessel flying the British flag and the arrest of one of its Chinese crew on a charge of piracy. The resident British agent demanded redress and, when this was refused, he summoned warships to attack Canton, which was defenseless. This was going too far for the House of Commons, which defeated the government on the issue. But Palmerston, who was prime minister, dissolved parliament, and the ensuing election proved again that, right or wrong, he was the national idol.

As this was the year of the Indian Mutiny, the Chinese war languished until the mutiny was suppressed. Then France, likewise exasperated with China, joined Britain in a military expedition that marched to Peking in 1860. There, as a reprisal for the ill-treatment of British prisoners, Lord Elgin, the former governor general of Canada and the future viceroy of India, ordered the burning of the Summer Palace, which his troops had already plundered. The allied occupation of Peking at last opened the eyes of the emperor and his advisers to the hopelessness of their long-protracted attempt to block the penetration of traders and missionaries. The treaty of 1860 confirmed and enlarged the rights of westerners in China, and it extended their British base by adding to Hong Kong a bit of the mainland half a mile away, the peninsula of Kowloon.

During the last five years of Palmerston's rule, Britain also joined the United States, France, and the Netherlands in a naval demonstration that brought the same lesson home to Japan. But at the same time, in 1863,[1] Palmerston's government freely gave Greece the Ionian Islands, whose inhabitants were Greek and desirous of political union

---

[1] The actual transfer occurred in the following year.

with their own people. Then too Palmerston sought to preserve the autonomy of Schleswig and Holstein, but he could not persuade his cabinet colleagues to run the risk of taking a firm stand against Prussia, which gobbled up these duchies in 1864.

Toward the United States, torn by civil war, the Palmerstonian policy was stiffer. Back in 1850, when he was foreign secretary, his minister, Bulwer, had negotiated with Clayton the conciliatory treaty that bound their governments in a joint guarantee of the neutrality of any canal that might be constructed across the isthmus joining the two Americas, and a mutual pledge that neither would ever gain exclusive control of it. These and other conditions of that treaty dispelled a cloud of suspicion between the two English-speaking powers. But now the conflict in the United States raised other issues that brought them to the verge of war.

The common American belief that Britain sided with the South contains much truth, but it needs serious qualification. Generally speaking, all the European powers that took any interest in the American conflict favored the South; and some of them, notably France under Napoleon III, were impatient with Britain for declaring her neutrality. They wanted her to take the lead in an intervention that would defeat the efforts of the North to crush the South; and Napoleon seized what seemed a good opportunity to erect a Latin empire in Mexico in defiance of the Monroe Doctrine, which had yet to wait many long years for any international recognition. Britain, however, did not even smile upon this venture; nor was there in Britain any body of opinion that desired intervention, either alone or at the head of a group of European powers. The people of Britain were divided over which side they wished would win, and the great majority actually backed the North, not the South. Instead of agitating for action to break the blockade of the South, which deprived them of work and wages, the Lancashire cotton operatives prayed for the success of the North. They bore their suffering patiently, for it was their conscious contribution to the cause of human freedom in America. Indeed, the whole working class of Britain was so hostile to slavery that its heart was solidly with the North.

Unfortunately for Anglo-American relations in this time of crisis, Britain had not yet adopted a democratic franchise, and the minority who controlled the government and the press felt strongly drawn toward the South. While the British did not believe in slavery, neither did they believe in democracy. The tone of their society was aristocratic, as was that of the South, whereas the society of the North was abandoned to democracy. They were also stout converts to free trade, which the South supported and the North would deny. More powerful in determining their attitude was the appeal of the constitutional principle on which the South had taken its stand, a principle then triumphing in Europe with Britain's active blessing, a principle for which Americans had once fought and won against Britain, a principle that Britain had since adopted for the remaining colonies but not for Ireland. It was that which a later American president formulated, with great acclaim, as "the self-determination of peoples." Not until 1863, when Lincoln thrust the issue of slavery into the forefront by issuing his emancipation edict, did the friendly feeling for the Confederate cause begin to cool in Britain; meanwhile the relations between London and Washington had been strained almost to the breaking point.

The serious friction did not come where it might be expected. Under the stress of war the American government reversed its position on two principles of international law over which it had quarreled with Britain in Napoleon's day. Then it had challenged the British blockade of the European coast from the Elbe to the Seine, on the ground that the line was too long for the blockade to be effective. Now it declared a blockade of the much longer coastline of the whole South, which the British government had just as much right to challenge. But London accepted it, though it caused acute distress in Lancashire. Similarly, the United States Navy now intercepted British vessels on the high seas and confiscated cargoes consigned to Nassau or other British ports on the principle that they were really destined for some Confederate port, though the American government had strenuously denied the existence of this "doctrine of continuous voyage" when the Royal Navy applied it against American vessels and cargoes during the struggle with Napoleon; and Britain, finding that this shoe too was now on the other foot, refrained from changing it.

The greatest danger to international peace arose from the American seizure of two Confederate envoys traveling in a British vessel on the high seas. It was a violation of international law and the flag, two things that were held as sacred in Britain as in the United States, and Palmerston was just the man to make the most of it. His government demanded redress, the American government refused, Britain began to prepare for war, and America yielded by releasing the illegitimate captives and disclaiming responsibility for their seizure. The crisis was turned when Prince Albert, Queen Victoria's consort, hastened his own death but probably averted war by rising from his sickbed to persuade Palmerston to be less peremptory, particularly not to insist upon an abject apology.

Less explosive but very bitter was another war-born dispute, for which the British government was to blame. As France under the great Napoleon had privateers built and fitted out in American ports to prey upon British commerce, so now the Confederacy turned to private British shipyards for raiders to harass the North. The British government stopped most of these vessels, but four of them escaped to sea. One was the notorious *Alabama,* which slipped out of Liverpool just before the arrival of an order for its arrest. The American minister had warned the Foreign Office of the supposed purpose of this specific vessel, but the laxity of the government in London had delayed the order. British official carelessness was therefore responsible for a breach of international law that was very costly to the commerce of the North and that poisoned Anglo-American relations for some years after the South was conquered and Palmerston was laid in his grave.

On Palmerston's death British foreign policy shed its excessive assertiveness and became more modest, more accommodating. The government was much less sensitive about British prestige abroad. Prussia soon astonished the world by overturning the European balance of power in two swift wars that smashed the imposing Austrian and French empires, but the British Foreign Office displayed little concern over the possible effect upon British interests. The government was also prepared to swallow its pride by a frank admission of the British fault in the *Alabama* affair and by the payment of whatever damages an international tribunal might award. Never before had a great power been willing to settle a major dispute in this fashion; and therefore the agreement to do so, made in the Washington Treaty of 1871, is an outstanding landmark in the history of international arbitration.

It was well that Palmerston's day was done. He had pandered to domestic national pride by fostering the delusion that Britain bossed the world, and his country had to pay for it in much more valuable coin than the money awarded to the United State for the depradations wrought by the *Alabama.* In the relations between sovereign states, unpopularity is the price of power, no matter how responsibly that power may be used. Britain could not have escaped it if "Palm" had never been born, and the way he made himself popular at home made his country more unpopular abroad. It is also a general rule of politics that a spirited foreign policy distracts domestic policy from seeking desirable reform, and here too Palmerston's activity was no exception. But if his departure thus appears to have been a double blessing for Britain, we must admit in fairness to him that he was the child of his age, that his foreign policy was on the whole what his people wanted and was probably a minor factor in dampening domestic reform.

By 1850 British society had just recovered from a spell of revolutionary fever that infected the working class. The democratic urge that burst the dikes of reaction in 1832, letting loose a flood of reforms, was really, as we have seen, a mass movement to capture parliament for the ulterior purpose of creating a new social order; and the discovery that the great Reform Bill did not democratize parliament soon produced among the masses and their leaders a bitter feeling of frustration. They saw, more or less clearly, that instead of escaping from their new economic masters they had substituted them for their old political masters. In desperation they turned to achieve their ends by more direct methods, and for a short while they flocked after Robert Owen, in whom they saw a Moses to lead them out of Egyptian bondage into the Promised Land.

It was nearly thirty years since this remarkable man, having worked his way up from the ranks of the wage earners to be the wealthy and philanthropic owner of a cotton factory, had persuaded parliament to investigate the evil conditions prevailing in most mills; meanwhile he had never ceased to be the prophet of an ideal industrial regime. Owen's idealism grew with the years, and now he was preaching socialism, though the word had not yet been invented. He advocated a nonpolitical cooperative communism. But it was not this that raised him up as a great prophet, though it drew many followers. What made his face shine as Moses' was his sudden championing of a new and revolutionary idea in the labor movement, which was to seize control of the machinery of production by direct action, a general strike. Here it is necessary to note a British distinction between a "trade union," which is limited to the workers in one trade or craft, and a "trades union." The new idea made little headway until Owen adopted it with his characteristic enthusiasm. It was in January 1834 that he announced the organization of the Grand National Consolidated Trades Union to include the whole of the working class of the nation. Half a million members joined in a few weeks, and through the spring and summer there was a plague of local strikes.

This rumbling of revolution alarmed the ruling class, but the Liberal government refused to pass repressive legislation, which its Tory predecessor would most certainly have done. Here and there, however, actions for conspiracy were started by employers against their workers. The most famous, or infamous, case was the prosecution of six agricultural laborers in the village of Tolpuddle, who had formed a lodge of the trades union. They were condemned to seven years' transportation, and despite a loud public outcry on their behalf the ministry allowed the sentence to be carried out. The heartless treatment of these poor victims, and the drastic nature of the new poor law, enacted in the same year, caused a flame of anger against the government to sweep through the working class. So also did the sudden collapse of the Grand National organization, which occurred at the same time as a consequence of its own weakness rather than as the result of any government action. These bitter experiences turned the laboring class back to seek the new social order through a radical reform of parliament, and so gave rise to the Chartist movement.

The People's Charter, designed to be a modern and democratic counterpart of the mediaeval Magna Carta, was born in 1836. It was a draft bill embodying six reforms, of which all but one have since become law. They were manhood suffrage, the secret ballot, the abolition of property qualifications for election to the House of Commons, the payment of members, equal electoral districts, and annual parliamentary elections. A nationwide agitation to press parliament to pass the Charter was getting well under way in 1838, when the anti-Corn Law League was founded; and from that time until the fall of protection, the League's drive for the more immediate and practical object of cheap food drained off much of the mass discontent. Nevertheless, the Chartist movement rapidly swelled to huge proportions and assumed a menacing aspect. While some of the leaders would confine it to peaceful agitation and petitions to parliament, others openly advocated violence. The Chartist press talked wildly of a general strike, of street barricades, of arming the people, and of bloody conflict after the continental fashion.

The danger of a revolutionary outbreak loomed very large in 1839. Delegates elected by mass meetings all over the country assembled in a national convention right by the Houses of Parliament, and they carried on their heated discussions without any interference by the authorities. Nowhere throughout the land was there any prosecution for sedition, though many an irresponsible orator urged excited hearers to appeal to arms. Many other irresponsible persons cursed the government for doing nothing, but Lord John Russell boldly defended the government and the right of the people to hold public meetings. "If they had no grievances," he said, "common sense would put an end to their meetings. It is not from free discussion that governments have anything to fear. There was fear when men were driven by force to secret combinations. *There* was the fear, *there* was the danger, and not in free discussion." The sane attitude of the government of the day appears also in its precautions against disorder—the dispatch of troops to towns where they might be needed, and a solemn warning to those troops that they must offer no provocation. The commander was Sir Charles Napier, who later conquered Sind; and when he found some Chartists saying that the soldiers were quiet out of fear, he graciously opened their eyes by having them inspect the guns. When the Chartist petition, bearing signatures that numbered a million and a quarter, was laid before parliament, that body discussed it gravely and rejected it overwhelmingly. Thereupon the convention, seeing no hope in armed revolt, tried to call a general strike; but the mass of the workers would have none of it.

Still Chartism lived, and in revenge for this defeat threw all its strength behind the Conservatives in the general election of 1841, only to discover that the new government was more hostile than the old one. In 1842 economic distress fanned the Chartist flame to a fiercer heat. This time the petition was bolder and gathered three and a third million signatures, and following its rejection by parliament a new call for a general strike brought much greater response. For some weeks it nearly tied up industrial Yorkshire and Lancashire. Though the strike collapsed of its own weight, the Conservative government acted more harshly than its Liberal predecessor. Most of the Chartist and trade union leaders were lodged in jail. About four score were transported, and five hundred were given prison terms. Such severity was quite unnecessary.

The Chartist movement was already broken. In 1848 it died after a last desperate revival under the stimulus of the many revolutions that convulsed Europe in that year. This time the monster petition to parliament was reputed to have five and a half million signatures. But examination reduced the number to less than two million, and revealed that many of them were spurious. Wags or rogues, or both, had appended a host of popular names—of characters in current novels and of people in high places, including Queen Victoria herself. When this wholesale fraud was exposed, Chartism expired to the accompaniment of laughter.

The revolutionary fever, which Britain then shook off, left its mark upon that generation. It had done much to educate the working class and also the other classes. To the former it gave a training in cooperative action, and it left them with a determination to improve their lot by methods that were more practical. To the latter it brought an equally needed realization that all was not well in the organization of society, and it made them think about how it could be improved. Much of the literature then appearing in England, all written for these other classes, reflects an uneasy social conscience. Moreover, it was Chartism that gave Disraeli the idea that grew into his concept of Tory democracy, a concept that reconciled his party to the advent of democracy.

The cause of parliamentary reform did not die with Chartism. In 1851 Lord John Russell pressed the question in the cabinet; and later in the session, when a private member of parliament proposed a reform bill, he opposed it, saying that the government would bring in its own bill on the subject. In 1852 he introduced a measure that would have enfranchised many industrial workers, but the fall of his government, turned out by Palmerston, stopped the bill after the first reading. He repeated his efforts in the next two years, only to see them blocked by the outbreak of the Crimean War. After the war John Bright made valiant attempts to stir the working class to demand a share of political power, but his eloquence then fell on deaf ears. Disraeli tried his hand with a bill in 1859, and the Commons threw it out. In the following year Russell again produced a bill, which he withdrew when it failed to rouse the interest of either parliament or the public.

The American Civil War greatly helped British democracy. The slow but sure victory of democracy over aristocracy in the United States had a considerable power of suggestion. On two definite counts it proved the British ruling class wrong and working class right. It demonstrated that democracy was not bound to fail, as the former had believed, and that laborers might have sounder political judgment than their social betters. Even the dire distress that it visited upon the cotton operatives and their families played its part. The suffering of these humble folk won them much sympathy, and, what was more important, the patience with which they bore it for the sake of others' freedom commanded widespread respect. But if the war created in Britain an atmosphere more favorable to the working class vote, the popular demand for it, which had sunk out of sight in 1848, was not yet very evident. Until this demand surged up again, parliamentary reform could be only an academic question.

With the final collapse of Chartism, the labor movement turned its back on politics, where it had floundered helplessly, and concentrated its attention upon the immediate task of improving working conditions. At the same time it began to show new signs of strength by developing a superior type of trade union. The old type, a small local organization managed by workmen in their off hours, was weak and shortsighted. Now powerful national organizations arose. The first was the Amalgamated Society of Engineers in 1851; and by the middle of the next decade the carpenters, the miners, the cotton spinners, the weavers, and other trades had each achieved consolidation on a national scale. These new trade unions had large funds at their disposal, and they had well-paid officers who devoted their whole time to their respective societies. The contrast with the old was like that between little business and big business, and that between untrained amateurs and trained professionals. Far from being a reversion to the extravagant ideas of 1834, the change was a great step forward. The new trade union leaders were men of much longer vision and more practical sense. Their goal was not the millenium, but a well-ordered industrial society in which the relations between labor and capital would be regulated by the leaders of both sitting down together as equals and settling their differences by negotiation or conciliation. They strongly discouraged all pressure from below to meddle in politics or to indulge in constant strikes, both of which activities they regarded as wasteful and injurious to the cause they were directing.

In becoming better organized and disciplined, trade unionism was preparing labor to bear the responsibility of sharing in the control of the state. So also was the cooperative movement, another new and remarkable development of the period. The opening in 1844 of a little retail shop by some two dozen workingmen, so that they could make their own domestic purchases without having to pay toll to middlemen, was the small beginning of great things. These Rochdale Pioneers were soon so successful that others followed their example, and cooperative stores sprang up all over England, particularly in the industrial north. From 1850 many "self-governing workshops" were also set up; but the cooperative movement made little inroad into the field of production, whereas it throve mightily in distribution. At the same time there was a rapid expansion of an older form of cooperation among workingmen, by which they were providing themselves with what we now call social insurance. Their Friendly Societies, which gave financial protection in the event of sickness or death, had a long and obscure history. For generations they had been poor and weak, their members commonly meeting in "pubs" where they dissipated much of their slender resources. From the thirties, however, these mutual benefit societies gathered strength under government inspection, which taught them how to manage their funds wisely; and now they were on their feet.

The advent of political democracy in Britain came swiftly and easily in 1867. After fighting shy of politics for half a generation, labor returned to the assault as a measure of self-defense. Most employers had always regarded trade unions with suspicion, and the rapid rise of the new great unions filled them with alarm. Thereupon they started a vigorous agitation against organized labor in general and these national unions in particular. When overspeculation caused a temporary financial crisis in 1857, employers cut wages, precipitating a rash of strikes that lasted for several years and played into the hands of the enemies of labor. On the whole, the strikes were the work of the older local unions, which still harbored the notion that the primary purpose of a union was to strike, and they were not successful. Facing defeat, some of the strikers resorted to violence. The worst was in Sheffield, the home of steel, where tools were destroyed, some workers were even murdered, and there was almost a reign of terror for a while. The leaders of the national unions, who stood firmly for industrial peace, publicly denounced the ugly business; but they could not stem the rising tide of hostile public opinion in the classes that controlled parliament.

Another ominous sign was the attitude of the law courts. Though the repeal of the combination laws in 1825 removed the statutory ban on trade unions, it did not give them legal recognition; and the common law, as interpreted by the judges, forbade their members to combine in a strike, on the ground that it was in restraint of trade and, therefore, an illegal conspiracy. Moreover, there was then no way for trade unions, as such, to get legal incorporation, without which they could have no legally enforceable rights to any funds they possessed or any property they owned. To protect these interests, they registered as Friendly Societies, which were incorporated under parliamentary legislation, but a court decision might at any time strip off this cloak and leave them naked. In 1867 such a decision was finally handed down, and in the same year the public agitation against trade unionism bore fruit in the appointment of a royal commission to investigate its doings. But already organized labor, realizing the necessity of getting some control over the law through its makers, had abandoned its aloofness from politics and had launched such a powerful drive for electoral reform that there was no stopping it.

The parliament that in 1867 enfranchised the workers of the towns had just demonstrated beyond all shadow of doubt that it was opposed to any such measure. On the death of Palmerston, Russell, now an earl and in the House of Lords, became prime minister, with Gladstone as leader of the Commons and the strongest force in the ministry. Naturally, following their past commitments, they prepared a reform bill, which was introduced in 1866. It was very mild, compared with the one that was passed in the following year, but it was much too extreme for the majority in the Commons. Robert Lowe,[2] a brilliant myopic lawyer who had returned from Australia where he was a vitriolic champion of responsible government, headed a secession of Liberal members who voted with the Conservatives against the bill even though they thereby drove their own party from power. The Conservatives, led by Lord Derby in the upper chamber and Disraeli in the lower, then tried to form a coalition government with the Liberal seceders in order to get a majority in the Commons. As Lowe and his fellows refused the offer, Derby formed a straight Conservative government, which avoided immediate defeat by performing the most surprising political somersault in British records.

The defeat of the 1866 bill, which had seemed to arouse not much more popular interest than the similar bills of preceding years, let loose a terrific clamor from the masses. They held huge public meetings and marched in great processions to demand electoral reform immediately. A monster demonstration to be held in Hyde Park was announced. The government forbade it and shut the gates. But the milling crowd burst through fifty yards of the heavy fence and poured into the park. This tumultuous preliminary added unexpected weight to the impressiveness of the demonstration. All over the country the stirring of the masses was reminiscent of Chartist days and of the popular pressure that forced parliament to reform itself in 1832. Now there was little talk of revolution, but little doubt that there would be something very like it unless parliament yielded.

Disraeli promptly mounted the storm, dragging many of his party after him. "If the people would have reform," he said, "we might as well give it to them and stay in power." Defying the recalcitrant wing of his own party and the antireform block of the other party, he calcu-

---

2 Later Lord Sherbrooke.

lated that he could draw sufficient parliamentary support from the liberal Liberals to carry reform. In this he was right. But he soon found that the combination of votes from opposite sides of the House was more than a little unmanageable. One amendment after another was added, and no one could tell what would next be urged. At one stage John Stuart Mill occasioned mingled anger and amusement by proposing votes for women—half a century before they got it. As the measure progressed, it bore less and less resemblance to the original bill, and every change made it more radical.

The act that emerged conferred the franchise in the urban constituencies upon every adult male who occupied a dwelling on which he paid local rates, a common condition for tenants, or occupied lodgings worth £10 a year. This practically doubled the electorate and definitely shifted the basis of political power to the industrial working class, who now possessed a majority of the votes. Derby called it "a leap in the dark," and Carlyle "shooting Niagara." Lowe said, "Now we must educate our masters." But these new masters were actually educating their old ones, and the process was bound to continue, for thenceforth Liberal and Conservative politicians had to compete for the support of the working class vote.

In the general election of 1868, Disraeli, who had just succeeded Derby as prime minister, went down to defeat, but he was not paying the penalty that Wellington paid in 1830 for jamming an unpopular reform through parliament. Gladstone won because he offered a more promising policy for dealing with Ireland, and his first attention as prime minister was absorbed by that perennial problem of British politics. Then he turned to domestic affairs and his government carried a number of reforms that were a logical sequel to the recent extension of the franchise and that echoed the reconstructive legislation following the great reform of 1832.

The first of these new reforms revolutionized elementary education and laid the foundations of the system that has since been erected. The policy adopted a generation before, of subsidizing voluntary schools, most of which were controlled by some religious society, had proved to be quite inadequate. Half the children of school age were attending no school, only a quarter were in schools efficiently run and inspected, and the three quarters who were thus neglected were the children of working class families. The warning uttered by Lowe could not go unheeded, but any attempt to meet the urgent need was sure to provoke heated controversy because it involved religion. The great majority of the existing schools were Church of England and taught the doctrines of that church, to which the great majority of the nation belonged; and as these doctrines were abhorrent to Dissenters, the latter had started nonsectarian schools. A battle royal followed between churchmen, to whom a godless education was equally abhorrent, and those who would divorce education from religion because one was a public matter and the other a private one. A national compulsory school system after the Prussian or the American model was politically impossible in England, with its established church; but the time had come when the government of the nation had to see that, in one way or another, the children of the whole nation got efficient schooling.

The Education Act of 1870 met the need by filling in the large gap. It established local school boards elected by the rate payers to maintain the necessary elementary schools under government supervision. For this purpose, it gave the boards power to levy rates and to collect fees, which they could waive for poor parents. It also provided government grants, and at the same time it increased the public grants to the voluntary schools. It compromised on the question of religious instruction in the new schools. The boards could require it if they so desired, but it had to be nonsectarian and put in the first or last period of the day so that children of objecting parents could be excused from exposure to it. In the following year another act abolished the religious tests that had made the universities close Church of England corporations.

Other reforms of this ministry included the adoption, in 1870, of competitive examinations for appointments to vacancies in the civil service. For years there had been a movement in this direction for the sake of greater administrative efficiency, and now it succeeded when the advent of democracy made it more urgent as a means of preventing deterioration under the influence of that disease of democracy known as the spoils system. Then too the army was made much more efficient and popular by a thorough reorganization, one feature of which was the abolition of the purchase of officers' commissions, an ancient relic of aristocratic privilege. Parliament balked at this particular reform, and to effect it the government had to fall back upon a royal warrant, which, though quite legal, drew vehement denunciations from the class that had long monopolized the officering of the army. In 1872 the Ballot Act gave protection to the democratic electorate by putting an end to open voting. In the following year another act vastly improved the administration of justice by revising legal procedure and reconstructing the principal courts. It was an energetic and intelligent housecleaning that swept out the debris of ages, some of which is reputed to have survived even in American courts.

Already the dubious legal position of trade unions had come under review, and the royal commission's investigation into their practices had vindicated organized labor as a whole against the common charge that it was responsible for such ugly incidents as had occurred in Sheffield. A statute of 1871 overrode the common law ruling that trade unions were conspiracies in restraint of trade, and it gave them legal recognition. As a result of recent experience, however, the labor victory was qualified by a legislative attempt to draw a line between lawful and unlawful actions in conducting strikes, and the definition of picketing was such that it was almost impossible to use the strike weapon without running foul of the criminal law. Though labor felt cheated, it was not exasperated. The rise in real wages was still operating to reduce the temptation to draw the sword, and the shaping of the law was no longer in the hands of men who could defy the will of the masses. At the next general election, in 1874, two workingmen won seats in the House of Commons, the property qualification for members having been abolished quietly in 1858. Though the public purse provided members with no salaries, this was no bar, for these two new members were paid by their fellow miners. Political democracy was beginning to function in Britain.

CHAPTER XXI

The Birth of the First Dominion

An outstanding feature of the development of the British Empire into the British Commonwealth of Nations has been the consolidation of adjacent colonies to form new British nations; and like the other essential feature in this development—the British North American Revolution which spread to other parts of the empire—it was first applied in British North America under the compelling influence of the United States.

The American Revolution planted the seed that the American Civil War brought to fruition in the establishment of the Dominion of Canada. It will be recalled that on the morrow of the Revolution the British government sent out Lord Dorchester to pull together the North American fragments that had survived the imperial wreck. Though the only means of communication were then so poor that he could not do it, the idea never quite died. From time to time some prominent individual in one or other of these colonies kept it alive by proposing a scheme to realize it. When Durham went to Canada he became a convert, and in his famous report he preached the gospel of salvation by unity. As the United States had unconsciously planted the seed, so also did the great Republic keep it watered. This was by the power of example and suggestion. One remarkable achievement of the American people that has since been mostly forgotten, even by themselves, is that they rehabilitated an ancient but long discredited form of government and thereby inaugurated the rather striking growth of federalism in the modern world. In other words, they demonstrated the practicability of the formula by which British North America, though divided by geography and by race, might be united. Then, too, the fact that the United States was striding like a young giant across the continent stirred the imagination of British North Americans. If the lost colonies could thus become a great nation, why could not the remaining ones unite and build another? And if they did not seek strength in union, what would be their fate? Sooner or later the young giant might swallow them up, one by one. Such hopes and fears inspired most of the advocates of federation for these colonies. But the agitation for it did not begin to win wide support until the middle of the nineteenth century.

The coming of the railway age lifted the union of British North America out of the land of dreams. In 1850 there were scarcely fifty miles of railway in the whole of British North America. Ten years later United Canada had two thousand of them. These included a trunk line that ran from Sarnia, at the foot of Lake Huron, to Rivière du Loup, on the south shore of the St. Lawrence a hundred and twenty miles below Quebec; and this Grand Trunk Railway had an outlet to the ocean through the United States at Portland, Maine. The Maritime Provinces had three little railways that had no connection with one another; if they could be linked up and joined with Rivière du Loup, British North America would at last be drawn together physically and therefore might be united politically. But who would pay for filling in the gaps? Private capital would not foot the bill, the railway mania had already strained the public finances of United Canada to the breaking point, and the much poorer governments of the Maritime Provinces could not find the money. In the end, after several years, the imperial government came to the rescue in order to make federation possible, and that was only when political considerations seemed to make federation imperative.

There is an old Canadian saying that federation was born of political deadlock. The reference is to an exasperating development in the old United Canada, where responsible government soon came to an impasse. The trouble arose from the coexistence of two peoples so deeply divided by race, religion, language, legal systems, and culture—each inhabiting a separate part of the country—that neither would submit to rule by the other. No cabinet could survive that did not have two heads and two distinct halves, one from Canada East (Quebec) and the other from Canada West (Ontario), and also the simultaneous support of a double majority in the assembly. A majority of members from Canada West could not make up for a minority from Canada East, or vice versa. Such conditions were impossible. Ten ministries fell in the ten years beginning with 1854. If self-government was to survive, the Union Act of 1840 had to go. The two parts of the country had to have separate administrations and legislatures, and yet they could not be completely severed. That would revive the financial difficulties of Upper Canada, and it would damage both sections of the country in more important ways. United Canada had undertaken responsibilities that could not well be divided. While each section had to have its own government to manage its own affairs, they also had to have a government to look after customs, railways, canals, and other interests that they had in common. In short, they could not go back to mere division; they had to go on to establish a federal system. But this did not mean that it must include any other colony. What stretched the solution to give it a much wider application?

The American Civil War is the answer to this question, but before we examine it we should observe some other developments that were conditioning the minds of men in British North America for the larger solution. Around the middle of the century the rapid expansion of settlement in Canada West ran up against the wilderness of rocks and lakes and Christmas trees that is known as the Pre-Cambrian Shield, whose southern edge is not a hundred miles north of Toronto. Blocked in this direction, the surplus population began to pour across the international boundary into the northern Middle Western States. The frontier movement that had once surged into Upper Canada had now passed beyond, into the newer and larger West of the United States. Immigrants were still crowding into Canada, but she could not keep them. Her growth was being cramped, and her public men were coming to feel that she must have a West of her own for expansion. Therefore they looked to the part of the Northwest that was still under the Union Jack; there they saw unlimited possibilities—and also an ominous shadow approaching them.

The Hudson's Bay Company was losing its hold over the huge empire of the west. Who would get possession of it? The advancing tide of American settlement strongly suggested that it might be the United States. Memories of what had recently happened on the Pacific coast were very fresh in Canada, and rather raw. The British government, reading the lesson of the Oregon crisis, had given all the land on Vancouver Island to the Hudson's Bay Company in 1849 for the purpose of building a colony that would solidify British possession of that exposed corner of the empire. But that was such a far corner of the earth that it attracted scarcely any British settlers. Therefore the colony of Vancouver Island, though endowed by London with a governor, a council, and an assembly, remained what it had been since the recent removal of the company's Pacific coast headquarters from Fort Vancouver on the Columbia, now in the United States, to the harbor of Victoria. It was only a little community of people who had been or still were connected with the company. The mainland remained a no man's land for another ten years. Then, in 1858, the discovery of gold on the Fraser River drew a swarm of fortune seekers, mostly from California. Thus a new and real colony sprang up overnight, but without a government until later in the year, when London formally made it a crown colony and christened it British Columbia. The name, however, was misleading, for the population was much more American than British.

Meanwhile the prairie region had attracted more attention in Canada. At its southeastern corner the little Red River colony had demonstrated the richness of its soil; but this colony too was so remote that its only growth was by natural increase and the settlement of people already in the country—retired company servants and a more numerous body of métis—until the middle of the century, when a new and easier way into the country was opened. The outside world had been creeping closer, through the United States; and at last—almost like an electric spark leaping across a narrowing gap—regular and rapidly growing communication was established between Fort Garry (Winnipeg) and St. Paul, Minnesota. It was over a prairie trail of five hundred miles along which Red River carts, soon by the hundred, creaked back and forth. The opening of this American door into the country built up the colony and pulled down its government. At last it began to attract immigrants from south of the border; the monopoly of trade, conferred by charter upon the company, became impossible; and the government, likewise vested in the company, lost its authority when the company tried to use it to preserve the monopoly. The restlessness of the settlers mounted as Americans and Canadians appeared in their midst, and they began to talk of getting a free government of their own by becoming a regular British colony, or by annexation to the United States, or by joining Canada. In the winter of 1856–57, nearly six hundred of them petitioned Canada to take over the country. On top of this encouragement from the West, Canada received more from England, where public criticism of the old company led to an investigation by a parliamentary committee, which recommended the same thing.

Then came the American Civil War, which profoundly altered the future of British North America as well as that of the United States. Had it not been for this war the United States, not Canada, might have been the heir of the Hudson's Bay Company. The vigorously expanding

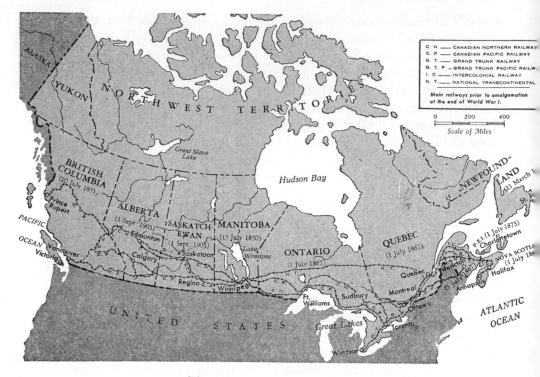

The Dominion of Canada

North was almost on the point of reaching farther north, into the empty prairie owned by the company, when the outbreak of the conflict with the South in 1861 turned the energies of the North in the opposite direction. In other words, the war pulled back the American arm that would seize what is now the Canadian Northwest. The war was also largely responsible for making this region permanently Canadian. It is doubtful if the old United Canada, however reorganized, would have been able to acquire and hold this huge territory, but the larger Dominion of Canada was able to do it, by how much margin we cannot say; and it is more than doubtful if there could have been a Dominion of Canada then or for a long time afterward, if at all, without the Civil War.

The Dominion of Canada was born, as it was conceived, in fear. The Civil War gave new and urgent force to the old argument that the great Republic would sooner or later devour the little adjoining British colonies if they did not seek strength in union. It raised the specter of an American war against Britain, a war in which the main attack would fall on British North America, as in 1812, but with infinitely greater chances of success. This time the United States was in a fighting mood; it was inured to fighting; and, what we sometimes forget, it was then for a short while the greatest military power of the world. The obvious menace welded British North America together.

The federation of British North America began to take definite shape in 1864, and this despite the failure of many strenuous efforts to find the necessary physical basis in a railway that would unite the Maritime Provinces with Canada. This failure then caused the Maritime Provinces to despair of any political union but one of their own, and so they made a move to achieve it by calling a conference to meet in Charlottetown, Prince Edward Island, September 1. Before it could meet, the prospect changed. The political deadlock in United Canada became so complete that opposing political leaders formed a coalition government pledged to find an escape through federation, and in taking this pledge they stretched the solution to include the provinces down by the sea. Only if this proved impossible would they fall back upon a federal reorganization of United Canada; and they were determined to press for the larger solution in the faith that, if they succeeded in reaching it, some way would then be found for getting the essential railway. Seizing the opportunity of the coming conference in Charlottetown, which was too good to miss, the Canadian government asked the Maritime Provinces for permission to send a delegation which would present the wider question. The request evoked a cordial invitation. The conference met, heard the Canadians, promptly shelved the project of a Maritime union, and immediately adjourned, for it was agreed to have a great conference in Quebec to work out the details of a federal scheme for all British North America.

The Quebec Conference, which assembled in October 1864, was Canada's constitutional convention. Almost everything in the British North America Act, which created the Dominion of Canada and became its written constitution in 1867, was settled in a series of seventy-two resolutions passed by this conference in about a fortnight. Such speed may seem astonishing, but there is no reason to believe that longer deliberations would have produced sounder conclusions. For years the best minds in the colonies had been focused upon the problem, and all its aspects had been discussed *ad nauseam* in public and in private. The leaders of the colonial governments who gathered in Quebec were thus thoroughly prepared for the work in hand. Also they were more or less familiar with the proceedings of the Philadelphia Convention of 1787, as well as with the subsequent history of the American Constitution, and some of them had made a close study of the American example. They therefore had an enormous advantage over their American predecessors, the advantage of hindsight. Finally, they felt that they had to reach an agreement, as the only step they could take to avert the peril looming just across the line; and the sooner this was done, the better.

In framing the constitution of the Dominion, the "fathers of confederation" copied from the American model, modifying it here and there in the light of American experience; but there were many things in it that they would not dream of adopting because, from their own experience with the British model and their own observation of how the American system worked, they were convinced that they already had something much better. It was a foregone conclusion that they would follow American precedent by establishing a federal form of government, and that they would split United Canada into two new provinces, Ontario and Quebec. In their allocation of powers between the Dominion and the provinces, they were so obsessed by the bloody tragedy being enacted next door that they would not allow the cloven hoof of state rights to appear in their work. Therefore they gave the residual powers to the Dominion, and they put in something else that Alexander Hamilton had tried to write into the American Constitution. They gave the Dominion the right to veto any provincial legislation. In these two provisions we see the indelible stamp of the American Civil War upon the Canadian constitution.

To improve upon the American model, the framers of the Canadian constitution also refused to let the provinces touch banking or criminal law, which they included in the list of subjects reserved for federal legislation; and they made an interesting innovation in their provision for the administration of justice, by which they married provincial and federal jurisdictions. Instead of repeating the American duplication, they decided to have the same courts administer both provincial and federal law, with the provinces responsible for the organization of the courts and the Dominion for the appointment and payment of the judges.

Another feature of the American Constitution these men at Quebec had to accept, but they liked it so little that they kept it to a bare minimum. One of the striking differences between the British and the American constitutions is that the former can be altered by the ordinary process of legislation. The two constitutions are therefore classified respectively as *flexible* and *rigid*. Because the authors of the Canadian constitution had to make it a federal one, and because rigidity is inherent in federalism, they had to make it rigid. This feature, however, they limited as far as possible. In contrast to the American Constitution, which is much more rigid than the federal principle necessitates, the Canadian is flexible to a degree that seems very strange to American eyes. In this respect it was a continuation of the constitutional system that the people of British North America already enjoyed and would not exchange for the American. They felt no need for a bill of rights, which therefore did not appear in the Canadian constitution; and they retained their freedom to amend their provincial constitutions by ordinary legislation.

The Quebec Conference departed from the tradition of bicameral government by giving one of the new provinces, Ontario, a unicameral legislature, which the people of that province wanted and have since retained. It was a prophetic innovation; for British Columbia followed the Ontario example on becoming a province, and within a generation all but one of the other provinces abolished their second chambers by simply legislating them out of existence. In framing the federal legislature, the Canadian "fathers" did not question the necessity, dictated by the federal principle, for two chambers. The lower one was made to resemble both the British House of Commons and the American House of Representatives, with the name of the former and the decennial redistribution of seats prescribed for the latter. The upper chamber was given the appearance of its American counterpart, being called the Senate and composed on a geographical basis intended to protect sectional interests. But the architects of the Dominion compromised the American principle of Senate representation, by dividing among the Maritime Provinces the same number of seats as they allotted to each of the other two provinces. They also decided against the election of senators. They feared that it would reproduce in Ottawa the deadlocks that had paralyzed Congress from time to time. They also felt that two elected houses would be incompatible with responsible government. If the houses disagreed, which would control the ministry? Therefore, after much debate, they chose appointment for life by the Dominion government. Here again they agreed that Alexander Hamilton had been right. Their decision of course meant that, in point of power, the upper chamber would resemble the British House of Lords rather than the American Senate.

The separation of powers, which Americans are taught to believe is one of the supreme virtues of their Constitution, was one thing that these men in Quebec would not borrow from the United States. It was not that they were unfamiliar with it, for they had grown up in the shadow of the great Republic. It was rather their firm conviction of the superiority of the opposite principle, the fusion of the executive and legislative in the cabinet, which they had been working for half a generation. They did not write it into the new constitution because they did not need to. It was the very heart of the provincial constitutions, which were to continue as they existed, and it was simply taken for granted that it would also be the heart of the federal government—the unwritten part that governs the operation of the written part.

By the letter of the law, the queen rules the Dominion through the governor general assisted by the federal cabinet, which he appoints; and the governor general rules each province through a lieutenant governor, whom he appoints (another echo of a Hamiltonian proposal) and who, in turn, appoints the provincial cabinet. The governor general and the provincial governors cannot do this, because they are constitutional monarchs and, like the queen, are the nominal but not the real heads of their respective administrations. The real head of each is, of course, the prime minister or premier, who is the majority leader in the legislature and selects his own cabinet colleagues. By the letter of the law, the legislature is elected for five years, subject to earlier dissolution by the representative of the Crown. But it is the premier who really decides this, and he may do it at any time. Here we come upon the unwritten yet inviolable principle of balanced checks in this system, which the people of France to their own grief have repeatedly ignored; for the power of the government to turn out the House, combined with that of the House to turn out the government, guarantees mutual responsibility and an immediate resolution of any deadlock between them by an appeal to the people in a general election.

To make federation possible, the Quebec Conference decided to bind the federal government to provide the railway communication that would tie the Maritime Provinces to the rest of the country; so the Canadian constitution has the peculiar distinction of having a railway written into it. The members of the conference also envisaged a Dominion that would extend right across the continent, for one of the great purposes of their meeting was to get the West before it was too late. Therefore, though they planned to include only United Canada and the Maritime Provinces in the original federation, they provided for the subsequent admission of the territory still under the government of the Hudson's Bay Company and the two Pacific colonies of British Columbia and Vancouver Island. They realized that such an addition would also have to be tied by adequate communications, but they hesitated to write this much bigger obligation into the constitution. Instead they passed a resolution stating that it was of "highest importance to the Federated Provinces" to undertake the task as rapidly as finances would permit.

The problem of how the written constitution might be amended did not bother its framers. Much of it could be altered by ordinary law passed by the appropriate legislature, federal or provincial, and for this they made the necessary provision. For the amendment of the rest, they made no provision of any kind, and this was no oversight. Neither did they prescribe a federal Supreme Court for the final judicial interpretation of the constitution, and this too was no oversight. The Dominion parliament created one in 1875, but it was not essential. The ordinary courts could hear constitutional cases, and appeal from these courts lay to the Judicial Committee of the Privy Council in London, the final court of appeal for all the empire except the British Isles. As for amendments, these could be made in the same manner as the original constitution was to be launched, by an act of the imperial parliament implementing the will of the federating colonies.

The next step was to get the consent of the several colonies to the plan prepared in Quebec. When submitted to the legislature of United Canada, it roused serious opposition only from Canada East, where the Roman Catholic Church and the French population were very apprehensive of what the English and Protestant majority in the new central government and parliament might do to them. There was some danger that the French might be stampeded into wrecking the proposal, but this was averted by their leaders, particularly the hierarchy. The church quickly reversed its attitude, fearing that the rejection of federation would lead to annexation, which seemed a much greater evil. As it was, nearly half the French members voted against the scheme.

It was not so easy to get the agreement of the Maritimes. They had been talking grandly of annexing Canada, but when they came face to face with the issue, it looked as if Canada was going to annex them, for its population was nearly four times that of all the Maritime Provinces. Would not they be the tail, and Quebec and Ontario the body of the proposed federation? Moreover, the mere fact that the doubtful provinces were maritime made their people less sensitive than the people of United Canada to the danger from their big neighbor. British sea power gave the former a feeling of security that the latter, being inland, could not share. The two island provinces, Newfoundland and Prince Edward Island, rejected the plan offhand. The New Brunswick government staked its existence on it in a general election, and lost. Neither the legislature nor the electorate of Nova Scotia were allowed to vote on the Quebec resolutions; for they too would have rejected them, and the government in Halifax, anxious for federation, stalled for time.

While federation was thus held up in the Maritime Provinces, strong forces worked quietly to bring them into line. The British government brought pressure to bear where it was most needed, chiefly through the lieutenant governors of New Brunswick and Nova Scotia. Each had backed the local opposition to the movement. Now the former had to go home for a visit that thoroughly converted him, and the latter was replaced by an enthusiastic advocate. Though the authorities in London had been reconciled to the prospect of the eventual independence of British North America, they could not tolerate the thought of its being swallowed up by a hostile United States. Torn between their anti-imperial revulsion from colonial commitments and their responsibility for defending these colonies against enemy attack, they saw no possible escape from the dilemma except through federation. That might come without the two island provinces, but not if New Brunswick and Nova Scotia held out. Hence the concentration upon these two.

More direct and more effective than this American-inspired British push were two other ways in which American hostility helped the reluctant colonies to jump over the stile. One was by giving them an economic kick. In January 1865, Congress voted to abrogate the Reciprocity Treaty of 1854. The people in the Maritime Provinces then saw themselves seriously injured by the loss of the American market for their produce. Federation offered them a substitute. On top of this blow came the immediate threat of a worse one—from the Fenians in the United States. These Irish Americans, who hated England with a consuming hatred, gathered on the border to invade and conquer British North America, and Washington winked at the enterprise. In 1866 they invaded Canada across the Niagara River, inflicting considerable damage before they were chased out. But their influence was greater where they did not actually appear—in New Brunswick. To defend the frontier against an army of four or five hundred Fenians—many of them veterans of the Civil War—who gathered on the American side of the St. Croix River, the New Brunswick militia was called out and a body of British regulars was rushed from Halifax. Meanwhile the threat of an invasion that never came off stirred a great wave of loyalty throughout the province, inclining many doubtful minds to seek strength in union. It also influenced public opinion in Nova Scotia.

The tide turned in the spring of 1866. The premier in Halifax proposed, and the assembly passed, a resolution that, without mentioning the Quebec plan, authorized the provincial government to arrange with the British government a scheme of union that would protect the rights of each province. A few weeks later, just as the fear of invasion was reaching its climax, the lieutenant governor of New Brunswick precipitated a general election by picking a quarrel with his ministry, and the voters upheld him by reversing their decision of the previous year. With these two provinces at last ready to proceed, their delegates joined representatives of the government of United Canada for a final conference at the end of the year. It was held in London, and there they adopted the Quebec resolutions with only slight changes.

One point had yet to be decided. What was the new country to be called? "The Kingdom of Canada" was the name chosen by John A. Macdonald, the Scottish immigrant who had become the outstanding political figure of United Canada and was the principal architect of the new federation. Many Canadians have since regretted that he could not persuade the British government to accept it, for they believe that it might have led to a much earlier recognition of the present status of Canada as an equal partner in the British Commonwealth. What made the British government veto it was the fear of offending republican sensibilities in the United States. Thereupon the colonial delegates fell back upon the old term *Dominion,* and substituted it for the dangerous word. In every other respect the British North America Act of 1867, the written constitution of the Dominion, was drafted exactly as they wished, and the "mother of parliaments" passed it without any question. It was also during this conference in London that the British government came to the financial rescue of the new Dominion so that it might build the essential railway as soon as possible. The rescue took the form of an imperial guarantee of interest on a Canadian loan.

Here it may be well to pause for a glance at a curious American irony. The last thing the United States wanted to see was the rise of a consolidated British power on its northern border. It was a revival of an old bogey, and it was something more. It was a defiance of American imperialism, better known as Manifest Destiny, and there was loud American talk of interfering to stop it. Yet it was the United States that provided, by its hostile attitude, the force that drove British North

America into federation, and this federation into an imperialist expansion. Americans, for example, thought that their denunciation of the Reciprocity Treaty would hasten annexation, but it had the very opposite effect. Likewise, the American purchase of Alaska, designed to head off the Dominion from reaching the Pacific, only stimulated the new Canadian imperialism and hurried on the Canadian annexation of the West right out to the Pacific.

When the Dominion of Canada came into existence in 1867, it was only one tenth as big as it is today. It had only four provinces; the two larger ones, Ontario and Quebec, were then a mere fraction of their present size, for all the land draining into Hudson Bay still belonged to the English fur-trading company; and of the other two provinces, New Brunswick and Nova Scotia, the latter straightway tried to pull out of the union.

The secession movement in Nova Scotia may suggest a parallel with the earlier movement of the same name in New England or in the South, but it had little in common with them. It was largely the work of one man who had preached federation when it was still a dream and then fought it when it became a practical issue—the eloquent, impulsive, and beloved Joseph Howe, the hoary champion of responsible government. He was passionately devoted to his native land, and he saw it being bound and delivered to Canada. Having lost the first round of the battle in 1867, he continued the fight more desperately and rallied behind him most of the people in his province. They had never voted for federation, and as soon as they had a chance, in the first election after the Dominion was created, they voted strongly against it. This was largely the result of Howe's fiery appeals by tongue and pen, reinforced by the geographical position of Nova Scotia, for the sea insulated her from the fear that operated in the provinces lying tight beside the United States. The antifederation government that was then established in Halifax sent Howe to London to demand the release of the province. But the British government turned a deaf ear to all his pleading. For safety's sake British North America had been united and must remain united. Nova Scotians grew angrier and angrier until the premier began to talk of finding an escape through annexation to the United States. His words frightened Howe into reversing his course again. Opening negotiations with the federal government in Ottawa, he secured better financial terms for his province, and thenceforth he courageously supported what he had so bitterly denounced.

For a short while the storm down by the sea raged furiously—and then blew itself out.

This whole affair is a striking manifestation of a Canadian phenomenon that has often puzzled American observers. It was the third time that a considerable body of Canadians openly talked in favor of annexation. The first was in Durham's day, when the English-speaking minority in Lower Canada boldly asserted that they would rather have annexation than allow the French majority to rule; and the second was in 1849, when a group of disgruntled English-speaking merchants and politicians of Montreal launched a public campaign to achieve annexation. The third was not the last time. Ever and anon, down to our own day, a Canadian annexation movement has raised its head and then subsided. The reason is really quite simple. The juxtaposition of the United States has made it a natural expression of sectional discontent, a stick to shake at the rest of the country; whenever it has seemed to become serious, it has provoked a stronger movement to suppress it. In the last analysis, Canadians love their own country no less than Americans do.

Canada's Louisiana Purchase was the acquisition of the Hudson's Bay Company's territory; and, as already suggested, Americans unwittingly rushed the conclusion of the bargain. They were openly talking of annexing the country north of the forty-ninth parallel, and in 1866 a bill to do this was actually introduced into congress and debated there. Then came the Alaska Purchase, coinciding with the birth of the Dominion. Canadians had hoped to get the West without paying for it, claiming that it had belonged to Canada since the days of the French explorers, that the company's charter was worthless, and that if the charter had given the company any territory this was only a strip of land around the shores of the bay. Such was the contention of the government of United Canada, but the government of the Dominion dropped it right away. It would have meant lawsuits that would drag on for years, and immediate action seemed urgent—to forestall the United States. As soon as the Canadian government was prepared to talk business, it found the English company ready to do the same. They came to terms in the spring of 1869, Canada agreeing to pay the company £300,000, and the company undertaking to return the territory to the Crown for transfer to Canada in December.

A rebellion on the banks of the Red River blocked delivery on the appointed date. For this the Canadian government was much to blame.

It had not consulted the inhabitants, who therefore felt that they had been sold like livestock with the land. The whites, numbering about fifteen hundred, took no part in the rising, which was the work of the métis, of whom there were nearly ten thousand, under the leadership of Louis Riel. Believing that the country was really theirs and that it was about to be taken from them, they rose to protect their rights and they set up a government that ruled the colony for eight months. Meanwhile they forced the Dominion to do what it should have done in the beginning—to negotiate an agreement with the people. This was then embodied in the Manitoba Act, passed by the Canadian parliament in May 1870, creating the Province of Manitoba with the same rights of self-government that the other provinces enjoyed. The act came into force in July, when the British government turned over the territory.

Meanwhile an American question mark still hung over the West. Riel's government included a Fenian, and it was known that some Fenians in the United States were scheming to capture this British colony. There were also doubts if Riel would be willing to surrender his authority when the time came. If he would not step down, some Americans might step in. Ottawa therefore decided to run no risk in taking over the country, and sent a military expedition of twelve hundred men to prevent possible resistance. Some of these men were Canadian militia. The others were British regulars, Ottawa having persuaded London that their presence would be a desirable discouragement to American temptation. When the expedition, which toiled over the old fur traders' route, approached its destination late in August, Riel and a few of his friends fled across the border. An amnesty had been granted for this almost bloodless rebellion; but, without knowing this, Riel had thrown it away by executing a young Canadian for defying his authority. As a consequence a price was set on his head.

The Province of Manitoba, thus prematurely born in an unnecessary convulsion, was then a tiny thing. It covered only a small corner of the territory acquired from the company. The remainder, having no population but wandering tribes of Indians, a few half-breeds, and a small number of fur traders, was placed under a lieutenant governor and council appointed and controlled by the federal government.

When the Dominion reached the Rockies in the summer of 1870, arrangements were already being completed to carry its borders over the mountains and down to the sea. Hard times had hit the two colonies on the Pacific coast. The alluvial gold deposits on the mainland had petered out, and the collapse of the gold rush had dragged down both British Columbia and Vancouver Island into such a pitiful condition that they could not support two governments. To cut expenses, London united the two colonies in 1866 under the name of the junior one. The people of both parts of the new British Columbia, who numbered about twelve thousand, were dissatisfied with their government and doubtful about their future. The island had lost its assembly, and the legislature of the united colony had more appointed than elected members. The people wanted self-government. They also wanted to shake off their stagnating isolation. They saw little chance of either in a separate colony lying in one of the far corners of the earth. Then why not join the United States? Would that not bring both freedom and prosperity? At once an annexation movement sprang up, and local conditions seemed to favor it. Most of the population on the mainland was American, and many British-born residents of the island argued that annexation would benefit the mother country by freeing her of a distant and awkward obligation. But other groups then started a strong countermovement to join the Dominion, which was opposed in turn by the appointed councilors, who feared for their offices, and the governor, who would lose his job. Heaven removed one obstacle in the summer of 1869, when the governor suddenly died. The other obstacle was overridden by his successor, who was picked for the purpose—the profederation governor of Newfoundland, whom Ottawa persuaded London to transfer to the other side of the continent.

In 1870 the legislative council voted for union with Canada and sent delegates to Ottawa to negotiate for the admission of British Columbia as a self-governing province of the Dominion. They found a warm welcome and a willingness to grant almost everything they sought. Realizing the futility of political union without a physical tie, and also the enormous outlay that this would entail, they asked for a wagon road within three years and the survey of a line along which a railway might be built when feasible. The Canadian cabinet promptly promised something better—to commence a railway within two years and to complete it in ten—for this would also develop the empty prairie region between Manitoba and the Rockies. When the Dominion and British Columbia agreed upon all the necessary terms of the union, their legislatures requested the British government to implement the union, and an imperial order in council was passed in 1871 making British Columbia another regular province of the Dominion—all in accordance with the procedure laid down in the British North America Act. Incidentally, the admission of Manitoba and British Columbia upset the geographical balance in the Senate by the addition of four senators for each of the new provinces.

Prince Edward Island joined in 1873. It had refused tempting offers by the Dominion of extra financial allowances to buy out the absentee proprietors, who had continued to be a millstone round the neck of the colony. But when a heavy load of steel was added, by the island's building of a railroad for which it could not pay, the federal government offered to assume this obligation too. That was what brought the shy one in. Newfoundland was still out, and it remained out despite flirtations from time to time, until 1949, when it became the tenth province, Alberta and Saskatchewan having been created out of the North West Territories in 1905.

CHAPTER XXII

Australian Gold and Maori Wars

GOLD TRANSFORMED Australia in the middle of the nineteenth century, and California was immediately responsible for this.

Men had been discovering the precious metal in New South Wales for a quarter of a century without starting any gold rush. The first to find it was a surveyor in 1823. He was ignored. The second was a convict in the same year. He displayed a nugget he picked up when he was doing road work. He was promptly flogged on the supposition that he had stolen the gold and melted it down. In 1839 a Polish geologist and explorer found it, and the governor warned him to keep quiet about it lest the discovery invert transportation from a deterrent to an inducement to crime. Two years later a scientific parson found it and showed a specimen to the same governor, who told him, "Put it away, Mr. Clerke, or we shall all have our throats cut." Nor were these all who picked the precious metal from the ground in the Bathurst region, across the mountains from Sydney. In 1848 one of the leading British pioneers of modern geology, Sir Robert Murchison, having examined the published work of the Pole, advised Lord Grey that there should be a mineral survey of Australia. The colonial secretary refused to consider it. He feared, he said, that the discovery of gold would embarrass a woolgrowing country. In addition to official apprehensions, there was another reason for the failure of these finds to produce any results. Nobody yet knew what a gold rush was.

The first outbreak of the highly contagious and disturbing gold fever was in 1849, when there was a stampede into California. The contagion affected Australia severely. That whole continent then had no more than about 150,000 men, and in fifteen months 3,000 of them sailed away from Sydney and Melbourne for San Francisco. It was a serious loss of man power in a country that had none too much of it;

and this, together with California's exciting gain, reversed the official attitude toward gold discoveries in Australia. It also happened that one of these emigrants, Edward Hargraves, was a sheep farmer from Bathurst who found little gold in California but a striking similarity between the auriferous rocks there and the formations back home in a little valley with which he was familiar. Becoming fired with the suggestion that he had run away from what he was seeking, he took the first ship he could for Sydney, rushed back to his old haunts, dug a panful of earth, washed it, and found gold. That was in February 1851; and within a month or so, four hundred men were digging furiously in his valley. The governments of New South Wales and Victoria later gave him a reward of £12,300; and well they might, for his discovery stopped the Australian exodus to California and started an influx of population such as the country had never seen.

This modern Ophir was only the first of several gold fields discovered in that most memorable of all years in Australian history. From other parts of the continent, and from New Zealand, men flocked to the mother colony where, for a while, all the new riches seemed to lie. The drain on the newly separated colony of Victoria, where there had also been sporadic finds, was heavy, and it inspired the organization of a local search that soon made the daughter outshine the mother. A mountain range and 150 miles separated Sydney from the best diggings in New South Wales, whereas there was no such barrier and scarcely more than 70 miles between Melbourne and ten times richer fields, notably those of Ballarat and Bendigo, which were discovered in the latter part of 1851. In September Ballarat had 2,500 people, and more were arriving at the rate of a hundred a day. Shepherds deserted their sheep, shearers their sheds, clerks their shops and offices, mechanics their trades, policemen their beats, and sailors their ships. All classes and conditions of men dashed off to the treasure hunt. Australia was so remote from the outside world that its new attraction produced little increase of immigration from overseas until September 1852.

Then the inrush of population began. During this month some 19,000 people landed in Melbourne, more than three times the number of the previous eight months; and by the end of December the total for the year was nearly 95,000, seven times the figure for 1851. The total population of Australia was 437,000 in 1851, about double what it had been ten years before, and this increase was largely the result of assisted immigration. By 1861 Australia had a population of 1,168,000, gold having trebled the increase during the decade of the discoveries. Those ten years saw the population of New South Wales rise from 187,000 to 350,000 and that of Victoria from 77,000 to 540,000, and their combined production of gold mount to £124,000,000.

The Australian gold rush displayed only some of the blatant features of the recent California rush, for the conditions were different. Law and order were already so well established in Australia that there was little need for vigilantes, extempore juries, or "Judge Lynch." Also, the throng that poured from the incoming ships and surged out to the gold fields of Victoria and New South Wales was much less cosmopolitan than the swarm that descended upon California. Though popular Australian tradition has supported the view that foreigners predominated in the early years of the rush, which of course swept in men of all nations, Australian scholars have found from the census records that the overwhelming proportion of the immigrants were British. An analysis of the population of 1861 shows that 92.5 per cent were born in Australia or in the United Kingdom. In the governors' dispatches of the time there are constant references to the general good order of the mining camps. Of course there was much heavy drinking and wild gambling; there were too few good women and too many bad ones; and swindlers, thieves, and robbers found too many victims. But the "cease work" gun, fired from the government commissioner's tent at nightfall, commanded obedience; and, strange as it may seem, officials and visitors alike bear witness to the regular observance of the Sabbath and the attendance of many diggers at divine service.

The one serious trouble was over diggers' licenses. From the beginning New South Wales and then Victoria required every digger to pay 30s. a month for a license. The purpose was to check the desertion of local labor from its accustomed employment and to tax the new activity for its own regulation. The exaction of this fee provoked growing resistance; for it took too little from the lucky and too much from the unlucky, it was taxation without representation, and it was administered badly—by policemen always prowling around to catch miners without licenses. The climax came in Ballarat toward the end of 1854. The miners made a grand bonfire of their licenses, the police chief ordered a "digger hunt" for licenses on the morrow, the fiery demonstraters stockaded themselves, hoisted a blue flag bearing the Southern Cross, proclaimed the Republic of Victoria, and took pot shots at a nearby military camp. Soldiers and police stormed the stockade, losing four men and killing thirty rebels. Thus ended Australia's one armed revolt. The licenses too were ended. The tax was changed to an export duty on gold, and the miners were required to pay £1 a year for the right to dig, in return for which they got the right to vote.

Very significant was a peaceful preliminary to this rising. It was the formation of the Ballarat Reform League which, in addition to the withdrawal of the hated licenses, demanded manhood suffrage, the abolition of property qualifications for members of the legislature, the payment of members, and frequent elections. It was no mere coincidence that these were four of the six reforms in the program of the English Chartists. There is also a connection between the abortive Republic of Victoria and the pitiful attempt at a revolution in Ireland in 1848. The commander of the Ballarat insurgents was an Irishman, and they included many other sturdy sons of Erin. Though the great majority of the immigrants came from the British Isles, they were no more a cross section of the society that they left behind them than were the English-speaking people who laid the foundations of the United States. These new Australians were largely representative of those sections of the population in their homeland whose spell of revolutionary fever had just collapsed in 1848.

Political discontent strongly colored the migration from the British Isles during these years. Then Irish republicanism took root and flourished in the United States, where the atmosphere was much more favorable to it than in any of the British colonies. Chartism, on the other hand, was not anti-British, and what was left of it migrated to Australia. One may wonder why it did not turn up in British North America too, but the explanation is simple. There democratic freedom was already established. In Australia this was not so.

By a coincidence that was quite fortuitous, the gold rush to Australia occurred at the very time when the Australian colonies had received from parliament, by an act of 1850, the power to make their own constitutions, and the squatter aristocracy were using this authority to perpetuate their own political control. It was a crucial turning point in the history of the continent. There might have been a very different story to tell if the constitutions that emerged from the squatter mold had had time to harden before the lure of gold swamped the country with a population that was strongly imbued with Chartist principles. Though gold did not give Australia responsible government, for that was bound to come soon anyway, it introduced a democratic force that quickly altered the shape of the new constitutions. By the end of the decade, New South Wales, Victoria, and South Australia had adopted manhood suffrage; these three colonies and Queensland, which became a separate colony in 1869, were the only parts of the British Empire in which voting was by secret ballot; South Australia and Victoria had limited the lives of their parliaments to three years; and in all these colonies constitutional amendments could be made by ordinary legislation. By 1890 all the Australian colonies had enacted most of the Chartist program.

When the principle of responsible government in Australia was conceded in 1852, to be implemented along with the new constitutions when they were completed, there was an interesting attempt to write into these constitutions a statutory definition of the distinction between reserved imperial powers and transferred colonial powers, and a prohibition of any imperial interference in the exercise of the latter. This question, as observed in an earlier chapter, had not been raised when British North American colonies got responsible government. But then those colonies were not drafting constitutions and there was no need to discuss the issue. It was William Charles Wentworth, the most forceful political figure in New South Wales, who now thrust it forward. His legalistic mind insisted on precision, and the idea was catching.

The first three draft constitutions that were sent to London—those of New South Wales, Victoria, and South Australia—all contained clauses that would divide sovereignty and make the colonial legislatures supreme in their own spheres. At first the Colonial Office was inclined to accept these clauses and ask parliament to sanction the drafts as they stood. They were then referred to the law officers of the Crown, and these cautious gentlemen pointed out that such parliamentary action would mean "a total abandonment by the Home Government of any right to interfere directly or indirectly with any colonial legislation whatever, except within the narrow circle" of the reserved imperial powers. The Colonial Office drew back and decided that the novel clauses must go. The South Australian draft was returned to its authors for this revision; and though they promptly obliged, this procedure put off promulgation for a year, until 1857. The other two drafts were not returned. New South Wales and Victoria were already so impatient over the delay caused by the hesitation over this question and by the distraction of the Crimean War that the home government deemed it wiser not to add to this delay by a reference to Sydney and Melbourne. Therefore the offending articles were deleted in London, and the bills, thus amended, were approved by parliament in 1856. Meanwhile

Tasmania, having received a hint from home, had rejected a proposal to insert similar clauses in its draft, with the result that it too was adopted by parliament in 1856. The problem did not arise in Queensland, whose constitution was copied from that of the mother colony.

The decision that was made in London and the acquiescence that it received in Australia were characteristically British. Responsible government in the colonies was then much more narrowly conceived than it is today. If it had been possible, which is more than doubtful, to work out and enact a legal formula that was mutually satisfactory in that day, it would not have fitted the needs of a later day. Wentworth was trying to insert into the constitutional relations between the colonies and the mother country a legal rigidity that was not necessary, and from this the British have instinctively shrunk. As the British constitution grew, so was the constitution of the British Commonwealth to grow, adjusting itself to conditions as they changed, and this so gradually that Britons themselves, to say nothing of other people, have often been unaware of the transformation that has taken place.

Gold did many things for Australia beside multiplying its population and democratizing its government. It stimulated the building of railways, which otherwise would have had to wait for many years; and it brought a sevenfold increase of overseas trade by 1861. It enormously enriched the country and reduced its geographical isolation. It made a new Australia. No longer was it a purely pastoral country.

The squatters greeted the gold discoveries with a curse, for the diggings robbed them of their labor. Their first impulse was to sell at a loss rather than see all their assets gradually waste away to nothing. The price of sheep runs tumbled, but soon recovered. Every immigrant who crowded in had a mouth to be fed, and this changed the outlook of the squatters. Instead of seeing only wool and ruin, they now saw meat and prosperity. During 1852 the price of a fat sheep in Melbourne jumped from 10s. to 30s., and it continued to rise. The price of cattle behaved similarly, and there was a swing to the raising of cattle because it was safer to let them run wild, an important consideration when labor costs soared. The result was that the total number of sheep in the two main colonies declined from 13,986,818 in 1851 to 11,854,312 in 1861, while the cattle population of these colonies rose from 1,766,180 to 2,900,015. Two factors prevented the swing from being more pronounced. One was a steady rise in the value of the wool clip from 1s. 1d. a pound in 1851 to 2s. 2¼d. in 1861. The other was a rapid fall in the freight rate on wool to England. After 1851 it dropped to ½ d. a pound, only a quarter of what it had been. Gold did it. When wool was the only export it required more shipping space than the incoming cargoes filled. The addition of gold meant little increase in the weight and almost none in the bulk of exported cargoes, while it attracted so many more ships, all packed with immigrants and goods, that shipping capacity went begging in Sydney and Melbourne.

The staple industy of the country was also helping itself by finding ways of overcoming the labor shortage and the doubling of wages. Wire fences crept around the "runs"; a few boundary riders replaced many shepherds and hutkeepers; and instead of the nightly folding, which covered the sheep with dust and trampled the pastures, the flocks were allowed to browse and lamb unmolested, which meant cleaner and heavier fleeces. Management was becoming easier, with less running around from station to station to check anything that had gone wrong and to distribute rations and newspapers, with fewer men to feed and keep in order, with less confusion with neighbors' flocks, and with fewer disputes over boundaries and watering places. A new pastoral age was dawning around 1860, and by the end of the decade Australia had added meat to its exports. But meanwhile the pastoralists had become engaged in a fight for existence against a new challenge.

This was the third challenge that the gold rush thrust upon the squatter aristocracy. They had lost the battle against political democracy in the fifties, they were winning the economic battle against strangling labor costs, and now in the sixties they had to fight a more strenuous battle over the possession of the land. The swollen population of the gold fields shrank in the late fifties. The surface deposits were being worked out, the digger's day was done, and that of the mining company had come. How could the stranded diggers make a living? The question was urgent and the answer seemed easy. It was by tilling the soil, an occupation that was little developed in Australia. On the eve of the gold discoveries, there were almost as many people in the country as there were acres under crop. The gold rush drew labor from the farms, causing a temporary reduction of the cultivated area. The new demand for food then made it expand. But at the end of the decade the balance was much the same as in 1850—little more than one acre per head of population—and the imports of grain had mounted with the number of mouths demanding bread. Why could not the country feed itself with bread as well as meat? The failure of the diggings made people look around for land on which they might support themselves, and what they found was that most of it was locked

up by the squatters. Then began a powerful political drive to unlock
the land, which belonged to the Crown and was only leased by the
squatters, and to throw it open for agricultural settlement on such easy
terms that any man might there establish his own independence—as
in North America.

The squatters lost the initial round of the battle over the land because they had lost the political battle of the fifties, when domocracy
triumphed. In 1861 the legislature of New South Wales passed an act
that broke open the squatters' leases. Anyone who wanted to farm
could now select from 40 to 320 acres of public land, and it became his
property on certain conditions. He had to pay the government £1 an
acre, one quarter on the completion of the survey and the rest as he
was able. He also had to reside on the land for three years. Other
colonies soon followed suit, but the main struggle between the squatters
and the "free selectors" was in New South Wales. There seems to have
been less violence and more fraud than in the corresponding conflict
that was later fought between the cattlemen and the dirt farmers in
the semi-arid American West.

The fraud was a notorious scandal, and the government did little or
nothing to stop it. Too many people were interested in the lax administration of the new law. Strangers wandered at will over squatters'
lands, to find choice patches which they "selected" for their strategic
rather than their agricultural value. Such rascals could ruin flock-
masters by depriving sheep of access to water, and in many other ways
they could be an intolerable nuisance. The squatters therefore bought
them out. To checkmate this racket, known as "peacocking," and also
to defeat honest selectors, the squatters developed a racket of their own,
called "dummying." Using hired "dummies" as well as their own
families—the New South Wales law allowed anyone over two years of
age to select—the squatters picked the "eyes" of their own runs. The
operation of these two rackets gave the squatters outright ownership of
the vital parts of their own holdings, and the impetus to gain security
commonly carried them on to take advantage of an earlier law that still
stood and permitted them to purchase what they were renting. So it
came to pass that the land was locked up more securely than ever.

While consolidating its position, the pastoral industry also extended
its geographical domain. Following on the heels of explorers, it invaded the interior of Queensland, where drought was a constant
menace. But cattle could travel farther than sheep for water, and the
pastures of the north were more suitable for cattle. Therefore Queens-

land then became what it has since remained, the chief cattle area of the continent. It was not until the eighties that the tapping of artesian wells made Queensland also a sheep country. For a while, also, danger lurked in the northern scrub. The natives fought the intrusion more strenuously than they had done elsewhere. They murdered isolated whites and even besieged large station households. But the "pest" declined with "the natural progress of the aboriginal race towards extinction," to quote the callous euphemism of a contemporary official.

The victory of the squatters was bought at a price. As the bitter contest dragged on through the sixties and seventies, the pastoral industry had to pay out a lot of cash in order to get security. In other words, it had to find additional capital. This the banks supplied, and so the industry emerged with a debt that has burdened it ever since. Another legacy of those unhappy years was the practical exclusion from public life of the squatters, the most substantial class of men in the country. Australia has missed the balancing influence that the small independent farmer gave to society in North America.

Australian society then became set in a pattern very different from that which is familiar in the United States and Canada, and the reason for it lies deeper than any squatter villainy or governmental stupidity. Even the strictest enforcement of the conditions that the selection laws prescribed could not have made Australia a land of democratic agriculture. Heaven had decreed otherwise, by withholding the necessary rainfall. Nature made the heart of North America one of the largest and richest and most solid agricultural regions in the world, and the heart of Australia a desert. The attempt to break up the great pastoral holdings for the sake of planting small farmers on the occasional pieces that could grow crops recalls the extravagant slaughter of North American buffalo for the sake of their tongues, then counted a delicacy. Only in South Australia was there any appreciable extension of tillage in this period, and that was because the highlands stretching north and northwest from Adelaide offered exceptional natural advantages for wheat culture. But even there the farmers soon reached the limit of the twelve-inch rainfall.

The population of Australia, unlike that of North America, has been predominantly urban since the early sixties. The failure to spread the people over the land forced the development of native manufactures, not for export but for domestic consumption, a development that had begun in New South Wales before the gold rush and that derived much benefit from it. Though the market was small, the distance from England was enormous and this added so much to the prime cost of many manufactured goods imported from the mother country that it was as cheap to produce them in Australia. How effective was this natural protection appears in a contrast between the two main colonies. Victoria was losing population and went protectionist in 1866, whereas New South Wales continued to recover its population lead without abandoning free trade. Victoria produced a greater variety of manufactured goods, but wages were just as good and opportunities were greater for workmen in the expanding industries of New South Wales. Even South Australia, without any tariff aid, turned out agricultural machinery, notably the "stripper." Pushed by two horses, this piece of machinery cut off the heads of the standing wheat and threshed them. It was a local invention that came into use in the forties and reduced harvesting costs from 3s. to 3½d. a bushel.

The cleavage between labor and capital was much more pronounced in Australia than in contemporary America. Even farming was more capitalist, while the grazing, mining, and manufacturing industries were wholly capitalist. The average Australian was not his own economic boss. He was a wage earner, like the average native of Britain, whence he had recently come. It was therefore doubly natural that the labor movement in the mother country should project itself into Australian society. Before the gold rush there was only a very little trade unionism in Australia. When the rush subsided there was much of it, and until the eighties it followed the same lines as in England. It was organized in crafts, conservatively led, shy of politics, and confined to the urban and mining population. In the lush coastal region of tropical Queensland, plantation agriculture appeared, and there the labor force was made up of Chinese coolies and Kanakas gathered by "blackbirders" from Southern Pacific islands.

Though the infant settlements of New Zealand lost some men in the Australian gold rush, this loss was as nothing when compared with the gain that the gold rush brought through the extraordinary demand it created for all kinds of farm produce, for New Zealand differed from Australia in being naturally a good agricultural country. There was a rapid expansion of cultivation and grain exports.

New Zealand was also an excellent grazing country, with pastures much richer than those of Australia, and the English market for wool offered greater possibilities than the Australian market for food. In 1853 New Zealand shipped out £19,000 of grain and £67,000 of wool. During the next two decades, with a fourfold increase of population to more than 300,000, the value of grain exports increased eightfold to £136,000 and that of wool fortyfold to £2,702,000, which though not so large as that of its much bigger neighbor was considerably greater in proportion to population. Wool was the mainstay of the colony. In Canterbury and Otago, adherence to Wakefield's principle of a "sufficient" price checked the growth of large pastoral holdings. But this was an exception to the general tendency of the period. Big estates multiplied to monopolize most of the available land. Economic forces favored them; and these forces were encouraged, quite unintentionally, by Sir George Grey on the eve of his departure in 1853, when he cut the sale price of public land to 10s. and, under certain circumstances, to 5s. an acre. He thought the Wakefield system was retarding settlement.

Most of this development, pastoral as well as agricultural, occurred in the South Island, though colonization had begun earlier in the North Island and nature smiled equally upon both islands. In 1858, at the time of the first census, the European population of New Zealand was 61,000, of which 58 per cent were in the North Island and 42 per cent in the South Island. The immigration of the next five years reversed the percentage almost exactly. The explanation is the Maoris. They cramped the extension of settlement in the North and gave it free scope in the South Island, for they had sold almost all the land in the latter and only a small fraction of it in the former.

An ugly storm was brewing in the North Island during the fifties. To sell or not to sell became the burning question among the Maoris. Their leaders saw that the Maori social structure was dissolving at the white man's touch, and they resolved to stop it. They would part with no more land, and they would consolidate their society in a great union of all the tribes under an elected great chief or king. So began the "king movement." Now and then a local Maori minority who were tempted to sell got munitions and other encouragement from land-hungry settlers; and then they fought the majority while the government, instead of intervening to preserve order, let the natives fight it out. This boded ill for the relations between whites and browns. So also did the strong inclination of the general assembly to pull the purse strings, by which it wrested control of native policy from the governor. Moreover, he lacked the ability and the strength of his predecessor, Sir George Grey, to understand the Maoris and win their confidence. In 1859 this successor of Grey reported home that the valuable lands in the island greatly exceeded the needs of the natives and that the

Europeans were determined to possess them, by fair means if possible and by some other method if necessary. He shares with them the responsibility for the tragedy that ensued.

From 1860 to 1872 a series of bitter guerilla wars plagued the North Island, threatened the government of New Zealand with bankruptcy, and strained the relations between the colony and the mother country. In January 1860 the governor, with the advice of his ministers, proclaimed martial law in the province of Taranaki to protect the recent purchase of a block of land from a local chief against the protest of a powerful chief who claimed that the land was part of his territory. Though the proclamation announced impending military operations against the natives, not a Maori had taken up arms and the powerful chief still confined his active opposition within peaceful bounds. He sent the ugliest old women of his tribe to kiss the surveyors. Soldiers were sent to guard the harassed surveyors, more troops were summoned from Australia and England, the white women and children were removed to safety, and hostilities began with an attack on the big chief's *pa*, or stronghold. Sir George Grey returned as successor to his own inept successor in the following year, but he could not undo the evil that others had done.

By the middle sixties about 10,000 imperial troops, nearly as many colonial troops, and a goodly number of "friendlies" (Maori allies) were campaigning against some 2,000 native warriors, who fought so gallantly that they won the admiration of the imperials but not the colonials. This sowed discord that prolonged the miserable struggle with the Maoris. The British officers and men felt that they were fighting for a sordid cause; and the mother country, which had to bear the chief cost of military operations, condemned the colony for dragging it into a land-grabbing war. Believing that the colonists, who now numbered a quarter of a million, should fight their own battles, London withdrew the imperial forces, the last of which departed in 1870.

The Maoris were crushed. Their numbers fell from 55,000 in 1861 to 37,000 in 1871, and they lost millions of acres by confiscation. But out of the protracted agony came two good results. One was a new attitude of the colonists toward the aborigines. In 1867 the latter were given direct representation in the general assembly, and five years later two of their chiefs were appointed to the upper house. From this beginning, the New Zealand government gradually evolved a native policy that became a just cause of great pride, for it has reconciled the Maoris without any race prejudice on either side. The other benefit was fortuitous. It was the opening of the land in the North Island to settlement at the very time when changing conditions were about to make small farming more profitable and its development was blocked by the land monopoly in the South Island. But this "drift to the north" did not become apparent until the census of 1881.

The Maori wars also left their mark on the government of the colony. They inspired a secession movement in the South Island, and strong protests against the location of the capital at distant and isolated Auckland. Therefore, in 1865, it was shifted to Wellington, at the southern extremity of the North Island. More important was another change. The quasi-federation system, under which the provinces enjoyed a considerable measure of autonomy, was not working well and the wars accentuated its weakness. For financial reasons alone, the central government had to withdraw resources that it had left to the provincial councils, and in 1876 it abolished the provincial system. Where a unitary form of government is politically possible, as in New Zealand, it has always been preferred to federalism.

CHAPTER XXIII

Readjustment in the Tropical Colonies

IN THE third quarter of the nineteenth century, when Britain was sitting on top of the world and much of her colonial empire was marching along the road of political freedom, her tropical colonies were in a sad plight. Economically they were passing through a painful period of readjustment to free labor and free trade; and their production, which had touched bottom, was rising again. But socially most of them sank to their lowest level, and politically their general movement was away from self-government. Not one of the crown colonies gained any political freedom, while most of the other group lost the right to govern themselves and were reduced to the status of crown colonies.

The black society of the British West Indies proved that the "saints" were no prophets. These enthusiasts had insisted that emancipation would precipitate its regeneration, but release from slavery plunged it into degeneration. Wherever possible, which was in most of the colonies except Barbados and some of the smaller crowded islands, the blacks displayed a lamentable tendency to relapse into barbarism. They squatted on public land and on derelict plantations that were reverting to jungle, and there they eked out a miserable existence. They had scarcely any more contact with white civilization than had their ancestors in Africa. Their state was utterly deplorable. They had no leaders, no education, no religion other than wild superstitions brought from Africa, no medical services, and no sanitation. Competent observers reported a general and serious retrogression of morals and decline of health since the days when their masters had an economic interest in preserving their lives and their working capacity. The conditions under which they lived were not primitive. They were primeval beyond words. The urban centers also had their stinking slums. Even in Kingston, the chief town of the chief island of the British West Indies, there was no scavenging. Small wonder frightful epidemics in the early fifties killed 20,000 in Barbados and more than twice that number in Jamaica. There was a small "carry over" of the wholesome restraints of civilization, but this died out with the slave generation, allowing black society to fall still lower.

The colonial governments did little or nothing to redeem the Negro from the degradation into which he slumped. Governor Harris of Trinidad early set his hand to the task by dividing the island into some forty wards, over each of which he appointed a warden empowered to levy local rates on all land and houses to pay for such essential things as roads, police, education, and relief for the aged and destitute. This was the most ambitious scheme that was attempted, and it soon failed. There, as elsewhere, the Negro would not submit to taxation, there was a lack of men as well as money for efficient local administration, and free elementary secular education ran into strong church opposition. To expect the whites to shoulder the burden was unthinkable. Most of them were in straitened circumstances, for which they blamed the mother country; and they felt not the slightest responsibility for the black problem which, as they fiercely believed, the British government had thrust upon them. As a result, social conditions in the British West Indies presented "a humiliating contrast with those existing in the French and Spanish West Indies."

White society in the British Caribbean colonies was also declining both in numbers and in character. It drew practically no recruits from the British Isles, though swarms of sturdy British emigrants were then leaving the old country. They were going to the United States, Canada, and Australia; but the attraction of these new lands diverted no part of this human stream from flowing to the West Indies. Such people would never dream of going there. They were much better off at home than they would be if they went to take up work that freed slaves rejected, or to compete with the "colored" population, mixed white and black, who formed the superior laboring class in the Caribbean. There opportunties for whites were dwindling. The islands were in the doldrums. Business was bad, estates were going bankrupt; those that were not abandoned were taken over by men on the spot, men who had not the quality of former plantation owners, men who belonged to a shrinking and sagging society. "The class of persons now filling the posts of attorneys, managers and overseers," the attorney general of St. Vincent reported in 1862, "is without doubt greatly inferior to the same class of persons in days gone by."

A great obstacle to economic recovery was the old English law of real property as it was applied in the colonies. By this law an estate when sold was still subject to all the liens that had been placed upon it, and the purchaser could get rid of them only by paying them off in full. As these charges often amounted to more than the property was worth, the creditors could then take the whole income that it might produce, with the result that the owner could neither work it nor sell it, and therefore he abandoned it. This old law was a veritable millstone around the neck of the old sugar colonies. The first to find relief from the intolerable burden was St. Lucia, on the very eve of emancipation. There, as we have noted previously, the French civil law survived, and legal ingenuity discovered in it a device, the *saisie réelle,* for judicial sales that gave the purchaser a free title. By 1843, sixty-nine of the eighty-one sugar estates in that island were thus cleared of mortgages amounting to more than a million pounds. But this French remedy was not available in the other British islands, and it was not until 1854 that a recent Irish precedent inspired a parliamentary offer of a rescuing hand to them. This was the first West Indian Encumbered Estates Act, later amended, which became operative in any colony whose legislature requested it. The act authorized sale by judicial decree, provided for the distribution of the proceeds among the creditors, and guaranteed the purchaser an unencumbered title. As the problem was already solved in St. Lucia and had not arisen in Trinidad or British Guiana, these colonies did not take advantage of the offer; but all the old sugar colonies, with the single exception of Barbados, invoked the remedy and profited by it. Within twenty years some 150 estates were thus redeemed, a number of them after lying idle for forty years or more.

The shortage of labor on the plantations was another serious problem, and this forced the development of an immigration policy. The Colonial Office resolutely and rightly resisted strong colonial pressure to draw a supply from Africa. As observed in an earlier chapter, blacks liberated from captured slave ships of other nations were introduced; but this immigration, which drew charges of hypocrisy from foreign countries, was so carefully regulated that it never became more than a trickle. The migration of Portuguese from Madeira and the Canaries to labor-hungry Trinidad and British Guiana also remained small. There was one inexhaustible source, and that was India. Mauritius had already solved the labor problem by recruiting from there. The Caribbean colonies, however, could not do it so easily. Two formidable difficulties stood in the way. One was the much heavier cost of the longer sea voyage; the other was the system of restrictive regulations imposed by official London. The first was largely overcome in 1848, when British Guiana and Trinidad—the two colonies where the labor shortage was by far the most acute—got a parliamentary loan for the purpose of subsidizing immigration. The other difficulty was more deeply rooted. The only practical way of getting labor from India was under contract, and there was a profound suspicion in England that slavery would return to its old haunts under this disguise. It took a lot of urging by colonial governors to persuade the authorities in London to lower the barriers. At first the Colonial Office would allow no contract with an immigrant laborer for more than a year. The period was stretched to three years, and later to five, as the governors unanimously insisted that longer contracts favored the welfare of the imported coolies themselves. London also blocked colonial legislation to prevent indentured laborers from wandering or running away, until repeated sad experiences demonstrated that it was better for them as well as for plantation owners to have carefully regulated laws against desertion.

Each colony was originally bound to pay the passage back to India of laborers on the completion of their engagements; but after a few years, by an agreement between the Colonial Office and the government of India, the obligation was lifted from Mauritius and modified in the West Indies. It was never much of a burden on the island in the Indian Ocean, and its removal imposed no great hardship upon the coolies there because they could manage to find their own way back if they so desired. On the other hand, it bore heavily on Caribbean colonies, and they could not be relieved of it without practically enforcing perpetual exile upon East Indians who had been brought thither. Therefore the qualifying period for a free passage home from the West Indies was lengthened to ten years, of which five had to be under indenture; and immigrants were tempted to remain by accepting a money bonus or a grant of land in lieu of a passage home. During the fifties a large proportion returned to their native land; but it was soon observed that the savings they carried with them tempted others to go to the West Indies, and from 1860 most of the immigrants from India preferred to settle in the colonies. Thus it came to pass that East Indians became an important element of the population in the British Caribbean, notably in Trinidad, where they form a third, and in British Guiana, where they are nearly half. They solved the pressing labor problem of these two colonies. But the strange assortment of races—East Indian, Negro, Portuguese, and even Chinese, of whom a few were also imported under indenture—was not always a harmonious one. The most serious friction was in British Guiana, where Negro mobs occasionally attacked one or another of the immigrant groups.

In the other British Caribbean colonies, imported coolies were never more than a small percentage of the population. Nevertheless, the presence of even a few immigrants, guaranteeing to planters a minimum of reliable workers, was often sufficient to prime the black labor pump. Strange as it may seem at first glance, this did not engender racial strife between the coolies and the creole Negroes. The latter rather welcomed the arrival of the former "as the instrument destined eventually to redeem them from the necessity of daily manual labour," to quote the words of one governor, in 1866; and the newcomers, who had to be fed, gave a much-desired tonic to the local market for the domestic produce of the natives.

Only two important colonies gained little or nothing from immigration. Barbados, being overpopulated and fully cultivated, suffered from no labor shortage. There economic compulsion operated to keep the blacks at work on the plantations for miserably low wages. Jamaica, which suffered most from the withdrawal of native labor from the plantations to support itself by a crude subsistence agriculture, received so few immigrants that their coming made scarcely any difference. A combination of circumstances peculiar to this colony explains its failure to attract substitutes. The island had a staggering debt; most of its planters were financially embarrassed, the majority of their estates being too small to produce as much as a hundred hogsheads of sugar a year, the recognized minimum for profitable operation; the current rate of wages was far below that of Trinidad or British Guiana, and the lack of medical supervision and hospital accommodation was the most notorious in the West Indies; there was a strong organized opposition to immigration, chiefly by the missionaries and the Negro members of the assembly; though some money was voted for immigration, most of it was wasted by carelessness and corruption; the obligation to repatriate East Indians was repeatedly dishonored, and many of them sank into a half-starved condition, too weak to work. It is small wonder that Jamaica was the laggard in the recovery that marked the third quarter of the century.

In some of the smaller islands a common method of readjustment to the new dispensation of free labor and free trade was for planters to take the laborers into partnership. Under this *métayage* system, the owner supplied the land and equipment, the *métayers* were responsible for all operations including the manufacture of the crop into sugar, and of this the tenants took one half while the proprietor took the other plus the skimmings and molasses. At best, however, *métayage* was a poor makeshift in the sugar industry, for which it was ill suited. It was much less efficient than owner-management and wage labor, and was preferable only to abandonment. It was the last desperate resort of planters who could not afford to run their own estates, but it enabled many of them to hang on until better times returned.

The price of sugar fell until 1854, and then began to rise. That was the year when the equalization of duties on foreign and British sugar was completed, and the worst had come. It was also the year when the Crimean War began, and it pushed the price up until the annual average reached £1. 15s. 7d. a hundredweight in 1857, which was 75 per cent above the 1854 level and the highest since 1841. There was no appreciable decline until 1861. During the next ten years the average was down 5s., but production increased in nearly all the British West Indies. Their staple industry had already gained an impetus that was regenerating it, the price recovery from 1854 having given a much-needed encouragement to improvements that lowered costs.

One of the major improvements was in the treatment of the soil. Until the middle of the century, planters depended on their stock to provide manure to preserve the fertility of the soil. Then the increasing substitution of steam for horses and mules as motive power began seriously to reduce the number of their beasts and consequently the supply of common manure. By a lucky stroke, birds long since dead saved the situation and improved it. At this very time, European agriculture was discovering the amazing value of what these birds had dropped on islands off Peru, and this suggested to sugar planters that they too might try this fertilizer. Their experiment with guano was an immediate success, and its adoption soon became pretty general. Though expensive, it paid for itself many times over, in richer crops. This was particularly true in the islands where the land had been cultivated for generations. Barbados imported large quantities of guano. Trinidad had little need for it, and British Guiana not much more; but Mauritius, where cultivation was already very intensive, throve on it.

The continued improvement in methods of cultivation, which had begun on the morrow of emancipation in order to get along with less labor, was another appreciable factor of recovery. The spreading dominion of the plow, and of horse hoes and harrows, cut costs. So did the introduction of the steam plow in the sixties. It proved to be such a success in the West Indies that it was later described as a "wonder-working implement." Deeper plowing, where feasible, was also practiced because it increased yield and profit.

There was an equally marked improvement of efficiency in the manufacture of the crop into sugar. Steam engines, which had long proved their worth in British Guiana, began to drive the mills in the other British colonies; further economies were introduced with more modern machinery for the various processes, from the expression of the juice from the cane to the preparation of the muscovado for shipment. The colonial production of refined sugar was relatively small, except in Mauritius and British Guiana, and there it meant a heavy additional investment in such equipment as the vacuum pan and the centrifugal machine. In one respect, the establishment of large central factories to take over the work of the estate mills, the British planters were behind their French fellows in Guadeloupe and Martinique. When Lord Grey headed the Colonial Office, he did his stubborn best to force this separation of disparate enterprises. The British planters listened to his preaching but went their own way. The evidence in favor of the differentiation of function in the French colonies was not conclusive, and the atrocious state of the roads in almost all the British colonies convinced British planters that the expense of transporting the cane to distant factories would eat up more than they might gain there. St. Lucia was the first British sugar colony to get a central factory, and that was not until 1874.

The first great expansion of sugar production occurred in Mauritius, which early took to guano and had an enormous advantage in importing labor from India. The annual export of sugar from this island, which had been 605,763 hundredweights in the early forties, was 1,951,000 during the three years from 1853 to 1855, an increase of more than 200 per cent. The corresponding figures for British Guiana, 537,132 and 931,000, and for Trinidad, 312,026 and 421,000, show a smaller gain. But in the late sixties the average annual export of British Guiana was 1,567,000 and of Trinidad 860,000, while that of Mauritius was no more than 1,984,000. Mauritius, however, was then staggering under the combined misfortunes of droughts, hurricanes, and malaria. By this time these three colonies were away in the lead, the two in the western hemisphere exporting more than all the rest of the British Caribbean put together. Of the latter, Barbados had achieved the most remarkable recovery. Its average export, which stood at 335,451 hundredweights in the early forties, leaped to 719,000 by a decade later, and reached 772,000 by the late sixties. The corresponding figures for Jamaica were 677,896, 459,000, and 551,000, though this had been the premier sugar colony before emancipation, when it shipped out nearly 1,400,000 hundredweights a year.

But the Jamaican economy was doing better than sugar statistics would indicate, for it was becoming more diversified. Jamaica rum, according to those who ought to know, is the best in the world. It was then fetching a higher price than its competitors, its production was gaining at the expense of sugar, and the gain was solid because the planters were devoting much attention to improving the quality of this precious liquid. In addition, the island was producing considerable quantities of such things as coffee, pimento, ginger, and logwood— largely the work of small cultivators. As such, the Negroes were at last finding their feet. By the late sixties, sugar was accounting for scarcely more than 40 per cent of the value of Jamaican exports.

Though most of the British West Indies continued to rely chiefly on sugar, rum, and molasses, Jamaica was not alone in turning to the cultivation of other crops than the cane. Cocoa was winning over sugar in Grenada, and becoming important in Trinidad and Dominica. During the American Civil War, several islands again found profit in growing cotton. This particular condition passed away when peace reopened the ports of the South. But already something else that was of immensely greater economic importance to all the old British sugar colonies had passed away. It was the black despair that overwhelmed them when the mother country deprived them of their slaves and of their monopoly market, the two main props of their old prosperity.

The neighboring British colonies that had never known the fattening stimulus of sugar and therefore had little to lose from the abolition of slavery or protection were all about as lean as ever, except during the American Civil War. Then the Bahamas, being most favorably located to serve as a center for blockade runners, reaped an enormous commercial harvest, only to lose it all when peace returned. The wrecking business was on the way out. The British government was building numerous lighthouses; the more valuable cargoes were deserting sail for steam, and steamships were less at the mercy of the wild gales that hurled sailing vessels on the rocks; and the trade routes were shifting to the north and the south of the islands. In the end the colony benefited, for wrecking had a demoralizing effect upon the population. As the spoils of the sea declined, the fruits of agriculture became more attractive. Bermuda also experienced a fictitious prosperity during the war, though to a much lesser degree: its little shipbuilding industry sickened and died as steam ousted sail; it lost its convict settlement but, thanks to its strategic position, it became a coaling station and its naval dockyard was improved; and at last this smallest of all British colonies began to utilize its meager agricultural resources by producing early vegetables for the New York market. British Honduras, by a convention of 1859 with contiguous Guatemala, got a definite boundary; and three years later the imperial government, finally brushing aside the fiction that Spanish sovereignty still lingered in that one corner of the mainland, erected this British settlement into a British colony. But there was little change in its restricted economy.

In tropical West Africa the only British trade of any account was in a region beyond British jurisdiction and felt no need for protection by the latter. This was the trade in palm oil, which had its principal seat in the delta of the Niger and was so prosperous that it exceeded £1,000,000 in 1860. The little British establishments on the Gambia, in Sierra Leone, and on the Gold Coast—especially the last two—were a financial liability and a cause of worry for the government in London.

Three nations, the Danes, the Dutch, and the British, had settlements on the Gold Coast, and they were uneasy neighbors because each contributed to the others' difficulties with the natives. Anxious to cut their losses, the Danes approached the British government with an offer to sell and a threat to make a deal with some other power if this offer was refused. The British bid £10,000, and the Danes delivered their posts in 1850. Some little time afterward the French appeared on the eastern horizon and began to use Lagos, in what is now the southwestern corner of Nigeria, as a base for recruiting Negroes to work on the plantations of Réunion in the Indian Ocean. Though under indenture the Negroes, collected in native wars, were practically slaves. Britain protested, and France retorted that Britain had provided a precedent in Sierra Leone. Mounting disorders in Lagos threatened the peace of the surrounding region, and the Colonial Office considered the occupation of Lagos but rejected it as an additional burden. Then French gunboats arrived, and London intervened by dispatching an expedition that overawed the native king into ceding to Britain the town of Lagos and its immediate vicinity in 1861.

Meanwhile serious trouble was brewing in the interior of the Gold Coast where the powerful king of Ashanti, growing more powerful with arms sold by the Dutch who abetted him, was preparing for war against the Fanti tribes and the neighboring British, allies since the days of George Maclean. The helpless governor appealed to London for military forces; London denied them out of a blind belief that there was no danger; and the fierce Ashantis descended in 1863, plundering and slaughtering at will. They retired from a ruined Gold Coast. Its merchants were bankrupt and, along with the surviving natives, were stricken with famine.

When the British at home heard of the disaster, the responsible public blamed the government and its predecessors for involving the country more deeply than they had intended in the awful tangle of Africa. Only the Church Missionary Society, seeking more protection for its work on the lower Niger, urged a forward native policy. The merchants trading to Africa were dumb. A Select Committee of the House of Commons, appointed in 1865 to survey the results of British rule in West Africa, began its investigations with the idea of pulling out everywhere except from Sierra Leone but was reluctantly driven to abandon the thought. Though the slave trade in this region was now nearly eradicated, the British government felt bound by other moral obligations to sustain its West African settlements. What, for example, would happen to the Fantis? They were in a terrible state, and apparently they were only temporarily saved from destruction by an impending outbreak of civil war in the Ashanti kingdom. In an attempt to remove an important cause of the recent catastrophe, London opened negotiations with the Dutch, some of whose posts were right beside the British. Following a recommendation of the Select Committee, a treaty was concluded to exchange Dutch establishments on the east for British on the west part of the Gold Coast. But the resulting excitement among the natives led to a new bargain in 1872, whereby the British bought out the Dutch. Thereupon the Ashantis descended again, but this time parliament voted £800,000 for a military expedition that in 1874 permanently subdued them and made their kingdom a British protectorate.

This is a startling sequel to a drab story, and it may seem to belong to the new age of imperialism that was then dawning. But there was no imperialist motive behind the decision to take such vigorous action. It was the work of Gladstone's government which, as we shall see in a later chapter, was notoriously pacifist and anti-imperialist; and Lord Derby, whose Conservative tenure of the Foreign Office was soon to be resumed, deplored the dispatch of the military expedition. He then said that he "had no great faith in that kind of moral influence which you acquire by burning a man's house over his head, and telling him he is to be your subject, whether he likes it or not." Britain, he added, had enough black subjects.

Ceylon was more prosperous in the third quarter of the nineteenth century than it had ever been in modern times. Coffee was now king, and by 1853 that monarch's health had completely recovered from the ill effects of overspeculation and the commercial crisis of six years before. Gone were the extravagance and the careless cultivation of the boom days. The planters had learned their lesson, and rising prices for their coffee swelled the profits made from sound financing and more scientific production. The industry expanded steadily, fed by new capital that it attracted from Great Britain and by Tamil labor from Southern India. Many native inhabitants had also taken to growing coffee, and they benefited by copying some of the improved methods of the British planters. Indeed, the exports of native coffee exceeeded those of plantation coffee until about 1856, when the balance began to swing heavily the other way. The peak of production was in 1870, when Ceylon shipped out 1,000,000 hundredweights, worth £2,750,-000. The area devoted to the crop continued to increase until the coffee trees covered some 430 square miles in the late seventies. But the yield was falling, and the days of King Coffee in that land were numbered. A blight, first noticed in 1868, was eating through the plantations, defying all efforts to control it. By 1875, however, it was not yet apparent that the battle was lost and that, for a second time, Ceylon was about to see the ruin of the single industry on which its prosperity depended.

The population of Ceylon could live without coffee but not without rice, their staple food. Its cultivation was confined to the natives and was their principal occupation. But if the production of coffee was the work mainly of immigrants, planters from Britain and laborers from India, this enterprise infused new life into the whole island. Perhaps the most important way in which it did this was by substituting a perennial surplus for the chronic deficit in the budget of the colony. In the late fifties, with money to spend on public works, the government began to restore the ancient irrigation system, the decay of which had deprived Ceylon of the capacity to feed itself, forcing it to import rice from India. From the beginning of British rule the government had seen the problem but had lacked the means of tackling it. Now coffee came to the rescue of rice. The task was arduous and long, much too long for coffee to see it through. But coffee provided the initial impetus, and the work has continued to our own day, progressing from restoration to further development.

There were thousands of small tanks to be repaired, for each irrigated only a patch of about fifty acres and an ordinary village had quite a number of tanks. They had to be fed by a network of canals from large storage reservoirs, and these had to be restored too. Nor was this all. The system would not work without continuous local cooperation among the individual cultivators. This vital feature, prescribed in minute detail by customary law which the village council enforced, had long since fallen to pieces when the supporting authority decayed. Now the government revived it by reviving the powers of the village council.

The government also spent large sums on extending and improving the roads, which made possible the further expansion of coffee production in the interior. As cultivation penetrated deeper into the highlands and the volume of the crop continued to swell, the strain on road transport, which was by ox carts, grew heavier and heavier, threatening a breakdown. The obvious solution was a railway, which had been seriously projected when the commercial crisis of 1847 swept the idea away. It reappeared in the middle fifties, when the government of the colony signed a contract with the original company; but a revision of the estimates multiplied the prospective cost to an alarming figure, and the colony was glad to buy off the contractor. Still the expense of maintaining the roads was mounting with the ever heavier traffic, and the life-giving industry was becoming choked on the highway. At last the government resolved to break the bottleneck. It advertised for tenders and accepted one. Work on the railway commenced immediately, in 1863, and four years later it was completed from Colombo to Kandy. It saved the goose that was laying the golden eggs and increased its productivity. The relief to the planters was more than physical. Their transportation costs went down and their profits up. The government also reaped its reward, for this publicly owned and operated railway was a financial success from the day of its opening.

The building of this railway contributed, incidentally, to the rise and the fall of a local movement for a more representative government in the colony. To finance construction as much as possible out of revenue, the governor cut down expenditure on public works, and the planters complained bitterly against retrenchment on the roads that they still had to use. When feeling was thus roused, it was exacerbated by a blow from London. After being a financial burden on Britain for half a century, Ceylon was at last in a sound financial position, and this welcome change suggested to the home government that the colony, now that it could afford it, should assume the cost of the military forces stationed there. The result was a protracted dispute between London and Colombo, which the former decided in its own favor in 1864. When the news reached Colombo, the unofficial members of the legislative council protested and resigned in a body; the following year saw the organization of the Ceylon League to agitate for a constitutional amendment that would give the unofficial members a majority in the council. They would then control the raising and the spending of the colony's revenue. The movement gathered strength from a temporary commercial crisis in 1866, only to lose it soon afterward. The Colonial Office would not listen to the Ceylon League, and it was submerged by the rising tide of prosperity that came when the railway solved the transportation problem.

No advance in the direction of self-government was then possible in any of the British tropical colonies. What the coffee planters in Ceylon demanded was really a step in the opposite direction. Britain would not shed any of her responsibility for the government of the crown colonies by transferring it to a small white minority whose economic interest would tempt them to abuse such a political concession. The government in London had enough worry over the tropical colonies that still had political constitutions modeled after that of the mother country. In these colonies the old representative system, which had degenerated under slavery, became unworkable after emancipation. Again and again the home government had to interfere in their internal affairs to protect the Negroes who formed the vast mass of the population.

The political plight of the old British West Indies was desperate. There only a rare black could acquire the property that qualified him to vote, and a much rarer black was able to win an assembly seat. On the other hand, the governing class, which clung for dear life to the principle of white supremacy, had so declined in number and in quality that almost everywhere its members were incapable of supporting the political institutions that they had inherited. In 1864 Jamaica had only nineteen hundred electors out of a population of nearly half a million. Its white community was so small and poor that it was impossible to get competent men to fill its legislature of sixty-eight in the two chambers, to say nothing of the other public offices of the colony. There and elsewhere the governors were powerless to effect any improvement in the laws or their administration. It was a hopeless situation. It was also a dangerous one.

A black explosion shook Jamaica in 1865. It was partly, but by no means wholly, a repercussion of the American Civil War. As the powerful armies of the North closed in on the South, freeing the last of the slaves and utterly crushing the slaveowning aristocracy, the news inflamed the Negroes of the island with wild visions of an approaching millenium for them. There was no general rising, but there was a serious riot in one locality. When fired upon, the rioters captured the courthouse and killed eighteen of its occupants. The disturbance spread, and for two or three days the southeastern corner of the colony was at the mercy of the insurgents; but they offered no resistance to the troops, who quickly restored order. Ten more people had been killed, seven of them rioters. Worse was soon to follow—from the whites, for they had suffered a bad scare and they exacted wholesale vengeance. Martial law was proclaimed; troops hunted down Negroes; nearly six hundred were executed, many of them without any trial; large numbers, including some women, were flogged; and a thousand Negro homes were burned. A reign of terror had taken the place of the expected millenium, and the cruel substitute evoked a loud cry of horror in Britain. The governor was recalled, but before he departed he persuaded the frightened legislature to surrender all its powers to the Crown. Parliament confirmed this act of abdication, and an imperial order in council of June 1866 promulgated a new constitution for Jamaica—as a crown colony, with a wholly nominated council to serve as its legislature.

The collapse of the old system had already begun elsewhere. In 1854 the Virgin Islands colony abolished its ridiculous council and assembly in favor of a single chamber with three nominated and six elected members. Five years later it reduced the elected members to four, and in 1867 it substituted appointment for election. An amusing story is told that illustrates the need for these reforms and explains how one of them was carried. The speaker of the assembly, dismounting from his mule to enter the legislative hall, turned the animal over to a Negro boy, and on adjournment came out to find the beast in a lather from violent galloping. He quickly recalled the house, which voted the boy guilty of a breach of privilege and condemned the boy's father to pay some dozens of rum. The fine was promptly paid by the father and consumed by the legislators, converting a hopeless minority into a jubilant majority for the constitutional reform, which was passed forthwith. Dominica followed more soberly, adopting in 1863 a single chamber with an elected majority and changing it two years later to give the governor a nominated majority.

But it was the fall of the assembly in Jamaica that induced a more general abdication, and it came rather quickly. In 1866 Antigua, St. Kitts, and Nevis chose crown colony government with a single chamber and a nominated majority; and in 1868 St. Vincent did the same. By the close of 1875, Barbados, Bermuda, and the Bahamas were the only colonies in the British West Indies that retained their old constitutions; and by 1878 all the elected members in the other colonies had disappeared from the single-chamber legislatures except the two little ones of Antigua and Dominica. Thus in the space of twenty years, ten out of thirteen colonial assemblies voted themselves out of existence. Financial pressure, applied by the Colonial Office, helped them over the stile; for most of the colonial governments were on the edge of bankruptcy and the home government refused to rescue them with funds from the imperial treasury unless they gave up their perverted rights of self-government. The general result was wholesome. Good government replaced bad government, there was a great outburst of much-needed legislative activity in the demoted colonies, the blacks began to feel the full benefits of emancipation, and the whites found that the new system speeded economic recovery.

CHAPTER XXIV

The Failure of British Policy in South Africa

By far the most fundamental problem of South Africa was that of the blacks, and it imperiously demanded a unified approach, which the political dismemberment of 1852 and 1854 made impossible. Motives of economy, suppressing instincts of humanitarianism, dictated the conclusion of the Sand River and Bloemfontein conventions. But just as the fear of another American Revolution had inspired the British government first to oppose and finally to grant colonial autonomy in North America, so did the British government's desire to shake off an imperial burden in South Africa force a reversal of the policy that it had dictated. Before the first diamond was picked up on the banks of the Vaal River, London had learned to regret the concession of independence to the Transvaal and the Orange Free State as a false step that defeated its own purpose and would somehow have to be reversed.

The black problem was indivisible because the two Boer republics were coterminous with the two British colonies and there were blacks everywhere: blacks whose land and labor the whites had acquired, blacks who were fragments of broken tribes engulfed by the white advance and who survived as squatters, and countless other blacks who hung like a cloud upon the borders of European settlement. In this preliminary analysis we may dismiss the outward thrust of the Boers upon the western and northern frontier of the Transvaal, though it should be noted that on the west it roused British concern by threatening to cut the Missionaries' Road, which ran from the Cape to the unknown interior. The country along the road was so poor and parched that it was very sparsely populated. On the northern frontier it was much better, and there were enough natives to put up a good fight. Yet the wars that the Boers waged there were of no immediate interest to the British. The indivisibility appears elsewhere—along the whole eastern side of South Africa.

On the far east, swarms of warlike Zulus were squeezed in between adjacent sides of Natal and the Transvaal, a joint menace to them. Between Natal, in which the blacks outnumbered the whites perhaps twenty to one, down to the eastern frontier of Cape Colony, where the blacks were thick, stretched the heavily populated Kaffirland, of which British Kaffraria was but the southern end. In the center of South Africa lay Moshesh's Basutoland, hemmed in by Cape Colony, the Orange Free State, Natal, and the eastern section of Kaffirland, known as Pondoland. The compression of population within these regions of black settlement had become so tight that any blow delivered on one side was liable to come out on the other, or even to cause a general explosion. Thus the black problem inexorably tied the republics and the colonies together, and yet it had divided them.

The Boers who turned their backs on British rule to go on the Great Trek did so because they could not stomach the British policy of protecting the blacks from white oppression. The trekkers were determined to have their own way with the natives, and later they were able to write into the conventions specific conditions that would guarantee them this free hand. The conditions were: no British alliance with natives north of the Orange River, no British traffic in arms with them, and no restrictions on the British sale of arms to the Boers in the republics. The result was that no matter how carefully the British might deal with the native tribes along their borders, war might break out there at any time as a repercussion of a distant Boer attack. The colonies were at the mercy of the republics through the black mass that united them.

The British, on the other hand, had a strategic advantage that they might use in an effort to bring the independent Boers into line, or at least to check their pressure upon the independent tribes. The annexation of Natal in 1843 blocked the Boer advance to the sea and condemned the republics to a landlocked existence. In that respect they were like Upper Canada, whose trade was taxed in Lower Canada; but they were in a worse position because they had severed their British connection and they had no alternative channel of communication with the outside world. Their imports, along with those of the colonies, had to pay customs duties in colonial ports, and they could not recover a penny of the proceeds. Here was the possibility of a bargain; but the legislatures of Cape Colony and Natal, which had the spending of this revenue, were not at all disposed to share it, and London would not coerce them. Neither was there any attempt to apply economic pressure by cutting off their trade. That was too small and, meager though it was, the colonies competed for it. Though the conventions also protected it, they would not have stood in the way if such a move had been otherwise feasible. Where the independent Boers were seriously vulnerable was in their dependence upon the British for arms and ammunition and for denying them to the natives. By signing the conventions, which guaranteed these things, the British had entered into a tacit alliance with the republics against the natives; but this was so counter to British interests and so abhorrent to British principles that it was bound to bring about a British modification or abrogation of the conventions.

Another important factor in the general situation was the key position held by the Orange Free State. It half surrounded Basutoland, with which it was chronically at war, and it was linked by more than geography with the Transvaal and Cape Colony. It had strong human ties with both—ties of blood, language, religion, and culture; and there was constant coming and going across the Vaal and Orange rivers. One might suppose that the two republics would draw together, and there were efforts to combine them in some sort of union. Marthinus Pretorius, who had succeeded to his father's position in the politically disjointed Transvaal, tried to do it by force of arms, only to meet defeat. Later the Orange Free State elected him president, only to reject him for a Boer of a very different stripe—J. H. Brand. He was an outstanding leader of the Cape bar who had studied in the Netherlands and England; his father was the speaker of the Cape assembly, his wife was English, and his children were given an English education. Until some time in the seventies, the Orange Free State felt a stronger affiliation with the south than with the north, for the center of gravity of the Boer population of South Africa was in Cape Colony. There was the main seat of the Boer race, of Boer wealth, of Boer culture. There, moreover, the Boers were living in harmony with the British, whom they outnumbered by about eleven to nine, and they had a lively sense of their close relationship with the people of the Orange Free State, though not with the wild men of the distant Transvaal.

To sum up, the policy of political division embodied in the conventions had to go because the native problem imposed upon South Africa a unity that would not be denied. Cooperation between Europeans in the country was imperative. Only through British leadership was there any possibility of achieving it, and this was the only way in which Britain could get rid of her South African incubus, which she would fain shake off. The tragedy was that it took so long to work out a solution.

Sir George Grey stands out as the man who was the first to catch a vision of the solution and the first to press toward it. His successful administration of New Zealand and his genius for handling the Maoris persuaded London to transfer him to South Africa to consolidate the new regime inaugurated by the conventions. But almost from the time of his arrival at the Cape, in December 1854, the harsh facts of South Africa made his views diverge from those of the Colonial Office.

The British withdrawal behind the Orange River, which gave birth to the Orange Free State, made peace impossible along its frontier with Basutoland. Moshesh had accepted a line the British drew on this frontier, but now he said that it had departed with them. The retirement of the only power for which he had any respect made him believe that he could recover the lands he had lost. He had no fear of the infant republic, unless it could get aid from the south, and to prevent this eventuality he dispatched emissaries to stir up the tribes on the eastern frontier of Cape Colony. By 1857 South Africa seemed about to blow up. The Kaffir tribes were ripe for another war, recent ravages of disease among their cattle having driven them to a new pitch of desperation; the Basuto war hung fire, Moshesh just waiting for the Kaffir outbreak to cover his contemplated attack in full force; and the Orange Free State, caught between this menace on the one side and actual invasion by Pretorius on the other, appealed to the Cape for help.

Grey saw that a fusion or alliance of the two republics would mean a concerted front against the natives, causing a terrific explosion of Zulus, Basutos, and Kaffirs. But what could he do to stop it? His hands were tied by the conventions and by monthly admonitions from the Colonial Office. He warned London of the awful danger to the colonies unless he forestalled Pretorius by seizing the opportunity to unite with the Free State. But all he got by way of concession was permission to offer his good services if the Orange Free State was in difficulties, and a suggestion that if any vital British interest necessitated pressure on the republics this could be applied through control of the ports and that meanwhile it might be useful if he could persuade the Cape legislature to hand over a share of the customs receipts. Otherwise, Grey was told, he must adhere to the strictest neutrality and the most scrupulous observance of the independence of the republics.

The immediate crisis passed, apparently because the desperation of the Kaffirs suddenly took a wild turn. Two of their number said they had seen the spirits of their dead warriors who told them that if they killed all their cattle and consumed all their corn, reserving none for seed, then a plentiful supply of fat cattle and bountiful crops would spring out of the earth and the white man would be swept into the sea. This wierd prophecy precipitated a mass madness of destruction that brought on a terrible famine. Untold numbers died of starvation and, to escape it, thirty thousand staggered into the colony to work for the farmers there. This Kaffir tragedy of course put off the Basuto war, with the result that the Orange Free State was able, without any assistance from the Cape, to repel the invasion from the Transvaal.

The Basuto war broke early in 1858, and it went hard with the Free State. The agile Basutos drove back the frontier commandos, and the government in Bloemfontein was too poor to pay for an effective military organization. The Cape legislature had twice rejected Grey's recommendation to hand over customs receipts on goods imported by the republic. Some colonists slipped north and joined the Free State forces, but this reinforcement was not appreciable because the governor, feeling bound to preserve neutrality, issued a proclamation forbidding the enlistment of British subjects under a foreign government. Again the Free State appealed to the Cape, and again Grey refused to intervene. His refusal threw the Free State back upon the Transvaal, to which it had also appealed, and a project for union with it was before the volksraad when Grey blocked its acceptance by threatening to alter the Convention of Bloemfontein. At the same time, in justice to the Free State, he offered to mediate in the war. Both sides gladly accepted. Moshesh feared a union of the two republics, and peace was restored on the basis of the old line slightly modified in favor of the Basutos. Grey, however, had no confidence that it would last unless he could underwrite it by a drastic revision of British policy, and he was thoroughly convinced that this could be postponed no longer. What convinced him was a decided swing of opinion in the Orange Free State.

Forbidden to unite with the Transvaal and rescued from a disastrous war, the Orange Free State turned to seek federation with the Cape as the best and possibly the only guarantee of security. Grey had already come to the conclusion that there was no solution for the exasperating problem of South Africa except by federating the whole country, and therefore he was eager to grasp the outstretched hand. The Free State was the key piece of the solution, and he could not throw it away. The salvation of South Africa was in his hands if only he could convert the home government before it was too late. "Nothing but a strong federal government," he wrote to the colonial secretary, "which unites, within itself, all the European races in South Africa can permanently maintain peace in this country and free Great Britain from constant anxiety for the peace of her possessions here."

But the times were most inauspicious for such a bold reversal of policy in Britain. From 1854 London had had its hands full of expensive and distracting troubles abroad—first the Crimean War, then the Indian Mutiny, and in this year a campaign in China and strained relations with France. In writing the above words, Grey did not know that a new government had come into office pledged to rigid economy. Indeed, the new colonial secretary sent Grey a plan to cut down imperial expenses in South Africa by merging Cape Colony, Natal, and British Kaffraria, and shifting the burden of defense onto the shoulders of the united government, which meant that most of it would fall on the taxpayers of the Cape.

Yet Grey's mind was so set on converting the home government to his own solution for South Africa that his reply was a curt dismissal of this proposal and a forceful presentation of his own. He was in thorough agreement with the British government's desire to reduce imperial commitments. Where he differed was in how to do it. He envisaged a United South Africa that would be fully capable of standing on its own feet. In conclusion he said:

> It is also hardly possible to help wishing, that if ever England should be compelled to retire from this country, and to throw its inhabitants entirely on their own resources, it should leave them in such a state that they could provide, at least tolerably, for their own safety, and ultimately attain to prosperity and greatness; so that blessings might follow the mother country as she withdrew, and it might hereafter be admitted that her rule had been beneficial and far-seeing. But if she is ever forced to retire from this country whilst South Africa is divided as it now is, a long period of anarchy, confusion, and trouble must prevail, and, it is to be feared, that sentiments of indignation will rather be felt against Great Britain, which forced such difficulties upon the people here, than those feelings of gratitude which it would be so desirable to see entertained.

Before he could learn what London thought of his scheme, Grey received from the government of the Free State a formal offer to negotiate a union with the Cape; and though it was contrary to his instructions, he submitted this offer, with his strong recommendation, to the colonial legislature when it met in March 1859. Then arrived such a categorical refusal from the home government that he had to withdraw the proposal he had just made. Three months later he was recalled for having violated his instructions. In the following year, after another change of government, he was restored and sent back, but only on the explicit understanding that federation was a dead issue. After another year he was transferred back to New Zealand, where he seemed to be urgently needed, as we have already seen.

By a tragic irony the Colonial Office finally came round to Grey's policy for South Africa and tried to thrust federation upon the country when conditions there were much less favorable to it, and this raised a question that is still warmly debated. Could Grey have succeeded if London had given him a free hand? It is very doubtful if it was then possible to create the strong central government that he desired. The territory was huge and the white population thinly scattered; the country was so poor that it could not think of building railways to unite it; the Transvaal was in a state of anarchy; the weakness of the Orange Free State was self-confessed; Natal was an infant; the solid black regions could not support themselves; Cape Colony would have had to bear the burden of all; and the Cape legislature had shown no sign of willingness to share its customs revenue. Even if Grey's federal government would have fallen far short of his ideal, it might have prepared the way for a much happier future by breaking down the political barriers that divided the country, by encouraging cooperation between Boer and Britain—before either of the republics had any solidity and long before they developed a common nationalism that drew them together against the British. This is the most fundamental consideration in passing any judgment on the statesmanship of the masterful governor and the adverse decision in London. If we grant, out of consideration for the times, that no other decision was then possible, this only makes the consequent suffering of all concerned—Bantus, Boers, and British—the working of blind fate, a Greek tragedy in real life and on a gigantic scale.

Once more the Orange Free State, rebuffed from the Cape, rebounded toward the Transvaal, choosing Pretorius as its president in 1860. Again the British intervened to avert the danger of a republican fusion, and this time the order came from London. The colonial secretary threatened to modify the conventions, meaning the regulations concerning the traffic in arms, if the personal union between the two republics became a political union. As long as the republics had no independent access to the sea, the British were in a position to strangle them and could, therefore, exercise some control over them. Now they made a few sly moves in the direction of the coast, and the British government determined to stop them even if this meant an extension of colonial boundaries. The secretary of state stretched Cape Colony and Natal toward each other and looked forward to their meeting across the lands of the Kaffirs, who had not recovered from their orgy of self-destruction. More than that, he said he was willing to annex Zululand to Natal if this was necessary to check the Transvaal, and, to the same end, he challenged the Portuguese claim to Delagoa Bay. "Events," he observed, "are taking much the same course as in India in the last century, and though we may deprecate them, the question is—are they within our power?" His answer was that they could not be prevented but might be controlled. But throughout, following the precedent of India and the current demand for imperial retrenchment, he insisted that Cape Colony and Natal should assume the responsibilities of government and the expenditures involved in their territorial expansion. He was consciously veering away from the policy of the conventions and heading toward full colonial self-government as a way of escape from an onerous and vexatious imperial burden.

The colonists were only too eager to manage their own affairs—as they conceived them, which did not include the cost of administering annexed tribal territories or of providing for defense. They would call the tune and make the British piper pay. To make things worse, Cape Colony, which had enjoyed prosperity in the fifties, suffered a protracted drought that caused a severe depression in the following decade, and this precipitated a bitter quarrel between the two parts of the colony. The East, centered on Grahamstown, was naturally jealous of the older, richer, more populous, and more solid West, centered on Cape Town. Moreover the East was largely English whereas the West was predominantly Dutch. The East was tolerably content with the consideration it received from the government in the West until hard times began to pinch. Then the East, complaining that it could not get its just share of public funds, angrily demanded complete separation, which the West would not tolerate. This sectional strife combined with the irresponsible demand for responsible government to produce a state of almost hopeless political confusion and deadlock that lasted through the sixties. It convinced the exasperated governor of the day that what was needed was less self-government, not more, and he urged a constitutional revision like that which had been adopted in Jamaica. Meanwhile he had more serious worries as high commissioner in South Africa.

The Orange Free State was still going round in circles. It gained nothing from its election of Pretorius, who thereupon lost his position in the Transvaal, which was his only value to the Free State. Too many turbulent Transvaalers disliked him on personal grounds, and too many more feared he would drive the British into withholding the vital supply of arms and ammunition. Therefore, in 1864, he returned to his old stamping ground and, with the aid of young Paul Kruger, recovered the Transvaal presidency. The Free State promptly replaced him with Brand, who immediately persuaded the high commissioner to arbitrate in the Basuto border dispute, which was flaming up again as the result of Basuto encroachments. The arbitrator redrew the old line; the jubilant Free Staters pushed up to it; and the Basutos, taken aback by the award, fell back. The retirement of the tribesmen was only temporary. They soon swarmed down again to occupy the huts they had built and to harvest the crops they had sown beyond the line.

So began another war, in June 1865. The Transvaal, more anarchic than ever, offered little hope of aid; but popular opinion in the Cape and Natal rallied strongly to the side of the Free State, and Brand appealed to them for volunteers. Again the high commissioner forbade the enlistment of British subjects in this foreign cause, and he threatened to cut off the stream of munitions to the republic. This time, with new tactics, the burghers were more successful. Within a year they imposed a treaty that gave them half the arable land of the Basutos. Moshesh repudiated it and appealed to the British to accept him as a subject and to annex his territory to Natal. London, which had been demanding a reduction of imperial troops in South Africa as elsewhere, thought this was an opportunity to consolidate the position of the colonies and make the colonists assume the responsibility for their own security. Therefore the Colonial Office sent word to accept the offer. On the map it looked like a good solution, but not on the ground. Natal with only a few thousand white settlers, with a recently introduced and growing population of Indian coolies working on sugar plantations, and with swarms of Zulus and Kaffirs all over, was wholly incapable of handling such an accession of territory and tribes. Yet something had to be done quickly to prevent the continuance of the Basuto war from stirring up the whole mass of blacks, Kaffirs and Zulus as well as Basutos. Thereupon the high commissioner took it upon himself to inform President Brand that Britain would annex Basutoland and guarantee peace on that border of the Free State. Brand demurred, arguing that the Convention of Bloemfontein bound the British to keep hands off. The argument and the war were cut short in March 1868 by a peremptory order stopping the supply of ammunition and a proclamation annexing Basutoland. London later gave a grudging consent to this *fait accompli.*

The Free State was furious at being robbed of the fruits of victory in violation of the convention, and the high commissioner admitted the necessity of negotiating some compromise. He rightly feared that the home government might repudiate his action if it dragged Britain into war with the republic. Therefore he met Brand on the Orange and placated the republic by agreeing to its annexation of a slice of the coveted lands. It was the price the Basutos had to pay to preserve what they retained under British protection. One may condemn the British intervention in the war and this compromise settlement. But what was the practical alternative? The war had gone so far that it is hard to see what else could have saved Basutoland from dismemberment and the whole of South Africa from the chain reaction that this would have released. The tragedy was deepening.

Meanwhile Pretorius recklessly tried to remake the map of South Africa by an enormous extension of the bankrupt and unruly Transvaal. Immediately after the British annexation of Basutoland, he proclaimed three annexations: on the west, the whole of Bechuanaland, where there were reports of treasure at different points along the Missionaries' Road; on the north, beyond the Limpopo River, a territory in which ancient gold workings had just been discovered; and on the east, to the north of Zululand, a corridor down to the sea in Delagoa Bay. Pretorius would make his country rich and assure its independence by procuring direct communication with the outside world. The news sent a shock through the two colonies. They protested vehemently. So also did Portugal and Britain, both of which still claimed Delagoa Bay. But, as a leading authority on South African history has pointed out, the London denunciation of the proclamation was inspired "almost entirely" by the belief that it meant an expansion of slavery and slave dealing through the annexed regions. The British denunciation, he observes, "was the virtual end of the Sand River Convention," from which the detested gunpowder clause was then struck.[1]

The Colonial Office was at last ready to welcome any overture that might restore the republics to the British fold, but with no idea of controlling them from London. The new policy differed from that of the conventions of 1852 and 1854 in method, not in object, which was still to relieve the imperial government of an imperial responsibility. This would be transferred to the South Africans themselves by the establishment of a federation that would pay its own way and manage its own affairs; and therefore the home government was impatient to lay the cornerstone of the new structure, which was responsible government in Cape Colony. Brand was distinctly favorable to federation, and the burghers of the Transvaal were turning against their too venturesome president, who had to eat his own proclamation. Moreover, the digging of the Suez Canal, completed in 1869, was undermining the British value of South Africa as a strategic base on the route to India. The contemporary examples of national unification in British North America, in Germany, and in Italy encouraged the hope that the solution of the South African problem, first advanced by Governor Grey and now sanctioned by London, might be achieved then or in the near future.

Diamonds destroyed this hope. The unlocking of the treasure house of South Africa began in 1868 with the discovery of these precious stones on the lower Vaal River in Griqualand West and in the following year with the finding of "The Star of South Africa," which first sold for £11,000 and then for £25,000. The territory was derelict. Most of the Griquas had disappeared when the game on which they lived moved northward, leaving only a few hundred squalid survivors on parched lands claimed by both the Free State and the Transvaal as well as the Griqua chief, and disputed by unscrupulous speculators. Such was the situation on the eve of the discoveries, which quickly made confusion worse confounded. As the brilliant news spread abroad, fortune hunters swarmed in. The mining town of Kimberley in the "dry diggings" was founded in 1870, and by the spring of 1871 there were more than ten thousand diggers in the diamond fields. Both Boer republics grasped at the prize, but neither was capable of exercising effective control; a miners' republic sprang up, the Union Jack was run

---

[1] C. W. De Kiewiet, *British Colonial Policy and the South African Republics, 1848–1872* (London, 1929), p. 264.

up, there was an appeal to the Cape, and the acting governor on his own authority sent in a magistrate under the Cape Punishment Act of 1836.

What was to be the future of this diamondiferous territory? Official dispatches from Cape Town piled up such a mass of evidence on conflicting claims that the Colonial Office could not unravel the tangle and was forced to rely on the advice they contained that the two Boer republics were trying to dispossess the poor natives. More pressing was the obvious need of the turbulent new community for some real government that could preserve order. But the British government could not be persuaded to step in and rule it, so strong was the anti-imperialist bias in the mother country. A new governor and high commissioner, Sir Henry Barkly, was dispatched in 1870 to force the adoption of responsible government in Cape Colony, which he succeeded in doing in 1872; and meanwhile he came to the conclusion, which he pressed upon London, that there was no alternative to annexation.

To this step the British government consented—on the condition that Cape Colony undertake the responsibility of governing and defending the disputed territory. In keeping with this policy of shifting the imperial burden to the colony, Barkly was expected to persuade the Cape legislature to take over Basutoland as well as Griqualand West. In the session of 1871 he got both chambers to pass the Basutoland bill, and he had the satisfaction of seeing a majority in the lower house override the strenuous objection of the minority to responsible government. But the upper chamber rejected this bill; and Barkly did not dare to introduce a measure for the annexation of the diamond fields because a preliminary skirmish in the assembly raised the prospect of certain defeat, which would kill the project, for in all probability the home government would then withdraw its qualified consent. Yet he managed to extract resolutions from the two houses in favor of his taking steps to provide better government in the diggings, and he reported home that this legislative pronouncement was a virtual pledge of annexation. Three months later, long before he could get the reply of the Colonial Office, which expressed trust in his discretion and hope that he would obey his instructions, Barkly cut the Gordian knot by proclaiming the annexation of Griqualand West.

This fateful action of October 1871 cut more than the Gordian knot. It thrust a knife into the heart of republican South Africa, and it split the Cape on racial lines. More serious than the angry reaction in the Transvaal was the effect on the Orange Free State, which held the key position in South Africa. The Free State had a patently just claim to at least a goodly part of the treasure-bearing territory and could never forgive such a highhanded denial of it. Many burghers in both republics cried out for President Brand to form a united republic and to strike for freedom by leading a bold drive down to the sea in Delagoa Bay. But this great South African turned the dangerous crisis by meeting his volksraad behind closed doors and persuading the members that war would wreck the whole country and that when the truth was known in England "all would come right." When the Cape legislature met in 1872, the government bill to establish responsible government was carried in spite of strong opposition from the English in the Eastern Province, but the government bill to annex the diamond fields had to be withdrawn in the face of an overwhelming opposition. Throughout the colony few of the English ventured to defend the proclamation; while the Dutch, deeply sympathetic with their exasperated republican brethren, condemned it in bitter terms. The proclamation poisoned South Africa. It bred in the minds of the Cape Dutch a stubborn belief that Britain was not to be trusted, and it fed a fierce anti-British nationalism into the veins of the republican Dutch.

Barkly had saddled the British government with the diamond fields, the very thing it had been most anxious to avoid; and what was of infinitely greater importance, he had utterly ruined all chance of achieving the federation of South Africa, which the British government wanted most of all. Why did he take such a fatal step? The answer deepens the irony. He thought that the Free State, if allowed to get the diamond fields, would become too strong and independent to enter the federal stable. By putting out his foot to hold the door open, he kicked it shut, and he did not know it. Neither did the home government. The result was that London pressed more eagerly for what had suddenly become impossible, and thereby accentuated the evil that had been done. The story of this belongs to a later chapter; for as the pressure continued, British policy in South Africa insensibly reversed its character and slid into a new era. From being anti-imperialist, the policy became imperialist, as will be seen when we examine the resurgence of imperialism.

Economically and socially, South Africa was revolutionized by the opening of its treasure chest. The new diamond fields quickly outshone all others in the world, and prosperity at last came to the country at the very time when the completion of the Suez Canal might have brought a depression. There was only a slight and temporary decline of shipping that called at Cape Town. Until the diamond rush there was so little promise of wealth in South Africa that it attracted practically no immigrants or capital. Well-watered Natal was still experimenting with sugar and other tropical produce with the aid of Indian coolies because the natives shunned labor on the plantations. Its white population was only 18,000 in 1865, and it gained no more than 2,000 in the next ten years. The rest of South Africa was predominantly pastoral, especially in the two republics; and its sheep industry, though considerable, was poor and small compared with that of the more spacious Australia. Wool was the only export staple, and it brought less than £2,000,000 a year until the end of the disastrous drought that persisted through the sixties. Wool passed this figure in 1871, and in that year diamonds appeared on the list of exports. The official value was some £400,000, but this covered only what was entered at the customs, and there is reason for believing that a far greater quantity of the gems slipped out unobserved by official eyes.

Riches begat riches in South Africa, as elsewhere. Capital poured in, providing the country with public works, particularly railways, which became a necessity because the primitive transportation system of ox carts over crude trails could not cope with the growing traffic. The slight trickle of immigration swelled into a stream—not a torrent, because South Africa was overpopulated with blacks and had no room for white labor unless it was skilled. Trade boomed. The export and import business of Port Elizabeth, which had already exceeded that of Cape Town since the newer port was much nearer the center of the country, leaped away ahead. The white population of Cape Colony reached 236,000 in 1875, having increased 55,000 in ten years. At this time the Orange Free State had nearly 30,000 whites and the Transvaal more than 40,000. Nobody knows how large the black population was, except in Cape Colony, where it was approximately half a million.

The native problem entered upon a new and more complicated phase. It was now industrial as well as rural, and tribal society was rudely shaken. From all over the country blacks swarmed to the diamond fields. There the government of the crown colony of Griqualand West tried to introduce the legal equality of whites and blacks that had been adopted in the Cape. But the independent diggers were as hostile to the idea as the Great Trekkers had been. They insisted on racial discrimination, and so the industrial society of South Africa, which was then born, assumed the split character that it has ever since retained. The whites were socially and economically a superior class separated by a great gulf from the toiling mass of blacks, none of whom could ever hope to rise above the ranks of unskilled labor. Though their wages were pitifully low by white standards, they were temptingly high by native standards. As a rule, the natives left their families behind them and, after a few months in the mines, returned to their kraals with money in their pockets, guns in their hands, and strange ideas in their heads. The constant ebb and flow of native population speeded the disintegration of tribal society, transforming it into an inexhaustible reservoir of labor to be drawn upon by the white man in his exploitation of South Africa's other resources. A generation after the Great Trek had destroyed all possibility of a geographical separation between Europeans and Africans, the coming of industrialism tied them together in a mutual dependence that was indissoluble.

CHAPTER XXV

The Indian Mutiny

THE INDIAN MUTINY of 1857 precipitated the completion of a process that had begun three quarters of a century before and was already nearly finished. Pitt's India Act, passed on the morrow of the American Revolution, and each subsequent renewal of the East India Company's charter at twenty-year intervals, cut down the power of the Company and enlarged the authority of the Crown over India until the last renewal, in 1853, left little more than the nominal sovereignty to be transferred from the Company to the Crown in 1858.

One of the most important factors in increasing the control of the British cabinet over the affairs of India was a revolution in communications. For a long time after parliament made the President of the Board of Control legally responsible for guiding the policy of the government in India, physical conditions made it impossible for him to exercise effective direction. The only communication between London and Calcutta was a voyage of five to eight months each way, and it often took two years to get an answer. By 1850, however, dispatches went in a month, via the Suez isthmus, and there were two services every month. Steam navigation had thus greatly subordinated the governor general to the President of the Board of Control, and an electric wire was soon to reduce still further the governor general's independence. In 1865, four years before the opening of the Suez Canal, the completion of an overland telegraph line to India brought Calcutta within a few hours of London.

During the passage of the act of 1853, it was taken for granted that the end of Company rule was not far off. This last renewal of the charter was not for the usual twenty years, nor for any definite period. The act merely stated that the Company should administer India as a trust for the Crown until parliament decided otherwise, which might be at any time. Meanwhile it pointedly prepared for the coming end, by reducing the number of directors and making a third of them nominees of the Crown, and by depriving the directors of the one remaining privilege that they valued—the patronage of India. Thenceforth the civil service in India was to be recruited by competitive examinations open to all natural-born British subjects—seventeen years before the same reform was enacted for the civil service in Britain.

Lord Dalhousie, who retired in 1856 and died in 1860, was long blamed for provoking the Mutiny by his extensive annexations, his bustling innovations, his disregard of native prejudice, his blindness to signs of Indian unrest, and his failure to take obvious military precautions. Not until the present century was justice done him, and it is easy to see why it was so long denied him. He died without uttering one word in his own defense, and he left his private papers under seal for fifty years. He silently bore the opprobrium of the day rather than run any risk of embarrassing his successor at a most trying time, and he was confident that the judgment of posterity would vindicate his own administration. It now appears that his chief fault was an excessive devotion to duty during the eight years he served as governor general.

Of Dalhousie's annexations, the first was the Punjab, which, as we have seen, was the completion of unfinished business left by his predecessor. It proved to be an asset rather than a liability in the crisis of the Mutiny. Dalhousie's second war, which brought another important annexation, was on the opposite frontier, in the southeast. The governor whom the independent king of Burma sent to rule Rangoon in 1850 had a habit, when drunk, of swearing that he would torture and behead the whole population and, when sober, of practicing extortion upon the inhabitants. These included a small group of British subjects. They had enjoyed the protection of a British resident who, under the treaty of 1828, was posted to the royal court of Ava, in the interior. But the Burmese government had got rid of him in 1840 by heaping insults upon him, and the people whom he had protected now had no recourse but to appeal to the governor general of India, which they did in 1851. He sent a frigate to demand the removal of the terrifying governor and compensation for two of his British victims. The king obliged with a new governor; but the guards of the latter, saying that he was asleep, refused admission to a deputation of British naval officers when they called to bring him greetings. Their commander thereupon declared a blockade and seized a ship. The governor retorted that the officers had been turned away because they were drunk, and his guns took up the argument by opening fire on the frigate.

The result was the Second Burmese War, of 1852. It surprised Dalhousie, but he lost not a moment in preparing an expedition that would make short work of it, and he went in person to Rangoon to superintend operations. By the end of the year the war was over and the province of Pegu was annexed, its inhabitants, only partly Burmese, having welcomed British delivery from the cruelties of their rulers. Independent Burma was thus shut off from the sea, and the whole of the coast of the Bay of Bengal down to Singapore was brought under British control, the acquisition of Pegu filling in the gap between Arakan and Tenasserim. These three Burmese provinces were administered as dependencies of the government of Bengal.

It was not this addition of territory, but Dalhousie's peaceful annexation of native states in India proper that attracted severe criticism, and then not until the Mutiny called for a scapegoat. All but one of these annexations were applications of the doctrine of lapse, by which sovereignty passed to the suzerain when a ruler died without a legal heir. It was an old and well-established Hindu doctrine that applied to estates as well as to principalities and has been preserved to our own day by the ruling Hindu princes. It recalls the right of escheat in the society of our feudal ancestors and the survival of this right in our modern legal disposition of property left by those who have no heirs and die intestate. In India it was complicated by a quirk of religious origin. The Hindu faith denied peace in the long hereafter to any man who died without a son to perform the customary funeral rites. Hence the peculiar importance attached to adoption by childless Hindus. Hindu law and custom, however, denied the right of succession by an adopted heir unless the permission of the suzerain had preceded the ceremony of adoption; and this permission was granted not as a matter of course but as a mark of favor, an act of grace. There were therefore two main legal points to be cleared up before the governor general could take over a native state under this doctrine. He could do it only if the Company was the immediate overlord, and if there was no legal heir.

In applying the doctrine of lapse, Dalhousie was simply carrying out a policy that the authorities in London had formally adopted seven years before he set foot in India, and he never acted until each case was examined thoroughly, referred to London, and officially sanctioned there. Seven native states thus came under direct British rule. Dalhousie proposed only one other such annexation, and he at once accepted the adverse decision of the home government, which held that the annexation would be illegal because the little state in question was not "dependent" but "a protected ally." Three of the seven cases deserve special mention: Satara, because it was the cradle of the Mahratta Confederacy; Jahnsi, because its widowed and embittered rani played an active part in the Mutiny; and Nagpur, because of its size, its strategic location, and the arguments with which some of Dalhousie's experienced advisers opposed its annexation. Nagpur, with its eighty thousand square miles and four million population, had the finest cotton lands in India and controlled the land route connecting Bombay with Calcutta. The arguments just referred to were chiefly that British rule was generally unpopular, that annexation would alienate the aristocracy by undermining their privileged position, and that a rigorous enforcement of the principle of lapse would have a vicious effect upon the government of other native states by suggesting to childless rajas that, as their states would disappear with them, they might as well enjoy to the uttermost the powers they possessed over their subjects. To Dalhousie and his other advisers, however, the only cure for the all too common evils of native despotism was to substitute British rule, which should therefore be extended whenever a legitimate opportunity occurred.

"The crowning act of Lord Dalhousie's administration was the annexation of Oudh." It had nothing to do with the doctrine of lapse, and was the one exception noted above. It was a desperate remedy for a desperate situation in the chief Moslem state of India. Oudh was being ruined by a progressively vile native government, and this had been going on for half a century in flagrant violation of a treaty of 1801. That treaty bound the ruler to reform his administration and to conduct it in accord with the advice of the Company's officers. Successive governors general had repeatedly warned him to mend his ways or there would have to be intervention, but he paid no attention to them, and he was able to do what he liked with his own subjects because he had a treaty contingent of the Company's army to keep them in order. Oudh was the running sore of India, and at last the British government decided to cut it out. Dalhousie was ordered to annex Oudh, though he had advised a less drastic remedy. Rather than depose the king, which he rightly feared would give a serious shock to the loyalty of other native rulers, he would leave him or his heir upon the throne and turn the administration over to British officials. But as

London determined otherwise, he obeyed, in one of his last acts as governor general. Unfortunately he was unable to complete the business, his successor having just arrived from England. After Dalhousie departed, his orders were disregarded. Though the king received a generous pension, no allowances were paid to his dependents for over a year; the chief commissioner appropriated a palace reserved for the royal family; and, most important of all in the light of what soon happened, Dalhousie's direction that Oudh should be completely disarmed was first neglected and then rescinded.

In addition to annexing native states, Dalhousie abolished a few titular sovereignties on the ground that they might serve as rallying centers for reactionary revolution; but the home government would not allow him to touch the only one of any great importance, that of the Mogul emperor in Delhi, with the result that he became a tool of the mutineers and thus precipitated the extinction of his hollow office. When the pensioned ex-Peshwa died, leaving an enormous fortune and an adopted son, Dalhousie allowed the latter to inherit the fortune but withheld the pension of £80,000, which was not hereditary but was also claimed by the adopted son, best known as the infamous Nana Sahib of the Mutiny.

This completes the tale of how Dalhousie shook the confidence of the princely houses of India. He undoubtedly created the impression among Indians that the existence of all native states was in jeopardy. The belief was absurd but natural, and it raises two serious questions. How much, if any, did this contribute to the Mutiny? That it was not much is suggested by the fact that, with rare exceptions, the ruling princes backed the British in the crisis, and their backing was of great value in checking and suppressing the outbreak. This governs the answer to the other question: Do the acts that inspired the belief merit condemnation? Taken as a whole and judged by themselves, these acts were overwhelmingly right; for whatever fault may be found with the British administration that supplanted the rule of Oriental despots, it was as dust in the balance when weighed against the oppression of millions of natives by the latter. If we then throw into the scale the contribution that these acts may have made to the Mutiny, we still do not begin to upset the balance.

The other innovations of Dalhousie's regime are a different matter, for they produced a more general disturbance in the society of India. In the Punjab, in Oudh, and elsewhere, there was a thorough revision of the land settlements in favor of the actual occupants of the land—

the tillers of the soil, as well as the government—at the expense of the old revenue-collecting aristocracy. Large sections of this wealthy, privileged, and influential class had therefore good reason for hating the British. The relentless pressing of the campaign against such social evils as suttee and infanticide, and new laws allowing Hindu widows to marry again and permitting converts to inherit property as freely as if they had not changed their religion, caused widespread unrest in an intensely conservative society. More provocative was the almost feverish activity of Dalhousie in pushing public works. He opened the first railway in India and made plans for a whole series of branch and trunk lines that formed the basis of the later network. He founded the telegraph system of the country, and had wires strung that connected Calcutta, Peshawar, Bombay, and Madras—"the accursed string that strangled us," according to one of the mutineers. Dalhousie swept away the miserable postal arrangements that had long satisfied the Company, and in their place he established a cheap and efficient public service covering the whole country. He fought famine by digging irrigation canals, and to do so he stole sacred water from the Ganges. He reviewed the whole problem of education and sent home recommendations that were embodied in a famous dispatch of 1854, calling for the erection of "a properly articulated scheme of education, from the primary school to the university," with scholarships to aid the needy, with frank support for female education, and with particular attention to practical knowledge throughout. He at once commenced to build on these orders, and the first universities of India were started at Calcutta, Bombay, and Madras in the year after his departure.

The impact of dynamic western civilization upon the static Oriental society of India was many times greater under Dalhousie than it had ever been before, and it was profoundly unsettling. Some of the oldest and shrewdest administrators who served under him feared that, in his impatience to bestow the benefits of western civilization upon the people of India, he was driving along at a dangerously fast pace; and it has since been generally admitted that he was not sufficiently mindful of the deleterious effect that his tireless reforming energy might have upon the spirit of India, which was the very antithesis of the spirit of the west with its restless change and relentless materialism.

A vague uneasiness permeated Indian society, and it found expression in all sorts of wild rumors of what the British were doing and were going to do. One of the most powerful of these, in a land ridden by ancient religions and religious feuds, was that the government was about to force Christianity upon all Indians, in the tradition of Moslem conquerors who had once compelled conversion to their faith at the point of a sword; and many a British officer innocently encouraged this rumor by openly preaching the Gospel of Christ to his troops. Another rumor of the time predicted that 1857, the century of Plassey, would see the crash of the British *raj,* and recent military reverses in Afghanistan and the Crimea lent color to the prophecy. In short, the atmosphere of India was surcharged with distrust and suspicion. This undoubtedly affected the native army, but according to the best informed opinion it favored rather than caused the uprising in 1857.

The prime causes of the Mutiny are to be found in the condition of the army in India. When Dalhousie departed, it numbered just over 278,000 soldiers, of whom less than one sixth were Europeans. This proportion had been falling, partly due to the withdrawal of two British regiments to serve in the Crimea. Far from being to blame for it, Dalhousie had vainly sought to redress the disparity by getting drafts from home to replace the units that had been removed. A much greater drain occurred shortly after his departure, when his successor, in obedience to urgent orders from London, shipped six British regiments to Persia to strike at the root of another Russian-inspired invasion of Afghanistan. There was also a growing deficiency of officers of the best type, and for this Dalhousie was more responsible, because he drew upon them to fill administrative posts, particularly those on the frontier. More serious was a decline in morale, which he saw clearly but was powerless to correct. "The discipline of the army," he reported home, "from top to bottom, officers and men alike, is scandalous." It was the officers who stood in the way of reform. They would not admit its necessity or that anyone outside the army knew anything about military affairs.

This defect of discipline was much more serious in the Bengal army than in the army of Madras or of Bombay. In the Bengal army, which was considerably larger than either of the other two, promotion went almost entirely by seniority and great deference was paid to high caste. A not unusual sight was that of a low-caste officer crouching meekly before a proud Brahman recruit. The Afghan War had caused a noticeable deterioration of morale. There the damage went far beyond the lowering of British prestige under the impact of military failure. There Moslem sepoys were deeply offended by having to fight men of their own faith. There Hindus suffered loss of caste, which cost them much to recover when they returned home; for in Afghanistan the cold climate interfered with their ritual ablutions, and both the food and the water were "unclean." Crossing the sea to fight in Burma also deprived Hindus of caste. One regiment refused to go in 1852, and the refusal was quite legal because it was one of the many units that had been recruited for service only in India. When none of the general service regiments were available to replace the garrison left in Burma, Dalhousie planned and his successor almost immediately issued a new regulation prohibiting the enlistment of any men who would not undertake to serve wherever they might be sent. Though it was not retroactive, the order excited much unrest because it cut across the character of the Bengal army, in which service was a hereditary occupation. Now high-caste sepoys saw their sons excluded from either their profession or their caste. Another cause of trouble was the enlistment of Sikhs, following the pacification of the Punjab, which suggested to the heated imagination of Bengal sepoys that a new army was being prepared to supersede their own.

A lascar met a Brahman sepoy near Calcutta in January 1857 and asked for a drink of water from his cup. The Brahman refused with the natural excuse that the low-caste lascar's lips would pollute the cup. Thereupon the sailor retorted that the proud soldier would soon lose his caste anyway, because, to load his rifle, he would have to bite the end off cartridges that would surely defile him. It was four years since the first greased cartridges, requiring this simple operation by the teeth, had reached India from England; they were now being manufactured in India, and the sepoys had accepted them without question until this minute. What the sailor said was true, for someone in England had blundered. In spite of a solemn warning from the adjutant general of the Bengal army against the use of either beef or pork fat to grease the cartridges, since the one would defile Hindus and the other Moslems, the new ammunition issued in India was contaminated by both ingredients.

The terrible story of the lascar's taunt spread like wildfire. Official orders promptly stopped the issue of the accursed cartridges but could not stop the mischief that had been done. At first there were local outbreaks, such as had occurred in previous years, with sepoys burning their officers' barracks. By May the mutinous disturbances were more general, and blood was flowing. Then it was that three native regiments at the great military station of Meerut murdered their officers and marched to Delhi, forty miles away. Not a single British regiment was there, and the native garrison joined the newcomers in seizing control of the city and slaying every European they could lay their hands on. The telegraph operator had barely time to flash warning signals to the authorities in the Punjab; and the British officer, who had only eight men to defend the large magazine against the raging mob, blew the place and hundreds of mutineers into the air.

So began the great Mutiny. It was largely confined to the upper Ganges valley, the heart of historic India, where there were scarcely any British troops; and the worst was over by the end of September, before the forces that were rushed from Britain had time to arrive. But this worst was terrible enough, particularly at Cawnpore. There Nana Sahib was taking his fiendish revenge. After a three weeks' siege under ghastly conditions, the garrison of four hundred British and some faithful sepoys surrendered on receiving his promise of honorable treatment. As they were departing in boats that he provided, a massacre began. Only four men escaped. The women and children who were not shot down, numbering about a hundred and twenty-five, were dragged ashore and reserved for a more horrible fate. Nana Sahib had them hacked to pieces and their severed remains dumped in a well near the slaughterhouse. At Lucknow, some forty miles away, a small body of British and of loyal sepoys took refuge in the Residency and held off swarms of assailants under the most trying conditions until reinforcements reached them in September, only to find that they had to sustain another siege that lasted into November.

But the back of the Mutiny was broken with the first relief of Lucknow and the recovery of Delhi, which occurred a few days before. Though 120,000 of the 128,000 men in the Bengal army revolted, the native armies of Madras and Bombay, the Sikhs of the Punjab, and the Gurkhas of Nepal fought wholeheartedly for the British. From two principal bases, the Punjab on the northwest and the strong fortress of Allahabad on the southeast, the successful advance was made on the seat of the Mutiny. There was still much hard fighting to be done against large bodies of rebel troops, one of which was ably led by the rani of Jahnsi. But British troops were now pouring in from England and by the next summer the last embers of the revolt were stamped out.

The nature of the Mutiny was not what some people of a later generation, who know nothing of India or the history of nationalism, have been prone to imagine. It was not a nationalist rising. The phenomenon of modern nationalism, which became a dynamic force in the French Revolution, had not yet penetrated beyond the confines of western civilization. That was a development that became noticeable only in the last quarter of the century. It is not known that the mutineers had any political aims of their own. Their movement, however, was exploited by a few interested schemers to give it a political direction. At first this was Moslem, when the insurgents in Delhi proclaimed the restoration of the Mogul Empire; and later on was Hindu, when the representative of the vanished Mahratta empire, Nana Sahib, was proclaimed Peshwa. These were the two clearest political ideas to emerge in the Mutiny, they were mutually incompatible, and the mutineers displayed little real interest in either. Except in Oudh and in the city of Delhi, the civilian population took little or no part in the rising. As the name implies, it was the work of soldiers who had lost all sense of discipline. They were uncoordinated, headless, military mobs furiously bent on destruction and utterly incapable of creating anything but anarchy. If they had succeeded in throwing off the British yoke, they would have thrown India back into frightful bloody chaos. Countless Indians saw it plainly, and they recoiled before the infernal vision. Their active support, particularly that of the princes, saved the British *raj* and India itself when they were in gravest peril.

"Clemency" Canning was the nickname applied in scorn to Lord Canning,[1] who succeeded Lord Dalhousie as governor general, because he effectively used his power and his influence to check the savage outcry of the British in India and at home, provoked by the horrors of the Mutiny, for a policy of wholesale vengeance. He insisted upon wholesale clemency, except for those who, by due process of law, were found guilty of murder; and with noble disdain he faced the storm of public abuse that this policy drew upon him. His firm stand was more than morally splendid. It was politically wise, for it saved the British from irretrievably alienating the peoples of India. As passions cooled, the fine sanity of his policy gradually won recognition and transformed the nickname, which stuck, into a title of honor.

The shock that the Mutiny administered to the self-complacency of Britain gave the deathblow to the dying East India Company. Palmerston introduced a bill to transfer the government of India from the Company to the Crown; and when, after the second reading of the measure, he fell from power, the Derby administration piloted through parliament another bill for the same purpose. By the Government of India Act of 1858, a Secretary of State for India replaced the President of the Board of Control, and the advisory function of the Court of

---

[1] Son of George Canning.

Directors was vested in a Council of India. This council, sitting in London, was so constituted that it would be independent of party politics and be possessed of the knowledge necessary for its task. During the members' term of office, at first for life but later reduced to a limited period of years, they enjoyed the same security of tenure as judges, being removable only on an address by both houses of parliament; and a majority of the members were required to have had at least ten years' recent experience in India. The revenues of India could be charged with the existing financial obligations of the Company, but otherwise they were to be devoted to the government of India; and, by way of check, orders of the secretary of state relating to expenditures and loans had to be submitted to the council for approval. Also, while placing under the Crown the army and navy of the Company, the act required the consent of parliament for the application of any Indian revenue to military operations outside India.

The new regime was inaugurated by a royal proclamation that had been rewritten to meet Queen Victoria's expressed wish that it "should breathe feelings of generosity, benevolence, and religious toleration." This oft-quoted document disclaimed any desire for "extension of our present territorial possessions"; it set forth a pledge to "respect the rights, dignities, and honour of native princes as our own"; it proclaimed the principle of religious freedom for all subjects, denying alike the right and the desire to impose the Christian faith on any, and declaring the "royal will and pleasure that none be in any wise favoured, none molested or disquieted, by reason of their religious faith or observances, but that all shall alike enjoy the equal and impartial protection of the law"; it enunciated the policy that "our subjects, of whatever race or creed, be freely and impartially admitted to office in our service, the duties of which they may be qualified by their education, ability, and integrity duly to discharge"; it offered to all rebels still in arms who were not guilty of the murder of British subjects a free pardon "on their return to their homes and peaceful pursuits"; and, in conclusion, it expressed an "earnest desire to stimulate the peaceful industry of India, to promote works of public utility and improvement, and to administer the government for the benefit of all our subjects resident therein. In their prosperity will be our strength, in their contentment our security, and in their gratitude our best reward." Noble as this proclamation is, it contained nothing really new. It was a timely and useful formulation of ideals that in one form or another—

instructions, orders, legislation, and administrative practice—had found scattered expression in the British government of India.

That the new regime was better than the old, as has been so often asserted, is open to serious question. For three quarters of a century the periodic renewal of the charter had been the occasion for a searching public inquiry into how the Company was managing the affairs of India and, as a consequence, for the intervention of parliament to remedy the defects that this grand inquest might disclose in the system. This automatic provision for the regular recurrence of a thorough overhauling of the government of India was now gone, and nothing took its place until the First World War. It may be said, on the other hand, that the transfer from Company to Crown subjected the government of India to continuous review by parliament. Such was the theory, but most members of parliament were incapable of translating it into practice. India was too remote, too strange, too vast, and too complicated. They left it to the experts. They likewise shrank from meddling in foreign policy, for understandable reasons; and this was also their general attitude toward colonial policy, which had never been easy for them to grasp intelligently and became more unfamiliar as the growth of colonial autonomy shifted the focus of this policy to the management of non-English and non-European societies.

To an even greater degree, and for a further reason, parliament was content to let the experts run India. Parliament had to pay the piper for the Colonial Department and the Foreign Office, but not for India. Though India resembled the colonies in not being taxed to provide revenue for the British Exchequer, it differed from them in receiving no subsidies from it. India bore the whole cost of its government, including the salary of the secretary of state in London, and all the expense of the army that protected it from enemies within and without. It may be urged that Britain paid for the naval defense of India. But this was a benefit shared by the self-governing colonies, and even by the United States. The annual naval estimates did not give the House of Commons the slightest prod to take a more active interest in this far-off land of teeming millions.

Though the negative attitude that parliament had displayed toward India, during the twenty-year intervals between the renewals of the charter, was now protracted indefinitely, there was no relaxation on the part of those who were directly responsible for the conduct of Indian affairs. They were as anxious as ever to fulfill the trust reposed in them. They executed important reforms, and they did much to improve conditions in India. The Indian Civil Service, which the Crown took over from the Company, comprised a superior breed of men; and their individual quality became finer as the system of recruiting by competitive examination from the ablest students in the British universities gradually filled its ranks, making it in many respects the best civil service in the world. Nevertheless, one can detect in the administration changes that were not for the better, changes that sprang not from the transfer to the Crown, which was relatively a superficial thing, but from the Mutiny itself and from the revolution in communications.

The Mutiny dealt a blow to British government in India from which it never recovered. It had been inspired by a noble vision, that of the gradual redemption of India by the westernizing and Christianizing of its whole society. This was now shattered. The fatalist doctrine that East is East and West is West dates from the Mutiny. Reform that might touch the hidden springs of religion in India was thenceforth taboo. The hideous experience of 1857 suddenly contracted the British sense of a mission to be carried out in that country, confining it to the preservation of peace and order, the strict enforcement of an impartial justice, and the provision of such physical and material developments as might be possible. It was a bleak prospect with no end in sight until, years afterward, the British began to think again in terms of training the people of India to govern themselves.

The Mutiny also damaged the British government in India by causing an immediate and permanent estrangement between the British in India and the people over whom they ruled. Before 1857 a large measure of mutual confidence had grown up between them, finding daily expression in countless personal relations of an easy, friendly, and kindly nature. This too was now shattered. The British in India never escaped from the haunting nightmare of the Mutiny. They were nervously conscious of being a small garrison amid a huge population that they could not trust. They withdrew from the society around them, shunning all contacts that were unnecesary. The Indians likewise drew in upon themselves; and with narrowing eyes they saw the British in a darker light, as more foreign, more formidable. The revulsion from Occidentalism, which had blazed forth so fiercely in the Mutiny, spread silently like an underground fire. The time was to come when Indians would cherish the memory of the Mutiny as a valiant outburst of their own nationalism against British imperialism, but they did not begin to mold this powerful myth until about a generation afterward. Meanwhile the suppression of the uprising marked the beginning of a defiant return to their old religions, of an idealization of their remote past, of a pride in an ancient India that was civilized long before Europe. The British in India, thus isolated by a double reaction, succumbed to the spirit of the land they had conquered and still ruled. They became a caste, the highest and tightest in that world of caste; and their austere aloofness robbed the government that they administered of the personal touch so dear to the Oriental. They might perform their functions with punctilious efficiency, but it was the efficiency of a machine.

The revolution in communications did further damage to the government in India, though it also brought much benefit to the country in various ways. By bridging the space between Britain and India, it terminated the long struggle between London and Calcutta over the effective control of policy in India, and this elimination of the pulling at cross purposes was good. Moreover, the very things that decided the issue—steam and electricity—also operated to banish the ignorance that had too often betrayed the home government into wrong decisions on matters of policy. Where, then, did the evil come in? It was in the concentration of power over India away from India—in London. This meant government of India by remote control, which widened the psychological gulf between rulers and ruled, increased the mechanization of the British administration in India, and weighed down its personnel under a heavy load of uninspiring "paper work."

With the transfer of formal sovereignty to the Crown, the title of viceroy was added to that of governor general, but the only change this made in the office was an exaltation of its dignity. The constitution of the government in India continued after the Mutiny with little important alteration save in one particular, and this was a development of a reform begun in 1853 by the last Charter Act. The reform was a separation of the executive and legislative functions of the governor general's council, which was then enlarged by the addition of other official members for legislative purposes. Dalhousie, who launched this new legislature, gave it an unexpected character that soon became more pronounced. It had an imposing set of parliamentary rules, it had a Hansard of its own, and its debates were open to the public. It definitely tended to regard itself as an independent legislative body, an embryonic parliament, to the embarrassment of Canning and of officials at home. They would have liked to undo what had been done, but they judged it wiser not to make the attempt. What stood in the way was not so much the natural desire of the Anglo-Indian colony for an independent legislature as it was the deep-rooted sympathy in England for free deliberation. After much heart-searching and consultation in official circles, a decision was reached to go on with the work.

In 1861 Canning transformed his executive council into a sort of cabinet by making its members severally responsible for the various administrative departments. This distribution of authority expedited the business of government, and it rescued the council from being cluttered up with a mass of detail that impeded its consideration of more important matters. In the same year parliament passed the Indian Councils Act, which reconstituted the legislative council. In addition to the five executive councilors, it was to comprise not less than six or more than twelve members nominated by the governor general, and at least one half of these additional members had to be men who held no other official position. Here entered the representative principle, which in later years was enlarged and extended to include elected members. The act also provided for provincial legislative councils. In the preparation of this measure it had been urged upon the government that the new legislative bodies would make fatal mistakes unless they included Indian members, and during the discussion of the bill in the House of Commons there was a motion to require this condition in the selection of the nonofficial members of the governor general's legislative council. The secretary of state successfully objected that it would be invidious to make such a statutory distinction between different classes of Her Majesty's subjects, but he let it be understood that natives of India would certainly be appointed, and they were.

More imperative were two other reorganizations in India at this time. The Mutiny had ruined the army and wrecked the finances of the country. With the transfer to the Crown, the Company's army and navy were amalgamated with the royal forces. The army in India was reconstituted on a smaller scale, but, for safety's sake, with a larger proportion of British and with the artillery and the arsenals in their hands. From 1857 to 1861 the deficits in the exchequer amounted to £36,000,000, approximately the normal annual revenue. But by the end of that period experts sent out from Britain succeeded in restoring the balance by cutting expenditures and increasing the revenue.

Another important effect of the Mutiny was a revolution of British policy toward the native states. Following their royal proclamation's pledge to the princes, the doctrine of lapse was openly renounced. The division of the country between British India and the native states was frozen from 1858. The former stopped eating up the latter. But while the six hundred odd native states were thus perpetuated as an integral part of the Indian system, their relations with the paramount power underwent a subtle change of a twofold nature.

The mere substitution of Queen Victoria for a chartered corporation inspired the princes with a sense of personal loyalty hitherto impossible, and so a personal touch was injected into the British management of the native states as the Company disappeared from the administration of British India. The native rulers felt that their subordinate position was now much more honorable; and judging by their repeated public assertions and actions, they proudly assumed the new obligation of loyalty to the imperial Crown. The British government reciprocated by cultivating the bond in various ways, notably by conferring titles and other honors upon leading princes. Hence the founding of the order of the Star of India in 1861.

The other part of the change in relations with the paramount power flowed from the revolution of communications within India itself, which made for increasing interference in the internal affairs of the native states. The improvement of communications—the construction of railways, the stringing of telegraph wires, the expansion of the postal system, and the rise of a public press—undermined the isolation of these principalities, exposing abuses in their government. Incidents that formerly would have passed unobserved in Calcutta now attracted attention and cried aloud for correction. To carry out the new British policy of preserving the princes and their dominions as bulwarks of the empire, it was necessary to check their misgovernment. In other words, the British had here to face the problem that had worried them and still worried them elsewhere in the empire. It was the conflict between the principles of autonomy and trusteeship. It was a dilemma that continually called for adjustment by choosing what seemed, on careful examination, to be the lesser evil. The solution that was gradually worked out concentrated largely upon the early education of the rulers, for which minorities provided the best opportunity, and upon advice and exhortation tendered through British residents at the native courts. When moral suasion was insufficient, there was recourse to a regency council, or temporary assumption of the administration by the resident, or, when all else failed, deposition of the reigning monarch in favor of a more reliable substitute. The consequence was that, as the years passed, British influence lifted the standard of government in the native states to approximate the rising standard in British India, and did it without impairing the loyalty of the princes.

The judicial system of British India was recast in the years around 1860, when the old Crown and Company jurisdictions were merged and the work of codification, begun by Macaulay nearly a generation before and requiring long labors by many legal experts, was at last completed and applied. There was also an overhauling of the land revenue system, or systems, in the interests of efficiency and of the peasant cultivators. Then too the government began to evolve a famine policy. From time out of mind famine had been a frequent occurrence in that land of monsoons, and the tragic consequences of the occasional failure of the monsoon rains had been accepted with the traditional fatalism of the Orient. This was no longer possible. Two severe visitations in the 1860's roused the government of India to its responsibility for meeting the danger, which was assuming larger proportions because the abolition of local war and endemic anarchy and the introduction of sanitary measures were allowing the fecund population to multiply as it had never done before, reaching 250,000,000 by 1871, when the first census was taken. The new famine policy was to push irrigation schemes and to rescue the people in stricken areas by sending in food from surplus districts with the aid of more railways and canals.

This was an age of marked material advancement in India. Railway construction was booming, fed by the stream of capital flowing out from Britain. What had been immense wastelands in Assam and along the slopes of the Himalayas, because no suitable productive crop was found for them until about 1850, became thriving tea plantations. The American Civil War greatly stimulated cotton growing in various regions, causing a lot of rather wild speculation and fictitious prosperity. The inevitable collapse came at the end of the war, when the Lancashire mills could again get long-staple cotton from the South instead of the short-staple cotton from India. But India as a whole was little dependent on the sale of her raw cotton abroad, and the financial panic produced by the collapse checked only temporarily the rapid flow of investment capital into India. The revolution in transportation was quickening internal commerce and helping to found new Indian industries—such as cotton in Bombay and jute in Bengal. The industrial revolution was invading India, enriching it and pulling its scattered parts together. Still the vast bulk of the people continued, as before, to live by agriculture; but now they could sell some of their produce, which was needed to feed the swelling population of the towns and cities, and with the proceeds they could buy cheap industrial products. If Indian industry thus completed the ruin of the old village handicrafts, it did so by supplying more efficiently the wants of the rural masses.

The process of unification then at work in India was much more than physical. Far from reversing the policy of leavening the Indian lump with western education, the Mutiny was followed by a more vigorous pursuit of this policy. The famous educational dispatch of 1854 and the establishment of the first Indian universities in 1857 were the foundation of the new effort. Like London University, after which they were modeled, the Indian universities were for a long time only examining and degree-granting bodies, but as such they performed a most valuable function. They set and maintained high standards to which the scattered colleges that were affiliated with them had to conform. These other institutions, government, missionary, and private, supplied the instruction to students admitted by university examinations and later tested by university examinations, first at the end of the second year in college, then for the bachelor's and finally for the master's degree, at each of which stages there was a heavy weeding out. As a university certificate was an open sesame to employment in the junior ranks of the government service, the rank depending on the grade of the certificate, and as the instructor was divorced from the examiner, there was keen competition between the colleges and within the colleges not to lower the quality of instruction but to raise it. There was also a rapid expansion of secondary education, public and private, to prepare youths for the university examination that would admit them to college. The whole movement left the masses untouched. It was confined to the traditionally literate classes. The language of college instruction was English, for the prescribed curriculum was basically English and a knowledge of that language gave preferment in the government service; therefore the schools were under pressure to provide training in the use of the favored tongue.

Macaulay's prophecy of thirty years before was being fulfilled with the rise of a new generation of Indians who found a new unity in their knowledge of English and in sharing the same outlook and ideas, literary and political, borrowed from England. Their number was relatively small, but their influence was out of all proportion to it. In every district they were the lawyers, the teachers, and the administrative officials who dealt most directly with the people. As yet there were no journalists among them, for the newspapers published in the country were all written by Englishmen for Englishmen and were scarcely read by Indians. But the time was near at hand—in the seventies—when the rise of a native press would magnify the influence of the Indian minority who had imbibed a western education.

VI THE HEYDAY OF IMPERIALISM

CHAPTER XXVI

The Rise of Modern British Imperialism

MODERN IMPERIALISM burst upon the world with tremendous energy in the last quarter of the nineteenth century, and many theorists have since tried to define and analyze this movement or force. Very significantly, it had no name until it began to manifest itself in the seventies. Lord Carnarvon, who had been colonial secretary in two Conservative cabinets, wrote in 1878, "we have of late been perplexed by a new word 'Imperialism,' which has crept in amongst us. . . . I have heard of Imperial policy and Imperial interests, but Imperialism, as such, is a newly coined word to me." He was not the only man whom the term has puzzled, for it has had more than one meaning. The confusion has been greatest in British minds because to them, and them alone, imperalism has meant two very different things that were unrelated in origin, in character, and in purpose. For a while the two meanings remained quite distinct, though in time they became tangled together. In fact, there were two British imperialisms, and it is necessary to draw a clear distinction between them. One was a reaction from the colonies, the other a reaction from continental Europe, and they appeared in this order.

The senior and purely British imperialism did not contemplate any extension of the empire. It was concerned almost entirely with the relations between the mother country and the colonies peopled by her, to the exclusion of India and the colonies inhabited by native races. To understand this imperialism we have to recall the mood in which official London yielded to the colonial demand for responsible government. Coming on top of free trade, which was a declaration of independence by the mother country against the colonies, the concession of responsible government was inspired by the belief that the colonies were of little if any use to the mother country and sooner or later were bound to become independent nations. In other words, Britain was consciously washing her hands of the troublesome and fruitless attempt to hold the maturing colonies within the empire. Liberals and Conservatives alike looked forward to the dissolution of the empire with a complacency tinged by an impatience that tended to grow with the years. "These wretched colonies will all be independent in a few years, and are a millstone round our necks." So said Disraeli in 1852, and he had a genius for catching the spirit of the age. Herman Merivale, Stephen's successor in the Colonial Office, summed up the colonial policy of his day when he wrote in 1870: "the object of our statesmen has been twofold: to encourage the colonies to prepare for independence for their own sake, and at the same time to relieve the people of this country from the share which they formerly bore in contributing towards their administration and defense." Impatience to get rid of the colonial burden mounted with the rise of colonial tariff walls against the mother country and with the failure of colonial autonomy to ripen into political independence. Therefore it is not surprising that during the sixties the British government proceeded to withdraw imperial troops from the colonies. Liberals began the move in 1862, Conservatives continued it, and Liberals pushed it to a conclusion in 1871, the year in which Bismarck created the German Empire.

The recall of the legions may suggest a Roman parallel, but this is misleading. The stimulus of startling power developments on the continent of Europe did not initiate, though it may have speeded, the policy of military concentration in Britain, which the War Office pressed as essential to the reform of the army. It was a small professional army dispersed all over the globe. The garrisons that Britain summoned home were puny things which the colonies were fully capable of replacing to meet any possible attack. Moreover, the military might of Britain did not, like that of Rome, reside in her army. Her armed strength was concentrated in her navy, the supremacy of which was absolute. That was her sure defense, and it enveloped her colonial empire. Far from approaching its fall, the British Empire was about to discover its strength.

The awakening began in the colonies and spread back to the mother country. It began with the grant of responsible government, which purged the imperial connection of its annoyance to the colonies. A cynic might say that the colonies simply wanted to eat their cake and have it too, that they insisted on the rights and refused to accept the responsibilities of independence. There is an element of truth in this, but it falls far short of explaining what happened. As the American Revolution had its roots in traditions of liberty that English people carried with them when they crossed the Atlantic to settle in America, so the later insistent demand of the British colonies for self-government sprang from the basic British character of their population. This British character was confirmed rather than undermined by the concession of responsible government, and it was reinforced by the stream of British emigration to the colonies. If Americans have sometimes missed the point, British statesmen long missed it too. Their cold logic could not reconcile colonial autonomy with imperial unity. They lacked Durham's warm faith that, when the people of the colonies entered into the possession of their British birthright, its magic influence would bind them to the parent state. Thus it came to pass that those who thought they were inaugurating the disruption of the colonial empire were actually inaugurating its salvation. By releasing the colonies from imperial restraints upon their governments, these men unwittingly released the colonies from a strain upon their British loyalty. As a consequence, faith in the British Empire was reborn in the colonies at the very time it was dying in Britain.

Not until the late sixties was there any indication that the colonial faith might prevail over the metropolitan skepticism. George Brown, the father of Canadian Liberalism, who joined Macdonald in the coalition of 1864, went to England immediately after the Quebec Conference to discuss federation with the home government. He was gratified to find an eager welcome for this idea and much enthusiasm about Canada's future. But, as he reported to Macdonald, he was "much concerned to observe . . . that there is a manifest desire in almost every quarter that, ere long, the British American colonies should shift for themselves, and in some quarters evident regret that we did not declare at once for independence." The same impression was gathered by another prominent Canadian politician on a visit to England in 1866. He was convinced, he said, that "the leaders on both sides, Gladstone and Disraeli included, would have been still more pleased if we had asked for our independence at once." Gloomier still were the words of one of the outstanding Canadian delegates to the London conference that drafted the British North American Act. Writing to his wife in January 1867, Alexander T. Galt remarked: "I am more than ever disappointed at the tone of feeling here as to the Colonies. I cannot shut my eyes to the fact that they want to get rid of us. . . . The connection between Canada and England is now one of sentiment, interest in both cases scarcely being in favor of it. Now the sentiment is becoming very weak here, and in Canada will not bear much longer the brunt of the ungenerous remarks continually made" (in England about Canada's being a burden and a weakness).

One of the first signs of the coming change in the tone of opinion in Britain was the founding in 1868 of the Royal Colonial Institute, or, as it was first called, the Colonial Society. The American Minister to the Court of St. James, Reverdy Johnson, was a guest at the inaugural dinner, and he had so little sense of the occasion that he tactlessly referred to the possibility "that some of the colonies which now flourish under the dominion of Her Majesty, and have so much reason to be proud of that dominion, may in the process of time find themselves under the flag of the United States." In uttering this note of American imperialism he knew he was in tune with his government, which made no secret of its desire to annex British North America. He may have thought he was also in harmony with the equally well-known British policy that sought withdrawal from colonial embarrassments. If so, he was sadly mistaken; for the British government, while ready to recognize Canadian independence if the Canadians wanted it, would never countenance annexation to the United States unless the Canadians clearly desired it, which they did not. The new society was a select body, a sort of club, whose purpose was to cultivate interest in the colonies. It collected a library that later grew to be the finest in the empire on the empire, and its meetings for the discussion of colonial questions attracted public attention from the very beginning. The general character of these meetings was in keeping with the motto of the organization, which was "United Empire." It was, however, more a symptom than a cause of the awakening British imperialism; for the movement found expression in other public meetings, in the press, and in parliament.

Gladstone's government was immediately responsible for this awakening. When he came into power in 1868, there was a widespread belief that he and his colleagues were bent on casting the colonies adrift, and the administration's insistence on withdrawing the garrisons confirmed the belief. The British public had viewed with indifference the prospect of colonial independence as the result of colonial demand, but independence thrust upon the colonies by the mother country was another matter. Protests arose and swelled into a chorus, particularly over the recall of the troops from New Zealand in the midst of a Maori war. The withdrawal policy had its supporters too, and the challenge made them speak out. Then, for the first time since the American Revolution, the colonies were the subject of a lively public debate in England.

Until 1871 the nascent imperialism was on the defensive, fighting to preserve the empire from impending dismemberment. As the danger lay in the general acceptance of the thesis that the colonies were a liability to Britain, the imperialists concentrated upon rebutting it. In trying to prove the material advantage of the connection, they stressed the value of the colonies chiefly as a market for British manufactures and as a field for British emigration. Thus the battle was joined on the hard ground of economic interest, the sole criterion of the Manchester School. There was almost no appeal to sentiment of any kind. Nor did party politics enter the conflict, for the division cut across parties. At first imperialism seemed to be a lost cause. The withdrawal of the garrisons proceeded inexorably, as the separatists desired. But this very move deprived them of their main proof that the colonies were a liability. Calculations of the balance between profit and loss were also affected by the fact that Britain was ceasing to be the only important industrial country and was beginning to feel the pressure of foreign competition. This suggested that colonial markets might, after all, become indispensable for the welfare of the parent state. There was no suggestion of returning to the old restrictive imperial trading system, or anything savoring of it. The imperialists were as firm believers in the gospel according to Adam Smith as were the separatists, and the colonies had tariff autonomy. There was complete confidence in the ability of British manufactures to meet foreign goods on equal terms, which might not be possible in colonies that left the empire; and there was a natural, if mistaken, hope that the colonies might be persuaded to abandon their protectionist heresy.

The next phase of this imperialist movement began in 1871, when it passed from the defensive to the offensive. Having won the battle against disruption, it began to fight for the consolidation of the empire by some constitutional scheme. The favorite was a political union of the mother country and the colonies in a great federation. Though this particular idea can be traced back for half a century and seems to have had its origin in the example of the American federation, now for the first time it gained wide publicity and considerable support. It had the most vociferous and best organized advocates, but their followers were only a minority of those who were anxious to see the empire held together more securely. To understand the strength of this growing desire, we have to glance at several new conditions that conspired to encourage it.

The contemporary revolution in communications was swinging British opinion from separatism to imperialism. Steam navigation, the opening of the Suez Canal in 1869, and the completion of the Atlantic cable in 1866 and the Australian cable in 1872, brought the colonies much closer to the mother country and thereby undermined the common notion that they were destined to drift apart. The great physical obstacle to the permanent unity of the empire was disappearing. It has been suggested that this annihilation of distance also affected British thinking about the empire by destroying the geographical isolation that had given the colonies immunity from attack by other powers, with the single exception of the United States. Yet it is doubtful if this consideration had much weight in a land whose people knew that they ruled the waves.

Another important factor in the changing British attitude was the extraordinary growth of settlement in British North America and Australasia. The rapid rise of new British nations overseas, fed by immigration from the crowded old land and nourished by the unlimited resources of the new lands they inhabited, nations resenting the thought that they would cease to be British, inspired visions of a maturing empire greater than any that had ever been seen. Already there was talk of the day when the daughter nations would collectively outgrow their mother in population and wealth.

The Reform Act of 1867 also contributed to the swelling tide of British imperialism. The industrial workers, then enfranchised and thenceforth the great majority of the electorate, did not share the separatist views that had long been fashionable. These views had been propagated by the Manchester School, which was basically an employers' movement and had shown little understanding of workingmen's interests, except in cheap bread, an issue now stale. The coming of democracy portended the passing of this school. The reaction against its exclusive emphasis on business profits, to the neglect of human values, found an expression in imperialism and also in an urge toward social reform, which was thus linked with imperialism and will be discussed in the next chapter. Here the point to note is that the extension of the franchise quickened and humanized public interest in the colonies. It did this by giving political power to the class that supplied almost all the emigrants to the colonies, the class in which the personal ties with the colonial empire were knotted. No longer was it politically possible to regard the colonies as mere ledger entries. More and more they were seen as flesh and blood, the same flesh and blood as that of the mother country, as integral parts of it rather than as external possessions. This new concept made the old question "What is the good of the colonies?" seem meaningless. It became common to compare them with the Isle of Man and outlying counties of England. Democracy fostered nationalism in Britain, as in other countries; and appeals to this irrational sentiment to bind the colonial empire together gradually replaced the material arguments against its dissolution.

The contemporary triumph of nationalism in other lands during the decade from 1861 to 1871 was yet another condition that greatly affected the attitude of the British toward the empire. It was then that the bloodiest of the national wars of the nineteenth century decided that the United States was to be one great nation instead of two smaller ones. It was then that both the Italians and the Germans, after centuries of political fragmentation, finally achieved national unity. These were world-shaking events, and they startled many Englishmen into thinking it was high time to unite the kindred people of the mother country and the autonomous colonies under one effective government representative of all, high time because the world seemed to be moving rather swiftly in the direction of the concentration of power based on the nationalist principle.

Disraeli's famous Crystal Palace speech of June 1872 is a landmark in the history of British imperialism. Among the early leaders of the movement there was a large proportion of colonials who had settled in England, and though they brought a welcome revelation that the colonies wanted to remain in the empire, these gentlemen were not otherwise distinguished. Of the English politicians who championed the cause, there were a few from each party, but none of them was of the first rank until the Tory chieftain delivered this famous speech at a party banquet. It gave British imperialism an enormous lift.

Blithely ignoring the fact that there had been no real difference between Liberals and Conservatives in colonial policy, and refraining from any reference to millstones, Disraeli branded the Liberals as the party that had done everything possible for forty years to shake off the empire and had nearly succeeded in doing it. "When those subtle views were adopted by the country under the plausible plea of granting self-government to the colonies, I confess that I myself thought that the tie was broken." He admitted that distant colonies had to have self-government for the management of their own affairs; but he declared that it "ought to have been conceded as part of a great policy of imperial consolidation," embodied in an imperial tariff, imperial control of unappropriated lands, an imperial code that would set forth the military responsibilities of the colonies, and a representative imperial council that would continuously coordinate the interests of the colonies and the parent state. It was a fine-sounding program that was entirely new to him, though not to other imperialists of the day; and never afterward did he make the slightest attempt to carry out any of it. Obviously he was trimming his political sails to catch the veering wind of public opinion.[1] In this he succeeded, for then began the popular tradition, which is by no means wholly true, that the Conservatives upheld the empire and the Liberals neglected it.

We now turn to examine the emergence of the other British imperialism which, by way of contrast, was largely a reaction from continental Europe, had an aggressive character, and found in Disraeli its first proponent and its unrelenting champion.

A new Europe, strange and disturbing, suddenly confronted Britain. One of the twin pillars of her security, the balance of power on the continent, was violently overthrown; and European nationalism, on which Englishmen were wont to smile as a natural and healthy movement that would stabilize peace, took an ominous turn. In quick succession the Prussian army smashed the Austrian and French empires and welded Germany into an empire much more powerful than any in Europe since Napoleon's day, an empire frankly based on Bismarck's ruthless policy of blood and iron. This was the red dawn of the age which we have since characterized as power politics. Might was enthroned as right, and its worshipers glorified its nakedness by chanting the doctrine of the new biological science, the survival of the fittest in the pitiless war of nature.

Nationalism began to wear an ugly mien as a consequence of Bismarck's triumph. German nationalism, having achieved its end through militarism, became married to it, and the example was contagious. Peacetime conscription spread from Prussia almost like an explosion—to the other states of the North German Confederation in 1867, to the Austrian empire in 1868, to the rest of the German empire when it was founded in 1871, to France in 1872, to Italy and Japan in 1873, and to Russia in 1874. The nations of Europe also took to arm-

---

[1] In the same speech he pledged his party to social reform, for he shrewdly saw that this too was a growing cause.

ing themselves economically, each seeking the greatest possible self-sufficiency; and the British dream of a coming millenium built on the universal adoption of free trade was rudely shattered. From the seventies the fateful movement of economic nationalism gathered momentum. A mad Old World was taking shape, and it was bound to affect Britain profoundly. It was separated from her not by a broad ocean but by a narrow strait only twenty miles wide.

A feeling of uneasiness spread through the country during the Franco-Prussian War. Gladstone's ministry was suspected of betraying more than the colonies, for it seemed to be oblivious to the momentous revolution that was taking place across the Channel. The government preserved a strict neutrality, being content with a warning to both belligerents that if either violated Belgian neutrality Britain would enter the conflict on the other side. That war, which she might have prevented by a more active foreign policy, seriously damaged her international position. It robbed her of the one thing that she had got out of the Crimean War—the European prohibition of a Russian fleet on the Black Sea. In 1870, under cover of the Franco-Prussian War, Russia tore up this provision of the Treaty of Paris of 1856; and there was nothing Britain could do about it, except to protest helplessly against a unilateral cancellation of a treaty obligation. Much more injurious was the blow that the Franco-Prussian War dealt to Britain by overturning the Old World. This blow reduced Britain's rank in the hierarchy of the powers, and it was effected in complete disregard of Britain who for generations had played a leading role in the affairs of Europe. In 1871, also, Gladstone's government concluded the Washington Treaty with the United States, which referred the *Alabama* claims to arbitration and bound Britain to pay whatever damages might be assessed. This agreement, to which a later generation of Britons looked back with pride, stirred bitter feelings in Britain at the time. Never before had a major dispute between great powers been submitted to arbitration; and as Britain was on the paying end of the agreement, it struck contemporary Britons as a national humiliation.

Disraeli damned the government for letting the country down in its relations with other powers, and the public discontent with the management of foreign policy undoubtedly weakened Gladstone's hold on the electorate. Yet it was domestic issues that played the major part in deciding the general election of 1874, which turned Gladstone out and brought Disraeli in; and more than a year passed before the new prime minister executed his first imperialist coup.

There is a tradition that the British annexation of the Fiji Islands in 1874, shortly after the Conservatives took office, was a conscious break from the Liberal policy of adding no more colonies to the empire. But recent research has shown that it was not. Ever since 1858 official London had wavered between accepting and rejecting repeated Fijian requests for annexation. Commissioner after commissioner was sent out, and their reports only made the problem more difficult. White settlers, mostly English from Australia, and anarchy were increasing in the islands, whose native population was about 150,000; and the whites were importing kidnaped labor for their plantations because the natives, who had a unique reputation for laziness, would not work on them. As the intervention of some civilized power became more imperative, the burden to be assumed appeared more formidable. For a while London looked around for some other government to undertake the task, but there was no such escape from the dilemma, which became more pressing by the time Disraeli became prime minister. Far from being eager for annexation, he left the matter to his Colonial Secretary, Lord Carnarvon, and urged him to handle it with caution. After months of hesitation, during which he squelched a move of British officials in Fiji to establish a protectorate over the islands, Carnarvon came to the conclusion that annexation was the lesser of two evils. He summed up the situation by saying that English settlers, English capital, and English crime wanted an English government. The strategic consideration that there was no naval base between North America and Australasia seems to have been a very minor item in his calculations. Apparently he attached more weight to clear suggestions from New South Wales and New Zealand—which, to his mortification, they later repudiated—that these colonies would help the mother country to bear the burden of the Fijian administration. It was a minor repetition of what had happened in South Africa. The Conservative administration was acting in the spirit of its Liberal predecessors when it reluctantly added this crown colony to the empire, as a liability rather than an asset. This is not at all surprising, for the international rivalries of Europe had not yet turned to seek an outlet in the scramble for colonies.

The master stroke of Disraeli's career was his purchase for the British government of the controlling block of the Suez Canal shares in 1875. The Frenchman who built the canal, Ferdinand de Lesseps, organized a French company for the purpose and gave half the shares to the khedive of Egypt in return for the franchise. From the launching of this enterprise, successive British governments were hostile to it, as well they might be, because it meant foreign control of the most vital link of communications of the British Empire. Even after the opening of the canal in 1869, Gladstone's government discouraged its use by British ships. But this suicidal attitude was soon abandoned, with the result that British shipping multiplied the traffic on the canal and the revenue of the French company. Four out of every five vessels that passed through were British. While the profits of the company mounted, the khedive plunged into hopeless bankruptcy, for he was a riotous spender who met his interest payments out of new loans. By 1875 his only remaining asset was the canal shares he had inherited, and he decided to sell them. In the summer of that year, rival French interests were bargaining for them and the French government was trying to make up its mind whether it should buy them or not. The whole business was kept secret, but Disraeli's long nose smelt it out. At once he moved swiftly and silently. Within a fortnight he scooped up the prize, with money privately advanced by his friends, the Rothschilds. The announcement of the coup burst like a bombshell. England was jubilant, France chagrined, and the whole world amazed. Disraeli's imperialism, on the alert to advance British interests, had won a mighty victory without shedding a drop of blood, without seizing an inch of territory, without impairing any sovereignty.

"The highway to India is now secure," said the triumphant prime minister. His remark was very characteristic. In harmony with the new spirit stirring in Europe, he thought of the empire in terms of power and influence and prestige; and this cast of mind made him cherish India above all other British possessions. In 1875 he sent the Prince of Wales on a regal tour through India, and in the following year he had parliament add "Empress of India" to the queen's titles.

Here appears another aspect of the Tory chieftain's imperialism: his emphasis on the outward trappings of British rule, on the spectacular side of the empire, its size and splendor, all of which was quite popular and somewhat vulgar. Though deplored by many Englishmen of finer instincts, it contained an inward something that was very sound. The Crown was the only visible symbol of the unity of the empire, with its heterogeneous peoples and governments. Parliament meant little or nothing to most of them. But in their own individual ways they could all understand allegiance to the queen, the personification of the empire, and they had nothing else in common. It was well for the empire that Victoria had rehabilitated the monarchy; and it was only just and natural that the spirit of the empire, rallying round its symbolic head, should exalt the Crown in public esteem.

Jingoism, a common feature of the imperialism that has infected the world since the seventies, got its name in England though it did not begin there. The origin and early use of the word, as will be noted shortly, reflects the dislike and even disgust aroused in many English minds by Disraeli's blustering and bellicose foreign policy in the Near East following a Balkan explosion in 1876. A Slav revolt against Turkish rule in Herzegovina precipitated Serbia and Montenegro into war against Turkey; the Turks defeated these two little independent states only to face a more dangerous rising of their Bulgarian subjects; this new revolt was crushed with wholesale slaughter, rape, and burning that horrified Europe. Russia raged and the western powers fumed. There was loud talk of joint intervention under the treaty of 1856, which gave the Ottoman Empire a European guarantee of its integrity in return for a solemn promise to treat its Christian subjects decently.

Gladstone's fiery tongue and pen led the hue and cry in England against "the unspeakable Turk." He published a pamphlet, *Bulgarian Horrors,* of which two hundred thousand copies were sold. He would expel the Turks "bag and baggage . . . from the provinces they have desolated and profaned." Disraeli pressed Constantinople to stop the atrocities and grant reforms, but he would not combine with the other powers to apply force to Turkey, whose sovereignty, he insisted, must be respected. As the sultan was also the caliph of the Moslem world, a British attack on him might shake the empire in India, where Britain had many millions of Moslem subjects. More important was the fear of playing into the hands of Russia, whose recent denunciation of disarmament on the Black Sea was an obvious step toward realizing her secular ambition of seizing the Dardanelles. The Liberal leader was furious with the government for blocking collective action. He cried out: "God's law should override calculations of political expediency." Disraeli called him an "unprincipled maniac." Never for generations had foreign policy been such a bitter party issue.

In 1877 Russia intervened alone, glad of an opportunity to settle the Balkan problem in her own way. Her army rolled back the Turks almost to the gates of Constantinople in 1878, when the sultan sued for peace and got it by ceding all but a narrow strip of his European territory and by recognizing the establishment of a big Bulgarian state through which Russia might dominate the Balkans. Meanwhile Gladstone looked upon Russia as God's instrument, Disraeli's eyes saw the devil broken loose, and the country was more sorely divided. As the Russian forces advanced toward their strategic goal, a wave of war fever swept through England, and the government rode perilously on the crest of it. Many people sang with great gusto a music hall ditty of the day:

We don't want to fight, but by Jingo if we do,
We've got the ships, we've got the men, we've got the money too.

Thereupon Liberals damned Disraeli and his enthusiastic followers as "jingoes." Nothing daunted, he brought Britain to the very verge of war with Russia. At his request parliament voted large sums for military and naval purposes, and he ordered the Mediterranean squadron to pass the Dardanelles. That was what stopped Russia short of Constantinople and made her negotiate peace. But it was not enough to prevent her from exacting from the Turk conditions that were intolerable to the British government, and so the crisis continued. Disraeli called out the army reserves, he rushed reinforcements to the Mediterranean, and he concluded a secret treaty with Turkey. The terms bound Britain to defend Asia Minor and gave her Cyprus, not as an outright possession but as a leased territory for which she would pay a stipulated annual tribute. In all likelihood war would have followed if the powers of Europe had not agreed with the government in London that there must be a drastic revision of the peace settlement that Russia had just imposed on Turkey.

The upshot was the Congress of Berlin in the summer of 1878, which forced Russia to accept a new settlement. It restored much of what Turkey had lost, it reduced the size of the new Bulgaria by two thirds, it allowed Austria to occupy the Turkish provinces of Bosnia and Herzegovina, and it confirmed the arrangement for the British occupation of Cyprus. From Berlin Disraeli returned home in triumph, bearing, as he said, "peace with honor." The tangible honor was the strategic Mediterranean island. As a potential naval base to guard the Suez Canal, his technical advisers thought less of it than he did, and four years later its value was reduced by the British occupation of Egypt—under Gladstone, who denounced the acquisition of Cyprus as an immoral deal. But there was a greater honor—an intangible one—that the Conservative prime minister brought home. He had recovered the international prestige that Britain had lost under his Liberal predecessor.

Long afterward Lord Salisbury, Disraeli's colleague at Berlin and his successor as head of the Conservative party, confessed "we put our money on the wrong horse," meaning Turkey, and it became fashionable to decry the work of the Berlin Congress. But this condemnation was inspired by developments that no one could foresee in 1878, and still later developments suggest a more charitable judgment. If the rest of Europe had then allowed Russia to control the Balkans, the subsequent history of the world might have been very different—and no better.

Two years after the people acclaimed Disraeli for the brilliant success of his imperialist foreign policy in Europe, they turned him out of power because his government got the country into difficulties in two other parts of the world—Afghanistan and South Africa.

The Second Afghan War, which broke out in 1878 and did not come to an end until 1880, was a product of the chronic hostility between Britain and Russia. For many years Russian policy had been following the line laid down by Alexander II, when he ordered the expansion of his empire in Central Asia as the only way of getting a free hand in Europe and the Near East, where Britain could always count on a European combination to check Russia. He would push his power to the point where he could threaten Britain in India and thereby coerce her into submission. The Russian advance toward India roused British suspicions, which Russian diplomatists tried to explain away by suggesting that this advance differed in no respect from the British expansion in India. There was some truth in the parallel, and Liberals swallowed it as the whole truth. The Conservatives were more wary. So also was the Amir of Afghanistan, Sher Ali. Seeing the British halted on his eastern frontier while the Russians were pressing down on him from the north, he turned to the British for protection. In 1869 and again in 1873 he asked for a defensive alliance, only to meet with a polite refusal. Trapped between two hostile empires, and denied support by the one he preferred, he naturally turned to make the best terms that he could with the other. The Russians were very obliging, for his about-face brought them to the position where they would dig their trap for the British.

The Conservatives came into office determined to checkmate Russia in Afghanistan. Gladly would they have grasped the outstretched hand of the amir to rescue him from the clutches of the bear, but the hand was already withdrawn. Therefore the new government sought security by two other moves. One had long been urged by advisers of the Indian administration. It was the occupation of Quetta, under a treaty signed with the khan of Kalat in 1876, which might enable the British to turn the flank of a hostile Afghanistan. The other move, designed to prevent that country from becoming hostile, was to get Sher Ali to accept a British resident and exclude a Russian one. This was more difficult, and it ultimately led to the British invasion of Afghanistan.

As the British government rallied Europe to thwart the czar's government in the Balkans, the Russians worked feverishly on their eastern trap and there too they encountered increasing British opposition. On the opening day of the Berlin Congress the governor general of Russian Turkistan dispatched a diplomatic mission to Afghanistan, and at the same time he sent off three columns of troops to follow the mission. When the Russian envoy reached Kabul, Sher Ali entered into a definite treaty of alliance with the Russian government. In the meantime, Russia had submitted to the terms set forth in the Congress of Berlin and counterorders had caught up with the troops marching on the Afghan border. But a message to the envoy, informing him that he was too late and warning him against making any promises to the amir, did not arrive until he had committed the Russian government. The result was the discomfiture of the Russians, the confusion of the British, and the undoing of Sher Ali.

On hearing of the arrival and obvious success of the Russian mission, the Viceroy of India, Lord Lytton, immediately persuaded London into letting him insist upon the amir's receiving a British mission also. When the announcement of the approach of this mission reached Kabul, the Russian envoy induced Sher Ali not to receive it, and the British envoy was turned back by threats of violence. This convinced Lord Lytton that he must smoke out the defiant amir with an ultimatum, to which the cabinet in London objected, fearing that bold action against Afghanistan would upset the Berlin settlement. After several stormy sessions, however, London agreed to let Lytton have his way. Sher Ali, vainly relying on the aid that the Russians had promised, continued his defiance, but on the approach of the British columns he fled to Russian territory, where he died early in 1879. In May of that year his son and successor, Yakub, a weak and shifty fellow, signed a treaty that placed Afghan foreign relations under British control and established a permanent British resident in Kabul. The British had got what they wanted—when it was no longer necessary—and soon they got what they did not want in Afghanistan.

On 3 September 1879, the day after the British resident reported by telegram that all was well, he and his whole escort were murdered in a riot of unpaid Afghan soldiers. We still do not know whether Yakub instigated the crime or was a helpless onlooker. The immediate result was another British invasion under Sir Frederick (later Lord) Roberts. Yakub joined him on the march, vowing that he would rather cut grass under the English than try to govern his own people. The would-be grasscutter was removed to India, where he lived on a British pension until his death in 1923. His departure, and the absence of any possible candidate for his throne, left the country without any government and allowed it to lapse into anarchy. Roberts was besieged by a hundred thousand tribesmen, and he was not secure until another British army fought its way in and joined him in Kabul in the spring of 1880. Even then the British occupied only a corner of the country; but they had become more deeply involved than they expected or liked, and they were anxious to extricate themselves.[2]

The debate among British historians over the wisdom of Lytton's Afghan policy still goes on, but British public opinion at the time ran strongly against it for sullying the honor of Britain by an act of unprovoked aggression. Disraeli's victory in Berlin turned sour in Afghanistan, where the war was still raging when the general election was held in the spring of 1880.

Developments in South Africa were even more responsible for the downfall of Disraeli's government. South African conditions, it will be recalled, had converted the Gladstone ministry to the idea of federating the two British colonies and the two Boer republics as the only means of escape from a baffling and burdensome imperial responsibility. The Conservatives thus inherited in 1874 what was in practice, though not in purpose, a forward policy; and they pushed it more vigorously than their predecessors, oblivious of the fact that the annexation of the diamond fields in Griqualand West had already made this policy impossible. In the determined pursuit of the elusive immediate object, the distant goal receded from view; and so occurred the transition from anti-imperialism to imperialism in South Africa.

The British annexation of the Transvaal in 1877 has struck many Englishmen, to say nothing of other people, as an act of naked imperialism. Actually the annexation was undertaken with the double motive of promoting federation and averting a disastrous native war. The Colonial Secretary, Lord Carnarvon, having failed to draw the

---

[2] The cost of this Afghan War was £20,000,000, of which the Indian exchequer bore three quarters and the imperial treasury one quarter.

governments of South Africa into a federal agreement which would then receive parliamentary sanction, reversed his tactics in 1876 by having parliament pass a law empowering them to unite. Local politics in the Cape, whose premier condemned this legislation as a blow aimed at responsible government, discouraged the hope of approaching the task from the south. At the same time circumstances in the northeast offered better prospects of success by an approach from that direction, and also revealed an urgent need for it.

President Burgers of the Transvaal visited Europe in 1875. In London he assured Carnarvon that he was strong for federation under the Union Jack. But he sang a different tune on the continent; there he tried to float a loan for a railway to Delagoa Bay that would assure independence to his country, with the aid of some outside power. Though he failed in this endeavor, the specter of foreign intervention invited preventive intervention by the British. There were, however, much more compelling reasons for the annexation.

Burgers could not govern his unruly people. Because they would not pay taxes, there were only twelve shillings and six pence in the treasury; and the very existence of the state was threatened because the Transvaalers would not submit to any authority and made war upon surrounding tribes, from which the British received appeals for protection. The anarchic republic was a grave danger to all South Africa; for the whole country, though divided politically, was tied together by the omnipresent black problem, and a bloody storm was then brewing in Zululand, on the frontiers of the Transvaal and Natal.

Zulu society bore a startling resemblance to that of ancient Sparta in military organization, discipline, and prowess. The Zulus had a regimental system of drilled soldiers who were not allowed to marry until they had "washed their spears" in enemy blood. Their army was forty thousand strong, and now it had firearms as well as assegais. Cetewayo, highly intelligent and utterly ruthless, had devoted twenty years to the perfecting of this remarkable fighting machine, and he was itching to launch it against his Boer neighbors. Apparently the only thing that had held him back was the personal influence of Sir Theophilus Shepstone, the missionary's son brought up with natives and just knighted for his extraordinarily able management of native affairs in Natal; and the Zulu king was already showing unmistakable signs of breaking loose from his white mentor.

Shepstone's reports on the Zulu menace and on the chaotic conditions in the Transvaal persuaded London that a crisis was at hand and he was the best man to deal with it. Therefore he was given a special commission and sent to Pretoria, where he was well received. As he expected, he found the republic bankrupt, the government helpless, and many responsible burghers, including the president and a majority of his executive council, so alarmed by the anarchy around them and by the dread Zulu war hanging over their heads that they implored him to take the country under British protection. Paul Kruger muttered a warning against tampering with independence, and Shepstone agreed to hold his hand if the Volksraad passed certain necessary reforms. The Volksraad rejected them, elected Kruger vice president, and repeated his warning. Thereupon Shepstone declared annexation inevitable. The Volksraad, alarmed by this pronouncement, adopted some of the rejected reforms and dispersed. Then Shepstone concluded the negotiation with Burgers.

These two men together framed the annexation proclamation. The president said he must issue a formal protest "to keep the noisy portion of the people quiet." The British agent objected, lest this encourage resistance, but he yielded to Burgers' persuasion that all opposition would disappear by the time British troops arrived, for they were to be sent in afterward to maintain order. Accordingly, in April 1877, Shepstone proclaimed the annexation and Burgers published his protest. Meanwhile the Zulu impis were mobilized for an attack; but on the receipt of a warning from Shepstone, dispatched on the eve of the proclamation, that it would be an attack on British territory, Cetewayo sent his soldiers home. He grumbled that he had called them out to fight the Dutch.

So far everything went well, without a single British soldier on Transvaal soil, and the future seemed propitious. The proclamation promised a separate government with its own laws and legislature; and Shepstone assumed the administration, as authorized by his commission, pending the preparation of a new constitution. He continued the old executive council as his new one, after it too made a formal protest against the annexation. Burgers, impoverished by his services to the republic, retired to the Cape; Kruger and another councilor set out for England to demand repeal; but a countermemorial, denouncing the mission and approving annexation, signed by six Volksraad members along with many other burghers, was also sent to England. There the annexation met with general approval, and Carnarvon had a pleasant interview with his two Boer visitors in January 1878. Though he brushed aside their demand as contrary to the wishes of the great majority, they seemed satisfied by his assurances that Dutch would be an official language and every consideration would be given to the desires and interests of the Dutch population. They thereupon offered, on their return, to support the new regime and asked for public employment under it.

Though Shepstone gave the Transvaal its first taste of efficient administration and the imperial government sweetened the dose with a loan of £100,000, a mixture that effected a rapid improvement of trade and public finances, there was growing resentment among the Boers. It was partly their own fault, for they had a congenital aversion to paying taxes and an inborn distrust of any authority but their own; partly Shepstone's fault, for he was too businesslike and autocratic, he issued his decrees without calling the Volksraad together, and he made no move to give the people another legislature; and partly nature's fault, for the new regime was almost immediately cursed by a South African drought more severe than any for a whole generation. By the time Kruger reached home, the fever of discontent had reached such a pitch that he soon turned round and sailed back to London, accompanied by his future general, P. J. Joubert, and bearing mass memorials against annexation. This second mission was no more successful than the first. In September 1878, Carnarvon's successor told the sullen delegates that the Transvaal would remain British and, as a self-governing colony, would be federated with the rest of South Africa for purposes common to all. But public opinion in England was splitting on the question of annexation. The Liberal opposition caught up the cries of the Boers, the agitation in England fed the agitation in the Transvaal, and in both countries it was violently inflamed almost immediately by war with the Zulus.

Cetewayo could not forgive the British for robbing him of his Boer prey, his impis were burning to "wash their spears," and raids across the border into Natal and the Transvaal plainly indicated the dangerous attitude of the Zulus. Sir Bartle Frere, governor of the Cape and high commissioner from 1876, thus faced a challenge which a distinguished career in India had taught him how to meet. In December 1878 he delivered an ultimatum to the Zulu king requiring him to dissolve his army, to substitute trial by law for trial "by rifle shots," and to accept a British resident. This precipitated the Zulu War in January 1879. On the day after it began, Kruger and Joubert presented their report from London to a congress of Transvaalers, who thereupon took a covenant to recover their lost independence. Nine days later the

British suffered a stunning military disaster at the hands of the Zulus. A British regiment encamped at Isandhlwana was surprised and annihilated. Though seven months later Cetewayo was captured and the Zulu military power was broken forever, the disgrace inflicted by the opening engagement could not be wiped out. Throughout South Africa, Isandhlwana seriously damaged the prestige of all white men in the eyes of the natives, and of the British in the eyes of the Boers. In England it raised a public howl against the ministry. Disraeli tried to escape by throwing Frere to the wolves, and the reputation of this devoted servant of the empire was torn to shreds; but this sacrifice did not appease the public. Disraeli's aggressive imperialism, with its wars and rumors of wars, dragged him down to defeat when the people went to the polls. He died in the following year, but his spirit did not die with him.

The general election of 1880 has an interesting significance in the history of British imperialism. It reveals that the British people were not converted to what the rest of the world has since come to recognize as imperialism. The country had the strength to ride roughshod over the difficulties encountered in Afghanistan and South Africa, but it lacked the will. That was why it recoiled before them instead of seeing in them a challenge to greater effort. That was why it turned the government over to Gladstone who lumped together the annexation of the Transvaal, the championing of Turkey against Russia, the acquisition of Cyprus, the invasion of Afghanistan, and the war against the Zulus as monumental proof of the essential immorality of imperialism. But his vehement anti-imperialism no longer envisaged the desertion of the colonies. That was a dead issue. His avowed policy was to avoid all dangerous foreign ventures and to withdraw from those that had embarrassed the fallen government.

The new government's efforts to liquidate these ventures were more fortunate in Central Asia than in South Africa. Lord Ripon, who replaced Lytton as viceroy, had merely to complete an arrangement that Lytton had begun when Abdur Rahman, Yakub's cousin and Dost Mohammed's grandson, appeared upon the scene early in 1880. He had spent the previous eleven years as a refugee and a Russian pensionary in Russian Turkistan, and the Russians now allowed him to return with an armed guard. His late hosts thought he would play their game, but he had fathomed enough of it to reject it in favor of British friendship, if this was still possible. On learning of his arrival, Lytton sent him conciliatory messages; the upshot was an agreement whereby the government of India recognized him as amir, paid him an annual subsidy, and got control of his foreign relations. By this last condition both sides understood that there would be no British interference in the affairs of Afghanistan so long as that country did not threaten to betray the security of India. Abdul Rahman saw to it that there was no interference. A much abler man than his grandfather, and "one of the greatest Asiatics of his day," he soon established and never relaxed his mastery over his unruly people, and he ever guarded the independence of Afghanistan by preserving the British friendship that had helped him to gain his throne.

In South Africa, Gladstone's second ministry made a bad situation worse. When the new government entered office in London, the Transvaalers were preparing to throw the British out. They no longer felt any need for British protection, since the British had smashed the Zulus; and they despised the British for their poor showing in the war against the Zulus. They were also encouraged by the sympathy of their fellows in the Free State and the Cape Colony. There the annexation of the Transvaal had given new life to old fears that the British were scheming to anglicize the whole country, with the result that the Afrikander Bond was organized in 1879. It was an anti-British nationalist movement inspired by the ideal of a Boer republic embracing all South Africa. The Transvaalers were also greatly encouraged by the reports that Kruger and Joubert brought back from London— of British embarrassments in Europe and Central Asia, of violent party strife over South African policy, and of the possibility that the Liberals who denounced the annexation might soon be in power. Subsequent Liberal speeches raised the hopes of the Transvaalers still higher. When they heard of the Liberal victory, their agitation subsided. Their independence seemed assured without their having to fight for it; and Kruger and Joubert wrote Gladstone urging him to satisfy the expectations that he had raised. Many of his supporters backed the request, but he hesitated and then refused, stating that the necessity of preserving order and of protecting the native population in the Transvaal made the continuance of British sovereignty imperative. At the same time Gladstone promised a large measure of self-government. The Transvaalers, who had already lost all faith in such a promise, were dumfounded by the prime minister's reply. To them it was final proof of British perfidy.

Meanwhile the ferment among the natives in South Africa was growing, for Isandhlwana was strong yeast. The most serious trouble with the blacks was in Basutoland where the Cape government, which had taken over the territory in 1871, provoked a rebellion that it could not suppress. The fighting began in September 1880 and ended in April 1881 with the nominal submission of the Basutos. This miserable affair, in which the Cape would brook no imperial interference, was a warning to the British government that it must walk warily in South Africa.[3] It was also a further blow to white prestige.

The whole of South Africa was quivering when the Transvaal storm broke in December 1880, on Dingaan's Day, the much-celebrated day of deliverance of the trekking forefathers of the Transvaal Boers. The old Volksraad, once more in session, decreed the restoration of the republic and elected a triumvirate to take charge of its affairs. The chosen leaders were Kruger, Joubert, and Marthinus Pretorius, the son of the man who had defeated Dingaan's host. On the same day a body of Boers under Piet Cronje opened fire on a British detachment. Soon the other British detachments on the wide veld were overwhelmed or besieged. But from the very beginning of the war both sides feared a fight to the finish. They saw it might spread to the rest of South Africa, and they were haunted by the nightmare of a general black uprising that seemed more imminent than ever and would certainly finish them all.

Negotiations therefore began almost as soon as hostilities commenced. Kruger offered to admit a British commission if the British troops withdrew from the Transvaal, a condition that was rejected. London promised a royal commission with full powers, and ordered the British commander, Sir Richard Colley, to arrange an armistice. He promptly obeyed by proposing terms that were acceptable to the Boers. But the very day before Colley's message reached Kruger, at the end of February 1881, the British commander and half his little force of some five hundred men were killed in the battle of Majuba Hill. The armistice was duly signed, in March, though Majuba had already made it gall and wormwood to the British. The Boer commandos dispersed, the British troops remained, and the commission arrived. It concluded the Convention of Pretoria in August, which guaranteed to the Transvaal "complete self-government, subject to the suzerainty of Her Majesty."

---

[3] By 1883, however, the Cape government sought to get rid of Basutoland by unloading it upon Britain; and the president of the Orange Free State, which was again stung by Basuto inroads, called upon London to intervene. The Basutos too desired the transfer, and early in 1884 their land once more became an imperial protectorate.

Some writers have made sport of this qualification as having only a vague meaning, but the articles of the convention were on the whole very precise. They gave Britain control of the foreign relations of the Transvaal, and for the first time they clearly defined its boundaries. They carefully protected native interests by a number of prescriptions, one of which provided that no enactment specially touching such interests should have any validity without the queen's consent. They made the Transvaal State liable for all the public debt incurred before annexation and much of it afterward. They prohibited discrimination against British goods, and safeguarded the rights of persons other than natives "conforming themselves to the laws of the Transvaal" regarding immigration, trading, property, residence, and taxation. They included nothing on political rights, but in the final negotiations Kruger definitely promised that British subjects would have the same privileges as Boers "so far as burgher rights are concerned" except possibly "in the case of a young person who has just come into the country." The convention was submitted to a newly elected Volksraad, which furiously opposed its ratification but yielded when Kruger bluntly told the members that the only alternative was another war. Thereupon the British troops marched out of the Transvaal down to Natal.

If Gladstone's acceptance of this solution was right, then his earlier refusal was wrong—horribly wrong because it added the curse of bloodshed. By yielding to the Boers on the morrow of the stinging defeat they inflicted on the British at Majuba Hill, he may have averted a horrible tragedy involving all the people in South Africa and many more; but he certainly wounded English pride, he lowered British prestige in the councils of Europe, and he injected new poison into South Africa. There he shattered all faith in the consistency of British policy, he made the British damn the power that had deserted them, and he inspired the Boers with a supreme contempt for this power. Boer nationalism became exalted, and it developed an aggressive imperialist spirit that would put the detested British and the despised blacks in their place. Paul Kruger, whose long term as president of the Transvaal commenced in 1883, aspired to make the Transvaal paramount over all South Africa. As a preliminary step in this direction, he once more sailed for England. There he confronted the colonial secretary with a demand for the recognition of the Transvaal as a sovereign state, and he got some concessions. The Convention of London, 1884, revised the Convention of Pretoria by eliminating the reference to suzerainty and the imperial right to veto native legislation, and by recognizing the Transvaal under its old name—the South African Republic.

By one of the striking ironies of history, Gladstone's second ministry, which had taken office pledged to a policy of withdrawing from new imperial ventures, was already being drawn into new imperial commitments far more extensive than Disraeli had ever dreamed of. No British government could stay out of the great international scramble for colonies that began in the early eighties. But this is such a large subject that we shall have to treat it in a separate chapter; here we may continue with a more general view of the growth of imperialism in Britain from 1880.

That year saw the nearest approach to a clear-cut party division over imperialism. Thenceforth though Conservatives and Liberals alike tried to make political capital out of the issue, and occasionally succeeded in doing so, the only difference between them on this question was that the latter were inclined to follow a more cautious foreign policy. It was a matter of degree rather than of kind, and it reflected a compromise between conflicting views within each party, the balance in Liberal councils being weighted more heavily on the side of caution. In the early eighties we begin to hear of "Liberal imperialists."

British imperialism gathered great momentum during this decade. It was stimulated by the international competition for overseas possessions. Then also the two imperialisms of diverse origin and character, the acquisitive and the consolidating, tended to run together into a many-sided movement that developed old ideas and added new ones. Some of these ideas provoked lively controversy, but this was largely between imperialists and served to popularize the general cause.

One new feature appeared in 1881 with the founding of the National Fair Trade League. It was a child of the depression that settled upon the country in the late seventies. British industry was feeling the pressure of foreign competitors sheltered behind rising tariff walls, and British agriculture was even harder hit because the combination of the revolution in transportation with the mechanization of American farming was at last flooding the British market with cheap food. Amid the encircling gloom many Englishmen lost their faith in free trade and sought salvation by an imperial application of the economic nationalism to which the rest of the world was turning. They demanded protective duties against foreign goods entering the mother country and the dependent parts of the empire, and a preferential trading system with the self-governing colonies, which might be persuaded to lower their tariffs on British manufactures in return for reciprocal advantages for their produce in the market of the mother country. They also urged a positive policy of building up the empire by channeling the outward flow of British capital, skill, and labor to British lands beyond the seas and away from foreign countries where it would develop anti-British strength.

The agitation of the "fair traders" did much to make imperialism the most popular movement of the day, but failed to capture it. There was poetic justice in this failure, for the fair traders were trying to use imperialism to foist protection upon a country of free traders. The most vulnerable point in their program was the fiscal preference for colonial produce because this meant taxes on foreign foodstuffs. That was enough to defeat them. It provoked a decisive outcry. The masses could not stomach the prospect of taxes on food, and their votes could turn out any government. Nevertheless, from this time forth, the idea of imperial preference as a bond of empire had its advocates in Britain, and they found considerable encouragement in colonial opinion. British imperialism thus acquired a protectionist taint. This was identified with a minority wing of the Conservative party, which was therefore split on the issue.

Another imperialist development in Britain at this time was the growth and widespread acceptance of the idea that the empire had a high moral mission to perform in the world. The idea had its roots in the old humanitarian movement, and though both parties cultivated it, Liberals contributed more than Conservatives to its nourishment. This was because, in the conduct of foreign policy, the Liberals were more inclined to be influenced by abstract principles of right and wrong, a characteristic well illustrated in the party strife over the Near Eastern crisis. Two of the leading preachers of the imperial gospel were the Liberal statesman, the Earl of Rosebery, and the outstanding Liberal journalist, W. T. Stead. In 1884 Rosebery declared that the welfare of the human race depended on the British Empire, the greatest potential instrument for civilizing the world; and in the same year Stead lauded British imperial power for offering the best practical hope of preserving the peace of warlike races, of wiping out the horrors of slavery, and of suppressing barbaric practices in vast regions of the earth. It was the call to take up the white man's burden. Kipling had not yet coined the phrase, but the call was clear and British ears were becoming attuned to it. British imperial responsibilities, which had long been an irksome burden, were becoming a noble duty.

This assumption of a lofty moral tone by British imperialism was offensive to people of other nations and provoked growing antagonism to the British Empire as the century drew to a close. To foreign observers Britain was guilty of flagrant hypocrisy. Their charges, which were partly inspired by jealousy of the most successful and by far the largest empire in the world, had some truth in them; but there was quite as much truth in the British justification of the empire. Every nation, seeing a coincidence of its own self-interest with the welfare of others, finds justification in the latter for the pursuit of the former; and the extent to which the actual coincidence is recognized is a measure of the genuineness of the justification. Perhaps the nearest parallel to this British example is the American discovery, at the close of the Second World War, that the United States had a very large interest in the recovery of a prostrate Europe.

J. R. Seeley's *The Expansion of England,* which was published in 1883, did more than any other single publication to popularize imperialism in Britain. It soon became a best seller and a classic; for it was a little book on a big subject that was already attracting much attention, it took current ideas and wove them together in a logical pattern with a large background, and it was remarkably well written. In bold outline it presented the growth of the British Empire as the crowning achievement of the English people who all the time were quite unconscious of what they were really doing. "We seem, as it were, to have conquered and peopled half the world in a fit of absence of mind." This remarkable accomplishment was due to no peculiar national virtue, said Seeley, who abominated jingoism and had no patience with the "bombastic school" of imperialists who were "lost in wonder and ecstasy" at the mere magnitude of the empire and "the energy and heroism which presumably have gone into the making of it." Englishmen could not have made it, he pointed out, if they had not been favored by special circumstances for which they could claim no credit. Because their country was an island, they were freer than their rivals from European entanglements. "Of the five States which competed for the New World, success has fallen to that one . . . which was least hampered by the Old World." In the long series of wars that England fought with them for room to expand overseas, their continental distraction gave her the victory. Incidentally, his emphasis on these struggles planted in the public mind of Britain and of foreign countries, where his book was also widely read, the distorted notion that the empire was largely the fruit of war and conquest.

Seeley's central thesis, however, was that the colonies were simply an extension of England and must be treated as such. Without glorifying English, or rather British, nationalism, he magnified it to imperial proportions as the essential basis for a constitutional reintegration of the empire. Like most of his contemporaries at home, he had no vision of the future commonwealth. Seeley knew so little about the existing colonial empire that he could not see the growth of dominion nationalism, and he completely ignored the existence of the French who formed a third of the Canadian population, and of the Boers who outnumbered the British in South Africa.

More realistic was Seeley's treatment of India. He dismissed as a childish indulgence in national vanity the statement of other writers that the Indian Empire was a monument to the innate superiority of the English people, and he gave a sound analysis of how British rule had been established and might be preserved. Why should it be preserved? This question, he remarked, was not on a parity with that about the value of the colonies. It had validity because no common nationality underlay the connection betweeen England and India, and therefore he faced it squarely. He first weighed the interest of England and found a doubtful balance. She got no tribute or any other direct pecuniary advantage to offset the fact that India locked up an English army and invited trouble with Russia. All she got was indirect—her share in the trade of India, which was open to all nations. If she withdrew, she might lose this through the relapse of India into anarchy or the seizure of the country by some other power. He concluded that it might have been better for England if she had never acquired her Indian Empire, but this he regarded as of little consequence. "Nothing is to be considered for a moment but the well-being of India and England, and of the two countries India, as being by much the more nearly interested, by much the larger, and by much the poorer, is to be considered before England." England had undertaken the momentous task of bringing western civilization to India, and she could not pull out in the middle of the experiment, for the simple reason that India was not yet capable of standing alone. If England were then to abandon India, her action would be "the most inexcusable of all conceivable crimes and might possibly cause the most stupendous of all conceivable calamities." Englishmen, warned Seeley, should not expect gratitude from India. Their rule, which rested on an army composed chiefly of Indians, could be maintained only as it had been established, by the tacit consent and the active support of Indians. "If by any process the population should be welded together into a single nationality," this support would disappear and the British Empire in India would come to an end.

Two other writers of international fame, the Anglo-Indian Rudyard

Kipling, and the American naval officer and historian A. T. Mahan, soon added still more to the impetus of British imperialism. It was in 1886 that the magic of Kipling's pen began to work upon the British public. His vivid tales and vigorous verses inspired myriads of readers with a feeling for the empire such as they had never experienced. Mahan's volumes, the first of which appeared in 1890, had no particular literary appeal; but his masterly interpretation of the governing role that sea power played in history was a penetrating revelation to the country that, more or less blindly, had surpassed all others in the development of sea power and, as a consequence, had attained an unprecedented imperial position.

From the formation of the Imperial Federation League in 1884 to its dissolution in 1893, British imperialism passed through an internal crisis over the question of closer constitutional union of the empire. The League was launched on a wave of imperialist enthusiasm. Its organizers included prominent politicians of both parties, other eminent Englishmen, and outstanding colonials in London; and the press of the country was almost unanimous in loud praise of their avowed purpose, which was to federate the empire. The original promoters thought that the main difficulty would be to persuade the people of the mother country to surrender their exclusive control over foreign policy by taking the people of the self-governing colonies into active partnership. But the inaugural meeting of the League revealed another obstacle that was no less formidable. It was colonial nationalism, which eyed with suspicion any attempt to curb colonial autonomy. When W. H. Smith, the news vendor who had "polished up the handle of the big front door" and become First Lord of the Admiralty in Disraeli's cabinet, proposed a resolution stating that the present relations with the colonies "must inevitably lead" either to the federation or to the disintegration of the empire, the Canadian High Commissioner, Sir Charles Tupper, stoutly denied the existence of this rigorous alternative. Unanimity was restored by the adoption of a compromise: "that, in order to secure the permanent unity of the empire, some form of federation is essential." Thenceforth the League had to be content with propagating the general idea of federation without giving it any concrete form. This discretion was necessary to hold together a membership whose particular views on the subject were widely divergent. Some members favored complete political federation immediately; some hoped for it in the uncertain future but feared defeat by the premature adoption of any definite plan; some would make less sweeping constitutional changes of various kinds; some thought in terms of combining the military resources of the empire; and some, principally colonials, sought to tie it together in a preferential trading system. They all talked volubly of federation, but the only meaning of the word upon which they agreed made it vaguely synonymous with imperial unity.

Harboring all shades of imperialist opinion, the League flourished greatly. Numerous branches sprang up in Great Britain and the colonies, meetings were held all over the empire, and a monthly review, *Imperial Federation,* was published from 1886. In this year there was an Indian and Colonial Exhibition in London, largely initiated by the League, which seized the opportunity to hold a conference that informally represented the whole empire. Immediately afterward the League urged the government to call an official conference or appoint a royal commission comprising accredited representatives of the United Kingdom and the self-governing colonies for the purpose of considering practical measures:

> (a) for placing upon a satisfactory basis the defense of the ports and the commerce of the empire in time of war, (b) for promoting direct intercourse, commercial, postal, and telegraphic, between the several countries of the empire in time of peace, and any other means for securing the closer federation or union of all parts of the empire.

This was the origin of the first Colonial Conference, which was held in the spring of 1887. The occasion was most auspicious; for the empire was then celebrating the golden jubilee of Queen Victoria's accession to the throne, and London was the scene of an imperial pageant that eclipsed any the world had ever seen, even in the most splendid days of Rome. The colonial secretary who called the conference was a leading member of the League, and so also was his successor who presided over the conference. The opening address by the prime minister, the Marquis of Salisbury, focused attention upon mutual defense and ruled out, as impractical for the time being, discussion of federation and of a customs union. Though the conference was only a deliberative body with no power to bind its constituents, it established a valuable precedent by bringing together the governments of the empire for mutual consultation.

To follow up this success, the League under the presidency of Lord Rosebery strove to make the Colonial Conference a permanent institution and to have it work out a practical scheme of closer constitutional union of the empire. To this end a delegation waited upon the prime minister in 1891. Salisbury was very sympathetic. He promised to broach the subject with the colonial governments, but he observed that it would be frivolous to ask their "statesmen to come together here without any definite idea of what ought to be done." His caution was a challenge to the League to abandon its caution, which had held it together, and to formulate a definite scheme.

After months of difficult deliberation the League evolved a tentative plan. As soon as South Africa and Australasia followed the Canadian example of national unification, a Council of Empire should be set up in London. It should be composed of one representative from each of the three dominions along with the most important members of the British cabinet. The development of its functions should be left to the dictation of time and experience. Its primary concern should be imperial defense, and it should supervise the application of the funds appropriated for this purpose by the various governments of the empire. The eventual if not the immediate adoption of a preferential trading system was also suggested, apparently at the behest of Tupper.[4] When this program was presented to the government, in 1893, Gladstone had replaced Salisbury; and though he too professed sympathy with the desire to consolidate the empire, he denounced the idea of abandoning free trade and he declared that the League had not produced the definite scheme that his predecessor had called for. This reply precipitated the dissolution of the League, which Salisbury's challenge had brought nearer; and the imperial federation movement collapsed.

There were later attempts to revive the movement, but they made less impression than the League upon public opinion. More vigorous but no more successful was the renewal of the agitation for an imperial *zollverein,* around the turn of the century when Joseph Chamberlain nearly wrecked the Conservative party over the issue. British free trade blocked the road to commercial unity, and the equal unwillingness of the British government and of the autonomous colonial governments to give up any of their powers barred the way to a constitutional reintegration. Yet the work of the Imperial Federation League had not been in vain. It opened a new path that the empire was to follow, that of consultation between the governments of the mother country and the colonies, the path of the present commonwealth.

---

[4] He claimed that he made this addition "almost singlehanded." It should be noted, however, that in 1887 Cape Colony proposed a duty of two per cent on foreign imports into every part of the empire to help pay for the Royal Navy.

CHAPTER XXVII

More Democracy and the Quest
for Social Justice

IN ENGLAND during the eighties, the adjective "unemployed" became also a noun and the word "unemployment" was coined. These two little developments of our language were surface ripples caused by a deep and growing public concern over the plight of the poor. Why this concern? Were the masses sinking, or was the social conscience rising, or were both changes at work?

One might conclude from what has been said in the previous chapter that the British economy was shrinking under the pressure from the outside world and that, as a consequence, the toiling massses were being squeezed as they had not been in the prosperous third quarter of the century. But before we accept this conclusion we should make a closer examination. The economic blight that settled upon British agriculture, for reasons already noted, was undoubtedly severe. Yet this was of relatively minor importance, since agriculture had become completely subordinate to industry in Britain. Of the male population over ten years old, farming operations employed only one sixth in 1851 and less than one tenth in 1881, a fraction that was to be cut in half during the next thirty years. It was the industrial life of the country that mattered.

The industrial primacy of Britain was obviously passing away, as we have observed and as Englishmen had predicted in the middle of the century. It was inevitable. The industrial resources of the little island were small compared with those of the much larger and newly united Germany, and they could not begin to compare with those of the United States. These two countries were beginning to exploit their resources so vigorously that they were becoming industrial giants. Their production of steel was quickly catching up to that of Britain, which fell behind the American in 1889 and the German shortly afterward. By the middle nineties the United States was mining more coal than Britain. In the new and rapidly expanding electrical and chemical industries, moreover, Germany was away in the lead from the very beginning. Other European countries also contributed, though in a lesser degree, to swing the balance of industrial power against Britain.

In this age of increasing international economic competition, Britain had the most vulnerable economy. Her vital dependence upon foreign trade far exceeded anything known in the previous history of great nations. The bulk of her food had to come from abroad; her people would starve without it. Much of the raw materials for her industries, of which cotton was only an outstanding example, also had to be imported; and to pay for them as well as the food, she had to export industrial products for sale in other lands. Indeed, as Professor Clapham has pointed out, a tight blockade of all her ports might force her into submission for lack of materials and markets before it could reduce her by a shortage of food.

To make things worse for Britain in her exposed position, world prices were falling lower and lower. The demand for gold had leaped far ahead of supply as a consequence of the continental adoption of the gold standard, which began with Germany in 1871 and occasioned heavy government buying, and of the enormous expansion of industrial and agricultural production in Europe and America. The general price level began to fall in 1873 and, with only an occasional and very partial recovery, it continued to decline until 1896—a long ebb tide. The total drop was 40 per cent, and more than half of this occurred between 1882 and 1887. British business lost its buoyancy. Its profits, once fat, became lean; and it had so little appetite for new capital that surplus funds accumulated on the Lombard Street market, depressing the rate of interest except in time of crisis. Moreover, in the late seventies, when Britain had to liquidate some of her foreign investments in order to pay her way, Englishmen began to worry over the adverse balance of trade, which had become chronic, and to fear that their country was doomed to live by eating into its capital.

Despite all these conditions, which drew many laments from British sons of Jeremiah, the British economy was not lapsing into a state of decline. The reduction of foreign assets was only slight and temporary. It came to an end in 1880 and was not resumed until after the outbreak of war in 1914. Meanwhile most of the earnings from investments abroad went to increase those investments. The adverse balance of trade was only in visible goods. The gap was filled by "invisible exports," such as the services of British ships, British bankers, and British insurance companies. London was still the financial center of the world and sterling was the great international currency. Britain owned a third of the world's ocean-going tonnage and five eighths of its ocean-going steam tonnage. Her shipping position was becoming stronger. In the middle seventies a third of the tonnage that entered her ports with overseas cargoes was foreign. In the middle eighties it was scarcely a quarter, when the total was larger. Her coasting traffic, which was proportionately much greater than that of any other nation because no part of the country was more than seventy miles from the sea, was open to ships of all nations, and yet the foreigner got less than half of one per cent of it.

World trade was expanding, and Britain's share of it was increasing absolutely, though not relatively. The causal effect between trade and prices was then the opposite of what has since become familiar. Falling prices, instead of causing a reduction of trade, were caused by an increase of trade that, as we have seen, exceeded the growth of the world's stock of gold. Thus even when the money value of British foreign trade did not increase, as sometimes happened, the real value did, because prices were lower. Britain's coal production was maintaining its lead over that of Germany, it was mounting at approximately the same rate as in the previous quarter of the century, and a larger proportion of it was going to the continent. As for industrial competition in international markets, the United States took little part in it; for the American industrial output, though now considerably greater than that of Britain, was almost wholly absorbed at home. German manufactures, however, were pushing their way in the world, even into England, where they became surprisingly common when a new law required goods to be labeled with the name of the country that made them. Yet many of these articles were of a kind that Britain did not produce, a fact that limited the impact of German competition abroad as well as in Britain. The industrial production of the rest of Europe was even more complementary to that of Britain.

The growth of the British population, which had long since committed the country to a crowded life of dependence on foreign trade, reached the thirty million mark in the early eighties, and the rate of growth continued with little change. Births practically doubled deaths, and emigration drained off much less than half the natural increase.

There was practically no distress emigration. That had ceased when the flight from stricken Ireland died down, and now it was observable that, on the whole, the fluctuating tide of emigration rose with good times and the export of capital.

That distress among the masses was not spreading is more clearly indicated by what we know about unemployment. Apparently there was no more of it in the fourth quarter of the century than in the third. Unfortunately the statistics of unemployment in the earlier period are so fragmentary and unreliable that they offer no basis of comparison with the latter period. Not until the beginning of the eighties was there any composite figure, and then only for trade union labor. Nevertheless, from trade union calculations and from other abundant evidence where they are weak, three years stand out as by far the greatest peaks of unemployment in the second half of the century, 1858, 1879, and 1886; of these the first was the worst and the second was worse than the third, when a group of trade unions reported that 10 per cent of their members were unemployed; and on an average, employment was about as good from 1881 to 1888 as it was from 1851 to 1858. Although economists are sometimes wrong, Alfred Marshall was usually right; and he told a royal commission in 1888 that he believed there had not been "a larger number of unemployed during the last ten years than in any other consecutive ten years." Yet two of the above three worst years were in this decade, and the air was heavy with gloomy talk of unemployment and trade depression, the subject of a full-dress inquiry by a royal commission in 1885–86.

When we turn to wages, we find that the average worker was better off than he had ever been. It is true that money wages, which had risen 60 per cent during the third quarter of the century, showed no such gain during the last quarter, and for a while they sank to a lower level. But this was never more than about 6.5 per cent below the previous high of 1874; from 1888 there was a rise to a new high; and, what is much more important, all this shifting has to be related to the movement of prices. California and Australia made them jump 35 per cent between 1851 and 1854 and for the next twenty years they remained fairly steady, with the result that real wages fell back at first and at the end of the next two decades registered much less than half the gain of money wages. Then prices passed their peak a year before money wages, and slid faster. Down and down they went while money wages slumped, wavered, and recovered; and the gap between them widened until prices hit bottom in 1896, 40 per cent below the high point of 1873. Meanwhile the average worker's real wage continued to go up and up through no effort of his own and almost without his realizing it. Not until 1900, when climbing prices overtook wage rates, did real wages begin to sag, ushering in a new phase of the labor movement. Their unbroken rise in the fourth quarter of the century equaled and may have exceeded the gain in the third quarter.

Even in agriculture—the one sector of the national economy that suffered a damaging blow from outside—wages improved after the initial shock. The continued and rather ineffectual effort to unionize agricultural labor seems to have contributed nothing to this improvement. The explanation of the apparent anomaly is to be found in the general prosperity of the country. Though American competition slashed the profits of British agriculture, causing much rural unemployment, and though British farmers then turned to improve their methods so that they could operate with less labor, the decline in the demand for agricultural labor was soon offset by the decline in supply, thanks to the opportunites for other employment that paid better. Thus labor escaped from the blow, which therefore fell on two other classes. British agriculture managed to survive by means of drastic cuts in farmers' profits and more especially in landlords' rents.

The conclusion to which all this leads is that the British economy, taken as a whole, was expanding rather than contracting in proportion to the population, that the toiling masses were not the victims of a new squeeze, and that the ferment of the time was the working of an awakened social conscience. But before we examine the stirrings of this conscience we should notice the advance of political democracy, which derived a stimulus from it and, in turn, imparted a greater stimulus to it.

In 1884 parliament gave the vote to workers in rural Britain on the same terms as in the towns. Though coming on top of the crisis in agriculture, this reform was not the result of it. From 1867, when both political parties cooperated to enfranchise urban labor, the extension of the electorate to include labor outside the towns was merely a matter of time. Justice demanded it, and neither party would deny it. Yet there was no great cry for it, such as had arisen in 1866; and when Gladstone introduced the bill to remove the anomaly, the Conservatives raised a loud cry against the proposal. Why the uproar?

Much more than the agricultural vote was at stake, for a large population engaged in other pursuits, notably mining, lived outside the legal boundaries of the towns. The measure would add two million to an electorate of three million. Some Liberals, even in the cabinet, thought this was going too far all at once, and more Conservatives were sure of it. The fight, however, turned on another issue. The Conservatives saw their safe country constituencies swamped by new voters attached to the Liberal cause, and therefore they demanded that a redistribution bill be attached to the franchise bill as the price for the passage of the latter. Gladstone insisted on dealing with redistribution later, and the Conservatives, beaten in the Commons, took their revenge in the Lords. The rejection of the bill by the upper chamber started a cry that has haunted British politics ever since, the cry of "ending or mending" the House of Lords.

As both parties shrank from throwing the Lords into the arena of a general election, their leaders met privately and dissolved the deadlock in generous cups of tea. Assured that Gladstone was not trying to play a party trick and would not spring an election before the adoption of a just redistribution, the Conservatives yielded and the bill became law during the autumn session. Early in 1885 the redistribution bill followed, merging small boroughs with the counties and dividing the latter into single-member constituencies according to population. The Chartist movement was dead and buried, but its principles were marching on.

The logical sequel to this extension of the democratic franchise for parliamentary elections was the parallel extension, from urban to rural Britain, of local self-government; and this soon followed almost as a matter of course, each party again making its own contribution. A Conservative ministry in 1888 passed an act establishing elected county councils and transferring to them the administrative powers that the appointed justices of the peace had long exercised in their quarter sessions; and in 1894 a Liberal government completed the system by an act that set up elective self-government in county subdivisions known as rural districts and also in the much smaller and older units, the parishes.

Labor legislation was one expression of the growing democratic spirit of the age. The law of 1871, which permitted strikes and at the same time the imprisonment of seven women for merely saying "Bah" to one blackleg, was a bitter parody of the nursery-rhyme mother's reply to her daughter who wanted to swim. It alienated working-class voters from the government that passed it. The lesson was not lost on Disraeli when he won the next general election, in 1874. Almost as soon as he became prime minister he appointed a royal commission on trade unions. Its report guided the government in preparing an enactment of 1875 that came to be regarded as organized labor's charter of freedom. It amended the criminal law so that it could not ensnare peaceful picketers. What is more important, because conspiracy "was still the sport of judicial indiscretion," it declared that nothing done by two or more persons in a labor dispute was punishable as a conspiracy, unless it would have been a crime if committed by one person. This has been called class legislation because it clipped the wings of the judges only when they would apply the law of conspiracy to labor disputes. For the liberty the government thus gave, it received an almost unanimous vote of thanks from the Trade Union Congress.

Another noteworthy piece of labor legislation of this time was, unlike the reform just mentioned, forced upon the government. It was the work of Samuel Plimsoll, a businessman who sat as an independent Liberal in the House of Commons. At one stage of his career he had fallen into such poverty that he had to live on less than eight shillings a week in London. From sharing the struggles of the poor, he rose with a crusading zeal on their behalf. He devoted himself chiefly to saving the lives of seamen in the merchant marine. It was he who exposed the scandal of "coffin-ships," unseaworthy and overladen vessels, often heavily insured, which brought their callous owners fat profits even when they were lost at sea with all hands on board.

Singlehanded and relentlessly, Plimsoll fought for a law to protect crews against these avoidable risks, and at last, in 1875, a member of the government brought in a bill for the purpose. Then Disraeli announced its withdrawal to make way for other business, and Plimsoll went wild. He shook his fist at the Speaker, denounced fellow members as villains, and damned shipowners who made fortunes out of drowned sailors. Far from losing his cause with his temper, he so startled the conscience of the country that the cabinet bowed before the storm. A temporary measure was pushed through parliament, and in 1876 it was replaced by a more carefully considered permanent one, the Merchant Shipping Act. One of the stringent regulations then imposed, and since improved, to protect seamen has left its mark on every British merchant vessel to this day—the circle with a horizontal line through the middle to show the limit of loading, very appropriately known as Plimsoll's mark or Plimsoll's line.

During the same administration a royal commission worked through the jungle of labor legislation that had grown since the thirties to cover practically the whole field of manufacturing industry. The task took two years but was worth it. The result was the great consolidating act of 1878, which revised, simplified, and codified the law on working conditions to protect life, limb, and health. Subsequent administrations added improvements here and there, but the main features of the 1878 law were admittedly so good that they were continued with little change in the next consolidation, which came in 1901.

The first Employers' Liability Act was passed in 1880. Hitherto the only law on the question was the common law, which applied also in the United States, and it denied employees the protection it gave to the public. It held the employer responsible for injuries to the public even if they were caused by an employee's negligence or disobedience, apparently on the assumption that an ordinary workman was not worth suing; whereas by the doctrine of "common employment," it made the employer liable to his employees only for injuries caused directly by his own negligence, which meant that for most injuries to workmen he was not liable at all. The trade unions had long pressed for the removal of this restriction, and now, as a consequence, statute law began to cut away the objectionable rule of the common law. The act of 1880 did nothing for seamen, domestic servants, and those who were not engaged in manual labor; but it qualified the old doctrine in its application to other classes of labor and practically abolished it for railroad employees.

As the law still turned on proof of negligence, employers evaded much of their new liability by taking advantage of legal technicalities; and many employers escaped entirely by contracting out of it, for there was nothing in the law to prevent their hiring men on the express condition that the latter waive their rights under the act. These two holes, which threatened to drain the law of its substance, were plugged in 1897 by the Workmen's Compensation Act. This measure wrought a legal revolution by casting out consideration of negligence, even on the part of the injured, and by establishing the principle, then novel but now common, that compensation for injury or death suffered by an employee at his work is due from the employer. It was a Conservative government that took this radical step, which compelled employers to be insurers against the risk of accidents to those in their service. At first there was much concern over the financial obligation thus thrust upon industry, but industry quickly found that the rates for such insurance were very reasonable. The act was a bold experiment and therefore did not cover all industry, but the experiment proved to be so successful that later its application was made general.

Britain was not the first country to adopt such a scheme. Bismarck's Germany was the pioneer in the field of social security legislation, having enacted the Sickness Insurance Law in 1883, the Accident Insurance laws of 1884 and 1885, and the Old Age Insurance Law in 1889. But the motives of the iron chancellor bore only a superficial resemblance to those of the government in London, and the German example had little more influence in England than in the United States.

Bismarck's prime object was to exalt the power of the state over its subjects, a concept that was utterly foreign to the British mind, steeped in ideals of individual liberty. Bismarck hated and feared the growing movement of social democracy, fostered by Germany's new industrialism, which would ruin his life's work. Therefore he launched harsh repressive laws to kill the movement and, failing in this, he tried to suck the life out of it by drawing off its followers with social legislation. He sought to bind the masses to the state by making the state pay the whole cost of their social security. But he had to compromise his program to get it through the Reichstag, which balked at the prospect of the enormous public expense, the dangerous concentration of control in the hands of the government, and the injurious effect upon the morale of the workers. All he could get by way of state payment was a minor contribution to old age insurance. The employers were compelled to carry the whole cost of accident insurance. The rest of the burden was divided between them and their employees, though the one thing that Bismarck had been most anxious to avoid was a compulsory contribution by the workers.

How little the British program of social security owes to that of Germany becomes apparent when we examine the background of the former. It was the fruit of an older and indigenous growth. A century before Bismarck introduced his famous insurance laws, the proliferation of little Friendly Societies in England inspired a Devonshire parson, John Acland, with the idea that the problem of social security was a national one, far too big for the nibbling efforts of these small clubs of poor men, and that the country as a whole should tackle it. Thereupon he worked out a comprehensive plan, which he published as a pamphlet and submitted as a bill to the House of Commons in 1786. It provided for insurance against sickness, unemployment, and old age, and also for marriage and maternity benefits, to be paid by a national organization supported by contributions from the state and from all adult workers of both sexes. It was an astonishingly accurate anticipation of what was to be enacted generations afterward, much too accurate for parliament to take it seriously. Parliament, however, began to encourage the formation of Friendly Societies because they helped to keep the poor rates down. By an act of 1793, the societies that registered got legal recognition and other privileges.

Thereafter, for many decades, this cooperative effort of the workers was the only conscious approach to the problem of social security; and as such, the government gave further encouragement to Friendly Societies. In 1819, at the height of the postwar reaction, parliament invited them, by a guarantee of high interest rates, to deposit their funds with the national debt commission, and it required the justices of quarter sessions, with whom they registered, to see that their regulations rested on sound principles. As this was a task beyond the capacity of the country squires who sat on the bench, an act of ten years later transferred control to a central authority. The previous act had brought the Friendly Societies to the door of the barrister of the debt commission, a remarkable man who was to lift them up and make them strong—John Tidd Pratt. He was appointed public examiner of Friendly Societies, and thenceforth he devoted himself to their cause until he died in 1870. A barrister of distinction and perhaps the best government expert of that reforming age, he administered the law and shaped it in their best interest. But it was not through the law that he did most for them. His statutory authority over them was as small as his influence was great. His numerous official reports and other publications inculcated the soundest principles of organization and management, and exposed incompetence and fraud. More particularly Pratt introduced the new actuarial science into the operation of the societies, giving them a financial strength that they had not possessed; and he did much to pull the movement away from the pubs and to concentrate its energies on social security.

The increasing importance of the Friendly Societies—by 1850 their membership included two thirds of the Lancashire working population—owed a great deal to a new feature that appeared in the middle of the century. It was the rapid rise of large fraternal orders of workingmen, such as the Odd Fellows, the Foresters, the Druids, and the Rechabites, some of which spread to the United States as well as to British lands beyond the seas. They attracted recruits by their affectation of mystery—after the fashion of the Masonic Order—by the advantages inherent in federal organizations, and by their advocacy of temperance. Here it is interesting to note that the temperance movement was making great strides in Britain, because organized labor had come to realize that overindulgence in alcohol drowned the working-man's future happiness along with his present miseries. In addition to the workingmen's fraternal orders there were, of course, the trade unions, which commonly sought legal protection by registering as Friendly Societies and operating as such. But for the most part all these mutual benefit organizations, new and old, large and small, did not reach below the level of skilled labor.

To meet the poorer people's needs for social security, another large development began in the years around the middle of the century, when collecting societies sprang up and some commercial companies commenced to cultivate the field of so-called industrial insurance. The leader in the latter was the Prudential Assurance Company, which would defray the funeral expenses of a whole household and make small payments to dependents and the aged. As both of these new services depended upon a house-to-house collection of small weekly premiums, often only a few pennies, the administrative expenses ate up a large proportion of the contributions, sometimes more than half. Indeed the cost would have been higher still if both agencies had not been able to count on a high percentage of lapse. Thus, on an average, the poorer people got less for their money and the poorest got nothing at all, their policies having been forfeited.

Such conditions induced the government, which could provide the same social insurance much more cheaply, to enter the business. As this was during the hard times created by the American Civil War, before the enfranchisement of the urban proletariate, there was no political ax to grind in the venture. Pure pity for the poor inspired the act of 1864, which authorized the national debt commission, using the post office as agent, to sell life insurance and annuities at cost. The result was very disappointing, even after the passage of an amending act in 1882. The public scheme languished while the collecting societies and the commercial companies flourished like a green bay tree. The people they served needed the insurance and were willing to pay a high price for it, yet they would not go after it. It had to go after them. As this was what made it so expensive, there could be no thought of the government's following suit. There seemed to be no possible solution for this particular phase of the problem until at long last, during the Second World War, after the state had arranged for other kinds of social security, the Beveridge Report proposed the nationalization of industrial life insurance.

One might suppose that, with the advent of democracy, organized labor would press parliament to enact a social security program. The democratic franchise, which was first exercised in 1868; the annual Trade Union Congress, or parliament of labor, which met for the first time in the same year; the Parliamentary Committee, elected in each Congress from 1871 to work for labor in the lobby of the House of Commons; and the general election of 1874, in which organized labor played a possibly decisive part and won its first two seats; all pointed toward the day when labor would be the strongest political power in the land. But it then had no such aspirations. The trade unions were little interested in politics, once they got their charter of liberty in 1875. Their finances were healthy and they had their own comprehensive provisions for social security; for they comprised only the aristocracy of labor, the well-paid ranks of the highly skilled. They were smug middle class, and they were not shaken out of their complacency until late in the eighties.

The plight of the poorer classes, who could not help themselves, began to dawn on the social conscience when the ghost of Acland came to life in the person of another Anglican parson, Canon William Blackley. In 1878 he published a proposal that soon aroused wide interest. It called for compulsory insurance with the state to provide sick benefits and old age pensions. The steep rise of unemployment to a peak in 1879 was undoubtedly a disturbing factor. But it was not until 1880, when economic conditions had much improved, that the great ferment began with the English discovery of a new American book, *Progress and Poverty* by Henry George.

Witnessing the orgy of land speculation in California and the "shocking contrast between monstrous wealth and debasing want" in New York, this unsuccessful sailor, printer, editor, and gold miner concluded that the economic ills of society sprang from the private ownership of land. This, he said, had no more justification in morality or reason than private ownership of air or sunlight would have. The land belonged by right to all the people of the country, who collectively gave it the value it possessed for the profit of the few who monopolized it. His diagnosis was not new, but his prescription was original. As the cancer was too deep-seated for removal by a major operation, he would cure it, as we might say, by financial X-ray treatment. While leaving the landlords in undisturbed possession of nominal ownership, the state should tax them to the full extent of what he was the first to label "the unearned increment." Because the yield would be more than sufficient to meet all the ordinary expenses of government, no other levy would be necessary and his would be the "single tax."

The popularity of the book—it was a best seller in England for about three years—was probably as much the effect as the cause of the growing interest in the problem it attacked. It focused attention more on the disorder than on the prescribed remedy, and it started people to think in terms of nationalizing the land and other means of production. The contemporary revival of socialism from its generation-long insular slumber was likewise both cause and effect of the awakening social conscience, and this revival also took the form of an intellectual rather than a working-class movement.

Two brands of socialism appeared, and they would have nothing to do with each other. The Social Democratic Federation, organized in 1881, preached the gospel of Karl Marx and directed its appeal to the masses, without making any impression upon them. Very different and much more important was the socialism of the Fabian Society, founded in 1883. The Fabians were a select group[1] of keen intellectuals who eschewed mass meeetings and all cheap propaganda and were utterly opposed to revolution. They were evolutionists who, in true British fashion, would gradually transform the existing order by wholly peaceful and constitutional means. Therefore they worked unceasingly to educate the influential members of the public. They undertook thorough investigations, the results of which they published in sober pamphlets and serious lectures, and they cultivated their not inconsiderable friendships with politicians and statesmen. They made British socialism respectable by divorcing it from violence and atheism and clothing it in sweet reasonableness.

More and more the educated classes were discussing what was wrong with society and how to set it right. Their conscience was sorely troubled by the discovery of the human misery in the swarming slums of the big cities. The outstanding revelation of the day was in the pages of *The Bitter Cry of Outcast London,* a pamphlet published in 1883 by a nonconformist divine named Reaney. No longer could the well fed sustain the old thesis that poverty was a crime that carried its own punishment. It was generally agreed that the poor law and charity were only palliatives, that destitution and its attendant degradation of

---

[1] Including the serious George Bernard Shaw, the more serious H. G. Wells, and the most serious Sidney Webb.

health and morals were preventable evils, that organized society should cure them and could cure them by action based on careful investigation. Early in 1884, when the opposition leader in parliament moved for a royal commission on the housing of the poor, the government promptly appointed one, with the result that there were more revelations. The same year saw the beginning of a social service movement that soon spread and invaded the United States. It was the founding of Toynbee Hall,[2] a settlement of Oxford men in the crowded eastern part of London.

In 1885 Joseph Chamberlain, the wealthy manufacturer who had practiced municipal socialism as mayor of Birmingham and was now the radical stalwart in the Liberal camp, delivered a number of speeches that reverberated throughout the land. One, in which he asked what ransom property would pay for the security it enjoyed under the law, was a straight sermon on the duties that possessors of property owed to society and a solemn warning that, if they did not discharge these duties, they might lose their privileges of ownership. In several speeches he attacked his party for its timidity and proposed his "unauthorized program," which would soak the rich to rescue the poor, particularly by providing every distressed, and now enfranchised, laborer with "three acres and a cow." In yet another he proclaimed, in words that have a familiar ring:

> Now that we have a Government of the people by the people, we will go on and make it the Government for the people in which all shall cooperate in order to secure to every man his natural rights, his right to existence, and to a fair enjoyment of it.
>
> I shall be told tomorrow that this is Socialism. I have learnt not to be afraid of words that are flung in my face instead of argument. Of course it is Socialism! The Poor Law is Socialism, the Education Act is Socialism, the greater part of municipal work is Socialism, and every kindly act of legislation by which the community has sought to discharge its responsibilities and its obligations to the poor is Socialism. But it is none the worse for that. . . . I do not pretend that for every grievance a remedy will be found. But we must try experiments, as we are bound to do. Let us continue to pursue our work with this object, and if we fail, let us try again and again till we succeed.

---

[2] In memory of Arnold Toynbee, the economic historian and social worker who died in 1883, six years before the birth of his nephew and namesake, the philosophical historian.

That was also the time when Lord Randolph Churchill, the brilliant and radical young Tory who would outliberal the Liberals, shot upward in the political firmament. As chancellor of the exchequer in 1886, he prepared a budget that would have shifted the weight of taxation upward in the scale of wealth. Some of his cabinet colleagues balked, and rather than compromise his principle he resigned his office. He never regretted his action, and he never recovered from it. He was a spent force, but the quest for social justice was stronger than ever.

It was in 1886 that the great merchant and shipowner Charles Booth commenced his monumental work, a scientific study of the London poor, for which he drew heavily on his own fortune and gathered a team of distinguished investigators.[3] No other social survey in any country has been so extensive, so thorough, and so impressive as this pioneer enterprise. The first of Booth's eighteen volumes on *Life and Labor in London* appeared in 1889. In the following year his namesake William Booth, who had launched the Salvation Army in 1878 and possessed intimate knowledge of metropolitan depravity, published his famous book *In Darkest London, and the Way Out,* from which we got the phrase "the submerged tenth." The title of William Booth's book was obviously, and wisely, cribbed from another work that had just created a popular sensation, Stanley's *In Darkest Africa.* The implied comparison was challenging, and it soon became apparent that William Booth's tenth was a gross underestimate. By 1891 Charles Booth demonstrated, to the general astonishment and his own surprise, that in the wealthiest city of the world a third of the whole population lived below "the poverty line" and that two thirds of the people in some large districts of the city were in this sad condition.

Meanwhile the rapid increase of unemployment in 1886 released an insurgent movement in the ranks of organized labor. Aggressive young leaders like John Burns attacked their staid elders for their "selfish and snobbish desertion" of their less fortunate nonunionized fellow workers and denounced their betrayal of organized labor by holding it aloof from the vital game of national politics. It was impossible to democratize trade unionism by reaching down and organizing the unskilled workers, among whom previous efforts at unionization had failed, without discarding what had become the major purpose of the union movement—the mutual provision of social security. The poorer

---

[3] Including Beatrice Potter, who later married Sidney Webb and the history of trade unionism.

workers could not afford it, and John Burns insisted that the existing unions could not afford it either. In 1887 he declared:

> Their reckless assumption of the duties and responsibilities that only the State or whole community can discharge, in the nature of sick and superannuation benefits, at the instance of the middle class, is crushing out the larger Unions by taxing their members to an unbearable extent. This so cripples them that the fear of being unable to discharge their friendly society liabilities often makes them submit to encroachments by the masters without protest. The result of this is that all of them have ceased to be Unions for maintaining the rights of labor, and have degenerated into mere middle and upper class rate-reducing institutions.

The British labor movement was approaching a serious crisis. The Front Bench or, as we might call them, the Old Guard, stubbornly resisted the demand for an aggressive policy, and the insurgent leaders threatened to break away. The latter had a growing following—and somewhere else to go, for Burns and others of them were then also members of the Social Democratic Federation. At the same time there were signs of an uneasy stirring among the unorganized workers. Therefore behind the struggle between the Old Unionism and the New Unionism loomed a larger and graver issue. It was whether trade unionism or militant socialism would capture the rank and file of labor.

Outside influences played an important if not a decisive part in settling the issue. In the summer of 1888 between six and seven hundred wretchedly paid women in the match factories of London went on strike. Their cause seemed to be as desperate as they were, for they had neither funds nor organization. But the very helplessness of these London "match girls" made a strong appeal to the sympathy of the general public. Hundreds of people in all classes subscribed money to help them, and in a fortnight the pressure of public opinion broke the obstinacy of their employers. It was the first victory of the New Unionism, and the lesson was not lost on other workers and employers. In the spring of 1889 Burns, who had just been elected to the London County Council, and others got the London gas-stokers to organize. Thousands enrolled, and in August they demanded an eight-hour instead of a twelve-hour day. The three gas companies yielded without a struggle. Immediately there was a successful drive to unionize the much larger army of unskilled dock laborers of London, who then struck for a wage of 6d. an hour, 8d. for overtime, and no hiring for less than four hours. The two powerful unions of the skilled stevedores struck in sympathy, and for five weeks the greatest port in the world was paralyzed. Labor was gaining solidarity, and again the public came to the aid of the strikers. With £18,000 collected at home and £30,000 cabled from Australia, Burns established an effective system of strike pay and bought off the East End loafers who were potential strike-breakers. Newspapers, clergymen, shareholders, shipowners, and merchants combined to force the dock companies to accept mediation and grant the dockers' demands.

The success of this great London dock strike of 1889 turned the crisis in the British labor movement. The triumphant New Unionism spread rapidly among the unskilled laborers and even among white-collar workers. Burns and Tom Man, the president of the dockers' union, left the Social Democratic Federation; the defection of the New Unionism scotched revolutionary socialism; and organized labor, though becoming more socialist, sought to gain its socialist ends only by the democratic process and constitutional means.

National insurance for social security was attracting more public attention. During the eighties, in parliament and elsewhere, there was much discussion of Blackley's scheme; and in 1891 Charles Booth came out with another. He would pay old age pensions out of taxes, and to everybody, rich and poor alike, on the avowed principle that the state should provide an honorable rather than a pauper maintenance for the aged. It was the most daring of the various proposals of the time, among which was that of Chamberlain, who urged voluntary insurance subsidized by the government. There ensued a long and loud "battle of the plans." A royal commission appointed by Gladstone, a committee of "experts" selected by Salisbury, and several parliamentary committees, all in turn wrestled with the problem—as vainly as Jacob did with the angel. Though the whole issue of social security was a very live one, it brought no positive government action until the first decade of the nineteenth century. Why were the earnest public discussions of the eighties and nineties so slow in producing legislative results?

One thing that stood in the way was, paradoxically, the social security that workingmen had already achieved for themselves. As Clapham has observed, there was a great and well-grounded reluctance to do anything that might weaken the voluntary efforts of the Friendly Societies and the trade unions, a reluctance that dictated circumspection and delay. Yet this was by no means the only paralyzing influence. A further explanation lies in the dynamics of politics.

The competition between the two historic political parties to win popular favor, which might have operated to speed the development of social security legislation, was sidetracked by other public issues that thrust themselves forward; and organized labor was still so shy of national politics that it shrank from playing an independent part in the great game. Thanks to the insurgent movement in trade unionism, eleven workingmen were elected to parliament in 1885; but like the original two of 1874, they did not form a separate party. They attached themselves as a sort of tail to the Liberals, and were therefore known as Lib-Labs. This little tail could not control the dog, and almost immediately, as we shall see in a later chapter, the dog began to chase a cat—Home Rule for Ireland—with the result that the Liberal party fell into a state of exhaustion that lasted until the early years of the next century. Meanwhile the Conservatives yielded to another temptation. They tried to ride high on the rising tide of imperialism, which was sweeping over the world to reach a British climax in the Boer War about the same time as it reached an American climax in the Spanish-American War. Labor was also to blame; for the tail still stuck to the Liberals, and the Conservatives could never have done what they did in these years if they had not been able to win a large proportion of working-class votes.

The first independent labor members of parliament, John Burns, Keir Hardie, and one other, were elected in 1892, along with twelve Lib-Labs; and the flaming red tie and the blaring brass band with which Keir Hardie arrived to take his seat in the House of Commons were loud symbols of a political movement that had a long uphill fight ahead. The Independent Labor Party, which he founded in the following year, never had much parliamentary success. Its frankly socialist program was too advanced for the ordinary British workingman. Every one of the twenty-eight I.L.P. candidates in the general election of 1895 was defeated. Failure at the polls, however, did not mean that the party had no political influence, for the vigorous agitation of its adherents leavened the lump of trade unionism to seek direct labor representation in parliament. In 1899 the Trade Union Congress adopted a resolution, drafted by members of the I.L.P., calling for joint action by the trade unions, the cooperative societies, and the socialist organizations for political purposes. In the following year this led to the birth of the Labor Party, which remained a rather sickly babe with no more than four representatives in parliament until the general election of January 1906.

Then the day of social security and advanced labor legislation dawned in Britain. The receding tide of imperialism had stranded the Conservatives, and Chamberlain's insurgent campaign for tariff reform completed the wreck. Meanwhile the Liberals, whose power he had helped to shatter twenty years before by his revolt against Gladstone's Irish policy, had dropped their pursuit of Home Rule and adopted a bold program of social reform, with which they swept the country. It was Liberal leadership, not Labor prodding, that provided the driving force in the new parliament; for the Liberals had a big over-all majority in the Commons and their government needed no support, though of course it got it, from the Labor members, whose number had jumped to more than fifty if we include the slightly enlarged Lib-Lab tail. Though in 1910 the Liberals lost so many seats to the Conservatives that the government became dependent on the votes of Labor members, the latter also suffered from the Conservative resurgence and had no choice but to uphold the Liberal policy.

Yet there was an appreciable pressure from below during these hectic years of reform before the First World War. It was a movement operating to destroy, not to strengthen, the Labor party. Marxian influences from America and syndicalist ideas from France were creeping in to feed upon the discontent in the rank and file of labor caused by the check upon real wages since 1900, by the meager accomplishment of labor in the political field, by a judicial decision to be noticed presently, and by the extremes of wealth and poverty. The discontent broke out in an epidemic of strikes that began in 1906 and reached a rather angry climax in 1912. This fever of labor unrest, accompanied by some delirious talk of direct action, injected a note of urgency into the Liberal program of reform.

As soon as the Liberals under Sir Henry Campbell-Bannerman were confirmed in office by the election of 1906, they rushed through the Trades Dispute Act to reverse a judicial decision that threatened the very existence of organized labor. The decision in question, delivered in 1901 by the House of Lords sitting as the highest court of appeal for cases arising in the British Isles, upheld a judgment for heavy damages against the union of the workers on the Taff Vale Railway in southern Wales for a strike in which the men had engaged and for deeds of violence they had committed during it, though the union had neither authorized the strike nor approved the violence. Again legal technicalities had wrought a grave miscarriage of justice, and throughout the land there arose a passionate demand for parliament to change the law. If the Conservatives, who were then in power, had heeded the cry, they might have fared better in January 1906. Their failure to wipe out the Taff Vale decision gave Labor many seats in the House of Commons and swelled the Liberal victory. It also seems to have been at least partly responsible, through the bitterness it bred, for pushing the new government into overcorrecting the fault. The first draft of the remedial measure left unions liable for actions done under their own direct authority in industrial disputes, but an amendment urged by Labor members and accepted by the prime minister abolished this liability too. The Conservative majority in the Lords, subdued by the blast of public opinion, did not dare to tamper with the altered bill, whose passage made trade unions privileged bodies. Another Liberal enactment of 1906, which should be noted in passing, is the Workmen's Compensation Act. It extended to all trades what the Conservatives had done for a few in 1897 to insure workmen against the hazards of their employment, and it added many occupational diseases to the recognized injuries for which compensation had to be paid.

The first social legislation of the new Liberal government, also passed in 1906, was for the care of children, and here we see the empirical process at work. The coming of free compulsory education had exposed a shocking condition. An alarmingly large percentage of pupils from poverty-stricken homes arrived at school in need of food and medical care. Thereupon inspired civil servants in the national Board of Education did their best to remedy the evil by working through the local education authorities. The public provision of cheap or free meals to needy school children was therefore no novelty introduced by the Provision of Meals Act of 1906. What that act did was to give parliamentary sanction and encouragement to an existing and growing practice, and to authorize the local authorities to recover the cost of the food from parents who could afford it. It also declared that the failure of parents to pay for meals supplied to their children should not entail any of the legal disabilities attached to the receipt of public relief. The Education Act of 1907 did much the same for the neglected health of school children. It imposed on every local education authority the duty of providing medical inspection, and to the same authority it gave power to arrange for treatment—again a statutory recognition of, and stimulus to, the good work that was already being accomplished.

More revolutionary was the enactment of old age pensions in 1908, and yet the need for such a reform had long been recognized by Conservatives as well as Liberals. The old "battle of the plans" had become bogged down in the matter of expense. During the Boer War a parliamentary committee, of which Lloyd George was a member, reported in favor of a definite scheme, and a departmental committee was assigned the task of working out the cost. It proved to be staggering. Toward the end of the Conservative regime Chamberlain baited the hook of tariff reform with old age pensions to be paid out of the revenue that his tariff would produce. When the Liberals came in they too shied at the cost. But after some hesitation they felt the urgency to be so great that they took the plunge with a simple and immediate noncontributory system to be paid for wholly out of public funds. The law of 1908 was Booth's plan with the upper and lower ends chopped off. It provided pensions for people over seventy years of age who were beneath a very modest income level and above the class of the socially undesirable, such as criminals, habitual drunkards, and recipients of poor relief.[4] It was admittedly experimental, and it has since been modified many times, mostly to make it more generous.

The Sweated Industries Act of 1909 introduced what was then a novel principle to relieve oppressed workers in certain badly paid industries where labor organization was nonexistent or ineffectual. Wage rates and working conditions in these industries were to be determined by trade boards comprising representatives of employers, workmen, and the government; and the awards of these bodies were to be legally binding if formally approved by the government. It was compulsory arbitration directed by the state in the interest of employees in private industry. By another act of the same year, the government established public labor exchanges in all the principal cities of the country. The object was more than the organization of the labor market for the benefit of those who needed work. It was also to collect information for a radical attack on the chronic problem of unemployment.

Though the House of Lords, in which the Conservatives had a huge majority, passed all the above measures, it did not hesitate to throw out some other government bills sent up from the Commons, beginning in 1906 with an education bill. This party sniping from above irritated the Liberal majority in the lower chamber, for it was notorious that the upper chamber registered automatic approval when the Conservatives were in power. Trouble was brewing as early as June 1907 when, on the motion of the prime minister, the Commons resolved: "That, in order to give effect to the will of the people as expressed by their elected representatives, it is necessary that the power of the other House to

---

[4] This particular disqualification disappeared at the end of 1910.

alter or reject Bills passed by this House should be so restricted by Law as to secure that within the limits of a single Parliament the final decision of the Commons shall prevail." The climax came late in 1909 when the Lords, in defiance of established precedent, threw out the budget. It was a fatal blunder that played into the hands of their enemies and brought on a protracted constitutional crisis, the like of which the country had not experienced since 1832.

The first three Liberal budgets, of which Asquith was the author, had been well received, for they departed little from tradition and contained only a slight suggestion of taxing wealth to relieve poverty. He raised the death duties, but not by much; and he introduced the principle, already applied in some European countries and in two Australian colonies, of taxing "unearned" incomes at a higher rate than "earned" incomes. When Asquith became prime minister on the eve of Campbell-Bannerman's death in 1908, he relinquished the office of Chancellor of the Exchequer to Lloyd George, and with it the task of finding a large additional revenue. There was a sudden demand for eight new battleships to meet the threat of German naval building, old age pensions now had to be paid for, and still more money was needed for more social reform that the government was determined to enact as soon as possible. Whoever presided over the Exchequer had to break with tradition, and Lloyd George did it with gusto. His first budget, that of 1909, would frankly make the rich contribute to the welfare of the poor. Though its battery of taxes may seem innocuous to the tax-ridden society in which we now live, its augmentation of succession duties on big estates, its addition to the regular rate on incomes with relief for those in the lower brackets and a supertax on the higher, and especially its 20 per cent levy on the "unearned increment," or increase in the value of land due to no labor or expenditure on the part of the owner, all made this historic budget appear quite revolutionary in those halcyon days of private wealth. It was the first time that the government of a modern state tried to use its taxing power to effect a redistribution of the national income.

Two general elections in 1910 were necessary to resolve the issues thrust forward by the Lords' rejection of the budget. The January election was inconclusive except on one point. Liberal losses and Conservative gains produced a balance between the two old parties in the Commons, but the Irish Nationalist and the Labor members gave the government a majority of 124. That persuaded the Lords to pass the reintroduced budget. To clip their wings so that they would never again be able to defy the popular chamber, Asquith brought in the Parliament Bill and the Commons adopted it. As the Lords were in no mood to submit to this operation, and believed they could avert it by reforming the composition of their own chamber, there was a complete deadlock. Hoping to find some basis of agreement, leaders of the opposing parties met in private conferences that lasted through the summer and autumn, only to reveal that neither side would budge without another appeal to the country. Thereupon the ten-months-old parliament was dissolved, and the second general election of the year was called. The Conservatives, encouraged by the strength they had recovered in January, counted on victory at the polls in December. But the standing of the parties in the new House turned out to be practically the same as in the old. In the spring of 1911 the Commons again passed the Parliament Bill with a good majority. In the summer the Lords were about to destroy it, and then the prime minister announced that he had the king's consent to create enough peers to ensure its passage. That made further resistance hopeless, and the Lords surrendered.

By the Parliament Act of 1911, the Lords cannot hold up a money bill for more than a month. If they have not passed it by that time, it becomes law on receiving the royal signature. The act defined money bills and made the speaker of the Commons the sole arbiter of whether a bill satisfies this definition. Any other bill, except one prolonging the life of parliament beyond five years, similarly becomes law if passed by the Commons in three successive sessions over a period of two years. The act also shortened the potential life of parliament from seven to five years. Though the Commons cannot extend this term without the free consent of the Lords, in everything else the elected chamber has been legally supreme over the hereditary chamber ever since 1911.

Immediately following this major democratic reform came a minor one, but minor only by comparison; and by a curious coincidence the need for it arose from a judicial decision of the House of Lords delivered in 1909 at almost the very time that that House made its fatal political decision to reject the budget. This was the Osborne judgment, which denied the legal right of trade unions to tax their members for the support of the Labor party, whose parliamentary members thus lost their only income. Voluntary collections provided a stopgap until the Commons were able, without the concurrence of the Lords, to vote themselves salaries in the summer of 1911 at the princely rate of £400 a year. As the Labor party had other financial needs, the government virtually reversed the Osborne judgment in the following year by an act that legalized any political levy imposed by a majority vote of a union. At the same time, as a polite gesture to the doctrine of individual liberty, it allowed any union member to claim exemption from the levy—if he had the temerity to do so. There were many other pieces of social and labor legislation enacted during this stirring Liberal regime, such as gave the miners an eight-hour day in 1908 and a minimum wage in 1911; but most of them are scarcely worth mentioning beside the greatest of all, which the government passed as soon as it had shorn the Lords of their veto.

This was the National Insurance Act of 1911, which established compulsory health and unemployment insurance financed by contributions from the state, the employers, and the workers. Like the Old Age Pension Act, it had been anticipated by an eighteenth century English parson; but, unlike the Pension Act, it had not been preceded by much public discussion in the nineteenth century. It derived some impetus from Germany, where Lloyd George by his own personal observation in 1908 was impressed with Bismarck's health insurance; but no country had yet undertaken compulsory unemployment insurance, if we except an ephemeral attempt in the Swiss canton of St. Gall, and the Welshman's main contribution was to provide the funds. The Board of Trade began to work upon the scheme of national insurance in the autumn of 1908, and much of the credit for it must be given to the remarkable cabinet minister who was then head of that government department— Winston Churchill. He had the vision and the courage to appreciate its value and to carry it through.

The health sections of the act inaugurated what is often erroneously called state medicine, and provided weekly cash payments in lieu of wages lost through illness. To solve the old problem of how the state could organize social security without injuring the trade unions and the Friendly Societies, their voluntary systems were incorporated in the statutory system, and they were adopted as machinery for administering this system. They had merely to become approved societies under the new law. As membership in them was not compulsory and they included only a minority of the people to whom the act applied—all manual workers between the ages of 16 and 70—provision was also made for insurance through the post office. However, when the operation of the act got under way, the popular preference for approved societies threw most of the work into their hands. This strengthened these voluntary organizations and rescued some of them from insolvency.

More definitely experimental was the provision for unemployment insurance, which applied to only a quarter of the number covered by the health clauses. Protection was confined to specified industries which, by their very nature, suffered more than others from seasonal or cyclical unemployment—men's trades, chiefly building and engineering. The benefits were lower than wage rates and were limited to fifteen weeks in any one year, which covered the familiar short periods of recurrent unemployment.

Viewed as a whole, the quest for social justice in Britain was humanitarian rather than doctrinaire, and was not a matter of party politics until Liberal leadership brought it into practical focus. Yet hosts of Conservatives agreed in principle with much of the labor and social legislation that their political opponents sponsored during the eight years before the First World War; and in that period of mounting party strife, the issues that generated the most heat were two that were only partly connected with social reform and one that had nothing to do with it. The one was Irish Home Rule, which we shall consider in a later chapter. The other two were the budget of 1909, which drew fire mainly on the ground that it was an attack against property, and the House of Lords, an entrenched stronghold of the Conservatives which even they admitted could not be defended against the advance of democracy without some radical change in its structure. Nevertheless, the establishment of the welfare state was an upheaval that stirred vehement political controversy and much class bitterness; and it shook Britain much more than, a generation later, the New Deal shook the United States. The arguments were fundamentally the same; but the British experience was that of a pioneer, and Americans did not have to go through the ordeal of two national elections in one year.

Turning to the overseas empire, we find Australians and New Zealanders, but not Canadians or South Africans, experimenting with social democracy. The underlying problem did not exist in South Africa, where whites were a privileged caste. Nor was it present in Canada, which shared with the United States the incomparable opportunities of the North American agricultural frontier. Conditions in the antipodes were quite different. Heaven decreed, as we have seen, that Australia could not develop as an agricultural democracy; and though nature was kinder to New Zealand, human obstacles there

seemed for a while to impose the same veto. When the people in these
two countries found that they were denied individual economic independence, they turned to bold social experiments by the state. They
did this half a generation before the mother country; but they got much
of their inspiration from the discussions that were current in England,[5]
and they were able to act more quickly because their society was
younger, simpler, and more democratic.

The £30,000 that the Australian unions sent to support the London
dock strike in 1889 reflected more than a lively Australian interest in
the British labor cause. It also reflected the strength that organized
labor had gained in Australia. Having recently spread from the mines
and the urban industries to include the migratory army of shearers on
the sheep runs,[6] it embraced a higher percentage of the population
than in any other country of the world. Prior to this time the Australian unions were fighting organizations that relied on the strike to
get what they wanted, and the dockers' victory in London reinforced
their confidence in this weapon on the very eve of a crisis in which it
failed them disastrously.

The crisis came with the collapse of a boom that sustained the
Australian economy until the end of the eighties. The discovery of
the rich gold deposits at Mount Morgan, Queensland, in 1882 was a
godsend to a country whose production of that precious metal had
dropped 50 per cent in twenty years. Falling prices of everything else
meant, of course, that the value of gold was going up. The growing
price disparity between manufactured goods and raw materials also
benefited the Australian economy, which depended on the export of
the latter; and the introduction of refrigerated shipping during this
decade gave further aid to producers of beef and mutton and at last
made it possible to put Australian butter on English tables. But the
chief factor in the Australian prosperity of the eighties was a heavy
importation of capital. Much of it was spent on ambitious public
works, much of it swelled bank deposits for the sake of a higher interest
than could be got in England, much of it was sunk in speculative urban
real estate, and all of it produced inflation.

The inevitable slump began in December 1889 with a big Mel-

---

[5] Henry George made a triumphal lecturing tour through New Zealand and Australia
in 1889–90, rousing great interest, as he had earlier done in England, in how legislation
could reform society.

[6] Whose occupation then made them the first to apply the word "scab" to a workman
who refused to join a union or who took the place of a striking union man.

bourne failure, and it was accelerated by the much bigger collapse, in November 1890, of the international banking house of Baring Brothers, London. Australian credit was paralyzed, only the soundest banks being saved from the general wreck; and public works came to a standstill, glutting the labor market when private employers were turning off hands. In the mad scramble for cover, a strike in the ports, which began in September 1890, started other strikes that soon became general. But picketing and violence, of which there was more than a little, were futile when there were plenty of strikebreakers eager for jobs and the colonial governments stepped in to protect them.

From the most disastrous defeat in Australian history, trade unionism emerged to fight on another field with another weapon. It plunged into politics, forming a Labor party in each of the colonies. The first test came in the New South Wales election of 1891, when a recent law for the payment of members came into force. The returns gave Labor 35 of the 125 seats and divided the remainder almost equally between the two old parties, thus placing the new party in a position to dominate the House. As the political movement spread throughout the country, Labor devised a system of party discipline more rigid and effective than any other party organization except that of the Irish Nationalists in the British parliament; and it forced the enactment of labor laws, some of which provided for public arbitration of industrial disputes. Practical experience rather than socialist theory dictated this labor legislation of the nineties. State intervention against the strikers had made Labor realize the power of the state and had made it determined to wield that power in its own interest. During this decade Australian trade unionism mastered the tricks of the political game and became the strongest political force in the land, though in only one colony did the party attain office, and that for scarcely a week.

After federation, in 1900, Labor was more successful politically, taking over the reins of state governments and playing a leading role in the new national parliament. There it rode the balance of power and dictated much legislation, including the enactment of old age and invalid pensions in 1908. Twice in this decade it formed short-lived administrations, which accomplished little; and gradually it drove the old parties into a fusion which was designed to check, but actually stimulated, the advance of the Labor party, whose inclination toward state socialism had become more marked. The general election of 1910 turned out the fusion government and put Labor in the saddle. The next general election, in 1913, gave the fusionists a majority of one in the House and again they took office, but only until the following year, when deadlock forced a dissolution and the voters restored the Labor government.

From 1900 Labor sought to fight its decisive battles in federal rather than state politics, which may seem strange in light of the fact that the constitutional distribution of powers left the states in control of their own industry, commerce, and other activities that also most nearly affected the economic life and social well-being of the country. But immigration and the tariff, in both of which Labor had a special interest, were federal matters; there was the possibility, suggested by the American example with which many Australians were quite familiar, that the balance of the constitution would swing in favor of the central government; and Labor was anxious to push this development because it offered both tactical and strategic advantages. Labor could, and presently did, win control of the elected Australian Senate, whereas it had been having difficulty with the nominated second chambers in the colonies which were carried over into the new regime; and what was of more importance, it was better to fight one overriding battle than six simultaneous and widely scattered engagements.

Though Labor's prime interest in immigration was the absolute exclusion of Orientals, the law which the first federal parliament promptly enacted for this purpose also squinted at white immigration, for it contained a clause that forbade the entry of "any persons," irrespective of color, "under a contract to perform manual labor." The party prized this provision as a protection against cheap European labor that employers might import. But Australia had little to fear on this score as long as Europeans could migrate freely to much nearer and richer America; and many Australians felt silly when attempts were made, under this clause, to bar respectable British artisans coming to fixed employment, particularly six English hatters who were soon dubbed the "mad hatters." The clause had its teeth pulled in 1905.

The tariff was a different matter, and Labor was divided over it until shortly after federation. Then it drew together on the issue and joined the manufacturers in demanding protection. In doing this, Labor was not just drifting with the tide of public opinion. There was a shrewd political calculation behind the move. It was that the government could not confer benefits on manufacturers, a small class, without forcing them to pass on most of these benefits to their employees. One device, that was called the New Protection and worked until the High Court of Australia declared it *ultra vires,* was to require domestic manufacturers to pay an excise tax that balanced the increase of the customs duty unless they could show that they paid "fair and reasonable" wages and observed other regulations for the benefit of their workmen.

More effective was the development of conciliation and arbitration for the settlement of industrial disputes by further state legislation and now by federal legislation too, the latter being specifically authorized by the constitution for disputes extending beyond the limits of any one state. To circumvent the laggard state legislatures, the Labor party determined to stretch the federal power, demanding that state employees, who included all railway workers, be expressly brought under the jurisdiction of the proposed national tribunal. This demand, which was plainly unconstitutional, and Labor's attempt to write into the projected law a considerable measure of preference for union members, such as was prescribed in New South Wales, delayed until 1904 the passage of an act on the subject, which embodied a compromise on the question of preference to unionists.

The act creating the federal Conciliation and Arbitration Court endowed it with extensive authority to fix wages and regulate working conditions. It consisted of a single member, called the president, chosen from the justices of the High Court of Australia; but he could appoint assessors to advise him on technical points, and he could delegate power to conduct inquiries. The choice naturally fell on the man who had inserted in the constitution the provision for this court, H. B. Higgins; for sixteen years he presided over it, making his name blessed to countless toiling Australians.

Clever lawyers found unsuspected ambiguities in the apparently clear wording of the act that confined the jurisdiction of the court to disputes extending beyond the limits of any one state, and the judgments of the court carried such weight that they influenced the decisions of state tribunals. "It may seem very shocking in some quarters," Higgins declared in one of his early judgments, "but it is my clear duty, in obedience to the law, to treat unionism as a desirable aid in securing industrial peace." In the beginning he laid down the principle of a minimum wage tied to the cost of living and defined this as what was necessary to meet "the normal needs of an average employee, regarded as a human being in a civilized country." Among such needs, in addition to food, shelter, and clothing, he recognized "frugal comfort," a certain amount of leisure, "provision for evil days," and the raising of a family of three children. For special strength or skill, the court awarded higher rates; but it tended to subordinate the claims of the favored few to those of the unskilled, thereby reflecting the egalitarian and class-conscious spirit that prevailed in Australia. Of course employers bitterly resented the sacrifice of a "free economy" on the altar of social justice, but Australians as a whole were proud of their achievement. They believed that by harnessing capitalism to serve the interest of the common man, instead of allowing it to run rampant as in America at that time, they were far ahead of all other peoples in the world, with the possible exception of the New Zealanders.

During the nineties New Zealand attracted wide attention in the outside world as the pioneer of social democracy. For this distinction, organized labor was less responsible than a fortuitous combination of circumstances and men. Trade unionism in New Zealand lagged far behind the Australian movement, being scarcely noticeable until 1890 and forming no political party of its own until 1909. In further contrast to Australia, which enjoyed prosperity until the end of the eighties, New Zealand entered upon a long period of economic prostration in 1879, when its credit collapsed after a spell of extravagant borrowing and spending. Unemployment piled up in the towns, depressing wages and working conditions. Immigration fell off and in the late eighties was exceeded by emigration. This seemed to be the only escape; for in the South Island, where most of the population still lived because of the troubles with the Maoris, the land was largely monopolized by the pastoral oligarchy whose influence had long dominated the government.

At last there was a political upheaval, born of desperation and released by a reform of the electoral system in 1889. This was the abolition of plural voting, which had enabled property owners to stultify the manhood suffrage adopted some years before. In the general election of 1890 the "continuous ministry," which had nothing constructive to offer, was routed by a newly formed progressive combination that cried out for state action to break the economic impasse. The victors were really a farmer-labor party, though it was called Liberal or Liberal-Labor because its leaders were Liberals. They constituted the cabinet that took office when the old government was forced to resign in 1891.

The electoral decision was less revolutionary than many outsiders have supposed. The appeal to state action was in harmony with a tradition already established in New Zealand, with its government railways, telegraphs, and telephones, all antedating 1890. Moreover, the state had long been serving the public in the capacity of a trust company and had developed the largest business of the kind in the country. Likewise, it had entered the business of life insurance, outdistancing all private competitors. Though the change of policy that followed 1890 was vigorous, it was one of tempo, of degree rather than of kind. For some of the experimental legislation enacted by the New Zealand parliament under the Liberals, precedents can also be found in the municipal socialism practiced in England and on the continent of Europe. But the departure of municipal bodies from "orthodoxy" is never so striking as that of a national government.

The first important measure of the new regime reversed the principle of taxation. In place of a property tax that was regressive in character and inelastic in yield, it substituted a land and income tax that was progressive in incidence and would produce an expanding revenue. This act of 1891 also provided for self-assessment and, as a check upon it, gave the government the right to purchase at the assessed value. The owners of one huge estate tried to bluff the administration into accepting a reduced assessment, and paid for it by the enforced sale of the property, which was then broken up and settled with small leaseholders, who thereby gained much from a transaction that cost the government nothing.

Thus began a rural transformation that, speeded by further enabling legislation in the early nineties, made New Zealand a nation of small farmers. The main driving force behind it was John McKenzie, minister for lands, immigration, and agriculture, who began life as the son of a Scottish Highland crofter and was honored with a knighthood shortly after he retired from office in 1900. Of course his policy could not have succeeded if conditions had not favored it. Nature provided an ideal soil and climate for close settlement; the contemporary development of refrigerated shipping made small farming profitable by opening the English market to New Zealand meat and dairy produce; and now an abundance of crown lands became available in the North Island, following agreements with the Maoris, whose earlier hostility had preserved that rich part of New Zealand from falling into the clutches of big sheepowners. What inspired McKenzie was not socialist theory but the typical crofter's passion for the soil and hatred of monopolizing landlords. His great work may be compared with the regeneration of rural Ireland, which Conservatives were then effecting.[7]

---

[7] See *infra*, p. 659–60.

Labor legislation, and its administration, was the special charge of William Pember Reeves. He was the most influential man in the cabinet until he left it in 1896 to represent his native New Zealand as high commissioner in England, where he later became head of the London School of Economics and a prominent Fabian. Fine scholar, brilliant writer, compelling debater, and very capable administrator, he was the chief intellectual inspirer of the Liberal-Labor program, and he still stands as its most authoritative and attractive historian. About the only criticism that can be made of his writings on the subject arises from his personal modesty, for they offer little suggestion of how great was his own contribution to the program.

During Reeves' few years as minister for labor, he gave New Zealand one of the most effective labor codes in the world. Almost single-handed he designed and pushed through parliament the most famous of all its measures: the Industrial Conciliation and Arbitration Act of 1894, which placed New Zealand in the forefront of the movement to preserve industrial peace by state intervention. "Frankly, the bill is but an experiment," he pleaded in the House, "but it is an experiment well worth the trying. Try it, and if it fail, repeal it." Employers hated it but were powerless to remove it from the statute book; while labor, which had not demanded the measure, rallied enthusiastically to its support and soon came to regard it as the Magna Carta of the workers.

New Zealand was the first British country to adopt old age pensions. As early as 1883, interest in the subject having been aroused by the discussions in England, the head of the old "continuous ministry" proposed a contributory scheme, but he did not press it. Outside parliament various other schemes were widely debated, and in 1894 a committee of the House recommended the appointment of a royal commission to study the question. The government did not act on this advice, and it seemed to have forgotten the matter until the eve of the general election of 1896. Then the premier, Richard Seddon, surprised parliament and the country by introducing a hastily drafted bill for old age pensions. It was a clever tactical move that helped him out of a difficult political position. The opposition had waxed strong and his cabinet had just been weakened by the departure of Reeves. A hostile amendment forced him to withdraw the bill, but he carried the issue to the hustings and the voters sustained him. Doubts of his sincerity disappeared when he reintroduced the bill in the following year. Again it encountered strenuous objections, principally because he insisted on paying the pensions out of tax receipts, and again he withdrew it. But in 1898 he carried it by a *tour de force;* he kept the House in committee without a break for nearly ninety hours, occupying the chair the whole time and reprimanding exhausted members who would join in the debate while still lying down.

Among other features of welfare legislation enacted by this ministry were government loans to small farmers struggling to establish themselves and to humble town dwellers for the purchase of homes, the assumption by the state of the whole responsibility for the treatment of mental diseases, and the provision of state maternity hospitals for working women. Of state socialism in the strict sense, there was little extension, and that little was mainly to curb real or threatened monopoly, notably in fire insurance and coal mining.

Quite illuminating is the way the government handled the country's leading private financial institution, the Bank of New Zealand. In 1894, after years of running in the red and concealing this fact by resorting to dishonest practices, it begged the government for aid to avert an immediate crash. The government rushed to the rescue in return for a controlling interest, which it might have used to dictate interest rates, exchange charges, and lending policy. But there was no attempt at any such interference. The bank was allowed to continue, under more careful management, as an ordinary commercial bank, which is a clear indication that state socialist ideals had not captured the community. Fortunately the government lost not a penny by this venture and ultimately made a good profit out of it, for the refloated bank was borne along by the tide of prosperity that began to flow joyously in 1896.

The socialistic trend in New Zealand, which was more apparent than real, slackened as the depression lifted, and it was reversed in the following decade. What caused this reaction was something more than the return of prosperity, which is a proverbial cure for radicalism. The very success of the Liberal-Labor party was its own undoing. As more and more people were settled on the land, they constituted a growing class of conservatives whose influence with the government gradually turned the balance against organized labor in the towns, and trade unionism lost some of the legislative and administrative favor that it had gained. Labor naturally broke away to form an independent and more radical party, which made little political impression because it represented a dwindling minority of the population. On the other hand, the rising demand of the small farmers to have their long leases transformed into freehold played into the hands of the opposition which, reconstituted as the Reform Party, won the election of 1912 and straightway satisfied this demand. But the fall of the Liberals was not the fall of liberalism or the end of social democracy. The Conservatives had to shed much of their conservatism and be converted into Reformers in order to get back into power; and the rural democracy of New Zealand was no less inclined than the urban democracy of Australia to operate the machinery of government in its own economic and social interest.

CHAPTER XXVIII

The Great Imperial Scramble

ONE OF the most extraordinary phenomena of modern times occurred in the last two decades of the nineteenth century, when western powers partitioned the huge continent of Africa, grabbed pieces of Asia, and gobbled up the countless islands of the Pacific. Why this mad scramble? Not until the turn of the century did a serious answer begin to take shape, and it was then the work of bourgeois liberals in America and England. Their work was later appropriated and developed by continental socialists, particularly the neo-Marxians, who propounded the full-blown theory that imperialism was simply the operation of predatory capitalism which, being cramped by limited opportunities at home, was seeking new worlds to exploit; that the government of each imperialist country was a tool of its capitalists who were using it to win for themselves wider markets, more raw materials, cheaper labor, and fresh fields for investment; and that the capitalist system was rushing to its own destruction by driving the international competition for these prizes toward an explosion of suicidal wars. This economic interpretation without its catastrophic conclusion, which was added by the apocalyptic vision of the communist prophets, gained wide acceptance among liberals in western civilization. It was so neat and clear, and it seemed so self-evident. This may explain the curious fact that there was almost no attempt to test its validity by a critical analysis of concrete examples of imperialist action.

A mere glance at the previous period is sufficient to expose the inadequacy of the theory. In the heyday of anti-imperialism, Britain was exporting great quantities of goods and capital to all parts of the globe, civilized and uncivilized, and from them she was importing food and raw materials. Her capitalism had burst the bounds of empire. Two thirds of her trade, by which she lived, was with countries that did not fly the Union Jack. Her best customers were the United States, Germany, and France; and she was pouring capital into Europe and America, where an extension of her political dominion was absolutely out of the question. Her own colonies, as they matured, were raising tariff barriers against her wares; and she was the only great trader in limitless regions of Africa and the Far East that belonged to no western power, and she was glad not to have these regions included in her empire. Apparently something more than mere capitalism is the explanation of why she joined the international race, when it began, to collect new colonies.

What drew Britain into the race, what kept her in it and put her in the lead, was the economic nationalism of her rivals. They imposed more or less severe restrictions upon foreign trade with their possessions, while she imposed none upon economic intercourse with hers. Annexations by other powers established exclusive national control over territories where traders of all nations had enjoyed equal opportunities and where free competition had given the lion's share of the trade to the lion—Britain. These other powers were wielding the sword of political sovereignty to slice off her trade, on the principle that trade follows the flag. In self-defense she then began to act on the principle that the flag follows trade, proclaiming her sovereignty over lands that rival nations threatened to appropriate at her expense. Her object, like theirs, was trade, but with an important difference. Theirs was to shut doors; hers was to keep them open, primarily for herself and incidentally for others. Hers was to forestall monopolization by other powers, not to gain a monopoly for herself, which she firmly believed was contrary to sound policy. The soundness of her free trade policy was more than economic. It was political too. Because she did not, like her rivals, play the dog in the manger, her annexations increased rather than diminished facilities for their trade. Therefore each of her rivals, on the whole, preferred to see her, rather than any other power, take over a new territory. That was the main, though not the only, reason why she won more than any other contestant in the race.

What produced the race is not so easy to explain, for there was a complexity of causes. One was the lifting of the veil from the dark continent, where the competitive urge for empire found its chief outlet. Though Europeans had been spreading round the globe since the days of Columbus, they had neglected Africa. Except at its northern and southern extremities, they had found little to attract and much to repel them. It was a land of tropical jungles and burning deserts, of disease

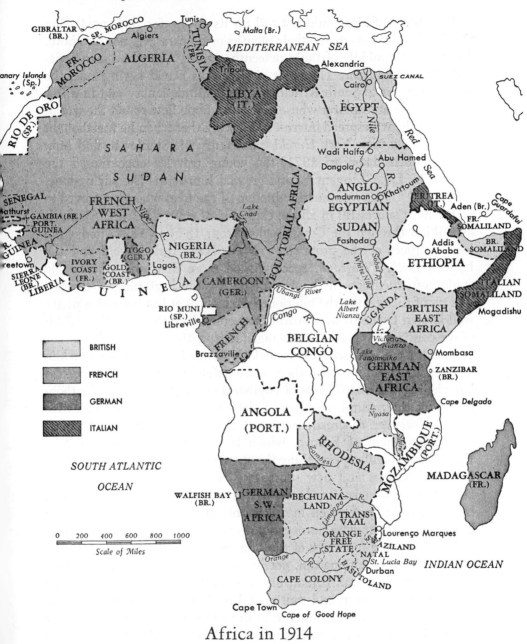

GIBRALTAR (BR.)
SP. MOROCCO
Algiers
Tunis
Malta (Br.)
MEDITERRANEAN SEA
Canary Islands (Sp.)
FR. MOROCCO
ALGERIA
TUNISIA (FR.)
Tripoli
LIBYA (IT.)
Alexandria
Cairo
SUEZ CANAL
EGYPT
RIO DE ORO (SP.)
S A H A R A
S U D A N
Nile
Red Sea
Wadi Halfa
Abu Hamed
Dongola
ANGLO-
Omdurman
Khartoum
EGYPTIAN
ERITREA (IT.)
Aden (Br.)
Cape Guardafui
FR. SOMALILAND
SENEGAL
Bathurst
GAMBIA (BR.)
PORT. GUINEA
FRENCH WEST AFRICA
Niger R.
Lake Chad
SUDAN
Fashoda
Addis Ababa
BR. SOMALILAND
GUINEA
Freetown
SIERRA LEONE (BR.)
LIBERIA
IVORY COAST (FR.)
GOLD COAST (BR.)
TOGO (GER.)
Lagos
NIGERIA (BR.)
CAMEROON (GER.)
EQUATORIAL AFRICA
Ubangi River
ETHIOPIA
ITALIAN SOMALILAND
RIO MUNI (SP.)
Libreville
FRENCH
Congo R.
Lake Albert Nianza
UGANDA
BRITISH EAST AFRICA
Mogadishu
BELGIAN CONGO
Lake Victoria Nianza
Mombasa
BRITISH
FRENCH
GERMAN
ITALIAN
Brazzaville
Lake Tanganyika
GERMAN EAST AFRICA
ZANZIBAR (BR.)
Cape Delgado
L. Nyasa
SOUTH ATLANTIC
OCEAN
ANGOLA (PORT.)
RHODESIA
Zambesi R.
MOZAMBIQUE (PORT.)
MADAGASCAR (FR.)
0 200 400 600 800 1000
Scale of Miles
WALFISH BAY (BR.)
GERMAN S.W. AFRICA
BECHUANA-LAND
Limpopo R.
TRANS-VAAL
Lourenço Marques
ORANGE FREE STATE
SWAZILAND
NATAL
St. Lucia Bay
Durban
INDIAN OCEAN
Orange
CAPE COLONY
BASUTOLAND
Cape Town
Cape of Good Hope

Africa in 1914

and death, of no civilization or accumulation of wealth such as had
been found in India, China, and Central and South America, and it
almost entirely lacked the obvious opportunities of North America for

white settlers. Ships could not sail up its rivers, for their navigation was blocked by bars across their mouths or by cataracts not far above. Not until the middle of the nineteenth century did white men penetrate its vast interior. The great pioneer was David Livingstone, the Scot who went to South Africa as a medical missionary and in a few years became an explorer whose name and fame flew round the world. Such was the widespread interest in his work that when he was thought to be lost the New York *Herald* sent Henry M. Stanley to find him. Many months later, in 1871, the young traveler encountered the veteran by Lake Tanganyika and greeted him with "Dr. Livingstone, I presume?" This was the introduction of the man who soon proved to be the most successful of all the explorers of central Africa. Stanley's expedition through the Congo region from 1874 to 1877, under the joint auspices of the proprietors of the New York *Herald* and the London *Daily Telegraph*, accomplished more than any other single exploring expedition in the continent. By the beginning of the last quarter of the century the interior of Africa was at last becoming pretty well known to the western world, and enough of the potential wealth of the continent was revealed to make it attractive to Europeans.

By this time, also, science was making Africa less forbidding to white men. They could now live there more safely, thanks to new medical knowledge; and the progress of engineering pointed the way for them to exploit the natural resources of the interior with the aid of native labor. Moreover, as already suggested, the growth of industrial society on the continent of Europe, which had lagged far behind that of Britain, was finally approaching the stage where it felt an urgent need for new markets and new sources of raw materials. Furthermore, according to western standards, Africa was a political vacuum. But even when we have taken into account all the above conditions, we have yet to explain why European powers rushed in to fill the vacuum.

The impelling force was of the same nature as the vacuum. It was political. It was nationalism, not just economic nationalism. Europe was tense with it, and Britain unconsciously encouraged it. She was the only world power, and continental nations envied her proud position. They generally attributed it to her industrial supremacy and her imperial possessions. Her example therefore stimulated them to develop their own industries as rapidly as possible by means of protective tariffs, which only intensified their national rivalries, and to acquire colonies, in which pursuit their own economic nationalism spurred them along. As the nations on the continent adopted protection to shield themselves against foreign, chiefly British, industrial competition at home, so also did they proclaim their sovereignty, as far as possible, over the markets and raw materials that they coveted abroad. It was to benefit their working classes no less than their capitalists. On the continent, as in Britain, the outburst of imperialism was an expression of the national will, a reflection of the democratic franchise, the popular press, and universal education, all of which were then becoming common.

The national will for national aggrandisement was concerned with more than economic gains. The Franco-Prussian War had smashed France, and her declining birth rate precluded any hope of ever being able to face Germany again except by supplementing her own manpower with what she might train and arm in Africa. It was principally for this purpose that she there added colony after colony to the one, Algeria, that she had held for half a century. Bismarck actually pushed France into her first new imperialist venture—the seizure of Tunis in 1881—to strengthen Germany's position in Europe by sowing the seed of discord between France and Italy and by diverting France from her dream of *revanche*.

Nationalism, now turned militant, had built up such conflicting pressures within the narrow confines of Europe that the only seeming alternative to explosion was expansion. Nationalism, by the internal law of its development, was being glorified into imperialism. Russia and Austria were so situated that their imperialist urge was directed toward contiguous territories; whereas other European nations, being mutually hemmed in, looked across the sea for the peaceful satisfaction of their aggressive impulse. Colonies gave prestige, and prestige is a most precious thing to a nation. In the outburst of imperial grabbing of territory in Africa, Asia, and the Pacific, the national ego of each competing power inflated itself.

Curiously enough, it was the ruler of a small power who started the scramble, Leopold II of Belgium. But if he had not done it, some other power would almost certainly have done it not long afterward. Before Leopold succeeded to his father's throne in 1865, he traveled much in distant lands, visiting India, China, and various parts of North Africa; he became inspired with a mission to lead the people of Belgium to enlarge their horizon by looking beyond the sea. After he became king, the progress of discovery in Africa focused his attention on that part of the world. His shrewd mind saw great possibilities in harnessing the missionary and commercial instincts for the development of the dark continent. On his invitation an unofficial international conference met in Brussels in 1876. The upshot was the founding of the Congo Free State, nominally under an international association but really under the private control of Leopold, who provided most of the capital and employed Stanley to direct the enterprise on the spot. As this Anglo-American explorer proceeded to build stations and to contract treaties with the natives, an agent of the French government was exploring in the northern Congo and he promptly proclaimed French sovereignty there; at the same time Portugal claimed that the whole Congo was hers by right of the discoveries her navigators had made centuries before. Leopold was embarrassed, for it was not as king of Belgium but as a private individual who headed a private corporation that he had launched his venture. Therefore he pulled diplomatic wires to get international recognition of his International Association as a sovereign state. The United States was the first power to oblige, by a convention of 1884, and the others soon followed suit.

European intervention in Egypt also began in 1876, but it was in no way connected with Leopold's Congo project or tainted with imperialism. The spendthrift Khedive Ismail defaulted in the payment of interest to the foreign bondholders, and a settlement was negotiated. The *Caisse de la Dette,* a board of trustees representing all the great powers, was established, and to it the khedive assigned specific revenues calculated to service the debt. To make sure that these revenues would continue to flow, it was also necessary to provide for a more efficient financial administration in Egypt; and as most of the debt was held in Britain and France, Ismail agreed to the appointment of two controllers general, one British and one French. Unfortunately for all concerned, he intrigued against this Franco-British Dual Control. Then the European powers, on the initiative of Germany, stepped in again; and in 1879 they got the sultan of Turkey, who was the suzerain of Egypt, to depose the uncooperative khedive in favor of his young son, Tewfik. He was honest but impotent; and the new regime was soon broken by a revolutionary movement headed by Arabi Pasha, a fanatical army colonel of fellah origin.

This movement, which seems to have been provoked by the monstrous misgovernment under which the country had long suffered, was nationalist in character. It was directed primarily against the Turkish ruling class and secondarily against Europeans. In 1882 there were mutinies in the Egyptian army, whose soldiers had commonly been defrauded of their pay; antiforeign rioting broke out, killing many

Europeans, chiefly Italians and Greeks; and the helpless khedive turned over the government to the revolutionaries, who had not the slightest capacity for directing it. Egypt was dissolving into anarchy, and the Dual Control was at an end.

The powers discussed armed intervention to restore order and to protect the Suez Canal, and a combined British and French fleet appeared off Alexandria. Gladstone's government, pledged against imperial ventures, shied away from an early French suggestion to use force; but when conditions in Egypt grew worse, France turned shy and Britain bolder. London favored Turkish action to quell the revolt, but Paris would not allow it. The sultan offered to give Egypt to Britain, but the prime minister and his foreign secretary rejected it offhand, without even consulting the cabinet. Finally, after both France and Italy refused a British invitation to join in military intervention, the government in London made up its mind to jump in alone. A few British regiments quickly overthrew Arabi on the battlefield of Tel-el-Kebir and restored Tewfik to his throne in the autumn of 1882. Thenceforth he was khedive by the grace of British bayonets.

Thus began the British occupation of Egypt, which still legally belonged to the Turkish empire and owed tribute to the sultan. Gladstone and his colleagues had not the slightest intention of annexing the country, or of declaring a protectorate over it. Neither could they contemplate immediate withdrawal, for that would mean letting Egypt relapse into anarchy, with grave peril to the Suez Canal. Yet they wanted to get Britain out of Egypt as soon as possible, because her presence there would antagonize other powers, particularly France, and restrict British freedom of action elsewhere. Therefore they decided that Britain should clean up the mess as quickly as she could, and London announced to the world that the occupation was only temporary. The task proved to be much bigger than expected, and the occupation much longer.

One of the first things that Britain had to do was to extricate Egypt from an impossible situation in the Sudan, and it was a painful experience. Back in 1820 Egypt had undertaken the conquest of that country. It was nearly completed under the grandiose Ismail, and its enormous expense completed his financial ruin. Success, however, seemed in sight when he employed two able English adventurers to command his armies and to organize the administration in the Sudan: first, Sir Samuel Baker, the explorer of the sources of the Nile; and then General Charles Gordon, famous as "Chinese Gordon" because he had led a Chinese army to brilliant victory over the formidable Taiping rebels a few years before. When this quixotic saint and hero resigned his appointment in 1879, he was succeeded by a wretched Egyptian whom he had dismissed from the service, and the Sudan became a huge den of iniquity. There, paralleling the rise of Arabi in Egypt, a religious fanatic who claimed descent from Mahomet proclaimed himself the Mahdi, or Moslem Messiah, and led a wild revolt that soon subjected most of the country to his own vile tyranny.

At the very outset the British government disclaimed any responsibility for what Egypt did in the Sudan, and the khedive sent an army of 10,000 men under a British officer to subdue the Mahdi. It was defeated and massacred in 1883. Tewfik and his prime minister were about to try again, when the British consul general in Cairo vetoed the project and London backed the veto. Too much Egyptian revenue had been poured down the Sudanese drain. Even in ordinary times it amounted to £200,000 a year. This had to be stopped if Egypt was ever to pay its own way.

Britain decided that Egypt must abandon the Sudan, and straightway assumed the responsibility for liquidating the burdensome legacy by extricating the Egyptian military and civilian personnel from the clutches of the Mahdi. The government called in Gordon and asked him if he would do it. He said yes, and that night he left London for Cairo, where, at his own request, he was again commissioned governor general of the Sudan. Rushing across the desert, he reached Khartoum in February 1884. The inhabitants welcomed him with open arms, believing he had come to save the country from the rebels. Their faith and the Egyptian commission may have infected him. Though he at once began sending out the women and children, he displayed little eagerness to get the soldiers out until it was too late. A month after his arrival he found himself besieged by a gathering host. Then the problem was how to rescue him and his garrison. Cairo and London wasted precious time over whether the relieving expedition should march straight across the desert or follow the longer but easier route up the Nile. The choice of the latter entailed boat building and further delay. The head of the advancing column approached Khartoum at the end of January 1885, and saw nothing but ruins. Only two days before, the savages had broken in and slaughtered Gordon and his garrison.

The tragic death of the hero who had captured the imagination of the British people nearly killed the Gladstone ministry. Fighting for its life against a blaze of public anger, the government refrained from casting any blame on Gordon, who was much to blame, and barely managed to defeat a hostile motion in the House of Commons.

The fate of the Sudan was terrible. The Mahdi, whose followers thought God had given him power to conquer the world, was planning the invasion of Egypt as his next step, but he did not live to take it. Five months after the fall of Khartoum he perished, the victim of disease or of poison administered by a woman of his harem. Under his fierce successor, the khalifa, who ruled until the British returned in 1898, captured Egyptians were enslaved, Europeans were loaded with chains and repeatedly flogged, and the whole country was a veritable charnel house, its population being reduced, it is said, from twelve million to two million.

The regeneration of Egypt was largely the work of Sir Evelyn Baring, later Lord Cromer, a scion of the great banking family who had chosen the army as his profession. From 1883 until his retirement in 1907, he was British adviser to the khedive's government, and though he received his orders from London he was almost invariably their real author. He was the consul general in Cairo who put his foot down on the attempt to reconquer the Sudan. For the first two years his task in Egypt seemed hopeless. Half the revenue, more than enough to pay the interest to the bondholders, had to be paid into the *Caisse.* Of the other half, some was already mortgaged, some had to go as tribute to the sultan, and what was left could not begin to meet the minimum needs of government. In 1884, on the recommendation of a British cabinet minister[1] who was sent out to examine the situation, a portion of the revenue assigned to the *Caisse,* where it was not needed, was diverted to the ordinary revenue fund, where it was sorely needed. But this move made matters worse instead of better, for all the other powers save Italy protested, and the abstracted money had to be restored. The international knot was loosened by the negotiation of the London Convention of 1885, whereby the powers agreed to release part of the *Caisse* surplus and to guarantee a new Egyptian loan of £9,000,000 paying only 3 per cent. This gave Baring just enough financial leeway to commence the performance of a seeming miracle. He managed to spend £1,000,000 of the loan on irrigation improvements, an investment that has paid a hundredfold, and by 1888 he balanced the budget.

Meanwhile expenditure other than on irrigation was cut to the bone, and the introduction of British officials into all administrative depart-

---

[1] Lord Northbrook, another Baring, uncle of Sir Evelyn.

ments cleansed them of their Oriental sloth and corruption. As the revenue increased, the tax burden on the peasants was lightened and more money was spent on public improvements, which in turn brought more revenue—and prosperity. Native officials grumbled over being driven or displaced; but the great mass of the six million population, the fellahin, no longer groveled, because at last they were treated like human beings. For centuries it had been the annual custom to force them, with whips and without pay, to toil for several months cleaning out the canals. Now a simple khedival decree abolished flogging, and wages were found for this necessary labor. Now, too, the fellahin finally got their fair share in the distribution of water, which from time out of mind the great landowners had manipulated in their own interest. The productivity of the ordinary peasant holding was doubled; new irrigation works, which were being pushed all the time, brought more and more wasteland into profitable cultivation.

Railways, of which there had been only a little construction, and roads, of which there were none when the occupation began, were now spreading all over the country. The department of public health, when established in 1884, could find not a sanitary house, hotel, or hospital in the whole land. The primitive town drains then emptied directly into the Nile or into canals that supplied the drinking water for the people living along their banks. The correction of such conditions took long laborious years. These and a host of other reforms gradually transformed Egypt into a modern prosperous country.

The British evacuation of Egypt, promised at an early date by Gladstone, remained a delicate international question. In 1887 the Conservative government of Lord Salisbury signed a convention with the sultan to end the occupation in 1890, with the proviso that it might be prolonged or renewed if there was a serious threat to the internal peace or external security of Egypt. The immediate purpose of the agreement was to heal a rift in the friendly relations between London and Constantinople. The convention was not at all to the liking of France and Russia. Therefore, using the proviso as a lever, they brought pressure to bear on the sultan; and he refused to ratify the convention.

The international status of the Suez Canal was also under lively discussion as a consequence of the British occupation of the country through which the canal ran. By the original concession the canal was to be open *"comme passages neutres"* to all merchant vessels without any national discrimination. But this condition was imposed by the old Egyptian government, not by international action, and the demand for the latter became acute in 1882 when the British general who was soon to smash the army of Arabi suspended navigation for four days. Finally, in 1888, Britain, France, Germany, Austria, Italy, Spain, the Netherlands, Russia, and Turkey signed the Suez Canal Convention, which declared that the canal should "always be free and open, in time of war as in time of peace, to every vessel of commerce or of war, without distinction of flag." In signing, however, Britain added a reservation that the convention should apply only in so far as it was compatible with her occupation of Egypt. This suspended the operation of the convention.

The crux of the matter was the defense of the canal, for which the Egyptian government was technically responsible and the British government, by reason of the occupation, was practically responsible. To financial control of the strategic waterway, Britain had added military control; and it was perfectly plain that the security of the canal was her main motive in going into Egypt and staying there. By thus entrenching herself on the crossroads of the world, she incurred the reproaches of the other powers. France was bitterly hostile. To the repeated charge that the British were not keeping their promise to get out of Egypt, the invariable reply was that the essential work of reform was not yet completed. It was the truth, though not the whole truth. In time the French gradually became reconciled, as they discovered that their investments in Egypt grew more valuable with every year that the British remained, and as fear of Germany stifled French hatred of England. By the Entente Cordiale of 1904, France formally recognized the British position in Egypt, and London agreed to put the principles of the 1888 convention into force. Thus it happened that the canal was closed to Spanish warships during the Spanish-American War in 1898, and open to Russian warships during the Russo-Japanese War six years later.

Turning from the occupation of Egypt to follow the international race for colonies, we should note an important connection. Though the British entry into Egypt was no part of that race, it greatly influenced the scramble for colonies. The entanglement of Britain on the Nile for the sake of the canal imposed a heavy handicap upon her, and it quickened the international jealousies that spurred her rivals on. But if her preoccupation with the land of the Pharoahs limited her liberty of action, it does not seem to have retarded her entry into the general competition.

The scramble for colonial territories is as bewildering as the croquet game of *Alice in Wonderland*. It occurred simultaneously in widely separated parts of the world, and all the participants were surprising one another in their interinvolved grabbing. A play-by-play account of the whole contest may seem to be necessary for a full understanding of Britain's part in it, but such a method would be very confusing and quite out of proportion here. Instead of jumping back and forth across the world and trying to keep an eye on every move of the other powers, it will be simpler to divide the subject geographically and to make specific reference to Britain's rivals only when they influenced her directly.

In 1884, while Gordon was besieged in Khartoum, Germany proclaimed a protectorate over Southwest Africa, stretching eight hundred miles between Cape Colony and Portuguese West Africa, but not including certain small islands or the harbor of Walfish (Walvis) Bay halfway up the coast of what was now German Southwest Africa. Back in 1867 Britain had annexed the small islands, rich in guano, and in the following year had rejected an invitation to annex the mainland. This invitation came from German missionaries who were laboring there, and the Prussian government backed their petition for British protection. In 1876, to pacify the warring tribes and to guard against Boer intrusion, the Cape government sent in a special commissioner, who reported that the chiefs wanted to be taken under British protection. Cape Town desired annexation, particularly of Walfish Bay because it was the only western entrance to the interior. London compromised in 1878 by allowing the Union Jack to be hoisted on Walfish Bay. In 1880 and again in 1881, Berlin complained to London that the natives were ill-treating the German missionaries, and London repeated the refusal to extend British jurisdiction beyond the fifteen-mile circle around Walfish Bay.

A Bremen merchant named Lüderitz then got some land from a native chief and proceeded to build a station at Angra Pequeña, halfway between Walfish Bay and the Cape border on the Orange River. Early in 1883, at his behest, Berlin once more approached London, this time inquiring whether Britain exercised authority there and would protect the new establishment, and intimating that otherwise Germany would have to extend to it the same protection as she gave to other German subjects in distant parts of the world "without the least design to establish a footing in Africa." Again London thought that Bismarck was suggesting British occupation or annexation. As this was out of the question unless Cape Colony would bear the cost, London replied that it would be necessary to consult Cape Town. Before an answer could be got from the Cape, where a change of government caused a long delay, the German protectorate was formally established, Bismarck having brusquely disposed of London's effort to stall by claiming that the region lay within the British sphere of influence. The proclamation of a German protectorate over Southwest Africa at once raised apprehensions lest Germany join hands with the Transvaal, which the London Convention at the beginning of the year had recognized as the South African Republic, or with the Portuguese in East Africa to hem in British South Africa from the north. It was a bitter blow to the Cape and a serious lesson to Britain. Walfish Bay was promptly handed over to Cape Colony.

The specter of a Teutonic belt across Africa just north of the Orange River was no mere figment of the British imagination. Almost as soon as the German flag was raised in the west, the survey of a railway to run eastward from Angra Pequeña was begun; the Volksraad of the South African Republic conferred upon a group of German and Dutch capitalists a monopoly of railroad construction in the Transvaal; Boer trekkers pushing westward into Bechuanaland had just set up two republics, and pushing eastward into Zululand now carved out another there, called the New Republic; and on St. Lucia Bay, a combination of Transvaalers and Germans prepared to repeat the coup of Angra Pequeña. The situation has been compared to that in North America when the French tried to confine the English colonies to the Atlantic seaboard.

Following the eighteenth century American precedent, the two British colonies were inclined to take a parochial view, while the responsibility for meeting the danger was actively assumed by a few British officials on the spot and by the home government. Then, too late, the Cape legislature voted unanimously for the British annexation of Southwest Africa, with the result that an embarrassed London had to placate an irate Bismarck, who had already threatened more trouble in Egypt if Britain made any trouble over Southwest Africa. From Bechuanaland, appeals of natives and whites for British protection reached the government of the Cape, but its prime minister would not entertain them. His treasury was almost bare, and he feared giving offense to his friends in the Transvaal. On the east, as for many years, Natal still impotently hankered after Zululand—which it finally got at the end of 1897.

To save Bechuanaland, through which ran the trade routes to the north, the British high commissioner for South Africa dispatched as resident commissioner a young man just turned thirty-one, Cecil Rhodes, who had made his fortune in diamonds and was beginning to make his mark in Cape politics; and the British government sent a military expedition of about 5,000 men. Rhodes' diplomacy and this show of force brought about a settlement without any bloodshed. Kruger withdrew his fighting commandos, over whom he had professed to have no control because they were violating the limits laid down in the London Convention; and in the spring of 1885 a British protectorate was proclaimed over Bechuanaland up to the twenty-second parallel of south latitude, which was just beyond the top of the Transvaal. Later in the year the southern portion of the new protectorate became the crown colony of British Bechuanaland.

On the east coast, a British warship was ordered to St. Lucia Bay, where a German agent of Kruger's government had got a large cession of land from a Zulu chief. The circulation of a rumor, which soon proved to be true, that the chief was about to sell to Lüderitz, persuaded the British government in December 1884 to annex, on behalf of Natal, the only possible harbor between Durban and the Portuguese Lourenço Marques on Delagoa Bay. The New Republic, having already claimed St. Lucia Bay, appealed to Holland, France, and Germany for help. Berlin added its protests to those of Pretoria, but this time Berlin was too late and Britain bought off German claims by making concessions in Cameroon. In January 1885 the Colonial Office warned the Cape ministry that, for safety's sake, it had better annex all it could of the coast right up to Portuguese East Africa. By the following year the last gap in the British coast between Natal and Cape Colony was closed; and in 1887, having recognized a restricted New Republic, Britain annexed what remained of Zululand and placed it under the governor of Natal.

Between Zululand and Portuguese East Africa lay Tongaland, less than fifty miles square but containing the mouth of the Kosi River which might be made into a harbor; back of Tongaland lay the larger Swaziland, whose independence was stipulated in Kruger's London Convention of 1884. His Boers, however, were penetrating Swaziland, and in 1887 they made a deal with native chiefs to give access to Kosi Bay, which he coveted as his one remaining chance to get a harbor of his own. Therefore, early in 1888, Tongaland was declared to be within the British sphere of influence. But Transvaal pressure on Swaziland continued and extracted from its drunken king a will making Kruger his heir. The British government refused to recognize this transaction, and then closed with an earlier offer by Kruger of a joint commission, which established a temporary joint administration of whites over whites in 1889. Transvaalers sabotaged this administration, and in 1893 the Volksraad denounced the agreement on which it rested. Rather than risk a war over Swaziland, London made a new agreement in 1894, by which it became a protectorate of the South African Republic with provisions to safeguard natives' interests.

All this jockeying for position has a twofold significance. Internally it was part of the complicated interplay of forces that culminated in the Boer War, to be treated in a later chapter. Externally it was keeping the northern door open for a British advance beyond the Transvaal. This advance had already begun, into what was soon to be known as Rhodesia. But before we follow it we should first look at what was happening elsewhere, because the further drive from the south aimed at linking British South Africa with other British territories being acquired from other bases.

On the great western bulge of Africa, fingers of French territory crept inland from Senegal and then down to the coast, isolating and confining the little British colonies of Gambia and Sierra Leone without causing any British concern because the country around was not very inviting. The French also shut in the British Gold Coast on the west and north without rousing any British jealousy.

It was different on the Niger, where the British had long enjoyed a thriving trade without claiming any territory. There a young Englishman named George Taubman Goldie appeared in 1877, and he conceived the idea of creating a British province. He would do it by reviving a method that his fellow countrymen thought had died in India, a chartered governing company. Two years later he succeeded in amalgamating the local British interests in the United African Company, which then pressed French rivals so hard that they sold out in 1884, when reverses in the Far East temporarily discouraged French imperial ambitions. At the very same time Dr. Gustav Nachtigal, who had won fame as an explorer of the northern interior, arrived in the neighborhood on a mission from Bismarck, which he promptly executed. He added two protectorates to the German empire. One was little Togoland, wedged in between the Gold Coast and French Dahomey, and the other was the much larger Cameroon, running back from the Bight of Bafria just east of what was presently to be Nigeria.

To regulate the scramble for Africa, which was now quite general and threatened to let loose all manner of international friction over conflicting claims, Bismarck called a conference in Berlin. There the representatives of fourteen powers, including the United States,[2] met in the winter of 1884–85 and drew up the Berlin Act. It recognized annexations already made and the existence of the Congo Free State; it prescribed free trade in the Congo basin and rules of navigation on the great rivers; and it laid down rules for imperial grabbing. These rules sanctioned the hitherto unrecognized right to declare spheres of influence; denied the validity of any occupation that was not "effective," thereby deflating Portugal's enormous claims; and required every power, on assuming a protectorate, to notify all the other powers.

When the conference discussed the Niger region, Goldie was there as an expert to advise the British representative, and the latter was able to assert without contradiction that the Union Jack was the only flag flying on the river and that none but British trading interests were there. In June 1885 London proclaimed a protectorate over the region from Lagos on the west to Cameroon on the east; and in the next year Goldie's company, renamed the Royal Niger Company, received a charter giving it the right of administering Nigeria, a precedent having been established in 1881 by the incorporation of the British North Borneo Company, to be noted later.

On the opposite side of Africa, around the great eastern horn of the continent, three European powers were busy as a consequence of the completion of the Suez Canal and the collapse of the Egyptian empire over the Sudan. On the adjacent corner of Arabia, the free port of Aden had been held by the British as an outpost of India ever since 1839; from this vantage point the Indian government had exercised considerable influence on the African Somali coast, though Ismail occupied ports upon it and claimed jurisdiction over it right out to Cape Guardafui, the tip of the horn. When the Mahdi destroyed the khedival empire, France took possession of one of these ports in 1883, and Britain three others in 1884. That was the beginning of French Somaliland and British Somaliland. About the same time Italy stepped in to create her colony of Eritrea on the Red Sea, and shortly afterward acquired Italian Somaliland by treaties with the Somali sultans.

Farther south, from Mogadishu to Cape Delgado, the Sultan of Zanzibar, Seyyid Bargash bin Said, was recognized as the ruler of the coastal region. He also claimed a vague overlordship of the vast

---

[2] The only signatory that did not ratify the agreement.

inland region stretching to the great lakes, but this claim had never been substantiated by any effective occupation. Almost the whole trade of this empire was in the hands of British and Indian merchants; and British influence had no rival in the capital town, also called Zanzibar, where an Anglican cathedral began to rise in 1873. Four years later Bargash offered a seventy-year lease of all his mainland dominions to a British shipowner and merchant, William (later Sir William) Mackinnon, and gave the resident British consul general a pledge that he would cede no territory to any power but Britain. London, however, would neither acknowledge the pledge nor allow an acceptance of the offer. That was when Disraeli was in power. In 1882 Gladstone's government rejected a proposal of Bargash to be taken under formal British protection; and when the English leader of a scientific expedition to Kilimanjaro, halfway up to Lake Victoria Nianza, got a concession of territory from a local chief in 1884, the consul general denounced the bargain as violating Zanzibar sovereignty, which Britain and France had recognized in a treaty of 1862. But the days of this sovereignty were numbered.

In November 1884 three deck passengers disguised as mechanics stepped ashore on the island; and in a few days they made their way to the nearby mainland with their stock-in-trade, which consisted of German flags and treaty blanks. One of the mysterious trio was Dr. Karl Peters, president of the German Colonial Society, and at the very time when the conference was assembling in Berlin he began to run up the flags and get the treaty forms filled out. Obliging chiefs formally repudiated the authority of their nominal overlord, the sultan, and accepted that of the kaiser. Peters kept his secret well. He carried his precious documents to Berlin while the conference was still sitting. As soon as it adjourned, however, the kaiser incorporated the German East Africa Company, headed by Peters, and proclaimed a German protectorate over the territory covered by the treaties, which were now divulged. Bismarck blustered, the German press shouted, and German warships appeared off the coast of German East Africa, the future Tanganyika.

British East Africa, now Kenya, was established slowly and cautiously as a reaction to this German surprise. A British claim to territory running back from Mombasa was ratified by an Anglo-German agreement of 1886, and in the following year Bargash turned over to a company formed by Mackinnon the administration of all his mainland beyond what Britain had recognized as German. London sanctioned this transfer, and in 1888 Mackinnon's organization blossomed forth as the Imperial British East Africa Company with a royal charter conferring governing rights in what was technically a British sphere of influence. In 1890 the shrunken sultanate of Zanzibar, now under a successor to Bargash, was declared a British protectorate, Germany and France having separately agreed to this in conventions of much wider import.

These two conventions, signed by Britain in the summer of 1890, resolved a tangled conflict of claims that straddled the continent. French imperial expansion, linking Senegal with Algeria across the Sahara Desert, pressed in a general southeasterly direction. It bore down upon the British in upper Nigeria and, what was more important, it aspired to stretch a broad French belt right across the widest expanse of Africa. One result was Anglo-French rivalry over the native kingdom of Uganda, which lay behind British East Africa and just north of Lake Victoria Nianza, the second largest lake in the world and the chief reservoir of the Nile. As this great river was the very life-blood of Egypt, it was already a cardinal principle of British policy to prevent any civilized power from getting control of its upper waters. Native rule over the land of these waters was incapable of blocking or diverting them, but Europeans could apply their engineering ability to stop the vital flow. Though the French were on the scene almost as soon as the British, it was the later appearance of the Germans that constituted the immediate threat. As in Southwest Africa and in East Africa, the German move came as a sudden surprise.

Following the Anglo-German agreement of 1886, which separated the British from the German sphere of influence by a line commencing on the coast and extending to the first degree of south latitude on the eastern shore of Lake Victoria Nianza, a supplementary agreement of 1887 gave Germany a free hand south of that lake and Britain north of it. Nevertheless, the redoubtable Karl Peters, early in 1890, slipped into Uganda and promptly got its king to sign a treaty making the country a German protectorate. When the news reached London it startled Salisbury into quick action. For some years Bismarck had been angling for Heligoland, which Britain had held since the Napoleonic wars and which he wanted as a guard for the entrance to the Kiel Canal, begun in 1887. Now his successor got it. It was the price that Britain paid for the convention of 1 July 1890, which defined unsettled Anglo-German boundaries in Africa. Germany recognized as lying within the British sphere of influence not only Uganda but also the whole territory northward to Egypt, eastward to the Italians in Somaliland, and westward to the Congo Free State and the watershed between the Nile and the Congo rivers. Germany also consented to a British protectorate in Zanzibar. A wit described the transaction by saying that Britain had exchanged a trouser button for a whole suit of clothes, and when the First World War came Britons added ruefully, "But what a strategic button!"

A British invitation to France to adhere to this convention followed immediately upon its conclusion. The result was a very limited bargain, completed in five weeks. France consented to a British protectorate over Zanzibar in return for a British recognition of the French protectorate over Madagascar and French influence over the western Sahara down to Lake Chad, where it would meet the British in Nigeria. There was no attempt to reach a comprehensive agreement comparable to that with Germany, for both parties knew that such an accord was then impossible. The French could not yet forgive the British occupation of Egypt, nor forego the dream of planting the tricolor on the banks of the Nile, somewhere, somehow, and sometime, which was to lead to the Fashoda crisis in 1898.

The British advance from South Africa, to which we now return, aspired to join the British penetration from the east coast and then push on to Egypt. This project of a continuous belt of British territory stretching through the whole continent from top to bottom and reinforced by a Cape to Cairo railway was even grander than that of France to fling a bridge across the greatest width of the continent. It was too ambitious for the British government but not for the master mind of Cecil Rhodes, whose name is written large on the map of Africa. It was he who conceived and directed the advance from the south, through the open door of Bechuanaland; though he was unable to carry it far enough to effect a junction with British East Africa, he added Rhodesia to the British Empire.

Immediately to the north of Kruger's South African Republic and of the British protectorate of Bechuanaland lay the fabled region of "King Solomon's Mines." There from time immemorial, natives had worked gold mines and had lived by agriculture, for the soil was fertile and the rainfall good. Moreover, the country was a high tableland and therefore, though within the tropics, had a healthy climate quite suitable for white colonization. The southern portion of this rich and tempting prize was known as Matabeleland because the Matabele, an offshoot of the Zulus, had conquered it and settled upon it when the

Boers of the Great Trek drove them north across the Limpopo River. Beyond Matabeleland and reaching to the Zambesi River was Mashonaland, which was inhabited by the less warlike Mashona tribes, whom the Matabele had reduced to subjection. Over all ruled the able and despotic Matabele chieftain or king, Lobengula. The kraal of this native potentate, at Bulawayo, began to attract concession-hunters in the seventies. The buzzing increased in the eighties, and it was wildly excited in 1886 by the discovery of gold on the Witwatersrand in the Transvaal. This was the greatest gold find of all history, and it suggested that even greater riches were to be found in the kingdom of Lobengula. There British and Boers from the south, Germans from the west, and Portuguese from the east staked out claims. Clearly the Matabele were about to lose the treasure house that they had conquered.

Kruger precipitated the coming crisis by dispatching an emissary who, in the summer of 1887, extracted from Lobengula a treaty that gave special privileges to Transvaalers north of the Limpopo under a resident Boer consul. The news reached Rhodes before the end of the year, and he urged the high commissioner, Sir Hercules Robinson, to proclaim Matabeleland-Mashonaland within the British sphere of influence. Robinson could not do this without instructions from London, but as time was short he rushed the Rev. J. S. Moffat, assistant commissioner in Bechuanaland, off to Bulawayo to protect British interests there. Moffat easily persuaded the Matabele king, in February 1888, to repudiate the Transvaal treaty, which he later said had been got from him by fraud, and to affix his mark to another with the "Great White Mother" binding him to enter into no foreign correspondence and particularly to cede no territory without the high commissioner's consent. In spite of angry Transvaal protests, Robinson ratified Moffat's treaty, which virtually made Lobengula's dominion a British protectorate.

Agents of Rhodes and his associates got Lobengula in October 1888 to assign to their syndicate all mineral rights in his kingdom in return for £1,200 a year, 1,000 rifles, 100,000 rounds of ammunition, and a steamboat on the Zambesi. Having gained this immense concession, Rhodes rushed to London to make arrangements for developing it. He had to float a company of commensurate size, and for it he sought a charter similar to those recently granted to the companies controlling North Borneo, Nigeria, and British East Africa. At first the government was unfriendly, and for some time he had to fight strenuous opposition from the Aborigines Protection Society, from imperialists advocating direct imperial rule, and from jealous rivals. But at last, in October 1889, he procured a royal charter for his British South Africa Company under certain conditions. The company was to be directly responsible to the Colonial Office for the handling of native affairs, it had to accept as some of its directors public men named by the government, it was obliged to buy out previous concessionaires, it was to exercise governmental powers only with the consent of the native ruler, and it was liable to have its charter revoked at any time. Meanwhile Rhodes was maturing his plans for the occupation of the country. The first white settlers arrived in 1890, the beginning of something that is unique. Here, but nowhere else in all the territories acquired by European powers during the great imperial scramble, a considerable white population took root in the soil. But this is a story that belongs to another chapter.

The geographical extent of the chartered company's dominion, christened Rhodesia by a royal proclamation in 1895, was at first very uncertain. The charter, adopting the vague terms of Rhodes' application, defined it as the region north of Bechuanaland and the Transvaal and west of Portuguese East Africa. There was no reference to limits on the north or the west, and nobody knew where this Portuguese territory ended. According to Portuguese claims that France and Germany had recognized by treaty in 1886, Portuguese East and West Africa extended without a break from the Indian to the Atlantic Ocean, leaving nothing for the new British company. On the other hand, Lord Salisbury in 1887 had registered with the Portuguese government a formal protest "against any claims not founded on occupation" because they were contrary to the Act of Berlin, adding that his government "cannot recognize Portuguese sovereignty in territory not occupied by her in sufficient strength to enable her to maintain order, protect foreigners, and control the natives."

After long and trying negotiations, a treaty was signed in June 1891 separating Portuguese territories on the east and west coasts by a broad wedge of British territory extending up to Lake Tanganyika. All but a little strip of this territory, a total of nearly half a million square miles, was the empire of the British South Africa Company. The little strip, running along the west side of Lake Nyasa and some distance down its effluence, the Shiré River, had been declared a British protectorate in 1889, when a force of armed Arabs under Portuguese leadership invaded it and with machine guns shot down natives who refused to submit. At the southern end of Lake Tanganyika, the British advance to the north was blocked by the Anglo-German convention of 1890. Salisbury had an offer from the Congo Free State to give Britain a narrow corridor running up to Uganda, but he did not hesitate to abandon this link in the "All-Red Route" when he found that it would probably wreck the negotiation with Germany.

The control of the upper Nile began to be a pressing issue shortly afterward, when King Leopold nearly stole a march on both France and Britain. His Congo Free State was expanding in this direction, and in 1892 an expedition led by Belgian officers reached the great river some distance below the Victoria Nianza while others penetrated into the Sudanese province of Bahr-el-Ghazal. London delivered warnings to Brussels, but the region at stake was still beyond the British reach. Uganda was too far inland to serve as a base for any effective operation, and the Mahdi's successor barred an approach from Egypt. Therefore a bargain was struck, by the Anglo-Congolese convention of May 1894. Leopold recognized the British sphere of influence as defined in the Anglo-German convention of 1890 and leased to Britain the corridor that Salisbury had then abandoned, and Britain allowed the Congo Free State to lease the disputed Sudanese province. But both parties quickly renounced their leases, London yielding to vigorous protests from Berlin against the British corridor along the west side of German East Africa, and Leopold bowing to excited pressure from Paris against the erection of a Congolese barrier across the French path to the Nile. In the previous year Paris had ordered an expedition to follow this path to the river and occupy Fashoda, only to call a halt on receiving word from Brazzaville that the Belgians threatened to stop the expedition by force. The wily Leopold was now turning to play along with the French.

What had fixed French eyes on Fashoda was a public address before the Egyptian Institute in January 1893 by Victor Prompt, an outstanding French engineer in the Egyptian service. Discussing certain hydrographic problems of the Nile, he observed that a barrage at the mouth of the Sobat, which flows into the Nile just above Fashoda, would be easy to construct and could be used, along with dams at the outlets of Lakes Victoria and Albert Nianza, to hold Egypt to ransom. Thence came half the summer supply of Egypt's water, he said, and the country would starve if this were withheld or be completely drowned if it were released in a flood. His words created a mare's-nest for the French and a nightmare for the British.[3]

France determined to seize this seat of power before Britain was ready to do it. The British plans called for indefinite delay until simultaneous thrusts could be launched from Egypt, when the government of that country had built up sufficient financial and military strength, and from Uganda, when it was connected with Mombasa by a railway that had yet to be built. While the British contemplated this north-south pincers movement, which they knew would be impossible for several years, the French planned a more immediate east-west pincers movement. Captain Marchand would lead a military mission from the French Congo to Fashoda, while Leopold from Brussels directed a parallel expedition through the Congo Free State, and at the same time another French expedition would approach the Nile through Abyssinia, which Italy, with secret French connivance, was then openly trying to conquer.

The key to what followed lies in Abyssinia, where the Italian army was floundering and finally suffered disastrous defeat at Adowa in March 1896. The Italian catastrophe was France's opportunity. It opened the door wide for a French advance through Menelik's empire, and it encouraged that triumphant King of Kings to send a large army to seize some of the Sudan on his own account, thus matching the design of Leopold. But Adowa also revolutionized the British plans. Already rumors of menacing French activity had shaken Lord Cromer's firm opposition to any Egyptian venture into the Sudan. Already the dervishes of the khalifa, whose hostility to Egypt had been held in check by hostilities with Abyssinia, were again swarming, this time not against their old Abyssinian foes but in cooperation with them against the Italians. Less than a fortnight after the battle of Adowa, the cabinet in London ordered an advance from the Egyptian border at Wadi Halfa to Dongola, more than two hundred miles up the river.

Who would pay for this expedition? Britain expected that Egypt would. Though Cromer had no money for it, the surplus controlled by the International Debt Commission was sufficient and Britain asked the other powers to sanction an advance of £500,000. London counted on a majority decision, but the Egyptian courts upheld the contention of

---

[3] When Marchand got to Fashoda, he found that Prompt was utterly wrong about the possibility of a barrage at the mouth of the Sobat.

France and Russia that a unanimous decision was necessary, with the result that the British government had to foot the bill and thereby became a partner in the enterprise, which was executed in the autumn of 1896.

That the occupation of Dongola was only a preliminary step to the recovery of the Sudan, the British did not try to conceal. In June 1896 Lord Salisbury, the prime minister, told the House of Lords: "We shall not have restored Egypt to the position in which we received her, and we shall not have placed Egypt in that position of safety in which she deserves to stand, until the Egyptian flag floats over Khartoum." But who would pay for this more expensive undertaking, which might cost as much as £2,000,000? Cairo could not and London would not—as yet. Nor was this the only formidable question. What forces were necessary to execute the larger operation? It was more than doubtful if the Egyptian army could do it alone. This meant that Britain would have to send a contingent of her own army to join in the reconquest of the Sudan, for which the British public was not prepared—as yet. Such considerations explain why, after Dongola, there was no further Egyptian activity in the Sudan until 1898, except the building of a strategic railway from Wadi Halfa across the desert to Abu Hamed and its occupation in August 1897. By that time Marchand had crossed the Nile watershed, and London was greatly worried over reports of a definite Abyssinian-dervish combination and a French expedition supported by Menelik. Two months later, in London, the British commander in chief urged an immediate advance from Abu Hamed to Khartoum and the government rejected it. At the end of the year, however, this decision was reversed and the order was issued.

From all sides there was a converging movement on the upper Nile in the first half of 1898, but only two of the opposing expeditions ever met, the others becoming bogged down. On July 10, Marchand, with half a dozen European officers and as many score Senegalese troops, reached Fashoda and there hoisted the tricolor. Sir Herbert Kitchener, sirdar (commander in chief) of the Egyptian army, was still hundreds of miles to the north and not yet near his objective, which was Khartoum, across the river from the khalifa's capital at Omdurman. It was not until 2 September that Kitchener's force of 22,000 British and Egyptian soldiers there met and destroyed the main dervish army of 40,000. This battle of Omdurman was so decisive that mopping-up operations were all that was needed to complete the conquest of the country.

But Kitchener, who was rewarded with a peerage for his smashing victory, had first to deal with Marchand, six hundred miles up the river. On the 7th a native steamer came down the river and was stopped near Khartoum. On being questioned, the crew said that white men had fired on them at Fashoda. That was Kitchener's first intimation that the French were there. On the 19th he was there too. His arrival probably saved the little French force from destruction. It had repelled one dervish attack but was expecting a fiercer one at any time. Now Marchand refused to retire or to haul down his flag without orders from home; Kitchener contented himself with hoisting the British and Egyptian flags; the two men agreed that it was not their business but that of their governments to resolve the clash of claims; and Kitchener ended the amicable meeting by inviting Marchand to join him in a whisky and soda.

The Fashoda crisis nearly plunged Britain and France into war. The tide of British imperialism, having reached a new height during the Diamond Jubilee of the previous year, rose higher still when the telegraph reported the triumph at Omdurman. The whole country seemed to have gone mad with glory. At the end of September, in the midst of the hysterical rejoicing, news of the Fashoda incident arrived, and the press began to rage against France for trying to steal the fruits of the British victory. The government, which had repeatedly warned France to keep hands off the Nile, flatly refused to discuss French claims until the Marchand mission had been withdrawn. France had to give in. She was in no condition to wage foreign war, for she was then trembling on the brink of civil war between the Dreyfusards and the Anti-Dreyfusards. But the abusive tone of the British press and the uncompromising stand of the British government made it almost impossible for the French government to back down. October was a month tense with naval and military preparations on both sides of the Channel. There was panic in France but not in Britain. To France it seemed that Britain was bent on provoking war to settle accounts, of which there were many, once and for all. France looked to her one ally, Russia, for support; and the heads of the czar's foreign, finance, and war ministries arrived in Paris for secret discussions. They departed leaving the French government hopeless. The French decision to capitulate came early in November. Discussions could then proceed, and in March 1899 the two governments signed an agreement that drew a dividing line between their spheres of influence north of the Congo Free State. The line excluded France from the whole basin of

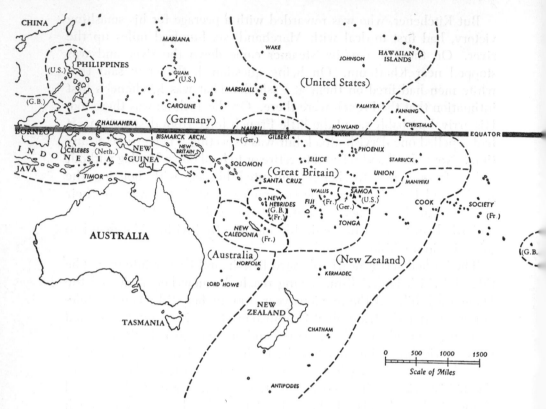

South Pacific Islands before First World War

the Nile. Already, in January, the status of the Sudan was formally
settled by the British and Egyptian governments. As the country was
conquered by "the joint military and financial efforts" of Britain and
Egypt, they were to share sovereignty over it. This condominium was
to be a bone of contention between the two governments when Britain
finally evacuated Egypt.

Compared with the partition of Africa, the contemporary partition
of the islands of the Pacific was a small business. Though countless in
number and sprinkled over an oceanic region that stretched for 6,000
miles east of the Philippines and the Dutch East Indies, the islands
in question were scarcely more than specks on the map. Their total
area was only some 70,000 square miles, and their total population
was probably less than a million. Europeans knew little and cared less
about them until the nineteenth century, when Christian missionaries
found them an inviting field for their labors. British Protestant mis-

sionaries, of various denominations, had the islands all to themselves for many years after the first thirty of them arrived shortly before 1800. The next to appear were French Roman Catholics, but the British Protestants continued to dominate the field. Of these Protestants, a goodly number were from Australia, the most noteworthy being the Presbyterians in the New Hebrides and the Wesleyans in Tonga.

On the heels of the missionaries came traders of many nations, including a large proportion of Americans. But in this activity, also, the British were far in the lead; most of the island trade, irrespective of the nationality of the traders, was conducted from the ports of Australia and New Zealand, because they were by far the most convenient. Therefore Australia and New Zealand acquired a special interest in the islands. The chief attraction at first was sandalwood for the Chinese market, where it was exchanged for tea to be sold in Australia. Then a profitable commerce in coconut oil and in copra sprang up; during the sixties a traffic in indentured labor began to reach great heights. This traffic raised a serious problem because, though it was often conducted quite respectably, it tended to degenerate into a veritable slave trade.

This evil was aggravated by the American Civil War, which encouraged the production of cotton in the tropical islands of the Pacific, notably in Fiji. In Queensland, also, cotton plantations arose along with the new sugar plantations, which together employed eleven hundred Polynesians in 1868. Though special colonial legislation protected these Polynesians and the governor reported that they were well treated, the home government was becoming worried over the situation. At the same time officers of the Royal Navy brought it home to the British government that this situation could not be isolated from the larger problem of the traffic throughout the islands, where there were increasing outrages committed by Europeans upon natives and retaliatory murders of white men. To facilitate their kidnaping operations, traders took to impersonating missionaries, which resulted in a tragic error in 1871, when the English bishop of Melanesia, mistaken for one of these scoundrels, was killed by natives. This shocking murder brought to a head a movement for intervention by imperial legislation.

Parliament passed the first Pacific Islanders Protection Act in 1872, which prohibited the transportation of native labor in British vessels without a special license for the purpose. But the wicked "blackbirding" throve more than ever—under the protection of other flags— because the agricultural exploitation of the islands by white settlers was gathering momentum and forcing up the price of labor. The next British action to cope with the evil was the annexation of the Fiji Islands in 1874, not to forestall other powers but, as we have seen in a previous chapter, because no other power would take them. Following this move, the British government had parliament pass the second Pacific Islanders Protection Act in 1875, which went a great deal further than the first. The new act provided for a high commissioner, with headquarters in Fiji, and a special court of justice to exercise jurisdiction over all British subjects in the islands of the Pacific outside the dominions of any civilized power. With the exception of the Marquesas Islands, Tahiti, New Caledonia, and the Loyalty Islands, which France had already annexed, all the archipelagos of Polynesia, Micronesia, and Melanesia thus passed under a qualified British protectorate, the qualification being that it affected only British subjects in these islands and that it made no claim to bar annexations by other powers. Still the nefarious traffic continued, as it was bound to do until the power vacuum was filled.

Germany started the scramble to divide up the islands, but the main pressure behind British participation in it came from Australia and New Zealand. Their interest in preserving their general trade in the islands, which annexation by other powers would cut down, and their concern for their own security, which might be seriously threatened if other powers established themselves in nearby islands, as France had done in New Caledonia, made them more and more impatient with the mother country's opposition to any British annexations in the Pacific. As in South Africa, so also in the South Pacific there was strong colonial pressure for British imperial expansion.

New Guinea, the second largest island in the world, is separated from the northern tip of Australia by the island-studded Torres Strait. Because its waters were perilous for navigation and were on the shortest route from New South Wales to India and China, the British Admiralty had the strait surveyed in 1846. The officer in charge of the work then took possession of the adjoining New Guinea coast for Britain, but London disavowed his action. In 1873 it was repeated, with the same negative result, by another British naval officer, Captain Moresby, who was engaged in trying to suppress the illegal labor traffic. By this time, however, there was a Queensland settlement on the southern side of the strait; the operations of pearl fishers were extending to the opposite shore; and Australians generally were beginning to display a lively interest in the great island. The west half had long belonged to the

Dutch, but the eastern half was still unappropriated by any power. Its annexation by Britain, to make sure it would not fall into foreign hands, was formally proposed by the government of New South Wales in 1875. The home government, having found Fiji a heavier financial burden than anticipated, refused to consider the proposal unless the Australian colonies would share the expense, which they declined to do. Therefore the subject was dropped, only to spring up again in 1878, when rumors of gold drew a flock of adventurers to eastern New Guinea and the high commissioner reported that the annexation of at least part was inevitable. This time the failure and withdrawal of the prospecting parties gave a respite to the Colonial Office.

Ominous rumors of an impending foreign occupation of eastern New Guinea began to fly around in 1882. Various powers were mentioned, particularly Germany, in which country there was a public agitation for the annexation and colonization of this "vacant" land. In February 1883 Queensland cabled London, urging British annexation before it was too late, and offering to bear the cost and to take formal possession on the receipt of authority by cable. Gladstone's colonial secretary replied that such an important question required careful consideration. Early in April the Queensland government had one of its officials proclaim at Port Moresby the annexation "pending decision" in London, hoping thereby to commit the home government. The home government not only declined to approve but it also rebuked the government of Queensland for assuming a power it did not possess. Moreover, the colonial secretary's crushing dispatch declared that the fears of foreign occupation were "indefinite and groundless"; that in any event annexation to Queensland would be open to objection, which was an intimation that the record of Queensland did not qualify her for taking charge of the native population in New Guinea; and that a forward policy in the Pacific must wait upon effective collaboration by the Australian colonies generally.

The last remark soon found an application in Victoria, when that colony urged the annexation of all the islands between New Guinea and Fiji, including the New Hebrides which were the special object of this proposal. For thirty years British and colonial missionaries had toiled in the New Hebrides which, lying close to New Caledonia, were under a French shadow. In 1878 the British and French governments agreed to respect the independence of these islands, but of late years there was a growing apprehension in Australia that France would seize them. Hence the Melbourne demand for their annexation by Britain.

The British response, in August 1883, was to persuade France to renew the mutual assurance.

Toward the end of 1883, an intercolonial convention met in Sydney and adopted unanimously a number of resolutions on Pacific questions. One of them was that the "further acquisition of dominion in the Pacific south of the equator, by any foreign power would be highly detrimental to the safety and well-being of the British possessions in Australasia, and injurious to the interests of the empire." On the basis of this broad principle, the delegates pressed for the immediate annexation of eastern New Guinea and requested the British government to open negotiations with France with the purpose of securing control of the New Hebrides in the interests of Australasia. They also undertook to recommend to their respective governments the appropriation of funds to support this Pacific policy.

The colonial governments whose representatives so eagerly called for the tune were much less eager to pay the piper, with the result that they lost part of the tune. In the late summer of 1884, when the British cabinet had just decided to establish a protectorate over eastern New Guinea with Australian financial support of £15,000 a year, Germany intervened with an intimation that she would take the northern side of the territory. As Bismarck had the whip hand in Egypt and in other parts of Africa, London shrank from offending Berlin and decided to limit the protectorate to the south side of the island. The British proclamation was issued in November, just in time to block a scheme under cover of the French flag. In December Bismarck announced the raising of the German flag in northern New Guinea. Australians raged at the mother country for being so blind and so timid, and London turned to negotiate with Berlin a delimitation of boundaries between British and German spheres in the Pacific. There the race was now on.

The British protectorate of New Guinea,[4] with an area of 90,000 square miles and a population of some 400,000, was annexed as a colony in 1888; in 1901 it was turned over to the newly federated Australia, which renamed it the Territory of Papua. In spite of continued Australian anxiety to get the New Hebrides, Britain would take no step to acquire them. By a convention of 1887, following a serious

---

[4] The British government appointed an administrator for New Guinea and put him under the governor of Queensland who, with the advice of his executive council, was to exercise general supervision over the protectorate subject to conditions prescribed for the protection of the natives. The £15,000 mentioned above was provided by Queensland, New South Wales, and Victoria, each paying £5,000.

native outbreak, they were placed under the protection of a joint Anglo-French naval commission.

Britain, Germany, and the United States made a somewhat similar arrangement for the Samoan Islands in 1889. For many years New Zealand had pressed Britain to annex them, but Britain would not; now a dangerous situation had developed in these islands. A disputed succession to the native throne led to a civil war in 1887, and Germany supported one claimant while Britain and the United States backed his rival. Heaven intervened at a crucial moment in March 1889. A German and an American squadron were apparently on the point of coming to blows when a terrific hurricane burst, sinking all the German and two American warships, and strewing the wreckage on the beach of Apia. It was under the sobering influence of this sudden disaster, which caused a heavy loss of life, that the three powers combined to stop the civil war and establish their collective control over the islands. But their partnership proved to be an uneasy one, the pacification of the islands was only partial, and the death of the native king in 1898 produced another civil war with the same division between the powers. In March 1899 British and American ships bombarded Apia, damaging the German consulate. Germany was intent on dividing the islands with the United States, and proposed compensation for Britain in the neighboring Tonga Islands; but London, mindful of New Zealand and Australian interests in Samoa, refused to agree, even when Germany threatened to form a European combination against Britain. Finally, in the autumn of 1899, the coming of the Boer War forced London to bow to Berlin in Samoa.

Elsewhere in the broad reaches of the Pacific, the international game of give-and-take had been regulated by fairly amicable agreement among the interested powers; and now, with the partition of Samoa, practically all the islands of this immense region were under the sovereignty of some western power. In total area and population, Germany gained most, with Britain a good second. Much behind came France and the United States, France collecting more square miles but less population than the United States. This, of course, is not counting the Philippines, which were the prize in a very different game and made American gains in the Pacific many times greater than those of Germany. More than a hundred Pacific islands, with a combined area of some 22,500 square miles and a population of approximately 330,000, were added to the British Empire between 1884 and the end of the century; many of these islands were placed under the control of New

Zealand, which thus became the seat of a sprawling minor island-empire.

Turning back toward southeast Asia, we come upon the third largest island in the world,[5] Borneo, where Dutch and English traders established themselves in the seventeenth century but neither nation got a real footing until the nineteenth century. Then the Dutch took three quarters of the island. The remainder, the north and the northwest, was formally placed under British protection in 1888, when it was already under effective British control. Most of this territory once belonged to the sultan of Brunei who, by successive grants, ceded it into British hands.

The first cession was to a remarkable Englishman, James (later Sir James) Brooke, a retired officer of the East India Company's army and the son of a wealthy member of the Company's civil service. A voyage to China through the Malay Archipelago fired him with an ambition to rescue the warring and piratical island tribes from their savage barbarism. Returning to England, this rich and practical Don Quixote fitted out and trained a private expedition, with which he sailed to Borneo. There he aided the sultan to suppress a tribal revolt in the province of Sarawak, and for this service the sultan made him raja of Sarawak in 1841. He spent all his private fortune in building up his little principality, introducing a civilized code of laws, recruiting a civil service of Englishmen, stamping out savagery, and, with the occasional assistance of British ships of war, suppressing the piracy that was a curse to the native tribes that engaged in it as well as to western shipping in the neighboring seas. His enlightened administration drew immigrants from other parts of Borneo and won him official recognition by the British government as an independent ruler. After his death in 1868, his nephew and heir, Sir Charles Brooke, proved to be a worthy successor. Under these two rajas, Sarawak grew to be many times its original size, the sultan of Brunei ceding the additional territory in return for annual money payments.

British North Borneo had a later and different origin. In 1881 the British North Borneo Company received a royal charter and acquired the territorial rights that the sultans of Brunei and Sulu had ceded to a syndicate three years before. It was the first of the new chartered Companies which, patterned somewhat after the defunct East India Company but without any monopoly of trade, were organized to de-

---

[5] Greenland and New Guinea are larger.

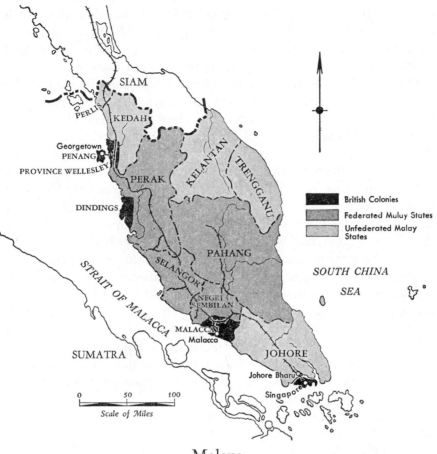

Malaya

velop and rule territories in which British traders were particularly
interested and in which the British government declined to assume
administrative responsibility. Subsequent concessions by the sultan of
Brunei extended the dominion of the Company, and in 1890 the British
government transferred to it the little neighboring island of Labuan,
which had become a crown colony in 1848.

When Sarawak, British North Borneo, and what was left of Brunei
became British protectorates in 1888, there was practically no change
in their administrations. Sarawak, the best governed of the three,
retained its complete independence in internal affairs. So did Brunei,
whose sultan was not saddled with a resident until 1906. The rule of
the company in British North Borneo was also left undisturbed, though
now the appointment of the governor had to receive the sanction of

the colonial secretary. The partition of Borneo between the Dutch and the British, completed by a boundary treaty of 1891, was unconnected with the international competition that carved up Africa and distributed the Pacific islands among the western powers.

On the Asiatic mainland, the expansion and consolidation of the British position in the Malay Peninsula likewise stands apart from the race between the imperial powers. Here the British advance was rather a repetition of what had happened in India during the days of the Company. When the Crown "took over" from the East India Company in 1858, the Straits Settlements, comprising Singapore, Malacca, Penang, and Province Wellesley, were virtually stranded. They had long been a heavy drain on the treasury of the Company, and now that they came under the new India Office with no change in the form of the administration, they were in a sorry plight. They had no money for fighting the local plague of piracy or for recruiting a competent civil service, to say nothing of providing for other immediate needs or future development. Their trade was with China, and they had practically nothing in common with India, except in the new department of government created in London to look after the affairs of India. Local agitation for freedom from this artificial tie became very strong, until in 1867 the Straits Settlements were transferred to the Colonial Office and became a crown colony with their own separate government. The nine years of stagnation were over.

The Straits Settlements were the foundation of British Malaya, and the next stage in the building was the addition of the Federated Malay States: Perak, Selangor, Negri Sembilan, and Pahang. The native states of the peninsula were seething with civil wars which spilled over their boundaries, and the Straits of Malacca were infested with pirates. The obvious cure for this growing anarchy, so dangerous to British life and property, was British intervention, and the Singapore Chamber of Commerce was eager for it. But the government of the colony informed the Chamber in August 1872 that it was contrary to British policy "to interfere in the affairs of the Malay States unless where it becomes necessary for the suppression of piracy or the punishment of aggression on our people or territories"; and the message added a warning "that, if traders, prompted by the prospect of large gains, choose to run the risk of placing their persons and property in the jeopardy which they are aware attends them in these countries under present circumstances, it is impossible for Government to be answerable for their protection or that of their property." Then fierce fighting broke out among 40,000 Chinese tin miners in Perak, who dyed their banners in the blood from the slit throats of their victims, defied the local Malay chief, and tried to blow up Chinese houses in neighboring Penang.

In the following year, 1873, London sent out a new governor to Singapore to inaugurate a new policy. He was instructed to employ British influence "with the native princes to rescue, if possible, these fertile and productive countries from the ruin which must befall them if the present disorders continue unchecked." To this end, he was directed to aim at the establishment of British official residents in the native states. Almost at once he found his first opening—an invitation to settle a dispute over the throne of Perak. Repairing thither he met some of the leading chiefs in January 1874; with them he concluded a treaty, making one of the claimants sultan and providing for a British resident at his court. Unfortunately the first resident assumed too much authority with too little tact. Malay spears thrust through the flimsy walls of a bathhouse soon disposed of him, necessitating a punitive expedition. The sultan, who was privy to the murder, was exiled, the actual murderers were hanged, a more discreet resident was installed, and Perak got a native government that was a model for that part of the world.

Selangor had a sultan who was more interested in horticulture than in ruling. While tending his princely garden with meticulous care, he allowed his rajas to run riot. In the autumn of 1873 retainers of one of these rajas seized a departing Malacca vessel, murdered the occupants, and then brazenly visited Malacca, where they were arrested. The aesthetic sultan was shocked and alarmed. He consented to have the criminals returned for trial and exemplary punishment, he sent his creese (Malay dagger) for their execution, he paid damages, and with the concurrence of his chiefs he accepted a British adviser, of whom he soon reported that the people rejoiced in his presence "as in the perfume of a flower." Thus, from 1874, Selangor ceased from troubling and settled down to enjoy peace and prosperity.

It took longer to settle affairs in Negri Sembilan, for it was then not a single state but a grouping of nine diminutive ones, all given to disorder. There British intervention began in 1874, and it was fifteen years before the little fragments were combined in a federation under one native ruler with a British resident to guide him in the way he should go.

Pahang, the largest state in the peninsula, was a more difficult problem. The ruler, who had seized the throne from his nephew, was a ruthless and grasping tyrant, and he was a danger to his neighbors as well as to his subjects. In 1887 he was persuaded to enter into a treaty with the governor of the Straits Settlements by which, in return for British recognition of his taking the coveted title of sultan, he admitted a British consular agent. But the new sultan was the same old sinner. In the following year, after instigating the murder of a Chinese British subject, he had to accept the tutelage of a British resident, who faced more than one rebellion before law and order were finally established. Much of his trouble arose from the suppression of slavery, upon which the British insisted in all four states. In 1895, Perak, Selangor, Negri Sembilan, and Pahang were federated with one civil service under a resident-general, whose seat was Kuala Lumpor, the capital of Selangor.

Johore, having a respectable government, was left without a British agent until 1914, though in 1885 its sultan placed himself under British protection. It is one of the Unfederated States. The others were added by treaty with Siam in 1909: Perlis, Kedah, Kelantan, and Trengganu. The treaty cleared up an anomalous situation in these states and also in Siam. These states were ancient dependencies of Siam but lay within a recognized British sphere of influence. The first three were administered for the native rajas by British officers in the service of Siam and were in a flourishing condition. Their population, mixed like that of most states of the peninsula, was predominantly Malayan. Trengganu was quite different. It had a population that was almost wholly Malayan and a government that had almost ceased to exist. The sultan was a religious recluse, there were neither written laws nor courts nor police, and everyone did what was right in his own eyes. It was the only peninsular state that was still sunk in hopeless anarchy. In Siam, as in other eastern lands, westerners were protected by treaty from being tried in any but their own consular courts. As this deroga- tion of sovereignty had grown irksome to the government in Bangkok, a bargain was struck in the treaty of 1909, by which British consular jurisdiction in Siam was abolished and Siam transferred to Britain "all rights of suzerainty, protection, administration, and control" of the four Malay states. The transfer took place without disturbance, and Britain installed an adviser in the court of each nominal ruler. The only important change was in Trengganu, and there it was most wholesome.

The British conquest and annexation of Upper Burma, in contrast to the British acquisitions in Borneo and the Malay Peninsula, had a

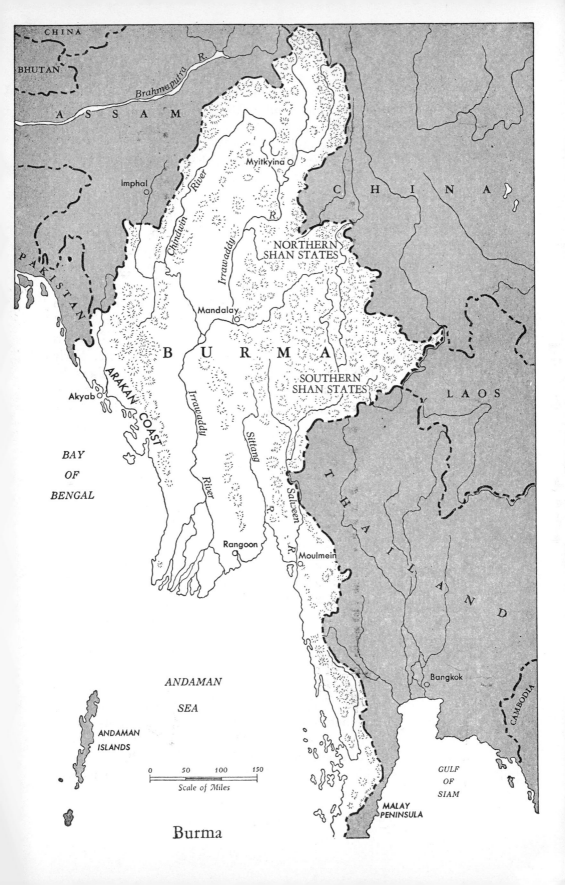

CHINA

BHUTAN

Brahmaputra R.

A S S A M

PAKISTAN

Imphal

Chindwin River

Myitkyina

C H I N A

NORTHERN
SHAN STATES

Irrawaddy R.

Mandalay

B U R M A

ARAKAN COAST

Akyab

BAY
OF
BENGAL

Irrawaddy River

SOUTHERN
SHAN STATES

Sittang R.

Salween R.

L A O S

T H A I L A N D

Rangoon

Moulmein

ANDAMAN

SEA

ANDAMAN
ISLANDS

0   50   100   150
Scale of Miles

Bangkok

CAMBODIA

GULF
OF
SIAM

MALAY
PENINSULA

Burma

direct connection with the scramble between the powers. Upper Burma was the truncated independent kingdom of Burma, which was cut off from the sea by the annexation of Pegu, or Lower Burma, to India at the close of the Second Burmese War in 1852. The king who lost that war straightway lost his throne to a shrewd brother, who kept him in captivity for the rest of his life. The British presented a peace treaty to the usurper, but he refused to accept it because he feared damnation as a king who signed away territory. Pegu thus passed from one sovereignty to another without any formal cession, and it was not until 1862 that the government of India was able to establish diplomatic relations with the government in Mandalay, the new capital of independent Burma. Then trade with Upper Burma was opened, and presently British steamers were running up the Irrawaddy River from Rangoon to Mandalay. The shrewd king died in 1878, leaving 53 wives, 110 children, and a will designating the succession. This was broken by a palace revolution, which put Thibaw on the throne. Early in 1879, to prevent his own overthrow by one of his royal brothers, he had nearly eighty princes and princesses murdered. Such massacres had stained the annals of Burma, but not since the coming of the telegraph; and the butchery did not stop in 1879. The outside world was horrified, and Burma groaned under the vicious rule of the monster. The government of India withdrew its representative, lest he too be murdered; and British Burma was menaced by the growing anarchy across the border. The unanimous cry of non-officials in Rangoon was for immediate intervention in, and annexation of, the nightmarish land.

British officialdom was deaf to this cry until France, having just carved out an empire in Indochina that approached the back door of Thibaw's kingdom, tried to dominate it by peaceful penetration. Thibaw was the tempter. He sent his envoys to Paris and there, in January 1885, the French foreign minister signed a treaty with them; in addition, he gave them a secret letter promising a supply of arms. Shortly thereafter, both in Paris and in Mandalay, French concessionaires negotiated the building of a railroad, the establishment of a bank, and the control of the royal monopolies in Burma, the revenues of the kingdom being pledged for the financial security of all these enterprises. Before the signature of the treaty in Paris, the British ambassador warned the French foreign minister that Britain had special interests in Upper Burma, and the latter assured him that he would never permit the import of arms into that kingdom. Seven months later there was a leak in Mandalay, and the viceroy of India telegraphed home the contents of the secret letter.

The crisis came toward the end of the year when the Burmese government, on a trumped-up charge, imposed an arbitrary fine of £250,000 on a British trading company and refused to submit the case to arbitration by the viceroy. A British ultimatum followed, demanding arbitration of the case, the admission of a British resident, and British control of Burmese foreign relations. Thibaw rejected the ultimatum and ordered his army to drive the British into the sea. A week later, on 14 November 1885, a British expedition crossed the border, advancing up the Irrawaddy, and on the 28th it took Mandalay with Thibaw in it. The royal captive was removed to a comfortable exile in India, and his kingdom was formally annexed on New Year's Day. The taking of Mandalay was easy, but the conquest of the rest of the country was hard. It required five years of mountain and jungle fighting. By a fateful irony, at the very time that the British plunged into Upper Burma, the French withdrew from it as a consequence of reverses in Tonkin.

To complete the tale of the British share in the great imperial scramble, we have merely to note two leases from China in 1898: the port of Weihaiwei for so long as Russia should retain Port Arthur, across the Gulf of Pechili; and, opposite Hong Kong, the extension of Kowloon territory for ninety-nine years.

In looking back over this global race for empire in the last quarter of the nineteenth century, we may conclude with a few general observations. The Marxians and others who have joined them in denouncing the western powers for indulging in this race have willfully or naïvely ignored some broad considerations that are very pertinent to any sane judgment of what these powers were doing. It is true that the iniquities perpetrated in the Congo Free State under Leopold became a byword; but these iniquities so scandalized the public opinion of the world that Leopold was driven to hand over his private empire to the government of Belgium, which could be held responsible for it. This experience suggests that it was much better for the natives in the appropriated territories in Africa and elsewhere to be brought under the rule of responsible western powers than to be exploited by private western interests operating in regions where no civilized government could control them. The missionaries who were devoting their lives to the welfare of the natives saw this very clearly. They also knew, as few other white men could know, how barbarous native society really was, and that the coming of white rule meant the suppression of unbridled savage wars, blood feuds, and the cruelest slavery, to say nothing of other inhuman practices that were likewise rampant. How Britain bore her share of "the white man's burden" that she shouldered in these years is a subject that we will examine later.

CHAPTER XXIX

The South African War, 1899-1902

THE ROOTS of the Boer War go back to the Great Trek. By doubling the area of European occupation in South Africa, the Great Trek committed the white population to live in the midst of an overwhelming majority of blacks; and by giving birth to the two Boer republics, it wrought a political dismemberment that bedeviled the relations between whites and blacks. It thus magnified the basic problem of South Africa, the mutual accommodation of white and black society; and it blocked a unified approach to the problem which could be solved in no other way. For this impasse the British government was partly responsible, the Boer withdrawal from the British colony being matched by Britain's desire to withdraw from imperial responsibilities in South Africa.

The plight of the country called desperately for the reintegration of what had been torn apart. Hence the impatience of Sir George Grey to federate the two republics and the two colonies. It was the anti-imperialist policy of the home government that first barred any attempt to achieve such a union; when London, still pursuing this policy, became converted to the view that only a united self-governing South Africa could relieve Britain of her South African burden, the British drive for federation was frustrated by political ineptitude. Whether it could have succeeded under more intelligent direction is an open question, for the obstacles in South Africa were many and great. Moreover, a consideration of these obstacles and how they grew suggests that even if a South African federation had then been formed it might have resembled the American Union in being unable to avoid a civil war.

The British annexation of the Transvaal in 1877, the rising of the Transvaalers to fight for their independence, their triumph over the British at Majuba Hill in 1881, and the British recognition of their republic in the same year, all gave a tremendous impetus to Boer nationalism throughout South Africa. It flared up in the Afrikander Bond, a bitterly anti-British organization. Though the fire could not catch in Natal, this mattered little because its white population— almost solidly British—was very small and the state did not get responsible government until 1893. In the three larger and self-governing states, the menace was very grave.

The Bond threatened to split the mother colony wide open. There the Dutch outnumbered the British two to one, but the latter had long dominated public affairs. The only official language was English, an incomprehensible tongue to the mass of the Dutch, who were mostly rural folk. Politics had interested them so little that a large proportion of those who were qualified to vote did not even bother to register. In the middle seventies only one quarter of the members of the Cape parliament had Dutch names, and these men were largely Anglicized. That such conditions should prevail so long may seem astonishing when we recall the history of British rule in French Canada. Fortunately for the peace of the Cape when Boer nationalism began to sweep through the land, a great Afrikander who has since been compared with Smuts had already arisen.

J. H. Hofmeyr came of a family that had farmed on the outskirts of Cape Town for more than a century, and for twenty years he had been an outstanding journalist. Early in his career he grasped the essential unity of South Africa, and he devoted the rest of his life to this ideal. He looked forward to the day when a united South Africa might stand on its own feet, apart from the empire. He loudly deplored the annexation of the Transvaal. To him it was an egregious blunder that might ruin his fondest hopes by inflaming Boer feeling against the British. His farseeing vision had revealed to him that only under the protection afforded by the empire's naval supremacy could Boer and Briton work out their common fate free from interference by foreign imperial powers. He also realized that the fullest cooperation of the two white peoples, upon which his heart was set, was unattainable until his own people shook off their political apathy and emulated the public activity of the British community. To this end, in 1878, he initiated the *Boeren Beschermings Vereeniging,* or Farmers' Protective Association, which was such an immediate success that several of its candidates won seats in the general election of 1879. He was of course the leader of the new Afrikander party in the House. Two years later he entered the cabinet. Though he soon left it, he and his followers continued to support the government long enough for him to secure, in 1882, a constitutional amendment recognizing the parliamentary use of the Dutch language and a provision that Dutch could also be employed as a medium of instruction in government schools.

This victory armed him to face the Bond, which threatened to leave his Vereeniging high and dry. Boldly throwing himself into the midst of the dangerous agitation, he captured the Bond in the Cape and led it away from its anti-British and republican course. By this remarkable feat he gained a commanding political position which enabled him to make and unmake ministries. He declined to form one of his own, for he feared that the appearance of Afrikander rule would consolidate the English members of the House in opposition to it and thus drive party politics down the road toward civil war. He preferred to work with this or that English premier of the Cape, and at the end of the decade he formed his famous alliance with Cecil Rhodes, who likewise cherished the ideal of a united self-reliant South Africa.

Meanwhile in the two republics Boer nationalism was unbridled and running wild. As might be expected, it was fiercest in the Transvaal. That had been the home of the wildest Boers from the very beginning, and in the early eighties their recent experiences had given them much more reason than their southern neighbors to hate and despise the British.

The embittered soul of the Transvaal was embodied in Paul Kruger, who as a lad had been one of the earliest trekkers from the Cape and had been present at the slaughter on Dingaan's Day. He grew up as a fighter, engaging in many savage attacks against native tribes, and on one occasion attempting by force of arms to bring the Orange Free State into subjection to the Transvaal. He headed the successful opposition to the liberal religious and political ideas of President Burgers, who sought to mitigate the bigotry and anarchy rampant in the Transvaal and espoused the cause of a united South Africa from the Cape to the Zambesi with equal rights for all civilized men. Kruger rose through the fall of Burgers and the republic. He rallied the Transvaal to revolt against the British occupation, and he conducted the peace negotiations for the Transvaal State. He was the Transvaal State. His election as president in 1883 was a recognition and a confirmation of that fact.

Kruger was the very antithesis of Hofmeyr. His ideal was a great and exclusive Afrikander republic gathered around the Transvaal, including the Orange Free State and as much more territory as he could lay his hands on, and built up with the aid of foreign powers. In other

words, he would erect a Transvaal empire by playing upon international rivalries, an old game that had brought many ambitious countries
to grief and was to drag South Africa into a disastrous war. He was a
stern fanatic who believed that God was on his side; for he had been
reared on the Old Testament and had become the champion of the
Doppers, the most bigoted sect of the Dutch church in South Africa.
He regarded his people as God's Chosen who had escaped from Egyptian bondage in the British Cape to conquer and enslave, with His
blessing, the Canaanite Bantus.

For the development and administration of the Transvaal, which
had never possessed an effective government, this determined Dopper
Boer had to import an able personnel. He might have found it among
the Boers of the Cape, but he turned his back upon them as infected
by a British bias. Instead he drew men from Holland and Germany
who were entirely free from this taint. He fed their personal ambitions
and they fed his. Coming from Europe where national cleavages were
most deep-seated and permanent, they brought with them stricter
notions of the division between national communities than had been
current in the South African family of states. Within that family
reciprocal rights of citizenship had not been much questioned. This
was strikingly illustrated by the election of three republican presidents
while they were undoubted British subjects and by the retirement of
one to enter the Natal legislature. A third became a British baronet.
Moreover, during the recent peace negotiations Kruger himself had
promised that in the Transvaal British subjects should have the "same
burgher rights" as the Boers. But this particular influence of Kruger's
foreign entourage should not be exaggerated. It merely gave a sharper
focus to a concept that was inherent in the growing Boer nationalism.

A more important contribution of these European adventures to the
increasing tension in South Africa was the encouragement that they
gave to Transvaal hopes of foreign aid and the consequent specter that
they raised in British minds. In 1883 an American promoter named
McMurdo got a concession from the Portuguese government to build a
railway from Lourenço Marques on Delagoa Bay to the Transvaal
border; and in the following year the extension of this line to Pretoria
was projected by the Dutch and German syndicate upon which the
Volksraad conferred a monopoly of railroad construction in the republic. Also in 1884, it will be recalled, the Germans annexed Southwest
Africa; they began the survey of a railway running eastward toward the
Transvaal; and some of them joined with Transvaalers in an effort to

repeat on the east coast, in St. Lucia Bay, the coup that had just been executed on the west coast, at Angra Pequeña. It seemed that the Transvaal might soon escape from its crippling dependence upon British colonial ports. But this venture required foreign capital, which shrank from such schemes. The political risks were too great and the prospective rewards too small. The republic was a poor weak thing whose potential wealth was yet hidden. Kruger had no sooner essayed to play the international game than he found that he could neither buy nor borrow the necessary chips. In desperation he turned to the British, who had forestalled him by annexing St. Lucia Bay in 1884, and he held out his hand.

A telegram from the president of the Transvaal to the government of the Cape at the end of July 1885 asked, "How about the Customs Union? Is there no chance that we take off the duty on colonial brandy and colonial-made wagons, and you the duty on our tobacco?" Early in 1886 the request was repeated with a suggestion that Pretoria should be linked with the Cape railway system by an extension of the line from Bloemfontein. It might be expected that these overtures would be warmly welcomed. Rhodes urged acceptance of the offer, but he was only a rising member of the Assembly. A more hopeful sign was a recent action of the Cape Bond. In 1884 Hofmeyr had persuaded that organization to come out in favor of a South African Zollverein, modeled on that which had knit Germany together, as the one immediately practical move to draw the country closer together. Moreover, the imperial government had forced the Cape to hand over a fair share of its customs receipts to Basutoland, and the competition between the high-tariff Cape and the low-tariff Natal for the trade of the interior had wrung from the parliament in Cape Town a temporary rebate of the difference on goods entering the Free State.

But in spite of all these tentative moves toward a customs union, with its implication of a closer union to follow, the Cape rebuffed the Transvaal. It was another instance of the blind selfishness of the coastal colonies in the matter of customs. By levying toll on the land-locked republics and refusing to share the receipts with them, Cape Colony and Natal were guilty of a grave injustice to the Orange Free State and the Transvaal, an injustice that naturally hardened republican Boer hearts against the British. The rejection of the Transvaal offer in 1886 was tragically final, for in this very year an amazing and disturbing development began in the northern republic—on the Witwatersrand.

The opening of the Witwatersrand gold field altered the whole face of things in South Africa. Indeed, it profoundly affected the whole world; for never in all history, ancient and modern, had there been a gold field to compare with this one, which soon leaped far ahead of all others in output and unlike them all has shown no sign of exhaustion. It reversed the secular movement of world prices, and it established the victory of gold over silver as the monetary basis of western civilization, William Jennings Bryan notwithstanding. But here we are not so much concerned with these two major effects upon the international economy, and their countless repercussions all over the globe, as we are with what the development of this gold field did to South Africa. It enormously enriched the country as a whole, and the Transvaal most of all; it tied black and white together as never before; and it so entangled the interests of Briton and Boer that the political disunity of the country had to be ended somehow, if not by peaceful means, then by war.

Technology thrust this issue upon South Africa. It had long been known that there was gold in the Transvaal, but the precious metal to be found there had attracted no attention because none of it was concentrated in nuggets or lodes. The Witwatersrand gold is all very thinly and quite evenly scattered in microscopic particles through uncommonly hard rock from which the Californian "forty-niners" and the Australian "diggers" could have got nothing. By 1886, however, the advance of applied science made possible the extraction of the treasure from this low-grade ore. What made the field so rich was, therefore, not the quality but the untold quantity of the ore. The geological formation of the gold-bearing reefs covers a surface area of about 170 by 100 miles, and it goes down obliquely to depths that have never yet been fathomed.

Mining in the Rand was profitable only if conducted on a large scale. It required huge machinery, a plentiful supply of cheap power to operate it, and a big investment of capital to launch and sustain the enterprise. Of course there was no water power in that parched land, but there was an abundance of good cheap coal so close that in one place the seams overlay the reefs. By another lucky coincidence, there was also at hand a group of men who had accumulated in Kimberley the essential capital and experience. Rhodes and his associates were thoroughly familiar with mining conditions in South Africa, and they were so wealthy that they could borrow heavily in England. Eagerly they threw all their resources into this new venture. Other speculators from near and far, little and big, did the same. Almost immediately the feverish competition to get at the treasure produced chaos on the Rand, as it had in Kimberley. Now the scale was much grander, and the tempo much faster. Order emerged in less than half the time, as the small fry abandoned the futile scramble and the larger companies pooled their interests. Within six years the Consolidated Gold Fields of South Africa, under the leadership of Rhodes, gained control of the gigantic mining industry of the Rand.

One important aspect of the new development should be noted in passing, though it contributed nothing to the coming of the Boer War and its seriousness was little appreciated until years after that conflict was over. The gold mines depended for their very existence upon an army of unskilled black labor many times larger than that of Kimberley—and no less unstable. Though the wages were far below the white level, they were high according to native standards of living, with the result that there was a constant turnover in the ranks—recruits were forever pouring in to earn a relative competence in a short period of intensive toil and then pouring out to live upon it. They came from all over South Africa, and even beyond. In other words, the Rand was pumping a human stream out of the exhaustless native reservoir and pumping it back again. But human beings are not like water. The native circulation through the gold mines greatly accelerated the disintegration of tribal society and left the blacks with nothing in its place.

Of more immediate concern was the new entanglement of Boer and Briton in the Transvaal. Hitherto that republic had been a Boer preserve, but no longer was it so. British capital rushed in, and a British population swarmed in, accompanied by a sprinkling of non-British adventurers. The Boers called the newcomers Uitlanders, or foreigners. Many were from the colonies, many more from the mother country. For the first time in its history, South Africa was drawing immigrants from England in large numbers. Gold had plunged the whole country into prosperity, and the favorite goal of the immigrants was the seat of that prosperity. All South Africa could not begin to supply the demand for skilled labor in and around the new mines; for skilled labor was a white monopoly in that land of the blacks, and up to this time the South African economy was overwhelmingly rural. There were also all sorts of other inviting opportunities for white people in the rapidly expanding community on the Rand, where almost overnight an untidy cluster of tin shacks on the high bleak veldt multiplied into a tawdry but wealthy city—Johannesburg.

Thus, after half a century, the industrial revolution caught up with the Great Trek. A bustling British urban society now shared the Transvaal with the stubbornly backward pastoral society of the Boers, which had in its own characteristic fashion replaced or subdued the much more backward society of native tribes. Would history repeat itself here? This momentous question took shape only gradually over a period of years, as the exploration of the gold field proceeded and the shafts penetrated deeper and deeper into the bowels of the earth. Not until 1895, when the Uitlanders had become twice as numerous as the burghers, was it fairly certain that the mines had an indefinitely long life ahead of them and that the populous community which served them would not presently wither and vanish, like so many other mining settlements, but would thrive as long as the industry that had called it into being. A crisis in the history of the Transvaal was clearly approaching, and it was bound to be a crisis in the history of all South Africa.

Meanwhile gold had lifted the Transvaal government out of its chronic bankruptcy into proud affluence with a twentyfold increase of revenue, and had revived its expansive policy that originated in the Great Trek. The renewed outward pressure was toward the north and the east, the way to the west having been recently barred by the British annexation of Bechuanaland in 1885. Kruger wished to concentrate on an eastward drive, but he had to compromise with the opposition party led by Joubert, who was his serious rival for the presidency and urged a northerly advance. Hence the race between Kruger and Rhodes, which the Boer began in 1887 and the Englishman won in 1888, to get control of Lobengula's tempting kingdom, the region of "King Solomon's Mines." Though one of these two protagonists was striving to split South Africa and get the lion's share for his own race while his opponent was aiming at a larger union based on the partnership of the country's two white races, this difference should not obscure the fact that both men were essentially South African imperialists.

On the east Kruger had already resumed his own and his predecessors' search for an independent outlet to the sea, a search that sprang from the shortsighted customs policy of the two British colonies. Visions of Transvaal gold resuscitated the McMurdo project. The survey was completed in 1887 and the railroad in 1889. The line to Delagoa Bay was not under British control, but neither was it under Transvaal control. Kruger would never be satisfied until his territory touched the sea, and by 1887 his people had made some headway in that direction. This, however, was through native states, it was in violation of the London Convention of 1884, and it ran into opposition by the British government. Hence the British annexation of Zululand in 1887, minus the New Republic which the Boers had carved out of it; the 1888 declaration of a British sphere of influence covering Tongaland, which became a British protectorate in 1895 under circumstances that will be noted presently; the joint administration in Swaziland from 1889 to 1893 and then, in 1894, the British concession that it should be a Transvaal protectorate. Though Kruger thus gained some territory because London was reluctant to become involved in a serious quarrel with him, he lost his great object—a coastal port—for the coast was now all British right up to the Portuguese boundary. Unable to break through without more powerful aid, he sought it in Berlin.

While all this was going on there was pulling and straining within South Africa over the issue of unity, which Transvaal gold made much more urgent; some progress was made toward the economic consolidation of the country by removing internal tariff barriers and by tying it together with railroads. In July 1886, only a few months after the rebuff administered to the Transvaal proposal of a customs union, the Cape turned penitent and issued invitations to a conference. It was then Kruger's turn to reject the advance, and in 1887 he countered with an attempt to effect a further disruption of South Africa. At a conference of the two republics in that year, he proposed that they should form a political federation of their own and should cooperate on railways, particularly to build a road to Bloemfontein as an extension of the Delagoa Bay line. President Brand would have none of it. Early in the new year, 1888, the governments of the Free State and the two colonies held a conference in Cape Town, and there they reached a specific agreement on a customs union of the three states and a policy of railroad construction that would link the southern republic with both colonies. But the Natal legislature refused to ratify the compromise on tariff rates and the Volksraad in Bloemfontein balked at the railway terms, so that the agreement came to nothing. Nevertheless, the fact that it had been made pointed in the direction of cooperation. On the other hand, the death of Brand in the summer of 1888 was not a good augury.

The Free State, long poised between the opposing policies of the Cape and the Transvaal, which were now coming to grips, thus lost the leadership of the Anglicized Boer from the Cape who had been president for twenty-four years. His successor was his opponent, F. W.

Reitz, a straight Boer nationalist and the father of the Bond in the Free State. In March 1889 Kruger met him and they concluded a defensive alliance of the two republics. But counsels in Bloemfontein were so divided that this political gravitation toward the north was almost simultaneously balanced by an economic gravitation toward the south. In this very month a conference of the three southern states met in the Free State capital, with two important results. One was the construction by the Cape government of a railroad from the Orange to the Vaal. The other was a customs union of the Free State and the Cape. The two neighboring protectorates of Bechuanaland and Basuto-land soon joined it, but Natal stayed out until 1898.

Even Kruger was willing in 1889 to discuss cooperation, for he was worried over the railways. Completion of the Delagoa Bay line was held up by the failure of the McMurdo company; Joubert, Kruger's domestic rival, opposed this outlet and wanted to make a connection with Natal; and Rhodes' activities in the north meant the extension of the railroad from Kimberley along the west flank of the two republics, unless arrangements could be made to run a line right through them to the Limpopo. Hofmeyr, ever seeking an opportunity to draw the northern republic into closer relations, approached Kruger with a wise suggestion. It was that the Transvaal should offer free trade in colonial produce on the condition that the Cape would prevent the extension of the Kimberley line and join the Transvaal in supporting the construction of the more direct through line to tap the resources of the Zambesi. Kruger replied that he was ready to negotiate this bargain. His Volksraad stopped him. The majority of that body would have no dealings with the colonies.

This decision of the Raad was a turning point in South African history. It greatly strengthened the hands of Kruger's Anglophobe advisers and made him more irreconcilable. It bound him to reject an 1890 offer from the British government to let him build a railway through Swaziland to Kosi Bay if he would enter the customs union. It repelled Hofmeyr into being a wholehearted supporter of Rhodes not only in Cape politics but also in his schemes for northern development, which might imprison the Transvaal and force it to reason. It also started Rhodes along the train of thought that led to the fatal blunder of the Jameson Raid. Rhodes became premier in the summer of 1890, and at once he set out to make a most strategic move on the South African chessboard. He proposed to purchase Delagoa Bay from the Portuguese. The British government refused to aid the design in any way, but he persisted and was almost on the point of buying it for £700,000 when Berlin objected and London bade him desist. In the west, however, the way was clear, and the railroad from Kimberley had already begun to climb up just outside the two republics toward the goal of Bulawayo. More and more Rhodes and Kruger stood out as opposing giants battling to determine the future of South Africa.

In the Cape the idea of cooperation between Briton and Boer now flourished as never before. The two elements were fused in the strongest government that the colony had ever had, and the Bond under Hofmeyr's leadership was soon attracting large numbers of English-speaking members. In the Orange Free State, President Reitz followed a cautious policy, while the customs union and railway construction were knitting ever closer ties with the mother colony. Until 1896 the cause of South African unity had nowhere more cordial supporters than in the southern republic. Natal, still jealous of the Cape and covetous of Transvaal trade, went its own way. Its railway reached the Transvaal border in 1891, but Kruger refused to admit it though he allowed the continuation of the Cape-Free State line, which ran through Johannesburg and entered Pretoria in 1892—two years before his capital had train connection with Delagoa Bay. London finally granted responsible government to Natal in 1893. The main purpose for doing so now was to curry favor with Kruger on the supposition that he would be more generous toward a colony whose rulers were no longer appointed by Britain. The extension of the Natal railway to the Rand was completed in 1895.

Within the Transvaal there was growing tension between the forces of reaction and progress. Modern industrial society, materialist and aggressive, threatened to overwhelm a static pastoral society whose members were resolved to preserve their way of life, which they believed was the way of God laid down in the Old Testament. Nor was this the only nature of the challenge, for here Briton was pitted against Boer. But the ensuing struggle was not so simple and clear-cut as this would imply, and until 1895 it was by no means certain that the conflict between the new order and the old could not be resolved without external interference or an appeal to arms. Neither side was solidly opposed to the other on the most burning questions of the day, which were monopolies, taxes, language restrictions, and the vote.

The proliferation of government-granted monopolies in the Transvaal was such that it recalls the plague of locusts in Egypt, one Biblical parallel that Kruger would deny for the simple reason that the voracious monopolists were his own foreign favorites. The railroad system of the republic was built, owned, and run by their Netherlands Railway Company, which squeezed all it could out of the mining industry, dictated rates and customs on traffic with the neighboring states, and in its own interests controlled the finances of the government, piling up the public debt. Another notorious example was the dynamite monopoly, which increased the cost of explosives, essential to the mining companies, by more than £750,000 a year—and also served Kruger's munitions factory. Taxes of all kinds were heaped upon the British community while the burghers, true to form, paid almost none. The English language was banned in the courts and the schools. Still worse in the eyes of most of the newcomers was the franchise law because it bolted the door against the redress of all other grievances. The residence requirement for the vote had been one year until 1882, when it was raised to five years. In 1890, just before the first batch of Uitlanders could qualify for the vote under this amendment, the prescribed term was increased to fourteen years.

How was it, then, that the British community was not firmly united against the Boers? The main reason was the attitude of the mining magnates. Much as they resented the arbitrary impositions that clogged their enterprise at almost every turn, these magnates were afraid to risk their huge vested interests by a quarrel with the government. They could grease official palms, for Kruger's courters were as corrupt as those of an absolute ruler. For the most part, also, the chiefs of the mining companies did not "care a fig for the franchise." Nor were all the other Uitlanders clamorous for it. Of those who came from the mother country, not a few shrank from the idea of shedding their British nationality for the sake of a vote in the republic, whereas the majority were less inhibited by such scruples in their growing impatience to grasp the political weapon with which they might mow down their galling disabilities. Those who came from the neighboring colonies, bringing with them their old-fashioned notions of a common South African citizenship, felt that this weapon was theirs by right. It was thus from the rank and file of the new industrial population, men who were accustomed to political freedom and decent administration until they came to live in a land where they were treated as an inferior breed, that a loud demand for reform and the franchise arose. Their repeated petitions to the president and the Raad brought only scornful replies. "Tell your people I shall never give them anything," were Kruger's blunt words to a delegation in 1892. It was not the capitalists but these people who, in their desperation, formulated the cry for intervention by the British government.

The Transvaal Boers were no less divided, and with good reason. Their president roused bitter feelings among them by surrounding himself with clever Europeans from Holland and Germany who filled him with their advice and their own pockets with the spoils of the economic privileges that he showered upon them. On occasion he had to fight hard to protect his monopolies against attack in the Volksraad. His repressive and isolationist policy also came under fire, and the issue between progress and reaction was joined, in that heart of the Boer community. Kruger sternly believed that any compromise would betray the republic, and there was much to be said for the franchise amendment in 1890. It seemed at the time to be damming a flood of foreign voters who would take only temporary possession of the Transvaal and then depart, leaving the burghers with a plundered country, an empty treasury, and a staggering debt. As the Uitlanders stayed and outgrew the burghers, the South African element in the former encouraged a liberal movement among the latter. Many of the more intelligent Boers, sensing the futility of resisting inevitable change, pressed for a policy of justice and liberality toward the Uitlanders and of friendship for the other members of the South African family. These men feared that Kruger would ruin the country by his blind perversity, while he was more than ever convinced that any concession to the new order would ruin him and everything for which he stood. Until 1895 his hold on political power was precarious. His old rival, Joubert, the candidate of the liberal opposition, nearly beat him in the presidential election of 1893, and the liberals were within striking distance of capturing control of the Volksraad.

The year 1895 was a fateful one for South Africa. Already the Rand was seething with unrest, which expressed itself in mass meetings, secret societies, and rifle clubs. Many Germans were employed in assisting Kruger to arm the republic, and the obvious approach of danger to the state was beginning to rally the Boer opposition behind the president. In January, addressing a banquet of Pretoria Germans on the kaiser's birthday, he declared that the Transvaal would secure its complete independence, by which he meant release from the London Convention and possibly a foot on the sea, with the aid of Germany. The British government replied in May with a proclamation establishing a protectorate over Tongaland. Kruger protested this as an unfriendly act. Berlin warned London that the Transvaal did not recognize the annexation, and presently declared that the independence of the republic was a German national interest.

The Transvaal trembled on the brink of a civil war that might involve Britain and Germany. In August the Raad received a monster petition from the Uitlanders and rejected it with derision after a debate in which they were damned as rebels and challenged to fight. At the same time Kruger outraged opinion in the Free State and the Cape by announcing that he would close the Vaal drifts, or fords. This was a nasty blow; for in the previous December a prohibitive trebling of rates by the Netherlands Railway Company had driven trade to abandon rail transportation over the forty miles between Johannesburg and the Free State border and to fall back upon the use of ox-drawn wagons which had to cross the Vaal at these fords. Kruger would thus cut off all trade with the Cape—in violation of the London Convention. It was a step toward war, and it led the Cape ministry, headed by Rhodes, to arrange secretly with the Colonial Office for troopships with drafts for India to call at the Cape for orders. When the ships arrived no troops were landed, for Kruger had bowed to an ultimatum and reopened the drifts.

Intervention or no intervention, a revolution was brewing in the Rand. Nobody could tell what the outcome would be, but everyone could see that it would be of grave moment to the whole of South Africa. Whether the Uitlanders by themselves could overthrow the Boer government was very doubtful, for they were poorly organized and armed. If they were crushed, the whole South African situation would become more explosive. It was therefore highly improbable that British South Africa could be restrained from rushing to the support of the embattled Uitlanders when they rose. If perchance their uprising did succeed without external aid, there were many indications that the revolution would merely replace the Boer government run in the interests of the Dutch-German clique by a cosmopolitan government managed by the mining industry and that the new regime would be no less objectionable, internally and externally, than the old one. Here was an additional reason for intervention by British South Africa. Yet such intervention might easily drag Britain and Germany into war over the Transvaal, which the Boers of that republic would welcome but the British in South Africa and the mother country were most anxious to avoid.

There was only one man who was in a position to steer South Africa through the dangers of the impending crisis: Cecil Rhodes, the premier of the Cape, the master of Rhodesia, the biggest mining magnate in the Transvaal, the greatest South African, and the only South African who had intimate relations with the British government. He leaped at the challenge, for he saw in it a wonderful opportunity to hasten the unification of the whole country from the Zambesi to the Cape of Good Hope in a federation of the two Boer republics and the three British colonies—a great South Africa that could stand on its own feet at last and relieve Britain of all responsibility for the native protectorates.

The first and most crucial step was to make sure that the outbreak on the Rand would be neither crushed nor perverted. For this purpose the agitation in Johannesburg was fed with money and arms, and a body of Chartered Company police was assembled on the Bechuanaland frontier—Rhodesia was too distant to serve as a jumping-off-place—ready for a dash to the golden city as soon as the inhabitants rose and called for aid. Then the British high commissioner would rush to Pretoria and preside over a conference that would confirm the independence of the Transvaal in return for a redress of Uitlander grievances. At the same time the reformed republic would agree to join in a customs and railway union and the establishment of a common court of appeal. From the moment of the rising these events would take place so swiftly that they would present the outside world with a *fait accompli*, which would lead in due course to the political federation of South Africa.

That some such scheme was afoot was no secret. The German government knew it; the British government knew it; and South Africans generally, Boer as well as British, knew it. But none outside the inner circle of the prime mover had any definite information of the actual plans. Rhodes did not take the British government into his confidence. He could not. He was conspiring against a neighboring state, and he realized that the home government would never enter into a plot of this kind even though the Transvaal was a serious threat to the peace of British South Africa. Yet he counted on the active cooperation of official London at the moment it became necessary for the success of the scheme, and until then he had to be sure that the imperial authorities would not interfere. Therefore he gave them enough hints of what was likely to happen to prepare them for action at the crucial moment and meanwhile to keep them quiet.

It has been strongly asserted and as strongly denied that the British government was privy to the plot, and such evidence as has come to light is not conclusive either way. There is nothing to prove that there was official complicity. The question is one of unofficial collusion. Joseph Chamberlain, who had become colonial secretary on the return of Salisbury to power in June 1895, is on record as confiding to a friend: "The fact is, I can hardly say what I knew and what I did not. I did not want to know too much." But before the plot was hatched his office was so apprehensive of dangerous rioting in Johannesburg that it had taken steps to meet the emergency. Bechuanaland police had been moved to the border, and the high commissioner had been instructed to go to Pretoria and mediate if this seemed necessary to preserve the peace and order of South Africa. These precautions were quite proper whereas those of Rhodes were not, but the former slid into the latter so obscurely that the rectitude of the British government is in doubt. Many important communications in this delicate affair were conveyed by word of mouth; even if they had all been transcribed, we still would not be able to tell if the recipient got the meaning intended by the tone of voice or the lifting of an eyebrow. About all that we can now say with any assurance is that the British government probably had a good idea of what Rhodes was up to, that it hoped he would snatch the thorn from the flesh of South Africa, that it was ready to do its part in tying up the wound and trusted that the whole operation would be over before Germany could stick a knife into the patient or the doctor.

The responsibility of Rhodes, as already suggested, is quite a different matter. He was the arch conspirator, and he was abusing his high position of public trust as head of the Cape ministry and as managing director of the Chartered Company when he plotted the use of force to overthrow the government of the Transvaal. Yet there is something to be said on his behalf. If the coup had come off as planned, it would have been a glorious climax to his career, which tuberculosis was soon to cut short; and the world would have acclaimed him as a great statesman whose end had justified the means, for such is the way of the world. But the expected revolution was not so well managed as that more artificial one which, only a few years later, was to give the United States the Panama Canal Zone.

At first Rhodes' prospects were bright. Kruger seemed bent on his own destruction, for his closing of the Vaal drifts united South Africans and the British government against him. It was not until 5 November 1895 that stern words from London made him open the drifts, by which action he retired from an impossible position. Within a fortnight Dr. Jameson, Rhodes' right-hand man who had been chosen to lead the incursion from Bechuanaland, visited Johannesburg. There he arranged for the rising to take place at the end of December, and he procured an undated letter signed by the local leaders calling upon him to rescue the women and children from the armed Boers. When he got back across the border to wait for the signal, he began to hear disquieting news from the gold-mining capital.

The promise of revolution was turning sour. While there was drilling in the streets, the leaders indoors were hesitant and divided. Booming business was spoiling the atmosphere for political agitation. The rising would interfere with the races, which always brought a welcome crowd to town. More serious was the split over the question of whether the revolutionary flag should be the Union Jack or the republican Vierkleur. It was referred to Rhodes, down at Groote Schuur, his estate just outside Cape Town. He said it did not matter. Then the Johannesburg conspirators were embarrassed by temptations that the wily Kruger held out: the offer of reduced railway rates, lower customs on foodstuffs, subsidies for English schools, and a special session of the Volksraad in January to consider the franchise. They put off the rising for ten days, sent a delegation to Groote Schuur to make new plans, and dispatched messengers to Jameson, who was champing at the bit, to prevent him from stirring.

Rhodes at once concluded that the revolution "had fizzled out like a damp squib," and so informed the high commissioner, who straightway passed the word on to Chamberlain. Rhodes felt a sense of relief when he came to this conclusion, for he thought he was casting off the shady burden that he had shouldered. Jameson, however, now judged that the time had come for him to act and that the revolution would break out as soon as he marched in. Therefore on 28 December he telegraphed Rhodes that unless he heard from him to the contrary he would ride on the night of the 29th. Rhodes replied ordering him not to move on any account. But this message did not get through, because meanwhile the wire to Mafeking had been cut; the result was an awful tragedy.

On receiving no word from Rhodes, the impetuous Jameson was naturally convinced that he had his chief's approval, and he proceeded accordingly. He inserted 20 December as the date of his undated invitation from Johannesburg, and with this in his pocket he set out at the head of five hundred men on his fatal Raid. That evening, down in Groote Schuur, Rhodes was distraught. He had just learned that his telegram had not been delivered and he could foresee the terrible consequences. Jameson, he burst out, "has ruined me and wrecked my life's work."

Hearing that the Raid was launched, the high commissioner publicly repudiated Jameson's march and peremptorily commanded him to retire; and the Johannesburg committee hastily declared themselves a provisional government and hoisted the Vierkleur upside down to show that all they wanted was reform. Kruger reacted by declaring that his government would consider all properly submitted complaints, by posting Piet Cronje to deal with the invasion, and by appealing to France and Germany for their intervention. The high commissioner's order reached Jameson on New Year's Day. Instead of obeying it, he pressed on. But on the morrow he was surrounded by Cronje's forces and obliged to capitulate. The Johannesburg committee agreed to an armistice, and as soon as they laid down their arms Kruger arrested them, but not for long. Reluctantly following a suggestion from Hofmeyr, he invited the high commissioner to Pretoria "to assist to prevent further bloodshed." There Jameson and his followers were turned over to be punished by British authority.

Meanwhile the invocation of foreign aid had stirred serious international repercussions. The kaiser, seeing a chance to establish a German protectorate over the Transvaal, sought to form a league with France and Russia against Britain, whose relations with the United States were then clouded by President Cleveland's threat to intervene in the Anglo-Venezuelan boundary dispute. A German cruiser lay in Delagoa Bay, another in Zanzibar was ordered to join it; the German consul in Pretoria asked Kruger for permission to bring in German marines from Lourenço Marques; and Berlin sent a semi-ultimatum to London. But France and Russia remained sullenly aloof, Kruger would not admit the marines lest he play mouse to the German pussy, and the news of Jameson's capitulation convinced the kaiser that all he could now do was to cable his congratulations to the Boer president on having preserved his independence[1] without the help of friendly powers. This famous telegram was an open insult to Britain. There the immediate effect was an outburst of intense indignation, the distraction of public attention from the guilt of the South African conspirators, and a government order for a partial mobilization of the fleet.

---

[1] The chancellor and the foreign minister knew better than to insert this unqualified word, which implied that the Convention of 1884 had no validity, but they yielded to the emperor's insistence.

The Jameson Raid laid a curse upon South Africa. It made extremely difficult, if not impossible, a peaceful achievement of what the country needed above all things—political unity. It split South Africa wide open. It broke the basis of harmony that had been laid in the Cape; where it destroyed the Rhodes-Hofmeyr[2] alliance, and it injected the poison of nationalism into the politics of the colony, arraying British against Dutch, the Progressives against the Bond, on the rights and wrongs of the Transvaal dispute. It abruptly pushed the Free State away from the Cape and into the arms of the northern republic, an alliance which was tightened in 1897. It greatly aggravated the evil situation in the Transvaal, for it immensely strengthened Kruger's power and his determination to keep the Uitlanders down, against whom new laws were passed. It gave an ugly twist to British policy, past, present, and future, as viewed by Boer eyes throughout the country and most particularly in the Transvaal.

In its broader aspects the Raid did incalculable harm. Throughout the world it raised cries of execration and derision. Britain's honor was sullied, supposedly by greed for gold; and the stain was rubbed in by many of her Liberals who, as soon as the patriotic tempest roused by the kaiser's telegram subsided, were stridently pro-Boer. The Raid revealed in a flash that Germany would intervene in the Transvaal if the occasion offered, and that Britain would fight to prevent it.

The status of the Transvaal now became a much more serious bone of contention between the republican government and the British government. It will be recalled that the 1884 London Convention dropped the preamble of the 1881 Pretoria Convention, which had guaranteed self-government subject to British suzerainty, but renewed the prohibition of any republican treaty with a foreign power and of differential duties on British goods. Thus the substance though not the name of suzerainty was preserved in a binding agreement signed by President Kruger, and his republic was really a British protectorate. By hook or by crook he was resolved to shake off this British yoke. The hook was negotiation with the imperial government, and Jameson's impetuous folly provided him with new bait for it: an enormous bill for damages caused by the Raid. The crook was of course foreign intervention, which the Raid made Kruger think was now easily within his grasp. On the other hand, the British government could not toler-

---

[2] Rhodes at once resigned his premiership of the Cape and his seat on the board of the Chartered Company. After two years he was restored to the latter.

ate a completely independent Transvaal because it would open the door of South Africa to foreign powers and imperil the colonies which she was bound to protect. The Raid had driven this lesson home. Compromise on the issue between London and Pretoria was impossible; and this, in the last analysis, meant war.

Neither side, however, could yet realize that the other would fight rather than yield; so both stumbled along the road of negotiation, sustained by false hopes of reaching an agreement. Chamberlain invited Kruger to London to discuss mutual difficulties, particularly Uitlander grievances, arbitration of claims arising from the closing of the drifts, and the question of the Raid. At the same time he made it clear that there would be no tampering with Article IV of the London Convention, which forbade treaties with foreign powers. Nevertheless, Kruger decided to go, apparently in the belief that his bargaining position was so strong that he could force the elimination of Article IV, and he selected the staff to accompany him. But he changed his mind when he received a mysterious message from Berlin suggesting that the proper procedure was for London to go to Pretoria. His refusal made little difference. While avoiding a head-on collision over the vital article, it added irritation on both sides, and this at a most awkward moment.

It was then that a Boer court condemned four of the Johannesburg committee to death and the others to imprisonment. War would probably have come quickly had not Kruger wisely commuted the sentences to fines, which Rhodes and his friend Alfred Beit paid, and an oath to abstain from political activity in the republic for three years. But the president and those around him were naturally incensed when an English court did no more to Jameson and his principal officers than send them to jail and deprive them of their commissions. Kruger and his supporters were no less angry, and they were more than ever convinced of British bad faith when, after long delays, a London parliamentary committee, appointed to investigate the Raid, submitted a report that roundly censured Rhodes and cleared the imperial authorities of any blame.

Neither did this report satisfy the enemies of Chamberlain and Rhodes in Britain. They shut their eyes and stopped their ears to anything that was against the Boer cause; this cause they championed so vigorously that they egged the Transvaal government on against their own government, and they built up the legend of the latter as the tool of the mining magnates. Meanwhile Europeans in Johannesburg, where a Frenchman was president of the Chamber of Mines, were complaining to their home governments against the unenlightened administration in Pretoria, and both French and German newspapers openly criticized Britain for taking no steps to safeguard financial interests in the Rand. Again and again Chamberlain tried to relieve the tension in South Africa by urging Kruger to redress Uitlander wrongs, and in this he was supported by numerous appeals from other sources, including the Canadian parliament. It was all of no avail. Kruger had set his price, and that price amounted to placing all South Africa at his mercy. Meanwhile confusion was becoming worse confounded as the Transvaal dispute created an enormous mass of bitterly controversial literature that is bewildering even today.

It has often been said that Chamberlain sent out Sir Alfred (later Lord) Milner as high commissioner in April 1897 to break the deadlock by forcing Kruger to submit, and that this new official was hand in glove with British capital. But there is no truth in these charges. For nearly a year after his arrival in Cape Town this silent, able man, who had completed his administrative training in Egypt and was to leave his stamp upon South African history, followed a passive policy. During this period he spent his time studying Dutch newspapers, traveling about the country, and trying to make up his own mind on how to handle the complicated situation. He distrusted the Rand capitalists, he regarded the Uitlanders with an eye that was more hostile than friendly, and he believed that liberal-minded burghers in the Transvaal might yet bring about reform and thus turn the crisis. Acting on this belief, he cautioned the British agent in Pretoria against irritating the irritable president.

One might suppose that the stimulus given to British imperialism by the celebration of Queen Victoria's Diamond Jubilee in 1897 would impose a new strain in South Africa. But there the Jubilee atmosphere, while it evoked great demonstrations of loyalty in the colonies, inspired good feelings in the republics toward the venerable monarch. Her portrait was displayed everywhere, Kruger telegraphed his congratulations to her, and out of respect for her he closed the public offices on the great day. All this was very encouraging.

Two events in February 1898 shattered Milner's hope that the Transvaal government, if left to itself, would gradually cease from troubling. One was the re-election of Kruger with an overwhelming majority. The other, which followed immediately, was the triumphant president's summary dismissal of the chief justice, who held office for life but had dared to insist on the principle of judicial review. This dismissal convinced the high commissioner that the Kruger regime was incorrigible except by external pressure. Thereupon Milner requested permission from London to insist upon the redress of Uitlander wrongs. Chamberlain refused it.

Milner's hardening attitude, which he took no pains to conceal, seemed to have a wholesome effect upon the truculent president. The latter received some good advice from friends in the Free State and the Cape, and he took some moderates into his government. Among them was a brilliant young Cape lawyer whom he made state attorney—Jan C. Smuts. Chamberlain's refusal to let Milner proceed more directly was simply out of fear of bringing things to a head in South Africa when clouds were gathering over Britain's relations with France, Russia, and Germany. The Fashoda crisis was approaching; Russia was taking possession of Port Arthur; Britain replied by moving into Wei-haiwei; and Germany was openly adopting a policy of naval construction designed to end the long era of Britain's unchallenged mastery of the sea.

Later in this year, 1898, when the imperialist fever raged in Britain as a consequence of what was happening on the Upper Nile, the British public displayed not the slightest interest in South Africa and the cabinet was so little worried over the suzerainty issue that Chamberlain and Milner, who had returned home for a few months, sent to Pretoria a mild dispatch that was intended to shelve it indefinitely. The fact that Kruger had been and still was preparing for a decision by force of arms was well known, but the only precaution that London took was to direct the Cape military authorities to prepare a plan that might be used if the Transvaal should suddenly make war on the colonies.

Negotiations, official and unofficial, continued while the ferment in the Rand boiled up more dangerously than ever. President Steyn of the Free State,[3] hoping to bring about a peaceful accommodation, invited his fellow president and the high commissioner to confer in Bloemfontein. There, in June 1899, Milner presented his terms for a settle-ment, and they were of such a nature that they won wide support among the Boers of the Cape. The vital feature was a demand for a five-year franchise for Uitlanders, which Kruger flatly rejected, though

---

[3] Steyn had been elected in 1896, following the resignation of Reitz on account of ill-health. Reitz joined Kruger's government in 1898 and threw his influence on the side of moderation.

the Free Staters and some of his own Transvaalers urged him to yield the point. In Britain it had been taken for granted that Kruger would sooner or later give way, and therefore the news that he was obdurate came as a great shock. Yet Chamberlain still believed that war could be avoided. He told the Commons that Uitlander grievances must be redressed but there must be no use of force for this purpose. To guard against a possible surprise attack from the Transvaal two thousand troops were sent to Natal, and Portugal was persuaded to stop the flow of munitions to the republic through Delagoa Bay.

At the end of August the Portuguese yielded to German counter-pressure, and the stream of arms poured in again, not to be stopped until after the outbreak of war, when London forced Lisbon to cut it off. Britain ordered 10,000 troops from the Mediterranean and India to protect the colonies from invasion. The first of them landed at Durban on 3 October. Already the two republics were mobilizing and had prepared their ultimatum, which was to have been sent on the previous day but was held up for a week by lack of transportation. It became effective on the 11th. Then the cheering Boer commandos struck southeast into Natal and west into the Bechuanaland extension of Cape Colony.

Thus began the war which Kruger thought would drive the British into the sea and make himself lord of South Africa. At first the odds were against the British, who had little more than 25,000 soldiers of varying quality to face nearly double that number of determined burghers in arms. For four months all the fighting was on British soil. In the west the republicans cut the railway line and invested Kimberley and Mafeking; on the south they invaded Cape Colony, occupying Colesburg and releasing in the border districts a rebellion that spread westward; and on the east they laid siege to Ladysmith, which contained most of the British forces in Natal.

The resistance of this town saved Natal from being completely overrun; and only the restraining influence of the Schreiner ministry, which had been formed as a result of the victory of the Bond in the general election of 1898, prevented the above revolt from becoming much more widespread in the Cape. The arrival of an army corps of 47,000 men, sent from England to bring the war to a swift close, barely sufficed to stem the tide of invasion. Actually the Boer advance had then spent its force. But this was not seen at the time, and the consequent alarm in the mother country led to the hasty collection and embarkation of the largest army she had ever put in the field, and the dispatch of the two best generals of the empire, Roberts and Kitchener.

The second phase of the war began in February 1900, when the new British forces were ready to strike. Roberts quickly relieved Kimberley,[4] captured the main western army of the Boers, and swept over the southern republic, taking Bloemfontein in March. Meanwhile the Free Staters trooped home in the vain hope of saving their own capital, and a relieving column broke the weakened siege of Ladysmith. Meanwhile, also, the two presidents, seeing the desperate military plight into which their boldness had led them, frantically called on France, Russia, Germany, and the United States for help, and offered to make peace on the basis of the *status quo ante bellum,* only to find that they had deceived themselves with dreams of foreign intervention and that the British would not allow them to play the game of "Heads I win, tails you lose." The Free State commandos dissolved, and Roberts, thinking they were out of the war, offered to allow all but the leaders to go home on parole. He proclaimed British sovereignty over the southern republic, renaming it the Orange River Colony. Pushing across the Vaal, he advanced through Johannesburg and took Pretoria early in June. Kruger and his government retreated eastward, along the railway, where, late in August, his army fought and lost the last pitched battle of the war. Thereupon the old and broken president abandoned his country and retired to Lourenço Marques, whence he sailed for Europe; while Roberts formally annexed the Transvaal, proclaimed that the war was over, and departed for England. But the end was not yet.

The third and last phase of the war was the most protracted and the most painful. It lasted for a year and a half, and it extended not only through the two republics but also into the western part of Cape Colony. In place of the Boer armies, which no longer existed, countless little mobile commandos waged a guerrilla war. They held the initiative until May 1901, when a new army of mounted infantry, then rather a novelty, had been prepared in England and now began to run down the elusive bands. One by one most of them were caught, with the aid of lines of blockhouses and of barbed wire. Early in 1902 the British government, declining mediation offered by the queen of the Netherlands, hinted at direct negotiation with the Boer leaders still in the field. This hint brought them together at Vereeniging. There Smuts

---

[4] Where Rhodes lived through the siege. His health was then broken, and he died in March 1902 on the eve of the peace negotiations.

suggested that present surrender was necessary to ensure a brighter future than South Africa had ever known, and they agreed to accept substantially the same conditions as Milner had offered more than a year before.

By the Peace of Vereeniging, signed in Pretoria on 31 May 1902, the republicans became British subjects; the Orange River Colony and the Transvaal were to be officially bilingual and to receive self-government in the near future; and the victors, far from exacting any war indemnity, undertook to make an outright gift of £3,000,000 to help re-establish the burghers on their farms, and also loans on easy terms for the same purpose. A further provision, which Milner later confessed was the greatest mistake of his life, postponed any decision on the native franchise until after full responsible government was established. White supremacy was thus virtually guaranteed by Britain for the sake of peace between the whites. Humanitarians have often condemned this surrender of their principle, but they have seldom tried to calculate what was the practical alternative.

The Boer War was the most serious ordeal that confronted the British Empire since the days of Napoleon. From first to last the British forces that were engaged in it numbered 366,000 regulars and other troops raised in the mother country; 52,000 South Africans, Boer as well as British; and 30,000 from Australasia, Canada, and various other colonies. But this military effort was not the full measure of the trial, for the war divided Britain sorely and subjected her to a hot blast of hostility from the European powers.[5] Foreign opinion vehemently denounced her as a greedy bully bent on conquering the two little republics of farmers in order to rob them of their mineral wealth, and gloated over the spectacle of a handful of burghers holding a mighty empire at bay. In Britain itself, a large minority likewise raised loud cries of shame against their government for going to war at the behest of the mining interests to crush the precious independence of the Boers. While these foreign and domestic critics spurred each other on and their combined shouts inflated the idea of capitalist imperialism, the majority of the British public, with little if any sounder knowledge of the deep and tangled roots of the war, rallied behind the British cause in South Africa.

---

[5] The American reaction was more moderate, being tempered by the fact that Britain had backed the United States in the recent Spanish-American War while all the other Old World powers openly sympathized with Spain.

When the Conservative ministry appealed to the country in the hotly contested "khaki election" of October 1900, Chamberlain blamed the Liberals for causing the war by encouraging Kruger to fight, and the counting showed that the opposition polled seven votes for every eight cast for the government. But these figures are misleading. Though the Liberals were united against the Conservatives, they were not united against imperialism or, for that matter, against the war. Rosebery, who had been eased out of the party leadership in 1896, headed a considerable group of imperialist Liberals. They charged the government with being caught unprepared for the war and with mismanaging it. Only a few outspoken Liberals cried for surrender to the Boer demand for complete independence, and between these two extremes there were various shades of opinion. Even David Lloyd George, then a rapidly rising young politician whose pro-Boer utterances so antagonized a public meeting that he had to escape from the angry crowd in the disguise of a policeman, was careful never to oppose the annexation of the two republics. The official leader of the party openly supported it.

The foreign reaction to the war administered a terrific shock to Britain. She suddenly saw that she was isolated in a jealous world and that, but for her naval supremacy, the conflict in South Africa might well have exposed her to a combined attack of hostile powers such as had completed the wreck of her First Empire. The revelation of her dangerous plight, now becoming more dangerous because Germany was preparing to challenge her upon the sea, moved her to find allies, which meant a reversal of her nineteenth century policy of having none. But meanwhile she was surprised and overjoyed to discover that she was not standing entirely alone. Her daughter nations beyond the ocean came to her aid. Of their own free will and simply out of sentimental attachment to her—not as in 1914 from any fear for her own safety—they sent contingents to fight by her side. It was a spontaneous demonstration of imperial unity in defiance of world opinion, and it seemed to be a portent of the organic reintegration and consolidation of the empire in days to come.

CHAPTER XXX

The Climax of British Imperialism

THOUGH THE Imperial Federation League, upon which Salisbury had smiled, a little icily perhaps, collapsed at a touch from the octogenarian Gladstone after he took office for the fourth and last time in 1892, the spirit of the League went marching on—even in the government, where Rosebery presided over the Foreign Office. When the veteran prime minister shot his final bolt for Irish Home Rule, which many Englishmen suspected as an attempt to break up the empire, he could no longer control his party, which had suffered the desertion of the Liberal Unionists on this very issue in 1886. Now his cabinet colleagues refused to let him call a general election as a protest against the Lords' rejection of his Home Rule bill. They also insisted on much larger naval estimates than his old-fashioned digestion would accept. Gladstone's day was done, and early in 1894 he resigned. It was significant that he had no say in the choice of his successor—Lord Rosebery, the father of Liberal imperialism. The change of leadership was a clear indication of the way the imperial wind was blowing. It blew harder in 1895, when Rosebery's tottering government resigned, Salisbury formed a Unionist ministry based on a fusion of Conservatives and Liberal Unionists, and a general election consolidated his position by giving the Unionists a large majority in the House of Commons. Though the new prime minister was not himself so keen an imperialist as his immediate predecessor, his cabinet was dominated by the strongest British imperial statesman since the elder Pitt—Joseph Chamberlain. He could have commanded almost any post in the administration, but his interest in the empire was so intense that he picked the Colonial Office, to which tradition had relegated second-rate or immature politicians; and he set out to remake the empire, as we shall presently see.

First it will be well to note that in one sense British imperialism reached its flood tide just before the Boer War and then began to recede. In Britain, as elsewhere, the imperialism that drove the western powers headlong in their late nineteenth century scramble for colonial territories grew by what it fed on. The national or racial pride that inspired each of the contestants tended to mount as the game of grab proceeded, because the plucking of every prize inflated the ego of the winner and inflamed the ego of at least one unsuccessful rival. The consequent international tension largely explains two incidents that occurred a few months after Salisbury entered upon his final term of office and how these incidents made the British imperial lion rage.

President Cleveland's message to Congress in the middle of December 1895, demanding forcible American intervention on behalf of Venezuela in its long-drawn-out dispute over the boundary with British Guiana, as Professor Langer has pointed out, used "unbelievably strong language and might very well have been regarded as tantamount to an ultimatum of declaration of war."[1] It stirred a furore of imperialist delight in the United States, and it cut British pride to the quick. Colonial Office officials urged Chamberlain to stop the impending uprising in Johannesburg lest it tie Britain's hands in dealing with the South American crisis; but he calculated that the latter would not come to a head until the impending Transvaal crisis was settled. Therefore the word was passed along that the Uitlanders should stick to their time schedule or postpone action for two years. When the revolutionary movement stalled and Jameson plunged ahead, Chamberlain did not wait to see if the Raid would succeed. He immediately denounced it in cables to the high commissioner and to Kruger. While the British government thus repudiated Jameson, the British public embraced him as a heroic British champion and with feverish excitement followed every cabled report of his advance until the news came that he had surrendered. This was a deadening blow. But on the following day the mood of the country was suddenly transformed from dejection to defiance by the publication of the kaiser's telegram to Kruger. As the flag-waving *National Review* observed, this was an "infinitely less offensive document" than Cleveland's recent message; but the pent-up feelings roused by the American seem to have found their chief vent in the violent popular reaction against Germany.

This deflection of British anger from the United States has been ascribed to the fact that Britain was feeling the pinch of German but

---

[1] William L. Langer, *The Diplomacy of Imperialism* (New York, 1935), p. 239.

not American industrial competition, to a sense of blood-brotherhood with the people of the great republic, and to a calculation that Germany was not likely to take up the challenge because she then had only a small fleet. But up to that time Englishmen also felt a closer relationship with the Germans than with any other European nation, and the United States too had only a weak navy. We may therefore suspect another effective influence was a more or less conscious realization that an important part of the empire, the Dominion of Canada, was a British hostage to the United States. Yet the order for a partial mobilization of the fleet, which foreign as well as domestic opinion believed was aimed only at Germany, was issued with an eye on Venezuela also.

Whatever may have caused the focusing of British wrath upon Germany, there was no mistaking the force of this outburst. Even the East End dockers replied to the kaiser's hard words with hard blows on the bodies of German sailors, while staid Londoners boycotted Germans in clubs and business, and the press blazed with indignation against the German empire and its ruler. Seldom if ever in time of peace had the whole nation displayed such a bellicose temper.

In the midst of the storm a new type of journalism was born in Britain. Alfred Harmsworth, later Lord Northcliffe, produced the first edition of the *Daily Mail* in April 1896. This was the first ha'penny newspaper to gain wide circulation, and its immediate success was as sensational as its contents. One of the original editors later wrote: "What sells a newspaper? is a question asked me. The first answer is 'War.' " After that he rated in descending order, a state funeral, a first-class murder, and any big public pageant or ceremony. The new organ was introduced with an imperial trumpet blast declaring that the *Daily Mail* would stand first of all:

> for the power, the supremacy, and the greatness of the British Empire. The *Daily Mail* is the embodiment and mouthpiece of the imperial idea. Those who launched this journal had one definite aim in view . . . to be the articulate voice of British progress and domination. We believe in England. We know that the advance of the Union Jack means protection for weaker races, justice for the oppressed, liberty for the downtrodden.[2]

By living up to this announcement the *Daily Mail,* which was founded and conducted to give the mass of the people what they wanted,

[2] Langer, op. cit., p. 84.

revealed and strengthened the hitherto unsuspected hold that imperialism had over the British masses.

The Diamond Jubilee in June 1897, already mentioned as a stimulus to British imperialism, was a repetition of the Golden Jubilee on a more impressive scale. Again the empire seized the occasion to worship itself in worshipping its own regal personification, now more venerable after sixty years on the throne. All over the world, in every land over which the Union Jack flew, there were appropriate ceremonies; and the celebration in the heart of the empire, still the greatest city in the world, was the most awe-inspiring that British people had ever experienced. Princes and potentates and colonial prime ministers and troops from every colony and dependency, white men, yellow men, brown men, black men, gathered in London for the imperial pageant. The dazzling formal procession was so long that the old lady who was the center of it all had to sit in her carriage for more than four hours without a break. Later she presided over a great military review at Aldershot; and the Prince of Wales, soon to be Edward VII, held a naval review at Spithead, where the war vessels were drawn up in four lines extending for thirty miles. From first to last the Diamond Jubilee was a most magnificent spectacle of imperial splendor and power. British people loved it, and they swelled with pride of empire as they had never done before. "Drunk with sight of power," they scarcely heeded the solemn words of the "Recessional," the penitential prayer that Kipling then wrote for them.

The fever mounted in the following year, as Kitchener moved up the Nile and the eyes of all Britain were upon him. When he demolished the khalifa's host at Omdurman, the people at home went wild with joy; when he met Marchand at Fashoda, they went wild with anger against France for daring to cross Britain's imperial path. They were itching to fight if France would not back down completely, and in their imperious mood they inflicted upon that proud country a humiliation more crushing than any great power has suffered without being disastrously defeated in war. It was the greatest triumph of British imperialism at its worst. In this resounding diplomatic triumph over England's most ancient foe, British imperialism of the competitive and grasping type reached its climax.

This kind of British imperialism was also noticeable in the Boer War. The crisis in South Africa naturally made the British exaggerate the opposing imperialism of Kruger, and this exaggeration reflected as well as stiffened British imperialism. But the bold united spirit that confronted France on the morrow of Fashoda was less in evidence when the republican Boers sprang to arms. As we have already observed, British opinion was sorely divided over the war. The British opposition to it, far from being drowned in a tidal wave of patriotism caused by the eruption of foreign hostility, persisted in championing the Boers. Moreover, the war was decidedly not a glorious one. Though Roberts redeemed the stunning defeats of the early months and London indulged in a night of delirious delight over the relief of Mafeking, the last and longest phase of the struggle advertised the valor of the Boers rather than that of the British.

From the very outbreak of the fighting the British conscience was troubled, and it expressed itself in much more than a still, small voice. Loud and strident were the British charges that British capital dictated the imperialist policy of the British government in South Africa. Those who made these charges were more encouraged than embarrassed by the fact that they were using the same language as their country's enemies, for these men believed that the government was betraying what they held most dear—the honor of Britain. They found much satisfaction in the peace terms accorded to the conquered, and more in the almost simultaneous publication of J. A. Hobson's *Imperialism, a Study,* the classic liberal exposition of the theory of economic imperialism.

Hobson argued that the great geographical expansion of the empire in the previous two decades, which had all been by the acquisition of backward territories, was primarily the work of capitalism seeking to exploit these territories and manipulating the forces of patriotism, and even of humanitarianism, to seize them; and that the process was operating to drag the empire to ruin by provoking wars and bloodshed. To many people the thesis was a penetrating and painful revelation, something similar to the great light that struck Saul of Tarsus and converted him into Paul the Apostle. This remarkable book, coming on top of the same author's well-informed *War in South Africa,* which appeared in 1900 and presented a strong case for the Boers, not only confirmed the opinion of those who had opposed the war but also did much to spread that opinion among those who had supported the war. For the British public at large, the war was a chastening experience that induced repentance for indulgence in a spree of jingoistic imperialism; and within a decade the average Englishman, without knowing much if any more about the issues at stake in South Africa, seems to have swung round to the view that his government had sinned when it went to war against the Boers.

But this, as already suggested, is not the whole story of British imperialism in the years around the turn of the century. The movement was also concerned with the reintegration and the regeneration of the existing empire. There was a strong revival of the desire to coordinate the autonomous portions of the empire, and there was a vigorous drive to inject new life into those parts of the colonial empire that were not self-governing. Chamberlain championed both causes with equal energy, though not with equal success, and he thereby made his tenure of the Colonial Office the most notable in its history. When he took charge of the department, he straightway had electric lights installed to replace the candles that still provided its only illumination. This was more than characteristic. It was symbolic of what was to follow. Never had a colonial secretary so inspired his staff and the whole colonial service even in the remotest corners of the empire. Now for the first time the minister responsible for the management of colonial affairs was a power in the cabinet and in the land.

Chamberlain inaugurated a new era in the history of the dependent empire. Many of these colonies, he pointed out, were "in the condition of undeveloped estates" which could be improved only by imperial assistance. The pinchpenny policy that had prevailed was morally wrong and economically stupid. It was Britain's bounden duty to foster the material welfare of populations under her care, and it was to her own business interest to invest some of her surplus wealth for this purpose. Commencing in British West Africa, Chamberlain pushed railway construction to open up backward areas. Some of the new railways were the straight product of state enterprise because private capital would not undertake the risk, while others were the work of private capital with various kinds of government support. He also found money for the construction of roads, bridges, buildings, harbors, and other public works in colonies that had not been able to afford them. Colonies that were better off but cramped for funds to make public improvements, he helped to borrow at low interest rates by imperial guarantees of specific loans and, more generally, by a special act of parliament that classified colonial bonds as trust securities.

One bold and imaginative plan on which Chamberlain's heart was set was to earmark the revenue from the government's Suez Canal shares, then amounting to £670,000 a year, for construction and development in the crown colonies. But he could not get this plan through the cabinet in face of the strenuous objections raised by the chancellor of the exchequer. In this proposal Chamberlain was more than a generation ahead of his time, for what he had in mind was substantially the Colonial Welfare and Development Fund which the government under his son created in 1940. But if the father failed in this large project, he persisted in loosening the imperial purse strings for his piecemeal projects to advance the welfare of the crown colonies.

The sagacious business instincts of the secretary of state moved him to circularize the colonial governors calling upon them for detailed reports on possible developments of intraimperial trade for the mutual benefit of the mother country and the colonies. What articles of foreign manufacture were supplanting British goods in the colonial market, and why, with specifications of prices, quality, design, packaging, freight costs, credit terms, and other conditions such as subsidies or bounties? Verbal descriptions were not enough. They had to be accompanied by actual specimens of the foreign articles sold in the colonies. Likewise, each governor was required to specify what products of his colony "might advantageously be exported to the United Kingdom or other parts of the British Empire, but do not at present find a sufficient market there, with any information with regard to quality, price or freight which may be useful to British importers."

The blight that had fallen on the British West Indies was a great challenge to the great colonial secretary. Protective tariffs excluded their staple produce, cane sugar, from the American and European markets, and export bounties paid by major European countries to encourage their own production of beet sugar flooded the British market with an article selling below West Indian costs. What could be done for the stricken colonies? Chamberlain provided them with temporary relief in the form of loans, for which parliament voted £3,300,000 in 1899, while he attacked the causes of the blight. He could not hope to breach the foreign walls that protected high-price markets. In adopting free trade Britain had thrown away the weapon with which tariff wars are fought. But foreign markets had never meant much to the British Caribbean colonies. The blow that was ruining them was the dumping of subsidized beet sugar on the British market. How could this be stopped? The prospect was not encouraging. Again and again the European powers had met in conference to consider how they might put an end to the vicious competition in export bounties, which was a notorious international scandal, and they had not been able to agree on any effective action. Here too the economic disarmament of Britain left her West Indian producers exposed. To the British masses free trade meant cheap food, and it required political daring on the part of their government to deprive them of the cheap sugar that foreign governments gave them. Their appetite had long since downed moral scruples against the free admission of slave-grown sugar. Nevertheless, in 1902, Chamberlain persuaded his colleagues to prohibit the import of bounty-fed sugar,[3] with the result that the old industry in the British Caribbean colonies got a new lease on life.

Already the British West Indian economy was experiencing healthy changes that sprang from Chamberlain's initiative and were to gather momentum, their full effect being felt in the years after he left office. The sugar industry itself was being rescued from an almost hopeless state of inefficiency, thanks to the search for better varieties of cane, the encouragement of better methods of cultivation, the construction of better roads, and the concentration of manufacture in larger and better mills than the old local ones that were very wasteful. There was also a shift in the West Indian economy to reduce its dependence upon sugar by substituting other crops suitable to the soil, the climate, and the plentiful supply of nonwhite labor. In 1890 Chamberlain had sent his son Neville to develop a new sisal plantation on Andros Island, the largest of the Bahamas. At the end of eight years, after sinking £50,000 of his own money in the venture, he abandoned it as a complete failure. But his personal loss seemed only to spur his public efforts to introduce new cultures that would be profitable in the West Indies. This was what they needed, according to a royal commission that reported in 1897, and this is what they gradually got. It was not easy to induce the dark-skinned peasants to adopt new ways, but Chamberlain accomplished much through the Imperial Department of Agriculture, which he established in the West Indies in 1898.[4] Not the least achievement of this new governmental agency was its control of insect pests.

The tropical colonies as a whole owe an immense debt to Chamberlain's promotion of the study of tropical medicine and sanitation. In 1897 he appointed Sir Patrick Manson medical adviser to the Colonial

---

[3] In this Chamberlain was assisted by the government of India, which had recently taken the same step because Indian consumption of sugar had outstripped Indian production and the latter was suffering from an invasion of European subsidized sugar.

[4] Chamberlain also set up a West African Department of Agriculture.

Office. Manson had made a name for himself by fighting parasitic diseases in Hong Kong, and he had already directed a younger colleague in the profession, Major (later Sir) Ronald Ross of the Indian Medical Services, to pursue the line of research that was soon to make him the leader in mastering malaria. Chamberlain was chiefly responsible for the founding, in 1899, of the London and Liverpool Schools of Tropical Medicine. With Manson teaching in the former and Ross in the latter, these two institutions quickly became world famous in the war on tropical disease.

But the crowning purpose of Chamberlain's career was the consolidation of the autonomous empire into a new organic union. It was he who persuaded his colleagues in the cabinet to make the Diamond Jubilee an imperial pageant, and in doing so he thought he saw a marvelous opportunity to draw the self-governing colonies into a more active partnership with the mother country. As in 1887, invitations from London drew official representatives from the colonies not only to participate in the imperial celebrations but also to deliberate with the home government on imperial problems. The Colonial Conference of 1897, however, was very different in size and character from its predecessor. The 1887 Conference was a large and motley gathering of ten dozen delegates, many of whom came from the crown colonies and the protectorates. The 1897 Conference, on the other hand, was a small body of a dozen men: the colonial secretary, who presided, and one delegate from each of the eleven self-governing colonies,[5] all of which now for the first time sent their prime ministers to sit in what had the semblance of an imperial cabinet. This was to be the model for the future.

Chamberlain opened the proceedings with a speech in which he proposed the creation of a permanent imperial council composed of plenipotentiaries formally empowered to commit their respective governments; and outside the Conference, in the whirl of lavish entertainment,[6] the colonial statesmen were subjected to all sorts of gracious social pressure to convert them to this idea. But these blandishments availed no more than Chamberlain's eloquence to persuade them that the empire ought to have a new constitution; with only the premiers of

---

[5] Canada, Newfoundland, the six Australian colonies, New Zealand, the Cape, and Natal.

[6] Which inspired Laurier's remark, in a letter to a friend, that he was not sure whether the British Empire needed a new constitution but he was certain that every Jubilee guest would need one.

New Zealand and Tasmania dissenting, they adopted a resolution affirming "that the present political relations between the United Kingdom and the self-governing colonies are generally satisfactory under existing conditions of things." Yet the cautious colonials who administered this rebuff to the eager imperialist in the chair were not entirely satisfied with these relations. Before the Conference ended they placed themselves on record, by a unanimous vote, in favor of Colonial Conferences at periodic intervals.

Here we catch a glimpse of the empirical process, which had shaped and was continuing to shape the unwritten British constitution, at work upon the unwritten constitution of the empire. For a second time a fortuitous event had brought together representatives of the autonomous empire to consult together on affairs common to all, and the experience taught them that the gathering of such an assembly should be a regular practice.[7] The upshot was that the Colonial Conference, renamed the Imperial Conference by its own resolution in 1907, became an established institution of the empire. Like the office of prime minister, no legislative action created it or invested it with authority, and no formal instrument regulated or restricted its functions. In characteristic British fashion, it was left to develop as the future might dictate. For the time being, at least, it was an outward manifestation of an inward desire of the various parts of the autonomous empire to draw closer together.

Chamberlain was already dreaming of commercial union, which had been specifically excluded from the discussions in 1887; but he intimated that for the present a British *zollverein* was impracticable. It was a subject of serious dissension within his government and party, as was well known; and no colonial representative had the temerity to champion it in defiance of the strong colonial adherence to protection and the intense English belief in free trade. However, there was one step that could be taken and, with Chamberlain's encouragement, the conference urged it to facilitate the development of preferential trade within the empire.

Canada pointed the way. After nearly a generation of vain endeavor to revive the reciprocity agreement with the United States, which Washington had ended in 1866, Canada turned to cultivate closer

---

[7] The Conference of 1902 passed a resolution favoring a meeting every four years. The next Conference, however, was postponed for a year because of a change of government in Britain. From 1907 the British prime minister was president and the colonial secretary vice-president.

commercial relations with the rest of the empire by initiating, only a few weeks before the Conference met, the policy of imperial preference. Though then committed to it, Canada could not apply it immediately because her hands were tied by old commercial treaties that Britain had signed and that were still in force. These guaranteed to a few foreign powers that there would be no tariff discrimination, even in favor of Britain, against their goods in British colonial markets; for at the time these treaties were negotiated Britain had the mistaken notion that she was leading the world to accept free trade and that her own colonies would fall into line. From 1881 Ottawa had repeatedly protested that the treaties were obsolete and should be revised or discarded to get rid of the above obligation, and in 1894 the Canadian protest was reinforced by a resolution of a special conference called by Ottawa and attended by representatives of Australia and Cape Colony to consider imperial cable communications and commercial relations. But London had consistently hesitated to touch the treaties out of fear of provoking foreign retaliation. Now, in order to implement the Canadian offer and to induce other colonies to emulate the Canadian example, the Conference of 1897 called upon the British government to denounce the treaties, and shortly thereafter that government gave the year's notice required for terminating them. The Canadian policy then became effective and other colonies gradually followed suit, hoping that sooner or later the mother country would return to protection and reciprocate their favors. Thus, half a century after the expiry of the "old colonial system," the colonies themselves began to revive it, and by so doing they quickened the agitation of the imperialist "fair traders" in Britain.

Another question aired in the Conference of 1897 was that of colonial contributions to imperial defense. Back in 1885, New South Wales, Victoria, and Canada had offered men for the Sudan campaign; and this practical expression of colonial devotion to the empire had suggested the possibility of working out some system of cooperative imperial defense. Hence Salisbury's direction to the conference of 1887 to concentrate upon it. The colonial representatives then accepted the principle of sharing the burden but gave little promise of applying it. The excuse offered by Canada was that she had already contributed much by providing, in her railways, a strategic line of transportation across the broad expanse of North America from the Atlantic to the Pacific. Jan Hofmeyr, who then represented the Cape, and Premier Griffith of Queensland proposed an imperial tariff on foreign imports to provide a revenue for imperial defense. The only concrete achievement of the 1887 Conference was an agreement of the Australian colonies and New Zealand to erect, on the advice of British authorities, local fortifications at their own expense, and to pay £126,000 a year toward the cost of an imperial squadron to protect trade in their waters.

More recent events had given new urgency to the problem and new hope of a cooperative solution. While Cleveland's message to Congress and the kaiser's telegram to Kruger startled Britain, they stirred in the colonies a wave of instinctive British loyalty which seemed to imply a willingness to match words with deeds. But history repeated itself in the Conference of 1897. Though Chamberlain's opening address asked if it was not advisable, or even vital, for the colonies to adopt some regular and comprehensive system of contributions to the naval power of the empire, and suggested a closer integration of the military forces of the empire by a periodic exchange of contingents between the mother country and the autonomous colonies, yet little was added to the accomplishment of ten years before. The Australasians raised their contribution to £200,000; Cape Colony promised a battleship, later compounded for £30,000 a year; and Natal offered £12,000 as her annual quota to the Royal Navy.

Against this uneven background of colonial reluctance to assume imperial commitments, the spontaneous reaction of the colonies to the Boer War stands out in bold relief. Their dispatch of troops to fight side by side with those of the mother country was, as we have observed, a demonstration of imperial unity in defiance of world opinion. It raised British imperial sentiment to an unprecedented peak. Blood is thicker than water; and the self-governing parts of the empire, though divided by oceans, were mingling their blood on the South African veldt. Never had there been such lively hopes as were inspired by this common sacrifice in a common cause that the autonomous empire, far from falling apart, was ready to draw closer together in an organic union that would grow with the years.

These hopes were centered on Chamberlain as the one man who could provide the leadership necessary to effect the reconsolidation of the empire. His political position was unique in the history of British cabinet government, for he is the only example of a statesman who dominated the cabinet without being either prime minister or government leader in the Commons.[8] He was by far the most dynamic figure

---

[8] A. J. Balfour was government leader in the Commons until July 1902, when he also became prime minister on the resignation of his uncle.

in British public life. He was also recognized as the outstanding British imperialist of the age, for on many occasions he had elaborated his vision of future imperial relations. Though opposed to Home Rule for Ireland as presented by Gladstone, Chamberlain favored "Home Rule all round." He would apply the principle to the whole of the British Isles, and federate their self-governing parts with the self-governing colonies to form a purely imperial government charged with responsibility for imperial foreign policy and defense. Along with this *kriegsverein*, he would also have a *zollverein* embracing the empire. In addition to his imagination, he possessed another quality essential in a statesman, or he could not have won the power he held. He was a keen realist.

Being the finest practical politician in Britain, Chamberlain knew full well that it would be impossible to build his magnificent pyramid in a day. The materials were living societies of the highest type, dedicated to the principles of individual and collective liberty, and any slip in handling them might spoil everything. Therefore, while openly expressing his belief that there should be free trade within the empire, he had frankly admitted that it was not yet a practical matter. When presiding over the Conference of 1897, he left in the minds of the colonial premiers no doubt of what he thought they should do; but he was always careful to put it in the form of a debatable question or his own personal suggestion, never as a proposition emanating from his government, for his shrewd political nose told him that colonial pride would balk at any hint of dictation. Toward the end of the Conference, when the president of the defense committee of the cabinet anxiously inquired about its progress, he replied with amused candor that the premiers personally favored union but feared to commit themselves lest they run foul of opinion back home.

> Our policy is to continue to impress our wishes and hopes for union and to leave the leaven to work. Union will not come in a hurry, and must follow the Federation of Australia and the South African Colonies. But the great thing is—to use a railway expression—to get the points right. If we do this, we shall go on on parallel lines for the future. If we make any mistake, we shall get wider and wider apart till the separation is complete.

Australian federation, which came in the midst of the Boer War and will be more fully considered in the next chapter, rejoiced the heart of Chamberlain and of other imperialists at the time because they regarded it as an essential simplification of the conditions for closer imperial union. There had been no such constructive event in the history of the empire since Canadian federation a generation before, which the intervening years had invested with this new imperial significance. That the addition of Australian unity to Canadian unity was preparing the way for the British Commonwealth of Nations, not for the erection of a crowning imperial edifice, was something which no one could see at that time. Later developments, by no means confined to the British world, determined the outcome; then the British Commonwealth was accepted by its members as a *pis aller* which, in characteristic fashion, they elevated into a sort of ideal more worthy than that of Chamberlain. Yet his ideal rested on the selfsame principle. He stated it clearly in May 1900, when he presented the bill to federate the Australian colonies.

> We have got to a point in our relations with our self-governing Colonies in which I think we recognize once for all that these relations depend entirely on their free will and absolute consent. The links between us at the present time are very slight. Almost a touch might snap them; but slender and slight as they are—although we wish and although I hope that they will become stronger—still if they are felt irksome in any one of our great colonies we shall not force them to wear them.

One clause in the measure as prepared in Australia tested the imperialist statesman's principle. The clause in question departed from Canadian precedent by cutting at the appellate jurisdiction of the privy council—one of the precious links. It barred appeals to London from Australian court decisions on constitutional matters, and it empowered the Australian parliament to limit appeals on other matters. The Australian delegates who had come to negotiate the passage of their new constitution were deaf to Chamberlain's argument that what was good enough for Canada should be good enough for Australia. Then he tried to postpone the issue by suggesting the ultimate creation of a new supreme court for the whole empire and, in the interim, the reform of the existing one by making it more representative; but they still insisted on "the Bill, the whole Bill, and nothing but the Bill." Finally he persuaded them to compromise on a substitute clause, which gave the High Court of Australia the final word on constitutional questions and provided that no Australian legislation to restrict other appeals should become effective without the consent of the home government. Though neither side got all it asked for, the important thing was the settlement of the difference by an exercise of mutual good sense.

South African unity, the third stout colonial pillar necessary to support the imperial superstructure envisaged by Chamberlain, could not be raised until a firm foundation was laid for it by a peace that would reconcile Boer and Briton. To make sure of it he had to deal firmly with Milner. During the war the proconsul repeatedly demanded an act of parliament to suspend the Cape constitution, for he was so alarmed by Boer sedition that he saw no hope of saving the colony except by a temporary spell of autocratic rule, such as had been applied to Lower Canada in 1838. But the keener insight of the colonial secretary saw that it would drive all the Boers of the Cape into the arms of the republicans and make reconciliation impossible. Moreover, as he told the cabinet, it was necessary to keep hands off the constitution of a self-governing colony in order to avoid alienating home supporters of the war and alarming opinion in Canada and Australia. Therefore he put his foot down and he kept it down. Milner was saved in spite of himself, and much more than Milner was saved by the firmness of his chief.

Though Chamberlain adjourned until some time after the war all larger plans for an imperial constitution, to be worked out by the self-governing colonies in collaboration with the mother country, it was hard for him—and for a host of others—to contemplate the passing of their comradeship in arms without leaving some result in concrete form. Early in April 1900 when a Liberal moved in the House of Commons "that the colonies should be admitted to some direct representation in the imperial parliament," Chamberlain at once discouraged the proposal as a bad approach toward the desired end. Even the discussion of it, he warned, would conjure up the disturbing specter of colonial taxation by the imperial parliament. Privately he was considering the possibility of a *zollverein* or a *kriegsverein*, and inclining toward the latter. He had recently sent confidential letters to the governor general of Canada and the governors of the Australian colonies asking them to sound out their ministers on the question of an imperial council to advise on imperial defense, and saying that if they were favorable to it he would much prefer the suggestion to come from them because he knew "the strong feeling of independence which exists in all the self-governing colonies." The replies were not very encouraging; and therefore he decided to hold his hand until the end of the war, when he could call another colonial conference and invite its overseas members to make their own proposals. In his deference to colonial opinion, he was beginning to think that perhaps the most, if not the only, effective approach would be the sacrifice of British free trade on the altar of imperial unity.

The Colonial Conference of 1902 met in a mixed atmosphere. The termination of the war released the revulsion against it in Britain, while the coronation of Edward VII inspired a fresh outburst of loyalty to the personification of imperial unity. Confident that the colonies were now ready to institutionalize their spontaneous cooperation in the war, Chamberlain again proposed the formation of an imperial council and the adoption of a general scheme of cooperative defense. Quoting words that Laurier had uttered in the Canadian House of Commons two years previously, "If you want our aid, call us to your councils," the colonial secretary affirmed Britain's willingness to close with what he assumed to be an open offer. The mother country, he said, would share the control of imperial policy in proportion to the colonies' willingness to share the burdens.

The quotation was correct but Chamberlain's interpretation of it was wrong. He had missed the context. Laurier was denying the charge of his former lieutenant, Henri Bourassa, that participation in the war had committed Canada to take part in all future British wars. Before Canada could be bound to such a course of action, Laurier asserted, it would be necessary to make the above statement to Britain and to work out new constitutional arrangements with her. He did not question the principle that a British declaration of war involved Canada in passive belligerency, but he insisted that Canada alone would decide whether she would be an active belligerent or not. From this stand he never wavered. He saw that Chamberlain ascribed his independence to his French blood and suggested that the colonial secretary have a private interview with the other four members of the Canadian delegation, all cabinet ministers of British stock. Chamberlain acted on the suggestion and found, to his surprise, that these Anglo-Saxons were equally firm in the same stand. Indeed, Australia joined Canada in rejecting, as derogatory to self-government, a New Zealand proposal that each colony should establish a special force for general imperial service in the event of an emergency. On the other hand, colonial contributions to the Royal Navy were increased, the new Commonwealth of Australia undertaking an annual payment of £200,000, New Zealand £40,000, Cape Colony £50,000, Natal £35,000, and Newfoundland £3,000. But the only step the Conference took to institutionalize imperial cooperation was to pass a resolution for a session every four years.

At this session Chamberlain also revived the question of closer commercial relations, and in doing so he was a little bolder than in 1897. On various occasions, both in and out of parliament, he had advanced the idea of a customs union of the empire without committing himself to it, for he feared the strength of free trade feeling at home and of protectionist feeling in the colonies. Now he presented free trade within the empire and a common tariff against the rest of the world as an ideal which, though not immediately practicable, might in time be realized. He saw a gleam of hope in a recent bit of domestic legislation. To help finance the war, his government had imposed a temporary tax of one shilling a quarter—3 cents a bushel—on the importation of wheat; and he counted on getting this tax continued on foreign wheat and lifted from colonial wheat as an initial step by the mother country along the road of imperial preference. Meanwhile he kept his own counsel; and the Conference passed a resolution declaring imperial free trade impracticable, approving imperial preference, and pressing it upon the British government.

Shortly afterward Chamberlain left for South Africa, where he spent several months helping that country back to its feet; when he returned to England in March 1903, he found that a majority of his cabinet colleagues had cut the ground from under his own feet by deciding to drop the duty on all wheat, foreign as well as colonial. Deeply chagrined over what he regarded as the betrayal of a high principle, he concluded that the time had come for more daring action. He determined to seize the free trade bull by the horns and throw it. Though his prime motive was imperial, he believed that a return to protection was also necessary for two other purposes: to provide a revenue that would meet the needs of social reform, notably the payment of old age pensions; and to rearm the country economically, so that it would no longer be at the mercy of its industrial rivals, which were all protectionists.

Being by far the most powerful politician in the land, Chamberlain commanded a large and enthusiastic following, which he organized in the Tariff Reform League, patterned after the old Anti-Corn Law League. At first he thought he could carry the government with him, but it was hopelessly divided over the issue. In the autumn he resigned from the cabinet so that he might be freer to mobilize public opinion. The battle between the Tariff Reformers and the Free Traders waxed hot and furious, but it was an unequal struggle. The political Titan who essayed to revolutionize the country's fiscal policy was fighting against a stronger impersonal force—the popular dread of taxes on food. The conflict rent his party and united the Liberals, who won a smashing victory in the general election of January 1906.

Though the Unionist Party went down to defeat, most of its successful candidates were Tariff Reformers, and this fact did more than console their champion. It encouraged him to continue his crusade relentlessly, in the confident hope that Tariff Reform would win the next election. Six months later a stroke of apoplexy laid him low. He never recovered. The next two general elections, both in 1910, saw his party still clinging to the cause of Tariff Reform and rejected by the majority of the voters. Not until the great depression did Britain abandon free trade and then solely for domestic reasons, though she also, now that she was able, adopted imperial preference.

Even if Chamberlain had persuaded the electorate to accept Tariff Reform he would have been little if any nearer his ultimate goal of a reconsolidated empire. True, he would have enacted imperial preference with an imperial purpose; but imperial preference was separated by a wide gulf from an imperial *zollverein,* his halfway house to imperial federation. Free trade within the empire surrounded by a common customs wall presupposed a surrender of tariff autonomy by the self-governing colonies, which was out of the question.

To return to the development of the Colonial Conference as an imperial institution, we should note the emergence of a rudimentary constitution during the session of 1907. In accordance with the resolution of 1902, there should have been a conference in 1906, and with this in view Chamberlain's immediate successor in the Colonial Office issued a circular dispatch in April 1905. This suggested that it might be well to discard the title of "Colonial Conference" for "Imperial Council" as more appropriate; that there should be a permanent secretarial staff, or commission, to prepare for and follow up the work of the periodic meetings; and that India should be represented at these meetings whenever her interests required it. The proposal to substitute the adjective "Imperial" for "Colonial" met with general approval. The old label was a misnomer because the great majority of the colonies—all but the few self-governing ones—were excluded from membership. To the change from "Conference" to "Council," the replies of the member governments, with one exception, raised no objection. The same was true of the proposal to establish a permanent secretariat in London. On both counts the objection came from Ottawa. The Laurier ministry detected a renewal of the design that Chamberlain had advanced in 1897 and repeated in 1902 to transform the periodic conference into a permanent imperial council invested with legislative and executive power.

When the Conference met in the spring of 1907—the political turnover in Britain having caused a year's postponement—the premier of Canada found a congenial colleague in the premier of the newly freed Transvaal. Botha openly shared Laurier's suspicion of an imperial council, and the French Canadian leader privately strengthened the Boer general's belief in racial and imperial cooperation. After much debate and careful picking of terms, the assembled statesmen agreed on the following resolution:

> That it will be to the advantage of the Empire if a Conference, to be called the Imperial Conference, is held every four years, at which questions of common interest may be discussed and considered as between His Majesty's Government and his Governments of the self-governing Dominions beyond the seas. The Prime Minister of the United Kingdom will be ex-officio President, and the Prime Ministers of the self-governing Dominions ex-officio members of the Conference. The Secretary of State for the Colonies will be an ex-officio member of the Conference, and will take the chair in the absence of the President. He will arrange for such Imperial Conferences after communication with the Prime Ministers of the respective Dominions.
>
> Such other Ministers as the respective Governments may appoint will also be members of the Conferences, it being understood that, except by special permission of the Conference, each discussion will be conducted by not more than two representatives from each Government, and that each Government will have only one vote.
>
> That it is desirable to establish a system by which the several Governments represented shall be kept informed during the periods between the Conferences in regard to matters which have been or may be subjects for discussion, by means of a permanent secretarial staff charged, under the direction of the Secretary of State for the Colonies, with the duty of obtaining information for the use of the Conference, of attending to its resolutions, and of conducting correspondence on matters relating to its affairs.
>
> That upon matters of importance requiring consultation between two or more Governments which cannot conveniently be postponed until the

next Conference, or involving subjects of a minor character or such as call for detailed consideration, subsidiary Conferences should be held between representatives of the Governments concerned specially chosen for the purpose.

Thus the Colonial Conference became the Imperial Conference, its composition was formalized, and its importance was exalted by the introduction of the prime minister of the United Kingdom as president. Yet it remained what it had been, a conference of governments, and the colonial premiers chose their new president to emphasize this fact. Such being the nature of the institution, the stipulation that each government had only one vote meant that the majority could overrule the minority on questions of procedure but not on substantive matters. On such matters not even a unanimous resolution could have any binding force. Another interesting innovation was the use of the word "Dominions" to designate this select group of colonies. The original draft, prepared in the Colonial Office, had "Colonies," to which the premiers of Canada, Australia, and New Zealand all objected. These gentlemen then cast about for a term that would distinguish the overseas members from colonies of an inferior status, and for want of a better they accepted the generic that Canada had adopted and popularized. It should also be observed that the resolution implicitly excluded India from membership.

The paragraph on the secretariat was a weak compromise. The Australian premier strongly supported the idea of a composite body quite distinct from the Colonial Office, whose jealousy was thereby aroused. This queered the pitch, but apparently not enough to defeat the project. It seems to have fallen a victim to misunderstanding. The Canadian premier, troubled by the ghost of Chamberlain and the specter of a new imperial bureaucracy, pointed out that the secretariat must have a head who would be responsible to some continuing authority. "To whom?" he asked. The Cape premier contended that he would be responsible to all the prime ministers. "How," demanded Laurier, " . . . when you are in South Africa and I am in Canada?" The upshot was a failure to agree on any concrete proposal to carry out the principle, and after the Conference adjourned a specialized Dominions Department was organized within the Colonial Office. Some have thought that this failure was unnecessary and unfortunate: unnecessary because the Conference turned its back upon an informal practice of mutual consultation that had grown up among the official representatives of the dominions resident in London,[9] who could have been charged along with some official of the British government with the duties specified in the resolution; unfortunate because this alternative would have given a clearer expression to the concept of imperial partnership.

The Conference of 1907 also differed from its predecessors in that it dealt with a wider range of topics and its resolutions were more effectively followed up. The liveliest discussions, apart from the constitutional issue, were again on defense and closer commercial relations. The Australian premier delivered an impassioned plea for reciprocal imperial preference by the mother country, and other overseas spokesmen expressed their desire for it, only to meet a stubborn resistance rooted in the recent popular mandate that had confirmed the British Liberal Party's belief in free trade. On the other hand, the government of the United Kingdom studiously refrained from any hint at dictation to the dominions on what they should do for imperial defense. It was agreed that there should be an Imperial General Staff drawn from the forces of the empire as a whole but without interfering with dominion autonomy in military matters. On the great question of naval defense, no uniform policy was possible. Australia wanted to terminate the agreement of 1902 in favor of building a fleet of her own. New Zealand was uncertain about this but for the time being preferred to continue her contribution of money and men to the Royal Navy. South Africans intimated that their country would move in the same direction as Australia. Canada was still unprepared to offer anything; therefore she blocked the passage of a Cape resolution stating that each dominion should make some appropriate provision, after consultation with the Admiralty.

The naval "scare" of 1909, when revelations of German plans to construct dreadnoughts caused a drastic increase of the British building program, evoked new offers of aid from the dominions. The House of Commons in Ottawa unanimously resolved that it would cordially approve any necessary expenditure for the speedy organization of a Canadian navy to cooperate with the Royal Navy in maintaining the naval supremacy of Britain which was "essential to the security of commerce, the safety of the empire, and the peace of the world." From

---

[9] The high commissioner of Canada and the agents-general of the other colonies. Australia had not yet appointed a high commissioner, but the Australian states continued the agents-general whom they had maintained before federation.

New Zealand and Australia came promises of dreadnoughts. South Africa could then do nothing new, being temporarily paralyzed by the birth throes of the Union. A subsidiary imperial conference met in London to coordinate defense plans; and there it was agreed that New Zealand should contribute a capital ship, Australia should create and control a squadron, and Canada should build cruisers and destroyers to guard her two coasts. Domestic difficulties, to be noted later, held up these Canadian plans; and South Africa, on becoming united, took over the subsidy obligations of the Cape and Natal. But Australia and New Zealand pushed their naval projects, and in 1912 the Federated Malay States presented a capital ship to the imperial navy.

The constitutional question loomed larger in the Imperial Conference of 1911. Sir Joseph Ward, the premier of New Zealand, had submitted in advance a proposal for a representative Imperial Council to advise the British government on imperial matters, but when the Conference met he overcalled his own bid by presenting an elaborate scheme of imperial federation. He was the first and last responsible statesman to do so. He would set up an imperial parliament charged with the conduct of foreign policy, including the supreme issues of peace and war. It would be composed of members drawn from the United Kingdom and the dominions, and it would choose an imperial executive. Out of regard for the principle of autonomy, Ward would allow his projected parliament no power of taxation, on the supposition that the existing parliaments of the empire would supply the necessary funds. The prime ministers of the other dominions would have none of his plan, and the president of the Conference, Mr. Asquith, flatly declared that the authority of his government over foreign policy "cannot be shared." At the same time he was more eager to consult his fellow prime ministers than they were to be consulted on such high matters. He had his Foreign Secretary, Sir Edward Grey, give them in secret session a survey of the international situation which, according to report, was fuller than any he had given to his own cabinet colleagues. It was a sobering revelation, and it left the dominion premiers with little or no desire to claim a voice in the management of high policy for the empire. They were then content to leave the responsibility where it lay, on the shoulders of the British government. The Australian premier, Andrew Fisher, wanted frequent discussions of the high commissioners with the foreign secretary on foreign policy, and the British government offered to gather the high commissioners in a standing committee of the Imperial Conference; but the dominions premiers were so divided on both points that no agreement on either was possible.

The main positive achievement of the Conference had to do with the negotiation of treaties. Fisher complained that Britain should have consulted the dominions before she joined other powers, as planned by the Hague Peace Conference of 1907, in drawing up and promulgating the code of international rules governing naval warfare known as the Declaration of London (1909). It mattered little that Asquith brushed aside the complaint, for the Declaration failed to get the ratifications necessary to put it in force; but what did matter was that the discussions produced an agreement for the future. Thenceforth the dominions were to be consulted in the preparation of instructions to British delegates to the Peace Conferences, conventions drafted by these conferences were to be circulated among the dominions before signature, and the same procedure was to be followed, as far as possible, in the negotiation of other international agreements. This reservation was inserted with the full consent of the members of the Conference. Botha said, "I want it clear. I do not want to handicap the British Government. I want them to undertake the full responsibility." Asquith asserted that his government did not wish "to shovel it off on the dominions." Fisher added, "I do not wish to handicap you either. We want to be associated as far as possible." Laurier would claim no right to be consulted except when Canada was immediately concerned. Turning to his Australian colleague he remarked, "We may give advice if our advice is sought," and he added a thinly veiled warning: " . . . if your advice is sought, or if you tender it, I do not think the United Kingdom can undertake to carry out that advice unless you are prepared to back that advice with all your strength."

Uncertainty clouded the future constitutional relations between the autonomous members of the empire. The old antinomy between imperial unity and colonial autonomy, having been dispelled as an illusion in the field of domestic affairs, was now thrusting itself into the field of foreign affairs; there the dominions shrank from pressing the issue because they were not mature enough to face it squarely.

The final, and in many respects the finest, phase of the imperial federation movement—the Round Table—sprang from seed sown by the publication, early in 1906, of an Englishman's brilliant and penetrating study of how the American Union was formed, F. S. Oliver's *Alexander Hamilton*. The concluding chapters drew from the rise of the United States cogent lessons on how the British Empire should be united in a great federation. Almost immediately the seed developed a vigorous root in the soil of Milner's "Kindergarten," a handful of extraordinarily able and public-spirited young graduates of Oxford University whom Milner had enlisted to help him in the reconstruction of shattered South Africa. Their work there being completed with the Union Act of 1909, which created the Union of South Africa whose constitution they largely drafted, they threw themselves into the task of reconstructing the empire. This task they approached with keener analytical minds and with shrewder sense than their predecessors. They were a devoted brotherhood devoid of personal ambition. The prime mover was Lionel Curtis. His principal lieutenant was Philip Kerr, later the eleventh Marquis of Lothian and ambassador to the United States.

Far from seeking to reverse the growth of colonial autonomy, the common mistake of previous imperialists, these new federationists pointed out that the existing distribution of governmental powers gave too little to the dominions and too much to the United Kingdom. The political development of the former could not be stopped at the point it had reached but was destined to press on into the very arcana of sovereign power. As these great British communities matured, it was inconceivable that they would remain content to be bound by the sole decision of the mother country on important questions of foreign relations and the vital issues of peace and war. At the same time, they would be loath to sever their British connection, and yet they would be forced to do it if that was the only way to satisfy their appetite for sovereignty.

This Round Table analysis of the imperial problem looming ahead was eminently sound. It adumbrated the British Commonwealth of Nations. But this solution, or rather dissolution, of the old dilemma has been only slowly evolved by an empirical process that defied the prevailing concept of sovereignty. According to the strict logic of sovereignty, there was only one solution of the dilemma that had wrecked the first British Empire, had later haunted the minds of those who yielded to the colonial demand for responsible government, and now inexorably called for a final decision because time had focused it upon the supreme issue of government. This solution the Round Table leaders presented in bold outline. It was that the mother country should admit the dominions to share with her the control of high policy for the whole empire; and, as a concomitant, that they should relieve her by assuming a corresponding share of the responsibility for defending the empire. This would, of course, impose an additional burden on them, but nothing like what they would have to bear if they chose the alternative of complete independence.

To achieve the federation of the empire, or rather, as they soon put it, to transform the empire into a genuine commonwealth, this little knot of men who had already accomplished great things set to work in a quiet and efficient manner. Instead of trying to propagate their idea by launching a general publicity campaign, with its attendant dispersion of energy, they founded in 1910 a high-class quarterly under the anonymous editorship of Philip Kerr, *The Round Table,* which was devoted to the publication of anonymous articles on the affairs of the empire and its various parts, "written with firsthand knowledge, and entirely free from the bias of local political issues." They also organized in many strategic centers throughout the empire small groups of intellectuals who were independent in their politics and could give a definite lead to public opinion. These groups of highly selected individuals met privately at more or less regular intervals to wrestle with the imperial problem as outlined above and elaborated by Lionel Curtis in challenging memoranda which the Round Table headquarters in London circulated; the reports of the group discussions were exchanged through this central office, thereby stimulating more fruitful discussion all round. Thus the movement expanded through the empire into a cooperative study of the imperial problem in all its aspects, and this at a time when the obvious approach of world war invested the problem with a more serious urgency.

When the final crisis came and the empire plunged into the fiery ordeal, this practical demonstration of imperial unity far exceeded anything that had gone before. Faith in the future of the empire had never burned so brightly as in the dark days that followed. The men of the Round Table eagerly seized upon the idea that the great war would act as a catalyst, speeding the transformation of the empire into their commonwealth, and for a while it seemed that perhaps they were right. The war did serve as a catalyst, but what it hastened was the emergence of a very different kind of commonwealth. The cause of imperial federation was one of the more important casualties in that gigantic clash of arms.

CHAPTER XXXI

The Formation of Two New Great Dominions: Australia and South Africa

THE FEDERATION of the six self-governing Australian colonies and the union of the four self-governing South African colonies in the first decade of the twentieth century were outstanding events in the growth of the imperial structure. Like the federation of British North America in the previous generation, these two new consolidations within the empire were formed without any conscious purpose of preparing the way for the federation of the empire or its transformation into the British Commonwealth of Nations. No one could then foresee that they were paving the road to the latter, because no one had yet any vision of what that might be. The other possibility was the only one that had been clearly set forth, but the colonies in each group were simply pulling together that they might better serve the interests they had in common.

The Australian story of political unification is far from being a mere repetition of the Canadian or an anticipation of the South African story. It is much simpler because the Australians were a homogeneous stock and the whole continent was theirs. The federation of the Australian colonies was favored by the fact that they were almost wholly peopled from the British Isles, but it was retarded rather than hastened by the fact that they had the continent to themselves. Long separated from one another by great distances over which there was no communication except by a sea journey, each colony became so engrossed in its own development that it felt little concern for the others or for its future relations with them. The centrifugal urge split the old New South Wales into four distinct colonies, as we have seen; and later it threatened the integrity of Queensland, which only federation seems to have saved from partition.

Meanwhile each colony levied its own customs duties, and inter-colonial tariff barriers arose. As the colonies grew and their trade increased, these barriers mounted, becoming quite formidable after the grant of responsible government. The effect was most serious along the Murray River where it divided New South Wales from Victoria and then pursued its course into South Australia. It was on this boundary that expanding settlement effected the first meeting of two Australian colonies. These were the outstanding rivals, by far the richest and most populous, and their fiscal policies were poles apart. New South Wales, alone among the Australian colonies, clung to the old-fashioned doctrine of free trade, and Victoria led the others in seeking salvation according to the new gospel of protection. Because there was a constantly swelling volume of trade crossing the river, and also moving up and down it, the collection of customs in this region became an exasperating nuisance. Repeated intercolonial efforts were made to remove it, but they foundered in intercolonial wrangling. Internal free trade was impossible without uniform tariffs against the outside world, and the clash of policies between Sydney and Melbourne barred any such uniformity.

In the building of railways, as in the erection of tariff walls but with more permanent results, the Australian colonies reinforced the divisions between themselves. Each colony was so anxious to develop its own hinterland and to make this tributary to its own principal port that the continent was provided with unrelated transportation systems. This disjointed design, together with the generally dry nature of the country, soon limited construction and operation to state enterprise, which in turn accentuated the uneconomic and separatist character of the design. To make matters worse, the colonies adopted different gauges, so that when systems did meet they could not be joined. More than half a century after federation, Australia still has not got a uniform gauge.

Another reason for the long continuance of Australian political disunity is that these colonies, sharing the whole continent and growing up under the protection of British naval supremacy, were absolutely immune from invasion by land or sea. The powerful backing that the close juxtaposition of the United States had given to the idea of federation in British North America had no parallel in Australia. Nor did Australia, being overwhelmingly white, have to face anything comparable to the black problem that inexorably called for political unity in South Africa.

What first made many Australians think seriously that they ought to have a common government was the appearance of foreign shadows on their horizon during the eighties. The international scramble to appropriate the islands of the southwest Pacific, which then began, squeezed growing Australian interests in these islands and raised the ominous prospect of foreign powers closing in on Australia. When the British government repudiated Queensland's annexation of eastern New Guinea and allowed Germany to share it, Australian blood boiled. The apparent betrayal by the mother country shocked Australian nationalism into angry consciousness. A united Australia might have won enough British support to forestall Germany. The lesson was too obvious to be ignored by the divided colonies. As the years passed and both Germany and France strengthened their holdings in the island-strewn sea, the anxiety of Australians over their exposed position provided the main impulse to unite their country under one government.

In the beginning the aim was wider—an Australasian union of some kind. New Zealand and Fiji felt the same apprehensions as the six Australian colonies and were therefore represented in the intercolonial convention that met at the end of 1883 to denounce further foreign annexations in the south Pacific. The premier of Victoria, who called the gathering, pressed for a federation of all eight colonies, but his government was the only one to support it. Thereupon the premier of Queensland came forward with a resolution, which was promptly adopted, for the creation of an Australasian council composed of delegates from each member government. From this resolution sprang the Federal Council of Australasia, authorized by imperial legislation in 1885, which sat every other year until 1899. At first there were hopes that it might lead to federation, but it could lead nowhere. It had no revenue, no executive power, only a modicum of legislative authority, and it was never joined by New South Wales or New Zealand.[1] It may suggest the mouse that the mountain in labor brought forth. But this is misleading, as we shall now see.

Intercolonial cooperation for greater security took a practical turn with the *ad hoc* agreement of Queensland, New South Wales, and Victoria to supply the annual £15,000 required of Australia as a condition for the British establishment of a protectorate in New Guinea; and this precedent was followed by the larger commitment undertaken in 1887, when New Zealand and the Australian colonies bound them-

---

[1] Representatives of Fiji appeared at only the first meeting.

selves to pay £126,000 a year toward the maintenance of a British naval squadron and to bear the whole cost of such local fortifications as expert British opinion would advise. The consequent report, submitted in 1889, on measures necessary to place these colonies in a proper state of defense heightened their anxiety over their military weakness. By this time, also, the idea of an Australasian federation was fading out. Two things discouraged it. One was the expanse of ocean—twelve hundred miles—that rolled between Australia and New Zealand. The other was the difference between the two lands and their people. New Zealand, however, participated in the first Australian drive for federation and the preparation of the initial draft of the Australian constitution.

This drive for federation was precipitated by the 1889 report, which postulated unified control as essential to Australian defense. Sir Henry Parkes, then premier of New South Wales for the fifth time, had been studying the movement of opinion toward Australian unity, and the startling effect of the above report convinced him that the hour had come for action. In October of that year he delivered a speech that reverberated throughout the country, calling for the creation of a national government. A few months later, in 1890, a conference representing all the Australian colonies and New Zealand met and passed a unanimous resolution for the summoning of a national convention. Accordingly all the legislatures elected bipartisan representatives who assembled in Sydney early in 1891 to frame the desired constitution. But before examining their work and its immediate results, we should note that influences other than the urgency of national defense were already pulling the country together.

Among these other influences was an old one—intercolonial migration. The great gold rush began it, and the collapse of that rush continued it. The struggle between squatters and selectors stimulated it, and so did the opening of the Queensland interior to pastoral development. There was nothing like this intercolonial movement of people in British North America until long after federation; though there was a parallel in South Africa, it there intensified the discord between Boer and Briton.

Organized labor likewise contributed unconsciously to Australian thinking in terms of continental unity. Labor early tended to join hands across colonial boundaries in order to strengthen its position in bargaining with employers and to get uniform laws touching its own immediate interests. In 1874 an intercolonial conference of miners tied together their separate unions in a national federation, the Amalgamated Miners' Association. In 1886 the Amalgamated Shearers' Union was formed. It was a national union of the hitherto unorganized army of migratory workers on the sheep runs—except in Queensland, which had its own Shearers' Union—and it soon became the largest, the strongest, and the most typical of all Australian unions. From 1879, also, there were frequent intercolonial congresses of trade unions. Labor thus blazed the trail for governments, which met from time to time in intercolonial conferences to deal with such common interests as navigation aids, mail services, cables, alien immigration, and defense. The intercolonial labor congresses were chiefly concerned with securing uniform legislation on such things as the eight-hour day, the legal status of unions, the protection of their funds, safety regulations for employees in mines and factories, and the exclusion of Chinese.

In pressing for this last object, labor espoused a lively national interest. Chinese immigration had been an Australian nightmare ever since the lure of gold began it in the early fifties. Almost at once there was a vigorous agitation to stop it; within a few years several colonies enacted severe laws against it, incidentally embarrassing Britain in her dealings with China. But there were already several thousand Orientals in the country, and others filtered in because other Australian colonies adopted milder measures to keep them out. Western Australia, for example, was tempted by the idea of speeding its slow development by using cheap yellow labor. There were doubts also in South Australia; and Queensland, where there were many Kanakas, showed signs of wavering on the exclusion of Asiatics. Unless all the bars were put up and kept up, Australia might in time be overrun by Chinese; for their number was legion, they were spreading out like a flood in southeastern Asia, they could thrive wherever white men could and in places where white men could not. So strong was the anti-Oriental agitation that in 1888 the premier of New South Wales called an intercolonial conference to discuss what could be done to check the yellow danger. All that the conference accomplished was to reveal more clearly than ever that, much as the majority of the people were determined to have a concerted and effective White Australia policy, they could not get it from six uncoordinated governments. But as this alarming fact struck home, it made Australians realize that they must have a national government for the sake of a White Australia. Thus racial exposure ranks with military exposure as a major cause of Australian federation. When the first national parliament met in 1901, it promptly enacted a stiff law against nonwhite immigration and initiated the repatriation of the Kanakas.

The 1891 draft of the Australian constitution, which emerged from the convention in Sydney, was based largely on a comparative study of the two most apposite examples, those of the United States and Canada—a study that was greatly facilitated by the recent publication of Bryce's famous classic, *The American Commonwealth*. Like the Canadians of a generation before, the Australians were so convinced of the superiority of their British cabinet system, with its fusion of powers, that they would not consider adopting the opposite American principle for their projected federal government; and this of course entailed the same provision for the office of governor general. They also followed Canadian precedent by providing that the federal government should pay annual subsidies to the states in return for the latter's surrender of the right to collect customs duties.

Otherwise the Australian plan was on the American side of the Canadian balance between the British and American constitutions. None of the delegates in Sydney sought, as Macdonald had done in Quebec, to set up a unitary government. All took for granted that it would be a federal one. Nor was there any copying of the Canadian deviations from strict federalism. The residual powers were to remain with the states, and their legislation was not to be subject to federal veto. The central government was not to appoint state governors or judges of state courts. There was to be equal representation of states in the senate. The Australians were more considerate of states' rights because they had to be. Australian federation was nothing so imperative as the Canadian had been.

When the draft of 1891 was submitted to the several colonies for their approval, the drive for federation became bogged down for some years. It was then that New Zealand dropped out. In Australia the leading colony balked and the others hesitated. The trouble was the projected surrender of governmental power to a central authority— states' rights. The strongest objections arose in New South Wales because it was the wealthiest and most populous Australian colony, and because it was the only one that had a free trade policy and a labor party in its legislature. Federation would enclose the whole country within a protective tariff; and the rotund leader of the free traders, who rejoiced in the nickname of "Georgie Porgy" even when he later became Sir George Reid, compared New South Wales to a teetotaler facing the prospect of keeping house with five drunkards. The Labor Party, which was divided on the question of fiscal policy, resented the intrusion of the federal issue as likely to interfere with the enactment of social reform.

What pulled the federation movement out of the morass and started it going again, this time to a successful conclusion, was the development of a severe economic depression. It set men to thinking how much better off they would be if the country were united and there were no internal tariff barriers to strangle trade. Federation at last began to have a widespread popular appeal. Local federation leagues were formed throughout Australia, and central leagues in the capital cities. They adopted a new plan of action calculated to tie the hands of bungling politicians while getting the fullest cooperation of the various legislatures. An enabling act was prepared for them to pass, and it was so drawn that once it became law each step in the process of constitution-making would follow automatically until the finished product was presented to the people, not the legislatures, for acceptance or rejection. The electorate would choose representatives to a new constitutional convention; this would draft a constitution and adjourn to let the legislatures examine its handiwork and propose amendments for consideration by the convention; it would reassemble and prepare a final draft, which would be submitted to a referendum in each colony. If the electorate in three or more colonies approved, the home government would be asked to have parliament enact it.

Bowing to popular pressure, New South Wales passed the Enabling Act at the end of 1895, and shortly thereafter Victoria, South Australia, and Tasmania did the same. Some months later Western Australia fell partly into line by providing for the selection of its representatives by the legislature but reserved the right to hold a referendum. After waiting a while for Queensland, which was distracted by an internal struggle over whether it should remain a political entity or be split up, the other five colonies decided to go ahead without their sister.

The constitutional convention, which met at Adelaide in March 1897, comprised the leading public men of the participating colonies. After a month's deliberation, they produced a document that was substantially the same as the draft of 1891. Then the legislatures got busy and turned out a sheaf of suggestions, which were presented to the convention in September. After three weeks of inconclusive debate, there was an adjournment occasioned by a general election in Victoria. The convention renewed its task of revision at Melbourne in January

1898 and completed it two months later. The four colonies that had committed themselves to a referendum on the amended draft voted in June, when the people of Victoria, Tasmania, and South Australia gave it an overwhelming majority. There was a majority also in New South Wales, but not large enough to satisfy the requirement of the law. To help this hesitant colony over the stile, a few concessions were necessary. The convention having ceased to exist, all six premiers met in January 1899 and negotiated a few changes in the convention's final draft. With this revision it was again submitted to a referendum, this time in Queensland as well as in the other four colonies, and the result was everywhere decisive in favor of the scheme. At the end of July 1900, after it was passed in London, a referendum was held in Western Australia. This too gave a favorable majority, and accordingly the sixth state was included in the Commonwealth of Australia when it came into being on 1 January 1901.

The constitution as finally adopted differs from the draft of 1891 in a few interesting respects. One was the method of choosing senators. The first convention, copying American precedent, prescribed election by the state legislatures; the second convention changed this to election by the people, thus anticipating the American amendment of 1913. A more important development was the insertion of provisions to break a deadlock between the Senate and the House of Representatives. If the upper chamber twice rejects a measure of the lower, the governor general dissolves both houses, and there is a general election. If the newly elected chambers repeat the deadlock it is resolved by a vote of the two houses sitting together as one. The ultimate decision was thus made to turn on the relative size of the two houses and on what majority should be required in the joint session. These two questions ranged the small states against the large ones, and called for compromise between them. They early agreed that the number of seats in the lower chamber, apportioned according to population and redistributed after each decennial census, should always be, as nearly as possible, twice the number in the upper chamber, where each state was given six seats. The settlement of this point produced greater disagreement on the other, the large states demanding a simple majority and the others insisting on a three-quarters majority. The latter was written into the draft submitted to the first referendum; New South Wales objected so strongly, however, that when the premiers met in conference for the last revision they agreed that a simple majority was all that should be required in a joint session, and so they made this change.

Here we may also note that the Australians, unlike the Canadians a generation before, drew up their constitution with a provision for its amendment without reference to London. The procedure laid down is passage by both houses and then a referendum in which the amendment, to become law, must have a majority of the voters in the whole Commonwealth and also majorities in more than half the states. Of course the several Australian states, like the Canadian provinces, retained the right that they had possessed as separate colonies to amend their own constitutions, the only exception being, again as in Canada, that they could no longer touch the powers surrendered to the national government at the time of federation.

Though New Zealand dropped out of the federation movement on the morrow of the 1891 convention, she returned for a moment at the very end—during the London negotiations over the Australian constitution. New Zealand then asked that the door be held open for her to enter at some later date as an original state. But this was the last suggestion that she might join. The gulf that separated her from Australia was too wide to be bridged by a common government.

The unification of the South African colonies, long dreamed of and long despaired of, was at last quickly achieved because it seemed to be the only alternative to a repetition of the bitter and bloody past that would drag the country down to self-destruction. The Boer War, which must be judged by its results as well as by its causes, provided the opportunity—by uniting for the first time under one sovereignty the autonomous white communities clinging to the tip of the black continent. But the application of external force that brought them together could not bind them together. Only a reconciliation of Boer and Briton could do that, for the peace treaty guaranteed self-government to the conquered republics.

The work of reconstruction in the two former republics, which Milner and his famous Kindergarten began before the war was over and then pushed forward at a feverish pace, laid the foundations of reconciliation. Speed was of the essence because so much had to be done and there was so little time to do it. The veldt was desolated; scarcely a farm home had escaped destruction, the native laborers were dispersed, and the stock was all gone. The towns too were mostly deserted, and four fifths of the houses on the Rand had been plundered. Society and government in the Transvaal and the Orange River Colony had to be rebuilt before the administration of these states could revert to their people, and any unnecessary delay in this transfer of authority would widen the breach between Boer and Briton.

For the rehabilitation of the conquered provinces, Milner was given a free hand. He was commissioned governor of each as a crown colony, and therefore he possessed dictatorial power over them. He was also provided with large funds from the British Treasury, which enabled him to pour out money like water. The £3,000,000 gift for resettling the burghers on their farms was not nearly enough and was accordingly increased. Uitlanders and natives were likewise compensated for war losses. Still greater was the amount spent on restoring and extending the railways and on a host of other public improvements. It all cost the British taxpayers more than £14,000,000, which some of them might consider cheap repentance for a war that had already cost them nearly £200,000,000. Milner also had at his disposal the proceeds of a big loan backed by the home government, and he made the mining industry pay heavier taxes than Kruger had ever exacted.

Milner's plans for the regeneration of South Africa turned on the mining industry. It could and should take over permanently the financial burden temporarily assumed by the imperial government, and it would do much more than that. The plundering of the treasure house might not last indefinitely, but meanwhile it would enrich the whole country as never before and place it on a surer footing by developing a more diversified and self-sustaining economy. The British high commissioner also looked forward to a South Africa so prosperous that it would attract immigrants from Britain in sufficient number to tip the balance of population against the Boers, who would then be gradually absorbed in a social synthesis predominantly British. Such being his vision, which time proved to be sound except for the large influx of British settlers and the consequent assimilation of the Boers, he was impatient to get the mines into full operation again.

The mines required an army of native labor, most of which had to be recruited in Portuguese East Africa by agreement with the authorities there, whose price was a share in the Transvaal trade. They exacted it in a modus vivendi that Milner negotiated with them in 1901. It provided that customs duties on Transvaal imports through Portuguese territory should be no higher than on similar goods imported through British territory, that railway rates would be approximately the same, that there would be no discrimination in the allocation of rolling stock, and that the provisions of a republican treaty of 1875 establishing free trade in local products should be continued. When the war was over, one of Milner's first concerns was to knit British South Africa together economically; in 1903 he gathered in Bloemfontein a conference which he persuaded to abolish intercolonial tariffs. Incidentally, it also introduced imperial preference after half a century of lapse. The terms of the new customs union fixed the rates levied at the ports to allow only a moderate protection and also gave the interior states the proceeds, minus a 5 per cent charge for collection, on imports consigned to them.

Half the prewar white population was back on the Rand and one third of the stamps were falling when hostilities ceased. But the return of the natives was disappointing, in spite of the fact that Milner effected much-needed reforms of their working and living conditions—reforms that cut the death rate in the compounds from fifty-four to thirty per thousand. In 1903 there were only 50,000 natives in the Johannesburg gold field, where 100,000 had toiled before the war. On the other hand, the demand for them was greater than ever before, some three hundred new mining companies having been organized during the first twelve months of peace. These figures give some measure of the acuteness of the labor problem that was holding up the progress of the country. Two solutions were then proposed, both very controversial.

One solution was the adoption of a white labor policy. It was urged by a small group on the Rand under the leadership of H. F. P. Creswell, a mining engineer and manager—later leader of the South African Labor Party—who, by overhauling the working of his own mine, was able to use well-paid white labor for unskilled tasks traditionally performed by cheap black labor. His radical experiment was somewhat marred by a strike of skilled employees against unskilled Europeans, and similar experiments in a few other mines failed completely. Nevertheless, he demonstrated that the substitution of white for black labor was not economically prohibitive. Thus fortified, he boldly assailed dependence on native labor as a menace to the integrity of European civilization in South Africa. Creswell struck at the very roots of South African society, which has ever since been riven by the controversy that he initiated. Almost immediately the bulk of mining opinion damned him and his idea. Milner did not. He believed that a white labor policy would attract British immigration which, while stamping a more definitely British character upon the country, would break down the unhealthy white prejudice against manual labor. But after much hesitation he rejected the proposal. It demanded a moral revolution that would take a long time and much trouble to work out. Milner faced a crisis that called for quick action, a temporary expedient.

The other solution was the importation of Chinese coolies, for which there was a strong popular demand. Indians were out of the question. There were already too many of them in Natal, where they outnumbered the whites; they were unpopular in the Transvaal, which had tried to prevent them from filtering in; and they would not go home to India when they completed their service. The Chinese were easier to handle. Yet Milner fought hard against using them. He yielded when he could see no alternative to meet the emergency. In 1904 some 23,000 coolies arrived, to be followed by others, the Chinese government having approved the indenture terms which restricted employment to the mines and provided for compulsory repatriation. The mining industry leaped ahead, pulling the country out of a postwar depression. Naturally the transformation was most striking in Johannesburg, which for the first time had just got real municipal self-government and an adequate water supply, and was now rebuilt as a modern city.

Neither in China nor in South Africa was there any serious objection to this solution of the labor problem on the Rand, but there was bitter criticism in Britain, Australia, and New Zealand. The premiers of these two dominions protested to London that it was an abuse of the military victory that their soldiers had helped to win, and the Liberals in the mother country raised such a hue and cry against Chinese slavery under the Union Jack that it contributed greatly to the smashing defeat of the Conservatives in the general election of January 1906. The new Liberal ministry stopped the issue of licenses for the importation of Chinese labor but did not interfere with existing contracts, with the result that the number of coolies in the mines reached a peak of 54,000 in 1907 and then steadily declined until the last of them were sent back to their native land in 1910. They had served their purpose, like the scaffolding that is removed when the construction of a building is completed. The employment of natives in the mines passed the prewar level in 1905 and continued to mount.

The reconstruction was more than economic, as already suggested. Neither of the two republics had known what a modern efficient administration was. As crown colonies they got it, and this new experience was in itself a valuable political education. Milner and his staff also laid a sound institutional foundation for self-government. Neither the Transvaal nor the Free State had possessed a public school system or local self-government. Now they got them, thanks to the energetic drive of these men. Three hundred specially selected teachers were brought from Britain and the dominions to help get the new schools going well; and instruction in the Dutch language, required by the treaty when the parents desired it, was first limited to five hours a week. Milner was plainly seeking to instill a British character into the rising generation of Boers. Boer nationalism countered by setting up some two hundred independent schools under local committees of parents. Milner offered a compromise of local committees with elected majorities, the right to pick teachers from the government list, and responsibility for providing half the expenses. The Boers refused and the scholastic war went on—against them. The superior teachers, equipment, and financial resources of the government schools prevailed. Meanwhile the competition did two good things. It advertised education and it led to a more liberal provision for the use of Dutch in the public schools.

Throughout the Herculean task of remaking the two conquered colonies, from which Milner retired exhausted in April 1905, his policy was not to rule them as an autocrat but to treat them as if they were already self-governing, to invite and follow the advice of their leading citizens. The principal Boers refused seats in his nominated legislative councils; but they also refrained, until a few months before his departure, from demanding even a voice in their own government. The peace treaty had set no date for the fulfillment of its promise of autonomy.

It was in the British, not the Boer, community that the Transvaal agitation for political emancipation began, with the forming of a public association to work for responsible government. The Boers soon followed suit, in January 1905, with the organization of a political party named Het Volk (The People) and pledged to the principle of self-government and conciliation. In the following month Steyn returned home to the Orange River Colony and started the movement there.

Milner and the home government cast about for a new policy to fit the ticklish time. The rising popular demand convinced them that a change from crown colony administration was urgent. On the other hand, they agreed that immediate self-government was out of the question. They feared what might happen to the leaven of British settlers recently introduced into the almost wholly agricultural society of the Orange River Colony; they were also uneasy over the failure of their cherished prospect that the population balance in the Transvaal would swing to the British side. They could not shake off their distrust of the Boers, and they could not cast off their responsibility for protecting the British. They concluded that the only thing to do was to feel their way by experimenting with a temporary compromise.

Accordingly, the Colonial Office announced that the Transvaal was to have a new constitution right away, with a curtailed gubernatorial authority, a unicameral legislature of which only one fifth would be nominated, and a wide European franchise for the election of the other members. The news intensified political activity in the colony. The majority of the British pulled together as the Progressive Party to support the scheme. The minority's responsible government association, broadened by the attraction of some Boer support, became the National Party which insisted that the new constitution would not work because it did not go far enough. Het Volk rallied the mass of the Boers and declared that any change short of complete self-government was undesirable. The National Party gravitated toward Het Volk, and the two eventually reached an understanding.

The election for which these parties prepared was never held. Balfour's weak cabinet hesitated until it fell in December 1905. Then the Liberals took over, and they too hesitated. Would they repeat Gladstone's betrayal of the Boers when he defeated Disraeli in 1880? Smuts hurried to England and pleaded with the new prime minister for the concession of self-government to the two former republics, explaining that Botha and he were anxious to cooperate with the British. After listening sympathetically to his visitor, Campbell-Bannerman said: "Smuts, you have convinced me."

It was a crucial turning point in the history of South Africa. The British government's decision to take the plunge broke the spell of mutual distrust that had long cursed that unhappy country. It was a great day for the aging Hofmeyr, who had spent his life to heal the white division in South Africa and had recently transformed the Bond into the South African Party in the hope of winning English moderates; and it was a greater day still for the two ex-republics, where the grant of responsible government evoked the spirit of reconciliation. In February 1907 the Transvaal voters went to the polls, Het Volk won a clear majority, and Botha became premier with Smuts as his right-hand man. Later in that year the corresponding party in the Orange River Colony was swept into office there. The political tide was also turning in the Cape, where in 1904 the temporary disfranchisement of the rebels had allowed the Progressive Party, whose cry was "Vote British!" to form a government with Jameson as premier. The inevitable reaction followed; then Jameson too pursued a conciliatory policy and renamed his party, calling it Unionist, to gain the backing of moderates. In February he had to resign, and the South African Party dominated the new government. Thus the three largest South African colonies passed under the control of Afrikanders.

This political turnover had a vital bearing on the question of South African unity. It cleansed Afrikander minds of the fear that federation was a British trick to perpetuate British domination. On the other hand it did not unduly alarm British South Africans over the possibility of Dutch domination through federation. The British were becoming reconciled to their numerically inferior position as the Afrikanders were being reconciled to the need for cooperation with them. But this removal of a serious psychological block could not induce the South African colonies to come together. Now that they were all again free to go their own way, there was grave danger that they would fly apart in the pursuit of their conflicting interests. What brought them together was a realization of this danger.

The native problem, which had long pointed to the necessity for the political unity of white South Africa and was the basic reason for its final achievement, assumed an ugly mein in 1906. The seat of the new trouble was Natal. That colony, enlarged by the annexation of Zulu-land in 1897, now had a European population of 97,000, almost entirely British, and nine times as many natives. The latter remembered Shepstone's paternal administration, while the former seemed to have forgotten it as European ownership ate into tribal lands and the blacks had to shoulder increasing burdens of labor, rent, and taxes. The imposition of a £1 poll tax was the last straw. In the old part of Natal, early in 1906, it provoked resistance that cost the lives of two white policemen. At once martial law was proclaimed and troops were summoned from the Transvaal.

Local forces quickly restored order but not the shaken nerves of the whites. A dozen natives were tried by court martial for the murder of the policemen and were condemned to death. London ordered the governor to stay execution pending further investigation; the Natal ministry resigned in protest; the Australian government pointedly asked why the imperial government thus interfered in a self-governing colony; the Colonial Office backed down; the Natal ministry resumed office; and the convicted natives were executed three days after the date originally set. Thereupon a serious rebellion blazed forth in Zulu-land,[2] and this time military reinforcements from the Transvaal and the Cape were needed to extinguish the fire in a bath of blood. The lesson was clear. Natal could not rule her natives without danger to them, to herself, and to the other colonies.

Natal was also the seat of another racial problem that had grown too big for it to handle and was already troubling not only its neighbors but also India and the government in London. There were more than 100,000 Indians, most of them now free and permanently settled in the little colony, where they throve better than in their native environment. Natal owed much of its economic development to them. As indentured servants they had built the sugar industry on the coast, and when they completed their contracts on the plantations they pursued many useful occupations in which they were reinforced by voluntary migration from India. Some were domestic servants or farm laborers; others were skilled mechanics or small tradesmen; some took up, and made pro-ductive, land that no one else would touch; while a few were pros-perous merchants. As there was no such increase in the local European population, Natal was becoming more an Indian than an English colony. Seeing this danger ahead, the European settlers had been try-ing, almost from the time they were granted responsible government, to get all the Indians in their midst, except the minority working under indenture, back to the land from which they had come. But the Indian government would not permit compulsory repatriation, and various devices of the Natal government, such as special taxes and restrictions, all failed to induce voluntary repatriation. Natal could have stopped importing Indian coolies under contract, but would not. It was the government of India that finally did it, in 1911.

The Indians spread beyond Natal in the eighties. Few went to the Cape, which had little attraction for them; and none to the Free State, which feared their intrusion and barred the entry of all Asiatics. It was to the booming Transvaal that they were drawn. Kruger's govern-ment also would have excluded them utterly but could not without violating the London Convention of 1884. Therefore the northern republic fell back on other means to discourage their entry: legislation

---

[2] The rising was not openly supported by Dinizulu, Cetewayo's son and successor, but he was suspected of complicity. Late in 1907, on rumors of an impending revolt led by him, martial law was again proclaimed and he was arrested. After some months' delay, during which the British government interceded to assure him of a fair trial, he was sentenced to a short term of imprisonment.

denying them the franchise and the right to live or trade or acquire real property outside locations set apart for them. This deterrent was not very effective and it was weakened by lax administration. The war chased the Indians out of the Transvaal, but they returned in greater numbers and the Boers hated them more than ever. The British community also resented their presence. Even before the end of hostilities Milner advised the home government that all Asiatics in the Transvaal should be registered and only those of the better class should be free from confinement to prescribed locations. London demurred, fearing unpleasant effects in India. When Milner retired in 1905, the question was still unsettled. In the following year an outbreak of plague in the filthy Indian quarter of Johannesburg intensified the local outcry against Indians and provided the legislative council with a sanitary excuse for action. An ordinance was then passed requiring all non-indentured Asiatics to register and to carry certificates bearing their fingerprints. Again the Colonial Office objected; this time on the ground that the settlement of the question should be left to the new regime.

When Botha became premier he promptly made the measure law, which immediately raised the much bigger question that London had been afraid to face. Led by Gandhi, then a barrister in Johannesburg, the Indians of the Transvaal adopted passive resistance and packed the jails. That was the beginning of an open and angry quarrel between two members of the empire which the imperial government was impotent to compose and which has continued to the present day. We shall later see how it inflamed Indian nationalism. What we should note here is the tangle in South Africa, where one colony had unwittingly involved another in an intractable problem that deeply concerned both the Indian and the British governments. Neither Natal alone nor the Transvaal alone could deal with it effectively. Only a united South Africa could do that.

Divided South Africa was also trembling on the brink of a suicidal economic war between the colonies over customs and railways. The customs union was subject to internal strains that threatened to break it. The coastal colonies wanted to raise the duties on imports in order to increase their revenues, which were in a sickly state, and to gain more protection for their own produce in the rich market of the Transvaal, to which it was now freely admitted; while the Transvaal farmers resented having to share this market, which they regarded as their own special preserve, and the mining community objected to all protective duties as a burden upon it.

Though the Transvaal was landlocked, it was not at the mercy of the coastal colonies. It had an alternative outlet to the sea through Mozambique, and there was a good guarantee that this northern route would remain open, for the Portuguese could paralyze the Rand by cutting off its vital supply of native labor. The customs union began to crack in 1906, when Natal denounced the convention, thereby forcing another conference to revise the tariff in the fiscal interests of Natal and the Cape. This in turn was attacked by the Transvaal on the ground that it raised the cost of living, and as soon as Botha took office he declared his intention of denouncing the revised convention.

The railways likewise threatened to be an instrument of strife instead of being a bond of union. One railway boundary had disappeared, Milner having early combined the railways of the former republics. That left three competing systems serving the four colonies. All were state-owned, and the prewar rivalry between the states for the life-giving trade generated on the Rand flared up more intensely than ever. In this, as in the tug-of-war over customs, the Transvaal had a great advantage over Natal and the Cape. Of the various lines from Johannesburg to the coast, the shortest was to Lourenço Marques. This line was also the only one that lay almost wholly within the Transvaal, whose revenue had therefore most to gain from its use. The line to Durban was nearly as short, but approximately two thirds of it belonged to Natal, and the revenue was divided accordingly. The lines to the Cape ports, East London, Cape Elizabeth, and Cape Town, were much longer and their ownership was more equally divided.

Mileage, however, was not the sole determining factor in channeling the external trade of the Transvaal. There was an appeal to patriotic sentiment. British trade should prefer British ports, and Afrikanders in the north should not desert their brethren in the south. Then too there was the old cutthroat railway game with which South Africa was already familiar. Rates and rebates could compensate for distance, and so could the manipulation of traffic facilities. Such tricks could also offset the effect of customs duties upon the direction of trade. Early in 1905, largely at Milner's behest, a conference in Pretoria agreed that the prized trade should be distributed equally between the three railway systems, which would require a renegotiation of the 1901 modus vivendi with the Portuguese. But rivalry between the Cape ports

blocked ratification by the Cape assembly, thereby upsetting the agreement. The dangerous problem, thus left unsolved, became more dangerous with the establishment of self-government in the Transvaal.
Lord Selborne, Milner's successor as high commissioner, reported in a
famous memorandum of 1907 that the problem presented such a conflict of interest between the separate colonies that they could resolve it
only by "arbitration or the sword." From this he drew a conclusion that
others also had reached and that was presented to an intercolonial
railway and customs conference at Pretoria in May 1908.

The conclusion was that the colonies should dissolve their conflict
in a political union. Of the many problems that called for the unification of South Africa, that of the railways was the most immediately
pressing; it brought to a head a movement initiated by the Kindergarten. These remarkable young men early fell into discussing among
themselves the future of the country. They could see no hope for it
unless the colonies were bound together in a federation, and that very
soon or it would be too late. Presently a bright light burst upon them
as they read the newly published *Alexander Hamilton* by F. S. Oliver.
This penetrating study of how Americans had formed a national union
in spite of great difficulties seemed to point the way for South Africans.
Under the leadership of Lionel Curtis, who for this purpose resigned
from the civil service, the group threw all its energies into the cause
of union.

Curtis' pen quickly produced two books that soon had a profound
influence in shaping the new South Africa. They presented a full and
compelling argument for federation, and a study of its successful
operation in other lands. The next step was to get the two white races
to study the question seriously. Therefore with tireless energy Curtis
and his associates traveled through the four colonies, organizing Closer
Union Societies, holding conferences, and enlisting the support of local
people. As there was no South African newspaper or magazine that
circulated throughout the country or represented more than a sectional
point of view, they filled the gap by establishing a monthly organ of
their own, *The State*, with Philip Kerr as editor. He is reputed to have
made it "the most important factor in creating the public opinion that
carried the Union through."[3]

Meanwhile on the persuasion of Jameson and with the consent of all
the governments concerned, Lord Selborne issued his famous mem-

---

[3] *The Round Table*, March 1941, p. 202.

orandum, which strongly advanced the case for a national government. Though it was not known publicly at the time, Curtis and his fellows had a good deal to do with the preparation of this important document. When the customs and railway conference assembled in May 1908, Smuts moved a series of resolutions, which were quickly passed, declaring that an early union of the South African colonies under the British Crown was essential, and inviting their legislatures to appoint delegates to a national convention which would frame a draft constitution. This turn of events brought such a sense of relief to the country that within two months the four legislatures accepted the invitation.

The national convention, which met at Durban in October 1908 and in the following month adjourned to Cape Town where it completed the draft constitution, was dominated by the Transvaal delegation. In addition to representing the wealthiest though not the most populous state, it was by far the best organized and prepared. It alone had composed all internal differences on the main questions to be considered. It alone was accompanied by a staff of expert advisers. It alone was armed with a constitution already drawn up, the work of Smuts and the Curtis group. As the other delegations had no definite plan of their own, they had to be content with offering amendments, which the convention threshed out or threw out until it reached a final agreement. The result was submitted to the four colonial legislatures, some of which proposed further amendments. In May 1909 the convention disposed of these in a short final session at Bloemfontein. The revised draft was then approved by the legislatures of the Transvaal, the Orange River Colony, and the Cape, and by a referendum in Natal. In September of the same year, it was enacted in London.

The speed with which the South African constitution was made and adopted offers a striking contrast with Canadian and Australian experience. It reflects the greater sense of urgency felt by South Africans, and it is all the more remarkable because they could get little guidance from what had been done in either of those dominions or in the United States.

The South African constitution differs fundamentally from the American, Canadian, and Australian constitutions in that it is not a federal one. The uniting colonies retained their identity as provinces, each with its own government but possessing no independent authority. The decision to establish a unitary form of government was made by the convention at the very outset, though until only a few months previously almost all South Africans had taken for granted that their country too would be a federation. It then seemed the best they could hope for. Indeed no country has ever adopted federation when the component states were willing, for the sake of unity, to surrender all their independence; and as late as February 1908 South Africans generally were still thinking in terms of a very limited surrender, a loose federation. Then the South African Party ousted Jameson from office, and at once Smuts wrote Merriman, the new Cape premier, saying that the time had come to push for federation. Merriman leaped at the proposal and replied that "the nearer to unification the better." Federation was only a partial cure for the grave evils inherent in continued political disunity, and fear of these evils was giving the movement such momentum as to suggest the possibility of driving straight on to get a more thorough cure in a more perfect union. Moreover, the divisions that cut deepest in South Africa were not territorial but racial—between Dutch and English, and between white and black—and these racial cleavages had little relation to intercolonial boundaries, which were largely artificial and accidental.

When the Transvaal delegation proposed union rather than federation, their Cape colleagues were ready to fall in with the idea. The colony they represented, being the oldest and the most populous, had least to fear from such a merger. The two little colonies had naturally more reason to fear that they would be submerged. But Orange River Colony was placated by the restoration of its old republican name, Orange Free State, and by the thought that Afrikanders outnumbered English South Africans in the whole country. This very thought, however, made Natal apprehensive of jeopardizing its peculiarly English character. When its delegates returned home, they were regarded as traitors. It alone demanded federation, which the other three rejected. Therefore Natal came face to face with the necessity of deciding whether to go in with them or stay out. Either alternative had its obvious dangers, and the government of Natal was so fearful of making the wrong choice that all it could do was to order a referendum. The result was a surprisingly large majority for joining the other colonies.

In the structure of the central government, South Africa bears a family resemblance to Canada and Australia, with its governor general, its two houses of parliament, and its cabinet system. The South African Senate was constituted much more like the Australian than the Canadian, with each province, irrespective of size, having the same number of senators—eight—and all elected. Their election, however, was made indirect, the electors being the representatives of the province in the lower house of the national parliament and the members of the provincial council, to be noted later, voting as one body. In addition to these thirty-two elected senators, the constitution provided for eight to be appointed as in Canada but holding their seats for only ten years, the term of the elected senators; and it required four of these eight to be chosen mainly for "their thorough acquaintance, by reason of their official experience or otherwise, with the reasonable wants and wishes of the coloured races." The allocation of seats in the lower chamber, the House of Assembly, is roughly in proportion to the European male adult population. As a sop to the two smaller provinces, they were originally much overrepresented. But the constitution provided for the progressive correction of this inequality.[4] The South Africans copied the Australian device of a joint session to break deadlocks between the two houses but eliminated the requirement of a prior dissolution. The final decision therefore comes sooner in South Africa, and it is more weighted against the upper house, which is little more than one quarter, instead of one half, the size of the lower house.

The structure of the South African provincial governments is entirely unlike that of the Canadian provinces or the Australian states. It is a distinct South African creation. The chief executive officer is an administrator appointed by the central government and responsible to it. His position is comparable to that of a governor who really governs. In place of the old two-chambered legislature there is an elected provincial council which sits for three years and cannot be dissolved during this period. At the first meeting after each election its members have to choose four persons, not necessarily from among themselves, to form, with the administrator as its head, an executive committee. The administrator and any other member of this committee who is not a member of the provincial council have the right to participate in the deliberations of the provincial council but not to vote in it. The council has authority to legislate and levy taxes, but every measure it passes has effect only when it receives the assent of the central government, and then only as long and as far as it is not repugnant to an act of the Union parliament. The provincial council is thus a sort of glorified county council, and the provinces are but the ghosts of the former self-governing colonies.

---

[4] By requiring an automatic redistribution of seats after each quinquennial census, beginning in 1911, and by prescribing that no seat should be taken from a province until the membership of the House, originally 121, reached 150, a size that has since been attained and was to remain fixed until the Union parliament decreed otherwise.

The judicial administrations of the uniting colonies were fused into one system. The highest court in each colony was continued as a provincial division of the Supreme Court of South Africa, from which appeal lies only in the Appellate Division of the Supreme Court. From this body the constitution barred all appeals to the Privy Council save by special leave of the latter. The Supreme Court of South Africa, unlike the corresponding courts of Canada and Australia, has been little troubled—until after World War II—by constitutional cases because South Africa has a unitary, not a federal, form of government and its parliament was endowed with almost absolute authority.

In point of power the South African parliament offers a marked contrast to the parliaments of Canada and Australia. The legislative authority that was divided between them and the provincial or state legislatures was concentrated in the Union parliament. In addition, it was given complete authority to amend the constitution by ordinary legislation or by a two-thirds majority of the two houses sitting together. The more difficult method was prescribed for any change in the establishment of Dutch and English on an equal footing as official languages of the Union, and for any alteration of the franchise based on race or color. The section (152) imposing this restriction was itself likewise "entrenched" to protect the other "entrenched clauses."[5]

The franchise was the thorniest question that the convention had to handle. The two ex-republics had white manhood suffrage and would make it uniform throughout the Union. The other two colonies objected strenuously. They had a property qualification that excluded poor whites. Natal also had special laws that denied the franchise to Indians and to all but a negligible number of colored people. The Cape too had an additional requirement, but this was an educational test that was applied without regard to race. The Cape was the only one of the four colonies in which the right to vote did not depend on the color of a man's skin. Here there were some 15,000 nonwhites on the electoral roll. Here too nonwhites were eligible for election to the legislature, though none of them had ever sought a seat. The Cape was proud of its enlightened policy of equal rights for all civilized men, and believed that the only way of salvation for the whole country was to follow this lead. But the Cape could not impose its system on the

---

[5] These also covered other matters, but with a time limit that has long since expired. For example, no province was to have its representation in the House of Assembly reduced by a redistribution of seats until they numbered 150.

other colonies, nor could they force theirs upon the Cape. Therefore, after a tough struggle, the convention agreed to leave the varied franchise as it stood and to bar non-Europeans from standing for election except to the provincial councils of the Cape and Natal. The provinces, however, were denied the control that they had exercised as self-governing colonies over their respective franchises.

Reviewing the South African constitution, one can see various features that suggest federalism. It designated Pretoria as the executive capital, Cape Town as the legislative capital, and Bloemfontein as the judicial capital. It transformed the several colonies into provinces, it gave them equal representation in the Senate and the two smaller ones a disproportionately large number of seats in the House of Assembly, and it continued in the provinces the existing colonial differences on the controversial question of political rights enjoyed by nonwhites. But all these concessions to colonial particularism, necessary as they were for the unification of South Africa, are no more than shadows of federalism.

The Union of South Africa was proclaimed on 31 May 1910. It was a fitting birthday because it was the anniversary of the Peace of Vereeniging, signed exactly eight years before.

CHAPTER XXXII

Dominion Nationalism

OF THE VARIOUS FORCES that have shaped and still govern the world of today, one of the most powerful is nationalism. During the last quarter of the nineteenth century and the opening years of the twentieth, it became the dominant political influence in western civilization and, spreading beyond, began to undermine western control of the rest of the world. Within the British Empire its growth was most pronounced in the great dominions, in Ireland, and in India.

Nationalism, which people commonly take for granted, is a mysterious thing, a subtle psychological power that defies exact analysis. What binds the members of a nation together is a feeling that they have something precious in common that distinguishes and separates them from any other people. Of what does this prized possession consist? One possible element is race, sometimes regarded as so important that a myth of racial unity has been created for national purposes. But race is not an essential component. Most nations are racial mixtures and different nations may have the same racial heritage. A more usual and much more potent element is language, which likewise is not essential though it comes near to being so. Though bilingual and multilingual nations exist, these are exceptions whose national unity is always handicapped and sometimes seriously strained by internal linguistic division, particularly when one language group tries to force its own tongue on the rest of the nation for the sake of closer national integration. On the other hand, many nations speak the same tongue as others, but there is a natural tendency to develop national variations of a common language, and sometimes this tendency has been artificially cultivated for national reasons. Irishmen have gone even further. They have revived a dead tongue out of national revulsion against England. Other elements, such as religion, or government, or country, or culture, have also contributed to the making of national consciousness. Yet, on the parallel of race and language, not one of them is essential.

The precious something is a compound as variable, as elusive, and as mysterious as that which makes a particular man fall in love with a particular maid. Their parents and friends may wonder what they see in each other that is so exclusively attractive, and so is it with nations. The average American finds it difficult to understand why Canadians, who seem to be so like himself, should prefer to remain a separate nation, for their preference is fundamentally instinctive rather than rational. The idea that Canada should join the United States is repellent to Canadians though natural to Americans for the obvious reason that the greater would absorb the lesser body, and self-preservation is the first law of a nation's existence and self-aggrandizement is the second.

Nationalism operates by external repulsion as well as by internal attraction, thus resembling the magnet with its opposite and inseparable poles, for the pulling together that makes a nation is essentially a pulling together against people outside itself. Nothing can rouse the national sentiment of a people more quickly or fiercely than a first-class quarrel with another nation. "My country right or wrong" is the natural language of nationalism, for it is of the essence of nationalism to exalt the nation in the hierarchy of human values, placing it at the top. Taking the world as a whole, one may question whether the noble brotherhood within the nation has been worth the price paid for it in the accentuation of the differences between nations. National sovereignty has become a commonly accepted ideal which, unless it is severely qualified, spells international anarchy.

Within the British Empire, nationalism was more or less tempered by a reluctance, rooted in sentiment and interest, to sever the British association or even to weaken it. This reluctance was naturally most marked in the parts of the overseas empire inhabited by people who sprang from the British Isles. In addition to being British originally, these colonies got self-government before they developed the consciousness of a separate nationality in their new environment. The situation was complicated in Canada and South Africa by the presence of the French and the Boers, who, being of alien stock brought under British rule by conquest, had awakened nationally out of resentment against this rule before self-government was introduced. But if each of these two dominions developed a dual nationality which distinguished them from the dominions peopled wholly from the British Isles, all the dominions were new countries, and all free to go their own way without any restraint imposed by Britain.

Ireland was different, and India much more so. In contrast to the dominions, Ireland was an old country with a glorious early history and a grievous later one. The Irish were a conquered people long held in subjection, and by the nineteenth century they did not have even a subordinate government of their own. Their nationalism was a struggle for self-government; it was so compromised by the existence of a Protestant minority population, transplanted from Great Britain centuries before and forming a solid block in the northeast of the island, that Ireland split completely instead of following the example of Canada and South Africa. Indian nationalism was also a reaction against foreign rule established by conquest, and it too split the country; but in other respects, as we shall see, it bears little resemblance to Irish and less to dominion nationalism.

The first dominion to develop a national consciousness was Canada, partly because it was the oldest, the biggest, and the wealthiest, and partly because it lay cheek by jowl with the United States. None of the others ever had such a close and powerful neighbor. Though the federation of British North America was conceived and born in fear of the United States, the people of the uniting colonies were not yet a nation. There was much talk among them that they would now form a nation, and there was no little pride in the anticipation of such an achievement. In this talk and this pride, we may see the first conscious stirring of Canadian nationalism. It was soon quickened by the enormous territorial expansion of 1870 and 1871, effected with an eager eye to forestall the United States. But the new dominion could not hope to survive, much less become really united, so long as it depended upon the United States for communication between its parts. The only all-year communication between the Maritime Provinces and Quebec was through Portland, Maine; there was no coming and going between Ontario and Manitoba except through Chicago and St. Paul; and the only way from central Canada to British Columbia was across the continent on American railways and up the coast on American vessels. Under such conditions, the pull of the great republic upon each of these widely separated parts would slowly but surely tear the dominion asunder.

That was why one of the terms of federation bound the Canadian government to build a railway that would join Halifax with Quebec. Begun in 1867 and completed in 1876, the Intercolonial Railway was constructed and operated as a government enterprise. It never paid; it could not pay; it was not intended to pay. It was a great public work designed to bind the Maritime Provinces to central Canada, and it achieved this purpose. Similarly, the Canadian Pacific Railway was undertaken in 1871 to rivet the newly acquired West to the East. The original plan was to build this too as a public work, and for some years this plan was followed without making much progress. Times were hard, and the magnitude of the task eclipsed that of the Intercolonial. Finally the government made a contract with a private corporation under which the latter completed the railway and became its owner. In addition to the sections already built and being built at public expense, the government gave the company huge subsidies in cash and land, and extensive exemption from taxation. This was the price paid for persuading private capital to invest in the road. The opposition cried out that the price was exorbitant, but the men who formed the company added little to their fortunes by this venture. With the driving of the last spike on the line across the Rocky Mountains in 1885, the steel rivet ran right through Canada from the Atlantic to the Pacific.

Something more than political federation and the building of these two vital railways was necessary for the people of Canada to become a nation. Provincial loyalties were old and strong. Federation had met with rejection in each of the Maritime Provinces. Nova Scotia even talked of annexation to the United States as a means of escaping from thraldom to Canada. Since the beginning of the century French Canadian nationalism had asserted itself loudly and sometimes very angrily. Its emphasis on race, language, and religion made it the most formidable obstacle to the cultivation of an all-Canadian nationalism. Protestant and English-speaking Ontario had grown up in opposition to Quebec; and the legacy of mutual suspicion between these two provinces was liable at any time to set them by the ears. The dominion had to develop a life and a spirit of its own if it was to be more than an artificial body that local loyalties might pull apart and deliver piecemeal to the United States.

This danger was so obvious that it evoked a conscious and widespread effort to make the different people of the country think and feel as one nation. The effort found its most interesting and probably its most effective expression in an organization that was formed not long after the dominion was born. It adopted the motto *Canada First*—not the old but the new Canada—and it attracted such support that it seemed about to become a regular political party. The challenge induced the two historic parties, Liberal and Conservative, to espouse the principles advocated by the Canada First movement which, as a consequence, began to break up in 1875. Already other influences were advancing the same cause.

The Washington Treaty of 1871, coinciding with the recall of the British garrisons, did much to rally the Canadians as a nation. By this treaty the United States agreed to arbitrate its *Alabama* claims against Britain in return for the opening of Canadian inshore fisheries to Americans. The prime minister of Canada, Sir John A. Macdonald, was one of five British commissioners sent to negotiate the treaty. His appointment to the commission is memorable as that of the first representative of any dominion or colony to participate in the conduct of foreign affairs. But the honor sat heavily upon him because, under combined British and American pressure, he had to yield the fisheries without getting what Canada demanded for them, which was a renewal of the 1854 reciprocity arrangement. The *Alabama* claims were a big stick in the hands of the American government, and until these claims were settled it could use them as an excuse for war. Macdonald knew full well that the brunt of the war would fall on his country and that he dare not withhold his signature from the treaty. Throughout the dominion there was bitter resentment against Britain for buying peace at Canadian expense, and still bitterer resentment against the United States for playing this game of power politics.

It was a ticklish time for Canada because the feud between Ontario and Quebec had just flared up over the solitary execution that marred the Manitoba rebellion early in 1870. The victim was an Ontario lad and an Orangeman. At once Ontario began to howl for the blood of the fugitive Riel, who had ordered the execution, and Quebec as passionately sprang to his defense. While the two major provinces were thus raging at each other, the Washington Treaty struck them a sobering blow that greatly helped to consolidate the country. It was not the last time that the United States unwittingly came to the rescue of a divided Canada.

Canadians still hankered after the lost American market, and the hankering increased with the onset of the long depression in 1873. A change of government then occurred in Ottawa, and the new Liberal administration spied a gleam of hope that a revival of reciprocity in natural products was not impossible. Thereupon Britain, at the request of Canada, commissioned another Canadian, this time with only the British ambassador as an associate, to negotiate the desired treaty. The business being wholly Canadian, the ambassador left its management to the Canadian, who actually worked out a treaty with the American secretary of state in 1874. It was promptly, but without any official recommendation, submitted to the United States Senate, and there it died without being even considered. Too many American interests were opposed to it, and too many American politicians believed that the refusal of commercial concessions would reduce Canada to such a desperate plight that it would beg to become part of the United States. This belief, the product of a blind nationalism, was to persist for many years and to contribute more than a little to the hardening of Canadian nationalism, as it did in 1874 through the rebuff administered to Canada.

This rebuff and the deepening depression drove the dominion along the road of economic nationalism in company with almost all other western countries except Great Britain. In 1878 Macdonald was returned to power on the issue of a self-sufficient economy, and in the following year his government passed a thoroughgoing protectionist measure. The Liberals fought stoutly against it, arguing that it was better to export what Canada could raise most cheaply, natural produce, and purchase from other countries what they could make more cheaply than Canada. But the opposition might as well have tried to prove that black was white. The people of Canada had awakened as a nation; and whether protection would be financially profitable or not, they felt that it would be nationally profitable because it would make them more independent economically and knit them together more securely. The change to protection coincided with the recovery of prices that continued for a few years, and the prosperous interlude confirmed the public faith in what Macdonald had shrewdly labeled the National Policy. It was soon commonly known by the initials N.P., and it was so popular that a smart manufacturer appropriated this abbreviation as the name of his product that became a perennial favorite with Canadian housewives—N.P. Soap.

The national unity of Canada was again shaken in 1885, when another execution in the West touched off an explosion in the East. This time the victim was Riel himself. Having returned to lead a rising of half-breeds living on the Saskatchewan, he was caught, tried, and condemned to death. The sentence split the country. French Canada raised an almost hysterical cry for the government to save him from the gallows, while Ontario grimly insisted that the noose be put around his neck. Macdonald and his cabinet colleagues, who were much to blame for the rebellion because they had paid no attention to the just grievances of the half-breeds, could not squirm out of the dilemma. They had to choose between pleasing Ontario or Quebec. After long and painful hesitation they chose Ontario; thus began the estrangement, which still persists, of Quebec from their party. When Riel mounted the gibbet, he became a French Canadian martyr whose life was sacrificed to appease an English Canadian demand for vengeance.

Very shortly another question arose that distracted public attention from this internal strife and tended to pull the country together again. The brief sun of prosperity had disappeared, and Canada was plunged into deeper economic gloom. As the Children of Israel had longed for the fleshpots of Egypt, so now did Canadians yearn for the American market. Once more Ottawa approached Washington, where the Canadian extremity seemed an American opportunity. The United States would not open its doors to Canadian raw materials unless Canada opened its doors to American manufactures. The Conservatives, who were still in office, would not listen to such a bargain. Many prominent Liberals, however, were convinced that Canada would have to pay this American price. They talked of free trade between the two countries, and of having one tariff wall around both. The Conservatives damned this suggestion of commercial annexation as the beginning of political annexation. "A British subject I was born, and a British subject I will die," cried Macdonald in the general election of 1891. He won. The Conservative victory, the last until twenty years afterward, is a nice illustration of how nationalism and imperialism, though commonly opposed throughout the British dominions, have frequently been allies in Canada, thanks to the near presence of the United States. The Liberals, learning their lesson, met in convention and formally repudiated the policy of unrestricted reciprocity.

To preserve the rhythm of Canadian nationalism, the family quarrel broke out again while the people of the country were demonstrating that they would not sell their national birthright for a mess of commercial pottage. Manitoba had early copied the dual public school system of Quebec, with Roman Catholic and French schools for one part of the population, and Protestant and English for the other. In 1890, immigration having made the new province mainly Protestant and English-speaking, the legislature abolished the separate schools of the minority and prescribed one uniform system of secular, and English, public schools. Quebec raged and Ontario rejoiced, and for six years the Manitoba school question was the storm center of Canadian politics. According to the constitution, education was a provincial matter but the federal cabinet could intervene to protect the rights of an aggrieved minority in a case of this kind. The responsibility for settling the ugly dispute, which turned on race, language, and religion, thus rested upon the dominion government, which did not know how to handle it. Old Macdonald died in 1891, worn out by the strenuous campaign, and the advantage of leadership passed to the Liberals under the young Laurier. He pleaded for a reasonable compromise with Manitoba, while the Conservative government blundered into ordering that province to restore its separate schools, hoping thereby to recover the strength it had lost in Quebec through the execution of Riel. By this maneuver, which antagonized Protestant Ontario, the Conservatives won the open backing of the Roman Catholic hierarchy. But this did neither of them any good, for in the next general election, in 1896, the majority of French Canadian voters defied their bishops' political dictation.

In that election Canadian national unity took a great stride forward without any aid from the United States. Laurier, now prime minister, quickly restored the national harmony by applying persuasion instead of coercion to the province of Manitoba, which kept its unified school system but modified its regulations by allowing voluntary religious instruction of Roman Catholic and Protestant children separately during school hours and by abandoning the requirement that all teaching must be in the English tongue. This amicable settlement of an angry question was typical of Laurier's more general achievement in drawing English Canada and French Canada together. In addition to being almost worshipped by his own people as their greatest son, he gained a personal ascendancy in English Canada which no English Canadian leader has ever paralleled in French Canada. For all his great charm and understanding, Laurier could not have done this had it not been for the fact that, though he was always a devout Roman Catholic, he would never tolerate the interference of his own church in the political field. He had openly fought it from the beginning of his public career. The climax came in 1896, when the bishops issued mandaments to be read from every pulpit directing the people to vote Conservative. On emerging victorious against such odds, Laurier and several other prominent Roman Catholics, irrespective of race, joined in an appeal to Rome against the political activity of the local hierarchy; the papal court sent out a prince of the church to investigate; and thenceforth the Roman Catholic clergy in Canada eschewed politics. All this, of course, saved Laurier from falling under English Canadian and Protestant suspicions as a possible tool of his church, and thereby enabled him to bridge the national gap.

Also in 1896 the Canadian nation commenced to grow in size, in strength, and in self-confidence at an amazing rate, for then the empty West began to fill with a rush and the dominion as a whole entered upon a period of abounding prosperity. The Liberals gleefully claimed all the credit for this great turn in the country's fortune, but these politicians had little to do with the splendid tide except to ride high upon it. What produced it was an astonishing combination of influences outside Canada.

The great westward flow of population in the United States, having at last occupied all the free American homestead land that was good for ordinary farming, began to spill over into the Canadian prairie at the very time when the long depression came to an end. Then manufactured goods lagged behind raw materials in the general recovery, causing the price of wheat in the world market of Liverpool to rise faster than Canadian production costs. Ocean freight rates continued their downward course for another dozen years, which meant a corresponding reduction of transportation charges on Canadian export and import trade across the Atlantic. To complete the tale of how blind forces cooperated in Canada's favor at the commencement of the Laurier regime, interest rates reached an all-time low, and capital was as plentiful as it was cheap. Britain was bursting with it, and found in Canada a preferred field for investment. When these fortuitous factors are added together, it is small wonder that immigrants flocked to Canada and the whole country filled out in a way that recalled the phenomenal growth of the United States in the nineteenth century. Before the First World War Canada was exporting more wheat than any other country except the United States and Russia; and the Canadian population, which had ceased to grow by 1891, when it was about 4,800,000, increased to nearly eight million.

Such vigorous growth gave a corresponding stimulus to Canadian national pride. It also exorcised a spell that had bewitched Canada for half a century—the spell cast by reciprocity with the United States—for the Canadian economy was now firmly oriented upon the international market of the Old World. At the same time the absorption of a large immigration was a healthy challenge to Canadian nationalism. There was some concern over the size of the influx from the United

States; but much of this was the re-emergence of a British stream that had flowed into the United States from the old country and from Canada, and as a general rule the Americans were more quickly assimilated than the newcomers from the British Isles. More difficult was the considerable body of immigrants from the European continent. Inevitably many of the older ones remained foreign, but Canadian society digested the younger generation and the task made Canadians more consciously Canadian.

A more important and most healthy influence in solidifying the nation was the internal migration set in motion by the rapid development of the country. It scattered sons and daughters of the Maritime Provinces all the way out to the Pacific coast and it spread large numbers of people from the old Canada all over the West, thereby multiplying the human bonds that held the dominion together. In addition, by mixing these migrants together in new surroundings, it gave them a broader national outlook, which they in turn imparted to the friends and relatives they had left behind.

When this dynamic development of the dominion was just getting nicely under way, the outbreak of the Boer War in 1899 imposed a new strain upon the growing national unity. The immediate and instinctive reaction in English Canada was an insistent demand that the government send a contingent to fight in South Africa, while French Canada just as naturally held back and was inclined to be apprehensive of this outburst of British imperialism in the rest of the country. The prime minister, who was thus pulled in opposite directions, had to yield to the majority cry, but at the same time he announced that the dispatch of troops from Canada was not to be a precedent. His disclaimer reassured most of his own race, but not Henri Bourassa, one of his ablest supporters, who turned on him and publicly accused him of betraying Canada by committing it to fight in a British war that was none of Canada's business. This was the beginning of a small political party and a large political movement known as Nationalist in Quebec and French Canadian Nationalist elsewhere. English Canada denounced Bourassa and his crowd as disloyal to the empire, and they retorted with charges of disloyalty to Canada. The issue was fundamental and the conflict confused it by making each side identify Canada with itself, French or British, which of course emphasized the racial schism.

Again the United States came to the rescue by administering a shock to the schizophrenic nationalism of Canada. The way the American

government got the Alaska Boundary Award of 1903 rankled so bitterly
that it blinded Canadians of that generation to the fact, now generally
accepted, that the award itself was substantially just. The dispute was
over the width, not the length, of the Alaskan panhandle. President
Theodore Roosevelt determined to use force if necessary, and in March
1902 he sent troops to the disputed region. He would not listen to the
Canadian request that the matter be referred to the Hague Court or
to arbitration by a neutral. A virtual ultimatum from Washington
forced Ottawa to agree to a settlement of the boundary by a joint
commission of "impartial jurists of repute," three American and three
British. Roosevelt flouted this agreement by picking men who were
notoriously anything but "impartial," and Canada urged Britain to
delay ratification as a protest. But London was anxious to avoid trouble
with Washington, and Canadian fears were not allayed by a British
refusal to let Canada name all the British panel. It was composed of
two Canadians and the Lord Chief Justice of England. He sided with
the United States commissioners to complete the award. Canada was
at once convinced that the British government, under American influence, had "tipped the wink" to him, to quote the words of "Teddy"
Roosevelt when he later declared that this was what had happened;
and a storm of indignation against both the United States and Great
Britain swept through the dominion, giving another clear demonstration of how nationalism feeds on wounds, real or supposed, inflicted
from without.

The naval scare of 1909 had the opposite effect, repeating the
experience of ten years before. The revelation that German naval
power was creeping up on the British left French Canada cold, for its
history made it more isolationist than any part of the United States; but
in the rest of the country there was warm concern over the danger
looming in the Old World. This reaction was not just a blind expression of British imperialism, like that of 1899. It was more national
and more responsible. Many English Canadians suddenly felt that
Canada was not playing the part of a self-respecting nation, that their
country was sponging on the mother country by enjoying the protection
of the Royal Navy without paying a penny for it, and that it was time
for this to stop. In 1910 Laurier's government introduced a bill for the
construction of a Canadian navy that, if need be, might serve as part of
the British fleet. The measure was attacked in French Canada because it
went too far, and in English Canada because it did not go far enough.
Bourassa and his followers cried out that the administration in Ottawa

had become the tool of London; while many English Canadians insisted on an outright gift of money to Britain, some because they were outright imperialists, more because the crisis seemed very urgent and this the quickest way to meet it. As might be expected, the crossfire between these extreme opinions, French on the one hand and English on the other, mutually exasperated those who held them.

The national confusion, which stalled the naval bill, became worse confounded when the government sprang a surprise by announcing the conclusion of an agreement with the United States to give Canada the reciprocity it had long desired. Farmers in the West, and also in the East, had revived the old demand; but the main pressure came from American publishers, who sought the free import of Canadian newsprint. Time, however, had brought changes in Canada too. The Conservatives discovered that they no longer wanted reciprocity, and not a few Liberals agreed with them that it would be the undoing of the country. They declared that Canada would become so dependent on the American market for the sale of its natural produce that it would be at the mercy of the United States. On the other side of the line, President Taft urged his people to seize this opportunity of establishing closer commercial relations with Canada because if they did not they might miss it forever through the tightening of imperial preference. When he summed up the situation by saying, "Canada is at the parting of the ways," he little realized how his words would reverberate in Canada as a powerful argument for choosing the British way. Likewise, when Speaker-designate Champ Clark blatantly advocated reciprocity as a step toward annexation, he dealt it a mortal blow in Canada.

From the Atlantic to the Pacific an outburst of patriotic sentiment such as had never been witnessed in the dominion came to a head in the general election of 1911. In Quebec the chief issue was the navy, and the Nationalists put up such a fight that Laurier lost many seats in his own province. But he still had a majority there, and he would have remained in office had he not suffered a much greater loss throughout the rest of the country, where the naval question was almost forgotten in the excited feeling over reciprocity and its danger to Canada, both as a nation and as a member of the empire. Again imperialism reinforced nationalism in Canada. It is doubtful if this time the action was reciprocal; for while Canadian experience had bred distrust of the United States, it had also bred distrust of Britain in her dealings with the United States. Canadian nationalism was a reaction against both powers, and it was still lacking in maturity.

Superficially Canadian nationalism had reached maturity in one section of the population, and that only: the Nationalists of Quebec, who loudly preached that Canada should command the undivided loyalty of all its own people and sever all but nominal ties with Britain. But if maturity means responsibility, the nationalism of Bourassa and his fellows was far from maturity. By flaunting their anti-British bias, they accentuated the divided loyalty that they deplored; and by insisting that Canada should stand alone on its own feet, they were behaving like children who would eat their cake and have it too. Most Canadians, even the French, had a sounder instinct that inhibited them from casting off the light imperial rein lest they fall under a heavier American yoke.

The nationalism of the majority, though sensibly qualified in this particular, was likewise lacking in responsibility, as appears clearly in the political paralysis that left the naval question up in the air. Laurier's measure, which had just become law, fell with him; and the Conservatives substituted a bill to give "immediate and effective aid" by appropriating money for three dreadnoughts to be built in Britain and added to the Royal Navy. It passed the Commons but was rejected by the large Liberal majority in the Senate inherited from the previous regime, and the government decided against appealing to the country on the issue. The result was that when war came in 1914 the dominion had only a "tin pot navy"—two obsolete cruisers that Laurier had got from Britain as training vessels. Canada was to reach maturity through the ordeal of the First World War.

Turning from the conditions that governed the growth of Canadian nationalism down to 1914, we should examine its constitutional effect in the evolution of what later became known as "dominion status." It was an enlargement of colonial self-government, which was originally limited to purely domestic affairs interpreted quite narrowly. The stretching of this interpretation began before federation, in the old Canada which could not be treated as an ordinary colony because it far surpassed all others in population and wealth and it lay too close to the United States. When it was merged in the dominion and the latter expanded from sea to sea, the new Canada stood out more prominently still in the imperial family and, as a consequence, blazed the trail toward constitutional equality with the mother country.

A sea change came over the office of governor general, making it more and more resemble that of the Crown in Britain. No governor general ever ventured to veto a bill passed by the dominion parliament, though the exercise of this prerogative was sanctioned by the British North America Act and was continued by governors in other parts of the empire enjoying responsible government. The British North America Act also recognized the discretionary right of the governor general to reserve bills for the home government to decide whether they should receive the royal assent or not; and his instructions required him to reserve all bills touching certain specified subjects such as divorce, legal tender, differential duties, the discipline of British forces, the rights of nonresidents, and British shipping. But the only reserved bill from which the Colonial Office withheld the royal assent was one that was passed in 1867, and Ottawa persuaded London to abandon mandatory reservation when new instructions were issued in 1878. On the eve of his retirement in 1872 the second governor general inadvertently assented to a bill that he should have reserved because it imposed discriminatory duties. This embarrassed the colonial secretary, who was then resisting pressure from the Australian colonies for the right to enact such duties. He yielded to their demand[1] rather than risk Canadian displeasure by disallowing the Canadian act, though he disallowed another Canadian act of 1872. But the latter was a partisan measure of doubtful legality which the new governor general had declined to veto or reserve lest he expose himself to the charge of interfering in the game of Canadian politics. This charge was leveled at the imperial government when the news reached Canada that the act was disallowed. There is no other example of imperial disallowance of legislation passed by the dominion.

The royal prerogative of mercy, exercised in Britain solely on the advice of the cabinet, was not so controlled in Canada. There the governor general had to consult the cabinet and then make his own independent decision. To this too the Canadian government objected, with the result that the new instructions of 1878 limited the gubernatorial discretion to cases involving imperial interests, which in practice meant that thenceforth the control was entirely in the hands of the Canadian cabinet. At the first Colonial Conference in 1887, a New Zealand proposal to extend the Canadian system to the other colonies failed to carry, having attracted little support except from the Canadian delegation.

In the conferring of titles and lesser honors, the role of the governor general is obscure for the simple reason that he did not bestow them.

---

[1] In the Australian Customs Duties Act of 1873.

That royal function had not been delegated and was performed on the advice of the British cabinet. But the governor general on his own authority made recommendations to the colonial secretary, and these recommendations were generally though not invariably followed. In the seventies the Canadian prime minister claimed the right to be consulted beforehand, and the governor general supported his contention. The argument was that Canada with a population of four million was not an ordinary colony, that English officials were not sufficiently familiar with the Canadian scene to make fair awards, that the Canadian people held their prime minister more or less responsible for the granting of honors to Canadians, and that an unsuitable choice might damage his political position. The colonial secretary rejected the claim. He professed a fear that honors would become prizes at the disposal of the party in power, a condition not unknown in England; he suggested that the size of the Canadian population had no bearing on the point; and he implied that the concession could not be made to Canada because then it would be claimed by the Australian colonies. Nevertheless, the Colonial Office paid more attention to the desires of the Canadian prime minister. In 1902 Laurier proposed that titles should be granted to Canadians only on the advice of the Canadian government, and Chamberlain agreed in so far as they were to be rewards for Canadian services. For imperial services rendered by Canadians, he said, the governor general should nominate the recipients after submitting their names to the Canadian government.

The governor general being the representative of the British government as well as of the Crown, the Canadian government early felt the need to balance the political function of this imperial official by establishing in London a Canadian official of ministerial rank, which none of the historic colonial agents had ever possessed. Accordingly, in 1879, the dominion parliament created the office of Canadian high commissioner, but not without some demur on the part of Downing Street. The opening of this independent channel of official communication with the British government more than two decades before the next dominion was formed, and could follow suit, may help to explain why Canada was not the pioneer in one particular of the evolution of the gubernatorial office—the selection of the man to fill it.

Until 1888 it was taken for granted that the colonial secretary should pick governors without consulting the governments over which they were to preside. Then Queensland raised the issue of these governments' right to have some say in the choice, and the colonial secretary issued a circular dispatch to the self-governing colonies requesting their opinions on whether they should be consulted beforehand. Most of the Australian colonies declared for it, but Canada did not. The Canadian government preferred the existing procedure because the proposed change might betray the governor general into favoring one party over the other and might eventually lead even to his election. The Colonial Office concluded the correspondence on the question by formally upholding the principle that governors owed their appointments to the Crown alone as a guarantee of political impartiality in the performance of their duties; but it thenceforth informally consulted the Australian colonies that had objected to the old system, and the new practice gradually became more general.

Another significant step in the development of dominion status came as a result of friction between the Ottawa cabinet and the commander in chief of the militia forces in the dominion. Following the withdrawal of the British troops in 1871, the governor general persuaded the Canadian government to get a major general from Britain to occupy this post. He and his successors, of similar background, filled it acceptably until shortly before the Boer War, when the incumbent of the day thought it his duty to teach the Canadian people their military duty to the empire. Laurier had him removed in 1900. His second successor was even more dictatorial. Thereupon, in 1904, he too was dismissed and the dominion parliament passed a new Militia Act providing for the appointment of a Canadian commander in chief and finally disposing of the idea, which had recently been mooted, that the imperial government had the right to call out and use the Canadian militia.

Dominion participation in the conduct of foreign affairs began, as we have seen, in 1871; and it is worthy of note that the appointment of a Canadian as one of the five British commissioners who negotiated the Treaty of Washington was conceded by London without any request for it from Ottawa. But North American circumstances dictated it; and if the British government was beforehand in proposing this radical innovation in diplomatic practice, Macdonald and his cabinet were not behindhand in insisting that until the dominion parliament ratified the treaty it would not bind Canada.

Three years later, when the British ambassador was the sleeping partner of the Canadian who negotiated an abortive reciprocity treaty with the United States, the propriety of this procedure was accepted without question in the mother country and the dominion. The precedent thus established in 1874, which was the direct result of the close

juxtaposition of Canada and the United States, governed the subsequent Canadian negotiation of commercial treaties with European
countries, of which there were several in the remaining years of the
century. Technically the Crown was acting on the advice of the British
government, which, having no interest in these particular transactions
other than to satisfy Canada, adopted as its own the advice of the
Canadian government. The diplomatic unity of the empire was preserved in theory. But how far was it still a fact?

That Canada had the power to make treaties with foreign countries
was asserted in a public address that the governor general, the Marquis
of Lorne—the son-in-law of Queen Victoria—delivered in 1883.
Apparently he was assuming that the imperial government's adoption
of the dominion government's advice had already withered to a mere
formality like the royal assent to parliamentary legislation. His words
tickled Canadian pride, which aspired to the possession of this power;
and they nettled the Colonial Office, which saw in them a false doctrine
that would disrupt the empire. The permanent undersecretary condemned Lorne's statement as "a considerable mistake . . . and a gratuitous one," but he could not make up his mind on what to do about it.
He was inclined to overlook it in view of the fact that Lorne was
completing a very successful term of office in Canada. What made the
undersecretary hesitate was the possibility that official silence would
be interpreted as official sanction. The secretary of state decided to run
this risk rather than face another. "Lord L. has certainly made a mistake," he remarked, "but I am afraid that we shall only make matters
worse if we call attention to it." So the issue was allowed to sleep
until it was awakened by developments during the First World War.

Meanwhile Canada negotiated and Britain signed a treaty with the
United States that provided for the joint regulation of certain Cana-
dian-American problems without even the formal participation of the
British government. This Boundary Waters Treaty of 1909 laid down
a new code of international law to govern the waters through which
the international boundary ran for more than half of its four thousand
miles. To administer this code, it set up a permanent body that is really
an international court, the Joint International Commission, composed
of six members, three Canadian and three American; in addition, the
treaty empowered the Commission to investigate any "question or matter of difference" submitted by the two neighboring governments "involving the rights, obligations or interests of either in relation to the
other or to the inhabitants of the other, along the common frontier."

The Commission has contributed to good relations between the two close neighbors much more than the public in either of them has realized. But here the significant point to note is an anticipation of future constitutional development, for the treaty stipulated that the Canadian members of the Commission were to be appointed by the king on the advice of the Canadian government.

Australian nationalism was a plant of different growth from Canadian nationalism. It was simpler, more natural, less forced, and not subject to violent reverses, largely because Australia was peopled almost wholly from the British Isles whereas Canada was peopled also from France and the United States. Demographic diversity in Canada required an exercise of will to form a nation in order to give life and strength to the newly created dominion, and from time to time the French-English schism disrupted national unity. These experiences had no parallel in Australia. There the people gradually discovered that they were a nation, and then they set up a federal government to meet its needs.

For generations the people of Australia had been British, and they were proud of it. Indeed, there is much truth in their later boast that they were more British than the population of the mother country. They were not a loose cross section of that society which contained a larger percentage of foreigners, was marked by class divisions, and was split by ancient national distinctions between England, Wales, Scotland, and Ireland. The Australians were a pretty solid segment of the working class in the old land, and in their new country they soon became fused into one racial stock. They were more homogeneous than the inhabitants of the British Isles or of any other British country except New Zealand. Therefore it is not surprising that they were a nation before they knew it.

The national consciousness of Australians was rooted in their class origin. Though intensely British in spirit, they heartily disliked many features of the society that they had left behind, and they were determined to improve upon it when they settled down after the hurly-burly of the gold rush. This determination and what it achieved gave them a sense of being differentiated from, and superior to, the people in the homeland. Here it will be recalled that they were strongly imbued with Chartism, which had vainly demanded the democratization of the state not as an end in itself but as a means of attaining social justice; that accordingly they wrested political power from the squatter aristocracy and established a real political democracy; that with this instrument they first strove to build a rural egalitarian society such as existed in North America; that they failed in this because physical nature was against them; and that they then succeeded in building an urban social democracy. Their growing pride in this growing accomplishment was a fundamental factor in their increasing awareness of being a nation.

This national pride was much enhanced by two other factors that were not present in Canada. The Australians had a whole continent to themselves, and they were separated by half a world from the land whence they had come and from all other countries of western civilization except the much smaller New Zealand. Canadian pride had to be content with half a continent, the much less populous half; and Canadians gave much less thought than Australians to the contrast, though it was equally striking, between their society and that of Britain. They gave less thought to it for the simple reason that their own society, in addition to being more molded by natural conditions, was overshadowed by a very much larger society of the same type in the United States. Moreover, Canadians were much less interested than Australians in experimenting with governmental action to shape their social structure because, as we have seen, the bounteous North American environment made immigrants from Britain shed their Chartism right away. The self-glorification that is inherent in nationalism could not be so pronounced in Canada as in Australia.

Thanks also to the exclusive possession of the continent and to its geographical remoteness from the rest of the western world, the growth of Australian nationalism was well started and was developing its own imperialist ambitions before it received any stimulus from a foreign power. Then the New Guinea episode produced an angry nationalist reaction against the mother country for allowing German imperialism to thwart what was really Australian imperialism. Hosts of Australians shared the dream of the Queensland premier who ordered the abortive annexation of New Guinea —"a united Australia ruling the south seas." And from London's repudiation of his bold action may be traced the rise of an Australian desire to become an independent British power. This ideal played a not inconsiderable part in the achievement of Australian federation, which quickened the development of Australian nationalism.

Meanwhile participation in the Boer War, which pulled Canada apart, was in Australia a unanimous expression of enthusiasm for the imperial cause. But this, though reflecting the immaturity of Australian nationalism, had the effect of strengthening rather than weak-

ening it, for Australians were justly proud of what they did in South
Africa. If Australians were uncritical of British policy in the Boer
War, they made up for it shortly afterward, when they openly and bitterly denounced the mother country for perverting the victory by
introducing Chinese coolies into the South African mines. Here we
touch upon the most deep-seated and explosive element in Australian
nationalism.

The anti-Asiatic feeling of Australians was a veritable phobia which
had been growing ever since white diggers clashed with Chinese on the
gold fields in the late fifties. The subsequent rise of the popular demand
for laws that would shut Chinese out of the country was perhaps the
first stirring of Australian national consciousness, and as the drive for
the exclusion of Asiatics gathered momentum it stood out as the main
force behind the development of Australian nationalism. It was not
until Australians were exasperated by the inadequacy of state legislation against the admission of Asiatics that they were finally converted
to federation as the only way to get a law that would forever guarantee
a White Australia. This, significantly enough, was the first thing they
demanded and procured from their first parliament. Everything that
they held most dear, from their advanced social democracy to their
racial integrity, impelled them to insist on a White Australia; for they
were obsessed by the fear that sooner or later they might be overwhelmed in their more than half empty continent by swarms of
Orientals.

Some outsiders may think this fear excessive, and even morbid; some
may criticize the Australian people for playing dog in the manger on a
gigantic scale; some may charge them with fanatical race prejudice and
arrogance. Indeed, among Australians themselves the issue roused
such passion that they commonly indulged in all manner of ignorant
statements, extravagant language, and wild arguments to push the
cause of absolute exclusion. Many of them, in the heat of discussion,
took generous liberties with God's will and the laws of science.

But the more responsible leaders had the intelligence, the honesty,
and the courage to keep their argument down on the solid ground of
practical necessity—the nation's self-preservation. Alfred Deakin,
who was soon to be prime minister, did it finely on the morrow of
federation, when Japanese infiltration had become a serious worry. "I
contend," he said, "that the Japanese need to be excluded because of
their high abilities. I quite agree . . . that the Japanese are the most
dangerous because they most nearly approach us, and would therefore

be the most formidable competitors." But more important than this consideration was another. "The unity of Australia is nothing, if it does not imply a united race." "A united race means not only that its members can intermarry and associate without degradation on either side, but implies . . . a people possessing the same general cast of character, tone of thought, the same constitutional training and traditions." He and his fellows were no less determined than the rank and file to plug all the holes left by state legislation; and in this the instinct of the masses was as sound as that of their leaders, who would purge the land and keep it pure of the exploitation of colored people by whites and all the many demoralizing influences of such exploitation.

It might be supposed that this dominant phase of Australian nationalism would impose a heavy strain on imperial relations. It made soft-headed humanitarians in Britain cry for their government's intervention to check the Australian enactment of racial discrimination. It embarrassed Britain in more than her dealings with China, for it wounded the pride of India, and it inspired Australia to speak sharply to the mother country on the subject of Chinese coolies in South Africa. But the South African incident soon blew over, and on no occasion did the British government oppose the White Australia policy. The only criticism that official London offered was a suggestion that the policy could be implemented just as effectively by legislation that did not bar Asiatics on the ground of race. Chamberlain advanced this at the Colonial Conference of 1897. He recommended the device that Natal had adopted—an educational test—to avoid giving unnecessary offense to the people of Asia. With good grace the first federal government followed suit in drafting the bill on which Australian hearts were set. Some crackpots damned the measure as "hypocritical" and "dishonest," but the responsible leaders would allow only one change in the proposed test. As originally framed it would have offended European nations by requiring a reading knowledge of English, and this was amended by the substitution of any prescribed European language, which evoked a Japanese protest. Japan's objections were not removed until after the conclusion of the Anglo-Japanese alliance, when an amendment of 1905 dropped the requirement of a European language and called for a test in "any prescribed language." This refinement of the law, which made it literally innocent of any offense to any race, left the law as effective as ever, for those who administered it always picked from the world's babel of tongues a language that the unwanted applicant for admission could not read.

Australian nationalism expressed itself also in military policy. Following Canadian precedent, the federal government in 1901 got a British general to organize and command the military forces of the country, and the officer selected was none other than the one who had been removed from Canada in the previous year. Apparently his North American experience had made him more discreet, but he was the same efficient soldier and again he encountered baffling obstruction. By an interesting coincidence, Australia took substantially the same action as Canada to assert its government's control over its own military policy and administration.

But the Australian policy was not to be that of Canada, for the two countries were very differently situated. The senior dominion could see no possibility of a hostile invasion except by the colossus next door and little sense in preparing to meet that, whereas the other dominion had several potential enemies to fear and could hope, with reasonable precautions, to repel the landing of any force that might slip through the British naval screen. Therefore the Australians, unlike the Canadians, were seriously interested in the development of their military strength. After looking around for a suitable democratic model, they copied the Swiss system of compulsory military training in peacetime, which gave them a national citizens' army four years before the outbreak of the First World War.

Naval defense likewise meant much more to seagirt Australia than to Canada with its long and indefensible land frontier; and this difference of conscious interest was accentuated by the imperial government's reluctance to further Australian imperial ambitions, which could have no counterpart in Canada. The motive behind Australian contributions to the Royal Navy was more national than imperial—to make sure that a British squadron would remain in Australian waters—and twenty years after these payments began, the newly formed Commonwealth of Australia served notice that it would substitute a navy of its own, thereby giving a more distinct expression to the national motive. Australia was thus much better prepared than Canada to face the dreadnought scare of two years later, and the younger dominion then plunged ahead with the construction of a national navy while the elder dominion floundered and did nothing. In this respect Australian nationalism was then demonstrably more mature than Canadian nationalism.

New Zealand was much less nationalist, so much so that it looked with pained disapproval upon the nationalism of the other dominions.

Though it developed its own individuality, and was quite conscious of this, New Zealand was the one British dominion that was anxious to see a constitutional reintegration of the empire. New Zealand pulled away from federation with Australia in the belief that the only proper federation was with the mother country, and in later years it viewed with sad regret the transformation of the empire into the commonwealth. The elevation of the daughter nations, including itself, to a position of constitutional parity with the parent state might cause the other daughters to rejoice, but not this one, for in the words of an outstanding New Zealand scholar, it had a real mother complex.[2]

The contrast is striking, particularly with Australia, and may seem surprising. New Zealand was even more British than Australia in the composition of its population, and was no less proud of it. New Zealand was an even more remote British—and white—outpost. It too developed an advanced social democracy, of which it could boast, and it likewise legislated against colored immigration. It too blamed Britain for allowing other powers to establish themselves in the South Seas, and it adopted universal military training at the same time as its neighbor. Moreover, it attained political unity long before Australia and had its own peculiar traditions of conflict with the Colonial Office, such conflict having marked the whole Wakefield period and darkened the period of the Maori wars. One might expect that all these conditions would create a national consciousness comparable to that of Australia.

Why were New Zealanders so lacking in national maturity, or, to put the question in another way, why did they not catch the current fever of nationalism? A clew may be found in the character of New Zealand society, which was quite distinct from that of Australia. It was more akin to that of the mother country, more, indeed, than any other in the world. "More English than England" is a phrase that many observers have applied to New Zealand. This use of the adjective "English" is of course the careless and common one which irritates Scots anywhere and not least in New Zealand, where they form an important 25 per cent of the population. Passing by this innocent inaccuracy, and accepting the meaning of the phrase as it was intended, we should note that it sums up a deep-rooted tradition. The founders of New Zealand sought to transplant a representative section of British society, not just a working class segment of it; they selected the colonists

---

[2] J. B. Condliffe, *New Zealand in the Making* (Chicago, 1930), p. 431.

with a keen eye for quality; and the original settlements contained an unusually large proportion of educated middle-class stock. Though the gold rushes of the sixties and the assisted immigration of the seventies introduced a mass of people out of sympathy with the early idealists, the earlier spirit leavened the lump.

Meanwhile, as we have seen, there was a rather sharp division into two classes: one comprising the holders of large estates who monopolized the land and controlled the government, and the other a landless proletariat. But New Zealand did not repeat the exasperating Australian sequel. Manhood suffrage broke the economic as well as the political power of the oligarchy; for nature worked with man in New Zealand, not against him as in Australia, to spread the population over the land in small family farms, mostly dairy farms. Nature cooperated by providing a climate that resembles that of southern England, with its mild temperature and well-distributed rainfall. Thus New Zealand developed as a rural democracy, the tone of which was more restrained than that of the urban democracy in Australia. The prevalence of family farms may suggest that New Zealand society became like North American society; but there was an important demographic difference, the New Zealanders being a homogeneous and relatively small block of British people who had only recently left their homeland. There were also important geographical differences.

New Zealand has often been called the Britain of the south because it has much the same shape and size as Great Britain and an even more temperate climate, and it is an insular rather than a continental country. These conditions made the outlook of New Zealanders very different from that of North Americans or Australians. Though Australia is nearly thirty times bigger than New Zealand, the disparity is not so great in land with a climate that favors close settlement. Yet Australia has five times as much of it, and this proportion is reflected in the relative size of their populations. On the eve of the First World War, Australia was approaching the five million mark while the New Zealand figure was about one million. This raises an intriguing and difficult question. How numerous must a people be before they think and feel as a distinct nation?

Size is undoubtedly a factor, but it is an extremely variable one because many other factors also govern the emergence of national consciousness. The French Canadians and the Afrikanders awoke as nations without being anything like so numerous as New Zealanders were in 1914. Yet these two examples are rare exceptions in the history of modern nationalism, and are explainable only by very special circumstances. Australians did not begin to feel that they were a nation until they numbered much more than a million, and this feeling did not grow strong enough to make them unite politically until they numbered nearly four million. It would rather seem that if their New Zealand cousins had been infected with the spirit of nationalism in the opening years of this century, we would have to look for special circumstances to explain it. What we find are conditions that had the opposite effect on such a people. Living in a small country in a remote corner of the earth twelve hundred miles from the nearest land mass, seeing foreign powers lick up the island crumbs in the surrounding seas, and knowing that international rivalries were threatening the peace of the world, they realized clearly that they could not stand alone without the support of the British Empire. It was of most vital importance to them. It commanded their supreme loyalty.

South Africa, like Canada, achieved political unity without possessing national unity. At the time each of these dominions was formed, the British element in the population had not acquired a distinct national spirit, whereas the descendants of the original colonists had developed a strong national consciousness of their own as a reaction against British rule and immigration. Yet experience had taught the two peoples in each country the need for conciliation and cooperation to build a dominion that would embody a new nation which, though retaining the dual character of its component parts, would have a united purpose.

The parallel is suggestive but may be misleading unless we recognize some important differences. British immigration had turned the balance of the population against the French in Canada but not against the Boers in South Africa, who, as a consequence, held a majority position in the government of the Union. Many of them still cherished the republican ideal, which had no appeal in French Canada; more of them nursed bitter memories of recent war against the British, which was impossible for French Canadians because they had fought no war against the British since the far-off days of 1760.

Yet Boer nationalism was not so solid as French Canadian. The French Canadians were a compact body and had defied all attempts to Anglicize them. The Boers on the other hand had been split by the Great Trek, when their intransigent minority wandered off into the wilderness where they cut themselves off from all contact with modern civilization, while their fellows remained behind in the parent colony where the best of them were more or less assimilated to British culture. The Boers had also to overcome a linguistic handicap from which the French were free. Though each people had inherited and modified a seventeenth century form of their language, the colonial divergence from the nineteenth century form in the homeland was as nothing in Canada to what it was in South Africa. From its very birth French Canadian nationalism found ample expression in literary French; but when the Boers awoke as a nation High Dutch was unintelligible to the mass of them. Their Afrikaans was a new though related language whose evolution is still a subject of controversy. It was only a spoken tongue, with simple vocabulary and construction, no standardized spelling or grammar, and no literature. Boer nationalists therefore bent their efforts to develop Afrikaans into a literary vehicle that could compete with English. The task was long and hard. Some progress was made in the last quarter of the nineteenth century, and more in the years immediately following the war of 1899–1902, but this was not enough to win official recognition instead of Dutch when the Union was framed. In 1914, however, the Cape, the Free State, and the Transvaal permitted the use of the new language as a medium of instruction in their primary schools.

Botha startled the Colonial Conference of 1907 by addressing it in Afrikaans before he proceeded in very good English; and it was characteristic of his broad outlook that he requested the home government to maintain a considerable garrison in South Africa and also carried a resolution, backed by Jameson and the Natalians, foreshadowing the provision of the South African constitution which limited appeals to the privy council. During the Imperial Conference of 1911, when he was head of the South African delegation, he frankly preferred to leave upon the shoulders of the British government the full responsibility for the foreign policy of the empire; unlike Laurier, he had no illusions about dominion freedom to choose between active and passive belligerency. It was at this time that a Pretoria daily argued that neither England nor "any other independent state of the empire" could have its neutrality broken save by its own "express declaration or act," and Botha replied curtly that "the enemy decides whether any part of the empire is to be left alone." In the following year Botha's government passed a Defense Act, which followed Australian and New Zealand precedent by providing for a citizen army something like the Swiss; during the debate on the measure Smuts remarked that however anxious the imperial government might be to withdraw its troops, the time for that had not yet come.

Unlike Canada, where the two-party system prevailed and the division between Liberals and Conservatives cut across racial lines, the Union began its existence with four parties between all of which the British vote was divided while the Afrikander vote, of dubious cohesion, was united in the largest of them. This held 66 of the 121 seats in the House of Assembly and was significantly named by Botha the South African National Party. The Unionist Party, which had 39 seats, was a combination of the Progressives in the Cape, the Free State, and the Transvaal under the leadership of Jameson. Its policy was to work for unity, and it tried to help Botha to contain his own extremists. There were 12 Independents. Eleven were from Natal, which had rejected Jameson's wooing. Finally, there was Creswell's rapidly growing Labor Party, which returned four members and had a working arrangement with Botha.

The honeymoon of the Union was obviously over in 1912, when friction within the government and within the majority party broke into the open. The main cause of the trouble was the coexistence of two cultures, British and Afrikander—one a world culture, rich, mature, and strong; the other a local product, poor, immature, and weak. Only by keeping the two apart could the latter be saved from absorption by the former. A Free State member of the cabinet, General Hertzog, saw this clearly; and as his first loyalty was to Afrikander culture, he publicly called for a "two stream policy" in opposition to the racial conciliation policy of Botha and Smuts, who put the unity of the country above everything else. Hertzog also asserted that South Africa must be ruled by "pure Afrikanders," and he pressed for an immediate and clear-cut decision that South African interests would always override imperial interests when they clashed. He was blowing upon smoldering racial fires. Among the rank and file of ex-republicans there were many who harbored dark suspicions that Botha and Smuts had sold out to British capitalism and imperialism. These leaders, whose hearts were set on healing the schism that had long tortured the country, were dismayed by Hertzog's anti-British outburst, and so were many other Afrikanders, while British South Africans raged.

A Natalian member of the cabinet resigned in protest. Botha tried to get Hertzog to resign too, as an alternative to submitting his inflammatory ideas to the ministry and accepting its judgment upon them.

Hertzog would do neither. Therefore the prime minister shook him out by tendering his own resignation to the governor general, which automatically dissolved the cabinet, and then by re-forming it. For some time there were hopes that Hertzog might be reconciled. Then he burned his boats in a blazing speech; a Labor motion of no confidence was supported by a majority of the Free State members; their constituencies buzzed with talk of a new party, which finally appeared in November 1913, when a considerable minority walked out of a South African Party congress. For all the storm that gave rise to Hertzog's Nationalist Party, it seemed to be sinking into the political background by the summer of 1914. But Afrikander nationalism was not to fade gradually into a larger South African nationalism. The First World War made this impossible.

CHAPTER XXXIII

Irish and Indian Nationalism

THE IRISH NATIONALIST MOVEMENT, which collapsed in the middle of the nineteenth century, was revived in America. Though the United States was too far from Ireland to have exercised there the unconscious influence that assured self-government to British North America, the potato famine started such a mass migration of Irish people to the United States that this country became what might be called, metaphorically, the arsenal of the Irish struggle against British rule. The resumed struggle was dominated first by the Fenians, successors to the violent republicans of 1798 and 1848, and later by the Home Rulers, heirs of the competing parliamentary tradition that goes back through the repeal agitation of O'Connell to the work of Grattan and Flood.

The Fenian Brotherhood, founded in New York in 1858, received a big impetus from the Civil War; for the Civil War gave military training, arms, and a martial spirit to large numbers of Irish-Americans, and it created an American atmosphere highly favorable to the anti-British scheming of the Fenians. Their organization spread rapidly and soon it had ramifications in almost every part of the world where Irishmen were to be found. But all their plans for a national revolution in Ireland came to naught. It was not so much because the British government, forewarned by their wild boasting, nipped their plots in the bud, as it was that they failed to gain any hold on the mass of the Irish peasantry. Fenianism offered no solution for grinding agrarian poverty other than shooting the landlords, and it was denounced by the priesthood. Yet there were quite a number of Fenian outrages in Ireland and England, the two most serious being in Manchester and London in 1867. In the former city, two Fenian leaders were rescued from a police van by a band of their fellows who killed the policeman inside by shooting him through the keyhole of the door. Three of the band were hanged for murder, and thus became the "Manchester martyrs" of Fenian hagiology. In London, Fenians blew up the wall of a prison in a vain endeavor to release an agent whom they had employed to purchase arms. The explosion killed twelve innocent persons and maimed a hundred and twenty others. Fenian methods of violence and intimidation thus operated to defeat their purpose, yet these methods unintentionally did something for Ireland. They jolted British statesmen out of their complacent and neglectful attitude toward that unhappy island.

"My mission is to pacify Ireland," said Gladstone when summoned to form his first ministry in December 1868. He and many of his followers believed that dangerous Irish discontent would wither away if they cut away its religious and economic roots—the privileged position of the Irish Church (Anglican), and the oppressive land system. Accordingly, in 1869 parliament disestablished the Irish Church, reducing it to a voluntary organization deprived of the right to collect tithes and of all endowments acquired before 1660; and in 1870 a Land Act was passed. The first measure removed a grave injustice long condemned by public opinion, but the second fell far short of what was needed.

Unlike English landlords, Irish landlords were commonly absentees who took as much money out of the land as they could get and put none into it. One of the most crying evils was that they took advantage of the law allowing arbitrary evictions in order to charge rack rents and to raise them still higher when tenants made improvements that increased the value of the property. Gladstone's bill required landlords to pay compensation to ejected tenants who were not in arrears with their rent or had not committed other legal faults. This proved to be small protection for tenants, because landlords frequently found it profitable to pay them the prescribed compensation for eviction. What the Irish desperately wanted was fair rents and security of tenure. They got neither, because public opinion in England, ill-informed on Irish conditions, would tolerate no tampering with the sacred rights of private property. Ireland was not pacified.

The Home Rule movement was launched in May 1870, when Isaac Butt, a Protestant barrister—who had defended Fenians in the courts—and former member of the House of Commons, addressed a large meeting in Dublin demanding an Irish parliament for local affairs; it got under way in the general election of the following year, when he found himself at the head of a Home Rule party of fifty-seven members in the new House. But he was an incompetent captain and they were an unruly crew. They got nowhere until after 1875, when they were joined by Charles Stewart Parnell, a young Protestant land-lord who inherited from his father's line a tradition of opposition to the Union, and from his mother, daughter of an American admiral in the War of 1812, a cold hatred of England. This frigid, calculating, and selfless man gradually ousted his leader and transformed the party into a close-fighting machine.

To coerce parliament, Parnell developed into a fine art the tactics of obstruction that some members of the Conservative opposition had recently invented to embarrass Gladstone; and the new parliamentary leader of the Irish allied himself with the Fenians and other revolution-ary organizations. As he explained to a New York audience in 1880, he would combine constitutional and illegal methods to win freedom for Ireland. Though a landlord himself, Parnell had a deep sympathy with the misery of the Irish peasantry, which he astutely recognized as the one force that was indispensable to victory.[1] This force, which the Fenians had neglected and the British government had failed to neu-tralize, he used to the utmost. In 1879, two years after the onset of the agricultural depression, the Land League was formed, with him as president, to fight evictions and rack rents. Through this society he rallied the Irish tenants on a national scale to wield a weapon that he devised for them and which they used so effectively that it soon ac-quired the name of a land agent who suffered under it, Captain Boycott. Evictions rose—they numbered ten thousand in 1880—and so did agrarian outrages, creating a reign of terror that lasted for several years. In parliament the Home Rule leader would have no alliance with either of the major parties, but negotiated with both and played each off against the other until his growing and well-disciplined following gained the balance of power.

Meanwhile the general election of 1880 turned out Beaconsfield and brought back Gladstone to face the growing uproar in Ireland at the same time as he had to deal with the crisis in the Transvaal. "The steps of crime dogged the steps of the Land League" and this had to be stopped, he told the House in January 1881. Accordingly, his govern-ment forced the passage of a Coercion Act, which virtually established martial law for a year. Parnell tried to block the measure but the sword of obstruction broke in his hands when the Speaker, with the approval

---

[1] In 1880 Parnell declared that he "would not have taken off his coat" to help the tenants if he did not believe that this was the way to legislative independence.

of the House, shut off debate. Ireland was thus responsible for introducing the closure into British parliamentary procedure.

Gladstone also made a heroic effort to redeem his failure of 1870 by pushing through the Land Act of 1881, which conceded the "Three F's" of the popular Irish demand: fair rents, fixity of tenure, and freedom of sale. It provided for the imposition of fair rents by an impartial tribunal; it prohibited the eviction of tenants who paid their rent; and it guaranteed to tenants the right to sell their interests in their holdings. The act struck at more than the crying grievance of the Irish peasants. It struck at Parnell's dependence on their support. In the autumn he was arrested and lodged in Kilmainham jail for inciting the intimidation of tenants who would take advantage of the new law. He warned the authorities that his removal from the scene would leave "Captain Moonlight" in charge. It was only too true. Agrarian outrages multiplied.

Parnell was released in the spring of 1882 on the understanding, known as the "Kilmainham treaty," that he would use his influence to check crime while the government would wipe out tenants' arrears of rent and end repressive measures. Four days later this hope of peace was brutally destroyed by assassins' knives that struck down a member of the cabinet, the chief secretary for Ireland, and his permanent undersecretary as they were walking in broad daylight through Phoenix Park, Dublin. Parnell denounced the murderers, as well he might, for they had dealt Ireland a foul blow. The English memory of it was a formidable obstacle when Gladstone tried to carry Home Rule. Meanwhile the shock inspired sterner legislation against the campaign of crime in Ireland, but it did not block the passage of a bill to prevent evictions by the payment of tenants' arrears out of public funds that the disestablishment of the Irish Church had provided. It was all in vain. The reign of terror continued in Ireland and spilled over into England, where Irish-Americans perpetrated various dynamite outrages and even tried to blow up the houses of parliament.

To find a solution for the anarchy in Ireland, some Liberals privately negotiated with Parnell—and so did a number of Conservatives—on such things as the dropping of coercion, the establishment of peasant proprietorship financed by the government, elected county councils similar to those that England was soon to get by the act of 1888, and an Irish central board chosen by these councils and charged with much of the responsibility for the administration of the country. The Irish education of English politicians was progressing when advanced wings of the two old parties thus bid for the Irish leader's support, and his bargaining position was strengthened by the Sudan tragedy, which was dragging the ministry down. Parnell calculated that he could get more from the Conservatives, and therefore the Irish vote in the Commons turned the balance against Gladstone in June 1885.

A general election was impossible for another six months because the recent extension of the franchise required new electoral rolls which were not yet completed. During the interim Lord Salisbury held office by grace of the Irish members; the Coercion Act expired; agrarian outrages, which had been declining, again increased; and the Conservative government passed an act appropriating money to purchase land for peasants who desired it. Parnell came out for an independent Irish parliament, the new lord lieutenant met him secretly and intimated his personal inclination to some form of home rule on the colonial model that would preserve imperial unity and security, and the prime minister remained mum on the subject. He hoped for Parnell's aid in the coming electoral contest, and he got it. In England the well-disciplined Irish vote rallied to the Conservatives. In Ireland not a single Liberal was returned, for the same influence made sure that the Protestant constituencies chose only Conservatives—seventeen of them—and every one of the other eighty-six seats were won by Nationalists,[2] thanks to the new rural franchise. The total result, known by mid-December, gave the Liberals a majority over the Conservatives, but not of the whole House. Parnell rode the balance of power.

Gladstone, already a secret convert to Home Rule, which he knew that many of his own party would not stomach, quietly approached Salisbury with an offer of support for legislation to set up an Irish parliament. The Liberal chieftain believed that Irish autonomy, though fraught with danger, was inevitable and that the safest way to grant it was with the backing of members on both sides of the House. The Conservative leader would have none of it. The resignation of his lord lieutenant and the announcement of a coercion bill showed his hand. The Irish phalanx deserted him, and he fell in January 1886. This forced Gladstone, on forming his third and shortest ministry, to take the plunge that Peel had taken in 1845 over free trade and Disraeli in 1867 over the franchise. Would enough opposition members come to his rescue to make up for defections in his own ranks? In June, 93

---

[2] More than a fourth of whom had been jailed under the Coercion Act.

Liberals—between a quarter and a third of the party—joined the opposition to reject his Home Rule Bill by a majority of 30. Nothing
daunted, he dissolved parliament and appealed to the country in July.
The result was decisive. The combined Conservative and Liberal Unionists got a majority of 118 over the combined Gladstonians and Par-
nellites. The Liberal party took twenty years to recover from the wreck.

What was denied to the Irish by the defeat of the bill was less than
what had been granted to British people overseas. In addition to foreign
affairs, the bill reserved the subjects of defense, foreign trade, and
customs to be controlled by imperial authority, and it required Ireland
to contribute one fifteenth of imperial expenses. Why, with these important limitations, was it more than the British public would tolerate?
Geography was a determining factor. Irish autonomy could compromise
British security as colonial autonomy could not. The proposed concession to Ireland called for a very much greater measure of trust on the
part of Great Britain than she had ever had to repose in any colony,
and of late years too many crimes had been committed in the name of
Irish liberty to commend that liberty to law-abiding Englishmen. Moreover, Protestant Ulster, which in former times had supplied leaders of
the Irish struggle for independence, suddenly blazed forth against
Home Rule. The reawakening of the old Orange feud against the
Green was largely the work of Lord Randolph Churchill, who crossed
to Belfast for this very purpose in February. Rather than submit to a
Dublin parliament, "Ulster will fight, and Ulster will be right," he
reported a few weeks later. These words almost immediately took wings
and flew about the British Isles as a fierce war cry. From June to
August, Belfast Orangemen demonstrated their loyalty by indulging in
savage riots that took at least thirty lives and destroyed much property.
Such wild lawlessness was proof positive that Home Rule would not
pacify Ireland, a house divided against itself.

Parnell seemed chastened. Having committed the Liberal party—
what was left of it, which was considerable—to Home Rule, his game
was to cultivate this alliance by generous cooperation, by playing the
statesman rather than the revolutionary. He also had the satisfaction
of seeing the Conservative government adopt remedial Irish measures
that he had proposed, of which more anon. But he had two vulnerable
points—one still a dark secret, the other more or less notorious. There
was no denying that he had been associated with criminal conspiracies
of Irish extremists, and in the spring of 1887 the London *Times* began
publishing a series of articles entitled "Parnellism and Crime" to prove

his guilt. He ignored these attacks until the newspaper published the facsimile of a letter purporting to be signed by him and virtually acknowledging his complicity in the Phoenix Park murders. He scornfully told the House of Commons that the letter was a forgery, and he was greeted with incredulous laughter from the ministerial benches. He could sue the *Times* for libel, but he would not. Feeling against him was running so high in England that it was more than doubtful if he could get justice from a London jury.

Things looked blacker for Parnell in 1888, when one of his followers who had been implicated in the *Times* charges sued and the newspaper produced more incriminating letters alleged to have been written by the Irish leader. Thoroughly roused, he declared to the House that these letters were forgeries too, and he demanded a select committee to investigate their origin. The government refused but passed a special act appointing a commission of three judges to examine the whole subject of the charges against Parnell and his party. What followed was in fact, though not in form, a state trial, the most famous of the century. It began in September and lasted for more than a year. Halfway through, a seedy Irish journalist confessed that he had forged the letters for mercenary reasons. He escaped arrest by fleeing the country and blowing out his brains in Madrid as police entered his room. The newspaper, which had bought the letters for some £2,500 without questioning their genuineness, had to pay much more for the use it had made of them—£5,000 damages to Parnell and £250,000 costs. His triumphant vindication lifted Home Rule out of the doldrums on the very eve of his fall, which dragged down his cause.

The dark secret, which at last came out, was that for nearly a decade Parnell had been living in sin with another man's wife. Toward the end of 1889 the other man, hitherto one of his most devoted followers, brought suit for divorce, naming him as corespondent. For months there were rumors that he would win another triumphant vindication, but such talk only heightened the tragedy when the case came up and no defense was offered. On the morrow of the Phoenix Park murders, of which he was innocent, Parnell had offered to resign and Gladstone had dissuaded him. Now their position was reversed. The Irish leader was guilty and he defied the Liberal leader's advice to retire for the sake of his cause. The nonconformist conscience of England strongly condemned the adulterer, and so did the Catholic conscience of Ireland. Several members of his parliamentary party were then in America on Home Rule business, and his two right-hand men cabled from Chicago opposing his continued leadership. The majority of the party deposed him to save the alliance with the Liberals and the support of the Catholic clergy, while the minority clung to him and the Fenians rallied back of him. So bitter was the schism that his death in 1891 could not heal it; and as the party broke up into factions, the majority led by Justin McCarthy and the minority now by John Redmond, the vital supply of American funds dried up.

Gladstone rushed to the rescue of dying Home Rule, raising it as the main issue in the general election of 1892. The government's majority over the Liberals in the new House dropped to forty, and once more the Irish members held the balance of power. They put their ally back in office, at the age of eighty-three, that he might give Ireland the parliament he promised. Against the will of many of his own followers, even in the cabinet, Gladstone brought in his second Home Rule bill and jammed it through the Commons in the summer of 1893. The Lords threw it out, whereupon the stubborn old man again declared for another dissolution of parliament on the issue. But his colleagues had had enough of it and of him. In the spring of 1894 he bowed out, and in the summer of 1895 his party was turned out by the electorate, this time more decisively than in 1886.

Irish nationalism quieted down under Conservative rule which, with the exception of this Liberal interlude, lasted for twenty years. In the beginning of this period agrarian lawlessness boiled up again, but not so seriously as in the past, and it presently subsided. Late in 1886 some Irish hotheads organized the "plan of campaign," a tenants' strike, which inevitably provoked violence. Tenants offered what they considered was a reasonable rent, and when it was refused they paid it to a national committee. Parnell did not approve; the Roman Catholic church disapproved; and the Salisbury administration, which had tried to govern Ireland under ordinary law, passed the Crimes Act of 1887, a permanent measure that strengthened the hands of the lord lieutenant and substituted trial by magistrates for trial by jury. These, however, were by no means the only reasons for the relative peace that descended upon Ireland. The disintegration of the Irish political movement, which was the real Parnell tragedy, was a veritable godsend to an administration thoroughly committed against Home Rule but willing to concede local self-government, which Ireland got in 1898 just ten years after England. Very important, also, was the continued operation of the legislation that Gladstone had passed to redeem the miserable lot of the peasants. Now the Unionists adopted this policy as their own and pushed it vigorously.

This policy, which one of its administrators aptly labeled "killing Home Rule with kindness," removed the main cause of mass discontent in Ireland—the oppressive land system. As soon as Salisbury took office in 1886, Parnell introduced a tenants' relief bill. The government promptly voted it down but later, in the very next session, passed a bill containing many of its leading provisions, including a reduction of judicially set rents. But the great achievement of the years that followed was the actual transfer of the ownership of the land to the peasants.

The idea of land purchase had originated with Bright, who inserted in the Disestablishment Act of 1869 provision for the sale of church lands to occupiers, the government lending them three quarters of the purchase price to be repaid with low interest over a long period. Some 6,000 tenants availed themselves of this offer. The Land Acts of 1870 and 1881 extended it to include other lands generally, but on such conditions that only some 1,600 tenants took advantage of it.

Land purchase gathered momentum from 1885, when Salisbury's interim administration appropriated £5,000,000 to advance, on the security of the land, the full purchase price and fixed repayment at 4 per cent of this price annually for forty-nine years. In 1889 another £5,000,000 was appropriated, the original sum having been exhausted; and the total number of purchases reached 25,000 by 1891, when parliament expanded the scope of the scheme by voting an additional £30,000,000 for it. Practically, though not technically, the government was expropriating the landlords to transform their tenants into free proprietors. The judicial protection of occupiers' rights as tenants depressed the market value of the land, making it that much easier for them to buy; and the Treasury, acting in its own as well as the purchaser's interest, often declined to advance a loan unless the landlord would accept less than the tenant was willing to pay, thereby forcing down the sale price.

The legal principle of compulsory sale was introduced in 1896, but only for bankrupt estates. This stimulated the creation of occupying owners and also an Irish cry for the general application of the principle because many solvent landlords refused to sell at ruinous prices. The government shrank from such undisguised confiscation, and yet was most anxious to speed the transfer of the land. Here was a nice dilemma from which an escape was sought by having the state assume the extra charge necessary to induce sale. Accordingly, an act was passed in 1903 offering vendors a bonus of 12 per cent on the purchase price for tenants, the bonus to be paid out of public funds. To balance this favor to landlords, the same act reduced the annual burden on purchasers from 4 to 3.25 per cent; and to preserve the solvency of the scheme, it lengthened the period of repayment to sixty-nine and a half years. The temptation of the bonus was so effective that the sale of estates proceeded rapidly, and Ireland became a country of peasant proprietors.

A very serious agricultural problem was solved along with, but independently of, the land problem. The Irish peasants were about the worst farmers in the civilized world, thanks to their own ignorance, which negligent landlords had done nothing to correct; and much of the miserable pittance that they wrung from the soil was gobbled up by middlemen, commonly local public house keepers, who had them in their clutches. The liquidation of the old landlords was no cure for these wretched conditions. What Irish agriculture sorely needed was a thorough revolution of farming and marketing operations. Such a revolution may be compared with that which English landlords had long since wrought. But there were two important differences. The state of Irish agriculture was much lower than English agriculture had been, and the English capitalist solution of the problem of efficiency was inapplicable in Ireland. The Irish agricultural revolution had to be more or less socialist in character.

One Irishman, a Unionist, was largely responsible for leading the multitude of Irish peasants in the way they should go to put Irish agriculture on its feet. He was Horace (later Sir Horace) Plunkett, a younger son of the sixteenth Lord Dunsanay,[3] a product of Eton and Oxford—and America. Ten years of ranching in Montana gave him a considerable fortune and an invaluable experience with which he returned to Ireland in 1889 to commence his lifework. His first step was to form local cooperatives. As they prospered and multiplied, he coordinated them nationally in the Irish Agricultural Organization Society, which he founded in 1894. It gave an enormous life to the cooperative movement and spread a knowledge of better farming, better business, and better living. From this he went on to enlist the aid of the government, and in 1899 he secured the passage of an Agricultural and Technical Instruction Act. This established a new governmental

---

[3] Grandfather of the literary Lord Dunsanay.

department which, with himself as active head, provided Ireland with colleges that trained agricultural scientists, schools that gave practical agricultural education, and itinerant agricultural instructors who conducted local classes and directed field demonstrations and experiments. The department enlisted the active support of local committees and fostered all kinds of cooperatives from creameries to banks. So it came to pass that Ireland was transformed into another Denmark, specializing in the dairy and poultry industries.

Meanwhile Irish nationalism was recovering from the hopeless state into which it had fallen by 1893. That year saw the founding of the Gaelic League by seven literary scholars in Dublin for the prime purpose of reviving the Irish language. Early in the nineteenth century it was still the native tongue of the majority of the population; but as the century drew to a close the mass of Irishmen spoke only English— thanks largely though not entirely to famine and heavy emigration, the effects of which were greatest in the purely Irish districts, and to the influence of the Roman Catholic clergy, who frowned on the use of Gaelic. Scottish Gaelic had been declining too, but not so rapidly, for Presbyterian Highlanders had been given the Bible in Gaelic and were taught to read it. The cognate Goidelic speech, long extinct in northwest and southwest England, survived only in Wales and there it was strong. It had gained a new lease of life in the late eighteenth century, when its adoption by Wesleyan preachers enabled them to sweep that part of the country into the Methodist fold, and in the nineteenth century from the revival of the mediaeval eisteddfod in 1819 as an annual national festival.

The founding of the Gaelic League under the presidency of Douglas Hyde, a Protestant of English extraction and the greatest living Celtic scholar, was the small beginning of a big movement commonly called the Celtic revival, or the Irish renaissance. In 1898 a national festival patterned after the Welsh was held, and it was so successful that thenceforth it was an annual event. The linguistic phase of the movement made slow but steady progress, while the literary phase, expressed in English with peculiar Irish grace, developed with almost explosive rapidity. Inspired by the rediscovery of ancient Irish literature, legends, and history, such poets and dramatists as W. B. Yeats, J. M. Synge, and Lady Gregory kindled a new spirit in Ireland and leaped into international fame. Everybody has heard of the Abbey Theater in Dublin, which was established in 1904 for the production of plays on Irish themes. There the very soul of Ireland seemed to sing.

The political aspect of this Irish reawakening was stimulated by the Boer War, but this influence was less striking than it was in the development of dominion nationalism. The schism that had paralyzed the Home Rule movement came to an end in 1899, when Justin McCarthy died and his followers accepted John Redmond as their leader. The reunion of the party, however, did not provide a single focus for Irish political aspirations. Within the Gaelic League there was a growing feeling that parliamentary agitation was futile, and in 1904 Arthur Griffith, the most brilliant journalist of the League, launched the Sinn Fein movement. The original and technical issue between Home Rulers and Sinn Feiners was that the former implicitly recognized what the latter utterly denied—the constitutional authority of the British parliament to legislate for Ireland. Griffith and his fellows asserted that the Irish members of that body were betraying Ireland by sitting in Westminster, that they should assemble in Dublin and there constitute themselves as an independent legislature. Practically and eventually this meant the application of revolutionary force to set up a republic. In 1905 Douglas Hyde toured the United States and brought back £11,000 for the Irish cause. But the reopening of the American purse was to have less influence than the exigencies of English politics upon the outcome in Ireland by determining whether the renewed drive for Home Rule would win the race against Sinn Fein.

When the Liberals returned to office at the end of 1905, they would not touch Home Rule, which had caused them so much grief, unless they had to in order to command a majority in the House of Commons. The general election at the beginning of 1906 relieved them of this necessity until the Lords' rejection of the 1909 budget forced an appeal to the country in January 1910. As there was every indication that the contest would be so close that the Irish Nationalists would again ride the balance of power, Asquith bid for Redmond's support by promising a Home Rule bill if the government was sustained. The Liberals lost a hundred seats and the Unionists gained even more, with the result that their standing in the new House was equal; Redmond then bound the prime minister to put Home Rule on the statute book as quickly as possible. Majority opinion in England was hostile to the project; but the Irish leader could count on the open sympathy of the dominions, which welcomed the prospect of Ireland's joining their ranks, and on the old pressure from the United States, whose friendship was becoming more valued in Britain.

Thus once more English politics had played into Irish hands, but it proved to be just a few months too late for Home Rule to win. As there was not the slightest chance of getting a Home Rule bill through the House of Lords, its enactment had to wait until the House of Commons acquired the constitutional right to override the veto of the upper chamber. This entailed another general election at the end of 1910, the passage of the Parliament Bill in 1911 after a memorable struggle, and a further delay prescribed by the Parliament Bill for legislation without the concurrence of the Lords. The Commons had to pass Home Rule in three successive sessions—in 1912, 1913, and 1914—before it could become law in defiance of the Lords. During this long process, party strife in Britain grew extremely bitter over Home Rule, and a storm blew up in Ulster that was more furious than the one of 1886.

To the ordinary Protestant in Ireland, "Home Rule meant Rome rule," an abominable thing. The dread of domination by a Roman Catholic government was also a cloak for economic fears. Ulster was the only industrial part of Ireland and, as a consequence, by far the richest. It possessed some of the biggest and most prosperous linen factories and shipyards in the world. Industrial Ulster was a juicy orange for a Home Rule government to squeeze. While the business community of Ulster recoiled in horror from the thought of crushing taxation, another nightmare haunted organized labor. It was Protestant, skilled, and well paid; whereas the unskilled workers were Catholic, unorganized, and poverty-striken. The skilled believed that a Roman Catholic government in Dublin would push their wages down by helping the unskilled up. Protestant Ulster rallied under the fiery leadership of a great lawyer, Sir Edward Carson, who thereby came to be known as "King" Carson, and resolved to resist Home Rule by force if necessary. Again the old cry was raised, "Ulster will fight, and Ulster will be right."

Though the Home Rule bill contained clauses that limited the power of the Irish parliament for the express purpose of safeguarding general imperial and specific Ulster interests, the announcement of these provisions in the spring of 1912 did not check the ominous movement that was centered in Belfast. Already it was creating its own army, the Ulster Volunteers; and in the autumn it produced the Ulster Covenant, modeled after the historic Scottish National Covenant, pledging its signers to fight to the death against Home Rule. To meet this threat in the north, southern Ireland began to arm and drill toward the end of 1913; thus a second illegal army sprang into existence, the Irish National Volunteers. The government forbade the importation of arms into Ireland; but they poured in from England for the Ulster Volunteers, and they trickled in from Germany for the Irish National Volunteers. Protestant Ulster was preparing to prove its loyalty to Britain by rebelling against the British government, and Nationalist Ireland was preparing to get national self-government with the aid of rifles aimed at Ulstermen and, if London did not keep its word, at British soldiers too.

Asquith was caught in a terrible plight. He could neither press on nor back out without incurring the grave risk of plunging Ireland into a bloody civil war. All he could do to ease the tension was to win Redmond's consent to an amendment that would allow any Ulster counties to stay out of Home Rule for six years, if they so decided by popular vote. But the only condition that the Ulster opposition would accept was the permanent exclusion of the counties with Protestant majorities. This was intolerable to the Nationalists because of the size of the Roman Catholic minorities, which ranged from 20 to nearly 50 per cent of the population in these counties. The Home Rule leader dared not make any further concession lest he lose his precarious hold on the Irish National Volunteers, who were really a Sinn Fein organization. To make matters worse, the Irish crisis demoralized the British Army. In the spring of 1914 there was a rash of resignations by officers who feared that they would be ordered to coerce "loyal Ulster."

On 25 May the Commons passed the bill for the last time, with a majority of 77 provided by Redmond's followers. But it was enacted too late to become operative. Before Ireland could blow up, the Old World blew up. Rather than face a civil war in Ireland that would cripple Britain as she entered the World War, Liberals and Home Rulers agreed, to the unspeakable relief of Unionists and Ulstermen, to suspend the operation of Home Rule until hostilities ceased. Though no one knew it at the time, that decision delivered Nationalist Ireland into the arms of the Sinn Fein leaders. Wisdom that looks backward has since condemned the lack of courage that dealt Home Rule the fatal blow, but no one can prove that the alternative would have been better.

Indian nationalism was more like Irish than dominion nationalism in that it was a reaction against foreign rule established by conquest, and it drew nourishment from roots that penetrated deep into the past of the country. Yet it owed much to what the British gave to India. The British gave political unity, which India had never possessed in all its long and confused history of previous conquests, and the British reinforced this political integration with physical integration. Every improvement in communication and transportation tended to break down the vertical and horizontal barriers—the divisions of geography, race, and caste—that had always prevented the people of India from having any sense of unity. The British also planted and watered the seeds of nationalism in the ground that they thus cleared for its growth. The educational policy inaugurated by Macaulay and pushed by the government even after the Mutiny—for the British scorned the idea of keeping the Indians down by keeping them ignorant—gave the literate classes a common language, English, that bound them together for the first time; and it indoctrinated them with British ideals of liberty, which sooner or later were bound to inspire a nationalist challenge to British rule. Moreover, quite apart from this formal education, individual Englishmen of scholarly bent explored the antiquities of India, which Indians themselves had long neglected, and thereby roused in them the proud consciousness of being the heirs of a civilization much more ancient and in many ways more splendid than that of England.

Though the Mutiny was a wild revulsion against Occidentalism as well as an outburst of anarchy, it was no expression of Indian nationalism, which did not arise until years afterward. There was, however, a causal relationship which Indian myth inverted. The blood spilled by the Mutiny manured the soil from which Indian nationalism sprang. As the reflex from the horrible shock of 1857 caused the British in India to withdraw from the society around them, and the Indians also to draw in upon themselves, a wide gulf opened between rulers and ruled, and the increased racial consciousness on both sides fed the growth of Indian nationalism.

The seventies saw the rise of a native press, both English-language and vernacular. Some of the latter seized the occasion of the Russo-Turkish War of 1877–78 to praise Russia and attack Britain, suggesting the assassination of British officials and the overthrow of the British *raj*. This was something new in India, and it looked like the beginning of Indian nationalist agitation. To the viceroy, Lord Lytton, and his council it was seditious incitement and too dangerous to tolerate. Therefore they passed the Vernacular Press Act of 1878, clamping censorship upon this class of newspapers. The response from the rising generation of western-educated Indians was an angry howl, another novelty in a land of traditional submission to authority. The act was also severely criticized in England, particularly by Gladstone. When he returned to power in 1880, he sent the Marquis of Ripon to replace Lytton. The new viceroy, a lifelong Liberal and a former secretary of state for India, repealed the Vernacular Press Act in 1882, an amendment of the penal code having provided penalties for seditious writing. But the injury to Indian feeling did not disappear with the act, and liability to prosecution did not deter native journalists from growing bolder.

In accordance with the repeatedly avowed British policy of no racial discrimination in the service of the government, Indians had risen to become magistrates and session judges, and it was decided under Ripon that the time had come to give them exactly the same jurisdiction as their British colleagues. The point was that only the latter had been allowed to try Europeans in some but not all of the courts. To remove this racial discrimination, the Ilbert Bill, so called after its legal author, was introduced into the legislative council in 1883. Indian opinion greeted it enthusiastically but was almost at once inflamed by the fierce fire it drew from British residents outside government circles, especially indigo and tea planters. Not since the Mutiny had there been such an outburst of bitter racial feeling. Bowing before the storm, the government withdrew the bill for another that protected Europeans by according them the right to be tried by a jury of which half had to be Europeans or Americans. This provision neutralized the main purpose of the act, but it did not leave things as they had been. The racial conflict was accentuated, and educated Indians had a practical lesson in the value of agitation.

Ripon established a large measure of local self-government in towns and rural districts. His object, as he explained when introducing this reform in 1882, was to train the people in self-government. He knew it would be a long and a hard process, and he cherished no hope that it would bring about an early improvement in administrative efficiency, but he had faith that improvement would follow in course of time. He also changed the educational system. Hitherto almost all the schools and colleges of western learning were under government or missionary control. He inaugurated a policy of encouraging, with the aid of public grants, district boards and private organizations to take over the work and expand it. Accordingly, there was an extraordinary increase in the number of such institutions under native management and with poorly paid native instructors; and there was a correspondingly rapid growth in the number of students, who thus acquired a ready knowledge of the English tongue and an ill-digested English literary education. As this became in a very few years the normal training for nearly all the members of the traditionally literate classes, and was confined to them, it posed a grave problem that slowly dawned on the British mind. Would the preparation of Indians for self-government keep pace with their demand for it?

The first Indian National Congress—the use of the word "National" was significant—met in 1885, and thenceforth there was an annual session of this unofficial and loosely-constituted body. Most of its members were delegates chosen by various societies, but almost any sympathizer was welcome and a few Europeans joined. Though the third Congress elected a Moslem president, and the fourth adopted a resolution that in effect would block any motion to which Moslems objected, the leaders of the Moslem community were openly suspicious of the movement and discouraged their followers from joining it. Moslems had not availed themselves of the opportunities to acquire a western education in anything like the degree that Hindus had done, and of course they were sensitively conscious of their minority position. The membership of Congress was therefore mostly drawn from the community of educated Hindus, in which Bengali and Brahmin influences predominated.

The express aim of the Congress movement from the very beginning was to evolve in India a system of self-government by the application of the principles that had prevailed in Britain and her autonomous colonies. "New light has been poured on us," said the president of the second Congress, "teaching us the new lesson that kings are made for the people, not peoples for their kings; and this lesson we have learned amid the darkness of Asiatic despotism only by the light of free English civilization." Such declarations of gratitude and loyalty to British rule commonly accompanied the demands of Congress for liberal reforms during the first twenty years of its existence, though it displayed through this period a growing tendency to be impatient with the administration's tardiness to make concessions, and to be dissatisfied with what was granted.

When the Earl of Dufferin succeeded Ripon in 1884, he brought with him a ripe experience of diplomatic dealing with Oriental peoples and also of service as a constitutional monarch while governor general of Canada. Although agreeing in the main with Ripon's policy, he won the confidence of the Anglo-Indian community without offending Indian opinion. Indeed, he encouraged the formation of Congress, for he felt the need implied by an old and able provincial governor who had regretted that the only way the people he ruled could make a complaint to him was by stirring up a riot. Before Dufferin retired in 1888, he worked out definite proposals to reform the viceroy's council and the provincial councils by the addition of new members who would represent as far as possible different Indian classes and interests, by the election of some of these new members, and by giving the councils greater freedom to discuss important government questions. Congress urged such changes as a step toward responsible government; but he was more cautious, and the ministry in London even more so. He disclaimed any intention of aiming at the introduction of the British parliamentary system, confining his object to greater Indian participation in the framing and conduct of policy. Salisbury's cabinet boggled at the proposed application of the elective principle because it was a western invention liable to perversion in the Orient. Nevertheless, in 1892 the Conservatives passed the Indian Councils Act to effect the reforms advocated by Dufferin and backed by his successor, including partial election. The reconstituted legislatures of the Indian governments still had official majorities, but whenever there was a difference of opinion the nonofficial members could often determine the issue. Moreover, they now acquired the right to criticize executive orders and the annual budget, and thenceforth the viceroy and the governors accorded a deferential hearing to their opinions.

Congress was grievously disappointed over the slowness and meagerness of the concession, but the great majority of its members realized that their country, with its multitude of ancient schisms and its 99 per cent illiteracy, was not at all prepared for anything like full self-government. Their methods were constitutional; their political ideals western. There was, however, one leader in Congress who represented a very different movement that was growing outside—a movement of revolutionary violence, of antiwestern hatred, of blind religious fanaticism.

The firebrand was B. G. Tilak, a highly educated Brahmin journalist of Bombay who never forgot that his ancestors had been numbered among the rulers of the Mahratta empire. He leaped into fame as the opponent of an Age of Consent Act, which was passed in 1891 following the death of a Calcutta child-wife and the prosecution of her husband for homicide. The act prohibited cohabitation with a wife less than twelve years old. This caused ignorant Hindus of Calcutta to cry out that their religion was in danger. Tilak caught up the cry and spread it broadcast, denouncing all Hindu supporters of the measure as traitors and renegades. His proclaimed hero was Sivaji, the seventeenth century robber chief who created the Mahratta state and killed Moslems in cold as well as hot blood. Tilak's preaching of murder was particularly popular among Bengalese worshipers of Kali, the goddess of destruction.

Two terrible scourges hit India almost simultaneously in 1896, famine and the bubonic plague. The former, affecting large sections of the country and believed to have been the worst it had ever known, was checked by the return of the rains in the following year. But only man could stamp out the plague; and the necessary sanitary measures, which the government promptly undertook, stirred such fierce opposition among the ignorant masses—two young British officers engaged in preventive work were deliberately murdered and there were sanguinary riots—that the authorities had to fall back upon milder methods which limited but could not eradicate the contagion. As might be expected, the popular opposition was inflamed by the native press, which blamed the British for both scourges, and the most incendiary articles were Tilak's. They cost him a year's imprisonment, after which he was more discreet for several years.

The charge that British rule was responsible for recurrent famines and the ravages of the plague was as natural as it was absurd. It was useful nationalist propaganda, which in every country plays on ignorance and appeals to prejudice. If the British had been more astute and less scrupulous, they might have used the educational system as a propaganda machine to solidify their rule; or at least they might have exercised their power to stop the native press from preaching, as it did, that British rule had done nothing but harm to India. In addition to famine and plague, the British were held responsible for the poverty of the peasants, supposedly by crushing taxation. The British were draining India of all her once enormous wealth. The reference of course was to salaries and pensions of British officials, a mere bagatelle, and to interest on British capital invested in the country, as in the United States and other lands, for the mutual benefit of borrower and lender. Britain was also to blame for the decline of Indian industry, which was actually growing and becoming more Indian in ownership, and for the progressive depreciation of the Indian currency, which was suffering from the world decline in the value of silver.[4]

The monetary standard of India, the rupee, had remained steady at about two shillings until 1873, when it began to fall, gathering momentum from 1885 until it touched bottom in 1893 at one shilling and a halfpenny. While the drop doubled the foreign debt, it gave a corre-

---

[4] Which caused a currency headache in the United States.

sponding stimulus to production for export; but this benefit was reaped by a relatively small class at the expense of the many, including the salaried and professional classes, who had to pay more for imported goods. To prevent a further drop, the government in 1893 stopped the free coinage of silver in the Indian mints; six years later it gave definite stability by introducing the gold standard and reducing the rupee to a token status at the rate of fifteen to the pound. Thereupon Indian nationalists cried out that their country was being bound to the chariot wheel of Britain, the pound sterling.

British bureaucracy reached its zenith and Indian nationalism entered upon a new and angrier phase during the viceroyalty of Lord Curzon, 1899–1905. As a ruler of India he alone among the viceroys ranks in stature with the greatest governors general in the days of the East India Company. Deep study and wide travel had made him an outstanding authority on the East. He had a genius for administration, a passion for efficiency, a lofty sense of duty, and a profound determination to give India a better government than it had ever known. He overhauled the whole administrative machinery, directing searching investigations and effecting drastic reforms. He did much to alleviate the lot of the peasantry, who formed the great mass of the population. The drought of 1899–1900 was nearly as bad as that from which the country was just recovering. The new famine, which cost about one million lives in British territory alone and £8,500,000 in relief, was the last such catastrophe until the end of British rule,[5] thanks to Curzon's vigorous expansion of irrigation and the railway system. He remitted taxes in distressed regions, freed cultivators from eviction by the ever-present native merchant and moneylender, introduced cooperative rural banks, and organized an imperial department of agriculture to encourage improved methods of tillage.

Excellent as were Curzon's many reforms when viewed singly, he drove too fast and too far for such a very old land, thereby repeating Dalhousie's mistake. Moreover, though he had piloted the Indian Councils Act through the Commons, all his reforms were administrative, none political. The most he would concede to Indian opinion was that the Indianization of the services—the total personnel numbered 6,500 British and 218,000 Indians—should be speeded, which he was impatient to see. But he seems to have enjoyed the support of most Indian nationalists until 1904.

---

[5] There was a serious drought in 1907–8, and another in 1918, but much less suffering.

It was then three years since the viceroy had summoned the principal officers of the educational system to hear his own penetrating analysis of what was wrong with the system and what was needed to make it right. It imitated English models too slavishly, concentrating too much on a literary at the expense of a technical education, and on English to the disadvantage of the vernaculars and the Oriental classics; it was too tolerant of lifeless instruction, cramming of indigested knowledge, and low academic standards; it neglected character building, the pride of all good schools in England; it lacked ideals and inspiration; it had grown piecemeal without intelligent direction and coordination. He observed that the greatest of all dangers in India was ignorance, and he impressed upon his hearers the fact that they were "handling the lifeblood of future generations." The speech stimulated action that reached down through the system, and he took more positive steps to improve it. His government made education a leading charge upon the public funds, advancing more liberal grants to local governments for it; an inspector general was imported from England; and a universities commission was appointed. Its findings led to the framing of the measure that loosed the storm.

The Universities Act of 1904 reconstituted the governing bodies of the universities, which were all state institutions, so that they would have majorities of educational experts; it left most of the undergraduate training to the colleges and provided that the universities should undertake advanced instruction; it tightened up the regulations for the inspection and the accrediting of schools and colleges; and it prescribed government appointment of university vice-chancellors (presidents), government approval of all appointees to their teaching staffs, and government supervision of some other details of university management. This direct government control may seem strange to Americans and was foreign to English practice; but then state universities did not exist in England, and they had long been the rule on the continent of Europe, where such control was almost universal. It seemed particularly desirable in India, where the inertia of society was so great, in order to build up the universities and through them to pull up the rest of the educational system. When the terms of the bill were published, the native intelligentsia, a product of the condemned system, reacted like a professional body whose monopoly position is in jeopardy. Even former moderates turned against Curzon and denounced him as the author of a sinister design to magnify the power of the executive and to destroy higher education.

The uproar mounted with the partition of Bengal in 1905. That province, which had an area of 189,000 square miles and a population of 78,000,000, was not only too large but was also too diverse in character to be administered as one. Eastern Bengal, where the Moslems were a majority, was a stagnant backwater in urgent need of a separate government. There was ample precedent for the partition. Assam, for example, had been cut off thirty years before. Now it and Eastern Bengal were combined to form a new province with an area of 106,000 square miles and a population of 31,000,000. The decision was the result of long deliberation, during which various alternatives were weighed and the plan was adjusted to meet outside criticisms. These gave no indication of the popular agitation that flared up in opposition to it at the last moment. Calcutta journalists and lawyers, who believed their vested interests were threatened by the readjustment of administrative boundaries, did their clever best by fair means and foul to defeat the change. But their influence can only partly explain the explosion of Hindu national fanaticism that shook much of India. The Bengali "nation" was being carved up in an effort to destroy its traditions, its language, and its religion! Tilak was again on the rampage, and revolution was in the air, striking here and there in political murder.

It happened that this crisis coincided with a clash between the viceroy and the commander in chief of the army in India, Lord Kitchener, over the matter of civilian control, on which the home government refused to take a stand against the popular soldier, who was in the wrong. Curzon resigned in protest. His departure and London's refusal to reconsider the partition did not assuage the storm that his reforms had provoked.

Events in the outside world contributed much to this storm, for they were feeding the fires of Indian nationalism. Like Irish nationalism and unlike dominion nationalism, it was little affected by the South African War. But the South African treatment of Indians as an inferior race was beginning to have serious repercussions in their homeland, and so also was Australian and Canadian legislation against the admission of Indians. Infinitely greater was the Indian excitement over the world-shaking Russo-Japanese War, 1904–5. The swift triumph of a comparatively small Asiatic state over an apparently mighty European empire reverberated "like a thunderclap through the whispering galleries of the East," heralding the doom of European domination in Asia. From one end of that teeming continent to the other, the effect of the Japanese victories was startling, and nowhere more than in India.

Less easy to assess is the influence of a Moslem religious revival that had spread from the African desert, had played a part in the Egyptian rising of Arabi, had run wild in the Sudan under the Mahdi, and had since penetrated the rest of the Islamic world under the direction of the crafty Abdul Hamid of Turkey who, as caliph, was nominally the spiritual and temporal ruler of Islam. Even before he captured the movement, it was political as well as religious, its missionaries preaching a spiritual regeneration that would restore the might of ancient days and throw off the yoke imposed by Christendom. Moslem India was now stirring uneasily. While the revival pushed it against British rule, the partition of Bengal had a restraining effect, for the creation of the new province pleased the Moslems. In 1906 they pulled away from the Indian National Congress and formed the Moslem League, thus adumbrating the complete split of 1947.

The moderates in Congress, already weakened by the furious agitation against the Universities Act and the partition of Bengal, were further weakened by the withdrawal of the Moslems; and they nearly lost control when the extremists tried to seize it with the aid of physical force in 1907. Outside Congress the cry for complete independence was rallying the professional classes, college students, schoolboys, industrial workers, and village headmen. Political crime multiplied, reaching even as far as London, where an Indian student assassinated the aide-de-camp of the secretary of state in 1909. That year saw the climax of the prewar wave of terrorism, which aimed at weakening the British *raj* and thereby hastening its end; it also saw the enactment by parliament of a statute designed to give Indians a greater voice in their own government.

The Morley-Minto reforms, an important stage in the political evolution of India, were a compound of the ideas of these two men and of specific claims that Congress advanced in 1904 and developed in the following year. One of these claims, borrowed from the French colonial system and later dropped, was for the direct representation of each Indian province in the House of Commons. The others called for larger representation in the Indian legislative councils, wider liberty of debate in these legislatures, and the admission of Indians to the executive councils.

The Earl of Minto, who had served in India and in other parts of the empire and was a great-grandson of a former governor general, was the Conservative appointee to succeed Curzon. John Morley (Viscount Morley from 1908), advanced Liberal and inveterate Home Ruler, was secretary of state for India in the Liberal cabinet that took office at the close of 1905. Though Morley and Minto belonged to opposite political parties, they were of one mind in seeking greater Indian participation in the administration of the country; and though separated by thousands of miles, they cooperated effectively to achieve this end. In 1906, while the one in England and the other in India quietly conducted preliminary examinations based on the above claims, Congress met and for the first time passed a resolution asking for the self-government that the dominions enjoyed; as initial steps in this direction, Congress prescribed a concession of the claims already mentioned, minus that for representation in Westminster, which then disappeared.

"The ingenious saying, that British rulers of India with a supreme parliament at home are like men bound to make their watches keep time in two longitudes at once, was now to be sharply tested."[6] Neither the viceroy nor the secretary of state saw how English political institutions could be adapted to the utterly foreign conditions of India. Yet both believed that the spirit of these institutions could and should be applied. Educated Indians were demanding it and, what was more decisive, the British public acting through parliament would insist upon it.

The most serious difference between the two great officials was that the man on the spot was inclined to combat the epidemic of political crime with more arbitrary methods than the distant cabinet minister thought prudent. But Minto and Morley agreed that the embarrassing campaign of revolutionary violence should not hold up their program of reform; they were also in accord on the wisdom of strengthening the leadership of the moderates in Congress by doing everything possible to meet their demands. Another delicate point that was early settled between them arose from Minto's recent experience as governor general of Canada, which taught him how easy it was to arouse, quite innocently, suspicions of dictation from England. Out of regard for Indian sensibilities, he insisted that the public and official initiative should come from the Indian government.

As soon as it was publicly known in India that organic changes were afoot, in October 1906, a Moslem deputation pressed Minto for a decision on a problem that was to bedevil the political development of India toward self-government. The deputation requested that a just proportion of Moslem representatives in the legislatures should be fixed by law and that these members should be elected by Moslem voters. The

---

[6] Morley, *Recollections,* II, 156.

problem was inherent in Indian society, and the Moslems had unwittingly aggravated it. By their neglect of the opportunities for acquiring a western education, they had failed to fit themselves for public life and office. Though they formed 23 per cent of the population of British India, only 12 per cent of the elected members of the viceroy's legislative council under the 1892 act were Moslems; in one province where they were were 14 per cent of the population not a single Moslem had been elected to the legislature. Minto's reply favored the principle of communal representation, but Hindus cried out against it as setting one religion against another. After much consultation in India and England, and much correspondence between the viceroy and the secretary of state, it was decided to give the principle a qualified application in a general revision of the electoral system to correct the underrepresentation not only of Moslems but of other important classes too, such as landowners and businessmen, under the law of 1892.

The machinery of western democracy, which takes for granted a fairly well-educated and united population in order to produce acceptable results, could not do this in India with its rigidly compartmented plural society. But the elective principle had been introduced, and there was no going back upon it. Hence the necessity to go on with it and, by trial and error, to evolve a tolerably satisfactory application of it.

The admission of Indians to membership in the Council of India— a council which had been established in London to advise the secretary of state and which possessed overruling authority on matters of finance —stirred little opposition from Europeans in India. In England, however, it roused strenuous objections from members of this council and from a powerful and well-informed section of the parliamentary opposition, and not a few Liberals were dubious about it. Morley forced the issue. He had the cabinet back of him, and he needed no new legislation for this particular innovation. In August 1907 he appointed two outstanding Indians, a Hindu who held the highest post yet attained by any Indian in the civil service and a Moslem who was the principal adviser of the Nizam of Hyderabad. He found them an invaluable reinforcement; but he was disappointed because their appointment could not be accompanied, as he had hoped, by the public promise of a more important appointment in India, which was the most contentious point in the whole program of reform.

This was the appointment of an Indian to the viceroy's executive council, for which, likewise, no new parliamentary enactment was necessary. In England, the Conservatives were not the only ones who fought against it. Some of Morley's cabinet colleagues, including Ripon, threw up their hands at the idea of allowing an Indian to share the innermost secrets of the government of India and the direction of that government's policy. In India, British officialdom was almost unanimously hostile to the proposal. Nevertheless, Minto and Morley persisted diplomatically, the British opposition in India weakened, and at home the resistance in the cabinet melted away. The king made the appointment in March 1909, and it proved to be an excellent one. The new executive councilor, chosen by Minto, was a Hindu barrister of highest repute, Mr. S. P. Sinha, whose supreme ambition, from which he never swerved, was to see his country a self-governing member of the empire.

The bill to reorganize the government of India was passed by parliament in May 1909 after three months of lively debate in both houses. When introducing it, Morley emphatically disclaimed any intention of aiming at the establishment of a parliamentary system in India. But he could not quiet opposition fears that the introduction of occidental machinery, however adapted, would lead to this very end; and on the second reading he boldly struck at these fears with the retort that "we ought to have thought of that before we tried occidental education; we applied that and occidental machinery must follow." The act of 1909 more than doubled the size of the various Indian legislatures to make them more representative and to do away with official majorities in all save the central one. A few of the additional members were to be appointed, but most were to be elected. The method of election was to be worked out by the government of India, which framed regulations that combined direct and indirect election and varied from province to province according to local conditions. Indians were also added to the provincial executive councils.

The Morley-Minto reforms delighted the responsible leaders of Congress as a definite step along the road toward self-government, and gave no little satisfaction to Moslems by guaranteeing them communal representation. On the whole, the new constitution worked quite well in the beginning. Two years after its adoption, when Minto and Morley had retired and Edward VII had been laid in his grave, there was a magnificent and unprecedented ceremony in Delhi before an assembled multitude of 80,000. George V, Queen Mary, the secretary of state, and the viceroy were all there for the coronation durbar of the first reigning British sovereign to visit India; throughout the country the occasion evoked great and spontaneous demonstrations of loyalty to the Crown, for India had inherited a deep reverence for exalted monarchy. From the throne in Delhi, the emperor made two dramatic announcements, all the more dramatic because his ministers had kept them a close secret. The seat of the government of India was to be moved from Calcutta to this ancient capital, which delighted Moslems; and Bengal was to be reunited, which made Hindus rejoice.

In the minds of most Indian politicians the reversal of the 1905 partition outweighed all other concessions of these years; for though the violent agitation against the severance of Eastern Bengal had pretty well died down, the reunion was interpreted in India as a yielding to clamor. This was unfortunate all round. It encouraged the revolutionary extremists, weakened the position of the Congress moderates, embarrassed the British, and embittered the Moslems. The continuing campaign of political outrage nearly reached a tragic climax in the following year, when an attempt on the life of Minto's successor severely wounded him and killed an attendant; already thoughts of violence were infecting Moslem heads as they wagged over the bitter jest "No bombs, no boons."

But the reunion of Bengal was by no means the only cause of the marked change that was coming over the attitude of the Moslems toward the government. They were gravely concerned over certain shifts in the international scene that affected the Islamic world. The Anglo-Russian agreement of 1907 on spheres of influence in Persia was a shock to Indian Moslems. They were also disquieted over the gravitation of Turkey into the German orbit, and they were seriously disturbed when Italy in 1911 and the Balkan League in 1912 made successful war on the Ottoman Empire. Indian Moslems organized and dispatched a medical mission to help the Turks, and they gave active support to the Red Crescent, the Islamic counterpart of the Red Cross. An anti-British spirit was growing in the Moslem community, and the Moslem League was shaking off its conservative character. In March 1913 it declared for self-government. The nationalist movement was not united, its two wings being irreconcilably opposed on the question of communal representation. But the advance of both wings was rendering the constitution of 1909 obsolete when the First World War broke out in 1914.

VII THE ERA OF WORLD WAR

CHAPTER XXXIV

The First World War: The Supreme Test

THE BRITISH ULTIMATUM to Germany on 4 August 1914 committed the whole British Empire to war on the sole authority of the government in London. With Ireland on the verge of civil war, India in a state of ferment, and the dominions maturing as individual nations, it seemed to the Germans that the British Empire had come to the brink of dissolution and that a British declaration of war would push it over. This illusion is incompatible with the later assertion of Germans and others that Germany would have preserved the peace had she known, before it was too late, that Britain would not remain neutral; but it is quite compatible with the fact, which has since been revealed, that the German general staff counted on Britain's plunging into the war when it broke out.

Empire or no empire, Britain could not stay out of the war. Her past was proof of that. She was a small island kingdom lying close to the continent of Europe where, from time to time through modern history, great military powers had arisen that would have overwhelmed her, had they been able to transport their land forces across the narrow intervening arm of the sea. What saved her from being conquered, first by Spain and on more than one subsequent occasion by France, was her fighting ships. Naval supremacy thus became the first law of her independent existence, and the balance of power in Europe the second law. A third was likewise dictated by geography. Any great power that controlled Belgium could hold a pistol at England's head. No other place on the continent had such natural advantages for launching a successful invasion of England. It was to prevent Spain from firing this pistol that England fought the great Armada in 1588, and since then she had fought every French move to seize Belgium. That was why she insisted at Vienna on giving this country to Holland. That was why she was the prime mover in the international neutralization of Belgium when the Belgians threw off the Dutch yoke. That was why she warned both belligerents in the Franco-Prussian War that, if either of them violated Belgian neutrality, she would join the other. Of course Britain would fight to defend her empire, as she had repeatedly done; but it should be remembered that these three basic conditions of her own security were established before her empire and that the security of the empire was vitally dependent upon her security.

Though the Franco-Prussian War destroyed the balance of Europe by making German military power dominant on the continent, Britain seemed to be little concerned for her security until nearly thirty years afterward. Her naval supremacy was absolute; she welcomed the achievement of German national unity not only on general principle but also as the removal of a cause of unrest in the heart of Europe; and Bismarck pursued a canny policy that, on the whole, placated rather than provoked the other powers. Unable to effect a reconciliation with France after what he had done to her in 1871, Bismarck was careful to keep her isolated. He did it by forming the Triple Alliance, which tied Austria and Italy to Germany; by a separate alliance with Russia, a rather delicate business because Austrian and Russian interests clashed in the Balkans; and by making the most of the Anglo-French quarrel over Egypt. Britain was so suspicious of France and Russia that she gravitated toward the Central Powers; but she refused to consider Bismarck's offer of an alliance in 1889, for she saw no point in abandoning her policy of "splendid isolation."

The European system lost its stability in 1890 when the new kaiser dismissed the old chancellor and began to steer German foreign policy along a disturbing course. William II straightway dropped the Russian alliance, with the natural result that Russia and France drew together in an alliance against the Central Powers. Germany thus came face to face with the prospect that Bismarck had dreaded, of a war on two fronts. Britain's position also deteriorated, because the combination of France and Russia increased the danger of friction with either; the kaiser took advantage of this to assume a more menacing attitude that reached an open climax in his startling telegram to Kruger and a secret climax in his effort to rally France and Russia behind Germany for the purpose of breaking British pride. In the previous year he had got their cooperation in the Far East, where together they forced Japan to return territory she had just wrested from China; and he continued to play with the scheme of uniting the divided European powers on a basis of common hostility to Britain.

In 1898 Britain began to turn from one side to the other with the object of securing an accommodation that would reduce the chances of becoming embroiled in war. The first approach was to Russia early in that year. Anglo-Russian relations were less strained than they had often been before the recent Armenian massacres killed the British policy of championing the Turk. Salisbury now proposed that the two powers should work out a mutual understanding on their problems in the Near East and the Far East. The Russian government discouraged the idea, and Chamberlain then opened discussions with the German ambassador to relieve the tension with Berlin. The kaiser's government dismissed the talk as premature, but suggested that it might be resumed at some future date.

Before the year was out, Britain was in a tighter position. In the Far East, the three powers that had intervened against Japan collected their commissions from China, Russia in Port Arthur, Germany in Kiaochow, and France in Kwangchow Bay. Britain countered by securing the lease of Weihaiwei for as long as Russia held Port Arthur, and by seeking the cooperation of the United States in China, which led to the declaration of the Open Door policy. In the Near East the kaiser made a spectacular visit, during which he picked up Britain's discarded friend, the sultan of Turkey, and proclaimed himself the champion of Moslems everywhere. At home he appointed Von Tirpitz to the Admiralty and got the Reichstag to pass the first Naval Law. Of less ultimate but more immediate consequence was the Fashoda crisis, which nearly plunged Britain into war with France.

Though this crisis passed in the spring of 1899, when France backed down because Russia would not support her, the autumn brought the Boer War and with it an alarming outburst of hostile opinion that bridged the gulf between the two armed camps of Europe. Britain's isolation had ceased to be splendid. It was perilous. Again a hand was held out toward Germany. This time Chamberlain openly suggested an alliance; but it met with little favor in England and much opposition in Germany, whose government bluntly repelled the offer in 1900 by passing the second Naval Law. This was most serious. The strongest military power in the world was building a navy to challenge the greatest sea power, and the kaiser made no secret of it.

In 1901 a third attempt to bring the two countries together pushed them farther apart. It was apparently the well-meaning work of the first secretary of the German embassy who, during the illness of the ambassador, reopened discussions with the British for a German alliance. As he did this in violation of instructions from Berlin, he deceived both governments, leading each to believe that the other had made the advance and was therefore willing to meet its terms. The break came when the British, who thought that the Germans were prepared to sign a bilateral treaty similar to the Russian one that the kaiser had dropped, at last discovered what the Germans expected of them. It was complete adherence to the Triple Alliance. Berlin had calculated that this was the necessary price for underwriting British risks of war with another European power, but London recoiled from a demand that would consolidate German mastery over Europe. The project of an Anglo-German alliance was buried deep under mutual suspicions that each country was trying to trap the other, and the important thing to note on the British side is that two of the three basic conditions of security were thrusting themselves forward.

The South African War drove home the lesson that Britain should reduce the dangers of isolation in a jealous world, and the failure of the negotiations with Berlin made London look elsewhere for friends. Chamberlain had warned the Germans that this would happen, but they were sure that Britain's bad relations with both members of the Dual Alliance left her no alternative. The British search gathered its first fruit in Tokyo; and Japan had reasons of her own for wishing to be friendly with Britain. She could not forgive Russia for stealing the spoils of her victory; she had good ground for fearing that Russian control was spreading from Manchuria to Korea; and she would fight if there was no other way to stop this penetration that jeopardized her security. If France then came to the aid of Russia, it might go hard with Japan, who therefore desperately needed the support of another great power. Germany would not give it, for the kaiser openly scorned the yellow race and sought to "nail down Russia in Asia." Only Britain could and would oblige.

Hence the Anglo-Japanese alliance of 1902, which was limited in scope to wars arising out of interests in China. It bound each party to benevolent neutrality in the event of an attack by one enemy and to active assistance only if two powers attacked. The treaty was revised in 1905 to cover India and all eastern Asia and to provide for active assistance against a single enemy; it was revised again in 1911 to relieve either party of the obligation to make war on a third power with whom it had signed a general arbitration treaty.[1] The alliance held the ring for Japan during the Russo-Japanese War of 1904–5; but neither in its original nor in its revised form did the Anglo-Japanese alliance contribute anything, except indirectly, to the coming of the 1914 catastrophe. The indirect influence, however, was considerable. The startling repulse inflicted by Japan made Russia seek compensation in the Balkans, thereby increasing the danger of war with Germany through Austria; it was a revelation of Russian weakness that, enhanced by the concomitant revolution of 1905, made Germany more willing to fight such a war; and it removed a major obstacle that had stood in the way of an Anglo-Russian entente, of which more presently when we have seen the other conditions that also led to this understanding.

It was not until the spring of 1904 that Britain broke through the ring of hostile powers in Europe, by concluding the Entente Cordiale with her most ancient and still most troublesome foe. Anglo-French discussions were initiated by Chamberlain and the French ambassador in 1902, and there was a lot of difficult ground to be covered. These discussions dealt with a trail of disputes that girdled the world from Newfoundland, over fishing rights, through the widest extent of Africa, down to Madagascar, on to southeast Asia, where French Indochina impinged on Siam, and beyond to the New Hebrides in the South Pacific. Over all these many controversies, big and little, old and new, hung the dark shadow of the Fashoda episode. But that was not the only deep humiliation that France had suffered in late years. Her hatred of Germany fought her hatred of Britain, and she now came to the conclusion that she could not continue the luxury of nursing both. She must either be reconciled with her ancient enemy or renounce all hope of recovering Alsace-Lorraine. The pull of the provinces torn from her body was decisive. An Anglo-French alliance of any kind was out of the question. Britain was as anxious to avoid new risks of war with a European power as she was to escape from old ones, and France was in no position to bargain with her for anything more than a settlement of the quarrels between them. This they achieved by

---

[1] The purpose of this condition was to release Britain from any obligation to assist Japan in a war against the United States. An Anglo-American general arbitration treaty was then being concluded. But the door of escape was unexpectedly barred by the United States Senate, which rejected the treaty. In 1914 the British government made another effort in this direction by informing Japan that it would regard the new Bryan conciliation treaty as fulfilling the condition prescribed by the qualifying clause of the alliance. Japan, however, does not seem to have agreed with this interpretation.

trading a concession here for a concession there. The thorniest problem was in Africa, which was solved by an exchange of promises of a free hand and diplomatic support for Britain in Egypt and for France in Morocco, if the latter disintegrated. The Entente paid its first dividend in the following autumn, when the Russian fleet nearly shot Japan's ally into the war by firing on British fishermen through the mists of the North Sea, and France mediated between her ally and her new friend. If this was all to the good, the next call for assistance was not.

The French in Algeria had an anarchic next-door neighbor in Morocco, and they were finding it intolerable. Early in 1905, assured of British backing, they began to negotiate with the sultan of Morocco for some reformation of his government. Germany seized this occasion to produce an international crisis and promptly protested against what was an obvious first step toward the establishment of French influence—an influence which might damage the commercial interests of other powers, including Germany, guaranteed by a convention of 1880. The kaiser went in person to Morocco, where he denounced any interference with its independence. But there was much more than Morocco at stake. By threatening France with war while her one ally was paralyzed by defeat in Manchuria and revolution at home, Germany was trying to break the Anglo-French entente. The threat forced the resignation of the French foreign minister who had signed the agreement; it also forced his government's consent to an international conference on the affairs of Morocco. Britain was not in the least intimidated. Sir Edward Grey, who had become foreign secretary on the resignation of the Conservative ministry, carried on his predecessor's policy of standing firmly behind France. At the Algeciras Conference of 1906, Germany embraced the shadow and France the substance of victory. The assembled powers provided for a Moroccan police force that was nominally international but really controlled by France.

Britain could not afford to let France down in this crisis. That would have thrown all Europe into the arms of Germany. Therefore, solely out of regard for her own security, Britain was ready to fight if France was attacked; and to coordinate the forces of the two countries in this eventuality, her naval and military chiefs entered into conversations with their French counterparts. Instead of being wrecked by the Moroccan crisis, the entente emerged from it stronger than ever. But the entente did not become an alliance until the outbreak of hostilities in 1914, for Britain would not let France commit her to war. This was the explicit understanding on which the above discussions were initiated and continued until the final crash. To the very end, London was loath to slam the door on a possible accommodation with Germany, whose suspicions and ambitions conspired to draw her ever farther away from Britain. Seeing Britain behind France, Germany stepped up her naval building in 1906 and at the same time undertook the widening of the Kiel Canal to allow the passage of the new and more powerful type of battleship then being introduced, the dreadnought.

Britain's next move on the international chessboard was to patch up her differences with Russia, the way having been prepared by other powers. The Armenian massacres had sickened Britain of her friendship with Turkey, the kaiser had supplanted the czar as the opponent of Britain in the Near East, in the Far East Japan had effectively quieted British fears of Russian encroachment upon China, and French influence combined with German behavior to bring London and St. Petersburg closer together. It was in 1905, when the Moroccan crisis was coming to a head and Russia was stricken by war and revolution, that the discussions between the two governments got under way; and it was in 1907, when Germany repeated at the Second Hague Conference her performance at the First in 1899 of obstructing proposals for a general limitation of armaments, that the Anglo-Russian entente was concluded. This was much less like an alliance than the Anglo-French entente, being simply a mutual agreement to keep hands off Tibet and Afghanistan and to separate the clashing interests of the two powers in Persia by recognizing a Russian sphere of interest in the northern third of that country and a British sphere of influence in the southern, with the central third a neutral zone between them. It discreetly avoided any reference to the contentious problem of the Dardanelles, and it did not resolve the conflict over Persia.

The conscience of the British public was sorely troubled by the bargain their government had made at the expense of that weak oriental state. *Punch* published its famous cartoon of the Persian cat between the Russian bear and the British lion, the last saying: "You CAN PLAY WITH HIS HEAD AND I CAN PLAY WITH HIS TAIL AND WE CAN *both* STROKE THE SMALL OF HIS BACK." The clear evidences of British uneasiness over the whole business, and the specter of British sea power in the Persian Gulf, may help to explain why Russia failed to keep faith with Britain in Persia despite Grey's repeated protests against Russian aggression there, which only increased the British embarrassment. But this was not the only embarrassment that the government in London had to face.

There was a deep division of opinion in the Foreign Office, in the cabinet, and in the public at large over relations with the European powers. Against entanglement in their quarrels, Labor stood solidly and so also did a large number of people in both old parties. Their motives ranged from a desire to push on with social reform and a detestation of armaments to a distrust of France and an abhorrence of the czarist autocracy. On the other hand, many were impatient to transform the ententes into positive alliances as the only way to prevent the great war toward which they believed Germany was resolutely driving. Grey could follow neither course without splitting the country, whose unity was essential for the success of any policy. He steered straight between the two extremes, clearly recognizing the dangers on both sides.

A return to isolation would destroy the newly-restored balance of power and tempt the two armed camps to bury their mutual hostility in a continental combination against Britain; whereas a substitution of alliances for the ententes, by giving free rein to aggressive tendencies in France and Russia and an open challenge to Germany, would be almost certain to bring on the great war, with Britain as a principal. Though Britain would not let France, and much less Russia, commit her to war, the ententes implied a moral obligation to stand by them if Germany attacked them. Whether she would then honor the obligation was a point on which Grey and Asquith, along with hosts of their fellow countrymen, were extremely sensitive, for until the very end of the precarious peace there was still a strong body of opinion in England that insisted on neutrality.

Meanwhile another factor of vital importance to British security was poisoning Anglo-German relations. The entente with Russia, coming on top of that with France to complete what is commonly, if erroneously, called the Triple Entente, was followed in 1908 by another acceleration of the German naval building program, which led to the "scare" of 1909. The naval race was now definitely on, the Germans trying hard to catch up with the British, and the latter to keep safely ahead with a two-to-one lead in capital ships. While the Germans saw that their own military might was checkmated by British sea power, the British saw no less clearly that their only sure means of defense was seriously threatened, which was a matter of life and death. If some of them feared that the construction of a big fighting fleet by the greatest land power on earth was designed to dominate Britain in order to dominate not only Europe but also the rest of the world, the horrid vision was no mere figment of a heated British imagination, for Germans themselves were then writing and talking of risking their own downfall by striking to achieve this very end.

As the competition in naval armaments continued, making each rival more fearful that the other was aiming at its destruction, the British put out feelers for an agreement to call the race off or even to halt it temporarily, but they only intensified it. The Germans misread the British anxiety as a sign of faltering, and refused to consider any terms short of a British desertion of the ententes with France and Russia. These negotiations, which began in 1909, came to a dead end early in 1912 when Lord Haldane, the German-educated British secretary for war, went to Berlin asking for a naval holiday in return for a pledge of nonaggression, and was confronted with a demand for a binding comitment to absolute neutrality if Germany should be "forced" into war. More than anything else, the German naval threat was convincing the government and the people of Britain that war was coming and that neutrality was impossible.

During the above negotiations, Europe was staggering from crisis to crisis. Britain had little to do with the first, which arose in the Balkans and coincided with the naval "scare." Back in 1878 the powers at the Berlin Congress had turned over Bosnia and Herzegovina to be administered by Austria, technically for Turkey, but had left their final disposition to be settled in the uncertain future. In 1908 Austria took it upon herself to settle the question by proclaiming the outright annexation of these provinces in order to kill a force that was pulling them away. This was their common nationalism with adjoining Serbia, which inspired that little kingdom's fond hope of acquiring them somehow and sometime. The sudden prospect of their being forever cut off enraged Serbia to the point of war. The issue hung on whether Serbia's big Slav brother would join in the fight against Austria, to whose support Germany would immediately come. Russia hesitated and Europe trembled. The crisis passed in 1909 when the czar's government bowed before an ultimatum from Berlin. This was the kaiser's last diplomatic triumph. His government might try to repeat it elsewhere, but could not in the Balkans because it had created a Russian resolve never again to submit to such a galling humiliation.

The next crisis, that of 1911, touched Britain more closely. France sent troops into Morocco to subdue some turbulent tribes, and Germany countered by dispatching a gunboat to Agadir, a closed Moroccan port on the Atlantic. The disintegration of the unruly sultanate was evidently at hand and partition imminent, which meant a new international agreement to replace that of 1906; and there was talk of a division of the territory between France, Spain, and Germany behind the backs of the other powers represented at the Algeciras Conference, including Britain. All this, particularly the possibility of a German naval base at Agadir, alarmed London. The British government declared it must have a voice in any new settlement; the German government replied with an ominous silence; and the tension mounted when Lloyd George, whose reputation as a leader of the peace party lent grave force to his words, delivered his startling Mansion House speech, in which he said that peace would be intolerable for Britain if the price was her exclusion from the regulation of affairs involving her vital interests. It was 1905 over again, now aggravated by the grimmer nature of the Anglo-German naval race. The Agadir crisis began to recede when Germany announced that she sought compensation outside Morocco; and an agreement was reached whereby Germany got a fat slice of the French Congo, and Morocco was divided into the international zone of Tangier, lying opposite Gibraltar, the Spanish protectorate, and the much larger French protectorate.

Europe recovered its breath but not its equipoise. The atmosphere of crisis had become a chronic condition that almost any incident might cause to flare up in a general war. Italy, though still hating France for the latter's seizure of Tunis in 1881, had since become a doubtful member of the Triple Alliance, her maritime exposure having forced her to serve notice on Berlin that she would not be drawn into war against Britain. In 1911 she went to war on her own account against Turkey, her understudy in that alliance, weakening the alliance still further and starting repercussions that led to the explosion of 1914.

The Tripolitan War was too good an opportunity for Balkan states to miss, and with the aid of Russian agents they formed a league that fell upon hard-pressed Turkey in 1912, conquering almost to the gates of Constantinople. It was a glorious victory for the Slavs. As it threatened to embroil Europe, Grey gathered a conference of the powers in London to impose a Balkan settlement. It failed, and the spring of 1913 saw the victors' quarrels over the spoils bring on the Second Balkan War, in which a new league that included Turkey closed in on Bulgaria and dictated a peace that left Balkan tempers boiling. The two Balkan wars were tantamount to a triumph for Russia and a defeat for Austria, qualified by the fact that Bulgaria, thirsting for revenge, was now ready to play Austria's game against Serbia, which was to crush that rising kingdom.

Meanwhile the British government's apprehensions of a surprise attack by the whole German fleet were so roused by the Agadir crisis and the failure of Haldane's mission to Berlin that a far-reaching Anglo-French agreement was made in 1912 to guard against this danger more effectively. Both French and British naval forces had been divided between the Mediterranean and the Atlantic. Now they were concentrated, the French in the Mediterranean and the British in home waters. This redistribution of vital defense strength gave Britain more security than France, and the French government naturally wished to redress the balance by formally binding the British to defend the northern shores of France against the German navy; but neither the British government nor the British public was ready for that, and France had to trust that Britain would live up to the much-increased moral obligation in the hour of peril.

In June 1914 the widening of the Kiel Canal was completed. In the same month Franz Ferdinand was murdered. This crime, committed by two Bosnians with Serbian backing, decided the government in Vienna that the hour had come to strike down Serbia lest the growing disaffection of the large Slav population of the old Hapsburg Empire cause its collapse. As Russia could not afford to desert Serbia a second time, nor Germany to lose her only real ally, nor France to let hers down, the moral obligation of Britain became painfully urgent. The prime minister, the foreign secretary, and other members of the cabinet had no doubt of what the country should do in its own interest; but they could not convince those among their colleagues who held out for neutrality, nor could they swing the large section of public opinion that insisted on remaining aloof from the impending war. Grey's desperate effort to escape from the dilemma by calling a conference of the powers to mediate between Vienna and Belgrade was blocked by a Berlin veto. Finally the Germans did for Britain what she could not do for herself. Their invasion of Belgium blew away her indecision, uniting the government and the country behind the ultimatum of 4 August 1914.

Far from falling to pieces under the impact of the mother country's momentous decision, as many Germans had confidently hoped, the empire at once displayed a solidarity that astonished the world, including the British themselves. Ireland recoiled from the civil war into which it had been about to plunge, Unionists and Nationalists being agreed on the postponement of Home Rule for the duration of the infinitely greater war against Germany which, if lost, would leave them nothing to fight about. Redmond called upon his fellow countrymen to enlist in the British army, and they responded in great numbers. India was swept by a tremendous wave, not of revolution but of loyalty to Britain, which astounded and embarrassed the government in Delhi. With one accord the ruling princes offered their personal services and the resources of their states for the prosecution of the war; while throughout British India there was a spontaneous and universal outburst of enthusiasm for the British cause. Tagore's publication of a poem abhorring the German violation of Belgium, Gandhi's eagerness to raise an ambulance corps, and the unsolicited declaration of the native members of the central legislature that India should share the heavy financial burden that the war was imposing on Britain, were but three expressions of this enthusiasm.

Less surprising, though no less gratifying, was the reaction of the dominions and colonies, which was to leap into the war under the leadership of the mother country. At once Australia turned over to the Admiralty the control of her navy, consisting of three capital ships and several destroyers and submarines; New Zealand followed up her gift of a dreadnought to the Royal Navy by placing at the disposal of the Admiralty her only cruiser, which had been commissioned just a fortnight before. But the naval effort of these two dominions was soon overshadowed by their military effort; and the other members of the overseas empire, having no navy to contribute, did all their fighting on land. We shall therefore pass by the war at sea,[2] though it played a most vital part in the outcome, and concentrate upon the military operations in which overseas troops engaged. First, however, it may be well to glance at the fighting strength that the principal members of the overseas empire contributed.

New Zealand, which most closely resembled the mother country, sent some 112,000 troops to fight overseas, which was 10.2 per cent of her population, while the British Isles sent approximately 5,000,000, or 10.9 per cent. Australia, likewise wholly British but more dominated

---

[2] The Australian and New Zealand war vessels served in many waters and on many missions without seeing much action. The presence of the battle cruiser *Australia* was an important factor in persuading Admiral von Spee to leave the western Pacific, the cruiser *Sydney* disposed of the weaker *Emden* in the Indian Ocean, another Australian craft assisted in the destruction of the *Königsberg* when it was trapped in an East African river, and two Australian submarines were lost.

by Labor, dispatched soldiers who numbered 6.6 per cent of her population; Canada, one third of whose people were French, 5.7 per cent; and white South Africa, more than half Afrikander, 5.4 per cent.[3] These figures become more impressive when we consider how these forces were recruited. It was entirely by voluntary enlistment—so deep-seated was the British antimilitarist tradition—until 1916, when the British parliament imposed conscription in the United Kingdom exclusive of Ireland, and the new Zealand parliament also adopted it. The Canadian parliament did the same in 1917, and Newfoundland followed suit in the critical spring of 1918. But nowhere else in the whole empire was it introduced even when, as had happened before and was to be repeated in 1940–41, all Britain's allies faltered or fell.

India on the outbreak of war had a population of about 320,000,000, and a fully trained army of some 80,000 European officers and men and some 230,000 Indians, combatant and noncombatant. It was organized on the principle that all the senior officers and one third of the rank and file of each division were Europeans. In the previous year it had been officially determined that India "should provide for her own defense against local aggression, and, if necessary, for an attack on the Indian Empire by a great power until reinforcements can come from home," but was not to be called upon to provide troops "for wars outside the Indian sphere." Nevertheless, in the early months of the war the Indian government dispatched almost all its army to serve beyond the sea and received from England, by way of exchange, half-trained territorials (voluntary militia). During the course of hostilities India supplied about as many fighting men as the four dominions. In the colonies, the whites did not lag behind their fellows elsewhere under the Union Jack, and the same was true of the other races.

This remarkable rallying of the overseas empire, which is a revealing commentary on the character of the empire as a whole, sprang from a variety of motives. The simplest was the instinctive loyalty to Britain that her sons and daughters had carried with them when they migrated; but its strength was diluted in each successive generation born abroad of such ancestry, and it was limited to British stock. More widespread and probably more influential was a firm belief in the righteousness of the Allied cause and the necessity to defeat Germany lest that mighty

---

[3] The fatal casualties suffered by the above forces during the war amounted to 17.8 per cent of the Australian, 15.2 per cent of the New Zealand, 14.1 per cent of the United Kingdom, 12.4 per cent of the Canadian, and 9.6 per cent of the South African.

militarist state enthrone its spirit in the world. This reasoned loyalty to a peaceful civilization based on law and order and personal liberty exerted a great power over people throughout the empire, irrespective of their racial origin. The German invasion of innocent Belgium and the immediate reaction in Britain epitomized the issue dramatically, and the various members of the overseas empire recognized that their security was vitally dependent upon British victory in the titanic struggle. The Indian urge to aid Britain in the war may have been partly inspired by a nationalist desire to earn the reward of full self-government, but local nationalism contributed nothing to the strenuous war effort of the colonies and dominions. Though the large part played by the dominions won for them an elevated status that transformed the British Empire into the British Commonwealth, this result was not what they fought for. It came upon them as a surprise.

In only one part of the empire—South Africa—did the outbreak of war precipitate a rebellion. It was the work of a handful of Boers and was quickly crushed by other Boers, as we shall see in the next chapter. Elsewhere in the empire, when the war dragged on, there were local anti-British outbursts. Ireland was convulsed by an armed uprising, India was the scene of violent disturbances, in Canada the old feud between English and French flared into a new crisis over conscription, and even solidly-British Australia was sorely split on this issue, all of which we shall also examine after surveying the military activities of the empire in the various theaters of war.

Strategic necessity rather than territorial covetousness dictated the seizure of all German overseas possessions, and with one exception they fell an easy prey to local forces of neighboring British or other Allied territories. In addition to being bases for possible attacks on these neighbors, the German colonies were particularly dangerous in the opening months of the war because German cruisers were loose on the high seas and might appear anywhere, their bunkers replenished in German colonial ports and their movements guided by German colonial signal stations. The *Emden* and the *Königsberg* were somewhere in the Indian Ocean and, what was more serious, the German Pacific squadron, under Admiral von Spee, had vanished from Kiaochow in June.

Australia and New Zealand, being inclined to imperial ventures on their own account, needed little encouragement from London to seize the German colonies within their reach, which they were able to do with their own naval covering. On 30 August 1914 a New Zealand expedition occupied German Samoa with its powerful wireless station at Apia. Already von Spee had turned up in German New Guinea, and after a visit at its naval base, Rabaul,[4] had vanished again. On 9 September the Australians took Rabaul, and on the following day they seized Nauru, the only other German signal station in the South Pacific. Shortly afterward the German admiral looked in at Apia and, finding the New Zealanders too strong for any landing party he could send ashore, he vanished once more over the blue waters. As Japan snapped up Kiaochow and forestalled Australia by seizing the German islands north of the equator, including the powerful Yap station, von Spee had no bases left in the Pacific, and he crossed to South America in search of prey. Off the coast of Chili his squadron destroyed a weaker British one, but on entering the South Atlantic was itself destroyed by a stronger one in the Falkland Islands Battle of 8 December 1914. Then the seas were clear of German raiders until the submarines began to prowl; for the Australian cruiser *Sydney* had disposed of the *Emden* in November at the Cocos Islands in the Indian Ocean and the *Königsberg* had been blockaded in October in the mouth of a German East African river,[5] where the crew took to land fighting under a brilliant general.

Of the four German colonies in Africa, the first to fall was Togoland. It contained the central wireless station for communication between Germany and all four colonies, and was seized in August 1914 by a Gold Coast force of natives commanded by British officers. It was not so easy to take the Cameroons, some six hundred miles to the east. This territory was much larger, and out of its warlike tribes the Germans had fashioned a rather formidable fighting body of Askaris. The capital, by the seacoast, fell in September 1914 to British-African and French-African troops; but the Germans and their native levies held out in the interior until February 1916.

The conquest of German Southwest Africa was reluctantly undertaken by the adjoining dominion. Though the South African act of 1912 created a defense force and provided that this could be used "anywhere in South Africa within or outside the Union," the government of the Union had not the slightest intention of employing it to attack the Germans next door until prompted to do so by London. Indeed, Botha hoped when war came that his newly united country, with its doubtful factor of Afrikander nationalism, would not be called upon

---

[4] The Bismarck Archipelago was part of the German protectorate of New Guinea. The German portion of the island of New Guinea was named Kaiser Wilhelm's Land.

[5] There units of the British and Australian navies destroyed it in July 1915.

to do more than defend itself by land—an obligation which he assumed at once by offering to release for duty elsewhere the garrison of 7,000 imperial regulars whose retention in South Africa he had previously favored. The British government gladly accepted Botha's offer. At the same time it requested his government to seize the two ports and destroy the three long-distance wireless stations of German Southwest Africa, since that colony constituted a threat not only to the Union but also to the British line of communications round the Cape when the Mediterranean route to the Far East might be closed by the war. Botha recognized the reasonableness of the request. The job had to be done, it could be most easily directed from the Union, and it was in the interest of the Union to do it with its own forces rather than leave it for imperial troops. Such considerations moved him to run the risk, which he of all men could best gauge, of dividing his own country. His decision touched off the rebellion, which delayed the invasion of German Southwest Africa. There all resistance ended in July 1915, when several thousand armed Germans surrendered to the forces of the Union led by Botha in person.

The war in German East Africa (now Tanganyika) is a very different story, the one heroic chapter in German colonial history. When hostilities began, this largest and richest of the German colonies possessed a military strength that was much more than a match for all the puny forces in the contiguous British territories, north, west, and south. General von Lettow-Vörbeck, a soldier of genius, had an army of 3,000 Europeans and 11,000 Askaris, which was soon reinforced by the men and light armament of the *Königsberg*. Meanwhile he drove into British East Africa (now Kenya), where he gained a position from which he threatened the railway from the port of Mombassa to Nairobi and was not driven out until 1916. Before he could descend upon the port, the arrival of a brigade from India made it secure, but it was not until the end of 1915 that the British were able to take the initiative against him, and some very hard fighting followed. The chief burden of the campaign, in which levies from the surrounding British, Belgian, and Portuguese colonies and more Indian troops participated, was borne by a strong contingent from the Union of South Africa. The last was sent at the request of London, as was also the commander in chief, General Smuts. He arrived in February 1916 and enhanced his military reputation by the masterly way in which he directed operations. When he was recalled in January 1917 to represent his government at the Imperial Conference, he had conquered all the best parts of the country. Yet neither he nor his successor in the command, another Afrikander, could catch the resourceful German general who, though having lost most of his men, was still fighting when the war ended in Europe. From first to last von Lettow-Vörbeck had managed to engage some 130,000 Allied troops, which meant that he had effected a successful strategic diversion of no mean proportions.

The war in the Near East was of very much greater magnitude and consequence than all the operations against the German colonies. By openly joining the side of Germany in the autumn of 1914, Turkey posed grave problems for the Allies, particularly the British. The old Ottoman Empire was still a major power, and it was strategically located to deliver crippling blows in several quarters; for it then extended from the Balkans and the Mediterranean to Persia and the Persian Gulf, and included the whole of the Arabian peninsula except the little British protectorates of Koweit, Bahrein, and Trucial Oman on the eastern fringe and Aden on the southern tip.

The control of the Dardanelles Strait became of supreme importance in the autumn of 1914. The huge conflict in Europe had reached a deadlock on the Western Front and was about to do the same on the Eastern Front, where a shortage of munitions was robbing the Russians of their great numerical advantage and their "steam roller" was grinding to a halt. The Western Allies had the industrial capacity that Russia lacked to supply her millions of soldiers, but the Turkish entry into the war bolted the door against delivery. Hence the Allied attempt to break through the Strait, the only way to save Russia from progressive military paralysis and to prevent Germany from throwing her whole weight against the Western Front.

The Suez Canal was another vital spot, and the British were also vulnerable in the Persian Gulf. For the security of the Canal, Britain had leased Cyprus from Turkey and was still occupying Egypt, which likewise was formally a part of the new enemy empire. She promptly rectified her anomalous position in both, by annexing the island and declaring a protectorate over the land of the Pharaohs; but paper instruments could not roll back the danger of an attack upon the Canal by the Turks who, though their border was a hundred miles away, quickly overran the intervening Sinai Peninsula. The British had to strengthen their forces in Egypt to guard their lifeline to the east.

The British interest in the Persian Gulf was originally the protection of India, for which purpose Britain had consistently kept other powers from gaining a foothold there—a policy somewhat comparable to that of the Monroe Doctrine. Moslem Turkey, backed by Germany, was more capable than Russia had ever been of striking at India through Moslem Persia and Afghanistan. In addition to the defense of India. Britain had a new and no less lively interest in the region of the Gulf, for Britain was beginning—in Persia—to be a large oil producer. The Royal Navy was being converted from coal, and to ensure a sufficient supply of the new fuel the government had bought, in May 1914, a controlling interest in the Anglo-Persian Oil Company, whose Abadan refinery was just across the river Shatt-el-Arab from Turkish territory. When war with Turkey was imminent, an Indian contingent was sent to secure the company's installations against the danger of an enemy attack. Here, as elsewhere in the fight against the Turk, troops from members of the British Empire lying east of the Suez were to play a leading part.

The assault on the Dardanelles, if successful, would have done much more than relieve Russia. It would have knocked Turkey out of the war because all Turkish munition production was concentrated in Constantinople. It was by far the bloodiest campaign of any in the Near East during the whole war. The attack on the Strait was first conceived as a naval operation, which began in February 1915 and failed miserably in March, forcing a decision to renew it as a sea-borne land operation with as many troops as could be spared from operations elsewhere. Two divisions of the Australian and New Zealand Army Corps (the Anzacs) were available, but only three others—two British and one French—were found for the new attempt in April, so imperious was the cry for Allied reinforcements on the Western Front. It was a tragedy of too little and too late. When the attackers landed on the Gallipoli peninsula, the Turks had six divisions on the heights above; and when the British sent in more divisions, the enemy was proportionately strengthened. In the autumn the British government abandoned as hopeless a venture that had cost 10,000 Anzac and 20,000 other lives. The surviving Anzacs rejoined their fellows in Egypt, where their corps was reinforced from home and reformed as two army corps. These, minus some mounted units retained for nearer service, were sent to the Western Front in the spring and summer of 1916, and there they fought through the rest of the war.

Turkey was to be taken not by a lunge at the throat but from the rear, and too late to save Russia from capitulation. The first offensive operation against the rear, the Mesopotamia campaign of 1915, began gloriously and ended disastrously. It grew out of the defensive move

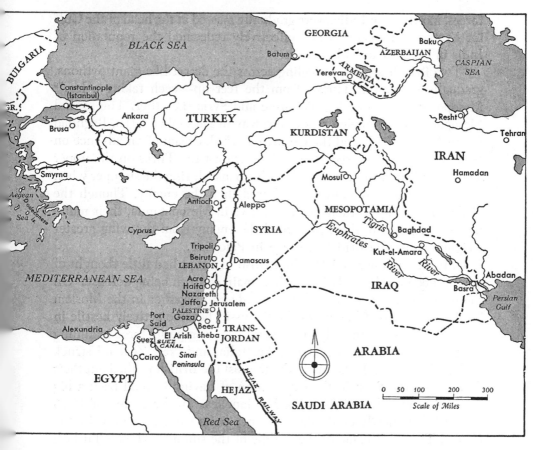

The Near East

at the head of the Persian Gulf, and was fed by a desire to offset the Dardanelles failure. In the late summer of 1915, after occupying Basra at the junction of the Tigris and the Euphrates, advancing Indian forces routed the Turks near Kut-el-Amara, two hundred miles up the Tigris, and this victory fired hopes of winning another higher up, at Baghdad. But the tide of war turned outside that ancient city and flowed back to Kut, where the Turks besieged what was left of the overbold expedition. It held out for five months while vain attempts were made to send relief. At the end of April 1916 the invested garrison of 2,000 British and 6,000 Indians surrendered. Other losses of this campaign brought the total to nearly 40,000. It was a heartbreak to India, whose military machinery had come perilously near a breakdown. But the defects thus disclosed were remedied; and much larger forces, mostly from India, were gradually massed at the head of the Gulf for another campaign, which effectively redeemed the reputation of India in her own and others' eyes.

"Two British armies, wriggling across the desert like giant pythons, gradually swallowed Turkey from the feet up—each taking a leg."[6] Mesopotamia was one leg, Palestine and Syria the other. The second Mesopotamian campaign was under way in December 1916, Baghdad fell in March 1917, and the German-Turkish dream of an advance on India was then shattered. Operations against the Turks on the upper Tigris and Euphrates continued, with a pause during the summer when the pitiless sun was more to be feared than the enemy. Though the victors had achieved their main objective in Mesopotamia, their maintenance of pressure there prevented the enemy from throwing greater weight against the British advance in Palestine.

Until the summer of 1916 the British in Egypt had little thought of an advance into the Holy Land, their main concern being defense. On the west the desert tribes, which were bound together in the Moslem brotherhood or sect known as the Senussi,[7] became actively hostile in November 1915. But early in the new year a composite force including troops from India, South Africa, Australia, and New Zealand struck back and defeated the Senussi. On the east the British pushed out their defenses of the Suez in the expectation of having to hold back a big Turkish army released from the Dardanelles. In the spring of 1916 some of their newly established advance posts were wiped out by the enemy. The crisis came in the middle of the summer when a Turkish force, strengthened by German units and led by a resolute German general, made a last desperate effort to gain the Canal and was compelled to withdraw, thanks largely to the mounted Anzacs.

In the ensuing campaign around the eastern end of the Mediterranean, this division of dominion cavalry continued to play a prominent part to the very last, and Indian units distinguished themselves too. Just before Christmas 1916 the British army leaped to El Arish, and three weeks later it drove the foe from the rest of northern Sinai. But Gaza, the fortress guarding the gateway of Palestine, was a harder nut to crack; and it defied capture until November 1917. The invasion and conquest of southern Palestine, which followed, was greatly assisted

---

[6] Liddell Hart, *The War in Outline*, p. 134.

[7] So called after their founder, the shiek who initiated the religious revival referred to on p. 672.

by the Arab revolt against Ottoman rule. This revolt, stimulated by the mysterious T. E. Lawrence, engaged more Turkish troops in guarding the long line of the Hejaz railway and territory south of it than did the defense of Palestine. There, however, the Turkish resistance stiffened as the British advanced; and during the rest of the winter of 1917– 18, the British offensive was almost entirely confined to probing operations. These were to have been followed by a vigorous drive in the spring of 1918, but the Germans then decreed otherwise by making a frantic effort to smash the British armies on the Western Front in Europe.

This crisis in the main theater of the war wrought a rapid transformation in the character of the British army in Palestine, which until then was chiefly composed of units formed in the United Kingdom. Most of these were at once withdrawn to France, and Indian units were substituted, which remade this army into one whose cavalry was one third and infantry two thirds Indian. Its size remained about the same, but its striking power took months to recover, and meanwhile hostilities on the Palestine front seemed to have sunk into a dull stalemate. The appearance was deceptive.

The last and most brilliant phase of the campaign opened on 19 September 1918 with a terrific assault that almost immediately broke through the enemy entrenchments, and from that moment the largely Indianized army swept on from victory to victory. Out of northern Palestine and on through Syria, the thoroughly disorganized Turks were chased, while those who could not escape surrendered in droves. The bag of prisoners swelled to 75,000 before Turkey capitulated on the last day of October. The Mesopotamian army was then only a dozen miles from Mosul. India had good reason to be proud of her martial achievement in the Near East.

On the Western Front, which absorbed by far the greatest military effort of the mother country, all parts of the empire were represented. The first troops from overseas to join the British forces facing the Germans were two infantry and two cavalry divisions of the Indian Army. They arrived in the autumn of 1914 and constituted one of the five British army corps then in France and Flanders. This reinforcement was proportionately the largest there received by the British from beyond the sea during the whole course of the conflict, and it came in the nick of time. The mother country had yet to raise and train the big armies that she was to pour across the Channel, and until the spring of 1915, when her sons who had enlisted in the first few weeks of the

The Western Front in World War I

war were ready to take the field, the small size of her professional army limited her expeditionary force to about 150,000 men. In October 1914 the Germans, with superior numbers, launched a fierce attack on the British line with the object of breaking through to the Channel ports and cutting Britain off from France. That catastrophe was not to occur until 1940, but it took many days of furious fighting to prevent the Germans from breaking through at this time. This first battle of Ypres cost the Indians 7,000 casualties and their British comrades 33,000.[8]

---

[8] These included 3,000 suffered by the British units of the Indian corps.

The number of British troops on French and Flemish soil was more than doubled by March 1915, when part of their line again became heavily engaged. The additions comprised regulars recalled from tropical stations, new soldiers enlisted at home, and the first Canadian division, which had spent the winter training in England. In the second Battle of Ypres, April 1915, the Canadians met the first gas attack in the history of warfare. Most of it fell on a French African division, quickly eating a hole four miles wide in the Allied front, right beside the Canadian division. In the days that followed, marked by more use of the horrible new weapon, the Canadians were nearly surrounded but they would not yield. By their firmness they prevented a disastrous breakthrough. Supports, including one of the Indian divisions, were rushed to the broken line, and contact with the French was re-established. This engagement cost many Canadian battalions more than half their men. In May, as part of a British offensive designed to aid the French farther south and to seize a commanding ridge a few miles south of Ypres, the Indians[9] and the Canadians again went into action. Both lost heavily and the Germans kept the ridge.

Here it may be well to observe an exasperating feature of the fighting on the Western Front. The novel combination of machine guns, barbed wire, and trenches gave the defensive such an enormous advantage over the offensive that the initial war of movement early became a war of stalemate, and the many attempts of each side to break the deadlock here and there along the line assumed the character of mass suicide. Air power was still in its infancy, and not until toward the end of the struggle did the tank, invented and developed by the British, herald a return to a war of movement.

By the beginning of 1916 the British had lost more than half a million men on the Western Front; yet their strength there had risen to a million, and from the hard-pressed French they had taken over more of the line. Their portion now extended from Ypres down to the Somme, and they had thirty-eight divisions to hold it. During the next six months these were increased to fifty-seven. Among the reinforcements was a South African brigade of four battalions, which had fought in Egypt and now formed part of a Scottish division that moved to the

---

[9] In the autumn the two Indian infantry divisions were transferred to Mesopotamia, where they could be more profitably employed and more easily kept up to strength by drafts from their homeland. The two cavalry divisions were retained in France until early in 1918 without getting much chance of serving as cavalry during the long and exhausting stalemate of trench warfare.

Somme in June for the opening of the greatest battle that the war had
yet seen. There, too, a company from Rhodesia, a battalion from Newfoundland, and the divisions from Canada, Australia, and New Zealand were to suffer terrific casualties along with their more numerous
comrades from the British Isles.

The Battle of the Somme was planned as a joint effort with the
French; it began according to schedule on 1 July 1916, with a tremendous artillery bombardment calculated to blast a way for masses of
infantry to break through on a twenty-five mile front and roll up the
German line. But the battle did not proceed according to the Allied
plan; for in this area the Germans had likewise massed men and guns,
and in addition they had developed marvelously strong field fortifications. The British right and the neighboring French pushed the enemy
back, but the British left was fought to a standstill. On one day alone
the British lost 60,000 men, their heaviest day's toll in the whole war.
The final attack, which occurred in November, was smothered in mud.
All in all, this four months' grim battle cost the various British forces a
total of 420,000 casualties, the French 194,000, and the Germans
440,000.

To understand the major British fighting on the Western Front in
1917, we should first glance at some broad features of the background.
In February Germany launched her unrestricted submarine campaign,
calculating that it would knock Britain out of the war before it could
bring the United States in. It nearly succeeded. On 9 April, three days
after the American entry, Admiral Jellicoe showed Admiral Sims the
list of sinkings and told him, "It is impossible for us to go on with the war
if losses like this continue." During that month the Allies lost nearly a
million tons of shipping. Meanwhile the Germans had improved their
military position by a skillful retirement to the much shorter and
stronger Hindenburg Line, and they planned to sit tight on the Western
Front while waiting for the outcome of the submarine warfare. April
also saw a terrifying tragedy on the French front in Champaigne, where
three whole armies were hurled and wrecked against the rocklike
German defenses. The shock to French morale started a mutiny that
spread to sixteen army corps and threatened a French military collapse.
On the other side of Europe, revolution toppled the czar from his
throne in March, and Russia was then on the way down and out. This
meant that large German forces would soon be freed from the Eastern
Front to be thrown into the Western Front, turning the numerical
balance against the combined British and French before the armies

that the United States had yet to raise and train could come to the rescue—in the summer of the following year.

Early in 1917 the British took over still more of the line on their south, so that the French could concentrate their strength for the mighty assault with which they hoped to win the war but nearly lost it; and to aid them further, the British agreed to deliver a smart blow in the Arras sector a week before the French were to strike. The British front of attack was a dozen miles long; and opposite the left of it was a key German position, Vimy Ridge, which had been transformed into a veritable fortress. The task of taking it was assigned to the Canadian Corps and executed so brilliantly, on the opening day, that when peace came their government crowned the commanding site with the principal Canadian war memorial. The seizure of Vimy gave the British a firm pivot on which they vainly tried to swing. The operation soon ran into such stiff resistance that the cost began to outweigh the local gain; but the French debacle decided the British to keep on hammering until May, by which time their whole advance had averaged no more than three miles.

For the rest of the year on the Western Front, the British fought practically alone against great odds. They were anxious to divert the attention of the enemy from the stricken French, and to make the most of the short time that Germany would still have to fight on two fronts. A further reason and a particular objective were supplied by the Admiralty. Jellicoe told the war cabinet that unless the army captured the submarine nests on the Belgian coast he thought it "improbable that we could go on with the war next year for lack of shipping."

The main effort was therefore to drive in a northeasterly direction from the left end of the British line at Ypres, but that base had first to be made more secure by clearing the Germans off a ridge that overlooked the town from the south. The ridge area was too strong to be taken by ordinary assault, and since 1914 it had seen no serious fighting; but underground an elaborate offensive had been proceeding for a year and a half. In the early dawn of 7 June 1917, along a front of about ten miles, a score of huge mines charged with a million pounds of high explosive blew up under the Germans, and, while the debris still hung in the air, three British army corps began to storm the heights. They were in firm possession of them by nightfall. A few days of stiff fighting followed, during which the Germans were pushed back until the line immediately south of the Ypres salient was straightened out. Of the various divisions that fought in this battle, two were Australian, one New Zealand, and two Irish—one from Ulster and the other from Southern Ireland.

The main offensive planned by the British high command began on 31 July after a fortnight's intense bombardment that only partly destroyed the enemy's field defenses and completed the ruin, already wrought by the guns on both sides, of the drainage system that was essential in that low-lying part of the country. Then the heavens opened and the whole battle area became an almost impassible quagmire. This third Battle of Ypres was a soldier's nightmare. It lasted until mid-November, and the farthest point to which the British penetrated was only seven miles from Ypres. It was high time that their commander in chief called off the offensive for which they had so little to show. They had paid a staggering price for it—a total loss of some 400,000 men.

The Allies were weaker and the Germans stronger on the Western Front at the end of 1917 than in the beginning of that year, and the downfall of Russia was swinging the military balance strongly in favor of the Germans. But other factors were operating against them. Though their submarines were taking a heavy toll of Allied shipping, it was much lighter than in the spring. The hunters were being hunted more effectively, and their prey guarded more carefully. The United States Navy had joined in the chase, the British had evolved the supersonic device for spotting submerged marauders, and ocean freighters had been herded in big convoys escorted by fighting ships. The Germans saw that they could no longer depend on the submarines to win the war, and also that they would lose it unless they won it quickly on the Western Front. The American entry had plugged the holes in the Allied blockade, which was at last beginning to strangle them, and within a very few months American manpower pouring into the battleline would decisively reverse the military balance. The German high command calculated that they could deliver victory over the combined British and French armies at a cost of one and a half million men, and their government agreed that it would be worth the price. German hopes soared high.

The Allies knew that heavy blows would fall upon them in the spring of 1918, but they were not unduly alarmed. They dug themselves in to wait on the defensive till the Americans arrived in the line; and they were confident that they could hold it against the Germans, who would then take their turn in paying the extravagant price of an offensive.

The first blow, which came on 21 March, shattered the Allied confidence. The British junction with the French had been shifted down to the Oise, and from there northward the whole British right for fifty miles caved under the weight of the enemy onslaught. This immediately swallowed a third of the British infantry on that part of the front, and in seven days it penetrated forty miles through open country to within ten miles of Amiens, a strategic communications center. There was very little left of the South African brigade when it was withdrawn at the end of the seventh day; but French and British reinforcements, including the Australian and New Zealand divisions and a Canadian machine gun brigade, had been thrown into the battle; and though it was not yet over, the enemy drive gained little more ground in this area. Meanwhile the Germans had given the Allies such a scare, by nearly tearing their armies apart, that the British and French governments at last established a unified command under Marshal Foch.

The second blow, launched on 9 April, broke through the British line some miles south of Ypres and threatened to undermine the entire British position. This crisis lasted for about ten days and left a bulge ten miles deep in the British line. Some of the reinforcements that rushed to the scene were got by sacrificing the precious Ypres salient. Among the others was the First Australian Division, called up from the Amiens sector where the fighting was still heavy. The South Africans were again in the battle from the beginning, their ranks refilled from their English base; and this time they were so cut up that for a while they ceased to be a brigade.

The third and most staggering blow began on 27 May. It struck the French on the heights north of the Aisne, and in three days it hurled them back thirty miles to the Marne, endangering Paris. No dominion troops were involved, but several British divisions were fighting beside the French, and then one of the double-sized American divisions came into action at Chateau Thierry. There the German advance was halted early in June, and ten days later the German pounding was suspended in preparation for another blow on a grand scale.

The Germans did not know that they had just lost their race against time. In these three blows they had thrown away their superior strength, and they could not recover it because their whole annual recruitment had been used up and it was less than the number of American troops that were landing every few weeks. Yet such was their scorn for Americans as fighters that they were still confident of victory in mid-July when they struck again on the Marne. Nine American divisions and a British army corps helped the French to strike back and retake some of the lost ground.

This thrust and counterthrust, which occupied only a few days, marked the great turn. The enemy did not see it, and Foch himself was not sure of it. To the premier of France he wrote: "The decisive year of the conflict will be 1919." Nevertheless, he had no thought of resting on the defensive while gathering strength for the final victory. He directed the three national commanders in chief to beat a tattoo along the German line so that the enemy would have no chance to regain the initiative. Foch's plan worked better than he expected.

This series of local surprise attacks with limited objectives began on 8 August, when the British struck to disengage Amiens. The Canadian corps, having been spared during the spring fighting, was chosen as the spearhead of the blow, and it was ably supported by the Australian corps. The assault achieved more than its purpose. It caused the first crack in the enemy's morale, already strained to the breaking point, and the shock soon reached up to the high command. Long afterward Ludendorff delivered his verdict: "August 8th was the black day of the German army in the history of the war. . . . It put the decline of our fighting power beyond all doubt." His first reaction was to declare for peace negotiations before things grew worse. Then he wavered between hope and despair. Some advisers urged him to strengthen his position by repeating the maneuver of a year and a half before; and as the menacing attacks continued he ordered a general withdrawal to the old Hindenburg Line.

Unlike the retirement in the beginning of 1917, which was executed with little interference by the Allies, this one was carried out under constant pressure. Troops of all the dominions were engaged in the fighting advance. The British in front of Arras, being close to the northern hinge of the Hindenburg Line, were most anxious to break it and the Germans to preserve it. There the fighting was intense, and there the Canadian corps was again used as a spearhead. Striking in the direction of Cambrai, it pierced twelve miles through strong defenses before it was stopped at the Canal du Nord early in September, when the Germans were completing their withdrawal to a stronger position. From the first beat of the tattoo to the last in mid-September,[10]

---

[10] By the American army on the St. Mihiel salient.

the French and the Americans together collected about 40,000 prisoners, while the British bag amounted to more than 70,000.

The Germans were back where they had started on 21 March, and meanwhile they had paid in casualties the full price for which their high command had promised to deliver victory. Now all they could hope for was to keep down the price of surrender by making a firm last stand. But Foch had revised his timetable, the success of the alternate attacks having fired him with the idea that he could win the war in 1918, and he was preparing to launch his grand offensive. His plan called for simultaneous converging attacks all along the great salient of the German front from Verdun to Ypres.

The main British task in this crushing operation was to smash the Hindenburg Line from St. Quentin northward, where the enemy was most strongly massed and entrenched. Accordingly on 27 September the Canadian corps jumped across the Canal du Nord on a narrow front, and the breach thus made was widened on both sides as more troops poured through and fanned out. By the next evening, when the attackers pushed to the outskirts of Cambrai, they had passed the northern end of the Hindenburg Line. Meanwhile a terrific bombardment was softening that line for a frontal assault, which was now released. There the forces of the other dominions went into action, the Australians in company with two American divisions lent to the British army for the occasion. By 5 October, when the sadly reduced Australian infantry was withdrawn from the fighting,[11] the British had driven right through to open country.

This achievement, together with the hammering on other parts of the enemy front, necessitated a general German retreat while negotiations for an armistice, which had just begun, proceeded. Many enemy soldiers were now surrendering, but not the machine gunners, who took a heavy toll of the advancing armies. There was still a lot of stiff fighting, though no set battles, and the dominion soldiers had their share of it until hostilities were ended by the Armistice on 11 November.

---

[11] "It had been attacking continuously for two months, until some of its battalions were now less than one company strong." Sir Charles Lucas, *The Empire at War*, III, p. 184.

CHAPTER XXXV

Nationalism in the Dominions, Ireland, and India under the Impact of the War

ONE OF THE MOST striking effects of the war was the intensification and spread of nationalism in the modern world—throughout western civilization and in other civilizations as well, among peoples who were self-governing and those who were not. In the British Empire it brought profound changes. Not the least of these was the emergence of the British Commonwealth, the subject of the next chapter, which can be better understood after an examination of nationalism, and its immediate effects, in the principal parts of the overseas empire under the impact of the war.

The revolt in South Africa, which the outbreak of the war precipitated, was inspired by Afrikander nationalism. It lasted for three months and might have blazed into a real civil war if it had not been ably handled. The rising began early in October 1914 when the Union was mustering its forces for the conquest of German Southwest Africa, which project Botha had carried in his parliament against the stout opposition of Hertzog and his Nationalist Party. They objected on principle to participation in Britain's wars, and they cherished the tradition dating from Kruger's day that Germany was the friend of the Boers. Hertzog, however, took no part in the rebellion. That was the work of a small minority of Boer military leaders who, thirsting for revenge on the British and convinced by the initial triumphs of the German juggernaut in Europe that the downfall of Britain was imminent, thought that at last their country could and, if they gave it a push, would easily break away from the empire and declare itself an independent Afrikander republic. They reckoned without Botha.

He would never repay with such treachery the trust that Britain had reposed in his people by giving them self-government shortly after she had conquered them; he could never countenance a move that would ruin South Africa by rekindling the civil war between its two white races; and he possessed the confidence of both races to a much greater degree than any other man. With characteristic statesmanship, he held back his levies of British extraction and used Afrikander troops to defeat the rebels with as little bloodshed as possible, so that the actual fighting assumed the appearance of a family quarrel; to prevent the bitterness of the conflict from eating into the country, he saw to it that the summary courts-martial, which tried the prisoners, tempered justice with healing mercy. Only one man was executed, a military officer who had revolted without taking the precaution of first resigning his commission. The rank and file were sent home, their sentences merely disqualifying them from the public service for ten years. In addition to this punishment, some of the leaders suffered fines and imprisonment for short periods. Never has armed rebellion been treated with greater clemency.

Though Hertzog did not support the revolt, neither did he condemn it. Sympathy for the rebels was widespread among Afrikanders, and it strengthened the political position of the Nationalists. In the election of October 1915 they doubled their representation in the House. Botha's South African Party still held a much larger number of seats, but no longer a majority. The government therefore became dependent upon the Unionists, who were wholly British. This in turn lent color to the Nationalist charge that Botha and Smuts had sold out to the British, which made it more difficult for these leaders to hold some of their Afrikander following.

Throughout the war the Nationalists fought South African participation in it as a betrayal of the country, and in 1917 they began openly to preach republicanism. Lloyd George's "rights of small nations" and President Wilson's "self-determination of peoples" were sweet music in their ears; they gleefully echoed the strident notes that Bourassa was raising in Canada; and the discord in South Africa grew. Botha's position was so delicate that he deemed it wiser to remain at home than to attend the Imperial Conference during the war; and when some of the British element suggested conscription, he immediately silenced such talk by declaring that he would have to recall the South African brigade from Europe to deal with the civil war it would produce. When the fighting in Europe ceased, Hertzog led a deputation to demand from the peace conference a recognition of independence for the whole Union or, if that was impossible, for the two former republics. Though the mission was foredoomed to failure in Paris, it succeeded at home in advertising the republican cause. Thus the war, coming so soon after the political unification of the country, revived and intensified Afrikander nationalism just when it seemed to be fading into a larger South African nationalism that would draw the two white races together.

Canadian national unity was also severely strained by the war, but not to the same degree as South African. In the senior dominion the French were scarcely half as numerous as the English-speaking population; the relations between them had never been poisoned by civil war; they had been cooperating in the business of self-government for two generations; and because they lived in the shadow of a great neighbor, their instinct of self-preservation had repeatedly pulled them together when they engaged in a family quarrel. In further contrast to South Africa, the call of the blood in French Canada was to Britain's closest ally, not to a neutral state like Holland or to Britain's archenemy. The initial reaction of Canada to the war betrayed no sign of racial cleavage. Even Bourassa proclaimed it a national duty to back Britain and France and applauded the dispatch of Canadian troops to Europe. But as the struggle wore on the conscription issue arose and it tore the two races apart.

French Canada fell behind English Canada in supplying recruits. French Canadians married much younger and had children as soon as possible, so that their young men were more bound by home ties and domestic responsibilities than other Canadians. French Canada was also much more cut off from the outside world. In 1914 English Canada contained a large number of people who had been born in the British Isles and relatively few who were removed from the mother country by more than a generation or two, whereas almost every French Canadian had to go back nearly two centuries and a half to find an ancestor who lived on the other side of the Atlantic. Moreover, two special circumstances of the time—one in France and the other in Ottawa—discouraged them from joining the colors. The strife between church and state in France, culminating in the separation of 1905, had sent refugee priests to Canada. From them and from their own clergy the French Canadians had been hearing bitter denunciations of the persecuting French Republic, and devout French Canadians were inclined to view Germany's attack as a judgment of God upon the irreligious and wicked French in Europe. At the same time, it was highly unfortunate that the cabinet minister responsible for raising and training the Canadian forces was an outstanding leader of the Orange

Order, which was notoriously hostile to Roman Catholicism and French Canada. In English Canada there was little understanding of these reasons and there was much open resentment against French Canada for not doing its duty, which of course angered French Canada, where Bourassa and his Nationalists revived their agitation against participation in Britain's wars.

Things came to a head in 1917, when Canadians were falling in France much faster than they were being recruited at home where, as we shall see, essential war production competed with the army for the manpower of the country as in no other dominion. Vehement cries for conscription were rising in English Canada, and against it in French Canada. When the United States entered the war and adopted the draft, Sir Robert Borden and his cabinet decided that conscription was necessary in order to keep faith with "the boys at the front" and to save Canada's honor. He was convinced, however, that a government composed of only one party should not force such an extreme measure upon the country, and he invited Laurier to join in forming a coalition government in which both parties would be equally represented. English Canada blindly believed that if the Liberal chieftain, the greatest French Canadian, would only take this step he would draw his people after him and unite the nation in a greater war effort. But Laurier knew his own people better and he was convinced that acceptance, by committing him to conscription, would destroy his influence over them and deliver them into the arms of Bourassa, which would surely wreck the country. He preferred to wreck his party, which in any event was past saving because it was hopelessly split between conscriptionists and anticonscriptionists. When he rejected the offer, most of the prominent English-speaking Liberals broke away from him and his French following.

The Conservative premier, thus assured of considerable Liberal support, introduced his conscription bill and proceeded to negotiate the formation of a coalition ministry. The bill was carried against the vote of almost every French Canadian in parliament, and the only French Canadians in the new bipartisan cabinet were two Conservatives whom most French Canadians regarded as traitors to their race. The general election that followed in December was perhaps the bitterest in the history of the dominion. Conscription was the main issue and it pitted race against race. It fused French Canada under Laurier into such a solid block as had not been seen since the first half of the previous century, and it left him with only a corporal's guard of

English-speaking followers in the House. After a few little riots, the
French submitted to conscription, but they hated it because it meant
coercion by the majority race. They were crushed under the steam
roller of English Canada, and they had horrid visions of being crushed
again in the dark uncertain future.

Over against this tragedy wrought by the war, we find in Canada
another and more permanent effect, one that stirred its people irrespective of race and tended to unite them. The nation rapidly matured
through being plunged into the war, much as a youth suddenly becomes
a man when he is thrust out into the world to fend for himself.
Canadians as a whole had felt little responsibility except for the internal development of their own country until the shock of 1914 turned
them face about. In bearing the new responsibility that they then
shouldered, they discovered their strength and were rather surprised
to find that they were taking their place as one of the nations of the
earth. Indeed, it was a source of secret pride that they sent their sons
away to fight while Americans stayed at home. This quickened the
anti-American feeling that has been such a strong stimulus to Canadian
nationalism; and though the consequent tension was relieved when the
United States at last entered the struggle, Canadians resented the subsequent boast of thoughtless Americans that they had "won the war."
Nor could Canadians forget that, though their country had only one
twelfth the population of the United States, more Canadians than
Americans were killed in action and nearly as many died of wounds.

The new national consciousness of Canada was also fed by a material
development that had no parallel elsewhere in the overseas empire. It
leaped ahead at a faster pace than the economy of the United States,
the only other country that was greatly enriched by the war. Soaring
prices swelled the production of food for export. The Prairie Provinces
doubled their wheat acreage and increased their livestock herds by
about a third. Never had there been such a demand upon the forest
regions of Canada for newsprint, and the value of Canadian exports of
pulp and paper was multiplied fivefold. The country's extensive mineral resources—mostly complex and low-grade ore bodies containing
nonferrous metals, the extraction of which presented difficult problems—were rapidly exploited as the war forced research that broke this
bottleneck. The war also made Canada one of the leading manufacturing countries of the world. During the final climax of the struggle in
Europe, one third of the expanded manufacturing capacity of the
dominion was employed by war orders from other countries— to say

nothing of Canadian war orders—for all sorts of material from munitions to ships and airplanes. All this, it may be noted in passing, laid such heavy demands upon the manpower of the country that it accentuated the failure of the voluntary enlistment system to preserve the strength of the Canadian fighting forces, and thus made conscription more urgent.

Another and healthier result of this material development, in which Canadian export production was quadrupled, was a revolution in the country's financial position. No longer was the national economy geared to a high rate of capital imports, almost entirely from London. The war stopped Canadian borrowing from Britain and made the dominion an important lender to the mother country. Nobody had dreamed that it would be possible to float a large loan in Canada, but now the domestic market absorbed all the loans raised by the federal government to cover war expenditures. It also provided much of the capital that built up the new productive capacity. The rest was supplied by the United States, for that was the time when American investments in Canada began to mount. Yet the proportion of Canadian ownership of Canadian industry grew apace, and it continued to grow after the war. Moreover, the United States now discovered a dependence upon Canada for forest products and nonferrous metals. Taking all these factors into account, it is not surprising that Canada gained greatly in wealth and economic independence.

None of the other dominions were so fortunate. Even in proportion to their smaller natural resources, they could not profit because their geographical position was a heavy handicap during the war. The total trade of each was actually cut back, and production with it, by the shortage of ships to carry it. Not only was tonnage reduced by sinkings, but most of what was available was taken off the longer runs and concentrated where it could serve best—on the shorter run across the North Atlantic, the lifeline of the Allies in Europe.

Australia, like Canada, was riven by the conscription issue, which seems to have stirred about as much bitter passion without the complication of racial antagonism. During 1915 a number of public men in Australia declared that voluntary enlistment was not producing adequate results, leagues were launched in the principal cities to drive for compulsory service in the war, and the question threatened the unity of the Labor Party. After a year in opposition, the Labor Party had won a sweeping victory in a general election that coincided with the outbreak of war. But it was losing its solidarity even before the shadow of conscription appeared, for in some sections of the party a revolt was brewing to get rid of its strongest leader, the attorney general in the new cabinet. In October 1915 the prime minister prudently retired before the impending domestic storm and his place was taken by the attorney general, William Morris Hughes. He was by far the ablest political leader in the land, and as pugnacious as his fellow Welshman, Lloyd George. On assuming office, Hughes announced that his government intended to adhere to the policy of voluntary enlistment, which was then providing enough men to repair the wastage overseas. In August 1916 he returned from a visit to England, where he was lionized, to find that enlistments had fallen badly and the cry for conscription had risen to a sharp pitch. He was now convinced that the country needed it and would support it if he could circumvent the growing opposition to it in his own cabinet and party. To do this, he got an act calling for a referendum on the issue, which was held in the following October.

All the leading newspapers and all the prominent public men in the country threw their weight behind conscription, but it was rejected by a small majority of the electorate. The strongest voice against it was that of a Roman Catholic prelate, an Irish newcomer who breathed Sinn Fein fire against Britain and branded the conflict in Europe as nothing but "a trade war." None of his fellow archbishops or bishops agreed with him, and many eminent Roman Catholic laymen denounced him. Yet he swayed the Irish vote, which in Australia alone among the dominions has played much the same political role as in the United States. Australia was also the only English-speaking country where the Marxian doctrine of class war had made much headway, and this heightened the hostility of the rank and file of Labor to conscription and its sponsors. Encouraged by the outcome of the referendum, the insurgent movement took command of the "official" Labor party and formally expelled the prime minister and other reigning chiefs. This purge inspired the contemporary jibe that the party had "blown out its brains." Actually it had blown itself out of power for a generation— except for a short spell at the onset of the world depression, 1929– 31—but not Hughes.

That irrepressible and indispensable man remained in office for another seven years. The opposition combined with his rump to form a new party, called Nationalist, which the country strongly supported in a general election of May 1917, when official Labor lost every seat in the Senate and retained only a futile minority in the House of Representatives. The public would not trust Labor to direct the affairs of Australia during such a crisis in its history, especially in view of the fact that a considerable element in Labor openly discouraged even voluntary enlistment, which was now scarcely more than half what was necessary to maintain the strength of the country's forces in the field. The verdict of May seemed to reverse that of the previous October, but during the election campaign Hughes had hobbled his government by a pledge that it would not attempt to enforce conscription without consulting the people again. Accordingly, a second referendum was held fourteen months after the first.

Meanwhile tempers mounted as Nationalists arrogated unto themselves the title of "Win-the-War Party" and hurled charges of disloyalty and pacifism at their opponents, while Labor fought back with all the bitterness of men who felt they were betrayed by their top leaders and a section of their own fellows. Exasperation born of unexpected political defeat found vent in a big strike that, reckless of the effect on the war effort, tied up the country's industries for ten weeks and was regarded by the government and its supporters as little short of organized rebellion. Hughes was so determined to get conscription that during the referendum campaign he repeatedly staked the existence of his administration upon it, thereby intensifying the opposition to it. The verdict of December 1917 was again adverse, the prime minister resigned, the governor general could not find anyone who could replace him, Hughes at once returned to office with the same cabinet, and a general sense of frustration settled down upon the land. The government was frustrated by its impotence to check the shrinkage of its valiant fighting divisions, the opposition party was frustrated by finding itself deeper in the political wilderness, and organized labor was frustrated by the bitter schism between the conscriptionist minority and the anticonscriptionist majority. Nevertheless, the Australian people as a whole took an immense pride in the war record of their soldiers, whose fatal casualties exceeded those of Canada or the United States; and this pride exalted their nationalism.

New Zealand entered the war and emerged from it the least nationalist and the most united of the dominions. The two parties, which were almost evenly balanced, turned their backs on political strife, and in 1915 buried it in a coalition government. In the following year, without any fuss, a draft law was enacted to remedy the inequities of voluntary enlistment, which was providing all the men that were needed. In proportion to population, the New Zealand expeditionary force was half as big again as that of Australia and almost double that of Canada. This fine showing, of course, reflects conditions that we have already observed. Though New Zealand resembled Australia and differed from Canada in having a solidly British population and a temporarily contracting economy that freed relatively more men for the fighting forces, New Zealand also differed from Australia in being more homogeneous socially and more akin in spirit to the mother country. Moreover, its small size and exposed position made it the most conscious of all the dominions that its fate was bound up with the empire. New Zealanders were justly proud of the part they played in the war and they derived national inspiration from it, but theirs was a muted nationalism.

In Ireland the fires of nationalism blazed up so fiercely during and right after the war that the country seemed to suffer the torments of the damned. When the outbreak of the World War persuaded Redmond and his parliamentary party to agree that the application of Home Rule should wait until the return of peace, the suspending act only postponed the impending civil war because of what this act did to Nationalist Ireland. There it shattered the dream of Home Rule just when it was at last becoming true, and the shock produced an ominous revulsion of feeling. Redmond and his fellows strove to rally their people behind the British cause in the World War, for they saw that this was the only way to win the confidence of England and Ulster, and thereby win self-government for Ireland without splitting it. But their following fell away from them. "Hope deferred maketh the heart sick," and the heart of Nationalist Ireland turned to Sinn Fein.

Again as in past generations, the Irish revolutionary leaders looked to England's archenemy for aid. Though Germany was no less eager than Spain and France had been to encompass England's fall by an Irish rising and was doing her best to foment it by intrigue, she was even less able to support it by a military invasion. The British authorities, after hesitating for some time to take preventive measures, began to hunt down the Sinn Fein leaders. By the spring of 1916 some five hundred of them were in jail and plans were afoot to catch all the others. Those who were still at large then decided that it was time to strike or their own plans would miscarry. At the last moment the commander of the Volunteers, having vainly expected the arrival of at least 40,000 Germans, judged the venture too foolhardy and held back most of his men.

Though the Easter Rebellion of 1916 was therefore the work of a small minority, it had enormous consequences. There was little fighting outside Dublin, where a republic was proclaimed and much blood was shed before the insurgents surrendered, which they did within a week. A thousand prisoners were taken, seventy were sentenced to death, and fifteen of these were shot. One of the principals, the son of a Spanish father and an American mother, was not executed because, having been born in the United States, he could claim American citizenship— Eamon de Valera. De Valera became the real national leader, the victims of the firing squad joined the roll of Irish martyr-heroes, and Irish nationalism was inflamed as never before into a fanatical religion. During the remainder of the war Nationalist Ireland was virtually an occupied country held down by British troops, and this only intensified Irish hatred of England. Meanwhile the British government, warned by the revolt and by Redmond that worse might follow if Home Rule were longer delayed, called a convention of Irish parties to work out an acceptable solution. Sinn Fein would have nothing to do with it; and the deliberations of the convention, which lasted for nearly a year, left the British government facing the old dilemma of 1914 aggravated by the proven "loyalty" of Protestant Ulster and "disloyalty" of Sinn Fein Ireland during the war.

Sinn Fein scored a political triumph on the morrow of the armistice, when the parliamentary election of December 1918 was held. Sinn Fein put up candidates pledged to sit in Dublin and never in Westminster; and in defiance of the British government, which had not yet begun to lose its physical mastery of the country, they won ten seats in Ulster outside the Protestant counties and every seat but two in all the rest of Ireland, a total of seventy-three. On election day more than half the successful candidates were in jail and others were in hiding. Only twenty-seven were able to gather on 21 January 1919 in the Mansion House, Dublin, as the Dail Eireann, or sovereign parliament of Ireland, which adopted a simple constitution and reaffirmed the 1916 proclamation of the republic. It was the Irish version of the contemporary European revolutions that established the "succession states" out of the fallen empires. But the British Empire was not one of these, the Irish emissaries knocked in vain at the door of the Paris Peace Conference, and the Dail was soon on the run from one secret meeting place to another.

Now there were two governments in Ireland, the republican and the British. Neither would recognize the existence of the other, except to fight it, and the war between them developed a savage fury that scorned the restraining laws of regular warfare. The British fought in uniform, but not the Irish Republican Army—the old Volunteers—who remembered that the wearing of uniforms had not saved their leaders from execution as criminals in 1916. The British commander in Ireland repeatedly called upon his government to admit officially that a state of war existed and to proclaim martial law, which would force armed Irishmen into uniform on pain of being shot when taken. But London would not give this recognition to Sinn Fein, and so the war of sniping, ambush, plunder, burning, and the seizure of hostages dragged on.

In a forlorn attempt to restore peace to Sinn Fein Ireland without wrecking it in Protestant Ulster, the British government substituted another Home Rule measure for the impossible act of 1914, the suspension of which was about to expire. This act of 1920 provided for two Irish parliaments, each independent of the other: a Northern Ireland parliament with jurisdiction over the six counties constituting the Protestant part of Ulster, and a Southern Ireland parliament for all the rest of the country. Certain subjects, such as the army, the navy, the currency, customs, and excise, were reserved for legislation by the imperial parliament; therefore Ireland was still to elect members to it, though in reduced number. If either Northern or Southern Ireland refused the offer of Home Rule, it was to be reduced to the status of a crown colony. If both accepted, the two parliaments were to elect a joint council for the management of such common affairs as they agreed upon, and might, by identical acts, supersede themselves by a single parliament for the whole island.

The new law was accepted in Northern Ireland, where the present semi-independent state was organized in 1921, but Southern Ireland would not even consider the offer. To Sinn Feiners the act was a mockery because it denied full independence, and a further crime against the Irish "nation" because it dismembered Ireland. The Partition Act, they called it, and Irishmen still dream of undoing this "wrong." The Dail claimed power over the whole of Ireland; when the time drew near for the election of the two Irish parliaments, the Dail resolved on the motion of its president, de Valera, to adopt the election for the purpose of replacing itself with a freshly chosen Dail. Trinity College, Dublin, returned four Home Rulers, who would not recognize the Dail, but all the 124 other members elected in Southern Ireland took the prescribed oath of allegiance to the republic and their seats as delegates in the second Dail.

As the irregular war continued more savagely than ever, the British government faced a new dilemma stated tersely by Sir Henry Wilson: "Go all out or get out." British prudence hesitated to "go all out," for the war in Ireland was stirring up dangerous trouble in Egypt and India, it was alienating the dominions, and it was poisoning Anglo-American relations. More effective was the revolt of the British conscience against the protracted horror in Ireland. "If the British Commonwealth can only be preserved by such means," declared the *Round Table,* "it would become a negation of the principle for which it stood." In the House of Lords the Archbishop of Canterbury cried out against calling in the aid of the devil to cast out devils. Many other leading Englishmen joined in the angry chorus, and the most responsible newspapers, irrespective of party, swelled it. The king himself, publicly and privately, used his influence in favor of peace; and overseas statesmen meeting in the Imperial Conference of 1921 helped to persuade the British cabinet, in which the revolt of conscience was gaining, to open negotiations for the pacification of Southern Ireland by the concession of dominion status. Accordingly, Lloyd George addressed de Valera as "the chosen leader of the great majority in Southern Ireland," and a truce was signed in July 1921, to be followed by a peace conference.

Why were the Irish leaders willing to negotiate? Apparently one of their number, the minister of defense, regarded the truce merely as a much-needed opportunity to rearm and reorganize the republican forces for a final and victorious drive against the British, whereas most of his colleagues distrusted his judgment of both the military and the political situation. The war was not going in their favor, and they could see little prospect of winning it. Their law courts had almost ceased to function, their government was at best only half-established, and not one foreign country had recognized it. What limited success they had achieved was largely owing to the British lack of moral support at home and abroad. If they refused to negotiate with a repentant Britain, they would throw away the chance of getting recognition from the one power that mattered most, they would reverse the balance of moral force, and they would commit their country to fight on against almost hopeless odds.

The negotiations split the Irish nationalists; and the treaty, which was signed on 6 December 1921, plunged them into a civil war that was no less bitter than the war against the British from which they had just emerged. The rock on which they split was the republic, to which they had sworn allegiance. The majority were prepared to abandon it, if necessary, to extract from the British a treaty, particularly one that embraced the whole of Ireland and conceded the substance of independence. They were naturally dubious about dominion status—a novel concept evolved to fit the needs of new nations overseas, not those of an old nation living so close to Britain. Geography guaranteed the dominions a freedom that was theirs by custom and constitutional convention but not by law. Allegiance to the British Crown, the mystic center of all government in the British world, meant no interference in the government of the existing dominions but might mean much in the government of an Irish dominion. The Irish delegation accepted the new treaty only when the British offered to insert in it wording that would ensure the new Irish Free State of the same liberty as possessed by Canada, or any other dominion; the British also had to agree to stretch the treaty by including Northern Ireland as an integral part of the Irish Free State, thus nullifying the hated partition. At the same time the British insisted, and the Irish delegation had to agree, on a further stipulation that Northern Ireland, which was not a party to the treaty, should not be bound by it if the parliament in Belfast so decided. The Dail accepted the treaty by a small majority after a stormy debate, the British parliament by an overwhelming vote, and the two houses of Northern Ireland rejected it offhand, thereby nullifying the nullification of the partition.

The stormy debate in Dublin was the prelude to civil war, for it turned on whether the Irish delegation, headed by Arthur Griffith and Michael Collins, had betrayed Ireland. As a protest against the vote, de Valera resigned his presidency of the Dail and withdrew from that body along with his irreconcilably republican following, while the pro-treaty majority formed a government under Griffith and including Collins. The Irish Republican Army, having inherited from Volunteer days an autonomous organization that antedated the Dail and had never fully recognized its authority, rose against the government, seized the famous Four Courts in Dublin, and threatened to embark on a war to subjugate Northern Ireland. The Free State government could not tolerate such defiance which, if not suppressed, would surely bring the British back in greater strength, and so a Free State army was organized to crush the insurgents. The British left the Irish to fight it out among themselves, which they did like the proverbial Kilkenny cats, only more destructively. The most intense fighting was in the capital, where more damage was done than in the previous war. Collins paid for the treaty with his own life, being killed in ambush; shortly afterward

Griffith's health broke and the founder of Sinn Fein died of heart failure. At last, in 1923, de Valera called off armed resistance; though he still claimed to be president of the Irish Republic, and the Irish Free State began to enjoy a peaceful existence.

In India on the outbreak of the World War, the enthusiasm for the British cause that swept like a tidal wave over the whole country had a national significance that was little perceived at the time. Never in the long history of India had there been such a spontaneous and universal outburst of feeling. When at last this subcontinent of peoples divided by race, language, religion, and culture instinctively throbbed as one, the potentialities of Indian nationalism became enormous. One may find a certain parallel in the Indian reaction to the Japanese triumph over the Russians, but that was a secret thrill and not nearly so impressive as the unanimous desire to assist Britain in the war against Germany. This pro-British enthusiasm of the Indians, which was a revealing commentary on the nature of British rule, caught the revolutionaries and the government unawares. It discouraged the former and embarrassed the latter. The bureaucratic mind, imbued with the idea of trusteeship for the Indian peoples, gave little or no guidance to the popular emotion. This therefore soon exhausted itself almost fruitlessly, and later had to be artificially revived to meet internal danger as well as the needs of the war in the Near East.

Meanwhile the revolutionary conspirators resumed their campaign of criminal violence, the politicians their agitation for self-government, and the British their efforts to suppress the one and satisfy the other. There were several small armed uprisings; political murder and robbery became almost a plague in Bengal and the Punjab; and a special committee appointed by the government and headed by a judge from England conducted an investigation during 1917 and 1918 that uncovered a widespread and dangerous revolutionary movement. The politicians, organized in the Indian National Congress and the Moslem League, were inspired by a more self-confident nationalism, which sprang from a just pride in India's magnificent military contribution to the war; and they brought the constitutional problem into clearer focus.

In 1915, for the first time, Congress and the League met in the same city, and they fraternized. In his presidential address to Congress, Sir Satyendra Sinha—he had been knighted since his appointment to the viceroy's executive council in 1909—made an eloquent plea for the British government to define the goal of its policy for India. This, he argued, would counteract the intoxicating effect of ideas of national freedom that educated Indian youths had imbibed. He also delivered a warning, which the president of the Moslem League echoed, that the road to complete self-government would be long and difficult. Sinha was not drawing his bow at random when he publicly uttered his plea. It was four years since Lord Hardinge, who was still viceroy, had privately proposed to the secretary of state a policy of gradually extending self-government in the provinces until they became autonomous, and the proposal had got bogged down in London; but he had won the confidence of the native political leaders, particularly by his bold advocacy of better treatment for Indians in the dominions. Later in 1915, he was succeeded by Lord Chelmsford who, at the first meeting of his executive council, propounded the questions: What was the goal of British rule in India, and what were the steps on the road to it? He and his advisers quickly concluded "that the endowment of British India as an integral part of the British Empire with self-government was the goal of British rule," but they could not formulate even the first step they would take toward it.

That the initial major change in the constitution should be in the field of provincial government, as suggested by Hardinge, seems to have been the consensus of opinion among British officials and Indian politicians alike. The difference between them was that Indian eagerness would outrun British caution in the transfer of authority. This difference, however, should not be exaggerated. The British had to allow for some abuse of what they conceded, this being insurance against worse trouble as well as the price of Indian education in self-government. On the other hand, the Indian leaders were restrained not only by a calculation of what the British were willing to yield but also by the realization that the vast majority of their own people were as yet incapable of self-government.

While the British were still groping for a concrete plan, representatives of Congress and the League worked one out, and the two main bodies adopted it in December 1916. This Lucknow Pact, as it has been called, provided for provincial legislatures based on communal electorates so arranged that Moslems would be somewhat overrepresented in provinces where they were a minority; and it limited majority rule by prohibiting the passage of any measure affecting either community, Moslem or non-Moslem, that was opposed by three quarters of the deputies of that community. The governor of each province was to be appointed, preferably from outside the regular civil service, half the members of his executive council were to be elected by the legislature, and with the advice of this council he could exercise a suspensive veto. The central government was to have exclusive control over certain specified heads of revenue and expenditure, the right to enact desirable uniform legislation for the whole country, and a vague general power of supervision over the provinces.

The British effort to accommodate the growing Indian nationalism owed much to Lionel Curtis, who went to India in the autumn of 1916. The Round Table groups, of which he was the coordinator, had been examining how India could be fitted into the project of a commonwealth with its cooperative control of foreign policy, and they had seen that the only way was through the development of self-government in India. From his own extensive studies and personal connections, Curtis already had some shrewd ideas of the way, which he now proceeded to explore on the spot, driven by an imperative larger than that of British officials or Indian politicians. With both classes, though a wide gulf separated them, he had intimate contacts, of which he made the most by working unobtrusively. Early in 1917 he published a letter to the people of India, which was widely circulated and helped to clarify the issue. Having found much confusion of thought in India from the common use of the word "self-government" with at least four different meanings, Curtis substituted the phrase "responsible government," with its definite concept of an executive chosen from and responsible to an elected legislature. He expressed the belief that this principle should be applied progressively, beginning with the transfer of certain subjects—such as public works, primary education, and local self-government—not to the provinces but to smaller and more homogeneous units into which the country should be divided, and concluding with the surrender of final authority to an Indian parliament.

British policy was at last officially defined in August 1917, when the secretary of state, Mr. E. S. Montagu, made the most momentous announcement since the termination of the company's rule in 1858. He declared:

> The policy of His Majesty's government, with which the Government of India are in complete accord, is that of the increasing association of Indians in every branch of the administration, and the gradual development of self-governing institutions, with a view to the progressive realization of responsible government in India as an integral part of the British Empire.

He continued by pointing out "that this policy can only be achieved by successive stages" and that the home government and the Indian government

> on whom the responsibility lies for the welfare and advancement of the Indian people, must be judges of the time and measure of each advance, and they must be guided by the cooperation received from those on whom new opportunities of service will be thus conferred, and by the extent to which it is found that confidence can be reposed in their sense of responsibility.

Thus in the midst of the World War, the coalition government of Liberals and Conservatives deliberately committed Britain to a scheme that had no precedent in the history of the world: the orderly devolution of governmental authority over a population comparable in size and diversity to that of all Europe. The secretary of state, with a small committee of experts, then sailed for India to confer with its government and politicians on how this colossal task should be undertaken. Six months after his arrival the famous Montagu-Chelmsford Report was signed, and in July 1918 it was published in England and India.

The authors of the report frankly faced the fact that the concession of the right to govern included the power to govern badly, and that this was necessary to develop the capacity for self-government. They also commended the stirring of Indian nationalism, saying:

> We believe that nationhood within the Empire represents something better than anything India has hitherto attained; that the placid, pathetic contentment of the masses is not the soil on which such Indian nationhood will grow, and that in deliberately disturbing it, we are working for her highest good.

They rejected the Congress-League plan as premature and as unworkable on other grounds, and they saw too many difficulties ahead of the new governmental units proposed by Curtis; but they took over his idea of a transitional dualism of power, and for want of a better practical alternative they fell back upon the field of provincial government to initiate the application of this dyarchy, as it soon came to be called.

The division between "transferred" and "reserved" powers would cut right through the middle of provincial government. The former, to be defined by category of subject, were to be handed over to ministers appointed by the governor from the legislature and responsible to it, while the remaining powers were to be exercised as heretofore under imperial authority. This "hybrid" executive was admittedly an experiment, the outcome of which would determine the further transfer of authority to responsible government. Meanwhile the governor, half constitutional sovereign and half autocrat, was to retain, for safety's sake in an emergency, the right to override the advice of his responsible ministers. The report also dealt with the problem of communal electorates, condemning them as undemocratic but advising their retention to protect the interests of the Moslems.

When the World War came to a close, the British government was preparing a bill that embodied the recommendations of the report and was designed to open a new and more liberal era in the history of India. This bill, it is interesting to note, was piloted through the House of Lords by an Indian, Sinha, who had been raised to the peerage and appointed undersecretary of state.[1] It became law in December 1919. In addition to introducing dyarchy, this Government of India Act reformed the Indian legislatures, central and provincial, and it provided that after ten years a parliamentary commission should review the working of the new constitution and report on how it could then be improved. India took a great step forward when the act came into operation in 1920, as we shall see in a later chapter.

Looking back, one may observe that the whole trend of British policy since 1858 had been toward some such experiment in trusting Indians to manage their own public affairs, and that the rise of Indian nationalism had accelerated the pace until the war brought on a race between the British tortoise and the Indian hare, or, to be more exact, between reform and revolution. The 1918 disclosure of a widespread terrorist conspiracy was a warning to the British *raj*; and the spring of 1919 saw ominous outbreaks, one of which was suppressed in a manner that betrayed British fear, inflamed Indian feeling, and attracted world-wide attention.

In the Punjab city of Amritsar the mob brutally murdered several Europeans, burned the banks and government buildings to the ground, and threatened to destroy the whole European community. The civil authorities called in the military, and General Dyer appeared with about a hundred native troops. On his orders they fired at the mass target, killing nearly four hundred and wounding some twelve hun-

---

[1] After its passage he returned to India as governor of one of the provinces; and in 1926, his health having failed, he went back to England to serve as a member of the judicial committee of the privy council. His death in 1928 was a great loss to the British and the Indians alike.

dred. Many British in India and at home applauded this ruthless action because they believed it averted a repetition of 1857, while others damned it as wholesale murder—"one of the worst outrages in the whole of our history," declared Asquith in parliament. Official judgment wavered until Dyer was dismissed from the service, his career broken; but the public controversy among the British continued, and from the beginning it was more like oil than water poured on the flames of Indian nationalism, which the news of the Amritsar "massacre" had spread through the land. When the Congress assembled in Amritsar on 27 December 1919, only four days after the Government of India Act received the royal assent in London, Indian nationalism threatened to sabotage the experiment that it had induced the British government to undertake. The Congress now condemned the act as "inadequate, unsatisfactory, and disappointing," and demanded "full responsible government in accordance with the principle of self-determination" and a statutory guarantee that this "should be established in the whole of British India within a period not exceeding fifteen years." But the British were determined to go through with the experiment before making any further commitment. Thus India emerged from the war to enter upon a new period of strain and stress, a period dominated by a new native leader whose spiritual force far surpassed that of any man whom India had produced for centuries.

CHAPTER XXXVI

The Emergence of the British Commonwealth

THE FIRST WORLD WAR killed the Round Table movement, but not in the beginning. Indeed, the amazing response that the challenge of 1914 drew from the overseas members of the empire suggested that they were ripe for the solution of the imperial problem sought by Lionel Curtis and his associates, and that the war would hasten the constitutional reconsolidation of the empire. When the dominions scorned the role of passive belligerents, which they were free to choose because the ultimatum of 4 August committed them to nothing more, and proudly assumed the heavy burden of active belligerency under the coordinating guidance of the mother country, were they not already paying of their own accord the price of admission to share proportionately with the mother country the control of high policy for the whole empire? Would they not have to be given what they were paying for? Their demand for it, inspired by their growing nationalism, became quite insistent, and the justice of their claim was freely admitted by the mother country.

The demand began, as one would expect, in the oldest and largest dominion—the only one in intimate contact with a foreign great power, and while that power was still a neutral. The prime minister of Canada, Sir Robert L. Borden, apparently the first statesman of the empire to sense the stimulation of dominion nationalism by the war, posed the question during a visit to England in the summer of 1915. He had an audience with the king, who admitted to him "that the dominions should have a voice in the determination of foreign policy." Borden also discussed the problem with the colonial secretary, who was still skeptical, and with Lord Bryce, who agreed that "the dominions must have a voice in foreign policy." "I told him," records the Canadian, "they would either have such a voice or each of them would have a foreign policy of its own." Already during this visit a significant precedent had been established when, in response to a formal summons, the dominion premier sat in the British cabinet and took part in its deliberations. A proposal to make cotton contraband was being considered, and he cautioned against any immediate action because, coming so soon after the *Lusitania* incident, it might have an unfortunate effect upon American opinion.

Four months after Borden's return home, the British government having meanwhile failed to consult his government and even to inform it concerning important decisions on the conduct of the war, he made it pretty plain to the authorities in London that it was dangerous for them to suppose that Canada would continue to throw her weight into the struggle and be content with no voice in its management. "Is this war being waged by the United Kingdom alone, or is it a war waged by the whole empire? If I am correct in supposing that the second hypothesis must be accepted, then why do the statesmen of the British Isles arrogate to themselves solely the methods by which it shall be carried on . . . ?" His prodding extracted from the British government a batch of pertinent secret documents. Before these documents were received by Borden, the prime minister of Australia, the redoubtable Mr. Hughes, passed through Ottawa on his way to England, and the two men discovered that they saw eye to eye on the right of the dominions to a voice in foreign policy. Thus encouraged, the Australian proceeded to England[1] and there drove the point home in a series of public speeches. But the British government gave no sign of yielding to the dominions' demand until December 1916, when Asquith resigned and Lloyd George took his place. Straightway the new prime minister organized a small war cabinet out of the regular cabinet and invited the dominion premiers to London for an Imperial War Conference, during which they would also serve as members of the war cabinet.

India was to be represented also, by two of her own leaders,[2] in recognition of her important contribution to the prosecution of the war. She did not qualify according to the constitutional resolution of 1907, which confined membership to the autonomous units of the empire;

---

[1] Where he too sat with the British cabinet.

[2] The maharajah of Bikanir, one of the ruling princes, and Sir S. P. Sinha, president of the Congress in 1915.

but the spokesmen of the mother country and the dominions vied with one another in welcoming her, and they unanimously amended the wording of 1907 so that thenceforth she could sit with them in her own right. Her admission was a sort of advance payment, an implicit pledge that she was destined to be another self-governing dominion.

From March until May 1917 the Imperial War Conference met on alternate days to discuss broad questions of imperial cooperation during and after the war. On the other days the overseas premiers sat with the five members of the British war cabinet in what was called the Imperial War Cabinet, where the immediate conduct of the war and other important matters came under confidential review. Legal purists have objected to this application of the term "cabinet" to a body of men who were responsible to no one legislature; but the growth of the British constitution has often given new meanings to old words, and the constitution of the empire was plainly in process of some fundamental change. This change was much debated, formally as well as informally, with the result that the following resolution was unanimously adopted:

> The Imperial War Conference are of opinion that the readjustment of the constitutional relations of component parts of the Empire is too important and intricate a subject to be dealt with during the War, and that it should form the subject of a special Imperial Conference to be summoned as soon as possible after the cessation of hostilities.
>
> They deem it their duty, however, to place on record their view that any such readjustment, while thoroughly preserving all existing powers of self-government and complete control of domestic affairs, should be based upon a full recognition of the Dominions as autonomous nations of an Imperial Commonwealth, and of India as an important portion of the same, should recognize the right of the Dominions and India to an adequate voice in foreign policy and in foreign relations, and should provide effective arrangements for continuous consultation in all important matters of common Imperial concern, and for such necessary concerted action, founded on consultation, as the several Governments may determine.

This resolution had its origin in Borden's "fixed purpose to set forth in terms that could not be misunderstood and by authority that must be respected a new conception of the status of the dominions in their relation to the governance of the empire." He discussed it with Smuts, who represented Botha at the conference, and they found themselves in wholehearted agreement. "At his suggestion," says the Canadian,

"I approached Australia and New Zealand, as well as Newfoundland, and in conjunction with Smuts I drafted a resolution which met with the approval of the other dominions." It was not submitted to the conference until it also had the approval of the British prime minister and his war cabinet, and was amended on the suggestion of Austen Chamberlain, then secretary of state for India, to include "a suitable reference to India," the insertion of which "had the concurrence of each dominion." In recording this story in his memoirs, which were not published until after his death, Borden modestly implied that his conspicuous position as prime minister of the senior dominion led him to take the initiative, and he paid high tribute to Smuts "whose wonderful intellectual powers, wide vision, and astonishing career gave him a commanding place in our deliberations."

In this resolution we may see a signpost indicating that the empire was rapidly approaching, if it had not already reached, the parting of the ways. The first paragraph, calling for a constitutional convention as soon as possible after the war, and the latter part of the second paragraph, asserting the right of the dominions and India to "an adequate voice in foreign policy and foreign relations" and postulating "effective arrangement for continuous consultation" and "concerted action," pointed toward imperial integration on some institutionalized basis and with one foreign policy directed by all. The first part of the second paragraph pointed in another direction, though by implication only, toward a looser imperial structure with potentially divergent foreign policies; for the control of foreign policy is inseparable from the power of taxation to pay for it, there could be no collective control without a collective decision to levy taxes, and such a decision would violate the sacred principle of dominion autonomy in domestic affairs.

When the empire was fighting for its very existence, its leaders deliberating in London could not be expected to choose between the two constitutional roads ahead. Indeed, they seem to have cherished the hope that somehow it would be possible to reconcile dominion autonomy with a collective foreign policy. In seconding Borden's motion to adopt the resolution, Smuts declared that it would rule out a federal solution of the imperial dilemma. Yet he clung to the idea of a united empire, saying:

> People talk about a league of nations and international government, but the only successful experiment in international government that has ever been made is the British Empire, founded on principles that appeal to the highest political ideals of mankind. Founded on liberal prin-

ciples, and principles of freedom and equality, it has continued to exist for a good time now, and our hope is that the basis may be so laid for the future that it may become an instrument for good, not only in the Empire but in the whole world. . . . How are we to keep this Empire together? . . . So far it has been possible for us each to go his own way, meeting once in so many years. In future it will be necessary for us to keep much more closely in touch with each other.

Some machinery operating on the principle of "continuous consultation," he remarked, would have to be devised. This, he added, would not be difficult "once we come to sit round the table and discuss the matter carefully." Borden was inclined to believe that the Imperial War Cabinet "should be held annually or oftener."

The proposed constitutional convention never met; the machinery to which Smuts referred as necessary was never designed; and the Imperial War Cabinet died with the war, no effort being made to transform it into a peacetime institution. Why? The usual answer is the further development of dominion nationalism. But this is not enough unless it is related to a radical change in the world outlook which, by sheer coincidence, began while the Imperial War Conference was sitting in 1917. What caused the change was the American entry into the war.

Until that time the British Empire offered to all its people who thought seriously about world peace the only visible hope of obtaining it. This fact, of which Smuts' words quoted above are a reminder, has since been largely forgotten; but in the early years of the war it governed British minds as they contemplated the future of the empire and the world. The prospect of a very different and much more attractive future, in which the British Empire would not have to shoulder the burden of Atlas, dawned as the United States, with its immense resources of wealth and manpower, stepped forth on "the great crusade" to fight "a war to end all wars" and "make the world safe for democracy." Then the idea of a league of nations, which had been mooted on both sides of the Atlantic, began to seem less visionary; and, what was of more practical value to Britons the world over, the American action began to hold out a promise that the United States would join in enforcing international law and order. League or no league, the United States and the British Empire working together could preserve world peace much more securely than the British Empire alone. That possibility was what really undermined the Round Table movement and all other efforts to achieve an imperial reintegration.

The imperial gathering of 1917 was repeated in 1918 on two separate occasions, the first being the alarming success of the Germans in breaking through the Western Front. The meetings lasted from the first part of June, when the military situation seemed desperate, to the middle of August, when ultimate victory seemed certain. In the beginning there was a grand inquest into the past functioning of the British high command, which was subjected to searching criticism by Borden in the British war cabinet and in the Imperial War Cabinet. He was speaking not for Canada alone but for all the dominions—Hughes of Australia not having yet reached England, Smuts[3] being discreetly doubtful of how such words would be received from a former enemy of Britain, and the other attending overseas ministers finding that the Canadian well expressed their own minds. Lloyd George himself welcomed the criticism, for it strengthened his hands in dealing with the military chiefs.

As the immediate crisis passed, attention shifted to a consideration of the future, and Hughes pressed the question of "continuous consultation." Then it was formally decided that "The prime ministers of the dominions, as members of the Imperial War Cabinet, have the right of direct communication with the prime minister of the United Kingdom and vice versa," and that "the prime minister of each dominion has the right to nominate a cabinet minister, either as a resident or visitor in London, to represent him at meetings of the Imperial War Cabinet to be held regularly between the plenary sessions." Here we may note, by way of anticipation, that the principle and practice of "direct communication" survived the war to become a rather useful ghost of the Imperial War Cabinet.

Among other matters that came under review was an Admiralty proposal of a single imperial navy at all times under one central authority. The dominion premiers replied that, however desirable this might be from the standpoint of naval strategy, it was "not practicable." Citing the Australian example of a dominion navy operating "with the highest efficiency as part of a united navy under one direction and command established after the outbreak of war," and anticipating the development of naval forces "upon a considerable scale by the dominions," they said "it may be necessary hereafter to consider the establishment for war purposes of some supreme naval authority upon which each of the dominions would be adequately represented." On returning

---

[3] Who again represented Botha.

to Canada, Borden was surprised to encounter an "impression that some great constitutional change was effected this year," which drew from him a public denial that there was any "departure from the decision of last year's conference that all constitutional changes should be postponed until after the war and should then be determined by a conference specially called for that purpose."

The second occasion for the summoning of the Imperial War Cabinet in 1918 was the impending military collapse of Germany. Early in the war it had been announced in the parliaments of the empire that the dominions would be fully consulted in the making of peace, and there was some preliminary discussion of peace terms during the meetings of 1917 and the summer of 1918. The time for decision was now at hand. From November to January the Imperial War Cabinet sat in London working out what the empire should do at the peace conference; and then, only slightly changed in personnel, it continued its labors in Paris as the British Empire delegation. This transformation of character was highly significant, as will now appear.

The British Commonwealth of Nations, after many long years of gestation, was finally born during these discussions in London and Paris, when the dominions and India acquired international status without separating from the empire. Canada forced the issue by rallying the dominions to demand international recognition, and they carried India with them as the prospective dominion of avowed British policy. To gain their end, the dominions had first to convince the British government and then, with the aid of its pressure, to get the consent of the Big Four, the great victorious powers who made the arrangements for the peace conference and dominated its proceedings.

Before sailing for England at the call of Lloyd George, Borden wrote him a letter on 29 October that caused some consternation in the Foreign Office, whose officials had hitherto assumed that the dominions could not be members of the peace conference because they had no international status. Now the Canadian premier urged serious consideration of their participation in the actual negotiations, serving notice that his country took for granted it would be a member of the conference. He also uttered a warning that any obstacles in the way would have to be surmounted in order to avoid "a very unfortunate impression" or even "a dangerous feeling" in Canada. While he was crossing the Atlantic, the armistice was signed; and at once his Australian counterpart, who had remained in England over the adjournment of the Imperial War Cabinet, gave a ruder jolt to London officialdom. Hughes protested violently against the British government's agreement, behind his back, to armistice terms that would govern the peace settlement. One of these terms, which roused his greatest ire, threatened his country's claim to annex conquered German territories in the Pacific. By the time Borden reached London, the lesson had begun to sink in; immediately Lloyd George and Bonar Law privately proposed to him that he, as spokesman of the dominions, should be associated with four leaders of the British government to make up the five representatives already allotted to each of the great powers by their own informal agreement. The Canadian demurred; and the Australian premier blasted the proposal when he heard of it, which was very shortly afterward. If any dominion other than Australia was to have a seat, he must have one too.

From mid-November the Imperial War Cabinet wrestled with the problem of dominion representation, which seemed to be almost as difficult as squaring the circle. How could five seats accommodate the whole empire? It was generally admitted that Great Britain required a minimum of four, because the prime minister could not be excluded, nor his second in command of the coalition government who was also leader of the Conservatives and the House of Commons, nor the foreign secretary, nor the colonial secretary. That left only one seat for five claimants—India and the dominions—none of whom could be left out. The British government suggested that the problem might be solved by choosing the five official plenipotentiaries from day to day, according to the nature of the subject under consideration, from a panel comprising representatives of all six governments. This was obviously not enough for the dominions because it meant, in practice, that each of them, along with India, would have only a fleeting turn in the fifth seat.

Finally the Canadian premier took the bit in his teeth and broke through the impasse. In addition to serving on the imperial panel, he declared, the dominions should have their own distinctive representation in the conference on the same basis as the smaller allied nations. He claimed it as a right that they had fully earned in the war, and he threw out dark hints of dire consequences if it were withheld from them. It would be intolerable for them to be refused what was accorded to states that had taken little or no active part in the fighting. The British government bowed to the will of the dominions, though it would compromise the principle of imperial unity, and Borden's resolution was adopted on the last day of the year.

When Britain appeared in Paris with her imperial family and

demanded seats for them in accordance with the agreement reached in
London, at once there was strong opposition on the logical ground that
the claimants were not independent sovereign states, the only entities
yet known to international law and usage. The crucial objectors were
Prime Minister Georges Clemenceau, of France, and President Woodrow Wilson, of the United States. Dominion status, which still puzzled
hosts of British people at home and abroad, was beyond the comprehension of Clemenceau, and he suspected a British trick in the apparition
of an empire that was both one and many at the same time. Woodrow
Wilson's constitutional studies had given him some understanding of
the strange anomaly that was growing in the British world; but he had
a legalistic mind and his country, like France, had a long-standing anti-
British bias. Lloyd George, however, was a powerful persuader, and
the dominions ably presented their case. The American scholar-states-
man waived his objection; and the French "Tiger" relented when told
that the dominions had put a million men in the field, had suffered
heavy casualties, and deserved international recognition for their sacrifices—which was precisely the argument on which he relied to win
for France the heavy peace terms he demanded.

In its immediate practical effect, this compromise of imperial unity
was more formal than real. It was in and through the British Empire
delegation, not as separate members of the conference, that the dominions found satisfaction for their natural ambition to share in the shaping of the peace settlement. The actual sessions of the conference were
few and short, their function being mostly confined to registering
decisions already concluded by negotiation between the great powers;
whereas the British Empire delegation, including the responsible
leaders of the dominions, met constantly to formulate the British stand
on all questions. It was at these meetings that the dominion statesmen
made their weight felt on a multitude of points, great and small. Also
as members of this delegation, they were assigned to international
commissions and committees that did much of the spade work for the
peace treaties. Smuts was one of the principal architects of the League
of Nations, the idea of which had been born on both sides of the
Atlantic. Moreover, he and his chief, Botha, were extremely useful in
helping to prevent Hughes from upsetting the applecart over the
disposition of the conquered German colonies. First in London and
now in Paris, the Australian premier was so obstreperous in his insistence on outright annexation of the territorial fruits his country had
gathered in the Pacific that the rest of the British Empire delegation

had grave difficulty in making him accept the League mandate system, which Smuts had conceived. Another fact worth noting is that Borden presided over meetings of the delegation when Lloyd George could not attend. Indeed, the dominions enjoyed a privileged position, for their membership in the British Empire delegation gave them an influence denied to other small powers, who were consulted only on questions directly affecting their interests.

Yet the compromise of imperial unity, expressed in the admission of the dominions to the conference in their own right, had practical results that extended far beyond the short life of the conference, for one act of international recognition led to another. The dual character of the empire—one and many—was written into the peace treaties. The preambles listed the British Empire, but not the dominions or India, among the high contracting parties; then, in proceeding to name the plenipotentiaries of each, the representatives of the dominions and India were listed separately. The same ambiguity is to be found at the end of the treaties, where the five plenipotentiaries appointed by the government of the United Kingdom signed for the whole empire, and immediately after them the plenipotentiaries of the dominions and India signed for their respective countries. It was Borden who, by rallying the dominions and working on the British government, got this much recognition of the dominions and India in the form of the treaty; and in doing so he had to be content with half the loaf he demanded. He tried hard to get an arrangement in which the dominions would not appear as subordinate and their signatures as supernumerary, but this was too advanced for the British government of that day. He did, however, make it clear to the British government that the dominions, as signatories, reserved the right to ratify the treaties.

As individual members of the peace conference, the dominions and India became, also in their own right, members of the League of Nations and of the International Labor Organization, which placed their international status on a more permanent footing. But in this there was nearly a slip that would have withheld from them a right enjoyed by all other ordinary members. According to the original drafts of the constitutions of these continuing international institutions, only independent states were to be eligible for election by the Assembly to the Council of the League, and by the General Conference to the Governing Body of the International Labor Organization. Borden detected this discrimination, which was implicit rather than explicit, and he protested against it. Again he encountered both French and American opposition, and this time it was stiffer.

Clemenceau was piqued because Morocco was left off the list of states invited to join the League. More serious was the prophetic fear that caused the United States delegation to balk at any further concession to the dominions. It was that the American people would gag when asked to swallow the Covenant with its provision for six British votes to one for the United States in the Assembly. But Borden persisted and he had the backing of the other prime ministers of the empire, including the dynamic Lloyd George to whom he supplied the argument that there were at least six Latin-American states over whom the United States could exercise more control than could Britain over the dominions in the operations of the League and the International Labor Organization. In the end, the drafts were amended to remove the bar; and to clear away all possible doubt, the Canadian got Clemenceau, Woodrow Wilson, and Lloyd George to sign a public affirmation that the dominions[4] were eligible for election to the League Council. The sequel shows that more than a theoretical right was at stake. Canada and India became members of the International Labor Organization Governing Body when it was formed in 1919, and in 1926 Canada was the first dominion chosen by the Assembly to serve a term in the League Council. Australia was the second, some years afterward.

In addition to the questions affecting constitutional relations between the mother country and the dominions that their assembled statesmen had to thresh out in the business of peacemaking, other questions of the same nature were explored by these gentlemen in private conversation with one another. They could not pass up such a good opportunity to exchange ideas on possible developments in the structure of the British Empire or, as some of them were now beginning to call it, the British Commonwealth of Nations. Two of these other questions were rather urgent. One concerned the office of governor general, the other the principle of diplomatic unity, and both foreshadowed important changes in the years to come.

A problem peculiar to South Africa called for a drastic acceleration of the speed with which the office of governor general had been evolving. On arriving in London, Botha met Borden for the first time; the

---

[4] For obvious reasons India was not mentioned in this document.

two men, though of very different backgrounds, soon became close friends who saw eye to eye on every issue that came up. The South African then sought the Canadian's help to undermine the perverse and dangerous belief of Boer farmers that they were still ruled by the British government through orders given to the governor general. If a native South African were appointed to this office, said Botha, naming a number who were well qualified for it, this would be an effective solution of the problem of schismatic Boer nationalism; and he asked Borden, as one who had great influence with Lloyd George, to approach him on the subject. Borden gladly interceded, but the only satisfaction he got from the British prime minister was a promise to think about it.

In Paris Botha renewed his plea, now fortified by a masterly memorandum prepared by Smuts on behalf of all the dominions, though it is doubtful if the author had the consent of any Australian or New Zealander. The main points of the document were as follows: the dominions were grateful for the concessions that the British government had so readily made to their "sentiment of independent nationhood," which the war had greatly stimulated. Yet one important step remained to be taken which would appeal more than anything else to them and "would have the most far-reaching effect in cementing together the members of the great British League of Nations." The end of the war afforded a uniquely fitting occasion to crown dominion status by relieving the governor general of his function as a channel of communication between dominion governments and the home government, so that he would be simply and solely a constitutional monarch, and by selecting for this highest office in each dominion an eminent citizen of that dominion. "If this important change were made now and announced in connection with the making of peace, it would be unnecessary to hold any special imperial conference to deal with constitutional relations, as was contemplated in the session of 1917." Again Borden pressed the British prime minister to grant Botha's request, and this time he "found Lloyd George's outlook more restricted than ever before." The little Welshman insisted that appointment from the British Isles was essential because it was "the last link" between the dominions and the mother country, to which argument the Canadian retorted that the unity of the empire was not very secure if it depended on that link. Then the question went to sleep until Ireland awakened it. Lloyd George's refusal, which may seem strange in light of his attitude during the Boer War, was very unfortunate for South Africa, but in none of the other dominions was public opinion yet ripe for such a drastic change as Smuts postulated.

What threatened the diplomatic unity of the empire was likewise a problem peculiar to one dominion. We have seen how the North American marriage of Canada to the United States was an embarrassment to Britain in her dealings with the United States, how Canadians were prone to accuse the mother country of sacrificing their interests under American pressure, how sometimes the Canadian government would not use the British ambassador in Washington except as a formal cloak to cover direct negotiations with the American government, and how these two governments set up their own International Joint Commission with a wide jurisdiction over the interests of each where they were inextricably interwoven along their common boundary. Apart from the function of this commission, over which the British government had renounced even formal control, and apart from the occasions when the British ambassador was the sleeping partner of a special Canadian envoy in negotiations with the American government, all official business between Ottawa and Washington was handled by the British ambassador; it had to pass back and forth through an official channel that crossed the ocean twice, the Canadian government communicating through the governor general with the Colonial Office, and the latter through the Foreign Office with the ambassador. Before the war the volume of the ambassador's Canadian business had greatly outgrown that of his other transactions. In 1912 when James (later Lord) Bryce was ambassador, he said: "About 90 per cent of all my official duties at Washington are purely Canadian," and he expressed the belief that a Canadian should assume them. The American entry into the war accentuated the need for direct contact between the governments of such close neighbors. By the beginning of 1918 Borden found it necessary to establish in Washington a Canadian War Mission, which was diplomatic in effect though not in form. Its usefulness in coordinating the war effort of the two countries was clearly demonstrated during the remaining months of the conflict.

London could not help seeing that the old method of conducting the foreign relations of the empire was obsolete in this one quarter and that Canada might not tolerate it much longer. An exchange of ministers between Ottawa and Washington was a simple and obvious solution, which both these governments had been contemplating; but that would break the diplomatic unity of the empire, which no responsible statesman of Great Britain was prepared to sacrifice. The British government therefore cast about for some way of preserving this precious principle while accommodating Canada in diplomatic relations with the United States. How could these two things be reconciled?

The only possible answer was in line with the suggestion made to Borden on the day of his arrival in London, when Lloyd George and Bonar Law proposed that he represent all the dominions at the peace conference. But his appointment as British ambassador to the United States was a very different and more difficult matter. It meant that a Canadian would take over the responsibilities of what had become the most important British diplomatic post, in which he would be charged with handling the affairs not only of all the dominions but also of the dependent empire and, much more important still, of Great Britain herself. The prospect of such self-denial on the part of the mother country was staggering. Nevertheless, after long deliberation, the British government decided to make the offer, which reflects the weight attached to the principle of diplomatic unity and to the need for satisfying Canada. A few days before the adjournment to Paris, an American newspaper man told the Canadian premier that he "had been spoken of as British Ambassador to Washington." Early in February Lloyd George asked him if he would accept the post, and Borden said he would "if political conditions permitted." He added that he could not give a definite reply until he returned to Canada and consulted his colleagues. Late in March, without returning to Canada, he declined the offer. Why, we do not know; but it is obvious that the proferred British solution for the Canadian problem could be only temporary, and we do know that in many conversations with Lloyd George and Arthur Balfour he explored the whole question of Canadian diplomatic representation in Washington, thus preparing the way for the agreement he reached with the British government a year later.

The dominions began to digest their new status when their statesmen returned home and sought public approval for what they had done during their long absence abroad. Opinion in each dominion was by no means unanimous, and the reaction varied from dominion to dominion. The great debate opened with the submission of the peace treaties to the dominion parliaments. Before this was done, however, there was a sharp and significant exchange of cables between London and Ottawa on whether submission to the dominion parliaments was necessary. The colonial secretary, whose government was eager for early ratification, would have had the king ratify for the whole empire without waiting for action by the dominion parliaments, which Borden admitted was legally permissible but insisted was politically dangerous. He had given a pledge to consult his parliament, which was in accord with precedent going back to the Washington Treaty of 1871 and was now essential to preserve his country's new international status as a separate signatory. When he promised an early session and quick parliamentary action, London agreed to wait. He won the point not only for Canada but also for the other dominions, and British ratification was delayed until all the dominion parliaments voted for it in September 1919.

The debate, which could not end with the hasty voting on ratification, was most confused in Canada, largely because of her dual nationality and her close ties with a great foreign power. At first the Liberals, who were rapidly recovering from their stunning defeat in 1917, declared that the government's claim to have elevated the country's position in the empire and in the world at large was "a colossal humbug," that the dominion was no more a sovereign state than it had been before, that therefore its participation in treaty making as a separate international entity was a hollow pretension and its ratification a mere sham. Then the critics lost their cohesion and began firing at cross purposes. While some continued to argue that nothing had happened, others asserted that something evil had happened and they could not agree on what it was. Imperialists attacked the government for wrecking imperial unity, nationalists of both races for drawing it tighter in an imperialist plot that invented the new status as an effective disguise. Some pointed to the Imperial War Cabinet in London, the British Empire delegation in Paris, and the constitutional imperial conference in the future as proof that Canada was being bound to fight in all Britain's wars; some feared that Canada's membership in the League and the World Court might commit her to war against Britain; some lamented the exposure to the perils of international rivalry from which the empire had shielded the dominion.

The government stuck to its guns and brought up a new one in May 1920, when the announcement was simultaneously made in London and Ottawa that, following an agreement now made with the United States, Canada was to have a resident minister of her own in Washington who would deal directly with the American government on all purely Canadian affairs. To paper over this crack in the diplomatic unity of the empire, the Canadian minister was to be associated with the British embassy and to take charge of it in the absence of a British ambassador. The opposition was shocked, but not into silence, for the war of words went on. Borden, who had led the struggle in London, Paris, and Ottawa, was now broken in health, and in July he retired. A year later his party was badly defeated at the polls, but the cause which was so dear to his heart triumphed. The Liberals espoused it when they returned to power, and the great debate died down to an occasional sally by an unregenerate imperialist or an extreme nationalist. The promised exchange of diplomatic representatives between Washington and Ottawa, however, was mysteriously held up for several years.

In South Africa the issue was much more clear-cut and even less capable of solution by a majority vote. There was no opposition on the ground that the government had betrayed the unity of the empire or the sheltered position of South Africa as a member of the empire. The debate was on only one front. The clash was between two kinds of nationalism, both anti-imperialist—one Afrikander, narrow and reactionary, the other South African, broad and forward-looking. Hertzog and his followers bitterly yearned to recover the republican independence that the British had taken from them, but they knew that public opinion in the country would not tolerate a disruption of the Union to release the Transvaal and the Orange Free State. Therefore they declared for secession of the whole Union from the empire—not right away, because they realized that this too would smash the Union, but whenever the Union decided for it. What they demanded immediately was an official recognition of the right to secede. Did the new status confer this right? "Yes or No?" demanded Hertzog. Smuts, who had become premier on Botha's death in August 1919, replied, " . . . absolutely and decisively, No!" and he went on to explain that, as the parliament of South Africa was composed of the king, the Senate, and the House of Assembly, the expulsion of the first by the other two would be unconstitutional. It "must be in the nature of a revolution."

The point of the debate may seem academic, but behind the spoken words there were unuttered thoughts of vital moment. The ultimate goal of Hertzog and his Nationalists was the transformation of the Union into an Afrikander republic purged of any British taint. On the other hand, Smuts and his supporters of both white races believed that neither of these should dominate over the other, or civil war would again break forth, and that their friendly cooperation was absolutely essential for the salvation of the country. Here was the fundamental issue back of all the talk about the right of secession. Both Hertzog and Smuts would unite their long-divided race, but for opposite ends:

Hertzog to work against, Smuts to work with, the other white race that shared the country with them. The premier reminded his opponents that he too, as their comrade in arms, had fought to preserve republican independence—until he came to see that it was gone forever and that the future promised a deeper and wider freedom. This, he emphasized, was what they now had as a partner in the British Commonwealth, "a league of free, equal states," and as a separate member of the League of Nations. He pleaded with his opponents to bury the dead past, to drop their agitation for what they themselves admitted was only an abstract principle, and to join in the task that lay ahead, of building a greater South Africa. But their ideal for South Africa was poles apart from his, and they would not abandon their precious symbolic right.

An appeal to the electorate in March 1920, far from reducing the strength of the Nationalists, made them the largest single party in the House. Still hoping to win them over, Smuts tried to negotiate a fusion with his own South African party, proposing that they should leave future constitutional change "to the natural course of events," and assuring them that he would admit of no obligation to any other part of the empire contrary to South African interests. It was likewise in vain. The continued intransigence of the Nationalists made him call on "all right-minded South Africans" to combine in one party, based on the principles of equal partnership in the commonwealth and the unity of the South African nation; and it also made the British party, the Unionists, who had supported him without sharing office, respond to his call by merging with his party. Thus reinforced, he brought on another general election, which was held in the beginning of 1921 and gave him a substantial majority. This, however, was at the expense of the Labor party, not of the Nationalists. The latter, pledging themselves to hold a referendum on secession before taking any step to effect it, got the same number of seats as before. Though South Africa was sorely split over what should be the relations between its two white races in the indefinite future, the actual line of cleavage was through the more numerous of the two, not between them; and though the dispute was over the new status, both sides were anxious to make the most of it for their opposite purposes.

Australians were much less concerned than Canadians or South Africans over their country's new status, which they seem to have taken for granted as the natural result of their contribution to the war. Being wholly British by blood, and self-confident in the possession of a continent to themselves, they knew that the empire was not breaking up and that they were the freest people in the world. But if they were little interested in theoretical speculation about the constitution of the British Commonwealth, they were very much interested in the concrete fact that their nation had become a mandatory power in the Pacific. The debate was almost entirely on national security. They had counted on outright annexation of their island conquests, but they had to be content with the substitute; and they resented Japan's acquisitions in what they imperially regarded as their own sphere, but they had to accept the equator as the dividing line.

New Zealand, on the other hand, was plainly worried over the constitutional and political implications of the new status. This dominion's solidly British character combined with her smallness and remoteness to make her suspicious of anything that might loosen the bonds of empire. Here, as in South Africa, there was a lively debate on only one front, but this was the opposite one. The government repudiated the suggestion that the separate signature of the peace treaty was an act of national self-assertion. The premier, Mr. W. F. Massey, declared: "We signed it as the representatives of the self-governing nations within the empire; we signed it as partners in the empire—partners, with everything the name implies." His reassurance, however, could not allay the uneasy feeling that the other dominions were dragging New Zealand out of the old imperial shelter and plunging her into the dangerous waters of international society. The announcement that Canada was to possess diplomatic individuality, which struck responsive chords in South Africa and Australia, was a disturbing shock to New Zealand.

The dominions were obviously out of step with one another. Smuts had quickly pushed ahead of Borden who held to his steady pace, while Hughes went his own self-satisfied gait and Massey hung back, each for reasons peculiar to his own country; and the divergent reactions, represented by these leaders, were accentuated by the American rejection of the peace settlement. This action crippled the League of Nations at its birth. What was the value of membership in it when the most powerful country in the world would have nothing to do with it? And what had happened to all the high hopes of the United States and the British Empire working together to enforce international law and order, now that the American government had hastily built up its navy to parity with Britain and the American attack on the League, with its "six British votes," had stirred up a storm of Anglophobia? Gone beyond recall was the *Pax Britannica,* upheld by a Royal Navy that was supreme; and the promise of a new and better system of maintaining world order, which would have made it much easier for the members of the British Commonwealth, as well as other nations, to march together, had collapsed in America.

The Imperial Conference of 1921 was the first effort of the British Commonwealth to function as a partnership. It promptly buried the idea of a constitutional conference anticipated by the resolution of 1917 and by Lord Milner, the colonial secretary, in a statement to the House of Lords in June 1920. He then looked forward to its meeting in the following year and expressed the hope that it would provide a central organ of government which, while recognizing the complete equality and independence of the dominions and the mother country, would enable them to act as one, promptly and efficiently, in their common interest. But New Zealand was the only dominion where there was any considerable body of opinion that agreed with him; the conference of 1921 was called for another purpose; and when its members came together they formally declared that "having regard to the constitutional developments since 1917, no advantage is to be gained by holding a constitutional conference." New Zealand was being dragged along by the other dominions.

The 1921 Conference met primarily to determine British foreign policy, and found little difficulty in reaching agreement except on one question. But that was the most urgent and the most momentous of all. Should the Anglo-Japanese alliance, which was up for review because it conflicted with the League Covenant, be revised and renewed, or should it be terminated?

The alliance had served its purpose as a protection against Russia and Germany in the Far East, and now Japan threatened to be the disturber of the peace in that part of the world. Her aggressive actions toward China during and after the war, which adumbrated her mad attempt of later years to conquer the whole of the Far East, roused grave misgivings in the British Empire and the United States. The American attitude toward the alliance, none too friendly at the time of the last renewal in 1911, was now so positively hostile that a further renewal would impose a severe strain on the relations between the two English-speaking powers. This prospect was even more intolerable to Canada than to the mother country, and the South African premier agreed that "The only path of safety for the British Empire is a path on which we can walk together with America."

Yet the American withdrawal from the system of world security made Britain wary of abandoning the alliance. It was her only check upon Japan, for Britain could not concentrate enough military and naval strength in the Far East to protect her interests there against a Japan alienated by being thrown over. The same considerations, unbalanced by any fear of the effect on Anglo-American relations, made Australia and New Zealand insist upon renewal.

The controversy became very heated when Mr. Arthur Meighen, Borden's successor, argued that "the empire's foreign policy in spheres in which any dominion is peculiarly concerned" should be governed by "the view of that dominion" in proportion to "the importance of the decision of that dominion," and he wound up by throwing a bombshell into the Conference: "In all questions affecting Canada and the United States, the dominion should have full and final authority." Hughes threw it back, saying that according to this principle "Australia should control the policy of the empire regarding the east, the Pacific, and the navy because they were more vital to her than to the other dominions." He and Massey would rather have the United States than Japan as an ally, but that choice was not offered to them. The only alternative for their countries was between a renewal of the alliance and exposure to Japanese hostility. Smuts tried to console his Australasian colleagues by assuring them that the League of Nations would promote international security; but he admitted that the support of the United States was essential for the maintenance of world order, and he recognized Japan as the greatest menace to world peace. Therefore, he contended, the empire must draw closer to the United States in order to face this danger. As the conference could reach no decision, since the dominions were deadlocked over the issue of Australian and New Zealand security versus Canadian security and the British government could not contemplate jeopardizing either, Meighen suggested a conference of Pacific powers as the only way out. London, however, could not take the initiative in summoning such a meeting because the current of isolationist and anti-British feeling was running too strong in the United States. Then a coincidence opened the door of escape from the impasse.

At this very time the American government was preparing to hold a conference of the principal naval powers to limit naval armaments. If this was at the secret prompting of the British government, as some writers have averred, the evidence for it is still lacking. Senator Borah, whose resolution called for this conference, denied that he had conferred with any representative of Britain or the State Department, and his whole career is eloquent proof that he was innocent of any desire to help the British Empire. It was at the behest of London, however, that Washington extended the scope of the proposed conference by adding the problem of the Far East to the agenda, with the result that one of the treaties concluded in the American capital resolved the British imperial dilemma. To the satisfaction of all concerned, the Anglo-Japanese alliance was buried by the Four Power Treaty of 13 December 1921, which bound the United States, the British Empire, Japan, and France to respect one another's "rights in relation to their insular possessions and insular dominions in the region of the Pacific Ocean" and to refer to a joint conference of all of them any dispute over these rights that could not be settled by diplomacy.

The representation of the dominions at this Washington Conference of 1921–22 was a sore point. The United States sent no invitation to them, though their international status had been recognized in the Paris conference and three of them were Pacific powers. With the exception of New Zealand, which was reluctant to assume the role of an international entity, the dominions deeply resented this American neglect, which came on top of the American condemnation of the League for including them as voting members. Lloyd George tried to soften the blow by promising to make room for them in the British delegation. But it was doubtful for some time whether any of them would stoop to enter "through a back door," as Smuts expressed it. The American affront hit him hardest of all because it played into the hands of Hertzog. Smuts guarded himself by declaring that his country would never attend a conference to which she was not invited in her own right; and he protected her interests by authorizing Balfour, the chief of the British delegation, to act for South Africa in the coming conference. Hughes had to swallow his pride because vital Australian interests were at stake in Washington. Being unable to go himself, he announced that he would send another Australian; but before he made this concession he burst out indignantly: "We did our utmost at the Imperial Conference to secure representation of the dominions, and it was only when the United States slammed the door in our face that we stopped." Massey likewise had to send a substitute. Meighen hesitated until he consulted Borden, who promptly advised that the dominions should overlook the American slight because the meeting in Washington "was of supreme international concern." Thereupon Sir Robert was asked, and he agreed, to represent Canada.

The British Empire delegation functioned in Washington precisely as it had in Paris, meeting as a whole to discuss every important question and threshing out differences of opinion, which were sometimes strong, until unanimity was reached. The Paris precedent was also followed in the signing of the treaties, Balfour signing twice, the second time for South Africa. But there was no agreement on what would have happened if the members had disagreed. The Canadian's report to his government stated that "any dominion delegate could, if convinced or instructed that his duty lay that way, reserve assent on behalf of his government"; whereas the New Zealander's report, based on the concept of an indivisible empire, asserted that the withholding of a dominion adherence "would have had no effect on the international operation and obligation of the treaty." Both these conflicting opinions were right, and both were wrong, during the transition from empire to commonwealth, when political reality was trampling on the heels of outmoded legal technicality.

The inherent weakness in one foreign policy for the whole empire, controlled jointly by the mother country and the dominions as demonstrated in the Paris and Washington conferences, was exposed by the Chanak crisis of September 1922. The revolutionary government of Mustafa Kemal having torn up the peace treaty imposed upon Turkey by the Allies, the Turks threatened the British forces still occupying the Dardanelles pending the negotiation of a new peace treaty. Should the British fight off an attack or offer no resistance at Chanak? A quick decision was imperative, precluding prior consultation of the dominions. At once Lloyd George announced that Britain would fight if her forces were attacked, and he cabled the dominions inviting them to back the mother country with the offer of military contingents. New Zealand and Australia promptly complied, the former with alacrity and the latter with some qualms over the brusqueness of the call and the prospect of another war. Canada politely but firmly refused, and South Africa did the same. The automatic solidity of the dominions on the supreme issue of peace or war had been tested and found wanting.

The lesson was confirmed by the new peace settlement with Turkey, which followed a change of government in Britain. Though the dominions were not invited, nor did they seek, to share in the negotiation of the Treaty of Lausanne, which was concluded in the summer of 1923, London presumed that they would formally accept it by adding their signatures and advising ratification. But when the time came, Canada declined and the others followed suit, on the ground that they had had no part in the transaction. They would neither assume any obligation under the treaty nor presume to prevent the mother country from binding herself by it. They regarded that as her business, not theirs. The treaty was not reworded to conform with this fact, but they were content to let it be. It restored their state of peace with Turkey, and they now knew that the future would fit technicality to reality. Already one of the dominions had contracted a treaty as an independent state, and this breach with the past had persuaded the members of the commonwealth to agree on new rules for the making of treaties.

When Canada and the United States signed the Halibut Fisheries Treaty in March 1923, the customary signature of the British ambassador was omitted because the Canadian government objected to it, and London yielded to the insistence of Ottawa. The change meant more than the dropping of an empty form. It meant the abandonment of the mother country's constitutional right to control the foreign relations of a daughter nation. This had been decided in principle when Canada was promised the right of legation, which had yet to be exercised. In characteristic British fashion the transfer of sovereignty, like the original concession of responsible government, required no legislative action; and in characteristic American fashion the treaty was held up a year and a half by a Senate reservation that would have undone the change and was so phrased as to give gratuitous offense to Canada. It stated that "none of the nationals, inhabitants, vessels or boats of any other part of Great Britain" were to engage in the fisheries contrary to the provisions of the treaty. The Senate was finally induced to withdraw this amendment by an undertaking of the government in Ottawa to enact a law prohibiting fishing from Canadian bases by non-Canadian nationals.

The new rules for the making of treaties were adopted by the Imperial Conference of 1923. They substituted separate for joint control and responsibility; but they also recognized the moral obligation of each member of the commonwealth, when acting alone, to avoid anything that might injure or embarrass another member. None was to commit another without its consent. Before entering upon any negotiation, the government concerned was to weigh carefully the possible effect on other parts, or the whole, of the commonwealth, and to consult with the governments of such as might be affected, so that they might express their views and be represented if the circumstances warranted. If two or more governments of the commonwealth were represented, they were to follow the pattern of Paris and Washington, and to keep those who were not represented fully informed of the progress of the negotiation.

These constitutional regulations of the commonwealth were essentially British in character. They were not legislation, for the body that promulgated them had no legislative authority; nor were they a legal compact, for the constituent governments did not adopt them as such. They were simply a set of voluntary rules that the British family of nations drew up because they wished to follow them in order to stick together. Good faith in the family relationship was the only sanction; and this was much stronger than outsiders could appreciate, because there was nothing quite comparable to this family relationship in the rest of the world.

In 1924, when the short-lived Labor government of Ramsay Mac-Donald recognized the U.S.S.R. without first consulting the dominions, this breach of faith with them provoked such criticism that he had to promise it would not happen again; and at Locarno in the following year, when the administration of Stanley Baldwin joined in guaranteeing the inviolability of the frontier between Germany and her western neighbors, this was with the tacit consent of the dominions and the treaty explicitly excluded them from any obligation under it unless they signified their acceptance of it. But to guard against future neglect or misunderstanding, the Imperial Conference of 1926 amended the rules by requiring each member of the commonwealth to give every other member prior notification of any intended negotiation. It also prescribed that every treaty be so framed and signed that the plenipotentiaries would bind only their respective governments, which was the very provision that Borden had tried to get at Paris in 1919.

Other developments of these years were likewise giving a clearer shape to the commonwealth. The Irish Free State took its seat as a dominion in the Imperial Conference of 1923; and though it was then "content to watch and follow," its fiery background soon thrust it forward as a bold leader. The newest dominion stole a march on the oldest by being the first to exercise the right of legation, with the appointment of an Irish minister to Washington in 1924, while Canada was still inhibited, by opposition within its cabinet, from acting on the promise of 1920. In taking the lead, the Irish effected a departure from the arrangement that had been contemplated. The idea of a dominion minister's close association with the British embassy, and of his taking charge of it in the absence of the ambassador, was dropped. The Irish minister was to handle affairs relating exclusively to the Free State, to settle by consultation with the ambassador, as the occasion arose, which of them should deal with Irish matters that might affect other commonwealth relations, and neither official was to be responsible for actions of the other. This precedent governed the exchange of ministers between Ottawa and Washington, which finally occurred in the beginning of 1927, when the United States at last reciprocated with the Free State by appointing a minister to Dublin.

In the League of Nations, the other dominions had acted independently, sometimes voting against the mother country and never meeting with her beforehand to coordinate their views. Now, in 1924, the Free State went further than they could go in this direction. In accordance with Article XVIII of the Covenant, the Dublin government registered with the League secretariat the treaty of 1921. The British government, as the other party to this treaty, formally protested, claiming that "the relations *inter se* of various parts of the British Commonwealth" were internal matters that did not come within the purview of the League. Dublin officially denied this contention, and London was unable to support it by adducing the agreement of the other dominion governments. The Free State won another point on the same principle during the 1925 session of the League Assembly. In the midst of a discussion of compulsory arbitration, one of the British delegation, after referring to the British Empire as "a partnership of six nations standing on a footing of equality," rashly went on to declare that in any matter affecting the vital interests of any one of these partners "there had to be solidarity of action" by all. At once the Irish representative challenged this assertion, and the British delegation hastened to disavow it.

Such incidents quickened the Irish anxiety for further clarification of the constitutional relations between the two countries, to make sure that the Free State was really free. It had been pacified, but not satisfied, by the formal concession that its status was precisely the same as that of Canada. This status had never been defined; and Irishmen, who had until so recently fought for their rights, were naturally more impatient than Canadians, who had never had to fight for theirs, to know exactly where they stood. Their different history also made them more intolerant of surviving limitations, whether real or only symbolic, upon their national freedom. For example, Dublin would stop all judicial appeals to the privy council in London, Ottawa only some; and the office of governor general, new to the people of the Free State but long familiar to Canadians, inspired peculiar resentment among the former. Their republican spirit made it hard for them to swallow the representative of the Crown, and their bitter war against the British government made them suspicious of the representative of that government. Their general attitude on the question of status was expressed by their Minister of External Affairs when, addressing the Dail in June 1926, he insisted that the Free State was a sovereign independent state and intimated that Britain should give notice of this fact to foreign powers that seemed to be ignorant of it.

South Africa, too, was inclined to be more importunate from 1924, when Smuts fell from power, victim of the postwar depression and a political pact between the Nationalists and Labor that matched his own absorption of the Unionist party. Though Labor, being predominantly British, served as a brake upon the extreme Afrikander urge of the much more numerous Nationalists, and constitutional issues played little part in the election of 1924, the new premier was the old Hertzog and his old following came within five seats of winning a majority in the new House. The anti-British and republican Boer tradition, paralleling the Irish tradition, would sweep away all vestiges of former subjection. Hertzog would never retract his principle of the right of secession, and he made no secret of his desire to see London inform foreign powers that the dominions were independent members of international society.

The utterance of such a desire was horrible to New Zealand, and it moved the premier of Australia to register a firm though polite dissent in his parliament, but it attracted little attention in Canada. Yet the senior dominion was not, as those "down under" seemed to be, satisfied to leave things as they were.

The Canadian government was nettled by two incidents that occurred in 1926. One was a decision of the privy council that invalidated an old and hitherto unquestioned Canadian statute barring appeals to the privy council in criminal cases, because the Canadian parliament was not invested with authority to abrogate a right that had been conferred by a statute of the superior British parliament. The other was the so-called "constitutional crisis" in Ottawa, where a third party temporarily controlled the balance in the House of Commons. The Liberal government of Mr. Mackenzie King, which had been in office for five years, lost its precarious majority and had to resign because the governor general refused the prime minister's request for a dissolution. What was thus denied to the Liberal was granted a few days later to the Conservative prime minister, who was no more able to command a majority. Within a few weeks the electorate returned the Liberals to power with an assured majority and a determination to strike a blow for Canadian equality of status with the mother country in the next Imperial Conference, which met that autumn.

When the Free State, South Africa, and now Canada were all prepared to do battle in the same cause, they found no adversary. Official London had been giving deep thought to the problem looming ahead; and the separation of the Dominions Office from the Colonial Office, which took place earlier in this year, was but a slight token of the large readjustment that the British government was willing to make in the relations between the mother country and the dominions. The result was a meeting of minds instead of a clash of wills when the conference got to work on this vital subject under the astute guidance of Lord Balfour. That ripe philosopher and veteran statesman served as chairman and draftsman of the committee, comprising all the dominion premiers, that really did the work which the full conference then adopted as its own. His report ranks with Durham's. It faced the same problem in the same spirit of liberty, and it was epoch-making. But the problem was now so much bigger and more complicated that the two reports may be likened to two treatises, one introductory and the other advanced. The Balfour Report also differed from the Durham Report in being promulgated as a solemn agreement between the responsible heads of governments.

The Imperial Conference of 1926, through the labors of the Balfour committee, gave the British Commonwealth intelligible form and intelligent motion. Hitherto the words "empire" and "commonwealth" had been used rather indiscriminately, often as if they were interchangeable, which reflected a confusion of thought. Now "commonwealth," which had been growing in popularity, at last became official and distinct to connote "the group of self-governing communities composed of Great Britain and the Dominions"; and their "position and mutual relation" were defined as follows:

> They are autonomous Communities within the British Empire, equal in status, in no way subordinate one to another in any aspect of their domestic or external affairs, though united by a common allegiance to the Crown, and freely associated as members of the British Commonwealth of Nations.

This simple yet comprehensive statement of what substantially had come to pass, not as the result of any conscious planning but rather as the consequence of an untidy empirical process operating over a long period of time, was of particular value for two reasons. It exorcised the inferiority complex that clouded the minds of hosts of people in the dominions; and it held up a glass in which the commonwealth could see its own inner nature, its own hidden ideal, so that it might more fully live up to this revelation.

While recognizing the essential character of the commonwealth, the report was careful to observe that equality of status did not necessarily mean equality of function. By way of illustration, it cited the obvious fact that, in the spheres of defense and foreign policy, the major responsibility "rests now, and must for some time continue to rest, with His Majesty's Government in Great Britain."

The surviving relics of inferior status were also frankly examined with the view of progressively eliminating them, and the result was a conscious shaping of the constitution of the commonwealth. This process began immediately and reached a central climax in 1931 with the passage of the famous Statute of Westminster. The Conference agreed that the official title of His Majesty the King was derogatory to the Free State because it contained the phrase "the United Kingdom of Great Britain and Ireland," and that it should be revised as follows:

> George V, by the Grace of God, of Great Britain, Ireland and the British Dominions beyond the Seas, King, Defender of the Faith, Emperor of India.

Parliament made this change in the following year, and by the same act altered its own title to "the Parliament of the United Kingdom of Great Britain and Northern Ireland." The Conference also agreed that equality of status called for a reform of the office of governor general so that its occupant would hold "in all essential respects the same position in relation to the administration of public affairs in a dominion as is held by His Majesty the King in Great Britain" and it was left to the governments concerned to arrange, according to their preference, for the performance of his old function as "the representative or agent" of the British government. The Free State pressed for abolition of all appeals to the privy council, but the other dominions, for various reasons to be noticed later, were not prepared to go so far. Therefore the report simply placed on record a declaration of the British government that it did not favor retention of appeals from any dominion against the wishes of that dominion. This opened the door for further exploration of the whole subject, some aspects of which were admittedly very complicated.

The Conference of 1926 also set in motion a train of action to cut away the legal vestiges of the old inferiority of dominion legislative power. These were referred to two special bodies of experts for careful scrutiny and later report. Meanwhile the Conference laid down two important principles: that it would not be in accord with constitutional practice for the British government to advise the Crown in any matter concerning the affairs of a dominion against the advice tendered by the government of that dominion; and that "legislation by the parliament at Westminster applying to a dominion would only be passed with the consent of the dominion concerned," which was simply a formal recognition of an informal rule that had been established by usage and convention. The task assigned to the legal experts was duly performed, and this led to the enactment of the Statute of Westminster in 1931.

CHAPTER XXXVII

The Statute of Westminster and the Shaping of the Commonwealth

THE STATUTE OF WESTMINSTER stands out as the "one great legal landmark in the history of the commonwealth."[1] It effected fundamental changes in the law governing commonwealth relations and thereby cleared the way for further fundamental changes that followed. Law, however, was not the only instrument that shaped the constitution of the British Commonwealth. Every constitution is more or less regulated by convention, which may supplement, or modify, or even paralyze the operation of law; and constitutional conventions have played a more important role in the British system of government than in any other. Such conventions owe their binding force to custom, or agreement, or both. It will also be observed that, as in the past, the individuality of each dominion affected its relations with the mother country, and that consequently the new constitutional pattern of the commonwealth was marked by considerable variations from dominion to dominion.

"Existing administrative, legislative, and judicial forms," said the Imperial Conference of 1926, "are admittedly not wholly in accord" with the equality of status which it postulated. What were these forms, and how could they be eliminated or altered to conform with the equality of status? As we have seen, one was the royal title, which the act of 1927 corrected; and another was the constitutional position of the governor general, which the conference of 1926 rectified by laying down the convention that it was to be the same as that of the king in Great Britain. A further convention, adopted by the Imperial Confer-

---

[1] Nicholas Mansergh, *Survey of British Commonwealth Affairs: Problems of External Policy, 1931–39*, p. 18.

ence of 1930, declared that the governor general of a dominion should be appointed by His Majesty on the advice of His Majesty's ministers in that dominion, thus formally completing the evolution of informal practice. Here we may also note that the agreement of 1926 led to the establishment of British high commissioners, representing the British government as distinct from the king, in the several dominion capitals on the analogy of the dominion high commissioners in London; that the dominions soon began to send high commissioners to one another; and that the office was diplomatic in character though not in name. The term "ambassador" could not be applied to it because international law defined an ambassador as the accredited agent of one sovereign residing at the court of another sovereign. The two additional conventions of 1926—no advice to the Crown by the British government contrary to the advice of a dominion government on the affairs of that dominion, and no imperial enactment applying to a dominion without the consent of that dominion—touched more complicated matters than the royal title or the gubernatorial position, and have to be related to other changes that were not yet worked out.

To examine the surviving imperial subordination of dominion parliaments, the conference of 1926 proposed the creation of an *ad hoc* committee of experts appointed by the commonwealth countries and the calling of a special subconference, the latter to deal with merchant shipping, and the former with all the rest of the subject. But the governments concerned decided that it would be better to combine these two bodies in a single technical conference, which accordingly prepared a report in 1929. This report set forth in precise terms the extent of imperial restrictions upon dominion legislation and made specific recommendations for remedial action by a combination of statute and convention. Here appeared for the first time the main substance of the Statute of Westminster. The Imperial Conference of 1930 adopted this report with little alteration, and it urged the enactment of the proposed statute after such further amendment as any dominion might require for the application of the statute to that dominion. Accordingly, the bill was submitted to the dominion parliaments, which made some changes in it and passed resolutions requesting the United Kingdom parliament to enact it, and it became law in December 1931. This long and meticulous care in the preparation of the statute was necessary because, though its scope was limited to the removal of legal vestiges of dominion legislative inferiority, some of these were embedded in vital constitutional organs. The surgeon's knife should make no slip when performing a complicated and delicate operation.

What the Statute of Westminster did, what it did not do, and why, can best be understood by considering the whole of which it was a part. The removal of the constitutional inequalities between the United Kingdom and the dominions was effected by a combination of constitutional convention and positive enactment, convention being employed where possible and enactment where necessary. The Statute of Westminster dealt with only some of the inequalities, and the equalizing process was continued by further legislation, dominion as well as imperial; but this was the crucial act.

Two of the new conventions were inserted in the preamble to the statute in order to give them the solemn sanction of the United Kingdom parliament because they imposed limitations on the exercise of its authority. One, which had just been adopted by the Imperial Conference of 1930 on the recommendation of the 1929 report and was based on the principle of a single indivisible Crown, required the concurrence of all the parliaments of the commonwealth, imperial and dominion, for any alteration of the law touching the royal titles or the succession to the throne. The other convention, of which this was a particular development, was that of 1926 barring imperial legislation applying to any dominion without the consent of that dominion.

The statute did not mention disallowance of dominion legislation, which was abrogation by the Crown on the advice of the British government. It was never a part of the Irish Free State constitution, which was drawn up in 1922 following the treaty of 1921. By that time disallowance had become obsolete, but it still applied in theory to the other dominions. Therefore the report of 1929 recommended, and the Conference of 1930 placed on record, another convention categorically stating that the power of disallowance could no longer be exercised over dominion legislation. As this formal nullification of a dead practice did not abolish the legal existence of the power, which remained as a ghostly shadow of bygone subordination, the report pointed out, and the Conference of 1930 repeated, that if the dominions wished they could get rid of the shadow too; for some could do it by simply amending their own constitutions, and the others by requesting the British parliament to delete it from their constitutions. All this was in line with the convention of 1926 that the advice of the United Kingdom government should never conflict with advice by a dominion govern‧ ment on a matter affecting that dominion.

So also was the treatment of reservation of dominion bills by the governor general for the assent or veto of the government in London. This limitation had likewise shrunk in practice, though not to a mere shadow. Legally the governor general could reserve any bill, and he was required to reserve bills touching a few special subjects. Discretionary reservation had pretty well died out, but mandatory reservation had not. It was still applied to some dominions by royal instructions, and to all by certain imperial statutes. Now, in 1930, it was formally recognized that, following the new definition of the governor general's constitutional position, his discretionary power could be exercised only on the advice of his ministers; and it was declared that "His Majesty's government in the United Kingdom will not advise His Majesty the King to give the governor general any instructions to reserve bills presented to him for assent." Convention thus disposed of reservation, except in so far as imperial statutes made it mandatory. The dominions might remove the remaining shadow, as they could that of disallowance, but not the remaining substance of reservation because the Colonial Laws Validity Act of 1865 stood in the way. By that act imperial statutes overrode dominion statutes. The consideration of this obstacle therefore merged in the much larger consideration of the whole inferiority of dominion legislative power; and the Conference of 1930 decided, on the recommendation of the 1929 report, that the surviving imperial limitations upon this power should be swept away.

Accordingly, section 2 of the Statute of Westminster—section 1 merely defined the dominions by enumerating them—freed all future dominion legislation from the restrictions of the Colonial Laws Validity Act and empowered the dominion parliaments to repeal or amend "any existing or future act of the United Kingdom parliament . . . in so far as the same is part of the law of the dominion." Section 3 conferred upon dominion parliaments "full power to make laws having extraterritorial operation," thereby clearing away many legal doubts of whether a dominion could legislate for its own people outside its own territorial limits, such legislation, of course, being applicable only in its own courts. Section 4 declared that no future act of the United Kingdom parliament would have the force of law in any dominion "unless it is expressly declared in that act that that dominion has requested, and consented to, the enactment thereof." This was a statutory application of the 1926 convention, and as such it became binding upon the courts, which conventions were not. Section 5 exempted the dominions from the operation of the Merchant Shipping Act, which had regulated merchant shipping for the whole empire, and section 6 did the same with the Colonial Courts of Admiralty Act.

This first half of the statute might be called the charter of the British Commonwealth because it constituted an imperial renunciation of all surviving legislative controls over the dominions. South Africa and the Irish Free State, however, were the only dominions in which sections 2 to 6 came into full force immediately. Potentially the new freedom applied to the other dominions too, but none of them would then accept it in its entirety. The meetings of 1926, 1929, and 1930 had disclosed considerable differences between these four dominions and the other two on the extent to which they desired or could take advantage of the contemplated legal equality with the mother country, and also considerable differences between the hesitant four. In accordance with their several requests, sections 7 to 10 were inserted, qualifying the applications of sections 2 to 6.

It was impossible to give unlimited authority to the parliaments of Canada and Australia because that would destroy their federal constitutions. Therefore section 7 excluded from the new power conferred upon the Canadian parliament anything that would extend its authority to amend the Canadian constitution or would allow the federal government to encroach upon provincial rights; and it made section 2 applicable to the provinces within the sphere of their competence as defined by the Canadian constitution. Sections 8 and 9 made analogous provisions for Australia. Section 8 also preserved existing limitations upon the power of New Zealand, though it had a unitary form of government, to amend its own constitution. Section 10 accommodated the further wishes of Australia, New Zealand, and Newfoundland by making sections 2 to 6 applicable to each only when and in so far as its parliament adopted them. The two remaining sections were purely formal, the first excluding the dominions and their provinces or states from the meaning of the word *colony* in all future acts of the United Kingdom parliament, and the second affixing to this act the title *Statute of Westminster*.

It will be observed that the statute said nothing about judicial appeals to the privy council or about foreign relations, the only other legal inequalities between the dominions and the United Kingdom. The Imperial Conference of 1930 had considered the question of appeals without reaching any definite conclusion, but the Statute of Westminster made a solution possible for each dominion by its own action or on its own initiative. As for the conduct of foreign relations, this was already regulated by the conventions of 1923 and 1926 in a manner satisfactory to the dominions until they saw the breakdown of international order, which did not begin until late in 1931. How this affected them and their relations with the mother country will appear later. It should also be noted that dominion status was never defined as such. It was merely surrounded by a number of constitutional conventions that applied to all dominions, and by the Statute of Westminster whose terms applied in varying degrees to the dominions.

Newfoundland got least from the statute—nothing more than formal recognition as a dominion. By far the smallest and poorest, it was once described by one of its own politicians as "a mouse with the trappings of an elephant." It took little interest in the statute, and no action to implement it during the short period when it had the power to act. In 1933 Newfoundland ceased to be a dominion in all but name. Overwhelmed by the depression, it voluntarily reverted to the position of a crown colony, subsidized by the mother country, to avoid financial bankruptcy. At the request of the Newfoundland legislature, the United Kingdom passed an act suspending the Newfoundland constitution and substituting government by a commission under the control of the government in London. The act was to remain in force indefinitely until the commission, with money supplied by the home government, restored the island's finances to solvency. The Second World War and Newfoundland's strategic location speeded the performance of this task, and then a constituent assembly was elected to determine the political future of this "oldest colony." Three alternatives were considered: revival of its dormant constitution, continuation of the commission government, and union with Canada. After two plebiscites and much negotiation with Ottawa, Newfoundland became a Canadian province in 1949.

It was New Zealand, suspicious of any weakening of imperial ties, that took the lead in adding section 10, which suspended the application of sections 2 to 6 to the three specified dominions; and New Zealand was the last to adopt these sections. A similar apprehension, though not quite so strong, postponed Australian action for more than a decade. Both dominions, however, experienced difficulties arising from their self-imposed lack of power. This was particularly true in the regulation of the whaling industry, which required them to get special legislation by the United Kingdom parliament in 1934; and when the Second World War necessitated emergency measures of various kinds, the old restrictions on the legislative power of these two dominions caused them serious embarrassment, which further *ad hoc* legislation by London could only partly relieve. Therefore in 1942 the Australian parliament passed the Statute of Westminster Adoption Act, which implemented sections 2 to 6. Early in 1944 the New Zealand government announced its intention of doing the same, but after some discussion with the British government it decided to wait until the war was over. New Zealand was also making up its mind to take full power to amend its own constitution. Accordingly, in 1947 the New Zealand parliament acquired the rights conferred in sections 2 to 6 and became free from the restriction imposed by section 8.

Canada held a middle position among the dominions under the Statute of Westminster. Like South Africa and the Irish Free State, it had sections 2 to 6 come into operation immediately; and like Australia and New Zealand, it inserted a provision exempting its constitution from this operation. Though the reason for this exemption was the same in the two federal dominions, there was a fundamental difference between their constitutions that left Canada inferior to Australia. The senior dominion could not amend its own constitution, whereas the junior could. It was partly a matter of age, and this in a double sense; for the basic Canadian document was drawn up a generation before the Australian, and Canadian national consciousness was much less mature in 1867 than Australian in 1900.

The Canadian disability was also rooted in the binational character of the country, and this was why it lasted so long. Constitutional guarantees of French and Roman Catholic minority rights were an essential feature of Canadian federation, and the World War had frightened French Canada by driving the English and Protestant steam roller over it. These minority rights would be at the mercy of the majority if Canada copied the American or Australian method of constitutional amendment, because French Canada was hived in one province. Quebec would have to be given a veto, which Ontario would not allow unless it got one too; and these two vetoes would freeze the constitution. That was not the way to free it from the necessity of going to London for every amendment other than those of minor detail. French Canada might feel no sentimental attachment to Britain, but it felt more trust in Britain than in English Canada as the custodian of the constitution. This trust also tended to preserve the judicial dependence of the senior dominion upon the mother country. An act of the Canadian parliament in 1933 barring criminal appeals to the privy council was now valid by reason of section 2 of the Statute of Westminster;

but civil appeals were still allowed, principally though not wholly,[2] because they involved judicial interpretation of the constitution, a well-known means of altering a constitution.

This judicial dependence disappeared first, and thereby it stimulated the search for a workable system of autonomous constitutional amendment that would terminate the need for the surviving legislative dependence. For a long time there had been a growing Canadian criticism of the privy council on the ground that its decisions were warping the constitution by a narrow legalistic interpretation of federal authority. The criticism became acute in 1937, when the privy council invalidated certain labor legislation of the dominion parliament implementing an international convention adopted by the International Labor Organization. The argument against this legislation was that it invaded the area of "property and civil rights" reserved for exclusive provincial legislation by one section of the British North American Act; the argument for it was that another section invested the federal parliament and government with "all powers necessary or proper for performing the obligations of Canada or of any province thereof" arising under treaties between the empire and foreign countries. The adverse decision hamstrung Canada as a treaty-making power, and this was not to be tolerated. Early in 1939 a bill was introduced into the Canadian House of Commons barring all appeals to the privy council. The debate on it was halted to clear up doubts of its constitutionality. This question was referred to the Supreme Court of Canada, which declared that the bill was *intra vires,* and an appeal from this decision was taken to the privy council, where the hearing was postponed because meanwhile the Second World War had broken out. In 1947 their Lordships upheld the judgment of the Canadian Supreme Court, which was based on the Statute of Westminster, and in 1949 the Canadian parliament passed a new measure abolishing all judicial appeals to London.[3]

Already the Canadian search for a formula by which Canada could

---

[2] Canadian professional opinion was divided on the question of carrying ordinary civil cases to the privy council. Popular opinion inclined to oppose it because only wealthy litigants could afford it.

[3] Australia and New Zealand were then free to do the same, but they did not. They lacked the Canadian incentive. From the very beginning, constitutional appeals from the High Court of Australia were prohibited except by special permission of that court, which granted it only once, in 1914. By an oversight in drafting the Australian constitution, constitutional appeals could bypass the High Court by going straight to the privy council from state courts, but this loophole was effectively plugged by federal legislation during the years 1903 to 1907.

amend its own constitution had found a partial solution and come within sight of completing it. The key to the solution was a system of differential rigidities, beginning with none, according to the varying nature of amendments that might be proposed. The federal and provincial governments were now agreed that the dominion parliament should have power, by ordinary legislation, to make any amendment that did not infringe upon existing provincial or treasured minority rights. Therefore the United Kingdom parliament passed a special act in 1949 investing the dominion parliament with this authority. The legal experts of the federal and provincial governments had yet to work out a satisfactory classification of other amendments with specifications of what further consent should be required for each class. It was a very complicated task that was still unfinished at the time of this writing.

Because South Africa was unencumbered by a federal constitution and uninhibited by imperialist scruples, the parliament of that dominion acquired immediately and without any qualification all the powers conferred by the Statute of Westminster, and the effect was far-reaching. That enactment pulled from the South African constitution an important linchpin that South Africans themselves had inserted as an essential condition of their own Union. It will be recalled that section 152 of the South Africa Act of 1909 gave the Union parliament power to amend the constitution by ordinary legislation in all save a few particulars—notably the equality of Dutch and English as official languages, and the nonwhite franchise in the Cape—for which it required a two thirds majority of both houses sitting as one body. Now that the Union parliament could override United Kingdom legislation, it was legally free to repeal section 152 by an ordinary act.[4] This possibility was clearly foreseen in Britain and South Africa, and in both countries the removal of the legal safeguard was considered inevitable. The prospect alarmed many South Africans of British stock, who pressed for a specific reservation in the Statute of Westminster to cover the entrenched clauses; but these people were an impotent minority, and their agitation irritated Boer opinion, particularly among the followers of General Hertzog, the prime minister. Nevertheless, he compromised when General Smuts raised the question during the debates on the resolution requesting the United Kingdom parliament to pass the Statute of Westminster. The compromise was an amendment, offered

---

[4] Though this was generally admitted at the time, there were a few legal doubts about it. They were finally buried by a decision of the Union Supreme Court in 1937.

by Smuts and inserted in the resolution, stating that the request was made "on the understanding that the proposed legislation will in no way derogate from the entrenched provisions of the South Africa Act." The moral obligation of the conventional safeguard, which was thus adopted to replace the legal safeguard, was respected for nearly two decades.[5]

Of more immediate importance was the fact that in 1934 the parliament of the Union exercised the power acquired in 1931 to shift the whole basis of the South African constitution, and in doing this it implicitly enunciated the heretical doctrine of a divisible Crown, which later became commonwealth orthodoxy. Because all the powers possessed by the parliament of South Africa, which were now complete, were conferred upon it by legislation of the United Kingdom parliament—and the latter body could *legally* repeal any of its own acts— the inequality between the two parliaments, though abolished in practice, still existed in theory. The ghost of subordination survived also in the formal conduct of foreign relations in the name of the king. This required the use of the Great Seal of the Realm of Great Britain, which was under the control of a United Kingdom secretary of state. The Union parliament now proceeded, by the passage of the Status of the Union Act and the Royal Executive Functions and Seals Act, to make the constitution of South Africa self-derived.

The Status Act of 1934 declared that the Union parliament was "the sovereign legislative power in and over the Union," that no act of the United Kingdom parliament of later date than the Statute of Westminster would be "part of the law of the Union, unless extended thereto by an act of the parliament of the Union," and that the Statute of Westminster "shall be deemed to be an act of the parliament of the Union and shall be construed accordingly." It repealed disallowance and reservation from the South Africa Act of 1909, thereby investing convention with the full force of law; and it did the same with the rule that in all South African affairs, internal and external, the king or his representative should act only on the advice of his South African ministers. It further amended the South Africa Act by deleting the words "of the United Kingdom of Great Britain and Ireland" from the reference to the king in the prescribed oath of allegiance. Here, as well as in the possibility that South African ministers might advise the king

---

[5] The Cape native, but not the colored, franchise was abolished in 1936 by the special procedure required by the South Africa Act.

to proclaim South African neutrality when he declared war on the advice of United Kingdom ministers, was the clear implication of a divisible Crown. It appeared also in the Royal Executive and Seals Act, which, following a precedent set by the Irish Free State in 1931, did away with the South African use of the Great Seal of the Realm by substituting the Great Seal of the Union under the custody of the Union prime minister or his deputy.[6]

Such legislation was dictated in South Africa by a political imperative that did not appear in the older dominions. They were either wholly or predominantly British; they had inherited constitutional traditions that were essentially pragmatic; they subordinated law to convention, and prized practice above theory; they were sure that they had full liberty to go their own way. It was very different in South Africa, where the Boers outnumbered the British three to two and had repeatedly fought in vain to escape from British imperialism, where republican freedom from British control had been won and lost again and again, where this experience bred Boer distrust of the British government and of the local British minority. Though such feeling was greatly weakened by the recognition of dominion equality, commencing with the 1926 Imperial Conference and culminating in the Statute of Westminster, it still haunted the political scene in South Africa.

Smuts had long feared this republican ghost as the enemy of unity in the Union, which he put above everything else; and though Hertzog, who no longer believed that the Afrikander lamb was in danger of being swallowed by the British lion, had come round to Smuts' view that the two white peoples of the country should cooperate and could do so only within the free brotherhood of nations now established as the British Commonwealth, there were ominous signs that more than a few extremists in Hertzog's own party would not continue to follow him on his reversed course. His Nationalist government was staggering under the weight of economic depression, and early in 1933 it was doomed when it lost the support of the few Labor members that had kept it in office since 1924. Thereupon Smuts called on Hertzog to resign and offered to serve under him in a coalition cabinet. The offer was an act of magnanimous statesmanship. Though Smuts knew that his binational South African party could win the coming election, he also knew that its majority would be slim and that its return to power would give

---

[6] Canada passed a corresponding act in 1939, but the other dominions did not follow suit.

new life to the old ghost, which he would avoid at any cost to himself and his party. Hertzog rejected his proposal; but Smuts repeated it, this time backed by a swelling public opinion in favor of a truly national government. It was then formed, with Hertzog as premier and Smuts as deputy premier; and it swept the country in a May election, winning 138 of the 150 seats in the House and, in addition, the support of six independent members.

In a land so long and so deeply divided, this grand victory for national unity provided an impetus toward a more perfect union through the fusion of the coalition into a single party; and to make this possible, the government had to reassure the Nationalists that South Africa was no longer constitutionally dependent upon Britain. Hence the further constitutional definition in the Status Act and its fellow. This was only partly successful, as became apparent later in 1934 when fusion created the United party and a considerable minority of the Nationalists, led by D. F. Malan, refused to follow Hertzog into it. They split off as the Purified Nationalist party. At the same time and as a protest against the assertion of national sovereignty, a much smaller English splinter calling itself the Dominion party broke away from Smuts. But the legislation that offended this extreme and failed to satisfy the other drew the great majority of both peoples closer together.

Turning to the Irish Free State, one may see many parallels with South Africa, but the underlying differences are more important. Though both dominions welcomed the full powers conferred by the Statute of Westminster, and both proceeded to place their national sovereignty beyond any question, the motive of South Africa was to make dominion status so acceptable to its own malcontents that it would reconcile them to continuing membership in the British Commonwealth of Nations, whereas the Irish purpose was to achieve by legislation what arms had failed to win—republican independence. Unlike the South African War, which had been fought to a finish and had been followed by the grant of self-government to the conquered, the Sinn Fein war against the British had ended in stalemate and a compromise treaty.

Dominion status was not what the Irish had fought for. It was conceded on terms that were in conflict with its very nature, and the bargain was repudiated by a large and determined minority. By the treaty of 1921 the British government imposed on Anglo-Irish relations a rigidity that bound no other dominion. The treaty prescribed how, and within what limits, the Free State would frame its own constitution, which was to remain subordinate to the treaty. By other provisions of the treaty, the Free State assumed responsibility for certain financial payments, such as pensions and land annuities, and the British government, for strategic reasons of defense, retained control of specified ports in the Free State.

When the British parliament was passing the Statute of Westminster, some right-wing Tories demanded amendments that would withhold from the Free State any power that might be employed to upset the treaty. Their fears had been roused by the political activities of de Valera. From the beginning he denied the validity of the treaty and the legal authority of the Free State government which was built upon it. When he called off the civil war, he refused to make peace with the new regime, which required every member of the legislature to take an oath of allegiance to the king. By 1926 he found that his policy of noncooperation and nonrecognition was no less futile than the appeal to arms, and he decided to fight the new regime from within. As the majority of the Sinn Fein congress objected, he organized the Fianna Fail party to carry out his plan. In 1927 they entered the Dail by swallowing the hated oath in order to get rid of it as soon as possible and thereby open the doors of the citadel for more inflexible republicans. De Valera dismissed the oath ceremony as an "empty formula." Then why, asked government supporters, had he split the nation by fighting against it, and why did he still agitate to abolish it? To uncompromising republicans, especially those of the I.R.A., he was now an apostate. But he was one of the most astute politicians of the age, and he pursued a careful course designed to rally all but the wildest elements of unappeased nationalism without alarming too many moderates. De Valera made great headway through the depression by promising a program of vigorous economic nationalism, and he won countless farmers by denouncing the payment of land purchase annuities to Britain.

The administration of W. T. Cosgrave, which did so much to consolidate the Free State during his decade of office, was already hard pressed by Fianna Fail in the autumn of 1931 when Tory talk of limiting the power to be conferred on the Free State threatened to destroy him and his protreaty party. At once he lodged a stout protest with the British government against the adoption of any such amendment which, he said, was unnecessary because the treaty could not be altered unilaterally. His protest was decisive, as it deserved to be, because it was in accord with the convention barring imperial legislation applying to a dominion without its consent. Here it may be observed that the effect of the Statute of Westminster upon the Anglo-Irish treaty was not on a parity with its effect on the entrenched clauses of the South African constitution because one set of obligations was external and the other internal.

In further contrast to South Africa, the Free State government that welcomed the Statute of Westminster and would use it to the full was almost immediately replaced by a government that spurned its use, scorned dominion status, and flouted the treaty; for the Irish election of February 1932 turned out Cosgrave and put de Valera in office. One of the last measures of the fallen government curbed a resurgence of republican terrorism by setting up a military tribunal that recalled British methods of dealing with Irish violence in the previous century; and two of the first things that the new government did were to release the republican prisoners and to suspend the tribunal.

De Valera was resuming the revolution which the treaty had halted in 1921. His goal then was his goal now—an independent republic in external association with the empire. Then he would have accepted a freely negotiated treaty that recognized reciprocal citizenship and Irish obligations in matters of common concern to the two countries, especially defense and external relations. Now it was doubtful if he would allow such qualifications of republican independence, and the steps he took toward his goal provoked British reactions that precluded a settlement of this nature.

The ensuing quarrel between the Free State and the United Kingdom governments, it should be observed, was enveloped in a juridical cloud. De Valera never retracted his denial of the validity of the treaty, and when the British charged him with violating the treaty he denied that too. Nor were the British always consistent. At times their appeal to the sanctity of treaties contradicted the stand they had taken, and from which they had never departed, when they protested the Free State registration of the treaty with the League of Nations. De Valera shrank from taking advantage of this inconsistency lest he commit himself to the binding character of the treaty.

The British were also embarrassed by the fact that though there was a recognized procedure for the settlement of international disputes there was none for intracommonwealth disputes. The optional clause of the international statute establishing the World Court, providing for compulsory arbitration by that court, had been discussed by the 1926 Imperial Conference; and it was then decided to put off for further discussion the question of accepting the clause which, without some reservation, would vitally affect intracommonwealth relations. The discussion was resumed in 1929 when the British Labor party, pledged to accept the clause, came into power; and an attempt was then made to find a common formula of acceptance for all the governments of the commonwealth. The Cosgrave government cut the discussion short by signing the clause without any reservation. The other commonwealth governments followed with identical reservations that excluded intra-commonwealth disputes. How were these to be handled? The 1930 Conference agreed "that some machinery for the solution of disputes which may arise between members of the British Commonwealth is desirable"; but the machinery it recommended fell far short of that which the member governments had already accepted for international disputes. There was to be no permanent tribunal and no compulsory arbitration. The reason for the contrast was that the member governments, including that of the Free State until de Valera came into power, trusted one another more, not less, than they trusted foreign governments. The underlying supposition was that family differences should and could be composed amicably, and that if an occasional difference called for more formal procedure this could be easily improvised on a temporary basis. This supposition was inherent in the very concept of the British Commonwealth of Nations. When the Anglo-Irish dispute arose, the British offered arbitration by a commonwealth tribunal such as had been contemplated in 1930. De Valera refused, demanding an international tribunal, which the British rejected and he, for reasons of his own, did not continue to urge.

In directing the new phase of the Irish revolution, de Valera had to combine caution with boldness. When he came into power, his party, though the largest that had yet appeared in the Dail, lacked a majority in that chamber—where he was obliged to lean on the support of the small Labor party until after he called a new election in January 1933, an election which gave Fianna Fail only a bare majority. In the upper chamber, the Senate, he always faced a hostile majority. To succeed, de Valera had to reach out in opposite directions—on the one hand catering to the republicans, of whom many hated him as a traitor, and on the other hand allaying the widespread fear that he would push the country back into civil war and anarchy, which he himself was determined to avoid at all costs. In 1932 he pleaded for the abolition of the oath on the ground that it would deprive wild republicans of any excuse for withholding willing obedience to the law of the land; and in 1936, following a new series of assassinations by members of the I.R.A., he outlawed that organization.[7] Gradually, as the country became more united behind him, de Valera pulled it along the road toward republican independence. In this he was helped by his quarrel with the British government, by the depression, and by the growing international anarchy, of which more anon.

The British government began to react in March 1932 with an official protest against the Free State government's declared intention to purge the oath from the constitution and to retain all the proceeds of the land annuities, the collection of which was continued.[8] Both actions, said the protest, would violate the treaty of 1921. De Valera denied it with tortuous reasoning, for he was in a rather awkward situation. Though he had long since committed himself thoroughly to the position that the treaty was neither legally nor morally binding on the Free State, he now recoiled from replying by an outright repudiation of it. That might encourage an outbreak of republican violence, and it would sully the honor of the Free State in the eyes of too many of its own citizens and of its friends abroad. Almost at once the prime ministers of South Africa, Australia, and New Zealand sent messages to de Valera deploring the deterioration of Anglo-Irish relations. But he rejected the implied rebuke and proceeded to implement his election promises. Payment was stopped when the next installment was due; the British government at once resorted to distraint by clapping duties on imports from the Free State; the government of the Free State retaliated as quickly in kind; and the summer of 1932 saw the two countries locked in a bitter tariff war that contributed to, and outlasted, their quarrel over the constitution.

In the Anglo-Irish dispute over de Valera's progressive moves to discard dominion status and to republicanize the constitution, the British wisely refrained from threatening sanctions; but they unwisely argued, in effect, that the treaty had frozen the status and the constitution of the Irish Free State, which therefore had to remain in this condition until British consent thawed it. Psychologically this argu-

---

[7] Which the Roman Catholic hierarchy in Ireland had condemned in October 1931 as "sinful and irreligious."

[8] De Valera's domestic position would have been stronger if he could have passed on to the peasants the relief gained by stopping payments to Britain. That was politically impossible because it would discriminate against those peasants who owed payments on money advanced by the Free State government, which had continued the land purchase policy.

ment was self-defeating. Legally, moreover, it was in conflict with the treaty guarantee of a status equal to that of any dominion, and it was demolished in 1935 by a privy council decision that the Statute of Westminster had given the Free State power to abrogate the treaty. Meanwhile de Valera, who could never admit the Irish validity of a British statute[9] of any kind or a definition of his country's status by reference to any dominion member of the commonwealth, consistently maintained that the Free State constitution was self-derived and wholly under the control of the people who had ordained it.

In 1932 the Senate emasculated de Valera's bill to amend the constitution by eliminating the oath and also the covering provision that the constitution could never contravene the terms of the treaty; but in the following year the unaltered bill became law by the vote of the lower chamber alone, the Senate's constitutional right of veto having expired.[10] Later in 1933 another Irish act forbade appeals to the privy council. There had never been more than a very few, Cosgrave's government had planned to end them in consultation with London, and the recent Canadian act was an encouraging precedent. The office of governor general, the highest monarchical symbol in the land and hitherto personified by Irishmen of distinction, was degraded in 1932 by de Valera's selection of a nonentity to succeed them. The new representative of the Crown continued to live in suburban seclusion, and a year after his appointment his theoretical right to reserve bills and to withhold assent to them was abolished by another constitutional amendment. A nationality act was passed in 1935, after a year of strenuous discussion, to differentiate between Free State citizens and British subjects. It was immediately followed by an aliens act which classified all British subjects as aliens, though it authorized the government to exempt from the practical effect of this law the nationals of any country, and the government promptly exempted those of all parts of the British Commonwealth. Then came the privy council decision, sweeping away the challenge, Irish as well as British, to the legal validity of all this contentious legislation. Already de Valera had started to get rid of the hostile Senate. It had thrown out a bill for its own aboli-

---

[9] The treaty and the constitution were enacted by the British parliament. It may also be observed that de Valera's government took no part in the privy council case that produced the above decision.

[10] The constitution provided for a senatorial suspensive veto of eighteen months. It also authorized its own amendment by ordinary legislation for a limited period, which an Irish act of 1929 extended to sixteen years, i.e., until 1938.

tion, and was soon to do it again, with the result that a resolution of the lower chamber put an end to the existence of the upper in May 1936.

The abdication of Edward VIII in December 1936 caught de Valera at an awkward moment. He was in the midst of working out, largely by himself, a constitution "new from top to bottom," and he was not nearly ready to produce it when the crisis called for immediate decisions on fundamental questions. On countless occasions he had pledged himself to remove the Crown from the constitution; and extremists were impatient for him to seize the opportunity to establish a republic, either by declaring it or by abstaining from action to replace the departing monarch.[11] But he turned his back on the temptation. The apple was not yet ripe.

While the other dominions acted in concert with the United Kingdom, according to the recently established convention, in merely substituting George VI for Edward VIII, de Valera passed, by guillotine procedure, legislation that recognized this change on the throne and at the same time carried the Free State one step further along the road of constitutional estrangement from Britain. There were two acts. The first, the Constitution (Amendment No. 27) Act, 1936, removed the Crown from the constitution. The second, the External Relations Act, 1936, immediately reinstated the Crown on a permissive basis for a limited purpose, and for so long as the Free State was associated with the other nations of the British Commonwealth and they recognized the king as the symbol of their cooperation and used him for the like purpose. This was "the appointment of diplomatic and consular representatives and the conclusion of international agreements" on the advice of the Free State government. Thus the parliament of the Free State, originally composed of king, Senate, and Dail on the British parallel of king, Lords, and Commons, was now reduced to the Dail alone.

On submitting this legislation, its author pointed out that it left untouched the first article of the 1922 constitution, which declared that the Irish Free State was "a coequal member of the community of nations forming the British Commonwealth of Nations." He also observed that this amendment of the constitution contained no proposition to sever "our connection with the states of the British Commonwealth," and that in view of the Free State's association with them "it is obvious that we ought to do our part to facilitate" their dealing with

---

11 It will be recalled that the anticipated British act to regulate the succession could not apply to the Free State without its consent.

the royal abdication. His language at the time plainly indicated a belief that Irish membership in the commonwealth was continuing, and yet it is no less plain that external association was implicitly adopted in December 1936.[12]

The enigma began to clear up in the late spring of 1937. The Free State government then declined[13] the invitation to attend the Imperial Conference that sat from May to July, and at the very same time the Irish were in the throes of adopting the new constitution. After a month of party wrangling over the draft, the Dail approved it by a vote of 68 to 42; and then the final decision was left to the electorate, who adopted the new constitution by a less favorable majority, 685,105 to 536,945.

The 1937 constitution was republican in all but name. In place of the two conflicting legal doctrines written into the old constitution—the delegation of governmental authority by the king and also by the people—it proclaimed that "all powers of government, legislative, executive, and judicial, derive, under God, from the people." For a powerless governor general formally appointed by the Crown, it substituted as head of the state a popularly elected president endowed with some independent authority. It revived the Senate in a more amenable form, de Valera having yielded to a public preference for bicameral government. In addition to placing a presidential and a senatorial check upon the Dail, it prohibited constitutional amendment by ordinary legislation alone. It repeated the provision of the External Relations Act noted above, but in vaguer language that avoided any mention of the king or commonwealth, by authorizing the government to use "any organ, instrument, or method of procedure used or adopted for the like purpose by the members of any group or league of nations with which the state is or becomes associated for the purpose of international cooperation in matters of common concern." Only by virtue of the continuance of the more explicit External Relations Act, which remained on the statute book, was it possible to maintain that Irish membership in the commonwealth was still a fact, and then only by a strained interpretation of that act as recognizing Irish allegiance to the common Crown.

Though de Valera succeeded in transforming the Irish dominion

---

[12] Mansergh, *op. cit.*, p. 290.

[13] With a bitter reference to Irish experience in the Imperial Economic Conference of 1932, where the Free State was the only dominion that got no tariff concession from Britain. See *infra* p. 783.

into what was virtually a republic standing outside the commonwealth, he refused to take the final step. He feared the effect on his own people, who had fought a fierce civil war on this very issue and were still deeply divided over it. He feared the effect on the British government, with whom he had yet to negotiate a termination of the tariff war, which was strangling the economic life of the country, and the surrender of the British treaty right to hold Irish ports. He also hoped to regularize external association by an amicable Anglo-Irish agreement. But what he feared most of all, by his own admission, was the effect on Northern Ireland, which might make partition irrevocable. Here was his one great delusion, the crowning tragedy of his career.

Though the Roman Catholic third of the population of Northern Ireland consistently opposed partition, the Protestant two thirds, who resented it in the beginning but accepted it as a sacrifice necessary for the sake of peace in the rest of the country, had since come to regard it as the rock of their salvation. This changed attitude was incomprehensible to de Valera. He was ever expecting the perverse majority in the North to repent of their sin against the Irish nation and to return to its bosom. Blinded by his own fanaticism, he could not see that his whole policy was greatly responsible for driving Ulster Unionists further away. Hard as their hearts were, the new constitution made them harder still; for it set up a new state named Eire, which in plain English is Ireland, and it boldly asserted that the national territory included all of Ireland, its islands and territorial seas. "Pending the reintegration of the National territory," the constitution continued, "and without prejudice to the right of the parliament and government established by this Constitution to exercise jurisdiction over the whole of that territory," the laws of Eire would apply only to the same extent as those of the former Irish Free State. When de Valera had settled his other accounts with Britain and another world war was impending, he swore that he would not depart from neutrality to win the inclusion of Northern Ireland; yet he still refrained from declaring a republic and repealing the External Relations Act lest he make the reunion of Ireland forever impossible. To complete the irony, the very success of his nationalist policy converted the opposition party which, on returning to power after the Second World War, carried that policy to its logical conclusion.

Though the Irish dominion ceased to exist when Eire superseded the Irish Free State, the rest of the commonwealth played make-believe over the departure of this dominion member by refusing to recognize the nature of what had just happened in Ireland. This, as an eminent authority had observed,[14] was "a revolution in law." Who *enacted* the new constitution? It was not the Free State parliament, which had the legal power to do so, under the Statute of Westminster as elucidated by the 1935 decision of the privy council. That parliament merely approved a slightly amended draft of the constitution and submitted it to a plebiscite without specifically authorizing the people to enact it. Nor was such power conferred by the Statute of Westminster upon the *people* of any dominion. Nevertheless, the preamble of the constitution stated categorically: "We, the people of Eire, . . . Do hereby adopt, enact, and give to ourselves this Constitution." Notwithstanding all this, when the new constitution came into force in December 1937, the government of the United Kingdom issued a statement saying that, having "considered the position created by the new constitution," it was "prepared to treat the new constitution as not affecting a fundamental alteration in the position of the Irish Free State, in future to be described under the new constitution as 'Eire' or 'Ireland,' as a member of the British Commonwealth of Nations"; and the statement went on to say that the overseas dominions, having been consulted, were "also prepared so to treat the new constitution." The only exception was a caveat added by the United Kingdom government that it could not recognize the application of the new name to include Northern Ireland, or anything else in the constitution that might affect that portion of the United Kingdom. Apart from this caveat, the statement was an exercise in self-deception that may be compared with de Valera's persistent mirage over Northern Ireland.

The British swallowing of the Irish constitutional revolution narrowed the area and reduced the tension of the Anglo-Irish dispute over the treaty of 1921, and now both parties were anxious for a settlement. The tariff war, which had begun while the Irish delegation was crossing the Atlantic to attend the 1932 Imperial Economic Conference in Ottawa, was a cruel contrast to the favorable trade agreements that the other dominions there concluded with the United Kingdom.[15] It bore much more heavily on the Irish economy than on the many times larger British economy because nature had securely tied the two together; and in spite of all that Dublin could do, the British government recouped

---

14 K. C. Wheare, *The Statute of Westminster and Dominion Status*, 3rd ed., p. 276.

15 Canada and South Africa signed trade agreements with the Irish Free State at the 1932 Conference, but these agreements were of no great importance.

from Irish exporters the treaty payments that the Irish government withheld. Meanwhile, as was natural under the circumstances, Irish national feeling became dangerously inflamed over the British retention of the treaty ports. On the other side, the damage to British trade with Ireland, though considerable, was not enough to break the deadlock. More powerful was a combination of political considerations. The overseas dominions, which had been disposed to regard the Irish repudiation of the treaty payments as justifying British retaliation, were now inclined to blame Britain for bullying her helpless little neighbor. In Britain, too, a large and growing body of public opinion damned the quarrel as a disgrace to British statesmanship. Most decisive was the perilous international situation. It convinced the Conservative prime minister, Neville Chamberlain, that the security of the United Kingdom necessitated a composition of the quarrel with Eire.

The two governments got together in London in January 1938, and before the end of April they worked out an agreement that wiped out what was left of the treaty and reopened trade between the two countries on an intracommonwealth basis of reciprocal preference. Eire undertook to pay £10,000,000 in final settlement of all financial claims, and Britain to deliver the treaty ports. It would be safer, the British government calculated, to turn them over to a friendly neutral than to hold them against a hostile Eire, particularly since the chiefs of staff had confidentially advised that the rejected alternative would require more forces than could be spared from other needs.

In the Dail debate on the agreement, Cosgrave declared that he could have got the ports with British consent six or seven years earlier but had hesitated to do so because the cost of maintaining them would have been too heavy for the Irish government; and in the House of Commons debate, Winston Churchill bitterly castigated the government for surrendering bases that were vital to the defense of the United Kingdom. Of course an ideal British solution would have been to sell the ports in return for a defensive alliance, but this was as impossible as what de Valera demanded during the negotiation— that Britain wipe out the partition. He told the Dail that the agreement was of advantage to Britain as well as Eire, because Eire was now fully responsible for her own defense and in defending herself she would be defending Britain; and he added that Britain would gain the full advantage on the day when "the whole of Ireland is recognized as a completely independent state." He did not mention the fact, obvious to all, that British interest guaranteed British aid against a foreign attack upon a virtually unarmed Eire. Such an admission would have been too humiliating.

The agreement was de Valera's greatest triumph as champion of Irish nationalism, and Britain's greatest moral victory over Irish nationalism. It was almost unanimously welcomed in Eire for its concrete achievement and also for giving convincing proof of British good faith. If it came too late to hold Eire in the commonwealth—an *if* that begs a very big question—it only confirmed the illusion of the remaining members that Eire was still one of their number.

In following the constitutional evolution of the commonwealth from the First World War, it will not have escaped attention that the Statute of Westminster, the climax of this revolution, coincided rather closely with the collapse of the world economy and the resurgence of international anarchy. The transition from a period of relative prosperity and security had a marked effect upon the shaping of the commonwealth, both constitutionally and otherwise. As long as the feeling of security prevailed, it gave free rein to the centrifugal urge of dominion nationalism in the field of constitutional relations. When this feeling gave way under the impact of great-power aggression, fear of another world war set up violently conflicting reactions in the dominions. On some people it operated to check the centrifugal urge, and on others to spur it on toward a complete break with Britain, as we shall see in the chapter on the coming of the Second World War. Meanwhile the economic depression, after starting a stampede of commonwealth countries down the road of economic nationalism, soon drove them together again in a scheme of mutual economic support. Here it will be well to go back to examine the problem of intracommonwealth economic relations as it developed from the First World War.

The old idea of imperial economic integration emerged from that struggle with new hope derived from the revelation of how strong the empire was when it stood together in face of the supreme test. The new hope, shared by the statesmen of the commonwealth, was focused in a program of three coherent policies: imperial migration, imperial investment, and imperial preference. The great stream of emigration from Britain, two thirds of which had poured into the United States, would thenceforth be made to flow into the dominions. In 1917 the members of the Imperial War Conference approved the principle, in the following year they discussed plans for its application, and shortly afterward the United States unwittingly favored it by moving to restrict immigration. No less natural was the supposition that surplus British capital, which had gone to develop foreign countries all over the world, would in future be channeled into the dominions—also with the unconscious assistance of the United States which, thanks to the war, had ceased to import capital and was now exporting it. As for all-round imperial preference, the British government had at last agreed to the principle in the 1917 Imperial War Conference and told parliament in the summer of 1918 that a plan to implement it was being prepared. Each of these policies would assist the others, and together they would transform the commonwealth by making the most of its human and material resources.

A foreign cynic might detect in this program a subtle scheme of the mother country to preserve dominion dependence, but he would be as wide of the mark as those suspicious foreigners of a later day who could see nothing but grasping imperialism in every American move. The mother country had long recognized the will and the right of the dominions to manage their own affairs, and, as we have seen, she encouraged their desire for equality of status with her. The threefold economic program was cooperatively formulated by the mother country and the dominions for their mutual benefit. It was designed to invigorate the economies of the dominions by supplying them with desired population, capital, and favors in the United Kingdom market; and to revitalize the economy of the parent state by solving her unemployment problem, by bringing profitable returns on new investments as well as old, and by rapidly expanding the preferred dominion markets for her products. These great expectations were only partly realized.

A special conference held early in 1921 brought to a head the discussion of assisted migration. The British government proposed to advance, through the dominion governments or voluntary organizations, sums up to £300 for each approved settler if the dominions would match these amounts, and to make £2,000,000 a year available for this purpose. South Africa was not interested because of its "limited field for white labor," but the other three overseas dominions found the offer attractive and closed with it. This led to the passage of the Empire Settlement Act of 1922, which placed an upper limit of £3,000,000 on the annual contribution of the British Treasury.

Though the project did not lack for money—Australia was positively extravagant—it pumped a disappointingly small number of settlers into the participating dominions. Emigration from the United Kingdom to British lands beyond the sea was not what it had been. The figure for the single prewar year of 1913 was 285,000, whereas the total for all the years from 1922 to 1930, when the net movement outward nearly disappeared to be followed by a net movement inward, was scarcely more than a million. Of this total, only 440,000 migrated with governmental assistance, and many of these might have undertaken the venture without it. The immediate absorptive capacity of the dominions was less than the planners had imagined, and, what was more important, the potential supply of settlers from the mother country was drying up. Though there was considerable unemployment in Britain during the twenties, the war had taken a heavy toll of the male age group desired by the dominions, and the outward pressure of population was being eliminated by the combination of social security and a fall in the birth rate below the replacement level. The reverse flow of migration from 1930 is explained by the depression, which hit staple-producing countries harder than industrial ones.

The migration of British capital to the dominions likewise fell far short of anticipation, and for corresponding reasons. The dominion economies, taken as a whole, were maturing and therefore capable of supplying their own capital needs to a surprising degree. South Africa was by far the greatest gold producer in the world. Canada was much richer than any other dominion, and financially more independent. Though New York had supplanted London as the market for Canadian loans, Canada was accumulating so much capital of her own that she was beginning to export some of it. Indeed, she was well on the way to becoming a creditor country. Australia was greedy for capital and borrowed heavily from the mother country, but this dominion was likewise able to finance more of her own development out of savings. New Zealand borrowed all she could without accumulating any significant domestic capital, but she was a small country with relatively little scope for large-scale investment.

The war seriously impaired Britain's financial as well as her demographic ability to assist dominion development. She was no longer the bountiful supplier of capital that she had been during the century before the war. In 1914 she was the greatest creditor country in the world, with external investments of nearly £4,000,000,000. Of these she lost about £1,000,000,000, mostly by sale to the United States to pay for war needs. During the war, also, she lent some £2,000,000,000 to her allies, from whom she could get scarcely anything back, and she borrowed £920,000,000 from the United States, on which she made annual payments until 1933. She emerged from the war with much of her capital gone and her economy badly shaken. Only by strenuous effort was she able to build up her overseas investment, foreign and imperial, to approximately £3,500,000,000 before the depression made her eat into capital again.

The adoption of imperial preference by the mother country in accordance with the promises of 1917 and 1918 could mean little until she abandoned her historic free-trade policy; and to this she clung, with some minor relaxations, until the depression stopped the outward flow of men and money. Her first departure from the old orthodoxy was in 1915, when she clapped 33⅓ per cent duties on the importation of certain "luxuries" such as musical instruments and private motor cars, for the sole purpose of meeting the wartime need for more revenue, strengthening sterling exchange, and relieving shipping. The effect was also protective, but this was incidental, because the new duties were not balanced by excise taxes on such articles of domestic manufacture. The British government's first concession of imperial preference was in the budget of 1919, and it was limited to duties already in force—on tea, coffee, cocoa, sugar, dried fruits, tobacco, and wine, in addition to the "luxuries" just mentioned. It gave substantial benefits to some dependent parts of the empire, but practically nothing to the dominions save a few sweet crumbs to South Africa and Australia. The first frankly protective British measure was the Safeguarding of Industries Act of 1921, which imposed antidumping duties and sheltered certain "key" industries behind a 33⅓ per cent tariff on such things as dyes. This act honored the pledges of imperial preference by extending the principle to the new duties—a polite but almost empty gesture. There was little scope for imperial preference by the mother country because she still adhered, in the main, to her policy of no taxes on the import of essential raw materials and food. Promising respect for this policy, the Conservatives won a general election late in 1922, and a year later the voters turned them out of office for seeking a mandate to abandon this policy.

Though the dominions were disappointed, they had little just ground for complaint. With the exception of South Africa, which had a low tariff of 15 per cent and granted a preference of 3 per cent, they protected their own manufacturers by such tall tariffs that a reduction of one third—their biggest preference—left British competitors with still a high barrier to scale. What the dominions wanted in return for their nominally generous preference was a real preference in the British market for their surplus products—principally wheat, wool, meat, and dairy produce—for which the people of the mother country would have to pay in higher costs of food and raw materials. If Canada was more willing than Australia or New Zealand to admit that the mother country had the same right as the dominions to decide her own fiscal policy in her own interests, and if Canada was also less vociferous in demanding reciprocal preference by the mother country, the senior dominion was in a very different position from that of her sisters "down under." They got most of their imports from Britain and they depended on her to take their chief exports, whereas Canada bought most heavily from the United States and was there finding a rich market for her rapidly expanding forest and mining industries.

The onset of the depression, with its collapsing markets, credits, and currencies, intensified economic nationalism in the dominions, as in other countries; and it converted the United Kingdom to the policy of protection, which incidentally closed the open circle of imperial preference. Her conversion was necessarily a mild one, because her economy had long since outgrown any possibility of even approximate self-sufficiency. But her extension of imperial preference went to the extreme limit of her new protection, which was inaugurated in February 1932 by the enactment of a general 10 per cent ad valorem duty on all foreign goods, with certain specified exceptions, hitherto admitted free. The exceptions, which included wheat, livestock, meat, wool, cotton, and some other raw materials, remained on the free list. The complete exemption of empire goods from this 10 per cent levy favored the dominions far more than they had favored the mother country with their preferences, and it was clearly intended to be tentative. It could be curtailed or enlarged according to the response of the dominions. Negotiations with them were to be opened that summer in Ottawa, where they were also to negotiate with one another.

The Imperial Economic Conference of 1932 was the scene of feverish and complicated bargaining. All the commonwealth countries were in a desperate plight, and while they agreed that together they could work their way out by a mutual adjustment of tariffs that would encourage more buying from one another, each strove to get a maximum and give a minimum of concessions. One participant remarked at the time that the most prominent member of the conference was "Mr. Gi'me," an observation that may be illustrated by the following exchange. The British suggestion that exemption from the 10 per cent tariff was conditional upon new dominion preferences irritated the Australian prime minister into declaring that this exemption was "a somewhat tardy response" to the favors his country had long conferred upon British industry. Prime Minister Stanley Baldwin retorted that "the greatest boon of all," free entry into the British market, was still enjoyed by the dominions on 90 per cent of their exports to the mother country in contrast to the 30 per cent enjoyed by foreign countries, and that British producers commonly found dominion preferences of little value because they were on top of such high tariff walls. As a matter of fact, Australia was one of the two dominions—the other was Canada—that had built the highest walls in the commonwealth and had recently piled them much higher still. But beneath the plain speaking and hard bargaining at Ottawa, there was a spirit of mutual sympathy and trust, which was inherent in the family relationship of the commonwealth.

During the conference the governments of the commonwealth concluded fifteen bilateral trade agreements, or treaties, known collectively as the Ottawa Agreements. There had been some reciprocity between the dominions, and now there was more of it. But this could not compare in importance with the bargains that the dominions severally made with the mother country. The gist of these was that the United Kingdom promised to continue the preferences already established and to extend them to other commodities—including wheat, meat, and some minerals—in return for an enlargement of dominion preferences, some by lowering tariffs on British goods and more by raising them on foreign goods. The dominions' desire to build up the dikes instead of removing obstacles from the channel was the counterpart of the mother country's determination, already announced, to work out some method of sheltering her own agriculture against dominion competition and still more against foreign competition. Taken as a whole, the agreements embodied a mutual compromise of economic nationalism.

The members of the commonwealth were pulling together to save themselves as best they could from the unprecedented economic calamity that had overtaken the world and was being aggravated by the individual efforts of other countries to save themselves, each reckless of the damage it was inflicting on others. The Ottawa Agreements were the combined response of the United Kingdom and the dominions to the Smoot-Hawley tariff of the United States and the prohibitive tariffs, quotas, and exchange controls of the principal European states.

The fact that the commonwealth was not self-sufficient was beside the point in Ottawa. What mattered there was that it was more self-sufficient than any of its members and they were determined to make the most of this advantage. There is no denying that they found valuable protection in the Ottawa Agreements, but all attempts to measure the value of this protection are futile. Statistical tables of United

Kingdom trade, export and import, empire and foreign, show a distinct recovery except in foreign imports. These remained about the same while empire trade was catching up on foreign trade, with imports from empire countries making the greatest gain.[16] But such tables have to be interpreted with the greatest caution. The shift in favor of empire trade had begun before the meeting in Ottawa, and no one can tell what would have been the effect upon it of a failure to get new concessions from the dominions. The trade of the United Kingdom with the Scandinavian countries increased more than that with the empire, and that with Australia less than Australian trade with Japan. Would either of these branches of foreign trade have grown more, or less, and by how much, if there had been no Ottawa Agreements? The one party to these agreements that seemed to gain relatively more than the others was Australia, despite the fact that wool got no protection, yet no one can calculate what this gain owed to a further depreciation of the Australian currency. Indeed, there was such a multiplicity of factors, domestic and foreign, affecting trade that we have to be content with the obvious general conclusion drawn above.

When the commonwealth governments pulled the old British Empire together against the rest of the world, they made pious professions of helping the world by their example of curbing suicidal economic nationalism. But foreign countries always resent preaching, especially by a big power, and the economic reintegration of the British Empire went far enough to stir alarm and hostility in other countries. Britain was particularly sensitive to this reaction and its attendant danger to her heavy foreign investments and her access to foreign markets for the sale of more than half her exports. Indeed, her recognition of this problem explains her adoption of a low rather than a high tariff; and from the beginning she regarded her new protection as a necessary counter with which to bargain for the preservation and, if possible, the advancement of her foreign financial and commercial interests. She began to use it for this purpose in 1933, when she concluded treaties with Sweden, Denmark, and the Argentine. After the Ottawa Conference the dominions discovered, some more easily than others, that the imperial market was not big enough for their surpluses and that they too needed commercial bridges with the outside world even at the cost

---

16 Foreign countries had been taking 60 per cent of United Kingdom exports and supplying nearly 80 per cent of United Kingdom imports. The dominions, India, and Southern Rhodesia accounted for about two thirds of the remainder in each category.

of sacrificing some of the imperial preferences, a condition that also suited the need of the mother country to repair her own foreign bridges.

With Britain's blessing Australia found in Japan a second-best customer for her wool clip, in return for the admission of Japanese textiles. But the most fruitful accommodation of the Ottawa system was in another quarter. The Smoot-Hawley tariff had dealt Canada a crippling blow, from which immediate Canadian tariff retaliation brought no relief and the Ottawa Agreements very little. Those agreements, however, contributed to American reason in the passage of the Reciprocal Trade Agreements Act of 1934, which enabled the two neighbors to call off their tariff war in the autumn of 1935. But this was not enough to satisfy Canada, whose natural market was next door. She wanted much freer access to it, and in this her interest coincided with that of the mother country, who also wanted much freer trade with the United States. Yet neither could make an acceptable offer of concessions to Washington until they worked out an agreement of their own to forgo some of the special privileges they enjoyed in each other's markets. This they did in 1937, with Canada taking the lead. Then Australia lent a helping hand, because she foresaw indirect gain through an Anglo-American agreement that would open the American door to English woolen manufactures. Thus prepared, Britain and Canada bargained side by side in Washington, and on the same day in November 1938 each signed a trade treaty with the United States, all three countries making large concessions for their mutual benefit. According to *The Economist*[17] of London, this was "the largest operation in trade liberalization that has ever been undertaken."

The depression left its mark on intracommonwealth economic relations—in national currencies wrenched apart and in commercial policies more closely integrated. This integration might be modified in favor of freer world trade as opportunity offered to accommodate the internal strain arising from the commonwealth's lack of self-sufficiency, but the preferential system was retained. It was the established policy of the dominions before the First World War, and it was solidified by the reciprocal action of the mother country when the crisis of the depression compelled her to abandon her old policy of economic internationalism.

---

[17] 31 December 1938.

CHAPTER XXXVIII

India's Advance Toward Dominion Status

BEFORE EXAMINING the constitutional progress of India during the period between the two World Wars, it will be well to look more closely at the Indian National Congress because it largely dominated the Indian political scene. Though its membership included only a sprinkling of Moslems and other minority elements, and its affairs were managed almost exclusively by high-caste Hindus of the professional class, it claimed more insistently than ever to represent all the people of India or, to use its own language, the whole Indian nation.

The Congress had just found a phenomenal leader in Gandhi, who gave it mass momentum. Never in world history has any other man exercised in his lifetime such a wide and powerful spell upon the popular imagination as Gandhi wielded from the end of the First World War. His leadership transformed what had been a movement of the intelligentsia into a movement of the people. In addition to its regular members, it could now count on the support of "millions of unregistered Congressmen," to quote Gandhi's own words. During the interwar years its fluctuating membership may have exceeded four million. It was open to anyone over eighteen years of age, regardless of race, religion, caste, or class, who professed a desire for national independence and paid the paltry annual subscription of four annas (4½ d.). Its activities, however, were chiefly financed by wealthy Indians.

There was a local, a provincial, and a central organization, the first being subject to control of the second, and the second under the command of the third. In each locality, such as a town, or municipal ward, or village, or little rural district, the primary members elected a primary Congress committee whose main function was propaganda and electioneering. In each of the twenty congressional provinces they elected delegates to the annual session of the Congress, which delegates also constituted a provincial Congress committee. Some weeks before the annual session the delegates, meeting in their respective provinces, elected the president of the Congress and selected one eighth of their own number to represent them on the All-India Congress Committee, commonly known as the A.I.C.C. This body also included the president, ex-presidents, and the treasurer of the Congress; and it regulated the business of the annual session, an assembly of more than two thousand persons which usually sat for no more than six days and was concerned only with matters of broad general policy. The A.I.C.C. was charged with carrying out the program laid down by the annual session and also with the management of new business that arose before the next session. As it was a body of several hundred and met only at irregular intervals a few times a year, the A.I.C.C. could not exercise continuous and close supervision. This task was performed by a small cabinet or executive committee of the A.I.C.C.

The Working Committee, as this small executive committee was called, comprised the president of Congress and about a dozen other members of the A.I.C.C. elected annually by the A.I.C.C., until an amendment of the Congress constitution in 1934 empowered the president to choose them on his entry into office. Though the president changed from year to year, the personnel of this "high command" remained much the same. Constitutionally it was the all-powerful executive authority of the Congress responsible only to the A.I.C.C. and the annual session, but practically it guided both of them. It was the controlling center of a great political machine, an oligarchy ruling over a nominal democracy.

Another and more vital feature in the operation of the Congress did not appear in its constitution at all. This was the supraconstitutional position of Gandhi. Officially he was president for one term only, 1924–25, and for some years he was a member of the Working Committee, but from 1934 he held no office whatsoever. Indeed, he then announced that he had ceased to be even a primary member. After his official withdrawal, however, he sometimes took a leading part in the discussions of the A.I.C.C. He often attended meetings of the Working Committee, and early in 1939 he forced the resignation of the president who had been re-elected by a slight majority over the official candidate. No important decision was made without consulting Gandhi, and in the last resort the will of the Congress was almost invariably his will. Pandit Jawaharlal Nehru has aptly described Gandhi's position as that of "permanent super-president." In short, he was the dictator because the masses worshiped him as the Mahatma, or great-souled one, and the whole Congress organization provided a well-nigh perfect instrument of concentrated power.

The policy of the Congress changed when Gandhi took hold of it, but this does not necessarily mean that the change was all his doing. The Congress movement, inspired by growing resentment against foreign rule, had reached a point where it was perhaps bound to repudiate the British *raj* and assert the inherent right of *swaraj,* or self-rule. Yet Gandhi undoubtedly hastened and sharpened the turn from an evolutionary to a revolutionary ideology, and he dictated the special character of the new policy—nonviolent noncooperation with the British. He believed that it would soon force the British to abdicate in favor of *swaraj,* and being a sincere pacifist he was convinced that this was the only way. By insisting upon it, he probably prevented the movement from bursting into wholesale violence. Even his enormous influence could not restrain the revolutionary urge in the rank and file of the nationalists from occasional local riots and bloodshed.

On the other hand, more than a few leading Congressmen broke away from the movement when it became revolutionary. They belonged to the class of Hindus who, as nominated or elected members of the legislative councils, had long worked with the British in the actual business of government. This experience convinced them that the quickest and only safe way for India to attain full self-government, which they desired as keenly as did Gandhi's followers, was by continued cooperation with the British in the program of constitutional reform. This was the origin of the All-India Moderate party, formed toward the end of 1918 and later renamed the National Liberal Federation. These Liberals eagerly welcomed the Government of India Act of 1919 and did their utmost to make its operation so successful that the British would speed the transfer of power and the elevation of India to a position of equal partnership with Britain in the commonwealth, whereas the Congress denounced the act and tried to make it such a complete failure that Britain would surrender the control of India to the Congress.

The Moslem League likewise lost its more conservative politicians in 1918, when they withdrew to form the All-India Moslem Association. Their attitude toward the act of 1919 was much the same as that of the Hindu Liberals, while the League became more radical under the leadership of M. A. Jinnah and inclined toward the position of the Congress except on the matter of communal electorates.

Various other circumstances, some of them extraneous, also contributed to the restless and uncertain mood of India that augured ill for the launching of the new and experimental regime. One was the Amritsar tragedy. Another was the postwar flu epidemic, which had attacked nearly three sevenths of the population and claimed more than six million lives. Yet another was the postwar economic depression, which precluded the adoption of ambitious social welfare schemes by the new ministers responsible to the provincial legislatures. More serious was a stirring among Moslems in India over what had just happened in the Near East. Their soldiers had fought valiantly against the Turks, but the fall of the Ottoman Empire, whose sultan was also the Moslem caliph, raised an Indian cry that Islam was in danger and that Britain would stand out as Islam's archenemy unless she promptly restored that empire with all its prewar power.

This anti-British caliphate movement played straight into the hands of Gandhi, who declared that the opportunity to unite Hindus and Moslems was such "as would not arise in a hundred years." Overriding some doubts in Hindu circles, he led the Congress into an alliance with the Moslem League to right "the caliphate wrong." It was an ominous anti-British combination which held firm until the summer of 1921, when a body of fanatical Moslems in southwest India, the Moplahs, rose against the government and massacred their Hindu neighbors. What little was left of the alliance was blown away by the Turkish abolition of the caliphate. But before the shattering Moplah blow, the coalition had threatened to wreck the new constitution; and as Hindu and Moslem fell apart again, their schism proved to be the principal stumbling block in the way of the country's constitutional progress.

Under the new constitution of 1919, the central legislature became bicameral. A slight majority of the upper chamber, the Council of State, and more than two thirds of the lower, the Legislative Assembly, were elected, the latter on a wider franchise than the former. The provincial legislatures, where the experiment in responsible government was to be tried, remained unicameral and retained the old name, legislative council; but now at least 70 per cent of the members had to be elected on a still wider franchise than previously, no more than 20 per cent could be officials, and the remainder were appointed from classes or communities that would otherwise be unrepresented. Outside the formal constitution, two other reforms underlined Britain's anxiety to implement the 1917 promise of equality with the dominions. The joint select committee of the two Houses of Parliament, when reporting on the bill in 1919, declared that India should have the same tariff autonomy as the dominions. This principle was promptly adopted in the so-called "Fiscal Convention," and its application was upheld by the British government against the loud protests of British manufacturers. The second reform was the progressive replacement of Britons by Indians in the upper grades of the civil and military services of the country.[1]

The Congress boycotted the first elections under the act of 1919, which were held in the autumn of 1920. Backed by attempts to interfere with the polling and by charges that all who accepted the act were traitors to the national cause, the boycott was part of Gandhi's first noncooperation campaign, which had begun earlier in the year. It collapsed in 1922, when his preaching of civil disobedience bore bloody fruit in the murder of a score of policemen in one province and landed him in jail. During his confinement—he was released on compassionate grounds of health in 1924—there was a hot dispute in the Congress over what it should do in the elections of 1923. Many Congressmen now condemned the boycott of 1920 as a major blunder because it had left the door wide open for the Liberals to enter the legislatures and take office as ministers in most of the provincial governments. Other Congressmen, however, insisted that it was still the right tactics. The dispute ended with a majority decision to run candidates for the purpose not of working the constitution but of obstructing its operation.

The sequel gives a rough indication of the political weight of the Congress. The percentage of the electorate who cast their votes in 1923 was 39.9, an increase from 29 in 1920; and a considerable number of Swarajists, as they were now called, won seats in every provincial legislature except that of Madras. In only two of the other provinces were they able to block the legislative passage of supplies and force the governors to resume control of "transferred" subjects, and there the deadlock was broken two years later. The elections of 1926 brought out 42.6 per cent of the registered voters and were the occasion of large-scale rioting between Hindus and Moslems, which destroyed much property and spilled more than a little blood.

Dyarchy was working and it continued to work until it was superseded by another British-made constitution in 1937. The Liberals got the system working while there was little internal opposition, thanks to the initial boycott; and they kept it going, thanks to the loyal support

---

[1] The lower grades of the civil service, comprising the vast majority of the personnel, had always been Indian.

of efficient British civil servants, who were now under Indian masters, and to the Swarajists in the legislatures, who were not always intransigent. Indeed, it was observed that these Congressmen tended to assume the role of a constitutional opposition, and that they not infrequently helped the administration by their keen criticism.

Though dyarchy had not been introduced into the central government, the viceroy's executive council now included three Indians instead of only one, and for the first time it was confronted by a large elected majority in the legislature, to which most of the ablest politicians gravitated. The result was rather surprising. Though the legislative majority had no constitutional control over the executive and might be overridden by the viceroy when they refused to pass any particular bill that he "certified" was essential, and though they were a permanent opposition pressing for the concession of responsible government, a large body of very useful legislation was enacted without recourse to certification,[2] for they listened to the government spokesmen usually with patience and often with assent, and their influence upon the executive was no less remarkable.

Yet the act of 1919 did not achieve its primary object of giving the people of India a real training in responsible government, and dyarchy was partly to blame for this failure. When put to the test of experience, a governor, half autocrat and half constitutional sovereign, an executive split into two compartments operating on opposite principles, a legislature controlling the policy of only one half of the administration while free to criticize and even to withhold supply from the other half—all made for political confusion rather than political education. Practical problems were forever arising that straddled the division between the "reserved" and the "transferred" subjects, and there was a chronic tendency of the politicians to magnify their functions on the "reserved" side at the expense of neglecting their opportunities on the "transferred" side.

The nature of Indian society was the fundamental reason for this failure of the act to serve its main purpose. The British authors of the act sincerely hoped but seriously doubted that responsible government, which their own very different kind of society had slowly evolved, could be applied in India as it had been in the colonies. Indian politicians, however, soon made it clear that this was what they wanted, but they did not develop the party system essential for its operation Responsible

---

[2] It was used only ten times during the life of the constitution.

government cannot work without political parties to organize the legislative majority, whose leaders form an administration, and an opposition to provide an alternative government. In India there was only one well-organized and disciplined party, that of the Swarajists. They alone had a definite policy but this was wholly negative. The Liberals were not a real political party. They lacked the necessary funds and cohesion, and they were inclined to break into shifting groups under different names and leaders. The Moslem League was wholly communal and comprised no more than a minority of politically-minded Moslems. In only two provinces did anything like a genuine political party appear: the Justice party, of anti-Brahmin Hindus, in Madras; and the National Unionist party, intercommunal, in the Punjab. It was perhaps inevitable in the plural society of India that party divisions generally followed communal lines instead of being based on political principle.

The line that cut the deepest was between Hindu and Moslem. It had been there for centuries before the British entered India, and now the prospect of national freedom from British control accentuated the antagonism between these two major communities by precipitating a struggle for place and power against the day of the foreign arbiter's withdrawal. Though the League and the Congress agreed that the country should have an Indian-made constitution with a parliamentary form of government, they parted company on two basic issues. The League accepted the commonwealth and sought equality within it, while the Congress rejected it as derogatory to Indian nationhood. The League demanded a federal constitution with the fullest possible provincial autonomy, so that Moslems would have the maximum freedom to rule the three provinces where they were in a majority; whereas the Congress, claiming to speak for British India as a whole, insisted upon a unitary constitution to consolidate the country and, incidentally, to deliver its rule into the hands of the over-all Hindu majority.

Leaders on both sides saw grave dangers ahead unless they could come together and work out some mutually acceptable constitution. Haste seemed necessary when, as a consequence of continual prodding by Liberals in the Legislative Assembly, the British government appointed the Simon Commission in the autumn of 1927 to review the working of the constitution—two years before the time set in 1919. A conference representing all Indian parties met in February 1928, only to be paralyzed by internal conflict between the Moslem League and the Mahasabha, a newly-formed organization of fanatical Hindus.

When the conference reassembled in May the breach was wider, and the task of preparing a constitution was referred to a small composite committee. Three months later it presented a penetrating and constructive report that far surpassed anything of the kind that Indian nationalists had yet produced.

This so-called Nehru Report[3] embodied the first attempt by Indians to draft a constitution for their country, the frankest effort they had ever made to deal squarely with the thorny problem of communalism, and a public warning to the princes of the native states. It postulated "full responsible government on the model of the constitutions of the self-governing dominions" not as the end of a gradual evolution which the British contemplated but "as the next practical step," because no party would be satisfied with less and this would not commit the Congress to renounce "the goal of complete independence." Communal dissensions, which "cast their shadow over all political work," had their root in mutual fear; and this could be banished only by a constitutional guarantee of full religious liberty and cultural autonomy to each community, so that none could domineer over another. Separate electorates, which violated the principle of responsible government and accentuated communal divisions, should be discarded. Legislative seats, however, should be reserved in strict proportion to population for Moslem minorities and for the non-Moslem minority in the North-West Frontier Province, but for none others. The North-West Frontier Province, to which, because of its dangerously exposed position, dyarchy had not been extended, was to have the same self-government as any other province; two new provinces were to be carved out of old ones, Moslem Sind to be separated from Bombay and a Hindu province to be erected in Southern India; and, in addition, a general revision of provincial boundaries to be more in accord with language divisions was recommended.

The allocation of powers between the central and the provincial governments was to be practically the same as the act of 1919 prescribed, and all unspecified subjects were to lie within the sphere of the central government. But this did not mean federalism. The British tradition of unitary government in India dominated the thinking of the committee. The Nehru Report merely suggested the possibility of federalism, particularly in reference to the future relations of the

---

[3] Pandit Motilal Nehru, president of the Congress, was the chairman, and his son, Pandit Jawaharlal Nehru, secretary general of the Congress and Motilal's successor as president, was the secretary of the Committee.

princely states to British India, or the Commonwealth of India, to use the name adopted in the draft constitution.

The problem of the ruling princes—autocrats who would not follow the British lead by conceding any measure of responsible government—was rapidly coming to the fore as a consequence of the nationalist drive in British India and the prospect of its becoming self-governing. The princes' suzerain and protector was the British Crown acting through the government of India, and they feared what would happen to them when the control of this government passed from British imperialists to Indian nationalists. The Montagu-Chelmsford Report had intimated that they could not remain aloof from the constitutional transformation in British India, and had adumbrated the ultimate inclusion of the native states in an all-India federation. Now the Nehru Report warned the princes that their own subjects would not "quietly submit to existing conditions forever," and that the people of British India would espouse their cause. A pertinent article in the draft constitution specifically transferred to the Commonwealth of India all the rights and duties of the existing government of India relative to the native states.

The all-India party conference, on reassembling at the end of August, accepted the Nehru Report with a few amendments, and ordered the draft constitution to be dressed in full legal form for submission at the end of the year to a constitutional convention likewise representing all parties. The convention never met, for almost at once the old feud flared up again. The Congress would have nothing less than the complete severance of the British connection, while the League insisted on a federal system with all residual powers vested in the provinces and the retention of communal electorates. Thus the promising work of the Nehru committee collapsed like a house of cards.

Meanwhile the Simon Commission was wrestling with the problem of how India could continue the advance along the road of self-government. Because the commission was appointed under the Government of India Act of 1919 to prepare the ground for a revision of that act, its members were chosen from parliament—two peers and four commoners, representing the three political parties, with Sir John Simon as chairman. The exclusion of Indians from this body stirred bitter feeling in India. "Simon, go back," was blazoned on banners that greeted the commission on its first visit to the country in the spring of 1928, and the hostility of the Congress rose to a dangerous pitch before the commission submitted its report. But a central India committee appointed by the viceroy from the two houses of the legislature, and provincial committees appointed by all but one of the provincial legislatures, sat and worked with the commission, which received numerous deputations and gathered an immense amount of information. During the course of the investigation its scope was enlarged by the British government, at the request of the commission, to include the relations between British India and the native states; likewise on Simon's recommendation an important change of procedure was announced. Between the submission of the commission's report and the framing of the government's policy for enactment by parliament, a new stage was to be inserted. The British government would meet representatives of British India and the princes in a Round Table Conference to seek the greatest possible measure of agreement.

The Simon Report, which was thus subject to revision by Indian leaders, was published in two volumes in June 1930. The first presented the most thorough analysis that had yet been made of the conditions underlying the problem of government in India, and the second set forth the conclusions and recommendations. The fundamental conclusion was that ultimately the constitutional framework of India must be federal in order to embrace the native states. The major recommendation was that parliament should abolish dyarchy in the provinces by turning over the whole of their administration to ministers responsible to their legislatures, free of any interference by governor or the central government except such as might occasionally be necessary for the safety of a province or the protection of minorities. The application of responsible government to the central executive should wait upon experience in the provinces; but the way should now be prepared for the federation of all India by refashioning the central legislature to represent the provinces rather than the people at large, and by associating the princes with British India in a consultative Council for Greater India. The commission deplored the divisive effect of communal electorates but could find no acceptable alternative. The report also declared that Burma, being very different from India, should no longer be under the government in Delhi, a point on which there was no controversy whatever.

That the advance toward the goal of full self-government should be gradual, a concept rooted in British domestic and colonial history, the Simon Report took for granted; but it rejected the method of advance that had been contemplated for India, which was simply a continuation of the process of shaping the government of that country by periodic inquiries and acts of parliament, and urged the adoption of the traditional British method by making the new constitution so elastic that it could develop by itself as the need arose. Whether this surrender of the constitutional initiative to Indians would lead to their assimilation of the British cabinet system, which the commission frankly admitted might not fit Indian conditions, or to the evolution of some other form of democratic government, should be left for Indian experience to decide.

India was seething with ferment by the time the commission completed its work. The Congress had boycotted its proceedings from the beginning, the announcement that the Round Table Conference would review the whole problem of government had evoked a statement signed by Gandhi and others that the proposed conference would fail unless the Congress was given "predominant representation" in it, the Congress had demanded "Complete Independence" at once, and another civil disobedience campaign was in full swing. It began with a "march to the sea" to extract salt, a government monopoly, and it soon developed into sporadic terrorism. The government declared the Working Committee an unlawful association; Gandhi, Pandit Jawaharlal Nehru, and multitudes of their disciples were lodged in jail; and the forces of law and order suppressed the incipient anarchy. But the civil disobedience campaign continued until the spring of 1931, when it was suspended in return for a release of "political prisoners." This bargain, which recalls Gladstone's "Kilmainham Treaty" with Parnell, was negotiated by the viceroy, Lord Irwin (later Earl of Halifax), with the incarcerated Gandhi, and it was only a truce that broke down at the end of the year.

The Round Table Conference held three sessions—in 1930, 1931, and 1932, all in London—and contributed much to the new constitution. Prime Minister Ramsay MacDonald presided, but the British delegation, which comprised Conservative, Labor, and Liberal members, was greatly outnumbered by the Indians. The Congress took part in only the second session, for it was in open revolt during the first and again during the third. A surprising concord soon carried the first session beyond the Simon Report. The distant prospect of dominion status, with its implication of a central government responsible to the electorate, and an all-India federation, in which the princes would provide "a stabilizing factor," seemed to move much closer to present possibility, as one after another Indian, Hindu or Moslem, politician or ruler, joined in the opening discussion. Thereupon a number of committees, each reflecting the variegated composition of the conference, got to work on the practical details of the new constitution; and the most important of these bodies devised a scheme for the central government that, in its essentials, was adopted by parliament in 1935. Another committee got bogged in the perennial dispute over communal electorates and emerged with nothing new except a demand of the depressed classes to be treated as a minority distinct from the rest of the Hindus.

Before the second session the world-wide depression had so impaired the credit of India that the British government warned parliament that it might have to vote financial assistance to the government of India, and during the session the financial crisis forced Britain off gold, thus emphasizing the precarious economic position of India. The session of 1931 also coincided with the passage of the Statute of Westminster, which sharpened the political impatience of India. But the outstanding feature of this session was the behavior of one member, Gandhi. As the sole spokesman of the Congress he asserted that he represented all the people of India, even the princes. He demanded complete and immediate surrender to his organization of all British control, including that of the British forces whose presence he tacitly admitted would be needed for some time. His only concession was that a free India would not necessarily use its freedom to secede from the British Commonwealth. His only constructive effort was an attempt to get his fellow Indian members to agree on a solution of the communal problem, and it was an utter failure. Nevertheless, the conference proceeded with its constructive task, giving more definite shape to the federal plan; and a proposal to establish full self-government in the provinces right away, without waiting for the completion of this plan, received little encouragement, the majority of the delegates preferring a single act of parliament for the whole constitution.

At the conclusion of the session Ramsay MacDonald warned the conference that its work must not be stalled by the communal deadlock, and that Indians should settle it among themselves or his government would feel compelled to impose a solution, unsatisfactory as that might be. After more than seven months of fruitless waiting, during which the Congress was again at war with the Indian government and Gandhi was once more in jail, the prime minister issued the "Communal Award" in August 1932. This followed the old system of separate electorates and reserved legislative seats for minorities, and extended it to cover the depressed classes, who soon gained official recognition as the Scheduled Castes. Their inclusion hit a tender spot in Gandhi, who

was ever a champion of the outcastes but could never tolerate a perpetuation of their schism from the rest of the Hindu population, for he
hoped to heal it by working on the conscience of the high castes. From
his prison in Poona he dictated a formula that reserved more seats for
the depressed classes and confined their separate voting to the pri-
maries; and by undertaking one of his famous fasts unto death, he forced
the reluctant leaders of the high castes and of the depressed classes to
accept this "Poona Pact." The British government adopted it as an
amendment to the Communal Award, and as such it became his one
contribution to the new constitution.

The third session, in the late autumn of 1932, was attended by none
of the major princes, and the conference could not throw off an uneasy
feeling that the rulers of the native states as a whole had lost their
federalist enthusiasm and were simply marking time. Yet the conference pressed on. Having pretty well settled the provincial constitutions,
it concentrated upon certain federal arrangements that its committees
had been studying since the previous session. One was the allocation
of residual powers. The Hindus wanted the central government to have
them, the Moslems the provinces; and there was a near deadlock until
it was suggested that the viceroy should decide each case as it arose.
The final session ended on Christmas Eve with mutual expressions of
peace and good will.

The British government outlined its proposals in a White Paper
based on the recommendations of the Simon Report as modfied by the
discussions of the Round Table Conference. The White Paper was
published in April 1933 and then referred to a joint select committee
of the two houses. This committee included most of the leading men
in British public life, among them three ex-viceroys, and was about the
strongest parliamentary committee ever appointed. As consultants who
took part in its discussions and its examination of witnesses, it had
almost all the ablest Indians of the Round Table Conference, from the
native states as well as from British India. With meticulous care the
committee went over the whole ground again, and with little amendment of consequence it confirmed the conclusions already reached. In
December 1934 its report was adopted by overwhelming majorities in
the two houses, and then the resulting bill was introduced. The only
serious opposition to the passage of the measure came from a small
group of die-hard Tories, led by Winston Churchill in the Commons
and the Marquis of Salisbury in the Lords, who fought it bitterly at
every stage.

The Government of India Act of 1935 was perhaps the most thoroughly digested piece of legislation in the history of the British parliament. To the provinces—including the North-West Frontier Province, the new ones of Sind and Orissa, and such others as might be carved out of existing provinces by agreement between the central government and the legislatures of the provinces concerned[4]—the act gave full responsible government subject to a few safeguards for the protection of such things as the peace of the land, "the legitimate interests of minorities," and the rights of native states and their rulers. In the event of a breakdown of the constitutional machinery, it empowered the governor to assume, with the consent of the governor general, the authority of government by a proclamation, which then had to be submitted to the secretary of state and laid before parliament. As in other federations, the provinces were to have exclusive jurisdiction over some matters and concurrent jurisdiction over others. In the latter field, federal legislation would override provincial, but there was provision for the reverse under certain circumstances. Following the Round Table Conference suggestion, the act made no specific allocation of residual powers but left the question to the discretion of the governor general.

For the old central government the act substituted "The Federation of India," which was to come into being when princely accessions brought half the total population of the native states into the union and filled half their full quota (two fifths) of seats in the Council of State, the upper chamber of the federal legislature. It members were to be chosen for nine years, one third every third year. The Federal Assembly was to be elected for five years, subject to earlier dissolution. Defense and foreign affairs were to remain under the control of the governor general, who was responsible for them to the secretary of state. Other federal subjects were to be entrusted to ministers responsible to the legislature under safeguards similar to those in the provinces. Thus dyarchy, expelled from the provinces, was to be introduced into the federal administration. This was in accord with a conclusion that the Round Table Conference had reached after a searching discussion which disclosed a purpose somewhat different from that of 1919. Flexibility was to replace rigidity, so that dyarchy might gradually work itself out in full responsible government.

---

[4] Under the same condition the act also authorized revision of provincial boundaries. Burma, however, was severed from India by the act itself, and not long thereafter another act provided it with an advanced colonial constitution.

The constitutional position of India as set forth in the act of 1935 was still inferior to that of the dominions in two substantial respects: the retention of British control over defense and foreign affairs, and the provision for safeguards against the abuse of self-government. As for defense and foreign affairs, it should not be forgotten that these were the last two fields of government that the dominions had taken over. It will be recalled that British troops had been kept for local defense in Canada, Australia, and New Zealand until 1871–72, and in South Africa until 1914; and that all these countries had refrained from asserting their right to control their own foreign policies until after the First World War. To attain equal status, India had to build up permanent forces of her own capable of defending the most dangerous frontier and the most difficult internal peace of any country in the commonwealth; but the Indianization of the army in India was being accelerated, and with it the shifting of the burden from British to Indian shoulders. Meanwhile, according to the idea put forward again and again in the discussions leading up to the act, the governor general would unofficially and progressively lean on the advice of responsible Indian ministers to guide his conduct in the reserved field, so that usage and convention would mold the constitution as in other British lands.

The safeguards, a revised version of "certification" which had no real parallel in the dominions, were regarded by the Hindu Liberals, the Moslems, and other minorities as essential during the period of transition for the protection of Indian rather than British interests. They were for use only in emergencies, any attempt to abuse them would defeat its own end by rousing hostile opinion, and it was within the power of Indians themselves to let them fall into desuetude along with the vestiges of imperial restraint upon the exercise of dominion self-government. To sum up, though the act of 1935 did not actually confer dominion status upon India, it conferred it potentially by giving India freedom to develop as the dominions had developed into a fully self-governing nation equal in status to the other partners of the British Commonwealth.

Now the great question was whether India was capable of becoming a nation. Irish nationalists had sacrificed unity for freedom. Indian nationalists were determined to attain both goals, but the problem of reconciling them was infinitely more complicated for Indians than it had been for Irishmen. To make things more difficult still, the resurgence of international anarchy, as will be related in the next chapter, injected a new urgency into Indian nationalism.

The federal part of the new constitution never came into operation because it required the voluntary adhesion of the princes, and this was not forthcoming. When they made their surprising declaration in favor of an all-India federation in the first session of the Round Table Conference, the precise terms on which they would join had yet to be threshed out; when these came under consideration, the princes shied at the extent of the authority they would have to surrender. British officials opened negotiations with them to allay their fears, while loud voices in the Congress damned the proffered British concessions as proof of a wicked design to reinforce the shaky structure of British rule. The reluctance of the princes hardened from 1937, when the official policy of the Congress, which was one of sympathy for their subjects but noninterference with their governments, gave way to an urge to revolutionize the native states. Their autocracy as well as their autonomy was at stake. If, as has been suspected, a main motive behind the new move of the Congress was to frighten the native rulers into causing a miscarriage of the federal scheme, then these rulers were the dupes of leading Congressmen. Be that as it may, the princes did not positively reject federation, their negotiations with the British continuing until after the outbreak of the Second World War, when they were formally suspended.

The princes' failure to seize the opportunity, which they themselves had raised, to become part of an all-India federation was ultimately to cost them their thrones; meanwhile it had the highly unfortunate effect of leaving the central government of British India to continue under the obsolete constitution of 1919, with no possibility of automatic growth into a national government comparable to that of a dominion. Here it is necessary to extend the blame to the authors of the 1935 act, Indian as well as British. It would have been much better if they had addressed themselves to the easier task of federating British India as a potential self-governing dominion which the native states might join. In short, they were too ambitious, too impatient.

In the provinces the act came into operation with the elections in the winter of 1936–37 and the reconstruction of their administrations at the beginning of April 1937. The interim was a period of tense uncertainty. The Congress had taken a firm stand against any British-made constitution, and in favor of one promulgated by a democratically elected constituent assembly. Now Pandit Jawaharlal Nehru, who was elected president in 1936, openly suggested that the opportunity for such an assembly would come as soon as the gathering international storm engulfed Britain, but like all other Congressmen he was eager to contest the elections under the act. That was as far as he would go in recognizing it. To accept office under it, he declared, would be a national betrayal. On this point Congress was sorely divided, other leaders stoutly maintaining that the refusal of office would be playing the imperialist game. The dispute was not confined to the question of tactics, for many of Nehru's opponents were impatient to take advantage of the act in order to pass social reform legislation which they believed should not be made to wait upon independence. The All-India Congress Committee temporized by issuing an election manifesto proclaiming the principle that Congressmen should enter the legislatures "not to cooperate in any way with the act, but to combat it and seek the end of it," and declaring that the issue of office should be decided after the elections. Meanwhile the Moslem League published its election manifesto, which was practically an offer of cooperation with the Congress if the latter would concede separate electorates, as in the Lucknow Pact of 1916. On this too the Congress leaders temporized, putting off a definite answer until after the elections, during which the two organizations worked in tacit agreement.

Fifty-four per cent of the total electorate, which the act had increased fourfold to about 30 million, went to the polls. The Congress candidates, including a few Moslems in Moslem constituencies, won a clear but not overwhelming majority in each of five provinces, and control in two provinces where none of the many parties secured a majority. In the other four provinces the elected Congressmen faced hostile majorities of Moslems alone or in combination with other groups. Taking all the provinces together, the Congress obtained 711 out of a total of 1,585 seats.[5] In March 1937, after two days of debate, the All-India Congress Committee resolved that the electorate had rejected the act and asserted their desire to frame their own independent constitution by an elected constituent assembly, that the act should therefore be withdrawn, that the Congress members of the legislatures must direct all their actions to this end, and that they must not take office in any province unless they had public assurance from the governor that he would not exercise "his special powers of interference or set aside the advice of ministers in regard to their constitutional activities."

This condition, privately dictated by Gandhi, prevailed over an

---

[5] In the unicameral legislatures and the lower chambers of the bicameral legislatures, the act having provided for two chambers in such provinces as desired them.

amendment to prohibit acceptance on any terms, and was inspired by a naïve belief that the governors would somehow find a loophole to accommodate the well-known anxiety of the majority leaders in the "Congress provinces" to take office. A more careful reading of the act would have revealed that there was no such loophole, and this soon became apparent when these gentlemen were invited to become premiers and had to refuse because no governor could give the prescribed assurance. Thereupon the governors of these provinces fell back upon the only immediate but essentially unstable alternative of appointing minority leaders to form cabinets; Gandhi, publicly admitting his sole paternity of the obstructive formula, declared that he had not intended to impose an impossible condition. Some Congressmen hailed the deadlock as hastening the day of deliverance from British rule, but they were a dwindling minority. The Congress legislative majorities grew more impatient to seize the reins of government that had been offered to them. How much they could do with these reins, they and other Congressmen saw in the non-Congress provinces, where full responsible government was operating. The viceroy also greatly helped to break the deadlock. In a strong appeal to the people of India to work the constitution for all it was worth, he pointed out that the safeguards were so limited in scope that they could not interfere with normal government. In July the A.I.C.C. waived the impossible condition, the interim ministries resigned, and Congress ministries took their place.

All eleven provinces now enjoyed a measure of self-government substantially equal to that of a Canadian province or an Australian state or, for that matter, of an American state; and their capacity to manage their own affairs was demonstrated during the period of more than two years before the Second World War. The parliamentary system worked, though not in precisely the same way as in other commonwealth countries, because Indian conditions were different. The governors, for example, commonly met with their cabinets and gave them the benefit of a longer and wider experience. Only once did a governor refuse to follow the advice of his responsible ministers, and they soon withdrew their consequent resignation. No governor attempted to legislate by ordinance. Only once did a governor block a bill, and that was on the advice of his ministers—to save their face. On several occasions governors reserved bills for consideration by the governor general, and of these measures only five were vetoed while others were returned with recommendations for amendment, which were then adopted.

The supreme test of the new system was the maintenance of law and order, which was no longer a "reserved" subject. In the performance of this task the provincial ministers had one distinct advantage over those who relinquished it. They were Indians, not foreigners. On the other hand, however, they lacked the experience of the British officials from whom they took over; and in various other respects their position was definitely weaker. Unlike their predecessors, they could not look to the central government for guidance nor, except in grave emergencies, could they call in British troops to restore order. Revolutionary nationalism, by its "civil disobedience" and other defiant behavior, had severely damaged the prestige of government generally, not just the British *raj*. In particular it had stirred dangerous agrarian ferment over just grievances, and it had exacerbated the endemic communal strife. The latter problem became much more difficult to manage when the responsibility for keeping the peace passed from neutrals, the British, to Indian ministers, who all belonged to one or other of the jarring communities.

From almost the beginning of the new regime there was a strong popular clamor for the repeal of the "repressive" laws inherited from the old regime, and for the release of all "political" prisoners, from simple *détenus* to convicted murderers. Presently the provincial governments freed the *détenus* and worked out varying policies for the progressive release of most "political" convicts. Contrary to widespread expectation, the "repressive" laws were not swept away. The only noticeable relaxation of these laws and their administration was in some Congress provinces, and there the resulting agrarian violence soon taught the lesson that if the government was going to govern it could not dispense with force. Gandhi underlined the lesson by declaring that Congress ministers, though pledged to nonviolence, were not thereby precluded from "resort to legal processes involving punishment." They could not, he asserted, "ignore incitement to violence and manifestly violent speeches." Their attitude stiffened and, apart from this temporary and far from general weakness, the provincial ministers loyally backed their administrative officers and police in the execution of their duty against the vicious attacks of a hostile press and irresponsible politicians. Responsible Indians thus used the old machinery of "repression" as resolutely as the British, and even put some new teeth in it. If these ministers did not maintain law and order quite so effectively as British officials had done, they may be excused because the times were more troublesome, and on the whole they must be credited with tolerable success. The Punjab government twice called in British troops to suppress communal riots that had got out of hand, but otherwise there was no recourse to this drastic remedy for disorder.

The legislative record of the provincial ministries resembled that of most democratic governments in that it fell short of election promises; but these were unusually extravagant in India, for obvious reasons, and no government in that terribly poor country could raise a tithe of the money needed for social reform. Yet much was accomplished by carrying further the work of the old regime to redeem the almost inhuman lot of the peasants, who constituted the vast majority of the population. New enactments extended security of tenure, cut down exorbitant rents, and pared the claws of the moneylenders who habitually preyed on the poverty-stricken tillers of the soil. If too many landlords sat in the legislatures to permit more radical measures on behalf of tenants, their public spirit appears in the relief for which they voted—and paid along with the rest of their class. All in all, the expenditures of the provincial governments on social services during the short period before the Second World War increased by about 14 per cent.

Some attempts were made to lift two other dark curses, alcoholism and illiteracy. The remedies prescribed by educated Indian opinion were prohibition and compulsory schooling, but financial considerations stood in the way. Where could the governments find substitutes for the considerable revenues derived from the liquor traffic, and the enormous funds for the necessary schools and teachers? The non-Congress governments passed only token legislation to satisfy the public demand, whereas the Congress ministries, pressed by their powerful central organization and the Mahatma himself, imposed prohibition on a limited scale, and also showed a greater eagerness to spread education. To cut the cost they experimented with "basic education"—schools centered around some form of productive manual work—and with flimsy shelters in place of traditional brick schoolhouses. One might suppose that the straitened circumstances of all the provinces would inspire some daring departures from orthodox financial policies; but there were none except a moderate tendency of Congress governments to budget for a deficit—as many governments in the western world were already doing.

More important was another difference between the Congress provinces and the others in the operation of responsible government. The non-Congress governments were coalitions, for the Moslems still lacked an effective party system and they did not attempt to govern without the support of other communities; and these coalition ministries were

wholly responsible to their legislative majorities and through them to
their constituents. The Congress governments, on the other hand, included only Congressmen and, along with their legislative majorities,
were largely the puppets of the centralized party machine, whose chiefs
held no public office. The Congress "high command" picked the ministers, dictated their policies, controlled the votes that kept them in
power, and often interfered in even minor matters. There was only one
exception to this rule by dictatorship from outside. It was in the backward and distant North-West Frontier Province, where Moslems constituted 92 per cent of the population and a considerable section of
them had appropriated the Congress organization without accepting its
ideology. There the "high command" could not rule as it did in the
other six provinces,[6] where an Indian autocracy replaced the British
autocracy.

The dictatorship established by the Congress leaders was but a partial
fulfillment of their great design to bring all India under the control
of their organization, and in their further pursuit of this end they
overreached themselves by trying to absorb or otherwise destroy all
rival political organizations. On the morrow of the elections to the new
provincial legislatures, they threw overboard their working alliance
with the Moslem League. This rejection of the League was the fateful
turning point in Indian politics which ultimately led to the dismemberment instead of the unification of the country.

At the next conference of the League, in the autumn of 1937, Jinnah
bitterly assailed the Congress for its exclusively Hindu policy which,
he declared, would surely stir more communal strife and thereby make
it more difficult for India to get rid of British imperial rule. Moslems,
he asserted, could "expect neither justice nor fair play under Congress
government." His words echoed through the land like a clarion call
rallying Moslems behind him and the League, with the result that he
quickly became the most powerful man in India, next to Gandhi, and
the League a national organization for the defense of the Moslem
community. The Congress leaders, whose mentality was slow to grasp
the full significance of the startling and dangerous Moslem reaction
that they had provoked, unwittingly inflamed it by reiterating the claim
of their organization to represent all Indians irrespective of race or
religion, and the assertion that minorities must seek protection within
its fold.

---

[6] Where the percentage of Moslems ranged from fourteen down to two.

Religious fanaticism was by no means confined to Moslems. It flared up among Hindus. The Mahasabha, growing in numbers and in truculence, attacked the Congress for chasing the mirage of an all-embracing Indian nationhood instead of frankly recognizing and championing the Hindu nation as the only nation whose fatherland and holy land was India. Most Moslems, however, suspected that the noncommunal professions of the Congress were only a cloak to hide a fundamental identity of purpose with the Mahasabha. As we have seen, the mere transfer from British to Indian hands of the responsibility for maintaining law and order was bound to magnify the danger of communal strife. Any possibility of checking this danger by cooperation between the leaders of the two great opposing communities was now thoroughly wrecked—"on the rocks of Congress Fascism," said Jinnah.

As the Hindu-Moslem tension mounted, breaking here and there into local rioting and bloodshed, all manner of angry charges were hurled back and forth, and quasi-military organizations sprang up. India was rushing toward a crisis in which the supreme issue was what should take the place of the admittedly stopgap central government. Before 1937 the League, like the Congress, had condemned the federal scheme of 1935 for not granting complete self-government at once. After 1937, the League denounced it as an instrument that would enable the Congress, by the regimentation of the Hindu majority as practiced in the Congress provinces to establish its tyranny over the whole country. The Congress campaign to rouse the people of the native states was, in the eyes of the League, a subtle design to enlist them for this very purpose. The Moslems would fight rather than submit to Hindu domination. Seized by a growing fear for the survival of their religion, their language, their whole culture, they no longer took for granted, as they did until 1937, the idea of Indian political unity in some sort of federation. Now a new idea was planted in their minds, which steadily gained in clarity and strength—the partition of India.

The concept of Pakistan has been traced to a small group of Indian students in England, who formulated it in a little leaflet that they privately circulated from Cambridge in 1933,[7] but the seed did not begin to take root in India until the Congress cast off the League in

---

[7] The authors of the above leaflet coined the name as *Pakstan* which, as they explained, meant "the five northern units of India — viz., Punjab, North-West Frontier Province (Afghan Province), Kashmir, Sind and Baluchi*stan*." The spelling was soon changed to Pakistan, which means "land of the pure."

1937. At first the Moslem leaders regarded it dubiously, but they were thinking in terms of adjusting the constitution of India to accommodate its multiple nationalism, upon which they placed increasing emphasis. One of these leaders, recognizing that Hindus and Moslems were so mixed up together that no mere revision of boundaries could separate them, went so far as to advocate a wholesale exchange of population. Suggestions of partition naturally evoked angry blasts from the Congress press, and these just as naturally tended to blow Moslem opinion away from the goal it was still officially seeking— a loose federation that would allow Moslem self-determination.

The Congress leaders, wedded to their plan of a democratically elected constituent assembly and a strong central government, could not think of compromising it. They looked forward with increasing confidence to the explosion of war in Europe and the opportunity it would give them to blow down the British *raj* and to build up a solid Congress *raj* over the whole of India. Little did they know how irrevocably they had split India.

CHAPTER XXXIX

Commonwealth Reactions to the Coming of the Second World War

THOUGH THE Nazi attack on Poland, like the German invasion of Belgium, precipitated Britain into a world war, her plunge in 1939 did not of itself commit the whole empire. With the exception of India, whose central government was still controlled by London, the other members of the commonwealth had each to make the supreme decision. Eire unhesitatingly took its stand as a neutral, Canada and South Africa waited a few days until their parliaments voted for war, while Australia and New Zealand declared that they were at war simultaneously with the mother country.

By these various actions the governments of the commonwealth finally settled a question that they had adumbrated in the Imperial Conference of 1926, when they formally recognized that the dominions' equality of status with the mother country did not mean equality of function, and that in matters of defense and foreign policy "the major share of the responsibility rests now, and must for some time continue to rest, with His Majesty's Government in Great Britain." Mutual consultation on such matters being then an accepted principle, the question was whether, in applying it, the coequal members of the commonwealth would cooperate in one high policy for all, or develop individual policies which they coordinated as best they could. This question did not much concern any of them so long as world peace seemed secure, an illusion that was first shaken and then shattered by the successive blows of great-power aggression beginning in the autumn of 1931.

As the storm clouds gathered on the horizon, foreign affairs became of paramount importance to the commonwealth, and this change in outlook made it painfully apparent that the dominions were still de-

pendent upon Britain in fact though not in constitutional theory. They
continued to hold her primarily responsible for preserving the commonwealth from the calamity of war. They had nothing like her long and
wide experience in the rough-and-tumble of international society, her
weight in the world was immeasurably greater than theirs, and their
interests were embraced by hers. True to the spirit of the commonwealth, she kept them fully informed of what she had to face, so that
she could take their reactions into account. These, however, were not
of much positive help to her.

The two Pacific dominions were profuse with advice, because they
felt they could not stay out of the dreaded war if Britain became involved in it; but they contradicted each other on the course that she
should pursue. Of the two binational dominions—each torn by internal division and fearing to be committed—South Africa was at times
quite emphatic in pressing her views on London, while Canada was
very chary of giving advice. The Irish dominion, being set on neutrality,
offered almost none; and, as we have seen, she stayed away from the
Imperial Conference of 1937, where the responsible heads of dominion
governments recorded their general approval of British policy. No other
Imperial Conference was held during the period of grave international
anxiety leading up to the outbreak of the Second World War. There
was not much point in having one when the United Kingdom government was in constant communication with the dominion governments
and none of them could tell when or how the next urgent crisis would
arise.

Though the fragile structure of international law and order commenced to crumble in the autumn of 1931 under the impact of Japan's
aggression in Manchuria, the commonwealth countries, in common
with all the other western democracies, were incapable of seeing what
was happening until long afterward. They were floundering in the
depths of the economic depression, the scene of the disturbance was a
remote corner of the globe, and they had little or no understanding of
what the local fighting was about. China appealed to the League of
Nations, which sent an international commission to investigate on the
spot the Sino-Japanese quarrel. Late in 1932 the commission submitted
its report, which recognized that Japan had legitimate grievances but
condemned her lawless actions against China; and in February 1933 a
special session of the League Assembly adopted the report, with only
Japan voting against it. Meanwhile, however, she had set up her puppet state of Manchukuo and had struck into China south of the Great

Wall. Now she withdrew from the League and defied the whole world.

No sanction was applied to Japan, except a futile nonrecognition of her conquest as a violation of the League Covenant, the Nine Power Treaty, and the Briand-Kellogg Pact. Repressive action was out of the question because the burden would fall on the great powers, and none was willing to run the risk of war with Japan. There were only two of them—one in the League and the other outside—that could have done anything effective to check or punish the aggressor; and Britain was physically incapable of undertaking it without the full backing of the United States, which condition was then utterly impossible, as Japan well knew.

Though the dominions were members of both the commonwealth and the League, they were little disturbed by this crisis. Australia and New Zealand might have been expected to betray some alarm comparable to what they had felt ten years previously over the British abandonment of the Japanese alliance. But they seem to have found relief in the fact that Japan had struck at China instead of them, and comfort in the thought that Japan was burying herself in a long war that would leave her either sated or exhausted. Neither dominion had taken the League very seriously. Both were so conscious of their dependence upon Britain for their security that they were prepared to follow her lead; and if Australia was more inclined to be independent, the Japanese market for wool gave her a special interest in preserving the good will of Japan. Canada too had a long Pacific coast line, but she felt less dependence on the Royal Navy and still less on the League. She lived in the sheltering shadow of the United States and had repeatedly raised an American voice in the League against the Covenant's provisions to maintain peace by collective force.

South Africa's two outstanding leaders, Hertzog and Smuts, were ardent supporters of the League, the failure of which would release dangerous domestic disputes over the republican issue; and the Union's high commissioner, Mr. C. T. te Water, made a strong plea in the Assembly for the great powers to uphold the authority of the League. But most South Africans, apparently, were little interested in what was happening in the Far East. The only other commonwealth statesman to speak out boldly was de Valera. As president of the League Council and acting president of the Assembly, he delivered a grave warning of the crucial test that the League was facing. Would it reveal "a weakness presaging ultimate dissolution" or would it allay the suspicion that "if the hand that is raised against the Covenant is sufficiently strong, it can smite with impunity"? What alarmed him was much more than the position of his own country. He was thinking of the fate of weak nations when left to the mercy of the strong; and his desperate cry was not an expression of Irish public opinion, whose chief interest in the League was its usefulness in furthering the cause of Irish national independence.

It was not until 1935 that the further disintegration of world order began seriously to shake the unity of the commonwealth on the question of foreign policy. From Hitler's overthrow of the Weimar Republic in 1933, a swift succession of startling developments was pushing Europe toward war. Before the year was out he pulled Germany out of the League. The Soviet government, having consistently denounced the League as a capitalist organization with which it would have no dealings, experienced a great change of heart when Germany fell under the control of the madman who had been screaming that he would carve out of Russia broad "living room" for the cramped German people. Moscow knocked at the door of Geneva and was admitted as a great power to a permanent seat on the Council of the League. Russia at once became the most outspoken champion of the League, thereby rousing in the western democracies a fear that tended to paralyze them—the fear that the devil had entered their system of collective security merely to save his own skin at their expense. In the same year, 1934, a group of Nazis murdered the chancellor of Austria in a vain attempt to seize that country. Mussolini then decided that he could safely climb on Hitler's back and leap on Ethiopia, where Italian imperialist ambitions had been buried by disastrous defeat in 1896. There, on the unmarked border of Italian Somaliland, the first clash occurred in December. Each side blamed the other for it, and Mussolini used this opportunity to push his quarrel with Ethiopia, while he pressed on with open preparations to strike with full force. To do this he had first to get through the Suez, and he was not quite sure that Britain would continue to respect the treaty guarantee that the canal would "be free and open in time of war as in time of peace, to every vessel of commerce or of war, without distinction of flag."

In March 1935, when these Italian preparations were spreading a general alarm, Hitler climbed on Mussolini's back and intensified the alarm by decreeing German conscription and full rearmament in defiance of the Versailles Treaty. In mortal terror of a rearmed Germany, France wooed Italy and got Britain to join in putting out feelers to see if the Duce would be satisfied with some territorial concessions, but he scorned them. In June, Hitler's threat of an all-out naval race persuaded Britain to accept his offer of a treaty limiting the German navy to 35 per cent of the British in surface ships and to parity in submarines. France regarded this agreement as a betrayal and pulled away from Britain toward Italy, while public opinion in Britain hardened against Italy and called for the League to check the would-be aggressor.

In September 1935 the British fleet was concentrated in the Mediterranean, and Europe held its breath. Little did the world know—for it could not then be told without encouraging Mussolini to strike boldly at Ethiopia—that the British naval display was not a preparation for the application of sanctions. It was, rather, a precaution against a surprise attack by Italian troops which were then mustering secretly in Libya, on the Egyptian border, to drive the British out of Egypt and from the Suez Canal. Britain of course had to pay for her discreet silence, because cynics in many lands accused her of trying to use the League to pull her chestnuts out of the fire.

Mussolini struck in October. Thereupon the League condemned the aggressor and proceeded to apply economic sanctions by calling upon its members to prohibit the sale of arms and specified raw materials and the lending of money to Italy and the purchase of her goods. Fifty nations responded loyally, and the clamp was applied in mid-November. It severely damaged but did not cripple the aggressor. Neither oil nor gas was on the banned list, and neither Germany nor the United States would cooperate with the League. Though Washington had worked hand in glove with Geneva in the Manchurian crisis, such cooperation was now out of the question, the appoaching shadow of the Ethiopian crisis having been enough to force the panicky passage of the Neutrality Act of August 1935. Early in November a member of the League committee on sanctions proposed the addition of oil in order to tighten the squeeze, and this was seriously considered until Mussolini shouted that it meant war. He need not have done so, for it was plainly impossible to stop the swelling stream of American oil that was pouring into Italy. But his outburst stimulated Italian pride and effort, and it emphasized the fact that the League powers would not fight Italy to save Ethiopia. Russia could not and France would not. There was only one other great power in the League capable of undertaking it, and Britain would not attempt it singlehandedly. In December the British and French foreign ministers, Sir Samuel Hoare and Pierre Laval, met in Rome and made a last-minute effort to prevent a complete conquest, by proposing that Mussolini settle for a slice of

Ethiopia in return for which he would give that landlocked country a port in Eritrea. He spurned the offer, and the British public were so enraged at the thought of compounding an international crime that they hounded their foreign secretary out of office. By May 1936 Mussolini had conquered practically the whole of Ethiopia.

Of the diverse reactions that the crisis of 1935 stirred throughout the commonwealth, perhaps the most surprising was New Zealand's strong championship of the League. That dominion suddenly discovered a vigorous faith in international law and morality upheld by collective security, and a confidence that the mother country would throw all her weight into the righteous cause. The New Zealand public saw clear proof of it in the concentration of the Royal Navy in the Mediterranean. Great, therefore, was the dismay and exasperation that swept New Zealand on the disclosure of the Hoare-Laval plan. The simultaneous explosion in Britain and the prompt repudiation of the plan by the British cabinet, which was itself surprised by the action of its absent member, brought consolation to the distant dominion. New Zealand came through the Ethiopian crisis with a stronger sense of dependence upon the mother country, and also with a stout belief that the League could and should be made to work. Only very reluctantly and out of deference to Britain did New Zealand consent to the lifting of sanctions some months after the fall of Ethiopia.

Australia had no confidence in the League and anxiously sought to restrain the mother country from venturing so far in support of it that she might find herself at war with the aggressor. The anxiety sprang from a shrewd calculation that a big European war was the opportunity for which Japan was waiting to embark on a career of grandiose conquest over the whole western Pacific region. Australians were acutely aware of "the vulnerability of our empty north," of the great disparity between the size of their continent and the size of their population, and of their utter dependence upon the strength of the British Empire for protection against a powerful foe. The Australian government therefore strongly favored a British policy of appeasement in Europe. It was also fearful of any British collaboration with Russia. The reason was not ideological but strategic, Russia being the only European power that impinged directly on Japan. Another matter of vital importance to Australia was the preservation of her lifeline through the Suez. During the crisis two of the three Australian cruisers were with the Royal Navy in the Mediterranean. Australia was bound to stick by Britain through thick and thin, but was more distrustful of sanctions and was the only commonwealth country that swallowed the Hoare-Laval pill without a gag. When a Labor voice in the Australian parliament asserted the country's right to decide on peace and war, the attorney general vehemently denied this "right to go mad."

The policy of the Irish Free State in this crisis was that of one man; and de Valera, though agreeing with many people in Britain and elsewhere that justice demanded an orderly new deal between the "haves" and the "have nots," insisted more strongly than in the Manchurian crisis that the League must enforce its authority because this was its "final test." His uncompromising stand drew bitter criticism from many of his own people. Roman Catholics attacked him for attacking Italy; and rabid nationalists accused him of betraying his country by trying to drag it into war at the heels of Britain, and by refusing to seize the occasion for a bargain with the British government over the treaty ports, or partition, or both. The failure of the League was a terrible blow to him, for he saw more clearly than most statesmen that international anarchy had triumphed. Australia and New Zealand might be content to sink or swim with the British Empire, but nationalist Ireland never. His policy thenceforth was strict isolation.

Though English Canada had pretty well come round to the position of French Canada that their country should not be drawn into other peoples' quarrels through membership in the commonwealth or the League, the Ethiopian crisis split the dominion wide open again, one part siding with Mussolini and the other against him. French Canada, being more intensely Roman Catholic than the Irish Free State, had stronger religious ties with Italy. It was also more drawn to Mussolini by ideology, not that French Canadians were inclined to be fascist— English Canadians suspected it and thereby widened the domestic breach—but because the Duce was the sworn foe of communism, which was anathema to devout French Canadians. That made them profoundly distrustful of the League, in which they saw the powerful hand of evil, Soviet Russia, working to destroy Christian civilization. They were anti-British as well as anti-League, because Britain was backing the League; and they echoed the angry cries that Italy was raising against Britain as the one power that Mussolini feared most. These cries, which were much resented in English Canada, reached a climax with the concentration of the Royal Navy in what Mussolini called his sea. English Canadians then hoped that British might would make him back down; but many held that Britain should not risk war when no part of the empire was being attacked.

When the invasion of Ethiopia began, the Canadian government did
not hesitate to join in the League condemnation of Italy and the League
resolution to apply economic sanctions; and in the general election that
followed almost immediately, the Canadian public were assured that
whichever party won it would not commit the country to armed intervention, even if the League were to call for such action. After five
years in opposition, the Liberals were returned to office with the support
of every French Canadian in the House, and the new Mackenzie King
government issued a careful statement of its policy in the crisis. It
would apply the sanctions agreed upon in Geneva; but it reminded the
people that successive Canadian governments had "opposed the view
that the League's central purpose should be to guarantee the *status quo*
and to rely on force for the maintenance of peace," and it declared
"that it does not recognize any commitment binding Canada to adopt
military sanctions, and that no such commitment could be made without the prior approval of the Canadian parliament."

In less than a week after this comforting communication, Canada
was startled by the news from Geneva that the addition of oil sanctions
was proposed, and by none other than the Canadian member of the
committee. The tension in the country mounted, and the government
was deeply embarrassed by the international discussion of "the Canadian proposal." The dominion seemed to have taken the lead in forcing
an issue for which it was not at all prepared to be responsible. Early
in December, after a month's hesitation, Ottawa publicly disclaimed
any intention of taking such an important initiative and explained that
the motion represented the views of the man who made it[1] and not those
of the Canadian government. This statement roused cheers in French
Canada and jeers in English Canada. The disclosure of the Hoare-Laval
agreement, which came in a few days, relaxed the internal tension of
the country and relieved the government's embarrassment. The whole
crisis taught Canada a lesson, which many Canadians found very hard
to learn: that until the dominion was much more united it could have
no positive external policy other than friendship with the United States,
whose extreme isolationism was for most Canadians more deplorable
than reassuring. The Canadian who took this lesson of unity most to
heart, and did most to apply it, was Prime Minister Mackenzie King.

Of all the dominions, South Africa was the one that reacted most

---

[1] He had cabled for consent but received no reply until two days after he formally
introduced the proposal.

violently against Mussolini and in favor of League action to stop him. Unlike French Canadians, Calvinist Afrikanders had no religious inhibitions about opposing Catholic Italy and no ideological fears of cooperating with Communist Moscow in support of the League. On the other hand, South Africa did not share New Zealand's idealist outlook. Its view of the crisis was as realistic as that of Australia—and much more alarming. What moved South Africans was the old fear from which they could never escape, the fear of a black upheaval. They dreaded the prospect of a European attack upon the last survival of African independence lest it start racial repercussions that would rumble all through the continent and shake the very foundations of South Africa. The rule of white over black could survive only if the black respected either the white man's honor or his power. The first condition would be damaged by successful Italian aggression in Ethiopia, and the second by a repetition of the Italian disaster of 1896. Te Water, speaking for "the one permanent and indigenous white civilization in Africa," warned the League Assembly in September against the dangers of a new partition of the continent: "danger to the adventuring nations themselves, danger to the black peoples of Africa, and menace to our own white civilization."

The crisis also focused the attention of Dutch as well as British South Africans upon the strategic position of their country. War in the region of the Suez Canal might close that busy artery and revive the importance of the Cape as a key point on the route between Europe and the Orient. Then South Africa, a small nation possessing the world's richest treasure house of gold and an immense seaboard but no navy to defend it, would be a tempting Naboth's vineyard. The country could not afford to desert the League or turn its back upon Britain, and few South Africans heeded the cry of Malan and his little minority that the League was the tool of wicked British imperialism.[2] Smuts proclaimed the peril in no uncertain words, and so did the prime minister. Hertzog told his fellow countrymen that they were at the beginning of

> a long and—if we must judge from what has gone before—one of the bloodiest and cruelest periods the world has ever known . . . yet we hear from the Opposition that we should cast off the friends we have and regard Great Britain as our enemy, as if we are not going to have enough

---

[2] Far from condemning Mussolini's aggression, Malan sympathized with Italian and German colonial ambitions and suggested the need for a general redistribution of colonial territories — except Southwest Africa.

enemies. And we must do that to a country which has handed to us our freedom to use as we think fit!

South Africa was the first country to respond to the League call for economic sanctions, and while the government promised to consult its parliament in the unlikely event of a League call for military sanctions, ministerial language implied a determination to back the League to the utmost. The Hoare-Laval pact shocked the South African public, embarrassed the government, and made Malan stand out, at least in his own eyes, as a Daniel come to judgment. But despite this heavy blow, which British repudiation only partly alleviated, and despite the continued success of Italian aggression, the South African government remained steadfast in its support of the League. The day after Addis Ababa fell, Hertzog asserted that the League should maintain sanctions even if it took years for them to accomplish their purpose. In the subsequent League debate over the lifting of sanctions, South Africa demanded their continuance, and the only support she got from any country was a qualified one from New Zealand. Though admitting the failure of the League, South Africans clung to the hope that it was not final.

India, impatient to reach the promised goal of dominion status, began to react like a dominion under the impact of the Ethiopian crisis. From the very beginning, Indians were hostile to Italy, for they had heard and could never forget Mussolini's scornful outbursts against colored races. Indian opinion rallied to the side of Britain in her declared intention to support the League, but soon became apprehensive of the outcome because the League took no preventive action while all the world could see that Mussolini was making full preparations to launch his aggression. The association of India in the application of sanctions was therefore gratifying, but at the same time it stirred resentment because the decision that committed India was made in London. There was no such mixture of feeling over what Sir Samuel Hoare did in Rome. That severely damaged British prestige in India. There the incident was made to appear in a particularly bad light because of the offending cabinet member's earlier career. Hoare's presumption to implicate Britain in a shameful bargain, said the nationalist press, had been fed by his years of autocratic rule over the India Office, and his forced resignation was due to his failure to realize the difference between matters on which the British public had strong feelings and those on which they had not—the affairs of India.

Another effect of the crisis that may be mentioned here was the breaking of an old and awkward Anglo-Egyptian deadlock. It will be recalled that when the sultan of Turkey, the legal suzerain of Egypt, entered the First World War as Germany's ally, the British formally covered their occupation by declaring a protectorate. The alternative, annexation, was rejected out of regard for Egyptian and French sensibilities, and for the same reason Britain promised Egypt to reconsider the whole question of that country's status when the war was over. As the tide of war receded from the Egyptian borders, the tide of Egyptian national feeling rose against the British. It broke into open rebellion in 1919. The rising was easily suppressed, and Lord Milner—a member of the British government and an old Egyptian "hand"—led a strong commission to examine the problem on the spot. He brought back a unanimous report urging the negotiation of a treaty that would recognize Egyptian independence in return for guarantees of British interests; but the majority in the cabinet, fearing the reproach of a surrender to Egypt while Ireland was still aflame, refused to accept the report. This refusal made the British position in Egypt more difficult. There was more rioting and the British high commissioner, Lord Allenby, sprang into action—against London. He demanded the immediate abolition of the protectorate and the negotiation of a treaty afterward. Backed by his principal colleagues, he rushed to London with his own and their resignations in his pocket, and the cabinet bowed to his ultimatum. On the last day of February 1922, a proclamation revoked the protectorate and declared Egypt an "independent sovereign state" with the reservation of four points to be settled by future agreement:

(a) The security of the communications of the British Empire in Egypt
(b) The defense of Egypt against all foreign aggression or interference, indirect or direct
(c) The protection of foreign interests in Egypt and the protection of minorities
(d) The Sudan

The British then gave up their forty years' task of reforming the administration of Egypt, but remained in the country pending the conclusion of negotiations on these four subjects. There the matter stuck, for the government of Egypt fell into such confusion that it was incapable of coming to terms with the British. Again and again the latter seemed to come within sight of an agreement only to have it blown away.

Now Mussolini unwittingly came to the rescue of the British by frightening Egypt into an accommodating mood. In January 1936 the king of Egypt forced the formation of a coalition ministry for the purpose of negotiating a treaty with Britain, which was concluded in August. It provided for the withdrawal of British troops to the Canal Zone and for their replacement there by Egyptian forces if, at the end of twenty years, the League of Nations found that these forces could protect the canal properly. Britain undertook to sponsor Egypt's application for membership in the League, which was granted almost immediately. She also undertook to get an international agreement of all the interested powers—which she did in the following year—to abolish the capitulations under which their nationals enjoyed immunity from Egyptian jurisdiction. The treaty also bound Egypt to Britain in a permanent defensive alliance. "In the event of war, imminent menace of war, or apprehended international emergency," the king of Egypt was to furnish "all the facilities and assistance in his power, including the use of his ports, aerodromes and means of communication." Another article confirmed the condominium over the Sudan, which the Egyptians had been insisting that Britain should evacuate and turn over to Egypt.

Australia was the only dominion that displayed any particular interest in the conclusion of this treaty. The Ethiopian crisis had made her so vitally concerned over the security of her lifeline through the Suez that she was impatient for an Anglo-Egyptian settlement, and she impressed her views on the Foreign Office throughout the negotiations. But there is no reason to suppose that Australian prodding hastened the treaty or influenced its terms. They were what Britain had sought for years. It was Mussolini's bold action that broke the deadlock, and this so effectively that Egypt welcomed the result as "the treaty of honor and independence." The agreement was no less welcome in Britain because the success of Italian aggression in Ethiopia had already started a rapid succession of alarming developments elsewhere.

Taking advantage of the Ethiopian distraction, Hitler overturned the balance of power in Europe and put Nazi Germany on top in March 1936, when without any warning and in flagrant violation not only of the Versailles Treaty but also of the Locarno Treaty—which Germany had voluntarily negotiated and signed—German troops rushed into the Rhineland to occupy and fortify it. With his western flank no longer exposed, the German dictator could do what he liked to France's eastern allies, for they were weak and he was strong; and France, shorn of their support, was like Sampson when Delilah cut his locks.

France could have blocked this master stroke of Nazi strategy, for the advancing German troops were under secret orders to retreat if France moved against them, as she had every right to do under the Locarno Treaty. But France was afraid to act alone, and the other three guarantors of that treaty would not commit themselves to back her up. Italy was estranged and otherwise engaged, Belgium shrank from incurring German hostility a second time, and Britain doubted the wisdom of armed intervention to prevent the recovery of German sovereignty over what was actually German territory. Lord Lothian expressed the prevailing view in the British Commonwealth, the United States, and other countries too, when he remarked, "After all, they are only going into their own back-garden." South Africa was particularly sympathetic with this German move, for Afrikanders still looked upon Germany as their old friend, and they regarded nazism as the inevitable result of the harsh terms the victorious Allies had imposed upon her. Therefore the Union government threw all its influence against any preventive action in the Rhineland.

The peace of Europe was also threatened by the outbreak of civil war in Spain, which began in July 1936 with the revolt of the army under General Franco. He knew he could count on the support of Hitler and Mussolini, and from the beginning these two declared enemies of democracy intervened to effect the destruction of the Spanish Republic. Thereupon Moscow intervened to preserve it, and there was widespread fear lest this barbarously waged struggle, which was rather appropriately called the Little World War, should suddenly flare up into a big one. Hitler's Russian backfire was working to paralyze the democracies. Opinion in France and Britain was so divided in sympathy, as it was in the United States and elsewhere, that all the governments of these two powers could do to avert the danger was to try to get an international agreement to prevent the sending of aid to either side in Spain. They succeeded in persuading almost all European governments, including the intervening dictators, to endorse this policy and to set up a nonintervention committee in London to enforce it. But the three intervening powers were so intent on a one-sided enforcement that the committee became a notorious farce. It checked but could not stop the flow of aid from Russia, and it looked on helplessly while Germany and Italy sent all they wanted to Franco. Thus the civil war assumed the character of an international war in which the Nazis and Fascists were fighting Communists.

In Britain, as in other democratic lands, feeling was hostile to both

protagonists, and opinion was divided over which was the more dangerous devil. Among the conservative-minded, whether economically or
politically, and among Roman Catholics generally, fear of communism
prevailed over hatred of nazism and fascism. The reverse was true of
liberals, labor, and socialists; and hosts of people, not knowing what to
think about the issue, cried out, "A plague on both your houses!" Even
if the British public had not been perplexed over the danger, the British
government could not contemplate any risk of becoming involved in
war over the Spanish struggle. Abhorrence of war, false confidence
that the League would preserve the peace, and economic depression had
conspired to reduce British expenditure on armaments to a perilously
low level from which they were just beginning to rise. Rearmament
was speeded by the sight of the aggressors' joining hands during the
Spanish war. The completion of the Berlin-Rome Axis was announced
in October 1936, the Berlin-Tokyo Anti-Comintern Pact a month
later, and Rome's adhesion to this in the following year. But Britain
had a long way to go to catch up.

The reactions of the other commonwealth countries to the struggle
in Spain displayed variations from the British policy in both directions.
India's fear of nazism and fascism was most pronounced, and her only
fear of communism was that it might drive Britain into an unprincipled
bargain with Hitler and Mussolini. To be associated automatically with
the nonintervention policy was galling to Indians. Nehru accused
Britain of having "hindered and obstructed the Spanish in their fight
for freedom." New Zealand, true to her idealism, wanted the League
to respond to the vain appeal of republican Spain for intervention
against aggression. Australia and South Africa were strictly neutral
toward the conflict and in firm accord with British policy. De Valera
too was stoutly noninterventionist, but Irish Catholic opinion and
ancient ties of sentiment with Spain were too strong for him to prevent
a voluntary Irish contingent from going to fight with Franco against
"anti-Christ."

The Canadian government had to stand aloof. French Canada
fervently believed that Franco was the champion of Christianity against
the godless republic, while English Canada was divided in much the
same way as Britain over the Spanish war. There was also a lively
debate over what the dominion should do if Britain became engaged
in war, the likelihood of which seemed much increased by her rearmament and the growing international tension. Some still argued that
Canada would then have to go to war too, while others insisted that

she should remain neutral. This policy, though favored by many French Canadians, found its strongest organized support in the semi-socialist C.C.F.[3] party, which had arisen during the depression and gained considerable following in the Prairie Provinces. Its leader, a Christian pacifist, introduced a motion in the House of Commons in January 1937 to commit Canada to strict neutrality. He said the country would be split from stem to stern if war came and Canada entered it. But the prime minister dealt firmly with the resolution. He saw that its adoption would produce this split immediately, and he placed the unity of the country above everything else. He declared he would commit the country to neither neutrality nor war, because either commitment would tie Canada's hands at the crucial hour, when her parliament should make the vital decision. His common-sense stand appealed to the bulk of the Canadian people, French and English alike. They were not swept off their feet by the doctrinaire isolationism, which was then hypnotizing the United States and thereby encouraging aggression; for though Canada was a North American country, its membership in the commonwealth and the League had cultivated a different outlook on the world.

In the Imperial Conference of 1937, which sat during the late spring and early summer of that year, the principal statesmen of the commonwealth exchanged views on the mounting danger of war and how they should meet it. Already the dominions were stepping up their own defenses, though not so feverishly as Great Britain because they were much farther from the seat of trouble, and now there was a general exchange of information on this important subject. Australia and New Zealand were particularly pleased with the plans to complete the great naval station of Singapore, and they urged the closest cooperation of all parts of the commonwealth in their common defense. Australia also spoke out for a nonaggression pact of Pacific powers, which she would gladly join, while New Zealand alone held fast to the belief in collective security under the League.

There was no attempt to bind the commonwealth together by mutual commitments, which in any event could not be effective until approved by the respective parliaments, as the conference formally recognized. The assembled statesmen also agreed that the way to deal with international tensions was by "cooperation, joint enquiry, and conciliation. It is in such methods, and not in recourse to the use of force between

---

[3] Cooperative Commonwealth Federation.

nation and nation, that the surest guarantee will be found for the improvement of international relations and respect for mutual engagements." A further testimony of belief in the efficacy of conciliation and compromise to relax existing friction appears in the last paragraph of the section on foreign affairs in the *Proceedings:*

> Finally the members of the Conference, while themselves firmly attached to the principles of democracy and to parliamentary forms of government, decided to register their view that differences of political creed should be no obstacle to friendly relations between governments and countries, and that nothing would be more damaging to the hopes of international appeasement than the division, real or apparent, of the world into opposing groups.

Here it is well to remember that the policy of appeasement, to which the conference gave general approval, was the British counterpart of the American policy of isolation, that each of these two policies lent support to the other, and that at this time there was more to be said for appeasement than against it. The patent failure of the League of Nations to solve the problem of "peaceful change" and to prevent naked aggression seemed to leave no alternative until Britain was prepared to fight if need be, and tragic experience had yet to brand appeasement as futile and hateful. Hope as well as desperation inspired the acceleration of British rearmament—hope that it would restrain the potential lord of Europe. On the morrow of the conference the Canadian prime minister, while visiting the capitals of western Europe to appraise the international situation for himself, met the German chancellor in a private interview and conveyed the warning that if he provoked war he would have to fight the whole British Commonwealth. Hitler must have reassured his guest, for when Mackenzie King returned home he said that the German dictator, though determined to gather into his Reich the German peoples in adjoining territory, would not risk a major war. Indeed, Hitler was fairly quiet during the whole of this year, and thereby he allayed fears that he harbored unlimited ambitions of conquest.

It was now Japan's turn to run amuck again. As Italy and Germany had profited by her example, and assisted each other to do it, Japan, at last in league with them, took advantage of the disturbances they created. In July 1937, at the Marco Polo Bridge just outside Peiping, she launched her full-scale war for the conquest of China. Once more China appealed to the League of Nations and the United States. The

League, having had its back broken in Ethiopia, could do little. In October it condemned Japan as an aggressor and called upon the signatories of the Nine Power Treaty to assemble and consider how to stop this major war. It was simply "passing the buck" to a group of interested powers, of whom the United States was the chief. They invited Japan to cooperate in settling her difference with China, and she replied that she alone would settle it because it was no business of others. Then all they did was to register their regrets, affirm their adherence to the principles of peace, and adjourn their conference. Britain and the other European democracies, paralyzed by the war still raging in Spain, dared not take any step ahead of the United States in the Far East; and the American government was paralyzed by the isolationist movement, which was rushing toward the hysterical climax of January 1938, when the House defeated by only a narrow majority (209 to 188) a resolution to prevent congress from declaring any war without a prior popular referendum in favor of it.

Indian opinion was exasperated by the British government's impotent attitude toward the renewed Japanese aggression, and by rumors that London was about to recognize the Italian empire in Ethiopia. Nehru, president of the Indian National Congress, begged New Zealand to speak out on behalf of international justice and order. India, he said, was "powerless to register a protest at the League Assembly through representatives who are nominated by the British government." New Zealand was herself so roused by the Japanese menace that she vigorously championed the Chinese cause. Her government clapped an embargo on the shipment of scrap metal to Japan and repeatedly pressed for compulsory League sanctions in direct opposition to the policy of London.

Australia was no less alarmed and much more prudent, for reasons already noted. Her government firmly refused to take any step to help China or hinder Japan and broke wildcat strikes of waterside workers who refused to load metal cargoes for Japan. Australia was more than ever conscious of being an imperial defense liability, and she determined to become an asset by developing a real air force and by strengthening her navy. The latter would help to keep a strong British fleet based on Singapore, her first and major line of defense against a Japanese invasion. But what would happen there if Europe blew up? That was Australia's nightmare. Therefore her government stoutly backed the British policy of appeasement and urged, in particular, the wooing of Mussolini by a recognition of his recent African conquest.

The other dominions displayed little concern over the new crisis in the Far East. Eire—if she could be called a dominion—saw in the tense international situation a good opportunity to get the treaty ports, and with them a better chance to stay out of Britain's wars. Canada, though bordering on the Pacific, felt no fear of far-off Japan. It was the European powder keg that made Canadians nervous. South Africans were generally less worried by the possibility of war in Europe and more sympathetic with Germany, but they were becoming very much disturbed by the Nazi shadow in their own back yard, their mandated territory of Southwest Africa.

Back in 1923, to confirm the German renunciation of this former German colony, the Smuts government had negotiated with the Weimar Republic an agreement whereby the latter recognized that "the future of Southwest Africa is now bound up with the Union of South Africa," in return for a guarantee that the Union, instead of exercising the treaty right to repatriate all Germans in the territory, would accept them as its own citizens with full political, linguistic, and cultural freedom, and would not make them or their children "liable in any circumstances for military service against the German Reich for a period of at least thirty years." Accordingly, in 1924, an act of the Union parliament declared all German inhabitants to be British subjects except such as might signify in writing that they did not wish to be naturalized. Only 221 out of 3,489 registered their refusal. German schools were established, an act of 1925 set up a legislative council of six nominated and twelve elected members, and prosperity attracted immigrants from the Union. The onset of the depression cast the Southwest African Germans down until they were lifted up by the news from their homeland that Hitler had come into power.

Almost at once the Germans in Southwest Africa responded to the call of the blood. In 1933 the German members of the legislature asserted that their naturalization in 1924 had not taken away their German nationality, and that "every decent German must now be a National Socialist." The Germans boycotted the regular courts in favor of arbitration courts under a German consular official; and they declared their allegiance to Hitler, by oath if they were not naturalized and without it if they were. In 1934 the Union administrator of the territory outlawed the Hitler Youth and other Nazi organizations, and he exiled their leaders. But new Nazi leaders arrived from Germany, and by 1936 practically every unwilling German in Southwest Africa was coerced into joining the Nazi cause. The Germans then constituted about half the European population, which numbered some 30,000, while most of the other half—the great majority of them Afrikanders— had come from the Union, and the blacks outnumbered the whites by nine or ten to one. In this same year Hertzog announced that his government, being responsible for the administration of the territory, could not tolerate within it the organization of a body prepared to seize control by force; and he tried to get it stopped by an order from Berlin, but the German government brushed off his approaches.

Afrikander opinion was caught in an awkward and painful conflict of its own making. Its nationalist bias against Britain had bred a fellow feeling for Germany which now threatened to undermine the security of South Africa. Leading Afrikanders had repeatedly denounced the Treaty of Versailles for imposing a Carthaginian peace upon Germany, and one of their major counts against that treaty was that it humiliated Germany by confiscating her colonial empire. When a resurgent Germany was obviously getting ready to right what Afrikanders had condemned as a wrong, Afrikander leaders began to sing a more British tune. In 1936 the minister of defense stated categorically: "In no circumstances can South Africa or Great Britain envisage the return of either Tanganyika or Southwest Africa to Germany. We are at work hand in hand with the rest of the British Empire in a common defense policy, and in this respect South Africa is to be the elder brother to the rest of British Africa." Early in 1937, as the Nazi infiltration into Southwest Africa continued in spite of Hertzog's suggestion of German compensation elsewhere and in defiance of his government's stiffer repressive measures in the territory, the prime minister publicly rebuked Malan for criticizing these measures as provocative; and toward the end of the year the deputy prime minister delivered a speech in which he stressed the binding character of the freely negotiated 1923 agreement.

These words of Smuts immediately drew a sharp protest from the German government, on the ground that the word *now* in the English version (*gegenwärtig* in the German) meant that the future of the territory was bound up with South Africa only at the time of the agreement, and not permanently. It was useless to reply by referring to the phrase "for a period of at least thirty years," because the feeble German quibble revealed a strong determination to recover Southwest Africa along with the other lost German colonies. As Hitler had not yet thrown all caution to the winds and still refrained from forcing the colonial issue, South Africa clung to the hope that he could be appeased by other colonial concessions. Official London hoped so too, and on 3 March 1938 the British ambassador broached the subject in an interview with the Führer by advancing a tentative proposal for a sort of international regime in central Africa which would have to be arranged by all the powers concerned. Hitler would have none of it. "Instead of establishing a new and complicated system," he replied, "why not solve the colonial problem in the simplest and most natural way, namely by returning the former German colonies?" He said he could wait four, six, eight, or ten years for the British and others to change their minds. The United Kingdom and South African governments accepted his refusal as final, and the internal strain in South Africa between sympathy for Germany and distrust of Nazi ambitions was increased rather than diminished by the wild course that Hitler now began to run in Europe.

British policy was sorely tried by the state of perpetual European crisis that commenced less than a fortnight after the above conversation in Berlin, when Hitler's legions rolled into terrorized Austria and he announced its annexation, in flagrant violation of his own repeated pledges to respect its independence. While British opinion found rough justice in this sudden solution of the age-old problem of German relations with Austria, whose people were really Germans, the roughness of the decision and its strategic implications were alarming. In Britain, as elsewhere, there were grave fears that the military might of Germany, having burst beyond her own boundary so easily, was stepping out on a career of conquering other peoples, and there was little doubt that the next on the list was Czechoslovakia.

There the German minority, who had never been German subjects but were descendants of mediaeval immigrants, had begun to stir up trouble at the bidding of Berlin. Though the Czechs had heavily fortified the mountainous barrier that separated them from Germany, their strong position was turned by the German seizure of Austria, which brought the Nazis up to the defenseless southern border. What would happen if the Nazi jaws closed on the head that was between them? Less than a fortnight after the annexation of Austria, Prime Minister Chamberlain addressed parliament on the ominous situation, uttering a warning that if Germany attacked Czechoslovakia "it would be quite impossible to say where it would end and what governments might be involved." In May, German armies maneuvered right beside Czechoslovakia, the German press and radio heaped abuse on that little country, the Czechs sprang to arms, France and Russia indicated willingness to help their threatened ally, and the Nazi menace touched Britain through the known weakness of France. Again Chamberlain cautioned Hitler, and shortly afterward the German threat subsided. Yet the whole affair was a warning of impending danger.

Britain faced something worse than a dilemma, for the thing had three hateful prongs—fascist, communist, and war—all totalitarian; and the appeasement policy, designed to avoid all three dangers, was now the subject of a fierce national controversy over whether this policy would actually save the country or betray it. Many people blamed the government for allowing international anarchy to break loose by letting the League of Nations down, and they insisted that it was not too late to save the day by a determined stand against all aggression. Others defended the government for refusing to take such a serious risk of plunging the country into war when no vital interest of the empire was clearly at stake. Left-wing opinion, supported by the fact that the three aggressors were openly bound together against Russia, accused the government of pursuing a pro-Fascist foreign policy out of fear of communism. Right-wing opinion, abhorring both ideologies, held fascism to be less dangerous than communism, and dreaded the prospect of war with the Berlin-Rome Axis lest it devastate western Europe and deliver the whole continent into the arms of Moscow, which was suspected to be the Soviet scheme. If there was to be war, the appeasers hoped it could be confined to eastern Europe, where the two devils might knock each other out and make the world safe for democracy. Others were sure that the Nazis would make short work of Russia and then, much mightier still, turn to devour the hapless west.

Above all, the British people prayed that they could avoid war—which would impose its own kind of totalitarianism upon them—at least for the duration of the struggle; but they were feverishly preparing to fight if they had to, for the outlook was black. In the new age of air warfare, Britain was terribly vulnerable. She had no more than half the airplanes and antiaircraft defenses that Germany possessed, and France not more than a third. Moreover, the mechanization of armies magnified the strategic value of industrial capacity, and in this there was the same disparity. To reduce it on both counts, Britain now agreed with France to correlate the armaments of the two countries.

The unprecedented danger to the heart of the empire deeply affected the other members of the commonwealth, where it stimulated domestic debate over the appeasement policy and also preparation against the possibility of war. It revealed to them that, in relation to commonwealth defense as a whole, they stood much more nearly on the same footing as Britain. While giving new emphasis to the old principle that they were severally responsible for their own local defense, it was a warning that they should not interpret this responsibility in the narrowest sense. They did not contemplate, nor did Britain expect or even desire, a repetition of what they did in the First World War when they sent large armies to serve on distant European battlefields. Not knowing if, when, or where they might have to fight—each in its own interest—but realizing that they would have to be prepared for any eventuality, each examined its own position and acted accordingly.

Though India had not yet reached the goal of dominion status and would therefore be committed automatically by a declaration of war on or by London, the act of 1935 had reaffirmed the principle that the army in India existed for India's own purposes. There were 55,000 men of the British army stationed in India, and that country had immense reserves of manpower for fighting. But the new conditions of warfare meant that manpower would count for much less and machine power for much more than in the past. Therefore the government of India started to make the country self-sufficient in high explosives. This was the beginning of that remarkable development of war industries in India which transformed that country into the principal supply base of all kinds of fighting equipment for the British campaigns in the Near East during the Second World War, with the incidental result of reversing the balance of financial indebtedness between Britain and India.

Australia nearly doubled her defense estimates, which were already considerable, and concentrated more on her air force and her munitions industry. New Zealand, likewise rearming, had to lean rather heavily on orders placed in Australia and England. The government of the little dominion still urged League action against all aggressors; to opposition criticism that this weakened the solidarity of the empire, it replied that moral principles should not yield to political expediency. But this independent stand on foreign policy, expressed in a refusal to "be prepared to swallow everything the British government cared to put forward," never interfered with New Zealand collaboration in defense; and in the middle of May 1938 the minister of finance declared, "If the Old Country is attacked, we are too. We hate all this war propaganda, but if an attack is made on Great Britain then we will assist her to the fullest extent possible." On this point the Australian government was in thorough agreement, but the advice it continually pressed upon the British government was to persist in the policy of appeasement as the only chance of averting war.

The South African government brought the same pressure to bear upon London, for reasons that had no existence in Australia. Afrikander sympathy for Germany was so strong that war between Britain and Germany would certainly wreck the Fusion government and seriously endanger the internal peace of South Africa. This being so, the South African government could not make active preparations to participate in such a war. The Simonstown agreement of 1921, by which Britain gave up her control of that naval base at the Cape in return for a South African guarantee to defend it with land and air forces and to make it available to the Royal Navy, was now a delicate embarrassment. It precluded neutrality in a war involving Britain, and thus confined South Africa to the old and objectionable choice between passive and active belligerency. Hertzog squirmed. On the one hand he had openly admitted the dependence of South Africa upon the Royal Navy, and on the other hand he had toyed with the idea that in the event of war his government could treat Simonstown as "foreign territory." Now he was publicly evasive on whether there might be a community of interest with Britain if war should come. His deputy, Smuts, was more forthright in the general election campaign of May 1938. He then said: "The policy of South Africa is to stand by our friends loyally and truly. If England is attacked, I think that our position is clear. There can be no doubt whatever that if England is in danger all the free dominions will do their duty as they did in 1914." He was not referring, as he later explained, to what the country should do if Britain became embroiled in hostilities arising from some dispute on the continent of Europe. But this qualification would apply in other dominions too.

Though the Canadian government resembled the South African in having to walk warily in order to preserve national unity in a binational country, and was therefore no less sympathetic with the British government's desire to preserve peace at almost any price, Ottawa studiously refrained from any attempt to influence British policy. It has been alleged that this restraint, which is in marked contrast to the pressures exerted by South Africa and the two Pacific dominions, was inspired by the prime minister's fear of moral commitments that would limit Canada's freedom of action in time of supreme crisis. But the South African prime minister was quite as eager to avoid any commitment, and yet he urged London along the path of appeasement. Perhaps it was that Mackenzie King was more sensitive than Hertzog to the inconsistency of telling London what to do when his own country would resent such advice from London, and it is certain that he had more confidence in the British government. He was also more cautious than Smuts, for he dared not say publicly what he had said privately to Hitler, with the knowledge of the British government: that if the dictator provoked war he would have to fight the whole British Commonwealth. Mackenzie King's policy was to prepare Canada to live up to this confidential warning—negatively by avoiding anything that would injure the cause of national unity, and positively by developing the defense program already initiated. In this development Canada stood between South Africa and the two Pacific dominions; for the senior dominion contained no body of population that shared the Afrikander fellow feeling for Germany, and was not so exposed to enemy attack as Australia and New Zealand. Here it should also be observed that the distinct upward turn of American defense preparations early in 1938 gave welcome encouragement to the government and people of Canada; and that President Roosevelt's Kingston speech in August, while increasing the Canadian sense of security, was a challenge to Canadian self-respect that rallied more support for the dominion's defense measures.

The world trembled in September 1938, for it seemed that the end had come. Hitler insisted on taking by force, if necessary, that part of Czechoslovakia where most of its German minority lived and constituted the local majority—the so-called Sudetenland, which comprised the layer of territory adjoining Germany and Austria. France was unconditionally pledged to aid Czechoslovakia against aggression; Russia was pledged to do the same if France honored her pledge; and though Britain had undertaken no such pledge, it was perfectly clear that she could not stand aside if France became engaged in war with Germany. Germany was all ready to strike, France was calling up her army, the British fleet was mobilized, and London parks were dug up for air-raid shelters. In a desperate effort to preserve the peace by personal interview with Hitler, the British prime minister, who had never ridden in an airplane before, flew to Germany—three times, inspiring the later caustic comment, "If at first you don't succeed, fly, fly again."

On the first occasion, at Berchtesgaden, Hitler threatened immediate invasion of Czechoslovakia unless Britain accepted the principle of self-determination in that country, in which event he was ready to discuss "ways and means." Chamberlain demurred until he could consult his cabinet colleagues and prepare a reply, and Hitler promised to refrain from active hostilities in the meanwhile, provided "nothing happened in Czechoslovakia of such a nature as to force his hand." The British and French governments then urged the Czech government to agree to the cession of all areas with over 50 per cent Sudeten German inhabitants, in return for a Franco-British guarantee of the new boundaries, and Prague concurred lest worse befall. Chamberlain hopefully presented this proposal to Hitler at Godesberg—their second meeting place—only to be met with increased demands, which included more territory and immediate German military occupation without plebiscite or provision for the withdrawal of Czech inhabitants. The Englishman balked. He would transmit this ultimatum to Prague but he would not sanction it. Before they parted, in deadlock, Hitler repeated what he had said at Berchtesgaden: that this was his last territorial ambition in Europe; and he added that he wanted England's friendship. Back in London, Chamberlain received the expected Czech refusal, he sent a personal message appealing to Mussolini to intercede with Hitler, and he related to a hushed House of Commons the whole story of these transactions, which pointed straight to war. As he was finishing, he paused to read a note just handed to him, and then he announced its surprising message: that he was invited, along with the Duce and the French prime minister, to meet Hitler at Munich in the morning.

At Munich the Führer got his three guests to join in a settlement of the crisis. The terms were those of his Godesberg ultimatum with some modifications in favor of Czechoslovakia. As an after flourish, he signed with Chamberlain a declaration that their two countries desired "never to go to war with one another again," they would consult together to remove differences between them, and "thus contribute to assure the peace of Europe." Immense was the rejoicing in Britain when the prime minister returned, waving this precious document and announcing that he brought back "peace with honor," "peace for our own time." He believed it, and so did the cheering crowds, for the country had suffered a terrible scare, hanging on the edge of an abyss. But other Britons—and their number was fast increasing—saw more cause for weeping than for rejoicing. Where, they asked, was the honor in throwing Czechoslovakia to the Nazi wolves? What was the value of peace bought at such a shameful price because Britain and France were afraid to stand up to Hitler? How was it possible to trust that wicked and dangerous man? Many critics found some consolation in the thought that Britain had bought more time to prepare for war, and though Chamberlain still pursued the mirage of appeasement—now more his than the nation's policy—the government accelerated the pace of rearmament.

All the dominion governments applauded Chamberlain's flights to Germany and prayed for peace at almost any price. The Australian prime minister even called Chamberlain out of bed to say that, if desirable, the Australian high commissioner in London would fly with a personal appeal to Mussolini; but the attitude of the dominions, while gratifying to Chamberlain as a confirmation that he was right, seems to have had little or no influence upon his policy during the critical month of September 1938. Whether they would have supported him in a bolder course that led to war with Germany is a different and more important question on which we have some light. If war had come in September 1938, three dominions would have backed Britain against Nazi aggression, and two would not.

Though facing a much greater peril of enemy attack than any other dominion, the two Pacific dominions would not have hesitated to take the plunge. "Wherever Britain is, we must be," were the words of the New Zealand prime minister when Chamberlain first took to the air. In Australia the government was less categorical at the time, and more pleased with the Munich settlement; but when the leader of the opposition asked for assurance that the government had not committed the country to war against Germany, the veteran Hughes, once more minister for external affairs, stated bluntly that if war had come "it would have required no committal. We should have been committed to war, and no power could have saved us from it."

The Canadian government made no such statement, for reasons already explained, yet it was fully prepared to summon parliament and recommend participation in the war. The French Canadian leaders in parliament—all Liberals—were pretty sure they could carry their people with them, and the Conservative opposition was bound to support the recommendation. The Canadian reaction to Munich was much like that of the United Kingdom: tremendous relief quickly followed by growing apprehension that the evil day had only been postponed. While many Americans loudly condemned Britain for not being willing to fight, some of their Canadian neighbors joined in the chorus, but many resented it as an outburst of irresponsible isolationism that would egg Hitler on.

Eire was all set to declare neutrality, now that the treaty ports were ceded. But the country's geographical position and military nakedness made de Valera fearful that its neutrality would not be respected by the Nazis and, as a consequence, by the British. He had great confidence in Chamberlain, arising from his recent dealings with him; and though the Irishman could not share the cool detachment with which the Englishman viewed the amputation of territory from Czechoslovakia, the two men were of one mind in believing that almost any peaceful settlement was better than the calamity of a general war which might well end in the subjection of all Europe to Russian domination. Therefore de Valera, braving the bitter criticism of many of his own country-men, worked in close and continuous cooperation with the British prime minister throughout the crisis; and after Munich he went out of his way to express his appreciation of what Chamberlain had done to preserve the peace.

The South African government, like the Canadian, kept its own counsel, but was prepared to hold aloof. Afrikander opinion was so strong in favor of the Sudeten Germans' cry for annexation to Hitler's Reich that the demand of Malan—who had gained much strength in the May election—for a prior declaration of neutrality exerted a power-ful pull on Hertzog's wing of the United party. The prime minister could not yield to the demand because it meant not only tearing up the Simonstown agreement but also splitting the government, the party, and the nation. On the other hand, he could not adopt a policy of even passive belligerency without grave risk of producing the same fatal split. Therefore he worked out a compromise formula designed to shelve, rather than resolve, the irreconcilable differences within the cabinet. In the event of war, he would declare that South African relations with belligerents would continue as if there were no war, that "relations and obligations between the Union" and other members of the common-wealth would remain unchanged in so far as they were "the result of contractual obligations concerning the naval base at Simonstown" or membership in the League or "the free association" of commonwealth nations, "and that nobody shall be permitted to make use of Union territory for any purpose calculated to infringe the said relations and obligations."

When war seemed most imminent, on the very day that Chamberlain explained to the House of Commons the failure of all his efforts to find a peaceful solution, Hertzog summoned his cabinet and presented his formula to it. As he invited no discussion and had privately got the concurrence of Smuts and two others, the rest raised no objection. He thereupon concluded that he had their unanimous consent. The acquiescence of Smuts, which was decisive, is still puzzling[4] and makes the agreement look like a South African Munich, for it was a well-known fact that his conception of South African interests was much broader than Hertzog's. Indeed, the bewildered public believed that the cabinet had been unable to reach any decision other than to call parliament on the outbreak of war; and Hertzog, relying on Smuts' agreement at this time, nearly trapped him and the country a year later, when the war finally came.

A few weeks after Munich a member of Hertzog's cabinet started on a tour of European capitals. He was Oswald Pirow, an Afrikander of German extraction, and he carried with him lively hopes of extracting the troublesome Nazi thorn from the side of South Africa. These hopes began to wither when he landed in Lisbon, and they died when he visited Berlin. The discovery that Hitler could not be budged from his claim to the restoration of Southwest Africa perceptibly stiffened the attitude of the Union. But at the same time Pirow reinforced Hertzog's determination to stay out of war, for the wanderer returned with two other disturbing convictions: that appeasement had little chance of success, and that Nazi military might, which fascinated him, was sure to triumph.

A revolution in British foreign policy was brewing as the reign of terror mounted in Europe during the fall and winter of 1938–39. Chamberlain grimly persevered in his quest for peace, that which he brought back from Munich having turned rotten, and the confidence of the British public in his leadership sank to a low ebb. London and provincial newspapers called for conscription and for a firm stand against the Nazi dictator, but the prime minister and his cabinet seemed like sleepwalkers on the edge of a precipice. Their awakening came in the middle of March, with Hitler's lightning seizure of helpless Czechoslovakia. The flash that struck down the Czech democracy revealed to Chamberlain and his colleagues the dire peril in which Britain stood along with the rest of the free world, and they resolved that Hitler must be stopped—by war if necessary but short of it if possible. Britain took the lead and France followed.

Within a fortnight Britain and France pledged full support to Poland against Nazi aggression, Hitler having launched a war of nerves that

---

[4] The explanation offered by Nicholas Mansergh, *Survey of British Commonwealth Affairs: Problems of External Policy, 1931–39*, p. 258, is not fully convincing.

plainly indicated that country as his next victim; similar guarantees were extended during the following weeks to Greece, Rumania, and Turkey, in reply to Mussolini's celebration of Good Friday by devouring little Albania. Britain had given no such pledges even to France before 1914, and now she broke another peacetime precedent by enacting conscription. The purpose of this was to cement the French alliance; for the French had suffered a million casualties in the First World War before one division of the newly formed British national army reached the front, and they were not prepared to shed their blood in such an unequal sacrifice again. Britain also recognized that France was in a more exposed position than in 1914, for now she had two additional hostile neighbors in Italy and Spain.

The one great weakness in the new British policy was the lack of any arrangement for Russian cooperation, without which it would be impossible to save either Poland or Rumania if Hitler ordered their subjugation, for then no British or French aid could reach them because they lay on the far side of Germany. If Moscow joined hands with London and Paris, that would almost certainly stop Hitler, who dreaded above all things a war on two fronts. The issue therefore turned on whether he or the western powers could make a deal with Russia. He was handicapped by his notorious hatred of communism and his much-published territorial designs on the Ukraine; they by their supposition that these two facts would in the last analysis force Moscow to stand with them against Hitler, and also by the gulf of mutual suspicion between them and the Soviet government. Russia negotiated with both sides simultaneously. Stalin's terms amounted to a free hand in the territories his country had lost at the end of the First World War, which Hitler promised and the western allies could not. The Berlin-Moscow pact, announced on 21 August and signed two days later, stunned the democratic world. Hitler put off the invasion of Poland for a few days in the hope that Britain would grasp the opportunity to crawl out of her pledge to that doomed country and pull France with her. The British response was a renewal of the pledge. The invasion began on 1 September. Britain promptly issued an ultimatum demanding a German withdrawal from Poland by the morning of the 3rd, and when the deadline came she declared war.

Meanwhile in the other commonwealth countries the rape of Czechoslovakia caused a more or less violent revulsion of feeling against appeasement, and this reaction prepared them to accept as inevitable the important decisions that London did not dare delay until it had consulted them: the desperate resolve to fight rather than stand aside while Nazi Germany picked off another victim, and the pledges to Poland, Greece, and Rumania. On the other hand, all save India were troubled by the British negotiations with Russia, on which they were kept informed. Catholic opinion, which represented almost the whole of Eire and half of Canada, abhorred communion with the devil. Most Afrikanders now held much the same view of the power that dwelt in the Kremlin. Australia and, to a lesser degree, New Zealand were apprehensive of repercussions through Russia upon Japan. Russian and British aid to the Chinese was exasperating Japan. The summer of 1939 saw an undeclared war, with heavy fighting between large bodies of Russian and Japanese troops on the border of Manchukuo. It also saw the Japanese siege of the British legation in Tientsin, followed by humiliating negotiations in Tokyo. If there was to be any Anglo-Russian cooperation, Australia insisted that it be confined specifically to Europe.

Indian nationalists were passionately anti-Nazi and harbored no suspicion of the U.S.S.R. until after the Berlin-Moscow pact. Indeed, the Soviet government's long professions of hostility to all imperialism harmonized with Indian impatience for freedom from British imperialism, and the prospect of war raised this impatience to a hysterical pitch. It did this by making London more cautious concerning the speed of India's advance toward dominion status, as well as by making Indians see that they were about to be committed to war again without having any say in the vital decision. Moreover, Indian opinion had been so greatly roused by aggression in Asia, Africa, and Europe, when Britain seemed to condone it, that the March revolution in foreign policy left many Indians wondering if the British sinner's change of heart was really sincere. The Nazi-Soviet pact, though banishing Indian fears of a German drive right through to the Persian Gulf, shocked Indian opinion by exposing Communist Russia as the accomplice of Hitler. The shock was a tonic to British prestige, but not to British rule, in India. Wholehearted as were Indian sympathies with Poland and her western allies when the war broke, Indian nationalists were bitterly opposed to any participation in the struggle while their country was still chained to the chariot wheels of Britain.

During the debate in the Irish Dail, which assembled on 2 September, not a single voice was raised against neutrality, and only one deputy, a prominent member of the opposition, went so far as to urge a resolution that neutrality was not incompatible with strong sympathies for the Allied cause. On 31 August, the German minister in Dublin had informed de Valera that Germany would respect Eire's neutrality if it were strictly enforced. This condition inspired doubts of how it would affect the country's economic dependence upon the United Kingdom, which supplied more than half Eire's imports and took all but two or three per cent of its exports. Would Germany tolerate this trade across the Irish Sea? The ships that carried it were British, and it was supplying Britain with essential food. Some deputies were deeply worried, but not J. M. Dillon, the opposition member just mentioned. "There is no more danger of submarines dominating the Irish Sea than there is of my going over to Germany to cut the mustache of Adolph Hitler," he said, and he boldly asserted that the surrounding sea was perfectly safe "thanks not to ourselves but thanks to God and the British Fleet." His confidence was not contagious.

Canada, Australia, and New Zealand were no less relieved than Eire by the news of the Berlin-Moscow pact, though it unquestionably meant war for them. Neither Australia nor New Zealand issued a declaration of war against Germany, for the governments of both dominions, still adhering to the principle of undivided sovereignty, simply accepted the British declaration as binding upon them, and they notified London accordingly. When the New Zealand parliament met two days later, the prime minister asked for its approval and the motion was immediately carried. Australia omitted this formality, though its parliament was then in session. Canada was much more deliberate. On 31 August the prime minister announced that parliament was being summoned for 7 September and that the government would ask it for authority to cooperate with the United Kingdom. On the following day, when the Germans burst into Poland, he made it clear that cooperation meant cooperation in war. Technically the senior dominion remained neutral until parliament met and approved the government's policy, and the delay allowed vast quantities of war material to be rushed in from the United States. When parliament came together the cabinet had not the slightest doubt of what the decision would be. Mackenzie King's great concern was, by free and full debate, to convince the country that there was no honorable alternative to joining the side of freedom and democracy against "a ruthless and tyrannical power which seeks world domination." After two days, during which a bare handful opposed the government's resolution for war, it was adopted without a division.

South Africa was the one dominion that hung in the balance. Like Mackenzie King, Hertzog was pledged to get the consent of his parliament before going to war, but he resembled de Valera in his determination to keep his country out of it, and like both these other national leaders he was sure that his policy would prevail. He honestly believed that participation in the war would wreck the Union. His plan was not quite so honest. It was to proclaim neutrality without consulting the cabinet or parliament. His repeated promises to call parliament had left a convenient loophole through which he could slip. He had never promised to call parliament if he decided against war. As for the cabinet, where he knew he would face determined opposition, he counted on acquiescence in a *fait accompli* supported by the pre-Munich agreement.

A wholly fortuitous coincidence upset this disingenuous scheme. In the middle of August, Hertzog found that he had overlooked an important fact: that the life of the Senate would expire on 5 September, making legislation impossible for some time to come unless he got an emergency act extending the life of the Senate. Thereupon he summoned parliament, solely for this purpose, to meet in special session on Saturday, 2 September. When it assembled on that date, the Senate bill was promptly passed, but there was such public excitement over the invasion of Poland, the British ultimatum, and the government's strange silence on what stand South Africa should take, that the prime minister had to promise a government statement to the House on Monday, and to consult his cabinet in the interval. That body met for three hours on Saturday afternoon, and he occupied the whole time with a speech on the necessity for declaring neutrality. Whether Nazi Germany won or lost, he said, South Africa would be secure, for he scouted the idea that Hitler aimed at world domination. The meeting was resumed on Sunday afternoon, when Britain was already at war, and he tried to commit his colleagues by reading the document they had accepted a year before. Smuts refused to be bound by an agreement made before the Nazi menace to the world had become so clear, and he declared he would carry the issue to the House. The cabinet split, five members supporting the prime minister and seven the deputy prime minister.

On the morrow the opposing leaders of a wrecked government appealed to the House, Hertzog opening with the argument that the country must adopt neutrality for the sake of national unity. But before he sat down he sullied his own cause by a bold defense of Hitler. This threw the advantage to Smuts, who at once pleaded that the national interest and honor called for participation in the war. The ensuing debate continued throughout the day and on into the evening. Then the House voted 80 to 67 in favor of Smuts. The issue was not yet settled, for that very night the defeated prime minister went to the governor general and asked for a dissolution so that the voters of the country could decide the question. Fortunately for the internal peace of the Union, His Excellency was not like his predecessors, a nobleman sent out from England, but a South African, Sir Patrick Duncan, and he refused the request. Hertzog resigned, Smuts became prime minister with an assured majority in the House, and a proclamation of 6 September severed the Union's relations with Germany.

CHAPTER XL

British Participation in the
Second World War

"WINSTON IS BACK," the Board of Admiralty signaled to the fleet on 3 September 1939. Britain was already at war, the Royal Navy was the one arm of her services fully prepared to fight, and the Admiralty had just learned that Churchill was returning, after a quarter of a century, to take charge of it. The news that he was back in the government, from which he had been excluded for years, and that he again occupied this key post, gave a much-needed confidence to countless Britons that at last they would have resolute leadership. In the following spring, when the Nazis overran Norway and easily drove out the British who had hastened to save that country, the shock to Britain raised an angry storm in the House of Commons against Chamberlain as prime minister; and almost immediately afterward the news that the Nazis had attacked neutral Holland and Belgium forced his resignation in favor of the one man for whom the whole country called. Churchill formed an all-party government, which he dominated; and his inspiring genius made him the greatest war prime minister in British history, the supreme leader of the British Empire and Commonwealth through more dangerous perils than the British world had ever known, and on to final victory.

Before examining the part that the British Empire and Commonwealth played in World War II, it will be well to compare the British outlook in September 1939 with that of August 1914. The enemy had bought off Russia; Italy and Japan were openly leagued with Germany; and though both were officially neutral, each was liable to strike without warning. France was the only British ally, but she was no longer the France of 1914. Her position was more exposed, with a hostile instead of a friendly Italy on her southern flank; and she had neither the strength nor the determination with which she entered the First World War. The United States was again neutral; and though Nazi behavior had stifled American sympathy for Germany, this change was offset by the isolationist resolve never to be "sucked" into another European war.

In contrast with 1914, when Germany possessed a battle fleet more powerful than any other in the world except the British, the Nazis had only five strong fighting ships ready for service—two battle cruisers and three "pocket battleships." They were also building four big battleships, but only two of these were ever completed. Over against this enormously increased disparity between British and German naval power stood the fact that a long-distance blockade by the Allies could not strangle Germany so long as her eastern and southeastern frontier was wide open. In the Mediterranean Mussolini had a formidable fleet, but it was no match for that of France or for the navy that Britain could concentrate there. In the Far East the British had long realized that they were unable to muster enough strength beyond Singapore to contain Japan if she became an open enemy; but they counted on the Singapore Naval Base, completed in 1938 at a cost of $100,000,000, to hold back any force that the Japanese could project over the three thousand ocean miles between their home base and Singapore.

The British prospect of land fighting alongside the French against the Germans, where there had been such frightful carnage in the First World War, was dominated by a concept derived from that experience: that the defensive would exhaust the strength of the opposing offensive, and thus win in the end. Though the Maginot Line mentality has since been an object of derision, it should not be forgotten that the Nazis had constructed the Siegfried Line to face the Maginot Line and that they took the latter not by frontal assault but from the rear by swarming past its northern end.

Some people have thought that the Maginot Line should have been extended northward to the sea, along the eastern border of either France or Belgium; but neither alternative was possible. The first would have thrown Belgium into the arms of Nazi Germany, and the second would have tied her to France. The Belgians were so nervously intent on maintaining their neutrality that they could contemplate no risk of compromising it. They secretly trusted that the Allies would rush to their aid against a Nazi attack. The only preparation that the Allies could make in this quarter was to develop field fortifications just inside the French border. How much farther forward they would be able to meet the enemy, they did not know; but they hoped it would be on the far side of Belgium so that they would be within striking distance of the industrial heart of Germany.

The British at once began to take over some of the French line opposite Belgium, with forces different from those of 1914. Like the Germans, but not to the same degree, they were mechanized, relying more on machines and less on manpower. On the other side of Germany the Nazis demonstrated the vast superiority of the offensive when supplied with proper equipment and coordinated by careful training for the new kind of warfare that was to startle the world—the Blitz-krieg. The *Luftwaffe* knocked out the Polish air force in two days, and then in little more than a fortnight the combination of planes, armored divisions (panzers), and motorized infantry crushed Polish resistance before the Russians marched in to take their slice of the conquered country. Yet in the west, where the suddenness of the Polish collapse was ascribed to insufficient Polish preparations, it was still supposed that the revolutionary effect of air power would, on the whole, aid the defensive by hampering the concentrations and communications of the offensive.[1] It was more and more certain that the Nazis would strike at France through the Low Countries, but quiet reigned on the Western Front until May 1940, when the storm broke. Within a week the Western Front was torn apart; and within three weeks the French army collapsed and what was left of the British army, all its equipment lost, was hurled into the sea at Dunkirk.

That was the beginning of Britain's darkest and finest hour. She had lost her footing on the continent and was herself threatened by invasion. From airfields right across the Channel in France and Belgium, the full fury of the *Luftwaffe* was loosed upon her ports and cities; and the Nazi submarines swarmed as they had never done before, for now they could operate from all the coasts on the northern side of Europe. The war had also spread southward, when Mussolini jumped to join in the kill of the French and British empires. His entry into the war extended it to include the Mediterranean area and a large section of Africa beyond. In addition to his armies in the Italian colonies of Eritrea and Somaliland and the newly conquered Ethiopia, he had more than 200,000 troops—soon to be increased to 300,000—in his African provinces that stretched from French Tunisia to Egypt.

---

[1] Winston S. Churchill, *The Second World War*, I, 475.

He was poised to seize the "glittering prize" of Egypt and to cut the British lifeline through the Suez. To non-British people all over the world, it seemed that the fall of Britain was at hand. Without an ally left, she stood alone save for the overseas members of the commonwealth, who could do little to succor her. But the spirit of her people was unbroken, and their desperate defiance rang out in the words of the new prime minister:

> Even though large tracts of Europe and many old and famous States have fallen or may fall into the grip of the Gestapo and all the odious apparatus of Nazi rule, we shall not flag or fail. We shall go on to the end, we shall fight in France, we shall fight in the seas and the oceans, we shall fight with growing confidence and growing strength in the air, we shall defend our island, whatever the cost may be, we shall fight on the beaches, we shall fight on the landing-grounds, we shall fight in the fields and in the streets, we shall fight in the hills; we shall never surrender, and even if, which I do not for a moment believe, this island or a large part of it were subjugated and starving, then our Empire beyond the seas, armed and guarded by the British Fleet, would carry on the struggle, until, in God's good time, the New World, with all its power and might, steps forth to the rescue and the liberation of the Old.

Churchill's shrewd instinct grasped the significance of the American reaction to the turn the war had taken. The fall of France had been unthinkable to Americans; and by exposing Britain as she had never been exposed—even when she stood alone against Napoleon, because then there was no air power and Britain ruled the waves—it startled the American people into realizing the awful danger that would face the United States if Britain fell too. She was the last fighting rampart of western civilization against the Nazi menace. This revelation in America brought more than moral support to Britain. In the midst of the Blitz the United States gave Britain fifty old but reconditioned destroyers lying unused in American naval yards, and Britain leased to the United States naval and air bases in Newfoundland and the West Indies. It was an exchange that added to the security of both parties. For the United States it meant pushing the defense line much farther from American shores. For Britain it bridged the crucial six-months' gap before the completion of the large new construction of destroyers undertaken at the beginning of the war.

The Battle of Britain, fought in the sky over England during the summer of 1940, was Hitler's first defeat in the war, and it was one of the decisive battles of the world. Though the Royal Air Force was inferior in numbers and suffered terrific casualties, it grew in strength and inflicted even heavier losses upon the enemy. The recent British invention of radar, then still called R.D.F. (Radio Direction Finding), helped the defenders; but this secret device was still in its infancy[2] and the protection it gave against surprise was less than the advantage of fighting at home from cannily concealed airports and of stepped-up aircraft production in scattered and camouflaged plants. The peak of the battle came in the mid-August week when 261 German planes were shot down and the British lost only 134. A month later, as the British learned long afterward, Hitler decided to call off his planned invasion because his air power had not blasted the way for it; but the heavy pounding continued—an average of two hundred bombers attacked London every night until November—because Goering believed that the *Luftwaffe* alone could compel British surrender. Well might Churchill say in the House of Commons, "Never in the field of human conflict was so much owed by so many to so few." The young men of the R.A.F. had saved Britain from conquest, and by saving Britain they had preserved the commonwealth—and much more.

Turning to what the overseas members of the commonwealth were doing, we may note that on the eve of the war there had been much doubt if the dominions would again send contingents to fight in Europe. They were much more aware of the seriousness of such an undertaking than they had been in 1914, their national self-consciousness had grown greatly since then, and the maturing of the commonwealth had developed the idea of specialized responsibilities distributed amongst its members according to the particular interest and capacity of each. The First World War had given birth to the idea: the United Kingdom pouring all its available manpower into the Western Front; Canada supplying food and munitions as no other dominion could; South Africa being most concerned with the enemy on her continent, India with the danger in the Middle East, Australia and New Zealand with communications through the Suez and also with the German possessions in the Pacific. The pattern, now partly altered, became more distinct as the war progressed.

The British Commonwealth Air Training Plan was a new and im-

---

[2] "The first five stations of the coastal radar chain, the five guarding the Thames Estuary, had watched Chamberlain's plane go and come on its peace missions of September 1938." Churchill, *The Second World War*, III, 45.

portant feature. It had been contemplated before the war and was adopted a few weeks after the outbreak of hostilities. Canada assumed the chief burden for obvious reasons: she could best afford to do it, she was next door to the huge aircraft industries of the United States, she had limitless space in which to train airmen far from any danger of hostile interference, and she was the only overseas member of the commonwealth from which a nonstop flight to England was possible. The United Kingdom, Canada, Australia, and New Zealand participated in the scheme whereby airmen—pilots, navigators, gunners, and wireless operators—of these four countries received their advanced training in Canada at the expense of the Canadian government and under the administrative control of the Royal Canadian Air Force. The product, which exceeded 130,000 fliers, was fed into the air forces of the participating countries. In addition, untold numbers of young men from the dominions found their own way into the R.A.F.

At sea the New Zealand *Achilles* was one of four cruisers that in December 1939 engaged the slower but more powerful pocket battleship *Graf Spee* off Montevideo and forced her to seek refuge in that port, where her captain scuttled her. Of the Australian cruisers, the *Sydney*, with a British destroyer flotilla, sank an Italian cruiser in the Mediterranean in July 1940, and the *Australia* disposed of a Vichy French destroyer off Dakar in the following September. In the following year, off the western coast of Australia, the *Sydney* came to a gallant end when she fought a German surface raider at point-blank range and both ships were sunk. Japan's entry into the war naturally drew the naval effort of these two dominions into close cooperation with the United States Navy in the Pacific. Along with three American cruisers, the Australian cruiser *Canberra* was sunk in an engagement near Guadalcanal in August 1942. To replace her the British government presented a similar ship, the *Shropshire,* to the Australian government.

South Africa had no navy, and at the beginning of the war Canada had almost none—six destroyers. But the senior dominion soon turned to develop a large fleet of small ocean-going vessels, mostly corvettes, that could be quickly constructed and were much in demand for the special purpose of hunting enemy submarines and protecting precious convoys from them on the North Atlantic passage. As the Canadian navy grew it took over more of this convoy duty—half of it by 1943 and most of it by the end of 1944.

Following the example of 1914, Canada sent an infantry division to England in December 1939 for further training preparatory to fighting on the continent. These troops were on the point of crossing the Channel when they were ordered back to camp because France had fallen and the British expeditionary force was escaping from Dunkirk as fast as possible. During the next three years these Canadians served as part of the British garrison waiting at first to repel an invasion that never came and then to take part in the invasion of the continent. During their long wait they were joined by many more from Canada—two additional infantry divisions, two armored divisions, and two armored brigades—to form two army corps.

Meanwhile the ground troops of the other overseas members of the commonwealth found scope for an active role elsewhere, along with United Kingdom forces, as a consequence of Italy's entrance into the war and France's departure from it. This sudden overturning of the whole situation in the Mediterranean was so alarming that the Admiralty, with a cautious eye on Mussolini's fleet and air force, contemplated abandoning the naval base at Alexandria and concentrating at Gibraltar. But Churchill promptly interposed his veto, and he rushed reinforcements to the fleet in the eastern Mediterranean and to the army stationed in Egypt. Though Britain herself was being pounded by the Blitz and threatened by invasion at any time, he drew on her defenses to send off air squadrons, anti-aircraft guns, and armored units to save the vital British position in the Near East.[3] At the same time he was worried lest Japan follow Italy's example—a possibility that gravely disturbed Australia and New Zealand, whose best soldiers were completing their training far from home, some in England and some in Palestine and Egypt. Therefore he cabled their prime ministers assuring them that his government calculated on being able to avoid war with Japan but would "cut our losses in the Mediterranean and sacrifice every interest, except only the defense and feeding of this island, on which all depends," to defend those dominions if Japan made a move to invade either of them. Their soldiers in England were naturally included in the reinforcements sent to Egypt, where they were united with more of their countrymen from home as well as Palestine.

Hostilities on a large scale in North Africa began in the middle of September 1940, when the main Italian army crossed the Egyptian border with eight times as many men and tanks as the British could then muster to oppose them. The British retired fighting, while the enemy advanced sixty miles to Sidi Barrani and then dug in. There,

---

[3] In July half the few tanks in England were dispatched to Egypt.

Northeast Africa

seventy-five miles short of the railhead at Mersa Matruh where the British expected to fight a desperate battle, the Italian movement stopped, not to be renewed for another three months—and then in the opposite direction.

This pause was a godsend to the British, for the Admiralty decided that it was too risky to send troops and supply convoys through the Mediterranean and therefore these had to go the long way round the Cape of Good Hope. But the delay brought its embarrassments. There were fears that Hitler might suddenly send enough of his armed might to North Africa to ensure a rapid Axis conquest of Egypt; and at the end of October the Italian army in Albania burst into neutral Greece, causing that country to call for British aid, which could come only from Egypt. At once a squadron of the R.A.F. flew north to Greece, where it assisted in driving back the invaders, and British troops landed in Crete to forestall a possible Italian attempt to seize that strategic island. This subtraction of strength from the attack being mounted against the Italian host in the western desert was painful at the time, but events soon showed that it was as nothing.

In the second week of December 1940 a small but completely mechanized army leaped forward from Mersa Matruh, fell upon Sidi Barrani, took it in two days, and chased the broken enemy across the frontier. An Indian division formed one third of this army until the fall of Sidi Barrani, when an Australian division relieved it for active duty elsewhere. In January 1941 the victors leaped again, first to Bardia and then to Tobruk, each time capturing a strongly fortified seaport in a two-day assault. By these swift strokes, the triumphant army reaped a harvest of 113,000 prisoners and more than 400 guns. This toll was raised to 130,000 prisoners, 1,290 guns, and 400 tanks by a further dash that took Benghazi in the first week of February 1941 and immediately thereafter stretched British control as far as Agheila on the border of Tripolitania, five hundred miles from the starting point.

Thus ended the Italian phase of the war in Libya. Indeed, the British nearly called off the pursuit when they took Tobruk, by which time they had nothing more to fear from Italians in that quarter and good reason to fear that they might soon have to throw all the fighting strength they could across the Mediterranean, because the Nazis were massing to overwhelm Greece. The impending crisis called for the assembling of the greatest possible strategic reserve in Egypt and lent urgency to the completion of a task already undertaken in another quarter.

This was the conquest of the Italian empire on the eastern side of Africa, held by a quarter of a million soldiers and swollen by the seizure of British Somaliland in December. The reduction of this empire began in January 1941, with a drive from the Sudan into Eritrea by two Indian divisions, including the one sent from Sidi Barrani, supported by six air squadrons. Other forces, including a South African division and air squadron, swept up from Kenya through Somaliland and into the heart of Ethiopia. Early in April the major task was finished, so that Indian and South African forces engaged in it could be moved to Egypt. These troops were sorely needed there to supplement the reinforcements that Britain, while suffering heavily from intensified U-boat attacks on her shipping and aerial bombing of her ports and cities, was continuing to send by the exasperatingly long sea route round the Cape.

Hitler had determined to clean up the Balkans before turning on Russia. He could not afford to let the British gain a foothold in Greece; to make this more difficult for them, he dispatched Rommel with fresh armored divisions and a strong air arm to retrieve the Italian disaster in Libya. When Rommel struck at Agheila on the last day of March 1941, the British had already sent so much of their Mediterranean fighting strength to succor Grece that their North African desert flank was too weakly held to withstand a powerful blow, and to cushion this they had to hold back units that were to have gone to Greece. The Greek venture and the defense of the desert flank crippled each other.

By mid-April Rommel was at the Egyptian border, having swept everything before him with the single exception of Tobruk. There, behind strong fortifications, a new Australian division and part of another held off the besiegers and were not cut off by sea. Again there was a pause. Tobruk was a thorn in Rommel's side, and he had spent most of his strength. To replenish this, he had to get reinforcements and supplies over a long and difficult route—via the port of Tripoli and a desert road that skirted the sea for hundreds of miles. The British Eastern Mediterranean Fleet tried to cut his communications by sinking convoys from Italy and smashing Tripoli. But these operations achieved only a limited success, and Rommel continued to build up his strength. As the defense of Egypt was desperately short of tanks but had a good reserve of trained crews to man them, three hundred tanks were loaded in England on fast transports and the Admiralty was persuaded to escort them through the perilous passage of the Mediterranean, over the middle of which the Nazi air force was flying. Though the loss of the convoy might have been fatal to the British position in the Near and Middle East, time was of the essence and the safer voyage round Africa would have taken forty days longer. The arrival of the tanks raised British hopes above the purpose of stopping Rommel, for these machines were expected to catch him off balance and throw him back in confusion. But he was prepared for the British challenge when it was delivered on 15 June 1941. For three days the desert battle raged, with heavy losses on both sides, and the action ended where it began.

Already the Greek venture had reached its tragic conclusion. It was a desperate undertaking. When first contemplated, it was part of a British plan to warn the Nazis off by drawing Turkey and Yugoslavia into a defensive alliance with Greece. The failure of that plan made the venture seem almost if not quite hopeless; but the British government went on with it, being bound by treaty to give Greece all assistance possible. It was also a delicate undertaking. Of the available forces, those that were best fitted for it were mostly Australian and New Zealand, and dominion troops could not be used as expendables without the consent of their respective governments. Both governments gave it freely, knowing the risk their soldiers would run. Australians formed a third, New Zealanders nearly a third, and United Kingdom troops the remainder of the expeditionary force, which numbered 53,000 and was supported by eighty fighters of the R.A.F. The storm burst upon it on 6 April, when a German army of fifteen divisions, four of them armored, and a German air force of more than eight hundred planes began the dreaded invasion.

As almost all the Greek army was off in Albania fighting the Italian enemy, the main burden of defending Greece against the Nazi foe fell upon the British. They fought with all their might, but the odds against them were enormous and they had to retire from each position where they tried to make a stand. At the end of a week the Greeks who had called them in suggested that they get out in order to spare the country from devastation. Greece capitulated on 21 April, and the British fought on to cover their own rescue—minus tanks, artillery, other equipment, and stores—by the Royal Navy from the small ports and beaches of southern Greece. Embarkation by day being impossible because the Nazis had complete control of the air, the evacuation was executed during a few nights commencing on the 24th, at the cost of three vessels. Nearly twelve thousand men, of whom more than half were United Kingdom troops, were lost in this Greek venture.

The month of May saw the more agonizing failure to save Crete from the Nazis. There the British, having paid their debt of honor by fighting on the Greek mainland, had a different object—to make the most of the strategic advantages of that island for offensive as well as defensive purposes. The troops evacuated from Greece in the best condition went straight to Crete—nearly 26,000 of them, representing equally their three countries—and they were reinforced from Egypt to provide a garrison of approximately 30,000. Because the possession of Crete was so valuable, there was no doubt that the Germans would soon strain every nerve to take it. At once they began to attack it from the air, where they were vastly superior; and soon they established a virtual daylight blockade of the island, depriving its defenders of all but a trickle of the vital munitions being sent from Egypt. The Germans could not conceal their preparations for a large-scale invasion by sea, but they had no fighting ships to protect it and the Royal Navy was counted on to blow the defenseless vessels back or down. It was from the air, not the sea, that Crete was taken, with a lavish expenditure of men and machines in the first air-borne invasion in the annals of warfare. On 20 May, after a night of paralyzing bombardment, more than 5,000 German soldiers descended from the sky and gained a foothold. Then began some of the fiercest fighting of the whole war. Swarms of other Germans followed by the aerial route and the British struggle became hopeless. Evacuation was ordered on the night of the 26th, but it was too late to rescue 5,000 of the 22,000 survivors. Crete cost the navy three cruisers and six destroyers sunk, severe damage to several other ships, and a loss of nearly 2,000 personnel. The New Zealanders suffered most. Of the 8,400 who were sent to the island from Greece, only 1,300 got out.

It seemed at the time that the British sacrifices in Greece and Crete were all in vain, but the British had unwittingly accomplished two things of inestimable value. They had delayed Hitler's invasion of Russia for several precious weeks, thus cutting down his chances of striking down that country before the winter set in; and they had destroyed the only parachute division that he had yet developed,[4] which he might have employed with decisive effect in either Russia or the Near East.

While British operations in the south (the conquest of Italy's East African empire), on the west (against Rommel), and in the north (the defense of Greece and Crete), were all proceeding simultaneously, the overstrained and undersupplied command in Egypt had also to deal with dangers in the east. Nazi agents were busy in Syria, which adhered to the Vichy regime, and also in Iraq, where, by a treaty of 1930, Britain maintained air bases and had the right of transit for military forces and supplies. In March 1941, the pro-Nazi Rashid Ali got control of the Iraq government, and the pro-British regent fled. At the same time, from Italian airfields in the Dodecanese, the *Luftwaffe* was attacking the Suez Canal and could easily jump into Syria, complete a Nazi bridge to Iraq, and reach on to Iran, India's next-door

---

[4] The British suspected that he had more.

neighbor. In April, Indian troops on the point of departure for Malaya were diverted to reinforce Basra for the double purpose of safeguarding Persian oil and keeping Rashid Ali in check. Their arrival made him go off at half cock before the Nazis were ready. Early in May he struck at a British air training center near Baghdad and he appealed to Hitler for aid. Almost immediately the Vichy commander in Syria received orders to admit the German air force and to turn over French war material for transportation to Iraq. On the 13th, Nazi aircraft got possession of the airfield at Mosul.

But Hitler was then mesmerized by Crete, and the British were increasing their strength in Iraq with planes from Egypt and a motorized column from Palestine. By the end of the month Rashid Ali and his fellow conspirators had escaped to Iran, the regent was restored, and the British occupied all the important points in the country. Meanwhile, amidst anxieties over the fall of Crete and the concentration against Rommel, preparations for a British expedition to Syria went ahead. It was a composite force comprising an Australian division, a motorized cavalry division, and some Free French units. Supported by the Royal Navy and a few R.A.F. squadrons, it advanced on 6 June. At the end of a week it faced such stout Vichy resistance that reinforcements were necessary. Accordingly, more troops from Egypt and from Iraq, including two Indian brigades, joined the fighting in Syria just a few days before Hitler's armies plunged into Russia. On 12 July, the Vichy commander gave up the struggle and Syria passed into Allied occupation.

The German attack on Russia brought some welcome relief to Britain. It was obvious that Hitler would not attempt an invasion of the island for some months, and the terror by night ceased to rain from the sky as he shifted his air force to the east. The last great raid on London was the worst. On the night of 10 May 1941, it caused more than 3,000 casualties, crippled the docks, smashed factories, knocked out all but one of the main railway stations for weeks, and destroyed the House of Commons, which luckily was empty. But there was no relief from the Nazi naval arm. It could not be used against Russia, and it threatened to strangle Britain.

Enemy planes ranging far out over the ocean assisted U-boats to find their prey, and also sank ships by air attack. Surface raiders added seriously to the loss while they played hide-and-seek with their pursuers on the high seas, and this game nearly reached a terrible climax at the time that Crete was falling. Then the newest and most powerful battleship afloat, the *Bismarck,* having slipped up the Norwegian coast, came down the Denmark Strait, between Iceland and Greenland, bent on wiping out Atlantic convoys. Fortunately, her fate was already being sealed by some of the strongest ships of the Royal Navy converging upon her course. The first to engage were the battle cruiser *Hood,* which she blew up with a lucky hit, and the battleship *Prince of Wales,* which she severely mauled. But the *Bismarck* herself was damaged in the encounter, and she had yet to fight more hunters as they closed in upon her and she tried to escape to Brest. Four hundred miles from that port, the *Bismarck* was sunk on 27 May. Though her elimination eased the strain on the British navy, the war in Russia soon increased it.

For more than a year after the Nazi invasion of Russia on 22 June 1941, that country was felt by Britain to be a burden, not a help. It seemed that Hitler was achieving a conquest which would make him mightier still, and that the relief mentioned above was only a temporary lull before a more terrific assault. Therefore it was a British imperative to send all possible aid to Russia. This meant sharing with Russia not only the Lend-Lease war supplies now arriving from the United States but also the output of British munition factories, all of which was sorely needed to build up the defenses of Britain against the danger of invasion, to strengthen the armies in the Near East with tanks and airplanes, and to guard the British position in the Far East against the growing Japanese menace. Moreover, it was on Britain that the burden fell of making deliveries to Russia, which meant more than the diversion of British shipping from other urgent uses, for the convoys required strong naval escorts on the route round the north of Nazi-occupied Norway to Murmansk and Archangel.

An additional route, safer though much longer, was opened through Iran in the late summer of 1941. The pro-Nazi Iranian government, isolated by British action in Iraq and Syria, capitulated quickly when, in accordance with a London-Moscow agreement, Russian forces moved in from the north and British (United Kingdom and Indian) from Iraq; and a few days later the Shah abdicated in favor of his pro-Ally son, who restored the constitutional monarchy. The British intervention was also designed to protect India and to preserve the flow of oil. But as soon as the friendly government was established in Teheran, the prime British objective became the development of communications from the Persian Gulf to the Caspian basin. This entailed an enormous amount of work on which the British army concentrated from September: enlarging ports, improving waterways, building roads, and reconstructing railways—an enterprise that Americans later took over and completed.

It is beyond the scope of this chapter to follow the operations of war in the Russian theater. The British had no part in the fighting there, and they exercised little influence upon it except by what they had unwittingly done in Greece and Crete and by the material aid they sent to Russia. It is well to remember, however, that their fighting elsewhere was more or less aided by the titanic conflict on the Russian plains.

London was impatient to clear the enemy out of North Africa in 1941 while Hitler was absorbed in Russia, where his armies advanced on a front of twelve hundred miles to a depth of about four or five hundred miles. Rommel was clinging to the border of Egypt, a thousand desert miles from his base at Tripoli. The British opposing him were inferior in tanks but superior in the air and in numbers; and Tobruk, which they nourished by sea, threatened his communications. As insurance against a repetition of the June fiasco, headquarters in Cairo clamored for more tanks and got them, though not so many as desired. Stalin was demanding them too, and the drain on Britain was serious, in view of a possible Russian collapse. "We have to be at concert pitch to resist invasion from September 1," said Churchill. Two other worries also beset the commander in chief of the Middle East.[5] He feared a German attack through Turkey, Syria, and Palestine, which the home government thought less likely; and along with that government he was embarrassed by the insistence of the Australian government, for domestic political reasons, upon the withdrawal of the Australian division from Tobruk. London pressed for a September offensive; Cairo said that was impossible and proposed postponement until November, to which Churchill reluctantly agreed.

The delay benefited Rommel, despite the British destruction of a large proportion[6] of the supplies and reinforcements being sent to him.

---

[5] Churchill said he "had always felt that the name 'Middle East' for Egypt, the Levant, Syria, and Turkey was ill-chosen. This was the Near East. Persia and Iraq were the Middle East; India, Burma, and Malaya the East; and China and Japan the Far East." In August 1942 he proposed "that the Middle East Command shall be reorganized into two separate Commands, namely: (a) 'Near East Command,' comprising Egypt, Palestine, and Syria, with its centre in Cairo, and (b) 'Middle East Command,' comprising Persia and Iraq, with its centre in Basra or Baghdad." The war cabinet objected to the change lest it cause "confusion and misrepresentation," and he agreed. Churchill, The Second World War, IV, 460–63.

[6] One third in August and nearly two thirds in October, on the passage across the Mediterranean, which was exposed by the transfer of the German air force from Sicily to the Russian front and by the paralysis of the Italian fleet for lack of oil withheld by Hitler for his machines in Russia.

The newly named Eighth Army, comprising about six divisions—of which half were United Kingdom, mostly armored, and the other half Indian, New Zealand, and South African—caught the German general by surprise on 21 November when he was shifting his troops for an attack on Tobruk which he intended to launch two days later. He had fewer tanks than the British, but nearly 50 per cent more than they estimated, and his were more powerful than theirs. For many days the battle raged and the issue was in doubt. By 10 December Rommel abandoned his garrisons in Bardia, Sollum, and Halfaya, and retreated westward, pressed by half the Eighth Army while the other half besieged the isolated garrisons. A three-day assault dislodged him from Gazala, and he continued his retreat, holding off his pursuers until they reached the end of their tether. Then, on 7 January 1942, he settled down in Agheila. Shortly afterward the isolated garrisons surrendered.

While this desert war was going in favor of the British, their position in the Mediterranean area was severely shaken. Early in November German U-boats invaded the Mediterranean, and a month later Hitler sent a whole air corps from Russia to Sicily and North Africa. These two months were disastrous for the British navy in this sea. German torpedoes sank an aircraft carrier, a battleship, and a cruiser; a new mine field off Tripoli claimed another cruiser; and time bombs placed by divers from an Italian submarine did such damage to two battleships in Alexandria harbor that they were long a useless burden. All that remained of the Eastern Mediterranean Fleet were three cruisers and a few destroyers; and Malta, which had become a veritable British hornets' nest between Italy and North Africa, was now threatened with destruction. But while this British reversal was occurring, it paled into relative insignificance under the glare of the eruption of the war on the other side of the globe.

The foundations of order in the Far East crumbled in 1940, when the Nazi conquest of Holland and France decapitated their empires and the British Empire was in grave danger of falling under the same fate. Almost immediately Tokyo forced concessions from Vichy and London. The French government let Japan get a foot inside the door of Indochina, and the British government agreed to close the Burma road for three months. In the autumn, when Japan was disappointed by Hitler's failure to encompass Britain's fall, London refused to renew the expiring closure order. But Vichy could not resist further demands from Tokyo; and as the months passed, Japan established herself firmly in Indochina, thereby gaining a strategic advantage of enormous value, as the western world fully realized after Pearl Harbor. Japanese influence spread from Indochina into neighboring Thailand, which bordered on British Malaya. Japan also intimidated the Dutch authorities in Batavia into giving her more oil. Obviously she was getting ready for a sudden spring on new prey.

The only visible hope of checking Japan was the United States, but at this time American material support of the war against Hitler was edging the United States ever closer to active belligerency in Europe, which American opinion was anxious to avoid. There is no need to retail here the long story of how the American government tried to restrain Japan, but it should be noted that Churchill repeatedly assured President Roosevelt that British policy would keep step with American policy, even if this meant war with Japan. There was, however, no guarantee that the United States would reciprocate if Japan made war on Britain; and it was recognized, with dark foreboding by American as well as British leaders, that Japan might astutely avoid the Philippines—the defense of which was the one definite commitment of the United States in the Far East—and seize secure control of British and Dutch possessions in that region while congress held up an American declaration of war. But on 7 December Japan took the vital decision out of the hands of the United States by blasting the American fleet in Pearl Harbor at almost the same moment as she attacked the British in Hong Kong. Four days later a repercussion of Pearl Harbor blew the United States into war against Nazi Germany and Fascist Italy, for on the 11th they declared war on the United States.

Though Pearl Harbor sealed the doom of the Axis, because the war potential of the United States was so much greater than that of Japan that it assured Allied victory, this was yet a long way off. Japan was fully girded for war, whereas the United States could not be for some time. Moreover, the destruction wrought at Pearl Harbor—coming on top of British naval disasters in the Mediterranean, and three days before Japanese aircraft sank the only two British capital ships in Far Eastern waters—meant that the Allies had suddenly lost the command of every ocean except the Atlantic. For an indefinite period Japan could strike where she willed in the Pacific and Indian oceans and gather a rich harvest of conquests.

Three Japanese divisions besieged Hong Kong which had a garrison of only six battalions, two of them Canadian, and no hope of relief. Nevertheless, the defenders held out valiantly until they reached the

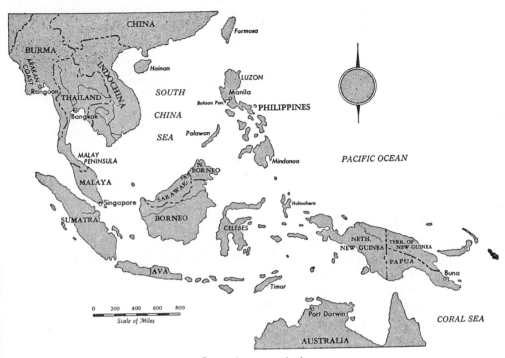

Southeast Asia

end of their endurance on Christmas Day. On the morrow of Pearl Harbor the Japanese began their invasion of Malaya and their air attacks on American installations in the Philippines preparatory to their landing two days later. In both countries the Japanese control of the sea and the air was decisive. The invaders worked down the Malaya peninsula, repeatedly outflanking all efforts to hold them back, and on 15 February 1942 they took Singapore as the Nazis had taken the Maginot Line, from behind. The garrison of 85,000, including a British division recently arrived from England and an Australian division brought back from the Middle East, became prisoners of war. It was the greatest single military disaster in British history. Meanwhile the remnants of the American air force in the Philippines withdrew to Port Darwin in Australia, and the American-Philippines army under General MacArthur retreated to the Bataan peninsula for a last desperate stand, which ended in April 1942. Without waiting for these two major capitulations, the Japanese began to overrun the Dutch East Indies, whose defenses were strengthened by British. American, and

Australian airmen and troops, of whom some 13,000 were taken prisoners when the conquest of the islands was completed by the surrender of the Dutch commander in Java on 8 March.

From Thailand, after more than a fortnight of air attacks on Rangoon, the Japanese invaded the southern strip of Burma in the middle of January. After the fall of Singapore heavy enemy reinforcements poured into Burma, and the only additional strength that the British could throw in was a British battalion from India and an armored brigade from the Middle East. Two Australian divisions from the Middle East were on their way to guard the outposts of their own country, and London begged for one of them to help hold Rangoon, the loss of which would entail the loss of Burma because there were no roads from India across the mountain chain in the north. The Australian government refused, and on 8 March the garrison of Rangoon barely escaped up the road to the north through the trap that was closing on them. Now the British had no port in which to land troops in Burma; the troops that remained performed the almost impossible feat of retiring overland to India; China was completely cut off; and the Japanese possessed naval bases on the Indian Ocean from which they threatened India and Ceylon.

Meanwhile in North Africa, too, the British suffered a severe reverse, for which the diversion of forces to the East was not responsible. The enemy had practically free passage across the Mediterranean, thanks to the crippling of the British fleet in those waters and the arrival of the Nazi air corps from Russia, and Rommel quickly recovered his strength. On 21 January 1942 he struck again. Catching the British by surprise, and displaying a genius for desert tactics that was now proverbial, he drove ahead for three weeks and three hundred miles until the embattled armies reached a new balance in the vicinity of Gazala. After a pause of a few months he was to drive the British back still farther; but by that time the main tide of the war was turning against the Axis.

This turn came slowly but surely as the result of high-level Anglo-American planning in Washington, which began as soon as Churchill could get there after Pearl Harbor. He arrived on 22 December, bringing with him a strong staff of top men in the armed services. Since his first personal message to President Roosevelt in May 1940, suggesting the transfer of destroyers, the two chiefs of state had developed, through frequent cable correspondence and a personal meeting in Newfoundland waters where they drew up the Atlantic Charter, a well-nigh perfect mutual understanding on the problems of the war; and the vital interest of the United States in the survival of Britain had caused American military experts to visit England and consult with British officials, even to the extent of suggesting that Britain should keep for her own security against invasion some of the fighting strength she was sending to the Middle East. All these prior contacts were a fine preparation for the closest cooperation between the two powers in the conduct of the war.

The combined chiefs of staff committee, which now sprang into existence, was a simple but remarkable device for the joint prosecution of the war. It was a permanent body with headquarters in Washington. There it comprised the American chiefs of staff and high officers who represented the British chiefs of staff and kept in constant touch with them in London. It also sat in any part of the world, sometimes for as long as a fortnight, where and when the chiefs of state held one of their frequent conferences, and there it comprised both British and American chiefs of staff. It worked as one team, and its recommendations became final when accepted by the British prime minister and the American president.

Some broad features of combined strategy were also settled at this Washington conference that lasted into January 1942. During their ten days at sea, Churchill and his staff had composed elaborate briefs on the problems ahead of them. The one that caused them the greatest anxiety was how to persuade President Roosevelt and his staff that the war in Europe should have priority over the war on the other side of the globe. It might go hard with Britain if she were left alone to face the danger of invasion and to fight Germany and Italy in Europe, Africa, and the Middle East, for Hitler might then decide to stabilize his Russian front in order to conquer Britain first. Great was the relief of the British mission to find that they did not need to press their argument. The American chiefs calculated that it was to the interest of their country to throw its main weight first along with that of Britain and Russia to crush Hitler, the more powerful foe, and meanwhile to check Japan wherever possible, for easier disposal afterward.

Australia, whose four combatant divisions were at this time serving abroad—one in Malaya and three in the Middle East—was deeply alarmed at the prospect of a Japanese invasion which Britain could do nothing to prevent; but Roosevelt promised Churchill to dispatch large American forces, land and air, without delay to defend that dominion, which would then become a major base for an assault upon the Japanese. New Zealand, not quite so nervous because not so close to the danger, was likewise assured of American aid. It was also estimated that repairs, new building being completed, and a redistribution of capital ships would restore the naval balance in the Pacific and Indian oceans by the summer.

Following the initial agreement to concentrate on Hitler first, the conference considered a plan that Churchill had originally conceived for British execution without American participation and had privately disclosed to Roosevelt in the previous October. It germinated from the rejection of his advice to the government of falling France to retire to North Africa and continue the war from there; and it grew with his determination to retrieve at the earliest possible opportunity what he and many others, including some prominent Frenchmen, regarded as a colossal French blunder. The closing of the western half of North Africa multiplied the difficulty of clearing the eastern half, and he believed that the commander of French North Africa might be persuaded to re-enter the war if sufficiently supported by British aid. For this purpose he held one armored and three field divisions ready, with shipping to transport them on short notice. Pearl Harbor naturally inspired him to revise this scheme and clarify his ideas of how to win the war against Hitler. Accordingly, on the voyage across the Atlantic, he drew up a general plan of joint Anglo-American operations in the Old World to lay before the conference.

French North Africa, the British prime minister pointed out, was the place for the first main offensive because there it could be most effective. He still hoped for a French invitation to enter, but if it was not forthcoming the combination of British and American forces would make it unnecessary. He asked for the dispatch of American bomber squadrons to strike at Germany from English bases, as British bombers had been doing for some time; and for American troops to be stationed in Northern Ireland, where they would serve as a deterrent against an attempted invasion by Germany and would release more mature British divisions for the campaign in French North Africa. President Roosevelt, whose mind was running along the same lines as Churchill's, granted both requests almost as soon as they were presented. As the Eighth Army was pursuing Rommel while Churchill was on the water, he added that it should be possible for Britain and the United States to have complete control of all North Africa out to the Atlantic by the close of 1942. Then, too, a footing might be established in Sicily and Italy.

If all this went well in 1942, the British prime minister continued, the task for 1943 would be the liberation of the captive countries of Europe. "It is impossible for the Germans, while we retain the sea power necessary to choose the place or places of attack, to have sufficient troops in each of these countries for effective resistance. In particular, they cannot move their armor about laterally. . . ." It would be necessary to land forty armored divisions of 600,000 men, of which Britain would supply about half, "capable of disembarking not at ports but on beaches, either by landing craft or from ocean-going ships specially adapted," and behind them "another million men of all arms."

Churchill's timetable was soon to be set back not only by a shipping shortage but also by Rommel and a decision of the German high command to transform what had been a diversion to rescue a weak ally into a strong effort to destroy British power in the Middle East. But the consequent year's delay of the cross-Channel invasion of France was highly fortunate because, as Churchill afterward admitted, it averted an almost certain disaster of the first magnitude. In sketching his master plan, however, he advised postponement of major decisions as long as possible, to gain the fullest advantage from unforeseen events and from secrecy. By the time he left Washington, the combined chiefs of staff had begun work on the North African project; and the conference had greatly stepped up the American program—already revised as a consequence of Pearl Harbor—for the production of tanks, aircraft, artillery, and merchant shipping to meet the needs of the enormous operations ahead.

The Japanese reached the limit of their conquests at the end of April 1942, when an American naval force, joined by two Australian cruisers, assembled in the Coral Sea to intercept an amphibious expedition that aimed at the capture of Port Moresby in New Guinea. The Japanese were turned back in the Battle of the Coral Sea, on 8 May, the first naval engagement to be fought wholly by planes, not a shot being exchanged between surface ships. Of like character, but a much more damaging defeat for the Japanese, was the Battle of Midway on 4 June. The tide had turned in the western Pacific, though the Japanese still had a more powerful battle fleet in those waters.

In the Indian Ocean the British collected a naval force which at first was not a match for what the Japanese sent in—nearly a third of their battle fleet and half their carriers. But the farthest advance that the enemy made was in the opening days of April 1942, when carrier-borne aircraft struck at Colombo and later at Trincomalee, the two

Ceylonese harbors that were the only good British bases in that ocean. Forewarned of the attack, the British had rushed in air reinforcements and had cleared out their shipping, with the result that the Japanese did relatively little damage and suffered heavy punishment. Though there is no telling what they might have attempted in this theater if their stab had not been so costly to themselves, they had no serious plans for an overseas invasion of either Ceylon or India. This of course was not known to the British, whose fleet withdrew toward the east coast of Africa, up which a stream of reinforcements from Britain for India and the Middle East was flowing at the rate of about 50,000 men a month—a limit imposed by the shortage of transports.

If the Japanese followed, as they were free to do, and seized Vichy-held Madagascar with its fine naval harbor at Diego Suarez, they could cut this vital British sea route and threaten South Africa. London had already suspected such a design, and Berlin had received definite reports of it. Nearly a fortnight before the attack on Colombo, an assault force bound for Madagascar sailed from Britain along with a troop convoy. Naval support was supplied from Gibraltar, and the whole expedition was assembled and organized in Durban late in April. On 11 May, after two days of stiff resistance by the French, the British secured control of strategic Diego Suarez. The Japanese navy had missed its chance and vanished from the Indian Ocean to face the Americans in the Pacific.

It was less easy to contain the more powerful foe, whose decision to wrest Egypt and the whole of the Middle East from Britain turned on communications by sea. The voyage from England round South Africa to Egypt took two or three months, the passage across the Mediterranean from Italy only two or three days. But Malta, with its British air and naval base, lay athwart this passage and was therefore the key to the British position that the Nazis would destroy. A terrific air battle was fought for the possession of this rocky little island, beginning in the winter and gaining in intensity through the spring and summer of 1942. Again and again it was on the point of falling from starvation or the depletion of its air force, when just enough relief got through to save it; and it would have fallen if the Axis had not diverted some of its available air power to cover the delivery of replenishments to Rommel. Though he was thus reactivated and able to win a startling success, it was at the expense of security to his own communications.

The last victorious desert campaign of the Axis began on 26 May 1942, and for some days the fighting swayed back and forth indecisively. By the middle of June the First South African and the Fiftieth British divisions, which had firmly held their ground at Gazala, were withdrawn to avoid being cut off and destroyed; and thirty miles to the east, Tobruk, containing the Second South African division, was threatened by the enemy pushing up from the south. On 19 June it was isolated, and two days later it fell. The surrender of the garrison of 33,000 men and of the port with its installations almost intact, to say nothing of the German capture of vast quantities of stores that supplied Rommel in the months to come, was a terrible blow to the British throughout the world. But reinforcements were on the way, including the New Zealand division from Syria, and the precipitate fall of Tobruk betrayed the Axis into a strategic blunder. Rommel was to have halted at the Egyptian border while a combined German and Italian air-borne and sea-borne assault took Malta. This was now put off, and Rommel received permission to drive deep into Egypt and occupy the narrow space between Alamein and the impassable Qattara Depression as an advanced base for operations against the Suez. The Eighth Army had not enough armor left to make a resolute stand at the border or at Mersa Matruh—where the New Zealanders were surrounded but brilliantly charged their way through with little loss to themselves—or at any other place west of Alamein. The army retired there in good order during the last days of June, and it was joined by the one Australian division remaining in the Middle East. At Alamein the British held a strong position. They also had the advantage of much-shortened communications, Alexandria being only forty miles away, while Rommel's communications were so strained that they could barely sustain him. There he came to a dead end.

Churchill was again in Washington on urgent business when Tobruk capitulated. The news nearly crushed him until Roosevelt asked, "What can we do to help?" The first few hundred of the powerful Sherman tanks had just come off the assembly line, and he asked for as many as could be spared. General Marshall, who was at once called in, agreed; and he offered, in addition, one hundred self-propelled guns. The guns and three hundred Shermans were loaded on fast ships and sent to the Suez.

Two grave issues had brought the prime minister flying across the Atlantic. One was the possibility of atomic warfare. By 1939 the basic research in Britain had gone so far that the government decided to press on with it in spite of competing claims on the country's scientific manpower for the prosecution of the war. By the summer of 1941 the work held out hopes of an atomic bomb before the end of the war; and in the autumn, on Roosevelt's suggestion, British and American scientists began to collaborate on the project. Now it had reached the stage where it seemed to justify the construction of large-scale production plants. It would be folly to erect them in Britain, under constant enemy air reconnaissance and danger of bombing. Therefore Churchill urged that the two countries pool all their information and undertake jointly the new phase of the project—in the United States. If the American government was not willing, he would turn to the Canadian government; and if it failed him, he was prepared to undertake the venture in some other safe part of the empire. He got the decision he wanted from Roosevelt.

High strategy was the other issue. The policy of "Germany first" had come under question in Washington, and there was no definite decision on where, when, and how American forces should engage in the task of smashing Hitler's might. For a year Stalin had been demanding, more or less truculently, the immediate opening of a second front in western Europe that would relieve the dangerous pressure on the Russian front; and during the spring both London and Washington, spurred by a visit from Molotov, began to toy with the idea of a cross-Channel invasion, at least to establish a bridgehead, in the late summer or early autumn of 1942. The more Churchill thought about it, the less he liked it. He had no relish for another military disaster, which he was sure would follow because not enough fully trained and armed forces would be available that year for a successful landing in France. He still thought that they would be ready in 1943 and that the best theater for Anglo-American operations in 1942 was French North Africa, which he feared might suddenly be seized by the Nazis. During his mission to Washington in June 1942, it was agreed that plans for the major cross-Channel invasion in 1943 should be prepared in London with all the energy and on the largest scale possible, that a minor crossing in 1942 should not be ruled out unless a more careful examination showed that it was not feasible, and that plans for the operation in French North Africa should be worked out fully and speedily in Washington.

The crucial decision did not come until late in July, a month after the prime minister returned home. The American chiefs of staff were set on a Channel crossing in 1942 and against the invasion of French North Africa. Then Roosevelt overruled them, to the great relief and joy of Churchill, and issued orders for the invasion to begin not later than 30 October. The wisdom of abandoning the attempt to effect even a lodgment on the French coast in that year was confirmed in the middle of August by the raid on Dieppe. This was a reconnaissance in force by 7,000 troops, of whom the Canadian Army, impatient for a chance to fight, supplied 5,000. The raiders had excellent air cover, which enemy dive bombers tried in vain to break, and they were able to maintain themselves on shore for nine hours. But the casualty rate was grim. Of the Canadians only 2,200 escaped, leaving behind 900 dead and the rest prisoners. On the other hand, the experience was of immense value, for it revealed unexpected strength in the German defenses and unknown weakness in the planning for the full-scale invasion of France, which otherwise might have been many times more costly.

Churchill flew to Egypt as soon as the Anglo-American invasion of French North Africa was settled. He feared that the counterpart of this operation, the next British drive in the desert, would be as futile as its predecessors unless there were some drastic changes. He found, as he had suspected, that the trouble was not in the morale of the troops or in their equipment—especially as the three hundred Shermans were then approaching through the Red Sea—but in the high command. Thereupon Generals Alexander and Montgomery were flown from England, the former to be the new commander in chief in the Middle East and the latter the new commander of the Eighth Army. Three weeks later Rommel made his last desperate thrust toward Cairo, and suffered heavily. This trial of strength convinced the British that when they were ready they would sweep on from victory to victory.

The Axis began to crack in the autumn of 1942. On 23 October, the reinforced Eighth Army, completely reorganized, equipped, and trained, began a furious assault upon the enemy position, which was fortified in depth and could not be turned because the flanks were protected by the sea on the north and the salt marshes on the south. Montgomery had undoubted air superiority, masses of powerful artillery such as had never been seen in the desert conflict, three armored and three infantry divisions from the United Kingdom, and four other infantry divisions from Australia, New Zealand, South Africa, and India respectively. After twelve days of violent fighting, this decisive Battle of Alamein ended with Rommel in full retreat, his armor almost all shattered and so much of his transport lost that he abandoned large numbers of his surviving troops. The British suffered 10,000 casualties and gathered 30,000 prisoners. Rommel could not face another serious

French North Africa

battle until he reached Tunisia, many weeks later. The next crack
came in Russia, just after the middle of November, when the Russian
pincers closed around the Nazi army in front of Stalingrad, though it
was not until the end of January that this defiant remnant of twenty-
one German and one Rumanian divisions surrendered.

The Anglo-American invasion of French North Africa, under General Eisenhower as commander in chief, began on 8 November and was
likewise ominous for the Axis, whose leaders were completely surprised
when they learned of the simultaneous landings at Casablanca, Oran,
and Algiers. At once there was a race between the Allies and the Axis

for the control of Tunisia, the central key of North Africa. There the first German and Italian troops arrived on the 9th, and they continued to arrive, chiefly by air; whereas the Allies, having to consolidate their widespread position in Morocco and Algeria, and having farther to go, did not begin to penetrate Tunisia until a few days later. Then both sides concentrated on throwing in all the strength they could for a final decision, which was delayed by the advent of the rainy season. It applied a muddy brake to road transport and it transformed the Allies' improvised airfields into quagmires, while the enemy operated from all-weather airfields. But Malta was revictualed and rearmed, and once more a strategic asset that interfered seriously with the enemy's communications.

In Libya Rommel paused at Agheila, where the old supply difficulty hampered Montgomery. But the diversion to Tunisia of reinforcements originally intended for Rommel, and a wide flanking movement of the New Zealanders who nearly cut him off, forced him to resume his disastrous retreat in the middle of December. Montgomery dismounted one of his two army corps and used all the vehicles to pursue with the other. On 23 January 1943 he took Tripoli, and on 4 February he crossed the border into Tunisia. The other half of his army had to wait for the return of its transport before it could move up to join him, which it did in the following month. Meanwhile, as arranged by Churchill and Roosevelt at their Casablanca conference in January, the Eighth Army passed under the command of Eisenhower; and Alexander, vacating the Middle East Command, became Eisenhower's deputy in direct charge of operations in Tunisia, with eleven British and four American divisions.

The first heavy fighting in Tunisia, where Rommel now commanded all the Axis troops, occurred during the third week of February, when two panzer divisions inflicted a severe defeat on the half-formed United States Second Corps and then ran into such stiff opposition that they were ordered back. Early in March, shortly after Alexander took command of the Allied front, Rommel again tried to break through it but was beaten back, his panzers taking terrific punishment from massed antitank artillery. This was his last action in Africa, from which he was soon invalided home, a sick man. Down in the south of Tunisia, the Eighth Army dislodged the enemy from the strongly held Mareth Line at the end of March, and from a second defensive position early in April. On the following day a patrol of the Indian division met one from the United States Second Corps, the first contact between the two armies that had started their African march nearly two thousand miles apart. The enemy withdrew up the coast, pushed by the Eighth Army, to make a resolute stand within a strong semicircular line about forty miles from Bizerte and Tunis.

All the Axis forces in Africa were trapped,[7] for they were so closely blockaded by sea and air as well as by land that they could neither get reinforcements nor execute a Dunkirk. Alexander launched the final assault on 22 April, and the fiercest fighting followed. It continued after the fall of Bizerte and Tunis on 7 May and died down only with the piecemeal surrender of the surviving enemy, which was completed on the 13th. The bag of prisoners amounted to nearly a quarter of a million. But this is a small measure of what the Allies gained. With the whole of North Africa now securely in their hands, the passage of the Mediterranean was at last reopened, and the "soft underbelly" of Axis Europe was fatally exposed.

Sicily came next, in accordance with an agreement reached at Casablanca, to clinch the control of the Mediterranean, and as a necessary step for the possible invasion of the Italian mainland. If the going was good in Sicily, the victors were not to stop there but to press on. In any event, however, it was settled that this stab on the underside of Europe was not to prejudice the preparations for the massive blow that was to descend upon the Nazis from across the English Channel in the following year. The attack on Sicily, the greatest amphibious operation that had ever been attempted, profited much from the experience gained in the North African landings, and it taught valuable lessons for the landings in Normandy. It was in the Sicilian venture, for example, that the Landing Ship, Tank (L.S.T.) was first used—a new type of craft of British origin in 1940, its design improved by subsequent British experience, and then built in large numbers in the United States. After a week of heavy aerial bombardment that firmly established air superiority over the island, the invasion began on 10 July. Thirty-eight days later the Italian garrison had wilted, and though the Germans had fought stoutly and taken every advantage of the difficult terrain, the conquest was complete. It was the work of the American Seventh Army of six divisions under General Patton, and the reconstituted British Eighth Army of seven divisions under Montgomery, which in this campaign included only one overseas division, the much-trained First Canadian. As in Tunisia, both armies were under the

---

[7] Only a few hundred managed to escape.

direct command of Alexander, while the supporting Allied naval force and air force were each likewise under a British commander, and all were under the general direction of Eisenhower, who temporarily moved his headquarters from Algiers to Malta for this operation. The inter-Allied dovetailing of command, begun in Africa and developed in Sicily, was another valuable contribution to the much greater allied campaign of 1944–45.

The invasion of the Italian mainland, under the direct command of Alexander, followed hard upon the conquest of Sicily. To help drive the enemy out of Sicily, the Allied air forces had raked the enemy's communications and airfields in Southern Italy up as far as Rome, thus preparing the way for the invasion of the Italian boot. During the Sicilian campaign, also, the long succession of Italian disasters bore fruit in the revolution that overthrew Mussolini on 25 July. That startling event, and secret feelers at once put out by the new government in Rome, clearly revealed that Italy yearned for the arrival of the Allies to rescue her from the Nazis, who had sixteen divisions in the country. No longer could there be any thought of stopping at Messina, and again time was of the essence because a firm Anglo-American agreement called for the withdrawal of most of the Allies' landing craft and seven of their best divisions in the autumn as part of the build-up for the invasion of northern France in the spring. Therefore the big question of the Italian campaign was how far up the peninsula the Allies could get before the Germans massed sufficient forces to block their advance.

Before dawn on 3 September 1943 Montgomery's Eighth Army crossed the Strait of Messina and began to work up the toe of the Italian peninsula. Six mornings later the United States Fifth Army, commanded by General Mark Clark and comprising two army corps, one of them British, landed in the Gulf of Salerno, just south of Naples, and had a tough time of it. On the previous evening the Italian armistice, signed secretly on the 3rd, was broadcast; and the Germans, then disarming the Italians, took complete charge of the defenses. They also got reinforcements more quickly. The near approach of the Eighth Army, toiling up from the south, saved the day for the Fifth Army. They joined hands on the 18th, and then together they pushed northward. A week later the Eighth occupied the great Foggia airfields, and on 1 October the Fifth entered Naples, its original objective.

The last three months of the year saw a considerable change in the composition of these two armies. In compliance with the agreement already noted, seven divisions were withdrawn to England to prepare for the cross-Channel invasion. By way of exchange, Alexander got six other divisions then in the Mediterranean area—two British, two Indian, and the other two New Zealand and South African—though not all immediately. Such a major substitution of forces in the midst of a campaign impeded its progress; and as there were not enough landing craft or troops to turn the enemy's flanks by sea, the fighting became a "slogging match" over terrain that favored the defensive. By the New Year the Italian campaign, now overwhelmingly British and definitely relegated to a secondary role, was deadlocked along a line running north-northeast across the peninsula from the mouth of the Garigliano, some forty miles up the coast from Naples. But what the Allies had gained in Italy was much more than three hundred miles of the boot.

The collapse of Italy wrought a strategic revolution. From 1940 the Italian fleet, though consistently shrinking from the risks of battle, had contained a watching British fleet. This was now freed because the Italian fleet, in obedience to its government's orders required by the armistice, had slipped out and gone to Malta, where it surrendered. More important still, the twenty Nazi divisions now tied down in Italy, and the elimination of thirty Italian divisions from the Axis garrisons in the Balkans and the Aegean, restricted the strength that Hitler could muster to repel the coming Anglo-American assault on Normandy.

Though the Italian campaign dragged until May, it gave further aid to the great Allied offensive soon to be launched across the Channel; for during this period there was heavy fighting that drew seven good German divisions from beyond Italy, as well as three from the north of that country. To break the deadlock by a blow in the rear and to hasten the liberation of Rome, an American and a British division landed on 22 January 1944 at Anzio, three quarters of the way to Rome; but the enemy soon sealed off this beachhead without being able to destroy it,[8] and the main Allied army pounded in vain at Cassino, the stout anchor of the Nazi line.

The break came in May, after Alexander got more forces and regrouped them. In addition to several French divisions from Africa and a Polish army corps, his reinforcements included the Fifth Canadian Armored Division from England. He packed more strength into the

---

[8] "As I said at the time, I had hoped that we were hurling a wildcat onto the shore, but all we got was a stranded whale." Churchill, *The Second World War*, V, 488.

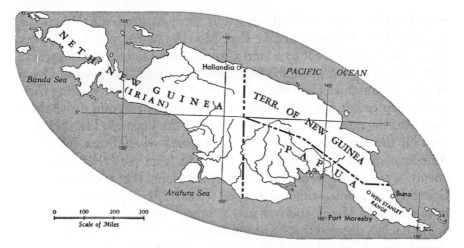

New Guinea

Anzio beachhead, where the Nazis expected the major thrust, and he carefully concealed from them the concentration of his weight against the southern end of the line from Cassino to the sea. There he struck on the night of the 11th. In a fortnight he was through, the Germans were in full retreat, and he gained contact with the forces breaking out from the Anzio perimeter. The Allies entered Rome on the evening of 4 June, and two days later, while they were pursuing the broken German armies, came the momentous turn of the war in the west— the Allied landing in Normandy.

But the Germans in Italy, far from abandoning that country, recovered their balance and offered stiffening resistance to cover their retreat to the so-called Gothic Line, which they had been fortifying for nearly a year and where they were soon reinforced by eight divisions from beyond Italy. The line ran across the peninsula from Pisa to Pesaro, and passed just north of Florence, which fell to the New Zealanders in the last week of July. Earlier in that month Alexander received orders to detach considerable forces—eventually seven divisions, American and French—to take part in the invasion of France from the south in August. It was the second time that his command was crippled, with the result that he had to fight in Italy until the very end of the war in Europe.

Meanwhile in the Pacific the power of the United States—chiefly naval and air—was beating back the Japanese. Only in New Guinea were British forces involved, and they were Australian.[9] When the attempt of the Japanese to take Port Moresby by sea was foiled, they determined to capture it by a land advance from the north coast, where they already had a good footing, over the almost impassable Owen Stanley Mountains. They started in July 1942 and were nearing their goal in September when the Australians stopped them and drove them back over the mountains. In January 1943 the Japanese lost their last hold on the southeastern tip of New Guinea when Buna fell to an American division that had been flown in from Australia. But the enemy were strongly established farther along the northern coast. General MacArthur, who had escaped from the Philippines to Australia in the previous March and was now supreme Allied commander in the South Pacific, decided that he must clean the enemy out of the northern shore before he could attack them in the Philippines. The struggle in New Guinea was long and arduous, for the country was wild and enormous, it abounded in mountains and tropical jungles, disease was rampant, and the Japanese fought so fanatically that few of them survived. There four Australian divisions, including the one that had been engaged at Alamein, bore the brunt of the fighting as one by one the enemy strongholds fell, commencing in September 1943 and continuing into 1944. Some Australians later lent a hand in the fighting in New Britain and Borneo, but in neither was their experience so grueling as it had been in New Guinea.

The war against the Japanese in Burma, under Lord Louis Mountbatten as supreme Allied commander in Southeast Asia, was the subject of a strong difference of opinion between the British and American governments and their respective chiefs of staff over strategy. When the Japanese overran Burma, cutting the road to China, the Americans substituted an airlift from the railhead at Ledo over the southern end of the Himalayas, "the Hump," to supply the Chinese armies and their own bomber force in China. As it was impossible to nourish major operations by this means of transport, American impatience to succor China and use it as a major base for the subjugation of Japan led to increasing pressure on Britain to reconquer northern Burma right away, for the purpose of opening a motor road from Ledo through five hundred miles of mountains and jungles into China. Churchill objected for several reasons: the probable passing of the need for the road before it could be completed, and the consequent waste of time and man-

---

[9] It will be recalled that the southeastern quarter of the island became an Australian colony in 1906 and the northeastern an Australian mandate after the First World War.

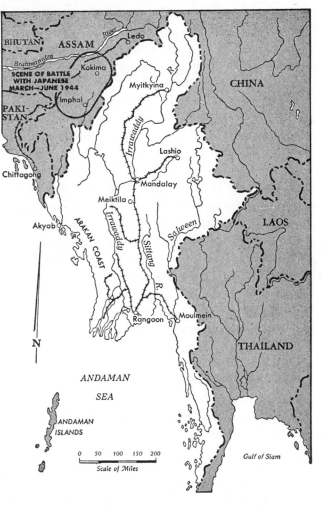

Burma during World War II

power; the easier approach to Japan by island hopping in the Pacific; the physical conditions in northern Burma, which made it about the worst place for fighting the Japanese; the much greater value and accessibility of southern Burma; and the advantage of strangling the Japanese by cutting their line of communication where, in the arc of islands around Malaya, it was exposed to amphibious attack. But he could not shake the American purpose, and therefore he agreed to further it by cooperating with what forces were available.

General Stilwell, Chiang Kai-shek's American chief of staff, opened the campaign in December 1943 with two Chinese divisions he had trained in India. He struck southward over the mountains from Ledo, driving back a Japanese division and being followed by the road-builders. Two British-Indian divisions advanced down the Arakan coast, where they tangled with two enemy divisions and disproved the legend that the Japanese were invincible in jungle fighting. Meanwhile the Chindits—brigades of British and Gurka troops whose specialized function was to fight far behind the enemy's front, where they were landed and supplied by air—had begun to threaten the communications of the Japanese that opposed Stilwell, whose advance was also assisted by reinforcements from China. Then came the main enemy assault upon the center of the Indian frontier. The immediate object of the Japanese was to capture a large stock of supplies which they sorely needed and to cut the railroad to Ledo, which would sever the route feeding Stilwell's army and the "Hump" traffic. The ulterior object was to break into India and revolutionize it. Stilwell and the Chindits plodded ahead while the main battle, on which the whole campaign turned, continued to rage from early in March 1944. To strengthen the defense the British-Indian divisions were flown from Arakan; and other reinforcements, British and Indian, also arrived. But still it seemed almost impossible to hold back the enemy. Late in June the ordeal came to an end when the Japanese broke and fled. India was saved from invasion, the Chindits took one of Stilwell's objectives, and he was besieging the other, Myitkyina, which fell in August.[10] The Japanese had lost about 100,000 men—and the initiative—in this Burma campaign, their largest land engagement in the war up to this time.

Hitler's doom was already being sealed by the tremendous fighting in Europe, where the fateful ring was closing in upon him. Though the Russian advance in the east and southeast assisted and was assisted by the Anglo-American advance in the west, Stalin was conducting his own war independently, and the western Allies were doing the same. Therefore, as previously noted, the operations of his much larger armies need not be recounted here. On the other hand, it is impossible to treat British apart from American operations against Hitler; for they were conceived jointly, they were planned by one directing body, and they were executed under an interlocking chain of command.

---

[10] The new road, after reaching Myitkyina, was continued south for a hundred miles and then east for another fifty miles before it joined the old road. The first convoy from Ledo arrived in China at the end of January 1945.

Eisenhower had returned to England at the beginning of 1944 to assume supreme command of the Anglo-American forces in Europe, with two British deputies as naval and air commanders in chief. Montgomery, who had left the Mediterranean at the same time, was appointed commander of the British, and General Omar Bradley of the American armies of invasion. During the invasion and afterward until Eisenhower took over direct command of all the forces in the field, which he did on 1 September, Montgomery served as deputy commander in chief in France; and later, when the campaign took an unforeseen turn, Eisenhower transferred large American forces from Bradley to Montgomery. Never in the history of warfare had there been anything like this fusion of allies to act as a single power. During the first few months each partner supplied about half their combined forces in France. Then the proportion changed as reinforcements gradually raised the British numbers to one million and the American to three million. Here we should also note that the only overseas commonwealth troops that participated in this campaign were Canadian. In the absence of the First Canadian Corps, which was not brought from Italy to join its fellow until March 1945, a British corps was added to the Second Canadian to complete the Canadian Army.

The landing in Normandy on 6 June 1944, D-Day, caught the Nazis off guard. They were expecting a great assault upon the northern coast of France, but not at the time nor the place that it occurred. Their meteorological service reported that the heavy weather in the Channel, which unknown to them had caused Eisenhower to postpone the operation for twenty-four hours, would make it impossible for several days. The German high command also made two crucial miscalculations. One was that an attempt at invasion across open beaches was bound to fail because it would lack the port facilities essential for landing and sustaining large forces, and that therefore the real assault would be concentrated on one or more of the heavily protected ports. The other was that the main attack would come across the Strait of Dover, the shortest sea passage and the most direct route to the heart of Germany. The German mind had not the slightest inkling of the plans that had been maturing in England for more than two years to tow prefabricated harbors across the Channel to the landing places; and even after D-Day the German belief in a heavier blow about to descend on Calais was so strong that it was six weeks before the reserves in that region were dispatched south to engage the invaders. What made the surprise of D-Day complete, and prevented a rapid concentra-

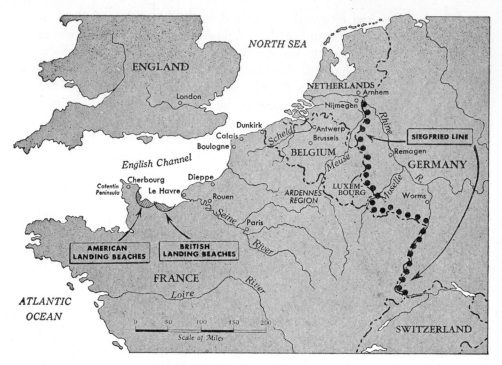

NORTH SEA

ENGLAND

London

Dunkirk

Calais

Boulogne

English Channel

Cotentin
Peninsula

Cherbourg

Le Havre

Dieppe

Rouen

Seine

Paris

AMERICAN
LANDING BEACHES

BRITISH
LANDING BEACHES

FRANCE

Loire

ATLANTIC
OCEAN

River

NETHERLANDS

Arnhem

Nijmegen

Antwerp

Brussels

Scheldt

Rhine

BELGIUM

Meuse

ARDENNES
REGION

LUXEM-
BOURG

SIEGFRIED LINE

Remagen

GERMANY

Moselle

Worms

SWITZERLAND

0   50   100   150   200
Scale of Miles

Allied Invasion, June 1944

tion of enemy forces to beat back the invasion, was the overwhelming superiority of the Allied air force. It had blinded the Germans by knocking out almost all their radar warning stations along the northern coast of France and had crippled the German power of movement by blowing up bridges and railways.

Thus it happened that, though the Germans had sixty divisions in France on D-Day and the Allies only fifteen a week later, that week of fighting gave the Allies a consolidated holding fifty miles along the coast west of Caen and inland up to a dozen miles. By August the Allies had thirty-five divisions in France, and Montgomery's long-prepared plan was working vigorously. While the British army group attracted the principal armored strength of the enemy by threatening to capture Caen and advance on Paris, the Americans overran the Cotentin peninsula and then wheeled round to the south of the German forces that the British were holding. Much of the enemy armor escaped from the closing trap, but it snapped shut on eight divisions, which were annihilated. Thus ended the great Battle of Normandy. The

German commander in chief in the west reported to Hitler: "The enemy air superiority is terrific and smothers almost all our movements."

When Eisenhower assumed direct command in France on 1 September, Paris was already liberated by a French division newly arrived from England; the three American and seven French divisions that had landed on the Riviera were chasing the Germans at top speed up the Rhone; and the main Allied forces had crossed the Seine and were pursuing a badly disorganized enemy who had lost much of their transport and nearly a quarter of a million prisoners. The next fortnight saw a rapid Allied advance on a widening front. The Canadian Army, forming the left flank, cleared the Channel ports and captured the launching sites of the flying bomb which, from its first use shortly after D-Day, had rained death and destruction on London comparable to what that city had suffered from the worst air raids of 1940 and 1941. The British pushed through the center of Belgium, taking the great port of Antwerp on the way and reaching the Dutch border. The Americans, freeing southern Belgium and Luxembourg, came up against the Siegfried Line down to the Moselle. Farther south they gained bridgeheads across that river, and on the extreme right flank the arrival of the forces that had come up the Rhone completed the line from Holland to Switzerland.

Now the campaign slowed down and the fighting grew intenser. Both sides were receiving heavy reinforcements; but the Germans had retired to a shorter and stronger position while the Allies were increasingly handicapped by lengthening and limited supply lines. They had yet only two large harbors that they could use, and both were far to the west. One was Cherbourg, which the Germans had so thoroughly demolished that it could not handle heavy loads until the end of August. The other was one of the two synthetic harbors that had been towed across the Channel to the original landing beaches—its mate had been early destroyed by a wild storm. Antwerp, though found almost intact, was cut off from the sea by the Germans who firmly held the lower reaches of the Scheldt. Instead of driving them out, which would entail heavy fighting, it was decided to cut them off by a daring stroke which, if successful, would accomplish much more. To punch a hole fifty miles deep across all the canals and rivers to the far side of the Rhine at Arnhem in Holland, one British and two American air-borne divisions were dropped at key points on the main road running north, and three British army corps followed to reinforce them and fill in the gaps.

The Germans fought fiercely against this dangerous thrust, and the weather turned bad for the Allied fliers, with the result that the operation failed just short of its goal. The British division, which had been flown to Arnhem, was isolated and recalled, but only a quarter of the men managed to escape back across the Rhine. The whole operation occupied the last two weeks of September. Then priority was given to the task of opening Antwerp by clearing the Scheldt estuary, which the Canadian Army undertook in October and completed during the first week of November. That month brought the heaviest rains in many years, bogging down the Allied offensive and persuading Eisenhower to put off the attempt to force the passage of the Rhine until the weather cleared. While the Allies were waiting, the Germans were busy preparing an unpleasant surprise for them.

The Battle of the Bulge, the last great offensive of the enemy in the west, was launched on 16 December with a furious attack by ten panzer and fourteen infantry divisions against four American divisions holding a seventy mile front in the Ardennes region. Breaking open a gap of about forty miles, the enemy struck in the direction of Antwerp, the seizure of which would sever the supply lines of the northern armies. The German penetration was more than sixty miles deep before it was held by the massing of superior forces; then, from Christmas Day, mounting counter-pressure gradually squeezed the bulge back until it disappeared at the end of January. Unlike the Allied thrust toward Arnhem, this desperate gamble of the Germans was a complete failure. It was also a ruinous one, for it cost them enormous quantities of material and 120,000 casualties.

But it should not be forgotten that the German losses were much heavier on the eastern front, where the Russians, with a numerical superiority of between two and three to one, faced two hundred divisions while the Americans and British in the west and in Italy encountered only some ninety. By the beginning of February 1945, when the western Allies had yet to breach the German frontier, the Russians were well inside it, on a line that cut down from the Baltic through Pomerania and Silesia to the southern tip of the latter. Moreover, this line extended across Czechoslovakia, through Hungary west of Budapest, and on into Yugoslavia. The Russians were in virtual control of the whole Balkan region except Greece, where British troops were curbing a fierce Communist insurrection that followed the German withdrawal from that country. This British intervention was hotly criticized in the United States; but after the war was over and the situation in Greece was more generally understood, the American government sent forces to complete what the British had begun.

Here we should also observe an important Anglo-American difference over high strategy, already decided in a way that was to be much regretted in later years. American insistence overruled Churchill's stout opposition to the sacrifice of the Italian campaign for the sake of the Riviera invasion. His heart was set on pushing that campaign to an early conclusion and on following it quickly with a drive through the Ljubljana Gap into Austria and Hungary to catch Germany in the rear. He feared what actually happened. The Riviera invasion contributed little to the success of the Allies in the north; against Alexander's weakened forces, the Germans were able to hold out in northern Italy until the very end of the war; their armies in the Balkans, instead of being cut off, effected an orderly retreat before the advancing Russians; and the door was left open for the Russians to sweep through Hungary and Austria.

The advance of the western Allies was resumed on 8 February with a Canadian blow directed southeastward from Nijmegen, and soon the whole line was in motion. Flooded rivers and sodden ground impeded progress, and so did the Germans, who were making their last great stand in the west—on their own soil. But the Allies were decisively superior in morale, in numbers, in equipment, in supplies and, above all, in the air. At the end of six weeks of continuous fighting along a front of more than two hundred and fifty miles, they had driven the enemy across the Rhine and, though it was not part of the plan, they had gained a foothold on the east bank at two points, Remagen and Worms. Now the sacred German river proved to be no obstacle to the Allies, so thorough were their preparations. They swarmed across at many points and then fanned out, meeting with little organized resistance. The Canadian Army, still on the left flank and at last joined by its First Army Corps from Italy, moved north into Holland and then along the coast into Germany, while the British and Americans advanced until they met the Russians. Meanwhile the Germans surrendered in droves. On 29 April, the day all the German forces in Italy surrendered, Hitler committed suicide in his Berlin bunker while the Russians were fighting in the streets of the city. The general capitulation of Germany was signed in Eisenhower's headquarters in Rheims on 7 May, eleven months and a day after the landing in Normandy.

The end of the war in Europe coincided with the final defeat of the Japanese in Burma. The liberation of that country had been subordinated not only to the opening of the road in China, which turned the campaign upside down, but also to the defeat of Germany, which absorbed reinforcements that were to have gone to Burma. Mountbatten was therefore instructed to do his best with the limited forces at his disposal. The Japanese hoped that the monsoon season, which was at its height in June 1944 when they lost their three-months' battle just inside the Indian frontier, would give them a respite to repair their broken strength; but there was no relaxation of the pressure upon them. Progress was slow while the torrential rains checked air activity and bogged down movement along roads that were never better than fair-weather trails. When the skies had cleared and the roads had dried, other difficulties loomed ahead.

The two best Chinese divisions and three squadrons of American transport aircraft were withdrawn because Chiang Kai-shek insisted that he needed them to meet a threatening Japanese advance. The departure of the aircraft, later replaced mostly by British machines, was the much more serious handicap because the Burma campaign depended largely upon air transport. As the remaining craft were short-ranged and were flying in supplies delivered at the end of steel by the much-overburdened Assam railway, another supply route was necessary if the army was to get much farther than four hundred miles from the railhead. To meet this need, a December drive down the Arakan coast opened new airstrips that were nearer the front and could get deliveries direct by sea from India. The heaviest fighting occurred in March around Mandalay and Meiktila, after which the enemy fell back, determined to hold the routes south along the Irrawaddy and the Sittang to the port of Rangoon. If the British could not recover that strategic key of the country before the return of the monsoon rains in May, the enemy could push them back. Rangoon fell on 3 May "with only a few hours to spare," as Churchill has recorded. This Burma campaign shares with the victorious American Philippines campaign the distinction of being one of the only two examples during the whole war of a major Japanese army being engaged and utterly defeated in the open field.

For the recovery of Malaya and Singapore, which came next in the British program, neither the troops nor the transports were available until the overthrow of German power. Then preparations were rushed for a landing in overwhelming strength; but just before everything was ready for this operation, it was forestalled by the action of the Japanese government when it sued for peace.

The collapse of Japan, coming so soon after that of Germany, also forestalled plans for a large redeployment of British fighting-strength to assist the United States in the reduction of Japan. In September 1944, at the second Quebec conference, Churchill offered to send, as soon as Germany was defeated, the main British fleet to take part in the major operations against Japan under the supreme American command, and Roosevelt at once accepted the offer. There were also plans to throw the Royal Air Force and British land forces into the Pacific war; but neither of these, apart from the Australian and New Zealand troops that were already there, had a chance to participate in it. The Royal Navy, however, was represented by a formidable division in the last stages of that war. In March 1945 it went into action as part of Admiral Spruance's fleet, and it suffered heavy casualties as well as severe damages from "suicide" bombers before the swift collapse of the enemy—with the blasting of Hiroshima by an atomic bomb on 6 August, the Russian declaration of war on the 8th, the destruction of Nagasaki by a bigger atomic bomb on the 9th, and Japan's acceptance on the 10th of the terms of surrender that the Allies had laid down at their Potsdam conference only a fortnight previously.

CHAPTER XLI

Less Empire and More Commonwealth

THE BRITISH renunciation of all imperial control over India and Ceylon, and the transformation of these two countries into three sovereign members of the commonwealth partnership, which occurred in the summer of 1947, meant an enormous shift from empire to commonwealth and a corresponding revolution in the character of the British Commonwealth. It was no longer an association of nations that had grown from British settlement overseas. It resembled the old empire in being multiracial, multicultural. It now extended beyond western civilization, beyond Christendom, to include three Asian powers whose combined population greatly exceeded that of all the other members added together. So radical was the change that the term "British Commonwealth of Nations" seemed a misnomer, particularly in the new India where the adjective "British" was associated with foreign rule, and it became the fashion to drop the adjective from the name. The idea also took root and grew that this shift from empire and the attendant revolution in the character of the Commonwealth might and should be carried further by colonial consolidations in Africa and the Caribbean to form still more self-governing dominions with non-British, non-European populations.

Here another significant change of nomenclature should be observed. The term "dominion," though alluring to people who aspired to rank in status with the senior members of the Commonwealth, was associated with memories of a status inferior to that of the mother country. For this reason the senior dominions were no longer so proud of the name as they had once been, and in India it seemed inappropriate. Therefore, in 1947, the titles of the Secretary of State for Dominion Affairs and the Dominion Office were altered to Secretary of State for Commonwealth Relations and Commonwealth Relations Office respectively.

The transfer of sovereignty in India was hastened but not caused by the Second World War; for Britain had already conceded the principle, and the constitution of 1935 had been consciously designed to let the people of India work out their own salvation as a fully self-governing nation equal in status to Britain and the dominions. The prospect of this transfer of sovereignty, however, had raised the vital question of whether the people of India were a nation or could become one. The divisions between French and English in Canada and between Boer and Briton in South Africa were as nothing compared with the major split in India between Hindu and Moslem; and the strain that the war imposed on the internal unity of the two dominions just mentioned— which we shall examine later—was likewise as nothing compared with the aggravation of disunity in India which irrevocably broke the constitution of 1935.

On the outbreak of the war the ruling princes rallied to the side of Britain, and the ministries of three of the four provinces in which the Moslems were a majority—the Punjab, Bengal, and Sind[1]—declared their support for the British cause. Jinnah and the League were non-committal at first, but presently they came out in favor of backing the war effort if Britain would give an assurance that the Moslems should be free to decide their own constitutional future.

The reaction of the Congress was very different. Having anticipated the coming of war as ushering in the day of independence for India, the Congress proclaimed its sympathy with democracy and freedom, and damned British imperialism for violating these principles in India. The last straw was the plunging of India into war against its will. The Congress demanded a British declaration in favor of independence and promised, if this were granted, a reconsideration of its refusal to cooperate in the prosecution of the war. Failing to get such a declaration, the working committee called out the eight Congress ministries in October 1939. Their resignations, which forced the provincial governors to assume the administration because no other ministry could command a legislative majority,[2] was celebrated by the Moslem League in a "day of deliverance and thanksgiving."

The British government sought to placate India at the outset of the

---

[1] The fourth, it will be recalled, was the North-West Frontier Province, which had a population that was 92 per cent Moslem and a Congress government composed of Moslems.

[2] Later in the war, however, cabinet government was restored with non-Congress ministries in three of the smaller provinces, including the North-West Frontier Province.

war by reaffirming the policy of dominion status for the country, by announcing that when the war was over the constitution of 1935 would be reconsidered in the light of Indian desires, and by offering as an interim measure the enlargement of the viceroy's executive council to include representatives of the Indian political parties. Acceptance of the offer of course required agreement between the parties, but this was not forthcoming. The breach between them became much wider in the spring of 1940, when the League finally committed itself to the establishment of Pakistan. It was the Congress that forced this step by insisting on the concession of Indian independence as pre-essential for the calling of a constituent assembly and for any communal agreement.

Outside the League the partition proposal met with general condemnation. There it was taken for granted, by British and Indians alike, that the political unity of the country must be preserved. To this end the viceroy issued a statement in the following August. It said that Britain, mindful of the minority problem, could not contemplate the surrender of "present responsibilities for the peace and welfare of India to any system of government whose authority is directly denied by large and powerful elements in India's national life," and that Indians themselves should be primarily responsible for drafting the new constitution. The League found comfort in the thought that the transfer of power would not subject Moslem India to Hindu domination; but the Congress found none in the suggestion of a constituent assembly, and did not heed the obvious warning that it must win the confidence of Moslem India. Congress leaders asserted that Indians could settle their own differences easily if Britain would leave the country, but the question of how they would settle them was darkened by increasing talk of civil war.

When the viceroy's continuing negotiations to draw opposing leaders into his executive council foundered on the League's demand that the Moslems have as many representatives as the Hindus, he reconstituted the council in July 1941 by appointing Indians who were personally distinguished but had little political backing in the country. The executive council now had, in addition to three British, eight instead of three Indian members, and by the end of the war the eight had increased to eleven. These changes, however, were of little moment when compared with other changes in the Indian political scene. When Japan entered the war and her conquering forces swept toward the gates of India, the internal tension became so dangerous that Britain made a much greater effort to effect a settlement with Indians and between Indians.

Churchill's coalition government sent out Sir Stafford Cripps in March 1942 with a draft declaration that soon became famous as the Cripps Offer. All departments of the central government, save that of defense, would be turned over immediately to Indian ministers selected in consultation with the political parties; as soon as the war was over, an Indian assembly would be elected to frame a constitution for India as a full-fledged dominion with liberty to secede from the Commonwealth. The British government would undertake beforehand "to accept and implement forthwith the constitution so framed," provided that any province or native state that so desired might refuse to join the new Indian Union, and that the constituent assembly sign a treaty with the British government covering "all necessary matters," including the "protection of racial and religious minorities," involved in "the complete transfer of responsibility from British to Indian hands." Cripps interviewed leaders of all the parties, but the outcome turned on the attitude of the Congress and the League. Both rejected the offer. Neither would budge from the stand it had taken, and they were wider apart than ever.

The Cripps Offer, which the British government left open, and its summary rejection by the two major Indian parties attracted wide attention in the outside world and disarmed many foreign critics who had condemned Britain for hanging on in India. This effect was important because Gandhi had won enormous moral support from public opinion in democratic lands, especially the United States. Now the Mahatma asserted that the immediate departure of the British would remove "the bait" attracting the Japanese to India; that if the British went and the Japanese came to conquer, India could easily defeat the latter by passive resistance; that Britain should "leave India in God's hands" from which, after a spell of anarchy and civil war, "a true India" would arise, united, strong, and free. One member of the Congress high command, the ex-premier of Madras who was to become the first native governor general of India in 1948, C. Rajagopalacharia, tried desperately to save the situation by persuading his party to accept the principle of Pakistan; but his well-meant crusade only embittered the Hindu-Moslem feud and he forestalled disciplinary action by resigning from the Congress.[3]

---

[3] He later rejoined it.

To force Britain to "quit India" immediately, the Congress launched, under Gandhi's leadership in August 1942, a mass movement of what was officially nonviolent noncooperation but was really violent sabotage of the war effort. Railways were torn up, telegraph and telephone wires pulled down, bridges and electric installations blown up. In-flamed mobs attacked police stations, revenue offices, and other government buildings. The nature of the destruction and its concentration in strategic areas suggested that Axis agents were behind the outbreaks, but it is doubtful if many of them were. The League denounced this "open rebellion," and the government took prompt countermeasures. In pursuance of a unanimous resolution of the viceroy's executive council, overwhelmingly Indian, Gandhi and other principal Congress leaders were clapped into jail, and their two central committees and their provincial committees were declared unlawful organizations. With rare exceptions, the Indian police were staunchly loyal, even unto death. In three weeks the rebellion died down, and by the end of the year most of the embers had been stamped out. The disturbances caused between two and three thousand casualties and property damages that amounted to a million pounds. With the Congress leaders in prison[4] and their organization outlawed, the political deadlock in India persisted through the rest of the war.

The hopelessness of this deadlock, together with a political upheaval in Britain, precipitated the end of the British Empire in India. Churchill's coalition government broke up in May 1945, when the reason for its existence was removed by the total defeat of Nazi Germany, and the prime minister formed a Conservative "caretaker" administration to fill the gap until the election of a new House of Commons. When the voters went to the polls in July, Churchill's government sustained a resounding defeat; and he had to exchange seats in the House with Clement Atlee, who had been his right-hand man in the coalition cabinet. For the first time the Labor party was in power with a majority in the Commons, where Labor outnumbered the Conservatives by almost two to one.[5]

Though both parties were committed by the Cripps Offer to grant Indian independence as soon as possible after the war, there was an

---

[4] In May 1944 Gandhi was released on compassionate grounds of ill-health. The other leaders were freed at the end of the war, when the ban on their organization was lifted.

[5] The liberals no longer counted for much in the political game. Their party had been broken by a split that dated from Lloyd George's ousting of Asquith during the First World War.

important difference between them in their attitude toward the problem. The Conservatives represented the class that had always supplied the men who ran the British government in India, and this background of knowledge and experience made them cautious. They wanted to be sure that there would be no betrayal of minorities or of the native princes. The Labor party, with less understanding of India and less fear of the chaos and bloodshed that might follow, had always championed Indian nationalism against British imperialism, and therefore approached the problem with impatience to get rid of it. But it is doubtful if Atlee's government could have done more than it did to bring about an agreement between the two great warring factions in India, or if there was much time to spare when it cut the Gordian knot that defied untangling.

The temper of India had become so inflamed that it was liable at any time to burst forth in a combined civil war and uprising against foreign rule; and Britain was so exhausted by her world war efforts that she had not the physical strength to face such a crisis, to say nothing of the moral revulsion that any such attempt would provoke at home and in the rest of the world. The British authorities in India reported that they could not maintain law and order much longer. Gone, too, was the old economic argument—so dear to right-wing politicians as a shield and to left-wing politicians as a target—that Britain should retain some political control over India in order to protect her large investment of capital there; for the war had reversed the balance of indebtedness between the two countries, Britain now owing India some £1,200,000.

For long weary months the Labor government strove to preserve the unity of India because the alternative seemed almost as bad as the operation that Solomon proposed when two women disputed the motherhood of one baby. Gandhi was right when he said that partition would be vivisection. In addition to the geographical intermingling of Hindus and Moslems, which would leave millions of people on the wrong side of any line, the very life of India was dependent upon material services that the British government of India had developed, such as the railway and irrigation systems, the armed forces and the whole organization of the defense of the country, which were so integrated that they could not be torn apart without inflicting incalculable harm. Moreover, the two halves of Pakistan would be separated by nearly a thousand miles.

At the end of the war, when Britain was bound to resume the search for a basis of agreement in India, there was only one definite step that the League and the Congress agreed should be taken, and that as soon as possible. It was the holding of elections for the central and provincial legislatures. They were long overdue, because the government had ruled out elections in wartime; and everyone knew that the central assembly elected in 1934 and the provincial bodies in 1937 no longer represented those who had chosen them. Therefore on 21 August 1945, only six days after the Japanese capitulation, the viceroy called for central and provincial elections without delay. He brushed aside Indian complaints against the restrictions of the existing franchise[6] by saying that any major revision would postpone the elections for at least two years.

The complex structure of Indian politics was much simplified by the appeal to the voters in the winter of 1945–46. With the single exception of the Sikh organization in the Punjab, the many minor parties lost heavily to the two major parties, whose mutual hostility was sharper than ever. The Congress strength in the provincial assemblies jumped from 704 to 930, and the League from 109 to 428 of the 492 seats allocated to Moslems. In eight provinces, including the politically anomalous North-West Frontier Province, the Congress now had an absolute majority and formed ministries; and it was the second largest party in the other three provinces. There the League had no absolute majority—at least partly because the communal award had given overrepresentation to minorities—but was able to take office with the support of fragmentary parties.[7]

Meanwhile exploratory discussions that the viceroy had pressed with leaders of Indian opinion ever since the spring of 1945 were getting nowhere, and in February 1946 it was announced in parliament that the government was sending three of its most important cabinet ministers—the secretary of state for India, the first lord of the Admiralty, and Sir Stafford Cripps—to help the viceroy work out with Indian leaders some way of setting up a constituent assembly and organizing an interim government backed by the main parties. The cabinet mission, which arrived in March, found that the League demand for Pakistan was too strident to be ignored without grave danger of civil war, and, on the other hand, that the concession of this demand would

---

[6] Both major parties had postulated the principle of adult suffrage, which would have enlarged the provincial electorates fourfold and the electorate of the central assembly (still constituted under the Act of 1919) tenfold.

[7] In the Punjab, but not in Bengal or Sind, the cabinet was a coalition.

do more violence to the principle of self-determination than a refusal. Of the two widely severed halves of the projected Pakistan, the western had a population that was 38 per cent non-Moslem, and the eastern 48 per cent; and in the rest of India there were twenty million Moslems. Outside the League no Indian opinion favored partition, and Congress leaders muttered threats of civil war to preserve the union. Yet the mission saw a ray of hope in a Congress reversal of its stand on federalism. The new formula provided for a rather loose federation of autonomous provinces invested with residuary powers, and for the strengthening of the federal government by the addition of such specified powers as any province might wish to confer upon it. The mission rejected the scheme for two reasons. One was that it would be difficult to work, with some ministers responsible to the whole federal legislature and others only to the members from particular provinces. The second was that it would be unjust to deny other provinces the corresponding right to combine among themselves for the management of common affairs.

Here was the key to the solution of India's constitutional problem that the cabinet mission proposed in the spring of 1946 after much consultation with Indian leaders. The central government, said the mission, should be organized on the basis of equality between the Hindu-majority provinces and the Moslem-majority provinces, and be confined to the control of foreign affairs, defense, communications, fundamental rights, and financial arrangements essential for these purposes; the provinces should possess residuary powers; and an intermediate governmental tier should be inserted by having the predominantly Moslem provinces set up an executive and a legislature for such matters as they wished to handle in common, and by having the predominantly Hindu provinces do the same. The constituent assembly should be elected by the provincial legislatures in proportion to population; after a formal opening, it should divide into sections to settle the provincial and group constitutions before coming together again to draw up a constitution for the central government. The native states should be fitted into the system by negotiation with them.

This plan devised by the cabinet mission was the best solution that was ever offered, and for a while there were encouraging signs that it might be applied. Both the Congress and the League accepted it, though with some equivocation; the constituent assembly was elected; and the viceroy was able to form an interim government in which both parties were equally represented and a few spokesmen of the lesser minorities held the balance. But the League entered the viceroy's new council only for self-protection against the Congress; the League members refused to take their seats in the constituent assembly, because Congress quibbles over how that body should proceed clearly indicated a determination to block the insertion of the intermediate tier of government; the League withdrew its acceptance of the mission's plan, asserting that Pakistan must have a completely separate constituent assembly; and the Congress bloc in the interim government declared that it would resign unless the British government forced the League either to withdraw its bloc or to enter the constituent assembly.

The British government could neither accept nor reject this ultimatum without wrecking not only the interim government but also the whole plan for having India provide itself with a constitution free from any British control. London then adopted a course designed to drive the League and the Congress into composing their differences and to silence forever their exasperated and exasperating charges that Britain was playing one party off against the other in order to retain her hold on the country. The Congress had long pressed Britain to back up her promises of full self-government by placing a definite time limit on her rule in India, and now the very reason for her past refusal became a compelling reason for granting the demand. On 20 February 1947 the British government announced that it would "take the necessary steps to effect the transfer of power into responsible Indian hands by a date not later than June 1948."

The attempt to drive the two great Indian factions together was no more successful than the previous efforts to draw them together, and failure now meant that partition was the only alternative to anarchy and civil war. The "Great Calcutta Killing," more horrible than any previous communal riot in all the years of British rule, had taken 4,000 lives and injured 10,000 people during four days in August 1946. Congress accusations that the League government of Bengal had incited the Moslems to this wholesale slaughter evoked counter-accusations that Congressmen had done it to discredit the provincial ministry. The Calcutta affair was the beginning of sporadic outbreaks of murderous communal hate on an alarming scale. India was like a vast human volcano.

The prospect of partition fed the communal rage because the League claimed too much territory for Pakistan, particularly the whole of Bengal and the Punjab, by far the most populous of the provinces that had Moslem majorities. According to the 1941 figures, the Moslem population of Bengal was 33,000,000 out of a 60,300,000 total, and the Moslems in the Punjab numbered 16,200,000 out of a 28,400,000 total. To make things worse for the League's claim, most of the Bengal Moslems were hived in the eastern half of the province, and most of the Punjab Moslems in the western half. The Congress insisted on the partition of these two provinces as the price for the partition of India, to which it was gradually being reconciled in spite of strong opposition by Gandhi. He declared as late as 31 May 1947 that "even if the whole of India burns, we shall not concede Pakistan, even if the Moslems demanded it at the point of the sword." Jinnah bitterly denounced the proposal to disrupt provincial unity; but in the end, which came rather swiftly, the League had to pay the Congress price for Pakistan.

British leadership was necessary to bring about this settlement, and one man supplied it in masterly fashion. He was Lord Louis Mountbatten, the last viceroy of India, who had won distinction as a naval and military leader in the late war. On arriving in March 1947 to take up his new duties, he found the country drifting into anarchy because nobody knew to whom the British would hand over the power of government when the narrow time limit ran out. It was a question for the Indians themselves to answer, and they had failed even under the shock administered by the setting of a date for British withdrawal. Mountbatten quickly got Gandhi and Jinnah to issue a joint appeal to the people of India, condemning the resort to violence for political ends; and he managed to preserve the bipartisan interim government. The two blocs in his council, which were scarcely on speaking terms and were directing mutually hostile administrative policies, he persuaded to work together in tolerable harmony.

Mountbatten's chief problem, of course, was the partitioning of India—not the general principle, which the Congress was resignedly admitting as inevitable, but its practical application. Jinnah vehemently asserted that the division of the country must follow provincial boundaries because if Bengal and the Punjab were to be broken up all the other provinces would have to suffer the same fate and the whole of India would be torn to pieces. The integrity of his Pakistan was also challenged by the Punjab Sikhs, who were crying for an independent Sikhistan, and by Congress Moslems in the North-West Frontier Province, who were agitating, with ominous encouragement from Afghanistan, for an independent Pathanistan.

From many deliberations with Congress, League, and Sikh leaders, singly and in groups, the viceroy pieced together a plan which they accepted early in June, and it was put into operation almost immediately. It contemplated the division of British India into Hindustan and Pakistan, each with its own constituent assembly; and it called for a vote by the people themselves or their representatives in each of the six territorial units claimed for Pakistan—British Baluchistan,[8] Sind, the North-West Frontier Province, the Punjab, Bengal, and Assam—to determine the territorial dispute. The first three chose to be included in Pakistan, the other three to be divided between Pakistan and Hindustan. Meanwhile a hierarchy of partition committees and subcommittees, in which Hindus and Moslems cooperated under a British chairman, got to work upon the immense task of dividing the army, navy, air force, civil service personnel, railways, post office, telegraph, finances, and the many other assets and liabilities of British India. Meanwhile, also, the Indian Independence Bill was drafted in London, submitted to the viceroy and by him to the Congress and the League leaders, and then rushed through parliament during the first fortnight of July.

The Indian Independence Act transferred sovereignty over British India on 15 August 1947 to the two new dominions of Pakistan and India. The latter name was substituted for Hindustan at the request of Congress leaders, who regarded the partition as a secession from the India that would still be a member of the United Nations and other international bodies. This made no practical difference to Pakistan which, after three days of independent existence, was elected to membership in the United Nations. To fill the legal gap between the transfer of sovereignty and the adoption of a new constitution by each dominion, the act endowed each with the office of governor general, conferred upon each constituent assembly the full powers of a dominion parliament, and, until each dominion provided otherwise, continued in force such parts of the Government of India Act of 1935 as might still be applicable. As for the native states, whose fate will be discussed shortly, the act simply renounced British suzerainty over them without conferring any of it upon either dominion. The act also provided for eliminating "Emperor of India" from the royal title, with the consent of the other dominions as required by the Statute of Westminster.

---

[8] Which was not a province. It was administered by a chief commissioner under the viceroy. The remainder of Baluchistan was a British protectorate with native rulers.

The Crown appointed Mountbatten[9] governor general of India and Jinnah governor general of Pakistan, following nomination by the Congress and the League respectively;[10] and the government of each dominion ensured a large measure of continuity between the old and the new regime by selecting members of the former ruling race to fill many of the highest offices. On 15 August and the following day, both declared public holidays, the birth of independence was celebrated with unbounded enthusiasm throughout the land. The burden of the past seemed to have rolled away. There were remarkable scenes of intercommunal fraternization, and the British were immensely popular. But the jubilations were soon hushed by the enormous human tragedy precipitated by the simultaneous partition of the country and removal of the neutral arbiter.

In the Punjab, even before 15 August, Sikhs and Hindus had begun to move eastward, and Moslems westward, to be under a government of their own kind. Now there was an orgy of communal plundering, burning, and killing that was both the cause and the effect of a huge panic flight in opposite directions, while the two new provincial governments looked on helplessly. In Bengal, the other explosive region, there was much less destructive fury, a contrast that some observers of Indian life might explain by saying that the Bengalis were more effete—or more civilized—and some by citing the influence of Gandhi, who rushed to the riot-ridden Calcutta and fasted for several days until sanity returned to that city. The governments of the two dominions, though exchanging bitter accusations, cooperated in checking the madness; and by mid-October it was stopped, but not its hideous accompaniment in the suffering and deaths from starvation, disease, and exposure. The refugees numbered about ten million—some estimates have run as high as twenty million—and the toll of human lives ran into the hundreds of thousands. Religious fanaticism claimed its most famous victim in the following January, when a Hindu assassinated Gandhi for backing peace with the Moslems.

The tragedy was a gruesome confirmation of the fears that had dictated the British policy of gradual transition to Indian self-rule. Atlee's government and Mountbatten have been blamed for not insist-

---

[9] Raised to an earldom as a reward for his remarkable achievement.

[10] In the absence of properly constituted dominion cabinets. On the day of his inauguration, Mountbatten told the Indian constituent assembly that he would ask for his release in the spring to make way for an Indian, which he did. Rajagopalacharia succeeded him. Jinnah died in September 1948.

ing on the temporary retention of some British control—at least in the Punjab—to preserve the peace and to assure an orderly exchange of population between the two dominions. But it will always be a moot question whether the consequence would have been better or worse than what happened, for the excitement of India had reached such a pitch that a British refusal to surrender all power might have lit a catastrophic war for Indian independence.

Both new dominions at the very beginning of their existence set up cabinet governments after the British model, but India outstripped Pakistan in the management of its own affairs. Pakistan was handicapped by being divided into two parts widely separated in character as well as by geography, and by having poorer physical and human resources. Moslems had lagged behind Hindus in acquiring a modern education, the Congress had given its leaders and followers a much better political training than the League, and the theocratic principle upon which Pakistan was founded was a weak support for the building of a democratically governed state.

The Pakistan constituent assembly soon became bogged down in the business of framing a constitution, the League began to disintegrate, and East and West Pakistan pulled against each other. A serious crisis developed in 1954 when the League ministry in the province of East Bengal, which comprised the whole of East Pakistan and contained a larger population than all the provinces of West Pakistan, appealed to the electorate for the first time since partition and was overwhelmingly defeated by the old United Front party, a coalition of Moslems and Hindus. The new provincial premier, who had been premier of the united province under the old constitution, flouted the League-dominated central government in Karachi, West Pakistan, and demanded the replacement of the provincial contingent in the constituent assembly. The central government dismissed his ministry and branded him as a traitor. It also dismissed ministries in several provinces of West Pakistan. Before the year was out the governor general stepped in, proclaiming a state of emergency throughout Pakistan, dissolving the deadlocked constituent assembly, forcing the prime minister, whom he later dismissed, to form a new cabinet on a national instead of a party basis, and enacting laws on his sole gubernatorial authority. This alarming swing from parliamentary government to dictatorship was halted when the highest court in Pakistan found that he had overstepped the legal bounds of his power and he recalled the constituent assembly in 1955.

When the dominion of India was born, the making of its constitution was already under way. Its constituent assembly had first met in December 1946 as the constituent assembly of British India, and as such it had held a second and a third session, in which it did essential work. The interparty agreement of June 1947 to accept partition removed the members who came from areas that would belong to Pakistan, lifted the ban on the attendance of Moslem members from Hindu-majority areas, and freed the assembly from the limitations imposed by the cabinet mission's plan. The fourth session, held in July, was therefore identical with the fifth—which began on 15 August—in composition and purpose, the purpose being the preparation of a federal constitution with a strong central government. As the drafting continued, it became morally certain that the long-cherished ideal of the Congress, "a sovereign independent republic," would be written into the constitution. This raised the question of whether it would not automatically sever the connection with the Commonwealth, which the leaders of the dominion were now very anxious to retain. When the clause was inserted, the question was referred to a special conference of Commonwealth prime ministers in London in April 1949. There Prime Minister Nehru, speaking for his government, declared that India desired to remain a full member and accepted the king as the head of the Commonwealth. All the other prime ministers agreed that India thereby remained a regular member of the Commonwealth, for which they had a good Irish precedent. Some cynics said that India's creditor position buttered her bread on the British side, which was true. But it should also be observed that there were larger political considerations behind the reluctance to break with Britain, and that India was repeating the nineteenth century experience of the colonies. India became a republic on 26 January 1950.

The native states could not long survive the withdrawal of Britain, whose antiannexationist policy had preserved them as museum pieces of a vanished age. They were scattered enclaves incapable of maintaining an independent existence, and their territories and inhabitants were the same in character as those of adjoining India or Pakistan, which they were expected to join on the best conditions they could get. It was not a pleasant prospect for the ruling princes; but there was a rough justice in their predicament because they had blocked the 1935 federal scheme to the great injury of the people in British India and because, with rare exceptions, they had ignored British prodding to set their own houses in order and were therefore in no position to negotiate on even terms with the heirs of British power in the two dominions. All but two big states joined India or Pakistan with astonishing celerity, the largest ones retaining their identity, others combining to form new political units, and many being simply annexed to neighboring provinces. India got the lion's share, thanks largely to combined affinity and propinquity.

Pakistan and India quarreled over the acquisition of only three states, Junagadh, Hyderabad, and Kashmir, where the people and their rulers were of opposite religions. The Moslem Nawab of Junagadh, a relatively small state of 4,000 square miles on the west coast some 300 miles from Pakistan, declared for accession to that dominion, as he had an undoubted right to do, and Pakistan accepted his offer. But internal trouble forced him to flee, troops of the other dominion entered to restore order, and a plebiscite gave an overwhelming decision for union with India. Hyderabad, by far the largest state, with an area about equal to that of Great Britain and a population of 16,000,000, mostly Hindus, was entirely surrounded by India. The Moslem Nizam saw that accession to Pakistan was not practical politics, and he opened negotiations with the government of India, hoping to gain a position of semi-independence as a member of that dominion. After long and fruitless negotiations, an armed invasion in September 1948 gathered Hyderabad into the Indian fold. Kashmir was likewise landlocked, but it bordered on both dominions. Its frontier with Pakistan was the longer, its only all-weather road communication with the outside word was through Pakistan, its river system was tributary to that of Pakistan, and its population of 4,000,000 was predominantly Moslem. On the other hand, the maharaja of Kashmir was a Hindu; so also were his officials and armed forces, and a not inconsiderable body of Kashmir Moslems favored the Congress party. The maharaja could not bring himself to declare for either dominion until some 2,000 Pathan tribesmen burst in from the west, looting, burning, and killing. Then he offered to join India and called upon it for military aid against the invaders. India obliged, Pakistan raged, and the two dominions were on the brink of war. India said that her acceptance of the accession would be subject to a referendum in Kashmir, which has been postponed indefinitely. Pakistan insisted that the Indian troops must first be withdrawn, which India refused, and the dispute still poisons the relations between the two neighboring countries despite repeated efforts of the United Nations to settle it.

Ceylon emerged as a sovereign dominion almost immediately after

India and Pakistan, but much more easily. Nationalism was of more recent growth in Ceylon and tensions arising from divisions of race, language, and religion were much less acute. The Singhalese constituted 70 per cent, and the Tamils 22 per cent of the population, which numbered 6,600,000 at the time of independence. The first step toward self-government had occurred in 1909 when, coincident with the Morley-Minto reforms in India, the Colonial Office directed a reform of the legislative council by the introduction of an elected element, chosen by a narrow and communal franchise. After the First World War, which stimulated nationalism in Ceylon as elsewhere, the elective principle was carried further until, in 1923, twenty of the twenty-three nonofficial members were elected.

During the twenties the demand for self-government in Ceylon continued to rise, encouraged by the demand in India, and the British government sent out a commission headed by Lord Donoughmore to examine the constitutional problem of Ceylon. The Donoughmore Report, submitted in 1928, pointed out that the existing representative government was heading for an impasse. It was bound to press on toward responsible government, for which the colony was not being prepared. Two obstacles blocked the way—communal tension, and the inexperience of the politicians. The commission recommended a new approach, which the government adopted. A single electoral roll with adult suffrage[11] replaced the communal system, and the council was reconstituted after the model of the London County Council instead of parliament. The council was to govern through seven standing committees, each electing its own chairman who would be the minister in charge of a particular department of government; and the seven chairmen, along with the heads of three "reserved" departments, would form the governor's cabinet. Intercommunal political cooperation followed in the wake of the abandonment of communal electorates; and the ingenious device, novel in British colonial experience, for combining the legislature and the executive worked so well that it was later copied in the West Indies. It gave the politicians of Ceylon a practical training in administration that prepared them for the full-blown responsible government that they demanded.

Late in the war Lord Soulbury led a commission to examine what should be done in Ceylon, and began to draw up a new constitution based on a draft prepared by the island's ministry. The result was a

---

11 Resident Indians were given a restricted franchise.

return to the parliamentary path at an advanced stage, just short of sovereignty. The first, and last, election under the Soulbury constitution was completed in September 1947, when the governor called upon the leader of the principal party to be prime minister and form a government. Already the Ceylon Independence Bill was being digested in London, and in December its final passage conferred full sovereignty upon the parliament of Ceylon, to come into effect on 4 February 1948. On the advice of the new dominion's prime minister, Lord Soulbury was commissioned governor general.

Burma's complete withdrawal from the empire on the morrow of the Second World War, far from encountering British resistance, had Britain's hopeful blessing, and was the logical consequence of Britain's failure to perform her supreme obligation to that country—of defending it against enemy attack and conquest. But this was not the only cause. Burma nursed a grievance against the British government that was of much longer standing. As a province of British India, Burma was opened to unrestricted Indian immigration, which built up an alien community of more than a million in a population of seventeen million. The average Burman could not compete with Indian coolies or artisans; and, what was many times more important because most Burmans were tillers of the soil, a swarm of Indian moneylenders preyed on the peasants and gobbled up a large proportion of their holdings by the foreclosure of mortgages.

During the war many of the Burmese people welcomed the Japanese as liberators and then turned against them as oppressors. Both reactions stimulated the desire for independence, which British policy had earlier encouraged by giving Burma the same measure of autonomy as any Indian province, though Burma was politically less mature. Only one sixth of the qualified voters were sufficiently interested in politics to go to the polls in the election of 1925. On being severed from India, Burma got responsible government under a constitution more liberal than that which operated in India, where the princely obstruction of the federal scheme automatically continued the central government under the obsolete constitution of 1919.

When the invaders were being chased out of Burma in the spring of 1945, Churchill's coalition government proclaimed that the self-government of the country should be developed to full dominion status, which implied the right to secede, and that as soon as constitutional government could be restored representatives of the people should draw up their own constitution. From the welter of native factions U (a

Burmese title of respect) Aung San, using strong-arm methods, emerged as premier of the interim government. In January 1947 he met Prime Minister Atlee in London and got his consent to the independence of the colony. In July a gang of assassins led by U Saw, a former premier who was later hanged for his crime, burst into the council chamber in Rangoon and machine-gunned leading members of the cabinet, including Aung San. His successor asked for and received a confirmation of Atlee's agreement. The constituent assembly hastily adopted a republican constitution which would cut all connection with Britain, and the British parliament implemented it in November by passing the Independence of Burma Act, which came into force on 4 January 1948.

As in the three new Asian partners of the Commonwealth, the peaceful withdrawal of Britain from Burma won local good will for the British, many of whom were retained in the service of the Burmese government. But the new regime was much less stable than that in any of these Commonwealth members, for in Burma the foundations of self-government had not been so securely laid and had been shattered by the Japanese conquest. A confused condition of multiple civil war ensued, with Communists split into two mutually hostile groups, both fighting the Rangoon government, which also fought to subdue the hitherto semi-independent hill peoples—the Karen tribes and the Shan States. Britain resolutely kept hands off.

Malaya, which Britain had likewise failed to protect from foreign attack and conquest, presented a different problem. Malaya was clearly incapable of standing on its own feet when the Japanese, as a consequence of defeats elsewhere, hastily departed, forestalling a British reconquest that was on the point of being launched. With the peaceful return of the British, which followed immediately, the pre-war governmental structure was restored, but radical changes were undertaken.

This structure, as we have seen, was a work of shreds and patches pieced together in untidy fashion: the island of Singapore, the island of Penang with Province Wellesley, the settlement of Malacca, and a few little island dependencies, all forming a crown colony officially known as the Straits Settlements; the Federated Malay States of Perak, Selangor, Negri Sembilan, and Pahang, British protectorates with a common civil service; and the Unfederated Malay States of Perlis, Kedah, Kelantan, Tregannu, and Jahore, also British protectorates but individually more independent. The natives of the crown colony were

British subjects; but those of the protectorates were the subjects of their respective sultans, whose sovereignty was qualified by the governor of the Straits Settlements in his capacity as high commissioner of the Malay States. There were thus ten more or less unrelated governments for a combined territory that was about the size of England and contained a population of nearly six million at the time the Second World War began. To make things more complicated, the easygoing Malays were already outnumbered in their own land, being only 42 per cent of the population. Immigration of more enterprising Hindus accounted for 14 per cent, of still more enterprising Chinese 41 per cent, and these Chinese were increasing so rapidly that they would soon be the largest racial group.

During the interwar years a Colonial Office effort to substitute a tidy union for the ramshackle system of government had foundered on the opposition of the unfederated sultans to a surrender of their autonomy, and of Singapore to the abandonment of its life-giving principle of free trade. The abortive plan included no provision for introducing self-government lest such a reform betray the Malays to the Chinese, most of whom aspired to return home with a competence gathered in Malaya. During the Japanese occupation, Malay national consciousness awoke, but the active resistance movement was wholly Chinese and dominated by Communists, whose ulterior motives were then little suspected.

On the morrow of the British restoration the colonial secretary, looking forward, as he said, to the preparation of Malaya "for self-government within the British Commonwealth," announced the intention of uniting all nine Malay protectorates and two of the three British settlements into one state, and of making Singapore a separate colony. The sultans quickly concurred and the union was formed in April 1946. At once a storm blew up among the Malay people, who feared that the balance of government was being turned in favor of the immigrant Chinese and who rallied against the demotion of their sultans. The surprised sultans then repented their precipitate surrender and assumed the leadership of the popular agitation.

Bowing before the storm, which spread to England, the British government reconsidered its own action and sought the advice of a committee in Malaya representing the sultans, British officials, and the United Malays National Organization. In April 1947 the island of Singapore, whose population was nearly four fifths Chinese, became a crown colony with its own governor, executive council, and legislative council, the last containing an elected element. The integral union of the nine Malay states and two British settlements came to an end on 1 February 1948, when they re-emerged in the rather loose Federation of Malaya, each with nominated executive and legislative councils, and the federal government with the same. All were promised elective councils "as soon as circumstances permit." In June of that year the peace of the country was shaken when a hard core of Communists, all Chinese, began to operate from secret lairs in the almost impenetrable jungle as terrorist gangs, much as they had done against the Japanese—and the Huks were doing in the Philippines. For several years they played a murderous game of hide-and-seek with greatly superior numbers of police and soldiers, who reduced them to a remnant by 1955.

Meanwhile in both Singapore and the Malayan Federation there was promising interracial political cooperation in the functioning of government and the rising demand for self-government, which led in 1955 to the inauguration of new constitutions, the holding of general elections, and a partial concession of responsible government. In Singapore a legislative assembly replaced the legislative council, almost all the seats were won by the nonracial Labor Front, and its lawyer leader, the native-born son of a Baghdad Jew, became chief minister. The legislative council of the Federation was continued, but more than half the seats were made elective and all but one of these were captured by a biracial alliance under the leadership of a Malayan prince, who likewise became chief minister. In both elections the wine of victory went to the heads of the victors. They demanded full responsible government immediately and independence in the near future. The colonial secretary flew from England and appeased them.

Though the two territories are politically separated, they are so interdependent that either would sink without the other. They have coordinated some of their affairs; but a political union, though urged by local politicians, is yet out of the question. What keeps them apart is their difference over fiscal policy and, still more, the mutual fear of the two chief races that one would dominate over the other; for the Malays have a slight numerical advantage in the Federation, the Chinese a big one in Singapore, and union would compromise both. Can two such disparate people be a nation? The answer to this question will govern the future of Malaya.

It has been suggested that a satisfactory answer may be found in a larger combination including Sarawak, which became a crown colony in 1946 when the last of the century-old Brooke dynasty ceded it,

North Borneo, which also became a crown colony in this year by transfer from the ruling company, and the Brunei protectorate—all three inhabited by people of the same stock as the Malays of the peninsula.[12] This larger combination has actually existed in shadowy form since the end of the war, when the high office of the Commissioner General in Southeast Asia was created. He resides in Singapore and has general supervision over the administration of all these territories.

Turning to the black man's continent, we see a serious movement for self-government in British East Africa, Central Africa, and West Africa, and an effort to develop each as a potential dominion. But first it should be observed that in each of these three groups of British dependencies, as in other parts of the colonial empire, there was a simultaneous economic and social revolution that was essential for their political progress.

Until 1940 the colonies were expected to bear the cost of their own administration, a condition that weighed heavily upon them. Though Joseph Chamberlain had done much for them, they continued to be "undeveloped estates" with meager revenues that provided little or no margin for expenditures that might bring social and economic improvement. Such an investment offered too little security and too distant returns for private capital, especially during the depression years, when the plight of the colonies became rather desperate and provoked native disturbances here and there. At last the British government decided to go to the rescue, and in 1940, just after the fall of France, the Colonial Development and Welfare Act was passed. It provided £5,000,000 a year for "any purpose likely to promote the development of the resources of any colony or the welfare of its people." In 1945, when the end of the war was in sight, another act of the same name multiplied the amount, and the process was repeated afterward. Some of the money was wasted in hasty and extravagant ventures, such as the abortive scheme for large-scale mechanized cultivation of groundnuts (peanuts) in Tanganyika, but the waste may be compared to the water spilled by an eager hand priming a pump. The important thing is that the pump was primed.

In British Central and East but not West Africa, physical conditions favored white settlement, and a white society had been planted amid a

---

12 So too are most of the inhabitants of Indonesia, whose postwar independence has had a marked effect on the outlook of the peninsular Malays.

many times larger black population. This combination of colors caused a serious conflict of interest that complicated the problem of government; and the problem was further complicated in East Africa by the presence of a third color—a considerable Indian community. It had begun generations before the British arrived, it had expanded under their protection, and it was more numerous than the European community.

In British West Africa, where the population was solidly black, the political awakening has been remarkably rapid and British policy has kept pace with it. Of the four territories that are collectively known as British West Africa, little Gambia whose population is some 275,000 has lagged behind; Sierra Leone, with a population of 2,000,000, got a considerable measure of representative government; while the Gold Coast, containing 4,000,000 people, and Nigeria 24,000,000, have rushed through the various stages of colonial constitutional development from nominated native members of their legislative councils to democratically elected legislative assemblies with cabinets and prime ministers—all since the Second World War. Though there is no common government for these four noncontiguous territories, there is the West African Council, which was set up in 1945 and serves as a useful agency for mutual consultation and the coordination of common affairs. It is composed of the colonial secretary and the four governors, and has a secretariat with permanent headquarters in Accra, the capital of the Gold Coast.

British Central Africa, comprising the three contiguous territories of Southern Rhodesia, Northern Rhodesia, and Nyasaland, was federated in 1953, and is of particular interest because this federation is designed to reconcile the interests of an advanced white society with those of a much larger black society inhabiting the same country. It was thirty years since the chartered company had ceased to rule and the old Rhodesia was divided into Northern and Southern Rhodesia with the Zambesi River as the boundary between them. Northern Rhodesia then passed under the direct control of the Colonial Office, and Southern Rhodesia was made a separate colony and endowed with responsible government. This, rather than incorporation as a province of the South African Union, where Afrikander nationalism was in the ascendant, was the choice, determined by a plebiscite, of the white settlers in Southern Rhodesia. They were mostly British immigrants from South Africa after the Boer War, and they numbered 34,000 amid a black population twenty times larger. Further immigration, also mostly from the Union, raised the white population to 160,000 by 1953.

Being an offshoot from the Union, Southern Rhodesia has applied a similar, though much milder, native policy. The difference is largely explained by the less crowded condition in Southern Rhodesia, by the reaction of the British settlers against the hard attitude of the Afrikanders, and by the constitutional provision that no legislation discriminating against Africans could become law in Southern Rhodesia without the permission of the imperial government. Though this veto has never been applied formally, it has operated informally by persuading the government of the colony to modify projected legislation in accordance with advice from London.

Northern Rhodesia was different, and Nyasaland still more so. In both, as in British West and East Africa, the Colonial Office insisted that the interests of the Africans must be paramount, and there was little European settlement in either territory until the 1931 discovery of the rich copper belt in Northern Rhodesia. The material development of the "new Rand" quickly repeated that of the original, with its characteristic color bar imposed by skilled white labor. But the African workers received official encouragement to form unions of their own, and African management boards and advisory councils were organized to look after the welfare of their own people in the mining towns. In the rest of the country, tribal councils and native courts remained the rule. In 1953 the European population numbered 42,000 and the African 1,700,000. By contrast there were then 2,400,000 Africans in the small and impoverished Nyasaland, whose chief export has been young men seeking work in the copper belt or farther south, even in Johannesburg, more than a thousand miles away. The representative principle was recognized in the composition of the legislative councils of both territories, but not to the same degree, Northern Rhodesia having a bloc of elected European legislative councilors who in turn elect several of their number to the executive council.

The pressure for federation, which began as early as 1931, came from the whites in the Rhodesias and was inspired by a mounting impatience to build a new self-governing dominion. The natives became alarmed lest Britain betray them as she had done in South Africa and also, to a certain extent, in Southern Rhodesia. But no British government would contemplate an amalgamation of the three territories until 1951, when it became clear that a new idea had taken hold of the European community—the conception of a white-black partnership in the proposed federation. One man was largely responsible for this wholesome development. He was Sir Godfrey Huggins (later Lord Malvern), a London doctor who had migrated for the sake of his health and was premier of Southern Rhodesia from 1933 until he became the first prime minister of the federation. He preached partnership as the only way of salvation for both races, because domination of either by the other would certainly lead to disaster. His own people harkened; but the natives, fearing a clever white trick to victimize them, cried out against any change unless it led along the all-black road the West Africa was traveling.

The issue that London faced was whether the welfare of the indigenous population would be better served in the long run by upholding or by overriding their opposition to federation, now that the European community offered to take them into partnership. The strong economic arguments for federation[13] could not be dismissed as merely materialistic, because they also spelled social, educational, and hygienic advancement. Another and most important consideration was the danger that a continued refusal of federation might start an anti-British and antiblack reaction that would drive the two Rhodesias into the arms of the South African Union. Then where would the blacks be? On the other hand, there was the risk that a wicked generation of whites might arise that would violate any constitutional guarantee of fair treatment for the Africans. On balance, it seemed safer to run this risk and trust the Europeans to realize that their own fate was sealed unless they carried their partners along with them in the development of the country. The decision was essentially that of a trustee.

The constitution of the Federation of Rhodesia and Nyasaland, which was worked out by the governments of the United Kingdom and the three territories in collaboration and was accepted by the electorate of Southern Rhodesia in a plebiscite, is not like that of any other federation. It left the different constitutions of the three territories as they were, and merely established a central government with a governor general and a federal assembly from which the cabinet is chosen and to which it is responsible. This federal legislature has exclusive control over such matters as external affairs, defense, foreign trade, immigration, currency, and the postal service. The assembly was established with twenty-nine white and six black members. These

---

13 Harnessing the immense power of the boundary river, the Zambesi, was only one of the alluring prospects for the country as a whole.

figures may suggest a betrayal of the huge native majority of the population, but they simply reflect the enormous disparity in political maturity between the two races. Because of this disparity the European community is the senior partner of the firm, the African the junior, and the promise of the senior to deal justly by the junior is underwritten by the British government. The two northern territories are still protectorates and governed as such, which means that London has direct control of their native policies; London has retained the constitutional check on Southern Rhodesian legislation affecting the natives; and three European members of the federal assembly are specially appointed or elected to represent African interests. In addition, the federal African Affairs Board, half white and half black, is charged with holding up, for final decision by London, any federal legislation that discriminates between Europeans and Africans. A good omen for the success of this novel experiment in interracial political partnership—which was fittingly inaugurated on the centenary of the birth of Cecil Rhodes whose steadfast ideal was equal rights for all civilized men—appeared in one of the first measures of the federal government. It was the establishment of a color-blind university.

British East Africa, which likewise comprises three contiguous territories each with its own government, has what may look like the beginning of a common government. During the war, when the enemy was next door, cooperation between these governments was imperative, and this experience led in 1948 to the establishment of the East Africa High Commission and the East Africa Central Assembly. The commission has three members, the governors of Kenya, Tanganyika, and Uganda, and is the executive charged with administering the services, such as postal, telegraph, customs, and income tax, which the participating governments have transferred to it. The assembly has two dozen members, some ex officio, some nominated, and some chosen by the three legislative councils. The majority of the assemblymen are Europeans—the others being Africans, Indians, and one Arab. Useful as is this administrative combination of the three territories, there is no present prospect of its becoming a political union—largely, though not entirely, because of the white settlement in the Kenya highlands, where the soil is fertile and the climate temperate.

The completion of the railway to Uganda in 1902 opened the door for white settlers, and the government invited them by offering grants of land in the highlands, which were almost empty of natives. But there was only a trickle of immigrants until the end of the First World

War, when the British government sent out more than a thousand demobilized soldiers who quickly made good as farmers. In 1920 the old British East Africa protectorate was divided into the protectorate of Uganda and the crown colony of Kenya, which thereby became more attractive to British colonists. Thus the highlands were developed as a white man's country. By 1952 Kenya contained a population of 40,000 Europeans, 150,000 Asiatics, and 5,500,000 Africans, all inhabiting only 40 per cent of the territory, because the rest was chiefly desert.

Self-government was already a lively issue when the colony was carved out of the old protectorate, the Europeans demanding responsible government for themselves to the exclusion of others, and the Indians demanding equal rights as British subjects. London was perplexed until 1923, when it dashed any hope of responsible government and decreed that each of the clamant communities should elect representatives to sit in the legislative council. It was then laid down that, though the highlands were reserved for white settlers, segregation was not to be the rule in the rest of the country, and that "Kenya is an African territory and the interests of the African natives must be paramount." No native had a seat in the legislative council until 1944. Other natives were added in 1947 and 1948, and their admission stirred fears among the white settlers that the avowed British policy of paramount African interests would soon culminate in the organization of Kenya as an entirely African self-governing state. The governor told them that their apprehension was "fantastic." Some constitutional change, however, was impending in 1952 when it was indefinitely postponed by the bloody Mau Mau crisis—a crisis which embittered white-black relations and was still plaguing the country in 1955.[14]

Tanganyika, taken from the Germans in the First World War, a

---

[14] The root of the trouble was not, as some have asserted, a repetition of the old story of natives being dispossessed of their lands by white settlers; for the area occupied by Europeans was being used by neither of the native races — the Kikuyu, who were primitive agriculturalists, or the Masai, more warlike pastoralists. As the Masai were not involved, a partial explanation may be found in what was happening to the Kikuyu. Their primitive method of agriculture used up the soil in a few years. Now the supply of virgin soil was running out because the British had stopped native wars, which had kept the population down. The consequent overcrowding of the Kikuyu on land they had half ruined naturally bred a desire to dispossess the whites of the land the latter had improved. British officials in the colony saw and tried to meet the urgent need to accommodate the growing pressure by teaching the Kikuyu more civilized ways of farming, but the outbreak of the treacherous campaign of murder waged by the Mau Mau secret society seems to have caught all the Europeans off guard.

British mandate under the League of Nations from 1919, and since 1946 administered by the British as a United Nations trust territory, is, like Kenya, only one third habitable.[15] It has also the same combination of races, though in a different proportion. In 1952 the Europeans numbered about 18,000, the Indians and Arabs 70,000, and the Africans 7,500,000. There is no entrenched white community comparable to that in the Kenya highlands. When Europeans sought to extend their holdings, they were barred by the rule that no land should be "allocated for nonnative settlement, unless it can be shown that it is not required for native occupation and is not likely to be so required in the foreseeable future." The government is less centralized than that of Kenya, much use being made of provincial councils in which there are more African than other nonofficial members.

Uganda, though much smaller in area than either of these other two territories, has a more prosperous and developed native population of some 5,000,000, and no real color problem. The few thousand European residents are mainly officials, missionaries, and their families—Uganda is a Christian country, with the only seat of higher learning in all East Africa. Trade is the chief occupation of the Asiatic community, which numbers about 38,000. Most of Uganda is well-watered grassland, and there the British found a superior form of native government which they continued and have improved. The most advanced people were the Baganda, on the west side of Lake Victoria. Their Kabaka (king) rules with the aid of a ministry and the Lukiko (parliament). The proposal to combine the three territories in a political union, first advanced by the governor of Kenya in the late twenties, has always encountered the stout opposition of the Baganda. Their proud independence inspired their young Cambridge-educated Kabaka in 1953 to defy the British governor, who thereupon deposed him and deported him to England. More than a year later the same spirit of independence, reinforced by a favorable court decision, brought about his restoration in a more amenable mood—after reforms which increased African representation to make it the majority of the legislative council of the protectorate and admitted the first Africans to the executive council.

The British West Indies, whose three million population is 90 per cent of African and slave origin, is the scene of a new political life

---

[15] More will be, with the progress of the scientific war against the deadly tsetse infestation.

that is driving toward the goal of democratic self-government and consolidation as a self-respecting dominion. It will be recalled that in the latter part of the nineteenth century self-government suffered a general reverse in the British Caribbean islands, when crown colony government was extended to the older colonies on the breakdown of their traditional constitutions.[16] Though some concession of the representative principle was later made, by the addition of elected council members, there was little if any prospect of British West Indian emancipation from crown colony rule until the very eve of the Second World War. In 1937 and 1938 the misery of the masses produced serious riots, which in turn moved the British government to send out a royal commission under Lord Moyne.

The Moyne Report, submitted in 1939, revealed desperate conditions[17] that called for desperate remedies. It is doubtful if any part of the world had been harder hit by the depression. The economy of the British West Indies was extremely vulnerable because it was entirely dependent upon the production of raw material for sale abroad; the already overcrowded population was piling up, and the social services were starved by the financial weakness of the colonial governments. About the only profitable resources were the pitch lake and the oil fields of Trinidad and the bauxite of British Guiana, and they gave employment to relatively few hands. On the whole, the British Caribbean colonies were the slum of the empire. As the revenues of the colonial governments could not begin to meet the urgent need for large expenditures on education, health services, decent housing, labor departments, social welfare agencies, and research, the commission recommended that the British government come to the rescue with an annual grant for the next twenty years. The Moyne Report was thus a major factor in initiating the series of Colonial Development and Welfare acts. For the British West Indies, the Development and Welfare Organization was established with headquarters in Barbados to assist, with expert advice, the various colonial governments in preparing their own schemes for improvement and then to channel the funds for the implementation of these schemes; for each of these

---

[16] In these colonies only two assemblies survived, those of Barbados and the Bahamas, and these two bodies were elected on a very narrow franchise. Bermuda, lying outside the Caribbean area and rarely classed as a West Indian colony, also retained its antiquated assembly.

[17] They were so bad that the report was withheld from the public until the end of the war, lest the enemy make valuable use of it for propaganda purposes.

colonies harbors an old and sturdy suspicion of outside interference in its internal affairs.

The political regeneration of the British West Indies, being tied to their social and economic regeneration, cannot reach full self-government until they are able to stand on their own feet without external support, a condition that will take years to fulfill. From 1938 there has been a most remarkable political awakening among the workers. Labor unions sprang up, fostered rather than opposed by the authorities and assisted by organized labor in Britain, to which pupils were sent from the West Indies for training. With the unions, and bearing various names, labor parties arose whose leaders likewise looked on the British Labor party as a model, which had the decisive advantage of universal suffrage. On this point the Moyne Report contained a pertinent comment: "some of us hold that the time has already come for the introduction of universal suffrage throughout the West Indies. We are not all satisfied that this is the case but we are unanimously of the opinion that universal suffrage should be the ultimate goal."

Constitutional reform began in Jamaica, the largest and most developed colony, where a bicameral legislature was established in 1944, with the house of representatives wholly elected by universal suffrage and empowered to elect five of the eleven members of the executive council. Similar reform soon became general even in the smaller and more backward islands, except that no unicameral legislature was split. There the change was in the franchise, in the number of elected members, and in their election of certain executive councilors. Labor thus gained control of the legislatures and an increasing share in the executives, under the leadership of surprisingly able and even distinguished men drawn from the small class of the colored intelligentsia.[18] The only setback occurred in British Guiana, whose constitution was suspended in 1953 when the newly victorious People's Progressive party, headed by an East Indian dentist trained in the United States, attempted to set up a Communist regime. Elsewhere the concession of semiresponsible government, with elected ministers in charge of

---

[18] A wealthy moneylender with a popular flair, Alexander Bustamente, was chief minister in Jamaica until 1955, when his party was defeated by that of his Rhodes Scholar cousin, Norman Manley, Q.C., the outstanding lawyer in the island. The Labor leader of Barbados, Grantley Adams, is another cultivated lawyer of wide vision. In 1948, as the first colonial member of a United Kingdom delegation to the General Assembly of the United Nations, he delivered an eloquent and pointed address that punctured an attack of the Soviet bloc on British colonial policy.

several executive departments, has spurred the Labor demand for full responsible government.

From the early twenties the Colonial Office had put out feelers to explore the possibility of a British West Indian federation,[19] but the result was not encouraging until Labor became politically conscious and caught the vision of a British Caribbean nation pulling together in a new dominion after the pattern of the old ones. In September 1947 delegates of the various legislatures held a conference at Montego Bay, Jamaica, with the colonial secretary himself in the chair, and set up a standing committee to devise a suitable scheme of federation. The committee's report, published in 1950, was approved by most of the legislatures and became the basis of a more finished draft constitution prepared in 1953 by a London conference of delegates meeting with the home government. British Guiana and British Honduras, both fearing a flood of surplus population from the islands, have turned thumbs down on the project. But it is doubtful if their rejection will deter the other colonies from combining to form a federal dominion that may help its members over the stile to full responsible government and would bring mutual support to all.

Of the senior dominions, the youngest had already departed from the Commonwealth. "We stand unequivocally for membership of the British Commonwealth," John Costello assured the voters in the general election campaign of early 1948, which ended by his replacing de Valera as prime minister. Later in the year he ate these words and got the Dail to pass an act repealing the External Relations Act of 1936 and transforming Eire into the Republic of Ireland. This measure, which came into operation in April 1949 on the anniversary of the Easter Rebellion, was a surrender to the extremist minority, a move to outflank de Valera, and a blind blow at Partition which it only reinforced. The British government responded by passing the Ireland Act of 1949, which gave legal sanction to the secession of "the part of Ireland formerly known as Eire and thenceforth as the Republic of Ireland," and declared that "in no event" would any part of Northern Ireland be severed from "the United Kingdom without the consent of the parliament of Northern Ireland." As a gesture of good will to the departing member of the Commonwealth, the same act also declared that in the United Kingdom and the colonial territories the eyes of

---

[19] A small and loose federation, that of the Leeward Islands, had been in existence since 1871, and its operation did not inspire much hope of a bigger and closer one.

the law would not regard the republic as a foreign country nor its citizens as aliens.

The Second World War brought great industrial development in South Africa but, like the First World War, it severely strained the unity of the country. Though Smuts, solidly backed by the British element of the population, gained more support from the people of his own blood as the war progressed, notably in the general election of 1943, the Nationalist opposition was deeply embittered. Both Hertzog and Malan repeatedly cried out for peace with Germany and the establishment of a South African republic. Both men were Nazis in spirit, and so were their followers. Hertzog died in the fourth winter of the war, still believing that Hitler would win it, and Malan clung to the same belief until nearly the end. In the beginning of the war the Nationalists were reunited under Hertzog as leader and Malan as deputy, but in November 1940 the latter became leader when the former was maneuvered out of the party for refusing to compromise the principle that English-speaking South Africans should have the same rights as Afrikaans-speaking citizens.

After the war the ever-present problem of white supremacy, aggravated by external influences, added more bitterness to the brew. The General Assembly of the United Nations arraigned South Africa for refusing to place the mandate of Southwest Africa, with its native population of 350,000, under the new trusteeship system of the United Nations, and, at the behest of India, for the treatment of Indians in the Union. South Africa, maintaining that the mandate had expired with the League of Nations and that the Indians in question were nationals of the Union, defied the General Assembly and accused it of violating the constitution of the United Nations by meddling in South African domestic affairs. Year after year the Assembly persisted in passing resolutions against South Africa, with the result that the South African delegation withdrew from the Assembly in the autumn of 1955. Though Britain abstained from voting against South Africa on these two contentious issues, her policy in other parts of the continent, particularly West Africa, angered South Africans, who feared it would ultimately subvert their own natives. For the same reason the Nationalists nursed another count against Britain. They demanded that she surrender to the Union the native protectorates that were enclaved in it—Bechuanaland, Basutoland, and Swaziland—and the British government refused on the ground that the people in these territories stoutly opposed the transfer.

All these issues combined to stir a reaction of feeling in South Africa that helped Malan to overthrow Smuts in the general election of 1948 and led to the adoption of severer measures to buttress white supremacy. One of these blew up a storm that rocked the country and shook the constitution. Malan would have abolished the colored vote, which still survived in the Cape province,[20] but he knew he could not get the constitutionally prescribed two thirds majority in a joint session of the two houses. Therefore he struck at the thing he abhorred by getting parliament to enact the removal of colored voters from the common electoral roll and the creation of a segregated roll for them to elect Europeans to represent them. The appellate division of the supreme court threw out the act as unconstitutional, and when he retaliated by passing an act making parliament itself the highest court in the land, the appellate division threw out that act too. Meanwhile he piped a new tune to beguile the English-speaking opposition. He no longer maintained that they were only British interlopers, not real South Africans. Their consent would be necessary for the establishment of a republic. He piped in vain, and the weight of four score years induced him to retire in 1954.

The new Nationalist leader and prime minister, J. G. Strijdom, resorted to more desperate means, which a group of Nationalist professors denounced in a published statement and many Nationalist women fought by picketing their legislators. But Strijdom had an iron grip on the party machine, and he jammed through parliament two revolutionary measures that came into force in December 1955. One packed the court that had defeated Malan, and the other the Senate, which it nearly doubled in size. The distribution of parliamentary seats, being strongly weighted in favor of the rural constituencies, had given the Nationalists a legislative majority though they represented less than half the electorate, and their chief was determined to use this advantage ruthlessly. Other measures restricted the freedom of speech and the press, heightening fears of a growing totalitarianism. The entrenched clauses of the constitution are now worthless paper, the English-speaking minority are in a precarious position, the pressure on the blacks is more intolerable than ever, and it would seem that only a break in the Nationalist ranks or a softening of hearts among Nationalist leaders can avert the peril that lies ahead.

During the war the other dominion with dual nationality, Canada,

---

[20] See *supra* p. 765, n. 5.

had some anxious moments over the internal unity of the country. The first came when the premier of Quebec, who had swept into power on an ultranationalist program in 1936, challenged the parliamentary decision to enter the war and backed up his challenge by calling a provincial election for October 1939. He paid for his folly by suffering a smashing defeat at the polls. The next test was precipitated by the fall of France in June 1940. There were whispered fears in parliament and elsewhere that the French of Canada might wish to follow the French of France out of the war, and that English-speaking Canadians might blindly push them in this direction by making disparaging remarks about the humiliated nation. But the children of France in the New World reacted proudly. As part of the fighting British Commonwealth they would help to restore the lost liberty of their fallen mother. The third ticklish time came a year later, when Hitler plunged his armies into Russia. Would French Canada, which had been reconciled to the war by the Nazi-Soviet combination that unleashed it, be willing to fight on the same side as Communist Russia? Again the answer was reassuring. Again, as in 1940, the swing of opinion in the United States, growingly hostile to the Nazis from the beginning of the war, was helping to weld Canada together, particularly since the Ogdensburg Agreement of August 1940 between President Roosevelt and Prime Minister King establishing the Permanent Joint Defense Board for the two countries.

The conscription issue seemed dead and buried before the "phony" phase of the war was over. The Liberals had repeatedly sworn they would never conscript men for overseas service, and when Mackenzie King held a general election in March 1940, the Conservative leader took the pledge too, in a vain effort to defeat the government. Under the shock soon administered by the Nazi invasion of Scandinavia, the Low Countries, and France, the government got from the new parliament full authority to mobilize all the manpower and material resources of the country, but at the same time the prime minister promised that he would not abandon the voluntary system for service overseas. Volunteers had been enlisting as fast as they could be handled, and this condition continued. Most of the draftees, though bound to serve only in Canada, offered themselves for duty abroad.

Nevertheless, the ugly ghost of 1917 began to rise from the grave, with increasing cries for and against the extension of the compulsory system to overseas service. Hot words flew back and forth. Racial feelings were not so dangerously inflamed as they had been in the previous war, but they were enough to cause grave concern for the national unity. To clear the air, a plebiscite was held in the spring of 1942 asking the people if they would release the government from its pledge not to conscript for service outside the country. Quebec voted no by almost three to one, and the other provinces yes by a majority of four to one, which only made matters worse by revealing how solidly French Canada and English Canada opposed each other on the issue. From this dangerous impasse the government found an escape for itself and the country by having parliament legalize conscription for overseas and by promising not to apply it until necessary. Not until the closing months of the war did heavy casualties in the Canadian army make it necessary, and then the dispatch of a small number of home servicemen sufficed. Meanwhile, though extremists on both sides fed the old racial feud, it failed to split the Liberal party, the only one that commanded wide support in both French and English Canada, thanks largely to Mackenzie King's political acumen and the influence of his French Canadian lieutenant, Louis St. Laurent, who succeeded him as prime minister in 1948.

In no other dominion was conscription an issue. It was utterly impossible in South Africa; New Zealand again adopted it early in the war with scarcely any question; and Australia shrank from repeating the bitter experience of the First World War. This Australian reluctance may seem surprising, in light of the fact that the country was exposed as never before to direct enemy attack. But the Labor party, which had been strongly infected by isolationism, began to recover from that paralyzing disease when the fall of the French and Dutch empires allowed the Japanese to creep southward toward Australia, and the saner outlook of the party enabled it to return to power in October 1941. Later, under the impact of the Japanese onslaught, the Labor government extended compulsory service from the confines of Australia and its dependencies to cover the area of the Japanese war up to the equator.

The war effected a profound reorientation of the two Pacific dominions, bringing them in line with the international position of Canada. All three, while still clinging as much as ever to their membership in the British Commonwealth of Nations, now recognized their vital dependence upon the United States for their security—as the United States discovered its dependence on British resistance when France fell. Australia had no direct diplomatic relations with any foreign country until 1940, when there was an exchange of ministers with

Washington. Early in 1941 the New Zealand government decided to follow suit, but the appointments were not made until the close of the year, after Pearl Harbor. Immense was the relief felt by these two dominions when the United States sent large forces, giving them the security that it was then impossible for Britain to give.

After the war, Australia and New Zealand sought a Pacific pact comparable to the Atlantic pact, of which Canada was a member; but the project hung fire until the United States led the United Nations and their forces in repelling Communist aggression in Korea. Then American policy turned to negotiate a peace treaty with Japan that would allow that country to rearm, and this prospect alarmed Australia and New Zealand. They objected that a rearmed Japan would be too dangerous to them unless the United States underwrote their security. The upshot was the ANZUS pact of 1951, binding Australia, New Zealand, and the United States together against a possible resurgence of Japanese militarism. There were some qualms in England over this independent action of the two distant dominions, though there had been no British objection to the permanent arrangement of Canada and the United States for their joint defense. But this was the first time that the two younger dominions exercised their right, as independent nations of the Commonwealth, to form their own foreign policy, and the government in London looked on as a friendly observer. Replying to doubters in and out of parliament, the Lord Chancellor of England said:

> The request to give our blessing to this arrangement came from Australia and New Zealand. The reason we are not in it is because it goes without saying we are in. For any attack made on Australia or New Zealand would find this country running to either country's aid with every man and every shilling we have.

These wise words are a reminder of the family relationship that holds the Commonwealth together, a relationship that has no parallel among other nations.

SOME SUGGESTIONS FOR FURTHER READING

THE most comprehensive work is *The Cambridge History of the British Empire,* eds. J. H. Rose, A. P. Newton, E. A. Benians, 8 vols. (Cambridge, 1929–): Vol. I, *The Old Empire from the Beginnings to 1783;* Vol. II, *The Growth of the New Empire, 1783–1870;* Vol. III, *The Empire Commonwealth, 1870–1921* (not yet published); Vol. IV, *British India, 1497–1858;* Vol. V, *The Indian Empire, 1858–1918;* Vol. VI, *Canada;* Vol. VII, Part I, *Australia,* Part II, *New Zealand* (bound separately); Vol. VIII, *South Africa.* Each volume of this series, henceforth referred to as *C.H.B.E.,* contains a full classified bibliography. A more selective and instructive guide to modern works on the empire and commonwealth is the series of review articles published in the September numbers of *The Canadian Historical Review* (University of Toronto Press).

A Historical Geography of the British Colonies, ed. Sir Charles P. Lucas, 7 vols. in 13 (Oxford, 1906–1925) is very useful. Ramsay Muir, *Short History of the British Commonwealth, Vol. II, The Modern Commonwealth, 1763–1933,* 8th ed. (London, 1954) covers the history of the British Isles as well as the history of the empire and commonwealth.

H. E. Egerton, *A Short History of British Colonial Policy,* 12th ed. revised by A. P. Newton (London, 1950) should be consulted. *The Cambridge History of British Foreign Policy,* eds. A. W. Ward, G. P. Gooch, 3 vols. (Cambridge, 1922–23); and L. C. A. and C. M. Knowles, *The Economic Development of the British Overseas Empire,* 3 vols. (London, 1928–36) are standard works.

CHAPTER I   How the American Revolution Released a British Revolution

T. E. May, *Constitutional History of England, 1760–1911,* ed. F. Holland (London, 1912); W. R. Anson, *The Law and the Custom of the Constitution,* 4th ed., 3 vols. (Oxford, 1935); and A. V. Dicey, *Introduction to the Study of the Law of the Constitution,* 9th ed. (London, 1939) are classics. Much new light on the political situation has been thrown by L. B. Namier, *The Structure of Politics at the Accession of George III,* 2 vols. (London, 1929) and *England in the Age of the American Revolution* (London, 1933). J. H. Rose, *Life of William Pitt,* 2 vols. (New York, 1924) is the best biography of that statesman. The same author's *A Short Life of William Pitt* (London, 1925) is not a mere abridgment. C. G. Robertson, *England under the Hanoverians,* 16th ed. (London, 1949) has a value reflected in its many editions. *The Oxford History of England,* Vol. XII (not yet published), will cover the reign of George III.

CHAPTER II   New Life in Old England

Herbert Heaton's article "The Industrial Revolution" in the *Encyclopaedia of the Social Sciences,* Vol. VIII (New York, 1932) gives an excellent lead, with a good bibliography, for further exploration of the subject. A more recent summary account is T. S. Ashton, *The Industrial Revolution, 1760–1830* (Home University Library, 1949).

J. L. and Barbara Hammond, *The Rise of Modern Industry* (New York, 1926) is interesting reading and contains good material, though it reflects a certain social bias. See also the same authors' three volumes, *The Village Labourer, 1760–1832, The Town Labourer, 1760–1832,* and *The Skilled Labourer, 1760–1832* (London, 1911–20). P. Mantoux, *The Industrial Revolution in the Eighteenth Century* (New York, 1928) and W. H. B. Court, *The Rise of the Midland Industries* (London, 1938) are important. For the agricultural revolution, consult R. E. Prothero (Lord Ernle), *English Farming, Past and Present* (London, 1913) and R. Curtler, *Enclosure and Redistribution of Our Land* (Oxford, 1920).

CHAPTER III   Fragments of Empire

Good works on the West Indies are W. H. Siebert, *The Legacy of the American Revolution to the British West Indies and the Bahamas* (Columbus, 1913); L. J. Ragatz, *The Fall of the Planter Class in the British Caribbean, 1783–1833* (New York, 1928); and Sir Alan Burn, *History of the British West Indies* (New York, 1954). On British North America, the reader might turn to A. L. Burt, *A Short History of Canada for Americans,* 2nd ed. (Minneapolis, 1944).

CHAPTER IV   Salvaging What Was Left of the American Wreck

Helen Taft Manning, *British Colonial Government after the American Revolution* (New Haven, 1933) is a masterly study. Various aspects of the subject are treated in the works of Burn and Ragatz and Vol. II of the *C.H.B.E.* already cited, and also in the following: R. L. Schuyler, *The Fall of the Old Colonial System* (New York, 1945); G. S. Graham, *Sea Power and British North America, 1783–1820* (Cambridge, Mass., 1941); A. L. Burt, *The Old Province of Quebec* (Minneapolis, 1933) and *The United States, Great Britain and British North America* (New Haven, 1940).

CHAPTER V   The Curse of the French Revolution

The works of Rose and Robertson mentioned above should be consulted, and some pertinent comments may be found in G. M. Trevelyan, *British History in the Nineteenth Century and After,* 2nd ed. (New York, 1938). The following biographies have a direct bearing on the subject: Moncure Conway, *Life of Paine* (New York, 1892); R. Coupland, *Wilberforce* (Oxford, 1923); J. L. Hammond, *Charles James Fox* (London, 1903); J. Morley, *Burke* (London, 1903); Graham Wallas, *Francis Place* (New York, 1919). There are also the following special studies: W. T. Laprade, *England and the French Revolution* (Baltimore, 1909); W. P. Hall, *British Radicalism, 1791–1797* (New York, 1912); G. S. Veitch, *Genesis of Parliamentary Reform* (London, 1913); and P. A. Brown, *The French Revolution in English History* (London, 1918).

CHAPTER VI   The Long French War

J. H. Rose, the biographer of Napoleon, covers the war in two chapters of the *C.H.B.E.*, Vol. II. A. T. Mahan, *The Influence of Sea Power upon the French Revolution and Empire, 1793–1812*, 2 vols. (London, 1892) is a famous classic. Very valuable also is his *Life of Nelson; the Embodiment of the Sea Power of Great Britain* (London, 1897), which goes into greater detail. Two volumes by A. Bryant, *The Years of Endurance, 1793–1802* (New York, 1942) and *The Years of Victory, 1802–1812* (New York, 1944), have received wide acclaim. E. F. Heckscher, *The Continental System* (London, 1922) and C. K. Webster, *The Foreign Policy of Castlereagh, 1812–1815*, new ed. (London, 1934) are standard works.

CHAPTER VII   How Ireland Nearly Became the First Dominion of the British Commonwealth of Nations

W. E. H. Lecky, *A History of Ireland in the Eighteenth Century*, 5 vols. (New York, 1893) is the authoritative work on the subject, which is also well discussed in Vincent T. Harlow, *The Founding of the Second British Empire, 1763–1793* (New York, 1952). Rose's *Pitt* is also useful.

CHAPTER VIII   The Establishment of the British Empire in India

P. E. Roberts, *History of British India under the Company and the Crown*, 3rd ed. (London, 1952) gives a good account, which may be supplemented by Vol. IV of the *C.H.B.E.* Other good references are C. H. Phillips, *The East India Company, 1784–1834* (Manchester, 1940); Marguerite E. Wilbur, *The East India Company and the British Empire in the Far East* (New York, 1945); Holden Furber, *John Company at Work, a Study of European Expansion in India in the Late Eighteenth Century* (Cambridge, Mass., 1948); and Keith Feiling, *Warren Hastings* (London, 1954).

CHAPTER IX   The Colonial Empire during the Long French War: (I) The Western Hemisphere

In addition to the works of Manning, Ragatz, Webster, and Burt cited above, see A. T. Mahan, *Sea Power in Its Relations to the War of 1812* (London, 1905); Douglas MacKay, *The Honourable Company, a History of the Hudson's Bay Company* (New York, 1936); and, what is more thorough than this, A. S. Morton, *A History of the Canadian West to 1870–71* (Toronto, 1939).

CHAPTER X   The Colonial Empire during the Long French War: (II) The Eastern Hemisphere

Eric A. Walker, *A History of South Africa*, 2nd ed. with additional corrections (London, 1947) is the fullest account by one author in a single volume. C. W. De Kiewiet, *A History of South Africa* (Oxford, 1941) is much shorter but very penetrating. L. A. Mills, *Ceylon under British Rule*

(London, 1933) is the standard study. W. K. Hancock, *Australia* (London, 1930) is perhaps the best introduction to the history of that country. See also the *C.H.B.E.*, Vols. VII and VIII.

CHAPTER XI   Overthrow of the Landed Oligarchy

Spencer Walpole, *A History of England from the Conclusion of the Great War in 1815,* 6 vols., revised ed. (London, 1890) is a classic. The first three volumes cover the period of this chapter. E. Halévy, *A History of the English People,* 3 vols. (New York, 1926) is the combined product of remarkable industry and insight. E. L. Woodward, *The Age of Reform* (Oxford, 1938), Vol. XIII of the new *Oxford History of England,* is by one of the leading English historians of the present day. More specialized studies are E. Porritt, *The Unreformed House of Commons,* 2 vols. (Cambridge, 1903), the outstanding authority; G. M. Trevelyan, *Lord Grey of the Reform Bill* (London, 1920); J. R. M. Butler, *The Passing of the Great Reform Bill* (London, 1914); and A. Brady, *William Huskisson and Liberal Reform* (London, 1928).

CHAPTER XII   The Rise of the Colonial Office and the Fall of Slavery

In addition to the works of Manning and Ragatz, and the *C.H.B.E.*, Vol. II, which have been cited above, the following authoritative studies should be consulted: H. L. Hall, *The Colonial Office* (New York, 1937); Paul Knaplund, *James Stephen and the British Colonial System, 1813– 1847* (Madison, 1953); and F. J. Klingberg, *The Anti-Slavery Movement in England* (New Haven, 1926). Frank Tannenbaum, "The Destiny of the Negro in the Western Hemisphere" in the *Political Science Quarterly,* March 1946, is a most enlightening article.

CHAPTER XIII   The Growth of Anti-Imperialism

The works of Brady, Graham, and Schuyler, cited above, have much to say on the subject, as also does Klaus E. Knoor, *British Colonial Theories, 1570–1850* (Toronto, 1944). The three best books on emigration to the colonies are Helen I. Cowan, *British Emigration to British North America, 1783–1837* (Toronto, 1928); W. A. Carrothers, *Emigration from the British Isles* (London, 1929); and Edwin C. Guillet, *The Great Migration* (Toronto, 1937).

CHAPTER XIV   The Flood of Reforms in Britain

In addition to the works of Schuyler, Walpole, and Woodward, already cited, the following should be mentioned: S. E. Finer, *The Life and Times of Sir Edwin Chadwick* (London, 1952); R. A. Lewis, *Edwin Chadwick and the Public Health Movement* (London, 1952); E. Hodder, *Life and Work of the Seventh Earl of Shaftesbury* (London, 1893); J. Morley, *Life of Richard Cobden* (Boston, 1881); G. M. Trevelyan, *Life of John Bright* (Boston, 1913); and Spencer Walpole, *The Life of Lord John Russell,* 2 vols. (New York, 1889).

CHAPTER XV   The British North American Revolution

Chester W. New, *Lord Durham, a Biography of John George Lambton, First Earl of Durham* (Oxford, 1929) is outstanding because of the subject and the author's treatment of it. W. P. M. Kennedy, *Statutes, Treaties and Documents of the Canadian Constitution, 1713–1929,* 2nd ed. (Oxford, 1930) is essential. For the Irish contrast, see Spencer Walpole, *History of England,* mentioned above, and Herbert Paul, *A History of Modern England,* Vol. I (London, 1904).

CHAPTER XVI   South Africa, a Workshop of Native Policy

The *C.H.B.E.,* Vol. VIII, and the works of Walker and De Kiewiet may be supplemented by documentary sources in K. N. Bell and W. P. Morrell, eds., *Select Documents on British Colonial Policy, 1830–1860* (Oxford, 1928).

CHAPTER XVII   Australasia and Systematic Colonization

Here, too, Bell and Morrell's volume is useful. The *C.H.B.E.,* Vol. VII, contains good chapters on the subject. For an introduction to New Zealand comparable to the volume by Hancock on Australia, see J. B. Condliffe, *New Zealand in the Making* (Chicago, 1930).

CHAPTER XVIII   The Tropical Colonies under the Impact of
Emancipation and Free Trade

See Bell and Morrell, as in the last two chapters; Burn, already cited; and the *C.H.B.E.,* Vol. II. For what happened to government in the British Caribbean, consult H. H. Wrong, *The Government of the West Indies* (Oxford, 1923).

CHAPTER XIX   Reform and Expansion in India

Roberts should be consulted before turning to the *C.H.B.E.,* Vols. IV and V. According to the title pages of these volumes, 1858 is the dividing date between them; but Vol. V contains much on the period before 1858. For "bare facts," V. A. Smith, *The Oxford History of India,* 2nd ed. (Oxford, 1923) is useful.

CHAPTER XX   Britain on Top of the World and Turning to
Democracy

J. H. Clapham, *An Economic History of Modern Britain,* 3 vols. (London, 1930–38) is a great authority. The subtitles of these volumes are: *Early Railway Age, 1820–1850; Free Trade and Steel, 1850–1886; Machines and National Rivalries, 1887–1914, with Epilogue, 1914– 1929.* C. A. Bodelson, *Studies in Mid-Victorian Imperialism* (New York, 1924) may be consulted with profit. H. C. F. Bell, *Lord Palmerston,* 2 vols. (London, 1936) and M. Hovell, *The Chartist Movement* (Manchester, 1918) are authoritative.

CHAPTER XXI   The Birth of the First Dominion

R. G. Trotter, *Canadian Federation: Its Origins and Achievement; a Study in Nation Building* (London, 1924) has not been superseded. There are some good chapters on the subject in the *C.H.B.E.*, Vol. VI. In addition to W. P. M. Kennedy's volume of documents, see his *The Constitution of Canada* (New York, 1922).

CHAPTER XXII   Australian Gold and Maori Wars

See references to Chapter XVII.

CHAPTER XXIII   Readjustment in the Tropical Colonies

See references to Chapter XVIII.

CHAPTER XXIV   The Failure of British Policy in South Africa

In addition to the *C.H.B.E.*, Vol. VIII, see C. W. De Kiewiet, *British Colonial Policy and the South African Republics, 1848–1872* (London, 1929).

CHAPTER XXV   The Indian Mutiny

T. R. Holmes, *History of the Indian Mutiny*, 5th ed. (London, 1913) may be consulted as well as Roberts and the *C.H.B.E.*, Vol. V.

CHAPTER XXVI   The Rise of Modern British Imperialism

Bodelson, cited above, and Seeley, mentioned in the text, are very important. For the revival of the imperial idea in the colonies, and specific proposals to reconsolidate the empire, see A. L. Burt, *Imperial Architects* (Oxford, 1913). Gladstone's role is elucidated in Paul Knaplund, *Gladstone and Britain's Imperial Policy* (London, 1927) and his *Gladstone's Foreign Policy* (New York, 1935), which supplement the classic J. Morley, *Life of Gladstone*, 3 vols. (New York, 1903). The standard biography of Disraeli is W. F. Monypenny and G. E. Buckle, *Life of Benjamin Disraeli*, 6 vols. (New York, 1910–20). An important aspect of foreign policy is treated by R. W. Seton-Watson, *Disraeli, Gladstone and the Eastern Question* (London, 1935). The essay by Ethel Drus, "The Colonial Office and the Annexation of Fiji," published in the *Transactions of the Royal Historical Society* (London, 1950), sheds new light on that subject. There is some good material in the *C.H.B.E.*, Vols. V and VIII.

CHAPTER XXVII   More Democracy and the Quest for Social Justice

R. C. K. Ensor, *England, 1870–1914* (Oxford, 1936), Vol. XIV of the *Oxford History of England,* is excellent. For further detail on England see Clapham, cited above; W. S. Churchill, *Lord Randolph Churchill,* 2 vols. (New York, 1906); A. W. Humphrey, *A History of Labor Representation* (London, 1912); Sidney and Beatrice Webb, *The History of Trade Unionism,* new ed. (London, 1920); G. D. H. Cole, *Short History of the*

British Working Class Movement, 3 vols. (New York, 1927). For Australasia, see *C.H.B.E.,* Vol. VII, and James Drummond, *The Life and Work of John Richard Seddon* (London, 1907).

CHAPTER XXVIII   The Great Imperial Scramble

Authoritative works by public men who participated in the scramble are: Lord Cromer, *Modern Egypt,* 2 vols. (New York, 1916); Sir H. H. Johnston, *The Opening Up of Africa* (New York, 1911) and *The Story of My Life* (London, 1923); and Sir Frederick J. D. (later Lord) Lugard, *The Rise of Our East African Empire* (London, 1923). W. L. Langer, *European Alliances and Alignments, 1871–1890,* 2nd ed. (New York, 1950) and his *The Diplomacy of Imperialism, 1890–1902,* 2nd ed. (New York, 1951) are indispensable. Among other useful works are Sir Charles P. Lucas, *Partition and Colonization of Africa* (New York, 1920); N. D. Harris, *Europe and Africa* (Boston, 1927); L. A. Mills, *British Rule in Eastern Asia* (London, 1942); Sir R. O. Winsted, *Malaya and Its History* (Home University Library, 1948) and *History of Malaya* (Singapore, 1935); and the *C.H.B.E.,* Vols. V and VIII.

CHAPTER XXIX   The South African War, 1899–1902

In addition to the works of De Kiewiet and Walker already cited, and the *C.H.B.E.,* Vol. VIII, see Jan H. Hofmeyr, *South Africa,* 2nd revised ed., ed. by J. P. Cope (New York, 1952), and J. L. Garvin, *Life of Joseph Chamberlain,* 3 vols. (London, 1932–34).

CHAPTER XXX   The Climax of British Imperialism

G. R. Parkin, *Imperial Federation* (New York, 1892) is by a leader of the movement. Richard Jebb, *The Imperial Conference,* 2 vols. (London, 1911) and his *Britannic Question* (New York, 1913), and A. B. Keith, *Imperial Unity and the Dominions* (Oxford, 1916) and his *Responsible Government in the Dominions,* 2nd ed., 2 vols. (London, 1928) are standard works.

The history of the Round Table movement has yet to be written. The historical approach of Lionel Curtis appears in his anonymous *The Project of a Commonwealth* (London, 1915), and his analysis in his anonymous *The Problem of the Commonwealth* (London, 1915). Though the latter was printed for private circulation only, it may be found in various libraries. *The Round Table,* published quarterly in London from 1910, has excellent articles on the subject.

CHAPTER XXXI   The Formation of Two New Great Dominions:
Australia and South Africa

See the Australian and South African volumes in the *C.H.B.E.,* and Hancock, Keith, De Kiewiet, Hofmeyr, and Walker, cited above. The constitutions are to be found in H. E. Egerton, ed. *Federations and Unions within the British Empire* (Oxford, 1924).

CHAPTER XXXII Dominion Nationalism

In addition to the works on the various dominions already cited, and articles from the dominions in *The Round Table,* see Gwen Neuendorf, *Studies in the Evolution of Dominion Status* (London, 1942); John S. Galbraith, *The Establishment of Canadian Diplomatic Status at Washington* (Berkeley, 1951); R. M. Dawson, ed. *Constitutional Issues in Canada, 1900–1931* (Oxford, 1933), with its sequel *The Development of Dominion Status, 1900–1936* (New York, 1937); and G. N. Tucker, "The Naval Policy of Sir Robert Borden, 1912–1914," *The Canadian Historical Review,* March 1947.

CHAPTER XXXIII Irish and Indian Nationalism

John, Viscount Morley, *Recollections,* 2 vols. (New York, 1917) is valuable because of the public part the author played. For Ireland, consult N. Mansergh, *Ireland in the Age of Reform and Revolution, 1840–1921* (London, 1940); M. MacDonagh, *The Home Rule Movement* (Dublin, 1920); J. L. Hammond, *Gladstone and the Irish Question* (London, 1928); and W. A. Phillips, *The Revolution in Ireland, 1906–1923* (London, 1923). For India, consult Roberts and the *C.H.B.E.,* Vol. V. There are good articles on Ireland and India in *The Round Table.*

CHAPTER XXXIV The First World War: The Supreme Test

The best reference is Sir Charles Lucas, ed. *The Empire at War,* 5 vols. (Oxford, 1921–26). For the general course of the war, see R. C. M. F. Crutwell, *A History of the Great War* (Oxford, 1934) and Liddell Hart, *The War in Outline, 1914–1918* (London, 1936), a pungent summary.

CHAPTER XXXV Nationalism in the Dominions, Ireland, and India under the Impact of the War

In addition to articles in *The Round Table* and Phillips, cited above, there are three outstanding works: W. K. Hancock, *Survey of British Commonwealth Affairs, Vol. I, Problems of Nationality, 1918–1936* (New York, 1937); Lionel Curtis, *Dyarchy* (Oxford, 1920); and R. Coupland, *The Indian Problem, 1833–1935* (London, 1942). See also the *C.H.B.E.,* Vol. V.

CHAPTER XXXVI The Emergence of the British Commonwealth

Hancock's *Survey,* just mentioned, and Keith's *Responsible Government,* cited earlier, are important. See also Sir Robert Borden, *Canada in the Commonwealth* (Oxford, 1929) and his *Memoirs,* ed. by Henry Borden, 2 vols. (Toronto, 1938).

CHAPTER XXXVII The Statute of Westminster and the Shaping of the Commonwealth

K. C. Wheare, *The Statute of Westminster and Dominion Status,* 5th ed. (Oxford, 1953) is the chief authority on the statute. Two more works by A. B. Keith, *The Government of the British Empire* (New York, 1935) and *The Dominions as Sovereign States; Their Constitutions and Governments* (London, 1938) are very useful. See also W. K. Hancock's *Survey*, Vol. I, already mentioned, and Vol. II, *Problems of Economic Policy, 1918–1939* (New York, 1942); N. Mansergh, *Survey of British Commonwealth Affairs: Problems of External Policy, 1931–1939* (New York, 1952); and G. F. Plant, *Oversea Settlement; Migration from the United Kingdom to the Dominions* (New York, 1951).

CHAPTER XXXVIII   India's Advance Toward Dominion Status

There is an excellent study of the subject in Coupland, cited above, and in his *Indian Politics, 1936–1942* (London, 1943). These are bound with a third volume, *The Future of India* (London, 1943), and published in New York, 1944. Coupland was a member of the Cripps Mission.

CHAPTER XXXIX   Commonwealth Reactions to the Coming of the Second World War

Mansergh's *Survey*, mentioned above, is a masterly analysis of the subject. G. M. Carter, *The British Commonwealth and International Security: The Role of the Dominions, 1919–1939* (Toronto, 1947) should also be consulted. C. L. Mowat, *Britain between the Wars, 1918–1940* (Chicago, 1955) is an excellent political, economic, and social survey.

CHAPTER XL   British Participation in the Second World War

There is nothing to compare with W. S. Churchill, *The Second World War*, 6 vols. (Boston, 1948–1953).

CHAPTER XLI   Less Empire and More Commonwealth

Besides articles in *The Round Table*, some good ones appear in *The Times British Colonies Review*, a quarterly first published in 1951. For India the best reference is E. W. R. Lumby, *The Transfer of Power in India* (London, 1954); for the West Indies, Mary Proudfoot, *Britain and the United States in the Caribbean* (New York, 1953). Vernon Bartlett, *Struggle for Africa* (New York, 1953) and *Report from Malaya* (London, 1954) are good reporting by a well-informed observer. C. H. Currey, *The British Commonwealth Since 1815, Vol. II, The Colonial Territories and the Anglo-Egyptian Sudan* (New York, 1952) is a useful survey. Apartheid is closely examined in Eugene Dvorin, *Racial Separation in South Africa* (Chicago, 1952). H. J. Harvey, *Consultation and Cooperation in the Commonwealth* (New York, 1952) is a good compilation. For an important subject not mentioned in the chapter, see Ronald Mendelsohn, *Social Security in the British Commonwealth* (London, 1954).

INDEX